This book
to Alvin E. "Monty" Montgomery
by the members of the
Professors' Sunday School
Class of the Burlingame
United Methodist Church.
as a token of the respect, and
affection in which he is held.
"Your intellectual and social
leadership has stimulated
our minds and lifted our
spirits." This sentence quoted
from the oral presentation
sums up the feelings of the
class and all are grateful.

BEQUEST

OF

ALVIN E. MONTGOMERY

SAN MATEO COUNTY GENEALOGICAL SOCIETY

INDEX TO
AMERICAN GENEALOGIES

*And to Genealogical Material Contained in All Works As Town
Histories, County Histories, Local Histories, Historical
Society Publications, Biographies, Historical
Periodicals, and Kindred Works.*

Compiled and Originally Published by

JOEL MUNSELL'S SONS

A REPRINT OF THE FIFTH EDITION, 1900

WITH SUPPLEMENT, 1900 TO 1908

GENEALOGICAL PUBLISHING CO., INC.
Baltimore 1984

Originally Published: Albany, New York, 1900 and 1908
Reprinted: Genealogical Publishing Co., Inc.
Baltimore, 1967, 1979, 1984
Library of Congress Catalogue Card Number 67-19607
International Standard Book Number 0-8063-0313-1
Made in the United States of America

INDEX

TO

AMERICAN GENEALOGIES;

AND TO

GENEALOGICAL MATERIAL CONTAINED IN ALL WORKS

SUCH AS

TOWN HISTORIES, COUNTY HISTORIES, LOCAL HISTORIES, HISTORI-
CAL SOCIETY PUBLICATIONS, BIOGRAPHIES, HISTORICAL
PERIODICALS, AND KINDRED WORKS,

ALPHABETICALLY ARRANGED

ENABLING THE READER TO ASCERTAIN WHETHER THE GENEALOGY OF ANY
FAMILY, OR ANY PART OF IT, IS PRINTED, EITHER BY ITSELF
OR EMBODIED IN OTHER WORKS.

FIFTH EDITION,

REVISED, IMPROVED AND ENLARGED, CONTAINING NEARLY 50,000 REFERENCES.

(First and Second Editions were Edited by Daniel S. Durrie.)

COPYRIGHTED, 1900.

ALBANY, N. Y.
JOEL MUNSELL'S SONS, PUBLISHERS
1900.

EXPLANATION.

This work indexes genealogical material by giving the titles of works containing references to the genealogies of American families, arranging the references to genealogical material alphabetically under family names or surnames. In most cases the references are to matter which consists of at least three or four generations.

The surname is given in **black type** followed by the titles of works containing information on each surname, with the number of the page on which the information is to be found. Look for the various spellings of a name. Most of the references are to town histories, and give the author's name followed by word Hist., for History of, and the name of town and State. This is the only work of the kind in the country.

These titles are given briefly, each occupying one line. For a full description of each genealogy the reader is referred to "The American Genealogist," a companion to this volume, published by us.

It has been the aim of the compiler to make it as thorough and complete as possible; hundreds of volumes of historical, biographical and miscellaneous publications have been minutely examined. But few persons have an adequate knowledge of the amount of genealogical material to be found in such volumes, from the fact that anything like a full collection of works in those departments can only be found in a few large cities, and without consulting them it is often an impossibility to prepare a family history, or to learn anything very definite of a particular family. With the assistance furnished by this volume no difficulty will be experienced in collecting needed information by any one interested in such investigations. It also affords instruction to the general reader, who may not know whether the history of his native county, town or village has been written and published. The work has been prepared with a view to facilitate the study of family history, and makes it unnecessary to visit the leading historical libraries, to learn by protracted search whether anything has been published on one's family.

ABBREVIATIONS.

Am.	American.	Dict.	Dictionary.	N. S.	Nova Scotia.
Anc.	Ancestry.	Epit.	Epitaph.	Proc.	Proceedings.
Anniv.	Anniversary.	Fam.	Family.	Rec.	Record.
App.	Appendix.	Gaz.	Gazetteer.	Reg.	Register.
Biog.	Biography.	Gen.	Genealogy.	Rem.	Reminiscences.
Can.	Canada.	Hist.	History.	Rep.	Report.
Cent.	Centennial.	Inst.	Institute.	Sett.	Settlers.
Ch.	Church.	Jour.	Journal.	Soc.	Society.
Co.	County.	Mag.	Magazine.	Supp.	Supplement.
Coll.	Collections.	Mem.	Memorial.	Tran.	Transactions.
		Narr.	Narrative.		

INDEX.

Aartse — N. Y. Gen. Record xxvi, 134-8
Abbe — American Ancestry ix, 44
Essex Mass. Antiquarian (1897) i, 14
Hinman's Puritan Settlers of Conn. 13
Savage's Genealogical Dictionary i, 6
Stiles' History of Windsor Ct. ii, 9, 831
Weaver's History of Windham Ct. 9-26
Abbett — Conrad Genealogy 34-6, 49-53
Abbey — Burleigh's Guild Genealogy 236
Smith's History of Sunderland Mass. 245
Abbot — Allison Genealogy 86
American Ancestry iii, 201
Anderson's Waterbury Ct. i, appendix 5
Barry's History Framingham Mass. 165
Bond's Watertown Mass. 1, 673, 901
Bouton's Sermons at Concord N. H. 59
Bouton's History of Concord N. H. 620-30
Brown's Bedford Mass. Families 1
Chandler Genealogy 4-9, 410-2
Dow's History of Hampton N. H. 583
Dudley's Arch. Collections plate 5
Eaton's History of Thomaston Me. 128
Essex Mass. Antiquarian (1897) i, 35-42,
  58-63, 79-84, 96-100, 103-8, 128-30, 141
Hayward's History of Hancock N. H. 297
Hazen's History of Billerica Mass. 2
Hill's History of Mason N. H. 199
Hinman's Connecticut Settlers 14-16
Hodgman's History of Westord Mass. 435
Hudson's History of Lexington Mass. 5
Lapham's History of Bethel Me. 458
Lapham's History of Rumford Me. 286-93
Lapham's History of Woodstock Me. 169
Livermore's Hist. of Wilton N. H. 526-55
Morrison's Hist. of Windham N. H. 300-5
Perkin's Old Houses of Norwich Ct. 407
Poor's History and Gen. Researches 84-5
Savage's Genealogical Dictionary i, 1-6
Secomb's History of Amherst N. H. 477-80
Smith's History of Peterborough N. H. 4-6
Stiles' History of Windsor Ct. ii, 10
Weaver's History of Windham Ct. 26
Abbott — Abbot Genealogy (1847) 197 p.
Abbott's History of Andover Mass. 28-35
American Ancestry i, 1; iv, 18, 93; v, 182;
  vi, 200; vii, 238; x, 66, 121
Austin's R. I. Genealogical Dictionary 234
Bass' History of Braintree Vt. 109
Bedford N. H. Centennial 278
Butler's History of Farmington Me. 349-60
Carter's History of Pembroke N. H. ii, 1-5
Cochran's History of Antrim N. H. 331

Cochrane's Hist. of Francestown N. H. 479
Coffin's History of Boscawen N. H. 462-6
Cogswell's Hist. of Henniker N. H 438-40
Eaton's History of Reading Mass. 52
Hammatt Papers, Ipswich Mass. 9
Hayward's History of Gilsum N. H. 253
Hubbard's Stanstead Co. Canada 261-3
Lapham's History of Norway Me. 454
Lapham's History of Paris Me. 492
Lincoln's History of Hingham Mass. ii, 8
Ogden Genealogy (1898) 100
Paige's History of Cambridge Mass. 477
Paige's History of Hardwick Mass. 321
Putnam's Historical Magazine vi, 41-6
Read's History of Swanzey N. H. 271
Ridlon's Harrison Me. Settlers 24
Runnel's Hist. of Sanbornton N. H. ii, 1-7
Saunderson's Hist. Charlestown N. H. 275
Selleck's Norwalk Ct. (1896) 345-7
Shourd's Fenwick Colony N. J. 28-34
Stearns' History of Ashburnham Mass. 581
Stearns' History of Rindge N. H. 423
Waldo's History of Tolland Ct. 128
Washington N. H. History 270, 695
Whitman Genealogy 457-60
Worcester's History of Hollis N. H. 363-4
Wyman's Charlestown Mass. Gens. i, 1
Abby — See under Abbe
Abeel — Abeel Genealogy (1899) 24 pages
Munsell's Albany Coll. iv, 93
Williamson Genealogy (1896) 15-20
Abel — Barrus' History of Goshen Mass.
  133
Bliss Genealogy 664-81
Caulkins' History of Norwich Ct. 209
Chambers' Early Germans of N. J. 227-9
Hines' Lebanon Ct. Address 143
Hinman's Connecticut Settlers 16
Hurd's History of New London Co. Ct. 509
Merrill's History of Acworth N. H. 178
Middlesex Ct. History 198
Power's History of Sagamon Co. Ill. 75
Savage's Genealogical Dictionary i, 6
Sedgwick's History of Sharon Ct. 61
Walworth's Hyde Gen. 1044-51, 1065-74
Whipple-Hill Families (1897) 90-2
Young's Chautauqua Co. N. Y. 307, 478
Abercromby — Sheldon's Deerfield 5
Temple's Whately 195
Abernethy — Davis' Wallingford 613
Hinman's Connecticut Settlers 17
Orcutt's History of Torrington Ct. 637

[iii]

Aborn — Daniel's Oxford Mass. 365
Essex Mass. Antiquarian i (1897), 161–4; iii (1899), 36
Waldo's Hist. of Tolland Ct. 130
Wyman's Charlestown Mass. Gens. i, 2
Abraham — Essex Antiquarian i
Abrahams — Wyman's Charlestown i, 3
Abram — Essex Antiquarian i
Abrams — Runnel's Sanbornton ii, 7–9
Abramse — Barton Genealogy 156
Achorn — Eaton's Thomaston Me. 128
Acie — Essex Antiquarian i
Acker — American Ancestry ii, 1
Raymond's Tarrytown Monument 101–9
Ruttenber's Newburgh N. Y. 282
Ackerley — Pelletreau's Westchester N. Y. Wills
See also under Akerly
Ackerman — Amer. Ancestry i, 1; vi, 33
Roe's Sketches of Rose N. Y. 206
Ackert — American Ancestry xii, 112
Smith's Rhinebeck N. Y. 194
Ackey — Egle's Hist. of Lebanon Pa. 233–5
Ackley — Field's Hist. of Haddam Ct. 43
Hinman's Connecticut Settlers 18–20
Lapham's History of Rumford Me. 293
Savage's Genealogical Dictionary i, 7
Sedgwick's History of Sharon Ct. 61
Smith Genealogy (1890) 37, 135
Whittemore's Middlesex Co. Ct. 198
Acly — American Ancestry ii, 1
Acres — Austin's R. I. Gen. Dict. 1
Fox's History of Dunstable Mass. 237
Savage's Geneological Dictionary i, 7
Acton — Shourd's Fenwick N. J. 18–27
Acy — Essex Mass. Hist. Coll. xix, 298
Adam — Adam Genealogy (1848) 16 pages
Chamber's Early Germans of N. J. 229
Adams — Adams' Fairhaven Vt. 281–4
Adams Fam. of Kingston Mass. (1861) 64 p
Adams Fam. of Franklin Mass. (1874) 139 p
Adams Fam. of Amherst Mass. (1880) 66 p
Adams Family of Ipswich Mass. (1881) 8 p
Adams Fam., Several Branches (1893) 84 p
Adams and Bradford Ancestry (1894) 11 p.
Adams Family of Derry N. H. (1899) 87 p
Adams Fam. of Charlestown Mass. (1894) 85
Adams Family of Newbury Mass. 1895) 6 p
Adams Family of Braintree (1898) 1238 p
Adams Family of Brookline (1899) 7 pages
Adams' Haven Genealogy 29
Adams' Quincy and Adams Mem. (1841) 9 p
Adams' Works of John Adams i, 6–12
Alden's Coll. of Am. Epitaphs iii, 5
Aldrich's History of Walpole N. H. 185
American Ancestry i, 1; ii, 1; iv, 76, 124, 157, 205; v, 37, 163; vi, 37, 98, 175; vii, 221; viii, 58; ix, 152, 213; x, 191; xi, 9
Anderson's Waterbury Ct. i, app. 5
Ballou's History of Milford Mass. 515–22
Bangor Me. Hist. Mag. vi, 78; viii, 225–7
Barry's Hist. of Framingham Mass. 166
Bass' History of Braintree Vt. 109
Bemis' History of Marlboro N. H. 395–8
Benedict's History of Sutton Mass. 582

Blake's History of Franklin Mass. 228–31
Bradbury's Hist. Kennebunkport Me. 224
Bond's Watertown Mass. 1–3, 547, 673, 946
Bronson's History of Waterbury Ct. 458
Brown's West Simsbury Ct. 7–10
Bulloch Genealogy
Butler's History of Farmington Me. 360–3
Butler's Hist. of Groton Mass. 384
Caulkin's Hist. of New London Ct. 486
Caverly's History of Pittsford Vt. 690
Chandler's History of Shirley Mass. 343
Chappell Genealogy (1895) 187–207
Chappell Genealogy (1900) 342–69
Chute Genealogy, appendix 5–9
Cleveland Genealogy (1879) 208–14
Cleveland Genealogy (1899) 239–41
Cleveland's Hist. Yates Co. N. Y. 610–12
Cochrane's History of Antrim N. H. 333–6
Cogswell's Hist. of Henniker N. H. 440–5
Cushman's Hist. of Sheepscot Me. 353.
Cutler's Hist. of Jaffrey N. H. 213–19
Cutter's Hist. of Arlington Mass. 183–9
Cutter Genealogy 50
Daniel's History of Oxford Mass. 365
Davis' Landmarks of Plymouth Mass. 3
Deane's Hist. of Scituate Mass. 211
Dearborn's Hist. of Salisbury N. H. 442–50
Drake's History of Boston Mass. (1856)
Draper's History of Spencer Mass. 159
Driver Genealogy 514
Eaton's History of Thomaston Me. 129
Eaton Grange (1890) 17–26
Emery's Newbury Mass. Remin. 54
Essex Antiquarian ii, 17–22, 40–5, 62–6, 76–80, 87–92, 111–3; iii, 46, 62, 79, 94; iv, 37
Evans Genealogy (1893) 73–6
Farrow's History of Islesborough Me. 166
Fox's History of Dunstable Mass. 237
Gold's History of Cornwall Ct. 312
Granite Monthly iv, 312
Greene's Todd Genealogy (1867)
Guild's Stiles Genealogy 341
Hale Genealogy 218
Hammatt Papers, Ipswich Mass. 9–11
Hayward's History of Gilsum N. H. 253
Hazen's Hist. of Billerica Mass. 3
Hemenway Genealogical Record 27–33
Hemenway's Vermont Gaz. v, 396
Herrick's History of Gardner Mass. 330
Heywood's Hist. Westminster Mass. 513–6
Hill's History of Mason N. H. 199
Hinman's Connecticut Settlers 20–6
Hodgman's History of Westford Mass. 436
Hollister's History of Pawlet Vt. 156
Hubbard's History of Springfield Vt. 200
Hudson's History of Lexington Mass. 6–8
Hudson's History of Sudbury Mass. 434
Huntington's Stamford Ct. Families 5
Jackson's History of Newton Mass. 231–3
Jameson's Hist. of Medway Mass. 443–51
Joslin's History of Poultney Vt. 197
Kidder's New Ipswich N. H. 289–93
Lancaster's Hist. of Gilmanton N. H. 255
Lapham's Hist. of Rumford Me. 294–300
Lapham's Hist. of Woodstock Me. 170

Leland Genealogy 192–6
Leonard's Hist. of Dublin N. H. 309–11
Lincoln's History of Hingham Mass. ii, 9
Little's History of Weare N. H. 713
Livermore's History of Wilton N. H. 297
Locke Genealogy 48, 60, 148–50
Loomis Genealogy (1880) 519–21, 697–700
Marvin's Hist. of Winchendon Mass. 445
Merrill's History of Acworth N. H. 178
Milliken's Narraguagus Valley Me. 18
Morse Memorial, appendix No. 32
Morse's Sherborn Mass. Settlers 1–9
Munsey's Magazine 1896
Muzzey's Reminiscences
N. E. Hist. and Gen. Reg. vii, 38–45, 351;
    viii, 41, 283–5; ix, 89, 127; x, 89–91;
    xi, 53–60; xiv, 360–3; xv, 244; xviii,
    244; xxxiii, 410–13; xxxiv, 66–9; xliv,
    209–11; xlviii, 190–6; liii, 214–6
N. Y. Gen. and Biog. Record xii, 9–12
Norton's Hist. of Fitzwilliam N. H. 453
Old Northwest Gen. Quarterly i, 21–3
Olin Genealogy by Nye (1892) 160–9
Orcutt's History of Stratford Ct. 1115
Paige's History of Cambridge Mass. 477–9
Parker's Hist. of Londonderry N. H. 254–5
Paxton's Marshall Genealogy 37
Pearson's Schenectady N. Y. Families 1
Pierce's History of Grafton Mass. 443–8
Poore Genealogy 58
Porter's Hartford Ct. Settlers 1–2
Power's History of Sangamon Co. Ill. 76
Putnam's Historical Mag vi, 85–97
Read's History of Swanzey N. H. 271
Richmond Va. Standard i, 44; iii, 15
Robinson's Items of Ancestry (1894) 34–9
Runnel's History of Sanbornton N. H. ii, 9
Salter's History of Monmouth Co. N. J. i
Saunderson's Charlestown N. H. 276
Savage's Genealogical Dictionary vi. 8–16
Sawtelle's Hist. of Townsend Mass. 427–48
Schenck's History of Fairfield Ct. 349
Secomb's History of Amherst N. H. 480
Shattuck's History of Concord Mass. 361
Sibley's History of Union Me. 430
Smith's Hist. of Sunderland Mass. 246
Stearns' Hist. of Ashburnham Mass. 582–94
Stearns' History of Rindge N. H. 523–9
Stiles' History of Windsor Ct. ii, 10–2
Stone's Hist of Hubbardston Mass. 219–21
Temple's Hist. of N. Brookfield Mass. 489
Thayer's Memorial (1835) 37–48, 173–4
Tilley's Mag. of N. E. History i, 237–40
Todd's History of Redding Ct. 173
Trubee Genealogy 93–6
Vinton Memorial 295–302
Vinton's Giles Genealogy 519
Vinton's Richardson Family 772, 884
Virginia Magazine of History iv (1897)
    448–50
Ward Genealogy (1851) 79
Ward's History of Shrewsbury Mass. 212
Washburn's History of Leicester Mass. 343
Washington N. H. History 271–5
Weaver's History of Windham Ct. 29
Wheeler's History of Newport N. H. 285

Whitmore's Copps Hill Epitaphs
Wight Genealogy 15, 58, 60
William and Mary Col. Quarterly v, 159–65
Worcester's History of Hollis N. H. 363
Wyman's Charlestown Mass. Gens. i, 4–14
Addington— Addington Gen. (1850) 5
Leverett Memoir 31–48
New Eng. Hist. and Gen. Reg. iv, 117–21
Savage's Gen. Dict. i, 17–8
Addleman — Young's Wayne Ind. 217
Adee — Baird's Hist. of Rye N. Y. 451.
Adford — Deane's Scituate Mass. 211
Adgate — Baker's Montville Ct. 498
Caulkins' History of Norwich Ct. 155
Hinman's Connecticut Settlers, 27
Perkins' Old Houses of Norwich Ct. 408–10
Perkins' Norwich Ct. Families 5–7
Savage's Gen. Dict. i, 18
Walworth's Hyde Gen. i, 588–96
Adkins — Hinman's Conn. Settlers 27–9
Savage's Gen. Dict. i, 18
Temple Genealogy (1887)
Temple's History of Whately Mass. 195
Timlow's Sketches of Southington Ct. i–iii
Wetmore Genealogy 28
Adrain — Clayton's Union Co. N. J. 507–9
Adsit — Amer. Ancestry ii, 2
Aersen — Nevius Genealogy 137–41, 663–5
Africa — Amer. Ancestry vi, 54
Agard — Orcutt's Torrington Ct. 638
Weaver's History of Windham Ct. 30
Ager — American Ancestry xi, 231
Stearns' Ashburnham Mass. 594
Stearns' History of Rindge N. H. 429.
See also Eager.
Agnew — Clyde's Irish Sett. of Pa. 9
Egle's Notes and Queries, 3d ser. ii, 28
Keith's Provincial Councillors (1883)
Scott Genealogy 19, 245, 312–7
Ahern — Smith's Sunderland 247–9
Aiken — American Ancestry, ii, 2, iv, 105
Bedford N. H. Centennial 279–84
Chase's History of Chester N. H. 462–4
Cochran's History of Antrim N. H. 336–9
Cochrane's Hist. of Francestown N. H. 480
Hemenway's Vermont Gaz. v
Hinman's Connecticut Settlers 29
Paige's History of Hardwick Mass. 322–4
Parker's Hist. of Londonderry N. H. 255–9
Runnel's Sanbornton N. H. ii, 10–12
Secomb's History of Amherst N. H. 481–3
Smith's History of Dutchess Co. N. Y. 498
Wheeler's History of Newport N. H. 286
Ainsworth — Ainsworth Gen. (1894)
Cutter's History of Jaffrey N. H. 211
Egle's Penn. Gens. 2d ed. 1–6
Hinman's Conn. Settlers 29
Longmeadow Mass. Centennial, app. 4
Savage's Gen. Dict. i, 19
Akerly — American Ancestry x, 130, 132
See also Ackerly
Akerman — Robinson's Ancestry 14–6
Akers — Lapham's Norway Me. 455
Akin — American Ancestry xi, 131
Akins — Salter's Monmouth Co. N. J.
Alban — American Ancestry xii, 110

Albee — Ballou's Milford Mass. 522–36
Eaton's History of Thomaston Me. 131
Machias Me. Centennial 152
Randall's Hist. Chesterfield N. H. 209–11
Read's History of Swanzey N. H. 273
Saunderson's Charlestown N. H. 277
Savage's Genealogical Dictionary i, 20
Albertse — Bergen's Kings Co. N. Y. 8
Albertson — Am. Ancestry ix, 72; xi, 66
Bunker's Long Island Genealogies 167–9
Clement's Newtown N. J. Settlers
Davis' Landmarks of Plymouth Mass. 4
Albeson — Deane's Scituate Mass. 211
Albin — Cogswell's Henniker N. H. 445
Albree — Am. Ancestry vii, 209; ix, 22
Brook's History of Medford Mass. 499–501
Albright — Egle's Pa. Gens. 2d ed. 558–61
Albro — American Ancestry xi, 67
Austin's R. I. Gen. Dict. 234.
Austin's Allied Families 1
Newport History Mag. iv, 238–42
Savage's Genealogical Dictionary i, 20
Alburtis — Riker's Newtown N. Y. 395–5
Alcock — Bronson's Waterbury 459–63
Ellis' History of Roxbury Mass. 90
Hayward's Hist. Hancock N. H. 298–300
Hinman's Connecticut Settlers 30
N. E. Hist. and Gen. Reg. xxxvi, 400–2
Prime's Sands Gen. 56–65
Savage's Genealogical Dictionary i, 21
Alcott — Lane Genealogy (1899) 46
Orcutt's Wolcott Ct. 425–38
Tuttle Genealogy (1883) 673
See also Allcott
Alcox — Anderson's Waterbury i, app. 6
Alden — Alden's Amer. Epitaphs ii, iii, iv
Alden Genealogy (1869) 184 pages
Alden Genealogy (1889) 429 pages
Alden Chart (1893) 2x3 feet
Alden-Fuller Record (1896) 1
American Ancestry i, 1; vi, 81; x, 176
Baker's History of Montville Ct. 600–2
Brownell Genealogy (1892) 9
Davis' Landmarks of Plymouth Mass. 4
Eaton's History of Thomaston Me. 131
Ellis Genealogy 364
Freeman's Cape Cod Mass. ii, 222–31
Hemenway's Vermont Gaz. iv, 163
Hines' Lebanon Ct. Address 143
Jennings Genealogy (1899)
Kingman's No. Bridgewater Mass. 443-6
Maine Hist. and Genealogical Rec. vii, 132
Mitchell's Hist. Bridgewater Mass. 85-90
N. E. History and Gen. Register xlvi,
  269–71; li, 427–31; lii, 54– 7, 162–7,
  326–6, 435–40; liv. 180–2
Paige's History of Hardwick Mass. 324–5
Pierce's History of Gorham Me. 153
Robinson's Items of Ancestry (1894) 41
Savage's Genealogical Dictionary i, 23
Sibley's History of Union Me. 430
Thatcher's History of Plymouth Mass. 157
Thayer's Memorial (1835)
Vinton Genealogy 289–95
Walworth's Hyde Genealogy 632
Whitman Genealogy 55

Alderman — Hinman's Ct. Settlers 31
Aldis — Savage's Genealogical Dict. i, 24
Aldrich — American Ancestry viii, 231;
  xi, 14, 164
Austin's R. I. Genealogical Dictionary 1
Austin's Allied Families 3–5
Ballou's History of Milford Mass. 537–9
Ballou Genealogy 350–3
Bassett's Hist. of Richmond N. H. 256–67
Capron Genealogy by Holden 192–8, 235–50
Daniel's History Oxford Mass. 366–8
Hayward's History of Gilsum N. H. 254
Herrick Genealogy (1885) 121
Hubbard's Stanstead Canada 318
McKeen's History of Bradford Vt. 310–8
Mitchell's History of Bridgewater Mass. 90
Mowry Gen. 209–20
Narragansett Historical Register iii, 33–9,
  119–25
Pierce's History of Grafton Mass. 448
Richardson's Woonsocket R. I. 205–20
Read's History of Swanzey N. H. 273–7
Roe's Sketches of Rose N. Y. 130
Savage's Genealogical Dictionary i, 25
Aldridge — Hull Genealogy 68–71
Alexander — Alexander Family of Penn.
  (1878) 220 pages
Alexander Family of New York (1881) 76 p.
Alexander Fam. of Maine (1898) 129 pages
American Ancestry i, 1; iv, 82, 208; vi,
  148; viii, 142; ix, 56; xii, 97
Bemis' Hist. of Warlboro N. H. 398–400
Cabell Genealogy 592–6
Cochrane's History of Antrim N. H. 339, 46
Cogswell's History of Henniker N. H. 445
Craft's History of Whately Mass. 354
Cunnabell Genealogy 69
Davis' Landmarks of Plymouth Mass. 5
De Bow's Review xxvi, 133
Egle's History Reg. Interior Penn. ii, 19–23
Egle's Notes and Queries (1897) 86–7
Essex Antiquarian iii (1899) 142
Foote's Sketches of Virginia ii, 100–2
Goode Genealogy 212, 482
Goodwin's Foote Genealogy 219
Green's Kentucky Families
Hayden's Virginia Genealogies 180, 192
Hayward's History of Gilsum N. H. 254
Hinman's Connecticut Settlers 31
Hyde's History of Brimfield Mass. 469
Janes Genealogy 377–82
Judd's History of Hadley Mass. 447
Merrill's History of Acworth N. H. 179
Morrison Genealogy 389
Morrison's Hist. of Windham N. H. 305–7
N. Y. Gen. and Biog. Record xii, 13–28,
  60–78, 111–23, 155–86
Norton's History of Fitzwilliam N. H. 454
Paxton's Marshall Genealogy 74–6, 248
Plumb's History of Hanover Pa. 387
Power's Sangamon Co. Ill. 76–8
Randall's History of Chesterfield N. H. 212
Read's History of Swanzey N. H. 272
Richmond Va. Standard i, 39; ii, 47–9; iii,
  2, 5, 7, 36, 37
Roe's Sketches of Rose N. Y. 287

Savage's Genealogical Dictionary i, 25
Secomb's History of Amherst N. H. 483
Sheldon's History of Deerfield Mass. ii, 6–8
Slaughter's Randolph Fairfax 2, 100
Smith's History of Sunderland Mass. 249
Stark's History of Dunbarton N. H. 252
Stiles' History of Windsor Ct. ii, 12
Temple's Hist. of Northfield Mass. 385–93
Waddell's AnnalsAugusta Co. Va. 193, 416
Wakefield Genealogy 219
Ward's History of Shrewsbury Mass. 212
Welles' Washington Family 183, 255–9
Wyman's Charlestown Mass. Gens. i, 15
Alford — Brown's West Simsbury 10
Eaton's Annals of Warren Me. 498
Wyman's Charlestown Mass. Gens. i 16
Alger — Alger Gen. (1876) 60 pages
Bemis' History of Marlboro N. H. 400
Boyd's History of Conesus N. Y. 139
Daniels' History of Oxford Mass. 368
Marvin's History Winchendon Mass. 44–5
Mitchell's Bridgewater Mass. 91–3
N. E. Hist. Reg. xxix, 270–2; xxxi, 161–2
Salter's History of Monmouth Co. N. J. ii
Savage's Genealogical Dictionary i, 27
Alison — Allison Genealogy 16–39
Alkire — Power's Sangamon Co. Ill. 78
Allaben — Bouton Genealogy 342–5
Allaire — Bolton's Westchester 676
Allan — Allan Fam. of Me. (1867) 32 pages
American Ancestry iv, 178; vi, 8
Dennysville Me. Centennial 101
Kidder's Mem. of Col. John Allan 25–32
Allard — Adams' Fairhaven Vt. 290
Adams' Haven Genealogy 38
Barry's History of Framingham Mass. 168
Temple's History N. Brookfield Mass. 493
Allcott — Allcott Gen. (1899) 48 pages
Allbe — Hubbard's Springfield Vt. 202
Allds — Cochran's Antrim N. H. 340
Smith's History of Peterborough N. H. 7
Alleman — Egle's Notes and Queries 4th
series, i, 32
Allen — Adams' Fairhaven Vt. 284–8
Aldrich's History of Walpole N. H. 186–9
Allen Family of Boston (1868) 14 pages
Allen Family of Medfield Mass. (1869) 88 p.
Allen Family of Braintree (1872) 251 pages
Allen Fam. of Windsor Ct. (1876) 76 pages
Allen Fam. of Sandwich Mass. (1882) 35 p.
Allen Fam. of Morristown N. J. (1883) 33 p.
Allen Fam. of New Bedford (1887) 21 pages
Allen Fam. of Manchester Mass. (1838) 47 p.
Allens of Manchester, Supp (1891) 24 p.
Allen Family of Boston (1891) 135 pages
Allen Fam. of Medfield Mass. (1896) 80 p.
Allen Fam. of Newbury Mass. (1896) 66 p.
Allen Fam. of Peru N. Y. (1897) 11 pages
Allen Fam. of Ashby Mass. (1898) 27 pages
Allen Fam. of New Haven (1899) 317 pages
American Ancestry i, 1; ii, 2; iv, 131, 171,
180, 208; v, 27; vi, 60, 154, 157; vii,
105, 225, 283; viii, 102, 107, 213; ix,
89, 119; xi, 164, 175, 199; xii, 23
Anderson's Waterbury Ct. i, app. 7
Austin's Ancestries 1

Austin's R. I. Gen. Dictionary 2
Austin's Allied Families 6–11
Babson's History of Gloucester Mass. 55–7
Baker's History of Montville Ct. 430–4
Ballou's History of Milford Mass. 539–42
Bangor Me. History Mag. v, 62–4, 181
Barry's History Framingham Mass. 167–8
Bass' History of Braintree Vt. 110
Bassett's Hist. of Richmond N. H. 267–71
Benedict's History of Sutton Mass. 583
Blake's History of Franklin Mass. 231
Bond's Watertown Mass. Gens. 3–8, 673
Boyd Genealogy 225–32
Boyd's History of Conesus N. Y. 140
Bulkley's Browne Memorial 91–3
Butler's History of Farmington Me. 363–8
Chandler Genealogy 563–6
Clarke's Old King Wm. Co. Va. Families
Cleveland Genealogy 204–12
Cleveland's Yates Co. N. Y. 332–4, 701
Clyde's Irish Settlement Pa. 10
Cogswell's History of Henniker N. H. 446
Corliss' North Yarmouth Me. 600
Cothren's History Woodbury Ct. ii, 1469–71
Craft's Genealogy 291–3
Crosby Genealogy 134
Cunnabell Genealogy 80
Cutter's History of Arlington Mass. 189
Daggett's Hist. of Attleborough Mass. 87
Daniel's History of Oxford Mass. 369
Davis' History of Reading Vt. 117
Davis' History of Bucks Co. Pa. 144
Davis' History of Wallingford Ct. 614;
Davis' Landmarks of Plymouth Mass. 5
Deane's History of Scituate Mass. 212
Dedham History Register xi, 41–4
Draper's History of Spencer Mass. 160
Driver Genealogy 190
Eaton's History of Thomaston Me. 131
Eaton's Annals Warren Me. 2d ed. 499
Egle's Penn. Genealogies 2d ed. 7–14
Essex Antiquarian ii, 135–40, 161–5, 176–81;
iii, 7, 17–25, 37, 174–6; iv, 14–6, 31
Essex Institute Hist. Collections i, 187–8;
xxiv, 223–40, 302–12; xxv, 44–59;
xxvii, 31–55
Freeman's Cape Code Mass. ii, 46, 163
Futhey's History of Chester Co. Pa. 462
Glover Genealogy 401–3
Green Genealogy (1894)
Green's Kentucky Families
Guild's Stiles Genealogy 397
Hammatt Papers, Ipswich Mass. 15
Hatch's History of Industry Me. 471–98
Hayden's Weitzel Genealogy
Hayden's Virginia Genealogies
Hayward's History of Gilsum N. H. 254
Hazen's History of Billerica Mass. 3
Hemenway Gen. Record 68
Heywood's Hist. of Westminster Mass. 517
Hill's History of Mason N. H. 199
Hollister's History of Pawlet Vt. 157–9
Hoyt's Salisbury Mass. Families 31–4
Hubbard's History of Springfield Vt. 198
Hubbard's Stanstead Canada 145
Hudson's History of Lexington Mass. 8

Hyde's History of Brimfield Mass. 367
Jackson's History of Newton Mass. 233
Jameson's History of Medway Mass. 451
Jennings Genealogy (1899)
Joslin's History of Poultney Vt. 198
Kingman's North Bridgewater Mass. 446
Knight's Deacon James Allen (1899) 67 p.
Lapham's History of Bethel Me. 460
Lapham's History Paris Me. 497-500
Leonard's History of Dublin N. H. 311
Littell's Passaic Valley N. J. 3-6
Loomis Genealogy (1880) 675
Maine Genealogist i, 9-14, 60
Merrill's History of Acworth N. H. 180
Middlefield Conn. History
Miner's History of Phelps Purchase 204
Missouri Pioneer Families 126, 237, 301
Mitchell's Bridgewater Mass. 93-9
Morrison's Hist. of Windham N. H. 307
Morse's Sherborn Mass. Settlers 10
Narragansett Hist. Register ii, 44, 279-86
Nevius Genealogy
Newport R. I. Magazine (1883) 191-3
New Eng. Histor. and Genealog. Register
    x, 225; xxv, 144-6; xxx, 444-55; xlvii,
    86; li, 212-4; liv. 349
Norton's History Fitzwilliam N H. 455-7
Orcutt's History of New Milford Ct. 639
Orcutt's History of Stratford Ct. 1115
Orcutt's History of Torrington Ct. 639
Paige's History of Hardwick Mass. 325-7
Pierce's History of Grafton Mass. 449
Power's Sangamon Co. Ill. Settlers 79
Putnam's Hist. Mag. i, 286-90; ii. 119-27
Rogers Genealogy (1897) 8-12, 31
Salem Press Hist. and Gen. Rec. ii, 102-6
Salem N. Y. Book of History 38-41
Salter's History of Monmouth Co. N. J. ii
Saunderson's Charlestown N. H. 278-80
Savage's Genealogical Dictionary i, 28-38
Sheldon's Hist. of Deerfield Mass. ii, 8, 25
Smith's History of Sunderland Mass. 250
Spooner Genealogy i, 359-84
Sprague's History of Gloversville N. Y. 107
Stearns' History of Ashburnham Mass. 594
Stearns' History of Rindge N. H. 429-32
Stiles' History of Windsor Ct. ii, 13-27
Stoddard's J. Allen Biog. (1883) 42-9
Stone's Hist. of Hubbardston Mass. 221-4
Strong Genealogy 967-70
Temple's Hist. of N. Brookfield Mass. 494
Temple's History of Brookfield Mass. 393
Temple's History of Palmer Mass. 408-12
Temple's History of Whately Mass. 196
Thompson Genealogy (1890) 236-8
Thurston's History of Winthrop Me. 172
Timlow's Sketches of Southington Ct. 13
Vinton Memorial 303-8
Wall's Remin. of Worcester Mass. 347-50
Ward's Rice Family 15, 16-29
Ward's History Shrewsbury Mass. 214-21
Washburn's History Leicester Mass. 343
Watkins Genealogy, 19
Weaver's History of Windham Ct. 30-9
Wheeler's History of Newport N. H. 287-9
Whipple-Hill Families (1897) 72

Whitman Genealogy 194-6, 208-13
Whittemore's Orange N. J. 380
Williams' Hist. of Danby Vt. 101
Wyman's Charlestown Mass. i, 16-9
Young's Chautauqua Co. N. Y. 350-2
Aller — Chambers' N. J. Germans 230
Allerton — Allerton Genealogy (1888) 166
Allerton Genealogy (1890) 7 pages
Allerton Genealogy 2d ed. (1900) 149 pages
American Ancestry iv, 128
Davis' Landmarks Plymouth Mass. 6
Hartwell Genealogy (1887) 39
Huntting's Hist. of Pine Plains N. Y. 316
Lee Genealogy (1895) 529
Mitchell's Hist. Bridgewater Mass. 356
N. E Hist. Reg. viii, 280; xliv, 290-6
Savage's Genealogical Dictionary i, 38
Taylor's Some Notable Families 38-43
Alley — Cogswell's Henniker N. H. 446
Essex Antiquarian iii (1899) 49-52
Lawrence and Bartlett Memorial 158
Savage's Genealogical Dictionary i, 39
Wyman's Charlestown Mass. Gens. i, 19
Alleyn — Savage's Geneal. Dict. i, 43-5
Alleyne — Winslow Memorial i, 286
Alline — Milliken's Narraguagus 15
Alling — Allen Genealogy (1883) 21-4
Alling Genealogy (1899) 317 pages
American Ancestry viii, 206
Chapman's Trowbridge Genealogy 33, 45
Davis' History of Wallingford Ct. 614
Dodd's History of East Haven Ct. 101
Hamden Ct. History 237-8
Nash Genealogy 19
Savage's Genealogical Dictionary i, 40
Tuttle Family of Conn. 620
Allis — American Ancestry ii, 2
Craft's History of Whately Mass. 354-64
Judd's History of Hadley Mass. 447
Hinman's Connecticut Settlers 48
Kellogg's Mem. Elder John White 101
Savage's Genealogical Dictionary i, 41
Sheldon's History of Deerfield Mass. 25-8
Smith's History of Sunderland Mass. 250-2
Temple's History of Whately Mass. 196-8
Allison — Allison Gen. (1893) 312 pages
Barlow Genealogy 346-95
Clyde's Irish Settlement Pa. 11
Egle's Notes and Queries 3d ser. iii, 164
Leonard's History of Dublin N. H. 312
Morse Memorial Appendix No. 11
Power's History of Sangamon Co. Ill. 80
Smith's History of Peterborough N. H. 8
Young's History of Chautauqua Co. N. Y.
Allmy — Salter's Monmouth N. J. iii
Allyn — Baker's Montville Ct. 514-7
American Ancestry xi, 231; xii, 76
Allyn Genealogy (1896) 20 pages
Candee Genealogy 121-40
Caulkin's History of Norwich Ct. 156
Doty Genealogy 41
Freeman's History Cape Cod Mass. ii, 274
Hinman's Connecticut Settlers 41-6
Hurd's History of New London Co. Ct. 533
Loomis Genealogy (1880) 365-7, 557, 805
Orcutt's History of Torrington Ct. 639-42

Stiles' History of Windsor Ct. ii, 27-34
Swift's Barnstable Families i, 5-12
Almy — Almy Genealogy (1897) 136 pages
American Ancestry iv, 189
Austin's R. I. Genealogical Dictionary 236
Spooner Genealogy i, 403
Alpock — Chambers' N. J. Germans 231-4
Alricks — American Ancestry vi, 93
Egle's Penn. Genealogies 2d ed. 15-26
New York Genealogical and Biographical
Record xxiv, 125
Alsobrook — Richmond Standard iv, 3
Alsop — N. E. Hist. Register xliv. 366-9
Lamb's History of New York City i, 740
Riker's Annals of Newtown N. Y. 334-8
Savage's Genealogical Dictionary i, 45
Whittemore's Middlesex Co. Ct. 156
Alston — Clute's Staten Island N. Y. 338
Alter—Egle's Notes and Queries 3d series
i, 521-4
Alverson — Daniels' Oxford Mass. 370
Alvord — American Ancestry xi, 165
Boyd's Winchester Ct. 62-5, 397
Burke and Alvord Genealogy (1864) 87-177
Eaton's Annals of Warren Me. 375
Hinman's Connecticut Settlers 32
Judd's History of Hadley Mass. 448
Kellogg's White Descendants 46, 72
Matthew's History of Cornwall Ct. 284
Nash Genealogy 85
Phœnix's Whitney Genealogy i, 712
Savage's Genealogical Dictionary i, 46
Stiles' History of Windsor Ct. ii, 34-7
Temple's History of Northfield Mass. 398
Whittemore's Hist. Middlesex Co. Ct. 199
Alward — American Ancestry vi 10
Bouton Genealogy 420-3
Littell's Passaic Valley Genealogies 7-11
Alworth — Aylsworth Genealogy 454
Amadon — Bassett's Richmond N. H. 271
Norton's History Fitzwilliam N. H. 457-9
Ambler — Ambler Gen. (1890) 23 pages
American Ancestry ii, 2; iv, 135
Hinman's Connecticut Settlers 48
Huntington's Stamford Ct. Families 5
Meade's Old Churches of Virginia i, 103
N. E. Histor. and Gen. Reg. xxxix, 333
Paxton's Marshall Gen. 42-5, 251, 262-6
Richmond Va. Standard i, 39; iii, 44
Roberts' Richland Families 128-31
Savage's Genealogical Dictionary i, 48
Ambrose — Bouton's Concord N. H. 631
Chase's History of Chester N. H. 464
Essex Antiquarian (1899) iii, 74
Hatch's History of Industry Me. 498
Hoyt's Salisbury Mass. Families 34
Savage's Genealogical Dictionary i, 48
Amerman — American Ancestry xii, 117
Bergen's Kings County N. Y. 10
Chambers' Early Germans of N. J. 234
Amery — Emery's Reminiscences 134-9
Ames — American Ancestry i. 2; iv, 43; xii
Ames Family of Mass. (1851) chart 2x4
Ames Family of N. H. (1890) 55 pages
Ames Ancestry (1898) 15 pages
Andrews' History of New Britain Ct. 188

Ball's Lake Co. Ind. 444
Bangor Historical Magazine v. 43-5
Bradford Genealogy (1898) 12-4
Butler's History of Groton Mass. 384, 468
Carter's History of Pembroke N. H. ii, 7-11
Coffin's History of Boscawen N. H. 466-8
Davis' Landmarks of Plymouth Mass. 6
Dearborn's History of Parsonfield Me. 365
Eaton's History of Thomaston Me. 132-4
Essex Antiquarian iii (1899) 88-90
Farrow's Hist. of Islesborough Me. 166-8
Hatch's History of Industry Me. 500
Hayward's Hist. of Hancock N. H. 300-9
Hill's History of Mason N. H. 199
Hinman's Connecticut Settlers 49-51
Joslyn's History of Poultney Vt. 199
Keith Genealogy (1889) 62-71
Kingman's North Bridgewater 437-43
Lapham's History of Norway Me. 455
Leonard's History of Dublin N. H. 312
Mitchell's Bridgewater Mass. 99-105
Montague Genealogy 553
New Eng. Historical and Gen. Reg. xvi,
255-7
Paige's History of Cambridge Mass. 479
Poor's Historical Researches 83, 120
Savage's Genealogical Dictionary i, 49
Smith's History of Peterborough N.H. 9-13
Stearns' History of Ashburnham Mass. 595
Sutliff Genealogy (1897) 27-32
Washington N. H. History 275
Weaver's History of Windham Ct. 39-41
Winsor's History of Duxbury Mass. 220
Worcester's History of Hollis N. H. 364
Amidon — Bass' Hist. of Braintree Vt. 110
Randall's Hist. of Chesterfield N. H. 212-6
Temple's North Brookfield Mass. 495.
Amidown — Daniel's Oxford 371
Ammidown — Ammidown's Coll. ii, 225
Ammidown Genealogy (1877) 54 pages
Child Genealogy 346-8
Hayward's History of Gilsum N. H. 256
Paige's History of Hardwick Mass. 328
Ammonet — Southern History Association
Publications iii (1899) 35-40
Amory — Amory Gen. (1856) 30 pages
New Eng. Hist. and Gen. Reg. x, 59-65
Whitmore's Heraldic Journal ii, 101-10
Wyman's Charlestown Mass. Gens. i, 20
Amos — Power's Sangamon Co. Ill. 81
Amrine — Parthemore Genealogy 101
Amsbury — Eaton's Thomaston Me. 134
Amsdell — See Amsden
Amsden — Davis' Reading Vt. 118-20
Hemenway's Vermont Gazetteer v, 161
Hudson's History of Marlboro' Mass. 308
Huron and Erie Counties Ohio 391
Judd's History of Hadley Mass. 448
New Eng. Hist. and Gen. Reg. xv, 21-3
Paige's History of Cambridge Mass. 479
Rice Genealogy 243
Savage's Genealogical Dictionary i, 50
Sheldon's History of Deerfield Mass. ii, 29
Temple's History North Brookfield Mass.
495
Amy — Hubbard's Stanstead Can. 192

Anable — American Ancestry xi, 18; xii
Anable Genealogy (1879) 20 pages
Anders — Kriebel's Schwenksfelders 46–69
Anderson — American Ancestry ii, 3; vii,
239; viii, 230; xi. 15, 197; xii
Amer. Hist. Mag. of Nashville iii, 240–59
Anderson's Waterbury Ct. i, app. 8
Anderson Family of Pa. (1880) 80 pages
Baird's History of Rye N. Y. 452
Champion Genealogy 48
Chase's History of Chester N. H. 464
Cincinnati Ohio Criterion (1888) ii, 313
Cleveland's History of Yates Co. N. Y. 512
Cochrane's Hist. Francestown N. H. 483
Cooley's Trenton N. J. Settlers 5–7
Crawford Family of Virginia 87–9
Eaton's Annals of Warren Me. 499–501
Eaton's History of Candia, N. H. 51–3
Egle's Penn. Genealogies 2d ed. 27–36
Egle's Notes and Queries 3d series iii, 366–8
Futhey & Cope's Chester County Pa. 463
Gilmer's Georgians 103
Green's Kentucky Families
Hanson's Old Kent Md. 367
Hyde's Hist. Address at Ware Mass. 52
Lincoln's History of Hingham Mass. ii, 10
Morrison's Hist. of Windham N. H. 307–14
New Eng. Histor. and Gen. Reg. xx, 198
Opdyck Genealogy 180–4
Parker's Hist. Londonderry N. H. 259–62
Paxton's Marshall Genealogy
Pompey N. Y. Reunion 251
Power's Sangamon County Ill. 83
Richmond Va. Standard ii, 49; iii, 24, 28,
31, 33, 35, 39, 48
Salisbury Family Memorials (1885) 535–60
Salter's History of Monmouth Co. N. J. iii
Savage's Genealogical Dictionary i, 50
Sheldon's History of Deerfield Mass. ii, 30
Stiles' History of Windsor Ct. ii, 37
Thomas Genealogy (1896) 556c–f
Weaver's History of Windham Ct. 41
Wheeler's History of Brunswick Me. 827
Wight Genealogy 129
Andress — Clyde's Irish Settlers Pa. 11
Andrew — Austin's R. I. Gen. Dict. 3
Burnham's Andrew Genealogy (1869)
Eaton Grange (1890) 65
Essex Antiquarian iii (1899) 136–8
Gold's History of Cornwall Ct. 320–3
Nason's Life of J. A. Andrew (1868) 76 p.
New Eng. History and Gen. Reg. xxiii, 11
Paige's History of Cambridge Mass. 480
Plumb's History of Hanover Penn. 387
Worthen's Hist. of Sutton N. H. 1087–1110
Andrews — American Ancestry i, 2; ii, 3;
iv, 80, 82, 188; vi, 40, 45; vii, 123; viii,
108; x, 36; xi, 165
Anderson's Waterbury Ct. i, app. 8
Andrews Fam. of Lancaster Pa. (1867) 8 p.
Andrews Family of Farmington Ct. (1872)
652 pages
Andrews Fam. of Taunton Mass. (1887) 86 p.
Andrews Family of Ipswich Mass. (1890)
234 pages
Andrews Fam. of Maryland (1893) 42 pages

Andrews Fam. of Taunton (1898) 8 pages
Andrews' New Britain Ct. 151, 195–7, 233
Austin's R. I. Gen. Dictionary 3
Babson s History of Gloucester Mass. 57
Ballou's History of Milford Mass. 542
Bangor Me. Historical Magazine viii, 104
Boyd's Annals of Winchester Ct. 105–7
Bunker's Long Island Genealogies 170
Cleveland's Hist. of Yates Co. N. Y. 485–7
Cochrane's Hist. of Francestown N. H. 484
Cogswell's History of Henniker N. H. 447
Cogswell's History New Boston N. H. 437–9
Davis' History of Wallingford Ct. 437–9
Dodd's History of East Haven Ct. 101
Eaton's Annals of Warren Me. 501–4
Eaton's History of Thomaston Me. 135
Eaton Grange (1890) 13–29
Egle's Penn. Genealogies 2d ed. 3–6
Essex Antiquarian iii (1899) 97–103, 113–9,
155
Goode Genealogy 93, 306–11, 475
Green's Kentucky Families
Hale's Lawrence Family 10–3
Hammatt Papers, Ipswich Mass. 11–3
Hinman's Connecticut Settlers 51–3
Huntington's Stamford Ct. Families 6
Hyde's History of Brimfield Mass. 368
Lapham's History of Bethel Me. 461
Lapham's History of Norway Me. 457
Lapham's History of Paris Me. 493–7
Lapham's History of Rumford Me. 300
Lapham's History of Woodstock Me. 170
Lincoln's Hist. of Hingham Mass. ii, 10–5
Loomis Genealogy (1880) 715–9
Machias Me. Centennial 152
Maine Historical and Genealogical Re-
corder iii, 194–9, 257–62; iv, 8–14,
77–83, 209–17, 236–44; v, 22–33, 162–7;
ix, 318
New Eng. Historical and Genealogical
Register xl, 21–6; li, 453–9; lii, 16–23
Perley's History of Boxford Mass. 24–7
Pierce's History of Grafton Mass. 450
Randall's Hist. of Chesterfield N. H. 216
Ransom Genealogy 40
Roe's Sketches of Rose N. Y. 141
Savage's Genealogical Dictionary i, 51–7
Schenck's History of Fairfied Ct. 350
Smith's History of Sunderland Mass. 252
Thomas Family (1896) 194
Timlow's Sketches Southington Ct. 3–12
Tuttle Genealogy 127–30
Vinton's Richardson Memorial 555
Walker Family 215
Ward's History of Shrewsbury Mass. 221–5
Wyman's Charlestown Mass. Gens. i, 21
Andries — Bergen's Kings Co. N. Y. 11
Andross — McKeen's Bradford 172–9
Stiles' History of Windsor Ct. ii, 38
Androvette — Clute's Staten Island 339
Andrus — American Ancestry ii, 3
Andrews' New Britain Ct. 139, 166–8, 172
Chandler Genealogy 310
Cleveland's Yates Co. N. Y. 521–4, 685–7
Hinman's Connecticut Settlers 54–6
Hollister's Pawlet Vt. 159

Joslin's History of Poultney Vt. 200
New England Hist. and Gen. Reg. xv, 242
Timlow's Sketches of Southington Ct. 3-12
Williams' History of Danby Vt. 103
Angell — American Ancestry ii, 3
Angell Genealogy (1872) 209 pages
Austin's Ancestral Dictionary 1
Austin's Ancestries 101
Austin's R. I. Genealogical Dictionary 4
Daniel's History of Oxford Mass. 372
Driver Genealogy 346
Savage's Genealogical Dictionary i, 57
Wheeler's History of Newport N. H. 289
Young's Chautauqua Co. N. Y. 416-8
Angeny — Wismer Genealogy 94-116
Angevine — Bolton's Westchester 706
Joslin's History of Poultney Vt. 200
Anger — Dodd's East Haven Ct. 102
Angier — Barry's Framingham 168
Baylie's History of New Plymouth iv, 89
Bond's History of Watertown Mass. 8, 674
Hudson's History of Lexington Mass. 8
Merrill's History of Acworth N. H. 180-2
Mitchell's Hist. of Bridgewater Mass. 105
Norton's Hist. of Fitzwilliam N. H. 459-62
Paige's History of Cambridge Mass. 481
Stearn's History of Ashburnham Mass. 595
Wyman's Charlestown Mass. Gens. i, 22
Angus — American Ancestry i, 2
Cleveland's Hist. of Yates Co. N. Y. 181-4
Annable — Deane's Scituate Mass. 213
Ellis Genealogy 92-6, 365-70
Essex Antiquarian iii (1899), 169
Freeman's Hist. of Cape Cod Mass. ii, 272
Hammatt Papers of Ipswich 12
Savage's Genealogical Dictionary i, 58
Swift's Barnstable Families i, 13-20
Annan — Smith's Peterborough 14
Annas — Lapham's Bethel Me. 462-4
Annes — American Ancestry vii, 193, 208
Annesley — American Ancestry i, 2
Annin — Annin Family Meet. (1866) 17 p.
Annis — Eaton's Annals Warren Me. 504
Essex Antiquarian iii (1899), 184-7
Morrison's History of Windham N. H. 314
Savage's Genealogical Dictionary i, 59
Anson — Clark Genealogy (1892) 77
Antes — Dotterer's Perkiomen Pa. i, 51; iii, 6-9
Egle's Notes and Queries (1898) 222-6
Anthoine — Cochrane's Antrim 341
Anthon — Anthon Genealogy (1872) 22 p.
Anthony — Austin's Ancestries 3
Austin's R. I. Genealogical Dictionary 4
Chambers' Early Germans of N. J. 235
Cooley's Settlers of Trenton N. J. 7
Gifford's Our Patronymics 23
Hayward's History of Hancock N. H. 310
Narragansett Historical Register i, 253
N. England Hist. and Gen. Reg. xxxi, 416
Peck and Earll's Fall River Mass. 223
Roome Genealogy 222-50
Savage's Genealogical Dictionary i, 59-60
Smith (Rev. Wm.) Life of ii, 546
Antill — Antill Genealogy (1899) 36 pages
N. Eng. Hist. Reg. xix, 165

Antle — Power's Sangamon Co. Ill. 84
Antonides — Salter's Monmouth N. J.
Antram — Savage's Geneal. Dict. i, 60
Antrim — Salter's Monmouth N. J. iv
Antrobus — Thomas Genealogy (1896) 196
Apgar — Chamber's N. J. Germans 236-43
Apley — American Ancestry ii, 5
Aplin — American Ancestry iv, 28
Apple — Davis' Bucks Co. Pa. 571
Eyerman Ancestors (1898)
Appleby — Daniel's Oxford 373
Applegate — Amer. Anc. viii, 41; xi, 59
Bergen's Kings Co. N. Y. Settlers 13
Salter's History of Monmouth Co. N. J. iv
Savage's Genealogical Dictionary i, 60
Appleman — Mellick Genealogy 705
Chambers' Early Germans of N. J. 243
Harris Family of New Jersey (1888) 180-97
Appleton — American Ancestry vi, 103
Appleton Fam. of Ipswich Mass. (1850) 183
Appleton Family Chart (1864) 24-30
Appleton Family Monuments (1867) 30 p.
Appleton Family of Boston (1873) 42 pages
Appleton Family of Boston (1874) 54 pages
Bangor Me. Historical Magazine vi, 273
Cutts Genealogy 112
Essex Antiquarian (1900) iv, 1-6, 26-30
Hammatt Papers, Ipswich Mass. 16-22
Heraldic Journal by Whitmore i, 97-9
Kidder's New Ipswich N. H. 294-329
Leonard's Hist. of Dublin N. H. 313-5
New England Hist. & Gen. Reg. xxv, 294; xxvii, 36-40
Paiges' History of Cambridge Mass. 482
Ridlon's Saco Valley Me. Families 445
Savage's Genealogical Dictionary i, 60-2
Secomb's History of Amherst N. H. 484
Temple's History of No. Brookfield Mass.
Applin — Bond's Watertown Mass. 9
Read's History of Swanzey N. H. 278-80
Savage's Genealogical Dictionary i; 62
Temple's History of Palmer Mass. 407
Apthorp — American Ancestry v, 4
Bridgeman's Kings Chapel Epit. 276-81
Wentworth Genealogy i, 519-21
Arbuckle — Secomb's Amherst 485
Archer — Am. Ancestry ii, 4; vi, 165
Bolton's Westchester County N. Y ii, 707
Driver Genealogy 217-29
Essex Antiquarian iv, 33-7
Heraldic Journal by Whitmore iii, 71
Meade's Old Families of Va. 198
Millikin's Narraguagus Valley Me. 19
Power's Sangamon Co. Ill. Settlers 85
Richmond Va. Critic (1888)
Richmond Va. Standard iii, 39
Robertson's Pocahontas Descendants
Savage's Genealogical Dictionary i, 62
Sullivant Genealogy (1874) 81-4
Archibald — Hayward's Hancock 311
Miller's Colchester County N. S. 34-108
Morrison's Hist. of Windham N. H. 315
Aree — Chambers' N. J. Germans 243
Arents — Bergen's Kings Co. N. Y. 11
Arey — Bangor Historical Mag. iv, 211
Dearborn's History of Salisbury N. H. 450

Eaton's History of Thomaston Me. 135
Freeman's Hist. of Cape Cod Mass. ii, 163
Armatage — American Ancestry i, 2
Armington — Amer. Anc. v, 150; xi, 138
New England Hist. and Gen. Reg. xxii, 54
Armistead — Armistead Gen. (1899) 23 p.
Carter Family Tree
Lee Genealogy (1895) 531
Hayden's Virginia Genealogies 530
Keith's Harrison Ancestry 13–21
Paxton's Marshall Genealogy 250, 316
Richmond's Standard ii, 38, 41; iii, 38
Slaughter's St. Mark's Parish 184
Wm. and Mary College Quar. vi, 31–234
Armitage — Savage's Gen. Dictionary i, 63
Armour — Morrison's Windham 315–7
Arms — American Ancestry iii, 147
Arms Genealogy (1877) 57 pages
Hubbard's Stanstead Canada 141
Hubbard's History of Springfield Vt. 203
Hudson's History of Lexington Mass. 9
Judd's History of Hadley Mass. 448
Kellogg's White Memorial 100
Nash Genealogy 43
Savage's Genealogical Dictionary i, 63
Sheldon's Hist. of Deerfield Mass. ii, 31–46
Smith's History of Sunderland Mass. 253
Strong Genealogy 1318–22
Armsbee — Savage's Gen. Dictionary i, 63
Armsby — Benedict's Sutton Mass. 583
Armstrong — American Ancestry iii, 3
Armstrong Gen. (1883) 19 p. reprint
Armstrong Genealogy (1895) 201 pages
Calnek's History of Annapolis N. S. 465
Cleveland's Hist. of Yates Co. N. Y. 740
Clyde's Irish Settlement, Pa. 12
Cope Family 90–9, 191–7
Davis' History of Buck's County Pa. 554
Eager's History of Orange Co. N. Y. 427
Hinman's Connecticut Settlers 57
Joslin's History of Poultney Vt. 201
Morrison's Hist. of Windham N. H. 317–26
Paxton's Marshall Genealogy
Power's Sangamon Co. Ill. Settlers 87
Roe's Sketches of Rose N. Y. 12
Savage's Genealogical Dictionary i, 63
Slaughter's St. Mark's Parish 164
Vail and Armstrong Genealogy (1894)
Walworth's Hyde Genealogy i, 665–9
Weaver's History of Windham Ct 41
Worthen's History of Sutton N. H. 600
Arnold — American Ancestry ii, 4; iv,
   110; vi, 31; viii, 160; ix, 210, 214; xi, 166
Aldrich's History of Walpole N. H. 189
Anderson's Waterbury Ct. i app. 9
Arnold Tree of R. I. (1877) 24–30
Arnold Genealogy (1880) 16 p., reprint
Austin's Ancestral Dictionary 2–4
Austin's R. I. Genealogical Dict. 240–7
Austin's Allied Families 12–20
Ballou Genealogy 107–9
Barry's Hist. of Framingham Mass. 170
Bartlett's Wanton Family 141
Bassett's History of Richmond N. H. 273
Benedict's History of Sutton Mass. 583
Boyd's History of Conesus N. Y. 141

Capron Gen. by Holden 198–200, 251–6
Collin's History of Hillsdale N. Y. app. 30
Daniel's History of Oxford Mass. 373
Eaton's History of Thomaston Me. 136
Field's History of Haddam Ct. 43
Freeman's Hist. of Cape Cod Mass. ii, 187
Futhey and Cope's Chester Co. Pa. 464
Glover Genealogy 338
Greene Genealogy (1894)
Hayward's History of Gilsum N. H. 256
Hemenway's Vermont Gazetteer v
Hinman's Connecticut Settlers 58–61
Hudson's History of Marlboro Mass. 309
Hudson's History of Sudbury Mass. 435
Jones' History of N. Y. in Rev. War 746
Loomis' Genealogy (1880) 683
Munsell's Historical Coll. of Albany iv, 94
Narragansett Hist. Reg iii, 43–7; v, 116–32
New England Hist. and Gen. Reg. xxxiii,
   432–8; xxxiv, 196–8
Orcutt's Hist. of Stratford Ct. 11–6
Paige's History of Hardwick Mass. 329
Perkins Old Houses of Norwich Ct. 411
Rhode Island Hist. Soc. Coll. iii, 294
Richardson's Woonsocket R. I. 187–220
Salter's History of Monmouth Co. N. J. v
Savage's Genealogical Dictionary i, 64–7
Thayer's Memorial (1835) 49–52
Tuttle Family 329
Weaver's History of Windham Ct. 42–4
Windsor's History of Duxbury Mass. 221
Wyman's Charlestown Mass. Gens. i, 23
Arnst — Anderson's Waterbury Ct. i, 9
Arp — Magennis Genealogy 115–7
Arnoux — American Ancestry vi, 23
Arrowsmith — Salter's Monmouth N. J.
Arser — N. Y. Gen. Rec. xxvi, 134–8
Artcher — American Ancestry i, 2
Arthur — Ely Genealogy 171–3
Asbury — Binney Genealogy 93–5
Welles' Washington Genealogy 241
Wyman's Charlestown Mass. Gens. i, 24
Ash — Lamborn Genealogy 297
Salisbury Mass. Families by Hoyt 35
Ashbridge — Futhey's Chester Pa. 465
Sharpless Genealogy 139
Ashby — Essex Inst. Coll. xvi, 88–90
Hartwell Genealogy (1895) 134–9
Hayden's Virginia Genealogies 449–53
Savage's Genealogical Dictionary i, 67
Temple's Hist. No. Brookfield Mass. 496
Ashcraft — Craft's Whately 364–5
Savage's Genealogical Dictionary i, 68
Temple's History of Whately Mass. 198
Ashe — Bellinger Genealogy 31
Wheeler's North Carolina 279
Asher — Smith's Rhinebeck N. Y. 196
Ashfield — N. Y. Gen. Rec. xxix, 92
Ashlett — Savage's Gen. Dictionary i. 69
Ashley — American Ancestry ii, 4; vi, 184
Ashley Genealogy (1896) 472 pages
Champion Genealogy 218
Dwight Genealogy 820–4
Goodwin's Olcott Family 44
Hinman's Connecticut Settlers 61–73
Joslin's History of Poultney Vt. 202–4

13

Longmeadow Mass. Centennial app. 4
N. E. Hist. Gen. Reg. ii, 394; xxxi, 318
Pond Genealogy (1875) 15-8
Savage's Genealogical Dictionary i, 68
Sheldon's Hist of Deerfield Mass. ii, 46-50
Smith's History of Sunderland Mass. 255
Weaver's History of Windham Ct. 44-7
West Springfield Mass. Centennial 114
Ashman — Egle's Notes and Queries 3d
   ser. ii, 418
Ashmead — Martin's Chester Pa. 441
Potts Genealogy (1895) 51
Wiswell's Ashmead Sermon (1870) 35
Ashton — American Ancestry iv, 231
Austin's Ancestries iii
Austin's R. I. Genealogical Dictionary 5
De Bows' Review xxvi, 131
Hayden's Virginia Genealogies 630-3
Salter's Hist. of Monmouth Co. N. J. vi
Savage's Genealogical Dictionary i, 69
Wm. and Mary College Quarterly vi, vii,
   115-9, 174-8
Askam — Plumb's Hanover Pa. 388
Askin — Hall Genealogy (1892) 88-91
Aspenwall — Montague Genealogy 445-7
Storrs Genealogy 463-5
Weaver's History of Windham Ct. 47
Wentworth Genealogy i, 464-6
Asper — American Ancestry ix, 229
Aspinwall — Amer. Ancestry ix, 240
Bowens of Woodstock Ct. 215-7
Breck Genealogy 57-9
Hinman's Connecticut Settlers 74
N. E. Hist. and Gen. Reg. xlvii, 342-8
N. Y. Gen. and Biog. Rec. xxvi, 26
Savage's Genealogical Dictionary i, 69-71
Wood's Brookline Mass. Sketches 70-8
Asten — Hill's Hist. of Mason N. H. 200
Astor — Green's Todd Genealogy
N. Y. Gen. Rec. xxii, 115-27; xxiii, 15-8
Astwood — Ellis' Hist. of Roxbury 91
Savage's Genealogical Dictionary i, 71
Atchinson — Longmeadow Centennial 5
Turner's Phelps Purchase N. Y. 419
Athern — Savage's Gen. Dict. i, 72
Atherton — Bassett's Richmond 273-6
Chandler's Hist. of Shirley Mass. 344-7
Hazen's History of Billerica Mass. 4
N. E. Hist. and Gen. Reg. xxxv, 67-72
Paige's History of Cambridge Mass. 579
Pope Genealogy 322
Randall's Hist. of Chesterfield N. H. 217-20
Savage's Genealogical Dictionary i, 72
Secomb's History of Amherst N. H. 486-8
Sedgwick's Hist. of Sharon Ct. 61
Sheldon's Hist. of Deerfield Mass. ii, 50-2
Warren's Hist. of Waterford M. 227-9
Wentworth Genealogy i, 195
Atkins — Am. Ancestry viii, 103; xii, 75
Anderson's Waterbury Ct. i, app. 9
Atkins Genealogy (1891) 154 pages
Atkin's History of Hawley Mass. 65
Craft's History of Whately Mass. 365-8
Eaton's Annals of Warren Me. 504
Emery's Newbury Mass. Reminiscences
Freeman's Cape Cod Mass. ii,164, 359

Middlefield Ct. History
Orcutt's History of Wolcott Ct. 439-45
Rich's History of Truro Mass. 519
Savage's Genealogical Dictionary i, 73
Sears Genealogy 60
Timlow's Sketches Southington Ct. 1-3
Vinton's Giles Genealogy 135-6, 146-8
Whitmore's Copps Hill Epitaphs
Atkinson — Atkinson Gen. (1890) 40 pages
Buxton Me. Centennial 183-8
Clarke's Old King Wm. Co. Va. Families
Coffin's History of Boscawen N. H. 468-76
Hatch's History of Industry Me. 501-7
Hinman's Connecticut Settlers 75
Little Genealogy 120-9, 281-4
Missouri Pioneer Families 198
Ridlon's Saco Valley Me. Families 447-52
Runnel's Hist. Sanbornton N. H. ii, 12-5
Savage's Genealogical Dictionary 74
Slaughter's Bristol Parish Va. 137-40
Smith's Genealogy of Wm. Smith 38-50
Wentworth Genealogy i, 318-22
Whitmore's Heraldic Journal 119-21
Atlee — American Ancestry xi, 15
Atlee Family (1884) 130 pages
Holstein Genealogy
Atterbury — Bakewell Genealogy 14-24
Attwater — Corliss' N. Yarmouth Me.
Atwater — Am. Ancestry iii, 3; ix, 232
Anderson's Waterbury Ct. i, app. 9
Atwater Genealogy (1851) 30 pages
Atwater Genealogy, new edition (1873) 64 p
Bagg and Atwater Ancestry (1895) 4 pages
Collin's Hist. of Hillsdale N. Y. App. 31
Davis's History of Wallingford Ct. 626-34
Dickerman Genealogy 158, 346, 574
Dwight's Strong Genealogy 83-6
Hinman's Connecticut Settlers 76
Orcutt's History of Torrington Ct. 642
Savage's Genealogical Dictionary i, 75
Timlow's Sketches Southington Ct. 14-7
Tuttle Family of Connecticut 31-3, 621-5
Wentworth Genealogy ii, 712-4
Atwell — American Ancestry v, 172
Atwell Genealogy (1896) 10 pages
Baker's History of Montville Ct. 278-88
Caulkin's History of N. London Ct. 305
Corliss' North Yarmouth Me.
Savage's Genealogical Dictionary i, 76
Vinton's Memorial Families 204
Worcester's History of Hollis N. H. 364
Atwood — Allison Genealogy 73-5
American Ancestry ii, 4; x, 183; xi, 67
Atwood Genealogy (1888) 42 pages
Ballou's History of Milford Mass. 544
Bangor Historical Magazine iv, 211
Bedford N. H. Centennial 284-5
Brownell Genealogy (1892) ii, 1-8
Cochrane's History of Antrim N. H. 342-4
Cochrane's Hist. Francestown N. H. 484-6
Cothren's Woodbury Ct. i, 490-9; ii, 1471
Daniel's History of Oxford Mass. 374
Davis' Landmarks Plymouth Mass. 7-9
Freeman's Cape Cod Mass. ii, 373, 635
Hammatt Papers, Ipswich Mass. 14
Little's History of Weare N. H. 716

Merrill's Hist. of Acworth N. H. 182
New Eng. Hist. and Gen. Reg. xv, 241
Ranney Reunion (1866) 48 pages
Rich's History of Truro Mass. 519
Savage's Genealogical Dictionary i, 77
Sears Genealogy 62
Temple's Hist. No. Brookfield Mass. 496
Walker Memorial 23
Washington N. H. History 277
Weaver's History of Windham Ct. 48
Whitmore's Copps Hill Epitaphs
Whittemore's Orange N. J. 440-2
Woodbury's Groveland Mass. Epitaphs 2
Wyman's Charlestown Mass. Gens. i, 16
Aubrey — Glenn's Merion (Pa.) 305-14
Auchmuty — Amer. Ancestry v, 175
Lamb's History of N. Y. City i, 751
Updyke's Narragansett R. I. Ch. 148-52
Audley — Austin's R. I. Gen. Dict. 5
Thomas Genealogy (1896) 197
Auger — American Ancestry xii
Savage's Genealogical Dictionary i, 78
Augier — Savage's Gen. Dict. i, 57
Augur — American Ancestry xii
Middlefield Ct. History
Augustine — Savage's Gen. Dict. i, 79
Aumack — Salter's Monmouth N. J. vi
Aungst — Brubacher Genealogy 171-4
Austin — Amer. Anc. i, 2; vi, 71; x, 202
Anderson's Waterbury Ct. i, app. 10
Austin's Ancestral Dictionary 5
Austin's Allied Families 20-5
Austin's R. I. Gen. Dictionary 246-9
Austin and Whittaker Chart (1881)
Baker's History of Montville Ct. 289-92
Boyd's Annals of Winchester Ct. 42
Cochrane's History of Antrim N. H. 344
Corliss Genealogy, Appendix
Cushman's History of Sheepscott Me. 353
Daniel's History of Oxford Mass. 375
Dodd's History of E. Haven Ct. 103
Dwight Genealogy 542
Dwight's Strong Genealogy 95
Eaton's History of Thomaston Me. 137
Ely Genealogy 184
Hayward's History of Gilsum N. H. 257
Hayward's Hist. of Hancock N. H. 311
Hinman's Connecticut Settlers 81-6
Hubbard's Stanstead County Canada 268
Joslin's Hist. of Poultney Vt. 204-6
Lapham's History of Rumford Me. 301
Loomis Genealogy (1880) 763-6
Newport R. I. Hist. Mag. iv, 227-36
Orcutt's History of Torrington Ct. 642
Penn. Mag. of Hist. and Biog. iv, 484-91
Roe's Sketches of Rose N. Y. 294
Savage's Genealogical Dictionary i, 80-2
Secomb's History of Amherst N. H. 489
Tuttle Family of Connecticut 625-7
Walworth's Hyde Genealogy 1006-8
Weaver's History of Windam Ct. 49
Whitney Genealogy (1860) appendix
Worcester's History of Hollis N. H. 364
Wyman's Charlestown Mass. i, 28-40
Avary — American Ancestry viii, 94
Avered — Boyd's Winchester Ct. 47-51

Averill — Amer. Anc. viii, 224; ix, 35, 49
Bradbury's Kennebunkport Me. 225
Cothren's Hist. of Woodbury Ct. 484-90
Cushman's History of Sheepscott Me. 354
Eaton's History of Thomaston Me. 137
Gregory's History of Northfield Vt. 78-81
Hemenway's Vermont Gazette iv, 618
Hinman's Connecticut Settlers 86
Livermore's History of Wilton N. H. 298
Machias Me Centennial Celebration 153
Savage's Genealogical Dictionary i, 182
Secomb's History of Amherst N. H. 489
Sharpe's South Britain Ct. Sketches 89-91
Topsfield Mass. Historical Coll. (1896) ii
Weaver's History of Windham Ct. 50
Avery — Allen's Worcester Assoc. 152
Amer. Ancestry ii, 4; v, 9; viii, 50; ix, 27
Avery Fam. of Groton Mass. (1888) 8 pages
Avery Fam. of Groton Mass. (1893) 20 pages
Avery Family of Dedham (1893) 366 pages
Avery Family of Groton (1894) 698 pages
Avery Family of Penn. (1898) 55 pages
Avery Family Magazine (1898) 104 pages
Babson's History of Gloucester Mass. 58
Baker's History of Montville Ct. 518-22
Blake's Mendon Association 124
Bridgman's King's Chapel Epit. 301-4
Calkin's History of New London Ct. 331
Cochrane's Hist. of Francestown N. H. 487
Ellis Genealogy 148
Freeman's History Cape Cod Mass. ii, 558
Hammatt Papers, Ipswich Mass. 15
Harris Genealogy (1878) 102-4
Hines' Lebanon Ct. Address (1880) 144
Hinman's Connecticut Settlers 88-90
Hurd's Hist. of New London Co. Ct. 474-6
Machias Me. Centennial Celebration 153
Morgan Genealogy (1851) 16 pages
N E. Hist. and Gen. Register xxvi, 197
Orford N. H. Centennial 103
Perkins' Old Houses of Norwich Ct. 412
Pompey N. Y. Reunion (1875) 253-8
Rich's History of Truro Mass. 520
Savage's Genealogical Dictionary i, 82
Sedgwick's History of Sharon Ct. 62
Smith Genealogy (1889) 99
Strong Genealogy 376-80
Upham Genealogy 40-2
Walworth's Hyde Genealogy 256-8
Wentworth Genealogy ii, 18-21
Wyman's Charlestown Mass. Gens. i, 40
Avis — Savage's Genealogy Dict. i, 183
Awl — Egle's Penn. Gens. 2d ed. 37-46
Axtell — American Ancestry vii, 29, 95
Axtell Genealogy (1899) 8 pages
Hudson's History of Marlboro' Mass. 310
Jameson's History of Medway Mass. 451
New Eng. Genealog. Register xxii, 143-4;
    xliv, 50-2; liii, 227-34
Pierce's History of Grafton Mass. 451-4
Savage's Genealogical Dictionary i, 84
Ayars — Sharpless Genealogy 327
Ayer — Am. Ancestry iv, 188; vi, 10. 24
Ayer (James) Biography (1892) 58 pages
Bouton's History of Concord N. H. 630
Chase's Haverhill Mass. 73, 216, 274, 615

Corliss Genealogy 240
Guild's Stiles Genealogy 380
Hoyt's Salisbury Mass. Families 36–43
Hubbard's Stanstead Co. Canada 195
Huntington's Stamford Ct. Families 7
Judd's History of Hadley Mass. 449
Lapham's History of Bethel Me. 464
Lapham's History of Norway Me. 458
Little's History of Weare N. H. 718
N. E. Reg. xv, 56; xvii, 307–10; xix, 28
Ridlon's Saco Valley Me. Families 452–4
Savage's Genealogical Dictionary i, 84
Titcomb's Early New Eng. People 279–85
Washington N. H. History 278–81
Wyman's Charlestown Mass. Gens. i, 40
Ayers — Chambers' N. J. Germans 244–8
See also Ayres
Aylesbury — Power's Sangamon 80
Aylett — Clarke's Old King Wm. Co. Va.
Lee Genealogy (1895) 172
Richmond Standard ii, 34, 40, 49
Slaughter's St. Mark's Parish Va. 189
Aylsworth — Austin's R. I. Dictionary 6
Aylsworth Genealogy (1840) 12 pages
Aylsworth Genealogy (1887) 496 pages
Bulkley's Browne Memorial 14
Ayrault — Austin's R. I. Gen. Dict. 7
Hinman's Connecticut Settlers 90
Savage's Genealogical Dictionary i, 85
Ayres — Austin's R. I. Gen. Dict. 8
Ayres Genealogy (1870) 55 pages
Bangor Me. Historical Magazine vi, 29
Caldwell Genealogical Record 66
Cleveland's History Yates Co. N. Y. 706
Egle's Penn. Genealogies 2d ed. 47–61
Egle's Notes and Queries i (1894) 387–9
Hammatt Papers, Ipswich Mass. 13
Merrill's History of Acworth N. H. 182
Montague Genealogy 613–5
Temple's North Brookfield Mass. 496
See also Ayers and Ayer
Babb — Daniels' Hist. of Oxford Mass. 375
Egle's Notes and Queries (1896) 205
Savage's Genealogical Dictionary i, 85
Babbidge — Corliss' N. Yarmouth Me.
Driver Genealogy 229–44
Eaton's History of Thomaston Me. 138
Farrow's History of Islesborough Me. 168
Wheeler's History of Brunswick Me. 828
Babbitt — American Ancestry xii, 10
Daniels' Oxford Mass. 375
Savage's Genealogical Dictionary i, 207
Thompson Genealogy (1890) 166
Babcock — American Ancestry i, 3; ii, 5;
    iv, 191; v, 170; ix, 197
Austin's Ancestries 7
Austin's R. I. Genealogical Dictionary 8
Babcock Genealogy (1861) 4 pages
Cleveland's History Yates Co. N. Y. 697–9
Dimock's Coventry Ct. Records 4–8
Douglas Genealogy 132–4
Greene Genealogy (1894)
Hinman's Connecticut Settlers 92–5
Hudson's History of Lexington Mass. 9
Irish's Sketch of Richmond R. I. 88
Joslin's History of Poultney Vt. 200

Narragansett Historical Reg. i, 61–4, 212
N. E. Hist. Gen. Reg. xiv, 23; xix, 215
Roe's Sketches of Rose N. Y. 95
Savage's Genealogical Dictionary i, 86
Sedgwick's History of Sharon Ct. 62
Stanton Genealogy 425, 561
Temple's Hist. of N. Brookfield Mass. 497
Weaver's History of Windham Conn. 50–8
Wight Genealogy 3, 79
Wyman's Charlestown Mass. Gens. i, 42
Babson — Babson's Gloucester 59–61
Poore Genealogy 62
Savage's Genealogical Dictionary i, 87
Slafter Genealogy 110
Bache — American Ancestry v, 162
Franklin Ancestry (1889) 8 pages
Meade's Old Churches of Virginia 374
New Eng. Hist. and Gen. Reg. viii, 374
Bachelder — Farrow's Islesborough 169
Washington N. H. History 281
Bacheldor — Waterbury Ct. i, app. 10
Bacheller — American Ancestry i, 3
Secomb's History of Amherst N. H. 496–9
Bachiler — Swift's Barnstable i, 39–44
Bachman — American Ancestry i, 5
Davis' History of Bucks Co. Pa. 389
Egle's History of Lebanon Co. Pa. 235
Backus — American Ancestry iii, 103; v,
    185, 235; vii, 247; viii, 159, 164
Backus Genealogy (1889) 376 pages
Butler's History of Farmington Me. 368–71
Caulkins' History of Norwich Ct. 157–61
Chapman's Pratt Genealogy 54–67
Goodwin's Genealogical Notes 303–5
Hinman's Connecticut Settlers 95
Huntington Genealogy 74
Munsell's Albany Collections iv, 99
Perkins' Old Houses of Norwich Ct., 414–6
Perkins' Norwich Ct. Families 7–22
Savage's Genealogical Dictionary i, 89
Walworth's Hyde Genealogy 419–21; 537–9;
    707–11; 920–8
Weaver's History of Windham Ct. 58–62
Bacon — American Ancestry i, 3
Ammidown's Historical Collections i, 455
Bacon Genealogy (1845) 41 pages
Barry's History of Framingham Mass. 170
Benedict's History of Sutton Mass. 584
Blake's History of Franklin Mass. 231
Brown's Bedford Mass. Families 2–5
Browne's W. Simsbury Ct. Settlers 11
Campbell's History of Virginia 311, 344
Champion Genealogy 339–43
Cogswell's History Henniker N. H. 448–50
Corliss' North Yarmouth Me.
Cothren's Woodbury Ct. 516–9; ii, 1471
Craft's History of Whately Mass. 368
Cutter's History of Jaffrey N. H. 220
Daniels' History of Oxford Mass. 376
Davis' Landmarks of Plymouth Mass. 9
Freeman's Cape Cod Mass. i, 352; ii, 264
Goode Genealogy 472
Hayward's History of Hancock N. H. 312–4
Hazen's History of Billerica Mass. 4
Herrick's History of Gardner Mass. 330
Heywood's Hist. of Westminster Mass. 520

Hinman's Connecticut Settlers 97-105
Hudson's History of Lexington Mass. 9
Hudson's History of Sudbury Mass. 435
Hyde's History of Brimfield Mass. 369-71
Jackson's History of Newton Mass. 234-6
Journal of Am.-Irish Hist. Soc. (1898) i
Keith's Harrison Ancestry 22-6
Kellogg's Memorial of Elder J. White 39
Lapham's History of Norway Me. 458
Leland Genealogy 210
Middlefield Ct. History
N. E. Hist. Reg. ii, 378; xxxvii, 189-98
Neill's Virginia Carolorum 243
Orcutt's History of Torrington Ct. 643
Paige's History of Cambridge Mass. 482
Pierce's History of Gorham Me. 154
Randall's Hist. of Chesterfield N. H. 220-3
Richmond Va. Standard i, 44; ii, 19, 20, 30, 38; iii, 5, 26, 43
Savage's Genealogical Dictionary i, 89-92
Sedgwick's History of Sharon Ct. 62
Sewall's History of Woburn Mass. 592
Swift's Barnstable Families i, 21, 38
Temple's Hist. N. Brookfield Mass. 502
Temple's History of Whately Mass. 198
Washington N. H. History 282-4
Woodbury's Sketch of Bradford Mass. 68
Woodbury's Groveland Mass. Epitaphs 4-7
Wyman's Charlestown Mass. Gens. i, 43
Bacot — Gregg's Old Cheraws 105
Badcock — Badcock Genealogy (1881) 11 p.
Hinman's Connecticut Settlers 106-8
Morse's Sherborn Mass. Settlers 10
N. E. Hist. and Gen. Register xix, 215-9
Norton's History of Fitzwilliam N. H. 462
Savage's Genealogical Dictionary i, 92
Badger — Am. Ancestry iv, 166, 208; v, 222
Badger (Rev. Joseph) Memoir (1841) 12 p.
Chase's History of Haverhill Mass. 615-7
Cogswell Genealogy 206-8
Lancaster's Gilmanton N. H. 256-8
Maine Genealogist i (1875-6) 70-4
N. H. Hist. Soc. Collections vi, 124-7
Runnell's Hist. of Sanbornton N. H. ii, 15
Savage's Genealogical Dictionary i, 93
Weaver's History of Windham Ct. 62-5
Wentworth Genealogy ii, 95-7
Whitmore's Copps Hill Epitaphs
Wyman's Charlestown Mass. Gens. i, 44
Badgley — Littell's Passaic Valley 12-6
Badlam — Whitman Genealogy 25
Bagby — N. E. Hist. Reg. xxxviii, 97
Bagg — American Ancestry vi, 11
Bagg Ancestry (1895) 4 pages
Loomis Genealogy (1880) 641-9
W. Springfield Mass. Centennial 109-14
Savage's Genealogical Dictionary i, 93
Bagley — Hayward's Hancock 314
Hoyt's Salisbury Mass. Families 43
Loveland Genealogy iii, 224-9
Savage's Genealogical Dictionary i, 93
Stackpole's History of Durham, Me. 149
Worcester's History of Hollis N. H. 365
Bagman — See Bogman
Bagnall — Davis' Plymouth Mass. 9
Bahan — Morrison's Windham 327

Bahl — Eyerman Ancestry (1899) 32
Bailey — American Ancestry i, 3; ii, 5; v, 177; vi, 73, 135; vii, 139; viii, 228; x, 148
Austin's R. I. Genealogical Dictionary 9
Bailey Family of Rowley (1858) 90 pages
Bailey Family of Hanover (1891) 26 pages
Bailey Family of Phila. (1892) 54 pages
Bailey Family Gathering (1894) 23 pages
Bailey Family of Newport (1895) 206 pages
Bailey Family Gathering (1896) 34 pages
Bailey Family Gathering (1897) 32 pages
Bailey Families of Mass. (1899) 479 pages
Baker's History of Montville Ct. 492-7
Ballou's History of Milford Mass. 545
Bangor Me. Historical Magazine vi, 260-6
Barry's History of Hanover Mass. 199-206
Bass' History of Braintree Vt. 111
Bolton's Westchester Co. N. Y. ii, 708
Butler's History of Farmington Me. 371-6
Calnek's History of Annapolis N. S. 468
Caulkin's History of New London Ct. 290
Chapman's Weeks Genealogy 128
Cochrane's Francestown N. H. 488-92
Coffin's History of Newbury Mass. 294
Corliss' North Yarmouth Me.
Cushman's History of Sheepscott Me. 355
Cutter's History of Jaffrey N. H. 222-6
Deane's History of Scituate Mass. 213-5
Dudley Genealogy
Dunster Genealogy 201-8
Egle's Notes and Queries 4th ser. i, 26
Essex Institute Hist. Coll. xix, 299-304
Field's History of Haddam Ct. 43
Futhey's History of Chester Co. Pa. 467-9
Hanover Mass. Records (1898)
Hanson's History of Gardiner Me. 72, 106
Hatch's History of Industry Me. 507-9
Hayward's History of Hancock N. H. 314
Heywood's History Westminster Mass. 522
Hine's Lebanon Ct. Address 144
Hinman's Connecticut Settlers 108-10
Hoyt's Salisbury Mass. Families 44-9
Hudson's History of Lexington Mass. 10
Joslin's History of Poultney Vt. 206-9
Kinne Genealogy 91-3
Littell's Passaic Valley N. J. Gens. 17
Little Genealogy 111-20
Little's History of Weare N. H. 719-25
Maine Hist. and Gen. Recorder ix, 367-70
Merrill's History of Acworth N. H. 183
Middlefield Ct. History
Mitchell's Hist. of Bridgewater Mass. 107
Morrison's History of Windham N. H. 378
Newport Historical Magazine iv, 146-50
Olin Genealogy by Nye (1892) 47-54
Poor Genealogy
Poor's Merrimack Valley 77-161
Read's History of Swanzey N. H. 281
Robinson's Items of Ancestry (1894) 25
Root Genealogy 515-8
Savage's Genealogical Dictionary i, 94
Sedgwick's History of Sharon Ct. 62
Sheldon's History of Deerfield Mass. ii, 52
Slaughter's St. Mark's Parish Va. 160
Washington N. H. History 285-91

Wheeler's History of Brunswick Me. 828
Whitman Genealogy 181-5
Woodbury's Groveland Mass. Epitaphs 8
Worthen's History of Sutton N. H. ii, 602-5
Wyman's Charlestown Mass. Gens. i, 45
Baillie — Baillie Genealogy (1898) 111 p.
Bulloch Genealogy
Baily — American Ancestry v, 195
Jackson Genealogy 228, 243-6
Potts Genealogy (1895) 369-75
Bain — American Ancestry ii, 5
Bainbridge — McMath Genealogy 65-119
N. E. Register xxii, 18-20
Baird — Capron Genealogy 240
Meginnes' Biographical Annals 64
Miller's Colchester County N. S. 167-84
Roe's Sketches of Rose N. Y. 72
Salter's History of Monmouth Co. N. J. vii
Bakeman — Bangor Hist. Mag. viii, 238
Baker — American Ancestry i, 3; ii, 6; iii,
    111, 126; iv, 169; vi, 51, 74, 93, 133;
    vii, 9, 24, 269; viii, 34, 113; x, 57; xi,
    16-17
Atkins' History of Hawley Mass. 45
Austin's R. I. Genealogical Dictionary 10
Baker Fam. of Lynn Mass. (1867) 99 pages
Baker Anc. of Ipswich Mass. (1870) 143 p.
Baker Family of Maine (1874) 18 pages
Baker Fam. of Dorchester (1889) 40 pages
Baker Family of New Eng. (1896) 12 pages
Baker's History of Montville Ct. 153-172
Bangor Historical Magazine iv, 211-3
Bemis' History of Marlboro N. H. 404-10
Binney Genealogy 17
Blackman's Susquehanna County Pa. 54
Blake's History of Franklin Mass. 232-4
Bond's Watertown Mass. Gens. 694
Bouton's History of Concord N. H. 632
Calnek's History of Annapolis N. S. 468
Carter's Hist. of Pembroke N. H. ii, 13-20
Caulkins' History of New London Ct. 362
Chandler's History of Shirley Mass. 347
Cochrane's History of Antrim, N. H. 346
Cogswell's History of Henniker N. H. 450-2
Corliss' North Yarmouth Me.
Cothren's History of Woodbury Ct. 502-4
Crafts Genealogy 282-4
Cutter's History of Jaffrey N. H. 226
Daniels' History of Oxford Mass. 377
Davis Genealogy (1888) 7
Dearborn's History of Salisbury N. H. 451
Dwight Genealogy 606-8
Eaton's History of Thomaston Me. 138
Ellis' History of Roxbury Mass. 91
Freeman's Cape Cod Mass. ii, 203, 707-14
Futhey's History of Chester Co. Pa. 469
Hammatt Papers, Ipswich Mass. 22-5
Harris Genealogy (1878) 77
Hayward's History of Gilsum N. H. 257
Hayward's Hist. of Hancock N. H. 315-20
Hedge's Hist. of East Hampton N. Y. 244-6
Herrick's History of Gardner Mass. 332-4
Heywood's Hist. Westminster Mass. 522-8
Hinman's Connecticut Settlers 110-2
Hollister's History of Pawlet Vt. 162
Hudson's History of Marlboro Mass. 311

Hyde's History of Brimfield Mass. 370-4
Jolliffe Genealogy (1893) 163-5
Leland Genealogy 57
Lewis' History of Lynn Mass. 116-8
Lincoln's History of Hingham Mass. ii, 18
Littell's Passaic Valley N. J. Gens.
Little's History of Weare N. H. 725
Loveland Genealogy iii, 260-7
Maine Hist. and Gen. Recorder viii, 154-68
Martin's History of Chester Pa. 408
Milliken's Narragaugus Valley Me. 24
Morse's Sherborn Mass. Settlers 11
N. E. Hist. Reg. xxxvii, 237; xliii, 279-90
Otis Genealogy (1851)
Pierce's History of Grafton Mass. 454
Pompey N. Y. Reunion (1875) 403-5
Pope Genealogy
Potts Genealogy (1895) 319-29
Power's Sangamon Co. Ill. Settlers 87-92
Rich's History of Truro Mass. 521
Roe's Sketches of Rose N. Y. 147
Runnel's Hist. of Sanbornton N. H. ii,15-9
Saunderson's History of Charlestown 281
Savage's Genealogical Dictionary i, 95-101
Sewall's History of Woburn Mass. 592
Smith's History of Peterborough N. H. 15
Smith's History of Sunderland Mass. 256-8
Stearn's History of Ashburnham Mass. 596
Stiles' History of Windsor Ct. ii, 39
Stone's History of Hubbardston Mass. 224
Swift's Barnstable Mass. Families i, 60-3
Waldo's History of Tolland Ct. 77-80
Walker Memorial 175
Ward's Hist. of Shrewsbury Mass. 238-40
Warren's History of Waterford Me. 229
Weaver's History of Windham Ct. 65-8
Wentworth Genealogy i, 396-8
Whitmore's Copps Hill Epitaphs
Williams' History of Danby Vt. 104-6
Winslow Genealogy ii, app. 34-48
Winsor's History of Duxbury Mass. 222
Wyman's Charlestown Mass. Gens. 47-9
Young's Hist. Chautauqua Co. N. Y. 352
Bakewell — Bakewell Gen. (1896) 99 pages
Balch — American Ancestry i, 4; iii, 217
Balch Family Leaflets (1895) 8 pages
Balch Genealogy (1897) 585 pages
Barry's History of Framingham Mass. 171
Cochrane's Hist. Francestown N. H. 492-7
Daniels' History of Oxford Mass. 378
Deane's History of Scituate Mass. 215
Essex Inst. Collections i, 151-3; xvii, 3-7
Hinman's Connecticut Settlers 112
Morrison's History of Windham N. H. 330
New Eng. Hist. and Gen. Reg. ix, 233-8
Poor's Merrimack Valley 86-8, 78
Savages Genealogical Dictionary i, 101
Stone's History of Beverly Mass. 23
Weaver's History of Windham Ct. 70
Wentworth Genealogy i, 272-5
Woodbury's Groveland Mass. Epitaphs 10-5
Balcom — American Ancestry ix, 203
Austin's R. I. Gen. Dictionary 10
Balcom Genealogy (1882) 12 pages
Boyd's Annals of Winchester Ct. 266
Calnek's History of Annapolis N. S. 469

18

Capron Genealogy by Holden 170-4
Daggett's Hist. of Attleborough Mass. 88
Hudson's History of Sudbury Mass. 435
Savage's Genealogical Dictionary i, 101
Weaver's History of Windham Ct. 68
Balcomb — Stone's Hubbardston 225
Baldey — Hubbell Genealogy 302
Baldridge — Hollister's Pawlet Vt. 163
Missouri Pioneer Families 134
Baldwin — American Ancestry i, 4; iv, 97;
vii, 125, 190; viii, 54, 69; x, 38; xi, 17
Anderson's Waterbury Ct. i, app. 11
Baldwin Lineage (1871) 7 pages
Baldwin Ancestry (1872) 15 pages
Baldwin Genealogy (1880) 68 pages
Baldwin Genealogy (1881) 974 pages
Baldwin Genealogy, Supp. (1889) 395 pages
Baldwin's Dennison Family 127-30
Barry's History of Hanover Mass. 206
Bond's Watertown Mass. Genealogies 11
Briggs' Hanover Mass. Records 7-10
Caulkins' Hist. of New London Ct. 303-5
Caulkins' Hist. of Norwich Ct. (1867) 161-3
Chambers' Early Germans of N. J. 249
Clark Ancestry (1891) 19-21
Cochrane's Hist. of Antrim N. H. 347-50
Cope Family of Penn. 40, 63, 144
Cutter's History of Jaffrey N. H. 227-9
Essex Inst. Collections xvii, 7
Draper's History of Spencer Mass. 174-6
Futhey's History of Chester Co. Pa. 471-3
Gold's History of Cornwall Ct. 275
Goodwin's Foote Genealogy 240
Hayden's Virginia Genealogies 504-6
Hayward's History Hancock N. H. 321-4
Hazen's History of Billerica Mass. 6-9
Heywood's History Westminster Mass. 528
Hibbard's History of Goshen Ct. 407-13
Hine's Lebanon Ct. Address 144
Hinman's Connecticut Settlers 113-7
Hodgman's Hist. of Westford Mass. 437
Hubbard's Stanstead Co. Canada 297-302
Judd's History of Hadley Mass. 449
Kitchell Genealogy 33-52
Littell's Passaic Valley Genealogies 26-30
Livermore's Hist. of Wilton N. H. 298-302
McKeen's History of Bradford Vt. 141-157
Morrison's History of Windham N. H. 331
New Eng. Register xxv, 153-6; xxvi, 295;
xxvii, 148-56; xxxviii, 160-70, 289-99,
372-6
New Jersey Hist. Soc. Suppt. vi, 107-39
Orcutt's History of Derby Ct. 693
Orcutt's History of New Milford Ct. 640-7
Orcutt's History of Stratford Ct. 1116
Orcutt's History of Torrington Ct. 643
Paxton's Marshall Genealogy
Perkins' Norwich Ct. Families 22-30
Peyton's History of Augusta Co. Va. 322
Pickering Genealogy
Power's Sangamon Co. Ill. Settlers 92
Prentice Genealogy 411
Prescott Memorial 121
Rice Genealogy 354-6
Richmond Va. Standard iii, 51
Rodman Genealogy 79

Saunderson's Charlestown N. H. 282
Savage's Genealogical Dictionary i, 101-5
Secomb's Hist. of Amherst N. H. 490-2
Sewall's Hist. of Woburn Mass. 388, 593
Sharpe's History of Seymour Ct. 157, 223
Sharpless Genealogy 290
Shaw's History of Essex Co. N. J. ii, 717-9
Sheldon's History of Deerfield Mass. ii, 54
Stearns' Hist. of Ashburnham Mass. 597
Strong Genealogy 906
Temple's Hist. of N. Brookfield Mass. 502
Temple's Hist. of Palmer Mass. 419-21
Tuttle Genealogy 157-63, 629-32
Vinton Genealogy
Vinton's Richardson Family 38-44; 51-4
Walworth's Hyde Gen. i, 338-47
Ward's History of Shrewsbury Mass. 246
Ward's Rice Family 354-6
Washburn's Hist. of Leicester Mass. 350
Weaver's History of Windam Ct. 70-3
Wheeler's History of Newport N. H. 292
Whittemore's Orange N. J. 42
Wyman's Charlestown Mass. Gens. i, 49
Young's Chautauqua Co. N. Y. 225, 535
Bale — Chambers' N. J. Germans 250
Bales — Livermore's Wilton 302-4
Balkam — Bangor Hist. Mag. iii, 203-5
Ball — American Ancestry i, 4; ii, 6; v,
221; vi, 105; viii, 72; x, 148; xii
Anderson's Waterbury Ct. i, app. 12
Austin's R. I. Genealogical Dictionary 11
Ball Family of Richmond (1853) Chart
Ball Fam. of Rhode Island (1891) 15 pages
Ball's Lake County Ind. (1884) 438-44
Ball's Maternal Ancestry of Washington
Ballou's History of Milford Mass. 549-53
Barry's Hist. of Framingham Mass. 171
Blood's History of Temple N. H. 203
Bond's History of Watertown Mass. 11-3
Carter Family Tree
Cochrane's History of Antrim N. H. 351
Cogswell's History of Henniker N. H. 452
Dodd's History of East Haven Ct. 104
Draper's History of Spencer Mass. 177-9
Ely Genealogy 243
Goode Genealogy 176
Goodyear Genealogy 175-7
Green's Kentucky Families
Hayden's Virginia Genealogies 45-144
Hayward's Hist. of Hancock N. H. 324-7
Heywood's Hist. of Westminster Mass. 530
Hill's History of Mason N. H. 200
Hinman's Connecticut Settlers 122
Lee Genealogy (1895) 545
Littell's Passaic Valley Gens. 31-4; 491
Meade's Old Families of Virginia ii, 126-8
Merrill's History of Acworth N. H. 184
Missouri Pioneer Families 136
New Eng. Histor. and Gen. Reg. ix, 158
Phœnix's Whitney Family, i, 285
Pompey N. Y. Reunion 267-9
Power's Sangamon Co. Ill. Settlers 93-5
Reed's History of Rutland Mass. 139
Richmond Va. Standard iii, 20
Roberts' Old Richland Pa. Families
Savage's Genealogical Dictionary i, 105-7

Sheldon's Hist. of Deerfield Mass. ii, 55-7
Smith's History of Sunderland Mass. 258
Southern Bivouac (1886) 727
Sylvester's History of Ulster Co. N. Y. 108
Temple's Hist. No. Brookfield Mass. 502
Tuttle Family of Connecticut 143-6; 628
Ward's Hist. of Shrewsbury Mass. 234
Washington N. H. History 291-3
Worcester's History of Hollis N. H. 365
Wyman's Charlestown Mass. Gens. i, 50-2
Ballance — American Ancestry vii, 245
Ballantine — N. E. Hist. Reg. vi, 371
Savage's Genealogical Dictionary i, 107
Ballard — Abbott's Andover Mass. 27
Adams' Haven Genealogy 28
American Ancestry iii, 186; vi, 75
Andrews Genealogy (1890) 140-2
Barry's Hist. of Framingham Mass. 172-5
Bouton's History of Concord N. H. 633
Chandler Genealogy 158
Daniel's History of Oxford Mass. 379-81
Lapham's History of Bethel Me. 465
Livermore's Hist. of Wilton N. H. 304
Locke Genealogy 56, 105
Montague Genealogy (1894) 160
Neill's Virginia Carolorum 317
Savage's Genealogical Dictionary i, 108
Smith's History of Sunderland Mass. 259
Weaver's History of Windham Ct. 73
Whitmore's Copps Hill Epitaphs
Wyman's Charlestown Mass. Gens. i, 52
Ballatt — Wyman's Charlestown i, 53
Ballenger — Lewis Genealogy (1893) 205-7
Ballentine — Hinman's Setts. 117-21
Balliet — Balyard Genealogy (1873) 28 p.
Balloch — American Ancestry viii, 101
Balloin — Wyman's Charlestown i, 54
Ballord — American Ancestry vi, 114
Browning's Magna Charta Barons 208
Ballou — Amer. Anc. iv, 222; vi, 129, 158
Austin's R. I. Genealogical Dictionary 12
Ballou Genealogy (1888) 1323 pages
Ballou's History of Milford Mass. 556-9
Bassett's Hist. of Richmond N. H. 277-98
Faxon Genealogy 101-6
Little's History of Weare N. H. 1023
Paige's History of Hardwick Mass. 330
Paxton's Marshall Genealogy 305
Pickering Genealogy
Read's History of Swanzey N. H. 283-6
Balsbaugh — Egle's Notes and Queries,
  2d series, ii, 373-5
Balsley — Keinadt Genealogy 58-60
Balstone — Savage's Gen. Dict. i, 109
Balyard — Balyard Gen. (1873) 28 pages
Bamberger—Parthemore Gen. 39-42; 75-8
Bame — American Ancestry ii, 153
Bamford — Runnel's Sanbornton ii, 19
Bancker — Munsell's Albany iv, 94
New York Gen. and Biog. Rec. ii, 68
Pearson's Schenectady N. Y. Settlers 4-6
Banckson — Martin's Chester Pa. 30-2
Bancroft — Allen Genealogy (1883) 28-30
American Ancestry i, 4; v, 156; viii, 200
Ballou's History of Milford Mass. 560
Benedict's History of Sutton Mass. 584

Butler's History of Groton Mass. 385
Calnek's History of Annapolis N. S. 471
Chandler Genealogy 469-72
Daniel's History of Oxford Mass. 381
Davis Ancestry (1897) 50-7
Driver Genealogy 340
Dwight Genealogy 885
Eaton's History of Reading Mass. 43-5
Ely Genealogy 33
Emery Genealogy (1890) 29
Fletcher Genealogy 60-3
Fox's History of Dunstable Mass. 240
Green's Early Groton Mass. Settlers 1
Green's Groton Mass. Epitaphs 235
Hayward's History of Gilsum N. H. 259
Herrick's History of Gardner Mass. 331
Hill's Old Dunstable Mass. 131-56
Hinman's Connecticut Settlers 123-5
Holton's Farwell Genealogy 41-3
Kellogg's Memorial of Elder J. White 57
Lapham's History of Norway Me. 459
Locke Genealogy 29, 51
Loomis Genealogy (1880) 707-9
Orcutt's History of Torrington Ct. 644
Salem N. Y. Book of History 55
Savage's Gen. Dict. i, 110-1
Stearns' Hist. of Ashburnham Mass. 598
Stearns' History of Rindge N. H. 433-8
Stiles' History of Windsor Ct. ii, 40-9
Temple's History of Northfield Mass. 399
Tyngsboro' Mass. Centen. Record 13-5
Vinton's Richardson Memorial 86
Vinton's Upton Genealogy 475
Wakefield Genealogy 51, 91
Wall's Remin. of Worcester Mass. 141
Wyman's Charlestown Mass. Gens. i, 54
Bandell — Brown's W. Simsbury 29
Bane — Jordan's Leighton Genealogy
Ridlon's Saco Valley Me. Families 114
See also Bean
Banghart—Chambers' N. J. Germans
Bangs — Amer. Ancestry iii, 99; iv, 128
Atkin's History of Hawley Mass. 48
Bangs Autobiography (1846) 311-9
Bangs Genealogy (1896) 360 pages
Baylie's New Plymouth ii, 220
Freeman's Cape Cod Mass. i, 639; ii, 512
Hubbard's Stanstead County Can. 117-9
Lapham's History of Norway Me. 459
Lincoln's History of Worcester Mass. 198
New Eng. Hist. Reg. viii, 369; x, 157-9
Paige's History of Hardwick Mass. 330
Pierce's History of Gorham Me. 155
Phœnix's Whitney Family i, 237-42
Pratt's History of Eastham 18-20
Preble Genealogy 57-9; 245
Rich's History of Truro Mass. 520
Savage's Genealogical Dictionary i, 111
Banister — Blair and Banister Gen. (1898)
Campbell's Virginia 724
Ely Genealogy 137-40; 286-90
Richmond Va. Standard ii, 15
Slaughter's Bristol Parish 143
Temple's History of N. Brookfield **Mass.**
  503
See also under Bannister

Bankhead — Hayden's Virginia Gens. 448
Page Genealogy 240
Banks — American Ancestry xi, 18
Baird's History of Rye N. Y. 395
Banks Genealogy (1890) 8 pages
Calnek's History of Annapolis N. S. 471-4
Chute Genealogy, appendix 9-17
Corliss' North Yarmouth Me.
Dearborn's Parsonsfield Me. 326-30; 365
Hinman's Connecticut Settlers 125
Jones Genealogy (1891) 92
New Eng. Hist. Gen. xliv, 258-64
Read's History of Swanzey N. H. 286
Saunders' Alabama Settlers 268, 443-8
Savage's Genealogical Dictionary 112
Schenck's History of Fairfield Ct. 351
Slaughter's Life of Fry 56
Todd's History of Redding Ct. 174
Wm. and Mary College Quar. vi, 113, 155
Banner — Washington N. H. Hist. 293
Bannister — American Ancestry viii, 207
Barrus' History of Goshen Mass. 134
Barry's History of Framingham Mass. 175
Bland Papers i, 27
Hudson's History of Marlboro' Mass. 312
Jameson's History of Medway Mass. 451
Savage's Genealogical Dictionary i, 112
Ward's History of Shrewsbury Mass. 247
See also under Banister
Banta — Amer. Ancestry iii, 65
Banta Genealogy (1893) 425 pages
Pearson's Schenectady N. Y. Settlers 6
Baptist — Goode Genealogy 234
Neill's Virginia Carolorum 377
Barager — American Ancestry, ii, 153
Barber — American Ancestry i, 4; iv, 192; vii, 25
Anderson's Waterbury Ct. i, app. 13
Austin's R. I. Genealogical Dictionary 13
Ballou's History of Milford Mass. 561-4
Barber Fam. of Lancaster Pa. (1890) 166 p.
Barber Family of Homer N. Y. (1893) 40 p.
Barber's Atlee Genealogy 92-5; 104-7
Barbour's Low Family Chart (1890)
Brown's West Simsbury Ct. 18-29
Burleigh's Guild Genealogy 57
Carter Genealogy by Potts (1883) 115-7
Clyde's Irish Settlement Pa. 14
Greene Genealogy
Hayward's Hist. of Hancock N. H. 327
Heywood's Hist. of Westminster Mass. 530
Hinman's Connecticut Settlers 126-9
Humphreys Genealogy (1884) 332
Irish's History of Richmond R. I. 89
Jameson's Hist. of Medway Mass. 452-4
Loomis Genealogy (1880) 264-75; 572, 751
Narr. Historical Register ii, 212-4
Orcutt's History of Torrington Ct. 645-58
Pompey N. Y. Reunion 283-6
Rockwood Family 23-6
Savage's Genealogical Dictionary 113
Smith's Hist. of Peterborough N. H. 16-8
Stiles' Hist. of Windsor Ct. ii, 50-8
Temple's Hist. of Northfield Mass. 400-2
Temple's History of Palmer Mass. 422
Whitmore's Copps Hill Epitaphs

Wight Genealogy 16-8
Wyman's Charlestown Mass. Gens. i, 55
Barberie — Whitehead's Perth Amboy
Barbour — Amer. Ancestry vi, 88; ix, 145
Barbour's My Wife and Mother (1885)
Barbour Genealogy (1898) 70 pages
Collin's Hist. of Hillsdale N. Y., app. 33
Daniel's History of Oxford Mass. 381
Faxon Genealogy 73-9
Green's Kentucky Families
Jour. of Smith and Dean of Portland 57
Kitchell Genealogy 17-53
Morse's Sherborn Mass. Settlers 12
Orcutt's History of Torrington Ct. 648
Slaughter's St. Mark's Parish Va. 118-21
Barbre — Power's Sangamon Ill. 95
Barcalow — Honeyman's Our Home 408
Barclay — Holgate's Amer. Gen. 122-35
New York Gen. Rec. iii, 21-3; xxvi, 121
Riker's Annals of Newtown N. Y. 319
Van Rensselaer's New Yorkers
Bard — Cochrane's Francestown 498
Van Rensselaer's New Yorkers
Bardelle — Barber's Atlee Gen. 70-2
Barden — American Ancestry ii, 6
Bassett's History of Richmond N. H. 299
Cleveland's Hist. Yates Co. N. Y. 184-94
Essex Institute Hist. Coll. vii, 213-5
Savage's Genealogical Dictionary i, 114
Barding — Porter's Hartford Settlers 13
Bardwell — Aldrich's Walpole 191
American Ancestry iii, 198; ix, 157, 175
Barrus' History of Goshen Mass. 134
Craft's History of Whately Mass. 369-85
Daniel's History of Oxford Mass. 382-5
Doolittle's Belchertown Mass. 266
Hollister's Pawlet Vt. 164
Judd's History of Hadley Mass. 450
Savage's Genealogical Dictionary i, 114
Sheldon's Hist. of Deerfield Mass. ii, 57-64
Smith's History of Sunderland Mass. 261
Temple's Hist. of Whately Mass. 199-203
Barents — Bergen's Kings Co. N. Y. 19
Barger — Keinadt Genealogy 64-6
Power's Sangamon Ill. Settlers 95
Barheit — Munsell's Albany Coll. iv, 95
Barheyt — American Ancestry i, 4
Pearson's Schenectady N. Y. Settlers 7-9
Baringer — American Ancestry ii, 6
Barkalow — Salter's Monmouth N. J.
Barkeloo — Bergen Genealogy 153-5
Bergen's Kings Co. N. Y. Settlers 20-2
Davis' History of Bucks Co. Pa. 201
Barker — Abbott's Andover Mass. 20
American Ancestry i, 5
Andrews Genealogy (1890) 109-12; 145-7
Austin's Ancestries 9
Austin's R. I. Genealogical Dictionary 14
Austin's Allied Families 26-35
Ballou's History of Milford Mass. 564
Bangor Me. Historical Magazine vi, 77
Barker Family of Charlestown (1871) 25 p.
Barker Family of Pomfret Ct. (1897) 36 p.
Barker Family of Plymouth (1899) 8 pages
Barker Colonial Families (1899) 4 pages
Barry's History of Hanover Mass. 206

Bemis' History of Marlboro, N. H. 410-12
Blood's History of Temple N. H. 203
Bolton's Hist. of Westchester Co. N. Y. 501
Buckingham Genealogy 215-7
Carter Genealogy by Potts (1883) 73
Cleveland's Yates Co. 398-400; 677-9
Cochrane's History of Antrim N. H. 352-7
Cogswell's History of Henniker N. H. 453
Cushman's Hist. of Sheepscott Me. 355-7
Davis' History of Wallingford Ct. 635
Deane's History of Scituate Mass. 216
Eaton's History of Thomaston Me. 139
Essex Institute Hist. Coll. xix, 304-7
Goodwin's Foote Genealogy 189
Guild's Stiles Genealogy 288
Hanover Mass. Records (1898)
Hanson's History of Gardiner Me. 156
Hayward's Hist. of Hancock N. H. 327-33
Hinchman's Nantucket Settlers 90-2
Kellogg's Mem. of Elder John White 90
Lapham's Hist. of Bethel Me. 475-8, 652
Lapham's History of Rumford Me. 302
Lincoln's Hist. of Hingham Mass. ii, 20-3
Livermore's Hist. of Wilton N. H. 305-7
Morrison's Hist. of Windham N. H. 331-3
N. Eng. Hist. and Gen. Reg. xxiv, 294; liii,
426-31
Newport R. I. Historical Mag. i, 37-50
Piper Genealogy (1889) 16
Pott's Carter Genealogy 73
Rodman Genealogy 127-9
Savage's Genealogical Dictionary i, 115
Secomb's History of Amherst N. H. 493
Smith Genealogy (1895) 53-8
Stearns' History of Rindge N. H. 438-41
Swift's Barnstable Families i, 64-7
Temple's History of Palmer Mass. 426
Warren's History of Waterford Me. 230
Washington N. H. History 691
Whitmore's Copps Hill Epitaphs
Winsor's History of Duxbury Mass. 223
Wyman's Charlestown Mass. Gens. i, 56-8
Young's Chautauqua County N. Y. 479
Barkley — Richmond Standard iii, 20
Barkman — Chambers' N. J. Germans
Barksdale — Goode Genealogy 78
Barksdale Genealogy (1895) 46 pages
Keim Genealogy 302-4
Lewis Genealogy (1893) 295-9
Barless — Roe's Sketches of Rose 272
Barlow — Amer. Ancestry viii, 211; ix, 88
Barlow Genealogy (1891) 508 pages
Beckwith's Creoles 15
Bolton's Westchester Co. N. Y. ii, 209
Freeman's Hist. of Cape Cod Mass. ii, 73
Hill and Barlow Genealogies (1880) 29 p.
Hinman's Connecticut Settlers 131
Hurd's History of Fairfield Co. Ct. 577
Orcutt's History of Stratford Ct. 1117
Paige's History of Hardwick Mass. 331
Savage's Genealogical Dictionary i, 116
Schenck's History of Fairfield Ct. 352
Todd's History of Redding Ct. 174-7
Wyman's Charlestown Mass. Gens. i, 589
Barnaby — American Ancestry v, 190
Barnaby Genealogy (1864) 3 pages, reprint

Davis' Landmarks of Plymouth Mass. 10
N. E. Hist. and Gen. Reg. xviii, 361-3
Pierce's (E. W.) Contributions 5-21
Savage's Genealogical Dictionary i, 117
Barnard — Abbott's Andover Mass. 20
American Ancestry ii, 6; iv, 83
Barnard Genealogy (1899) 40 pages
Barry's Hist. of Framingham Mass. 175
Benedict's History of Sutton Mass. 584
Bond's Watertown Mass. Gens. 14-6, 676
Carter Gen. (1883) 37-40, 50-3, 71-4, 100-2
Caverly's History of Pittsford Vt. 692
Craft's History of Whately Mass. 385-7
Daniel's History of Oxford Mass. 385
Eaton's History of Thomaston Me. 139
Futhey's Hist. of Chester Co. Pa. 473-7
Heywood's Hist. of Westminster Mass. 531
Hinman's Connecticut Settlers 132-41
Hoyt's Salisbury Mass. Families 49-53
Hubbard's Hist. of Springfield Vt. 206-13
Hudson's History of Marlboro Mass. 313
Judd's History of Hadley Mass. 450
Leach's Morton Ancestry 138-42
Little's History of Weare N. H. 726-9
Loomis Genealogy (1880) 635
Maris Genealogy 62
Martin's History of Chester Pa. 407-10
Merrill's History of Acworth N. H. 184
New Eng. Hist. and Gen. Reg. xv, 269
Norton's History of Fitzwilliam N. H. 462
Pierce's History of Grafton Mass. 455
Savage's Genealogical Dictionary i, 118-21
Secomb's History of Amherst N. H. 494
Sheldon's Hist. of Deerfield Mass. ii, 65-75
Smith's History of Delaware Co. Pa. 44
Smith's History of Sunderland Mass. 262
Stiles' History of Windsor Ct. ii, 58
Strong Genealogy 1465-8
Temple's Hist. of No. Brookfield Mass. 504
Temple's History of Whately Mass. 203
Waldo's History of Tolland Ct. 88
Wentworth Genealogy i, 110
Whitmore's Copps Hill Epitaphs
Whitmore's Heraldic Journal iii, 106
Worthen's History of Sutton N. H. 629
Wyman's Charlestown Mass. Gens. i, 59
Barnes — American Ancestry i, 5; ii, 6;
iv, 3, 172; v, 152, 162; ix, 20
Adams' History of Fairhaven Vt.
Anderson's Waterbury Ct. i, app. 13
Austin's R. I. Genealogical Dictionary 15
Baird's History of Rye N. Y. 453
Bangor Historical Magazine iv, 212
Bedford N. H. Centennial 286-9
Caverley's History of Pittsford Vt. 691
Chardon, Ohio, Newsp., Oct. 3, 17, 24, 1883
Chute Genealogy, appendix 17-21
Cleveland's Hist. of Yates Co. N. Y. 129-32
Cochrane's History of Antrim N. H. 357
Cogswell's Hist. of Henniker N. H. 453-7
Clute's History of Staten Island N. Y. 341
Daniel's History of Oxford Mass. 385
Davis' Landmarks of Plymouth 10-3
Dawson Genealogy 90-2
Dodd's History of East Haven Ct. 104-6
Douglas Genealogy 330

Draper's History of Spencer Mass. 173
Driver Genealogy 117-9
Eaton's History of Thomaston Me. 139
Hanson's History of Gardiner Me. 111
Hayden's Virginia Genealogies 719
Hedge's East Hampton N. Y. 246-9
Heywood's Hist. Westminster Mass. 532-5
Hinman's Connecticut Settlers 141-3
Howell's Hist. of Southampton N. Y. 202
Hoyt Genealogy 123, 132
Hudson's Hist. of Marlboro Mass. 314-20
Lincoln's Hist. of Hingham Mass. ii, 23-32
Livermore's Hist. of Wilton N. H. 307
Middlefield Ct. History
Missouri Pioneer Families 313
Mitchell's Hist. of Bridgewater Mass. 356
Montague Genealogy 427
Morris Genealogy (1853) 37
Norton's History of Fitzwilliam N. H. 462
Orcutt's History of New Milford Ct. 648
Orcutt's History of Wolcott Ct. 446-8
Paige's History of Hardwick Mass. 331-3
Power's Sangamon Co. Ill. Settlers 97
Ridlon's Saco Valley Me. Families 455
Roe's Sketches of Rose N. Y. 200
Savage's Genealogical Dict. i, 121, 123
Sedgwick's History of Sharon Ct. 62
Stiles' Hist. of Windsor Ct. ii, 59
Stone's History of Hubbardston Mass. 226
Temple's History of No. Brookfield Mass.
  505
Timlow's Sketches of Southington Ct. 17-26
Tuttle Genealogy 632
Ward's History of Shrewsbury Mass. 243
Washington N. N. History 294
Wentworth Genealogy i, 247
Williams' History of Danby Vt. 110
Wyman's Charlestown Mass. Gens. i, 60
Young's History of Wayne Co. Ind. 337
Barnett — Aldrich's Walpole N. H. 190
American Ancestry ii, 7
Egle's Penn. Genealogies 2d ed. 63-77
Gilmer's Georgians 130
Hayward's History of Hancock N. H. 333
Power's Sangamon Co. Ill. Settlers 96
Stiles' History of Windsor Ct. ii, 60
Walworth's Hyde Gen. 498-500, 505
Young's History of Warsaw N. Y. 264
Barney — American Ancestry vi. 17; xii
Bassett's History of Richmond N. H. 306
Hayward's History of Hancock N. H. 334-6
Merrill's History of Acworth N. H. 185
Savage's Genealogical Dictionary i, 123
Washington N. H. History 295-300
Barnhart — Herrick Genealogy (1885) 234a
Barnhill — Cunnabell Genealogy 109
Miller's Colchester Co. N. S. 184-99
Barnitz — Spangler Genealogy 195-204
Barns — See Barnes
Barnum — Amer. Ancestry vi. 196; xii, 42
Barnum Genealogy, reprinted article
Cleveland Genealogy 235
Emery's Taunton Mass. Ministry ii, 8-10
Hinman's Connecticut Settlers 144
Orcutt's History of Stratford Ct. 1117-21
Roe's Sketches of Rose N. Y. 163

Savage's Genealogical Dictionary 1, 124
Selleck's Norwalk Ct. (1896) 340-4
Barnwell — American Ancestry v, 89
Barnwell Chart (1898)
Bellinger Genealogy 94
Barr — Bedford N. H. Centennial 289
Driver Genealogy 263
Lancaster Pa Historical Papers ii, 216
Temple's Hist. of N. Brookfield Mass. 511
Barradale — Meade's Virginia i, 198
Barraud — Hanson's Old Kent Md. 171
Richmond Va. Standard ii, 45
Barre — Van Brunt Genealogy 44
Barrel — Barry's Hanover Mass. 208
Stearn's Hist. of Ashburnham Mass. 599.
Barrell — Cutts Genealogy 170-4
Deane's History of Scituate Mass. 217
French's History of Turner Me. 53
Heywood's Hist. Westminster Mass. 535-7
Mitchell's Hist. of Bridgewater Mass. 106
Savage's Genealogical Dictionary i, 124
Wyman's Charlestown Mass. Gens. i, 60
Barrett — American Ancestry i, 5; ii, 7;
  iii, 68, 72; vi, 167; x, 99, 203
Barrett Genealogy (1888) 8 pages reprint
Barrett Fam. of Braintree (1888) 296 pages
Barry's History of Framingham Mass. 175
Chandler's History of Shirley Mass. 348
Cochrane's History of Antrim N. H. 357
Cochrane's Hist. of Francestown N. H. 500
Dwight Genealogy 602-4
Eaton's History of Thomaston Me. 140
Goss' Melrose Mass. Address 13
Hayward's History of Gilsum N. H. 260
Hill's History of Mason N. H. 200
Hinman's Connecticut Settlers 145
Hodgman's History of Westford Mass. 437
Hubbard's History of Springfield Vt. 214-8
Hudson's History of Lexington Mass. 10
Kidder's Hist. of New Ipswich N. H. 330-4
Little's History of Weare N. H. 729
Livermore's Hist. Wilton N. H. 308-12
Locke Genealogy 107
Munsell's Albany Collection iv, 94
New Eng. Hist. Gen. Reg. xlii, 257-64;
  liii, 400
Paige's History of Cambridge Mass. 483
Potter's Concord Mass. Families 5, 108-18
Randall's Hist. of Chesterfield N. H. 223-5
Salisbury Family Memorials (1885) 31
Savage's Genealogical Dictionary i, 124-6
Secomb's History of Amherst N. H. 495
Shattuck's History of Concord Mass. 363
Sheldon's Hist. of Deerfield Mass. ii, 75
Sibley's Hist. of Union Me. 431
Smith's History of Sunderland Mass. 263
Stearn's Hist. of Ashburnham Mass. 600-5
Stiles' History of Windsor Ct. ii, 60
Swain Genealogy 64-71
Temple's History of No. Brookfield Mass.
  511
Temple's History of Northfield Mass. 402
Virginia Magazine of History vi, 205
Washington N. H. History 301, 691
Williams' History of Danby Vt. 109
Wyman's Charlestown Mass. Gens. 61-3

Barringer — Wheeler's No. Car. ii, 67
Wheeler's Eminent No. Carolinians 967
Barritt — American Ancestry ix, 25
Barron — American Anc. v, 53; vii, 111
Bedford N. H. Centennial 290–2
Bond's Watertown Mass. 17
Butler's History of Groton Mass. 386
Green's Early Groton Mass. Settlers 2
Green's Groton Mass. Epitaphs 236
Hayward's History of Gilsum N. H. 260
Heywood's Hist. of Wetsminster Mass. 537
Hodgman's History of Westford Mass. 437
McKeen's History of Bradford Vt. 180–93
Saunderson's Charlestown N. H. 282–4
Savage's Genealogical Dictionary i, 126
Secomb's History of Amherst N. H. 493
Washington's N. H. History 302
Welles' Amer. Family Antiquity i, 25–40
Worcester's History of Hollis N. H. 365
Wyman's Charlestown Mass. Gens. i, 63
Barrons — See Barnes
Barrows — Am. Anc. vi, 22; ix, 139; xii
Barrus' History of Goshen Mass. 138–42
Daggett's Hist. of Attleborough Mass. 87
Davis' Landmarks of Plymouth 13–5
Eaton's Annals of Warren Me. 504
Eaton's History of Thomaston Me. 140–2
Hinman's Connecticut Settlers 146
Hyde's History of Brimfield Mass. 469
Lapham's History of Norway Me. 459
Lapham's History of Paris Me. 501–3
Maine Hist. and Gen. Recorder vii, 134–45,
   198–206; viii, 27–32
Pompey N. Y. Reunion 258
Power's Sangamon Co. Ill. Settlers 98
Savage's Genealogical Dictionary i, 125
Sedgwick's History of Sharon Ct., 62
Thurston's History of Winthrop Me. 173
Weaver's History of Windham Ct. 74, 90
Wyman's Charlestown Mass. Gens. i, 63
Barrus — Bassett's Richmond 300–6
Barry — American Ancestry x, 200
Barry's Hanover Mass. 419–41
Bass' History of Braintree Vt. 110.
Lincoln's History of Hingham Mass. ii, 33
Temple's Hist. of N. Brookfield Mass. 511
Wyman's Charlestown Mass. Gens. i, 63
Barsham — Bond's Watertown 17
Savage's Genealogical Dictionary i, 127
Barstow — American Ancestry ii, 7
Barry's History of Hanover Mass. 208–43
Bond's Watertown Mass. 18, 677–9
Briggs' History of Shipbuilding 97–120
Corliss' North Yarmouth Me.
Cushman's History of Sheepscott Me. 356–8
Daniels' History of Oxford Mass. 386
Deane's History of Scituate Mass. 218
Hanover Mass. Records (1898)
Lincoln's History of Hingham Mass. ii, 34
Savage's Genealogical Dictionary i, 128
Sedgwick's History of Sharon Ct. 63
Smith's Hist. of Sunderland Mass. 264
Temple's History of No. Brookfield Mass.
   572
Walworth's Hyde Genealogy 44
Wheeler's History of Brunswick Me. 829

Whipple-Hill Families (1897) 96–9
Winsor's History of Duxbury Mass. 224
Bartholomew — American Ancestry vi,
   192; vii, 46; x, 14, 185; xii
Anderson's Waterbury Ct. i, app. 14
Austin's Allied Families 35
Bartholomew Reunion (1882) 37 pages
Bartholomew Genealogy (1885) 753 pages
Bartholomew Lineage (1899) 60 pages
Collin's History of Hillsdale N. Y. App. 32
Daniels' History of Oxford Mass. 387
Davis' History of Wallingford Ct, 650
Hammatt Papers, Ipswich Mass. 25
Hibbard's History of Goshen Ct. 413–7
Orcutt's History of Wolcott Ct. 449
Paige's History of Hardwick Mass. 336
Savage's Genealogical Dictionary i, 129
Sheldon's History of Deerfield Mass. ii, 76
Tucker's History of Hartford Vt. 408–10
Bartin — Winsor's Duxbury Mass. 225
Bartles — Chambers' N. J. Germans
Bartlett — American Ancestry i, 5; ii, 7;
   viii, 40–3, 229; xii
Austin's Ancestral Dictionary 6
Bangor Me. Hist. Magazine iv, 214; vi, 104
Bartlett Family Sketches (1876) 114 pages
Bartlett Fam. of Weymouth (1892) 112 pages
Bartlett's Russell Genealogy
Benedict's History of Sutton Mass. 584
Bond's Watertown Mass. 899–901
Bradford Genealogy (1898) 9–11
Capron Genealogy by Holden 46–8
Chapman's Weeks Genealogy 129
Chase's History of Haverhill Mass. 620
Cleveland's History of Yates Co. N. Y. 397
Cochrane's Hist. of Francestown N. H. 502
Coffin's History of Newbury Mass. 295
Cogswell's History of Henniker N. H. 457
Cogswell's History Northwood N. H. 622–5
Cogswell's Nottingham N. H. 167–70
Collin's History of Hillsdale N. Y. app. 34
Corliss' North Yarmouth Me.
Craft's History of Whately Mass. 387–9
Cutts Genealogy 162–6
Daniels' History of Oxford Mass. 388
Davis' Landmarks of Plymouth 15–22
Dearborn's Hist. of Salisbury N. H. 452–64
Eaton's History of Thomaston Me. 142
Ellis Genealogy 370
Emery Genealogy (1890) 11–3
Emery's Newbury Mass. Reminisc. 31
Guild's Stiles Genealogy 25
Hayward's History of Hancock N. H. 336–8
Herrick Genealogy (1885) 155–60
Heywood's Hist. of Westminster Mass. 537
Hine's Lebanon Ct. Address 144
Hinman's Connecticut Settlers 147, 151
Hoyt's Salisbury Mass. Families 54–9
Hubbard's Stanstead County Canada 197
Hudson's History of Marlboro Mass. 320
Jackson's History of Newton Mass. 238–40
Judd's History of Hadley Mass. 451
Kidder's History of New Ipswich N. H. 334
Lapham's Hist. of Bethel Me. 466–74, 651
Lapham's History of Norway Me. 460–3
Lapham's History of Rumford Me. 303

Lapham's History of Woodstock Me. 174
Lawrence and Bartlett Genealogy (1888) 224 pages
Lincoln's History of Hingham Mass. 34
Little's History of Weare N. H. 730-2
Loomis Genealogy (1880) 689-93
Mitchell's Bridgewater Mass. 109, 357
Morse Memorial (1896) 76-9
Narr. Historical Register vi, 30-6
Nealley Chart
N. E. Hist. and Gen. Reg. xl, 192-204
Norton's History of Knox County Ohio 320
Old Eliot Me. Monthly iii (1899) 65-76
Paige's History of Cambridge Mass. 484
Paige's History of Hardwick Mass. 334
Pierce's (E. W.) Contributions 22-5
Savage's Genealogical Dictionary i, 130-3
Stiles' History of Windsor Ct. ii, 61-7
Strong Genealogy 582, 766, 770, 789
Temple's History of No. Brookfield Mass. 512
Temple's History of Whately Mass. 204
Titcomb's Early N. E. People 185-200
Todd's History of Redding Ct. 177
Wheeler's History of Newport N. H. 296
Williams' History of Danby Vt. 106-9
Winsor's History of Duxbury Mass. 225
Worcester Mag. and Hist. Jour. ii, 184
Wyman's Charlestown Mass. Gens. 64-6
Young's History of Warsaw N. Y. 235
Bartley — Chambers' N. J. Germans
Morrison's Windham N. H. Hist. 334-6
Pearson's Schenectady N. Y. Settlers 10
Bartlit — Foote Genealogy (1867) 21-3
Bartol — Corliss' North Yarmouth Me.
Savage's Genealogical Dictionary i, 133
Barton — American Ancestry ii, 7; ix, 129; xi, 200; xii
Austin's Ancestries 11
Austin's Genealogical Dictionary 250
Baetjer's Carteret Genealogy 17
Baird's History of Rye N. Y. 396
Barry's History of Framingham Mass. 176
Benedict's History of Sutton Mass. 586
Daniels' History of Oxford Mass. 389-99
Draper's History of Spencer Mass. 173
Jackson's History of Newton Mass. 236
Lapham's History of Bethel Me. 474
Lapham's History of Norway Me. 459.
New York Gen. and Biog. Rec. iii, 30-2
Paxton's Marshall Genealogy 256, 353-6
Rittenhouse Genealogy (1897) 16-40
Washburn's History of Leicester Mass. 345
Wheeler's Croyden N. H. Centen. 73-7
Wheeler's History of Newport N. H. 294
Whitman Genealogy 153-5
Whitmore's Heraldic Journal iv, 130-2
Whittemore's Middlesex County Ct. 200
Bartow — American Ancestry iii, 4
Bartow Genealogy (1875) 60 pages
Bartow Genealogy 2d ed. (1878) 318 pages
Bartow Family in England (1890) 44 pages
Bolton's Westchester County N. Y. ii, 350
N. Y. Gen. and Biog. Rec. iii, 30-2; v, 147
Penn. Mag. of Hist. and Biog. xiv, 214
Whitehead's Perth Amboy N. J. 138-41

Bartram — Bartram Family Chart (1893)
Maris Genealogy 73
Savage's Genealogical Dictionary i, 134
Schenck's History of Fairfield Ct. 353
Smith's History of Delaware Co. Pa. 44
Todd's History of Redding Ct. 178-81
Barziza — Carter Family Tree
Bascom — Bascom Genealogy (1870) 79 p.
Edward's Southampton Mass.
Freeman's Hist. Cape Cod Mass. ii, 727
Harris' Ancestry of W. C. Harris
Savage's Genealogical Dictionary i, 134
Sheldon's Hist. of Deerfield Mass. ii, 77-9
Temple's History of Northfield Mass. 403
Wheeler's History of Newport N. H. 296-9
Basford — Chase's Chester N. H. 405-7
Bashaw — Power's Sangamon Ill. 98
Bashford — American Ancestry ii, 7
Bashore — Egle's Queries (1897) 180
Baskerville — Goode Genealogy 233
Richmond Va. Standard iii, 44
Thomas Genealogy (1896) 198
Baskin — Goode Genealogy 300
Bass — Arber's John Smith's Works
Barry's History of Hanover Mass. 244
Bass' History of Braintree Vt. 111-5
Bass Family Ancestry (1896) 14 pages
Calnek's History of Annapolis N. S. 474
Crane's Rawson Genealogy 30
Hanover Mass. Records (1898)
Hayward's History of Hancock N. H. 338
Herrick Genealogy (1885) 117-9
Hinman's Connecticut Settlers 159
Mitchell's Hist. of Bridgewater Mass. 110
Neill's Virginia Carolorum
Neill's Virginia Vetusta
Richmond Va. Standard ii, 46
Robinson's Items of Ancestry (1894) 40
Savage's Genealogical Dictionary i, 135
Thayer Memorial (1835) 53-66
Washburn's Hist. of Leicester Mass. 344
Weaver's History of Windham Ct. 93
Whitmore's Copps Hill Epitaphs
Bassett — Am. Anc. ii, 8; xi, 167; xii, 29
Anderson's Waterbury Ct. i, app. 15
Andrew's History of New Britain Ct. 380
Baird's History of Rye N. Y. 396
Bassett Chart by Leeds (1886) 18x24 inches
Bassett Reunion (1897) 40 pages
Bassett Reunion (1898) 23 pages
Bassett Reunion (1899) 30 pages
Bassett's Hist. of Richmond N. H. 307-10
Carter Family Tree
Cleveland's Hist. of Yates Co. N. Y. 155-9
Davis' Landmarks of Plymouth Mass. 22
Dickerman Genealogy 156-61
Ellis Genealogy 407
Freeman's Cape Cod Mass. i, 333; ii, 142
Goodyear Genealogy 61-3
Hamden Ct. History 228-36
Hayward's History of Hancock N. H. 339
Hinman's Connecticut Settlers 159-62
Keith's Harrison Ancestry 27-33
Lewis' History of Lynn Mass. 184
Lincoln's Hist. of Hingham Mass. ii, 35-7
Mitchell's Hist. of Bridgewater Mass. 111-3

Munsell's Albany Collections iv, 95
Orcutt's History of Derby Ct. 695-9
Orcutt's History of Stratford Ct. 11, 21-3
Paige's History of Hardwick Mass. 334
Preble Genealogy 260
Savage's Genealogical Dictionary i, 136
Sharpe's History of Seymour Ct. 205
Shourd's Fenwick Colony N. J. 45-9
Swift's Barnstable Families i, 45-51
Walker Genealogy 179
Weaver's History of Windham Ct. 93
Welles' Washington Gen. 187, 199, 219
Wilkes-Barre Pa. Historical Record i, 23
Wyman's Charlestown Mass. Gens. i, 67
Baster — Austin's R. I. Gen. Dict. 15
Baston — Corliss' North Yarmouth Me.
Batchelder — American Ancestry iii, 139;
  vi, 41; viii, 16; xii, 42
Austin's Allied Families 36-8
Batchelder Genealogy (1898) 623 pages
Chase's History of Chester N. H. 467
Cochrane's Hist. Francestown N. H. 502-8
Cogswell's Nottingham N. H. 333, 626-38
Dearborn's History of Salisbury N. H. 465
Dow's History of Hampton N. H. 588-600
Eaton's History of Reading Mass. 45-7
Fisk Genealogy 135
Fullonton's Hist. of Raymond N. H. 303-8
Herrick Genealogy (1885) 20-2, 255
Hubbard's Stanstead Co. Canada 209, 285
Kidder's History of New Ipswich N. H. 235
Leland Magazine 88, 125
Livermore's History of Wilton N. H. 312-4
McKeen's History of Bradford Vt. 374-7
Morrison's History of Windham N. H. 226
Morse Genealogy, Appendix No. 24
Morse's Sherborn Mass. Settlers 14
Runnell's Hist. Sanbornton N. H. ii, 20-7
Smith Genealogy (1895) 83-5
Whitmore's Batchelder Genealogy (1873)
Batcheller — Benedict's Sutton 587-90
Cushing's Biog. T. Batcheller (1864) 30-2
Daniels' History of Oxford Mass. 399
Dwight Genealogy 1000-6
Leland Magazine 81
New Eng. Hist. and Gen. Reg. xxvii, 364
Norton's History of Fitzwilliam N. H. 463
Pierce's History of Grafton Mass. 455-8
Sanborn Genealogy (1894)
Temple's Hist. of No. Brookfield Mass. 515
Batchelor — Bass' Braintree Vt. 115
Freeman's Cape Cod Mass. ii, 179
Savage's Genealogical Dictionary i, 87-9
Bate — Barry's Hanover Mass. 245-58
Chapman Genealogy 254-7
Hudson's History of Lexington Mass. 10
See also Bates
Bateman — American Ancestry ii, 8
Hinman's Connecticut Settlers, 151
Hoar Family Lineage (1898) 25
Savage's Genealogical Dictionary i, 137
Wyman's Charlestown Mass. Gens. i, 67
Bates — American Ancestry i, 5; ii, 8; vi,
  68, 195; ix, 130; xii
Aylsworth Genealogy 464-8
Ballou's History of Milford Mass. 569

Barry's History of Hanover Mass. 245-58
Bates and Fletcher Gen. (1892) 58 pages
Bates Genealogy (1900) 145 pages
Butler Genealogy (1888) 76-85
Clement's Newtown N. J. Settlers
Cutter's History of Jaffrey N. H. 231
Davis' Landmarks of Plymouth 23-5
Deane's History of Scituate Mass. 219
Field's History of Haddam Ct. 45
Hanover Mass. Records (1898)
Hayward's History of Gilsum N. H. 262
Heywood's Hist. of Westminster Mass. 538
Hinman's Connecticut Settlers 152-5
Hubbard's Hist. of Springfield Vt. 218-21
Huntington's Stamford Ct. Families 8
Hurlbut Genealogy 407
Hyde's History of Brimfield Mass. 387
Leland Genealogy 161
Lincoln's Hist. of Hingham Mass. ii, 38-51
Loomis Genealogy (1880) 681
Missouri Pioneer Families 130
Mitchell's Hist. of Bridgewater Mass. 113
New Eng. Hist. and Gen. Reg. xxxi, 141
Norton's History of Fitzwilliam N. H. 797
Power's Sangamon County Ill. Settlers 99
Richmond Va. Standard ii, 44
Savage's Genealogical Dictionary i, 137-9
Sedgwick's History of Sharon Ct. 63
Sheldon's History of Deerfield Mass. ii, 79
Stearn's History of Ashburnham Mass. 605
Stiles' History of Windsor Ct. ii, 68
Swift's Barnstable Mass. Families i, 145
Temple's Hist. of No. Brookfield Mass. 518
Todd's History of Redding Ct. 182
Whitman Genealogy 159, 245-53
Bath — Calnek's Annapolis N. S. 475
Pearson's Schenectady N. Y. Settlers 13
Bathrick — American Ancestry ii, 8
Champion Genealogy 133-6
Cutter's History of Arlington Mass. 191
Paige's History of Cambridge Mass. 485
Wyman's Charlestown Mass. Gens. i, 68
Bathurst — Jones Gen. (1891) 143-9
Richmond Va. Standard iii, 5, 24
Batson — Chamber's N. J. Germans
Savage's Gen. Dictionary i, 139
Batte — New Eng. His. and Genealogical
  Reg. xxxviii, 199; xxxix, 164; li,
  181-8, 348-57; lii, 44-51, 321-2
Richmond Va. Standard iii, 33, 40
Savage's Genealogical Dictionary i, 140
Slaughter's Bristol Parish Va. 206
See also under Bates
Battell — American Ancestry iii, 134
Cothren's History of Woodbury Ct. 1471
Dickerman Genealogy 548-51
Leland Magazine 178
Orcutt's History of Torrington Ct. 649
Savage's Genealogical Dictionary i, 140
Battelle — Battelle Genealogy (1889) 20 p.
Batten — Cochrane's Francestown 508-10
Batter — Savage's Gen. Dict. i, 141
Batterson — Am. Ancestry iii, 4; v, 181
Hinman's Connecticut Settlers 155-7
Stiles' History of Windsor Ct. ii, 68
Batterton — Power's Sangamon 100-5

Battey — Austin's R. I. Gen. Dict. 16
Daniel's History of Oxford Mass. 400
Battle — American Ancestry viii, 217
Wheeler's History of North Carolina
Battles — Ballou's Milford Mass. 570-3
Bass' History of Braintree Vt. 115-7
Davis' Landmarks of Plymouth Mass. 25
Dickerman Genealogy 42-5
Heywood's Hist. of Westminster Mass. 538
Kingman's N. Bridgewater Mass. 457-60
Lincoln's History of Hingham Mass. ii, 51
Mitchell's Hist. of Bridgewater Mass. 113
Norton's Hist. of Fitzwilliam N. H. 464
Pickering Genealogy
Porter Genealogy (1878) 68
Wheeler's Eminent North Carolinians 162
Bauder — Montgomery N. Y. Hist. 152
Baulstone — Austin's R. I. Dict. 16
Savage's Genealogical Dictionary i, 109
Baum — Egle's Notes and Queries, 3d ser. ii, 24-6
Baumann — Bowman Genealogy
Bavis — Bavis Ancestry (1880) 4 pages
Baxter — Amer. Ancestry i, 5; vi, 53
Baxter Genealogy (1879) 114 pages
Bergen's Kings Co. N. Y. Settlers 23
Bradbury's Kennebunkport Me. 224
Childs Genealogy 460-4
Cleveland's Hist. of Yates Co. N. Y. 746
Cochrane's Hist. of Francestown N. H. 510
Dedham Hist. Register viii, 97-104
Draper's History of Spencer Mass. 181
Hinman's Connecticut Settlers 162
Hubbard's History of Stanstead Can. 148
New Eng. Hist. and Gen. Reg. xx, 157
New York Gen. and Biog. Record xxxi, 3-8, 74-9, 178-80
Read's History of Swanzey N. H. 287
Savage's Genealogical Dict. 141
Wyman's Charlestown Mass. Gens. i, 69
Bay — Willard's Med. Annals 213-7
Bayard — American Ancestry iii, 78
Bayard Genealogy (1885) 24 pages
Bolton's Westchester County N. Y. ii, 709
Cleveland's Hist. of Yates Co. N. Y. 694
Lamb's History of N. Y. City i, 343, 696
Mallery's Bohemia Manor 46-75
McKean Genealogy 142
Messler's Hist. of Somerset Co. N. J. 59
New York Gen. Rec. x, 36-8; xvi, 49-72
Valentine's N. Y. Manual (1853) 390
Bayles — American Ancestry vi, 10
Bayley — Bangor Hist. Mag. iv, 137
Bradbury's History of Kennebunkport Me. 226
Gage's History of Rowley Mass. 438
Lincoln's Hist. of Hingham Mass. ii, 52
Porter's Hartford Ct. Settlers 4
Redfield Genealogy 7
Savage's Genealogical Dictionary i, 142
Wise Biography
Baylies — American Ancestry v, 44
Baylor — Clarke's Old King William Co. Va. Families
Meade's Va. Churches ii, 464
Page Genealogy 64

Richmond Va. Standard iii, 2, 23
Virginia Mag. of History vi, 197-9, 307-9
Bayne — American Ancestry viii, 95
Walker Genealogy (1896) 252-7
Baynton — Salisbury Gen. (1885) 551-6
Baytop — Richmond Va. Standard iii, 31
Beach — American Ancestry ii, 9; vii, 5; ix, 68, 136; x, 72
Anderson's Waterbury Ct. i, app. 15
Boltwood's Noble Genealogy, 319-23
Boyd's Annals Winchester Ct. 33-5, 186
Burleigh's Guild Genealogy 64
Davis' History of Wallingford Ct. 635-50
Ely Genealogy 385-7
Hall's Genealogical Notes 156-8
Hibbard's History of Goshen Ct. 418-33
Hinman's Connecticut Settlers 163
Humphreys Genealogy 278
Littell's Passaic Valley Genealogies 35-7
Loomis Genealogy (1880) 740-2
Orcutt's History of Derby Ct. 699-701
Orcutt's History of New Milford Ct. 648
Orcutt's History of Stratford Ct. 11, 23-9
Orcutt's Hist. Torrington Ct. 649, 663-6
Power's Sangamon Co. Ill. Settlers 202-4
Savage's Genealogical Dictionary i, 144
Sharpe's History of Seymour Ct. 158
Strong Genealogy 836-8
Tanner Genealogy 10-2
Temple's History of Northfield Mass. 404
Todd's History of Redding Ct. 182
Vinton's Giles Genealogy 82
Walker Family 163
Beacham — Selleck's Norwalk 97-101
Wyman's Charlestown i, 70
Beachey — Bitsche Genealogy 53-60, etc.
Beadle — Davis' Wallingford Ct. 651
Hinman's Connecticut Settlers 164
Savage's Genealogical Dictionary i, 144
Wyman's Charlestown Mass. Gens. i, 70
See also Bedell
Beal — Ballou's Milford Mass. 573-5
Beal Genealogy (1865) 8 pages
Futhey's History of Chester Co. Pa. 479
Hobart's History of Abington Mass. 243
Jackson's History of Newton Mass. 240
Kingman's No. Bridgewater Mass. 447
Lapham's History of Norway Me. 463
Lincoln's Hist. of Hingham Mass. ii, 53-77
Maine Hist. and Gen. Recorder v, 241
Martin's History of Chester Pa. 264
Mitchell's History of Bridgewater Mass. 113-5
Paxton's Marshall Genealogy 311
Porter Genealogy by J. W. Porter 36
Randall's Hist. of Chesterfield N. H. 225
Read's History of Swanzey N. H. 288
Redfield Genealogy 90
Stackpole's History of Durham Me. 150
Vinton's Giles Genealogy 483
Wyman's Charlestown Mass. Gens. i, 71
Yates Family Memoir
Beale — American Ancestry ii, 9
Butler's Hist. of Farmington Me. 376
See also under head of Beal
Beall — Balch's Brooke Fam. of England

Beals — Bassett's Richmond N. H. 360
Bouton Genealogy 169
Calnek's History of Annapolis N. S. 475
Craft's Hist. of Whately Mass. 389–91
Dyer's History of Plainfield Mass. 126–30
Hudson's History of Lexington Mass. 11
Joslin's History of Poultney Vt. 211
Savage's Genealogical Dictionary i, 145–7
Smith's History of Sunderland Mass. 267
Stearns's Hist. of Ashburnham, Mass. 606
Temple's Hist. of Whately Mass. 205
Beam — American Ancestry viii, 135–7
Chambers' Early Germans of N. J. 256–8
Power's Sangamon Co. Ill. Settlers 104
Roome Genealogy 11–5
Beaman — Adam's Fairhaven Vt. 300–3
Heywood's Hist. of Westminster Mass. 539
Hudson's History of Marlboro Mass. 322
Joslin's History of Poultney Vt. 212
Keyes Genealogy 10–3
Savage's Genealogical Dictionary i, 147
Smith's History of Sunderland Mass. 268
Temple's History of Northfield Mass. 405
Ward's History of Shrewsbury Mass. 248
Beamond — Stiles' Windsor Ct. ii, 69
Beamsley — Savage's Gen. Dict. i, 147
Bean — Amer. Ancestry iv, 119; vi, 53
Baker Genealogy (1867) 22–4
Bangor Me. Historical Mag. i, 159–64
Bean Family Reunion (1896) 152 pages
Bean's Hist. of Montgomery Co. Pa. 554–6
Cassel Genealogy 265–9
Chase's History of Chester N. H. 467
Cogswell's History of Henniker N. H. 458
Cogswell's Hist. of Nottingham N. H. 334
Dearborn's Hist. of Salisbury N. H. 466–78
Eaton's History of Thomaston Me. 143
Fullonton's Hist. of Raymond N. H. 187–92
Guild's Stiles Genealogy 121
Lancaster's Hist. of Gilmanton N. H. 257
Lapham's Hist. of Bethel Me. 478–87, 652
Lapham's History of Rumford Me. 304
Otis Genealogy
Poore Genealogy 88
Potts Genealogy (1895) 237–41
Ridlon's Saco Valley Me. Families 456–64
Runnel's Sanbornton N. H. ii, 27–31
Wentworth Genealogy ii, 15–8
Worthen's Hist. of Sutton N. H. 606–25
Beane — Austin's Allied Families 39
Beans — Bowie Genealogy 54–7
Bearce — Lapham's Norway Me. 464
Lapham's Hist. of Woodstock Me. 175
Mitchell's Hist. of Bridgewater Mass. 115
See also under Bearss
Beard — Cogswell's New Boston 380–3
Hazen's History of Billerica Mass. 9
Heywood's History of Westminster Mass. 541
Livermore's Hist. of Wilton N. H. 314
Loveland Genealogy, Supp. to vol. ii, 1–35
Nevins Genealogy
Norton's Hist. of Fitzwilliam N. H. 464
Orcutt's Hist. of Stratford Ct. 1129
Savage's Genealogical Dictionary i, 148
Sedgwick's History of Sharon Ct. 63

Washington N. H. History 302
Young's Hist. of Wayne Co. Ind. 237, 325
Beardsley — Am. Anc. i, 5; vi 56; vii, 40
Anderson's Waterbury Ct. i, app. 16
Beardsley Genealogy (1867) 32 pages
Leavenworth Genealogy 104
Norton's History of Knox Co. Ohio 359
Orcutt's History of Derby Ct. 701
Orcutt's Hist. of New Milford Ct. 649
Orcutt's Hist. of Stratford Ct. 1130–42
Savage's Genealogical Dict. 148
Sedgwick's Hist. of Sharon Ct. 63
Bearss — Bearss Gen. (1871) 16 pages
Boyd's History of Conesus N. Y. 143
Freeman's Cape Cod Mass. ii, 297–300
Savage's Genealogical Dictionary 149
Swift's Barnstable Mass. Families i, 52–9
See also under Bearce
Beath — Beath Genealogy (1898) 20 pages
Beaton — Morrison's Windham 337–45
Beattie — Eaton's Thomaston Me. 143
Lapham's History of Bethel Me. 487
Beatty — Beatty Gen. (1873) 120 pages
Chambers' Early Germans of N. J. 258–60
Cooley's Trenton N. J. Gens. 8–13
Egle's Penn. Gens., 2d ed., 78–97
Egle's Notes and Queries, 1st ser., i, 456; (1898) 29
Beauchamp — Hinman's Puritans 168
Savage's Genealogical Dictionary i, 149
Beaumont — Davis' Wallingford 635
Beautiette — North Brookfield 523
Beauvelt — Cole Genealogy 32–4, 74–7
Beavay — N. E. Hist. Reg. xxxvii, 236
Beaver — Amer. Anc. i, 6; ii, 9; iii, 191
Beavers — Chambers' N. J. Germans
Bebout — Littell's Passaic Valley 37
Bechtel — Penn. Magazine xix, 148–51
Beck — Goode Genealogy 257
New Eng. Hist. and Gen. Reg. xi, 256
Pearson's Schenectady N. Y. Settlers 10
Savage's Genealogical Dictionary i, 150
Becker — American Ancestry ii, 9
Bouton Genealogy 246–8
Brubacher Genealogy 181–3
Collin's Hist. of Hillsdale N. Y. app. 35–8
Munsell's Albany Colls. iv, 95
Pearson's Schenectady N. Y. Settlers 11
Becket — Essex Inst. Coll. viii, 139–44
Life of Rev. Wm. Smith
Savage's Genealogical Dictionary i, 151
Beckford — Driver Genealogy 245–50
New Eng. Hist. and Gen. Reg. v, 451
Savage's Genealogical Dictionary i, 151
Beckley — Andrew's New Britain 297
Hinman's Connecticut Settlers 175
New Eng. Hist. and Gen. Reg. xvi, 20–1
Randall's Hist. of Chesterfield N. H. 226
Savage's Genealogical Dictionary i, 151
See also under Bickley
Beckman — Runnell's Sanbornton ii, 32
Beckwith — American Ancestry ii, 10; vi, 63; viii, 21, 67; xi, 205
Beckwith Genealogy (1891) 384 pages
Beckwith Genealogy (1899) 88 pages
Beckwith Notes (1899) 55 pages

Bulkley's Browne Mem. 66, 101-4
Caulkins' History of New London Ct. 298
Champion Genealogy
Hayward's History of Gilsum N. H. 262
Hemenway's Vermont Gaz. v, pt 3, 39-41
Lane Genealogy (1899) 40-5
Merrill's History of Acworth N. H. 186
Savage's Genealogical Dictionary i, 151
Slaughter's Bristol Parish Va. 131
Walworth's Hyde Genealogy 967, 1003-5
Beckworth — Hinman's Settlers 177
Beddoe — Cleveland's Yates Co. 465-7
Bede — Cleveland's Yates Co. N. Y. 516
Bedell — Bedell Gen. (1885) 22 pages
Bunker's Long Island Genealogies 172-6
Clute's Hist. of Staten Island N. Y. 342
Hoyt's Salisbury Mass. Families 61
Keith's Harrison Ancestry 34
Littell's Passaic Valley N. J. Gens. 39-44
Savage's Genealogical Dictionary i, 152
See also Beadle
Bedford — Kulp's Wyoming Families
Littell's Passaic Valley N. J. Gens. 45
Ormsby Genealogy 21
Bedinger — Lee Genealogy (1895) 471
Powers Sangamon Co. Ill. Settlers 105
Welles' Washington Genealogy 243
Bedle — Salter's Monmouth Co. N. J.
Bedlow — Nevins Genealogy 81-4, 665-9
N. Y. Gen. and Biog. Record xxxi, 51
Beebe — American Ancestry ii, 10, 153;
vi, 196; vii, 188; viii, 24
Anderson's Waterbury Ct. i, app. 16
Caulkin's Hist. of New London 338-40
Field's History of Haddam Ct. 47
Griffin's Journal, Southold L. I. 200
Hinman's Connecticut Settlers 172
Litchfield Co. Ct. History (1881) 166
Orcutt's History of Stratford Ct. 1142
Paul's History of Wells Vt. 64
Phœnix's Whitney Family 170
Savage's Genealogical Dictionary i, 153
Wilbraham Mass. Centennial 292
Beecher — Am. Anc. i. 6; v, 105; vii, 176
Ammidown Family 26
Anderson's Waterbury Ct. i, app. 17
Dawson Genealogy 83-6
Dickerman Genealogy 192-8
Goodwin's Foote Genealogy 155
Morris Genealogy (1853) 11-8
Orcutt's Hist. of New Milford Ct. 650
Orcutt's History of Wolcott Ct. 450-2
Savage's Genealogical Dictionary i, 153
Strong Genealogy 144-50
Sharpe's History of Seymour Ct. 221
Tuttle Family of Conn. 153-7, 634-7
Beede — Hatch's Industry Me. 509-12
Livermore's Wilton N. H. 253-60, 315-7
Otis Genealogy 8, 51
Beedle — See Bedell and Beadle
Beedy — Crosby Genealogy 69-72
Beeford — Babson's Gloucester, 61-2
Beekman — American Ancestry iii, 4
Beekman Genealogy (1888) 12 p. reprint
Bergen's Kings Co. N. Y. Settlers 25
Hoffman Genealogy 502-5

Holgate's American Genealogies 66-86
Honeyman's Our Home Magazine 490-4
Lamb's History of New York City i, 416
Munsell's Albany Colls. iv, 96
Nevins Genealogy
New Eng. Hist. and Gen. Register li, 337-9
N. Y. Gen. Biog. Rec. xvi, 133-6; xvii,
281; xix, 41-52; xxviii, 52-4; 156-8;
xxx, 83-5
Pearson's Schenectady N. Y. Settlers 12
Smith's History of Dutchess Co. N. Y. 389
Schoonmaker's Hist. Kingston N. Y. 472
Sylvester's Hist. of Ulster Co. N. Y. 171
Talcott's N. Y. and N. E. Families 1-8
Beeman — American Ancestry xi, 16
Beere — Austin's R. I. Gen. Dict. 17
Salter's Hist. of Monmouth Co. N. J. ix
Beers — Bartow Gen., appendix, 197
Bennett Genealogy (1899) 38-49
Bond's Watertown Mass. Gens. 19, 679
Cothren's History of Woodbury Ct. 513-6
Draper's History of Spencer Mass. 180
Gold's History of Cornwall Ct. 313-5
Hinman's Connecticut Settlers 174
Mansfield Genealogy 49
Orcutt's Hist. of New Milford Ct. 651
Orcutt's Hist. of Stratford Ct. 1143-6
Power's Sangamon Co. Ill. Settlers 113
Savage's Genealogical Dictionary i, 154
Schenck's Hist. of Fairfield Ct. 353
Trubee Genealogy 97-9
Washburn's Hist. of Leicester Mass. 344
Beerup — Power's Sangamon Ill. 113
Beeson — Beeson Genealogy (1898) 27 p.
Young's Wayne Co. Ind. 327
Behee — Plumb's Hanover Pa. 389
Beidler — American Ancestry xii, 127
Beiteman — Perkiomen Region ii, 185-7
Belcher — Am. Anc. ii, 10; iv, 211; v, 120
Barry's Hist. of Framingham Mass. 177
Bass' History of Braintree Vt. 117
Belcher Genealogy (1873) 8 pages, reprint,
Butler's History of Farmington Me. 377-87
Cochrane's Hist. Francestown N. H. 511-3
Goode Genealogy 232
Hammatt Papers, Ipswich Mass. 26
Hinman's Connecticut Settlers 177
New Eng. Hist. Reg. xi, 335; xxvii, 239-45
Paige's History of Cambridge Mass. 486
Temple's Hist. No. Brookfield Mass. 524
Temple's History of Northfield Mass. 405
Thayer's Memorial 21
Thornton's Tabular Pedigree (1850)
Vinton's Giles Family 263
Wyman's Charlestown Mass. Gens. i, 73
Belden — American Ancestry ii, 10; viii,
213; xi, 19
Andrew's Hist. of N. Britain Ct. 184, 236
Goodwin's Foot Family 49
Hinman's Connecticut Settlers 179-82
Nash Genealogy 67
N. E. Hist. and Gen. Reg. xv, 746; 905-7
Savage's Genealogical Dictionary i, 157
Selleck's Norwalk Ct. (1896) 383-98
Smith's Hist. of Dutchess Co. N. Y. 498
Sprague's Hist. of Gloversville N. Y. 108

Temple's Hist. of Northfield Mass. 405–8
Temple's Hist. of Whately Mass. 205–9
Belding — American Ancestry i, 6; ii, 10
Craft's History of Whately Mass. 390–402
Ellis Genealogy 117, 170–3; 186–8; 371–3
Hemenway's Vermont Gazette v, 310–2
Huntington's Stamford Ct. Families 10
Judd's History of Hadley Mass. 452
Read's History of Swanzey N. H. 288–90
Sheldon's Hist. of Deerfield Mass. ii, 80
Temple's History of Whately Mass. 26
Belfield — Jones Gen. (1891) 182–4
Richmond Va. Standard iv, 19
Belknap — American Ancestry x, 80
Barry's Hist. of Framingham Mass. 178–9
Bemis' History of Marlboro N. H. 414
Cleveland's Hist. of Yates Co. N. Y. 321
Cutter's History of Arlington Mass. 192
Hemenway's Vermont Gazette v, 107
Hubbard's Stanstead County Canada 326
Leonard's History of Dublin N. H. 316
New Eng. Hist. and Gen. Reg. xiii, 17–9;
  xliv, 400; xlix, 68
Ruttenber's Newburgh N. Y. 267–72
Ruttenber's Orange Co. N. Y. 357–62
Savage's Genealogical Dictionary i, 158
Stiles' History of Windsor Ct. ii, 70
Vinton's Richardson Genealogy 488
Wentworth Genealogy ii, 111
Wheeler's Hist. of Newport N. H. 300–3
Whitney Genealogy (1860)
Winchester Mass. Record ii, 272–82
Wyman's Charlestown Mass. Gens. i, 73
Bell — Amer. Ancestry i, 6; ii, 11; xi, 131
Chambers' Early Germans of N. J. 261
Chase's History of Chester N. H. 468–71
Cochrane's History of Antrim N. H. 360
Cochrane's Hist. Francestown N. H. 513–6
Cogswell's Hist. of Henniker N. H. 469
Craft's Genealogy 104–9
Cunnabell Genealogy 33
Dwight Genealogy 237–40
Egle's Notes and Queries, 3d ser., iii, 366–8;
  (1898) 71–3
Ellis' History of Roxbury Mass. 91
Green's Kentucky Families
Hayward's Hist. of Hancock N. H. 340–2
Hinman's Connecticut Settlers 186–8
Huntington's Stamford Settlers 10–2
Kilbourne Genealogy 441
Munsell's Albany Colls. iv, 96
New Eng. Hist. and Gen. Reg. xxiii, 253
New York Gen. and Biog. Rec. xxviii,
  153–5, 201–7; xxix, 59–68
Parker's Hist. Londonderry N. H. 262–4
Paxton's Marshall Genealogy 297
Peyton's History of Augusta Co. Va. 311
Power's Sangamon Co. Ill. Settlers 106–9
Richmond Va. Standard iii, 16
Savage's Genealogical Dictionary i, 159–60
Scott Genealogy 71–9, 238–40
Secomb's History of Amherst N. H. 500
Slaughter's St. Mark's Parish Va. 125
Spooner Genealogy i, 269–73
Temple's Hist. of No. Brookfield Mass. 524
Temple's History of Palmer Mass. 422

Timlow's Sketches of Southington Ct. 26
Waddell's Annals of Augusta Co. Va. 430 3
Washington N. H. History 303
Wyman's Charlestown Mass. Gens. i, 75
Young's Hist. of Chautauqua Co. N. Y. 593
Bellamy — Cothren's Woodbury 507
Davis' History of Wallingford Ct. 652
Hinman's Connecticut Settlers 182–5
Paul's History of Wells Vt. 64
Savage's Genealogical Dictionary i, 160
Bellas — American Ancestry x, 24
Bellinger — Bellinger Gen. (1895) 109 p.
Bellingham — Essex College xix, 307
Savage's Genealogical Dictionary i, 161
Bellis — American Ancestry iv, 134
Chambers' Early Germans of N. J. 262–4
Bellows — Aldrich's Walpole 193–213
American Ancestry i, 6; ii, 11; xi, 57
Barry's Hist. of Framingham Mass. 180
Bellows Family Meeting (1855) 125 p.
Bellows Fam. Narratives (1888) 383 pages
Bellows Genealogy (1898) 657 pages
Bond's Hist. of Watertown Mass. 532–9
Daniel's History of Oxford Mass. 401
Densmore's Hartwell Genealogy
Heyward's Hist. of Westminster Mass. 541
Hubbard's Stanstead County Canada 327
Hudson's Hist.of Marlborough Mass. 322–4
Saunderson's Charlestown N. H. 284–6
Savage's Genealogical Dictionary i, 162
Stone's History of Hubbardston Mass. 227
Strong Genealogy 1162–75
Temple's Hist. of No. Brookfield Mass. 524
Ward's History of Shrewsbury Mass. 244
Bellowsfelt — See Bellis
Belscher — Goode Genealogy 232
Belshaw — Ball's Lake Co. Ind. (1884)
Beman — Buckingham Genealogy 145
Bemas — Caulkins' New London 283
Bement — Hinman's Settlers 188–90
Bemis — American Ancestry ii, 11; vi,
  132; ix, 100; xii
Barry's Hist. of Framingham Mass. 180
Bemis' History of Marlboro N. H. 414–20
Bond's Watertown Mass. Gens. 20–6, 677
Cutter's History of Arlington Mass. 193
Draper's History of Spencer Mass. 161–73
Dunster Genealogy 146–58
Hemenway's Vermont Gazetteer v, 62–4
Heywood's Hist. Westminster Mass. 542–7
Hinman's Connecticut Settlers 190
Lapham's History of Paris Me. 504
Leonard's History of Dublin N. H. 316–8
Norton's History of Fitzwilliam N. H. 465
Savage's Genealogical Dictionary i, 163
Stearns' Hist. Ashburnham Mass. 607–10
Stearns' History of Rindge N. H. 441
Temple's Hist. of No. Brookfield Mass. 525
Vinton's Richardson Genealogy 97
Westminster Mass. Centennial 17
Wyman's Charlestown Mass. Gens. i, 76
Bemus — Bemus Genealogy (1894) 7 pages
Young's Chautauqua Co. 320
Benade — Keim Genealogy 506
Bendall — Savage's Genealogical Diction-
  ary i, 163

Bender — American Ancestry i, 6
Eyerman Ancestors (1898)
Hudson's History of Marlboro' Mass. 325
Roe's Sketches of Rose N. Y. 120
Benedict — American Ancestry i, 6; ii,
11; iv, 29; vi, 110, 199, 202; viii, 56–7;
ix, 62, 186; x, 9; xi, 19
Anderson's Waterbury Ct. i, app. 18
Bailey Ancestry (1892) 14–8, 32–7
Benedict Genealogy (1849) 4 pages
Benedict Genealogy (1870) 474 pages
Bolton's Westchester Co. N. Y. ii, 501
Boyd's Annals of Winchester Ct. 71
Bronson's History of Waterbury Ct. 463–6
Chapman's Trowbridge Family 128
Cleveland's Yates County N. Y. 484–6, 539
Hall's Records of Norwalk Ct. 308–20
Hinman's Connecticut Settlers 190–5
Huron and Erie Counties Ohio 173–5
Lamb's History of New York i, 202–27
Loomis Genealogy (1880) 787
Morris Bontecou Genealogy 95–6, 160–2
Savage's Genealogical Dictionary i, 164
Selleck's Norwalk Ct. (1896) 365–70
Todd's History of Redding Ct. 183
Young's Hist. of Chautauqua Co. N. Y. 321
Beney — Binney Genealogy
Benezet — Davis' Bucks Co. Pa. 149
Benge — Lewis Genealogy (1893) 70–5
Benger — Va. Magazine ii (1895) 340
Benham — Amer. Ancestry ii; x, 109
Anderson's Waterbury Ct. i, app. 18
Davis' Hist. of Wallingford Ct. 653–6, 941
Dimond Genealogy 87
Hamden Ct. History 236
Hinman's Connecticut Settlers 195
Morris' Bontecou Genealogy 41–3, 149
Power's Sangamon Co. Ill. Settlers 109
Savage's Genealogical Dictionary, 155
Tuttle Family 641
Benjamin — Am. Anc. v, 227; viii, 110
Bond's Watertown Mass. Gens. 26–9, 680
Burke and Alvord Genealogies 187–94
Heywood's Hist. of Westminster Mass. 547
Hinman's Connecticut Settlers 196
Kewaunee Wis. Owl (1900) i
Norton's History of Fitzwilliam N. H. 466
Orcutt's History of Stratford Ct. 1146
Paige's History of Hardwick Mass. 336
Roe's Sketches of Rose N. Y. 43
Savage's Genealogical Dictionary i, 165
Stearns' Hist. of Ashburnham Mass. 610–2
Stiles' History of Windsor Ct. ii, 71
Swift's Barnstable Families i, 143
Washburne's Hist. of Livermore Me. 17–21
Whitman's Genealogy 563–9
Wyman's Charlestown Mass. Gens. i, 77
Benner — Barry's Hanover Mass. 258
Dennysville Me. Centennial 102
Eaton's Annals of Warren Me. 504
Perkiomen Region vol. ii, 78–82
Smith's History of Rhinebeck N. Y. 172–7
Bennett — American Ancestry i, 7; ii, 11;
vi, 176; xii
Austin's R. I. Genealogical Dict. 18
Babson's History of Gloucester Mass. 62

Ballou's History of Milford Mass. 577
Barry's History of Framingham Mass. 180
Bassett's Hist. of Richmond N. H. 311–13
Bennett Family of Ipswich (1875) 8 pages
Bennett Fam. of Weymouth (1899) 50 pages
Bergen's Kings Co. N. Y. Settlers 27–30
Bolton Genealogy (1889) 44
Buckminster's Hastings Family 101–6
Butler's History of Groton Mass. 386
Caverno Genealogy 26–8
Champion Genealogy 27
Chandler's History of Shirley Mass. 351–6
Cleveland's History of Yates Co. N. Y.
688–92
Cogswell's Hist. of Northwood N. H. 639-41
Craft's History of Whately Mass. 402
Eaton's History of Thomaston Me. 143
Futhey's History of Chester Co. Pa. 480
Hammatt Papers, Ipswich Mass. 27
Hayward's Hist. of Hancock N. H. 342–5
Hazen's History of Billerica Mass. 11
Hemenway's Vermont Gaz. v, 99, 187, 398
Hinman's Connecticut Settlers 198–200
Hollister's History of Pawlet Vt. 165
Hudson's History of Lexington Mass. 11
Kulp's Wyoming Valley Families
Lapham's History of Bethel Me. 488
Lapham's History of Norway Me. 465
Maris Genealogy 77
Neill's Virginia Carolorum 304
N. E. Hist. and Gen. Reg. xxix, 165–70
Norton's History of Fitzwilliam N. H. 466
Orcutt's History of New Milford Ct. 651–8
Orcutt's History of Stratford Ct. 1148
Plumb's History of Hanover Pa. 391–5
Power's Sangamon Co. Ill. Settlers 110–12
Read's History of Swanzey N. H. 290–3
Ridlon's Harrison Me. Settlers 25
Salter's History of Monmouth Co. N. J. ix
Savage's Genealogical Dictionary i, 166–8
Secomb's History of Amherst N. H. 501
Sedgwick's History of Sharon Ct. 64
Slaughter's St. Mark's Parish Va. 38
Smith's History of Delaware Co. Pa. 44
Stearns' History of Ashburnham Mass. 613
Stearns' History of Rindge N. H. 442–4
Stowe's Hist. of Hubbardston Mass. 228
Tyngsboro' Mass. Centennial Record 16
Virginia Magazine of History iii (1895) 53–6
Ward's History of Shrewsbury Mass. 229
Washington N. H. History 304
Weaver's History of Windham Ct. 94–6
Whitmore's Copps Hill Epitaphs
Wood Genealogy 12
Worcester's History of Hollis N. H. 366
Wyman's Charlestown Mass. Gens. i, 78
Benney — American Ancestry viii, 92
Binney Genealogy
Benning — Wentworth Genealogy i, 65
Benninger — Salem N. Y. Book 56
Bennock — Bangor Hist. Mag. iii, 236–8
Benoit — Munsell's Albany Colls. iv, 97
Temple's Hist. of No. Brookfield Mass. 526
Bensen — American Ancestry i, 7
Munsell's Albany Colls. iv, 96
Pearson's Schenectady N. Y. Settlers 13

Benson — American Ancestry i, 7; ii, 11
Barry's History of Framingham Mass. 181
Bassett's History of Richmond N. H. 313
Benson Genealogy (1872) 65 pages
Bergen Genealogy 80
Bradbury's Kennebunkport Me. 227
Calnek's History of Annapolis N. S. 477
Davis' Landmarks of Plymouth 26
Deane's History of Scituate Mass. 220
Dearborn's History of Parsonfield Me. 453
Hatch's History of Industry Me. 512
Hoffman Genealogy 487-9
Lapham's History of Norway Me. 466
Lapham's History of Paris Me. 506-8
Mitchell's Bridgewater Mass. 115
Riker's History of Harlem N. Y. 480-91
Savage's Genealogical Dictionary i, 168
Talcott's N. Y. and N. E. Families 8-22
Williams' History of Danby Vt. 111
Bent — American Ancestry x, 140
Barry's Framingham 181-4, 453
Bent Genealogy (1894) 10 pages, reprint
Bent Genealogy (1900) 313 pages
Calnek's History Annapolis N. S. 477-9
Glover Genealogy 340
Hudson's History of Marlboro Mass. 324
Lapham's History of Paris Me. 508
N. E. Hist. Reg. xlviii, 288-96; xlix, 65-7
Norton's Hist. of Fitzwilliam N. H. 467-70
Savage's Genealogical Dictionary 169
Bentley — Austin's R. I. Gen. Dict. 19
Bennett and Bentley Gen. (1899) 30-7
Bentley Family of Ohio (1897) 20 pages
Eaton's History of Thomaston Me. 145
Potts Genealogy (1895) 377-80
Robertson's Pocahontas' Descendants
Savage's Genealogical Dictionary 160
Stanton Genealogy 129
Thomas Genealogy (1896) 200
Wyman's Charlestown Mass. Gens. i, 79
Young's Hist. of Chautauqua Co. N. Y. 233
Benton — American Ancestry i, 7; iv, 236;
vii, 173; x, 198; xii
Bass' History of Braintree Vt. 117
Benton's History of Guildhall Vt. 265
Cleveland's History of Yates Co. N. Y.
262-70
Green's Kentucky Families
Gregg's Old Cheraws S. C. 104
Hart Family of Virginia (1882) 78-82
Hinman's Connecticut Settlers 201-3
Hubbard's Stanstead Co. Canada 125
Matthew's History of Cornwell Vt. 284
Missouri Biographical Dictionary 5
New Eng. Hist. and Gen. Reg. xvi, 18;
liv. 175-9
Paxton's Marshall Genealogy 64
Peyton's History of Augusta Co. Va. 305
Richmond Va. Standard ii, 7
Ridlon's Saco Valley Me. Families 464
Savage's Genealogical Dictionary i, 169-70
Stiles' History of Windsor Ct. ii, 71
Talcott's N. Y. and N. E. Families 485-92
Waldo's History of Tolland Ct. 80-3
Washington N. H. History 305
Bentzen — Green's Todd Genealogy

Bergen — American Ancestry v, 199; vi,
151
Bergen Genealogy (1866) 302 pages
Bergen Genealogy 2d ed. (1876) 658 pages
Bergen's Settlers Kings Co. N. Y. 31-4
New York Gen. and Biog. Record x, 152
Power's Sangamon Co. Ill. Settlers 114-6
Berger — Chambers' N. J. Germans
Bergey — Cassel Genealogy 95-8
Bergh — N. Y. Gen. Record xix, 122-5
Smith's History of Rhinebeck N. Y. 178-81
Berkley — Carter Family Tree
Evelyn's Life of Mrs. Godolphin 148
Page Genealogy 144, 149
Richmond Va. Standard i, 47, 49; iii, 4, 48;
iv, 2
Bernaben — Bartow Genealogy 2d part
Bernard — Eaton's Thomaston Me. 145
Richmond Va. Standard iii, 26
Robertson's Pocahontas' Descendants
Tiernan Genealogy 193-5, 205-22
Bernhard — Chambers' N. J. Germans
Bernon — Ammidown's Colls. i, 125
Austin's R. I. Genealogical Dict. 19
Baird's Huguenot Emigration to America
Rhode Island Hist. Soc. Colls. iii, 315
Savage's Genealogical Dictionary i, 170
Berrien — Bergen's Kings Co. N. Y. 34
Bolton's Westchester ii, 799
Riker's Annals Newtown N. Y. 338-44
Berringer — Munsell's Albany iv, 97
Smith's Hist. of Rhinebeck N. Y. 190-2
Berry — Am. Ancestry vi, 17; viii, 137
Bangor Me. Historical Magazine viii, 104
Barry's History of Framingham Mass. 184
Bowie Genealogy 371-9
Chase's History of Chester N. H. 471
Clayton's History of Bergen Co. N. J. 232
Cogswell's History of Henniker N. H. 460
Dow's History of Hampton N. H. 600
Eaton's History of Thomaston Me. 145
Freeman's Cape Cod Mass. ii, 198, 207
Guild's Stiles Genealogy 37
Hanson's Hist. of Gardiner Me. 79, 81
Hinman's Connecticut Settlers 204
Lane Genealogy (1891) 40, 109-11
Lapham's History of Bethel Me. 488
Lapham's History of Norway Me. 469
Lapham's History of Paris Me. 510-12
Lapham's History of Woodstock Me. 176
Lawrence and Bartlett Memorial 23
Lincoln's History of Hingham Mass. ii, 78
Machias Me. Centennial Celebration 154
Maine Genealogist ii, (1876) 6-14
Morrison's History of Windham N. H. 336
N. Y. Gen. and Biog. Record xv, 49-57
Oneida Hist. Soc. Trans. ii 127-32
Paige's History of Hardwick Mass. 336-9
Roome Genealogy 7, 24-95
Savage's Genealogical Dictionary i, 170
Shotwell Genealogy 37-9
Swift's Barnstable Families i, 136-9
Wheeler's History of Brunswick Me. 829
Berteaux — Calnek's Annapolis N. S. 480
Berthold — Beckwith's Creoles 62
Bertine — Bolton's Westchester ii, 710

Bertolet— Keim Family 107-10, 267-9
Perkiomen Region 96
Bertram — Hurd's Fairfield Ct. 578
Bertrand — Hayden's Va. Gens. 334
Besbedge—Savage's Gen. Dictionary i, 171
See Bisbee
Bessac — Bessac Genealogy (1863) 22 pages
Besse — Freeman's Cape Cod ii, 74
Lapham's History of Bethel Me. 489
Bessee — Mitchell's Bridgewater 116
Bessey — American Ancestry xi, 132
Lapham's Paris Me. 513-6
New Eng. Hist and Gen. Reg. xxxvii, 377
Best — Am. Ancestry ii, 11, 153; x, 97
Keep Genealogy
Bethune — Bethune Gen. (1866) 54 pages
Bethune Genealogy 2d ed. (1894) 55 pages
Duffield Golden Wedding (1867) 58 pages
Morrison's Hist. of Windham N. H. 337-45
Bettis — Temple's No. Brookfield 526
Betton — Dickey Genealogy 26-31
Morrison's Windham 337-45
Betts — American Ancestry ii, 153; v, 43; vii, 205
Bergen's Settlers of Kings Co. N. Y. 33
Betts Genealogy (1888) 132 pages
Boardman Genealogy (1895) 138-49
Hall's Records of Norwalk Ct. 274-7
Hinman's Connecticut Settlers 205-7, 440
Hollister's History of Pawlet Vt. 166
New York Gen. and Biog. Rec. xvi, 1-6, xix, 164
Paige's History of Cambridge Mass. 488
Riker's Annals of Newtown N. Y. 373-8
Savage's Genealogical Dictionary i, 172
Sedgwick's History of Sharon Ct. 64
Selleck's Norwalk Ct. (1896) 225-50
Smith's Genealogy of Wm. Smith 57, 73
Swift's Barnstable Families i, 88
Todd's History of Redding Ct. 184
Betz — American Ancestry xii, 34
Bevan — Glenn's Welsh Tracts 154-86
Martin's Chester Pa. 42-4
Bevans — Orcutt's Stratford Ct. 1149
Power's Sangamon Co. Ill. Settlers 117
Beveridge — Eaton's Thomaston 146
Beverley — Beverley Chart (1890)
Beverly — Carter Family Tree
Lee Genealogy (1895) 319
Meade's Old Churches of Va. ii, 481
Neill's Virginia Carolorum
Virginia Magazine of History ii, 405-13; iii, 47-52, 169-76, 261-71, 383-92
Beverstock — Hayward's Gilsum 264
Bevier — American Ancestry vi, 58
Bevin—Hinman's Connecticut Settlers 207
Whittemore's Middlesex County Ct. 201
Bevoise — Bergen's Kings Co. N. Y. 85
Beyer — Kriebel's Schwenkfelders 17-35
Magennis Genealogy 172-4
Beyerly — Egle's Notes and Queries 3d series, iii, 532-6
Parthemore Genealogy 153-6, 169-75, 204-10
Bezer — Potts Genealogy (1895) 125-34
Bibb — Gilmer's Georgians 108
Saunder's Alabama Settlers 433-42

Bibbins — Hinman's Conn. Settlers 207
Weaver's History of Windham Ct. 96-9
Bibbitt — Temple's No. Brookfield 500
Bibighaus — Bibighaus Gen. (1888) 44 p.
Bice — Power's Sangamon Co. Ill. 117
Bickford — Bradbury's Kennebunkport
Cogswell's History of Henniker N. H. 462
Cogswell's Hist. of Nottingham N. H. 641-5
Eaton's Annals of Warren Me. 505
Herrick's History of Gardner Mass. 335
Piper Genealogy (1889) 48
Runnell's Hist. Sanbornton N. H. ii, 33-5
Wentworth Genealogy ii, 519-21
Bickley — William and Mary College Quarterly v, 28-30, 124-7
See also under Beckley
Bicknall — Wyman's Charlestown 81
Bicknell — Am. Ancestry v, 182; vi, 83
Ballou's History of Milford Mass. 578
Bicknell Reunion (1880) 96 pages
Bicknell Memorial (1880) 48 pages
Bicknell Reunion (1883) 56 pages
Lincoln's History of Hingham Mass. ii, 79
Bickwell — Savage's Gen. Dict. i, 174
Biddle — Am. Anc. iii, 212; vi, 44; xi, 20
Biddle Autobiography (1883) 376
Biddle Genealogy (1883) 16 pages
Biddle Genealogy (1892) 87 pages
Biddle Genealogy Additions (1895) 95 pages
Boogher's Miscellaneous Americana 101-6
Savage's Genealogical Dictionary i, 174
Biddlestone — Savage's Gen. Dict. 187
Bidlack — Ransom Genealogy 34
Weaver's History of Windham Ct. 99-102
Bidlake — Hinman's Conn. Settlers 208
Bidwell — American Ancestry ix, 3-18
Andrews' History of New Britain Ct. 384
Bidwell Genealogy (1884) 123 pages
Brown's West Simsbury Ct. Settlers 13
Hinman's Connecticut Settlers 209
New Eng. Hist. Gen. Reg. xxvii, 192
Read's History of Swanzey N. H. 293
Stiles' History of Windsor Ct. ii, 72-4
Bigelow — Adam's Fairhaven Vt. 313
Allen's Worcester Mass. Association 95
American Ancestry i, 7; ii, 12; iv, 192, 205; v, 126; vii, 94; viii, 76, 85
Barry's Hist. of Framingham Mass. 184-8
Bass' History of Braintree Vt. 117
Bemis' History of Marlboro N. H. 421
Bigelow Genealogy (1877) 10 pages
Bigelow Genealogy (1890) 517 pages
Bigelow Reunion (1887) 46 pages
Bigelows in Revolution (1877) 15 pages
Bond's Watertown Mass. Gens. 29-41, 682
Craft's History of Whately Mass. 402-4
Daniels' History of Oxford Mass. 402
Draper's History of Spencer Mass. 181
Hayward's History of Hancock N. H. 345-8
Heywood's Hist. Westminster Mass. 547-54
Hinman's Connecticut Settlers 210-4
Hudson's Hist. of Marlboro' Mass. 325-30
Hurd's Hist. of New London Co. Ct. 399
Keyes' West Boylston Mass. Reg. 14
Loveland Genealogy i, 77-80
Missouri Pioneer Families 128

Morse's Sherborne Mass. Settlers 15
N. E. Hist. Gen. Reg. x, 297; xlii, 79–81
Norton's Hist. of Fitzwilliam N. H. 470–4
Pierce's H.story of Grafton Mass. 458–62
Savage's Genealogical Dictionary i, 175
Stearns' History of Ashburnham Mass. 615
Sylvester's History of Ulster Co. N. Y.
Temple's No. Brookfield Mass. 526–8
Tuttle Genealogy 444–6
Vinton's Richardson Genealogy 644
Wall's Reminis. of Worcester Mass. 44–8
Ward's History of Shrewsbury Mass. 230–3
Westminster Mass. Centennial 22
Bigg — Bigg Genealogy (1875) 8 pages
New Eng. Hist. and Gen. Reg. xxix, 253
Biggs — Hinman's Conn. Settlers 214–6
Missouri Pioneer Families 129
Neff Genealogy 266–76
Savage's Genealogical Dictionary i, 176
Bignal — Merrill's Acworth N. H. 187
Bigod — Thomas Genealogy (1897) 202
Bigsby — American Ancestry i, 8
Biles — Jolliffe Genealogy 155–60
Bill — Am. Ancestry v, 21; vii, 138; viii, 98
Bass' History of Braintree Vt. 118
Bill Genealogy (1867) 368 pages
Caulkins' History of New London Ct. 320
Hayes' Wells Genealogy 111
Hayward's History of Gilsum N. H. 265
Hine's Lebanon Ct. Address (1880) 145
Huntington Genealogy 110
Hurd's Hist. of New London Ct. 509
Savage's Genealogical Dictionary i, 177
Spooner Genealogy i, 271
Vinton's Richardson Memorial 374
Whittemore's Middlesex County Ct. 201
Billings — Ames' Redman Farm
Austin's R. I. Gen. Dict. 21
Ballou Genealogy 527–9
Bangor Me. Historical Magazine i, 13
Barrus' History of Goshen Mass. 137
Cochrane's Hist. of Francestown N. H. 516
Dana's History of Woodstock Vt. 589–98
Dunster Genealogy 60–2
Dwight Genealogy 763
Hayward's Hist. of Hancock N. H. 348–50
Hinman's Connecticut Settlers 216
Hurd's History of New London Co. Ct. 415
Judd's History of Hadley Mass. 454
Lapham's History of Bethel Me. 489
Lapham's History of Paris Me. 516
Lapham's History of Woodstock Me. 49
Loomis Genealogy (1880) 650
New Eng. Hist. and Gen. Reg. xxxi, 319
Paige's History of Hardwick Mass. 337
Perkins' Old Houses of Norwich Ct. 417
Pompey N. Y. Reunion 286–8
Power's Sangamon Co. Ill. Settlers 118
Savage's Genealogical Dictionary i, 177–9
Sheldon's Hist. of Deerfield Mass. ii, 82–4
Smith's Hist. of Sunderland Mass. 269–73
Stearns' History of Ashburnham Mass. 615
Thayer's Memorial (1835) 67–73
Warren's History of Waterford Me. 231
Weaver's History of Windham Ct. 102
Whitmore's Copps Hill Epitaphs

Billington — Bangor Hist. Mag. iv, 216
Davis' Landmarks of Plymouth Mass. 28
Hayden's Virginia Genealogies 84
Savage's Genealogical Dictionary i, 169
Bills — Savage's Gen. Dictionary i, 179
Secomb's History of Amherst N. H. 501–3
Billups — Saunder's Alabama 367
Bilyeu — Power's Sangamon Co. Ill. 118
Binder — Egle's Notes (1898) 217
Bingham — Amer. Ancestry i, 8; x, 155
Bingham Genealogy (1898) 249 pages
Caulkins' History of Norwich Ct. 164
Granite Monthly (1882) v, 353–7
Hayward's History of Gilsum N. H. 266–8
Hine's Lebanon Ct. Address 146
Hinman's Connecticut Settlers 218–21
Matthew's History of Cornwall Vt. 284
New Eng. Hist. and Gen. Reg. xlix, 333–5
Perkins' Norwich Ct. Families 31–50
Randall's Hist. of Chesterfield N. H. 226–8
Savage's Genealogical Dictionary i, 180
Walworth's Hyde Gen. 57, 203, 1039–44
Binney — American Ancestry viii, 35
Binney Genealogy (1886) 278 pages
Ballou's History of Milford Mass. 579
Bridgeman's Granary Epitaphs 119–22
Life of Rev. Wm. Smith
Lincoln's Hist. of Hingham Mass. ii, 80–2
Savage's Genealogical Dictionary i, 180
Wyman's Charlestown Mass. Gens. i, 83
Birch — Roome Genealogy 288–92
Savage's Genealogical Dictionary i, 181
Birchard — Caulkin's Norwich 165–7
Hine's Lebanon Ct. Address 146
Hinman's Connecticut Settlers 221–3
Perkins' Old Houses of Norwich Ct. 419–21
Savage's Genealogical Dictionary i, 181
Walworth's Hyde Genealogy 41
See also under Burchard
Bird — American Ancestry iv, 85
Baird's History of Rye N. Y. 453
Bird Family of Hartford (1855) 24 pages
Bird Family of Dorchester (1871) 40 pages
Blake Genealogy
Bond's Watertown Mass. Gens. 41
Chambers' Early Germans of N. J. 265
Deane's History of Scituate Mass. 221
Eaton's History of Thomaston Me. 147
Eaton's Annals of Warren Me. 505
Fisher Genealogy 77
Glover Genealogy 370–3, 425–7
Hinman's Connecticut Settlers 223–7
Lapham's History of Bethel Me. 490
Lapham's History of Norway Me. 466
Lapham's History of Paris Me. 518
New Haven Colony Collections i, 114–7
N. E. Hist. Gen. Reg. xxv, 21–30, 151
Pope Genealogy
Power's Sangamon County Ill. 119–22
Savage's Genealogical Dictionary i, 182
Temple's Hist. of No. Brookfield Mass. 529
Underwood's Pollard Genealogy
Wyman's Charlestown Mass. Gens. i, 84
See also under Byrd
Birdsall — American Ancestry ix, 71
Baird's History of Rye N. Y. 454

Bolton's Hist. of Westchester N. Y. ii, 710
Bunker's Long Island Genealogies 177–83
Cleveland's History of Yates Co. N. Y. 650
Collin's History of Hillsdale N. Y. 45
Ruttenber's History of Orange N. Y. 368
Birdsey — Hinman's Conn. Settlers 227
Middlefield Ct. History
Orcutt's History of Stratford Ct. 1149–51
Pompey N. Y. Reunion (1875) 273–82
Savage's Genealogical Dictionary i, 183
Birge — Amer. Ancestry ii, 12; x, 200
Goodwin's Foote Genealogy 113
Hinman's Connecticut Settlers 228–31
Kilbourne Family 72
Loomis Genealogy (1880) 363–5
Orcutt's History of Torrington Ct. 650–2
Savage's Genealogical Dictionary i, 183
Stiles' History of Windsor Ct. ii, 74–6
Birney — Green's Kentucky Families
Orcutt's History of Torrington Ct. 652
Biron — Stearns' Ashburnham 617
Birrell — Stearns' Ashburnham 617
Bisbee — American Ancestry iii, 157
Bassett's History of Richmond N. H. 14
Bisbee Genealogy (1876) 48 pages
Dyer's History of Plainfield Mass. 127
Eaton's Annals of Warren Me. 205
Hubbard's History of Springfield Vt. 223–9
Lapham's History of Bethel Me. 489
Lapham's History of Paris Me. 517
Lapham's History of Woodstock Me. 180
Lawrence and Bartlett Mem. 95–9, 134–6
Lincoln's History of Hingham Mass. ii, 82
Mitchell's Hist. of Bridgewater Mass. 117
Ridlon's Settlers of Harrison Me. 25
Vinton's Giles Memorial 197–9
Warren's History of Waterford Me. 232
Wheeler's History of Brunswick Me. 829
Winsor's History of Duxbury Mass. 227
Bisco — Lapham's Hist. Paris Me. 519
Biscoe — Aldrich's Walpole N. H. 213
Bond's Watertown Mass. 42–4, 683–5
Draper's History of Spencer Mass. 176
Bishop — American Ancestry x, 157; xii, 27
Bassett's Richmond N. H. 315
Brook's History of Medford Mass. 501
Calnek's History of Annapolis N. S. 482
Coffin's History of Boscawen N. H. 476
Cogswell Genealogy 21
Cutts Genealogy
Daggett's History of Attleboro' Mass. 88
Davis' Landmarks of Plymouth Mass. 28
Dickerman Genealogy 473
Dodd's History of East Haven Ct. 170
Hammatt's Papers, Ipswich Mass. 28–30
Hinman's Connecticut Settlers 232–5
Howell's Southampton N. Y. 2d ed. 203–5
Huntington's Stamford Ct. Settlers 12–5
Maltby Genealogy (1895) 51
Morris' Bontecou Genealogy 115
Norton's Hist. of Fitzwilliam N. H. 474–6
Pompey N. Y. Reunion 259
Putnam's Historical Magazine v, 241–50, 288–90, 311–6; vi, 15–20, 53–7, 114–20, 169–75, 199–206, 239–45, 271–9
Read's History of Swanzey N. H. 293

Roe's Sketches of Rose N. Y. 117
Savage's Genealogical Dictionary i, 183–6
Temple's History of Palmer Mass. 429
Thurston's Hist. of Winthrop Me. 174
Walworth's Hyde Gen. 369
Whitehead's Perth Amboy N. J. 364
Whitman Genealogy 1056
Winsor's History of Duxbury Mass. 228
Bispham — Bispham Gen. (1890) 348 pages
Wyman's Charlestown Mass. Gens. 85
Bissell — American Ancestry iii, 125; iv, 106; v, 112; xi, 167
Anderson's Waterbury Ct. i, app. 19
Bissell Genealogy (1859) 16 pages
Burleigh's Guild Genealogy 61
Dwight Genealogy 412–6
Goodwin's Gen. of Olcott Family 29
Hine's Lebanon Ct. Hist. Address 146
Hinman's Connecticut Settlers 235–40
Kellogg's White Descendants 30
Litchfield County Ct. History (1881)
Loomis Genealogy (1880) 289–91, 669
Norton's Hist. of Fitzwilliam N. H. 475
Orcutt's History of Torrington Ct. 653–5
Orford N. H. Centennial 103
Savage's Genealogical Dictionary i, 186
Stiles' History of Windsor Ct. ii, 76–106
Strong Family 1473–5
Bitgood — Worden Genealogy 73–84
Bitley — Cleveland's Yates County 531
Bitsche — Bitsche Genealogy (1892) 205 p.
Bitting — Perkiomen Region Pa. 59
Bittinger — Egle's Notes and Queries, 2d series, ii, 337–9
Bittletone — Paige's Cambridge 488
Bixby — Adam's Haven Genealogy 37
American Ancestry xii
Barry's Hist. of Framingham Mass. 188
Benedict's History of Sutton Mass. 590
Bond's Watertown Mass. Gens. 78–83
Cochrane's Hist. Francestown N. H. 517–25
Dudley Genealogy 115
Guild's Stiles Genealogy 385
Hodgman's History of Westford Mass. 438
Jackson's History of Newton Mass. 242
Leonard's History of Dublin N. H. 318
Marvin's Hist. of Winchendon Mass. 447
Perley's History of Boxford Mass. 28
Savage's Genealogical Dictionary i, 188
Stearns' Hist. of Ashburnham Mass. 618
Ward's History of Shrewsbury Mass. 240
Washington N. H. History 692
Blachley — Clayton's Bergen N. J. 359
Blachly — Huntington's Stamford 12
Black — Amer. Ancestry ix, 166; xii, 131
Bangor Me. Historical Magazine iv, 61–5
Barry's History of Framingham Mass. 189
Eaton's History of Thomaston Me. 147
Egle's Notes and Queries, 3d ser., iii, 505
Hanson's Old Kent Md. 175, 183
Lapham's History of Paris Me. 520
Penn. Magazine of Hist. and Biog. i, 121
Power's Sangamon Co. Ill. Settlers 122–4
Randall's Hist. of Chesterfield N. H. 229
Read's History of Swanzey N. H. 294
Ridlon's Saco Valley Me. Families 465–7

Savage's Genealogical Dictionary i, 188
Slaughter's Bristol Parish Va. 170
Stearn's Hist. of Ashburnham Mass. 618
Blackbeach — Savage's Gen. Dict. i, 189
Blackburn — Hayden's Va. Gens. 633-8
Meade's Old Families of Virginia ii, 208
Paxton's Marshall Genealogy 365
Thomas Genealogy (1896) 556, f-h
Blackfan — Davis' Bucks Co. Pa. 299
Blackford — Freeman's Cape Cod 298
Paxton's Marshall Genealogy 385
Swift's Barnstable Families i, 99-103
Wyman's Charlestown Mass. Gens. i, 86
Blackington — Cutter's Arlington 193
Daggett's History of Attleboro Mass. 88
Eaton's History of Thomaston Me. 148-50
Blackleach — Orcutt's Stratford 1155
Raymond's Burritt Sketch
Blackler — Sheldon's Deerfield ii, 84
Blackman — American Ancestry iv, 238
Blackman Genealogy (1894) 22 pages
Boyd's Annals of Winchester Ct 131
Davis' Landmarks of Plymouth Mass 28
Hinman's Connecticut Settlers 244
Loomis Genealogy (1880) 533-5
Plumb's History of Hanover Pa. 398-402
Savage's Genealogical Dictionary i, 190
Sedgwick's History of Sharon Ct. 64
Blackmar — Austin's R. I. Dictionary 21
Temple's Hist. of No. Brookfield Mass. 529
Blackmore — Dawson Genealogy 267
Deane's History of Scituate Mass. 221
Savage's Genealogical Dictionary i, 190
Blackshear — American Ancestry xi, 58
Blackstock — American Ancestry xii
Blackstone — Austin's R. I. Dict. 21
Blackstone Genealogy (1857) 43 pages
Blaxton Biog. by Amory (1886) 25 page
Corliss' North Yarmouth Me.
Blackwell — Freeman's Cape Cod 164
Hayden's Virginia Genealogies 265-77
Riker's Annals of Newtown N. Y. 354-8
Savage's Genealogical Dictionary i, 190
Spooner's Mem. of W. Spooner 60
Blackwood — Dennysville Me. 102
Blagg — Life of Mrs. Godolphin 142
Orcutt's Stratford Ct. 1156
Blaine — Egle's Hist. Reg. Int. Penn. ii,
    145-50
Robinson and Blaine Family (1867) 142 p.
Blair — American Ancestry iv, 42
Blair Genealogy (1898)
Bolling Genealogy 33
Cleveland's Hist. of Yates Co. N.Y. 599, 601
Clyde's Irish Settlement Pa. 17
Green's Kentucky Families
Gibbs' Blanford Mass. History 56-60
Miller's Colchester County N. S. 167-84
Page Genealogy 72
Richmond Va. Standard ii, 7
Saunders' Alabama Settlers 395-8
Smith's Hist. of Peterborough N. H. 18
Strong Genealogy 1322-5
Blaisdell — Cogswell's Henniker 462
Corliss' North Yarmouth Me.
Dearborn's Hist. of Salisbury N. H. 478-81

Eaton's History of Thomaston Me. 150
Hoyt's Salisbury Mass. Families 63-6
Palmer Genealogy (1886) 42-7
Runnel's Hist. of Sanbornton N. H., ii, 35
Savage's Genealogical Dict. i, 19
Worthen's History of Sutton N. H. 630-3
Blake — American Ancestry, i, 8; ii, 13;
    iv, 86, 115; v, 29, 200; ix, 238, x, 201;
    xi, 168
Babson's History of Gloucester Mass. 62
Ballou's History of Milford Mass. 581-3
Bangor Historical Magazine ii, 1-18; vi, 79
Barrus' History of Goshen Mass. 135
Bellinger Genealogy 26
Blake Family of Dorchester (1857) 140 p.
Blake Family of Dorchester (1881) 64 pages
Blake Family of Middletown Ct. (1895) 39 p.
Blake Family of Boston (1898) 147 pages
Blake's History of Franklin Mass. 234-6
Blake's History of Hamden Ct. 237-40
Boyd's Annals of Winchester Ct. 208-10
Brown's Bedford Mass. Families 5
Butler's Hist. of Farmington Me. 387-92
Chandler Genealogy 827-9
Chase's History of Chester N. H. 472
Cleveland Genealogy (1899) 241-6
Cogswell's Hist. of Northwood N. H. 645-7
Crafts Genealogy 110
Dow's History of Hampton N. H. 601-12
Eaton's Annals of Warren Me. 506
Farrington Memorial (1899) 11-3
Fullonton's Hist. of Raymond N. H. 185-7
Glover Genealogy 427
Hayward's History of Gilsum N. H. 268
Hemenway's Vermont Gazetteer v, 29-31
Hinman's Connecticut Settlers 246-8
Hobart's History of Abington Mass. 351
Jameson's History of Medway Mass. 455
Lapham's History of Bethel Me. 491
Lapham's History of Norway Me. 467
Lapham's History of Paris Me. 521-3
Lincoln's Hist. of Hingham Mass. ii, 83-5
Little's History of Weare N. H. 735
Maine Genealogist ii, (1877) 129
Middlefield County History
New Eng. His. Gen. Reg. xi, 181; xv, 110;
    xxi, 292-4; xlv, 35-8
Norton's Hist. of Fitzwilliam N. H. 476
Orcutt's History of Torrington Ct. 655
Pierce's My Ancestors (1864) 48 pages
Pope Genealogy 67-72, 319
Read's History of Swanzey N. H. 294
Rice Genealogy
Runnel's Hist. of Sanbornton N. H. ii, 36-9
Sanborn Genealogy (1894)
Savage's Genealogical Dictionary i, 192-4
Sibley's History of Union Me. 432
So. Carolina Hist. and Gen. Mag., i 153-66
Stearns' History of Rindge N. H. 444-50
Temple's Hist. of No. Brookfield Mass. 530
Vinton's Richardson Family 179
Whittemore's Orange N. J. 266
Worthen's Hist. of Sutton N. H. 625
Wyman's Charlestown Mass. Gens. i, 87
Blakely — Cothren's Woodbury Ct. 504
Hollister's History of Pawlet Vt. 167

Blakeman — Goodwin's Gen. Notes 1–7
Orcutt's History of Stratford Ct. 1151–5
Savage's Genealogical Dictionary i, 194
Blakeslee — Amer. Ancestry viii, 40
Anderson's Waterbury Ct. i, app. 19–21
Bronson's Hist. of Waterbury Ct. 469–77
Davis' History of Wallingford Ct. 656
Tuttle Family of Connecticut 27, 639–41
White Genealogy (1892) 9–11
Blakesley — Savage's Genealogical Dictionary i, 189
Blakeway — Thomas Gen. (1896) 204–7
Blakey — Watkins Genealogy 37
Blakiston — Holstein Genealogy
Blanchard — Abbott's Andover 39
Amer. Ancestry i, 8; viii, 95; ix, 26, 27, 29
Barbour's My Wife and Mother App. 27
Bass' History of Braintree Vt. 118
Bemis' History of Marlboro N. H. 422–4
Blanchard Memorial by Hudson (1899)
Brook's History of Medford Mass. 502–4
Chase's History of Chester N. H. 472
Cochrane's History of Antrim N. H. 363–5
Cochrane's Hist. of Francestown N. H. 526
Cogswell's Hist. of Henniker N. H. 462
Corliss' North Yarmouth Me. 1089–92
Crosby Genealogy 137–41
Daniel's History of Oxford Mass. 403
Dearborn's Hist. of Salisbury N. H. 481–4
Fox's History of Dunstable Mass. 237–9
Hanson's Hist. of Gardiner Me. 128
Hazen's History of Billerica Mass. 12
Hinman's Connecticut Settlers 249–50
Hobart's Hist. of Abington Mass. 353–6
Hudson's History of Lexington Mass. 12
Huntington's Stamford Ct. Settlers 16
Lapham's History of Rumford Me. 305–7
Livermore's Hist. of Wilton N. H. 317–23
Merrill's History of Acworth N. H. 187
Miller's Colchester County N. S. 254–8
Mitchell's Hist. of Bridgewater Mass. 118
Morrison's Hist. of Windham N. H. 345–7
Morse's Sherborn Mass. Settlers 16
New Eng. Hist. and Gen. Reg. x, 152
Pierce Genealogy (1894)
Runnell's Hist. of Sanbornton N. H. ii, 39
Salem N. Y. Book of History 35–7
Savage's Genealogical Dictionary i, 195–207
Secomb's History of Amherst N. H. 503–71
Temple's History of Palmer Mass. 428
Thayer's Memorial (1835) 14
Washington N. H. History 306–9
Wheeler's Croydon N. H. Centennial 79
Worcester's History of Hollis N. H. 366
Worthen's History of Sutton N. H. 626
Wyman's Charlestown Mass. Gens. 88–92
Young's History of Wayne Co. Ind. 412
Blanck — American Ancestry i, 8
Bland — Bland Papers 13–5, 145–9
Campbell's History of Virginia 670
Goode Genealogy 54
Lee Genealogy (1895) 137–40
Meade's Old Churches of Va. i, 446
New Eng. Hist. and Gen. Reg. xxvi, 34
Robertson's Pocahontas' Descendants
Richmond Va. Critic (1888)

Richmond Va. Standard ii, 14; iii, 38
Slaughter's Bristol Parish Va. 147–63
Blanden — Jackson's Newton Mass. 243
Blandford — Savage's Gen. Dict. i, 197
Blandin — Daniel's Oxford Mass. 404
Blanding — American Ancestry x, 70
Bassett's Richmond 316–8
Blanding Family Chart (1895) 13x16 in.
Norton's Hist. of Fitzwilliam N. H. 477
Blaney — Daniel's Oxford Mass. 405
Essex Inst. Coll. xvi, 90–4
Johnston's History of Bristol Me. 388–92
Wyman's Charlestown Mass. Gens. 381
Blank — Hertzler Genealogy 280–2
Blankenbaker — Garr Genealogy 68, 521–3
Blanshan — Schoonmaker's Kingston
Blasdel — Chase's Chester N. H. 474
Hudson's Hist. of Lexington Mass. 12
Blashfield — Corliss' North Yarmouth
Hyde's History of Brimfield Mass. 381
Blass — American Ancestry ii, 13
Blatchford — Amer. Ancestry ix, 190
Blatchford Genealogy (1871) 104 pages
Savage's Genealogical Dictionary i, 198
Blatchley — Hinman's Puritans 240–2
Savage's Genealogical Dictionary i, 198
Blauvelt — Cole Genealogy 74–7
N. Y. Gen. and Biog. Rec. xxviii, 158–61
Blaxton — Armory's Wm. Blaxton
Savage's Genealogical Dictionary i, 198
Blay — Hanson's Old Kent Md. 313
Blazo — Dearborn's Parsonfield 366
Bleecker — Bolton's Westchester 810
Holgate's American Genealogies 87–98
Munsell's Collect. of Albany i, 277; iv, 98
Blethen — Stackpole's Durham Me. 151
Whitman Genealogy 197–202
Blickensderfer — Amer. Ancestry xi, 20
Blin — Hinman's Connecticut Settlers 250
Blincoe — Goode Genealogy 205
Blinman — Savage's Gen. Dict. i, 199
Blinn — American Ancestry ii, 13
Hudson's History of Lexington Mass. 12
New Eng. Hist. and Gen. Reg. xvi, 19
Blish — Hayward's Gilsum N. H. 269
Hollister Genealogy 291–3
Savage's Genealogical Dictionary i, 200
Bliss — Amer. Ancestry iv, 119; v, 131
Austin's R. I. Gen. Dict. 22
Baker's History of Montville Ct. 523–7
Barbour's My Wife and Mother App. 62
Bliss Genealogy (1881) 808 pages
Caulkin's History of Norwich Ct. 167
Dwight Genealogy 882–5
Eaton Genealogy (1895)
Evans' Fox Genealogy 206–9
Freeman's Cape Cod Mass. ii, 276, 292
Hayward's History of Gilsum N. H. 270–2
Hine's Lebanon Ct. Address 147
Hinman's Connecticut Settlers 253–8
Hyde's History of Brimfield Mass. 371–4
Joslin's History of Poultney Vt.
Kellogg's White Descendants 47–66
Longmeadow Mass. Centennial, app. 6–15
McKeen's History of Bradford Vt. 223–9
Morris and Flynt Ancestors (1882) 25–30

Morris Genealogy (1887) 58–60
New Eng. Hist. and Gen. Reg. xxxi, 320, 417–20; xxxii, 67, 175–8
Perkins' Old Houses of Norwich Ct. 422
Savage's Genealogical Dictionary i, 200–2
Spooner Genealogy i, 391
Stebbins Genealogy 10
Stiles' Hist. of Windsor Ct. ii, 107
Temple's Hist. of N. Brookfield Mass 530.
Warren-Clarke Genealogy 28–33
West Springfield Mass. Centennial 124
Wetmore Genealogy 257
Wilbraham Mass. Centennial 296–7, 304
Bliven — Am. Ancestry v, 117; xi, 199
Narragansett Historical Register i, 65
Block — American Ancestry x, 12
Blodgett — Am. Ancestry ix, 69, 77, 82
Bemis' History of Marlboro N. H. 424–6
Cutter's History of Jaffrey N. H. 234
Guild's Stiles Genealogy 39–41
Hayward's Hist. of Hancock N. H. 350–2
Heywood's Hist of Westminster Mass. 555
Hinman's Connecticut Settlers 258
Hodgman's History of Westford Mass. 438
Hudson's History of Lexington Mass. 13–5
Hyde's History of Brimfield Mass. 382–4
Life of Rev. Wm. Smith
Penn. Magazine of Hist. and Biog. iv, 382
Loomis Genealogy (1880) 672–5
Norton's Hist. of Fitzwilliam N. H. 479–82
Paige's History of Cambridge Mass. 489
Plumb's History of Hanover Pa. 390
Randall's History of Chesterfield N. H. 229
Savage's Genealogical Dictionary i, 202
Sewall's History of Woburn Mass. 593
Sheldon's History of Deerfield Mass. ii, 85
Stearns' Hist. of Ashburnham Mass. 618
Stiles' History of Windsor Ct. ii, 108–11
Temple's History of Palmer Mass. 425
Wyman's Charlestown Mass. Gens. i, 93
Bloemendal — Munsell's Albany iv, 98
Blois — Savage's Genealogical Dict. i, 203
Blood — American Ancestry iii, 6
Blood's History of Temple N. H. 203–6
Butler's History of Groton Mass. 387–9, 468
Daniels' History of Oxford Mass. 405
Dunster Genealogy 209–15
Eaton's History of Thomaston Me. 151
Green's Early Groton Mass. Settlers 3
Green's Groton Mass. Epitaphs 237
Hayward's History of Gilsum N. H. 272
Hayward's History of Hancock N. H. 352
Hill's History of Mason N. H. 198–200
Livermore's History of Wilton N. H. 323
Merrill's History of Acworth N. H. 188
Orford N. H. Centennial 104
Potter's Concord Mass. Families 6
Savage's Genealogical Dictionary i, 204
Shattuck Genealogy 368–72
Shattuck's History of Concord Mass. 364
Stone's History of Hubbardston Mass. 229
Temple's Hist. of No. Brookfield Mass. 530
Washington N. H. History 309
Worcester's History of Hollis N. H. 366
Bloodgood — Am. Ancestry iv, 118; v, 235
Bloom — Bergen's Kings Co. N. Y. 37–9

Chambers' Early Germans of N. J. 266
Flint's Peters Lineage 49–51
Bloomer — Baird's Hist. of Rye N. Y. 396
Bloomfleld — Savage's Gen. Dict. i, 203
Hinman's Connecticut Settlers 260
Bloomingdale — Amer. Ancestry i, 8
Bloss — American Ancestry v, 40
Bloss Genealogy (1886) 5 pages
Bloss Genealogy 2d ed. (1887) 19 pages
New Eng. Hist. and Gen. Reg. xli, 298–301
Wentworth Genealogy i, 364–6
Blossom — American Ancestry vii, 183
Freeman's History of Cape Cod ii, 260
Hollister's Pawlet Vt. 169
Lincoln's History of Hingham Mass. ii, 85
Mitchell's Hist. of Bridgewater Mass. 118
Paul's History of Wells Vt. 65
Savage's Geneological Dictionary i, 205
Swift's Barnstable Mass. Families i, 75–9
Blott — Savage's Gen. Dict. i, 205
Blount — American Ancestry viii, 100
Hubbard Stanstead County Canada 229
Thurston's History of Winthrop Me. 175
Wheeler's N. Carolinians lvii–lxi, 130–2
Blow — American Ancestry xi, 69
Blowers — Paige's Cambridge 489
Savage's Genealogical Dictionary i, 206
Bloys — Bond's Watertown 685
Blue — Power's Sangamon Co. Ill. 124
Blunt — Amer. Ancestry ii, 13; v, 134
Bangor Me. Historical Magazine viii, 105
Brewster's Portsmouth N. H. ii, 90–2
Butler's History of Farmington Me. 392–4
Savage's Genealogical Dictionary i, 206
Secomb's History of Amherst N. H. 508
Sibley's History of Union Me. 433–5
Blush — Swift's Barnstable 89–98
Bly — Savage's Genealogical Dict. i, 206
Blye — Eaton's Thomaston Me. 151
Blythe — Essex Inst. Colls. xvi, 95
Boardman — American Ancestry vii, 15
Boardman Memoir (1849) 478 pages
Boardman Log-Book (1885) 44–6
Boardman Genealogy (1895) 778 pages
Butler's History of Farmington Me. 394
Cochrane's Hist. of Francestown N. H. 527
Farrow's Hist. of Islesborough Me. 169–72
Hatch's History of Industry Me. 513–6
Hinman's Connecticut Settlers 261
Lane Genealogy (1891) 66
New Eng. Hist. and Gen. Reg. xv, 244–6
Paige's History of Cambridge Mass. 490–93
Salisbury's Fam. Histories (1892) i, 235–46
Savage's Genealogical Dictionary 207
Sedgwick's History of Sharon Ct. 64
Timlow's Sketches of Southington Ct. 27
Whitney's Lawrence Wills (1860) 48 pages
Boas — Egle's Penn. Gens. 2d ed. 98–106
Bobb — Plumb's Hist. Hanover Pa. 388
Bobbit — Savage's Genealogical Dict. i, 207
Bockee — Bockee Genealogy (1897) 167 p
Smith's Dutchess Co. 124
Bockes — Munsell's Albany Colls. iv, 99
Boden — Driver Genealogy 114–7
Bodfish — Freeman's Cape Cod Mass. ii, 142, 300, 329, 471

Savage's Genealogical Dictionary i, 211
Swift's Barnstable Families i, 68–74
Bodge — Wyman's Charlestown 95–7
Bodie — Hubbard's Stanstead Co. 244
Bodine — Clute's Staten Is. N. Y. 344
Chambers' Early Germans of N. J. 267–9
Maginnes' West Branch Valley Pa. 522
Salter's History of Monmouth Co. N. J. x
Thompson Genealogy (1889) 14–6
Bodle — Riker Genealogy 12
Bodman — Savage's Gen. Dict. i, 207
Bodwell — Bodwell (J. R.) Biog. 39–41
Bond's Watertown Mass. Gens. 893–5
Cochran's History of Antrim N. H. 365
Emery Genealogy (1890) 15
Hubbard's Stanstead County Canada 220
Humphrey Genealogy (1884) 323–8
Lapham's History of Norway Me. 469
Maine Hist. and Gen. Recorder viii 195–7
Runnell's Hist. Sanbornton N. H. ii, 40–4
Boehm — Boehm Memorial 27 pages
Boerman — See Bowman
Boerum — See Van Boerum
Boey — Bowie Genealogy 242–4
Bogardus — American Ancestry ii, 13
Gale Genealogy (1866) 182–7
Munsell's Albany N. Y. Collections iv. 99
Schoonmaker's Hist. of Kingston N. Y. 473
Sedgwick's History of Sharon Ct. 65
Bogart — Amer. Ancestry iii, 174; iv, 226
Calnek's History of Annapolis N. S. 482
Clute's History of Staten Island N. Y. 346
Munsell's Albany Collections iv, 100
Nevius Genealogy
Talcott's New York Families 22–63, 417
Bogert — American Ancestry iv, 134
Cole Genealogy (1876) 104–15
New York Gen. and Biog. Rec. ix, 191
Riker's History of Harlem N. Y. 491–4
Roome Genealogy 144
Boggess — Lindsay Genealogy 114–20
Boggs — American Ancestry vii, 22
Eaton's History of Thomaston Me. 152
Eaton's Annals of Warren Me. 507–9
Hayden's Virginia Genealogies 362–4
Norton's History of Knox Co. Ohio 370
Bogle — Daniels' Oxford Mass. 405
Hudson's History of Sudbury Mass. 436
Bogman — Bogman Genealogy (1890) 36 p.
Bogue — American Ancestry iv, 202
Caverly's History of Pittsford Vt. 693
N. Y. Gen. and Biog. Record iii, 62–8
See also under Booge
Bohonon — Bohonon Genealogy (1888) 6 p
Worthen's History of Sutton N. H. 634
See also Buchanan
Boice — American Ancestry ii, 13
Boiden — Temple's Palmer Mass. 427
Boies — American Ancestry ii, 13
Ely Genealogy 236
Gibbs' Blandford Mass. Address 55
Strong Genealogy 459–62
Boland — Sedgwick's Sharon Ct 65
Boll — Power's Sangamon Ill. 125
Bolles — American Ancestry iii, 6
Baker's History of Montville Ct. 111–23

Bassett's Hist. of Richmond N. H. 318–28
Bolles Genealogy (1865) 64 pages
Caulkins' Hist. of New London Ct. 368–70
Hinman's Connecticut Settlers 285–7
Read's History of Swanzey N. H. 295
Savage's Genealogical Dictionary i, 208
Tuttle Genealogy 707
Wyman's Charlestown Mass. Gens. i, 97
Bolling — American Ancestry v, 32
Bolling Genealogy (1868) 68 pages
Clarke's Old King Wm. Co. Va. Families
Goode Genealogy 64
Hayden's Virginia Genealogies
Lapham's History of Paris Me. 525–9
Meade's Old Churches of Virginia i, 78
New Eng. Hist. and Gen. Reg. xxvi, 35
Richmond Standard ii, 12, 32; iii, 33, 36
Robertson's Pocahontas' Descendants 31
Slaughter's Bristol Parish Va. 140–7
Bolmer — Roome Genealogy 225–7
Bolster — Daniels' Oxford Mass. 406
Lapham's History of Norway Me. 468
Lapham's History of Rumford Me. 307–9
Ridlon's Settlers of Harrison Me. 26–8
Bolton — Am. Ancestry iii, 63, 109; ix, 45
Bangor Me. Hist. Magazine iv, 212
Bass' History of Braintree Vt. 119
Bolton Family of Phila. (1862) 222 pages
Bolton Fam. of Reading Mass. (1888) 8 p
Bolton Fam. of Reading 2d ed. (1889) 98 p
Bolton Genealogy (1895) 524 pages
Bolton's Westchester Co. N. Y. ii, 711–3
Chandler's History of Shirley Mass. 357–9
Douglass Genealogy 175–80
Heywood's Hist. Westminster Mass. 555–8
Martindale's Hist. of Byberry Pa. 233–42
Mitchell's Hist. of Bridgewater Mass. 118
Olin Genealogy by Nye (1892) 426–41
Roberts' Richland Pa. Families 101–5
Savage's Genealogical Dictionary i, 208
Whitmore's Heraldic Journal ii, 110–3
Wyman's Charlestown Mass. Gens. i, 98
Boltwood — American Ancestry i, 8
Hinman's Connecticut Settlers 288
Judd's History of Amherst Mass. 455–8
Noble Genealogy 276–87, 342–52
Savage's Genealogical Dictionary i, 208
Temple's History of Northfield Mass. 409
Bomberger—Brubacher Genealogy 113–37
Egle's Penn. Genealogies 2d ed. 107–12
Harris' History of Lancaster Co. Pa. 62
Bomgardner — Bretz Genealogy 8–12, 45–7
Bond — American Ancestry i, 8; v, 62; vi, 104; viii, 12
Benedict's History of Sutton Mass. 590
Bond Family of Watertown (1826) 8 pages
Bond and Price Gen. (1872) 35 pages
Bond Genealogy (1896) 201 pages
Bond's Watertown Mass. 45–83, 686–9
Bradbury's Kennebunkport Me. 228
Chase (Ira) Memorial 97
Harris' Watertown Mass. Epitaphs 6
Hastings Genealogy
Hatfield's History of Elizabeth N. J. 69
Hayden's Virginia Genealogies 167, 184
Hayward's History of Hancock N. H. 353

Haywood's History of Gilsum N. H. 273
Heywood's Hist. of Westminster Mass. 558
Hinman's Connecticut Settlers 288–90
Hoyt's Salisbury Mass. Families 66
Hudson's History of Lexington Mass. 16
Hyde's History of Brimfield Mass. 384
Lapham's History of Bethel Me. 493
Life of Rev. Wm. Smith
New Eng. Hist. and Gen. Register lii, 464
Paige's History of Hardwick Mass. 340
Pearson's Schenectady N. Y. Settlers 15
Salisbury's Family Histories (1892) ii, 353
Saunderson's Charlestown N. H. 287–9
Savage's Genealogical Dictionary i, 209
Sharpless Genealogy 145–8, 203–5, 320–4
Sigourney Genealogy
Stearns' History of Ashburnham Mass. 619
Temple's Hist. of No. Brookfield Mass. 31-3
Temple's History of Palmer Mass. 427
Washburn's Hist. of Leicester Mass. 347–9
Washburne's Notes on Livermore Me. 30
Young's History of Wayne Co. Ind. 202
Bondurant — Power's Sangamon 124
Bonesteel — Smith's Rhinebeck 213-6
Bonham — Savage's Gen. Dict. i, 210
Bonine — Sharpless Genealogy 415
Bonnell — American Ancestry x, 108
Baetjer's Carteret Genealogy 23
Bradbury's Bonnell Family (1875)
Littell's Passaic Valley Gens. 46–53
Bonner — Hayward's Hancock 353-8
New Eng. Hist. and Gen. Register v, 174
Paige's History of Cambridge Mass. 489
Bonnett — Bolton's Westchester 713
Bonney — Barry's Hanover Mass. 259
Bonney Chart (1878)
Bonney Genealogy (1898) 178 pages
French's History of Turner Me. 51
Lapham's History of Norway Me. 468
Lapham's History of Paris Me. 523-5
Mitchell's Hist. of Bridgewater Mass. 119
Savage's Genealogical Dictionary i, 211
Thurston's History of Winthrop Me. 175
Winsor's History of Duxbury Mass. 228
Bonnycastle — Slaughter's St. Marks
Bonsa — Daniels' Oxford Mass. 406
Bonsall — Smith's Delaware Co. Pa. 447
Bonte — American Ancestry xii, 43
Bontecou — Bontecou Gen. (1885) 271
Bontecou Ancestry (1887) 29 pages
Cunnabell Genealogy 119
Bonython—Bonython Genealogy (1884) 7 p.
Folsom's History of Saco Me. 113–6
New Eng. Hist. Register xxxviii, 50–6
Booden — Bangor Historical Mag. iv, 215
Boodey — Boodey Genealogy (1880) 297 p.
Hayward's History of Gilsum N. H. 273–5
Booge — Booge Genealogy (1872) 6 pages
Field's History of Haddam Ct. 47
Hinman's Connecticut Settlers 291
New York Gen. and Biog. Rec. iii, 62-8
Booker -- Stackpole's Durham Me. 153
Virginia Mag. of History vii, 94–100, 208, 322–4
Wheeler's Brunswick Me. History 830
Boom — Munsell's Albany Colls. iv. 101

Boomer — Austin's R. I. Gen. Dict. 23
Joslin's History of Poultney Vt. 219–21
Boone — American Ancestry v, 72
Jenkin's Hist. Gwynedd Pa. 2d ed. 369–71
Penn. Mag. of Hist. and Biog. xxi, 112–6
Slaughter's St. Marks Va. iii, 17, 21
Boorem — Salter's Monmouth N. J. 10
Boorn — Bassett's Richmond 322-5
Boorse — Cassel Genealogy 67, 87, 121-6
Boosey — Hinman's Conn. Settlers 292
Savage's Genealogical Dictionary i, 211
Booth — Am. Ancestry vi, 48, 150; ix, 75
Andrew's New Britain Ct. 126, 182–7
Bond's Watertown Mass. Gens. 812
Booth Fam. of Stratford Ct. (1862) 64 pages
Booth Family of Milwaukee (1877) 56 pages
Booth Fam. of Stratford Ct. (1892) 27 pages
Booth Association (1868) 40 pages; (1869) 19 pages
Cothren's Woodbury Ct. 508–10, 1474
Deane's History of Scituate Mass. 222
Dwight's Life of E. G. Booth
Goode Genealogy 50 e
Hinman's Connecticut Settlers 293–6
Longmeadow Mass. Centennial app. 14–16
New Eng. Hist. and Gen. Reg. xxxii, 176–8
Orcutt's History of New Milford Ct. 802
Orcutt's History of Stratford Ct. 1156–61
Pierce's (E. W.) Contributions 26–30
Saunders' Alabama Settlers 12
Savage's Genealogical Dictionary i, 212
Sharpe's History of Seymour Ct. 156
Sharpe's South Britain Ct. Sketches 150
Stiles' History of Windsor Ct. ii, 111–4
Trubee Genealogy 100-9
Wetmore Genealogy 112
Boothby — Dearborn's Parsonsfield 366
Lapham's History of Norway Me. 469
Ridlon's Saco Valley Me. Families 468–514
Borden — Am. Anc. iii, 136; ix, 241; xii
Austin's R. I. Genealogical Dictionary 23
Borden Genealogy (1899) 348 pages
Davis Genealogy 80
Fowler's Sketch of Fall River Mass.
Jennings Genealogy (1899)
McKean Genealogy 15-7
Pell's Howland's Journal (1890) 54
Peck and Earll's Fall River Mass. 224–43
Salter's History Monmouth Co. N. J. xi
Savage's Genealogical Dictionary i, 213
Swift's Barnstable Mass. Families i, 64–7
Waddell's Annals of Augusta Co. Va. 398
Walker Genealogy 156
Bording — Potts Genealogy (1895) 85
Bordley — Bordley Gen. (1865) 158 pages
Hanson's Old Kent Maryland 81
Thomas Genealogy (1896) 207
Bordman — Savage's Gen. Dict. i, 213
Boreel — Green's Todd Genealogy
Boreman — Hammatt Papers 30
Savage's Genealogical Dictionary i, 214
Borie — McKean Genealogy 192-4
Boright — American Ancestry ii, 14
Borland — Cushman's Sheepscott 358
Cutts Genealogy 60-2
Giles Genealogy 335-7

Paige's History of Cambridge Mass. 493
Wyman's Charlestown Mass. Gens. i, 99
Borman — Hinman's Settlers 265–80
Borneman — Borneman Gen. (1881) 114 p.
Boroughs — Hubbard's Stanstead 314
Borrough — Clement's Newtown N. J.
Borthwick — Am. Ancestry i, 8; viii, 95
Bortle — American Ancestry ii, 153
Borton — Cregar's Haines Ancestry 20–2
Bos — Munsell's Albany Colls. iv, 101
Boss — American Ancestry i, 8; ix, 128
Austin's R. I. Genealogical Dict. 24
Boss Family (1900) 96 pages
R. I. Historical Magazine vii, 59–61
Bosson — Pickering Genealogy
Boston — Guild's Stiles Genealogy 38
Ridlon's Saco Valley Me. Families 514–6
Bostwick — Amer. Ancestry ii, 14; xi, 66
Bostwick Genealogy (1851) 50 pages
Hinman's Connecticut Settlers 297–301
Huntting's Hist. of Pine Plains N. Y. 317
Orcutt's History of New Milford Ct. 659–68
Orcutt's History of Stratford Ct. 1161
Ruggles Genealogy
Savage's Genealogical Dictionary i, 215
Whitney Genealogy i, 553
Winsor's History of Duxbury Mass. 229
Boswell — Hinman's Ct. Settlers 301
Ripley's Ingersoll Genealogy 60–2
See also Buswell
Bosworth — Child Genealogy 125–34
Davis' Landmarks of Plymouth Mass. 29
Dennysville Me. Centennial 102
Eaton's Annals of Warren Me. 509
Hammatt Papers, Ipswich Mass. 31
Hine's Lebanon Ct. Hist. Address (1880)
Joslin's History of Poultney Vt. 219
Lincoln's History of Hingham Mass. ii, 86
Mitchell's Hist. of Bridgewater Mass. 119
Norton's History of Fitzwilliam N. H. 482
Savage's Genealogical Dictionary i, 215
Strong Genealogy 590–2
Bothwell — American Ancestry i, 9
Temple's Hist. of No. Brookfield Mass. 534
Botolph — Stiles' Windsor Ct. ii, 114
Botsford — Bartholomew and Botsford
    Records (1899) 48–58
Cleveland's Yates Co. 122–4
Savage's Genealogical Dictionary i, 217
Sedgwick's History of Sharon Ct. 65
Bottam — Walworth's Hyde Gen. 368
Botting — Lincoln's Hingham Mass. ii, 87
Botts — Austin's Allied Families 39
Goode Genealogy 367, 424–6
Bottum — American Ancestry vi, 96
Boucher — American Ancestry ii, 14
Boude — Atlee Genealogy 87–9
Boudinot — Alden's Epitaphs i, 101–5
Boughey — N. E. Hist. Reg. v, 307
Boughton — American Ancestry vi, 14, iv,
    221; vi, 194, 201
Anderson's Waterbury Ct. i, app. 21
Bouton and Boughton Gen. (1890) 684 pages
Leavenworth Genealogy 190
Smith Genealogy (1870)
Bouker — Ward's Shrewsbury 225

Bouldin — Goode Genealogy 121, 195
Hayden's Virginia Genealogies 312
Richmond Va. Standard iii, 14, 16, 45
Boulter — Dow's Hampton N. H. 612
Ridlon's Saco Valley Me. Families 516
Savage's Genealogical Dictionary i, 217
Boulton — N. E. Register xxxviii, 199
Bound — Daniels' Oxford Mass. 406
Bourke — Bulloch Genealogy
Bourman — Swift's Barnstable i, 80–4
Bourn — Bourn Genealogy (1875) 32 pages
Read's History of Swanzey N. H. 296
Bourne — American Ancestry v, 141
Bourne's History of Welles Me. 756
Freeman's Cape Cod i, 677; ii, 128, etc.
N. E. Hist. Gen. Reg. xiv, 82; xxvii, 26
Savage's Genealogical Dictionary i, 218
Spooner's Memorial of W. Spooner 117
Swift's Barnstable Families i, 104–26, 140
Tanner Genealogy 22–4
Whitman Genealogy 138–40
Winsor's History of Duxbury Mass. 229
Bourquin — Bellinger Genealogy 93
Boutell — American Ancestry v, 150
Benedict's History of Sutton Mass. 591
Cochrane's Hist. of Francestown N. H. 528
Hayward's Hist. of Hancock N. H. 359–72
Secomb's History of Amherst N. H. 509–14
Boutin — Newport Hist. Magazine iv, 138
Bouton — Amer. Ancestry i, 9; viii, 198
Bouton Recollections (1870) 55 pages
Bouton Family of Meredith (1886) 10 pages
Bouton Genealogy (1890) 684 pages
Hall's Records of Norwalk Ct. 182, 306
Hinman's Connecticut Settlers 304
Huntington's Stamford Ct. Settlers 16
New Eng. Hist. and Gen. Register li, 330–4
Savage's Genealogical Dictionary i, 220
Sedgwick's History of Sharon Ct. 66
Selleck's Norwalk Ct. (1896) 348–52
Boutwell — Barry's Framingham 188
Cochrane's History of Antrim N. H. 366–70
Eaton's History of Reading Mass. 47
Hayward's History of Hancock N. H. 373
Norton's History of Fitzwilliam N. H. 483
Runnell's Hist. of Sanbornton N. H. ii, 44–6
Savage's Genealogical Dictionary i, 219
Bouvé — Lincoln's Hingham ii, 88
Bovie — Munsell's Albany Colls. iv, 101
Pearson's Schenectady N. Y. Settlers 17
Bow — Coe-Ward Memorial 55
Hinman's Connecticut Settlers 301
Bowden — Howell's Southampton 205
Bowditch — American Ancestry iv, 94
Mallmann's Shelter Island N. Y. 197–203
Mitchell's Hist. of Bridgewater Mass. 119
New Eng. Hist. and Gen. Register l, 436–8
Savage's Genealogical Dictionary i, 220
Bowdoin — Bowdoin Genealogy (1887) 28 p.
Bowdoin Genealogy 2d ed. (1894) 52 pages
Bridgman's Granary Epitaphs 1–7
Hyde's Hist. Address at Ware Mass. 53
Knox Co. Me. Hist. Magazine i, 77
Maine Hist. Soc. Colls. i, 185
Mass. Hist. Soc. Colls. 3d series, ii, 49
Meade's Old Churches of Virginia i, 259

New Eng. Hist. Reg. viii, 247; x, 78; xi, 43
Savage's Genealogical Dictionary i, 221
Whitmore's Temple and Bowdoin Family
Whitmore's Heraldic Journal ii, 136
Winthrop's Address at Bowdoin Coll.
Wyman's Charlestown Mass. Gens. i, 101
Bowe — Savage's Genealogical Dictionary
    i, **222**
Stiles' History of Windsor Ct. ii, 114
Bowen — Adam's Fairhaven Vt. 283
American Ancestry viii, 97, 114; xii
Austin's Ancestral Dictionary 7
Barry's History of Framingham Mass. 190
Bassett's Hist. of Richmond N. H. 325–32
Bowen Family of Wales (1884) 107 pages
Bowen Fam. of Woodstock Ct. (1893) 272 p.
Bowen Family of Woodstock Ct. (1897) 245 p.
Chandler Genealogy 312–4
Cincinnati Ohio Criterion (1888) iii, 750
Davis Genealogy 157
Hinman's Connecticut Settlers 281
Hughes and Allied Families 185–232
Johnson Genealogy (1891) 16–9
Montague Genealogy 518–20
Morris and Flynt Ancestors (1882) 18
Morris Genealogy (1894) 26
N. E. Hist. and Gen. Register xlvii, 453–9
Power's Sangamon Co. Ill. Settlers 126
Saunderson's Charlestown N. H. 289
Savage's Genealogical Dictionary i, 222
Shroud's Fenwick Colony N. J. 517–20
Wyman's Charlestown Mass. Gens. i, 101
Young's History of Wayne Co. Ind. 285
Bower — Bower Genealogy (1879) 8 pages
Howell's Southampton 423
Kilborne's Bower Family (1856)
Sharpe's History of Seymour Ct. 186–88
Stiles' History of Windsor Ct. ii, 115
Bowerman — American Ancestry xii
Freeman's Cape Cod 151
New Eng. Hist. and Gen. Reg. xxxi, 281
Spooner Genealogy i, 60, 367
Swift's Barnstable Mass. Families i, 80–4
See also Bowman
Bowers — American Ancestry ix, 190
Bangor Me. Historical Magazine ii, 119
Butler's History of Groton Mass. 389, 469
Eaton's History of Thomaston Me. 152
Hayward's Hist. of Hancock N. H. 373–81
Hazen's History of Billerica Mass. 14–6
Heywood's Hist. of Westminster Mass. 559
Hinman's Connecticut Settlers 302
Johnson Genealogy (1872) 17 pages
Merrill's History of Acworth N. H. 189
Paige History of Cambridge Mass. 493
Runnell's Hist. of Sanbornton N. H. ii, 46
Savage's Genealogical Dictionary i, 223
Sawin Genealogy 16–8
Smith's History of Peterborough N. H. 21
Stearns' History of Rindge N. H. 431
Wyman's Charlestown Mass. Gens. i, 102
Bowes — Heraldic Journal i, 109
New Eng. Hist. and Gen. Reg. x, 82, 129
Paige's History of Cambridge Mass. 494
Bowie — Bowie Genealogy (1899) 523 pages
Slaughter's St. Marks Va. 149

Stackpole's History of Durham Me. 155
Thomas Genealogy (1877) 39
Bowker — American Ancestry iv, 152
Ballou's History of Milford Mass. 588–91
Barry's History of Hanover Mass. 259
Deane's History of Scituate Mass. 223
Hudson's History of Marlboro' Mass. 330
Hudson's History of Sudbury Mass. 436
Lapham's Hist. of Paris Me. 529–31
Machias Me. Centen. 155
Norton's Hist. of Fitzwilliam N. H. 483–7
Salter's History of Monmouth Co. N. J. xi
Saunderson's Charleston N. H. 289
Temple's Hist. of No. Brookfield Mass. 534
Bowlby — Calnek's Annapolis N. S. 483
Bowler — American Ancestry iv, 105
Bowles — Bangor Hist. Magazine v, 28
Bowles Genealogy (1851) 8 pages
Dorr Genealogy
Hinman's Connecticut Settlers 282
Missouri Pioneer Families 129, 243
New Eng. Hist. and Gen. Register ii, 192
Savage's Genealogical Dictionary i, 224
Thomas Genealogy (1877) 39
Wyman's Charlestown Mass. Gens. i, 103
Bowling — Power's Sangamon Ill. 126
See also Bolling
Bowman — American Ancestry x, 94
Bond's Watertown Mass. Gens. 689–702
Bowman Genealogy (1886) 258 pages
Chambers' Early Germans of N. J. 269–72
Cogswell's Hist. of Henniker N. H. 464–9
Cutter's History of Arlington Mass. 195
Daniels' History of Oxford Mass. 407
Green's Kentucky Families
Hayden's Memorial of Ann E. Sweitzer
Hazen's History of Billerica Mass. 16
Heywood's Hist. Westminster Mass. 560
Hinman's Connecticut Settlers 303
Hudson's Hist. of Lexington Mass. 17–20
Huntting's Hist. of Pine Plains N. Y. 318
Morris Genealogy (1894) 130–4
North's History of Augusta Me. 807–9
Paige's History of Cambridge Mass. 494–6
Pierce's History of Grafton Mass. 462
Roy's Thrall Sermon (1894) 24–32
Ruttenber's History of Orange N. Y. 390
Saunderson's Charlestown N. H. 290
Savage's Genealogical Dictionary i, 224
Smith's Hist. of Sunderland Mass. 275–7
Stearns' History Ashburnham Mass. 620
Wheeler's History of Newport N. H. 306
Wyman's Charlestown Mass. Gens. i, 103
Bowne — American Ancestry x, 74
American Historical Register iii, 37–42
Bergen's Kings Co. 441–5
Bunker's Long Island Genealogies 184
Field Genealogy (1895) 112–6
New Eng. Hist. and Gen. Register xxv, 294
New York Gen. and Biog. Rec. iv, 24–7
Shotwell Genealogy 133
Thomas Family (1896) 209–13
Thomas Genealogy (1896) 209–13
Thompson's History of L. I. N. Y. 385–90
Bowyer — Sharpe's Seymour Ct. 185–9
Bowzer — Page Genealogy 163

Box — Bellinger Genealogy 61
Boyce — Bassett's Richmond 332–6
Essex Mass. Institute Hist. Colls. xix, 308
Goode Genealogy 301
Hayward's History of Hancock N. H. 382
Hemenway's Vermont Gazetteer iv, 179
Montague Genealogy 210
Norton's History of Fitzwilliam N. H. 487
Savage's Genealogical Dictionary i, 225
Williams' History of Danby Vt. iii, 12
Boyd — Am. Ancestry iii, 74; vi, 30, 174
Baird's History of Rye N. Y. 397
Bangor Historical Magazine i. 113; ix, 71
Boyd Genealogy (1884) 318 pages
Boyd's Annals of Winchester Ct. 312–7
Boyd Convention (1882) 42 pages
Boyd's History of Conesus N. Y. 144
Brewster's Portsmouth N. H. ii, 166–8
Chase's History of Chester N. H. 475
Cleveland's Yates Co. N. Y. 299, 505–7
Clyde's Irish Settlement Pa. 18–22
Cochrane's History of Antrim N. H. 370–6
Cochrane's Hist. Francestown N. H. 529–31
Egle's Penn. Genealogies 2d ed. 113–9
Egle's Notes and Queries 3d series, iii,
    190–2, 249; annual vol. (1896) 142;
    (1897) 24–5
Futhey's History of Chester Co. Pa. 485
Goode Genealogy 142
Jameson's History of Medway Mass. 456
Meginness' West Branch Valley Pa. 34–6
Missouri Pioneer Families 129–136
Power's Sangamon Co. Ill. Settlers 127
Richmond Va. Standard iii, 27, 43
Smith Genealogy (1900) 135–7
Temple's Hist. of No. Brookfield Mass. 534
Young's Hist. of Wayne Co. Ind. 227, 238
Boyden — American Ancestry ix, 142
Bemis' History of Marlboro N. H. 426–8
Bond's History of Watertown Mass. 90
Boyden Genealogy (1879) not in N. E.
Hatch's History of Industry Me. 516–20
Hemenway's Vermont Gazetteer v, 37–40
Hill's Dedham Mass. Records i
Savage's Genealogical Dictionary i, 225
Sheldon's History of Deerfield Mass. ii, 86–8
Wall's Reminis. of Worcester Mass. 353
Boyer — Keim Genealogy 462
Power's Sangamon Ill. 128
Boyington — Boynton Genealogy 262
Boykett — Savage's Gen. Dict. i, 226
Boykin — Baptist Encyclopedia
Boyle — Littell's Passaic Valley 53–5
Boyles — Eaton's Thomaston Me. 153
Hayward's History of Hancock N. H. 382
Boylston — Bond's Watertown 702–5
New Eng. Hist. Gen. Reg. vii, 145–50, 351
Savage's Genealogical Dictionary i, 226
Vinton Memorial 308–11
Wyman's Charlestown Mass. i, 105–8
Boynton—Am. Anc. ii, 15; vi, 172; xi, 132
Ballou's History of Milford Mass. 592
Bedford N. H. Centennial 292–4
Blood's History of Temple N. H. 206
Boynton Family Directory (1884) 147 pages
Boynton Genealogy (1897) 386 pages

Butler's History of Groton Mass. 469
Buxton Me. Centennial 175–7
Cochrane's Hist of Francestown N. H. 531
Dwights' Strong Genealogy 429
Eaton's History of Thomaston Me. 153
Emery's Reminis. of Newbury Mass. 321–5
Essex Institute Hist. Colls. xx, 63–72
Hayward's History of Hancock N. H. 383–5
Hodgman's History of Westford Mass. 439
Hoyt's Salisbury Mass. Families 67–9
Hubbard's Hist. of Stanstead Can. 187–90
Little's History of Warren N. H. 554
Little's History of Weare N. H. 737–9
Livermore's History of Wilton N. H. 324
Machias Me. Centennial 155
Marvin's History of Winchenden Mass. 448
Morrison's History of Windham N. H. 347
Norton's History of Fitzwilliam N. H. 488
Roe's Sketches of Rose N. Y. 144
Runnell's Hist. of Sanbornton N. H. ii, 470
Savage's Genealogical Dictionary i, 226
Secomb's History of Amherst N. H. 514–6
Smith's History of Petersborough N. H. 22
Temple's Hist. of No. Brookfield Mass. 535
Worcester's History of Hollis N. H. 367
Bozart — Eyerman Ancestors (1898)
Brace — Hinman's Ct. Settlers 307–11
Kellogg's White Descendants 66
Leavenworth Genealogy 65–8
Loomis Genealogy (1880) 742–6
Orcutt's History of Torrington Ct. 656
Pompey N. Y. Reunion 263
Tuttle Genealogy 89
Bracken — American Ancestry xii, 37
Egle's Notes and Queries (1896) 163
Brackenbury — Malden Mass. Cen. 239
Savage's Genealogical Dictionary i, 228
Wyman's Charlestown Mass. Gens. i, 108
Brackett — American Ancestry ix, 242;
    xii, 6, 8
Anderson's Waterbury Ct. i, app. 22
Austin's Allied Families 40–2
Bass' History of Braintree Vt. 120
Brackett Genealogy (1860) 56 pages
Bracketts of Portsmouth N. H. (1896) 2 p.
Bracketts of Portsmouth 2d ed. (1897) 8 p.
Chapman's Weeks Genealogy 129–31
Cochrane's History of Antrim N. H. 376–8
Cochrane's Hist. of Francestown N. H. 543
Dearborn's History of Parsonsfield Me. 451
Dow's History of Hampton N. H. 614
Eaton's Annals of Warren Me. 509
Gibb's History of Blandford Mass. 65
Hazen's History of Billerica Mass. 17
Hill's Dedham Mass. Records i
Hughes and Allied Families 235–9
Johnston's History of Bristol Me. 384
Odiorne Genealogy
Paige's History of Cambridge Mass. 496–8
Richardson Genealogy
Ridlon's Harrison Me. Settlers 34–7
Ridlon's Saco Valley Me. Families 520–3
Savage's Genealogical Dictionary i, 228
Smith and Deane's Journal 365
Smith's Hist. of Peterborough N. H. 23–5
Wentworth Genealogy i, 461–4; ii, 135–7

Bracy — Milliken's Narraguagus 15
Savage's Genealogical Dictionary i, 227
Bradbrook — Savage's Dict. i, 227
Bradbury — American Ancestry iii, 132; iv, 39-40; viii
Bradbury Genealogy (1890) 320 pages
Buxton Me. Centennial 231-42
Corliss' North Yarmouth Me. Mag. 718-22
Cutts Genealogy 193
Dawson's Historical Magazine (1858) 214-8
Eaton's History of Thomaston Me. 154
Goodwin's History of Buxton Me. 384-90
Hatch's History of Industry Me. 520
Heywood's Hist. of Westminster Mass. 560
Hoyt's Salisbury Mass. Families 69-72
Lapham's History of Norway Me. 470
Lapham's History of Paris Me. 531
New Eng. Hist. and Gen. Reg. xxiii, 262
North's History of Augusta Me. 810
Ridlon's Saco Valley Me. Families 106
Savage's Genealogical Dictionary i, 229
Smith's Founders of Mass. Bay 251-6
Worcester's History of Hollis N. H. 368
Wyman's Charlestown Mass. Gens. i, 109
Young's History of Wayne Co. Ind. 239
Bradford — American Ancestry v, 34. 223, 237; vi, 137; vii, 229, 241; viii, 103-9; ix, 106; xii
Baker's History of Montvillee Ct. 391-403
Bond's Watertown Mass. Gens. 77
Bradford Family of New Eng. (1850) 27 p.
Bradford Fam. of New York (1873) 8 pages
Bradford Fam. of New Eng. (1895) 29 pages
Bradford Fam. of Duxbury (1896) 27 pages
Butler's History of Farmington Me. 395-7
Caulkins' History of Norwich Ct. 169
Cleveland Genealogy (1899) 350-4
Cochrane's Hist. Francestown N. H. 532-40
Cogswell's Hist. of New Boston N. H. 132
Davis' Landmarks of Plymouth 30-9
Dudley's Archæolog. Collections pl. 4
Dwight Genealogy 208
Dwight's Strong Genealogy 294, 959
Eaton's History of Thomaston Me. 154
Egle's Notes and Queries (1898) 128
Foster Pedigree (1897-8) ix, 1-7
French's History of Turner Me. 57
Futhey's History of Chester Co. Pa. 486
Gold's History of Cornwall Ct. 303-7
Hartwell Genealogy (1895) 128-34
Hayward's History of Hancock N. H. 385-8
Hine's Lebanon Ct. Histor. Address 147
Hinman's Connecticut Settlers 311-6
Lincoln's History of Higham Mass. ii, 90
Mitchell's Bridgewater Mass. 358-61
Moore's American Governors i, 88-91
Morrison's History of Windham N. H. 348
Morse's Genealogy of Richards Family 14
Morton's New Eng. Memorial 180
New Eng. Hist. and Genealogical Register iv, 39-50, 233-45; ix, 127, 218; xiv, 174, xlviii, 196-8
N. Y. Gen. Biog. Record iv, 183-8
Perkins' Old Houses of Norwich Ct. 424
Power's Hist. of Sangamon Ct. Ill. 129-31
Rice Genealogy

Savage's Genealogical Dictionary i, 230-2
Secomb's History of Amherst N. H. 516-9
Slaughter's St. Marks Parish Va. 122
Spooner Genealogy i, 436-62
Stebbins Genealogy 11
Thacher's Hist. of Plymouth Mass. 108-11
Washington N. H. History 310-3
Waters Genealogy (1882) 22-7
Whittemore's Mayflower Descendants 5-32
Winsor's History of Duxbury Mass. 230-4
Bradfute — Carter Family Tree
Bradish — Barry's Framingham 190
Collin's Hist. of Hillsdale N. Y. app. 39-43
Paige's History of Cambridge Mass. 496-8
Paige's History of Hardwick Mass. 341
Temple's Hist. of No. Brookfield Mass. 535
Wyman's Charlestown Mass. i, 110-3
Bradley — American Ancestry i, 9; ii, 15; v, 13, 210, 228; viii, 145, ix, 36
Anderson's Waterbury Ct. i, app. 22
Bass' History of Braintree Vt. 119
Bouton's History of Concord N. H. 634-6
Bradley Fam. of Dorchester (1878) 45 pages
Bradley Family of Guilford (1879) 46 pages
Bradley Family of Fairfield (1894) 69 pages
Caulkin's History of New London Ct. 278
Dickerman Genealogy 174-9, 376-80, 575-84
Dodd's History of East Haven Ct. 106-10
Fiskes of Amherst N. H. 136-8
Goodyear Genealogy 146
Hamden Ct. History 240
Hemenway's Vermont Gazetteer v
Hinman's Connecticut Settlers 316
Kilbourn's Litchfield Ct. History 154
Maine Hist. and Gen. Recorder iii, 35-7
Meade's Old Families of Virginia
Mitchell's Hist. of Bridgewater Mass. 120
Montague Genealogy 133-6
Morris Genealogy (1853) 19-25
Orcutt's History of Derby Ct. 703
Orcutt's History of Torrington Ct. 656
Orcutt's History of Wolcott Ct. 453-5
Power's Hist. of Sangamon Co. Ill. 16, 131
Redfield Genealogy 19
Savage's Genealogical Dictionary i, 233
Schenck's History of Fairfield Ct. 354-8
Sharpe's South Britain Ct. Sketches 73-5
Sharpless Genealogy 191, 307-9
Timlow's Sketches of Southington Ct. 28 31
Titcomb's Early N. E. People 256-64
Tuttle Genealogy 148-50, 643
Bradshaw — Brook's Medford 504
Hudson's History of Lexington Mass. 21
Paige's History of Cambridge Mass. 498
Savage's Genealogical Dictionary i, 234
Temple's Hist. of No. Brookfield Mass. 535
Wyman's Charlestown Mass. i, 113-5
Bradstreet — Abbott's Andover 17-9
Amer. Ancestry v. 117; vii, 187, 195; x, 159
Brook's Hist. of Medford Mass. 505
Chase's History of Chester N. H. 475
Drake's History of Boston Mass. (1856)
Dudley Genealogy (1848) 116-20
Essex Mass. Inst. Hist. Colls. xxiv, 64-71
Hammatt Papers, Ipswich Mass. 32
Hanson's History of Gardiner Me. 131-3

Hinmann's Connecticut Settlers 317–9
Moore's American Governors i, 388
New Eng. Hist. and Gen. Reg. viii, 312–24; ix, 113–21; xlviii, 168–71
Paige's History of Cambridge Mass. 498
Ridlon's Saco Valley Me. Families 523
Savage's Genealogical Dictionary i, 235
Wyman's Charlestown Mass. Gens. 115
Bradt — American Ancestry i, 9
Bradway — Shoud's Fenwick 35–41
Brady — Cogswell's Henniker N. H. 469
Meginness' West Branch Valley Pa. 568–83
Orcutt's History of Torrington Ct. 657
Bragaw — Riker's Newtown N. Y. 370–3
Bragdon — Goodwin's Buxton Me. 378
Leighton Genealogy
Ridlon's Saco Valley Me. Families 523
Bragg — American Ancestry x, 131
Ballou's History of Milford Mass. 595–9
Hammatt Papers, Ipswich Mass. 34
Hubbard's History of Springfield Vt. 240–2
Stiles' History of Windsor Ct. ii, 116
Temple's Hist. of No. Brookfield Mass. 536
Ward's History of Shrewsbury Mass. 227
Wheeler's Croydon N. H. Centennial 78
Wheeler's Eminent N. Carolinians 456–9
Wheeler's History of N. Carolina ii, 441
Bragham — Pearson's Schenectady 19
Brailey — Ballou Genealogy 378–81
Brainerd — American Ancestry i, 9; v, 230; vi, 47; ix, 18, 165; x, 179; xi, 143; xii.
Brainerd Genealogy (1857) 303 pages
Butler's History of Farmington Me. 397
Field's History of Haddam Ct. 44
Hinman's Connecticut Settlers 329
Huntington Genealogy 203
Phœnix's Whitney Family of Ct. i, 147
Savage's Genealogical Dictionary 237
Temple's History of Palmer Mass. 422–4
Thurston's History of Winthrop Me. 175
Washington N. H. History 313
Whittemore's Middlesex 202, 323, 406
Braisted — Clute's Staten Island N. Y. 347
Braithwaite — Thomas Gen. (1896) 214
Brakenridge — Hyde's Ware Mass. 49
Braley — Braley Genealogy (1878) 8 pages
Braman — Clark's Norton Mass. 76
Bramhall — Davis' Landmarks 39
Hurlbut Genealogy 424
Lincoln's History of Hingham Mass. ii, 90
Branch — Am. Ancestry vii, 162; xi, 180
Goode Genealogy 468
Little's History of Weare N. H. 739
Meade's Old Families of Virginia
Robertson's Pocahontas' Descendants
Savage's Genealogical Dictionary i, 238
Brand—Savage's Genealogical Dict. i, 238
Brandige — Andrew's New Britain 130
Brandow — Greene Co. N. Y. 418–21
Brandt — American Ancestry ii, 15
Dotterer's Perkiomen Region Pa. 37
Temple's Hist. of No. Brookfield Mass. 536
Branham — Jolliffe Genealogy 201–8
Brann — Eaton's Thomaston Me. 155
Brannin — Va. Mag. of Hist. v. 336

Bransford — Amer. Anc. xi, 98, 142, 168
McFerrin's Tenn. Methodism iii, 481
Branson — American Ancestry xi, 21
Branson Genealogy (1898) 57 pages
Power's Sangamon 132–4
Brant — Egle's Notes and Queries 3d series ii, 490–3
Braose — Thomas Genealogy (1896) 216
Brashear — Green's Ky. Families
Brasier — N. Y. Gen. Rec. xxvii, 37–42
Wyman's Charlestown 117–9
Brassey—Boddington's Brassy Genealogy
Brastow — Bangor Historical Magazine ii, 135–7; vii, 237
New Eng. Hist. Gen. Reg. xiii, 249–51
Bratt — Munsell's Albany iv, 101–4
Pearson's Schenectady Settlers 19, 26
Brattle — Brattle Genealogy (1867) 90 p.
Bridgman's Granary Epitaphs 317–9
Bridgman's King's Chapel Epitaphs 259
Hinman's Connecticut Settlers 321
Paige's History of Cambridge Mass. 499
Savage's Genealogical Dictionary i, 238
Wyman's Charlestown Mass. Gens. i, 119
Brawner — Power's Sangamon Ill. 135
Braxton — Blair, Banister and Braxton Genealogy (1898)
Campbell's Spotswood Papers 21
Carter Family Tree
Clarke's Old King Wm. Co. Va. Families
Meades' Old Families of Virginia
Richmond Va. Standard iii, 29
Bray — Adams Genealogy (1895) 42
American Ancestry xi, 21
Andrew's New Britain Ct. 303
Babson's History of Gloucester Mass. 63
Corliss' North Yarmouth Me. Magazine
Driver Genealogy 251–64
Essex Institute Hist. Colls. vii, 244–7; viii, 82–9
Maine Hist. Recorder iii, 248–56; iv, 25–8
Meade's Old Churches of Virginia i, 199
New Eng. Hist. Gen. Reg. xxxviii, 67
Parthemore Genealogy 206
Poore Genealogy 65
Ridlon's Harrison Me. Settlers 28–30
Salter's History of Monmouth Co. N. J. xi.
Savage's Genealogical Dictionary i, 239
Sharpe's South Britain Ct. Sketches 59
Brayton — Austin's Ancestral Dict. 8
Austin's R. I. Genealogical Dictionary 251
Mowry (Richard) Genealogy 198
Savage's Genealogical Dictionary i, 240
Swain Genealogy 78–97
Brazleton — Iowa Historical Atlas 263
Bread—Hinman's Connecticut Settlers 321
Breakenridge — Breakenridge Family of Palmer Mass. (1887) 65 pages
Temple's History of Palmer Mass. 415–9
Brearley — American Ancestry xii.
Brearley Chart (1886)
Cooley's Trenton N. J. Genealogies 13–7
Brechin — American Ancestry iv, 218
Breck — Allen's Worcester Mass. 36
American Ancestry v, 16; ix, 178
Barry's History of Framingham Mass. 190

Breck Genealogy (1889) 281 pages
Hudson's History of Marlboro Mass. 332
Morse's Sherborn Mass. Settlers 16–8
New Eng. Hist. and Gen. Reg. v, 396
Savage's Genealogical Dictionary i, 240
Wheeler's Croydon N. H. Centen. 80–3
Wheeler's History of Newport N. H. 307–9
Breckenridge — American Ancestry xi, 22
Cabell Genealogy 489–515
Collin's Kentucky 214
Egle's Notes and Queries 4th series i, 282
Green's Kentucky Families
Meade's Old Families of Virginia ii, 474
Paxton's Marshall Genealogy 71–3
Peyton's History of Augusta Co. Va. 304
Power's Sangamon Co. Ill. Settlers 136–8
Preston Genealogy (1870) 6–20
Richmond Va. Standard ii, 7
Waddell's Annals Augusta Va. 140–2, 401–4
See also Breakenridge
Brecknoch — Clarke's Old King Wm. Co.
    Va. Families
Breed — American Ancestry vi, 14
Breed Family Meeting (1872) 22 pages
Breed Family Chart (1888) 7x14 inches
Breed Genealogy (1892) 229 pages
Cochrane's History of Antrim N. H. 378
Cogswell's History of Henniker N. H. 470
Dwight Genealogy 1108–11
Little's History of Weare N. H. 740–6
Savage's Genealogical Dictionary i, 241
Stearns' History of Rindge N. H. 452
Washington N. H. History 315
Wyman's Charlestown Mass. i, 120–4
Breen — Lincoln's Hingham ii, 91
Breese — Am. Ancestry v, 158; ix, 178
Oneida Historical Society Trans. ii, 97–9
Salisbury Fam. Memorials (1885) 475–532
Salter's History of Monmouth Co. N. J. xii.
Breeze — Munsell's Albany iv, 104
Brennan — Smith's Peterborough 25
Brenneman — Brubacher Genealogy 102
Brent — Cincinnati Criterion iii, 751
De Bow's Review for May 1859
Goode Genealogy 239
Hanson's Old Kent Md. 17
Meade's Old Families of Virginia
Old Northwest Gen. Quarterly iii (1900) 64
Paxton's Marshall Genealogy 377
Richmond Va. Critic (1888)
Richmond Va. Standard ii, 49
Brenton — Austin's R. I. Dict. 252–7
Dwight's Strong Genealogy 359
Hall's Genealogical Notes 104
R. I. Hist. Society Collections iii, 265–8
Savage's Genealogical Dictionary i, 242
Whitmore's Heraldic Journal iii, 173
Brereton — American Ancestry xii.
Brett — Kingman's No. Bridgewater 452–7
Lapham's History of Paris Me. 532–5
Mitchell's Hist. of Bridgewater Mass. 120–2
Richmond Va. Standard iii, 36, 43
Savage's Genealogical Dictionary i, 243
Bretz — Bretz Genealogical (1890) 142 p.
Egle's Notes and Queries 3d series i, 35
Brevard — Wheeler's N. Car. ii, 237

Brevoort — Greene's Todd Genealogy
Navarre Genealogy 151–6
N. Y. Gen. and Biog. Rec. vii, 58–60
Riker's History of Harlem N. Y. 494–7
Roome Genealogy 227
Brewer — Am. Ancestry x, 135, 203; **xi, 93**
Andrew's New Britain 206
Bangor Me. Historical Magazine i, **131–3**
Barry's History of Framingham Mass. 191
Bemis' History of Marlboro N. H. 428
Bolton's Westchester Co. N. Y. ii, 711
Bond's Watertown Mass. Genealogies 92
Draper's History of Spencer Mass. 179
Ellis' History of Roxbury Mass. 92
Ely Genealogy 93, 215–9
Fowler's Chancery Genealogy 196
Hammatt Papers, Ipswich Mass. 39
Hinman's Connecticut Settlers 32–7
Kellogg's White Descendants 73
Lincoln's History of Hingham Mass. ii, **93**
Locke Genealogy 35
Morris Genealogy (1894) 37
New Eng. Hist. and Gen. Reg. xxx, 424–6
Norton's Hist. of Fitzwilliam N. H. 489–91
Savage's Genealogical Dict. i, 243, 444
Stearns' History of Rindge N. H. 453
Strong Genealogy 1284–7
Temple's Hist. of No. Brookfield Mass. 537
Ward's History of Shrewsbury Mass. 245
Ward's Rice Family 11
Wilbraham Mass. Centennial 293–6
Brewster — Am. Ancestry vii, 33; **xii, 28**
Brewster Golden Wedding (1860) 28 pages
Brewster Chart (1872) 18x24 inches
Caulkins' History of New London Ct. 276
Caulkins' Norwich Ct. (1867) 211–3
Cochrane's Hist. of Francestown N. H. 541
Davis' Landmarks of Plymouth 40–5
Davis Genealogy (1888) 58
Dudley's Archæological Coll. plate 4
Eaton's History of Thomaston Me. 156
Elderkin Genealogy 90–103
Foster Genealogy (1889) 58
Frisby's History of Middlebury Vt. 24
Gold's History of Cornwall Ct. 272
Hine's Lebanon Ct. Historical Address 147
Hinman's Connecticut Settlers 327–31
Hurd's History of New London Co. Ct. 510
Mitchell's Hist. of Bridgewater Mass. 361
New Eng. Hist. Reg. l, 360; liii, 109–14,
    283–8, 439–46
Savage's Genealogical Dictionary i, 214
Steele's Life of Brewster (1857) 350
Strong Genealogy 131, 606, 623
Watson's Some Notable Families 47–50
Wetmore Genealogy 552–72
Whittemore's Mayflower Descendants 15
Winsor's History of Duxbury Mass. 234–7
Briant — Cutter's Jaffrey N. H. 236
See also under Bryant
Brice — Hanson's Old Kent Md. 83
Brick — Breck Genealogy 143–5, 150–3
Shroud's Fenwick N. J. 42–4
Bricker — Lancaster Pa. Historical Papers
    iii, 20
Norton's Knox Co. O. 348

Brickett — Chase's Chester N. H. 480
Bridge — Allen's Worcester Mass. 86-8
American Ancestry i, 9-10; vi, 140
Bond's Hist. of Watertown Mass. 93-5, 705
Bridge Genealogy (1884) 120 pages
Bridgman's King's Chapel Epitaphs 260-3
Green's Groton Mass. Epitaphs 337
Green's Early Settlers of Groton Mass. 3
Hayward's History of Gilsum N. H. 275
Hudson's History of Lexington Mass. 21-6
North's History of Augusta Me. 811-6
Paige's History of Cambridge Mass. 500
Paige's History of Hardwick Mass. 341
Stearns' History of Ashburnham Mass. 62.
Temple's History of Northfield Mass. 410-2
Wakefield Genealogy 38
Whitney Genealogy (186.) appendix
Willis' Law and Lawyers of Maine 462-8
Wyman's Charlestown Mass. Gens. i, 425
Bridgeham — Savage's Gen. Dict. i, 249
Bridgen — Savage's Gen. Dict. i, 250
Wyman's Charlestown Mass. i, 126-30
Bridger — Meade's Virginia i, 305
Richmond Va. Standard ii, 45; iii, 37
Bridges — Barry's Framingham 193
Dennysville Me. Centennial 103
Draper's History of Spencer Mass. 179
Eaton's History of Thomaston Me. 157
Hammatt Papers of Ipswich Mass. 36
Livermore's History of Wilton N. H. 325
New Eng. Hist. and Gen. Reg. viii, 252
Power's Hist. of Sangamon Co. Ill. 138-40
Rockwood Genealogy 129-34
Savage's Genealogical Dictionary i, 247-9
Sheldon's History of Deerfield Mass. ii, 88
Stickney Genealogy 451
Temple's Hist. of No. Brookfield Mass. 537
Bridgman — Bridgman Gen. (1894) 168 p.
Chardon Ohio Newspaper July 14, 1880
Doolittle's Belchertown Mass. 255
Hammatt Papers of Ipswich Mass. 37
Hinman's Connecticut Settlers 336
New Eng. Hist and Gen. Reg. xvi, 135
Savage's Genealogical Dictionary i. 250
Strong Genealogy 826-8
Temple's History of Northfield Mass. 412
Bries — Munsell's Albany Coll. iv, 104
Brigden — Heywood's Westminster 563
Briggs — Adam's Fairhaven Vt. 310
American Ancestry i, 10; ii, 15; iii, 70; v,
18; vi, 55; vii, 13; ix, 135
Austin's Allied Families 43
Austin's R. I. Genealogical Dictionary 25
Barry's History of Hanover Mass. 259
Briggs' History of Shipbuilding 178-81,
183-9, 287-98, 382
Brigg Family of Westchester N. Y. (1878) 51
Briggs Family Archives (1880) 278 pages
Briggs Fam. of Halifax Mass. (1887) 144 p.
Clark's History of Norton Mass. 77
Cleveland's Hist. of Yates Co. N. Y. 655-7
Daniels' History of Oxford Mass. 409
Davis' Landmarks of Plymouth Mass. 45
Deane's History of Scituate Mass. 225
Ely Genealogy 190
Essex Mass. Institute Coll. vi, 171-4

Freeman's Cape Cod Mass. ii, 68, 608
Guild's Stiles' Genealogy 313-21
Hayward's History of Gilsum N. H. 276
Hinman's Connecticut Settlers 337
Huntington's Stamford Ct. Settlers 17
Lapham's History of Norway Me. 471
Lapham's History of Paris Me. 535-9
Lapham's History of Woodstock Me. 182
Livermore's Block Island R. I. 321-5
New Eng. Hist. and Gen. Register lii, 14
North's History of Augusta Me. 816
Roe's Sketches of Rose N. Y. 125
Saunderson's Charlestown N. H. 291-3
Savage's Genealogical Dictionary i, 251
Sears Genealogy 162
Temple's Hist. of No. Brookfield Mass. 537
Vinton's Giles Genealogy 216
Washburne's Notes on Livermore Me. 41
Winsor's History of Duxbury Mass. 237
Brigham — American Ancestry i, 10; **x,**
59; xi, 207
Bemis' History of Marlboro N. H. 429
Brigham Family Meeting (1896?)
Brown's History of Whitingham Vt. 168-72
Davis Ancestry (1897) 31-5
Hayward's History of Gilsum N. H. 276
Hemenway's Vermont iv, 181; v, 715
Hudson's History of Lexington Mass. 26
Hudson's Hist. Marlborough Mass. 332-46
Merrill's History of Acworth N. H. 191
Morse's Gen. of Grout Family 15-20
Morse's Gen. Register i, 87-104; ii, 1-110
Norton's Hist. of Fitzwilliam N. H. 491-6
Paige's History of Cambridge Mass. 501
Pierce's History of Grafton Mass. 462-8
Savage's Genealogical Dictionary i, 252
Stearns' History of Rindge N. H. 454-6
Stone's History of Hubbardston Mass. 230
Temple's Hist. of No. Brookfield Mass. 538
Ward's Rice Family 11
Ward's Hist. of Shrewsbury Mass. 234-8
Warren's History of Waterford Me. 232
Worcester Magazine ii, 151
Young's Hist. of Chautauqua Co. N. Y. 537
Bright — Bond's Watertown 96-9, 706-9
Bright Genealogy (1848) 7 pages
Brights of England (1858) 345 pages
Harris' Watertown Mass. Epitaphs 7-9
Holton's Farwell Genealogy 113
Richmond Va. Standard iii, 6
Savage's Genealogical Dictionary i, 253
Whetmore's Heraldic Journal 81-3
Brightman — Austin's R. I. Dict. 27
Brill — Smith's Dutchess Co. 499
Brimblecorn — Pierce's Grafton 468
Brimhall — See under Bramhall
Brimmer — Bangor Me. Mag. iv, 73
Ely Genealogy 193
Sigourney Genealogy 22-4
Brinckerhoff — American Ancestry iii, 73,
222, 224; iv, 16
Bergen's Kings County N. Y. Settlers 48
Brinckerhoff Genealogy (1887) 188 pages
Hoffman Genealogy 490
Riker's Annals of Newtown N. Y. 290-9
Winfield's Hist. Hudson Co. N. J. 526-30

Bringhurst — Claypoole Gen. 64, **152**
Sharpless Genealogy 391
Brink — American Ancestry ii, 15
Schoonmaker's Hist. of Kingston N. Y. 473
Sylvester's History of Ulster Co. N. Y. 337
Brinley — Austin's Ancestral Dict. 9
Austin's R. I. Genealogical Dict. 256-9
Bridgeman's King's Chapel Epit. 219-28
Salter's Hist. of Monmouth Co. N. J. xii.
Savage's Genealogical Dictionary i, 255
Tyngsboro Mass. Centennial Record 5
Wentworth Genealogy i, 529-34
Whitmore's Heraldic Journal ii, 31
Brinsmade — Cothren's Woodbury 1474
Dickerman Genealogy 384
Hinman Connecticut Settlers 338
Orcutt's History of Stratford Ct. 1163
Savage's Genealogical Dictionary i, 254
Walworth's Hyde Genealogy 945
Brintnal — Barry's Framingham 194
Savage's Genealogical Dictionary i, 255
Willard Genealogy 289, 390
Wyman's Charlestown Mass. Gens. i, 131
Brintnell — Clark's Norton Mass. 78
Brinton — American Ancestry ii, 15
Brinton Genealogy (1879) 60 pages
Cope Genealogy 242-4
Futhey's History of Chester Co. Pa. 486-7
Life of Rev. Wm. Smith
Smith's History of Delaware Co. Pa. 449
Brisbin — American Ancestry v, 57
Lindsay Genealogy
Briscoe — Aylsworth Genealogy 91
Hanson's Kent Md. 121-4
Hayden's Virginia Genealogies 185
Savage's Genealogical Dictionary i, 255
Stone's History of Beverly Mass. 36
Brise — Ruggles Genealogy
Bristed — Greene's Todd Genealogy
Bristol — Adams' Fairhaven Vt. 303-7
American Ancestry ii, 16
Aylsworth Genealogy 90
Davis' History of Wallingford Ct. 657
Goodyear Genealogy 80-2
Guild's Stiles Genealogy 26
Hamden Ct. History 241
Morris' Bontecou Genealogy
Redfield Genealogy 36
Wheeler's Croydon N. H. Centennial 83
Young's History of Warsaw N. Y. 238
Britt — Power's Sangamon Co. Ill. 141
Britten — Sewell's Woburn Mass. 594
Brittin — Littell's Passaic Valley 55-9
Britton — Clute's Staten Island 348
Hubbard's History of Springfield Vt. 231
Power's Sangamon Co. Ill. Settlers 140
Randall's Hist. of Chesterfield N. H. 232-4
Read's History of Swanzey N. H. 299
Smith (Rev. Wm.) Life of
Stearns' History of Ashburnham Mass. 620
Wards History of Shrewsbury Mass. 249
Broadnax — Meade's Old Fams. of Va.
Slaughter's History of Bristol Parish Va.
Broadus — Slaughter's St. Marks 194
Broadwell — Littell's Passaic 59-61
Power's Hist. of Sangamon Co. Ill. 142-4

Broady — American Ancestry ix, 125
Brock — American Ancestry vii, 153
Norton's History of Fitzwilliam N. H. 496
Savage's Genealogical Dictionary i, 257
Wentworth's Genealogy i, 205, 671-3
William's History of Danby Vt. 116
Brockenbrough — Goode Gen. 402
Hayden's Virginia Genealogies 110
Meade's Old Churches of Va. ii, 474-7
Paxton's Marshall Genealogy 106-10
Richmond Va. Standard ii, 34; iii, 29
Virginia Mag. of History v, 447; vi, 82-5
Brockett — Anderson's Waterbury 22
Davis' Wallingford 658-61
Orcutt's History of Wolcott Ct. 456
Savage's Genealogical Dictionary i, 257
Timlow's Sketches of Southington Ct. 31
Tuttle Genealogy 546-9, 642
Whittemore's Orange N. J. 425
Brockholst — N. Y. Gen. and Biog. Record ix, 115-8, 188
Brocklebank — Brocklebank Genealogy
Essex Collection xx, 138-51
Gage's History of Rowley Mass. 439
Savage's Genealogical Dictionary i, 258
Stearns' History of Ashburnham Mass. 621
Stearns' History of Rindge N. H. 456
Brocks — Munsell's Albany iv, 105
Brockway — American Ancestry iii, 222;
iv, 133; v, 100; vi, 61; xi, 58
Andrews' History of New Britain Ct. 309
Brockway Genealogy (1887) 22 pages
Brockway Genealogy (1888) 34 pages
Brockway Genealogy new ed. (1890) 167 p.
Clark Ancestry (1891) 23-5
Hinman's Connecticut Settlers 340
Morris Genealogy (1853) 41-6
Savage's Genealogical Dictionary 258
Sedgwick's History of Sharon Ct. 66
Washington N. H. History 315-21
Worthen's History of Sutton N. H. 636
Young's Hist. of Chautauqua Co. N. Y. 519
Brodhead — Am. Ancestry iii, 165; v, 204
Brodhead's Delaware Water Gap 240-50
Schoonmaker's Hist. of Kingston N. Y. 473
Sylvester's History of Ulster Co. N. Y. 114
Whitmore's Heraldic Journal iii, 1-4
Brogden — Hanson's Old Kent Md. 88
Wheeler's Eminent N. Carolinians 466
Bromfield — Bridgman's Kings Chapel
Bromfield John, Reminis. (1852) 210 pages
Bromfield Gen. (1871) 10 pages reprint
New Eng. Hist. and Gen. Register xiii, 35;
xxv, 182-5, 329-35; xxvi, 36-43, 141-3
Salisbury's Fam. Memorials (1885) ii, 610-2
Savage's Genealogical Dictionary i, 258
Whitmore's Heraldic Journal iii, 187
Bromley — Hollister's Pawlet Vt. 171
Williams' History of Danby Vt. 112-5
Bronaugh — Hayden's Virg. Gens. 534
Bronck — Greene Co. N. Y. History 421-3
Munsell's Albany N. Y. Collections iv, 104
Bronk — American Ancestry i, 10
Bronson — American Ancestry viii, 62
Anderson's Waterbury Ct. i, app. 23-9
Andrews' Hist. of New Britain Ct. 184, 340

Boyd's Annals of Winchester Ct. 109–12
Branson Family Magazine (1899) 29
Bronson's History of Waterbury Ct. 469–77
Brown's West Simsbury Ct. Settlers 12
Cothren's History of Woodbury Ct. 503–7
Goodwin's Olcott Genealogy 25
Hinman's Connecticut Settlers 341–7
Morris and Flynt Ancestors (1882) 31
N. E. Hist. and Gen. Register xxxv, 361–3
Orcutt's History of Stratford Ct. 1164
Orcutt's History of Wolcott Ct. 458–63
Savage's Genealogical Dict. i, 279, 801
Timlow's Sketches of Southington Ct. 32–4
Tuttle Genealogy 15–8, 65
Van Rensselaer's New Yorkers
Young's History of Warsaw N. Y. 239
Brooke — American Ancestry iv, 128
Bowie Genealogy 351–70
Brooke Family of Maryland (1899) 661
Glenn's Merion in Welsh Tract 355–63
Goode Genealogy 314
Meade's Old Families of Virginia
Page Genealogy 129
Paxton's Marshall Genalogy 143
Thomas Genealogy (1896) 218–23
Brooker — American Ancestry 11, 16
Orcutt's History of Torrington Ct. 657–60
Brookins — Paul's History of Wells Vt. 66
Brooks — American Ancestry i, 10; iii, 77;
  v, 127; vi, 134, 206; viii, 20, 49, 172;
  ix, 122; x, 167; xi, 23
Anderson's Waterbury Ct. i, app. 29
Austin's R. I. Genealogical Dictionary 27
Bangor Historical Mag. i, 154–8; vii, 22
Barry's History of Hanover Mass. 260–3
Bond's History of Watertown Mass. 719–27
Briggs' History of Shipbuilding 381–4
Brook's History of Medford Mass. 506–9
Buxton Me. Memorial 156–62
Chapman's Folsom Genealogy 170
Cochrane's History of Antrim N. H. 379
Cochrane's Hist. of Francestown N. H. 1005
Cogswell's History of Henniker N. H. 470
Cutter's History of Arlington Mass. 197
Deane's History of Scituate Mass. 223
Essex Mass. Institute Colls. xxi, 24–32
Field's History of Haddam Ct. 44
Foster Pedigree (1897) vi, 1–7
Freeman's History of Cape Cod Mass. i, 666
Garrard Genealogy 73–6
Hanover Mass. Records (1898)
Hayward's Hist. Hancock N. H. 388–403
Hazen's History of Billerica Mass. 18–20
Herrick's History of Gardiner Mass. 338
Heywood's Hist. Westminster Mass. 563–7
Hibbard's History of Goshen Ct. 433–5
Hinman's Connecticut Settlers 348–50
Lapham's History of Norway Me. 472
Lapham's History of Woodstock Me. 183
Livermore's History of Wilton N. H. 326
Locke Genealogy 37, 73
Merrill's History of Acworth N. H. 191
New Eng. Hist. Reg. v, 355–7: xxix, 153–7
North's History of Augusta Me. 817–9
Norton's History of Fitzwilliam N. H. 496
Orcutt's History of Stratford Ct. 1164

Orcutt's History of Torrington Ct. 660
Orcutt's History of Wolcott Ct. 457
Pierce's History of Grafton Mass. 469–71
Porter Genealogy 209–11
Potter's Concord Mass. Families 6
Power's Sangamon Co. Ill. Settlers 144
Prentice Genealogy 404
Randall's Hist. Chesterfield N. H. 234–6
Ransom Genealogy 37
Savage's Genealogical Dictionary i, 259–63
Secomb's History of Amherst N. H. 519
Sewall's History of Woburn Mass. 594
Shattuck's History of Concord Mass. 364
Sheldon's Hist. of Deerfield Mass. ii, 90–2
Stearns' Hist. of Ashburnham Mass. 621–7
Stearns' History of Rindge N. H. 456–8
Temple's History of Northfield Mass. 413
Upham Genealogy 44–51
Walworth's Hyde Genealogy 322–4
Washington N. H. History 322
Wyman's Charlestown Gens. i, 132–6
Broom — Babson's Gloucester Mass. 281
Martin's History of Chester Pa. 281–5
Broomall — American Ancestry iv, 140
Maris Genealogy 57, 141, 220
Quisenberry Genealogy 129–37
Sharpless Genealogy 375
Bross — Amer. Ancestry iv, 71; viii, 209
Brothwell — Orcutt's Stratford 1350
Broughton — Broughton Gen. (1883) 7
Hinman's Connecticut Settlers 351
Joslin's History of Poultney Vt. 221–5
New Eng. Hist. Gen. Reg. xxxvii, 298–304
Paul's History of Wells Vt. 67
Savage's Genealogical Dictionary i, 263
Sheldon's History of Deerfield Mass. ii, 92
Stearns' History of Ashburnham Mass. 627
Brouwer — Munsell's Albany iv, 105
New York Gen. and Biog. Rec. ix, 126–9
Pearson's Schenectady N. Y. Sett. 26, 30
Roome Genealogy 160–4
Browder — Montague Genealogy 660
Brower — Amer. Ancestry i, 18; iv, 20
Bergen's Settlers of Kings Co. N. Y. 51–5
Davis' History of Bucks Co. Pa. 670
New York Gen. Rec. viii, 132; ix, 126–9
Salter's Hist. of Monmouth Co. N. J. xiii
Brown — American Ancestry i, 10; ii, 16;
  iv, 182, 215; vi, 182, vii, 71, 176; viii,
  78, 152, 242; ix, 23, 39, 190–1; x, 160;
  xi, 10, 23, 70, 169; xii, 111, 132
Alexander Genealogy 123
Ammidown Genealogy 345
Anderson's Waterbury Ct. i, app. 29–31
Andrews' History of New Britain Ct. 225
Austin's Ancestries 13
Austin's R. I. Genealogical Dict. 27, 258–63
Babson's History of Gloucester Mass. 64
Bailey Genealogy (1895) 110–28
Baird's History of Rye N. Y. 399–403
Ball's Lake County Ind. 422
Ballou's History of Milford Mass. 602–4
Ballou Genealogy 195–9, 453–68
Bangor Historical Magazine ii, 43, 224; iv,
  213; vi, 142; ix, 207
Barry's Hist. of Framingham Mass. 195–7

Barbour's My Wife and Mother 68-70
Bass' History of Braintree Vt. 120
Bassett's History of Richmond N. H.
Blood's History of Temple N. H. 207-10
Bolton's Westchester Co. N. Y. ii, 713-5
Bouton Genealogy 474-6
Bradbury's Kennebunkport Me. 229
Bronson's History of Waterbury Ct. 478
Brown Family of Rhode Island (1851) 16 p.
Brown Fam. of Stonington (1860) 12 pages
Brown Fam. of Nottingham Pa. (1864) 18 p.
Brown Association of Vermont (1866) 8 p.
Brown Association of Vermont (1868) 126 p.
Brown Family of Northampton (1879) 38 p.
Brown Family of Penn. (1882) 22 pages
Brown Family of Penn. (1885) 134 pages
Brown Family of Washington (1893) 26 p.
Brown Family of Dutchess Co. (1895) 18 p.
Brown Fam. of Bucks Co. Pa. (1896) 35 p.
Browne Family Letters (1871) 4 pages
Browne Family Notes (1887) 111 pages
Browne Fam.of Rhode Island (1888) 173 p.
Brown's Bedford Mass. Families 5
Brown's History of Whitingham Vt. 154-62
Brown's West Simsbury Ct. Settlers 14-8
Cabell Genealogy 425-31
Capron Genealogy by Holden 187-9
Carter Family Tree
Caverly's History of Pittsford Vt. 693
Chambers' Early Germans of N. J. 272
Chandler's History of Shirley Mass. 359-63
Chase's History of Chester N. H. 476-9
Chase's Hist. of Haverhill Mass. 248, 624
Clarke Family of Watertown 46, 82
Clarke's Old King Wm. Co. Va. Families
Cleveland's Yates Co. N. Y. 306-10, 462-5
Clyde's Irish Settlement of Pa. 22-5
Cochrane's History of Antrim N. H. 380-5
Cochrane's Hist. Francestown N. H. 545-9
Cogswell's Hist. of Henniker N. H. 471-5
Cogswell's Hist. of Nottingham N. H. 335
Cogswell Genealogy 163
Corliss' North Yarmouth Me. Magazine
Craft's History of Whately Mass. 404-11
Crane's Rawson Family Genealogy 58
Cushman's Hist. of Sheepscott N. H. 359
Cutter's History of Arlington Mass. 197
Daniels' History of Oxford Mass. 410-3
Davis' Landmarks of Plymouth Mass. 45
Davis' History of Wallingford Ct. 662
Dearborn's History of Parsonsfield Me. 367
Dodd's History of East Haven Ct. 110
Douglass Genealogy 143-7, 158-60
Dow's History of Hampton N. H. 615-30
Eaton's History of Candia N. H. 53-5
Eaton's History of Thomaston Me. 158, 162
Egle's Hist. Reg. of Interior Pa. ii, 47-53
Egle's Notes and Queries 4th series i, 246
    (1897) 141
Farrow's History of Islesborough Me. 173
Fiske Genealogy 138
Foote's Sketches of Va. 2d series 99
Freeman's Hist. of Cape Cod Mass. ii, 371
Fullonton's Hist. of Raymond N. H. 178-85
Greene Genealogy
Green's Kentucky Families

Hammatt Papers of Ipswich Mass. 38
Hatch's History of Industry Me. 521
Hayden's Oliver Brown Biog. (1882) 22 p.
Hayden's Virginia Genealogies 147-201
Hayward's History of Gilsum N. H. 278
Hayward's Hist. of Hancock N. H. 403-5
Hazen's History of Billerica Mass. 18-21
Hemenway's Vermont Gazetteer v, 710-3
Heywood's Hist. Westminster Mass. 567-70
Hine's Lebanon Ct. Address (1880) 148
Hinman's Connecticut Settlers 357
Hoar Family Lineage (1898) 32
Hobart's History of Abington Mass. 357-60
Hollister's History of Pawlet Vt. 171
Hoyt's Salisbury Mass. Families 72-8
Hubbard's History of Springfield Vt. 233-40
Hubbard's Stanstead County Canada 194
Hudson's Hist. of Lexington Mass. 27-30
Hudson's History of Marlboro' Mass. 346
Hudson's History of Sudbury Mass. 35
Hull's Genealogy 64-6
Humphreys Genealogy 301-18, 464
Huntington's Stamford Ct. Settlers 17-9
Jackson's History of Newton Mass. 245
Johnston's History of Bristol Me. 236-9
Jolliffe Genealogy (1893) 113
Kidder's Hist. New Ipswich N. H. 339-42
Kirk Genealogy 56-8, 116-21
Lapham's History of Bethel Me. 494-6, 652
Lapham's History of Norway Me. 473-5
Lapham's History of Paris Me. 539
Littell's Passaic Valley Genealogies 61-4
Little's History of Weare N. H. 747-9
Livermore's Hist. of Wilton N. H. 327-30
Loomis Genealogy (1880) i, 166-79; ii, 703-7
Maine Historical Society Colls. iv, 280
Mallmann's Shelter Island N. Y. 307-9
Marvin's History of Winchenden Mass. 450
Merrill's History of Acworth N. H. 192
Miller's Colchester Co. Nova Scotia 262-6
Mitchell's Hist. of Bridgewater Mass. 122
Morse's Sherborne Mass. Settlers 18
Muzzey's Reminiscences
Narr. Weekly Westerly R. I. 1897 May June
Nash Genealogy 81
New Eng. Hist. and Gen. Register vi,
    232-4; vii, 312; ix, 219; xx, 243; xxv,
    352
New York Gen. and Biog. Record xxvi, 1;
    xxviii, 1-7
Norton's History of Fitzwilliam N. H. 497
Orcutt's History of Stratford Ct. 1116
Orcutt's History of Torrington Ct. 660
Paige's History of Cambridge Mass. 502
Paige's History of Hardwick Mass. 341
Perkins' Old Houses of Norwich Ct. 426
Peyton's History of Augusta Co. Va. 304
Pierce's History of Grafton Mass. 471
Plumb's History of Hanover Pa. 395-7
Potter's Concord Mass. Families 7, 118-21
Power's Sangamon Co. Ill. Settlers 151-3
Preston Genealogy (1870) 20-30
Randall's History of Chesterfield N. H. 236
Read's History of Swanzey N. H. 300
Reed's History of Rutland Macs. 144
Richmond Va. Standard ii, 7, 10; iii, 6

Ripley's Ingersoll Genealogy 93
Rockwood Genealogy 104-8
Runnel's Hist. of Sanbornton N. H. i, 471
Ruttenber's Hist. of Orange Co. N. Y. 389
Salter's Hist. of Monmouth Co. N. J. xiii
Sanderson's Hist. of Charlestown N. H. 293
Savage's Genealogical Dictionary i, 264-79
Sheldon's History of Deerfield Mass. ii, 92
Slafter Genealogy 62
Slaughter's St. Ann's Parish Va. 183
Secomb's History of Amherst N. H. 520
Smith's History of Rhinebeck N. Y. 203
Smith's History of Sunderland Mass. 278-80
Stark's History of Dunbarton N. H. 252
Stearns' Hist. of Ashburnham Mass. 628
Stearns' History of Rindge N. H. 458-61
Stiles' History of Windsor Ct. ii, 117-22
Stone's Hist. of Hubbardston Mass. 231-5
Temple's Hist. No. Brookfield Mass. 539
Temple's History of Palmer Mass. 412-5
Temple's History of Whately Mass. 211-3
Thomas Genealogy (1877) 45
Thomas Genealogy (1896) 224
Thurston's History of Winthrop Me. 176
Tuttle Genealogy 637-9
Warner's History of Waterford Me. 234-7
Washburn's Hist. of Leicester Mass. 345-7
Washington N. H. History 322
Welles' Washington Genealogy 247
Wentworth Genealogy 134-6, 237
Wheeler's History of Newport N. H. 309-12
Whitman Genealogy 123-6
Whitmore's Copps Hill Epitaphs
Whitmore's Heraldic Journal ii, 24-8, 95
Wight Genealogy 114
Williams' History of Danby Vt.115
Winsor's History of Duxbury Mass. 238
Worcester's History of Hollis N. H. 368
Worthen's History of Sutton N. H. 627-9
Wyman's Charlestown Mass. i, 136-46
Brownback — Rittenhouse Gen. 237-43
Browne — American Ancestry vii, 55
Bond's Watertown Mass. 116-47, 727-32
Browne Genealogy. See Brown
Driver Genealogy 296
Eaton's History of Reading Mass. 49-52
Egle's Notes and Queries 1st series i, 134-6
Essex Institute Coll. viii, 33-48, 225; xx, 151-5; xxxii, 211-9
Hughes Genealogy 65
Meade's Old Families of Virginia
Morrison's Hist. Windham N. H. 348-51
N. E. Hist. Reg. xxv, 352-5; xliv, 281-5
New York Gen. and Biog. Record xxxi, 65-70, 166-70
Richmond Va. Standard ii, 17; iii, 7
Slaughter's Bristol Parish Va. 170
Welles' Washington Genealogy 219
Brownell — Am. Ancestry iv, 153; vii, 115
Austin's Ancestral Dictionary 10
Austin's R. I. Genealogical Dictionary 29
Brownell Genealogy (1892) 53 pages
Pierce's Genealogical Contributions 30-5
Savage's Genealogical Dictionary i, 279
Browning — Am. Anc. v, 145; xi, 169-70
Austin's R. I. Genealogical Dictionary 262

Baker's History of Montville Ct. 223-30
Hyde's History of Brimfield Mass. 380
Jones Genealogy (1891) 192-4
Lewis Genealogy (1893) 131-5
Orcutt's Hist. New Milford Ct. 668-70, 802
Reed's History of Rutland Mass. 152-4
Savage's Genealogical Dictionary i, 279
Stone's History of Hubbardston Mass. 235
Whittemore's Orange N. J. 317
Brownson — Boyd's Winchester 109-12
Joslin's History of Poultney Vt. 226
Keith's Harrison Ancestry 68-70
Brubacher — Brubacher Gen. (1884) 243 p.
Bruce — Am. Anc. ii, 17; vi, 36; xi, 170
Bangor Me. Historical Magazine iii, 91
Barry's History of Framingham Mass. 197
Bass' History of Braintree Vt. 121
Blake Genealogy 47-8, 69-71
Cabell Genealogy 335
Green's Todd Genealogy
Hayward's History of Gilsum N. H. 278
Heywood's Hist. of Westminster Mass. 575
Hudson's History of Marlboro Mass. 347
Jolliffe Genealogy (1893) 99
Locke Genealogy 43, 151-8
Norton's History of Fitzwilliam N. H. 498
Paige's History of Hardwick Mass. 342
Pierce's History of Grafton Mass. 472
Power's Sangamon Co. Ill. Settlers 153
Richmond Va. Standard ii, 47
Runnell's Hist. of Sanbornton N. H. i, 472
Savage's Genealogical Dictionary 280
Secomb's History of Amherst N. H. 521-3
Smith's History of Peterboro N. H. 267
Temple's No. Brookfield Mass. 539-41
Upton Memorial (1874) 504-18
Washburn's History of Leicester Mass. 344
Washington N. H. History 323
Wm. and Mary College Quar. vi, 113, 155
Bruen — Am. Ancestry v, 37; xi, 24, 70
Babson's History of Gloucester Mass. 65-7
Baldwin Genealogy 841-3
Bruen (John) Biog. (1857) 116 pages
Davenport Genealogy 251
Hinman's Connecticut Settlers 331-4
New Jersey Hist. Society Collections vi, 112
Savage's Genealogical Dictionary i, 280
Whittemore's Orange N. J. 449
Brundage — Baird's Rye N. Y. 398
Bruner — Neff Genealogy 310
Penn. Magazine of History xxi, 415
Brunk — Power's Sangamon Ill. 153
Brunson — Andrews' New Britain 225
Steele Family of So. Car. (1900)
Brush — Mead's Greenwich Ct. 315
Phœnix's Whitney Family i, 274
Savage's Genealogical Dictionary i, 281
Sewall's History of Woburn Mass. 595
Smith's History of Dutchess Co. N. Y. 125
Wallbridge Genealogy 278
Whittemore's Orange N. J. 378
Brusie — American Ancestry ii, 17
Brussy — Munsell's Albany iv, 105
Bruyn — American Ancestry iv, 213
Hoffman Genealogy 485-7
New York Gen. and Biog. Rec. xx, 26-9

Schoonmaker's Hist of Kingston N. Y. 473
Sylvester's History of Ulster Co. N. Y. 259
Bryan — American Ancestry ii, 17
Baldwin Genealogy (1889) 1813-33
Bellinger Genealogy 75-9
Bryan Genealogy (1889) 27 pages reprint
Bulloch Genealogy
Hayden's Virginia Genealogies 201-20
Magennis Genealogy 82
Missouri Pioneer Families 132
Power's Sangamon Co. Ill. 154-7
Savage's Genealogical Dictionary 281
Slaughter's Bristol Parish Va. 169
Bryant — American Ancestry i, 11; vi, 193;
vii, 131; viii, 120; ix, 226; x, 133
Baker Genealogy (1867) 73
Bassett's Hist. of Richmond N. H. 338-41
Black Hawk County Iowa Hist. (1886) 261
Carteret and Bryant Gen. (1887) 56 pages
Cochrane's History of Antrim N. H. 385
Cochrane's Hist. Francestown N. H. 549-52
Cushman's History of Sheepscott Me. 359
Davis' Landmarks of Plymouth Mass. 46
Deane's History of Scituate Mass. 227
Eaton's History of Reading Mass. 56
Eaton's History of Thomaston Me. 162
Hatch's History of Industry Me. 523
Hayward's History of Gilsum N. H. 279
Hinman's Connecticut Settlers 360-2
Hudson's History of Lexington Mass. 30
Jaquett Genealogy 177-9
Kingman's N. Bridgewater Mass. 448-51
Lapham's History of Bethel Me. 496
Lapham's History of Paris Me. 540
Lapham's History of Woodstock Me. 185
Lawrence and Bartlett Memorial 118
Lincoln's History of Hingham Mass. ii, 95
Machias Me. Centennial Celebration 156
Mitchell Genealogy (1894)
Mitchell's Hist. of Bridgewater Mass. 123-5
New Eng. Historical and Gen. Register
xxiv, 315-8; xxxv, 37-9; xlviii, 46-53
Pfeiffer Genealogy 42-5
Read's History of Swanzey N. H. 299
Ridlon's Saco Valley Me. Families 525-46
Savage's Genealogical Dictionary i, 282
Stanton Genealogy 276-9
Swift's Barnstable Mass. Families i, 146
Temple's Hist. of No. Brookfield Mass. 541
Whitehead's Hist. of Perth Amboy N. J. 145
Winsor's History of Duxbury Mass. 238
Wyman's Charlestown Mass. Gens. i, 146
Bryer — Austin's R. I. Gen. Dictionary 30
Cutts Genealogy 28
Savage's Genealogical Dictionary i, 283
Buch — Heinecke Genealogy 29-31
Buchanan — American Ancestry vi, 23
Buchanan Genealogy (1849) 240 pages
Buchanan Reunion (1892) 55 pages
Chambers' Early Germans of N. J. 273
Clarmont Co. Ohio History 367
Dearborn's Hist. Salisbury N. H. 485-503
Lamb's History of New York City i, 740
McKean Genealogy 128-33
Hanson's Old Kent Maryland 49
Roe's Sketches of Rose N. Y. 88

Salisbury's Family Histories (1892) i, 208
Van Rensselaer's New Yorkers
See also Bohonon
Bucher — Brubacher Genealogy 19-21
Egle's Penn. Genealogies 2d ed. 120-142
Egle's History of Lebanon Co. Pa. 236
Buck — Am. Anc. i, 11; iii, 93, 144; xi, 71
Aylsworth Genealogy 123-5
Bangor Hist. Mag. ii, 21-4 142; vi, 51-6
Blackman's Susquehanna Co. Pa. 58-60
Buck Family of Conn. (1889) 273 pages
Buck Family of Penn. (1893) 142 pages
Buck Family of Conn. (1894) 54 pages
Caverly's History of Pittsford Vt. 695
Crane's Rawson Genealogy 190-2
Davis' History of Bucks Co. Pa. 542
Deane's History of Scituate Mass. 229
Hinman's Connecticut Settlers 364-7
Hollister Genealogy 277
Lapham's History of Norway Me. 476
Lapham's History of Paris Me. 542
Lapham's History of Woodstock Me. 185-7
Mitchell's Hist. of Bridgewater Mass. 125
Montague Genealogy 567
New Eng. Hist. Reg. xv, 297; xxxviii, 69
Orcutt s History of New Milford Ct. 671-3
Paige's History of Cambridge Mass. 503
Parthemore Genealogy 164, 182-6
Penn. Mag. of Hist. and Biog. xii, 496
Savage's Genealogical Dictionary i, 283
Sewall's History of Woburn Mass. 596
Timlow's Southington Ct. Sketches 34-8
Walworth's Hyde Genealogy 1117
Buckalew — Salter's Monmouth 13
Buckbee — American Ancestry ii, 17
Buckingham — Bronson's Waterbury
Buckingham Genealogy (1872) 384 pages
Buckinghams of Ohio (1892) 256 pages
Cothren's Hist. of Woodbury Ct ii, 1472
Hinman's Connecticut Settlers 371-5
Orcutt's Hist. of New Milford Ct. 673-7
Savage's Genealogical Dictionary i, 284
Buckland — American Ancestry x, 94
Eaton's Annals of Warren Me. 380
Hinman's Connecticut Settlers 275-7
Hubbard's Stansted Co. Canada 324
Joslin's History of Poultney Vt. 227
Savage's Genealogical Dictionary i, 285
Stiles' History of Windsor Ct. 11, 122-6
Buckley — American Ancestry ii, 17
Bulkeley Genealogy
Morris Genealogy (1898) 569
Savage's Genealogical Dictionary i, 286
Roe's Sketches of Rose N. Y. 48
Thomas Genealogy (1896) 225-37
Whitmore's Copps Hill Epitaphs
Bucklin — Eaton's Thomaston Me. 162
Eaton's Annals of Warren Me. 510
Knox Co. Me. Hist. Mag. i, 17-9
Williams' History of Danby Vt. 117
Whipple-Hill Families (1897) 93-5
Bucklyn — American Ancestry vii, 162
Buckman — Benedict's Sutton Mass. 591
Cutter's History of Arlington Mass. 198
Fell Genealogy 89
Hudson's History of Lexington Mass. 31

Jameson's History of Medway Mass. 456
Power's Sangamon Co. Ill. Settlers 157
Buckmaster — Dickerman Gen. 360–2
Cochrane's Hist. of Francestown N. H. 552
Buckminster — Alden's Am. Epitaphs ii
Allen's Worcester Mass. Assoc. 81
Barry's Hist. Framingham Mass. 199–203
Clark Family of Watertown Mass. 22–72
Cochrane's History of Antrim N. H. 387
Savage's Genealogical Dictionary i, 286
Wood's Brookline Mass. Sketches 103
Wood Genealogy 217–23
Bucknam — American Ancestry xi, 171
Bangor Historical Magazine viii, 95
Corliss' North Yarmouth Me. 111–4, 1119–21
Wyman's Charlestown Mass. i, 147–9
Buckner — Goode Genealogy
Meade's Old Families of Virginia
Buckwalter — Futhey's Chester 484
Budd — American Ancestry v, 59
Baird's History of Rye N. Y. 403–6
Bolton's Westchester County N. Y. ii, 715
Chambers' Early Germans of N. J. 274–7
Neff Genealogy 196
Savage's Genealogical Dictionary i, 287
Buddington — Savage's Gen. Dict. 287
Budley — Savage's Gen. Dictionary i, 287
Budlong — American Ancestry ii, 16
Austin's R. I. Genealogical Dictionary 264
Savage's Genealogical Dictionary i, 288
Buel — American Ancestry i, ii; xii, 104
Hine's Lebanon Ct. Historical Address 149
Hinman's Connecticut Settlers 368–71
Loomis Genealogy (1880) 301–18
Sedgwick's History of Sharon Ct. 66
Stiles' History of Windsor Ct. ii, 126
Walworth's Hyde Genealogy 1128–31
Buell — Barbour's My Wife app. 63
Brown's West Stimsbury Ct. Settlers 30
Buell Genealogy (1881) 404 pages
Cleveland's Hist. of Yates Co. N. Y. 207–13
Eager's History of Orange Co. N. Y. 338
Hibbard's History of Goshen Ct. 435–42
Kilbourne Genealogy 113
Savage's Genealogical Dictionary i, 288
Welles' Amer. Family Antiquity i, 45–64
Wheeler's Hist. of Newport N. H. 312–21
Buffam — American Ancestry v, 229
Daniels' History of Oxford Mass. 414
Buffer — Bassett's Richmond N. H.
Buffington — Egle's Pa. Gens. 223–5
Futhey's History of Chester Pa. 489
Savage's Genealogical Dictionary i, 289
Buffum — Aldrich's Walpole 216–8
American Ancestry vi, 192
Austin's Allied Families 43–5
Ballou Genealogy 451–3
Bassett's Hist. of Richmond N. H. 340–9
Richardson's Hist. of Woonsocket R. I. 207
Savage's Genealogical Dictionary, i 289
Williams' History of Danby Vt. 118
Buford — Goode Genealogy
Greene's Kentucky Families
Paxton's Marshall Genealogy 179, 291–3
Bugbee — Amer. Ancestry iii, 75; iv, 175
Austin's Allied Families 45–8

Hayward's Hist. of Hancock N. H. 405–7
Livermore's History of Wilton N. H. 330
Tucker's History of Hartford Vt. 411
Bugby — Bugby Genealogy (1877) 17 pages
Savage's Genealogical Dictionary i, 289
Bulfinch — Bulfinch Genealogy (1895) 15 p.
Bulgar — Austin's R. I. Gen. Dict. 30
Bulkeley — Amer. Ancestry viii, 208
Bulkeley Genealogy (1875) 289 pages
Champion Genealogy 351–3
Fowler's Chauncey Genealogy 233
Hall's Genealogical Notes 82–91, 168–70
Kulp's Wyoming Valley Families
New Eng. Hist. and Gen. Reg. xlii, 82
Potter's Concord Mass. Families 8
Prentice Genealogy 278–80
Ruggle Genealogy
Bulkley — Am. Ancestry v, 134; xi, 197
Bulkley's Browne Memorial 143
Fowler's Chauncey Memorial
Hinman's Connecticut Settlers 378–86
Loomis Genealogy (1880) 726–32
N. E. Hist. Reg. xvi, 135; xxiii, 299–304
Redfield Genealogy 55
Savage's Genealogical Dictionary i, 290–2
Schenck's History of Fairfield Ct. 358
Smith Genealogy by Wellington Smith
Trubee Genealogy 110–2
Whitmore's Heraldic Journal i, 81–3
Bull — American Ancestry i, 11; ii, 17; xii
Austin's Ancestries 15
Austin's R. I. Genealogical Dict. 30, 264–7
Barbour's My Wife and Mother app. 41
Bellinger Genealogy 73
Chapman Genealogy 188
Cothren's History of Woodbury Ct. 511–3
Dickerman Genealogy 584
Eager's History of Orange Co. N. Y. 483
Futhey's History of Chester Co. Pa. 489–92
Greene's Todd and other Families
Hayden's Virginia Genealogies 206
Hinman's Connecticut Settlers 386–402
Narr. Historical Register iv, 250–2
Newport Historical Magazine iv, 134
Orcutt's History of New Milford Ct. 677
Paige's History of Cambridge Mass. 504
R. I. Historical Magazine v, 12–7
R. I. Hist. Society Collections iii, 307, 398
Savage's Genealogical Dictionary i, 292–4
Sheldon's History of Deerfield Mass. ii, 93-5
South Car. Hist. and Gen. Mag. (1900) i, 76–90
Williams' History of Danby Vt. 119
Young's History of Wayne Co. Ind. 338
Bulla — Young's Wayne Co. Ind. 338
Bullard — American Ancestry v, 142
Ballou's History of Milford Mass. 606–8
Barry's History of Framingham Mass. 203
Benedict's Hist. of Sutton Mass. 592–611
Bond's Watertown Mass. 147–9, 732
Bullard Genealogy (1878) 22 pages
Cochrane's History of Francestown N. H. 553
Hayward's Hist. of Hancock N. H. 407–10
Hill's Dedham Mass. Records
Hill's History of Mason N. H. 200

Jameson's Hist. of Medway, Mass. 457–60
Leland Magazine or Genealogy 181
Morse's Sherborn Settlers 22, 57 a–g
Power's Sangamon Co. Ill. Settlers 158
Read's History of Swanzey N. H. 302
Savage's Genealogical Dictionary i, 294–6
Secomb's History of Amherst N. H. 522
Slafter Genealogy 69
Smith Genealogy by Wellington Smith
Wight Genealogy 23
Wyman's Charlestown Mass. Gens. i, 149
Bullen — Barry's Framingham 205
Butler's History of Farmington Me. 398
Crane's Rawson Genealogy 52
Hinman's Connecticut Settlers 402
Jameson's History of Medway Mass. 460
Lapham's History of Norway Me. 477
Morse's Sherborn Mass. Settlers 19–21
Savage's Genealogical Dictionary i, 296
Stiles' History of Windsor Ct. ii, 127
Bullington — Neill's Va. Carolorum 46
Bullis — American Ancestry ii, 17
Bullitt — Green's Kentucky Families
Hayden's Virginia Genealogies 597–9
Richmond Va. Standard iii, 16
Slaughter's Fry Genealogy
Bullman — Doty Genealogy 379
Bulloch — American Ancestry, vii, 75
Baillie Genealogy 24–9
Bellinger Genealogy 69–73
Bulloch Genealogy (1892) 171 pages
Bulloch's Baillie Genealogy (1898)
Bullock — Adam's Fairhaven Vt. 295–8
Am. Ancestry i, 11; ii, 18; vi, 21; vii, 46
Baird's History of Rye N. Y. 406
Ballou Genealogy 290–3
Bassett's Hist. of Richmond N. H. 349–52
Driver Genealogy 294
Eaton's History of Thomaston Me. 163
Hubbard's Stanstead Co. Canada 236–9
Ridlon's Saco Valley Me. Families 546–50
Savage's Genealogical Dictionary i, 297
Bulmer — Chambers' N. J. Germans
Bulsen — Munsell's Albany Coll. iv, 106
Pearson's Schenectady N. Y. Settlers 30
Bump — Bassett's Richmond N. H. 35
Bumpas — Savage's Gen. Dict. i, 297
Swift's Barnstable Mass. Families i, 857
Bumpus — Lapham's Paris Me. 542–4
Winsor's History of Duxbury Mass. 239
Bumstead — New Eng. Hist. Reg. xv, 193.
Savage's Genealogical Dictionary i, 298
Bunbury — Wentworth Gen. i, 325–8
Bunce — Hinman's Conn. Settlers 403–5
Savage's Genealogical Dictionary i. 298
Tuttle Genealogy 618
Bundy — Aldrich's Walpole N. H. 218
Savage's Genealogical Dictionary i, 298
Bunker — American Ancestry xi, 133
American Gen. Rec. ii, 177–80
Austin's Allied Families 49–51
Eaton's History of Thomaston Me. 163
Farrow's History of Islesborough Me. 174
Lapham's History of Rumford Me. 309
Paige's History of Cambridge Mass. 504
Runnel's Hist. of Sanbornton N. H. ii, 57

Savage's Genealogical Dictionary i, 298
Sinclair Genealogy 276–9
Wyman's Charlestown Mass. i, 150–3
Bunn — Chamber's N. J. Germans 278–80
Savage's Genealogical Dictionary i, 299
Bunnel — Davis' Wallingford Ct. 633–5
Dwight's Strong Genealogy 319
Hinman's Connecticut Settlers 405
Bunnell — Anderson's Waterbury 31
Bunt — American Ancestry ii, 18
Bunten — Stark's Dunbarton N. H. 213
Bunting — Bunting Family Chart (1895)
Burbank — American Ancestry iii, 194
Benedict's History of Sutton Mass. 611
Bradbury's Hist. of Kennebunkport Me. 231
Burbank Genealogy (1880) 26 pages
Clute's Hist. of Staten Island N. Y. 349
Coffin's History of Boscawen N. H. 476–9
Davis' Landmarks of Plymouth Mass. 47
Dearborn's Hist. Parsonfield Me. 367, 451
Hinman's Connecticut Settlers 406–8
Hudson's History of Lexington Mass. 32
Lapham's History of Bethel Me. 497
Lincoln's Hist. of Hingham Mass. ii, 97–9
Little Genealogy 95
Morrison's Hist. of Windham N. H. 351
Norton's Hist. of Fitzwilliam N. H. 498, 799
Savage's Genealogical Dictionary i, 300
Slaughter's St. Mark's Parish Va. 160
Temple's Hist. of N. Brookfield Mass. 541
Washington N. H. History 323–9
Woodbury's Sketch of Bradford Mass. 70
Burbeck — American Ancestry vii, 79
Glover Genealogy 312–7
Whitmore's Copps Hill Epitaphs
Burbee — Norton's Fitzwilliam 500
Burbeen — Burbeen Gen. (1892) 52 pages
Sewall's History of Woburn Mass. 595
Burch — American Ancestry ii, 18
Orcutt's History of Stratford Ct. 1166
Power's Sangamon Co. Ill. Settlers 159
Burchan — New Eng. Hist. Reg. xl, 406
Burchard — Ely Genealogy 166–8, 351
See also **Birchard**
Burd — Egle's Notes and Queries 3d ser.
    iii, 231–4
Egle's Pa. Hist. Reg. ii, 214–30
Burden — Green's Kentucky Families
Savage's Genealogical Dictionary i, 300
Burdett — American Ancestry x, 163
See also **Burditt** below
Burdge — American Ancestry iii, 66
Bangor Me. Historical Mag. iii, 88
Cope Genealogy 92, 192
Burdick — American Ancestry i, 12
Austin's R. I. Genealogical Dictionary 31
Greene Genealogy
New Eng. Hist. and Gen. Reg. xiv, 24
Savage's Genealogical Dictionary i, 301
Walworth's Hyde Genealogy 516
Burdine — Missouri Pioneer Families 134
Burding — Eaton's Thomaston Me. 147
Burditt — Caverly's Pittsford Vt. 694
Wyman's Charlestown Mass. i, 154–6
Burdon — Benedict's Sutton 611–3
Daniel's History of Oxford Mass. 414

Burdoo — Hudson's Lexington Mass. 33
Burgaart — Munsell's Albany iv, 106
Burge — Hodgman's Westford 440
Savage's Genealogical Dictionary i, 302
Burger — American Ancestry ii, 18
Bockee Genealogy 29–32
Burgert — American Ancestry ii, 18
Munsell's Albany N. Y. Collections iv, 106
Burgess — Am. Ancestry v, 213; viii, 214
Austin's R. I. Genealogical Dictionary 31
Barrus' History of Goshen Mass. 136
Barry's History of Hanover Mass. 263
Burgess Genealogy (1865) 196 pages
Cleveland Genealogy 159–65
Davis' Landmarks of Plymouth 48–50
Eaton's Annals of Warren Me. 511
Farrow's History of Islesborough Me. 175
Freeman's Hist. of Cape Cod ii, 91, 150, 228
Hayward's Hist. of Hancock N. H. 410–3
Hinman's Connecticut Settlers 409
Hubbard's Hist. of Springfield Vt. 243
Paige's History of Hardwick Mass. 343
Savage's Genealogical Dictionary i, 302
Sinclair Genealogy 229
Stearns' Hist. of Ashburnham Mass. 628–30
Winsor's History of Duxbury Mass. 239
Burghardt — Great Barrington 107–10
Burgher — Clute's Staten Island 351
Burgis — Kirby Genealogy
Burgner — Burgner Gen. (1890) 172 pages
Burgwin — American Ancestry vii, 223
Burhans — American Ancestry iii, 162
Burhans Genealogy (1894) 844 pages
Schoonmaker's Hist. of Kingston N. Y. 474
Sylvester's Hist. of Ulster Co. N. Y. 298
Burk — Baird's History of Rye N. Y. 454
Burke — Burke Genealogy (1864) 240 p.
Hubbard's Hist. of Springfield Vt. 245
Temple's Hist. of No. Brookfield Mass. 541
Burkett — Eaton's Thomaston Me. 164
Burkhart — Power's Sangamon 160–2
Burkholder — Brubacher Genealogy 53–6
Burks — Hemenway's Vt. Gaz. v
Burleigh — Bond's Watertown 77
Childs Genealogy 165–9
Daniel's History of Oxford Mass. 415
Guild Genealogy by Burleigh 252
Runnel's Hist. of Sanbornton N. H. ii.58–77
Temple's Hist. of Palmer Mass. 430–2
See Burley
Burleson — Hinman's Settlers 409–19
Saunders' Alabama Settlers 72
Burley — Burley Gen. (1880) 200 pages
Caldwell Genealogy 70
Chapman's Weeks Genealogy 131
Dearborn's Hist. of Salisbury N. H. 508
Hurd's Hist. of Rockingham Co. N. H. 402
Hammett's Papers of Ipswich Mass. 35
Burling — Field Genealogy (1895) 117
Thomas Genealogy (1878)
Thomas Genealogy (1896) 237–9
Burlingame — Austin's R. I. Dict. 32
Savage's Genealogical Dictionary i, 303
Burnap — Benedict's Sutton 613–5
Daniel's History of Oxford Mass. 415
Eaton's History of Reading 568–8

Hemenway's Vermont Gazetteer v
Hinman's Connecticut Settlers 410
Savage's Genealogical Dictionary i, 303
Stearns' Hist. of Ashburnham Mass. 631
Burnell — Savage's Gen. Dict. i, 304
Burnet — Hinman's Conn. Settlers 411
Burnett — American Ancestry xii, 28
Daniel's Oxford Mass. 415
Dod Genealogy 88
Egle's Penn. Genealogies 2d ed. 679
Howell's Hist. of Southampton N. Y. 206–9
Temple's Hist. of No. Brookfield Mass. 542
Burnham — Am. Anc. i, 12; iii, 87; xi, 184
Andrews Genealogy (1890) 177–83
Andrews' History of New Britain Ct. 23
Bangor Me. Historical Magazine v, 182
Barry's Hist. of Framingham Mass. 204
Bradbury's Hist. Kennebunkport Me. 231
Burnham Fam. of Ipswich (1869) 546 p.
Burnham Fam. of Hartford (1884) 292 p.
Cochrane's Hist. of Antrim N. H. 388–91
Cochrane's Hist. of Francestown N. H. 55–7
Crowell's History of Essex Mass. 313
Davis' History of Reading N. H. 121–3
Dearborn's Hist. of Parsonsfield Me. 368
Eaton's Hist. of Thomaston Me. 164
Frisbie's History of Middlebury Vt. 40–2
Gold's History of Cornwall Ct. 252
Hammatt's Papers of Ipswich Mass. 41–3
Heywood's Hist. of Westminster Mass. 572
Hinman's Connecticut Settlers 412–8
Huntington Genealogy 149
Kellogg's White Genealogy 118
Lapham's History of Bethel Me. 499
Leland Genealogy 181
Livermore's History of Wilton N. H. 330
Loomis Genealogy (1880) 224–64
Machias Me. Centennial 156
Morrison's Hist. of Windham N. H. 352–4
New Eng. Hist. and Gen. Reg. xvi, 22
Ridlon's Harrison Me. Settlers 31–4
Savage's Genealogical Dictionary i, 304
Stark's History of Dunbarton N. H. 238
Stearn's History of Rindge N. H. 461
Stiles' History of Windsor Ct. ii, 128–32
Tanner Genealogy 39–42
Tuttle Genealogy xxxv
Wood Genealogy 62
Burnley — Barksdale Genealogy 24
Burns — Cochran's Antrim N. H. 391–4
Eaton's History of Thomaston Me. 164
Lancaster's History of Rowley Mass. 258
Lincoln's Hist. of Hingham Mass. ii, 100
Livermore's History of Wilton N. H. 331
Secomb's History of Amherst N. H. 523
Wyman's Charlestown Mass. Gens. i, 156
Burpee — Chase's Chester N. H. 480
Eaton's History of Candia N. H. 57
Eaton's History of Thomaston Me. 165
Essex Mass. Institute Colls. xx, 215–8
Heywood's Hist. of Westminster Mass. 572
Stickney Genealogy 501–4
Worthen's History of Sutton N. H. 638–40
Burr — Amer. Ancestry vii, 7, 105; xii, 35
Bangor Historical Mag. iii, 87; vi, 80
Burr Genealogy (1878) 437 pages

Burr Genealogy 2d ed. (1891) 535 pages
Freeman's Hist. of Cape Cod Mass. i, 694
Hinman's Connecticut Settlers 427-36
Hubbard's Hist. of Springfield Vt. 246
Hurd's History of Fairfield Co. Ct. 580
Jameson's History of Medway Mass. 461
Lincoln's Hist. of Hingham Mass. ii, 100-8
Loomis Genealogy (1880) 565-72
Mitchell's Hist. of Bridgewater Mass. 125
New Eng. Hist. and Gen. Register v, 472
Olcott Genealogy (1845) 57
Orcutt's History of Torrington Ct. 661-3
Paige's History of Cambridge Mass. 505
Redfield Genea ogy 56
Savage's Genealogical Dictionary i, 305-8
Schenck's History of Fairfield Ct. 359-62
Sedgwick's History of Sharon Ct. 67
Sprague's History of Gloversville N. Y.
Stiles' History of Windsor Ct. ii, 132-4
Temple's History of Northfield Mass.
Todd's History of Redding Ct. 184-6
Tuttle Genealogy 385-407
Wyman's Charlestown Mass. Gens. i, 157
Burrage — Amer. Ancestry v, 23, 87
Burrage Genealogy (1877) 265 pages
Savage's Genealogical Dictionary i, 308
Wyman's Charlestown Mass. i, 157-9
Burrall — Hinman's Settlers 418-24
Burrell — Lincoln's Hingham ii, 109-12
Burridge — Bass' Braintree Vt. 122
Burrier — Plumb's Hanover Pa. 389
Burrill — Ballou's Milford Mass. 608
Lewis' History of Lynn Mass. 116, 492
Pickering Genealogy (1897)
Savage's Genealogical Dictionary i, 308
Burrington — Austin's Anc. Dict. 12
Austin's R. I. Genealogical Dictionary 33
Burris — Quisenberry Genealogy 53-5
Burritt — Andrews' New Britain 199
Burritt Genealogy (1892) 52 pages
Cothren's History of Woodbury Ct. 510
Fairfield Hist. Soc. An. Rep. (1892) 3-43
Foster Pedigree (1897) v, 1-48
Hinman's Connecticut Settlers 436
Morris' Bontecou Genealogy
Orcutt's History of Derby Ct. 705
Orcutt's History of Stratford Ct. 1168
Plumb's History of Hanover Pa. 397
Todd's History of Redding Ct. 187
Tuttle Genealogy 123-6
Burroughs — Burroughs Gen. (1894) 24 p.
Caulkins' History of New London Ct. 301
Cooley's Trenton N. J. Genealogies 17-23
Davis Genealogy (1889) 93
Hayward's History of Gilsum N. H. 279
Hinman's Connecticut Settlers 424-7
Maine Historical Society Colls. i, 175
Orcutt's History of Stratford Ct. 1167
Riker's Annals of Newtown N. Y. 283-5
Stiles' History of Windsor Ct. ii, 134
Wyman's Charlestown Mass. Gens. 159
Burrow — Smith Genealogy (1889) 93
Burrows — American Ancestry i, 12; ii,
    18; viii, 199; xi, 172; xii, 68
Burrows Genealogy (1872) 76 pages
Cunnabell Genealogy 110

Davis' History of Bucks County Pa. 235
Hurd's Hist. of New London Co. Ct. 476-8
Littell s Passaic Valley Genealogies 64
Salter's Hist. of Monmouth Co. N. J. xiv
Savage's Genealogical Dictionary i, 310-312
Wentworth Genealogy ii, 445
Bursley — Freeman's Cape Cod 290-6
Savage's Genealogical Dictionary i, 312
Swift's Barnstable Families i, 127-35
Burt — Am. Anc. i, 12; vi, 60; viii, 77, 79
Aldrich's History of Walpole N. H. 219-22
Burt Genealogy (1892) 347 pages
Burt, Henry, Life of (1893)
Butler's History of Groton Mass. 391
Chandler's History of Shirley Mass. 364
Davis' Landmarks of Plymouth Mass. 50
Eager's History of Orange Co. N. Y. 425
Ely Genealogy 91
Hayward's Hist. of Hancock N. H. 413-23
Hyde's History of Brimfield (Mass.) 385-7
Kellogg's White Descendants 118, 216
Longmeadow Mass. Centen. app. 16-23
Loomis Genealogy (1880) 521
Morris Genealogy (1853) 48
New Eng. Hist. Gen. Reg. xxxii, 302-5
Power's Sangamon Co. Ill. Settlers 162
Randall's Hist. of Chesterfield N. H. 237
Savage's Genealogical Dictionary i, 312-4
Sheldon's Hist. Deerfield Mass. ii, 96-9
Temple's History of Northfield Mass. 414
Winslow Genealogy i, 460
Wyman's Charlestown Mass. Gens. i, 160
Burton — Amer. Anc. iii, 158; v, 180, 237
Austin's Allied Families 51
Austin's R. I. Genealogical Dict. 267
Cogswell Genealogy 258
Collin's History of Hillsdale N. Y. app.
    43-5
Eaton's Annals of Warren Me. 512-4
Eaton's History of Thomaston Me. 165
Hinman's Connecticut Settlers 437
Livermore's History of Wilton N. H. 332-9
Maine Bugle for July, 1898
North's History of Augusta Me. 820-2
Orcutt's History of Stratford Ct. 1169-71
Our Ancestors 8-12
Power's Sangamon Co. Ill. Settlers 163
Savage's Genealogical Dictionary i, 314-6
Slafter Genealogy 25, 27
Sprague's Hist. of Gloversville N. Y. 109
Wheeler's History of N. Carolina ii, 163
Wyman's Charlestown Mass. Gens. i, 160
Burtt — Livermore's Wilton N. H. 339
Burwell — Amer. Ancestry iv, 67
Burwell Family Proceedings (1870) 26
    pages
Campbell's History of Virginia 550
Carter Family Tree
Chase's History of Chester N. H. 480
Goode Genealogy 63
Hinman's Connecticut Settlers 438-40
Keith's Harrison Ancestry 34-8
Jones Genealogy (1891) 45
Meade's Old Churches of Va. i, 353; ii, 290
Page Genealogy 64, 144
Paxton's Marshall Genealogy 102, 252

Richmond Va. Standard i, 40; ii, 38; iii, 42–5; iv, 2
Savage's Genealogical Dictionary i, 316
Busby — Savage's Gen. Dict. i, 316
Busecot — Austin's Allied Families 52
Austin's R. I. Genealogical Dictionary 33
Busenberry — Chambers' N. J. Germans
Bush — Am. Anc. iv, 163; v, 111; xii, 77
Bolton's Westchester County N. Y. ii, 509
Caulkin's History of Norwich Ct. 213
Cleveland's Yates Co. N. Y. 314, 529–31
Clute's History of Staten Island N. Y. 351
Draper's History of Spencer Mass. 182
Ely Genealogy 120
Hinman's Connecticut Settlers 441–3
Hudson's History of Marlboro' Mass. 349
Loomis Genealogy (1880) 637–41
Meade's History of Greenwich Ct. 306
Paige's History of Cambridge Mass. 505
Paxton's Marshall Genealogy 269
Quisenberry Genealogy 77–95
Savage's Genealogical Dictionary i, 316
Temple's Hist. of No. Brookfield Mass. 543
Ward's History of Shrewsbury Mass. 242
Bushell — Potts Genealogy (1895) 639
Bushman — Corliss' No. Yarmouth Me.
Bushnell — American Ancestry ii, 18; iv, 145; ix, 207; x, 199
Bushnell Family Chart
Caulkins' History of Norwich Ct. 213–5
Collins' History of Hillsdale N. Y. app. 45
Hine's Lebanon Ct. Hist. Address 149
Hinman's Connecticut Settlers 444–52
New Eng. Hist. and Gen. Reg. iv, 19; lii, 446–8; liii, 208–14
Norwich Conn. Jubilee 202
Perkins' Old Houses of Norwich Ct. 428–31
Savage's Genealogical Dictionary i, 317
Tuttle Genealogy 367
Walworth's Hyde Genealogy 7, 919
Bushrod — Hayden's Virginia Gens. 636
Buskirk — Boyd's Conesus N. Y. 145
Buss — Bemis' Hist. Marlboro N. H. 431–3
Livermore's Wilton N. H. 339–43
Savage's Genealogical Dictionary i, 319
Smith's History of Peterborough N. H. 27
Bussell — Bangor Historical Mag. iii, 136
See also Buzzell
Bussey — Dedham Hist. Register x, 75
Bussing — American Ancestry vi, 6, 29
Riker's History of Harlem N. Y. 497–500
Roome Genealogy 117–27
Buswell — Driver Genealogy 151–5
Eaton's History of Candia N. H. 57
Guild's Stiles Genealogy 14–9
Hoyt's Salisbury Mass. Families 80–2
Merrill's Hist. of Acworth N. H. 193
Runnel's Hist. Sanbornton N. H. ii, 77–9
Savage's Genealogical Dictionary i, 519
Stearns' History of Rindge N. H. 462
See also Buzzell and Boswell
Butler — American Ancestry ii, 19; iii, 7; viii, 69, 214; ix, 122, 191; x, 41, 170; xi, 24; xii, 11, 22, 43
Anderson's Waterbory Ct. 1, app. 32
Andrews Genealogy (1890) 183

Andrews' Hist. New Britain Ct. 275, 280
Austin's Allied Families 53
Barry's History of Framingham Mass. 205
Bass Ancestry 8
Bemis' History of Marlboro N. H. 433
Bridgman's Granary Epitaphs 260, 271
Buckingham Genealogy 205
Butler Fam. of Pelham N. H. (1849) 16 p.
Butler Family of Ohio (1881) 8 pages
Butler Fam. of Nottingham N.H. (1884) 4 p.
Butler Family of Berwick Me. (1886) 192 p.
Butler Family of Pelham (1887) 36 pages
Butler Family of Saybrook Ct. (1887) 61 p.
Butler Family of Boston (1888) 162 pages
Butler Family of Dorchester (1895) 26 p.
Butler's Hist. of Farmington Me. 399–407
Carter Genealogy by Potts (1883) 91
Caulkin's History of New London Ct. 342
Clarke's Old King Wm. Co. Va. Families
Clute's History of Staten Island N. Y. 353
Cochrane's History of Antrim N. H. 395–9
Coffin's History of Boscawen N. H. 481
Cogswell's History of Henniker N. H. 475
Coggswell's Nottingham 170–9, 336–9
Collin's History of Kentucky ii, 120
Corliss' North Yarmouth Me. Magazine
Cothren's Hist. of Woodbury Ct. ii, 1472
Cutt's Genealogy 72–5, 139–43, 261–4
Daniels' History of Oxford Mass. 417–20
Eaton's History of Thomaston Me. 166–70
Egle's Hist. Reg. Interior Penn. i, 1–17
Emery Genealogy 473–5
Freeman's Cape Cod Mass. ii, 68, 485, 772
Futhey's History of Chester Co. Pa. 492
Green's Kentucky Genealogy
Hammatt's Papers of Ipswich Mass. 40
Hatch's History of Industry Me. 525–39
Hayward's History of Gilsum N. H. 280
Hayward's Hist. of Hancock N. H. 423–6
Hemenway's Vermont Gazette v, 89
Hinman's Conn. Settlers 454–60
Howell's History of Southampton N. Y. 209
Kulp's Wyoming Valley Families
Maine Hist. Gen. Rec. iii, 134; iv, 226
Meade's Old Families of Virginia
McKeen's History of Bradford Vt. 359–61
New Eng. Hist. and Gen. Reg. i, 167–70; ii, 355–60; iii, 73–6, 353–8; xvi, 17
Norton's History of Fitzwilliam N. H. 500
Paxton's Marshall Genealogy 227
Penn. Magazine of History vii, 1–7
Perkins' Old Houses of Norwich Ch. 432
Pompey N. Y. Reunion 271–2, 405–9
Poore's Genealogy 14–33
Potts Genealogy (1895) 209–18
Power's Sangamon Co. Ill. Settlers 164
Randall's History of Chesterfield N. H. 239
Savage's Genealogical Dictionary i, 320–2
Sibley's History of Union Me. 435–8
Sigourney Genealogy
Stearns' History of Ashburnham Mass. 631
Stiles' History of Windsor Ct. ii, 135
Swift's Barnstable Mass. Families i, 144
Walworth's Hyde Genealogy i, 522–8
Ward's History of Shrewsbury Mass. 241

Wentworth Genealogy i, 665-71
Whitmore's Copps Hill Epitaphs
Butman — Babson's Gloucester 66
Guild's Stiles Genealogy 384
Butrich — Shattuck's Concord 366
Butterfleld — American Ancestry ix, 68
Brown's Bedford Mass. Families 6
Butler's History of Farmington Me. 407-20
Butterfield Genealogy (1890) 11 pages
Chandler Genealogy 330
Chase's History of Chester N. H. 480
Cochrane's Hist. Francestown N. H. 557-64
Cutter's Hist. of Arlington Mass. 199-201
Dunster Genealogy 253
Emery Genealogy (1890) 345
Hayward's History of Hancock N. H. 427
Hemenway's Vermont Gazette v, 189
Haywood's Hist. of Westminster Mass. 573
Hodgman's History of Westford Mass. 440
Livermore's History of Wilton N. H. 343
Locke Genealogy 78
New Eng. Hist. Gen. Register xliv, 33-43
Norton's History of Fitzwilliam N. H. 500
Paige's History of Cambridge Mass. 505
Phœnix's Whitney Family i, 299
Savage's Genealogical Dictionary i, 322
Sewall's History of Woburn Mass. 597
Tyngsboro Mass. Centennial 5-12
Washington N. H. History 329
Wyman's Charlestown Mass. Gens. 161
Butters — Am. Ancestry xi, 73, 134, 172
Butters Genealogy (1896) 466 pages
Hudson's Lexington Mass. 34
Sewall's History of Woburn Mass. 596
Butterworth — N. E. Reg. xli, 191-4
Savage's Genealogical Dictionary i, 323
Buttolph — Hinman's Ct. Settlers 461
Savage's Genealogical Dictionary i, 323
Whitney Genealogy i, 115
Button — American Ancestry xii, 44
Button Genealogy (1889) 16 pages
Paul's History of Wells Vt. 68
Savage's Genealogical Dictionary i, 324
Williams' History of Danby Vt. 120
Buttrick — Bemis' History of Marlboro
  N. H. 436
Heywood's Westminster 573
Morrison's History of Windham N. H. 854
Potter's Concord Mass. Families 8
Stearns' History of Ashburnham Mass. 631
Stearns' History of Rindge N. H. 463
Butts — American Ancestry viii, 59
Austin's R. I. Genealogical Dictionary 34
Keith's Harrison Ancestry, Addenda 6
Paul's History of Wells Vt. 70
Savage's Genealogical Dictionary i, 322
Butz — Eyerman Ancestors (1898)
Buxton — Benedict's Sutton Mass. 615
Cleveland's History of Yates Co. N. Y. 676
Cochrane's Hist. of Francestown N. H. 564
Cogswell's History of Henniker N. H. 476
Cogswell's Hist. of New Boston N.H. 401-4
Corliss' North Yarmouth Me. Magazine
  1146-53, 1200-8
Eaton's Annals of Warren Me. 514
Hayward's Hist. of Hancock N. H. 427-9

Hemenway's Vermont Gazette v
Huntington's Stamford Ct. Families 20
Little's History of Weare N. H. 751-3
Paul's History of Wells Vt. 70
Ridlon's Saco Valley Me. Families 518-20
Temple's Hist. of N. Brookfield Mass. 54
Williams' History of Danby Vt. 121
Young's History of Warsaw N. Y. 242-4
Buzby — Potts Genealogy (1895) 343
Buzzell — American Ancestry xi, 72
Caverno Genealogy 20
Cogswell's Nottingham N. H. 650-4
Dearborn's History of Parsonfield Me. 369
Guild's Stiles Genealogy 371
See also Bussell and Buswell
Byam — Norton's Fitzwilliam 501-3
Byard — Dunster Genealogy 175-9
Byers — Egle's Pa. Gens. 2d ed. 765-7
Hayden's Weitzel Genealogy 67-71
Johnston Genealogy (1897) 135-9, 162-5
Byfield — Savage's Gen. Dict. i, 325
Byington — Anderson's Waterbury 32
Boynton Genealogy 262-86
Orcutt's History of Wolcott Ct. 465
Byles — Babson's Gloucester Mass. 66
Savage's Genealogical Dictionary i, 326
Byley — N. E. Hist. Register lii, 44-50
Byram — American Ancestry iii, 8; xii
Corliss' North Yarmouth Me. Mag. 1174-7
Hanson's History of Gardiner Me. 156
Littell's Passaic Valley Genealogies 65
McElroy's Abby Byram, Indian Captive
Mitchell's History of Bridgewater Mass.
  127-9
Savage's Genealogical Dictionary i, 326
Byrd — Balch's Prov. Papers 128-31
Campbell's History of Virginia 420, 712
Clarke's Old King Wm. Co. Va. Families
Glenn's Colonial Mansions 54-8
Meade's Old Fams. of Va. i, 315; ii, 290
New Eng. Hist. and Genealogical Register
  xxxiv, 162; xxxviii, 306
Paxton's Marshall Genealogy 312
Prescott's Page Genealogy
Richmond Va. Critic (1888)
Sketches of Lynchburg Va. 299-305
Slaughter's Bristol Parish Va. 296, 291
See also under Burd and Bird
Byrne — Driver Genealogy 270
Byron — Corliss' No. Yarmouth Me.
Bythewood — N. E. Hist. Reg. xl, 299
Cabanne — Beckwith's Creoles 71-7
Cabell — American Ancestry iv, 65; v, 97,
  98; viii, 204
Cabell Genealogy (1895) 641 pages
Campbell's History of Virginia 626
Meade's Old Families of Virginia i, 60-3
Sketches of Lynchburg Va. 206-19
Eaton's History of Thomaston Me. 170
Richmond Va. Standard i, 37, 41; ii, 12, 17,
  19, 40; iii, 14, 34
Robertson's Pocahontas' Descendants
Schenck's History of Fairfield Ct. 362
Slaughter's Fry Genealogy 23
Cable — Tilley's Magazine of N. E. History iii, 135-40

Cabot — Dwight Genealogy 579–82
Pickering Genealogy
Cadman — American Ancestry ii, 19
Austin's R. I. Genealogical Dictionary 268
Cadmus — Winfield's Hudson 555–61
Cadwalader — Cooley's Trenton 23–9
Glenn's Merion in Welsh Tract 252–60
Life of Rev. Wm. Smith
Morris Genealogy (1898) 198–201
Penn. Mag. of History vi, 209–12; x, 1–3
Cadwell — Andrews' New Britain 252
Hinman's Connecticut Settlers 465
Kellogg's Memorial of John White 102
Savage's Genealogical Dictionary i, 327
Stiles' History of Windsor Ct. ii, 135
Cady — Adams' Fairhaven Vt. 322–6
American Ancestry ii, 18
Bass' History of Braintree Vt. 122
Bond's Watertown Mass. Gens. 733
Butler's History of Groton Mass. 391
Cleveland Genealogy (1899) 1573, 1981
Hayward's History of Gilsum N. H. 280
Little's Genealogy 56–8
Savage's Genealogical Dictionary i, 327
Stiles' History of Windsor Ct. ii, 136–40
Caen — See under Bain
Cahill — Norton's Fitzwilliam 503
Cain — Lincoln's Hingham ii, 113–6
Temple's No. Brookfield 547
Calaway — Dawson Genealogy 101
Calbreath — See Galbraith
Calder — Wyman's Charlestown 164
Calderwood — Eaton's Warren Me. 514
Eaton's History of Thomaston Me. 170
Caldwell — Am. Ancestry v, 187; ix, 32
Caldwell's Genealogy (1873) 80 pages
Caldwell Letter (1885) 8 pages
Cochrane's History of Antrim N. H. 399
Cogswell's History of Henniker N. H. 477
Dwight Genealogy 436–45
Egle's Penn. Gens. 2d ed. 683
Egle's Notes and Queries 4th ser. i, 4
Hammatt's Papers of Ipswich Mass. 44–6
Hudson's History of Lexington Mass. 34
Lapham's History of Paris Me. 545
Little's History of Weare N. H. 754
North's History of Augusta Me. 822
Powers' Sangamon Co. Ill. Settlers 165–7
Richmond Va. Standard ii, 34
Savage's Genealogical Dictionary i, 328
Secomb's History of Amherst N. H. 525
Smith's Hist. of Petersborough N. H. 28, 30
Stark's History of Dunbarton N. H. 248
Stearns' History of Ashburnham Mass. 632
Temple's History of Northfield Mass. 416
Welles' American Family Antiquity (1881)
Wyman's Charlestown Mass. Gens. i, 165
Calef — American Ancestry v, 143; xi, 172
Chase's History of Chester N. H. 481–3
Dearborn's Hist. of Salisbury N. H. 511–8
Drake's Witchcraft Delusions ii, 28
Hammatt Papers of Ipswich Mass. 46
Heywood's Hist. of Westminster Mass. 574
Runnell's Hist. Sanbornton N. H. ii, 79–84
Savage's Genealogical Dictionary i, 329
Wyman's Charlestown Mass. Gens. i, 166

Calhoun — Childs Genealogy 809
Gold's History of Cornwall Ct. 276
Marshall Genealogy (1884) 64
Powers' Sangamon Co. Ill. Settlers 167–9
Stearns' History of Rindge N. H. 464–6
Calkins — Am. Ancestry ii, 20; xii, 137
Anderson's Waterbury Ct. i, app. 32
Babson's History of Gloucester Mass. 67
Boltwood's Noble Genealogy 364
Hemenway's Vermont Gazette iv, 850
Hines' Lebanon Ct. Hist. Address 150
Read's History of Swaney N. H. 305
Sedgwick's History of Sharon Ct. 67
Temple's History of Palmer Mass. 438
Walworth's Hyde Genealogy 956–9, 1011
Wentworth Genealogy i, 354
Williams' History of Danby Vt. 121
Call — Bangor Hist. Magazine vii, 172
Daniels' History of Oxford Mass. 420
Dearborn's Hist. of Salisbury N. H. 518–22
Malden Mass. Bi-Centennial 240
Morrison's History of Windham N. H. 355
Runnel's Hist. of Sanbornton N. H. ii, 84–7
Savage's Genealogical Dictionary i, 329
Wheeler's History of Newport N. H. 322
Wyman's Charlestown Mass. i, 166–73
Callaway — Cabell Genealogy 366–9
Meade's Old Families of Virginia
Richmond Va. Standard 17, 21
Callender — American Ancestry ii, 20
Savage's Genealogical Dictionary i, 330
Temple's History of Northfield Mass. 416
Caller — Southwick Genealogy 481–3
Callerman — Powers' Sangamon 169
Calley — Wyman's Charlestown 173
Calnek — Calnek's Annapolis N. S. 485–7
Calthorpe — William and Mary College
Historical Register ii, 106–12, 160–8
Calverly — Runnell's Sanbornton 87–6
Calvert — Heraldic Journal iii, 18, 21
Neill's Terra Mariæ
Richmond Va. Standard iii, 50
Virginia Magazine of History v, (1898)
436–9; vi, (1898) 73–5
Calvin — N. E. Hist. Reg. xxvii, 136
Caman — See under Cain
Camburn — Salter's Monmouth xv
Came — Ridlon's Saco Valley 550–5
Cameron — American Ancestry i, 12
Quisenberry Genealogy 127–9
Camfield — See Canfield
Cammann — American Ancestry v, 68
Cammet — Swift's Barnstable i, 249
Camn — William and Mary College Historical Register iv, 61, 275–8
Camp — American Ancestry iv, 22; v, 172;
x, 48, 183; xi, 86
Anderson's Waterbury Ct. i, app. 32
Andrews' Hist. of New Britain Ct. 207, 376
Baldwin Genealogical Supp. 1262
Boyd's Annals of Winchester Ct. 330
Camp Genealogy (1897) 2 vols.
Coe and Ward Memorial 46–50
Hinman's Connecticut Settlers 470–2
Hubbard's Stanstead Co. Canada 169
Littell's Passaic Valley Genealogies 66

Middlefield Ct. History
Norton's History of Fitzwilliam N. H. 503
Orcutt's History of New Milford Ct. 678
Savage's Genealogical Dictionary i, 331
Sedgwick's History of Sharon Ct. 67
Selleck's Norwalk Ct. (1896) 350, 402-8
Campbell — Aldrich's Walpole 222-4
Alexander Genealogy (1898)
Am. Anestry iv, 49; vi, 87; viii, 156; ix, 190
Ammidown's Historical Collections i, 240
Bakewell Genealogy 82-7
Bangor's Historical Magazine i, 79-81; iii,
 181-4; iv, 90; vii, 166-70
Barry's History of Framington Mass. 205
Bellinger Genealogy 99
Butler Genealogy (1888) 52, 69
Campbell Genealogy (1878) 8 pages reprint
Campbell Family of N. Orleans (1887) 4 p.
Campbells of Kishacoquillas (1894) 48 p.
Campbell's Spotswood Papers 25
Cochrane's History of Antrim N. H. 400-2
Cochrane's Hist. Francestown N. H. 565-7
Cogswell's Hist. of Henniker N. H. 478-87
Cogswell's Hist. of New Boston N. H. 412-5
Cushman's Hist. of Sheepscott Me. 360-2
Daniels' History of Oxford Mass. 421-32
Douglass' Genealogy of Campbell (1878)
Dyer's History of Plainfield Mass. 131-4
Eaton's History of Thomaston Me. 170
Egle's Penn. Genealogies 2d ed. 581
Egle's Notes and Queries 1st ser. i, 385,
 419, (1896) 142
Ely Genealogy 269-71
Foote's Sketches of Va. 2d series 117
Green's Kentucky Families
Hayden's Virginia Genealogies 17-9
Hemenway's Vermont Gazette v. 244
Hepburn Genealogy 98
Johnson Genealogy (1895) 94-7
Joslin's History of Poultney Vt. 229
Keith's Harrison Ancestry 79-81
Meade's Old Churches of Va. ii, 160
Merrill's History of Acworth N. H. 194-7
Milliken's Narraguagus Valley Me. 9-11
Morrison's Hist. of Windham N. H. 356-74
Munsell's Albany Collections iv, 107
New Eng. Hist. Gen. Reg. xxxii, 275-80
New York Gen. and Biog. Record xvi, 6-10
Pearson's Schenectady N. Y. Settlers 32
Peyton's History of Augusta Co. Va. 307
Power's Sangamon Co. Ill. 16, 170-6
Randall's History of Chesterfield N. H. 240
Richmond Va. Standard i, 30, 32, 35, 38;
 ii, 39, 45, 47, 49; iii, i, 5, 7, 39, 44; iv, 3
Roe's Sketches of Rose N. Y. 264
Savage's Genealogical Dictionary i, 331
Secomb's History of Amherst N. H. 526-8
Slaughter's St. Mark's Parish Va. i, 188
Waddell's Annals of Augusta Co. Va. 396-8
Whitmore's Heraldic Journal iii, 151
Wyman's Charlestown Mass. Gens. i, 174
Campfield — N. J. Historical Soc. vi, 141
Selleck's Norwalk Ct. (1896) 286-8
See Canfield
Campsey — Jameson's Medway 462
Canada — Hinman's Conn. Settlers 472

Canby — American Ancestry vii, 158
Canby Genealogy (1883) 59 pages
Davis' History of Bucks County Pa. **274**
Morris Genealogy (1898) 660
Thomas Genealogy (1896) 383-5
Candage — American Ancestry iii, 156
Bangor Me. Hist. Mag. iv. 129-37; v, **182**
Candage Genealogy (1899) 9 pages
Eaton's History of Thomaston Me. 171
Candee — American Ancestry viii, 115
Anderson's Waterbury Ct. i, app. 33
Candee Genealogy (1882) 240 pages
Candell — Roome Genealogy 108
Candish — Bangor Magazine iv 129-37
Candler — Am. Anc. vi, 188, 197; vii, 228
Cane — Paige's Cambridge Mass. 506
Canedy — Power's Sangamon Ill. 177
Canfield — American Ancestry vi, 153
Buckingham Genealogy 239-41
Canfield Genealogy (1897) 200 pages
Cothren's History of Woodbury Ct. ii, **1490**
Humphrey's Genealogy 197-9
Joslin's History of Poultney Vt. 230
Orcutt's History of Derby Ct. 706
Orcutt's History of New Milford Ct. 679-86
Power's Sangamon Co. Ill. Settlers 176
Savage's Genealogical Dictionary i, 332
Sedgwick's History of Sharon Ct. 67-9
Sharpe's History of Seymour Ct. 193-6
Sharpe's South Britain Ct. Sketches 157-9
Smith Genealogy by Wellington Smith
Whittemore's Orange N. J. 48
Canney — New Eng. Hist. Register v, 452
Cannon — Clute's Staten Island 354
Davis's History of Wallingford Ct. 665
Hearne Genealogy 50
Orcutt's History of Stratford Ct. 1172
Page's History of Hardwick Mass. 344
Selleck's Norwalk Ct. (1896) 408-20
Swift's Barnstable Mass. Families i, 250
Trowbridge Genealogy 102-4
Canterbury — Power's Sangamon 177
Savage's Genealogical Dictionary i, 333
Cantine — Schoonmaker's Kingston
Sylvester's History of Ulster Co. N. Y. 252
Cantrall — Power's Sangamon 183
Sheldon's History of Deerfield Mass. ii, 99
Cantzon — Saunders' Alabama 394-518
Capehart — Goode Genealogy 243
Wheeler's Eminent N. Carolinians 220
Capell — Cleveland's Yates Co. 707
Hudson's History of Lexington Mass. 35
Capen — Adams' Fairhaven Vt. 346-8
New Eng. Hist. and Gen. Register xx, 246
Clapp Genealogy 15
Clapp's Jones' Hill Mass. 59-64
Draper's History of Spencer Mass. 186
Glover Genealogy 373-6
Lapham's History of Bethel Me. 499
N. E. Hist. and Gen. Reg. v, 397; xx, 246-8
Savage's Genealogical Dictionary i, 333
Thayer Memorial (1835) 75-80
Washburn's History of Leicester Mass. 350
Whitmore's Copps Hill Epitaphs
Wyman's Charlestown Mass. Gens. i, 175
Capewell — Cothren's Woodbury 1475

Capp — Egle's Notes and Queries (1896) 155–8

Capps — Power's Sangamon Ill. 185

Capron — Bassett's Richmond N. H. 383

Bemis' Hist. of Marlboro N. H. 436–9

Capron Genealogy (1859) 263 pages

Chapin's Uxbridge Mass. Address 165–9

Daggett's History of Attleboro' Mass. 89.

Oneida Co. Hist. Soc. Trans. ii, 120–4

Read's History of Swanzey N. H. 305

Richardson's Woonsocket R. I. 308–12

Card — Austin's R. I. Gen. Dictionary 270

Austin's Allied Families 55

Babson's History of Gloucester Mass. 67

Cardell — Walworth's Hyde Gen. 529

Carder — Austin's R. I. Dictionary 270–3

Savage's Genealogical Dictionary i, 334

Cardwell — Baker's Montville Ct. 537

Cardwill — American Ancestry xii, 31

Carew — Perkins' Norwich Ct. 433

Walworth's Hyde Genealogy 1038

Carey — Alden's Am. Epitaphs ii, 251–3

Daniels' History of Oxford Mass. 432

Dudley's Archæological Coll. plate 5

Evan's Fox Genealogy 143–9

Heywood's Hist. of Westminster Mass. 575

Hinman's Connecticut Settlers 485

Morrison's History of Windham N. H. 374

Plumb's History of Hanover Pa. 403–5

Poole Genealogy 126–39

Smith's History of Peterborough N. H. 30

Temple's History of Northfield Mass. 417

Thomas Family (1877) 52

Thomas Genealogy (1896) 239–41

Ward's History of Shrewsbury Mass. 262

Washington's N. H. History 329

Wyman's Charlestown Mass. i, 176–81

Cargel — Daniels' Oxford Mass. 433

Cargill — Cushman's Sheepscott 362

Richardson's Woonsocket R. I. 308–12

Carhart — Am. Anc. i, 12; ii, 20; x, 140

Baird's History of Rye N. Y. 455

Carhart Genealogy (1880) 142 pages

Chambers' Early Germans of N. J. 280–3

Carkin — Livermore's Wilton N. H. 344

Carle — Hall's Trenton N. J. 231.

Little's History of Warren N. H. 67

Hanson's Old Kent Maryland 232

Ridlon's Saco Valley Me. Families 555–67

Carleton — American Ancestry viii, 236

Bangor Me. Historical Magazine v, 183

Carleton Genealogy (1897) 6 pages

Eaton's History of Thomaston Me. 171, 672

Essex Mass. Inst. Historical Colls. (1883)

Hazen's History of Billerica Mass. 21

Merrill's History of Acworth N. H. 197

Poor's Historical Researches 89, 134–6

Secomb's History of Amherst N. H. 528

Stearns' History of Rindge N. H. 466–8

Wyman's Charlestown Mass. Gens. 181–4

See also Carlton

Carley — Brown's Whitingham Vt. 189–92

Hayward's Hist. of Hancock N. H. 430–4

Hemenway's Vermont Gazette v, 721

Smith's Hist. of Peterborough N. H. 31

Washington N. H. History 330

Carlin — Goode Genealogy 267

Carlisle — Aldrich's Walpole 224–7

Chambers' Early Germans of N. J. 283

Fell Genealogy 84–6

Green's Kentucky Families

Carll — Shroud's Fenwick N. J. 521–4

See also Carle

Carlton — Essex Hist. Coll. xx, 249–61

Cochrane's Hist. of Francestown N. H. 568

Hayward's Hist. of Hancock N. H. 434–6

See also Carleton

Carman — American Ancestry xi, 74

Bunker's L. I. Genealogies 164–6

New York Gen. & Biog. Rec. xiii, 48

Carmer — Carmer Family (1893) Chart

Carnahan — Nevins Genealogy

Carnes — American Ancestry xi, 134, 203

Cogswell's Henniker 487

Lincoln's History of Hingham Mass. ii, 117

Wyman's Charlestown Mass. Gens. i, 184

Carney — Cushman's Sheepscott 363

Eaton's History of Thomaston Me. 172

Caroll — American Ancestry ii, 20

Carpenter — Adams' Fairhaven 344–6

Aldrich's History of Walpole N. H. 227

Am. Ancestry ii, 20; iii, 214; v, 152; ix, 73; x, 102, 159, 198; xii, 116

Andrews' History of New Britain Ct. 334

Austin's R. I. Genealogical Dictionary 35

Austin's Allied Families 56–9

Bailey Genealogy (1895) 150–61

Baird's History of Rye N. Y. 455–67

Ballou's History of Milford Mass. 610–2

Ballou Genealogy 554–8

Barrus' History of Goshen Mass. 143

Benedict's History of Sutton Mass. 615

Blanding Family Chart (1895)

Bliss Genealogy 646

Bockee Genealogy 88–96

Bolton's Westchester County N. Y. ii, 716

Carpenter Fam. of Weymouth (1877) 10 p.

Carpenter Estate by Usher (1883) 70 pages

Carpenter Reunion (1885) 15 pages

Carpenter Family Circular (1893) 7 pages

Carpenter Genealogy (1898) 908 pages

Carpenter Abstracts (1899) 3 pages

Caverly's History of Pittsford Vt. 694

Clement's Newtown N. J. Settlers

Daggett's History of Attleboro, Mass. 89

Dawson Genealogy 60

Futhey's History of Chester Co. Pa. 494

Greene Genealogy (1894)

Guild's Stiles Genealogy 378

Harvey Genealogy 925–7

Haywood's Hist. of Gilsum N. H. 281–3

Hinman's Connecticut Settlers 487–9

Hoogland Genealogy 269

Hughes Genealogy 88–92, 135–9

Huron and Erie Counties Ohio 514

Jillson Genealogy 169–71

Johnson Genealogy (1895) 124

Lapham's History of Paris Me. 548

Loomis Genealogy (1880) 618–20

Mott Genealogy 252–6

New Eng. Hist. and Gen. Reg. ix, 52–4

Paige's Hist. of Hardwick Mass. 344

Penn. Mag. of Hist. and Biog. vi, 453-7
Perkins' Old Houses of Norwich Ct. 435
Power's Sangamon Co. Ill. Settlers 187
Queen's County N. Y. History
Read's History of Swanzey N. H. 307-9
R. I. Historical Magazine vi, 205
Rodman Genealogy 116-8
Ruttenber's Hist. of Newburgh N. Y. 293
Ruttenber's Hist. of Orange Co. N.Y. 380-2
Savage's Genealogical Dictionary i, 335-8
Smith's Hist. of Dutchess Co. N. Y. 125-9
Smith's Lloyd and Carpenter Gens. (1870)
Strong Genealogy 952
Vinton Genealogy 480-4
Wentworth Genealogy i, 469-73
Wyman's Charlestown Mass. Gens. i, 185
Carr — Am. Ancestry vii, 68; viii, 215
Austin's Ancestries 75
Austin's R. I. Genealogical Dictionary 37
Bangor Me. Historical Mag. i, 9-12
Bradbury's Hist. Kennebunkport Me. 233
Carr Genealogy (1894) 540 pages
Chase's History of Chester N. H. 483-5
Clyde's Irish Settlement Pa. 383-6
Cochrane's History of Antrim N. H. 402-7
Cochrane's Hist. of Francestown N. H. 569
Currier's Ould Newbury Mass. 76-9
Davis' History of Bucks County Pa. 421
Eaton's History of Candia N. H. 58-60
Eaton's History of Thomaston Me. 172
Hayward's History of Hancock N. H. 436
Heywood's Hist. of Westminster Mass. 576
Hinman's Connecticut Settlers 489
Hoyt's Salisbury Mass. Families 84-7
Hudson's History of Sudbury Mass. 438
Kingman's North Bridgewater Mass. 469
Little's History of Weare N. H. 755-7
Meade's Old Families of Virginia
Mitchell's Hist. of Bridgewater Mass. 129
N. H. Historical Soc. Collections vii, 377
Newport Historical Magazine iii, 243
Otis Genealogy
Richmond Va. Standard iii, 19
Runnell's Hist. Sanbornton N. H. ii, 96-9
Savage's Genealogical Dictionary i, 338
Shotwell Genealogy 15, 196
Tilley's N. E. Notes and Queries i, 65-8
Virg'a Mag.Hist.ii,225-8; iii,208-17; v.440-2
Washington N. H. History 330-3
Wentworth Genealogy i, 62-6
Wheeler's Hist. of Newport N. H. 324-6
Carriel — Benedict's Sutton Mass. 616
Dwight Genealogy 949-53
Saunderson's Charlestown N. H. 297
Sibley's History of Union Me. 439
Carrier — American Ancestry ix, 19
Hazen's History of Billerica Mass. 22
Hinman's Connecticut Settlers 490
Nash Genealogy 75
Sedgwick's History of Sharon Ct. 69
Walworth's Hyde Genealogy 554-6
Carrington — American Ancestry xii, 27
Andrews' North Britain 338
Cabell Genealogy 558-71, 605-10
Campbell's History of Virginia 624
Davis' History of Wallingford Ct. 661-71

Foote's Sketches of Virginia series ii, 575
Goode Genealogy 128-30, 249-51
Green's Kentucky Families
Hinman's Connecticut Settlers 491
Meade's Old Families of Virginia ii, 29
Orcutt's History of New Milford Ct. 686
Paxton's Marshall Genealogy 104
Richmond Va. Standard i, 45; ii, 7, 35, 37;
  iii, 14, 15, 26, 27
Slaughter's St. Mark's Parish Va. 164
Sullivant Biography 247-55
Tuttle Genealogy 69
Watkins Genealogy 28
Carroll — Daniel's Oxford Mass. 433
Eaton's Annals of Warren Me. 515
Glenn's Colonial Mansions 361-3
Hanson's Old Kent Maryland 137-58
Lee Genealogy (1895) 385-8
Munsey's Magazine, xvi (1896), 22-32
Rowland's Life of Charles Carroll
Thomas Genealogy (1896) 242
Worthen's History of Sutton N. H. 643-5
Carrut — Temple's North Brookfield 547-9
Carruth — Carruth Gen. (1880) 12 pages
Carsley — Ridlon's Harrison Me. 43-50
Swift's Barnstable Families i, 147-50
Carson — Cochrane's Francestown 569-74
Green's Kentucky Families
Power's Sangamon Co. Ill. Settlers 188
Wheeler's Eminent N. Carolinians 88-93
Carswell — Little's Weare N. H. 757
Carter — Amer. Anc. vi, 148; xi, 163, 174
Andrew's Hist. of New Britain Ct. 200
Atkins' History of Hawley Mass. 60
Ballou's History of Milford Mass. 612
Bangor Me. Historical Magazine v, 183
Benedict's History of Sutton Mass. 617-20
Boardman Genealogy (1895) 131-7
Bond's History of Watertown Mass. 150
Bouton's History of Concord N. H. 636-8
Campbell's Spotswood Papers 22
Campbell's History of Virginia 412
Carter Family of Penn. (1883) 304 pages
Carter Family of Mass. (1887) 272 pages
Carter Family of Virginia (1884) Chart
Carter Family of Va. 2d ed. (1897) Chart
Coffin's Hist. of Boscawen N. H. 482-4
Cogswell's Hist. of Henniker N. H. 487-90
Cope Genealogy 30, 38, 57-62, 130-44
Cregar's Haines Ancestry 54
Cutter Genealogy 44-8
Cutter's History of Arlington Mass. 201
Cutts Genealogy 154-6
Daniel's History of Oxford Mass. 434
Davis' History of Wallingford Ct. 665
Futhey's History of Chester Co. Pa. 494
Glenn's Colonial Mansions 288-94
Hartwell Genealogy (1895) 56
Hayden's Virginia Genealogies 130, 140
Heywood's Hist. Westminster Mass. 577-9
Hinman's Connecticut Settlers 492-6
Hoyt's Salisbury Mass. Families 87-9
Hyde's History of Brimfield Mass. 388
Jones Genealogy (1891) 159-67
Keith's Harrison Ancestry 87
Kellogg's White Descendants 40

Lapham's History of Bethel Me. 499–501
Lapham's History of Norway Me. 478
Lapham's History of Paris Me. 546
Lee Genealogy (1895) 356–62
Meade's Old Churches of Va. ii, 110–3
Morris Genealogy (1894) 48
New Eng. Hist. and Gen. Reg. xvii, 51–3
Norton's Hist. of Fitzwilliam N. H. 504–7
Orcutt's History of Wolcott Ct. 467–70
Potts Genealogy (1895) 105–15
Power's Sangamon Co. Ill. Settlers 189
Prescott's Page Genealogy 59, 74, 133
Read's History of Swanzey N. H. 310
Richmond Va. Critic (1888)
Richmond Standard ii, 16, 42; iii, 38; iv, 2
Ruttenber's Newburgh N. Y. 297–300
Ruttenberg's Orange Co. N. Y. 384–6
Savage's Genealogical Dictionary i, 340–2
Secomb's Hist. of Amherst N. H. 530
Sewall's Hist. of Woburn Mass. 124–7, 597
Sharpless Genealogy 293
Sheldon's Hist. of Deerfield Mass. 100
Slaughter's St. Mark's Parish Va. 121
Smith's Hist. of Peterborough N. H. 33
Stearns' History of Rindge N. H. 468
Timlow's Southington Ct. Sketches 38–43
Virginia Magazine of History v (1898), 408–
   28; vi (1898), 1–22, 88–90, 145–52, etc.
Vinton's Richardson Family 574, 663
Welles' Washington Genealogy 176–200
Whittemore's Orange N. J. 287–9
Wyman's Charlestown Mass. i, 186–93
Carteret — Carteret Gen. (1887) 56 pages
Hatfield's Elizabeth N. J. 110
N. J. Hist. Soc. Proceedings 2d series i
Wyman's Charlestown Mass. i, 193–9
Carthrae — Green's Kentucky Fams.
Cartland — Dearborn's Parsonsfield
Little's History of Weare N. H. 758
Cartmell — Power's Sangamon Ill. 193
Cartwright — Power's Sangamon 190
Savage's Genealogical Dictionary i, 343
Sedgwick's History of Sharon Ct. 70
Caruthers — Green's Kentucky Fams.
Paxton's Marshall Genealogy 158
Richmond Va. Standard iii, 2, 25
Carver — Davis' Plymouth Mass. 51
Davis' History of Bucks Co. Pa. 279
Hodgman's Hist. of Westford Mass. 441
Hollister's History of Pawlet Vt. 173.
Martindale's Hist. of Byberry Pa. 243–50
Mitchell's Bridgewater Mass. 129, 362
Power's Sangamon Co. Ill. Settlers 193
Savage's Genealogical Dictionary i, 343
Sheldon's Hist. Deerfield Mass.ii,101–4, 398
Smith Genealogy (1879) 99
Smith Genealogy (1895) 102–5
Symmes Genealogy 104
Washburn's Notes on Livermore Me. 17
Winsor's History of Duxbury Mass. 240
Cary — Am. Ancestry iii, 8, 142; ix, 49
Cary Genealogy (1874) 306 pages
Collin's Hist. of Hillsdale N. Y. app. 46–9
Goode Genealogy 281–5
Green's Todd Genealogy
Jameson's History of Medway Mass. 462

Keith's Harrison Ancestry 39–41
Kingman's N. Bridgewater Mass. 463–9
Lapham's History of Paris Me. 549, 559
Lawrence and Bartlett Memorial 109
Meade's Old Churches of Va. i, 455
Mitchell's Hist. of Bridgewater Mass. 130–4
Perley's History of Boxford Mass. 72
Prescott's Page Genealogy 93, 239
Richmond Va. Critic (1888)
Richmond Va. Standard ii, 41; iii, 31
Robertson's Pocahontas Descendants
Savage's Genealogical Dictionary i, 344
Slaughter's Life of Fairfax 67, 72
Southern Bivouac for May (1886) 733
Temple's Hist. of N. Brookfield Mass. 550
Ward's History of Shrewsbury Mass. 263
Welles' Amer. Fam. Antiquity i, 69–119
Winsor's History of Duxbury Mass. 241
Caryl — Dedham Historical Register i, 149
Hemenway's Vt. Gazetteer v, 163
Wight Genealogy 80
Casad — American Ancestry, xi, 217
Case — American Ancestry iii, 161; v, 153,
   221; viii, 81; xi, 174; xii, 37
Austin's R. I. Genealogical Dictionary 273
Brown's W. Simsbury Ct. Settlers 35–55
Case, Life of John, 1635–1704 (1898) 22–4
Chambers' Early Germans of N. J. 284–8
Cochrane's History of Antrim N. H. 407
Cochrane's History of Francestown N. H.
   574
Eaton's History of Thomaston Me. 173
Goodwin's Genealogical Notes 275–300
Griffin's Journal of Southold L. I. 175
Hinman's Connecticut Settlers 497–502
Hollister Genealogy 540
Humphreys Genealogy 116–8; 246–52
Lapham's History of Norway Me. 478
Mallmann's Shelter Island N. Y. 321
Narragansett Hist. Register i, 208–10
Perkins' Old Houses of Norwich Ct. 437
Rhode Island Hist. Society Colls. iii, 309
Savage's Genealogical Dictionary i, 345
Sprague's Hist. of Gloversville N. Y. 112
Stiles' History of Windsor Ct. ii, 140–3
Casey — American Ancestry iii, 8
Austin's Ancestral Dictionary 13
Austin's R. I. Genealogical Dictionary 40
Bartlett's Wanton Family 121
Casey Families of R. I. (1893) 46 pages
Lincoln's Hist. of Hingham Mass. ii, 119
Tilley's Mag of New Eng. Hist. iii, 83–128
Cash — Driver Genealogy 253, 265–8
Savage's Genealogical Dictionary i, 347
Stickney's History of Minisink N. Y. 170
Cashow — American Ancestry ix, 243
Caskie — Welles' Washington Gen. 230
Casley — Freeman's Cape Cod ii, 208
Cass — Amer. Ancestry i, 13; xi, 93
Bassett's Hist. of Richmond N. H. 356–68
Dow's Hist. of Hampton N. H. 632, 1064
Palmer Genealogy (1886) 51
Runnels' Sanbornton N. H. ii, 99–102
Cassel — American Ancestry ix, 164
Cassel Genealogy (1896) 465 pages
Casson — Wheeler's Eminent N. Car. 88

Cast — Eaton Hist. of Candia N. H. 60
Hubbard's Stanstead Co. Canada 184-6
Power's Sangamon Co. Ill. Settlers 195-7
Savage's Genealogical Dictionary i, 347
Cassity — Power's Sangamon Ill. 195
Castle — American Ancestry ix, 65; xii
Anderson's Waterbury Ct. i, app. 34
Bronson's Hist. of Waterbury Ct. 481-3
Cothren's Hist. of Woodbury Ct. ii, 1486
Temple's History of Whately Mass. 213
Castner — Cleveland's Yates Co. 667
Chambers' Early Germans of N. J. 88-90
Jenkins' Hist. Gwynedd Pa. 2d ed. 422-4
Caswell — Clark's Norton Mass. 79
Eaton's Annals of Warren Me. 515
Frisby's History of Middlebury Vt. 66-8
Hubbard's Hist. of Stanstead Canada 172
Pierec's Biographical Contributions 36-42
Ridlon's Harrison Me. Settlers 50-4
Savage's Genealogical Dictionary i, 348
Wyman's Charlestown Mass. Gens. i, 194
Catchpole — Roe's Rose N. Y. 139
Cates — Caverno Genealogy 334
Cogswell's Hist. Nottingham N. H. 339
Eaton's History of Thomaston Me. 173
Runnels' Hist. Sanbornton N. H. ii, 102-9
Catesby — Jones Genealogy (1891) 117-21
Richmond Va. Standard ii, 51
Catland — Eaton's Thomaston Me. 173
Catlett — Carter Family Tree
Hayden's Virginia Genealogies 244
Meade's Old Families of Virginia
Slaughter's St. Mark's Parish Va. 156
Catlin — American Ancestry ix, 204
Candee Genealogy 141-7
Hinman's Connecticut Settlers 503-10
Savage's Genealogical Dictionary i, 348
Sheldon's Hist. of Deerfield Mass. ii, 104-8
Smith's Hist. of Sunderland Mass. 284
Tuttle Genealogy 617
Cattell — Shroud's Fenwick Col. 61-3
Sheldon's Hist. of Deerfield Mass. iii, 104-8
Caudebec — See under Cuddeback
Cauffman—Rodenbough's Autumn Leaves 13-24
Cauldwell — Littell's Passaic 68-74
Caulkins — Bill Genealogy 196
Caulkin's Hist. New London Ct. (1895) vii
Caulkins' History of Norwich Ct. 171-3
Hinman's Connecticut Settlers 511-3
Savage's Genealogical Dictionary i, 349
Smith Genealogy (1889) 95-8
Cave — Hayden's Virginia Gens. 13
Slaughter's St. Mark's Parish Va. 122-5
Cavender — Hayward's Hancock 437
Heywood's Hist. of Westminster Mass. 579
Cavendish — Bangor Mag. iv, 129-37
Caverley — Strong Genealogy 859
Caverly — American Ancestry vi, 69
Brown's West Simsbury Ct. Settlers 56
Caverly Genealogy (1880) 196 pages
Runnels' Sanbornton N. H. ii, 109-11
Caverno — Caverno Genealogy (1874) 36 p.
Cavins — American Ancestry ix, 40
Cawley — Runnels' Sanbornton 87-96
Cazier — Egle's Penn. Genealogies 453-5

Center—Barbour's Low Fam. Chart (1890)
Hinman's Connecticut Settlers 513
Livermore's History of Wilton N. H. 345
Wyman's Charlestown Mass. Gens. i, 195
Chace — Amer. Ancestry ii, 21; x, 40
Spooner Genealogy i, 46-8
Chadbourne — Eaton's Thomaston 174
New Eng. Hist. Gen. Reg. xiii, 339-41
Pierce's History of Gorman Me. 159
Ridlon's Settlers of Harrison Me. 38-43
Ridlon's Saco Valley Me. Families 567-77
Savage's Genealogical Dictionary i, 350
Wentworth Genealogy i, 389
Chaddock — Barry's Hanover 263
Roe's Sketches of Rose N. Y. 67
Chadsey — Aylsworth Genealogy 143
Chadwell — Bond's Watertown 150-2
Savage's Genealogical Dictionary i, 350
Chadwick — American Ancestry ii, 21
Bass' History of Braintree Vt. 124
Bond's Watertown Mass. 150-2, 734
Champion Genealogy 54
Coffin's History of Boscawen N. H. 485
Cogswell's Hist. Nottingham N. H. 340-5
Cutts Genealogy 138
Hinman's Connecticut Settlers 514
Platt's Greenough Ancestry 11
Salter's Hist. of Monmouth Co. N. J. xvi
Savage's Genealogical Dictionary i, 351
Stearns' History of Rindge N. H. 470-2
Thurston Genealogy (1892) 210-3
Wentworth Genealogy ii, 282-4, 501-3
Worthen's History of Sutton N. H. 645-9
Wyman's Charlestown Mass. Gens. 196
Chafee — Stiles' Windsor Ct. ii, 143
Chaffee — Amer. Ancestry ii, 13; vii, 93
Caverley's History of Pittsford Vt. 696
Daniel's History of Oxford Mass. 434
Davis Genealogy 478
Hinman's Connecticut Settlers 516
Morris Genealogy (1894) 33
Morris and Flint Ancestors (1882) 23-5
Sedgwick's History of Sharon Ct. 70
Walker Genealogy 181
Chaffin — Aldrich's Walpole N. H. 228
Stearns' Hist. of Ashburnham Mass. 634
Chalfant — Futhey's Chester Co. Pa. 495
Chalker — Hinman's Conn. Settlers 517
Savage's Genealogical Dictionary i, 352
Chalkley — Sewall's Woburn 599
Challis — Hoyt's Salisbury Families 89-91
Chalmer — Machias Me. Centennial 158
Chaloner — Me. Historical Mag. viii, 137
Chamberlain — American Ancestry xi, 173
Austin's Allied Families 59-61
Bangor Me. Historical Magazine vi, 81-3
Barry's History of Hanover Mass. 264-6
Chamberlain, John, Biography (1838) 14 p.
Chamberlain Golden Wedding (1877) 74 p.
Chamberlain Genealogy (1897) 16 pages
Chamberlain Family Meeting (1898) 28 p.
Chamberlain Family Meeting (1899) 63 p.
Child Genealogy 244-50
Cleveland Genealogy (1879) 184-204
Daniel's History of Oxford Mass. 434-7
Hanson's Old Kent Md. 288

Hazen's History of Billerica Mass. 23
Hinman's Connecticut Settlers 518
Jackson's History of Newton Mass. 253
Lincoln's Hist. of Hingham Mass. ii, 121
Meade's Old Families of Virginia
Morse's Sherborn Mass. Settlers 58
Paige's History of Hardwick Mass. 345
Randall's Hist. of Chesterfield N. H. 242-5
Salter's Hist. of Monmouth Co. N. J. xvii
Saunderson's Charlestown N. H. 304-8
Savage's Genealogical Dictionary i, 352-5
Sedgwick's History of Sharon Ct. 70
Sewall's History of Woburn Mass. 599
Sharpless Genealogy 165
Shattuck Genealogy 372
Stearns' Hist. of Ashburnham Mass. 634
Stiles' History of Windsor Ct. ii, 143
Temple's History of Northfield Mass. 418
Washington N. H. History 333
Wheeler's History of Newport N. H. 328
Whitman Genealogy 420, 452-7

Chamberlin — Amer. Ancestry ix, 146
Austin's R. I. Genealogical Dictionary 40
Brown's Bedford Mass. Families 6
Butler's History of Groton Mass. 392
Chamberlin Fam. Newbury Vt. (1894) 11 p.
Dunster Genealogy 197-200
Dwight Genealogy 510
Futhey's History of Chester Co. Pa. 496
Hodgman's Hist. of Westford Mass. 441
Hubbard's Stanstead Co. Canada 131, 275
Mitchell's Hist. of Bridgewater Mass. 134
Palmer and Trimble Gen. 101-7, 125-30
Roe's Sketches of Rose N. Y. 60
Wyman's Charlestown Mass. i, 197-9

Chambers — American Ancestry vii, 252
Barber Genealogy (1890) 39-56
Chambers' Early Germans of N. J. 290-4
Cooley's Trenton N. J. Genealogies 29-39
Futhey's History of Chester Co. Pa. 496
Hall's Trenton N. J. Presb. Church 158
Lee Genealogy (1895) 101-3
New York Gen. and Biog. Rec. iii, 57-62
Wyman's Charlestown Mass. Gens. i, 199

Champe — Richmond Standard iii, 11

Champernon — Essex Inst. xvii, 17

Chambless — Shroud's Fenwick 57-60

Champion — Amer. Ancestry vii, 17, 42
Champion Genealogy (1891) 558 pages
Clement's Newtown N. J. Settlers
Ely Genealogy 164-6; 347-9
Field's History of Haddam Ct. 47
Hinman's Connecticut Settlers 520-3
Savage's Genealogical Dictionary i, 355
West Springfield Mass. Centennial 114

Champlain — Amer. Ancestry v, 90

Champlin — Austin's R. I. Dict. 274
Austin's Ancestral Dictionary 14
Baker's History of Montville Ct. 350-9
Cleveland's History of Yates Co. N. Y. 539
Livermore's Hist. of Block Island R. I. 325
New Eng. Hist. and Gen. Reg. xiv, 24
Savage's Genealogical Dictionary i, 355
Sylvester's Hist. of Ulster Co. N. Y. 141
Updyke's Narragansett R. I. Ch. 111-4
Worthen's History of Sutton N. H. 660-4

Champney — Champney Gen. (1885) 36
Champney Genealogy (1867) 76 pages
Chapman's Trowbridge Genealogy 239
Kidder's Hist. of New Ipswich N. H. 343-8
Paige's History of Cambridge Mass. 506-8
Savage's Genealogical Dictionary, i, 356
Wyman's Charlestown Mass. Gens. i, 200

Chandler — Abbot's Andover Mass. 32
American Ancestry vii, 214; ix, 103, 179;
    xi, 60, 173
Backus Genealogy 141-5
Bedford N. H. Centennial, 294-7
Bouton's Hist. of Concord N. H. 638-41
Bowens of Woodstock Ct. 174-7
Butler's History of Farmington Me. 420-2
Chandler Genealogy (1872) 1212 pages
Chandler Genealogy 2d ed. (1883) 1315 p.
Chandler's History of Shirley Mass. 365
Chapman's Trowbridge Genealogy 48
Cochrane's History of Antrim N. H. 409
Cochrane's Hist. of Francestown N. H. 575
Coffin's History of Boscawen N. H. 487-9
Coggswell's Hist. of Henniker, N. H. 491
Corliss' North Yarmouth Me. 1095-9
Davis Ancestry (1897) 66-72
Davis' Landmarks of Plymouth Mass. 53
Dodd Genealogy 113
Eaton's History of Thomaston Me. 174
Futhey's History of Chester Co. Pa. 497
Granite Monthly of Concord N. H. iv, 129
Hayward's History of Gilsum N. H. 283
Hazen's History of Billerica Mass. 24
Hill's History of Mason N. H. 201
Hinman's Connecticut Settlers 530-2
Hodgman's History of Westford Mass. 442
Hudson's Hist. of Lexington Mass. 35-40
Kidder's Hist. of New Ipswich N. H. 348
Lapham's History of Bethel Me. 501
Larned's History of Windham Ct.
Livermore's History of Wilton N. H. 346-9
Longmeadow Mass. Centen. app. 23-6
Loomis Genealogy (1880) 709-12
Mitchell's Hist. of Bridgewater Mass. 136
Nash Genealogy 149
N. E. Reg. xv, 339-44; xxxiii, 68-70, 202
North's History of Augusta Me. 823-5
Norton's Hist. of Fitzwilliam N. H. 507
Old Eliot Me. Monthly ii (1898) 152
Penn. Mag. of Hist. and Biog. ix, 234-6
Savage's Genealogical Dictionary i, 356-9
Secomb's History of Amherst N. H. 531
Sheldon's Hist. of Deerfield Mass. ii, 108
Sinclair Genealogy 205
Stiles' Hist. of Windsor Ct. ii, 144
Thurston's History of Winthrop Me. 177
Virginia Magazine of History iii (1896), 321
Wall's Remin. of Worcester Mass. 62-78
Walworth's Hyde Genealogy 891-6
Whitmore's Heraldic Journal i, 72
Winslow Genealogy ii, 715-24
Winsor's History of Duxbury Mass. 241-4

Channell — Hubbard's Stanstead 147

Channing — Austin's Ancestries 17
Salisbury's Family Histories (1892) i, 84
Walworth's Hyde Genealogy 753

Chapel — Baker's Montville Ct. 474-85

Chapin — Amer. Ancestry ii, 21; vii, 27, 110; viii, 67; xi, 181
Ballou's History of Milford Mass. 614–32
Barbour's My Wife and Mother 52, 64
Boyd's History of Conesus N. Y. 146
Briggs' Hanover Mass. Records 15–20
Chapin Family Meeting (1862) 97 pages
Chapin Family of Springfield (1862) 368 p.
Chapin Family of Roxbury (1889) 59 pages
Chapins in the War (1895) 15 pages
Cochrane's History of Antrim N. H. 410
Dwight Genealogy 334–6, 341–58
Ellis Genealogy 374
Ely Gen. 50, 54, 94–6, 105–7, 116–20, 238
Hayward's History of Gilsum N. H. 284
Morris and Flint Genealogy 87
Nash Genealogy 87
New Eng. Hist. and Gen. Reg. iv, 352
Roe's Sketches of Rose N. Y. 36
Savage's Genealogical Dictionary i, 359
Stiles' History of Windsor Ct. ii, 145–7
Temple's Hist. of Northfield Mass. 419–22
Temple's History of Palmer Mass. 433
Temple's History of Whately Mass. 213
Thurston Genealogy (1892) 360
Wall's Worcester Mass. Reminis. 337–40
Washington N. H. History 334
West Springfield Mass. Centennial 115
Wheeler's History of Newport N. H. 330–5
Wilbraham Mass. Centennial 297
Young's History of Warsaw N. Y. 246
Chaplain — American Ancestry xii
N. E. Hist. Reg. iv, 175
Chapler — Eaton's Thomaston Me. 174
Chaplin — Chandler's Shirley 365–9
Davis' History of Reading Vt. 126–30
Essex Mass. Inst. Hist. Coll. xx, 219–22
Gage's History of Rowley Mass. 439
Herrick Genealogy (1885) 284–6
Norton's Hist. of Fitzwilliam N. H. 507–10
Paige's History of Cambridge Mass. 508
Paige's History of Hardwick Mass. 347
Poor's Merrimac Valley Hist. Researches 97
Ridlon's Harrison Me. Settlers 37
Savage's Genealogical Dictionary, i 360
Stearns' History of Rindge N. H. 472–6
Waterford Me. Centennial 240
Chapline — Nourse Genealogy 77–92
Chapman — American Ancestry i, 13; iii, 9; iv, 201; ix, 65
Austin's R. I. Genealogical Dictionary 41
Baker's History of Montville Ct. 532–6
Ballou's History of Milford Mass. 632
Barry's History of Hanover Mass. 266
Buckingham Genealogy 167–70
Burleigh's Guild Genealogy 99
Caulkin's History of New London Ct. 340
Chapman Genealogy (1864) 413 pages
Chapman Family of Duxbury (1876) 86 p.
Chapman Family of Ipswich (1878) 34 p.
Chapman Family of Ipswich (1893) 139 p.
Chapman's Weeks Genealogy 132
Cushman's History of Sheepscott Me. 364
Cutts Genealogy 149
Daniels' History of Oxford Mass. 437
Davis' History of Bucks Co. Pa. 252–7, 701

Dow's History of Hampton N. H. 633
Eaton's Annals of Warren Me. 516
Eaton's History of Thomaston Me. 175
Essex Mass. Inst. Hist. Coll. xvi, 95–7
Fell Genealogy 68–70
Fields' History of Haddam Ct. 47
Fiske Genealogy 138–41
Freeman's Cape Cod Mass. ii, 220, 711
Goode Genealogy 346
Hayward's History of Gilsum N. H. 286
Hammatt's Papers of Ipswich Mass. 48
Hubbard's Stanstead Co. Canada 327
Kellogg's White Genealogy 62
Lapham's History of Bethel Me. 503–12
Lyman's History of Easthampton Mass. 187
Maine Genealogist iii, 129–62
New Eng. Hist. and Gen. Register iv, 20
Orcutt's History of Stratford Ct. 1172
Perkins' Old Houses of Norwich Ct. 439
Rich's History of Truro Mass. 521
Richmond Va. Standard ii, 47; iii, 35–7
Robinson's Items of Ancestry (1894) 47
Runnel's Hist. Sanbornton N. H. ii, 111–4
Savage's Genealogical Dictionary i, 361–3
Sedgwick's History of Sharon Ct. 71
Sheldon's History of Deerfield Mass. ii, 109
Smith's History of Peterboro N. H. 34–6
Stiles' History of Windsor Ct. ii, 147–9
Strong Genealogy 1084–6
Swift's Barnstable Mass. Families i, 151–3
Temple's History of Whately Mass. 213
Thurston Genealogy (1892) 180–3, 294
Timlow's Southington Ct. Sketches 43–9
Waldo's History of Tolland, Ct. 62–8
Washington N. H. History 334
Wentworth Genealogy i. 245
Whittemore's Hist. of Middlesex Co. Ct. 573
Winsor's History of Duxbury Mass. 244
Wyman's Charlestown Mass. Gens. i, 201
Chappell — Am. Ancestry xi, 133; xii, 90
Caulkins' New London 325, 352
Chappell Genealogy (1893) pamphlet
Chappell Genealogy (1895) 209 pages
Chappell Genealogy (1900) 382 pages
Hines' Lebanon Ct. Historical Address 150
Hinman's Connecticut Settlers 546–8
Loomis Genealogy (1880) 816, 919–21
Savage's Genealogical Dictionary i, 363
Sedgwick's History of Sharon Ct. 72
Virginia Magazine of History iii, 416–20
Chard — Savage's Gen. Dictionary 41
Chardavoyne — Roome Genealogy 109–11
Charles — Hyde's Brimfield Mass. 389
Charlescraft — Craft's Genealogy 732–7
Charlot — American Ancestry ii, 21
Charlton — Calnek's Annapolis N. S. 487
Perkins' Norwich Ct. 440
Stiles' Windsor Ct. ii, 149
Charnock — Heraldic Journal iii, 107–10
Charruand — Carteret Genealogy 28
Chase — Aldrich's Walpole N. H. 229
American Ancestry i, 13; iii, 9; v, 92, 184; vii, 217; viii, 126; x, 8, 85, 122, 184, 185; xii, 45
Ballou's History of Milford Mass. 634
Barlow Genealogy 227–9

Bass' History of Braintree Vt. 123
Bemis' History of Marlboro N. H. 440
Benedict's History of Sutton Mass. 620-7
Brown's History of Whitingham Vt. 172-8
Burleigh's Guild Genealogy 248
Chandler's History of Shirley Mass. 369-74
Chase Family of Newton (1865) 94 pages
Chase Pedigree (1867) 1 page
Chase Family of Hampton (1869) 19 pages
Chase Family of Swanzey (1874) 86 pages
Chase Family of Maine (1878) 18 pages
Chase Family of Yarmouth (1886) 31 pages
Chase Family of Newbury (1894) 19 pages
Chase Prof. Ira Memorial, appendix
Chase's History of Chester N. H. 485-9
Chase's History of Haverhill Mass. 624-6
Cleveland's History of Yates Co. N. Y. 560
Coffin's History of Newbury Mass. 297
Cogswell's Hist. of Henniker N. H. 492-6
Cogswell's Hist. Nottingham N. H. 347-53
Conn. Quarterly iii (1897) iv (1898)
Corliss' North Yarmouth Me. Magazine
Cushman's History of Sheepscott Me. 365
Davis' Landmarks of Plymouth Mass. 53
Dearborn's History of Salisbury N. H. 522
Dow's History of Hampton N. H. 634-7
Driver Genealogy 263
Ely Genealogy 191-3
Emery Genealogy 29, 505
Evans Genealogy (1893) 26-8
Freeman's Hist. Cape Cod Mass. ii, 188-97
Hammatt's Papers of Ipswich Mass. 49
Hayward's History of Gilsum N. H. 286
Hemenway's Vermont Gazetteer, v, 716-8
Hill's Lawrence and Townley Estate
Hoyt's Salisbury Mass. Families 91-5
Hubbard's Hist. of Springfield Vt. 248-52
Lapham's History of Bethel Me. 502
Lapham's History of Norway Me. 478
Lapham's History of Paris Me. 552-6
Lapham's History of Woodstock Me. 190-3
Little's History of Weare N. H. 759-67
Machias Me. Centennial 157
Mowry Genealogy 217-9
New Eng. Hist. and Gen. Register i, 68-70
Norton's Hist. of Fitzwilliam N. H. 510-2
Peck and Earll's Fall River Mass. 244-52
Pierce's History of Gorham Me. 158
Poor's Merrimac Valley Researches 138
Prescott Memorial 553-5
Runnel's Hist. Sanbornton N. H. ii, 114-22
Savage's Genealogical Dictionary i, 364-6
Spaulding Memorial 522-5
Stark's History of Dunbarton N. H. 228
Stiles' History of Windsor Ct. ii, 149
Temple's History of No. Brookfield Mass. 552
Titcomb's Early New Eng. People 286-8
Updyke's Narragansett R. I. Church 109
Usher's Lawrence and Townley Estate
Washburn's History of Livermore Me. 25-7
Washington N. H. History 335-7
Wheeler's History of Newport N. H. 329
Whitmore's Heraldic Journal iv, 153-67
Williams' History of Danby Vt. 123
Wood Genealogy 43

Worthen's History of Sutton N. H. 670
Wymans' Charlestown Mass. Gens. i, 209
Chastain — Virg. Hist. Society v, 193-204
Chatfield — American Ancestry x, 124, 152
Anderson's Waterbury Ct. i, app. 34
Chatfield Genealogy (1896) 32 pages
Dwight Genealogy 678
Hedge's History of Easthampton L. l. 249
Hinman's Connecticut Settlers 550
Howell's History of Southampton N. Y. 210
Loomis Genealogy (1880) 67
Orcutt's History of Derby Ct. 709
Savage's Genealogical Dictionary i, 366
Chatterson — Roe's Rose N. Y. 17
Chatterton — Dickerman Genealogy 395-8
Hamden Ct. History 242
Merrill's History of Acworth N. H. 198
Chauler — Green's Todd Genealogy
Chauncey — Brewster's Rambles 280-5
Chauncey Family Table (1787)
Chauncey Genealogy (1858) 336 pages
Cutts Genealogy 101
Darling Memorial (1888)
Fowler's History of Durham Ct. 110
Goodwin's Olcott Genealogy (1845) 52
Hall's Genealogical Notes 87
Hinman's Connecticut Settlers 524-30
Judd's History of Hadley Mass. 459
New Eng. Hist. and Genealogical Register
    x, 105-21, 251-62, 323-37; xi, 148-53
Orcutt's History of Stratford Ct. 1173
Paige's Hist. of Cambridge Mass. 108, 508
Savage's Genealogical Dictionary i, 336-9
Stiles' History of Windsor Ct. ii, 150
Strong Genealogy 1279-91
Tuttle Genealogy 109-11
Whitmore's Heraldic Journal i, 187-90
Chauvin — Beckwith's Creoles 141-5
Cheatham — Goode Genealogy 100
Checkley — Checkley Genealogy (1848) 6 p.
Dorr Genealogy
Drake's History of Boston Mass. 459
New Eng. Hist. Register ii, 349-54; xv, 13
Savage's Genealogical Dictionary i, 369
Chedsey — Dodd's East Haven 111-4
Hinman's Connecticut Settlers 551
Savage's Genealogical Dictionary i, 370
Cheeney — Hinman's Ct. Settlers 552-5
Cheesebrough —Savage's Dictionary i, 373
Steele Genealogy (1896)
Wetmore Genealogy 113
Cheeseman — See Chesman
Cheever — Bill Genealogy 68
Cheever Family Pedigree (1878) 1 sheet
Cheever Family of Boston (1879) 42 pages
Cheever Family of Boston (1882) 11 pages
Cheever Family of Boston (1884) 26 pages
Cheever Family of Boston (1896) 54 pages
Cutts Genealogy
Driver Genealogy 435
Essex Mass. Inst. Historical Colls. v, 236
Freeman's Hist. of Cape Cod Mass. ii, 403
Hammatt's Papers of Ipswich Mass. 54
New Eng. Hist. Register xxviii; xxxii, 90;
    xxxiii, 164-202; xxxvi, 305-13; xxxviii,
    170-93

Paige's History of Cambridge Mass. 509
Savage's Genealogical Dictionary i, 370–2
Temple's Hist. of No. Brookfield Mass. 552
Chellis — Dearborn's Salisbury 523
See also under Challis
Chenault — American Ancestry x, 18
Quisenberry Genealogy 96–122
Chenery — American Ancestry viii, 68, 70
Damon Genealogy 124–7
Montague Genealogy 512
Chenevard — Hinman's Settlers 555
Cheney — Am. Anc. ii, 21; viii, 36; x, 177
Ballou's History of Milford Mass. 634–45
Bond's Watertown Mass. Gens. 152
Cheney Genealogy (1897) 582 pages
Chute Genealogy, appendix 21–7
Cochrane's History of Antrim N. H. 411–3
Cochrane's Hist. Francestown N. H. 576–8
Coffin's History of Newbury Mass. 298
Cogswell's History of Henniker N. H. 496
Ellis' History of Roxbury Mass. 93
Goodwin's Olcott Genealogy 20
Harris' Watertown Mass. Epitaphs 11
Hayward's History of Hancock N. H. 438
Jackson's History of Newton Mass. 255–7
Little's History of Weare N. H. 767
New Eng. Hist. and Gen. Register xxii, 139
Norton's History of Fitzwilliam N. H. 511
Paige's History of Cambridge Mass. 509
Pope Genealogy
Runnell's Hist. Sanbornton N. H. ii, 122–9
Smith's Hist. of Peterborough N. H. 36–40
Stearns' History of Ashburnham Mass. 635
Washington N. H. History 337–41
Wheeler's History of Newport N. H. 335–41
Worthen's History of Sutton N. H. 649–60
Young's History of Chautauqua N. Y. 438
Chesebrough — American Ancestry vii,
133, 247; viii, 205; ix, 195, 198; x, 178
Baldwin's Denison Genealogy 10
Chesebrough Wm. Biography (1893) 22–5
Hinman's Connecticut Settlers 566–8
Stanton Genealogy 483–552
Stonington Ct. Centen. 289–93
Wetmore Genealogy 113
Chesholme — Paige's Cambridge 509
Chesley — Calnek's Annapolis N. S. 488
Chapman's Weeks Gen. 133
Hatch's History of Industry Me. 539
Lapham's History of Paris Me. 556
New Eng. Hist. and Gen. Register v, 453
Otis Genealogy
Paxton's Marshall Genealogy 310
Savage's Genealogical Dictionary i, 375
Temple's Hist of No. Brookfield Mass. 553
Wentworth Genealogy i, 221; ii, 90
Chesman — Am. Ancestry x, 141, xi, 60
Chesman Genealogy (1893) 103 pages
Lincoln's History of Hingham Mass. ii, 122
Chester — Alden's Am. Epitaphs iv, 145
American Ancestry i, 13; iv, 157; viii, 5
Baker's History of Montville Ct. 240–3
Bond's History of Watertown Mass. 735–40
Caulkin's History of New London Ct. 353
Chester Family of Wethersfield (1868) 8 p.
Chester Family of Wethersfield (1886) 29 p.

Chester Family of Wethersfield (1893) chart
Chester Family of Boston (1896) 11 pages
Goodwin's Genealogical Notes 8–22
Hinman's Connecticut Settlers 557–66
Huntington Genealogy 167
New Eng. Hist. and Gen. Reg. xxii, 338–42
Paige's History of Cambridge Mass. 510
Savage's Genealogical Dictionary i, 375
Talcott's Gen. Notes of N. E. Fams. 492–4
Walworth's Hyde Genealogy 442–4
Chestney — American Ancestry i, 13
Cheston — Thomas Genealogy (1877) 53
Thomas Genealogy (1896) 244–7
Chetwood — Wetmore Genealogy 421
Chevalier — Penn. Magazine vii, 483
Salisbury Family Memorials (1885) 540–60
Chew — Bel Air, Md. Times for March 2,
1887, and March 16, 1888
Bowie Genealogy 380–91
Morris Genealogy (1898) 907–11
Richmond Va. Critic (1888)
Thomas Genealogy (1877) 55–65, 170
Thomas Genealogy (1896) 247–84
Cheyney — Futhey's Chester Pa. 497
Chichester — Hayden's Virginia Gens. 92
Huntington's Stamford Ct. Settlers 21
Savage's Genealogical Dictionary i, 376
Chickeley — Southern Bivouac (1886) 649
Chickering — American Ancestry vi, 194
Dedham Hist. Register iii, 117–23; iv, 44
Kidder's History of New Ipswich N. H. 349
Savage's Genealogical Dictionary i, 376
Secomb's History of Amherst N. H. 532
Sewall's History of Woburn Mass. 461
Wight Genealogy 25
Wyman's Charlestown Mass. Gens. i, 212
Chidell — Leland Genealogy 162
Chidsey — Cleveland's Yates Co. 699
Dickerman Genealogy 169–73
Rodenbough's Autumn Leaves 37–44
Childs — American Ancestry iii, 200; v.
106; vii, 144; xi, 24, 92
Barry's History of Framingham Mass. 206
Blood's History of Temple N. H. 211
Bond's Watertown Mass. 152–7, 740
Bridgman's Granary Burial Ground 200–2
Butler's History of Farmington Me. 422–4
Childs Family Chart (1869) 30x40 inches
Childs Genealogy (1881) 842 pages
Cogswell's Hist. of Henniker N. H. 497–502
Cutter's History of Arlington Mass. 203
Daniels' History of Oxford Mass. 438
Dwight Genealogy 515–22
Freeman's Hist Cape Cod Mass. ii, 303–19
French's History of Turner Me. 52
Guild's Stiles Genealogy 291–4
Herrick's History of Gardner Mass. 339
Heywood's Hist. of Westminster Mass. 580
Hinman's Connecticut Settlers 571–4
Hubbard's Stanstead Co. Canada 144, 308
Hudson's History of Lexington Mass. 41
Jackson's History of Newton Mass. 361
Keyes' West Boylston Mass. Register 15
Morris Genealogy (1887) 23–5, 30
North's History of Augusta Me. 826
Paige's History of Hardwick Mass. 347

Pierce's History of Grafton Mass. 473
Power's Sangamon Co. Ill. Settlers 198
Orcutt's History of Torrington Ct. 666
Ripley's Ingersoll Genealogy 77–9
Savage's Genealogical Dictionary i, 377–9
Sheldon's History of Deerfield Mass.110–20
Spooner Genealogy i, 198–207
Swift's Barnstable Families i, 183–8
Wyman's Charlestown Mass. Gens. i, 213
Chiler — Stearns' Ashburnham 636
Chillingsworth — Foster Gen. (1889) 49
Chilson — Middlefield Ct. History
Southwick Genealogy 191, 307
Chilton — Pilgrim Rec. Society Bulletin
Chinery — Bond's Watertown Mass. 157
Chinn—Hayden's Virginia Genealogies 75
Chipman — American Ancestry xi, 60
Anderson's Waterbury 35
Calnek's History of Annapolis N. S. 489–91
Chipman Family Sketch (1861) 4 pages
Chipman Family Lineage (1872) 59 pages
Chipman Family of Maine (1897) 44 pages
Chute Genealogy, appendix 27–36
Essex Institute Collections xi, 263–319
Freeman's Cape Cod Mass. ii, 164, 289
Hemenway Genealogy 68
Hinman's Connecticut Settlers 514–8
Hubbard's History of Springfield Vt. 252
Kilbourn's History of Litchfield Ct. 70
Lapham's History of Paris Me. 557
N. E. Hist. Gen. Reg. xv, 79–81; xviii, 90
Peirce Genealogy (1894)
Poland Me. Centennial 102
Roy's Thrall Sermon (1894) 19–23
Savage's Genealogical Dictionary i, 380
Stone's History of Beverly Mass. 271
Swain Genealogy 58–61
Swift's Barnstable Mass. Families i, 153–65
Chipp — American Ancestry ii, 21
Chisman — William and Mary College
Hist. Register, i, 89–98
Chisolm — American Ancestry v, 69
Cleveland's Hist. Yates Co. N. Y. 215–20
Chittenden—Am. Anc. ii, 22; v, 16; viii, 47
Baldwin Genealogy 530
Chittenden Genealogy (1882) 262 pages
Deane's History of Scituate Mass. 232
Hinman's Connecticut Settlers 578–81
Kellogg's White Memorial 38
Savage's Genealogical Dictionary i, 381
Worden Genealogy 62–5
Choate — Am. Anc. v, 122, 211; vi, 146, 185
Choate Genealogy (1896) 474 pages
Coffin's History of Boscawen N. H. 489
Cogswell Genealogy 82
Hammatt's Papers of Ipswich Mass. 50–3
New Eng. Hist. and Gen. Register xv, 293
Savage's Genealogical Dictionary i, 383
Sheldon's History of Deerfield Mass. 120
Stearns' History of Ashburnham Mass. 636
Washburn's Hist. Leicester Mass. 351
Wyman's Charlestown Mass. Gens. i, 214
Chouteau — Beckwith's Creoles 7–70
Chrisler — American Ancestry i, 14
Chrisman — Green's Kentucky Families
Plumb's History of Hanover Pa. 402

Christian — Green's Kentucky Families
Meade's Old Families of Virginia
Pearson's Schenectady N. Y. Settlers 35
Peyton's History of Augusta Co. Va. 313
Richmond Va. Standard ii, 43
Slaughter's St. Mark s Parish Va. 188
William and Mary College Quar. v, 261–3
Christie — Banta Genealogy 107–11
Cochrane's Antrim 413–7
Hubbard's Stanstead County Canada 241
Miller's Colchester Co. Nova Scotia 243–7
Morrison Genealogy 252
Christlieb — Christlieb Gen. (1895) 52 p.
Christopher — Clute's Staten Island 354
Christophers — Caulkins' New London
Hinman's Connecticut Settlers 582
Savage's Genealogical Dictionary i, 383
Chrysler — American Ancestry ii, 22
Chrystie — American Ancestry v, 152
Freeman's Hist. of Cape Cod Mass. ii, 144
Morrison's Hist. of Windham N. H. 409–13
Chubbuck — Lincoln's Hingham ii, 122–5
Savage's Genealogical Dictionary 384
Stiles' History of Windsor Ct. ii, 151
Church — Adams' Fairhaven Vt. 326
American Ancestry iii, 203; vi, 12, 46; xi,
183; xii, 34
Austin's R. I. Genealogical Dictionary 41
Baker's History of Montville Ct. 505–13
Barbour's My Wife and Mother app. 42
Barry's History of Hanover Mass. 267
Baylie's New Plymouth iv, 123, 129, 230
Bond's Hist. of Watertown Mass. 158, 741
Brownell Genealogy (1892) 15–8
Butler's History of Farmington Me. 424–8
Church Family of Hartford Ct. (1878) 6 p.
Church Family of Dover N. H. (1879) 5 p.
Church Family of Rhode Island (1887) 85 p.
Church's King Phillip's War xliv–vii
Collin's History of Hillsdale N. Y. app. 51
Cothren's History of Woodbury Ct. 526
Davis' Landmarks of Plymouth Mass. 54
Deane's History of Scituate Mass. 233
Fell Genealogy 47
Field's History of Haddam Ct. 46
Freeman's Hist. of Cape Cod Mass. ii, 357
Goodwin's Olcott Genealogy 56
Hinman's Connecticut Settlers 583–9
Hudson's Hist. of Marlborough Mass. 350
Judd's History of Hadley Mass. 460–2
Lincoln's History of Hingham Mass. ii, 125
Little Genealogy 154–6
Mack Genealogy 53–8
Mitchell's History of Bridgewater Mass.
363
Montague Genealogy (1886) 64–6
New Eng. Hist. and Gen. Reg. xi, 154–6
North's History of Augusta Me. 828
Orcutt's History of Torrington Ct. 667
Paige's History of Hardwick Mass. 348
Porter's Hartford Ct. Settlers 2
Reed's History of Rutland Mass. 135
Savage's Genealogical Dictionary i, 384–6
Sedgwick's History of Sharon Ct. 72
Stone's History of Hubbardston Mass. 237
Wheeler's History of Newport N. H. 342

Winslow Genealogy ii, 975-86
Winsor's History of Duxbury Mass. 245
Churchill — American Ancestry i, 14; vii, 44; xi, 109
Andrews' New Britain Ct. 164-6, 211-6
Churchill Genealogy (1887) 18 pages
Cogswell's Hist. of Nottingham N. H. 353
Dana's History of Woodstock Vt. 599-603
Davis' Landmarks of Plymouth 54-9
Dearborn's History of Parsonsfield Me. 369
Hayden's Virginia Genealogies 253
Hinman's Connecticut Settlers 590-6
Hurlbut Genealogy 405
Kilbourn Genealogy 254
Lapham's History of Norway Me. 479
Lapham's History of Paris Me 557
Lapham's History of Woodstock Me. 193
Lincoln's History of Hingham Mass. ii, 126
Mitchell's Hist. of Bridgewater Mass. 136
New Eng. Hist. and Gen. Reg. xxxiv, 301-4
Orcutt's History of Wolcott Ct. 471
Power's Sangamon Co. Ill. Settlers 198-205
Savage's Genealogical Dictionary i, 386
Sprague's History of Gloversville N. Y. 113
Churchman — Futhey's Chester Pa. 497
Johnston's History of Cecil Co. Md. 525
Rodenbough's Autumn Leaves 47-50
Chute — American Ancestry iii, 62
Calnek's History of Annapolis N. S. 491-3
Chute Family of Maine (1882) 12 pages
Chute Genealogy (1894) 517 pages
Gage's History of Rowley Mass. 440
Hammatt Papers of Ipswich Mass. 53
Maine Hist. and Gen. Rec. iii, 290; vii, 54
New Eng. Hist. and Gen. Register xiii, 123
Savage's Genealogical Dictionary i, 387
Thurston Genealogy (1892) 17, 40
Waters Genealogy (1882) 13
Whitmore's Heraldic Journal 142-4
Cilley — Am. Anc. v, 138; vi, 194; ix, 168
Cilley Genealogy (1893) 47 pages
Cogswell's History of Henniker N. H. 502
Cogswell's Nottingham N. H. 175-97, 354
Dow's History of Hampton N. H. 637
Eaton's History of Thomaston Me. 176
Little's History of Weare N. H. 768-73
Maine Gens. ii, 77-9, 121-8; iii, 65-107
Nealley Chart
Sinclair Genealogy 371-3
Cist — American Ancestry vii, 48
Harvey Genealogy 791-806
Claas — Bergen's Kings Co. N. Y. 61-3
Claflin — American Ancestry xii, 28
Ballou's Milford Mass. 646-53
Barry's History of Framingham Mass. 207
Daniels' History of Oxford Mass. 439
Hudson's History of Lexington Mass. 42
Morse's Sherborn Mass. Settlers 59
Clagett — Bowie Genealogy 392-421
Claggett — Hayden's Virginia Gens. 169
Secomb's History of Amherst N. H. 533
Wheeler's History of Newport N. H. 343
Claghorne — Savage's Dictionary i, 388
Swift's Barnstable Mass. Families i, 180-2
Claiborne — Campbell's Virginia 324
Carter Family Tree

Clarke's Old King Wm. Co. Va. Families
Goode Genealogy 65
Lewis Genealogy (1893) 92
Meade's Old Families of Virginia
Neill's Virginia Carolorum 43
New York Gen. and Biog. Rec. xxvi, 149
Richmond Va. Standard ii, 4, 52; iii, 38; iv, 3-4
Slaughter's Bristol Parish Va. 164-72
Virginia Magazine of History i, (1894) 313-24, 436-40; ii, 216-8
Clap — Blake Genealogy 58
Bolton's Hist. of Westchester N. Y. ii, 509
Bridgeman's King's Chapel Epit. 239-53
Deane's History of Scituate Mass. 234-7
Emery's Taunton Mass. Ministry i, 292-5
Hinman's Connecticut Settlers 598
Judd's History of Hadley Mass. 462
Lyman's Hist. Easthampton Mass. 141-52
N. E. Gen. Reg. xiv, 275; xv, 215, 225-34
Pope Genealogy 323-6
Savage's Genealogical Dictionary i, 388-91
Swift's Barnstable Mass. Families i, 249
Trumbull Genealogy 15-24
Clapp — Am. Ancestry i, 14; ii, 22; iii, 75
Baird's History of Rye N. Y. 457
Bemis' History of Marlboro N. H. 442
Chardon, Ohio, Newspaper Mar. 10, April 7, 21, 1886
Clapp Family Meeting (1870) 67 pages
Clapp Genealogy (1876) 516 pages
Hayes' Wells Genealogy 192
Hill's Dedham Mass. Records i
Leach's Morton Ancestry 118-20
Loomis Genealogy (1880) 753
Mott Genealogy 366
New Eng. Hist. and Gen. Register xliii, 429
Pompey N. Y. Reunion 295
Pope Genealogy
Ransom Genealogy
Sheldon's Hist. of Deerfield Mass. ii, 120-3
Stiles' History of Windsor Ct. ii, 151-3
Strong Genealogy 339-44, 389-96, 574, 1239
Wright's History of Easthampton Mass. 28
Wyman's Charlestown Mass. Gens. i, 216
Clapper — American Ancestry i, 14; ii, 22
Roe's Sketches of Rose N. Y. 190
Clare — Thomas Genealogy (1896) 323-7
Clark — Aldrich's Walpole N. H. 230
Alexander Genealogy 78-88
American Ancestry i, 14; ii, 22; iii, 94; v, 212, 236; vi, 95; viii, 24, 63, 153, 203; ix, 137, 159, 185; x, 121, 139, 196, 198; xi, 182; xii, 24, 41
Anderson's Waterbury Ct. i, app. 36-8
Andrews' Hist. of New Britain Ct. 193, 253
Avon N. Y. Record 30-2
Aylsworth Genealogy 70
Babson's History of Gloucester Mass. 68
Baird's History of Rye N. Y. 499
Ball's Lake County Ind. 404
Ballou's History of Milford Mass. 653-61
Barbour's My Wife and Mother app. 35
Barry's History of Framingham Mass. 206
Barry's History of Hanover Mass. 268-70
Bemis' History of Marlboro N. H. 443

Blake's History of Franklin Mass 236–8
Bolton's Westchester County N. Y. ii, 717
Bond's Watertown Mass. Gens. 159–62, 741
Boyd's History of Conesus N. Y. 147
Bridgeman's Granary Epitaphs 307–13
Briggs' History of Shipbuilding 123
Bronson's History of Waterbury Ct. 483–5
Brown's Bedford Mass. Families 7
Brown's West Simsbury Ct. Settlers 55
Calnek's History of Annapolis N. S. 493
Camp Genealogy ii, 28–30
Champion Genealogy 50
Chapin Genealogy
Chase's History of Haverhill Mass. 275
Clark Family of Northampton (1857) 13 p.
Clark Family of Watertown (1866) 260 p.
Clark Family of Plymouth (1869) 43 pages
Clark Family of Milford Ct. (1870) 11 pages
Clark Ancestry (1876) 25 pages
Clark Family of Connecticut (1877)
Clark Family of Boston (1879) 8 pages
Clark Family of Haddam Ct. (1880) 11 p.
Clark Family of Rhode Island (1881) 49 p.
Clark Family of Farmington Ct. (1882) 94 p.
Clark Family of Amherst Mass. (1883) 7 p.
Clark Family of Newbury (1883) 120 pages
Clark Family of Plymouth (1884) 183 pages
Clark Fam. of Newbury 2d ed. (1885) 216 p.
Clark Families of Essex Mass. (1889) 10 p.
Clark Family of N. Y. City (1891) 32 pages
Clark Fam. Hempstead N. Y. (1891) 106 p.
Clark Fam. Hempstead N. Y. (1892) 122 p.
Clark Family of Dorchester (1896) 176 pages
Clark Family of Colerain Mass. (1898) 74 p.
Cleveland's Hist. of Yates Co. N. Y. 481–3
Cochrane's History of Antrim N. H. 417–9
Cochrane's Hist. Francestown N. H. 579–88
Cogswell's New Boston N. H. 369–73
Cogswell's Hist. Nottingham N. H. 654–6
Collin's History of Hillsdale N. Y. app. 48
Cooley's Trenton N. J. Genealogies 39–41
Cutts Genealogy 177
Daniels' History of Oxford Mass. 439
Davis' Landmarks of Plymouth 59–63
Deane's History of Scituate Mass. 237
Dickerman Genealogy 258–61
Draper's History of Spencer Mass. 183
Dwight Genealogy 274–8
Dyer's History of Plainfield Mass. 134–7
Eaton's Annals of Warren Me. 517
Eaton's History of Candia N. H. 61
Eaton's History of Thomaston Me. 176
Egle's Notes and Queries 3d ser. ii, 461;
    iii, 37–9, 262–5
Elderkin Genealogy
Essex Mass. Inst. Hist. Coll. xxvi, 59–68
Farrow's History of Islesborough Me. 188
Field's History of Haddam Ct. 44
Foster Genealogy (1889) 116–9
Freeman's Cape Cod Mass. ii, 524, 756–71
Frisbie's History of Middletown Vt. 74–9
Gage's History of Rowley Mass. 440
Gifford's Our Patronymics 19
Gold's History of Cornwall Ct. 273
Goodwin's Genealogical Notes 23–39
Greene Genealogy (1894)

Guild's Stiles Genealogy 209–11, 241
Hanson's History of Gardiner Me. 137
Harris' Watertown Mass. Epitaphs 12
Hatch's History of Industry Me. 540–2
Hayward's History of Gilsum N. H. 287
Hayward's Hist. of Hancock N. H. 439–49
Hemenway's Vermont Gazetteer v, 95
Herrick's History of Gardner Mass. 340
Heywood's Hist. of Westminster Mass. 581
Hinman's Connecticut Settlers 600–16
Hollister's History of Pawlet Vt. 175–7
Howell's History of Southampton N. Y. 211
Hubbard's Stanstead County Canada 198
Hudson's History of Lexington Mass. 42–5
Huntington Genealogy 86
Jackson's History of Newton Mass. 257–60
Jameson's History of Medway Mass. 462–8
Jenning's Bennington Vt. Memorial
Joslin's History of Poultney Vt. 231–40
Judd's History of Hadley Mass. 462
Kellogg's White Memorial 27, 51, 70, 111
Kidder's History of New Ipswich N. H. 353
Lancaster's History of Gilmanton N. H. 260
Lapham's History of Bethel Me. 512
Lapham's History of Paris Me. 550–2
Lapham's History of Woodstock Me. 193
Leland Genealogy 164
Leonard's History of Dublin N. H. 322–4
Lincoln's History of Hingham Mass. 11, 129
Littell's Passaic Valley Genealogies 75–80
Little's History of Weare N. H. 773
Livermore's History of Wilton N. H. 349–51
Locke Genealogy 58, 141–4, 300
Lyman's Hist. Easthampton Mass. 152–61
Mack Genealogy 48–53
Magazine of Am. History xxii, 246–9
McKeen's Bradford 162–5, 361–5, 382–7
Merrill's History of Acworth N. H. 199–202
Middlefield Ct. History
Missouri Pioneer Families 395
Mitchell's Hist. of Bridgewater Mass. 365
Morris Genealogy (1887) 91–3
Morrison's Hist. of Windham N. H. 377–9
Morse Memorial appendix No. 15½
Morse's Sherborn Mass. Settlers 59–62
N. E. Register xiv, 25; xvi, 140; xxxiii, 119
New York Gen. and Biog. Record xix,,176;
    xxviii, 65–71
North's History of Augusta Me. 829–35
Norton's Hist. of Fitzwilliam N. H. 512–4
Orcutt's History of Derby Ct. 710–13
Orcutt's History of New Milford Ct. 794
Paige's History of Cambridge Mass. 510
Paige's History of Hardwick Mass. 348–50
Palmer and Trimble Genealogy 130–6
Parker's Hist. of Londonderry N. H. 264–6
Paul's History of Wells Vt. 71–4
Pierce's History of Grafton Mass. 473
Pierce's History of Gorham Me. 191
Randall's Hist. of Chesterfield N. H. 247–50
Read's History of Swanzey N. H. 311
Rice Genealogy
Richmond Va. Standard iii, 39
R. I. Historical Society Colls. iii, 313
R. I. Historical Magazine vii, 125–36
Robinson Genealogy (1837) 36 pages

Runnell's Sanbornton N. H. ii, 129, 151
Salem N. Y. Book of History 41
Saunders' Alabama Settlers 455-7
Saunderson's Hist. Charlestown N. H. 309
Savage's Genealogical Dict. i, 388, 405
Sears Genealogy 86-8, 193
Secomb's History of Amherst N. H. 534-8
Sewell's History of Woburn Mass. 509
Sheldon's Hist. of Deerfield Mass. ii, 123-5
Shourd's Hist. of Fenwick Colony N. J. 525
Sinclair Genealogy 374-89
Slaughter's St. Mark's Parish Va. 190
Smith Genealogy by Wellington Smith
Smith's Hist. of Sunderland Mass. 287-98
Stanton Genealogy 206
Stearns' Hist. of Ashburnham Mass. 636-9
Stearns' History of Rindge N. H. 476
Stephens Genealogy 45-9
Stickney's Minisink Region N. Y. 121
Stiles' History of Windsor Ct. ii, 153-7
Stoddard Genealogy (1865) 13, 26-32
Stone's Hist. of Hubbardston Mass. 238-52
Strong Genealogy 1439-73
Temple's Hist. of N. Brookfield Mass. 554
Temple's History of Palmer Mass. 434
Thomas Genealogy (1896) 285
Timlow's Southington Ct. Sketches 49-61
Topsfield Mass. Hist. Collections 1896 ii
Tuttle Genealogy 2-15
Vermont Historical Gazetteer v, 95
Washington N. H. History 341
Wentworth Genealogy i, 222
Wheeler's History of Brunswick Me. 830
Wheeler's Eminent North Carolinians xii
Whitmore's Copps Hill Epitaphs
Whittemore's Hist. Middlesex Co. Ct. 204
Wight Genealogy 13
Williams' History of Danby Vt. 125
Winsor's History of Duxbury Mass. 246
Wood's Brookline Mass. Sketches 215-9
Wright's History of Easthampton Mass. 29
Wyman's Charlestown Mass. Gens. i, 217
Clarke — American Ancestry i, 14; iii,
122, 133; iv, 143; v, 155; vii, 51, 73; ix,
32; x, 159; xi, 185, 222; xii, 41, 118
Atkins' History of Hawley Mass. 52
Austin's Ancestries 126
Austin's R. I. Genealogical Dictionary 43-8
Austin's Allied Families 61-5
Bingham Genealogy 241-8
Chapman's Weeks Genealogy 134
Clarke Genealogy, see Clark
Cogswell Genealogy 205
Cushman's History of Sheepscott Me. 366-8
Cutter's History of Arlington Mass. 204
Essex Inst. Coll. xvi, 270-9; xx, 222-6
Foster Genealogy (1889) 95
Gedney and Clarke Genealogy (1880)
Goode Genealogy 230, 375-8
Greene Genealogy (1894)
Green's Kentucky Families
Hammatt Papers of Ipswich Mass. 62-4
Hemenway's Clarke Papers 8, 18-20
Irish's History of Richmond R. I. 129-55
Lane Genealogy (1891) 64, 67
Meade's Old Families of Virginia

Newport R. I. Hist. Mag. i, 75-96, 129-55
O'Callaghan's Clarke Voyage to Am. 71-81
Orcutt's History of Stratford Ct. 1174-6
Pompey N. Y. Reunion 291-5
Poore Genealogy 50-2
Pope Genealogy
Preble Genealogy 253
Richmond Va. Standard ii, 39
Salisbury's Fam. Histories (1892) iii. 215-42
Sims, Clarke and Ross Families (1870)
Stiles' History of Windsor Ct. ii, 834-6
Tuttle Genealogy 359-73
Warren and Clarke Genealogies 42-8
Whitmore's Heraldic Journal ii, 75-7
Clarkson — Clarksons of N. Y. (1875)
Clarksons of Charleston S. C. (1877) 4 p.
Clarksons of Philadelphia (1890) 259 pages
Cogswell's Hist. of Henniker N. H. 502-5
Lamb's History of New York City 385
New York Gen. and Biog. Rec. xi, 156-8
Paxton's Marshall Genealogy 99
Clary — Judd's Hist. Hadley Mass. 464
Kidder's New Ipswich N. H. 351, 385
Savage's Genealogical Dictionary i, 405
Sheldon's History of Deerfield Mass. ii,
125
Smith's Hist. of Sunderland Mass. 298-301
Temple's History of Northfield Mass. 423
Wentworth Genealogy ii, 104
Clason — American Ancestry viii, 81
Clason Genealogy (1892) 160 pages
Clauson — Stickney's Minisink 139
Clauw — Munsell's Albany Coll. iv, 107
Clawson — American Ancestry ix, 88
Huntington's Stamford Ct. Settlers 22
Clay — American Ancestry xii
Bangor Me. Hist. Mag. v, 184
Chase's History of Chester N. H. 492
Clay Genealogy (1895) 51 pages
Colton's Life of Henry Clay i, 17-9
Green's Kentucky Families
Hanson's History of Gardiner Me. 170
Hart Family of Va. (1882) 15-20
Holstein Genealogy
Ridlon's Saco Valley Me. Families 577-80
Runnel's Sanbornton N. H. ii, 152-6
Saunders' Alabama Settlers 270-91
Stearns' History of Rindge N. H. 477
Walker Genealogy 131
Clayes — Cunnabell Genealogy 13
Norton's Hist. of Fitzwilliam N. H. 514
Temple's Hist. Framingham Mass. 506-9
Claypoole — Claypoole Gen. (1892) 4 pages
Claypoole Gen. (1893) 196 pages
Claypoole Gen. app. (1894) 15 pages
Clayton — Butler's Farmington 428-30
Futhey's History of Chester Co. Pa. 498
Potts Genealogy (1895) 117-23
Power's Sangamon Co. Ill. Settlers 16, 205
Slaughter's St. Mark's Parish Va. 125-7
Clearwater — Amer. Ancestry iii, 95
Cleary — Roe's Sketches of Rose N. Y. 41
Cleaver — Futhey's Chester Pa. 498
Jenkins' Hist. Gwynedd Pa. 2d ed. 411
Cleaves — Chandler Genealogy 23
Corliss' North Yarmouth Me. Magazine

Lapham's History of Norway Me. 480
Secomb's History of Amherst N. H. 539
Cleeman — Richmond Standard ii, 32
Cleeves — Austin's Allied Families 65
Clemans — Paul's Hist. of Wells Vt. 75-7
Clemence — Austin's R. I. Dict. 48
Clemens — American Ancestry xii, 25
Kratz Genealogy 198-205
Clement — Ballou's Milford Mass. 661
Chase's History of Haverhill Mass. 275
Clement's Newtown N. J. Settlers
Dearborn's Hist. of Salisbury N. H. 525-7
Hayward's History of Hancock N. H. 449
Hoyt's Salisbury Mass. Families 95-8
Hubbard's Stanstead County Canada 313
Little's History of Weare N. H. 774-6
Pearson's Schenectady N. Y. Settlers 37
Pompey N. Y. Reunion 289-91
Poor's Merrimac Valley Researches 142
Runnel's Hist. of Sanbornton N. H. 156-9
Savage's Genealogical Dictionary i, 407
Stark's Hist. of Dunbarton N. H. 241
Clements — Dow's Hampton N. H. 638
Eaton's Annals of Warren Me. 517
Ely Genealogy 323
Power's Sangamon Co. Ill. Settlers 206
Wentworth Genealogy i, 125
Clemmons — Hinman's Ct. Settlers 617
Clemons — Ridlon's Saco Vall. 580-4
Clendennen — Clyde's Irish Settlers 28
Egles' Historical Reg. of Penn. i, 36
Morrison Genealogy 254
Clesson — Sheldon's Deerfield 126-8
Cleveland — Adam's Fairhaven 316-21
American Ancestry i, 15; iii, 10, 186; v, 41
Ballou's History of Milford Mass. 662
Bass' History of Braintree Vt. 125
Champion Genealogy
Child Genealogy 807-9
Cleveland's Hist. of Yates Co. N. Y. 206
Cleveland Genealogy (1879) 260 p.
Cleveland Family of Woburn (1881) 48 p.
Cleveland Lineage (1884) 4 pages
Cleveland Lineage (1885) 14 pages
Cleveland Genealogy (1899) 2,894 pages
Crafts Genealogy 226-30
Ely Genealogy 323
Gifford's Our Patronymics 10-6
Hinman's Connecticut Settlers 618-20
Hollister's History of Pawlet Vt. 177
Hubbard's Stanstead County Canada 303
Joslin's History of Poultney Vt. 241
Kelly Genealogy (1892)
Lindsay Genealogy
New Eng. Hist. and Gen. Reg. xxxix, 212-7
Paige's History of Hardwick Mass. 350
Perkins' Old Houses of Norwich Ct. 441
Putnam's Historical Magazine i, 153-66
Richardson Genealogy 192
Walworth's Hyde Genealogy 399-410
Wyman's Charlestown Mass. i, 219-21
Young's Hist. of Chautauqua Co. N. Y. 300
Clever — Cochrane's Antrim N. H. 419
Cleverly — American Ancestry v, 95
Bass' History of Braintree Vt. 125
Binny Genealogy 59

Clifford — Aylesworth Genealogy 303
Bangor Me. Historical Magazine viii, 95
Caverly's History of Pittsford Vt. 696
Chase's History of Chester N. H. 493
Dow's History of Hampton N. H. 638-40
Hoyt's Salisbury Mass. Families 99
Hubbard's Stanstead County Canada 310
Lancaster's Hist. of Gilmanton N. H. 259
Lapham's History of Paris Me. 558
Smith's Founders of Mass. Bay 349-53
Stark's History of Dunbarton N. H. 249
Stone's Hist. of Hubbardston Mass. 252
Clift — American Ancestry iii, 10; xi, 25
Mitchell's Hist. of Bridgewater Mass. 137
Clifton — Austin's R. I. Gen. Dict. 48
Clinch — Pearson's Schenectady 28
Cline — Power's Sangamon Ill. 206-8
Clinton — Alden's Am. Epitaphs v, 276
American Ancestry vi, 52; xi, 182
Campbell's Life of Gov. Clinton 19-39
Doty Genealogy 556-8
Eager's Hist. of Orange Co. N. Y. 628-33
New York Genealogical and Biographical
    Record xii, 195-8; xiii, 5-10, 139, 173-80
Niven's Little Britain N. Y. Church (1859)
Valentine's N. Y. City Manual (1853) 415
Clock—American Ancestry xi, 11
Huntington's Stamford Ct. 23
Clogston—New Eng. Gen. Reg. lii, 25-7
Washington N. H. 342
Clopton — N. E. Hist. Reg. xviii, 184
Clore — Garr Genealogy 88
Close — Bolton's Westchester ii, 717
Hollister Genealogy 526-9
Mead's History of Greenwich Ct. 307-9
Closs — Roe's Sketches Rose N. Y. 111
Closson — Hubbard's Springfield Vt. 254
Cloud — Futhey's Chester Co. Pa. 500
Potts Genealogy (1895) 141-64
Cloues — Barbour's Low Chart (1890)
Clough — Bangor Me. Hist. Mag. v, 185
Champion Genealogy
Cogswell's Hist. of Henniker N. H. 506-8
Eaton's History of Thomaston Me. 177
Eaton's Annals of Warren Me. 517
Hoyt's Salisbury Mass. Families 99-102
Little's History of Weare N. H. 776-8
New Eng. Hist. and Gen. Reg. viii, 79
Niven's Little Britain N. Y. Church (1859)
Runnels' History of Sanbornton N. H. ii,
    159
Savage's Genealogical Dictionary i, 410
Whitmore's Copps Hill Epitaphs
Wyman's Charlestown Mass. Gens. 222
Cloutman — Pierce's Gorham Me. 161
Clow — American Ancestry ii, 24
Clowes — American Ancestry xi, 3
Bunker's L. I. Gens. 186-8
Cloyes — Barry's Framingham 210-3
See also under Clayes
Clum — American Ancestry ii, 24
Hall's Trenton N. J. Presbyt. Church 249
Clute — Amer. Ancestry i, 15; x, 100
Munsell's Albany N. Y. Colls. iv, 108
Pearson's Schenectady Settlers 38-45
Cluxton — Sedgwick's Sharon Ct. 72

Clyde — Clyde Family of Pa. (1880)
Clyde's Irish Settlement in Pa. 29–34
Hayward's History of Gilsum N. H. 288
Hayward's History of Hancock N. H. 449
Martin's History of Chester Pa. 267
Morrison's Hist. Windham N. H. 380–90
Washington N. H. History 343
Clymer — American Ancestry v, 45
Penn. Mag. of History and Biog. ix, 353–5
Coale — McKean Genealogy 149
Thomas Genealogy (1877) 65
Thomas Genealogy (1896) 286–91
Coalter — Slaughter's Bristol Va. 160
Coan — Am. Ancestry v, 116, 128; ix, 189
Avery Genealogy (1893) 231–3
Coates — American Ancestry viii, 111
Cleveland's Hist. of Yates Co. N. Y. 495
Coates Genealogy (1885) 171 pages
Crane's Rawson Genealogy 201
Cunnabell Genealogy 83
Futhey's History of Chester Co. Pa. 501
Glenn's Some Colonial Mansions 119
Holstein Genealogy
Pierce's History of Gorham Me. 157
Plumsted Genealogy 61
Power's Sangamon Co. Ill. Settlers 209
Savage's Genealogical Dictionary i, 412
Cobb — Adams' Fairhaven Vt. 341–3
American Ancestry iv, 179; v, 91; vi, 64;
    vii, 251; x, 182; xi, 64
Ballou's History of Milford Mass. 662
Bangor Historical Magazine iv, 1–8
Bass' History of Braintree Vt. 125
Bond's Watertown Mass. Gens 847–9
Clark's History of Norton Mass. 79
Cleveland Genealogy (1899) 44–6
Cobb (Sylvanus) Life of (1867)
Cobb Ancestors (1897) 8 pages
Davis' Landmarks of Plymouth 63–6
Deane's History of Scituate Mass. 238
Eaton's History of Thomaston Me. ii, 178
Eaton's Annals of Warren Me. 518–20
Freeman's Cape Cod ii, 274, 340, 763
Hayward's History of Hancock N. H. 450
Heywood's Hist. of Westminster Mass. 582
Hobart's Hist. of Abington Mass. 360–3
Hollister's History of Pawlet Vt. 178
Hubbard's Hist. of Springfield Vt. 255–7
Jillson Genealogy 167
Kingman's N. Bridgewater Mass. 475
Lapham's History of Norway Me. 481
Lincoln's Hist. of Hingham Mass. ii, 131–4
Morse's Sherborn Mass. Settlers 62
New Eng. Hist. and Gen. Reg. ii, 389; xviii
Paige's History of Hardwick Mass. 351–3
Perkins' Old Houses of Norwich Ct. 443
Pierce's History of Gorham Me. 158
Pratt's History of Eastham Mass. 27
Rich's History of Truro Mass. 523
Richmond Va. Standard ii, 23
Runnels' History of Sanbornton N. H. i,
    473
Savage's Genealogical Dictionary i, 412–4
Slaughter's Bristol Parish Va. 45
Swift's Barnstable Families i, 166–70
Virginia Magazine of History iv (1897), 332

Waldo's History of Tolland Ct. 97–9
Williamson and Cobb Gen. (1896) 37–55
Cobbett — Hammatt Papers 54–9
Hinman's Connectict Settlers 626
Savage's Genealogical Dictionary i, 414
Cobbs — Ala. Historical Society Trans.
Hoyt's Salisbury Mass. Families 102
Cobia — Pierce Genealogy (1894)
Cobleigh — Norton's Fitzwilliam 514–6
Randall's Hist. of Chesterfield N. H. 251–3
Stearns' History of Ashburnham Mass. 639
Cobourne — Smith's Delaware Pa. 454
Coburn — American Ancestry ii, 24; v, 228
Bass's History of Braintree Vt. 126
Daniel's History of Oxford Mass. 441
Eaton's History of Thomaston Me. ii, 179
Eaton's History of Warren Me. 520
Farrow's History of Islesborough Me. 189
Hinman's Connecticut Settlers 627
Lapham's History of Norway Me. 482
Livermore's History of Wilton N. H. 351
Worthen's History of Sutton N. H. 664–6
Cochran — Adams Gen. (1894) 75, 79–87
Aldrich's History of Walpole N. H. 231
American Ancestry ii, 24; iv, 194; vi, 80
Carter's Hist. of Pembroke N. H. ii, 34–49
Cochrane's History of Antrim N. H. 421–9
Cochrane's Hist. Francestown N. H. 588–92
Cochrans of Halifax (1899) 18 pages
Cogswell's New Boston N. H. 356–69
Cothren's History of Woodbury Ct. 519–25
Dickey Genealogy 48–50
Eaton's History of Thomaston Me. ii, 179
Futhey's History of Chester Pa. 500
Haywood's History of Hancock N. H. 451
Hinman's Connecticut Settlers 730–3
Martin's History of Chester Pa. 319–23
Morrison's Hist. Windham N. H. 390–402
Marshall Genealogy (1884) 62–70
Peyton's History of Augusta Co. Va. 312
Secomb's History of Amherst N. H. 539
Smith's (Rev. Wm.) Biography
Cock — Amer. Ancestry ix, 75; x, 73, 81
Bolton's Westchester Co. N. Y. ii, 718
Bunker's Long Island Genealogies 188–90
Miller's Colchester Co. Nova Scotia 151–8
N. Y. Gen. Biog. Rec. iv, 188–90; viii, 9
Shotwell Genealogy 233–5
Cocke — Amer. Hist. Mag. of Nashville ii
    (1897) 152–71
Jones Genealogy (1891) 121–43
Hanson's Old Kent Md. 172
Richmond Va. Standard ii, 31, 35, 37, 40,
    44, 52; iii, 8, 20, 40
Slaughter's Bristol Parish Va. 173, 184
Virg. Hist. Soc. Colls. v (1886), 194–204
Virginia Magazine of History iii, 282–92,
    405–14; iv, 86–96, 212–7, 322–32, 430–
    50; v, 71–89, 181–94, 449
Watkins Genealogy 21
Cocker — Strong Genealogy 728–30
Cockrell — Richmond Standard iv, 3
Cockrill — American Ancestry xi, 185
Amer. Hist. Mag. of Nashville iii, 331–45
Cocks — American Ancestry ix, 73; xi, 9
Coddin — Gorham's Purchase 436

Coddington — Amer. Anc. vii, 103; ix, 131
Austin's R. I. Genealogical Dict. 276-9
Bartlett's R. I. Hist. Tracts iv, 7-60
Mott Genealogy 227-35
New York Gen. and Biog. Rec. xxiii, 190-2
Savage's Genealogical Dictionary i, 415
Turner's Wm. Coddington Inquiry 9-16
Updyke's Narragansett Church R. I. 164
Codman — Amer. Ancestry iii, 133; vi, 91
Hoyt's Salisbury Mass. Families 102
Joslin's History of Poultney Vt. 242
Pierce's History of Gorham Me. 161
Savage's Genealogical Dictionary i, 416
Washington N. H. History 349
Wyman's Charlestown Mass. Gens. 224-6
Codmer — Savage's Gen. Dict. i, 417
Codrington — Richmond Va. Standard ii, 35, 37
Cody — Hughes Genealogy 183
Coe — American Ancestry vii, 100; xii
Babson's History of Gloucester Mass. 69
Baird's History of Rye N. Y. 407
Barlow Genealogy 245-7
Bent's History of Whiteside Co. Ill. 261
Bolton's Westchester County N. Y. ii, 717
Boyd's Annals of Winchester Ct. 51-6
Boyd's History of Conesus N. Y. 148
Coe Genealogy (1856) 14 pages
Coe Genealogy 2d ed. (1859) 16 pages
Coe Ancestry (1897) 136 pages
Cogswell's Hist. Nottingham N. H. 656-9
Davis Genealogy (1888) 106
Hinman's Connecticut Settlers 627-31
Litchfield County Ct. History (1881) 724
Middlefield Ct. History
Orcutt's History of Stratford Ct. 1176
Orcutt's History of Torrington Ct. 668-75
Riker's Annals of Newtown N. Y. 400
Savage's Genealogical Dictionary i, 417
Coely — N. Y. Gen. and Biog. Rec. ix, 53
Coerte — Bergen Genealogy 61
Coeyeman — Messler's Somerset N. J. 19
Coeymans — Munsell's Albany iv, 109
Coffeen — Hale Genealogy 197
Coffey — Parthemore Genealogy 103
Coffin — American Ancestry i, 15; ii, 15; viii, 125; xi, 194
American Gen. Record (1897) ii, 192-4
Amory's Life of Sir Isaac Coffin
Austin's Allied Families 67-71
Babson's History of Gloucester Mass. 69
Buxton Me. Centennial 211-7
Champion Genealogy 369
Coffin Memoir (1855) 181 pages
Coffin Early Generations (1870) 17 pages
Coffin Grandchildren (1881) 261 pages
Coffin Family of Nantucket (1881) 64 p.
Coffin Armorial Bearings (1881) 8 pages
Coffin Ancestors (1886) 141 pages
Coffin Early Wills (1893) 86 pages
Coffin Genealogy (1896) 53 pages
Coffin's History of Boscawen N. H. 491-5
Coffin's History of Newbury Mass. 298
Crane's Rawson Genealogy 39
Dow's History of Hampton N. H. 640-3
Emery Genealogy (1890) 61

Hoyt's Salisbury Mass. Families 103
Lapham's History of Bethel Me 513
Maine Hist. Society Collections iv, 240-9
Morse Memorial, appendix 89
Mott Genealogy 321
New Eng. Historical and Genealogical Register ii, 336-41; xxiv, 149-55, 305-15; xxv, 90 (1881)
Savage's Genealogical Dictionary i, 418-20
Stearns' History of Rindge N. H. 478-80
Wheeler's History of Newport N. H. 346
Whitmore's Heraldic Journal iii, 49-56
Wyman's Charlestown Mass. Gens. 226
Coffman — Palmer Gen. (1875) 169
Coggan — Savage's Gen. Dict. i, 420
Coggeshall — Austin's R. I. Dict. 49
Bailey Ancestry (1892) 44-6
Coggeshall Reunion Address (1884) 25 p.
Newport R. I. Hist. Mag. (1883) 145
R. I. Historical Magazine vi, 173-89
Ripley's Ingersoll Genealogy 84
Savage's Genealogical Dictionary i, 421
Tilley's Mag. of N. E. History ii, 99-105
Coggin — American Ancestry vi. 34
Bangor Me. Historical Magazine 186
Foster Pedigree (1897) ii, 1-11
Freeman's Hist. of Cape Cod Mass. ii, 260
Secomb's History of Amherst N. H. 541
Swift's Barnstable Families i, 189-91
Symmes Genealogy 82
Coggshall — Coggshall Chart (1876)
Coghill — Coghill Genealogy (1879) 193 p.
Cogshall — Stamford Ct. Settlers 24
Cogswell — Am. Anc. i, 15; iv, 108; viii, 200
Andrews' History of New Britain Ct. 342
Baker Genealogy (1867) 26-8
Chase's History of Haverhill Mass. 226-8
Chute Genealogy, appendix 37-40
Coffin's History of Boscawen N. H. 495
Cogswell Genealogy (1884) 683 pages
Cogswell's Hist. of Henniker N. H. 509-16
Cogswell's Nottingham N. H. 659-75
Granite Monthly of Concord N. H. ix, 185-7
Hammatt Papers of Ipswich Mass. 59-62
Hinman's Connecticut Settlers 635-9
Kelley's W. Cogswell Sermon 10-6
Kellogg's White Memorial 108
Knight's Memorial of Frederick Knight
Lancaster's Hist. of Gilmanton N. H. 258
Montague Genealogy 462-4
Morrison's Hist. of Windham N. H. 403
Orcutt's History of New Milford Ct. 687
Otis Genealogy (1851)
Runnel's Hist. of Sanbornton N. H. ii, 161
Savage's Genealogical Dictionary i, 422
Timlow's Southington Ct. Sketches 61-3
Wentworth Genealogy ii, 92-5
Cohoon — Hayward's Hancock N. H. 452
Stiles' History of Windsor Ct. ii, 157
Coiner — Keinadt Genealogy 78-93
Coit — American Ancestry v, 10
Babson's History of Gloucester Mass. 71
Bartlett's Wanton Genealogy 151
Bill Genealogy 180
Caulkins' History of New London Ct. 275
Chandler Genealogy 53-7

Coit Genealogy (1874) 341 pages
Coit Book by Gilman (1895) 19 pages
Hinman's Connecticut Settlers 630–53
Perkins' Old Houses of Norwich Ct. 444–6
Prentice Genealogy 280
Savage's Genealogical Dictionary i, 422
Walworth's Hyde Genealogy 1112–4
Coker — Little Genealogy 196
Colbath — Lincoln's Hingham ii, 134
Colborn — Roe's Rose N. Y. 200
Colburn — Adams' Fairhaven Vt. 330–4
American Ancestry iv, 136, 187; x, 7
Ballou's History of Milford Mass. 665–7
Bangor Me. Historical Magazine v, 186
Bassett's History of Richmond N. H. 369
Cochrane's Hist. Francestown N. H. 592–4
Dedham Mass. Historical Register ii, 108–
 12; v, 53–61, vi, 53–8
Fox's History of Dunstable Mass. 240
Hanson's History of Gardiner Me. 71
Heywood's Hist. of Westminster Mass. 583
Hill's Dedham Mass. Records i
Hubbard's Hist. of Springfield Vt. 258–60
Little's History of Weare N. H. 778
Norton's Hist. of Fitzwilliam N. H. 516–8
Power's Sangamon Co. Ill. Settlers 211–5
Randall's Hist. of Chesterfield N. H. 254–6
Savage's Genealogical Dictionary i, 423
Stearns' History of Rindge N. H. 480–2
Worcester's History of Hollis N. H. 369
Colby — Chase's Chester N. H. 493–5
Child Genealogy 586, 796–9
Cochrane's Hist. of Francestown N. H. 594
Cogswell's Hist. of Henniker N. H. 516–25
Colby Genealogy (1897) 130 pages
Dearborn's Hist. of Salisbury N. H. 527
Eaton's History of Candia N. H. 63
Eaton's History of Thomaston Me. 180
Hayward's Hist. of Hancock N. H. 452–8
Hoyt's Salisbury Mass. Families 103–10
Hubbard's Hist. Stanstead Co. Can. 151–53
Lapham's History of Rumford Me. 312
Little's History of Weare N. H 779–90
McKeen's History of Bradford Vt. 282–5
Runnel's Hist. Sanbornton N. H. ii, 161–76
Savage's Genealogical Dictionary i, 444
Whittemore's Orange N. J. 420
Worthen's History of Sutton N. H. 666–70
Colcord — Cogswell's Nottingham 198
Dearborn's Hist. of Parsonfield Me. 370–2
Dow's History of Hampton N. H. 643
Hayward's History of Hancock N. H. 459
Savage's Genealogical Dictionary i, 424
Colden — Alden's Epitaphs v, 268–74
Colden Genealogy (1873) 24 pages, reprint
Lamb's History of New York City i, 521
New York Gen. and Biog. Rec. iv, 161–83
Ruggles Genealogy
Ruttenber's Hist. of Orange Co. N. Y. 355
Coldwell — Amer. Ancestry vii, 148
Cole — American Ancestry i, 15; ii, 25; iii,
 11; vii, 274; viii, 58, 144; ix, 74; x, 46,
 68, 196; xi, 25; xii, 6
Anderson's Waterbury Ct. i, app. 38
Austin's Ancestral Dictionary 15
Austin's R. I. Genealogical Dictionary 50

Bangor Me. Historical Magazine iv 216
Barry's Hist. of Framingham Mass. 213
Bassett's History of Richmond N. H. 370
Benedict's History of Sutton Mass. 627
Boyd's History of Conesus N. Y. 149
Brown's Bedford Mass. Families 7
Clarke's Old King Wm. Co. Va. Families
Clement's Newtown N. J. Settlers
Cleveland's Yates Co. N. Y. 203–6, 496–9
Clute's History of Staten Island N. Y. 356
Cochrane's History of Antrim N. H. 431
Cole Family of New York (1876) 269 pages
Cole Family of New Eng. (1887) 308 pages
Corliss' North Yarmouth Me. 965–7
Davis' Landmarks of Plymouth Mass. 66
Deane's History of Scituate Mass. 238
Dearborn's Hist. of Salisbury N. H. 527
Dow's History of Hampton N. H. 644
Freeman's Hist. Cape Cod Mass. ii, 373–87
Guild's Stiles Genealogy 325
Gumaer's History of Deerpark N. Y. 73
Hemenway's Vermont Gazetteer v
Hinman's Connecticut Settlers 653–7
Hoyt's Salisbury Mass. Families 111
Hubbard's Hist. Stanstead Co. Can. 197
Kingsman's N. Bridgewater Mass. 477–9
Lapham's History of Norway Me. 483
Lapham's History of Paris Me. 560
Lapham's History of Woodstock Me. 195
Leland Genealogy 253
Littell's Passaic Valley Genealogies 80–3
Mitchell's Hist. of Bridgewater Mass. 137
Narragansett Historical Reg. ii, 179–92
Pope Genealogy
Resseguie Genealogy 55–9
Rich's History of Truro Mass. 523
Richmond Va. Standard ii, 4, 31, 32
Savage's Genealogical Dictionary i, 425
Schoonmaker's Hist. Kingston N. Y. 475
Sewall's History of Woburn Mass. 605
Smith's Hist. of Dutchess Co. N. Y. 497
Thurston's History of Winthrop Me. 178
Timlow's Southington Ct. Sketches 64–72
Updyke's Narragansett Ch. R. I. 105–7
Winsor's History of Duxbury Mass. 247
Wyman's Charlestown Mass i, 228–30
Colebath — See Galbraith
Colegrove — American Ancestry xii, 29
Aylsworth Genealogy 66, 100, 190
Colegrove Genealogy (1894) 792 pages
Coleman — Boyd's Conesus N..Y. 149
Chambers' Early Germans of N. J. 294–7
Clarke's Old King Wm. Co. Va. Families
Cleveland's Hist. of Yates Co. N. Y. 246–8
Coleman Family Lineage (1867) 24 pages
Coleman Lineage 2d ed. (1898) 36 pages
Cooley's Trenton N. J. Genealogies 41
Egle's History of Lebanon County Pa. 237
Ely Genealogy 23, 47
Freeman's Hist. of Cape Cod Mass. ii, 286
Hollister Genealogy 159–64
Judd's History of Hadley Mass. 464
Meade's Old Families of Virginia
N. E. Hist. Gen. Reg. xii, 129; xvi, 141
Paxton's Marshall Genealogy 130–2; 236–40
Power's Sangamon Co. Ill. Settlers 209

Robertson's Pocahontas Descendants
Runnel's Hist. of Sanbornton N. H. ii, 176
Saunders' Alabama Settlers 514
Savage's Genealogical Dictionary i, 430
Sedgwick's History of Sharon Ct. 72
Slaughter's Bristol Parish Va. 202
Slaughter's St. Mark's Parish Va. 128
Stearns' Hist. Ashburnham Mass. 639-41
Stone's Hist. of Hubbardston Mass. 254-7
Swift's Barnstable Families i, 195-9
Temple's History of Whately Mass. 27
Coles — Amer. Ancestry ix, 77, 80; x, 82
Cole Genealogy (1887)
Davis' History of Wallingford Ct. 719
Meade's Old Families of Virginia ii, 15
Middlefield Ct. History
Richmond Va. Standard iii, 26
Shourd's Fenwick's Colony N. J. 64-9
Slaughter's St. Mark's Parish 186
Thompson's Hist. of Long Island i, 510
Virginia Magazine of Hist. vii, 101, 326-9
Colesworthy — N. E. Reg. xv, 330
Coley — American Ancestry viii, 131
Power's Sangamon Co. Ill. Settlers 210
Schenck's History of Fairfield Ct. 362
Colfax — Hinman's Conn. Settlers 657
Savage's Genealogical Dictionary i, 432
Colie — American Ancestry vi, 30
Whittemore's Orange N. J. 414
Colgate — Norwich Ct. Jubilee 200
Whittemore's Orange N. J. 281
Colgrove — American Ancestry ii, 25
Collamer — Collamer Gen. (1887) 44 p.
Collamore — Deane's Scituate 239
Eaton's History of Thomaston Me. 181
Savage's Genealogical Dictionary i, 432
Whittemore's Orange N. J. 340
Coller — Barry's Framingham 214
Boyd's History of Conesus N. Y. 150
Collester — See McAllister
Colley — Eaton's Thomaston Me. 181
Collicott — Savage's Gen. Dict. i, 432
Collier — Amer. Ancestry i, 16; ii, 25
Daniel's History of Oxford Mass. 442-6
Dudley's Arch and Gen Coll. plate 4
Goode Genealogy 50, 276-8
Hinman's Connecticut Settlers 661-4
Lincoln's Hist. of Hingham Mass. ii, 135
Missouri Pioneer Families 141
Munsell's Albany Collections iv, 109
Roe's Sketches of Rose N. Y. 291
Savage's Genealogical Dictionary i, 432
Winsor's History of Duxbury Mass. 248
Collin — American Ancestry ii, 26
Collin's Hillsdale N. Y. 16-22, app. 1-29
Collingswood — Davis' Landmarks 68
Collins — American Ancestry i, 16; ii, 26;
  iv, 189; vii, 172; ix, 84, 196, 199; x,
  146; xi, 161; xii
Austin's R. I. Genealogical Dictionary 51
Babson's History of Gloucester Mass. 72-4
Bemis' History of Marlboro N. H. 444-9
Clement's Newtown N. J. Settlers
Cleveland's Hist. Yates County N. Y. 317
Cochrane's Hist. of Francestown N. H. 594
Cogswell's Nottingham N. H. 355-7

Collins Assoc. of Vt. (1865) 15 pages
Collins Fam. of New Jersey (1871) 54 pages
Collins Fam. of New Jersey (1871) 13 p.
Collins Fam. of Milford Ct. (1872) 124 p.
Collins Family Gathering (1892)
Collins Family of Phila. (1893) 164 pages
Davis' Landmarks of Plymouth Mass. 68
Dearborn's Hist. of Salisbury N. H. 527-9
Dodd's History of East Haven Ct. 114
Eaton's History of Thomaston Me. 182
Farrow's History of Islesborough Me. 189
Freeman's History of Cape Cod ii, 373, 598
Goodwin's Foote Genealogy 240
Hall's Genealogical Notes (1886) 76
Hatch's History of Industry Me. 542-62
Hayward's Hist. of Hancock N. H. 460-2
Hibbard's History of Goshen Ct. 442
Hinman's Connecticut Settlers 664-71
Hough's History of Lewis Co. N. Y. 230
Hoyt's Salisbury Mass. Families 111
Hubbard's Hist. of Stanstead Co. Can. 200
Huntington Genealogy 129
Irish's History of Richmond R. I. 91-3
Little's History of Weare N. H. 796
Morris Genealogy (1853) 58-70
N. E. Hist. Reg. v, 95; ix, 335; xvi, 141
Norton's Hist. of Fitzwilliam N. H. 518-21
Orcutt's History of New Milford Ct. 688
Paige's History of Cambridge Mass. 511
Paige's History of Hardwick Mass. 353
Putnam's Historical Mag. iii, 30; v, 30-2
Rich's History of Truro Mass. 522
Roe's Sketches of Rose N. Y. 269
Savage's Genealogical Dictionary i, 433-6
Stackpole's History of Durham Me. 159
Stiles' History of Windsor Ct. ii, 158
Walworth's Hyde Genealogy i, 297-338
Washington's N. H. History 344-6
Wyman's Charlestown Mass. Gens. i, 231
Collis — Hyde's Brimfield Mass. 391
Temple's History of Palmer Mass. 433
Collord — Am. Ancestry xi, 62-4; xii, 121
Collord Ancestors (1899) 44 p.
Collyer — Baird's Hist. of Rye N. Y. 407
Colman — Dawson Genealogy 155-9
Deane's History of Scituate Mass. 241
Dimock's Coventry Ct. Records 27-9
Emery's Reminisc. Newbury Mass. 151-6
Essex Mass. Inst. Hist. Colls. xx, 226
Hinman's Connecticut Settlers 658-60
New Eng. Hist. and Gen. Register xii, 129
Savage's Genealogical Dictionary i, 437
Sturges and Colman Families of Maine
  (1898) 16 pages
Sturges Genealogy (1900) 35-40
Thurston Genealogy (1892) 80-3
Colmery — Scott Genealogy 53-63
Colquitt — Goode Genealogy 98
Colquhoun — Richmond Standard ii, 32
Colson — Eaton's Thomaston Me. 182
Milliken's Narraguagus Valley Me. 2
Colston — Hanson's Old Kent Md. 131
Paxton's Marshall Gen. 45-7, 105-15, 218
Colt — Colts of Gartsherrie Scotland 250-6
Hinman's Connecticut Settlers 672-8
Loomis Genealogy (1880) 149-65

Orcutt's History of Torrington Ct. 657-7
Savage's Genealogical Dictionary i, 437
Tuttle Genealogy 182
Walworth's Hyde Genealogy 101-6
Colton — Adams' Fairhaven Vt. 327-30
American Ancestry ii, 26
Chandler Genealogy 83
Cothren's Woodbury Ct. ii, 1478-81, 1605
Ely Genealogy 46, 101-4
Hinman's Connecticut Settlers 678-82
Longmeadow Mass. Centennial, app. 27-46
Morris and Flint Ancestors (1882) 39-41
New Eng. Historical and Genealogical
Register xxxiii, 202-4, 319-22, 416-9;
xxxiv, 31-4, 187-90
Old Northwest Gen. Quart. i, 180-2; ii, 9-11
Savage's Genealogical Dictionary i, 438
Stiles' History of Windsor Ct. ii, 159
Wentworth Genealogy ii, 55
Colver — Chambers' N. J. Germans 297-9
Colville — American Ancestry ii, 26
Colvin — American Ancestry i, 16
Austin's R. I. Genealogical Dictionary 52
Roe's Sketches of Rose N. Y. 30
Wight Genealogy 175
Williams' History of Danby Vt. 125-8
Colwell — American Ancestry iv, 104
Austin's R. I. Genealogical Dictionary 53
Mitchell's Hist. of Bridgewater Mass. 138
Combs — Cochrane's Antrim N. H. 431
Temple's Hist. of N. Brookfield Mass. 556
Comee — Herrick's Gardner Mass. 340
Hudson's History of Lexington Mass. 46
New Eng. Hist. and Gen. Reg. l, 210-9
See also under Comey
Comegys — Hanson's Kent Md. 224-9
Comer — Cleveland's Yates Co. 720
Comerford — Sanbornton N. H. 177
Comery — Eaton's Warren Me. 520
Comey — Comey Gen. (1896) 50 pages
See also under Comee
Comfort — Fell Genealogy 75-7
Comings — Hodgman's Westford 443-5
Comly — Martindale's Byberry 250-84
Commons — Young's Wayne Ind. 174-6
Compton — Chappell Gen. (1895) 106-17
Comstock — American Ancestry i, 16; v,
88; vii, 155; xi, 202
Austin's R. I. Genealogical Dictionary 280
Austin's Ancestral Dictionary 16
Baker's History of Montville Ct. 132-52
Ballou's History of Milford Mass. 667
Bangor Historical Mag. iv, 125; vii, 119
Bassett's History of Richmond N. H. 378
Bulkley's Browne Memorial 19
Caulkin's History of New London Ct. 205
Champion Genealogy 57
Cleveland's Hist. of Yates Co. N. Y. 460-2
Hall's History of Norwalk Ct. 185-96
Hayward's History of Gilsum N. H. 289
Hayward's History of Hancock N. H. 461
Hinman's Connecticut Settlers 682-91
Morris Genealogy (1887) 111 116-8
Narr. Historical Register iv, 63-5
Orcutt's History of New Milford Ct. 689
Richardson's Woodsocket R. I. 242-8

Savage's Genealogical Dictionary i, **439**
Sedgwick's History of Sharon Ct. 73
Selleck's Norwalk Ct. (1896) 250-65
Turner's Phelps Purchase N. Y. 223
Wheeler's History of Newport N. H. 348-80
Conable — Cunnabell Genealogy
Conant — American Ancestry iv, 101, 111,
167; vii, 106
Cochrane's History of Antrim N. H. 434
Conant Chart (1884) 18x38 inches
Conant Genealogy (1887) 640 pages
Conant Lineage (1890) 18 pages
Daniels' History of Oxford Mass. 449
Eaton's History of Thomaston Me. 182
Herrick's History of Gardner Mass. 342
Heywood's Hist. Westminster Mass. 583-5
Hinman's Connecticut Settlers 691-3
Hollister's History of Pawlet Vt. 180
Hudson's History of Sudbury Mass. 438
Mitchell's Bridgewater Mass. 138-41
Paige's History of Hardwick Mass. 354
Potter's Concord Mass. Families 8
Power's Sangamon Co. Ill. Settlers 216
Savage's Genealogical Dictionary i, 440
Stearns' Hist. of Ashburnham Mass. 641-3
Stone's History of Beverly Mass. 18
Whitman Genealogy 101-5
Worcester's History of Hollis N. H. 370
Wyman's Charlestown Mass. Gens. i, **232**
Conard — Conrad Genealogy
Montgomery Genealogy (1897) 59-61
Conary — Eaton's Thomaston Me. 184
Conde — American Ancestry i, 16
Condict — Chambers' N. J. Germans
Condit — Condit Genealogy (1885) 410 p.
Dodd Genealogy 91, 182
Shaw's History of Essex Co. N. J. ii, 722-4
Whittemore's Orange N. J. 51
Condon — Eaton's Thomaston Me. 183
Condy — Caulkin's New London Ct. 353
Pearson's Schenectady N. Y. Families 47
Cone — American Ancestry iv, 25; ix, 134
Andrews' History of New Britain Ct. 249
Field's History of Haddam Ct. 44
Hemenway's Vermont Historical Gaz. v
Hinman's Connecticut Settlers 693-6
Humphrey Genealogy 344
Hurlbut Genealogy 413
Loomis Genealogy (1880) 523-6
Paul's History of Wells Vt. 78
Savage's Genealogical Dictionary i, 441
Smith Genealogy (1890) 19-29
Walworth's Hyde Genealogy 783
Whittemore's Hist. Middlesex Co. Ct. 321
Conelly — Power's Sangamon Ill. 217
Coney — Breakenridge Genealogy 63-5
Congdon — Austin's R. I. Gen. Dict. 53
Austin's Allied Families 71-4
Baker's History of Montville Ct. 124-8
Newport Historical Magazine iv, 236-8
Conger — Williams' Danby Vt. 129
Conkey — Salem N. Y. Book 58
Conklin — American Ancestry i, 16; ii, 26
Cleveland's Hist. of Yates Co. N. Y. 491-5
Davis Genealogy (1888) 103-5
Frey Genealogy 34

Hedge's East Hampton N. Y. History 250-3
Littell's Passaic Valley 83-9, 499-501
Mallmann's Shelter Island N. Y. 300-4
Pompey N. Y. Reunion 288
Power's Sangamon Co. Ill. Settlers 215
Savage's Genealogical Dictionary i, 441
Conkling — American Ancestry x, 63
Essex Inst. Hist. Collection xxxi, 43-53
Hayes' Wells Genealogy 89
New York Gen. and Biog. Rec. xxvii, 152-9
Sedgwick's History of Sharon Ct. 73
Conn — Cochrane's Antrim N. H. 435
Stearns' Hist. of Ashburnham Mass. 643-5
Connable — Cunnabell Genealogy
Conner — Clute's Staten Island 357
Dearborn's History of Parsonsfield Me. 372
Hanson's Old Kent Md. 79
Runnell's Sanbornton N. H. ii, 178-82
Savage's Genealogical Dictionary i, 443
Wheeler's History of N. Carolina ii, 82
See also under Connor
Connet — American Ancestry vi, 144
Conant Genealogy 563-71
Littell's Passaic Valley Genealogies 89
Connor — American Ancestry iv, 14
Bell's History of Exeter N. H. 7-9
Cogswell's Hist. of Henniker N. H. 525-33
Hoyt's Salisbury Mass. Families 113
Welles' Am. Family Antiquity ii, 193-236
See also under Conner
Conover — Bergen Genealogy 140
Roome Genealogy 175
Salter's History of Monmouth Co. N. J. xx
Welles' Am. Family Antiquity iii, 113-62
Conrad — Am. Ancestry vii, 197; viii, 78
Conrad Genealogy (1891) 128 pages
Conroy — Temple's No. Brookfield 556
Worcester's History of Hollis N. H. 370
Consaulus — Munsell's Albany iv, 127
Pearson's Schenectady N. Y. Settlers 48
Constable — Bartow Genealogy 197-200
Hanson's Old Kent Md. 85
Hough's History of Lewis Co. N. Y. 238-42
Constant — Power's Sangamon 218-24
Contee — Bowie Genealogy 430-45
Contesse — Richmond Standard i, 49
Constantine — Ashburnham 645-8
Converse — American Ancestry i, 16; x, 67
Bemis' History of Marlboro N. H. 450-3
Convers Family of Bedford (1897) 97 pages
Converse Genealogy (1887) 241 pages
Draper's History of Spencer Mass. 188
Haywood's History of Gilsum N. H. 280
Hemenway Genealogy 55-8
Hubbard's Stanstead County Canada 302
Hyde's History of Brimfield Mass. 391
Morris Genealogy (1899) 41-6
New Eng. Hist. and Gen. Register l. 346-52
Randall's Hist. of Chesterfield N. H. 256-8
Roe's Sketches of Rose N. Y. 195
Saunderson's Charlestown N. H. 311
Savage's Genealogical Dictionary i, 443-5
Secomb's History of Amherst N. H. 543-5
Sewall's History of Woburn Mass. 72, 176
Stearns' History of Rindge N. H. 482-91
Temple's Hist. of N. Brookfield Mass. 557

Temple's History of Palmer Mass. 437
Timlow's Sketches of Southington Ct. 72
Vinton Genealogy 23
Vinton's Richardson Genealogy 248
Walworth's Hyde Genealogy 633
Washburn's Hist. of Leicester Mass. 353
Winchester Mass. Record i, 233
Wyman's Charlestown Mass. Gens. i, 234
Conway — Am. Ancestry iv, 204; xii, 41
Bassett's History of Richmond N. H. 370
Carter Family Tree
Clarke's Old King Wm. Va. Families
Hayden's Virginia Genealogies 222-90
Meade's Old Families of Virginia
Norton's History of Knox Co. Ohio 297
Slaughter's St. Mark's Parish 129, 158
Conyers — N. Y. Gen. Dict. xxvi, 24-6
Cony — Butler's Farmington 430-4
Cony Genealogy (1885) 39 pages
Guild Genealogy 29-32
Maine Hist. and Gen. Recorder i, 207-9
North's History of Augusta Me. 836-9
Conyn — Munsell's Albany iv, 109
Conyngham — Kulp's Wyoming Valley
Penn. Mag. of History and Biog. vii, 204
Cook — American Ancestry i, 16; ii, 27;
vi, 21; ix, 196, 214; x, 91; xi, 186
Anderson's Waterbury Ct. i, app. 39
Andrews' History of New Britain Ct. 207
Austin's R. I. Genealogical Dict. 54, 282
Babson's History of Gloucester Mass. 74
Ballou's History of Milford Mass. 668-82
Ballou Gen. 163-9, 193-5, 348-50, 396-407
Bassett's History of Richmond N. H. 371-6
Beckwith Genealogy (1899) 36, 52, 71
Bond's Watertown Mass. 163, 743
Boyd's Annals of Winchester Ct 302-4
Bronson's History of Waterbury Ct. 485-7
Capron Genealogy 46-53, 217-21
Chapman's Trowbridge Genealogy 39-41
Cook Family of Plymouth (1870) 20 pages
Cooke Family of Mass. and Ct. (1882) 36 p.
Cooke Family of Virginia (1896) 48 pages
Cooley's Trenton N. J. Genealogies 42-4
Cope Genealogy 44, 78-82, 157, 175
Daniels' History of Oxford Mass. 449
Davis' History of Wallingford Ct. 671-718
Davis' Landmarks of Plymouth Mass. 69
Dyer's History of Plainfield Mass. 138
Fox's History of Dunstable Mass. 242
Freeman's Cape Cod ii, 366, 389, 642
Hazen's History of Billerica Mass. 25
Hemenway's Vermont Hist. Gaz. v, 36
Hibbard's History of Goshen Ct. 448-52
Hinman's Connecticut Settlers 698-703
Hobart's History of Abington Mass. 363
Hollister's History of Pawlet Vt. 179
Howell's Hist. of Southampton N. Y. 212-7
Hubbard's Hist. Stanstead Co. Canada 288
Hubbard's History of Springfield Vt. 260-3
Humphrey Genealogy 281-3
Judd's History of Hadley Mass. 465-71
Kellogg's White Genealogy 77
Kidder's History of New Ipswich N. H. 352
Mitchell's Hist. of Bridgewater Mass. 141
Nash Genealogy 33

Orcutt's History of Torrington Ct. 677-80
Paige's History of Cambridge Mass. 513-6
Pearson's Schenectady N. Y. Settlers 49
Poole Genealogy 92-4
Poore Genealogy 29, 52-5
Randall's Hist. of Chesterfield N. H. 258
Read's History of Swanzey N. H. 313-5
Rich's History of Truro Mass. 424
Richardson's Woonsocket R. I. 224-33
Stearns' History of Ashburnham Mass. 648
Stiles' History of Windsor Ct. ii, 161-6
Strong Genealogy 339-44, 1380-7
Temple's History of Northfield Mass. 424
Timlow's Sketches of Southington Ct. 63
Tuttle Genealogy 645-8
Williams' History of Danby Vt. 130-2
Wyman's Charlestown Mass. Gens. 235-7
Cooke — American Ancestry iv, 92
Baldwin's Candee Genealogy 149-58
Bartlett and Russell Families
Cooke Genealogy, see Cook Genealogy
Cutter Genealogy 290-5
Cutter's History of Arlington Mass. 205-8
Driver Genealogy 508
Hanson's Old Kent Md. 244
Jackson's History of Newton Mass. 247-50
Kellogg's White Genealogy 48
Nourse Genealogy 44-57
Slaughter's St. Mark's Parish Va. 155
Temple's History of N. Brookfield Mass. 558
Tompkins Genealogy 36
Welles' American Fam. Antiquity ii, 31-87
Cookery — Wyman's Charlestown 237
Cooks — Paul's History of Wells Vt. 75
Cookson — Farrow's Islesborough 189
Cool — Chambers' N. J. Germans
See also Kool and Cole
Coolbroth — See Galbraith
Cooledge — Cochrane's Antrim 436-8
Hudson's History of Lexington Mass. 47
Morse Memorial appendix
Savage's Genealogical Dictionary i, 451-3
Cooley — American Ancestry i, 16
Atkins' History of Hawley Mass. 56
Buckingham Genealogy 260-2
Caverly's History of Pittsford Vt. 697
Chapman Genealogy 53
Cooley's Trenton N. J. Genealogies 44-54
Craft's History of Whately Mass. 415-7
Ely Genealogy 150, 321
Goodwin's Olcott Genealogy 26
Guild's Stiles Genealogy 193-6
Hinman's Connecticut Settlers 704
Longmeadow Mass. Centennial app. 47-56
New Eng. Historical and Genealogical Register xxv, 25-7, 159; xxxiv, 386-9
Saunderson's Charlestown N. H. 312
Savage's Genealogical Dictionary i, 453
Sheldon's Hist. of Deerfield Mass. ii, 129-33
Smith's History of Sunderland Mass. 302-9
Stiles' History of Windsor Ct. ii, 166
Strong Genealogy 1325-9
Temple's History of Palmer Mass. 435-7
Warren and Clarke Genealogy 49
West Springfield Mass. Centennial 115

Coolidge — American Ancestry x, 92
Barry's Framingham Mass. History 215
Bemis' History of Marlboro N. H. 453
Bond's Watertown Mass. 165-86, 743-9
Clark Genealogy (1866) 73, 124
Converse Genealogy
Coolidge Family Chart (1899)
Greene's Todd Genealogy
Harris' Watertown Mass. Elitaphs 14-8
Hayward's History of Hancock N. H. 462
Heywood's Hist. Westminster Mass. 586-9
Jackson's History of Newton Mass. 251
Leland Genealogy 270
Morse's Sherborn Mass. Settlers 62-4
Norton's Hist. of Fitzwilliam N. H. 521-3
Paige's History of Cambridge Mass. 516
Randall's History of Chesterfield N. H. 259
Stearns' History of Ashburnham Mass. 649
Washburne's Notes on Livermore Me. 31
Waterford Me. Centennial 56
Coombs — Bangor Historical Mag. vii, 174
Coombs Manuscript in Me. Gen. Soc. Lib. 50 pages
Eaton's History of Thomaston Me. 184-6
Farrow's Hist. of Islesborough Me. 175-87
Knox Co. Me. Hist. Mag. i, 19-23, 33
White and Coombs Genealogy (1872) 81 p.
Coomes — Longmeadow Centennial 56
New Eng. Hist. and Gen. Reg. xxxv, 161
Coon — American Ancestry ii, 27
Greene Genealogy (1894)
Marshall Genealogy (1884) 142-4
Munsell's Albany Collections iv, 138
Coons — American Ancestry ii, 27
Cooper — American Ancestry i, 17; ii, 27; iv, 80; v, 212; vii, 231; viii, 56; ix, 149
Austin's R. I. Genealogical Dict. 54
Bangor Historical Mag. ii, 40; v, 45-7
Bolton's Westchester Co. N. Y. ii, 718
Chambers' Early Germans of N. J. 302
Cochrane's Hist. of Francestown N. H. 596
Clement's Newtown N. J. Settlers
Cooper Family Ancestors (1879) chart
Cooper Family of Rowley (1885) 11 pages
Cooper Family of Boston (1890) 11 pages
Cooper Family of New Jersey (1896) chart
Cushman's History of Sheepscott Me. 369
Daniels' History of Oxford Mass. 449
Davis' Landmarks of Plymouth Mass. 70
Dickerman Genealogy 142-4
Eaton's Annals of Warren Me. 521
Eaton's History of Thomaston Me. 186
Essex Inst. Coll. xx, 226-9; xxv, 119-23
Freeman's Hist. of Cape Cod Mass. ii, 276
Futhey's History of Chester Co. Pa. 502
Goode Genealogy 156
Hanson's History of Gardiner Me. 137
Heywood's Hist. of Westminster Mass. 589
Hinman's Connecticut Settlers 705-8
Howell's Southampton N. Y. 217-26
Hudson's History of Lexington Mass. 47
Leland Genealogy 117-9
Littell's Passaic Valley Genealogies 90-2
Machias Me. Centennial 158
Maine Hist. and Gen. Recorder ii, 85-93
Morrison Genealogy 248

Munsell's Albany Collections iv, 110
New Eng. Hist. and Gen. Reg. xliv, 53-61
New York Gen. and Biog. Record xv, 9-11
Paige's History of Cambridge Mass. 516
Power's Sangamon Co. Ill. Settlers 224-8
Preble County Ohio History 192
Reily's Life of Cardinal Gibbons v, 128-30
Richmond Va. Standard iii, 36
Roome Genealogy 135
Savage's Genealogical Dictionary i, 543-5
Swift's Barnstable Mass. Families 192-4
Walker Genealogy (1896) 219-21
Washington N. H. History 347
Wheeler's Croydon N. H. Centennial 84
Wyman's Charlestown Mass. i, 238-40
Coote — Whitmore's Heraldic Journal i, 166-8; iii, 24-6
Cope — Am. Ancestry iv, 137; v, 24; ix, 183
Cope Genealogy (1861) 251 pages
Cope Ancestral Chart (1879) 12x18 inches
Futhey's History of Chester Pa. 502-4
Copeland — Bangor Hist. Magazine i, 137
Bass' History of Braintree Vt. 126-8
Binney Genealogy
Burleigh's Guild Genealogy 67
Cochrane's Hist. of Francestown N. H. 597
Deane's History of Scituate Mass. 242
Eaton's Annals of Warren Me. 521-4
French's History of Turner Me. 52
Hayward's History of Hancock N. H. 463
Kingman's N. Bridgewater Mass. 470-3
Merrill's History of Acworth N. H. 202
Mitchell's Hist. of Bridgewater Mass. 141
Savage's Genealogical Dictionary i, 455
Thayer Memorial (1835)
Washington N. H. History 347
Coperthwait—Cregar's Haines Genealogy
Copley — Hinman's Conn. Settlers 709
Whitmore's Heraldic Jour. (1868) iv, 175-82
Copp — American Ancestry vii, 152
Baker's History of Montville Ct. 528-30
Daniels' History of Oxford Mass. 450
Hubbard's Hist. Stanstead Co. Canada 233
Morrison's History of Windham N. H. 304
New Eng. Hist. and Gen. Register x, 369
Runnell's Sanbornton N. H. 11, 182-7
Savage's Genealogical Dictionary i, 456
Whitmore's Copps Hill Epitaphs
Coppock — Potts' Carter Genealogy 169
Sharpless Genealogy 149, 287
Corbett — Ballou's Milford Mass. 682-8
Butler's History of Farmington Me. 434-7
Calnek's History of Annapolis N. S. 494
Collins' History of Hillsdale N Y. app. 50
Hinman's Connecticut Settlers 712
Lincoln's History of Hingham Mass. ii, 138
Miller's Colchester Co. Nova Scotia 211-5
Sedgwick's History of Sharon Ct. 73
Corbin — American Ancestry i, 17
Bemis' History of Marlboro N. H. 455
Bowens of Woodstock Ct. 169
Boyd's Annals of Winchester Ct. 113
Carter Family Tree
Crafts Genealogy 238
Daniels' History of Oxford Mass. 490
Davis Genealogy 16, 60, 70

Dwight Genealogy 592
Hinman's Connecticut Settlers 711
Lee Genealogy (1895) 83-9
Meade's Old Families of Virginia ii, 145
Richmond Va. Standard iii, 20, 38
Sanderson's Charlestown N. H. 313-5
Wheeler's History of Newport N. H. 351-3
Wight Genealogy 69-71
Cordell — Hayden's Virginia Gen. 638
Richmond Va. Standard iii, 6
Cordis — Pierce Genealogy (1894)
Wyman's Charlestown Mass. Gens. i, 240-2
Corey — Ammidown Genealogy 53
Bassett's History of Richmond N. H. 376
Bemis' History of Marlboro N. H. 455
Bond's Hist. of Watertown Mass. 187, 749
Brown's Bedford Mass. Families 7
Cogswell Genealogy 142
Foster Genealogy (1889) 91-4
Hayward's History of Gilsum N. H. 290
Hodgman's History of Westford Mass. 443
Leonard's History of Dublin N. H. 325
Norton's Hist. of Fitzwilliam N. H. 523-5
Savage's Genealogical Dictionary i, 459
Stearns' Hist. of Ashburnham Mass. 650-5
Walker Genealogy 52
Washington N. H. History 448-50
Woods' Brookline Mass. Sketches 181-5
Coriell — Littell's Passaic Valley 92-5
Corlet — Cutter Genealogy 14-8
Corlett — Paige's Cambridge Mass. 517
Corlew — Deane's Scituate Mass. 243
Corley — Hudson's History of Lexington 35
Corlies — American Ancestry xi, 63
Corliss — American Ancestry vi, 101; vii, 84, 210, 226; xi, 74; xii
Corliss Genealogy (1875) 337 pages
Corliss' North Yarmouth 285-93, 326-33
Hoyt's Salisbury Mass. Families 113
Little's History of Weare N. H. 797-9
McKeen's History of Bradford Vt. 287-91
Morrison's Hist. of Windham N. H. 405-8
Orford N. H. Centennial 105-8
Poor's Merrimac Valley Researches 104
Corneilisen — Bergen's Kings Co. 69
Cornelius — American Ancestry ii, 27
Bunker's Long Island Genealogies 192-5
Cornell — American Ancestry i, 17; iii, 123, 139; iv, 33, 145
Austin's R. I. Genealogical Dictionary 54
Baird's History of Rye N. Y. 454
Bergen's Kings Co. N. Y. Settlers 71-4
Bolton's Westchester Co. N. Y. ii, 719-24
Cornell Genealogy (1896) 1 page 7x14 inches
Cornell's Westchester N. Y. (1890) 47 pages
Hazen's History of Billerica Mass. 26
Hinman's Connecticut Settlers 725
Mott Genealogy 327-69
New York Gen. and Biog. Record xxxi, 180
Prime's Sands Genealogy 69-72
Cornforth — Hatch's Industry 562-5
Corning—American Ancestry i, 17; ix, 210
Bliss Genealogy 691-701
Dodge Ancestry (1896) 19
Hinman's Connecticut Settlers 713-22

Cornish — Davis' Landmarks 70-2
Hinman's Connecticut Settlers 722-4
Savage's Genealogical Dictionary i, 458
Cornu — Stearns' Ashburnham 655
Cornwall — Andrews' New Britain 229
Goodwin's Foote Genealogy 245
Hall's Genealogical Notes (1886) 152
Hinman's Connecticut Settlers 724
New Eng. Hist. and Gen. Reg. xlix, 39-45
Cornwallis — Neill's Carolorum 99
Cornwell — American Ancestry ii, 28
Coe and Ward Memorial 52-5
Kellogg's White Genealogy 27
Middlefield Ct. History
Savage's Genealogical Dictionary i, 459
Corp — Austin's R. I. Gen. Dictionary 56
Corr — Clarke's King Wm. Va. Fams.
Correll — Power's Sangamon 228-30
Corse — Morris Genealogy (1898) 629
Sheldon's Deerfield 133-6, 388
Temple's Northfield Mass. 425
Corsen — Clute's Staten Island 358-62
Corser — American Ancestry x, 43
Coffin's History of Boscawen N. H. 497-509
Corson — American Ancestry, ix, 163
Davis' History of Bucks County Pa. 357
Dearborn's History of Salisbury N. H. 531
Neff Genealogy 316
Corss — American Ancestry ix, 54
Corteis — Barry's Hanover 272-88
Cortelyou —Bergen Genealogy 90, 128, 150
Bergen's Kings Co. N. Y. Settlers 74-6
Clute's History of Staten Island N. Y. 363
Honeyman's Our Home Magazine 242
Nevius Genealogy
Van Brunt Genealogy 18
Corthell — Barry's Hanover Mass. 271
Hobart's History of Abington Mass. 365
Lincoln's History of Hingham Mass. ii, 140-4
Whitman Genealogy 141
Cortlandt — Heraldic Journal iii, 70, 150
Cortright — Gumaer's Deer Park 69
Corwin — Cleveland's Yates County 556
Chambers' Early Germans of N. J. 303-8
Corwin Genealogy (1872) 284 pages
Corwin Parentage (1881) 19 pages
Essex Inst. Hist. Collections xvii, 331-48
Hinman's Connecticut Settlers 788
Corwith — Howell's Southampton 226
Cory — American Ancestry xii
Austin's R. I. Gen. Dict. 56
Littell's Passaic Valley Genealogies 94-8
Stearns' History of Rindge N. H. 469
Cosed — Chambers' N. J. Germans
Cosgrove — Barlow Genealogy 249-346
Cosmore — Hinman's Settlers 727-9
Cossart — N. Y. Gen. Rec. xxviii, III, 131, 243; xxix, 114
Cossett — Cossett Gen. 16 mo. (1885)
Hinman's Connecticut Settlers 727-9
Cost — Turner's Phelps Purchase 228
Coster — American Ancestry viii, 240
Munsell's Albany Collections iv, 110
Cotelle — Swift's Barnstable i, 250
Cotheal — American Ancestry ix, 141

Cothren — American Ancestry v, 215
Butler's History of Farmington Me. 437-9
Cothren's History of Woodbury Ct. ii, 1482
Hinman's Connecticut Settlers 730-3
Cotter — Gold's Hist. of Cornwall Ct. 275
Cotting — Cutter's Arlington Mass. 208
Hudson's Hist. of Marlborough Mass. 351
Cottle — American Ancestry viii, 206
Hatch's History of Industry Me. 565-7
Hoyt's Salisbury Mass. Families 114
Morrison's History of Windham N. H. 408
Poor's Merrimac Valley Researches 169
See also under Cottrell
Cotton — Allen's Worcester Asso. 154-6
American Ancestry viii, 128; ix, 124, 170
Cotton Pedigree by Drake 13x21 inches
Cotton Ancestry (1868) 12 pages, reprint
Davis' Landmarks of Plymouth Mass. 72
Dorr Genealogy
Dow's History of Hampton N. H. 646-9
Dudley Genealogy 121
Durant's Hist. of Lawrence Co. Pa. 180-2
Freeman's Cape Cod Mass. i, 361; ii, 276
Hinman's Connecticut Settlers 734-6
Hoyt's Salisbury Mass. Families 117
Jackson's History of Newton Mass. 251-3
Kellogg's White Genealogy 52
Lapham's History of Woodstock Me. 196
N. E. Hist. and Gen. Reg. i, 164-6; iv, 92; xlix, 180-2
Norton's History of Knox Co. Ohio 297
Pierce's History of Gorham Me. 158
Savage's Genealogical Dictionary i, 462-5
Scott Genealogy 143-67
Sewell's History of Woburn Mass. 337-40
Vinton's Giles Genealogy 77
Wetmore Genealogy 327
Whitmore's Heraldic Journal iv, 49-57
Cottrell — American Ancestry i, 17
Austin's R. I. Genealogical Dictionary 57
Farrow's History of Islesborough Me. 190
See also under Cotlle
Cottrill — Hemenway's Gazetteer, iv, 520
Cottymore — Dunstable Bi-Cent. 171-3
Couch—American Ancestry xii, 35
Coffin's Boscawen N. H. 510-6
Dearborn's Hist. of Salisbury N. H. 532-5
Hinman's Connecticut Settlers 737
Jessup Genealogy 97-104
Nash Genealogy 117
Richmond Va. Standard i, 46
Schenck's History of Fairfield Ct. 363-6
Todd's History of Redding Ct. 187-9
Young's Hist. Chautauqua Co. N. Y. 596
Coues — Brewster's Portsmouth 245
Coughlan — Lincoln's Hingham ii, 744
Coughlin — Stearns' Ashburnham 655
Coughtry — American Ancestry i, 17
Counce — Eaton's Thomaston Me. 188
Eaton's Annals of Warren Me. 524
Wyman's Charlestown Mass. Gens. i, 244
Council — Power's Sangamon Ill. 230-2
Courtenay — Amer. Ancestry vi, 171
Richmond Va. Standard iii, 6
Courter — American Ancestry viii, 138
Couse — Chambers' N. J. Germans 310

Cousins — Corliss' North Yarmouth Me.
Hinman's Connecticut Settlers 739
Morse's Sherborn Mass. Settlers 65
Ricker's Poland Me. Centennial 104
Ridlon's Saco Valley Me. Families 590-7
Coutant — Sylvester's Ulster N. Y. 250
Couwenhoven — Roome Genealogy 139
Covel — Freeman's Cape Cod ii, 597
Covell — Roe's Sketches Rose N. Y. 157
Covenhoven — Meginnes' History of West
    Branch Valley Pa. 618-20
Covert — American Ancestry i, 17
Calnek's History of Annapolis N. S. 495
Covey — Austin's R. I. Gen. Dict. 58
Covil — New Eng. Hist. Reg. xxxi, 280
Covington — Baldwin Genealogy 1056
Davis' Landmarks of Plymouth Mass. 73
Coward — Salter's Monmouth N. J. 21
Cowden — Egle's Pa. Gens. 2d ed. 143-7
Cowdrey — American Ancestry iii, 121
Eaton's History of Reading Mass. 58-60
Hodgman's Hist. of Westford Mass. 443
Cowdrick — American Ancestry vi, 14
Cowdry — Cogswell's Henniker 533
Hazen's History of Billerica Mass. 26
Paul's History of Wells Vt. 79
Wyman's Charlestown Mass. Gens. i, 245
Cowee — Heywood's Westminster 590-3
Cowel — Herrick's Gardiner Me. 344
Cowell — American Ancestry i, 18
Anderson's Waterbury Ct. i, app. 41
Hall's Trenton N. J. Presb. Church 233
Savage's Genealogical Dictionary i, 466
Cowen — Deane's Scituate Mass. 243
Cochrane's Hist. of Francestown N. H. 597
Cowenhoven — Bergen Gen. 133, 146-8
Bergen's Kings Co. N. Y. Settlers 76-82
Riker's Annals of Newtown N. Y. 362-5
Cowing — Cleveland's Yates Co. 549
Eaton's History of Thomaston Me. 188
Mitchell's Hist. of Bridgewater Mass. 143
Cowland — Austin's R. I. Gen. Dict. 58
Cowles — American Ancestry i, 18; vii,
    218; viii, 225; ix, 23
Andrews' Hist. of New Britain Ct. 230
Cole Genealogy (1887)
Cowles Family Chart (1893) 1x1 1-2 feet
Davis' History of Wallingford Ct. 719
Doolittle's Hist. of Belchertown Mass. 270
Hubbard's Stanstead Co. Canada 138
Judd's History of Hadley Mass. 471-3
Morse Genealogy 166
Orcutt's History of Torrington Ct. 680
Savage's Genealogical Dictionary 466
Timlow's Sketches of Southington Ct.64-72
Cowley — Cowley Genealogy (1881) 35 p.
Olin Genealogy by Nye (1892) 69-79
Cowman — Thomas Genealogy (1877) 67
Thomas Genealogy (1896) 291-3
Cowpland — Martin's Chester 271-3
Cox — American Ancestry i, 18; ii, 28; vi,
    113; ix, 81; xi, 26; xii
Bond's Watertown Mass. Genealogies 188
Cox Genealogy (1898) 40 pages
Cox Association Proceedings (1899) 8 pages
Davis' Landmarks of Plymouth Mass. 73

Eaton's Annals of Warren Me. 525
Futhey's History of Chester Co. Pa. 505-8
Greenlaw's Gen Advertiser (1898) i, 81-90
Joslin's History of Poultney Vt. 241
Lapham's History of Norway Me. 484
Malden Mass. Bi-Centennial 245
Maris Genealogy 110
McAllister Genealogy 73-1
Miller's Colchester Co. Nova Scotia 299-308
North's History of Augusta Me. 840-2
Paige's History of Cambridge Mass. 518
Paige's History of Hardwick Mass. 355
Potts Genealogy (1895) 341
Preble Genealogy 240-2
Preble's Life of John Cox (1871) 24 pages
Savage's Genealogical Dictionary i, 466
Sawin Genealogy 21-4
Sharpless Genealogy 296
Young's History of Wayne Co. Ind. 340
Wyman's Charlestown Mass. Gens. i, 245
Coxe — American Ancestry ii, 28
Hall's Trenton N. J. Presb. Church 236
Penn. Mag. of History and Biog. 457
Coy — Barry's Framingham Mass. 215
Coye — Hyde's Brimfield Mass. 391
Coyner — Keinadt Genealogy 102-41
Cozens — Morse Genealogy app. 49
Savage's Genealogical Dictionary i, 460
Cozzens — Barry's Framingham 216
Hinman's Connecticut Settlers 739
Spooner Genealogy i, 405
Crabb — Egle's Pa. Gens. 2d ed. 351-4
Savage's Genealogical Dictionary i, 468
Thomas Genealogy (1896) 556 h-j
Cradock — New Eng. Hist. and Gen. Reg-
    ister viii, 25-8; ix, 122-6; x, 231
Roberts' Cradock Biog. (1856)
Whitmore's Heraldic Journal (1865) i
Craft — American Ancestry xi, 3
Hinman's Connecticut Settlers 741
Hodgman's History of Westford Mass. 443
Jackson's History of Newton Mass. 263
Judd's Hist. of Hadley Mass. 473
Roe's Sketches of Rose N. Y. 214
See also Crafts
Crafton — Power's Sangamon Ill. 233
Crafts — Chandler Genealogy 275-7
Cothren's Woodbury Ct. 525; ii, 1476-8
Crafts Genealogy (1893) 803 pages
Craft's History of Whately Mass. 418-43
Dows Genealogy 185-8
Driver Genealogy 305
Ellis' History of Roxbury Mass. 94
Kingman's No. Bridgewater Mass. 473
Mitchell's Hist. of Bridgewater Mass. 143
Ruggles Genealogy
Savage's Genealogical Dictionary i, 469
Sheldon's History of Deerfield Mass. ii, 136
Temple's History of Whately Mass. 216-23
Cragbore — Paige's Cambridge 518
Cragen — Kidder's New Ipswich 353-5
Cragin — American Ancestry i, 18; viii, 87
Blood's History of Temple N. H. 213
Cragin Genealogy (1860) 38 pages
Hayward's History of Hancock N.H. 465-7
Livermore's History of Wilton N. H. 353

Sewall's History of Woburn Mass. 607
Smith's History Peterborough N. H. 42-4
Stearns' History of Rindge N. H. 492
Craig — American Ancestry x, 51; xi, 136
Bass' History of Braintree Vt. 128
Burleigh's Guild Genealogy 51
Butler's History of Farmington Me. 440-4
Chambers' Early Germans of N. J. 311
Chase's History of Chester N. H. 496-8
Clyde's Irish Settlement in Pa. 35-8
Cogswell's History of Henniker N. H. 534
Draper's History of Spencer Mass. 189
Egle's Penn. Genealogies 2d ed. 541-55
Hayward's History of Hancock N. H. 468
Littell's Passaic Valley Genealogies 98-100
Missouri Pioneer Families 244
North's History of Augusta Me. 842-4
Prentice Genealogy 414
Waddell's Ann. of Augusta Co. Va. 388-92
Washburn's History of Leicester Mass. 352
Washington N. H. History 350
Craighead — Craighead Genealogy (1876)
    173 pages
Craigue — Hayward's Hancock 469
Craik—Hayden's Virginia Genealogies 341
Slaughter's Fry Memoir 76
Crain — Egle's Pa. Gens. 2d ed. 148-55
Hubbard's History of Springfield Vt. 263-5
Washington N. H. History 352-62
Cralle — Hayden's Virginia 117-20
Cram — American Ancestry xii
Bass' History of Braintree Vt. 128
Cochrane's History of Antrim N. H. 439
Cochrane's Francestown N. H. 598-602
Cogswell's Nottingham N. H. 358-68
Dow's History of Hampton N. H. 649-51
Fullonton's Hist. of Raymond N. H. 193-7
Hayward's History of Hancock N. H. 470
Hurd's History of Rockingham Co. N H.
    446
Lane Genealogy (1891) 160-2
Little's History of Weare N. H. 800-4
Livermore's History of Wilton N. H. 353-6
Morrill's History of Acworth N. H. 203
Poor's Merrimac Valley Researches 104
Runnel's Hist. Sanbornton N. H. ii, 187-9
Savage's Genealogical Dictionary 570
Washington N. H. History 350-2
Cramer — Chambers Early Germans of
    N. J. 312
Smith's Rhinebeck N. Y. 198
Crampton — American Ancestry ix, 220
Savage's Genealogical Dictionary i, 471
Stone Genealogy 16
Crance — American Ancestry ii, 28
Cranch — Alden's Am. Epitaphs iii, 13
Crandall — Am. Ancestry ii, 28; iv, 95
Austin's R. I. Genealogical Dictionary 58
Austin's Allied Families 74-7
Crandall Family of R. I. (1860) 8 pages
Crandall Family of R. I. (1888) 63 pages
Greene Genealogy (1894)
Hayward's History of Gilsum N. H. 293
Longmeadow's Mass. Centennial app. 57
Roe's Sketches of Rose N. Y. 203
Stanton Genealogy 490

Waldo's History of Tolland Ct. 86
Williams' History of Danby Vt. 132
Crandon — Davis' Landmarks 74
Crane — American Ancestry i, 18; iii, 11,
    119; iv, 20; v, 157; vi, 68; viii, 33; ix,
    129
Bassett's History of Richmond N. H. 377
Cothren's Hist. of Woodbury Ct. ii, 1483-6
Crane Family of Milton (1893) 26 pages
Crane Genealogy (1895) 2 vols.
Daniels' History of Oxford Mass. 451
Eaton's Annals of Warren Me. 526
Goode Genealogy 152, 291
Herrick Genealogy (1885) 124
Hinman's Connecticut Settlers 742-51
Jameson's History of Medway Mass. 468
Lane Genealogy (1899) 13
Littell's Passaic Valley Gens. 100-10, 498
Longmeadow Mass. Centennial, app. 57
Maine Historical Magazine viii, 177
Mitchell's Hist. of Bridgewater Mass. 143
New Eng. Hist. and Gen. Register xxvii.
    76-8; xli, 176; xlvi, 216-8; xlvii, 78-81,
    325-9
Norton's History of Fitzwilliam N. H. 524
Orcutt's History of New Milford Ct. 689
Orcutt's History of Stratford Ct. 1177
Perkins' Old Houses of Norwich Ct. 447
Savage's Genealogical Dictionary i, 471
Smith's History of Peterborough N. H. 445
Smith's Life of Zenas Crane 55
Stiles' History of Windsor Ct. ii, 167
Thayer Memorial (1835) 36
Trubee Genealogy 113
Washington N. H. History 352-62
Cranmer — Cregar's White Genealogy
Morris Genealogy (1898) 313
Crannell — American Ancestry i, 18
Munsell's Albany Collections iv, 110
Cranston — American Ancestry v, 83
Austin's Ancestries 87
Austin's R. I. Genealogical Dictionary 60
Cranston Genealogy (1889) 52 pages
Draper's History of Spencer Mass. 187
Hudson's Hist. of Marlborough Mass. 352
Martin's History of Chester Pa. 108-10
Montague Genealogy 432-4
Narr. Historical Register vii, 342-56
Savage's Genealogical Dictionary i, 472
Whitmore's Heraldic Journal iii, 59-61
Crapo — Spooner Genealogy i, 176
Crapser — American Ancestry ii, 29
Crary — Hinman's Conn. Settlers 752
Savage's Genealogical Dictionary i, 472
Crater — American Ancestry x, 41, xii, 108
Crater Genealogy (1894) 27 pages
Chambers' Early Germans of N. J. 312-6
Crathorne — Penn. Mag. iv, 491-500
Cravens — Nourse Genealogy 89-92
Craver — American Ancestry i, 19; ii, 29
Crawford — Am. Ancestry v, 71; x, 184
Austin's R. I. Genealogical Dictionary 61
Bangor Hist. Magazine i, 144-6
Chase's History of Chester N. H. 498
Crawford Genealogy (1883) 194 pages
Daniels' History of Oxford Mass. 452

Eaton's Annals of Warren Me. 527–9
Egle's Notes and Queries 2d ser. ii, 165–7
Gilmore's Georgians 123
Hayden's Weitzel Genealogy (1883) 58–60
Hemenway's Vt. Hist. Gazetteer v, 245
Johnson Genealogy Supp. (1896) 204–26
Lapham's History of Paris Me. 353
Meade's Old Families of Virginia
New York Gen. and Biog. Rec. xvi, 110–4
Pearson's Schenectady N. Y. Settlers 51
Peyton's History of Augusta Co. Va. 314
Reed's History of Rutland Mass. 155
Richmond Va. Standard ii, 6; iii, 28
Ruttenber's Newburgh N. Y. 311–3
Waddell's Annals of Augusta Va. 423–30
Ward's History of Shrewsbury Mass. 262
Crawley — Chappell Genealogy (1895) 41–6
Creamer — Driver Genealogy 276
Creetman — Miller's Colchester 365–9
Cregar — Chambers' N. J. Germans
Cregier — Munsell's Albany iv, 111
Crego — American Ancestry ii, 29
Morris' Bontecou Genealogy 164
Crehore — Aldrich's Walpole N. H. 232
American Ancestry vi, 106
Crehore Genealogy (1887) 45 pages
Stearns' History of Ashburnham Mass. 655
Creigh — American Ancestry vi, 202
Creigh Family (1893) 7 pages
Egle's Penn. Genealogies 2d ed. 594
Egle's Notes and Queries 4th ser. i, 211
Creighton — Eaton's Warren 529–31
Eaton's History of Thomaston Me. 190
Odiorne Genealogy
Crenshaw — Goode Genealogy 78
Richmond Va. Standard ii, 30; iii, 29
Cresap — American Ancestry v, 27
Cressey — Cogswell's Henniker 534
Cochrane's Hist. Francestown N. H. 602–8
Cressey Genealogy (1877) 10 pages reprint
Guild's Stiles Genealogy 87
Huntington's Stamford Ct. Settlers 26
New Eng. Hist. and Gen. Register xxxi, 197–206
Pierce's History of Gorham Me. 159
Randall's Hist. of Chesterfield N. H. 260–2
Cresson — Cresson Genealogy (1888) 2 p.
Read's History of Swanzey N. H. 316
Creswell — Lincoln's Hingham ii, 146
Creter — Chambers' N. J. Germans 167
See also Crater
Crie — Eaton's Thomaston Me. 190
Crigler — Garr Genealogy 81
Crippen — American Ancestry i, 19
Caverly's History of Pittsford Vt. 698
Hinman's Connecticut Settlers 754
Loomis Genealogy (1880) 693–5
Sedgwick's History of Sharon Ct. 73
Cripps — Clute's Staten Island N. Y. 364
Crisler — Garr Genealogy 66, 76–80
Roe's Sketches of Rose N. Y. 276
Crispe — Bond's Watertown 188, 750
Crispell — Hoffman Genealogy 487
New York Gen. Record xxi, 83–6
Schoonmaker's Hist. of Kingston N. Y. 476
Crispin — Davis' Bucks County Pa. 300

Crissey — Am. Ancestry ix, 72; xii,115
Boyd's Annals of Winchester Ct. 270
Timlow's Southington Ct. Sketches 72–8
Young's Hist. of Chautauqua Co. N. Y. 563
Critchett — Chase's Chester N. H. 499
Critchfield — Norton's Knox Ohio 322
Crittenden — American Ancestry vi, 206
Atkins' History of Hawley Mass. 67
Green's Kentucky Families
Hinman's Connecticut Settlers 755
Joslin's History of Poultney Vt. 243
New Eng. Hist. and Gen. Reg. lii, 466–9
Richmond Va. Standard ii, 7·
Croasdale — Potts Genealogy (1895) 25–9
Crocker — Am. Ancestry ii, 29; xi, 135
Baker's History of Montville Ct. 531
Bangor Me. Historical Magazine v, 27
Barry's Hist. of Hanover Mass. 271
Caulkins' History of New London Ct. 361
Daniels' History of Oxford Mass. 453
Eaton's Annals of Warren Me. 531
Eaton's History of Thomaston Me. 195
Emery's History of Taunton Ministry i, 330
Freeman's Cape Cod Mass. ii, 281–304
Hinman's Connecticut Settlers 755–7
Hollister's History of Pawlet Vt. 181
Holton's Winslow Genealogy i, 264–71
Kingman's No. Bridgewater Mass. 480
Lapham's History of Paris Me. 563
Machias Me. Centennial 159
New Eng. Hist. and Gen. Register ii, 389
Savage's Genealogical Dictionary i, 474
Sedgwick's History of Sharon Ct. 74
Smith Genealogy (1895) 22–6
Smith's History of Sunderland Mass. 310–3
Swift's Barnstable Families i, 200–48
Young's History of Warsaw N. Y. 251
Crockett — Cogswell's Nottingham
Hayward's History of Hancock N. H. 471
Lapham's History of Norway Me. 484–7
Lapham's History of Woodstock Me. 197
Eaton's History of Thomaston Me. 191–5
Lane Genealogy (1891) 56–8
Peyton's History of Augusta Co. Va. 288
Pierce's History of Gorham Me. 160
Runnell's Sanbornton N. H. ii, 189–96
Wentworth Genealogy ii, 5–9, 91
Croff — Crafts Genealogy 751–68
Williams' History of Danby Vt. 133
Crofoot — Hinman's Conn. Settlers 767
Hough's History of Lewis Co. N. Y. 231
Croft — Crafts Genealogy 755–64
Orcutt's History of Derby Ct. 731–5
Savage's Genealogical Dictionary i, 475
Croll — Egle's Notes and Queries 3d ser. iii, 361
Crombie — Blood's Temple N. H. 215
Chase's History of Chester N. H. 500
Cogswell's New Boston N. H. 374–7
Cochrane's Hist. Francestown N. H. 608–10
Crommelin — N. Y. Gen. Rec. xxiv, 67–70
Crompton — Dawson Genealogy 143
Cromwell — American Ancestry x, 192
American Historical Register i, 867–73
Baird's History of Rye N. Y. 458
Bolton's Westchester Co. N. Y. ii, **724**

Dwight Strong Genealogy 160
Savage's Genealogical Dictionary i, 476
Tompkins Genealogy 38
Wentworth Genealogy i, 157
Cronise — American Ancestry iv, 241
Croode—Savage's Genealogical Dict. i, 473
Walker Genealogy 144
Crook — Evans' Fox Genealogy 108–18
Crooker — American Ancestry xi, 186
Barry's Hanover Mass. 271
Bassett's History of Richmond N. H. 378
Hinman's Connecticut Settlers 758
Lapham's History of Bethel Me. 514
Lapham's History of Norway Me. 487
New Eng. Hist. and Gen. Register xii, 68
Secomb's History of Amherst N. H. 545–7
Cropley — Calnek's Annapolis N. S. 496
Cropper — Hamilton's Wise Biography
Crosby — Adams' Haven Genealogy 23
American Ancestry i, 19, iii, 11; iv, 236;
    vi, 67; xi, 187
Atkins' History of Hawley Mass. 62
Ballou's History of Milford Mass. 690
Bangor Me. Hist. Mag. i, 81–3; ii, 105–17
Cleveland's History of Yates Co. N. Y. 143
Cochrane's Hist. of Francestown N. H. 610
Crosby Genealogy (1877) 143 pages
Crosby Family of N. Y. (1899) 24 pages
Cutter's History of Jaffrey N. H. 257–60
Dow's History of Hampton N. H. 651
Dudley's Arch. and Gen. Collection plate 4
Essex Mass. Institute Coll. xx, 230
Foster Genealogy (1889) 120–2
Freeman's History of Cape Cod ii, 213, 365
Gibb's History of Blandford Mass. 61
Hazen's History of Billerica Mass. 27–32
Hemenway's Vermont Hist. Gaz. v, 86
Hinman's Connecticut Settlers 759
Hudson's History of Lexington Mass. 47
Locke Genealogy 112
Maine Hist. and Gen. Recorder iv, 160
Martin's History of Chester Pa. 208–18
New York Gen. and Biog. Rec. xviii, 87–9;
    xxix, 190; xxx, 5–10, 73–9, 146–52
Norton's History of Fitzwilliam N. H. 525
Paige's History of Cambridge Mass. 519
Saunderson's Charlestown 245–7, 315–8
Savage's Genealogical Dictionary i, 476
Secomb's History of Amherst N. H. 547–51
Stearns' Hist. Ashburnham Mass. 656–60
Ward's History of Shrewsbury Mass. 255–8
Warren-Clarke Genealogy 51–3
Croscup — Calnek's Annapolis N. S. 496
Crosley — Sharpless Genealogy 232, 363
Crosman — American Ancestry vi, 197
Cross — American Ancestry viii, 169
Daniels' History of Oxford Mass. 453
Dearborn's History of Salisbury N. H. 535
Goode Genealogy 157
Hammatt Papers of Ipswich Mass. 66
Hayward's Hist. of Hancock N. H. 471–3
Hinman's Connecticut Settlers 761
Lapham's History of Bethel Me. 515
Little's History of Weare N. H. 804
Mitchell's Hist. of Bridgewater Mass. 144
Orford's N. H. Centennial 108

Paul's History of Wells Vt. 82
Pierce's History of Gorham Me. 160
Power's Sangamon Co. Ill. Settlers 236
Preble Genealogy 242
Read's History of Swanzey N. H. 316–8
Runnell's Sanbornton N. H. ii, 196–200
Savage's Genealogical Dictionary i, 477
Stiles' History of Windsor Ct. ii, 168
Crossett — Chase's Chester N. H. 500
Read's History of Swanzey N. H. 319
Crossman — Benedict's Sutton 628
N. Y. Gen. and Biog. Rec. xxii, 77–80
Savage's Genealogical Dictionary i, 478
Stackpole's History of Durham Me. 162
Croswell — Butler's Farmington 444–6
Davis' Landmarks of Plymouth Mass. 75
Hinman's Connecticut Settlers 760
Wyman's Charlestown Mass. Gens. 249
Crotcheron — Clute's Staten Island 364
Crouch — Cleveland's Yates Co. 388
Eaton's History of Thomaston Me. 195
Egle's Penn. Genealogies 2d ed. 145
Hayward's History of Gilsum N. H. 294
Hyde's History of Brimfield Mass. 393
Randall's History of Chesterfield N. H. 263
Read's History of Swanzey N. H. 319
Richmond Va. Standard iv, 2
Wyman's Charlestown Mass. i, 250–2
Crouse — Everhart Genealogy 103
Ross and Highland Co. Ohio
Crouss — Chute Genealogy, app. 41
Crow — Barbour's Wife and Mother 32
Dwight Genealogy 112–4
Hinman's Connecticut Settlers 763–7
Judd's History of Hadley Mass. 474
Miller's Colchester Co. N. S. 199–210
Porter's Hartford Connecticut Settlers 3
Power's Sangamon Co. Ill. Settlers 234
Savage's Genealogical Dict. i, 479
Stiles' History of Windsor Ct. 576
Talcott's N. Y. and N. E. Families 495–8
Crowder — Power's Sangamon 237–40
Crowell — American Ancestry iv, 210
Atkin's History of Hawley Mass. 61
Austin's Allied Families 78
Bangor Me. Historical Magazine iv, 216
Freeman's Cape Cod ii, 192–9, 708–14
Hinman's Connecticut Settlers 768
Middlefield Conn. History
Morrison's History of Windham N. H.
    414–6
Paige's History of Hardwick Mass. 355
Sears Genealogy 41, 143–5
Wheeler's Eminent N. Carolinians 203
Wheeler's History of N. Carolina ii, 199
Wheeler's History of Newport N. H. 354
Yarmouth Mass. Reg. May 9, 1850, 4 col.
Yarmouth Register July 4, 1896, reprint
Crowfoot — Savage's Gen. Dict. i, 480
See also under Crawford
Crowl — Power's Sangamon Ill. 235
Crowley — Williams' Danby Vt. 133
Crowninshield — Am. Ancestry iv, 126
Driver Genealogy 268–72, 327
Hudson's History of Lexington Mass. 48
Crozer — Crozer Genealogy (1866) 29 pages

Crozier — Cleveland's Yates 339-42
Davis' Hist. of Bucks Co. Pa. 109
Martin's History of Chester Pa. 454
Cruger — Cruger Chart (1892) 2x3 feet
Lamb's History of New York City i, 517
New York Genealogical and Biog. Record
  vi, 74-80, 180-2; xxiii, 147-9
Cruikshank — Salem N. Y. Book 48-51
Crumbie — Stearns' Rindge N. H. 493
Crump — Temple's Whately Mass. 223
Crumrine — American Ancestry vi, 153
Cruser — Clute's Staten Island N. Y. 366
Crutcher — American Ancestry ix, 20
Cruttenden — N. E. Hist. Reg. lii, 466-9
Savage's Genealogical Dictionary 481
Cubberly — Clute's Staten Island N. Y. 368
Cuddeback — Am. Anc. vii, 31, 171, 213
Gumaer's History of Deerpark N. Y. 41-50
N. Y. Gen. and Biog. Rec. xxvii, 145-52
Stickney's History of Minisink N. Y. 133
Cudworth — American Ancestry iii, 170
Bemis' History of Marlboro N. H. 456
Daniels' History of Oxford Mass. 453-5
Deane's History of Scituate Mass. 245, 251
Guild's Stiles Genealogy 474
Savage's Genealogical Dictionary i, 481
Stearns' History of Rindge N. H. 494
Swift's Barnstable Families i, 252-75
Culbertson — Am. Ancestry v, 39; viii, 124
Culbertson Genealogy (1893) 316 pages
Culbertson Genealogy Supp. (1896) 38 p.
Egle's Notes and Queries 2d ser. ii, 331-4
Culin — Carter Genealogy (1883) 85, 111-3
Cullen — Richmond Va. Standard iv, 3
Cullick — Hinman's Conn. Settlers 769-72
Porter's Hartford Ct. Settlers 4
Savage's Genealogical Dictionary i, 482
Culp — Kolb Genealogy
Culver — American Ancestry i, 20, x, 204;
  xi, 26; xii, 21
Anderson's Waterbury Ct. i. app. 41
Caulkins' History of New London Ct. 309
Davis' History of Wallingford Ct. 720-2
Hine's Lebanon Ct. Historical Address 151
Hinman's Connecticut Settlers 762-4
Howell's Hist. of Southampton N. Y. 228
Hurd's Hist. of New London Co. Ct. 511
Joslin's History of Poultney Vt. 244
Paul's History of Wells Vt. 83
Savage's Genealogical Dictionary i, 482
Smith's History of Dutchess Co. N. Y. 247
Strong Genealogy 915-7
Cumins — Hall's Trenton N. J. Ch. 194
Cumming — American Ancestry iv, 242
Goode Genealogy 192
Cummings — Alden's Epitaphs v, 215
American Ancestry vi, 55, 178
Bemis' History of Marlboro N. H. 457-61
Benedict's History of Sutton Mass. 629
Butler's History of Groton Mass. 393
Chambers' Early Germans of N. J. 317-20
Cochrane's History of Antrim N. H. 441
Cochrane's Hist. Francestown N. H. 610-2
Corliss' North Yarmouth Me. Magazine
Cummings Manuscript in Me. Gen. Soc.
  Lib. 23 pages

Cummings Family of Merrimack (1881) 8 p.
Cummings Family of Ipswich (1889) 3 p.
Cummings Family of Topsfield (1899) 39 p.
Daniels' History of Oxford Mass. 446-8
Densmore's Hartwell Genealogy
Draper's History of Spencer Mass. 186
Fox's History of Dunstable Mass. 240-2
Green's Kentucky Families
Hayward's Hist. of Hancock N. H. 473-81
Hazen's History of Billerica Mass. 32
Heywood's Hist. of Westminster Mass. 593
Hinman's Connecticut Settlers 774
Hudson's History of Lexington Mass. 278
Hyde's Hist. Address at Ware Mass. 48
Kidder's History of New Ipswich N. H. 355
Lapham's History of Bethel Me. 516
Lapham's History of Norway Me. 488-90
Lapham's History of Paris Me. 564-8
Lapham's History of Woodstock Me. 198
McKeen's History of Bradford Vt. 390
Merrill's History of Acworth N. H. 204
Morrison Genealogy 231
New Eng. Hist. and Gen. Reg. xxxiv, 344
Norton's Hist. of Fitzwilliam N. H. 525-7
Paige's History of Hardwick Mass. 356
Perley's History of Boxford Mass. 29
Power's Sangamon Co. Ill. Settlers 241
Read's History of Swanzey N. H. 320-2
Richmond Va. Standard iii, 2
Ridlon's Harrison Me. Settlers 54
Savage's Genealogical Dictionary i, 433
Sibley's History of Union Me. 441
Spooner Genealogy i, 356-8
Stearns' History of Ashburnham Mass. 660
Temple's Hist. of N. Brookfield Mass. 560
Temple's History of Palmer Mass. 432
Topsfield Hist. Society Colls. v, (1899)
Tyngsboro Mass. Centennial 18
Worcester's History of Hollis N. H. 371
Worthen's History of Sutton N. H. 676
Cummins — Cleveland's Topsfield 27
Cunnabell — Cunnabell Gen. (1886) 187
Cunningham — American Ancestry v, 65
Cochrane's Hist. of Francestown N. H. 612
Cushman's History of Sheepscott Me. 370
Davis' Landmarks of Plymouth Mass. 77-9
Draper's History of Spencer Mass. 183-5
Egle's Notes and Queries (1897) 2-3
Futhey's History of Chester Co. Pa. 508
Hinman's Connecticut Settlers 775
Missouri Pioneer Families 200
Smith's Hist. of Peterborough N. H. 45-8
Stark's History of Dunbarton N. H. 243
Temple's Hist. of N. Brookfield Mass. 561
Waddell's Annals of Augusta Co. Va. 442
Wyman's Charlestown Mass. Gens. i, 252
Cunred — Conrad Genealogy (1891) 128 p.
Cunyngham — Roberdeau Genealogy 9-39
Currie — Hayden's Virginia Gens. 239
Paxton's Marshall Genealogy 180
Richmond Va. Standard v. 20
Currier — American Ancestry iii, 12
Butler's History of Farmington Me. 446-8
Chase's History of Chester N. H. 501
Cogswell's History of Henniker N. H. 535
Cogswell's Nottingham N. H. 369-72

Dearborn's History of Salisbury N. H. 536
Fullonton's History of Raymond N. H. 192
Hazen's History of Billerica Mass. 33
Hoyt's Salisbury Mass. Families 118-24
Hubbard's Stanstead County Canada 277
Lancaster's History of Gilmanton N.H. 260
Little's History of Weare N. H. 806-8
Merrill's History of Acworth N. H. 205
Poor's Merrimac Valley Researches 115
Runnel's Hist. of Santornton N. H. ii, 201
Savage's Genealogical Dictionary i, 484
Smith's Founders of Mass. Bay 353
Thurston's History of Winthrop Me. 179
Wentworth Genealogy ii, 99
Curry — Egle's Notes and Queries 3d ser. i, 309
Eldredge Genealogy 31-3
Runnel's Sanbornton ii, 202-5
Curtenius — Oneida Hist. Society ii, 132-4
Curtin — American Ancestry vii, 81
Egle's Penn. Genealogies 2d ed. 296-301
Curtis — American Ancestry i, 20; ii, 29; iii, 69; ix, 240; xi, 213
Anderson's Waterbury Ct. i, app. 42
Barry's History of Hanover Mass. 272-88
Bass' History of Braintree Vt. 128
Bradbury's Hist. of Kennebunkport Me. 235
Brown's W. Simsbury Ct. Settlers 31-4
Cochrane's History of Antrim N. H. 442-5
Corliss' North Yarmouth Me. Magazine
Cothren's History of Woodbury Ct. 531-9
Craft Genealogy 84-6
Curtis Family of Roxbury (1869) 29 pages
Curtis Family of Wethersfield (1899) chart
Cushman's History of Sheepscott Me. 371
Daniels' History of Oxford Mass. 456
Davis' Landmarks of Plymouth Mass. 75
Davis' History of Wallingford Ct. 722-5
Deacon's Stoddard Genealogy
Deane's History of Scituate Mass. 251
Dodd's History of East Haven Ct. 115
Draper's History of Spencer Mass. 183
Eaton's History of Thomaston Me. 197
Ellis' History of Roxbury Mass. 94
Guild's (Calvin) Ancestry 8
Hall's Genealogical Notes (1886) 168
Hanover Mass. Records (1898)
Heywood's Hist. Westminster Mass. 594-6
Hinman's Connecticut Settlers 776-88
Huntington's Stamford Conn. Settlers 27
Kingman's No. Bridgewater Mass. 476
Lapham's History of Paris Me. 569
Lapham's History of Woodstock Me. 200
Lincoln's History of Hingham Mass. ii, 148
Livermore's History of Wilton N. H. 356
Loveland Genealogy i. 199-202
Mead's History of Greenwich Ct. 309
Meade's Old Churches of Virginia i, 262
Mitchell's Hist. of Bridgewater Mass. 144
New Eng. Hist. and Gen. Reg. xvi, 137; li, 166-8
Orcutt's History of Derby Ct. 715-7
Orcutt's History of Wolcott Ct. 472
Perley's History of Boxford Mass. 35
Ransom Genealogy 46
Read's History of Swanzey N. H. 322

Rodman Genealogy 112-4
Runnel's Hist. of Sanbornton N. H. ii, 205
Savage's Genealogical Dictionary i, 484-8
Secomb's History of Amherst N. H. 522
Sedgwick's History of Sharon Ct. 74
Upham Genealogy 52
Wall's Reminis. of Worcester Mass. 33-40
Walworth's Hyde Genealogy 599
Washington N. H. History 362
Winsor's History of Duxbury Mass. 249
Wyman's Charlestown Mass. Gens. i, 253
Curtiss — American Ancestry ix, 195
Andrews' History of New Britain Ct. 247
Cothren's Hist. of Woodbury Ct. ii, 1486-90
Foster Pedigree (1897)
Hubbard's Stanstead County Canada 168
Montague Genealogy 539-41
New Eng. Hist. and Gen. Register xliii, 321
Orcutt's Hist. of Stratford Ct. 1178-88, 1351
Orcutt's History of Torrington Ct. 681
Timlow's Sketches of Southington Ct. 73-8
Trubee Genealogy 115-7
Wheeler's History of Brunswick Me. 831
Curwen — Drake's Hist. of Boston Mass.
Essex Institute Hist. Collections ii, 228-30
Whitmore's Heraldic Journal i, (1865) 144-9
Vinton's Giles Gen. 339-44
Curwin — New Eng. Hist. Reg. x, 304
Savage's Genealogical Dictionary i, 488
Cushing — American Ancestry vii, 70; x, 6, 202; xi, 26
Bangor Me. Historical Magazine v. 185
Barry's History of Hanover Mass. 288-90
Binney Genealogy
Bond's Watertown Mass. Genealogies 189
Bridgeman's Copps Hill Epitaphs 223
Bridgeman's Granary Epitaphs 13
Buckingham Genealogy (1872) 242-5
Buckingham Genealogy (1892) 44-51
Carter's History of Pembroke N. H. ii, 53-8
Cushing Genealogy (1877) 117 pages
Cushing Lineage (1884) 19 pages
Davis' Landmarks of Plymouth Mass. 76
Deane's History of Scituate Mass. 254-60
Dearborn's Hist. of Salisbury N. H. 537-41
Eaton's Annals of Warren Me. 531
Freeman's Hist. of Cape Cod Mass. ii, 628
Hanover Mass. Records (1898)
Hoyt's Salisbury Mass. Families 124
Lincoln's Hist. Hingham Mass. ii, 150-85
Mitchell's Hist. Bridgewater Mass. 366-72
N. E. Hist. and Gen. Reg. viii, 41; xix, 39-41
Page Genealogy 197
Saunderson's Charlestown N. H. 318-21
Savage's Genealogical Dictionary i, 489-91
Smith Genealogy (1895) 60-73
Stackpole's History of Durham Me. 164
Stearns' Hist. of Ashburnham Mass. 661-8
Sumner Genealogy (1854) 57
Temple's Hist. of N. Brookfield Mass. 561
Turner Genealogy (1852)
Ward's History of Shrewsbury Mass. 252-4
Wheeler's History of Brunswick Me. 831
Whitmore's Heraldic Jour. ii, 123; iv, 55-7
Whitmore's Copps Hill Epitaphs
Winsor's History of Duxbury Mass. 249

Cushman — Adams Genealogy (1861) 23-6
Adams' History of Fairhaven Vt. 334-6
Am. Anc. i, 20; iii, 12; v, 39; ix, 99; xi, 75
Barrus' History of Goshen Mass. 142
Bass' History of Braintree Vt. 129
Butler's History of Farmington Me. 448-51
Corliss' North Yarmouth Me. Magazine
Cushman Genealogy (1855) 665 pages
Cushman Celebration (1855) 76 pages
Cushman Monument Proc. (1859) 96 pages
Davis' Landmarks of Plymouth Mass. 77-9
Eaton's Annals of Warren Me. 531
Lapham's History of Bethel Me. 517-9
Lapham's History of Norway Me. 490
Lapham's History of Paris Me. 570-3
Lapham's History of Woodstock Me. 202
Mitchell's Hist. of Bridgewater Mass. 372
Savage's Genealogical Dictionary i, 491
Stearns' History of Ashburnham Mass. 633
Thurston's History of Winthrop Me. 179
Winsor's History of Duxbury Mass. 249
Custis — Custis' Reminiscences 113
Lee Genealogy (1895) 456-61
Meade's Old Churches of Virginia i, 262
Neill's Virginia Carolorum 208
Paxton's Marshall Genealogy 264
Potter's American Monthly vi, 85
Richmond Va. Standard iii, 150
Cuthbert — Hayward's Gilsum 294
Ogden Genealogy (1898) 64, 85-7, 132-6
Cutler — American Ancestry i, 19; iv, 87; xii
Am. Genealogical Record (1897) ii, 182-4
Avon N. Y. Genealogical Record (1871)
Barry's History of Hanover Mass. 291
Benton's History of Guildhall Vt. 217-9
Bond's History of Watertown Mass. 189-92
Brown's Bedford Mass. Families 7
Butler's History of Farmington Me. 451-4
Cochrane's Hist. of Francestown N. H. 612
Cutler Genealogy (1867) 80 pages
Cutler Genealogy (1889) 665 pages
Cutler Genealogy (1897) 20 pages
Cutler's History of Arlington Mass. 211
Daniels' History of Oxford Mass. 456
Driver Genealogy 421
Dunstable Mass. Bi-Centennial 160
Eaton's History of Reading Mass. 60
Eaton's History of Thomaston Me. 197
Hatch's History of Industry Me. 567-9
Hemenway's Vermont Hist. Gaz. v. 393
Heywood's Hist. of Westminster Mass. 596
Hubbard's History of Springfield Vt. 265-7
Hinman's Connecticut Settlers 790-3
Hudson's Hist. of Lexington Mass. 48-54
Hudson's History of Sudbury Mass. 438
Judd's History of Hadley Mass. 474
Kidder's History of New Ipswich N. H. 356
Morrison's Hist. of Windham N. H. 417-22
Morse's Sherborn Mass. Settlers 67-71
Morse Genealogy, appendix 64
Morse's Genealogical Register ii. (1859) 237
N. E. Hist. and Gen. Reg. iv, 175; vii, 298-300
Norton's History of Fitzwilliam N. H. 527
Paige's History of Cambridge Mass. 521-6

Paige's History of Hardwick Mass. 357
Pierce's History of Grafton Mass. 474-7
Rockwood Genealogy 62-94, 102
Savage's Genealogical Dictionary i. 493-6
Sewall's History of Woburn Mass. 607
Smith's History of Peterborough N. H. 48
Stearns' Hist. of Ashburnham Mass. 669-72
Stearns' History of Rindge N. H 498-500
Temple's Hist. of N. Brookfield Mass. 562
Upham Genealogy 38
Ward's History of Shrewsbury Mass. 260
Whitney Genealogy (1860)
Wyman's Charlestown Mass. i, 254-60
Cutter—American Ancestry iv, 112; vii, 54
Bond's Watertown Mass. Gens. 102
Corliss' North Yarmouth Me. 764-73
Crosby Genealogy 53-5
Cutter Genealogy (1871) 420 pages
Cutter's History of Jaffrey N. H. 261-97
Cutter's History of Arlington Mass. 211-25
Draper's History of Spencer Mass. 188
Eaton's Annals of Warren Me. 532
Heywood's Hist. of Westminster Mass. 597
Hudson's History of Sudbury Mass. 439
Paige's History of Cambridge Mass. 519-21
Power's Sangamon Co. Ill. Settlers 240
Wyman's Charlestown Mass. i. 260-71
Cutting — American Ancestry iv, 142; v. 110; viii. 46; ix, 169
Barry's History of Framingham Mass. 216
Bemis' History of Marlboro N. H. 461-3
Bond's Watertown Mass. Gens. 193-6
Eaton's Annals of Warren Me. 532
Heywood's Westminster Mass. 599-601
Hubbard's Stanstead County Canada 330
Norton's History of Fitzwilliam N. H. 528
Savage's Genealogical Dictionary i, 496
Stearns' Hist. of Ashburnham Mass. 672
Ward's History of Shrewsbury Mass. 259
Washburn's History of Leicester Mass. 351
Washington N. H. History 363
Westminster Mass. Centennial 29
Wheeler's Croydon N. H. Centennial 90-3
Wheeler's History of Newport N. H. 358-61
Cutts — American Ancestry iv. 138
Brewster's Portsmouth N. H. ii, 142-6
Cutts Genealogy (1892) 658 pages
Hatch's History of Industry Me. 569
Maine Hist. and Gen. Recorder iv. 294-7
New Eng. Hist. and Gen. Register ii, 276
Richmond Va. Standard iii, 6
Savage's Genealogical Dictionary i. 494
Slaughter's St. Mark's Parish Va. 186
Wentworth Genealogy i, 312-4
Wheeler's History of Newport N. H. 357
Cuyler — American Ancestry v, 133
Munsell's Albany Collections iv, 111
New York Gen. Rec. iii, 81-3; iv. 77-83
Pearson's Schenectady N. Y. Settlers 52
Dabney — American Ancestry vi. 91, 166
Dabney Genealogy (1888) 206 pages
Daniels' History of Oxford Mass. 457
Gilmer's Georgians 166
Meade's Old Families of Virginia
Page Genealogy 163
Richmond Va. Standard ii, 34; iii, 24

Sketches of Lynchburg Va. 245
Slaughter's St. Mark's Parish Va. 186
Dade — Dade Genealogy (1891) 3 pages
Hayden's Virginia Genealogies 731-4
Savage's Genealogical Dictionary ii, 1
Slaughter's St. Mark's Parish Va. 158
Dadey — Wyman's Charlestown 271-3
Dadnum — Barry's Framingham 217
Daggett — Benedict's Sutton Mass. 630
Bemis' History of Marlboro N. H. 463
Daggett Genealogy, see Doggett
Daggett's Hist. of Attleborough Mass. 89
Eaton's History of Thomaston Me. ii, 197
Hatch's History of Industry Me. 570-89
Hinman's Connecticut Settlers 793
Savage's Genealogical Dictionary ii, 2
Sibley's History of Union Me. 443-6
Tuttle Genealogy 648
Dailey — Austin's R. I. Gen. Dict. 62
Whitman Genealogy 22
Dain — Jameson's Medway Mass. 468
Dains — Cleveland's Yates Co. 132-5
Dakin — Trowbridge Genealogy 189
Hill's History of Mason N. H. 201
Daland — Driver Genealogy 273-8
See also under Dealand
Dale — Ballou's Hist. Milford Mass. 693
Coffin's History of Newbury Mass. 300
Egle's Notes and Queries (1897) 162
Livermore's Hist. of Wilton N. H. 356-8
Meade's Old Families of Virginia i, 278
N. Eng. Hist. Gen. Reg. xxvii, 427
Penn. Mag. of History and Biog. iv. 494
Daley — American Ancestry ii, 29
Lincoln's Hist. of Hingham Mass. ii, 185-7
Norton's Hist. of Fitzwilliam N. H. 529
Dallas — Dallas Gen. (1877) 19 pages
Dallicker — Chambers' N. J. Germans
Dalrymple — Dalrymple Gen. (1878) 68 p.
Daniel's History of Oxford Mass. 458
Pickering Genealogy
Dalton — Am. Anc. iv, 216; v. 79; ix, 37
Dalton Pedigree (1873) 6 pages, reprint
Dearborn's Hist. of Parsonsfield Me. 372
Dorr Genealogy
Dow's Hist. of Hampton N. H. 653-6
Driver Genealogy 135-7, 437
New Eng. Hist. Gen. Reg. xxvii. 364
Runnel's Hist. Sanbornton N. H. ii, 207-9
Savage's Genealogical Dictionary ii. 3
Timlow's Southington Ct. Sketches 87-90
Daman — Deane's Scituate Mass. 260
Hill's Dedham Mass. Records
Dame — Amer. Ancestry vii, 189; xii, 79
Dodge Ancestry (1896) 55
New Eng. Hist. and Gen. Register v, 456
Page Genealogy 198
Savage's Genealogical Dictionary ii, 3
Wentworth Genealogy i. 450
Wheeler's History of Newport N. H. 362
Damen — Bergen's Kings Co. N. Y. 83
Dameron — American Ancestry iv, 58
Damon — Barry's Hanover Mass. 291-4
Bolton Genealogy 26
Cutter's History of Arlington Mass. 226-9
Damon Genealogy (1882) 148 pages

Damon Family of Phila. (1896) 39 pages
Davis' Landmarks of Plymouth Mass. 79
Eaton's History of Reading Mass. 60-2
Fisk Genealogy 141-5
Heywood's Hist. Westminster Mass. 601-3
Hubbard's Hist. of Springfield Vt. 267-70
Hudson's History of Lexington Mass. 55
Lincoln's Hist. of Hingham Mass. ii, 187
Norton's Fitzwilliam N. H. 529-32, 801
Savage's Genealogical Dictionary ii, 4
Secomb's History of Amherst N. H. 553
Temple's Hist. of N. Brookfield Mass. 562
Wakefield Genealogy 50
Wyman's Charlestown Mass. Gens. i, 273
Dana — American Ancestry ix, 169
Bowens of Woodstock Ct. 170
Brighton Mass. Item, March-April, 1899
Chandler Genealogy 104-7, 293
Chapman's Trowbridge Genealogy 262
Dana Genealogy (1865) 64 pages
Dana Memoir (1877) 46 pages
Dana Chart (1870) 18x24 inches
Dana Manuscript in Me. Gen. Lib. 325 p.
Dana's History of Woodstock Vt. 604-9
Daniels' History of Oxford Mass. 458-60
Darling Memorial (1888) 101-3
Dwight Genealogy 665, 796, 800
Hill's Dedham Mass. Records i
Hinman's Connecticut Settlers 795
Hubbard's Hist. of Springfield Vt. 270-2
Jackson's History of Newton Mass. 264
Joslin's History of Poultney Vt. 244
Larned's History of Windham Co. Ct.
Leland Genealogy 21
May Genealogy 51
Munsey's Magazine 1896
Orford N. H. Centennial 110-6
Paige's History of Cambridge Mass. 526-9
Savage's Genealogical Dictionary ii, 4
Secomb's History of Amherst N. H. 554
Stearns' Hist. of Ashburnham Mass. 673
Strong Genealogy 400-2
Wyman's Charlestown Mass. Gens. i, 274
Dandridge — Clarke's King Wm. Va. Fams.
Meade's Old Families of Virginia
Richmond Va. Standard ii, 10, 12, 21
Robertson's Pocahontas' Descendants
Spotiswood Genealogy 23
Welles' Washington Genealogy 259
William and Mary College Quar. v, 33-9
Dane — Abbott's Andover Mass. 96
Babson's History of Gloucester Mass. 324
Chandler Genealogy 108
Cogswell's Hist. New Boston N. H. 421-3
Cochrane's Francestown N. H. 613, 1006
Dean's John Dane of Ipswich (1854) 16 p.
Dodge Ancestry (1896) 9-14
Hammatt Papers of Ipswich Mass. 67-70
Hayward's Hist. of Hancock N. H. 482
N. E. Hist. Gen. Reg. viii, 148; xviii, 263
Poor's Merrimack Valley Researches 81
Savage's Genealogical Dictionary ii, 5-7
Spalding's F. Dane Sermon (1875) 36 pages
Temple's Hist. N. Brookfield Mass. 563-5
Danforth — American Ancestry xi, 189
Baylie's N. Plymouth 79

Bond's Watertown Mass. Gens. 196, 752
Bradbury's Kennebunkport Me. 236
Cochrane's Hist. Francestown N. H. 615-7
Coffin's Hist. of Boscawen N. H. 516-8
Danforth Family Meeting (1886) 40 pages
Danforth Family Meeting (1893) 44 pages
Davis' Landmarks of Plymouth Mass. 79
Emery's Taunton Mass. Ministry i, 177
Farmer's Historical Collections ii, 269-71
Hayward's History of Hancock N. H. 483
Hazen's History of Billerica Mass. 34-8
Hudson's History of Lexington Mass. 55
Lapham's History of Norway Me. 491
Little's History of Weare N. H. 808
New Eng. Hist. Gen. Reg. vii, 315-21
Paige's Hist. of Cambridge Mass. 529-32
Paige's History of Hardwick Mass. 358
Perkins' Old Houses of Norwich Ct. 448
Perry's Jones' Book of Minutes (1894) 11
Runnel's Sanbornton N. H. ii, 209-11
Savage's Genealogical Dictionary ii, 7-9
Secomb's Hist. of Amherst N. H. 556-9
Sinclair Genealogy 124-6
Stearns' Hist. of Rindge N. H. 500
Symmes Genealogy 49
Tyngborough Mass. Centennial 19
Washington N. H. History 364-6
Worcester's History of Hollis N. H. 372
Wyman's Charlestown Mass. Gens. i, 275
Dangerfield — Meade's Va. i, 405
Richmond Va. Standard iii, 6
Daniel — Baldwin Genealogy 362
Bond's Watertown Mass. Gens. 197
Goode Genealogy 49, 104
Hayden's Virginia Genealogies 292-330
Hinman's Connecticut Settlers 796-9
Montague Gen. (1894) 127-32
Morse's Sherborn Mass. Settlers 71-4
Page Genealogy 104
Richmond Va. Standard i, 32; iii, 51
Daniell — American Ancestry v, 149
Ballou's Hist. of Milford Mass. 694-703
Daniell Genealogy (1874) 19 pages
Jameson's Hist. of Medway Mass. 468-71
N. E. Hist. and Gen. Reg. xxviii, 185-94
Paige's History of Cambridge Mass. 532
Runnel's Hist. Sanbornton N. H. ii, 211-5
Daniels — Amer. Anc. v, 31; vi, 5; xi, 11
Austin's Allied Families 79-83
Blake's History of Franklin N. H. 238
Bond's Watertown Mass. Gens. 752
Boyd's History of Conesus N. Y. 151
Calnek's History of Annapolis N. S. 497
Caulkins' History of New London Ct. 351
Daniels' History of Oxford Mass. 461
Jameson's Hist. of Medway Mass. 471-80
Lapham's History of Paris Me. 573-5
Leland Genealogy 215, 269-71
Livermore's Hist. of Wilton N. H. 358
Montague Genealogy 379-504
Munsell's Albany N. Y. Collections iv, 112
Norton's History of Knox Co. Ohio 326
Savage's Genealogical Dictionary ii, 9
Sibley's History of Union Me. 446
Smith's Founders of Mass. Bay 243-51
Temple's Hist. of N. Brookfield Mass. 565

Danielson — Hyde's Brimfield 393-6
Putnam's Historical Magazine v, 47-9
Whitman Genealogy 633-45
Dann — Bouton Genealogy 442
Huntington's Stamford Ct. Settlers 27
Darby — Heywood's Westminster 605-11
Westminster Mass. Centennial 29
Darkin — Shourd's Fenwicks Col. 224-6
Perkins' Old Houses of Norwich Ct. 450
Darley — Kingsman's N. Bridgewater
Washburn's Notes on Livermore Me. 221
Darling — Am. Anc. iii, 13; iv, 42; xi, 75
Ballou's History of Milford Mass. 703-5
Bangor Me. Historical Magazine v, 187-9
Barry's Hist. of Framingham Mass. 219
Benedict's History of Sutton Mass. 631
Blake's History of Franklin Mass. 240
Bradbury's Kennebunkport Me. 237
Clarke's Kindred Genealogies (1896) 41-64
Cogswell's Hist. of Henniker N. H. 535-42
Darling Genealogy (1888) 112 pages
Hudson's Hist. of Marlborough Mass. 353
Jameson's History of Medway Mass. 480
Kulp's Wyoming Valley Families i
Leland Genealogy 89
Little's History of Weare N. H. 809
Marvin's History Winchendon Mass. 452
Randall's Hist. of Chesterfield N. H. 266-8
Runnel's Hist. Sanbornton N. H. i, 215-7
Stearns' History of Rindge N. H. 501
Temple's History of Palmer Mass. 444
Wyman's Charlestown Mass. Gen. i, 276
Young's History of Warsaw N. Y. 253
Darlington — Amer. Ancestry ix, 212
Cope Genealogy 68, 148, 208
Darlington Gathering (1853) 52 pages
Futhey's Hist. of Chester Co. Pa. 509-15
Maris Genealogy 153
Sharpless Genealogy 262, 401-3
Smith's History of Delaware Co. Pa. 455
Darnall — Power's Sangamon 242-4
Darragh — American Ancestry vii, 214
Davis' History of Bucks Co. Pa. 553
Penn. Magazine of History xxiii, 86-91
Saunderson's Charlestown N. H. 320-33
Darrah — Bedford N. H. Centennial 297
Hayward's History of Hancock N. H. 484
Darrin — American Ancestry vii, 49
Champion Genealogy 88-90
Darrow — American Ancestry ii, 29
Anderson's Waterbury Ct. i, app. 43
Baker's History of Montville Ct. 102-10
Caulkins' History of New London Ct. 347
Dodd's History of East Haven Ct. 116
Walworth's Hyde Genealogy 762-5
Dart — American Ancestry vii, 248
Baker's History of Montville Ct. 455-7
Dart Genealogy (1888) 16 pages
Hayward's History of Gilsum N. H. 295-7
Hubbard's Hist. of Springfield Vt. 278
Savage's Genealogical Dictionary ii, 10
Darwin — Champion Genealogy
Dascomb — Livermore's Wilton 359-62
Daskom — Orcutt's Stratford Ct. 1189
Dassett — Savage's Gen. Dict. ii, 11
Davault — Missouri Pioneer 254

Davenport — Amer. Ancestry ii. 30; iii, 192; vi, 41; viii, 99; x, 192; xi, 190
Ballou's History of Milford Mass. 705-8
Benedict's History of Sutton Mass. 631
Bolton's Westchester Co. N. Y. ii, 513
Cutts Genealogy 232-4
Davenport Genealogy (1851) 398 pages
Davenport Genealogy Supp. (1876) 432 p.
Dodd's History of East Haven Ct. 116
Goodwin's Genealogical Notes 306
Hemenway's Vermont Hist. Gaz. v, 34
Hinman's Connecticut Settlers 1st ed. 205
Hough's History of Lewis Co. N. Y. 148
Huntington Genealogy 96
Huntington's Stamford Ct. Settlers 28
Jackson's History of Newton Mass. 265-7
Maltby Genealogy (1895) 58
Meade's Old Families of Virginia 36
New. Eng. Hist. and Gen. Reg. iii. 351; iv, 111-6; ix, 146-8; xxxiii, 25-34
Power's Sangamon Co. Ill. Settlers 244
Preble Genealogy 255
Randall's Hist. Chesterfield N. H. 268-70
Ransom Genealogy 49
Richmond Va. Standard ii, 26
Savage's Genealogical Settlers ii, 11-4
Thurston's History of Winthrop Me. 179
Tuttle Genealogy 354-8
Walworth's Hyde Genealogy 1060-2
Ward's History of Shrewsbury Mass. 265
Waterford Me. Centennial 262
Whitmore's Heraldic Journal i. 36-8
Daves — Daves Biography (1892) 16 pages
Davey — Adam's Fairhaven Vt. 355-8
David — Secomb's Amherst N. H. 559
Davids — Raymond's Tarrytown 172
Davidson — American Ancestry viii, 61, 129; ix, 121; xii, 20, 29
Collin's Hist. of Hillsdale N. Y. app. 51-3
Cutter's History of Jaffrey N. H. 298-300
Daniels' History of Oxford Mass. 462
Davidson Chart (1887) 5 pages
Hayward's History of Hancock N. H. 485
Iowa's Historical Atlas 264
Merrill's Hist. of Acworth N H. 206
Morrison's Hist. of Windham N. H. 425-35
Wyman's Charlestown Mass. Gens. i, 277
Young's History of Warsaw N. Y. 254
Davie — Butler Genealogy 34
Caulkins' History of New London Ct 415
Davis' Landmarks of Plymouth Mass. 80
Savage's Genealogical Dictionary ii, 14
Slaughter's Bristol Parish Va. 203
Wheeler's History of N. Carolina 188, 198
Davies — Am. Ancestry iii, 14; ix, 161
Anderson, Davies and Wersler Gen. (1880)
Calnek's History of Annapolis N. S. 498
Cabell Genealogy 285-7
Davies Genealogy (1895) 138 pages
Egle's Notes and Queries 3d ser. iii. 99
Power's Sangamon Co. Ill. Settlers 245
Davis — American Ancestry i, 20; ii, 38; iii. 14. 206; iv. 5, 46, 90, 209, 215; vi. 13. 33, 191; vii. 156, ix, 114, 123; x, 105, 153; xi, 27, 187, 188
Ammidown Genealogy 19

Anderson's Waterbury Ct. i, app. 44
Austin's R. I. Genealogical Dict. 62-4
Aylsworth Genealogy 102, 201-3
Babson's Hist. Gloucester Mass. 75-9, 253
Ballou's History of Milford Mass. 709-11
Barnstable Patriot 1863
Bemis' History of Marlboro N. H. 464-6
Bond's Watertown Mass. Gens. 516
Bowens of Woodstock 168
Bouton's History of Concord N. H. 641
Bowie Genealogy 92-5
Bradbury's Hist. Kennebunkport Me. 237
Brown's Bedford Mass. Families 8
Bullock Genealogy
Butler's Hist. of Farmington Me. 454-60
Butler's History of Groton Mass. 394
Chambers' Early Germans of N. J. 321
Chandler's Hist. of Shirley Mass. 375-84
Chase's History of Chester N. H. 503
Chase's History of Haverhill Mass. 276
Cleveland's Yates Co. 322, 467-72, 718
Cochrane's History of Antrim N. H. 446
Cochrane's Hist. of Francestown N. H. 617
Cogswell's Hist. of Henniker N. H. 542-4
Cope Genealogy 102, 200-2
Corliss' North Yarmouth Me. Magazine
Crafts Genealogy 147-9
Cunnabell Genealogy 100
Daniel's History of Oxford Mass. 463-82
Darling Memorial (1888)
Davis Family Monthly (1867) 64 pages
Davis Family of Cambridge (1881) 46 p.
Davis Family of Mass. (1884) 610 pages
Davis Family of L. I. (1888) 197 pages
Davis Ancestry (1897) 94 pages
Davis' Landmarks of Plymouth Mass. 81-3
Dearborn's Hist. of Parsonsfield Me. 373
Dow's History of Hampton N. H. 656-8
Driver Genealogy 407-9, 416-9
Eager Chart (1859)
Eaton's Annals of Warren Me. 533-5
Eaton's History of Thomaston Me. ii, 198
Egle's Notes and Queries 3d series ii, 52 (1897) 232
Freeman's Hist. Cape Cod i, 578; ii, 321-6
Futhey's History of Chester Co. Pa. 515-7
Greene Genealogy (1894)
Hammatt Papers of Ipswich Mass. 70
Hanson's History of Gardiner Me. 67
Hatch's History of Industry Me. 589-601
Hayden's Weitzel Genealogy (1883) 33
Hayward's Hist. of Gilsum N. H. 297-9
Hayward's Hist. Hancock N. H. 486-510
Hazen's History of Billerica Mass. 39
Herrick Genealogy (1885) 283-7
Heywood's Hist. of Westminster Mass. 604
Hill's History of Mason N. H. 201
Howell's Southampton N. Y. 2d ed. 424
Hoyt's Salisbury Mass. Families 124-31
Hubbard's Hist. of Springfield Vt. 272-4
Hubbard's Stanstead Co. Canada 202-4
Hudson's History of Lexington Mass. 55
Hyde's Hist Address at Ware Mass. 48
Hyde's History of Brimfield Mass. 470
Johnson Genealogy (1895) 56
Jones Genealogy (1891) 60-3

Keyes' West Boylston Mass. Register 16
Kidder's Hist. of New Ipswich N. H. 356
Lapham's History of Paris Me. 576
Lapham's History of Woodstock Me. 203
Lincoln's Hist. of Hingham Mass. ii, 189
Littell's Passaic Valley Gens. 110-2
Little's History of Weare N. H. 809
Martin's History of Chester Pa. 146-8
McKeen's History of Bradford Vt. 387-90
Merrill's History of Acworth N. H. 207-9
Missouri Pioneer Families 252
Montague Genealogy 522-5
Morris Genealogy (1887) 68
Morrison's History of Windham N. H. 435
Morse's Richards Genealogy 121, 131
New Eng. Hist. and Gen. Reg. iii, 84; ix,
    195; xx, 212-7, 299-307; xxi, 65-8
North's History of Augusta Me. 845
Norton's Hist. of Fitzwilliam N. H. 533-5
Ogden Genealogy (1898) 95-7
Pearson's Schenectady N. Y. Settlers 53
Penneypacker's Phœnixville Pa. 268
Potter's Concord Mass. Families 9, 72
Power's Sangamon Co. Ill. Settlers 246
Randall's Hist. of Chesterfield N. H. 270-8
Reed's History of Rutland Mass. 109-19
Rich's History of Truro Mass. 524
Ridlon's Saco Valley Me. Fams. 597-612
Runnel's Sanbornton N. H. ii. 217-9
Savage's Genealogical Dictionary ii, 15-24
Secomb's History of Amherst N. H. 561
Sedgwick's History of Sharon Ct. 75
Sewall's History of Woburn Mass. 608
Sharp's History of Seymour Ct. 170
Sharpless Gen. 205-13, 328-36, 541-62
Shattuck's History of Concord Mass. 368
Shourd's Fenwick Colony N. J. 528-34
Speed Genealogy 125-8
Stackpole's History of Durham Me. 166
Stearns' History Ashburnham Mass. 674-9
Stearns' History of Rindge N. H. 502-5
Stickney Genealogy 504
Stickney's History of Minisink N. Y. 168
Stone's Hist. Hubbardston Mass. 259-61
Strong Genealogy
Swift's Barnstable Families i, 276-303
Temple's Hist. of No. Brookfield Mass. 565
Temple's History of Palmer Mass. 440
Thompson (Ebenezer) Memoir
Warren and Clarke Genealogies 55
Washington N. H. History 366-84
Wheeler's History of Newport N. H. 363
Whitmore's Copps Hill Epitaphs
Wood Genealogy 45, 147-52
Wood's Brookline Mass. Sketches 41-9
Worcester Magazine ii, 182
Worthen's History of Sutton N. H. 678-85
Wyman's Charlestown Mass. i, 278-83
Wyman's Hunt Genealogy 103
Davison — Amer. Anc. vii, 194, 264; xii, 46
Davis Genealogy 50 141
Davison Genealogy (1887) 8 pages
Hammatt Papers of Ipswich Mass. 71
Norton's Hist. of Fitzwilliam N. H. 535-7
Savage's Genealogical Dictionary ii, 24
Smith's Hist. of Peterborough N. H. 50-3

Sullivan Genealogy 187-91
Walworth's Hyde Genealogy 536
Wyman's Charlestown Mass. Gens. i, 283
Davol — Austin's R. I. Gen. Dict. 284
Peck's Fall River Mass. Industries 253-60
Dawes — American Ancestry xi, 27
Barry's Hanover Mass. 294
Bridgman's King's Chapel Epitaphs 293
Cutter Genealogy 117
Dawes Genealogy (1878) 158 pages
Lincoln's Hist. of Hingham Mass. ii 190
May Genealogy 9
Mitchell's Hist. of Bridgewater Mass. 145
Pierce Genealogy (1894)
Savage's Genealogical Dictionary ii, 24
Winsor's History of Duxbury Mass. 251
Dawson — Amer. Anc. iii, 87, 102; x, 112
Dawson Genealogy (1874) 572 pages
Dawson Gen. Extract (1874) 115 pages
Dodd's History of East Haven Ct. 115
Goode Genealogy 85
Power's Sangamon Co. Ill. Settlers 244
Savage's Genealogical Dictionary ii, 25
Tuttle Genealogy 47-59
Day — American Ancestry v, 84; ix, 52;
    xi, 37, 135, 212; xii, 121
Babson's History of Gloucester Mass. 79
Ballou's History of Milford Mass. 711
Bangor Me. Historical Magazine v, 186
Benedict's History of Sutton Mass. 632
Boltwood's Noble Genealogy 102-7
Chandler's Hist. of Shirley Mass. 384-6
Cochrane's Hist. of Antrim N. H. 446
Daniels' History of Oxford Mass. 482
Davis Genealogy 57
Day Family of Hartford (1840) 44 pages
Day Family Hartford 2d ed. (1848) 129 p.
Day Family of Gloucester (1879) 11 pages
Dodd's History of East Haven Mass. 115
Dolbeare Genealogy 23
Doty Genealogy 75-9
Dwight Genealogy 908-15
Eaton's History of Thomaston Me. ii, 198
Ely Gen. 113-6, 155, 168, 205, 246-8, 273-5
Hammatt Papers of Ipswich Mass. 70
Hayward's History of Gilsum N. H. 299
Hill's Dedham Mass. Records i
Hodgman's History of Westford Mass. 445
Lapham's History of Woodstock Me. 205
Leland Genealogy 178
Littell's Passaic Valley Genealogy 113-23
Little's History of Weare N. H. 810
Loomis Genealogy (1880) 383-9, 607-16
Marvin's History of Winchendon Mass. 453
Olin's Olin Genealogy 161-5
Paige's History of Cambridge Mass. 532-4
Poor's Merrimack Valley 85-91, 144-8
Power's Sangamon Co. Ill. Settlers 247
Randall's Hist. of Chesterfield N.H. 279-82
Read's History of Swanzey N. H. 324
Savage's Genealogical Dictionary ii, 25-8
Sedgwick's History of Sharon Ct. 74
Stackpole's History of Durham Me. 167-70
Stiles' History of Windsor Ct. ii, 170
Temple's History of Northfield Mass. 428
Timlow's Southington Ct. Sketches 78

West Springfield Mass. Centennial 116
Whittemore's Orange N. J. 57
Young's History of Warsaw N. Y. 255
Dayton — American Ancestry i, 21
Anderson's Waterbury Ct. i, app. 44
Hedge's Hist. of Easthampton N. Y. 253-7
Howell's Southampton N. Y. 229-36
Mead's History of Greenwich Ct. 311
Orford N. H. Centennial 109
Orcutt's History of Stratford Ct. 1189
Orcutt's History of New Milford Ct. 691
Timlow's Sketches of Southington Ct. 79
Tuttle Genealogy 193
Deacon — American Ancestry x, 147
Deacon Genealogy (1895) 19 pages
Deady — Roe's Sketches of Rose N. Y. 37
Deake — American Ancestry iii, 76
Dealand — Driver Genealogy 273-8
Felton Genealogy 249
Dean — American Ancestry i, 21; ii, 30
Ballou's History of Milford Mass. 712-4
Bunker's Long Island Genealogies 195
Cleveland's Yates Co. N. Y. 302-6, 409
Cooley's Trenton N. J. Genealogies 54
Dean Family of N. H. (1883) 12 pages
Dean Family of Oakham Mass. (1889) 29 p.
Driver Genealogy 266-8
Essex Institute Hist. Coll. xiii, 263-317
Green's Todd Genealogy
Hammatt Papers of Ipswich Mass. 67-70
Hayward's History of Gilsum N. H. 300
Heywood's Hist. of Westminster Mass. 605
Hill's Dedham Mass. Records i
Huntington's Stamford Ct. Settlers 30
Kelley Genealogy (1897) 54-6
Lapham's History of Paris Me. 576-8
New Eng. Hist. and Gen. Register xli, 261
Paige's History of Hardwick Mass. 360
Pierce's Life of Gardner Dean (1883) 307 p.
Raymond's Tarrytown Monument 60-78
Richmond Va. Standard iii, 17
Ridlon's Saco Valley Me. Families 127
Saunderson's Charlestown N. H. 323
Sewall's History of Woburn Mass. 609
Spooner Genealogy i. 266-77
Stearns' History of Rindge N. H. 505-7
Swift's Barnstable Mass. Families i, 327
Temple's Hist. of N. Brookfield Mass. 566
Titcomb's New Eng. People 129-32
Deane — American Ancestry vi, 88; ix, 186
Bangor Me Historical Magazine iv, 218
Briggs' History of Shipbuilding 327-30
Cochrane's Hist. Francestown N. H. 618-22
Deane Family of Taunton (1849) 16 pages
Deane Family of Maine (1887) 70 pages
Deane Family of Taunton (1893-7) 40 pages
Dwight Genealogy 1007-9
Emery's Taunton Mass. Ministry i, 49-56
Faxon Genealogy 57
Freeman's Hist. of Cape Cod Mass. ii, 629
Hinman's Connecticut Settlers 1st ed. 206
Holton's Winslow Genealogy i, 435-8
Morse Genealogy, appendix 60½
New Eng. History and Gen. Register iii,
375-87; ix, 93; xviii, 263; xxv, 358-62;
xxxvii, 228-95

Savage's Genealogical Dictionary ii, 28-31
Strobridge Genealogy 25-7, 42-8, 68-74
Ward's History of Shrewsbury Mass. 269
Whitman Genealogy 127-9
Wyman's Charlestown Mass. Gens. i, 285
Dear — Hammatt Papers of Ipswich 76
Dearborn — Adams' Haven Genealogy 14
American Ancestry v, 82; vi, 90; xi, 76
Carter's Hist. Pembroke N.H. ii, 59-67, 331
Chase's History of Chester N. H. 503-9
Cochrane's Hist. of Francestown N. H. 622
Cogswell's Nottingham N. H. 199, 372-4
Dearborn's Hist. of Parsonsfield Me. 374-6
Dearborns of Exeter N. H. (1884) 56 pages
Dearborns of Hampton N. H. (1893) 16 p.
Dow's History of Hampton N. H. 659-72
Eaton's History of Candia N. H. 64
Fullonton's Raymond N. H. Hist. 197-200
Granite Monthly of Concord N.H. vii, 124-7
Hanson's History of Gardiner Me. 340
Lawrence and Bartlett Memorial 176-80
Little's History of Weare N. H. 811-4
Maine Hist. and Gen. Rec. iii, 1-8, 69-70
N. E. Hist. and Gen. Reg. ii, 81-98, 297-305
New Hampshire Hist. Soc. Coll. vii, 382
Richardson's Vinton Genealogy 396
Ridlon's Saco Valley Me. Families 612
Runnels' Sanbornton N. H. 219-26
Savage's Genealogical Dictionary ii, 31-3
Deardorff — Power's Sangamon 248
Dearing — Bradbury's Kennebunkport
Dearth — Hyde's Brimfield Mass. 396
Death — Barry's Framingham 220
Morse's Sherborn Mass. Settlers 74
Savage's Genealogical Dictionary ii, 33
Deats — Chambers' N. J. Germans 322-5
De Beelen — Gazzam Genealogy 57-60
De Benneville — Egle's Notes (1898) 181-3
Keim and Allied Families i, 180-5
Debevoise — Queens Co. N. Y. 317-21
Riker's Annals of Newtown N. Y. 406-10
Temple's Hist. of N. Brookfield Mass. 566
De Blois — American Ancestry vii, 209
De Bouchelle — Mallery's Bohemia
De Bow — American Ancestry viii, 138-40
De Bruyn — Lamb's N. Y. City i, 350
New York Gen. and Biog. Rec. x, 856
De Camp — Chambers' N. J. Germans
De Camp Family of Ohio (1896) 177 pages
De Camp Genealogy (1900) 74 pages
De Carteret — Corliss' Yarmouth
Decker — American Ancestry ii, 30
Clute's History of Staten Island N. Y. 369
Farrow's History of Islesborough Me. 190
Gumaer's History of Deerpark N. Y. 61-3
New York Gen. and Biog. Rec. xxvii, 131-3
Ridlon's Saco Valley Me. Families 613-21
Stickney's History of Minisink N. Y. 136
Whittemore's Orange N. J. 289
De Cou — Chambers' N. J. Germans
Dederer — Roome Genealogy 344-6
Dederick — American Ancestry i, 21; ii, 31
Greene County N. Y. History 423-30
Deem — Keim Genealogy 281
Deering — American Ancestry vi, 23; xi, 28
Lapham's History of Norway Me. 492

Lapham's History of Paris Me. 579-81
Preble Genealogy 162
Ridlon's Saco Valley Me. Families 621-31
Savage's Genealogical Dictionary ii, 33
Wentworth Genealogy i, 316
Deeth — Norton's Fitzwilliam 537-9
Defoe — Johnston's Cecil County 526-34
Deforest — Amer. Ancestry i, 21; iii, 184
Bronson's History of Waterbury Ct. 487-91
Cothren's Hist. of Woodbury Ct. ii, 1491-4
Dwight Genealogy 1112
Munsell's Albany Collections iv, 113
Orcutt's History of New Milford Ct. 691
Orcutt's History of Stratford Ct. 1190-4
Riker's History of Harlem N. Y. 571-4
Talcott's N. Y. and N. E. Families 429
De Garmo — Munsell's Albany iv 114
De Graffenried — Saunders' Alabama
    Settlers 309-16
De Graaf — Holgate's Am. Gen. 99-102
Montgomery and Fulton Co. N. Y. 150
Munsell's Albany Collections iv, 114
Pearson's Schenectady Settlers 54-8
De Groof — N. Y. Gen. Rec. xxvii, 101-3
De Groot — Clute's Staten Island 371
Robinson's Items of Ancestry (1894) 56-8
Degrove — Ruttenber's Newburgh 294
Ruttenber's Hist. of Orange Co. N. Y. 382
De Hart — Bergen Genealogy 108
Bergen's Kings County N. Y. Settlers 89
Clute's History of Staten Island N. Y. 373
De Haven — Atlee Genealogy 108-10
De Haven Genealogy (1895) 31 pages
Holstein Genealogy
Deininger — Egle's Notes and Queries 3d
    ser. iii, 381-6
De Kraft — Richmond Stand. iii, 6, 8
De Labeaume — Bingham Gen. 209-12
De La Grange — American Ancestry i, 21
Munsell's Albany Collections iv, 115
Delafield — N. Y. Rec. vii, 91, 118
Van Rensselaer's New Yorkers
Delamater — American Ancestry i, 21; ii,
    31, 153; viii, 22
Delamater Genealogy (1882) 229 pages
New England Hist. and Gen. Reg. xiv, 41-7
N. Y. Gen. and Biog. Record xx, 131
Riker's History of Harlem N. Y. 500-5
Walworth's Hyde Genealogy 988
Willard's Albany Medical Annals 272
Delamont — Pearson's Schenectady 59
De Lancey — Bolton's Westchester 297
Calnek's History of Annapolis N. S. 499
Holgate's American Genealogy 114-21
Jones' N. Y. City in Rev. War i, 649-53
Lamb's N. Y. City i, 444-7, 532, 536, 626
New York Gen. and Biog. Rec. iv, 181-3
Deland — Driver Genealogy 273-8
Temple's No. Brookfield Mass. 566-70
Winsor's History of Duxbury Mass. 251-5
Wyman's Charlestown Mass. Gens. i, 287
De Lane — Temple's N. Brookfield 570
Delano — American Ancestry v, 11; xii, 45
Briggs' History of Shipbuilding 223-7
Davis' Landmarks of Plymouth 83-5
Delano Genealogy (1899) 561 pages

Doty Genealogy 271
Marshall's Grant Ancestry 161
Mitchell's Hist. of Bridgewater Mass. 373
Savage's Genealogical Dictionary ii, 33, 45
Saunderson's Charlestown N. H. 324
Sedgwick's History of Sharon Ct. 76
Smith's History of Sunderland Mass. 315-8
Spooner Memorial 71
Swift Genealogy 24
Thurston's History of Winthrop Me. 180
Tucker's History of Hartford Vt. 412-4
Waldo's History of Tolland Ct. 114
Washburne's Notes on Livermore Me. 22
Delap — Calnek's Annapolis N. S. 499
Swift's Barnstable i, 304-14
Delaplaine — Alden's Epitaphs v, 173
Delavan — Bolton's Westchester 514
Huntington's Stamford Ct. Settlers 30
Delhonde — Essex Inst. Coll. vii, 205-7
Dell — Sharpless Genealogy 158-60
Delong — Aylsworth Genealogy 471-7
Lindsay Genealogy
Delvey — Temple's N. Brookfield 570
Demarest — Cole Genealogy 49, 230-2
Roome Genealogy 15-8
Demary — Stearns' Rindge N. H. 507
Demeritt — Coggswell's Nottingham 678
Thompson (Ebenezer) Memoir
De Meyer — N. Y. Gen. Rec. ix, 13-6
De Mille — American Ancestry iii, 138
Deming — American Ancestry i, 21; ix, 187
Andrews' History of New Britain Ct. 308
Champion Genealogy 271-3, 288, 303-5
Ely Genealogy iii, 241
Glastenbury Ct. Centennial 162
Goodwin's Genealogical Notes 233-6
Howell's Southampton N. Y. 2d ed. 411
New Eng. Hist. and Gen. Reg. xvi, 264-8
Savage's Genealogical Dictionary ii, 35
Sedgwick's History of Sharon Ct. 76
Talcott's N. Y. and N. E. Families 499-505
Timlow's Sketches of Southington Ct. 80-2
Demitt — Lamb's Hist. of N. Y. City i, 343
Demond — Hyde's Ware Mass. 52
Demorest — American Ancestry ii, 32
De Mott — American Ancestry viii, 140, 142
Dempsey — Stearns' Ashburnham 679
De Mun — Beckwith's Creoles 92
Demuth — Eaton's Thomaston Me. 201
De Myer — Schoonmaker's Kingston
Denegar — American Ancestry ii, 32
De Neve — Nevius Genealogy
Denham — American Ancestry iii, 127
Denio — American Ancestry vii, 185
Sheldon's History of Deerfield Mass. 138-41
Denison — Aldrich's Walpole N. H. 223
American Ancestry i, 21-2; vii, 277, xii
Austin's R. I. Genealogical Dictionary 64
Baker's History of Montville Ct. 539-41
Benton's History of Guildhall Vt. 255
Denison Fam. of Stonington Ct.(1881) 423 p.
Denison Fam. of Ipswich Mass. (1882) 52 p.
Denison Family of Floyd N. Y. (1884) 72 p.
Lapham's History of Norway Me. 496-8
New Eng. Hist. and Gen. Reg. xlvi, 352-4
Norton's History of Fitzwilliam N. H. 539

Paige's History of Cambridge Mass. 534
Perkins' Old Houses of Norwich Ct. 451
Prentice Genealogy 404-6
Savage's Genealogical Dictionary ii, 36-8
Stanton's Genealogy 75, 483
Stonington Ct. Bi-Centennial 296-9
Whittemore's His. of Middlesex Co. Ct. 487
Denman — Matthews and Denman Families (1897) 16 pages
Denn — Shourd's Fenwick Colony 142
Dennet — Buxton Me. Centennial 227-9
Dennett — Bangor Hist. Magazine v, 64
Lapham's History of Paris Me. 579
Dennie — Pearson's Schenectady 60
Denning — Babson's Gloucester 80
Mason and Denning Families (1898) 16 p.
New York Gen. and Biog. Record xxx, 140
Dennis — American Ancestry xi, 130
Austin's R. I. Gen. Dictionary 65
Caulkins' History of New London Ct. 351
Eaton's History of Thomaston Me. ii, 201
Freeman's Hist. of Cape Cod Mass. ii, 700
Hammatt Papers of Ipswich Mass. 75
Hayward's History of Hancock N. H. 510-8
New Eng. Hist. and Gen. Reg. xlix, 441-4
Paige's History of Hardwick Mass. 361
Savage's Genealogical Dictionary ii, 38
Whitehead's Perth Amboy N. J. 364
Dennison — American Ancestry ix. 153
Caulkins' History of New London Ct. 332-5
Cochrane's Hist. of Francestown N. H. 624
Corliss' North Yarmouth Me.
Dodd's History of East Haven Ct. 117
Ellis' History of Roxbury Mass. 95
Hammatt Papers of Ipswich Mass. 72-5
Hughes Genealogy 8-10
Hyde Genealogy i, 196-201: ii, 1015-26
Denniston — Eager's Orange Co. 617
Denny — Amer. Ancestry iv, 216; viii, 172
Breck Genealogy 25-7
Denny Genealogy (1886) 267 pages
Egle's Penn. Genealogies 2d ed. 587-91
Fisher Genealogy (1896) 201-7
Futhey's History of Chester Co. Pa. 518
Richmond Va. Standard iii, 7
Schenck's History of Fairfield Ct. 366
Spooner Genealogy i, 350
Washburn's Hist. of Leicester Mass. 354-8
Worcester Mag. Hist. Journal ii. 100
De Normandie — Amer. Ancestry vii. 98
De Nottbeck — Greene's Todd Genealogy
Denslow — Austin's Allied Families 84
Savage's Genealogical Dictionary ii. 39
Stiles' History of Windsor Ct. ii. 171
Densmore — Am. Ancestry iii, 116, vii, 82
Densmore, see Dinsmore
Milliken's Narraguagus Valley Me. 3
Denton — American Ancestry x, 187
Eager's Orange Co. N. J. 411
Huntting's Hist of Pine Plains N. Y. 328
Savage's Genealogical Dictionary ii, 39
Stickney's History of Minisink N. Y. 168
Denyo — See Denio
De Peyster — American Ancestry iii, 83
De Peyster Genealogy (1854) 249 pages
De Peyster Memorial (1881) 80 pages

De Peyster Reference (1886) 8 pages
De Peyster Antiquity (1881) 52 pages
Lamb's Hist. of New York City i, 420, 517
New Eng. Hist. and Gen. Register li, 334-6
New York Gen. and Biog. Recorder ix, 124
Valentine's N. Y. Common Council Manual (1853) 392, (1861) 556-76
Welles' Am. Family Antiq. (1881) 9-52
De Potter — Nevius Genealogy
De Puy — Brodhead's Water Gap, 235
Clute's History of Staten Island N. Y. 373
Schoonmaker's Kingston N. Y. 476
Sylvester's History of Ulster Co. N. Y. 228
Dequindre — Hall Genealogy (1892) 102-5
Derby — Am. Anc. i, 22; v. 109; vi, 31, 105
Austin's R. I. Genealogical Dictionary 65
Austin's Allied Families 84-6
Driver Genealogy 279-90
Essex Institute Historical Collections iii, 154-67, 201-7, 283-9
Heywood's Hist. of Westminster Mass. 605
Joslin's History of Poultney Vt. 245
Locke Genealogy 66. 122
Paul's History of Wells Vt. 85
Savage's Genealogical Dictionary ii, 40
Sawin Genealogy 14
Stearns' History of Ashburnham Mass. 680
Stearns' History of Rindge N. H. 509
De Ridder — Munsell's Albany iv. 116
De Riemer — N. Y. Gen. Rec. vii, 61-4
Roome Genealogy 235-43
Dering — American Ancestry iv, 51
Dotterer's Perkiomen Region Pa. iii. 21
Mallman's Shelter Island N. Y. 177-80
Savage's Genealogical Dictionary ii, 41
Wood's History of Long Island 194-8
De Rose — Chambers' N. J. Germans
Derr — American Ancestry vii, 204
Derrick — American Ancestry ii. 32
Derthick — Harris Gen. (1878) 46, 72, 121-5
Desborough — Savage's Dictionary ii, 41
Desbrosses — Lamb's N. Y. City i, 760
De Shong — Martin's Chester Pa. 246
De Sille — Lamb's N. Y. City i, 167
New York Gen. and Biog. Rec. viii, 128
Despeaux — Ballou's Milford Mass. 715
Deterick — Plumb's Hanover Pa. 407
Deturk — Egle's Pa. Hist. Register ii, 92-8
Detweiler — Cassel Genealogy 415-21
Eyerman Ancestors
Hertzler Genealogy 98-107
Moyer Genealogy 266-76
Deuel — Harvey Genealogy 92
DeVeaux — Bellinger Genealogy 7, 49
De Veaux Genealogy (1885) 302 pages
Devens — American Ancestry iii, 194
Bridge Genealogy 82-7
Wyman's Charlestown Mass. i, 289-92
Devereau — Dearborn's Parsonsfield
Driver Genealogy 329
Pickering Genealogy
Tuttle Genealogy 725-7
Walworth's Hyde Genealogy 523-5
Devoe — American Ancestry ii, 32; vi, 159
De Voe Genealogy. see De Veaux

Munsell's Albany Collections iv, 116
Richmond Va. Standard iii, 47
Devol — American Ancestry i, 22
Devotion — Brookline Historical Pub.
Soc. No. 14, 1898, 35-46
Ruggles Genealogy by Bailey (1896) 11-3
Savage's Genealogical Dictionary ii, 42
De Wandelaer — Munsell's Albany iv
Dewees — Maris Genealogy 158
Dewell — Humphreys Genealogy 194
De Wever — Munsell's Albany iv. 117
Dewey — American Ancestry xi, 224; xii
Andrews' New Britain Ct.
Bennington Vt. Centennial (1869)
Dewey Genealogy (1898) 1117 pages
Dwight Genealogy 692-5
Follett Genealogy (1896) 113-24
Hemenway's Vermont Hist. Gaz. iv, 61
Hine's Lebanon Ct. Hist. Address 152
Joslin's History of Poultney Vt. 246-54
Loomis Genealogy (1880) 655-8, 695-7
New York Gen. and Biog. Record vi, 63-73,
129-49, 166-80; viii, 108-16, 153-64
Savage's Genealogical Dictionary ii, 434
Stiles' History of Windsor Ct. ii, 172
Strong Genealogy 370-2
Tanner Genealogy 20-2
Taylor's Great Barrington 111-3, 160
Temple's History of Palmer Mass. 441
Wallbridge Genealogy 279-86
Walworth's Hyde Genealogy 720-3
Wright's Williams Genealogy 32
Young's Hist. of Chautauqua Co. N. Y. 549
Dewing — Hill's Dedham Mass. Record i
Temple's Hist. of N. Brookfield Mass. 571
De Witt — American Ancestry i, 22; ii,
32; iii, 160; xi, 196
Bergen's Kings County N. Y. Settlers 97
Daniels' History of Oxford Mass. 483-5
De Witt Genealogy (1886) 18 pages reprint
Eager's History of Orange Co. N. Y. 396
Gregg's History of Old Cheraws S. C. 97
Gumaer's History of Deerpark N. Y. 65-7
Harvey Genealogy 820-31
New York Genealogical and Biographical
Record v, 165-8; xvii, 251-9; xviii,
13-21; xxi, 185-90; xxii, 3-6
Schoonmaker's Hist. of Kingston N. Y. 477
Stickney's History of Minisink N. Y. 137
Sylvester's History of Ulster Co. N. Y. 102
De Wolf — American Ancestry iv, 48; xi, 77
Champion Genealogy
Eaton Genealogy (1895)
Salisbury Family Histories (1892) ii, 123-65
Savage's Genealogical Dictionary ii, 44
Sheldon's Hist. of Deerfield Mass. ii, 141-3
Dexter — Am. Anc. i, 23; iii, 180; vi, 121
Austin's Ancestral Dictionary 18
Austin's R. I. Genealogical Dictionary 288
Brook's History of Medford Mass. 510
Dexter Chart (1857) 2x2½ feet
Dexter Genealogy (1859) 108 pages
Freeman's Hist. Cape Cod Mass. ii, 78, 446
Hemenway's Vermont Hist. Gaz. v, 356
Hudson's Hist. of Marlborough Mass. 354
Malden Mass. Bi-Centennial 246

New Eng. Hist. and Gen. Reg. viii, 248
New York Gen. and Biog. Rec. xxii, 6
Oneida N. Y. Hist. Soc. Trans. ii, 124-6
Paige's History of Hardwick Mass. 362-4
Savage's Genealogical Dictionary ii, 44-7
Shafter Genealogy 46
Stiles' Hist. of Windsor Ct. ii, 172-4
Swift's Barnstable Families i, 315-26
Whitman Genealogy 444-50
Wyman's Charlestown Mass. i, 292-4
Dey — Nevius Genealogy
New York Gen. and Biog. Record vii, 57
Deyarmond — Miller's Colchester 187-9
Deyo — Sylvester's Hist. of Ulster Co. N. Y. 308
Deyoe — Hist. of Greene Co. N. Y. 451
De Zeng — N. Y. Gen. Rec. ii. 53; v, 8-12
Thomas Genealogy (1877) 68
Thomas Genealogy (1896) 293
Diamond — American Ancestry i, 23
Hammatt Papers of Ipswich Mass. 77
Howell's Southampton N. Y. 2d ed. 236
Hudson's History of Lexington Mass. 56
Smith's Hist. of Peterborough N. H. 53-5
Dibble — Chapman's Trowbridge Gen.
Gold's History of Cornwall Ct. 258
Huntington's Stamford Ct. Settlers 31
Huntting's Hist. of Pine Plains N. Y. 329
Jessup Genealogy 85-8, 277-83
Orcutt's History of Torrington Ct. 682
Sedgwick's History of Sharon Ct. 76
Stiles' History of Windsor Ct. ii, 174
Wakefield Genealogy 205
Dibblee — American Ancestry ii. 153
Huntting's Hist. Pine Plains N. Y. 325-8
Dick — American Ancestry ii, 32
Carter Gen. (1883) 54. 75-81. 102-8
Martin's History of Chester Pa. 394-7
Dicke — Eaton's Annals Warren Me. 391
Dickens — Austin's R. I. Gen. Dict. 66
Livermore's Hist. Block Island R. I. 326
Dickerman — American Ancestry v, 145
Blake's History of Hamden Ct. 242-5
Dickerman Genealogy (1897) 651 pages
Kingman's No. Bridgewater Mass. 487
Mitchell's Hist. of Bridgewater Mass. 146
Savage's Genealogical Dictionary ii, 47
Tuttle Genealogy 166-9, 649-51
Dickerson — Chandler's Shirley 386-8
Chambers' Early Germans of N. J. 328-31
New York Gen. and Biog. Record xxii, 22;
xxx, 180, 247-53
Power's Sangamon Co. Ill. Settlers 249
Dickey — Aldrich's Walpole N. H. 235
American Ancestry xi, 190
Clarke's Old King Wm. Co. Va. Families
Cochrane's Hist. of Antrim N. H. 449-53
Cochrane's Hist. Francestown N. H. 626-9
Dickey Genealogy (1898) 322 pages
Eaton's Annals of Warren Me. 535
Futhey's Hist. of Chester Co. Pa. 520-2
Merrill's Hist. of Acworth N. H. 209-12
Miller's Colchester Co. N. S. 309-11
Morrison's Hist. of Windham N. H. 436
Parker's Hist. of Londonderry N. H. 267-9
Secomb's History of Amherst N. H. 562
Dickie — Chappell Genealogy (1895) 71-7

Dickinson — American Ancestry vii, 220;
  ix, 50; xi, 188, 191
Blake's Mendon Association 130
Clayton's History of Union Co. N. J. 201–9
Cooley's Trenton N. J. Gens. 55–64
Crafts' History of Whately Mass. 445–57
Dickinson Genealogy (1897) 145 pages
Dickinson Reunion (1884) 206 pages
Essex Institute Hist. Colls. xxi, 69–72
Gage's History of Rowley Mass. 441
Goodwin's Foote Genealogy 270–5
Goodwin's Genealogical Notes 6
Hemenway's Vermont Historical Gaz. v
Heywood's Hist. of Westminster Mass. 611
Humphreys Genealogy 285–7
Judd's History of Hadley Mass. 472–88
Kellogg's White Genealogy 32, 103
Leach's Morton Ancestry 132–7
Lyman Genealogy (1865) 32 pages
Middlefield Ct. History
Montague Genealogy 504–9
Morse's Sherborn Mass. Settlers 75–7
New Eng. Hist. and Gen. Reg. xvi, 263
Orcutt's History of Stratford Ct. 1194
Penn. Mag. of History and Biog. v, 480
Read's History of Swanzey N. H. 325–8
Redfield Genealogy 45
Savage's Genealogical Dictionary ii, 47–9
Sheldon's Hist. of Deerfield Mass. ii, 144–9
Smith's Hist. of Sunderland Mass. 319–22
Stearns' Hist. of Ashburnham Mass. 681
Swift's Barnstable Mass. Families i, 347
Temple's Hist. of Northfield Mass. 429–32
Temple's History of Palmer Mass. 442
Temple's History of Whately Mass. 223–6
Timlow's Sketches Southington Ct. 82–4
Whittemore's Middlesex Co. Ct. 487
Dickman — Dickerman Genealogy 561–7
Dicks — Sharpless Genealogy 226, 351
Dickson — Cutter's Arlington Mass. 231
Dickson Genealogy (1889) 223 pages
Dunster Genealogy 54–60
Green's Kentucky Families
Miller's Colchester Co. N. S. 248–51, 384
Paige's History of Cambridge Mass. 534–6
Savage's Genealogical Dictionary ii, 49
Wyman's Charlestown Mass. Gens. 295–7
Didier — American Ancestry i, 159
Didlake — Richmond Standard ii, 46
Diehl — Diehl Genealogy (1891) 60 pages
Dies — Greene Co. N. Y. History 430
Dieterly — Borneman Genealogy 26–33
Dietrich — Heffner Genealogy 41–3
Dietz — Eyerman Ancestors (1898)
Diffenderfer — Wolff Family 101
Digby — Heraldic Journal ii, 92
Diggens — Stiles' Windsor Ct. ii, 175
Digges — Lee Genealogy (1895) 311
Meade's Old Churches of Virginia i, 238
Richmond Va. Standard ii, 24
Reily's Conewago Pa. History (1886) 21–6
Southern Bivouac (1886) 732
Wm. and Mary College Historical Register
  i, 80–8, 140–54, 208–13
Dighton — Me. Hist. Recorder vi, 362–6
Dihm — Keim Genealogy 281

Dike — American Ancestry iii, 173
Babson's History of Gloucester Mass. 81
Benedict's History of Sutton Mass. 633
Caverly's History of Pittsford Vt. 698
Heywood's Hist. Westminster Mass. 611–3
Kingman's N. Bridgewater Mass. 488–90
Noyes Genealogy (1861) 7–9
Dill — Barry's Hist. of Hanover Mass. 294
Brown's West Simsbury Ct. Settlers 59
Lincoln's Hist. of Hingham Mass. ii, 192
Whittemore's Orange N. J. 442
Dillard — Power's Sangamon Ill. 250
Dillaway — Eaton's Thomaston Me.
Dillenback — New York Gen. and Biog.
  Record xxix, 115
Diller — Diller Genealogy (1877) 56 **pages**
Koiner Genealogy 171 pages
Dilley — Plumb's Hanover Pa. 408
Caldwell Genealogy (1873) 9
Dillingham — Eaton's Warren Me.
Hammatt Papers of Ipswich Mass. 77
Hollister's History of Pawlet Vt. 183
North's History of Augusta Me. 847
Savage's Genealogical Dictionary ii, 50
Dillon — Power's Sangamon Ill. 251
Dilts — Chambers' N. J. Germans
Dilworth — Futhey's Chester Co. Pa.
Diman — Davis' Landmarks 86
Pickering Genealogy
Wight Genealogy
Dimick — Ellis Genealogy 375
Turner Genealogy (1877)
Dimmick — Amer. Ancestry i, 23; ii, 32
Freeman's Cape Cod Mass. i, 618, 647
Hyde's History of Brimfield Mass. 470–2
Dimmock — Amer. Ancestry iv, 189
Morrison's History of Windham N. H. 437
Savage's Genealogical Dictionary ii, 51
Swift's Barnstable Families i, 328–45
Dimock—Walworth's Hyde Genealogy 987
Dimon — Hedge's East Hampton 273–5
Howell's Southampton 236–8
See also Dimond
Dimond — American Ancestry vi, 15
Bouton's History of Concord N. H. 641–3
Cochrane's History of Antrim N. H. 453
Dearborn's History of Salisbury N. H. 541
Dimond Genealogy (1891) 179 pages
Schenck's History of Fairfield Ct. 367
Dinehart — American Ancestry ii, 32
Dingley — Maine Hist. Gen. Rec. 120–5
Savage's Genealogical Dictionary ii, 52
Stackpole's History of Durham Me. 170
Winsor's History of Duxbury Mass. 255
Dingman — American Ancestry ii, 33
Munsell's Albany Collections iv, 117
Pearson's Schenectady N. Y. Settlers 62
Dinsmore — Chase's Chester N. H. 509
Cochrane's History of Antrim N. H. 453–7
Cochrane's Hist. Francestown N. H. 629–33
Cogswell's History of Henniker N.H. 544
Dinsmore Golden Wedding (1867) 24 pages
Dinsmore Genealogy (1891) 48 pages
Eaton's History of Thomaston Me. ii, 202
Hayward's History Hancock N. H. 518–21
Keyes' W. Boylston Mass. Gen. Reg. 17

Little Genealogy 159–61
Morrison's Hist. Windham N. H. 437–510
Morrison's Among the Scotch-Irish (1891)
Paige's History of Hardwick Mass. 364
Washington N. H. History 384
Dinwiddie — American Ancestry vi, 15, 89
Ball's History of Lake Co. Ind. 425–32
Dinwiddie Papers iii, 21–8
Disbrow — Baird's Hist. of Rye N. Y. 408
Bolton's Westchester County N. Y. i, 499
Cleveland's Hist. of Yates Co. N. Y. 153–5
Porter's Hartford Ct. Settlers 5
Savage's Genealogical Dictionary ii, 52
Diser — Wyman's Charlestown 297
Disosway — Clute's Staten Island 375
Ditmars — Bergen's Kings Co. N. Y.
Calnek's History of Annapolis N. S. 501
Queens County N. Y. History 250
Riker's Annals of Newtown N. Y. 390
Williamson Genealogy (1896) 21
Ditson — Hazen's Billerica Mass. 40
Divelbiss — Power's Sangamon Ill. 253
Divoll — Heywood's Westminster 613
Dix — American Ancestry iii, 135
Bond's Watertown Mass. 198–201, 753
Coffin's History of Boscawen N. H. 518–20
Dix Chart by Bokes (1882) 20x24 inches
Dwight's Strong Genealogy 362
Eaton's History of Reading Mass. 62
Farrow's History of Islesborough Me. 191
Hammett Papers of Ipswich Mass. 76
Richmond Va. Standard ii, 47
Savage's Genealogical Dictionary ii, 53
Dixey — Savage's Gen. Dictionary ii, 54
Dixon — American Ancestry v, 83
Daniels' History of Oxford Mass. 485
Dickson Genealogy (1889) 223 pages
Egle's Penn. Genealogies 2d ed. 156–8
Goode Genealogy 417
Harvey Genealogy 379–511
Hubbard's Stanstead Co. Canada 142
Marshall Genealogy (1884) 28
Power's Sangamon Co. Ill. Settlers 252
Richmond Va. Standard iii, 16
Savage's Genealogical Dictionary ii, 54
Dixwell — Hinman's Conn. Settlers (1846)
Savage's Genealogical Dictionary ii, 54
Di Zerega — American Ancestry vi, 83, 97
Doan — Maris Genealogy 189
Penn. Mag. of History and Biog. ix, 236
Sharpless Genealogy 411
Doane — Am. Anc. i, 23; iii, 14; xii, 91
Atkin's History of Hawley Mass. 63
Bangor Me. Hist. Mag. iii, 65; iv, 219
Chapman Genealogy 52
Maine Hist. Rec. ii, 250; iv, 119–27, 286–9
Pratt's History of Eastham Mass. 17
Savage's Genealogical Dictionary ii, 55
Temple's Hist. N. Brookfield Mass. 572–4
Walworth's Hyde Genealogy 470
Dobson — Futhey's Chester Co. Pa. 524
Dockham — Eaton's Warren Me. 533
Dodd — Baldwin Gen. 1118–20, 1155–64
Dodd Genealogy (1839) 24 pages
Dodd Genealogy (1864) 221 pages
Dodd Ancestry (1889) 11 pages

Dowd Genealogy (1865)
Heywood's Hist. of Westminster Mass. 614
Hinman's Connecticut Settlers 1st ed. 209
Littell's Passaic Valley Genealogies 125–36
Savage's Genealogical Dictionary ii, 56
Whittemore's Orange N. J. 59
Doddridge — Hayden's Va. Genealogy 662
Dodds — Power's Sangamon Ill. 253–7
Dodge — American Ancestry iii, 76, 136;
    vi, 144, 185, 192; vii, 242, 247; ix, 91,
    138; xi, 76; xii, 107
Atkin's History of Hawley Mass. 62
Austin's R. I. Genealogical Dictionary 66
Bangor Me. Historical Magazine v, 189
Benedict's History of Sutton Mass. 634
Calnek's History of Annapolis N. S. 501–3
Chandler's History of Shirley Mass. 389
Cochrane's History of Antrim N. H. 457–60
Cochrane's Hist. Francestown N. H. 633–9
Cogswell's Hist. of Henniker N. H. 545–50
Cogswell's New Boston N. H. 379–95
Cushman's History of Sheepscot Me. 373–6
Daniels' History of Oxford Mass. 486
Dodge Early Records (1879) 12 pages
Dodge Reunion (1879) 53 pages
Dodge Address (1879) 30 pages, reprint
Dodge Family of Worcester (1880) 20 pages
Dodge Family of Rhode Island (1886) 233 p.
Dodge Family of Essex Mass. (1894) 448 p.
Dodge Ancestry (1896) 76 pages
Dodge Lands at Cow Neck L. I. (1896) 32 p.
Dodge Family of Block Island (1898) chart
Dodge Family of Essex, vol. ii (1898) 218 p.
Dow's History of Hampton N. H. 674
Driver Genealogy 271
Eaton's History of Thomaston Me. 202
Farrow's Hist. Islesborough Me. 192–200
Fiske Genealogy 145
Greene's Todd Genealogy 100–7
Hammatt Papers of Ipswich Mass. 78
Harris Genealogy (1878) 67
Hayward's Hist. of Hancock N. H. 521–31
Hemenway's Vermont Hist. Gazette v, 136
Heywood's Hist. of Westminster Mass. 615
Herrick Genealogy
Little's History of Weare N. H. 815
Livermore's Hist. of Block Island R. I. 327
New Eng. Hist. Reg. xv, 254; xlvi, 383–91
Pickering Genealogy
Pompey N. Y. Reunion 296–300
Prime's Sands Genealogy 73–7
Savage's Genealogical Dictionary ii, 56
Secomb's History of Amherst N. H. 564–9
Sheldon's Hist. Deerfield Mass. ii, 149–51
Stearns' History of Ashburnham Mass. 682
Temple's Hist. N. Brookfield Mass. 574–6
Walworth's Hyde Genealogy 404
Washington N. H. History 385
Wyman's Charlestown Mass. Gens. i, 298
Dodson — Deane's Scituate Mass. 263
Savage's Genealogical Dictionary ii, 57
Doe — Dearborn's Parsonsfield 376–8
Lapham's History of Norway Me. 493.
Lapham's History of Paris Me. 581
Runnel's History of Sanbornton N. H. ii,
    226

Doggett — Briggs' Shipbuilding 38, 52
Davis' Landmarks 87
Doggett Genealogy (1894) 686 pages
Dolbeare — Baker's Montville Ct. 333-42
Dolbeare Genealogy (1893) 32 pages
New Eng. Hist. and Gen. Reg. xlvii, 24-7
Dolbeer — American Ancestry xii
Dolber — Palmer Genealogy (1886) 62-4
Dolby — Chase's Chester N. H. 511
Cogswell's History of Henniker N. H. 551
Dole — Bangor Me. Hist. Mag. iv, 217
Chandler's History of Shirley Mass. 390
Dow's History of Hampton N. H. 675
Guild's Stiles Genealogy 339-41
New Eng. Hist. and Gen. Reg. xxxviii, 74-9
Poore Genealogy 16-9, 118-20
Savage's Genealogical Dictionary ii, 58
Washington N. H. History 386-8
Wilder Genealogy 291-3
Woodbury's History of Bedford N. H. 298
Dolley — Lapham's Rumford Me. 316
Dolliver — Babson's Gloucester 81
Putnam's Historical Magazine vi, 157-68
Dolloff — Bell's Hist. of Exeter N. H. 10
Guild's Stiles Genealogy 329-31
Lapham's History of Rumford Me. 315
Runnel's Hist. of Sanbornton N. H. ii, 227
Doloff — Hubbard's Stanstead Can. 191
Dolovan — Austin's R. I. Gen. Dict. 67
Dolph — American Ancestry vii, 118
Dolsen — Stickney's Minisink 167
Dominick — American Ancestry iv, 181
Dominy — Hedge's Easthampton N. Y.
Donahue — Eaton's Thomaston Me.
Donaldson — Donaldson Genealogy
Freeman's Cape Cod 467
Donerly — American Ancestry ii, 33
Dongan — Lamb's N. Y. City i, 299
Donnell — Barry's Hanover Mass. 294
Savage's Genealogical Dictionary ii, 59
Donner — Power's Sangamon Ill. 258
Donovan — Craft's Whately 457
Eaton's Thomaston Me. ii, 203
Runnel's Hist. of Sanbornton N. H. ii, 229
Doolan — Stearns' Ashburnham 682
Doolittle — Anderson's Waterbury Ct. i, app. 45
Andrews' New Britain Ct.
Boyd's Annals of Winchester Ct. 272
Davis' History of Wallingford Ct. 726-41
Dawson Genealogy 93-5
Doolittle Belchertown Mass. 273-7
Doolittle Genealogy (1893) 38 pages, reprint
Hull Genealogy 16a
New Eng. Hist. and Gen. Reg. vi, 293-6
Oneida N. Y. Hist. Society Trans. ii, 76
Orcutt's History of Torrington Ct. 682-5
Savage's Genealogical Dictionary ii, 59
Temple's History of Northfield Mass. 433-5
Tilley's Mag. of N. E. Hist. iii, 151-87
Tuttle Genealogy 217, 651
Door — Hanson's Gardiner Me. 75
See also under Dorr
Dorchester — Savage's Dictionary ii, 60
Temple's History of Palmer Mass. 443
Warren and Clarke Genealogy 58

Dore — Wentworth Genealogy 1, 278-82
Doremus — Am. Anc. viii, 141-3, 183-5
Clayton's History of Bergen Co. N. J. 201
Doremus Genealogy (1897) 232 pages
Whittemore's Orange N. J. 402-4
Dorland — Am. Ancestry ii, 33; xii, 62
Bergen's Kings Co. N. Y. Settlers 101
Chambers' Early Germans of N. J. 335
Dorland Genealogy (1898) 320 pages
Egle's Notes and Queries (1898) 74
Dorman—Bradbury's Kennebunkport 239
Hammett Papers of Ipswich Mass. 79
Milliken's Narraguagus Valley Me. 2
Perley's History of Boxford Mass. 96
Savage's Genealogical Dictionary ii, 61
Thayer Memorial (1835) 5
Dorr — Amer. Ancestry i, 24; ii, 33; iv, 15
Blake's Mendon Association 84-6
Chamberlain's Lebanon Me. Soldiers 15-7
Champion Genealogy 51
Crane's Rawson Genealogy 8, 40, 82-4
Dorr Genealogy (1879) 84 pages
Hudson's History of Lexington Mass. 56
North's History of Augusta Me. 847-9
Savage's Genealogical Dict. ii, 61
Walworth's Hyde Gen. 194-6; ii, 960-98
Dorrance — Buckingham Genealogy 224
Kulp's Wyoming Valley Families
Power's Sangamon Co. Ill. Settlers 260
Dorrington — Seagrave Genealogy, app. 9
Dorsey — Dorsey Family (1898) chart
Phelps Purchase 392
Doten — Barry's Hanover Mass. 294
Doty Genealogy 147-166
Spooner Genealogy i, 441-5
Dotey — Sedgwick's Sharon Ct. 76
Dotterer — Perkiomen Region Pa. 57
Doty — Am. Ancestry ii, 33; ix, 22; x, 33
Baird's History of Rye N. Y. 462
Davis' Landmarks of Plymouth 87-91
Doty Genealogy (1897) 1035 pages
Eaton's Annals of Warren Me. 2d ed. 536
Heywood's Hist. of Westminster Mass. 615
Littell's Passaic Valley Genealogies 139-44
New York Gen. and Biog. Rec. xxvi, 83
Paige's History of Hardwick Mass. 365
Savage's Genealogical Dictionary ii, 61
Doubleday — Hine's Lebanon Ct. 153
Wyman's Charlestown Mass. Gens. i, 300
Doude — See Dowd
Dougherty — Barry's Framingham 221
Doughty — Amer. Ancestry ix, 63; x, 118
Bunker's Long Island Genealogies 198
Doty Genealogy 281
N. Y. Gen. and Biog. Rec. xxx, 122, 254
Douglas — American Ancestry iii, 194
Caulkins' History of New London Ct. 300
Douglas Family of Middleboro (1874) 8 p
Douglas Genealogy (1879) 563 pages
Douglas Family of Middleboro (1890) 226 p
Douglas Family of Virginia (1894) chart
Gold's History of Cornwall Ct. 241-3
Goode Genealogy 354
Hinman's Connecticut Settlers 1st ed. 209
Mallmann's Shelter Island N. Y. 312-5
New Eng. Hist. and Gen. Reg. xxviii, 69-75

Power's Sangamon Co. Ill. Settlers 261
Richmond Va. Standard iii, 6
Savage's Genealogical Dictionary ii, 63
Stackpole's History of Durham Me. 172-4
Wheeler's History of Brunswick Me. 831
Douglass — Am. Ancestry iv, 67; ix, 198
Bullock Genealogy
Egle's Notes and Queries 4th ser. i, 262
Hamilton's Wise Biography
Meade's Old Families of Virginia i, 458
Ransom Genealogy
Robertson's Pocahontas' Descendants
Dougrey — Morris' Bontecou Genealogy
Douthat — Paxton's Marshall Genealogy
Richmond Va. Standard iii, 23
Douthett — Am. Ancestry iv, 102; ix, 96
Douthett and Ward Genealogy (1889) 36 p.
Douty — American Ancestry viii, 45
Douw — American Ancestry i, 24; iii, 155
Hoffman Genealogy 495
Munsell's Albany Collections iv, 117
New Eng. Hist. and Gen. Reg. li, 339-44
New York Gen. and Biog. Rec. iii, 82-4
Talcott's N. Y. and New Eng. Gens. 64-79
Dow — Allison Genealogy 55
American Ancestry iii, 204; v, 170; xi, 193
Bouton's History of Concord N. H.
Cochrane's History of Antrim N. H. 462
Cochrane's Hist. of Francestown N. H. 641
Cogswell's History of Henniker N. H. 550
Cogswell's Hist. Nottingham N. H. 679-81
Daniels' History of Oxford Mass. 487
Dimock's Coventry Ct. Records 38-40
Dow's History of Hampton N. H. 676-88
Dowd Genealogy (1885)
Eaton's History of Thomaston Me. ii, 204
Hayward's History of Hancock N. H. 531
Hoyt's Salisbury Mass. Families 133-7
Hudson's History of Lexington Mass. 278
Little's History of Weare N. H. 816-24
Morrison's Hist. of Windham N. H. 510-2
Savage's Genealogical Dictionary ii, 63
Stackpole's History of Durham Me. 174
Stiles' Stranahan Genealogy 103-7
Titcomb's Early New Eng. People 238-43
Washington N. H. History 389
Wheeler's History of Newport N. H. 366
Worcester's History of Hollis N. H. 372
Dowd — Am. Anc. v, 96; vi, 35; vii, 144
Dowd Genealogy (1885) 355 pages
Savage's Genealogical Dictionary ii, 64
Dowell — Sharpless Genealogy 370
Dower — Lincoln's Hingham ii, 195
Downe — American Ancestry ix, 203
Downer — American Ancestry iii, 149
Downer Genealogy (1900) 244 pages
Hoyt's Salisbury Mass. Families 138
Savage's Genealogical Dictionary ii, 65
Downes — American Ancestry xi, 189
Cochrane's Hist. Francestown N. H. 641-6
Sedgwick's Sharon Ct. 77
Sharpe's So. BritainCt. Sketches 152-4, 161
Downie — Carey's Bridgewater Mass.
Downey — Temple's N. Brookfield 577
Downing — American Ancestry ii, 34
Bradbury's Kennebunkport Me. 240

Clarke's Kindred Genealogies (1896) 143-55
Cochrane's History of Antrim N. H. 463-7
Deacon's Stoddard Genealogy
Futhey's History of Chester Co. Pa. 525
Hayward's History of Gilsum N. H. 302
Miller's Hist. Colchester Co. N. S. 338-40
Montague Genealogy 34-42
Palmer and Trimble Gen. 345-9, 406-10
Plumb's History of Hanover Pa. 406
Poor's Merrimac Valley Researches 82
Read's History of Swanzey N. H. 328
Ruttenber's Hist. of Orange Co. N. Y. 398
Savage's Genealogical Dictionary ii, 65-7
Downman — Hayden's Virg. Gens. 72
Downs — Anderson's Waterbury 46
Orcutt's History of New Milford Ct. 692
Orcutt's History of Stratford Ct. 1195
Ransom Genealogy
Savage's Genealogical Dictionary ii, 65
Swift's Barnstable Families i, 34-58
Wentworth Genealogy i, 254-6
Dows — American Ancestry iv, 137
Dowse — American Ancestry iv, 139
Cregar's White Genealogy
Daniels' History of Oxford Mass. 487
Dowse Genealogy (1890) 348 pages
Hazen's History of Billerica Mass. 41
Morse's Sherborn Mass. Settlers 78
Savage's Genealogical Dictionary ii, 68
Wyman's Charlestown Mass. i, 301-8
Dowst — Pickering Genealogy
Dox — Munsell's Albany Colls. iv, 118
Talcott's N. Y. and N. E. Families 166-71
Doyen — Carter's Pembroke N. H. 70-2
Doyle — Davis' Bucks County Pa. 668
Temple's Hist. of N. Brookfield Mass. 577
D'Oyley — American Ancestry vii, 232
Dozier — Power's Sangamon Ill. 262
Dragoo — Jolliffe Genealogy 195-8
Drake — American Ancestry iv, 204
Barbour's My Wife and Mother 64-7
Bass' History of Braintree Vt. 129
Bolton's Westchester Co. N. Y. ii, 726
Chambers' Early Germans of N. J. 335-42
Dow's History of Hampton N. H. 688-94
Drake Genealogy (1845) 51 pages
Drake Family Chart (1861)
Drake Family Chart (1867)
Drake Genealogy (1896) 364 pages
Eaton's History of Thomaston Me. ii, 204
Green's Kentucky Families
Hurd's Hist. of Rockingham Co. N. H. 425
Kingman's No. Bridgewater Mass. 490
Kirby Genealogy
Lane Genealogy (1891) 110, 117
Littell's Passaic Valley Genealogies 145
Loomis Genealogy (1880) 865-9, 390-3
New York Gen. and Biog. Rec. xxvii 176-82
Orcutt's History of Torrington Ct. 682-5
Preble Genealogy 263
Salisbury's Fam. Histories (1892) ii, 215-24
Savage's Genealogical Dictionary ii, 69-71
Stiles' History of Windsor Ct. ii, 177-91
Temple's History of N. Brookfield Mass. 578
Whitney Genealogy i, 100

Drakely — Cothren's Woodbury 539
Savage's Genealogical Dictionary ii, 71
Tuttle Genealogy 574
Draper — American Anc. i, 24; viii, 96, 158
Ballou's History of Milford Mass. 719-23
Chandler Genealogy 51-3
Cochrane's History of Antrim N. H. 467
Cochrane's Hist. Francestown N. H. 646-9
Draper Golden Wedding (1871) 32 pages
Draper Genealogy (1892) 312 pages
Draper's History of Spencer Mass. 190-4
Guild's (Calvin) Ancestry 3
Hill's Dedham Mass. Records i
Hudson's History of Lexington Mass. 57
Randall's History of Chesterfield N. H. 283
Savage's Genealogical Dictionary ii, 71
Temple's Hist. of N. Brookfield Mass. 578
Washington N. H. History 389-91
Wyman's Charlestown Mass. Gens. ii, 308
Dreisbach — Egle's Notes (1898) 48
Drennan — Power's Sangamon 262-8
Dresher — Kriebel's Schwenfelders 4
Dresser — American Ancestry v, 79
Ammidown Genealogy 29
Ammidown's Historical Collections ii, 220
Barrus' History of Goshen Mass. 144
Daniels' History of Oxford Mass. 488
Essex Mass. Institute Hist. Colls. xxi, 73-7
Gage's History of Rowley Mass. 441
Heywood's Hist. of Westminster Mass. 616
Hubbard's Stanstead Co. Canada 317
Power's Sangamon Co. Ill. Settlers 268
Ridlon's Saco Valley Me. Families 631
Savage's Genealogical Dictionary ii, 72
Washington N. H. History 391
Worthen's History of Sutton N. H. 688-92
Dret — Munsell's Albany Colls. iv, 119
Drew — Am. Anc. ii, 34, 154; iv, 144; ix, 129
Carter's History of Pembroke N. H. ii, 73-6
Davis' Landmarks of Plymouth 91-5
Dow's History of Hampton N. H. 694
Eaton's History of Thomaston Me. 205
Hubbard's Stanstead Co. Canada 230, 309
Savage's Genealogical Dictionary ii, 72
Thompson Genealogy (1890) 132
Wentworth Genealogy ii, 292-4
Winsor's History of Duxbury Mass. 256
Drinker — Bartow Genealogy 135
Drinker Genealogy (1893) 30 pages
Morris Genealogy (1898) 888-92
Savage's Genealogical Dictionary ii, 72
Wyman's Charlestown Mass. Gens. i, 309
Drinkwater — Corliss' North Yarmouth
    Me. Magazine, 123-8 386-93, 397-403,
    1142-6
Eaton's History of Thomaston Me. ii, 205
Maine Hist. and Gen. Recorder iii, 265-7
Orcutt's History of New Milford Ct. 692
Stackpole's History of Durham Me. 175
Driscoll — Temple's N. Brookfield 580
Driver — Driver Genealogy (1889) 556 p.
Drody — Freeman's Cape Cod 145
Drown — Roe's Sketches of Rose N. Y. 212
Drowne — American Ancestry ii, 34
Bartlett's Russell Genealogy 119-24
Brewster's Portsmouth N. H. ii, 139-43

Drowne Genealogy (1879) 16 pages
N. Y. Gen. and Biog. Record xvii, 215-8
Savage's Genealogical Dictionary ii, 74
Whitmore's Copps Hills Epitaphs
Druce — Jackson's Newton Mass. 271-3
Paige's History of Cambridge Mass. 536
Savage's Genealogical Dictionary ii, 74
Drumm — Am. Ancestry ii, 34; iii, 193
Drummond — American Ancestry vi, 161
N. Y. Gen. and Biog. Record xvii, 35-7
Drury — Aldrich's Walpole N. H. 241
American Ancestry ii, 34; iii, 179
Barry's Hist. of Framingham Mass. 222-5
Caverly's History of Pittsford Vt. 699
Draper's History of Spencer Mass. 194
Drury Chart (1880) 11x17 inches
Drury Genealogy (1900)
Heywood's Hist. Westminster Mass. 616-8
Norton's Hist. of Fitzwilliam N. H. 539-43
Pierce's History of Grafton Mass. 475
Savage's Genealogical Dictionary ii, 72
Temple's History of N. Brookfield Mass.
    580
Temple's Hist. Framingham Mass. 527-9
Turner Genealogy (1852)
Ward's Rice Genealogy 13
Ward's History of Shrewsbury Mass. 266-9
Worcester's History of Hollis N. H. 372
Dryden — Missouri Pioneers 253
Duane — Lamb's History of N. Y. City
Valentine's N. Y. Common Council Man-
    ual (1853) 410-2, (1861) 547-9
Dubbs — Bretz Genealogy 83-90
Du Bois — American Ancestry i, 24; ii, 34;
    iii, 211; vi, 25; vii, 192
Bass' History of Braintree Vt. 130
Blackman's Susquehanna Co. Pa. 66
Du Bois Genealogy (1860) 76 pages
Du Bois Chart (1876)
Du Bois Reunion (1876) 157 pages
Greene County N. Y. History 109-13
Hoffman Genealogy 491, etc.
New York Gen. and Biog. Rec. xxiv, 153-9;
    xxvii, 190-4; xxviii, 13-6
Sahler Genealogy 7-9
Schoonmaker's Hist. Kingston N. Y. 477-9
Shourd's Fenwick Colony N. J. 75-7
Sylvester's History of Ulster Co. N. Y. 180
Dubose — Gregg's Old Cheraws 91-5
Duboys — Clute's Staten Island N. Y. 376
Dubs — Penn. Mag. of History xviii, 371-6
Perkiomen Region Pa. by Dotterer 21
Duche — Penn. Mag. of History xii, 486
Dudley — American Ancestry iv, 146; vii,
    166; viii, 11, 26
Bangor Me. Historical Magazine vi, 174
Barbour's My Wife and Mother, app. 56
Barry's History of Framingham Mass. 225
Benedict's History of Sutton Mass. 635-8
Chase's History of Chester N. H. 511-13
Daniels' History of Oxford Mass. 489
Davis' History of Wallingford Ct. 741
Drake's History of Boston Mass. (1856)
Dudley Genealogy (1848) 144 pages
Dudley Genealogy (1862) 160 pages
Dudley Genealogy (1886) 1201 pages

Dudley Reunion (1892) 52 p.; (1893) 103 p. (1895) 53 pages
Dudley Gen. Supplement (1898) 96 pages
Dunstable Mass. Bi-Centennial 177
Emerson's History of Douglas Mass. 212-4
Fullonton's Hist. Raymond N. H. 202-15
Hammett Papers of Ipswich Mass. 80
Hoyt's Salisbury Mass. Families 139-41
Hudson's History of Lexington Mass. 58
Lancaster's History of Gilmanton N. H. 260
Lapham's History of Paris Me. 584
Lapham's Hist. of Woodstock Me. 707-10
Moore's Am. Governors i, 273, 294, 402
Nealley Chart
N. E. Hist. Gen. Reg. i, 71; x, 130-42, 337-44
Paige's History of Cambridge Mass. 536
Randall's Hist. of Chesterfield N. H. 283-5
Ruggles Genealogy
Runnels' History of Sanbornton N. H. ii, 230
Saunders' Alabama Settlers 386-91
Savage's Genealogical Dictionary ii, 75-8
Shattuck's History of Concord Mass. 369
Smith Genealogy (1890) 189
Strong Genealogy 756-64
Waterford Me. Centennial (1879) 244
Wheeler's History of Newport N. H. 367-9
Whitmore's Heraldic Journal i, 185-7
Due — Hayward's Hancock N. H. 532
Duel — American Ancestry xi, 154
Ely Genealogy 188
Duer — Van Rensselaer's New Yorkers
Duey — Bretz Genealogy 4, 16-24
Duff — Power's Sangamon Co. Ill. 269
Duffie — Green's Todd Genealogy
Duffield — Davis' Bucks Co. Pa. 203
Duffield Golden Wedding (1867) 58 pages
Green's Todd Genealogy 122-6
Martindale's History of Byberry Pa. 284-9
Neill Genealogy (1875) 65-93
Neill's Ancestry of Henry Neill 29-33
Dufford — Chambers' N. J. Germans
Duggan — Temple's No. Brookfield 580
Duhamel — American Ancestry ix, 66
Duke — Green's Kentucky Families
Paxton's Marshall Gen. 178-83, 282-90
Prescott's Page Genealogy 209
Richmond Va. Standard iii, 20
Dulany — Meade's Old Families of Va.
Dumaresq — American Ancestry vi, 170
Dumaresq Genealogy (1863) 23 pages
New Eng. Hist. Register xvii, 189-96
Whitmore's Heraldic Journal iii, 97-104
Dumas — Temple's No. Brookfield 580
Dummer — Coffin's Newbury 301
Dummer Genealogy (1881) 29 pages
Dummer Academy (1865) (1888)
Essex Mass. Institute Hist. Colls. xxi, 77
Hoyt's Salisbury Mass. Families 141
Hammett Papers of Ipswich Mass. 83
New Eng. Hist. Reg. xxxv, 254-71, 321-31
North's History of Augusta Me. 849
Salisbury's Family Mems. (1885) 260-80
Savage's Genealogical Dictionary ii, 79
Whitmore's Heraldic Journal ii, 34

Dumond — American Ancestry vi, 12
Schoonmaker's Hist. of Kingston N. Y. 479
Sylvester's History of Ulster Co. N. Y. 102
Du Mont — Life of Rachel Du Mont 93
McPike Genealogy 43-172
Messler's History of Somerset Co. N. J. 60
New York Gen. and Biog. Record xxix, 104-9, 240; xxx, 36-40
Sylvester's History of Ulster Co. N. Y. 102
Dun — Swift's Barnstable Families i, 348
Dunbar — Anderson's Waterbury 46
Barry's History of Hanover Mass. 295
Clarke's Old King Wm. Co. Va. Families
Daniels' History of Oxford Mass. 489
Davis' Landmarks of Plymouth Mass. 95
Deane's History of Scituate Mass. 264
Dow's History of Hampton N. H. 695
Dunbar Genealogy (1886) 35 pages
Eaton's Annals of Warren Me. 537
Eaton's History of Thomaston Me. ii, 205
Hayward's History of Hancock N. H. 533
Hobart's History of Abington Mass. 366
Kingman's No. Bridgewater Mass. 481-7
Lincoln's Hist. Hingham Mass. ii, 195-205
Livermore's History of Wilton N. H. 362
Milliken's Narraguagus Valley Me. 17
Mitchell's Hist. Bridgewater Mass. 147-50
Munsell's Albany Collections iv, 119
Orcutt's History of Torrington Ct. 685
Pearson's Schenectady N. Y. Settlers 63
Slaughter's St. Mark's Parish Va. 175
Temple's History of Palmer Mass. 444
Washburn's History of Leicester Mass. 358
Welles' Amer. Family Antiquity i, 217-53
Whitman Genealogy 367-70
Winslow Genealogy ii, 689-93
Duncan — American Ancestry ix, 144
Babson's History of Gloucester Mass. 82
Barry's History of Hanover Mass. 295
Bartow Genealogy 140
Chase's History of Haverhill Mass. 628
Cochrane's History of Antrim N. H. 468-75
Daniels' History of Oxford Mass. 490
Eaton's History of Candia N. H. 65
Eaton's History of Thomaston Me. ii, 206
Hayward's Hist. of Hancock N. H. 534-42
Hemenway's Vermont Gazetteer v, 92-4
Merrill's History of Acworth N. H. 212-4
Parker's Londonderry N. H. 269-72
Power's Sangamon Co. Ill. Settlers 270-2
Savage's Genealogical Dictionary ii, 80
Smith's History of Peterborough N. H. 60
Temple's Hist. N. Brookfield Mass. 580-8
Dunckle — Hazen's Billerica Mass. 42
Duncklee — Cochrane's Francest'n 649-53
Secomb's Amherst 570-3
Wyman's Charlestown Mass. Gens. i, 311
Dundore — American Ancestry iv, 15
Dundore Genealogy (1881) 58 pages
Dungan — Austin's R. I. Gen. Dict. 67
Austin's Allied Families 86
Austin's Ancestries 126
Davis' History of Bucks Co. Pa. 359
Dunham — American Ancestry i, 25; ii, 35
Andrews' Hist. of New Britain Ct. 157, 232
Bass' History of Braintree Vt. 130

Cleveland Genealogy (1899) 434-6
Daniels' History of Oxford Mass. 490
Davis' Landmarks of Plymouth 96-8
Guild's Stiles Genealogy (1892) 190
Hanson's History of Gardiner Me. 158
Hobart's History of Abington Mass. 367-72
Hyde's History of Brimfield Mass. 396
Lapham's History of Bethel Me. 519
Lapham's History of Norway Me. 495-6
Lapham's History of Paris Me. 585-9
Lapham's History of Woodstock Me. 210-2
Littell's Passaic Valley Genealogies 146
Loomis Genealogy (1880) 515
New York Gen. and Biog. Rec. xxvii, 94
Pompey N. Y. Reunion 301
Randall's Hist. of Chesterfield N. H. 285-7
Savage's Genealogical Dictionary ii, 80
Sedgwick's History of Sharon Ct. 77
Spooner Genealogy i, 392-400
Swift's Barnstable Mass. Families i, 346
Timlow's Sketches of Southington Ct. 84-7
Dunklee — Caverley's Pittsford 700
Denny Genealogy
Hayward's History of Hancock N. H. 543
Hudson's History of Lexington Mass. 59
Dunlap — Caverley's Pittsford Vt 700
Chase's History of Chester N. H. 513
Cochrane's History of Antrim N. H. 476-81
Dearborn's Hist. of Salisbury N. H. 542-5
Maine Hist. and Gen. Recorder iv, 72-6
Miller's Colchester Co. Nova Scotia 111-8
Orcutt's History of Stratford Ct. 1195
Power's Sangamon Co. Ill. Settlers 272
Wheeler's History of Brunswick Me. 832
Dunlevy — American Ancestry xii
Dunn — American Ancestry ix, 173
Austin's R. I. Genealogical Dictionary 68
Buxton Me. Centennial 173
Eaton's History of Thomaston Me. ii, 206
Heywood's Hist. of Westminster Mass. 618
Lincoln's History of Hingham Mass. ii, 205
Meginnes's Historical Journal ii, 24-6, 175
Norton's History of Fitzwilliam N. H. 543
Power's History of Sangamon Co. Ill. 272
Ridlon's Saco Valley Me. Families 119
Saunders' Alabama Settlers 377-86
Sharpless Genealogy 237, 366
Temple's Hist. of N. Brookfield Mass. 581
Dunnell — Bartlett's Wanton Family 137
Buxton Me. Centennial 168-70
Dunnell Genealogy (1862) 87 pages
Ridlon's Saco Valley Me. Families 632-4
Dunning — American Ancestry vi, 171
Bangor Historical Magazine vi, 159-62
Eaton's History of Thomaston Me. ii, 207
Knox Co. Me. Hist. Magazine i, 45, etc.
New Eng. Hist. and Gen. Reg. lii, 38-41
Slafter Genealogy 23-5
Sprague's History of Gloversville N. Y. 115
Stickney's History of Minisink N. Y. 120
Wheeler's History of Brunswick Me. 832
Dunshee — Aldrich's Walpole N. H. 244
Dunsmore — Saunderson's Charlestown
Dunspaugh — American Ancestry ii, 154
Dunster — Cutter's Arlington Mass. 234
Dunster (Henry) Life of (1872)

Dunster Genealogy (1876) 333 pages
Freeman's History of Cape Cod Mass. ii, 522
Heywood's Hist. Westminster Mass. 619-21
New Eng. Hist. and Gen. Reg. xxvii, 307-11
Paige's History of Cambridge Mass. 537-9
Savage's Genealogical Dictionary ii, 82
Stearns' History of Ashburnham Mass. 683
Titcomb's New England People 82-91
Wyman's Charlestown Mass. Gens. i, 312
Dunton — American Ancestry x, 104
Barry's History of Framingham Mass. 226
Cleveland's History of Yates Co. N. Y. 378
Eaton's History of Reading Mass. 63-6
New Eng. Hist. and Gen. Reg. liv, 286-8
Norton's History of Fitzwilliam N. H. 543
Duntz — American Ancestry ii, 35
Dunwoodie — Am. Ancestry vi, 62, 115
Dunwoody — Baillie Genealogy 92-8
Bellinger Genealogy 105-7
Bulloch Genealogy
Bulloch's Stewart Genealogy 20
Dupee — Heywood's Westminster 621-3
Du Pont — American Ancestry iii, 180
Smith (Rev. Wm.) Biography
Dupuy—Am. Anc. vii, 263; viii, 197; x, 29
Dupuy Genealogy (1880) 8 pages
Goode Genealogy 173
Meade's Old Churches of Virginia i, 467
Virg. Hist. Soc. Collections v, (1886) 151-82
Watkins Genealogy 25
Duran — Stackpole's Durham Me. 176-8
Durand — Adams' Fairhaven Vt. 348
American Ancestry vii, 227; ix, 199
Orcutt's History of Derby Ct. 718
Sharpe's History of Seymour Ct. 159
Durant — American Ancestry i, 25
Hazen's History of Billerica Mass. 43-5
Hubbard's History of Springfield Vt. 277
Jackson's History of Newton Mass. 268-70
Knox Co. Me. Hist. Magazine i, 110-2
Secomb's History of Amherst N. H. 573
Temple's History of Palmer Mass. 443
Durell — Jackson's Newton Mass. 270
Lapham's History of Paris Me. 590-2
Wentworth Genealogy ii, 101
Duren — American Ancestry vii, 5
Hudson's History of Lexington Mass. 60
Locke Genealogy 96
Durfee—American Ancestry ix, 121; xii, 25
Austin's Ancestries 19
Austin's R. I. Genealogical Dictionary 68
Davis' Landmarks of Plymouth Mass. 98
Fowler's History of Fall River Mass. 67
Jennings Genealogy (1890)
Peck's Fall River Mass. Industries 261-76
Turner's Phelps Purchase N. Y. 382
Walker Genealogy 155-7
Durgee — Babson's Gloucester Mass. 82
Durgin — Coffin's Boscawen N. H. 520
Cogswell's Hist. Nottingham N. H. 681-7
Dearborn's History of Parsonsfield Me. 378
Farrow's History of Islesborough Me. 200
Folsom Genealogy by Chapman 193
Lancaster's History of Gilmanton N. H. 261
Runnels' Sanbornton N. H. ii, 231-45

Durham — Champion Genealogy 90-5
Cleveland's Hist. of Yates Co. N. Y. 472-6
Williamson's History of Belfast Me. 93-5
Durkee — American Ancestry iii, 15
Hammett Papers of Ipswich Mass. 84
Walworth's Hyde Genealogy 92
Wheeler's History of Newport N. H. 371
Durland — Calnek's Annapolis N. S. 503
Stickney's Minisink 172
See also under Dorland
Durling — See Dorland
Durpee — Wheeler's Newport N. H.
Durrant — Bedford Families 9
Durrell — Bradbury's Kennebunkport
Emery Genealogy (1890) 104
Durrie — Durrie's Steele Genealogy 41
Duryea — Am. Ancestry ix, 77; x, 187
Bergen's Kings Co. N. Y. Settlers 103-5
Bunker's Long Island Genealogies 200
New York Gen. and Biog. Rec. xi, 62-70
Riker's Annals of Newtown N. Y. 371
Dusenbury — American Ancestry ii, 35
Baird's History of Rye N. Y. 461
Dustan — Clute's Staten Island 377
Dustin — Chase's Chester N. H. 513
Cochrane's History of Antrim N. H. 481
Cochrane's Hist. Francest'n N. H.654-8
Corliss Genealogy
Eaton's History of Candia N. H. 66
Hayward's History of Hancock N. H. 544
Heywood's Hist of Westminster Mass. 623
Runnels' Sanbornton N. H. ii, 245-7
Duston — Cogswell's Henniker 552-5
Lapham's History of Bethel Me. 520-2
Little's History of Weare N. H. 825
Morrison's Hist. of Windham N. H. 520-3
Dutch — Babson's Gloucester Mass. 83
Dearborn's History of Parsonsfield Me. 378
Hammett Papers of Ipswich Mass. 81-3
Herrick Genealogy (1885) 21, 273-5
Savage's Genealogical Dictionary ii, 84
Dutcher — Ballou's Milford Mass. 723-5
Raymond's Tarrytown Monument 89-100
Dutton — Anderson Waterbury 47
Bangor Historical Magazine ix, 71
Bass' History of Braintree Vt. 131
Brown's Bedford Mass. Families 9
Cochrane's Hist. Francest'n N. H. 658-60
Davis' History of Wallingford Ct. 741-3
Douglas Genealogy 209-11
Dutton Genealogy (1871) 112 pages
Hayward's History of Hancock N. H. 545
Hazen's History of Billerica Mass. 45
Hemenway's Vermont Gazetteer v, 41, 213
Hill's History of Mason N. H. 201
Hodgman's History of Westford Mass. 445
Maris Genealogy 60, 130
Martin's History of Chester Pa. 247, 251
Power's Sangamon Co. Ill. Settlers 273
Stearns' Hist. of Ashburnham Mass. 683
Stearns' History of Rindge N. H. 510
Temple's Hist. of Northfield Mass. 435
Temple's History of Palmer Mass. 445
Timlow's Southington Ct. Sketches 87-90
Tucker's History of Hartford Vt. 414-21
Du Vall — N. Y. Gen. Rec. xxii, 105

Duyckinck — Bergen's King Co. 105
N. Y. Gen. and Biog. Record xxiii, 33-7
Dwelley — Barry's Hanover Mass. 296
Deane's History of Scituate Mass. 265
Hanover Mass. Records (1898)
Savage's Genealogical Dictionary ii, 85
Winsor's History of Duxbury Mass. 257
Dwight — American Ancestry i, 26, iv,
    232, 244; ix, 57; xi, 12
Benedict's History of Sutton Mass. 638
Chandler's History of Shirley Mass. 391-4
Doolittle's Belchertown Mass. 260-3
Dwight Genealogy (1874) 1144 pages
Eaton's History of Thomaston Me. ii, 207
Goodwin's Genealogical Notes 40-7
Larned's History of Windham Co. Ct.
Longmeadow Mass. Centennial, app. 58
N. Y. Gen. Rec. iv, 151-5; xvii, 23-32
Savage's Genealogical Dictionary ii, 85-7
Stearns' History of Ashburnham Mass. 684
Strong Genealogy 365-76, 402-4
Temple's Hist. of N. Brookfield Mass. 582
Tuttle Genealogy 409-17
Dwinel — Lapham's Rumford Me. 316
Dwinell — Vt. Hist. Gaz. iv, 161-3
Dwinnel — Benedict's Sutton Mass. 638
Dunnel and Dwinnel Gen. (1862) 84 pages
Poor's Merrimac Valley Researches 117
Savage's Genealogical Dictionary ii, 87
Dyckman — Bolton's Westchester 727
Munsell's Albany Collections iv, 119
N. Y. Gen. and Biog. Record xxi, 81-3
Riker's History of Harlem N. Y. 505-12
Dye — Greene Genealogy (1894)
Joslin's History of Poultney Vt. 254
Young's Hist. of Chautauqua Co. N. Y. 581
Dyer — American Ancestry i, 26; iv, 20, 52
Austin's Ancestries 21
Austin's R. I. Genealogical Dictionary 290
Bangor Me. Hist. Mag. vii, 182; viii, 233
Barry's History of Hanover Mass. 300
Bass' History of Braintree Vt. 131
Brown's West Simsbury Ct. Settlers 57-9
Davis' Landmarks of Plymouth Mass. 99
Dyer Genealogy (1884) 130 pages
Dyer's History of Plainfield Mass. 139-48
Eaton's History of Thomaston Me. ii, 208
Freeman's Hist. of Cape Cod Mass. ii, 551
Hobart's History of Abington Mass. 372-8
Lincoln's History of Hingham Mass. ii, 207
Milliken's Narraguagus Valley Me. 8
Mitchell's Hist. of Bridgewater Mass. 150
Olin's Olin Genealogy 71-89, etc.
Poole Genealogy 89-91
Rich's History of Truro Mass. 525-7
Runnel's Hist. of Sanbornton N. H. ii, 248
Savage's Genealogical Dictionary ii, 88
Stackpole's History of Durham Me. 178
Swift's Barnstable Mass. Families i, 346
Wheeler Ancestors (1896) 11
Wyman's Charlestown Mass. Gens. i, 315
Dyke — Davis Plymouth Mass. 85
Jackson's History of Newton Mass. 271
Mitchell's History of Bridgwater Mass. 146
Dymond — Savage's Gen. Dictionary ii, 50
Dymont — Dimond Genealogy 112-33

Dynn — Driver Genealogy 281
Dyson — Slaughter's Bristol Parish 7
Eader — Richmond Standard iii, 31
Eager — Caulkins' Norwich Ct. 174
Cogswell's History of Henniker N. H. 555
Eager and Davis Chart (1859) 20x50 inches
Eager's History of Orange Co. N. Y. 302
Hayward's History of Gilsum N. H. 303
Heywood's Hist. of Westminster Mass. 624
Hudson's Hist. Marlborough Mass. 355-7
Paige's History of Cambridge Mass. 539
Pierce's History of Gorham Me. 163
Savage's Genealogical Dictionary ii, 105
Ward Genealogy 45
Ward's History of Shrewsbury Mass. 272-4
Worcester Mag. and Hist. Journal ii, 152
See also under Ager
Eagle — Egle's Pa. Gens. 2d ed. 159-86
Eagley — Egle's Pa. Gens. 2d ed. 767
Eames — Adams' Haven Gen. i, 38; ii, 24
American Ancestry i, 26; xii, 29
Ballou's History of Milford Mass. 726
Bangor Me. Historical Magazine v, 47
Barry's Hist. of Framingham Mass. 227-33
Brown's West Simsbury Ct. Settlers 69
Butler's History of Islesborough Me. 201
Hudson's Hist. Marlborough Mass. 357-9
Hudson's History of Sudbury Mass. 440
Keyes' West Boylston Mass. Register 17
Kingman's North Bridgewater Mass. 496
Lapham's History of Bethel Me. 521-3
Leland Genealogy 27
Mitchell's Hist. of Bridgewater Mass. 105
Morse's Sherborn Mass. Settlers 79-81
Morse Mem. appendix 50
Paige's History of Cambridge Mass. 539
Perley's History of Boxford Mass. 30
Read's History of Swanzey N. H. 330-2
Savage's Genealogical Dictionary ii, 89-91
Sewall's History of Woburn Mass. 609
Sheldon's History of Deerfield Mass. 151
Sutliff Genealogy (1897) 27-32
Wight Genealogy 104
Earl — Cleveland's Yates Co. 179-81
Prime Genealogy (1895) 47
Stearns' History of Rindge N. H. 511-3
Earle — Am. Anc. iii, 168; vii, 65; xi, 100
Austin's R. I. Genealogical Dictionary 69
Clayton's History of Bergen Co. N. J. 247
Earle Chart (1860)
Earle Genealogy (1888) 492 pages
Hinchman's Nantucket Settlers 98-100
Jennings Genealogy (1899)
Savage's Genealogical Dictionary ii, 91
Stone's Hist. Hubbardston Mass. 262-4
Temple's Hist. of N. Brookfield Mass. 582
Washburn's Hist. Leicester Mass. 359-65
Earll — Hughes Genealogy 201-5
Early — Early Genealogy (1896) 53 pages
Egle's History of Lebanon Co. Pa.
Egle's Notes and Queries (1897) 48-50
Morrison's History of Windham N. H. 523
Page Genealogy 162
Parthemore Genealogy 132-4
Wheeler Ancestors (1896) 18-20
Earnest — Power's Sangamon Ill. 274

Easley — Power's Sangamon Ill. 276
Easson — Calnek's Annapolis N. S. 504
East — Savage's Genealogical Dict. ii, 92
Easterbrook — Amer. Ancestry viii, 53
Lincoln's Hist. of Hingham Mass. ii, 208
Swift's Barnstable Mass. Families i, 358
Wyman's Charlestown Mass. Gens. i, 316
Eastlack — Clement's Newtown N. J.
Eastman — American Ancestry iv, 244;
   vii, 187; viii, 3; ix, 189; x, 148, 197;
   xii, 35
Bouton's History of Concord N. H. 645-50
Chapman's Weeks Genealogy 135
Chase's History of Haverhill Mass. 276
Cleveland's History of Yates Co. N. Y. 741
Coffin's History of Boscawen N. H. 521
Cogswell's Hist. of Henniker N. H. 556-9
Cogswell's Hist. of Nottingham N. H. 374
Corliss Genealogy 239
Corliss' North Yarmouth Me. Magazine
Cothren's History of Woodbury Ct. 541
Dearborn's Hist. of Salisbury N. H. 545-51
Dennysville Me. Centennial 103
Eastman Chart (1858) 11x18 inches
Eastman Genealogy (1867) 11 pages, reprint
Eaton's Annals of Warren Me. 538
Eaton's History of Thomaston Me. ii, 208
Evans Genealogy (1893) 77-82
Fletcher Genealogy 242
Granite Monthly of Concord N. H. 387-90
Hoyt's Salisbury Mass. Families 141-7
Judd's History of Hadley Mass. 489-92
Kellogg's White Genealogy 47
Lancaster's History of Gilmanton N. H. 262
Lapham's History of Rumford Me. 317
Little's History of Weare N. H. 825-9
New Eng. Hist. and Gen. Reg. xxi, 229-37
Paige's History of Hardwick Mass. 368
Power's Sangamon Co. Ill. Settlers 276
Ridlon's Saco Valley Me. Families 162
Runnel's Sanbornton N. H. ii, 249-56
Savage's Genealogical Dictionary ii, 92
Secomb's History of Amherst N. H. 574
Thurston's History of Winthrop Me. 181
Wheeler's History of Newport N. H. 373
Worcester's History of Hollis N. H. 372
Easton — Am. Anc. viii, 167; ix, 215; xi, 14
Austin's Ancestral Dictionary 19
Austin's R. I. Genealogical Dictionary 292
Easton Genealogy (1899) 245 pages
Guild's (Calvin) Ancestry 19
Hammett Papers of Ipswich Mass. 91
Locke Genealogy 102
Savage's Genealogical Dictionary ii, 93
Eaton — American Ancestry iii, 151, 191;
   iv, 11, 144, 215; v, 82; vi, 11, 101; viii,
   130; ix, 176
Ammidown Genealogy 54
Barry's Hist. of Framingham Mass. 233-7
Benedict's History of Sutton Mass. 639
Blake's History of Hamden Ct. 256
Bond's Hist. Watertown Mass. 202-4, 754
Bowens of Woodstock Ct. 182
Brown's West Simsbury Ct. Settlers 62
Butler's History of Farmington Me. 461-7
Chase's History of Chester N. H. 514

Cleveland Genealogy 221-3
Cochrane's History of Antrim N. H. 482
Cochrane's Hist. Francest'n N. H. 661-5
Cogswell's Hist. of Henniker N. H. 559-61
Corliss' North Yarmouth Me. Magazine
Currier's Castleton Vt. Epitaphs 11-3
Davidson College Magazine (1899) 14-9
Davis Genealogy 52
Davis' Landmarks of Plymouth Mass. 99
Davis' History of Wallingford Ct. 940
Dedham Historical Register xi, 67-80
Dearborn's Hist. of Salisbury N. H. 551-3
Draper's History of Spencer Mass. 196
Eaton Family of Dedham (1889) 8 pages
Eaton Family of Nova Scotia (1884) 128 p.
Eaton Family Reunion (1888) 21 pages
Eaton Family of N. H. (1890) 88 pages
Eaton Family Reunion (1891) 35 pages
Eaton Family of Nova Scotia (1895) 29 p.
Eaton Family of Nova Scotia (1899) 20 p.
Eaton's Annals of Warren Me. 538-40
Eaton's History of Candia N. H. 67
Eaton's History of Reading Mass. 63
Eaton's History of Thomaston Me. 209
Hayward's Hancock N. H. 546-52, 1051
Hemenway's Vermont Hist. Gaz. iv, 160
Heywood's Hist. Westminster Mass. 626-9
Herrick's History of Gardiner Mass. 345
Hill's Dedham Mass. Records i
Hoyt's Salisbury Mass. Families 147-51
Hubbard's History of Springfield Vt. 280
Hudson's History of Sudbury Mass. 439
Lapham's History of Rumford Me. 318
Lincoln's History of Hingham Mass. ii, 209
Little's History of Weare N. H. 830-3
Livermore's History of Wilton N. H. 363
Mitchell's Hist. of Bridgewater Mass. 373
New Eng. Hist. and Gen. Register xxvii,
    195; xxxviii, 29-31
New Haven Hist. Soc. Papers iv, 185-92
N. Y. Hist. Soc. Colls. new series ii, 490
Norton's History of Fitzwilliam N. H. 545
Paige's History of Cambridge Mass. 539
Poore Genealogy 84-91
Potts Genealogy (1895) 89-100
Power's Sangamon Co. Ill. Settlers 280
Read's History of Swanzey N. H. 332
Runnel's Sanbornton N. H. ii, 256-61
Savage's Genealogical Dictionary ii, 95-8
Secomb's History of Amherst N. H. 575-7
Stearns' Hist. of Ashburnham Mass. 684-7
Stiles' History of Windsor Ct. ii, 191-4
Temple's Hist. of N. Brookfield Mass. 583
Vinton Genealogy 64-6
Waldo's History of Tolland Ct. 84-6
Wall's Reminisc. of Worcester Mass. 360
Washington N. H. History 392-4
Wheeler's History of Brunswick Me. 833
Winsor's History of Duxbury Mass. 257
Worthen's Hist. Sutton N. H. 693-5, 1052-86
Wyman's Charlestown Mass. Gens. 317
Wyman's Hunt Genealogy 105
Young's Hist. of Chautauqua Co. N. Y. 506
Eavenson — Palmer and Trimble Gene-
    alogy 49-50, 67-71, 188-90
Ebbing — Lamb's Hist. of N. Y. City i, 260

Eberhart — American Ancestry vii, 18
Eberhart Genealogy (1891) 263 pages
See also under Everhart
Eberle — Lancaster Pa. Historical Society
    Papers (1900) iv, 75-85
Eberly — Hess Genealogy (1896) 159-74
Ebersole — Bretz Genealogy 121-6
Egle's Notes and Queries 3d ser. i, 65
Ebey — Power's Sangamon Co. Ill 277
Ruttenber's Hist. of Orange Co. N. Y. 373
Eby — Brubacher Genealogy 18-72
Eckel — Chambers' N. J. Germans 345
Eckerson — N. Y. Gen. Record vii, 119
Eddy — Adams' Fairhaven Vt. 571
American Ancestry viii, 112; xi, 30
Andrews' New Britain Ct. 221, 275-9
Austin's Allied Families 87-90
Bangor Me. Historical Magazine iv, 53
Bond's Watertown Mass. Gen, 203, 754
Clark's History of Norton Mass. 80
Clute's History of Staten Island N. Y. 378
Cunnabell Genealogy 76
Cutter's History of Arlington Mass. 235
Daniels' History of Oxford Mass. 491-6
Davis' Landmarks Plymouth Mass. 100-2
Eddy Family of Maine (1877) 72 pages
Eddy Family Tree (1880) 16x22 inches
Eddy Genealogy (1881) 180 pages
Eddy Family Reunion (1881) 265 pages
Eddy Family Reunion (1884) 304 pages
Greene's Todd Genealogy 129
Jackson's History of Newton Mass. 273
Joslin's History of Poultney Vt. 225
Maine Genealogist ii, (1877) 113-20
New Eng. Hist. and Gen. Reg. viii, 201-6
Norton's History of Fitzwilliam N. H. 545
Savage's Genealogical Dictionary ii, 98
Sheldon's History of Deerfield Mass. 152
Stearns' History of Ashburnham Mass. 687
Stearns' History of Rindge N. H. 513
Wakefield Genealogy 109
Walworth's Hyde Genealogy 436
Ward's History of Shrewsbury Mass. 274
Williams' History of Danby Vt. 141
Edes — Bangor Hist. Magazine iv, 235-7
Cochrane's History of Antrim N. H. 484
Savage's Genealogical Dictionary ii, 100
Smith's History of Peterborough N. H. 62-6
Wheeler's History of Newport N. H. 374
Whitmore's Copps Hill Epitaphs
Wyman's Charlestown Mass. i, 319-24
Edgarton — Chandler's Shirley 394-9
Edgcomb — Smith Genealogy (1889) 83
Edge — Futhey's Chester Pa. 527-9
Sharpless Genealogy 100
Edgecomb — Eaton's Thomaston 209
Hatch's History of Industry Me. 601
Ridlon's Saco Valley Me. Families 635-76
Edgecombe — Brown's Simsbury 62
Caulkins' History of New London Ct. 366
Caulkins' History of Norwich Ct. 227
Savage's Genealogical Dictionary ii, 100
Edgell — Heywood's Westminster 629-33
Edgerly — Am. Ancestry iv, 107; xi 181
Edgerly Genealogy (1880) 8 pages, reprint
Kelley Genealogy (1892)

N. E. Hist. Reg. xv, 337-9; xxxiv, 282-7
Runnel's Hist. of Sanbornton N. H. ii, 26-3
Edgerton — Am. Ancestry iii, 113; xii, 32
Atkins' History of Hawley Mass. 101
Ball's History of Lake Co. Ind. 385
Caulkins' History of Norwich Ct. 173
Eaton's History of Thomaston Me. ii, 209
Hollister's History of Pawlet Vt. 184-7
Joslin's History of Poultney Vt. 256
Mitchell's Hist. of Bridgewater Mass. 157
Plumb's History of Hanover Pa. 411
Waldo's History of Tolland Ct. 99
Walworth's Hyde Genealogy 613, 625
See also Egerton
Edgett — Stanton Genealogy 326
Edison — N. E. Hist. Register xlviii, 199
Edmunds — American Ancestry vii, 146
Converse Genealogy
Denny Genealogy
Temple's Hist. N. Brookfield Mass. 583-5
Edmiston — Alexander Genealogy 18
Edmond — Chandler Genealogy 512-4
Edmonds — American Ancestry xi, 28
Austin's R. I. Gen. Dictionary 70
Cothren's History of Woodbury Ct. 542
Savage's Genealogical Dictionary ii, 101
Sharpe's South Britain Ct. Sketches 93
Wyman's Charlestown Mass. i, 324-30
Edmonston — Eager's Orange Co. 620
Edmunds — Barry's Framingham 237
Little's History of Weare N. H. 833
Meade's Old Families of Virginia
Olin's Olin Genealogy 38
Slaughter's St. Mark's Parish Va. 140
Watkin's Genealogy 32
Williams' History of Danby Vt. 136-8
Edrington — American Ancestry vii, 238
Edsall — American Ancestry iii, 15
Bergen's Kings Co. N. Y. Settlers 107
Haines' Hardyston N. J. 73-5
N. Y. Gen. and Biog. Rec. xiii, 194-6
Riker's Annals of Newtown N. Y. 341
Edson — Craft's Whately 457
Daniels' History of Oxford Mass. 496
Edson Genealogy (1864) 62 pages
Kingman's No. Bridgewater Mass. 492-6
Mitchell's Hist. of Bridgewater Mass. 151-7
Noyes Genealogy (1861) 11-3
Savage's Genealogical Dictionary ii, 102
Sinclair Genealogy (1896) 147
Stearns' History of Ashburnham Mass. 688
Temple's Hist. of N. Brookfield Mass. 585
Temple's History of Whately Mass. 227
Young's Hist. of Chautauqua Co. N. Y. 258
Edwards — American Ancestry ii, 35; vi, 54, 135; vii, 163, 164; viii, 13; ix, 216; x, 166, 169, 180; xi, 78
Anderson's Waterbury Ct. i, app. 47
Blood's History of Temple N. H. 217
Chapman's Trowbridge Genealogy 192
Clarke's Old King Wm. Co. Va. Families
Cogswell's History of Henniker N. H. 561
Corliss' North Yarmouth Me. Magazine
Daniels' History of Oxford Mass. 496
Dimock's Coventry Ct. Records 41
Dwight Genealogy 1035-43

Dwight's Strong Genealogy 1419-21
Edwards Family Meeting (1871) 206 **pages**
Edwards Family of Springfield (1886) 28 p.
Edwards Family of Virginia (1894) 38 p.
Edwards Fam. of Cromwell Ct. (1891) 12 p.
Futhey's History of Chester Co. Pa. 527
Goode Genealogy 205
Goodwin's Genealogical Notes 48-68, 301-8
Gregg's History of Old Cheraws S. C. 82
Hammett Papers of Ipswich Mass. 95
Hatch's History of Industry Me. 602
Hayden's Virginia Genealogies 98
Hedges' Hist. East Hampton N. Y. 258-72
Hinman's Connecticut Settlers 1st ed. 219
Howell's Southampton N. Y. 238-40
Lapham's History of Bethel Me. 523
Little's History of Weare N. H. 834
Meade's Old Families of Virginia
Morris Genealogy (1898) 717
Ogden Genealogy (1896) 13, 24-9, 47-51
Orcutt's History of Stratford Ct. 1195-7
Paxton's Marshall Genealogy 122
Potts Genealogy (1895) 333
Power's Hist. of Sangamon Co. Ill. 278-80
Roberts' Old Richland Pa. Families
Savage's Genealogical Dictionary ii, 102-4
Smith's Genealogy by Wellington Smith
Stiles' History of Windsor Ct. ii, 194-8
Stoddard Genealogy (1865) 4-8
Stoughton's Windsor Farms Ct. 146-8
Talcott's N. Y. and N. E. Families 506-9
Tuttle Genealogy 374-85
Wetmore Genealogy 546-51
Wight Genealogy 174
Wyman's Charlestown Mass. Gens. 330
Eells — Andrews' New Britain Ct. 258
Barlow Genealogy 223-7
Barry's History of Hanover Mass. 301-5
Hanover Mass. Records (1898)
Hinman's Connecticut Settlers (1846)
Kellogg's White Genealogy 49
Lincoln's History of Hingham Mass. ii, 209
Phœnix Whitney Genealogy i, 403
Savage's Genealogical Dictionary ii, 104-9
Egbert — Clute's Staten Island 379
Egberts — American Ancestry v, 37
Munsell's Albany Collections iv, 119
Talcott's N. Y. and N. E. Families 182
Ege — Chambers' N. J. Germans 345-8
Egerton — Swain Genealogy 100-7
Vermont Historical Gazetteer iv, 623
Vinton's Giles Genealogy 223
See also Edgerton
Egery — Paige's Hardwick Mass. 367
Eggleston — American Ancestry v, 3
Barbour's My Wife and Mother, app. 72
Goode Genealogy 279-81
Goodwin's Olcott Genealogy 51-3
Loomis Genealogy (1880) 547, 679
Meade's Old Churches of Virginia ii, 20
Orcutt's History of Torrington Ct. 686
Savage's Genealogical Dictionary ii, 105
Stiles' Windsor Ct. ii, 198-207, 836
Talcott's N. Y. and N. E. Families 510
Williams' History of Danby Vt. 141
Egle—Egle's Pa. Genealogies 2d ed. 159-86

Egleston — N. Y. Rec. xxiii, 122-7
Egley — Egle's Penn. Genealogies 129-50
Egmont — Munsell's Albany iv, 120
Ehle — Whitmore Genealogy 75-9
Eich — Chambers' N. J. Germans 347-9
Eichar — Bowie Genealogy 422-6
Eichelberger — Rupp Genealogy 61-5, 68
Eigenbrodt — N. Y. Rec. xviii, 122-6
Eighmy — American Ancestry ii, 35
Eire — Bond's Watertown Mass. 204
Ekel — Egle's Penn. Genealogies 129-50
Ela — American Ancestry v, 213
Ela Genealogy (1897) 44 pages
Parker's History of Londonderry N. H. 272
Elbridge—Salisbury's Memorials i, 103-44
Elden — Buxton Me. Centennial 149-5
Egle's Notes and Queries (1898) 17
Goodwin's History of Buxton Me. 359
Ridlon's Saco Valley Me. Families 108
Elder — Craft's Whately Mass. 459
Egle's Penn. Genealogies 2d ed. 187-213
Hatch's History of Industry Me. 603
Mack Genealogy 69-75
Maine Hist. and Gen. Recorder iv, 161-7
Marshall Genealogy (1884) 13-5
Pierce's History of Gorham Me. 164
Power's Sangamon Co. Ill. Settlers 282-4
Temple's History of Whately Mass. 228
Elderkin — American Ancestry ix, 62
Caulkins' History of New London Ct. 117
Caulkins' History of Norwich Ct. 215
Elderkin Genealogy (1888) 223 pages
Elderkin Family of N. Y. (1896) 14 pages
Kellogg's White Genealogy 88
Savage's Genealogical Dictionary ii, 108
Eldred — Austin's R. I. Gen. Dictionary 71
Austin's Allied Families 90
Cleveland's History of Yates Co. N. Y. 735
Newport Historical Magazine iv, 242-8
Savage's Genealogical Dictionary ii, 107
Eldredge — American Ancestry xi, 29
Eldredge Genealogy (1896) 35 pages
Lawrence, Hughes and Eldredge Families of N. J. (1891)
Lincoln's Hist. of Hingham Mass. ii, 211-3
New Eng. Hist. Register li, 46-54
Eldridge — Aldrich's Walpole N. H. 245
Bangor Me. Hist. Magazine iv, 219, 236
Cogswell Genealogy 263
Freeman's Cape Cod ii, 598, 601, 710
Futhey's History of Chester Co. Pa. 530
Meade's Old Churches of Virginia
Richmond Va. Standard ii, 10, 36
Robertson's Pocahontas, Descendants
Savage's Genealogical Dictionary ii, 107
Sharpless Genealogy 223
Elerby — Gregg's Old Cheraws 64
Eliot — Amer. Ancestry iii, 16; iv, 26, 111
Atkins Genealogy (1891) 80-4
Caverley's Eliot Memoir (1881)
Dorr Genealogy
Drake's History of Boston Mass. (1876)
Dwight Genealogy 179
Dwight's Strong Genealogy 359, 502
Eliot Family of Beverly (1854) 4 pages
Eliot Family of Roxbury (1854) 184 pages

Eliot Family of Beverly (1857) chart
Eliot Family of Beverly (1887) 157 pages
Ellis' History of Roxbury Mass. 117
Hall's Genealogical Notes (1886) 104, 107
Hill's History of Mason N. H. 201
Jones' History of Stockbridge Mass. 131
Maltby Genealogy (1895) 70
Mass. Hist. Society Colls. 2d series ii, 228
New Eng. Historical and Gen. Register
    viii, 45, 259; x, 355-8; xxvii, 124; xxviii,
    144-6; xxxiii, 144; xxxix, 365-71
Paige's History of Cambridge Mass. 540
Stiles' History of Windsor Ct. ii, 207
Walker Genealogy 26
Whitmore's Copps Hill Epitaphs
Elithrop — Essex Institute Colls. xxi, 78
Elkenburg — American Ancestry ii, 35
Elkin — Power's Sangamon Ill. 281
Elkins — American Ancestry vii, 9
Dow's History of Hampton N. H. 697-702
Essex Mass. Inst. Hist. Colls. 197
Leach's Reading Genealogy 237-60
Leavenworth Genealogy 141
Runnel's Hist. Sanbornton N. H. ii, 263-5
Smith's Founders of Mass. Bay 163-5
Ellenwood — Secomb's Amherst 577
Ellery — Babson's Gloucester 84-7
Bartlett's Wanton Family 125
Bartlett's R. I. Hist. Tracts iii, 125
Ellery Chart (1881) 2x3 feet
Muzzey's Reminiscences
New Eng. Hist. and Gen. Reg. xliii, 313-5
Newport Historical Magazine iv, 183-96
Savage's Genealogical Dictionary ii, 112
Wyman's Charlestown Mass. Gens. i, 331
Whitmore's Heraldic Journal i, 177-82
Ellet — Clarke's King Wm. Va. Families
Lloyd and Carpenter Gen. (1870) 66-80
Ellice — Jameson's Medway Mass. 480
Ellicott — Thomas Genealogy 69-75, 177
Fox, Ellicott and Evans Gen. (1882) 281 p.
Thomas Genealogy (1896) 294-302
Ellingwood — Bethel Me. 523-5
Dodge Ancestry (1896) 18, 69
Roe's Sketches of Rose N. Y. 247
Savage's Genealogical Dictionary ii, 113
Elliot — Babson's Gloucester Mass. 299
Benedict's History of Sutton Mass. 639-41
Bouton's History of Concord N. H. 560-4
Chase's History of Chester N. H. 515
Cope Genealogy 86, 190
Cushman's History of Sheepscott Me. 377
Daniels' History of Oxford Mass. 496
Hoyt's Salisbury Mass. Families 151
Lapham's History of Rumford Me. 319-23
New Eng. Hist. and Gen. Reg. xliv, 112-4
Penn. Mag. of History and Biog. vi, 333
Pierce's History of Grafton Mass. 477
Ridlon's Saco Valley Me. Families 677
Saunders' Alabama Settlers 365
Savage's Genealogical Dictionary ii, 108-12
Secomb's History of Amherst N. H. 579
Sedgwick's History of Sharon Ct. 78
Walworth's Hyde Gen. ii, 754-9, 937-45
Elliott — American Ancestry v, 130, 205
Bulloch's Stewart Genealogy 13-9

Calnek's History of Annapolis N. S. 505
Coffin's History of Boscawen N. H. 523
Cutts Genealogy 26, 50
Dwight Genealogy 987–96
Eaton's History of Thomaston Me. ii, 210
Egle's Penn. Genealogies 2d ed. 653
Hazen's History of Billerica Mass. 46
Hine's Lebanon Ct. Historical Address 153
Leonard's History of Dublin N. H. 328
Miller's History of Colchester Co. N. S. 911,
Power's Sangamon Co. Ill. Settlers 284
Whitmore's Heraldic Journal iv, 183–91
Wyman's Charlestown Mass. Gens. i, 322
Ellis — Adams' Fairhaven Vt. 368–70
American Ancestry i, 26; iii, 151; v, 130;
  vi, 8, 193; vii, 23, 73; viii, 219; ix, 109;
  x, 179; xi, 188
Andrews' History of New Britain Ct. 717
Ballou's History of Milford Mass. 726–9
Bangor Me. Historical Magazine v, 190
Barry's History of Hanover Mass. 305–7
Bassett's History of Richmond N. H. 384
Clement's Newtown N. J. Settlers
Cochrane's Hist. of Francestown N. H. 665
Davis' Landmarks Plymouth Mass. 102–5
Dedham Historical Register xi, 81–6
Ellis Family of Virginia (1849) 11 pages
Ellis Family of Mass. (1888) 483 pages
Ellis Family of Boston (1893) 6 pages
Freeman's Cape Cod Mass. ii, 72, 133, 164
Glenn's Merion in Welsh Tract 205–34
Hatch's History of Industry Me. 603
Hayward's History of Gilsum N. H. 304
Hemenway Genealogy 35–7
Hemenway's Vermont Hist. Gazetteer v
Heywood's Hist. of Westminster Mass. 633
Hill's Dedham Mass. Records i
Hubbard's History of Springfield Vt. 281–5
Humphreys Genealogy 433
Jameson's History of Medway Mass. 480–2
Lawrence and Bartlett Genealogy 108
Loomis Genealogy (1880) 779
Machias Me. Centennial 159
Meade's Old Churches of Va. ii, 460–3
Morris Genealogy (1898) 651–4
Nevius Genealogy
Norton's History of Fitzwilliam N. H. 546
Paige's History of Hardwick Mass. 367
Penn. Mag. of History and Biog. xiv, 199
Power's Sangamon Co. Ill. Settlers 285–7
Read's History of Swanzey N. H. 333
Savage's Genealogical Dictionary ii, 113
Sharp's History of Seymour Ct. 164
Sheldon's History of Deerfield Mass. 153
Smith's History of Delaware Co. Va. 458
Spooner Genealogy i, 483–8
Stearns' Hist. of Ashburnham Mass. 689–92
Titcomb's New England People 5–37
Wheeler's Hist. of Brunswick Me. 833
Whitmore's Copps Hill Epitaphs
Wight Genealogy 18
Ellison — Allison Genealogy 243–51
Rodman Genealogy 149
Ellmer — Savage's Gen. Dictionary ii, 115
Ellmes — Deane's Scituate Mass. 266
Ellms — Eaton's Thomaston Me. 209

Ellsworth — American Ancestry xii
Aylsworth Genealogy 436–54
Essex Institute Hist. Colls. xxi, 79, 97
Goodwin's Genealogical Notes 302
Howell's Southampton N. Y. 2d ed. 241
Kellogg's White Genealogy 31
Loomis Genealogy (1880) 300
Marshall's Grant Ancestry 107
New Eng. Hist. and Gen. Register v, 458
Paige's History of Hardwick Mass. 368
Runnel's Hist. Sanbornton N. H. ii, 265–8
Savage's Genealogical Dictionary ii, 114
Secomb's History of Amherst N. H. 580
Stiles' History of Windsor Ct. ii, 208–34
Strong Genealogy 299–302
Young's Chautauqua Co. N. Y. 419, 643
Elmendorf — American Ancestry i, 26
Hoffman Genealogy 517–9
Huntting's Hist. of Pine Plains N. Y. 330
Munsell's Albany Collections iv, 120
N. Y. Gen. and Biog. Record xx, 101–6
Schoonmaker's Hist. of Kingston N. Y 479
Sylvester's History of Ulster Co. N. Y. 102
Elmer — Allison Genealogy 212, 218–29
American Ancestry ix, 173, 223
Ellis Genealogy 373
Elmer Family of N. J. (1860) 64 pages
Elmer Family of Conn. (1899) 96 pages
Heywood's Hist. of Westminster Mass. 634
Hyde's History of Brimfield Mass. 397
Littell's Passaic Valley Genealogies 148–50
Orcutt's History of Stratford Ct. 1197
Orcutt's History of Torrington Ct. 687
Sedgwick's History of Sharon Ct. 78
Stiles' History of Windsor Ct. ii, 234–9
Temple's History of Northfield Mass. 437
Elmore — American Ancestry i, 26; v, 28
Power's Sangamon Co. Ill. Settlers 287
See also under Elmer
Elricks — Marshall Genealogy (1884) 43
Elster — Buckingham Genealogy 112–4
Elsworth — American Ancestry v, 154
Roome Genealogy 104–9
Elting — American Ancestry iv, 151
New York Gen. and Biog. Rec. xvi, 25–31
Schoonmaker's Hist. of Kingston N. Y. 479
Sylvester's History of Ulster Co. N. Y. 54
Elton — Anderson's Waterbury 48
Cregar's White Genealogy
Eltonhead — Neill's Va. Carolorum 254
Elwell — American Ancestry xi, 29
Anderson's Waterbury 48
Babson's Gloucester Mass. 87–90
Corliss' North Yarmouth Me. 1067–75
Eaton's History of Thomaston Me. ii, 211
Farrow's History of Islesborough Me. 203
New Eng. Hist. and Gen. Reg. liii, 25–32
Savage's Genealogical Dictionary ii, 116
Shourd's Fenwick Colony N. J. 78
Elwes — N. Y. Gen. Rec. xvii, 233
Elwood — American Ancestry x, 42
Elwyn — Wentworth Genealogy i, 337
Ely — American Ancestry iii, 78; vii, 137
Darling Memorial (1888)
Ely Reunion (1879) 158 pages
Ely Genealogy (1885) 525 pages

Goodrich's Recollec. of a Lifetime i, 533
Goodwin's Olcott Genealogy 16
Hall's Genealogical Notes (1886) 106
Hill's Gen. Table of Lee Family, app. C.
Kellogg's White Genealogy 65
Kitchell Genealogy 52
Longmeadow Mass. Centennial, app. 58–61
Montague Genealogy (1886) 83–5
New Eng. Hist. Gen. Reg. xxxv, 236–8
Orcutt's History of Stratford Ct. 1197
Saunderson's Hist. Charlestown N. H. 333
Savage's Genealogical Dictionary ii, 116
Selleck's Norwalk Ct. (1896) 225
Walworth's Hyde Genealogy ii, 838–47
West Springfield Mass. Centennial 117
Embree — Futhey's Chester Co. Pa. 53–6
Price's Embree Biography (1881) 67 pages
Embry — Meade's Old Families of Va.
Emerick — American Ancestry ii, 36
Emerson — Aldrich's Walpole N. H. 245
American Ancestry v, 87; vi, 185; xi, 29
Babson's History of Gloucester Mass. 197
Bemis' History of Marlboro N. H. 469–71
Blake's Hist. of Mendon Association 271–4
Chapin Genealogy
Chapman's Trowbridge Genealogy 309
Chase's History of Chester N. H. 516–8
Cochrane's Hist. Francest'n N. H. 666–8
Cogswell's History of Henniker N. H. 562
Crane's Rawson Genealogy 87–90
Daniels' History of Oxford Mass. 497
Dearborn's History of Parsonsfield Me. 378
Eaton's History of Candia N. H. 69–72
Eaton's History of Thomaston Me. ii, 213
Eaton's History of Reading Mass. 68
Emerson Maternal Ancestors (1887) 151 p.
Emerson Genealogy (1900) 537 pages
English Emersons (1898)
Fletcher Genealogy 63–70
Fullonton's Hist. of Raymond N. H. 215–9
Hammatt Papers of Ipswich Mass. 85, 90
Hayward's Hist. of Hancock N. H. 553–63
Heywood's Hist. of Westminster Mass. 634
Kidder's Hist. of New Ipswich N. H. 445
Little's History of Weare N. H. 835–9
Livermore's History of Wilton N. H. 363–5
Malden Mass. Bi-Centennial 244
Morrison's Hist. of Windham N. H. 524–7
New Eng. Hist. and Gen. Register li, 359
New Hamp. Hist. Society Colls. vii, 378
Poore Genealogy 75–8
Poor's Merrimac Valley Research 100, 171
Ridlon's Harrison Me. Settlers 57–9
Runnel's Hist. of Sanbornton N. H. ii, 268
Savage's Genealogical Dictionary ii, 117
Secomb's History of Amherst N. H. 581
Thompson's Memoirs of Eben Thompson
Turner Genealogy (1852)
Walker Genealogy (1861) 24
Washington N. H. History 394
Wheeler's History of Newport N. H. 376–9
Williams' History of Danby Vt. 142–4
Worcester's History of Hollis N. H. 373
Wyman's Charlestown Mass.Gens. i, 334
Emery — Am. Anc. iv, 37; vii, 121; ix, 212
Austin's R. I. Genealogical Dictionary 72

Bangor Me. Historical Magazine vi, 138–43
Benton's History of Guildhall Vt. 219
Buxton Me. Centennial 220-6
Carter's Hist. of Pembroke N. H. ii, 82–9
Chase's History of Chester N. H. 518
Cochrane's History of Antrim N. H. 485
Cogswell's History of Henniker N. H. 564
Coffin's History of Newbury Mass. 301
Cutter's History of Jaffrey N. H. 309–15
Dow's History of Hampton N. H. 702–5
Dudley Genealogy 122
Eaton's Hist. of Thomaston Me. ii, 211–3
Emery Family of Saco Me. (1869) 6 pages
Emery Family Reunion (1888) 18 pages
Emery Family of Newbury (1889) 22 pages
Emery Fam. of Newbury (1890) 610 pages
Farrow's History of Islesborough Me. 203
Freeman's Hist. of Cape Cod Mass. ii, 605
Guild's Stiles Genealogy 32–5
Hatch's History of Industry Me. 604–14
Hoyt's Salisbury Mass. Families 152
Little's History of Weare N. H. 840–2
Maine Hist. Society Collections iv, 289
N. E. Reg. xxiii, 414; xxvii, 423; liv, 313
Palmer Genealogy (1886) 56–9
Poor's Merrimac Valley Researches 119
Ridlon's Saco Valley Me. Families 678–81
Runnel's Sanbornton N. H. ii, 269–72
Savage's Genealogical Dictionary ii, 118
Emes — Leonard's Dublin N. H. 330
Sutliff Genealogy (1897) 27–32
Emlen — Futhey's Chester Co. Pa. 536
Emmans — Bergen's Kings Co. N. Y. 108
Emmerson — Williams' Danby Vt. 142–4
Emmerton — Driver Genealogy 343
Emmerton Genealogy (1881) 244 pages
Emmes—Whitmore's Copps Hill Epitaphs
Emmett — Heraldic Journal i, 95
Memoir of J. P. Emmett (1898)
Van Rensselaer's New Yorkers
Whitmore's Temple Genealogy
Emmons — Babson's Gloucester Mass. 90
Blake Genealogy 48
Blake's History of Mendon Association 109
Bradbury's Kennebunkport Me. 242
Chambers' Early Germans of N. J. 350
Daniels' History of Oxford Mass. 497
Mack Genealogy 16–9, 35–42
North's History of Augusta Me. 850
Savage's Genealogical Dictionary ii, 119
Spooner Genealogy (1871) 210
Temple's Hist. of N. Brookfield Mass. 587
Whittemore's Middlesex County Ct. 321
Emory — Stearns' Ashburnham 692
Stearns' History of Rindge N. H. 514–9
Empie — American Ancestry ii, 36
Welles' Washington Genealogies 281
Empy — Pearson's Schenectady N. Y. 65
Emrie — Emery Genealogy (1890) 106
Enders — Egle's Notes and Queries 3d
ser. ii, 195–8
Endicott — Dedham Mass. Historical
Register vi, 45–50, 145–7
Dunstable Bi-Centennial 176
Felton Genealogy (1886) 20
Moore's American Governors i, 363–6

New Eng. Hist. Gen. Reg. i, 263-75, 335-43
Perley's History of Boxford Mass. 98
Savage's Genealogical Dictionary ii, 120-3
Endle —Wilson Genealogy (1898) 67-72
Engell — Chambers' N. J. Germans
England — Austin's R. I. Gen. Dict. 72
Cregar's Haines Ancestry 60-2
Futhey's History of Chester Co. Pa. 538
Power's Sangamon Ill. Settlers 289-92
Engle — Cregar's Haines Genealogy 18-20
Penn. Mag. of History and Biog. iv, 353-5
Sharpless Genealogy 306
English — Am. Anc. v, 81; vi, 28; viii, 89
Cogswell Genealogy 232
Cunabell Genealogy 36
Savage's Genealogical Dictionary ii, 123
Tuttle Genealogy 195-9
Ennall — William and Mary College Hist.
Register ii, 98-105, 135
Eno — Andrews' New Britain Ct. 127
Barber Genealogy (1893) 32
Barbour's My Wife and Mother, app. 76
Bidwell Genealogy 55
Hayden's Virginia Genealogies 24-8
Huntting's Hist. of Pine Plains N. Y. 331-5
Marshall's Grant Ancestry 109-13
Orcutt's History of Torrington Ct. 687
Savage's Genealogical Dictionary ii, 124
Stiles' History of Windsor Ct. ii, 239-48
Enos — Powers' Sangamon Co. Ill. 288
Ensign — Am. Ancestry vii, 119; viii, 214
Deane's History of Scituate Mass. 266
Savage's Genealogical Dictionary ii, 124
Stiles' History of Windsor Ct. ii, 248
Winsor's History of Duxbury Mass. 257
Ensor — Mallery's Bohemia Manor
Ensworth — Cleveland Gen. (1899) 140-2
Enterline — Egle's Notes and Queries 3d
ser. i, 229-33
Enyard — Clute's Staten Island 380
Enyart — Power's Sangamon Ill. 292
Eoff — Chambers' N. J. Germans 351
Epes — Hammatt Papers of Ipswich 93
Eppes — Meade's Old Church of Va.
New Eng. Hist. and Gen. Register xiii, 115
Page Genealogy 105
Richmond Va. Standard ii, 32; iii, 16, 40
Savage's Genealogical Dictionary ii, 125
Slaughter's Bristol Parish Va. 172
Virginia Mag. of History iii, (1896) 393-401
Epps — Cochrane's Francestown 668-71
Erb — Harris' Lancaster Co. Pa. 194-7
Erichzon — Pearson's Schenectady 65
Errington — Paige's Cambridge 540
Erskine — Life of Rev. Wm. Smith
Erving — Bowdoin Genealogy (1887)
New York Gen. and Biog. Rec. xxx, 209-12
Esling — American Ancestry iii, 16; vi, 30
Cath. Hist. Society Colls. ii, 333-66
Esmond — Collins' Hillsdale N. Y. 53
Espy—Egle's Pa. Genealogies 2d ed. 214-27
Kulp's Wyoming Valley Families
Plumb's History of Hanover Pa. 410
Esselstyn — American Ancestry ii, 36
Munsell's Albany Collections iv, 120
Zabriskie's Claverack N. Y. Church 45

Estabrook — American Ancestry vi, 62
Bond's Watertown Mass. Genealogies 204
Cutter's History of Arlington Mass. 236
Estabrook Genealogy (1891) 359 pages
Fowler's Chauncey Memorial 299
Hayward's Hist. of Hancock N. H. 563-5
Hemenway's Vermont Hist. Gaz. v, 146
Heywood's Hist. Westminster Mass. 635-8
Hudson's History of Lexington Mass. 61-4
Norton's History of Fitzwilliam N. H. 547
Paige's History of Cambridge Mass. 541
Reed's History of Rutland Mass. 159
Savage's Genealogical Dictionary ii, 126
Washington N. H. History 394
Westminster Mass. Centennial 32
Estaugh — Clement's Newtown N. J.
Esten—Austin's R. I. Gen. Dictionary 294
Esterbrook — American Ancestry vii, 56
Estes — American Ancestry iii, 153, 205;
iv, 42; x, 28, 180
Barry's History of Hanover Mass. 307-10
Bassett's History of Richmond N. H. 386
Estes Family of Maine (1892) 17 pages
Estes Genealogy (1894) 401 pages
Lapham's History of Bethel Me. 525-9
Lapham's History of Woodstock Me. 213
Savage's Genealogical Dictionary ii, 126
Spooner Genealogy i, 484-7
Stackpole's History of Durham Me. 179-81
Estey — American Ancestry viii, 100
Hemenway's Vermont Gazeteer v, 144
Heywood's Hist. of Westminster Mass. 638
Estherbrooks — Hodgman's Westford
Estill — Waddell's Augusta Va. 407
Esty — Essex Institute Hist. Collections
xvi, 104-6; xxxvi, 129-40
Morrison's History of Windham N. H. 527
Morse Memorial, appendix 20
Thurston's History of Winthrop Me. 181
Eustace — Hayden's Virginia Gens. 261
Eustis — American Ancestry xii
Eustis Genealogy (1878) 27 pages
New Eng. Hist. Gen. Reg. xxxii, 204-31
Reed's History of Rutland Mass. 127
Wyman's Charlestown Mass. Gens. i, 336
Evan — Smith's Delaware Co. Pa. 459
Evans — Alexander Genealogy 111-3
Am. Anc. iii, 65; vii, 235; ix, 201; xi, 216
Austin's R. I. Genealogical Dictionary 73
Carter Genealogy (1883) 63, 85-7, 113-5
Dearborn's History of Salisbury N. H. 553
Eaton's History of Reading Mass. 69
Egle's Notes and Queries 3d ser. iii, 407-27
Evans Family of N. H. (1893) 107 pages
Evans Family of Penn. (1895) 20 pages
Fox, Ellicott and Evans Gen. (1882) 287 p.
Futhey's History of Chester Co. Pa. 538-44
Gregg's Hist. of Old Cheraws S. C. 75-100
Holton's Winslow Memorial 475-80
Hoyt's Salisbury Mass. Families 154
Jackson Genealogy 188, 193-5
Jenkins' Hist. Gwynedd Pa. 2d ed. 146-95
Johnston's History of Cecil Co. Md. 485-95
Lapham's History of Norway Me. 499
Little's History of Weare N. H. 842
Maris Genealogy 224

Montgomery Genealogy (1897) 50–3
Morrison's History of Windham N. H. 528
Rhoad's Clover-Croft Chronicles (1893)
Runnel's Hist. Sanbornton N. H. ii, 273
Saunderson's Charlestown N. H. 334
Savage's Genealogical Dictionary ii, 127
Sheldon's History of Deerfield Mass. 153
Smith's History of Peterborough N. H. 66
Temple's History of Northfield Mass. 438
Timlow's Sketches of Southington Ct. 90
Worthen's History of Sutton N. H. 696–9
Wyman's Charlestown Mass. Gens. i, 336
Evarts — Adams Genealogy (1894) 22–39
American Ancestry x, 123
Litchfield County Ct. History 557
Savage's Genealogical Dictionary ii, 128
Eveleth — Babson's Gloucester 91–3
Hammatt Papers of Ipswich Mass. 94
Hatch's History of Industry Me. 614–7
Hayward's History of Hancock N. H. 565
Leonard's History of Dublin N. H. 331
North's History of Augusta Me. 851
Savage's Genealogical Dictionary ii, 129
Stackpole's History of Durham Me. 182
Evelyn — Life of Mrs. Godolphin 151
Everard — Meade's Old Families of Va.
New Eng. Hist. and Gen. Reg. xxxviii, 66
Southern History Assoc. Pubs.
Everden — Austin's R. I. Gen. Dict. 73
Everest — American Ancestry ii, 37
Brown's West Simsbury Ct. Settlers 59
Everett — American Ancestry iv, 185, 217
Boyd's Annals of Winchester Ct. 47–51
Cochrane's Hist. Francest'n N. H. 671–3
Crawford Genealogy 79–84
Eaton's History of Thomaston Me. ii, 213
Everett Genealogy (1860) 7 p. reprint
Heywood's Hist Westminster Mass. 639–42
Hill's Dedham Mass. Records i
Jameson's History of Medway Mass. 482
Lapham's History of Norway Me. 498
Morse's Sherborn Mass. Settlers 81
New Eng. Hist. and Gen. Reg. xiv, 215–9
Norton's History of Fitzwilliam N. H. 548
Richmond Va. Standard iv, 5
Savage's Genealogical Dictionary ii, 130
Sedgwick's History of Sharon Ct. 79
Temple's History of Northfield Mass. 439
Everhart — American Ancestry xii, 108
Everhart Genealogy (1883) 142 pages
See also under Eberhart
Everingham—Humphreys Genealogy 587
Everitt — Orcutt's New Milford 693
Orcutt's History of Torrington Ct. 688
Whittemore's Orange N. J. 267
Eversfield — Bowie Genealogy 446–57
Everton—Savage's Gen. Dictionary ii, 132
Wyman's Charlestown Mass. Gens. i, 337
Everts — American Ancestry ii, 26
Goode Genealogy 171
Joslin's History of Poultney Vt. 256
Evertsen — Bergen's Kings County 111
Munsell's Albany Collections iv, 120
Ewell — Cochrane's Francestown 673
Deane's History of Scituate Mass. 267
Ewell Genealogy (1878) 78 pages

Freeman's Hist. of Cape Cod Mass. ii, 257
Hayden's Virginia Genealogies 333–54
Savage's Genealogical Dictionary ii, 132
Swift's Barnstable Mass. Families i, 359
Ewer — Austin's Allied Families 92
Freeman's History of Cape Cod ii, 151–64
Savage's Genealogical Dictionary ii, 132
Swift's Barnstable Mass. Families i, 360–4
Ewing — Cooley's Trenton N. J. 64–6
Egle's Hist. Reg. Interior Penn. ii, 206–13
Ewing Genealogy (1858) 38 pages
Penn. Mag. of Hist. and Biog. vii, 94–100
Ewings — Caverley's Pittsford Vt. 701
Ewins — Worthen's Sutton N. H. 1020–3
Eyerman — American Ancestry xi, 198
Eyerman Ancestry (1898) 50 pages
Eyerman Ancestry (1899) 62 pages
Eyre — Bascom Genealogy 25, 69
Martin's History of Chester Pa. 49–53
Meade's Old Churches of Virginia i, 259
New Eng. Hist. Reg. xv, 13, 58; xxxviii, 67
Savage's Genealogical Dictionary ii, 133
Sharpless Genealogy 215
Smith's History of Delaware Co. Pa. 462
Eyster — Egle's Pa. Gens. 2d ed. 351
Fabens — Essex Inst. Coll. xviii, 49–72
Fabens Genealogy (1881) 26 pages reprint
Faddis — Palmer and Trimble Gen. 359
Fagan — Power's Sangamon Co. Ill. 293
Fahnestock — American Ancestry vi, 18
Fahnestock Genealogy (1879) 69 pages
Harris' History of Lancaster Co. Pa. 202
Fairbanks — Am. Anc. v, 122; viii, 152
Austin's Allied Families 93
Barry's Hist. of Framingham Mass. 239–41
Blake's History of Franklin Mass. 240
Butler's Hist. of Farmington Me. 467–70
Cochrane's History of Antrim N. H. 487
Cochrane's Hist. Francest'n N. H. 674–8
Fairbanks Family of Dedham (1885) 55 p.
Fairbanks Family of N. H. (1886) 30 pages
Fairbanks Family of Dedham (1892) 72 p.
Fairbanks Family of Vermont (1896) 2 p.
Fairbanks Family in America (1897) 967 p.
Hayward's History of Gilsum N. H. 305
Herrick's History of Gardner Mass. 347
Hill's Dedham Mass. Records i
Hubbard's Hist. of Springfield Vt. 286–91
Hudson's History of Sudbury Mass. 441
Hyde's History of Brimfield Mass. 398
Jameson's History of Medway Mass. 483
Keyes' West Boylston Mass. Reg. 18–20
Leland Genealogy 239–41
Leonard's History of Dublin N. H. 331
Morse's Sherborn Mass. Settlers 82–5
Norton's History of Fitzwilliam N. H. 549
Rockwood Genealogy 109–27
Savage's Genealogical Dictionary ii, 135–7
Smith's History of Peterborough N. H. 67
Stearns' Hist. of Ashburnham Mass. 692–8
Thurston's History of Winthrop Me. 181–3
Washington N. H. History 395
Wood Genealogy 116–9
Fairchild — American Ancestry i, 27; iii, 121; vii, 254; x, 158
Conn. Quarterly iii, (1897) 352

Dwight's Strong Genealogy 105
Hall's Records of Norwalk Ct. 222, 290
Hurds' History of Fairfield Co. Ct. 581, 795
Orcutt's History of Derby Ct. 719
Orcutt's History of Stratford Ct. 1197–1202
Power's Sangamon Co. Ill. Settlers 294
Savage's Genealogical Dictionary ii, 137
Todd's History of Redding Ct. 190–2
Faircloe — Chambers' N. J. Germans
Fairclough — Orcutt's Wolcott Ct. 473
Fairfax — American Ancestry v, 114
Driver Genealogy 350
Fairfax Genealogy (1868) 234 pages
Goode Genealogy 114, 378, 456
Lee Genealogy (1895) 147
Lindsay Genealogy 112
Meade's Old Churches of Va. ii, 106–10
New York Gen. and Biog. Record xxiv, 39
Richmond Va. Standard iv, 20
Slaughter's Life of R. Fairfax 62–6
Smith's History of Sunderland Mass. 327–9
Thomas Genealogy (1877) 74–8, 178
Thomas Genealogy (1896) 303–13
Fairfield — Austin's R. I. Dictionary 73
Bradbury's Kennebunkport Me. 243
Eaton's History of Reading Mass. 70
Hammatt Papers of Ipswich Mass. 105
Hayward's History of Hancock N. H. 565
Hudson's History of Lexington Mass. 64
Maine Hist. Gen. Rec. iii, 118–22; iv, 1–6
New York Gen. and Biog. Record xxix, 102
Savage's Genealogical Dictionary ii, 137
Fairlamb — Buckingham Genealogy 253
Sharpless Genealogy 371
Fairly — Pearson's Schenectady 66
Fairman—Fairman Genealogy (1898) 36 p.
Fairn — Calnek's Annapolis N. S. 506
Fairweather—Savage's Dictionary ii, 138
Falconer — Bolton's Westchester 731
See also Faulkner
Fales — Ballou's Milford Mass. 737–40
Calnek's History of Annapolis N. S. 507
Eaton's Hist. of Thomaston Me. ii, 214–21
Hill's Dedham Mass. Records i
Temple's Hist. of N. Brookfield Mass. 587
Ward's History of Shrewsbury Mass. 281
Falis — Stone's Hubbardson Mass. 265
Falkinburg — Salter's Monmouth N. J.
Falls — Durant's Lawrence Pa. 183–5
Fancher — Anderson's Waterbury 49
Ball's History of Lake County Ind. 403
Bouton Genealogy 35
Huntington's Stamford Ct. Families 33
Faneuil — Heraldic Journal ii, 121
Weisse's Bethune and Faneuil Genealogy
(1866) 54 pages (1884) 55 pages
Fannin — Baillie Genealogy 98–103
Fanning — Caulkins' New London Ct. 306
Cleveland's Southold N. Y. Record 103
Dorr's Life of J. F. Watson 60–2
Howell's Southampton N. Y. 2d ed. 241
Savage's Genealogical Dictionary ii, 140
Wheeler's History of N. Carolina ii, 332
Fanton — Schenck's Fairfield Ct. 367
Farden — Bergen's Kings Co. N. Y. 112
Farewell — Lapham's Bethel Me. 529–31

Fargo — Baker's Montville Ct. 129–31
Caulkins' History of New London Ct. 373
Pompey N. Y. Reunion 373–87
Young's History of Warsaw N. Y. 257–60
Farley — Am. Ancestry iv, 223; v, 112
Carter Family Tree
Chambers' Early Germans of N. J. 352–6
Choate Genealogy 45–8
Cogswell Genealogy 155
Cushman's History of Sheepscott Me. 378
Fisher Genealogy 149–85
Foster Pedigree (1897) iii, 1–63
Hammatt Papers of Ipswich Mass. 96–100
Hazen's History of Billerica Mass. 47
Hubbard's Stanstead County Canada 173
Hudson's History of Lexington Mass. 65
Meade's Old Churches of Virginia
Mellick's Story of an Old Farm 683–5
Richmond Va. Standard ii, 14, 44
Savage's Genealogical Dictionary ii, 140
Sewall's History of Woburn Mass. 611
Tuttle Genealogy xxxv
Worcester's History of Hollis N. H. 373
Farmer — Am. Ancestry vii, 221; xii, 49
Ball's History of Lake Co. Ind. 292
Coffin's History of Boscawen N. H. 524
Farmer Genealogy (1813) 12 pages
Farmer Genealogy 2d ed. (1828) 20 pages
Hayward's History of Hancock N. H. 566
Hazen's History of Billerica Mass. 49–51
Hudson's History of Lexington Mass. 65
Le Bosquet's Life of J. Farmer (1884) 138 p.
Lincoln's Hist. of Hingham Mass. ii, 214
Morrison's History of Windham N. H. 529
New Eng. Hist. Gen. Reg. i, 22–34, 360
Savage's Genealogical Dictionary ii, 141
Secomb's History of Amherst N. H. 582
Whitehead's Perth Amboy N. J. 92–8
Farnam — American Ancestry vii, 227
Whitman Genealogy 545
Farnham — Aldrich's Walpole 246–8
Am. Anc. ii, 37; iv, 177, 221; vi, 133; vii, 63
Barry's History of Hanover Mass. 310
Eaton's History of Thomaston Me. ii, 221
Farnham Genealogy (1886) 91 pages
Farnham Genealogy 2d ed. (1889) 141 p.
McKeen's History of Bradford Vt. 377–80
Morris Genealogy (1853) 81
Redfield Genealogy 64–7
Runnel's Hist. Sanbornton N. H. ii, 274–6
Savage's Genealogical Dictionary ii, 142
Stiles' History of Windsor Ct. ii, 249
Wentworth Genealogy i, 443–5
Farnsworth — Am. Ancestry vi, 44; x, 172
Bass' History of Braintree Vt. 132
Butler's History of Groton Mass. 395–9
Calnek's History of Annapolis N. S. 507
Chandler's History of Shirley Mass. 409–12
Chute Genealogy, appendix 41–51
Farnsworth Genealogy (1891) 122 pages
Farnsworth Genealogy (1897) 514 pages
Farrow's History of Islesborough Me. 204
Green's Groton Mass. Epitaphs 239–41
Green's Groton Mass. Settlers 4–7
Heywood's Hist. Westminster Mass. 642–4
Norton's History of Fitzwilliam N. H. 550

Saunderson's Charlestown N. H. 333-45
Savage's Genealogical Dictionary ii, 143
Washington N. H. History 396–406
Woodward's History of Bordentown N. J.
Wyman's Charlestown Mass. Gens. i, 340
Farnum — Abbot's Andover Mass. 34
American Ancestry x, 17, 176
Barry's History of Hanover Mass. 310
Bouton's History of Concord N. H. 655-61
Cochrane's Hist. Francest'n N. H. 678–81
Dearborn's History of Salisbury N. H. 555
Hayward's History of Gilsum N. H. 306
Joslin's History of Poultney Vt. 257–9
Lapham's History of Rumford Me. 324–9
Lapham's History of Woodstock Me. 215
Leonard's History of Dublin N. H. 333
Pierce's History of Grafton Mass. 477–9
Secomb's History of Amherst N. H. 582
Smith's History of Peterborough N. H. 68
Whitmore's Copps Hill Epitaphs
Farquhar — Sharpless Gen. 202, 317–9
Thomas Genealogy (1877) 78
Thomas Genealogy (1896) 313
Farr — American Ancestry iv, 218; xi, 30
Dunster Genealogy 195
Eaton's History of Thomaston Me. ii, 222
Farr Family of Utah (1898) chart
Paige's History of Hardwick Mass. 369
Randall's Hist. Chesterfield N. H. 292-306
Read's History of Swanzey N. H. 336
Savage's Genealogical Dictionary ii, 144
Farrabus — Paige's Cambridge 541
Farrah — Clary's Farrah Discourse (1847)
Farran — Temple's Palmer Mass. 445
Farrand — Cothren's Woodbury 544
Harris Genealogy (1883) 99
Kitchell Genealogy 35–42
Farrar — Am. Ancestry ii, 154; xii, 106
Barry's History of Framingham Mass. 241
Bemis' History of Marlboro N. H. 472–9
Blood's History of Temple N. H. 218
Bond's Watertown Mass. Genealogies 728
Farrar Genealogy (1853) 45 pages
Hayward's History of Gilsum N. H. 306
Hayward's History of Hancock N. H. 567
Hemenway's Vermont Hist. Gaz. v, 85
Humphreys Genealogy 448
Kidder's Hist. New Ipswich N. H. 358–73
Lancaster's History of Gilmanton N. H. 264
Lapham's History of Paris Me. 596
Lapham's History of Woodstock Me. 216
Neill's Virginia Carolorum 182
N. E. Hist. Gen. Reg. iii, 212; vi, 313–28
Norton's Hist. of Fitzwilliam N. H. 551–5
Old Northwest Gen. Quarterly iii, 111
Potter's Concord Mass. Families 9, 107
Richmond Va. Standard
Savage's Genealogical Dictionary ii, 144
Sewall's History of Woburn Mass. 611
Stackpole's History of Durham Me. 183
Stearns' Hist. of Ashburnham Mass. 698
Stearns' History of Rindge N. H. 519
Southern Bivouac (1886) 646
Virginia Magazine of History vii, 319–22
Ward's History of Shrewsbury Mass. 279

Washington N. H. History 407
See also under Farrow
Farrell — Anderson's Waterbury 49
Pearson's Schenectady N. Y. Settlers 67
Temple's History of Palmer Mass. 458
Farren — Dodd's East Haven Ct. 118
Farrington — Abbott's Andover 39
American Ancestry x, 171; xii, 25
American Historical Register i, 440
Bangor Me. Historical Magazine vi, 102
Bolton's Hist. of Westchester Co. N. Y. 732
Cochrane's History of Antrim N. H. 489
Cochrane's Hist. Francestown N. H. 681
Eaton's Annals of Warren Me. 540
Eaton's History of Thomaston Me. ii, 222
Farrington Genealogy (1880) 24 pages
Farrington Genealogy 2d ed. (1899) 64 p.
Groton Historical Series xix, 22
Hill's Dedham Mass. Records i
Livermore's History of Wilton N. H. 365
Ruttenber's Hist. Orange Co. N. Y. 405–7
Savage's Genealogical Dictionary ii, 145
Washington N. H. History 406
Whipple-Hill Families (1897) 100
Farris — Davis' Plymouth Mass. 105
Farrow — Bangor Magazine v, 173-7, 236
Chambers' Early Germans of N. J. 356–8
Deane's History of Scituate Mass. 268
Farrar Memoir (1853) 2
Farrow's Hist. of Islesborough Me. 205–8
Lincoln's Hist. Hingham Mass. ii, 215–7
See also under Farrar
Farwell — American Ancestry iii, 109; iv, 188; vii, 222
Bangor Me. Hist. Magazine v, 36
Butler's History of Groton Mass. 399
Chandler's History of Shirley Mass. 413–5
Dunstable Mass. Bi-Centen. 95–118, 122–30
Eaton's History of Thomaston Me. ii, 222
Farwell Family (1878) chart
Farwell Genealogy (1879) 254 pages
Farwell Family of Concord Mass. (1888) 2 p.
Fox's History of Dunstable Mass. 242
Hammatt Papers of Ipswich Mass. 101
Hayward's History of Hancock N. H. 568
Heywood's Hist. of Westminster Mass. 644
Joslin's History of Poultney Vt. 259
New Eng. Hist. and Gen. Reg. xxxv, 275
Norton's History of Fitzwilliam N. H. 555
Randall's Hist. of Chesterfield N. H. 306–9
Saunderson's Charlestown N. H. 345–52
Savage's Genealogical Dictionary ii, 147
Stearns' Hist. of Ashburnham Mass. 698
Washington N. H. History 408–11
Fassaur — N. Y. Gen. Rec. xvi, 41
Fassett — Brown's Bedford Families 9
Caverly's History of Pittsford Vt. 701
Follett Genealogy (1896) 124–59
Hazen's History of Billerica Mass. 51
Hodgman's History of Westford Mass. 446
Hudson's History of Lexington Mass. 66
Jenning's History of Bennington Vt.
Montague Genealogy 350-3, 434
Norton's Hist. of Fitzwilliam N. H. 556–60
Paige's History of Hardwick Mass. 370
Wallbridge Genealogy 286–9

Faulkner — Bangor Hist. Magazine v, 191
Hazen's History of Billerica Mass. 52
Morrison Genealogy 175
Randall's Hist. of Chesterfield N. H. 309
Savage's Genealogical Dictionary ii, 147
See also Falconer
Faunce — Davis' Plymouth Mass. 106
Freeman's Hist. of Cape Cod Mass. ii, 153
Lapham's History of Norway Me. 500
Lapham's History of Paris Me. 597
Mitchell's Hist. of Bridgewater Mass. 373
Savage's Genealogical Dictionary ii, 148
Spooner Genealogy i, 442. 456-8
Fauntleroy — De Bow's Review xxxvi
Jones Genealogy (1891) 167-81
Meade's Old Churches of Va. ii, 478-81
Favor — Hayward's Hancock N. H. 569
Lapham's History of Norway Me. 500
Little's History of Weare N. H. 843-5
Fawcett — Norton's Knox Co. Ohio
Faxon — Durrie's Steel Genealogy 66
Faxon Genealogy (1843) 24 pages
Faxon Genealogy 2d ed. (1860)
Faxon Genealogy (1880) 377 pages
Kingman's North Bridgewater Mass. 509
Savage's Genealogical Dictionary ii, 149
Sheldon's History of Deerfield Mass. 154
Tuttle Genealogy 92-4
Vinton Genealogy 311-7
Vinton's Richardson Genealogy 426
Washington N. H. History 411-3
Fay — Aldrich's Walpole N. H. 248-50
American Ancestry xi, 192; xii, 6
Ballou's History of Milford Mass. 741
Buckminster's Hasting Genealogy 116-8
Fay Genealogy (1898) 420 pages
Follett Genealogy (1896) 184-93
Hazen's History of Billerica Mass. 148
Hill's History of Mason N. H. 202
Hudson's Hist. Marlborough Mass. 359-61
Hyde's History of Brimfield Mass. 399
Jennings' Hist. of Bennington Vt. 255-63
Norton's Hist. of Fitzwilliam N. H. 560-2
Paige's History of Hardwick Mass. 370-5
Pierce's History of Grafton Mass. 479
Rice Genealogy
Savage's Genealogical Dictionary ii, 149
Spooner Genealogy i, 94, 299-322
Walworth's Hyde Genealogy 479
Ward's History of Shrewsbury Mass. 281
Young's Hist. Chautauqua Co. N. Y. 507
Fayreweather — Orcutt's Bridgeport
Orcutt's History of Stratford Ct. 1202
Feake — N. Y. Gen. Rec. xi, 12-24, 70-4,
168-70
Shotwell Genealogy 134-6
Fearing — American Ancestry viii, 143
Bliss' Colonial Buzzards Bay
Davis' Landmarks Plymouth Mass. 106-8
Lincoln's Hist. of Hingham Mass. 217-29
Savage's Genealogical Dictionary ii, 150
Fearne — Smith's Delaware Co. Pa. 462
Fears — Babson's Gloucester Mass. 281
Featherly — American Ancestry i, 27
Fee — Lincoln's Hingham ii, 229
Feeks — American Ancestry x, 77

Feeney — Temple's Palmer Mass. 459
Feero — Munsell's Albany Colls. iv, 121
Feeter — American Ancestry x, 127
Feild — Goode Genealogy 244
Slaughter's Bristol Parish Va. 173-7
Feke — Bunker's Long Island Gens. 202
Felch — American Ancestry ix, 140
Babson's History of Gloucester Mass. 93
Cochrane's Hist. Francest'n N. H. 682-5
Cogswell's History of Henniker N. H. 506
Eaton's History of Reading Mass. 71
Felch Genealogy (1881) 98 pages
Hayward's History of Hancock N. H. 570
Little's History of Weare N. H. 845-8
Norton's Hist. of Fitzwilliam N. H. 562-4
Paige's History of Cambridge Mass. 542
Piper Genealogy (1889) 34-6, 43-5
Savage's Genealogical Dictionary ii, 150
Worthen's History of Sutton N. H. 702-10
Fell — Babson's Gloucester Mass. 323
Davis' History of Bucks County Pa. 278
Fell Genealogy (1891) 555 pages
Kulp's Wyoming Valley Families
Orcutt's History of Torrington Ct. 689
Savage's Genealogical Dictionary ii, 151
Waldo's History of Tolland Ct. 75
Fellows — American Ancestry i, 27; ii,
37; iv, 188; x, 128
Baker's History of Montville Ct. 346-50
Calnek's History of Annapolis N. S. 509
Coffin's History of Boscawen N. H. 526
Corliss' North Yarmouth Me. Magazine
Dearborn's Hist. of Salisbury N. H. 556-62
Dow's History of Hampton N. H. 706
Essex County Mass. Register i, (1894)
177-9; ii, (1895) 20-2
Hammatt Papers of Ipswich Mass. 100
Hoyt's Salisbury Mass. Families 155
Stearns' Hist. of Ashburnham Mass. 699
Worthen's History of Sutton N. H. 710-4
Felmley — Chambers' N. J. Germans
Felshaw — Davis Genealogy 48
Felt — American Ancestry iii, 127
Blood's History of Temple N. H. 219
Corliss' North Yarmouth Me. Magazine
Driver Genealogy 471
Felt Genealogy (1893) 568 pages
Hammatt Papers of Ipswich Mass. 103
Lapham's History of Woodstock Me. 217
Savage's Genealogical Dictionary ii, 151
Smith's History of Peterborough N. H.
70-2
Felthousen — Pearson's Schenectady
Felton — American Ancestry v, 74
Ballou's History of Milford Mass. 742
Bemis' History of Marlboro N. H. 479
Cunnabell Genealogy 75
Felton Family of Salem Mass. (1877) 19 p.
Felton Genealogy (1886) 260 pages
Hudson's Hist. Marlborough Mass. 361-4
Norton's Hist. of Fitzwilliam N. H. 564-6
Savage's Genealogical Dictionary ii, 151
Secomb's History of Amherst N. H. 583
Feltz — American Ancestry ii, 38
Fendall — Bowie Genealogy 467-70
Fenderson — Dearborn's Parsonsfield

Fenimore — American Ancestry i, 27
Penn. Mag. of History and Biog. xvi, 377
Fenn — American Ancestry ii, 38; iii, 210
Anderson's Waterbury Ct. i, app. 49
Baldwin Genealogy 50, 510
Davis' History of Wallingford Ct. 743
Grigg's Life of Elam Fenn (1884) 87–93
Jessup Genealogy 315–8
Savage's Genealogical Dictionary ii, 152
Tuttle Genealogy 516
Fenner — Am. Hist. Register iv, 263-8
Austin's Ancestries 23
Austin's R. I. Genealogical Dictionary 74
Fenner Genealogy (1886–7) 43 pages
Pompey N. Y. Reunion 302–4
R. I. Hist. Mag. vii, 161-83
Savage's Genealogical Dictionary ii, 153
Fennick — Am. Hist. Register iii, 221–3
Fenno — Fenno Gen. (1898) 11 p., reprint
Guild's Stiles Genealogy 89
Heywood's Hist. of Westminster Mass. 644
Jackson's History of Newtown Mass. 277
Lapham's History of Bethel Me. 531
New Eng. Hist. and Gen. Reg. lii, 448–57
Stearns' History of Rindge N. H. 520
Fenton — Cleveland's Yates County 145
Fenton Genealogy (1867) 34 pages
Hyde's History of Brimfield Mass. 400
Paul's History of Wells Vt. 86
Temple's History of Palmer Mass. 446
Wales Mass. Centennial 20
Young's Chautauqua Co. N. Y. 248, 358
Fenwick — Savage's Gen. Dict. ii, 153
Ferguson — Am. Ancestry ii, 38; xi, 193
Bedford N. H. Centennial 299
Cleveland's Hist. of Yates Co. N. Y. 334
Egle's Penn. Genealogies 2d ed. 228–31
Gibb's History of Blandford Mass. 62
Marshall Genealogy (1884) 44–7
Old Eliot Me. Monthly iii, (1899) 46–54
Power's Sangamon Co. Ill. Settlers 295
Robertson's Pocahontas' Descendants
Smith's Hist. of Peterborough N. H. 73–8
Temple's History of Whately Mass. 228
Fernald — Am. Anc. iii, 193; vi, 157, 180
Dearborn's Hist. of Parsonsfield Me. 379
Jordan's Leighton Genealogy 53
Old Eliot Me. Monthly i, (1897) 21–3
Feroe — American Ancestry ii, 38
Ferrand — Eaton's Thomaston Me. 224
Ferrar — Neill's Virg. Carolorum 42
Ferrell — Temple's Palmer Mass. 458
Ferris—Am. Anc. iii, 155; vii, 270; ix, 208
Bolton's Westchester Co. N. Y. ii, 422
Clark Genealogy (1892) 96–9
Ferris Genealogy (1899) 60 pages
Huntington's Stamford Ct. Settlers 33
Meade's History of Greenwich Ct. 312
Orcutt's History of New Milford Ct. 694–9
Ransom Genealogy
Savage's Genealogical Dictionary ii, 155
Sharpless Genealogy 251, 392–5
Smith's History of Dutchess Co. N. Y. 500
Thomas Genealogy (1895) 314
Ferry — Bass' Hist. of Braintree Vt. 132
Cochrane's History of Antrim N. H. 489

Hyde's History of Brimfield Mass. 402
Lyman's Hist. of Easthampton Mass. 185
Montague Genealogy 276–81, 290–8
Savage's Genealogical Dictionary ii, 155
Temple's History of Palmer Mass. 457
Ferson — Knox Co. Me. Mag. i, 112–8
Fessenden — Aldrich's Walpole 250–2
Bond's Watertown Mass. Gens. 757
Cutter's History of Arlington Mass. 237
Daniel's History of Oxford Mass. 499
Eaton's History of Thomaston Me. 224
Freeman's Cape Cod i, 461, 618; ii, 154
Hemenway's Vermont Hist. Gaz. v, 110
Heywood's Hist. Westminster Mass. 645–7
Hudson's Hist. of Lexington Mass. 66–9
Locke Gen. 27 43–6 89–91, 146, 313–6
Maine Hist. Society Collections iv, 289
Morrison's Hist. of Windham N. H. 530
Morse Memorial 166
Paige's Hist. of Cambridge Mass. 542–4
Pope Genealogy
Ridlon's Saco Valley Me. Families 681–6
Savage's Genealogical Dictionary ii, 155
Spooner's Memorial of W. Spooner 113
Ward's History of Shrewsbury Mass. 281
Fetrow — Parthemore Genealogy 106–8
Fetter — American Ancestry vii, 61
Fetterhoff — Egle's Notes and Queries 3d
ser. i, 548
Fetterman — Fisher Genealogy 211–34
Few — Potts Genealogy (1895) 357–63
Feyler — Eaton's Thomaston Me. 225
Ficklin — Slaughter's St. Mark's 164
Fidler — American Ancestry ii, 38
Field — American Ancestry ii, 38; iii, 97;
v, 93; vi, 96; vii, 279; viii, 157; ix,
181; xii, 18
Austin's R. I. Genealogical Dict. 75–7
Baird's History of Rye N. Y. 463–5
Ballou's History of Milford Mass. 744
Bangor Historical Magazine vi, 92
Bolton's Westchester Co. N. Y. ii, 728–31
Bond's Watertown Mass. Genealogies 207
Cooley's Trenton N. J. Genealogies 66–71
Corliss' North Yarmouth Me. 448-52
Crafts' History of Whately Mass. 461–4
Doty Genealogy 681–3
Field Family of Stockbridge (1860) 105 p.
Field Family of Flushing (1863) 9 pages
Field Family of Newfane Vt. (1871) 10 p.
Field Family of Flushing (1874) 14 pages
Field Family of Providence (1878) 65 pages
Field Family of Stockbridge (1880) 147 p.
Field Family of Flushing (1895) 132 pages
Field Genealogy (1900) 1300 pages
Hemenway's Vermont Historical Gaz. v
Hollister Genealogy 167–75
Hubbard's Hist. of Springfield Vt. 291–7
Hyde's Hist. of Brimfield Mass. 403
Judd's History of Hadley Mass. 492–4
Kingman's North Bridgewater 409–503
Lapham's History of Paris Me. 599
Lincoln Genealogy (1899) 72–88
Longmeadow Mass. Centen. app. 61–3
Martin's History of Chester Pa. 296
Mead's History of Greenwich Ct. 312

Meade's Old Churches of Virgina
Mellick's Story of an old Farm N. J. 650
Mitchell's Hist. of Bridgewater Mass. 158
Morris and Flynt Ancestors (1882) 33
New Eng. Hist. and Gen. Reg. xvii, 106-12; xviii, 260; xxii, 166-73; xxx, 406-9; xxxv, 239, 356-8; xlviii, 331-6; li, 359
Newfane Vt. Centennial 155-7
Paige's History of Hardwick Mass. 375
Randall's Hist. Chesterfield N. H. 309-11
Read's History of Swanzey N. H. 337
Ridlon's Saco Valley Me. Families 686-9
Savage's Genealogical Dictionary ii, 155-7
Sheldon's Hist. of Deerfield Mass. 155-63
Slaughter's St. Mark's Parish Va. 130-2
Smith's Hist. Peterborough N. H. 79-83
Smith's Hist. of Sunderland Mass. 330-9
Talcott's N. Y. and N. E. Families 561-6
Temple's Hist. of Northfield Mass. 441-50
Temple's History of Whately Mass. 228
Thayer Memorial (1835) 46
Whittemore's Hist. Middlesex Co. Ct. 408
Fields—Chambers' N. J. Germans
Eaton's Thomaston Me. 225
Fife — Cutter's Jaffrey N. H. 276-8
Bemis' History of Marlboro N. H. 481-3
Carter's Hist. of Pembroke N. H. ii, 92-7
Norton's Hist. of Fitzwilliam N. H. 566
Fifield — Bouton's Concord N. H. 705
Dearborn's Hist. of Salisbury N. H. 563-75
Dow's History of Hampton N. H. 707-9
Joslin's History of Poultney Vt. 261
Lapham's History of Bethel Me. 531
Little's History of Weare N. H. 849
Runnel's Sanbornton N. H. ii, 276-8
Savage's Genealogical Dictionary ii, 158
Washington N. H. History 413
Worthen's History of Sutton N. H. 716
Wyman's Charlestown Mass. Gens. 345
Filbrick — Hammatt Papers 109
Filer — Doolittle's Belchertown 137
Hedge's Easthampton N. Y. History 272
Savage's Genealogical Dictionary ii, 158
Strong Genealogy 1305-11
Talcott's N. Y. and New Eng. Families 511
Files — Eaton's Thomaston Me. 225
Pierce's History of Gorham Me. 615
Fillebrown—Amer. Ancestry xii, 48
Cutter's Arlington 238
Paige's History of Cambridge Mass. 544
Wyman's Charlestown Mass. Gens. i, 346
Filley — Humphreys Genealogy 181-3
Loomis Genealogy (1880) 318-26
Savage's Genealogical Dictionary ii 159
Stiles' Hist. of Windsor Ct. ii, 250-8
Fillmore — Caulkins' Norwich Ct. 229
New Eng. Hist. and Gen. Reg. xi, 141-7
Walworth's Hyde Gen. 398, 654, 727-9
Fillow — Fillow Gen. (1888) 274 pages
Finan — Stearns' Ashburnham 699
Finch — American Ancestry ii, 38
Anderson's Waterbury Ct. i, app. 50
Cleveland's Hist. of Yates Co. N. Y. 731-3
Dodd's History of East Haven Ct. 118
Eager's History of Orange Co. N. Y. 401-3
Goodyear Genealogy 81

Greene County N. Y. History 309
Huntington's Stamford Ct. Settlers 34
Orcutt's History of Wolcott Ct. 475
Savage's Genealogical Dictionary ii, 159
Smith's Hist. of Peterborough N. H. 83
Stickney's Hist. of Minisink N. Y. 154-7
Timlow's Sketches Southington Ct. 91-3
Fincher — Literary Era, June 1899
Findlay — Harrison Ancestry 58
Findley — Marshall Gen. (1884) 158-60
Finel — Joslin's Hist. of Poultney Vt. 261
Fingar — American Ancestry ii, 39
Finkle — American Ancestry ii, 39
Ainsenberry Genealogy 138-54
Finlay — Egle's Penn. Gens. 2d ed. 87
Harris Family of New Jersey (1888) 203-9
Merrill's History of Acworth N. H. 214-9
Finley — American Ancestry xii, 29
Littell's Passaic Valley 151
Finney — Amer. Ancestry ii, 40; xii, 13
Davis' Landmarks of Plymouth 109-11
Futhey's History of Chester Pa. 547
Hine's Lebanon Ct. Historical Address 153
McKean Genealogy 10
Penn. Magazine iv, 234-40; vii, 466-71
Timlow's Southington Ct. Sketches xci
Watkins Genealogy 39
See also under Phinney
Finton — Cleveland's Yates Co. 145-7
Firly — Power's Sangamon Ill. 296
Firman—Fairman Genealogy 5-7
Norton's Fitzwilliam 566
Firmin — Essex Inst. Coll. xvii, 34-9
Hammatt Papers of Ipswich Mass. 102
Savage's Genealogical Dictionary ii, 160
New Eng. Hist. Gen. Reg. xxv, 51-5
Fish — Amer. Ancestry ii, 40; v, 201
Austin's R. I. Genealogical Dictionary 78
Austin's Allied Families 95-7
Ballou's History of Milford Mass. 746
Bass' History of Braintree Vt. 133
Cooley's Trenton N. J. Gens. 71-4
Daniel's History of Oxford Mass. 500-6
Davis' Landmarks of Plymouth 111
Eaton's History of Thomaston Me. ii, 226
Freeman's Cape Cod ii, 51, 161, 337, 478
Hatch's History of Industry Me. 617-21
Hayward's History of Gilsum N. H. 306
Hubbard's Stanstead Co. Canada 256
Morrison's Hist. of Windham N. H. 531
Read's History of Swanzey N. H. 338
Riker's Annals of Newtown N. Y. 365-70
Savage's Genealogical Dictionary ii, 161
Smith's Hist. of Sunderland Mass. 339
Stiles' History of Windsor Ct. ii, 258
Van Rensselaer's New Yorkers
Walworth's Hyde Genealogy 803-6
Welles' Amer. Family Antiquity iii, 141-62
Wentworth Genealogy i, 232
William's History of Danby Vt. 144-7
Winsor's History of Duxbury Mass. 258
Fisher — Aldrich's Walpole N. H. 255
American Ancestry ii, 40; iv, 195; vii, 237; x, 71, 114, 178; xi, 109
Austin's R. I. Genealogical Dictionary 79
Bangor Hist. Magazine v, 65-7; vi, 93, 110

Bassett's History of Richmond N. H. 387
Blake's History of Franklin Mass. 241-9
Chambers' Early Germans of N. J. 360-70
Clark's History of Norton Mass. 81
Cleveland's Hist. of Yates Co. N. Y. 419
Cochrane's History of Antrim N. H. 491
Cochrane's Hist. of Francestown N. H. 685-701
Cogswell Genealogy 394-6
Cogswell's Hist. of Henniker N. H. 567-9
Corliss' North Yarmouth Me. Magazine
Cregar's White Genealogy
Dedham Historical Register i, 24-6, 57; iii, 187-92, iv, 17-21, 61-5, 103-7; v, 34-7, 137, 162-5; vi, 65-8; vii, 38, 76, 117-9, 154-6; viii, 25, 50, 85, 131; ix, 22-4, 60-2, 90-3, 113-7; x, 15-9, 83-6, 118; xi, 26
Dotterer's Perkiomen Region Pa. 26
Eaton's Annals of Warren Me. 541
Egle's Notes and Queries 3d ser. ii, 162-4
Fisher Family of Delaware (1889) 24 p.
Fisher Family of New Jersey (1890) 243 p.
Fisher Family of Penn. (1896) 245 pages
Fisher Family of Dedham (1898) 466 pages
Garr Genealogy 72-6
Hayward's Hist. of Hancock N. H. 571-3
Hill's Dedham Mass. Records i
Hubbard's Hist. of Springfield Vt. 297-9
Hudson's History of Sudbury Mass. 441
Jameson's History of Medway Mass. 484-6
Lamborn Genealogy 270
Miller's Colchester Co. Nova Scotia 323-7
Morris Genealogy (1898) 752-5
Norton's Hist. of Fitzwilliam N. H. 566-8
Page Genealogy 104
Parthemore Genealogy 25, 55-67
Plumb's History of Hanover Pa. 415
Potts Genealogy (1895) 221-7
Power's Sangamon Co. Ill. 144, 297-9
Richmond Va. Standard ii, 2
Rodman Genealogy 94-6
Savage's Genealogical Dictionary ii, 161-4
Stearns' Hist. of Ashburnham Mass. 700
Temple's History of Northfield Mass. 450
Washington N. H. History 414-20
Wentworth Genealogy i, 555-8
Wheeler's History of N. Carolina ii, 392
Whipple-Hill Families (1897) 67-70
Worthen's History of Sutton N. H. 715
Young's History of Warsaw N. Y. 261-4
Fisk — Adams' Haven Genealogy 53-5
Ballou's History of Milford Mass. 748
Blake's Mendon Mass. Association 151-3
Blood's History of Temple N. H. 220
Bouton's History of Concord N. H. 661
Daniel's History of Oxford Mass. 506
Dunster Genealogy 62-4
Eaton's History of Thomaston Me. ii, 225
Hammatt Papers of Ipswich Mass. 104
Haven Genealogy 43-5
Hemenway's Vermont Hist. Gaz. iv, 789
Johnson's Genealogy (1876) 14-6
Leonard's History of Dublin N. H. 335-7
Montague Genealogy 437
Morse's Sherborn Mass. Settlers 85-7

Norton's Hist. of Fitzwilliam N. H. 568
Paige's History of Hardwick Mass. 376
Quincy Mass. Church Anniversary 104-6
Randall's Hist. of Chesterfield N. H. 311-4
Ruttenber's Hist. of Newburgh N. Y. 306
Ruttenber's Hist. of Orange Co. N. Y. 391
Secomb's Hist. of Amherst N. H. 584-7
Timlow's Sketches of Southington Ct. 93
Washington N. H. History 420-3
Williams' History of Danby Vt. 145-7
Worthen's History of Sutton N. H. 701
Fiske — Am. Anc. iii, 219; iv, 21; v, 175
Ballou Genealogy 565-8
Barry's Hist. of Framingham Mass. 242-4
Bradford Genealogy (1898) 15-8
Bond's Watertown Mass. 208-19, 758-62
Butler's History of Groton Mass. 401, 471
Cochrane's Hist. Francestown N. H. 702-4
Cutter's History of Arlington Mass. 240-2
Essex Mass. Inst. Hist. Colls. viii, 175-89
Fiske Sermon at W. Cambridge (1843) 40 p.
Fiske Genealogy (1865) 151 pages
Fiske Lineage (1867) 20 pages
Fiske Genealogy 2d ed. (1867) 209 pages
Fiske Genealogy (1896) 654 pages
Hudson's Hist. of Lexington Mass. 69-75
Jackson's History of Newton Mass. 277
Leland Genealogy 29-31
Livermore's History of Wilton N. H. 365-7
New Eng. Hist. Gen. Reg. iv, 180; xi, 221
Paige's History of Cambridge Mass. 545
Pierce's History of Grafton Mass. 480
Saunderson's Charlestown N. H. 333
Savage's Genealogical Dictionary ii, 164-8
Spooner's Memorial of W. Spooner 202-5
Stiles' History of Windsor Ct. ii, 259
Symmes Genealogy 28-30
Temple's History of Palmer Mass. 447-9
Vinton's Giles Genealogy 262
Whitmore's Heraldic Journal iii, 120-5
Wyman's Charlestown Mass. Gens. i, 348
Fisler — Bretz Genealogy 116-9
Egle's Notes and Queries 1896 An. vol. 119
Fitch — Alden's Amer. Epitaphs iv, 139
American Ancestry i, 27; iv, 28; xii
Babson's History of Gloucester Mass. 93
Baker's History of Montville Ct. 377-90
Bemis' History of Marlboro N. H. 484-7
Brown's Bedford Mass. Families, 10-2
Caulkins' Hist. of Norwich Ct. 148, 153
Cogswell Genealogy 243
Dimock's Coventry Ct. Records 43-5
Eaton's History of Reading Mass. 72
Hall's Norwalk Ct. Records 189, 191, 213
Hayward's History of Hancock N. H. 573
Hazen's History of Billerica Mass. 53
Hine's Lebanon Ct. Historical Address 154
Hollister's History of Pawlet Vt. 188-90
Hudson's History of Lexington Mass. 75
Huntington Genealogy 107
Loomis Genealogy (1880) 540-5
Mayflower Descendants 20
Morris Genealogy (1853) 11-3
Morse's Sherborn Mass. Settlers 87-9
Perkins' Old Houses of Norwich Ct. 452-6
Salem N. Y. Book of History 31-3

Savage's Genealogical Dictionary ii, 168–70
Selleck's Norwalk Ct. (1896) 193–224
Stearns' History of Rindge N. H. 521–3
Stiles' History of Windsor Ct. ii, 261–70
Stranahan Genealogy (1868) 49–91
Strong Genealogy 311, 320–30
Thayer Memorial (1835) 41–3, 90–102
Van Hoosear's Norwalk Ct. Epitaphs 24
Walworth's Hyde Genealogy 262
Westcott's Life of John Fitch 27–9, 413
Fithian—Hedge's East Hampton 275–7
Howell's Southamptton 242–5
Fitler — Pfeiffer Genealogy 21–37
Fitts—Bangor Me. Hist. Magazine vi, 91
Bass' History of Braintree Vt. 133–5
Benedict's History of Sutton Mass. 641
Chase's History of Chester N. H. 519–21
Cochrane's Hist. of Francest'n N. H. 704
Daniel's History of Oxford Mass. 507–10
Dearborn's Hist. of Salisbury N. H. 575–8
Eaton's History of Candia N. H. 77
Fitts and Fitz Genealogy (1869) 91 pages
Fitts and Fitz Genealogy (1897) 170 pages
Hoyt's Salisbury Mass. Families 156–8
Lane Genealogy (1891) 164–7
New Eng. Hist. Reg. xxii, 70–2, 161–5
Paige's History of Cambridge Mass. 546
Fitzgerald — Eaton's Thomaston Me. 226
Eaton's Annals of Warren Me. 541
Meade's Old Churches of Virginia
Fitzhugh — Carter Family Tree
De Bow's Review xxvi, 133
Lee Genealogy (1895) 89
Meade's Old Churches of Virginia ii, 192
Richmond Standard ii, 3, 24, 35, 51; iii, 2
Thomas Genealogy (1890) 315
Turner's Hist. Phelps Purchase 365, 396
Virginia Magazine of History i, 412–5; vii, 196–9, 317–9
Welles' Washington Genealogy 252
Fitzpatrick — Blake's Franklin 249–91
Fitzpen—See under Phippen
Fitz-Randolph — Am. Anc. vi, 22; xi, 81
Calnek's History of Annapolis N. S. 510
Fitz-Randolph Family (1895) 7 pages
Joliffe Genealogy 217–21
New York Gen. and Biog. Rec. xxx, 106–9
Paxton's Marshall Genealogy 235
Swift's Barnstable Mass. Fams. 368–70
Fitzwater — Cleveland's Yates Co. 669
Flack — American Ancestry ii, 40
Flagg—American Ancestry xi, 136
Andrews' New Britain Ct. 218
Ballou's History of Milford Mass. 749
Barry's Hist. of Framingham Mass. 244
Bass' History of Braintree Vt. 143
Beckwith Genealogy (1899) 64
Bond's Watertown Mass. 219–25, 762–4
Chase's History of Chester N. H. 521
Draper's History of Spencer Mass. 197
Flagg Genealogy (1877) 8 pages, reprint
Hayward's History of Hancock N. H. 574
Heywood's Hist. of Westminster Mass. 647
Maine Genealogist ii, 80–7
New Eng. Hist. Reg. xxvii, 246; xxx, 112
North's History of Augusta Me. 852–69

Norton's History of Fitzwilliam N. H. 569
Pierce's History of Grafton Mass. 480–3
Platt's Greenough Ancestry 12
Saunders Genealogy
Savage's Genealogical Dictionary ii, 171
Sewall's History of Woburn Mass. 611
Stone's History of Hubbardston Mass. 266
Wall's Reminis. of Worcester Mass. 106–8
Ward's Hist. of Shrewsbury Mass. 278
Worcester's History of Hollis N. H. 375
Flanders — Bouton's Concord N. H. 705
Coffin's History of Boscawen N. H. 527–30
Cogswell's History of Henniker N. H. 569
Dodge Ancestry (1896) 56
Flanders Genealogy (1873) 8 pages
Futhey's History of Chester Co. Pa. 549
Hoyt's Salisbury Mass. Families 159
Little's History of Weare N. H. 851
McKeen's History of Bradford Vt. 367–70
New Eng. Hist. Gen. Reg. xxvii, 170–6
Poor's Merrimac Valley Researches 122
Ridlon's Saco Valley Me. Families 690
Runnel's Hist. of Sanbornton N. H. ii, 278
Savage's Genealogical Dictionary ii, 172
Flansburgh — American Ancestry ii, 40
Pearson's Schenectady N. Y. Settlers 69
Fleet — American Ancestry ix, 233; xi, 4
Virg. Mag. of Hist. and Biog. ii (1895)
Fleisher — Egle's Notes and Queries 1896, Annual volume, 127
Fleming — American Ancestry ii, 40
Bolling Genealogy 25
Chambers' Early Germans of N. J. 371
Egle's Penn. Genealogies 2d ed. 232–45
Fleming Genealogy (1868) 64 pages
Goode Genealogy 211
Lowry Genealogy 8
Meade's Old Churches of Virginia
Paxton's Marshall Genealogy 337
Richmond Va. Standard ii, 20, 23; iv, 1
Robertson's Pocahontas' Descendants 33
Savage's Genealogical Dictionary ii, 172
Temple's History of Palmer Mass. 449
Flemly — Mellick Genealogy 686
Flemming — Bond's Watertown 225, 764
Flensburgh — Munsell's Albany iv, 121
Fletcher — Aldrich's Walpole 253–5
Am. Anc. vi, 140, 203; vii, 3, 85; ix, 138
Ballou's History of Milford Mass. 750
Bates and Fletcher Genealogy (1892) 58 p.
Bradbury's Hist. Kennebunkport Me. 244
Butler's History of Groton Mass. 401
Chandler's History of Shirley Mass. 416
Cochrane's History of Antrim N. H. 492–5
Cochrane's Hist. of Francestown N. H. 705
Dunstable Mass. Bi-Centennial 157
Eaton's History of Thomaston Me. ii, 227
Farrow's History of Islesborough Me. 209
Fletcher Family Chart (1848) 20x24 inches
Fletcher Family Notes (1849) 24 pages
Fletcher Genealogy (1871) 279 pages
Fletcher Family Reunion (1878) 12 pages
Fletcher Family Sketches (1878) 10 pages
Fletcher Genealogy (1881) 563 pages
Fletcher's Hatch Genealogy 22–4
Fox's History of Dunstable Mass. 243

Hayward's History of Hancock N. H. 575
Hazen's History of Billerica Mass. 53
Hill's Old Dunstable Mass. 147–62
Hodgman's Hist. of Westford Mass. 446–50
Kidder's Hist. of New Ipswich N. H. 374–6
Leland Genealogy 61–3
Lincoln's Hist. of Hingham Mass. ii, 231
Livermore's History of Wilton N. H. 367
Morse's Memorial appendix 51½
New Eng. Hist. and Gen. Reg. xxii, 389–93
Pierce's History of Grafton Mass. 483
Power's Sangamon County Ill. 299–303
Randall's Hist. of Chesterfield N. H. 314–6
Reed's History of Rutland Mass. 115
Ridlon's Saco Valley Me. Families 102
Savage's Genealogical Dictionary ii, 172–4
Saunderson's Charlestown N. H. 354
Secomb's History of Amherst N. H. 587–91
Stearns' Hist. of Ashburnham Mass. 700–2
Stearns' History of Rindge N. H. 523–5
Vinton's Richardson Genealogy 111
Wakefield Genealogy 162, 165, 168
Washington N. H. History 423–8
Wheeler's Hist. of Newport N. H. 386–8
Wood Genealogy 70–7
Wyman's Charlestown Mass. Gens. i, 348
Flewwelling — Orange County 365
Flinn — Littell's Passaic Valley 153
Morris Genealogy (1894) 97–102, 125–9
Flint — American Ancestry vi, 84; viii, 54
Bass' History of Braintree Vt. 135–41
Bassett's History of Richmond N. H. 388
Bemis' History of Marlboro N. H. 487
Brown's Bedford Mass. Families 12
Butler's History of Farmington Me. 470
Cochrane's History of Antrim N. H. 495–9
Cochrane's Hist. Francestown N. H. 706
Cogswell's History of Henniker N. H. 570
Driver Genealogy 291–307
Eaton's History of Reading Mass. 72–9
Eaton's History of Thomaston Me. ii, 227
Essex Mass. Inst. Hist. Colls. xvi, 106–9
Flint Genealogy (1860) 150 pages
Flint Genealogy, see Flynt
Hayward's Hist. of Hancock N. H. 575–8
Heywood's Hist. Westminster Mass. 648–50
Lapham's History of Norway Me. 501
Lincoln's Hist. of Hingham Mass. ii, 231
Livermore's Hist. Wilton N. H. 368–71
Marvin's Hist. Winchendon Mass. 454
New Eng. Hist. Gen. Reg. xiv, 58–60
Pompey N. Y. Reunion 304
Potter's Concord Mass. Families 10
Read's History of Swanzey N. H. 339
Saunders' Alabama Settlers 398
Savage's Genealogical Dictionary ii, 174
Secomb's History of Amherst N. H. 591–3
Shattuck's History of Concord Mass. 371
Stearns' History of Ashburnham Mass. 703
Vinton's Richardson Genealogy 553
Ward's History of Shrewsbury Mass. 275
Washburn's History of Leicester Mass. 365
Worthen's History of Sutton N. H. 699
Wyman's Charlestown Mass. Gens. 349
Flintner — Hanson's Gardiner Me. 82
Flitner — American Ancestry x, 10

Cutts Genealogy 202
Maine Hist. Gen. Rec. vi, 285–92, 341–8, 417–21
Flock — Chambers' N. J. Germans
Flood — Chandler's Shirley Mass. 417
Bemis's History of Marlboro N. H. 487–9
Savage's Genealogical Dictionary ii, 175
Flora — Egle' Queries 3d ser. i, 328
Florida — Hemenway's Vt. Gaz. v, 162
Florville — Powers Sangamon 303
Flounders — Austin's R. I. Dictionary 79
Flournoy — Cabell Genealogy 354–64
Richmond Standard i, 37; iii, 14
Virginia Mag. of Hist. and Biog. ii, 81–90, 190–213, 318–27, 437–47; iii, 67–79, 414–6; iv, 97–101
Flower — Carter Gen. (1883) 107, 156–9
Clarkson Memoirs (1890)
Ellis Genealogy 112, 152–4, 373
Martin's Hist. of Chester Co. Pa. 436–44
N. E. Hist. and Gen. Reg. xliv, 399
Sharpless Genealogy 287
Smith's History of Delaware Co. Pa. 436
Welles' Amer. Family Antiquity ii, 133–65
Floyd — Aldrich's Walpole N. H. 252
Bangor Me. Historical Magazine v, 191
Carter Family Tree
N. E. Hist. and Gen. Reg. xxxviii, 74
New York Gen. and Biog. Rec. xv, 41
Preston Genealogy (1870) 48
Richmond Va. Standard ii, 7
Strong Genealogy 604–6
Thompson's Long Island N. Y. ii, 431–7
Wyman's Charlestown Mass. Gens. i, 350
Flucker — Wyman's Charlestown 350
Flumervelt — Chambers' N. J. Germans
Flynt — American Ancestry iv, 176
Morris and Flynt Ancestors (1882) 48–53
Fobes — Lapham's Paris Me. 601–4
Mitchell's Bridgewater Mass. 159–63
Savage's Genealogical Dictionary ii, 176
Wallbridge Genealogy 289
Winsor's History of Duxbury Me. 258
Fogerty — Eaton's Thomaston Me. 228
Fogg — American Ancestry xi, 78
Corliss' North Yarmouth Me.
Dearborn's Hist. of Parsonsfield Me. 380
Dow's History of Hampton N. H. 709–16
Eaton's History of Thomaston Me. ii, 228
Fogg's Eliot Me. Settlers 1–9
Fullonton's Hist. of Raymond N. H. 223 6
Hayward's Hist. of Hancock N. H. 579–81
Lane Genealogy (1891) 86–90
Maine Hist. Rec. i, 70–80; viii, 149, 214–8; ix, 41–8
Old Eliot Me. Monthly ii, (1898) 77–85
Runnel's Hist. Sanbornton N. H. ii, 279
Savage's Genealogical Dictionary ii, 177
Wheeler's History of Newport N. H. 388
Foland — Amer. Ancestry i, 27; ii, 41
Foley—Lincoln's Hingham Mass. ii, 232
Temple's Palmer Mass. 462
Folger — Am. Ancestry i, 28; ii, 41; vi, 17
Folger Genealogy (1862) 10 pages
New Eng. Hist. Gen. Register xvi, 269–78
Savage's Genealogical Dictionary ii, 177

Folk — Chambers' N. J. Germans 375
Follansbee—Cochrane's Francest'n 706-8
Follansbee Assoc. Reports (1865) 28 pages
(1869) 8 pages
Little's History of Weare N. H. 853
Smith's History of Peterborough N. H. 84
Follansby — Benton's Guildhall Vt. 270
Follett — American Ancestry iv, 127
Austin's Allied Families 99
Follett Genealogy (1896) 248 pages
Hatch's History of Industry Me. 621
Huron and Erie Counties Ohio 406
Morse Memorial appendix 60
Stone's History of Hubbarston Mass. 268
Follmer — Meginness' Jour. ii, 383
Folsom — American Ancestry iii, 193
Bell's History of Exeter N. H. 12-4
Chapman's Weeks Genealogy 51, 136-8
Chase's History of Chester N. H. 522-4
Cochrane's Hist. of Francestown N. H. 708
Cogswell's History of Henniker N. H. 571
Folsom Gen. (1876) 29 p. (1879) pamphlet
(1882) 297 p.
Fullonton's Hist. of Raymond N. H. 226-8
Lancaster's Hist. of Gilmanton N. H. 262
Montague Genealogy 348
New Eng. Hist. Gen. Reg. xxx, 207-31
New Hampshire Hist. Soc. Colls. vi, 191
Orcutt's History of Stratford Ct. 1205
Palmer Genealogy (1886) 48-51
Runnels' Hist. Sanbornton N. H. ii, 280-3
Savage's Genealogical Dictionary ii, 178
Fonda—Am. Anc. i, 28; vii, 29; x, 101; xi, 232
Munsell's Albany N. Y. Colls. iv, 122
Pearson's Schenectady N. Y. Settlers 70-2
Fondey — American Ancestry i, 28
Fones — Austin's R. I. Gen. Dict. 79
Savage's Genealogical Dictionary ii, 179
Shotwell Genealogy 136
Fontaine — Bergen's Kings Co. 115
Clarke's Old King Wm. Co. Va. Families
Green's Kentucky Families
Maury's Huguenot Memoirs (1853)
Meade's Old Churches of Virginia i, 465
Perkins' Old Houses of Norwich Ct. 457-9
Saunders' Alabama Settlers 293-7
Slaughter's Fry Memoir 48
Slaughter's St. Mark's Parish Va. 184, 189
Welles' Washington Genealogy 251
Virginia Hist. Soc. Colls. v, (1886) 119-50
Virginia Magazine of History vi, 305-7
Foote—Am. Anc. iv, 88, 191; v, 231; x, 205
Anderson's Waterbury Ct. i, app. 51
Barbour's My Wife and Mother app. 62-4
Bingham Genealogy 235-40
Brown's West Simsbury Ct. Settlers 53-6
Caulkins' History of New London Ct. 308
Cochrane's Hist. Francest'n N. H. 709-13
Davis' History of Wallingford Ct. 745
Dearborn's History of Salisbury N. H. 579
Dickerman Genealogy 502-9
Felton Genealogy (1886) 247
Foote Genealogy (1849) 360 pages
Foote Family of Arlington Vt. (1867) 32 p.
Foote Family of Colchester Ct. (1886) 26 p.

Hall's Genealogical Notes 104, 149-52
Hoyt's Salisbury Mass. Families 161
Humphrey Genealogy 261-5, 346-9
Judd's History of Hadley Mass. 494
Loomis Genealogy (1880) 573-8
Mathew's History of Cornwall Vt. 285
Nash Genealogy 42
N. E. Hist. Gen. Reg. ix, 272; xxvii, 448
Orcutt's History of Stratford Ct. 1202-4
Savage's Genealogical Dictionary ii, 179-82
Virginia Mag. of History vii, 73-5, 201-3
Walworth's Hyde Genealogy 276
Young's Chautauqua Co. N. Y. 359-61
Footman — Bulloch Genealogy
Forbes — Am. Anc. iii, 147; x, 102; xii
Bangor Me. Historical Magazine iv, 20
Daniel's History of Oxford Mass. 510
Dodd's History of East Haven Ct. 119
Dudley's Archæological Coll. plate 5
Forbes Genealogy (1892) 199 pages
N. Y. Gen. and Biog. Rec. xxi, 159-62
Sill Genealogy (1897) 14-7
Forbush — Forbes Genealogy
Heywood's Hist. Westminster Mass. 650-2
Hubbard's Hist. of Springfield Vt. 302
Hudson's Hist. of Marlborough Mass. 364
Paige's History of Hardwick Mass. 377
Pierce's History of Grafton Mass. 484-8
Sheldon's History of Deerfield Mass. 164
Smith's Hist. of Peterborough N. H. 85-8
Temple's Hist. N. Brookfield Mass. 588-91
Ward's Rice Genealogy 21
Force — American Ancestry vi, 80; xi, 219
Chambers' Early Germans of N. J. 375
Ford — American Ancestry ii, 41; v, 115
Anderson's Waterbury Ct. i, app. 52
Baldwin Genealogy 1108, 1113
Barbour's My Wife and Mother app. 24
Bass' History of Braintree Vt. 141-3
Blake's History of Hamden Ct. 245
Collin's Hist. of Hillsdale N. Y. app. 54-6
Davis' Landmarks of Plymouth Mass. 111
Dawson's Historical Magazine (1871) 91
Deane's History of Scituate Mass. 269
Ford Genealogy (1890) 293 pages
Goode Genealogy 291
Hobart's Hist. of Abington Mass. 378-83
Kingman's N. Bridgewater Mass. 503
Kitchell Genealogy 50
Maine Hist. and Gen. Recorder iii, 229
Mitchell's Bridgewater Mass. 163, 373
Poole Genealogy 78-80
Pope Genealogy
Power's Sangamon Co. Ill. Settlers 304
Randall's Hist. of Chesterfield N. H. 316
Runnel's Hist. Sanbornton N. H. ii, 283-5
Savage's Genealogical Dictionary ii, 182-4
Stiles' History of Windsor Ct. ii, 270
Strong Genealogy 17
Temple's History of Whately Mass. 229
Whitman Genealogy 370
Winsor's History of Duxbury Mass. 259
Wyman's Charlestown Mass. Gens. i, 352
Fordham — Howell's Southampton 245
Savage's Genealogical Dictionary ii. 184
Fordyce — Aylsworth Genealogy 182

Forehand — Amer. Ancestry ix, 220
Forman — Leaveuworth Gen. 338-43
Paxton's Marshall Genealogy 229-33
Salter's Hist. of Monmouth Co. N. J. xxvii
Forney — American Ancestry x, 172
Forney Genealogy (1895) 59 pages
Wheeler's History of N. Carolina 241
Forrest — American Ancestry iv, 146
Cincinnati Ohio Criterion (1888) ii, 474
Clyde's Irish Settlers in Pa. 45
Daniel's History of Oxford Mass. 511
Forrest Genealogy (1897) 141 pages
Power's Sangamon Co. Ill. Settlers 305
Richmond Va. Standard iii, 37
Runnel's Hist. of Sanbornton N. H. i, 474
Forrer — See Forry
Forristall — Fitzwilliam N. H. 570-4
Forry — Forry Genealogy (1898) 9 pages
Wagenseller Genealogy 172-80
Forsaith — Chase's Chester N. H. 524
Wheeler's History of Newport N. H. 389
Forshee — Cole Genealogy 86-90, 171-203
Forster — American Ancestry vi, 204
Caulkins' History of New London Ct. 312
Egle's Penn. Gens. 2d ed. 247-63
Forster Genealogy. See Foster
Wyman's Charlestown Mass. Gens. i, 353
Forsyth — Am. Ancestry iii, 150; vii, 87
Cope Genealogy 39, 61, 141
Forsyth Genealogy (1888) 29 pages
Forsyth Genealogy (1897) 40 pages
Granite Monthly Concord N. H. viii, 251
Richmond Va. Standard iii, 23
Ruttenber's Hist. of Orange Co. N. Y. 394
Sylvester's Hist. of Ulster Co. N. Y. 106
Fort — Munsell's Albany Colls. iv, 123
Schuyler's Colonial New York ii, 367-75
Whittemore's Orange N. J. 430
Forth — N. E. Hist. Reg. xxiii, 184
Fortune — Power's Sangamon Ill. 306
Forward — Holton's Winslow Gen. 341
Stiles' History of Windsor Ct. ii, 271
Fosdick — Amer. Ancestry x, 143, 161
Caulkins' History of N. London Ct. 343
Mallmann's Shelter Island N. Y. 250
Savage's Genealogical Dictionary 185
Wyman's Charlestown Mass. i, 354-60
Fosket — Cleveland Gen. (1899) 73
Hyde's Brimfield Mass. 403
Temple's History of Palmer Mass. 453
Wyman's Charlestown Mass. Gens. i, 360
Foskett — Heywood's Westminster 652-5
Foss — Chase's Hist. of Chester N. H. 525
Little Genealogy 290
Machias Me. Centennial 161
Ridlon's Saco Valley Me. Families 690
Fossett — Johnston's Bristol Me. 442
Fossey — Hammatt Papers 108
Foster — Abbott's Andover Mass. 38
Aldrich's History of Walpole N. H. 256-9
American Ancestry i, 28; ii, 42; iv, 140,
   230; v, 186; vi, 40; x, 174, 196; xii, 36
Ammidown Genealogy 33
Austin's R. I. Genealogical Dictionary 80
Babson's History of Gloucester Mass. 94
Bangor Me. Historical Magazine ix, 32

Barry's Hist. of Framingham Mass. 245
Bemis' History of Marlboro N. H. 490-2
Blood's History of Temple N. H. 221
Briggs' History of Shipbuilding 227-40
Caldwell Genealogy 64
Calnek's History of Annapolis N. S. 510-3
Capron Genealogy by Holden 28-37
Chute Genealogy, appendix 52-66
Claremont Ohio History 435
Cochrane's History of Antrim N. H. 499
Cogswell's Hist. of Henniker N. H. 572-5
Collin's History of Hillsdale N. Y. app. 56
Corliss' North Yarmouth Me. Magazine
Cutter's History of Arlington Mass. 243
Daggett's Hist. of Attleborough Mass. 90
Daniel's History of Oxford Mass. 511-3
Davis Genealogy 95-8
Davis' Landmarks of Plymouth Mass. 112
Deane's History of Scituate Mass. 270
Dearborn's Hist. of Salisbury N. H. 580-2
Dedham Mass. Hist. Register vi, 22-6
Dennysville Me. Centennial 103
Driver Genealogy 275
Dwight Genealogy 634-60, 671-4
Eaton's History of Candia N. H. 80
Eaton's History of Reading Mass. 79
Eaton's History of Thomaston Me. ii, 229
Essex County Mass. Hist. and Gen. Reg.
   (1894) 20-3, 54-7, 81-3
Foster Fam. of Charlestown (1870) 25 pages
Foster Fam. of Charlestown (1871) 6 pages
Foster Family of Ipswich (1872) 35 pages
Foster Family of Ipswich (1876) 24 pages
Foster Fam. of Gloucester Mass. (1885) 32 p.
Foster Family of Billerica (1889) 139 pages
Foster Pedigree (1897) 384 pages
Foster Ancestry (1898) 26 pages
Foster Fam. of Dorchester (1898) 22 pages
Foster Genealogy (1899) 1081 pages
Freeman's History of Cape Cod ii, 111, 765
Goodwin's Olcott Genealogy 31
Green's Todd Genealogy
Guild's Stiles Genealogy 286-8, 353-7
Hammatt Papers of Ipswich Mass. 105-8
Hartwell Genealogy (1895) 89-94
Hayward's Hist. of Gilsum N. H. 308-10
Hayward's Hist. of Hancock N. H. 581-5
Hazen's History of Billerica Mass. 54
Herrick's History of Gardner Mass. 348
Heywood's Hist. of Westminster Mass. 655
Hill's History of Mason N. H. 202
Holton's Winslow Genealogy i, 148-62
Howell's Hist. Southampton N. Y. 247-56
Hubbard's Stanstead Co. Canada 137
Hyde's History of Brimfield Mass. 404
Kidder's Hist. of New Ipswich N. H. 376
Kilbourne Genealogy 126
Lapham's History of Bethel Me. 532-4
Lapham's History of Norway Me. 502
Leach's Morton Ancestry 148-52
Little's History of Weare N. H. 855.
Livermore's History of Wilton N. H. 371
Locke Genealogy 64, 145, 300
Machias Me. Centennial 160
Maine Hist. Magazine (1893) viii, 152-5
Merrill's History of Acworth N. H. 216

Milliken's Narraguagus Valley Me. 13
Morse Sherborn Mass. Settlers 89
Narragansett Historical Reg. i, 222-5
N. E. Hist. Gen. Reg. i, 352-4; xx, 227,
  308; xxv, 67-71, 394-9; xxvi, 394-9;
  xxx, 83-102; lii, 194-203, 336-40
Newport R. I. Mercury for June 10, 1899
Norton's History of Fitzwilliam N. H.
  574-6
Paige's History of Cambridge Mass. 547
Paige's History of Hardwick Mass. 377-9
Perley's History of Boxford Mass. 31
Poore Genealogy 177-82
Power's Sangamon Co. Ill. Settlers 307-10
Read's History of Swanzey N. H. 340
Ridlon's Harrison Me. Settlers 59-63
Rodenbough's Autumn Leaves 56-71
Saunders' Alabama Settlers 366
Savage's Genealogical Dictionary ii, 185-91
Sedgwick's History of Sharon Ct. 79
Sewall's History of Woburn Mass. 612
Sheldon's Hist. of Deerfield Mass. 164
Spooner's Memorial of W. Spooner 215
Stearn's Hist. Ashburnham Mass. 703-10
Stearns' History of Rindge N. H. 525
Stiles' History of Windsor Ct. ii, 272
Stoddard Genealogy (1865) 48, 73
Svift's Barnstable Families i, 388-90
Temple's N. Brookfield Mass. 591-3
Temple's History of Northfield Mass. 451
Temple's History of Palmer Mass. 450-3
Thurston's Hist. of Winthrop Me. 183-5
Washington N. H. History 428
Whitman Genealogy 432-7
Wood Genealogy 47-57
Worcester's History of Hollis N. H. 375
Wyman's Charlestown Mass. i, 362-6
Young's History of Warsaw N. Y. 264
See also under Forster
Fotler — Lincoln's Hingham ii, 234
Foulke — Claypoole Genealogy 88, 154
Hayden's Virginia Gens. 658
Jenkins' History Gwynedd Pa. 2d ed.
  233-81
Penn. Mag. of History and Biog. xii, 369
Robert's Old Richland Pa. Families 142-60
Fountain — Bolton's Westchester 518
Clute's Hist. of Staten Island N. Y. 381
Conn. Quart. iii (1897) 106, 234, 351, 353, 480
Perkins' Old Houses of Norwich Ct. 457-9
Fournier — Howell's Southampton 256
Foutch — Power's Sangamon Ill. 310
Fowke — Clarke's King Wm. Va. Fams.
Fowke Genealogy (1891) 4 pages
Hayden's Virg. Gens. 155-61
Meade's Old Churches of Virginia ii, 482
N. E. Hist. and Gen. Reg. xxxviii, 320
Southern Bivouac (1886) 727
Fowkes — Power's Sangamon Ill. 311
Fowle — American Ancestry xii
Bond's Watertown 108, 225
Hudson's History of Lexington Mass. 279
Savage's Genealogical Dictionary ii, 192
Secomb's History of Amherst N. H. 594
Sewall's History of Woburn Mass. 612-4
Wyman's Charlestown Mass. i, 367-72

Fowler — American Ancestry ii, 43, 154;
  iii, 17; v, 91; vi, 96; vii, 280; ix, 140;
  x, 169; xii, 12
Anderson's Waterbury Ct. i, app. 53
Baird's History of Rye N. Y. 465
Ball's History of Lake Co. Ind. 375
Bangor Me. Historical Magazine iv, 237
Bartow Genealogy part 2
Bolton's Westchester Co. N. Y. ii, 519
Burleigh's Guild Genealogy 88-91
Carter's Hist. of Pembroke N. H. ii, 100-7
Champion Genealogy
Chapman's Weeks Genealogy 137
Chase's History of Chester N. H. 525
Coffin's History of Boscawen N. H. 531
Douglas Genealogy 206-8
Dow's History of Hampton N. H. 716
Driver Genealogy 316, 370
Essex Mass. Inst. Hist. Colls. xxvi, 85-7
Fowler Family of Windsor Ct. (1857) 27 p.
Fowler Family of Milford Ct. (1867) 12 p.
Fowler Family of New Haven (1870) 42 p.
Fowler Family of Ipswich (1883) 269 p.
Fowler Family of New York (1889) 78 p.
Fowler's Chauncey Genealogy 190
Granite Monthly Concord N. H. iv, 1-5
Guild's Stiles Genealogy 324-7, 651-3
Hammatt Papers of Ipswich Mass. 108
Herrick Genealogy 258-305
Hine's Lebanon Ct. Historical Address 154
Howell's Southampton N. Y. 2d ed. 257
Hoyt's Salisbury Mass. Families 162-5
Hurd's History of New London Ct. 511
Loomis Genealogy (1880) 688
Maltby Genealogy (1895) 75
Montague Genealogy 203
N. E. Hist. Gen. Reg. vii, 131; xi, 247-54;
  liii, 310-6
Orcutt's History of Torrington Ct. 690-3
Power's Sangamon Co. Ill. Settlers 312
Ruttenber's Hist. of Newburg N. Y. 274-7
Ruttenber's Hist. Orange Co. N. Y. 365-7
Savage's Genealogical Dictionary ii, 193-5
Stickney Genealogy 505
Stiles' History of Windsor Ct. ii, 274
Walworth's Hyde Genealogy 709-11
Warren and Clarke Genealogy 65
Washington N. H. History 429-31
Worthen's History of Sutton N. H. 717-20
Fowles — Eaton's Warren Me. 542
Fownes — N. E. Hist. Reg. xviii, 185
Fox — Alden's Epitaphs i, 229-31
American Ancestry v, 66
Baker's History of Montville Ct. 365-76
Bond's Watertown Mass. Genealogies 765
Brown's West Simsbury Ct. Settlers 62
Caulkins' History of New London Ct. 370
Cleveland's Hist. Yates Co. N. Y. 339-401
Cochrane's History of Antrim N. H. 500-3
Crafts' History of Whately Mass. 465-6
Crosby's Obituary Notices (1858) 403
Cutter's History of Jaffrey N. H. 326-8
Dwight's Strong Genealogy 1199
Fox, Ellicott and Evans Gen. (1882) 281 p.
Fox Family of Haddam Ct. (1890) 31 pages
Hayden's Virginia Genealogies 60

Hayward's Hist. of Hancock N. H. 585-91
Hubbard's Stanstead Co. Canada 175
Kidder's Hist. of New Ipswich N. H. 337
Montgomery and Fulton Cos. N. Y. 151
Norton's History of Fitzwilliam N. H. 576
Paige's History of Cambridge Mass. 547
Palmer and Trimble Genealogy 190, 261-3
Richmond Va. Standard iii, 23
Rodman Genealogy 154
Savage's Genealogical Dictionary ii, 195-7
Sewall's History of Woburn Mass. 139-43, 331
Stiles' History of Windsor Ct. ii, 274
Strobridge Genealogy 27, 48
Swain Genealogy 74-6
Temple's History of Whately Mass. 230
Washington N. H. History 431
Wentworth Genealogy ii, 85-7
Foxcroft — N. E. Reg. viii, 171-60
Paige's History of Cambridge Mass. 548-50
Savage's Genealogical Dictionary ii, 197
Vinton Genealogy 124
Foxwell — Deane's Scituate Mass. 272
Folsom's History of Saco Me. 116
N. Eng. Hist. Gen. Reg. xxxix, 343
Savage's Genealogical Dictionary ii, 198
Swift's Barnstable Families i, 365-7
Foye — Wyman's Charlestown 372
Frace — Chambers' N. J. Germans
Frairy — See Frary
Fraleigh — Am. Ancestry i, 29; ii, 43
Smith's History of Rhinebeck N. Y. 210-8
Frame — Guild's Stiles Genealogy 22
France — American Ancestry i, 29
Francis — Am. Anc. iii, 18 iv, 59 v, 16
Andrews' History of New Britain Ct. 162
Balch's Provincial Papers of Pa. 41-50
Bergen's Kings County N. Y. Settlers 116
Boardman Genealogy (1895) 687-92
Brooks' History of Medford Mass. 512-4
Cutter's History of Arlington Mass. 244
Essex Inst. Hist. Coll. xxv, 123, 288-90
Francis Genealogy (1900) 24 pages
Hanson's Old Kent Md. 296
New Eng. Gen. and Hist. Register xvii, 262; xxvii, 136; xlviii, 345
Paige's History of Cambridge Mass. 550
Paul's History of Wells Vt. 86-9
Power's Sangamon Co. Ill. Settlers 313-7
Savage's Genealogical Dictionary ii, 199
Stiles' History of Windsor Ct. ii, 274
Wyman's Charlestown Mass. Gens. i, 374
Francisco — American Ancestry ii, 43
Frank — Corliss' North Yarmouth Me.
Lapham's History of Norway Me. 503
Pearson's Schenectady N. Y. Settlers 73
Young's Chautauqua Co. N. Y. 235-8
Franklin — Bridgeman's Granary Burial Ground 323-32
Cleveland Genealogy (1899) 2079-83
Franklin Fam. Woodbury Ct. (1839) 103 p.
Franklin Family of Phila. (1889) 8 pages
Franklin Family of Phila. (1899) 24 pages
Hammatt Papers of Ipswich Mass. 110
Hayden's Virginia Genealogies 658
Morris Gen. (1898) 371-4, 563-9, 709-16

New Eng. Hist. and Gen. Register viii, 374; xi, 17-20; xvi, 273; xxvii, 246
N. Y. Gen. and Biog. Rec. xxiii, 127-30
Penn. Magazine of History xxiii, 1-22
Phœnix's Whitney Genealogy i, 723
Plumb's History of Hanover Pa. 412
Ransom Genealogy 33, 68, 71-3
Savage's Genealogical Dictionary ii, 199
Spark's Life of Benj. Franklin 546
Whitmore's Heraldic Journal ii, 97-9
Frary — Crafts Whately Mass. 466-71
Judd's Hist. of Hadley Mass. 496
Kellogg's White Genealogy 39
Leach's Morton Ancestry 112-6
Morris Genealogy (1894) 135
Morse's Genealogical Reg. ii (1859) 177-80
Savage's Genealogical Dictionary ii, 201
Sheldon's Hist. of Deerfield Mass. 165-7
Temple's History of Whately Mass. 230-2
Fraser — American Ancestry x, 93, 141
Hubbard's Stanstead Co. Canada 242
Fravor — American Ancestry i, 29
Frazee — Littell's Passaic Valley 154-7
Power's Sangamon Co. Ill. Settlers 317
Frazer — Am. Ancestry iv, 235; v, 18
Cothren's Hist. of Woodbury Ct. 1494-7
Futhey's History of Chester Co. Pa. 552
Martin's History of Chester Pa. 275
Washington N. H. History 433
Winsor's History of Duxbury Mass. 259
Frazier — Lamborn Genealogy 290
Dearborn's Hist. of Salisbury N. H.
Huntting's Pine Plains 335
Richmond Va. Standard iv, 2
Whittemore's Orange N. J. 282
Fredenburgh — Amer. Ancestry ii, 43
Cleveland's Yates Co. N. Y. 712-4
New York Gen. and Biog. Rec. xix, 178
Fredenrich — American Ancestry i, 29
Frederick — Plumb's Hanover Pa. 413
Freeborn — Austin's R. I. Gen. Dict. 296
Freeborne — Savage's Gen. Dict. ii, 202
Freeland — Benedict's Sutton 642-6
Freeman — American Ancestry i, 29; vii, 81; viii, 63, 219; xii
Ammidown Genealogy 36
Bangor Me. Historical Magazine v, 4
Bassett's History of Richmond N. H. 389
Bouton Genealogy 545-7
Capron Genealogy by Holden 252-63
Clarke's Old King Wm. Co. Va. Families
Daggett's History of Attleborough Mass. 90
Daniel's History of Oxford Mass. 513
Dudley's Archæological Coll. plate 4
Foster Genealogy (1889) 50-4
Freeman's Genealogy (1860) 92 pages
Freeman Genealogy (1875) 456 pages
Freeman's Cape Cod ii. 151, 380-5, 757-65
Huntington Genealogy 103
Journal of Smith and Dean 135, 363
Lapham's History of Norway Me. 504
Livermore's History of Wilton N. H. 367
New Eng. Gen. Reg. xx. 59-63, 353-5
Paige's History of Hardwick Mass. 379-81
Pearson's Schenectady N. Y. Settlers 74
Pierce's History of Gorham Me. 168

Pratt's History of Eastham Mass. 124
Rich's History of Truro Mass. 527
Ridlon's Saco Valley Me. Families 128
Ryder's Life of Mrs. A. F. Ryder 44 pages
Savage's Genealogical Dictionary ii, 203–5
Swift's Barnstable Families i, 385–7
Timlow's Sketches of Southington Ct. 94
Whittemore's Orange N J. 67
Winsor's History of Duxbury Mass. 260
Wyman's Charlestown Mass. Gens. i, 375
Freer — American Ancestry vii, 135
Freese — Dow's Hampton N. H. 716
Frelinghuysen — Chambers' Life of Frelinghuysen (1863)
Chambers' Early Germans of N. J. 378–84
Honeyman's Our Home Magazine 56–8
McPike Genealogy
Thompson's Readington N. J. Church 133–6
Fremont — Richmond Standard ii, 7
French — Alden's Am. Epitaphs ii, 6–8
American Ancestry ii, 44; iii, 145; iv, 50;
    v, 157; vi, 11, 198; vii, 281
Ballou's History of Milford Mass. 752–4
Bangor Me. Historical Magazine iv, 209
Bass' History of Braintree Vt. 144
Bedford N. H. History 701–5
Carter's Hist. of Pembroke N. H. ii, 107–10
Chapman's Weeks Genealogy 138–40
Chase's History of Chester N. H. 525–9
Coffin's History of Boscawen N. H. 532
Cogswell's History of Henniker N. H. 576
Cogswell's Hist. of Nottingham N. H. 379
Corliss' North Yarmouth Me. Magazine
Crosby Genealogy 35–7
Cutter's Hist. of Jaffrey N. H. 338–43
Daggett's Hist. of Attleborough Mass. 91
Dearborn's Hist. of Salisbury N. H. 584
Dow's History of Hampton N. H. 717
Eaton's Annals of Warren Me. 542
Eaton's History of Thomaston Me. ii, 231
Fillow Genealogy 98
Fox's History of Dunstable N. H. 243–5
French Family of Stoughton (1870) 12 p.
French Reunion at Dunstable (1879) 24 p.
French Family of Braintree (1885) 15 p.
French Family of Milford (1890) 8 pages
French Family Ancestry (1894) 186 pages
French Family (1897) 4 pages
French's History of Turner Me. 52
Hayward's Hist. of Hancock N. H. 591
Hemenway's Vermont Gazetteer v, 42, 213
Hill's Dedham Mass. Records i
Hoyt's Salisbury Mass. Families 166–70
Hurlbut Genealogy 428
Kellogg's White Genealogy 44
Kingman's N. Bridgewater Mass. 504–7
Lancaster's Hist. of Gilmanton N. H. 263
Lane Genealogy (1891) 138–40
Lapham's History of Norway Me. 505
Leonard's History of Dublin N. H. 338
Lincoln's Hist. of Hingham Mass. 235–41
Littell's Passaic Valley Genealogies 157
Livermore's History of Wilton N. H. 372–5
Mitchell's Hist. of Bridgewater Mass. 163–5
Morris Genealogy (1894) 30
Morris' Bontecou Genealogy 174

New Eng. Hist. and Gen. Reg. xliv, 367–
    72; xlvii, 357–61
New York Gen. Biog. Rec. ix, 118–20
Orcutt's History of Derby Ct. 720–3
Orcutt's History of Stratford Ct. 1204
Paige's History of Cambridge Mass. 551
Penn. Mag. of History iv, 108–12, 234–40
Runnel's Hist. Sanbornton N. H. ii, 285–7
Savage's Genealogical Dictionary ii, 205–9
Sharpe's History of Seymour Ct. 154
Sharpe's South Britain Sketches 69–71
Sheldon's Hist. of Deerfield Mass. 167
Smith's Hist. of Petersborough N. H. 88
Temple's Hist. of N. Brookfield Mass. 593
Temple's History of Palmer Mass. 459–61
Thayer Memorial (1835) 90–9
Valentine's N. Y. Manual (1853) 400
Vinton Genealogy 89–91, 193–6, 317–23
Walker Genealogy 140–7
Walworth's Hyde Genealogy 41
Washington N. H. History 433–8
Whitman Genealogy 25–8
Whitmore's Copps Hill Epitaphs
Worcester's History of Hollis N. H. 375
Worthen's History of Sutton N. H. 720–3
Wyman's Charlestown Mass. Gens. i, 376
Fretz — American Ancestry xi, 79
Fretz Genealogy (1896) 607 pages
Frew — Young's Chautauqua Co. 248
Frey — Amer. Ancestry v, 161; ix, 19
Frey Genealogy (1870) 35 pages
Levering Genealogy (1897) 107
Montgomery and Fulton Cos. N. Y. 151
See also under heading of Fry
Friar — American Ancestry ii, 44
Friend — Bangor Me. Hist. Mag. v, 191
Washington N. H. History 428–40
Frink — Ballou's Milford Mass. 754
Read's History of Swanzey N. H. 342
Reed's History of Rutland Mass. 98
Sheldon's Hist. of Deerfield Mass. 168
Temple's History of Palmer Mass. 453
Frisbee — American Ancestry ii, 44; ix,
    191, 219; x, 180
Sedgwick's History of Sharon Ct. 80
Frisbie — Anderson's Waterbury 53
Frisbie's Hist. of Middlebury Ct. 65
Harvey Genealogy 835–41
Frisby — Hanson's Old Kent Md. 80–2
Joslin's History of Poultney Vt. 262–4
Orcutt's History of Wolcott Ct. 477–9
Phœnix's Whitney Genealogy i, 184
Thomas Genealogy (1877) 153
Timlow's Sketches of Southington Ct. 95
Frissell — Chandler Genealogy 129
Mack Genealogy 39–42
Fritchey — Egle's Queries 3d ser. i, 540
Fritz — American Ancestry ii, 44
Chambers' Early Germans of N. J. 385
Frizell — Savage's Gen. Dict. ii, 209
Frizzell — Barry's Framingham 246
Morris Genealogy (1887) 44
Frogg — Green's Kentucky Families
Frohock — Me. Hist. Rec. ix, 124–8
Frone — Chambers' N. J. Germans
Frost — Am. Ancestry ii, 44; ix, 83; x, 79

Anderson's Waterbury Ct. i, app. 54
Ballou's History of Milford Mass. 755-9
Baird's History of Rye N. Y. 409
Barlow Genealogy 441-59
Barry's Hist. of Framingham Mass. 246-8
Bemis' History of Marlboro N. H. 492-8
Blake's Mendon Mass. Association 87-9
Bunker's Long Island Genealogies 204
Chandler's History of Shirley Mass. 417-20
Chapman's Weeks Genealogy 140
Clute's History of Staten Island N. Y. 383
Corliss' North Yarmouth Me. Magazine
Cutter's Hist. of Arlington Mass. 244-50
Cutter's History of Jaffrey N. H. 334-42
Cutts Genealogy 287
Daniel's History of Oxford Mass. 514
Eliot Me. Hist. Soc. Exercises (1897) 34-43
Essex Inst. Colls. vi, 113; xxv, 284-7
Frost Genealogy (1852) 27 pages
Frost (Charles) Memoir and Genealogy
Hatch's History of Industry Me. 622
Hazen's History of Bellerica Mass. 60-3
Jordan's Leighton Genealogy (1885) 80-82
Lapham's History of Bethel Me. 535-7
Lapham's History of Norway Me. 507-11
Lapham's History of Rumford Me. 330
Leland Genealogy 172
Leonard's History of Dublin N. H. 339
Morse's Sherborn Mass. Settlers 90
New Eng. Hist. and Gen. Reg. iii, 249; v,
   165-70; x, 45; xvii, 425; liii, 245-7
New York Gen. and Biog. Rec. xi, 169-71
Old Eliot Me. Monthly (1897) i, 85-103,
   122, 173-85
Oneida Hist. Society Trans. ii, 118-20
Orcutt's History of Stratford Ct. 1205
Orcutt's History of Wolcott Ct. 480
Paige's History of Cambridge Mass. 552-6
Paige's History of Hardwick Mass. 381
Pierce's History of Gorham Me. 167
Redfield Genealogy 12
Robinson's Items of Ancestry (1894) 8-13
Saunderson's Hist. Charlestown N. H. 355
Savage's Genealogical Dictionary ii, 210-2
Schenck's History of Fairfield Ct. 368
Stearns' History of Ashburnham Mass. 710
Stiles' History of Windsor Ct. ii, 275
Stone's History of Hubbardston Mass. 269
Temple's History of Palmer Mass. 449
Thurston's History of Winthrop Me. 185
Timlow's Southington Ct. Sketches 96-8
Tuttle Genealogy 25-9
Welles' Amer. Family Antiquity i, 177-90
Wentworth Genealogy ii, 49-55
Wyman's Charlestown Mass. Gens. 377-80
Frothingham — Am. Anc. i, 29; viii, 46
Kelley Genealogy (1897) 46-51
Lapham's History of Paris Me. 604
May Genealogy 63
Savage's Genealogical Dictionary ii, 212
Wyman's Charlestown Mass. Gens. 381-5
Fry — Am. Ancestry i, 29; v, 183; xii, 14
Austin's R. I. Genealogical Dictionary 298
Fry Genealogy (1880) 112 pages
Goode Genealogy 119
Meade's Old Churches of Virginia i, 405

Paul's History of Wells Vt. 90
Paxton's Marshall Genealogy 124
Richmond Va. Standard iii, 16, 20, 28
Slaughter's St. Mark's Parish Va. 132-4
Speed Genealogy 80-6
See also under Frey and Frye
Frye — Abbott's Andover Mass. 23-5
American Ancestry xi, 215; xii, 32
Carter's Hist. of Pembroke N. H. ii, 110-5
Eaton's History of Thomaston Me. ii, 231
Guild's Stiles Genealogy 16
Lapham's History of Bethel Me. 537
Livermore's History of Wilton N. H. 375-8
Maine Hist. Society Colls. iv, 284
Morrison's History of Windham N. H. 532
New Eng. Hist. and Gen. Reg. viii, 226-8
Ridlon's Saco Valley Me. Families 691-4
Savage's Genealogical Dictionary ii, 213
Wight Genealogy 84
Fryer — Babson's Gloucester Mass. 94
Munsell's Albany Colls. iv. 124
Fulford — Anderson's Waterbury 55
Fulham — Bond's Watertown 227, 766
Fulkerson — Missouri Pioneer 256
Fullam — Norton's Fitzwilliam 577-9
Randall's Hist. of Chesterfield N. H. 318
Temple's Hist. of No. Brookfield Mass. 594
Fullenwider — Amer. Ancestry vi, 193
Fuller — American Ancestry i, 29; xi, 31,
   79; xii, 12, 15
Andrews' History of New Britain Ct. 194
Atkins' History of Hawley Mass. 46
Babson's History of Gloucester Mass. 362
Ball's History of Lake County Ind. 397
Bass' History of Braintree Vt. 145
Bemis' Hist. of Marlboro N. H. 498-501
Benedict's History of Sutton Mass. 646
Bond's Watertown Mass. 227, 666, 766-71
Chapman's Trowbridge Family 247
Cochrane's Hist. Francestown N. H. 713-9
Daniel's History of Oxford Mass. 514
Davis' Landmarks of Plymouth 113-6
Dawson Genealogy 59
Dedham Historical Register iv, 156-62; v,
   38-40, 83-93, 127-34
Dow's History of Hampton N. H. 718
Eaton's Annals of Warren Me. 543-5
Eaton's History of Thomaston Me. 232
Field's History of Haddam Ct. 47
Fiske Genealogy 136
Freeman's Hist. of Cape Cod ii, 154, 485
Fuller Family of Salem (1859) 16 pages
Fuller Family of Newton (1869) 16 pages
Fuller Family of Lebanon (1880) 8 pages
Fuller Family of Dedham (1888) 8 pages
Fuller Family of Dedham (1893) 8 pages
Fuller Family of Gloucester (1894) 49 pages
Fuller Family of Salem (1895) 8 pages
Fuller Family of Salem (1896) 47 pages
Fuller Family of Plymouth (1896) 68 pages
Fuller Family of Plymouth (1896) 8 pages
Fuller Fam. Middleton Mass. (1897) 101 p.
Fuller Family of Salem (1898) 50 pages
Fuller Family of Ipswich (1899) 7 pages
Hammatt Papers of Ipswich Mass. 111-3
Hanson's History of Gardiner Me. 133

Hayward's Hist. of Hancock N. H. 592
Heywood's Hist. of Westminster Mass. 656
Hill's Dedham Mass. Records
Hine's Lebanon Ct. Hist. Address 155
Hoyt's Salisbury Mass. Families 170
Humphreys Genealogy 410
Hurd's History of New London Ct. 512
Jackson's Hist. of Newton Mass. 277–88
Jameson's History of Medway Mass. 480
Joslyn's History of Poultney Vt. 264
Kingman's N. Bridgewater Mass. 507
Knox Co. Me. Hist. Mag. i. 88–91
Lapham's History of Paris Me. 605–8
Lapham's History of Woodstock Me. 220
Lincoln's Hist. of Hingham Mass. ii, 241
Livermore's History of Wilton N. H. 378
Mitchell's Hist. of Bridgewater Mass. 165
New Eng. Hist. and Gen. Reg. iii, 85; xiii,
   351–63; xlviii, 345; liii, 335–41
North's History of Augusta Me. 869–74
Noyes Genealogy (1861) 10
Paige's History of Cambridge Mass. 556
Paige's History of Hardwick Mass. 382
Pearson's Schenectady N. Y. Settlers 75
Pond Genealogy (1875) 21
Robinson's Items of Ancestry (1894) 65–7
Runnel's Hist. of Sanbornton N. H. ii, 287
Savage's Genealogical Dictionary ii, 215–20
Secomb's Hist. of Amherst N. H. 595–7
Sedgwick's History of Sharon Ct. 80
Sewall's History of Woburn Mass. 614
Sheldon's Hist. of Deerfield Mass. 169–71
Stiles' Hist. of Windsor Ct. ii, 275
Swift's Barnstable Families i, 371–84
Temple's History of Palmer Mass. 454–7
Thurston's History of Winthrop Me. 185
Titcomb's New Eng. People 274–8
Vinton's Richardson Genealogy 555
Wheeler Ancestors (1896) 9
Wight Genealogy 115
Wilbur Life and Genealogy appendix
Winsor's History of Duxbury Mass. 261
Fullerton — Eager's Orange Co. 413
Kingman's No. Bridgewater Mass. 508
Whitman Genealogy 329–33
Fullinwider — Power's Sangamon 318
Fullonton — Chase's Chester N. H. 529
Fullonton's Hist. Raymond N. H. 219–23
Fulton — Egle's Pa. Gens. 2d ed. 264–8
Egle's Notes and Queries 3d ser. i, 492–4;
   3d ser. iii, 266–8
Ellis Genealogy 119–26
Futhey's Hist. of Chester Co. Pa. 555–8
Miller's Colchester Co. N. S. 259, 312, 361
Richmond Va. Standard iii, 2
Smith's History of Rhinebeck N. Y. 199
Wheeler's History of Brunswick Me. 834
Funderburk — Power's Sangamon 319
Funk — Moyer Genealogy 288–326
Funkhouser — American Ancestry xi, 80
Funston — Boyd Genealogy 232–5
Furber — American Ancestry xii, 15
Cogswell's Nottingham 687
Furbish — American Ancestry xii, 134
Eaton's Thomaston Me. 233
Wentworth Genealogy i, 477–9; ii. 37

Furbur — Whitmore's Copps Hill Epit.
Furbush — Hatch's Industry Me. 623
Old Eliot Me. Monthly iii (1899) 1–4
Rice Genealogy
Furman — Am. Anc. vii, 184; viii, 65, 72
Cooley's Trenton N. J. Genealogies 74–8
Riker's Annals of Newton N. Y. 399
Furnald — Cogswell's Nottingham 379
Cutts Genealogy 180–2
Old Eliot Me. Monthly ii (1898) 89–91
Wentworth Genealogy i, 309–12, 313–15
Furnell — Savage's Gen. Dict. ii, 220
See also under Furnald
Furness — American Ancestry iv, 206
New Eng. Hist. and Gen. Reg. xxx, 63
Fussell — Dawson Genealogy
Futhey — Futhey's Chester Pa. 558
Fyfe — Perry Memoranda (1878) 28 p.
Fyler — Boyd's Winchester Ct. 188
Hinman's Connecticut Settlers 1st ed. 212
Orcutt's History of Torrington Ct. 694–9
Stiles' History of Windsor Ct. ii, 275–7
Gaar — Young's Wayne Co. Ind. 418
See also Garr
Gaasbeck — Sylvester's Ulster Co. 106
Gachet — N. E. Hist. Gen. Reg. i, 344
Gadsden — Bellinger Genealogy 100
Gage — Aldrich's Walpole N. H. 259
American Ancestry iii, 18, 155; iv, 212,
   220; v, 67; vi, 69
Ballou's History of Milford Mass. 769–71
Cleveland's Hist. of Yates Co. N. Y. 230–7
Coffin's History of Boscawen N. H. 534–6
Corliss' North Yarmouth Me. 1024
Dodge Ancestry (1896) 16
Gage Genealogy (1882) 4 pages, reprint
Gage Genealogy (1889) 16 pages
Gage Genealogy (1894) 62 pages
Gage Ancestry (1899) 8 pages
Gage's History of Rowley Mass. 442
Granite Monthly Concord N. H. vi, 62–4
Hoyt's Salisbury Mass. Families 171
Lapham's History of Bethel Me. 538
Livermore's Hist. Wilton N. H. 378–81
Loomis Genealogy (1889) 848
New Eng. Hist. and Gen. Reg. liii, 201–6
Norton's History of Fitzwilliam N. H. 579
Runnel's Sanbornton N. H. ii, 288–92
Savage's Genealogical Dictionary ii, 220
Secomb's History of Amherst N. H. 597
Washington N. H. History 440–5
Whitmore's Heraldic Journal iii, 148–51
Wyman's Charlestown Mass. Gens. i, 397
Gager — Caulkins' Hist. Norwich Ct. 103
Heywood's Hist. of Westminster Mass. 657
Hine's Lebanon Ct. Historical Address 155
Savage's Genealogical Dictionary ii, 221
Sedgwick's History of Sharon Ct. 81
Wallbridge Genealogy 290
Walworth's Hyde Genealogy 675–7, 732
Gagnon — Temple's N. Brookfield 594
Gaige — American Ancestry i, 30
Gaillard — South Car. Huguenot Society
   Transactions v, 91–101
Gaines — American Ancestry vii, 191
Cunnabell Genealogy 85

Goode Genealogy 124, 290, 470
Hammatt Papers of Ipswich Mass. 117
Meade's Old Churches of Virginia
Nourse Family of Virginia 45-7
Power's Sangamon Co. Ill. Settlers 321
Richmond Va. Standard iii, 14
Slaughter's St. Mark's Parish Va. 149, 164
Southern Histor. Assoc ii, (1898) 168
Galbraith — Egle's Penn. Gen. 269-88
Ridlon's Saco Valley Me. Families 584-90
See also under Colbath
Gale — American Ancestry i, 30; vi, 9
Barry's History of Framingham Mass. 249
Benedict's History of Sutton Mass. 647-9
Bond's History of Watertown Mass. 229-31
Bouton's History of Concord N. H. 662-4
Cochrane's Hist. Francestown N. H. 720
Daniels' History of Oxford Mass. 515
Dearborn's Hist. of Salisbury N. H. 585-92
Denny Genealogy
Gale Genealogy (1863) 9 pages
Gale Genealogy (1866) 254 pages
Huntington's Stamford Ct. Settlers 36
Jameson's History of Medway Mass. 487
Lancaster's Hist. of Gilmanton N. H. 265
Little's History of Weare N. H. 857
Morse's Grout Genealogy 24-34
New Eng Hist. Gen. Reg. xviii, 189-97
Perkins' Old Houses of Norwich Ct. 460
Pickering Genealogy
Runnel's Sanbornton N. H. ii, 292-6
Savage's Genealogical Dictionary ii, 221
Stearns' History of Ashburnham Mass. 711
Whittemore's Hist. Middlesex Co. Ct. 241
Gales — Wheeler's North Carolina ii, 416
Galespy — Gregg's Old Cheraws S. C. 62
Gallatin — Gallatin's Works iii (1879)
Gallaudet — Bolton's Westchester 734
New York Gen. and Biog. Rec xix, 118-21
Gallaway — Balch's Prov. Papers 75
Galliger — Temple's Palmer Mass. 473
Gallison — Lapham's Norway 511
Winslow Genealogy ii, 745-8
Gallop — Babson's Gloucester Mass. 94
Caulkins' History of New London Ct. 291
Eaton's History of Thomaston Me. ii, 233
Temple's History of Palmer Mass. 468
Gallow — Sedgwick's Sharon Ct. 81
Galloway — Thomas Genealogy (1877) 78
Thomas Genealogy (1896) 317-21
Gallup — Am. Ancestry i, 30; ix, 111, 113
Barry's History of Framingham Mass. 249
Davis Genealogy (1888) 48-51
Gallup Genealogy (1893) 329 pages
Gregory's History of Northfield Vt. 220
Harvey Genealogy 914
Huron and Erie Counties Ohio 179
Hurd's History of New London Co. Ct. 478
Savage's Genealogical Dictionary ii, 222
Smith Genealogy (1889) 123 pages
Galpin — American Ancestry ix, 189
Baird's History of Rye N. Y. 410
Baldwin Genealogical Supp. 1047
Cothren's History of Woodbury Ct. 544
Orcutt's History of Stratford Ct. 1206
Savage's Genealogical Dictionary ii, 223

Galt — Power's Sangamon Co. Ill. 19
Richmond Va. Standard iii, 32
Galusha — American Ancestry x, 147
Huntington Genealogy 99
Gamage — American Ancestry ix, 71
Gambel — Chase's Chester N. H. 530
Gamble — Cabell Genealogy 256
Eaton's Annals of Warren Me. 545
Eaton's History of Thomaston Me. 234
Gilmer's Georgians 34
Goode Genealogy 402
Huntting's Hist. Pine Plains N. Y. 336-8
Knox County Me. Hist. Magazine i, 1-188
Richmond Va. Standard ii, 2, 51
Waddell's Annals Augusta Co. Va. 187-90
Gamblin — Ellis' Roxbury Mass. 118
Gamby — Cleveland's Yates Co. 528
Gammell — Hudson's Lexington 75
Gammett — Miller's Colchester County
Gammon — Lapham's Norway Me. 512
Ridlon's Harrison Me. Settlers 64
Gamwell — Temple's Palmer Mass. 469
Gannett — Deane's Scituate Mass. 273
Harris' Bascom Genealogy 45-50
Mitchell's Hist. of Bridgewater Mass. 166
Savage's Genealogical Dictionary ii, 224
Gano — American Ancestry vii, 229
Ganong — American Ancestry viii, 144
Ganong Genealogy (1893) 27 pages
Gansevoort — Munsell's Albany iv, 124
New York Gen. and Biog. Record iii, 84
Roseboom Genealogy 42-55
Ganung — Cleveland's Yates Co. 299
Gar — See Garr
Gara — Washington Co. Ohio 717
Garber — Goode Genealogy 407
Gardener — Peirce Genealogy (1894)
Gardenier — American Ancestry ii, 44
Munsell's Albany Collections iv, 125
Gardiner — American Ancestry xii
Austin's R. I. Genealogical Dictionary 81
Babson's History of Gloucester Mass. 95
Bunker's Long Island Genealogies 336-41
Chandler Genealogy 57
Clement's Newtown N. J. Settlers
Cregar's White Genealogy
Gardiner Papers (1883) 102 pages
Gardiner Genealogy (1890) 210 pages
Gilmore's Gardiner Me. Church (1893)
Hanson's History of Gardiner Me. 83, 105
Hedge's Hist. Easthampton N. Y. 277-85
Heraldic Journal iii, 81; iv, 97-102
Hinman's Connecticut Settlers 212
Holgate's American Genealogy 58-65
Judd's History of Hadley Mass. 497
Lamb's History of N. Y. City 570
Narragansett Register i, 211-3; ii, 306-9
N. Y. Gen. and Biog. Rec. xxiii, 159-90;
xxvii, 213
Peck's Rochester N. Y. Centennial 653-6
Pierce's Biog. Contributions 43-51
Preble Genealogy 259
Ruttenber's Hist. Newburgh N. Y. 301-3
Ruttenber's Orange Co. N. Y. 387-9
Savage's Genealogical Dictionary ii, 225
Thompson's Long Island ii, 378-81

Updyke's Narragansett 125–30; 330
Waddell's Annals of Augusta Co. Va. 438
Gardner — Allen's Worcester Assoc. 52
Allen Genealogy (1883) 5
Am. Anc. i, 31; ii, 44, 154; ix, 126; xii, 51
Austin's Allied Families 100–3
Aylsworth Genealogy 136, 278
Baker's History of Montville Ct. 543–53
Bangor Me. Historical Magazine ix, 87
Barry's History of Hanover Mass. 311
Blood's History of Temple N. H. 222
Cleveland's History of Yates Co. N. Y. 659
Cochrane's Hist. Francestown N. H. 721
Collin's History of Hillsdale N. Y., app. 57
Cutter's History of Arlington Mass. 251
Dennysville Me. Centennial 104
Essex Institute Hist. Coll. i, 190; vi, 161–3
Gardner Genealogy (1858) 14 pages
Gardner Family of Maine (1898) 29 pages
Greene Genealogy
Hyde's History of Brimfield Mass. 404
Kitchell Genealogy 412–4
Lee Genealogy (1895) 477–80
Lincoln's Hist. Hingham Mass. ii, 242–63
Machias Me. Centennial 162
Morse's Sherborn Mass. Settlers 90
New Eng. Hist. Gen. Register xxv, 48–51
Paige's History of Cambridge Mass. 557
Peirce's Life of Gardner Dean (1883) 307 p.
Pickering Genealogy
Poole Genealogy 144–6
Power's Sangamon Co. Ill. Settlers 321
Prime Genealogy (1895) 50
Rhode Island Hist. Society Colls. iii, 308
Rhode Island Historical Magazine 217–20
Savage's Genealogical Dictionary ii, 226–31
Secomb's History of Amherst N. H. 589
Sewall's History of Woburn Mass. 614
Shotwell Genealogy 24–35
Stearns' History of Rindge N. H. 527
Temple's History of Palmer Mass. 469–71
Walworth's Hyde Genealogy 253–5, 520–2
Whitman Genealogy 90–2
Whitmore's Copps Hill Epitaphs
Winchester Mass. Record i, 244–6
Wood's Brookline Mass. Sketches 284–93
Worden Genealogy 59–62
Wyman's Charlestown Mass. i, 398–402
Garfield — American Ancestry i, 31; iii, 163, 181; ix, 190; x, 45
Bemis' History of Marlboro N. H. 502
Bond's Watertown Mass. Gens. 231–5, 771
Bridge Genealogy 77
Draper's History of Spencer Mass. 198–200
Garfield Family Ancestry (1881) 15 pages
Garfield Family Ancestry (1882) 16 pages
Heywood's Hist. Westminster Mass. 657–9
Hudson's History of Sudbury Mass. 442
Montague Genealogy 123
N. E. Hist. Gen. Reg. xxxvii, 253–63; xlix, 194–204, 449
Norton's History of Fitzwilliam N. H. 580
Savage's Genealogical Dictionary ii, 231
Thurston Genealogy (1892) 32
Ward's History of Shrewsbury Mass. 290–2
Young's Hist. Chautauqua Co. N. Y. 238

Garges — Kratz Genealogy 66–73
Garit — Power's Sangamon Ill. 322
Garland — Amer. Ancestry v, 195; x, 21
Caverno Genealogy 12
Cogswell's History of Henniker N. H. 577
Dearborn's Hist. of Parsonsfield Me. 380
Dearborn's Hist. of Salisbury N. H. 592–5
Dow's History of Hampton N. H. 720–6
Garland Genealogy (1897) 214 pages
Goode Genealogy 240
Lane Genealogy (1891) 150
Meade's Old Churches of Virginia
Power's Sangamon Co. Ill. Settlers 324
Savage's Genealogical Dictionary ii, 232
Garlick — Orcutt's New Milford 795
Roe's Sketches of Rose N. Y. 127
Trubee Genealogy 118–20
Garlington — Chappell Genealogy 177–83
Chappell Genealogy (1900) 330–41
Garner — American Ancestry ii, 44, 154
Lincoln's Hist. Hingham Mass. ii, 242–63
See also under Gardner
Garnet — See under Garnett
Garnett — Meade's Old Fams. of Virginia
Richmond Standard iii, 11, 14, 23, 26, 93
Slaughter's St. Mark's Parish Va. 134–6
Garnsey — Anderson's Waterbury Ct. i, app. 58
Andrews' New Britain Ct. 208
Baird's History of Rye N. Y. 411
Bassett's History of Richmond N. H. 391–5
Huntington's Stamford Ct. Settlers 36
Garr — American Ancestry xii, 33
Garr Genealogy (1894) 608 pages
Garrabrant — Hudson Co. N. J. 520–4
Garrard — Garrard Genealogy (1898) 134 p.
Garratt — Barry's Hanover Mass. 312
Garrett — Brown's West Simsbury 66–8
Deane's History of Scituate Mass. 274
Egle's Notes and Queries 4th ser. i, 255–7
Futhey's History of Chester Co. Pa. 560
Hayden's Life of Major John Garrett 20–4
Maris Genealogy 160
Savage's Genealogical Dictionary ii, 233
Sharpless Genealogy 153–6, 221–5, 345–9
Smith's History of Delaware Co. Pa. 464
Swift's Barnstable Mass. Families i, 449
Garretson — Harvey Genealogy 843–55
Power's Sangamon 323
Garrigues — Thomas Gen. (1877) 80
Garringer — Plumb's Hanover 420–2
Garrison — American Ancestry i, 31; iii, 19, 83; iv, 161
Clute's Hist. of Staten Island N. Y. 384
Garrison Genealogy (1876) 4 pages, reprint
New Eng. Hist. Gen. Register xxx, 418–21
Plumb's History of Hanover Pa. 419
Garvey — Power's Sangamon Ill. 325
Garvin — Wentworth Genealogy ii, 88–90
Gary — Andrews Genealogy (1890) 130
Lapham's History of Norway Me. 512
Norton's History of Fitzwilliam N. H. 580
Wyman's Charlestown Mass. Gens. i, 402
Gaskerie — Schoonmaker's Kingston
Gaskill — Ballou's Milford Mass. 162–4
Bassett's History of Richmond N. H. 395

9

Richard Mowry Genealogy 219, 222
Southwick Genealogy 586–90
Gaskins — Hayden's Virginia Gen. 440
Gasley — American Ancestry vii, 27
Gasque — Roome Genealogy 115c–115i
Gassett — Hayward's Gilsum N. H. 310
Hayward's History of Hancock N. H. 592
Morse Memorial, appendix 53
New Eng. Hist. and Gen. Register i, 344
Gaston — American Ancestry v, 86, 103
Bay State Monthly ii, 246
Mellick's Story of an Old Farm N. J. 635
Wheeler's Eminent N. Carolinians 137–9
Wheeler's History of N. Carolina ii, 114
Gasue — Futhey's Chester Co. Pa. 562
Gatchett — Futhey's Chester Pa. 561
New Eng. Hist. Register i, 344
Savage's Genealogical Dictionary ii, 234
Gately — Heywood's Westminster 659
Gates — American Ancestry i, 31; ii, 45;
v, 15; viii, 10, 212; xii, 13
Barry's Hist. of Framingham Mass. 250–2
Bemis' History of Marlboro N. H. 503–6
Calnek's History of Annapolis N. S. 513–5
Chapman's Trowbridge Genealogy 258
Chute Genealogy, appendix 66–77
Cochrane's History of Antrim N. H. 503
Daniels' History of Oxford Mass 517
Davis Ancestry (1897) 27–9
Draper's History of Spencer Mass 198
Dwight Genealogy 449
Eaton's Annals of Warren Me 545
Eaton's History of Thomaston Me ii, 234
Field's History of Haddam Ct. 45
Gates Genealogy (1877) 2 pages, reprint
Gates Genealogy (1887) 4 pages
Gates Genealogy (1898) 372 pages
Goodwin's Foote Genealogy 78
Haywards' History of Gilsum N. H. 311
Hayward's History of Hancock N. H. 594
Hemenway's Vermont Hist. Gaz. v, 55
Herrick's History of Gardner Mass. 349
Heywood's Hist. Westminster Mass. 660–3
Hudson's Hist. Marlborough Mass. 366
Lincoln's History of Hingham Mass. ii, 264
Merrill's History of Acworth N. H. 217
New Eng. Hist. and Gen. Reg. xxxi, 401
Paige's History of Cambridge Mass. 557
Phœnix's Whitney Family i, 603
Power's Sangamon Co. Ill. Settlers 326
Savage's Genealogical Dictionary ii, 235
Sheldon's History of Deerfield Mass. 171
Smith Genealogy (1890) 155–9
Stearns' Hist. of Ashburnham Mass. 711–4
Stone's Hist. of Hubbardston Mass. 270–2
Temple's History of Palmer Mass. 463–6
Turner's Phelps Purchase 206
Walworth's Hyde Genealogy 756
Whittemore's Middlesex Co. Ct. 207
Whittemore's Orange N. J. 444
Young's History of Warsaw N. Y. 271–3
Gatewood — Richmond Standard iii, 31
Welles' Washington Genealogy 237
Gatton — Power's Sangamon Ill. 326
Gaul — American Ancestry ii, 45
Temple's Hist. of N. Brookfield Mass. 595

Gault — Burleigh's Guild Genealogy 233
Carter's Hist. Pembroke N. H. ii, 118–22
Chase's History of Chester N. H. 530
Granite Monthly Concord N. H. ix, 71
Temple's Hist. of N. Brookfield Mass. 595
Gaunt — American Ancestry v, 59
Gause — American Ancestry xi, 82
Gaut — Heywood's Westminster 663
Gautier — N. Y. Gen. Record iii, 1–3
Winfield's Hist. Hudson Co. N. J. 549–65
Gavit — Collin's Hillsdale N. Y. App. 58
Gay — Am. Ancestry i, 31; ii, 154; xi, 31
Blake's History of Franklin Mass. 249–51
Butler's History of Farmington Me. 471–6
Cochrane's Hist. Francest'n N. H. 721–6
Eaton's History of Thomaston Me. ii, 235
Gay Genealogy (1879) 15 pages
Hanson's History of Gardiner Me. 156
Hill's Dedham Mass. Records i.
Hine's Lebanon Ct. Hist. Address 156
Jameson's History of Medway Mass. 487
Lincoln's History of Hingham Mass. ii,
262–6
Loomis Genealogy (1880) 794
Meade's Old Churches of Virginia
New Eng. Historical and Genealogical
Register vi, 373; xxxiii, 45–57
Paige's History of Cambridge Mass. 558
Phœnix's Whitney Genealogy i, 147
Read's History of Swanzey N. H. 344
Robertson's Pocahontas' Descendants
Savage's Genealogical Dictionary ii, 236
Sedgwick's History of Sharon Ct. 81
Sibley's History of Union Me. 451
Stone's History of Hubbardston Mass. 273
Washington N. H. History 445
Gayer — Amory's Life of I. Coffin 83–5
New Eng. Hist. Gen. Reg. xxxi, 297–302
Gaylord — Amer. Ancestry v, 127; vi, 48
Anderson's Waterbury Ct. i, app. 55
Davis' History of Wallingford Ct. 747–50
Gaylord Genealogy (1872) 64 pages
Harvey Genealogy 837–9
Hibbard's History of Goshen Ct. 452–5
Judd's History of Hadley Mass. 497
Litchfield Co. Ct. History 354
Loomis Genealogy (1880) 579–83
Orcutt's Hist. of New Milford Ct. 699–702
Orcutt's History of Torrington Ct. 699
Savage's Genealogical Dictionary ii, 238
Stiles' Hist. of Windsor Ct. ii, 277–84, 837
Gazley — Champion Genealogy 130
Gazzam — American Ancestry v, 69
Gazzam Genealogy (1894) 72 pages
Geary — Savage's Gen. Dictionary ii, 240
Gebhard — American Ancestry ii, 45
Gedde — Egle's Notes and Queries 3d series
iii, 197–9
Gedney — Baird's Rye N. Y. 468–70
Essex Mass. Inst. Hist. Colls. xvi, 241–79
Gedney and Clarke Genealogy (1880) 52 p.
Hammatt Papers of Ipswich Mass. 118
Savage's Genealogical Dictionary ii, 240
Sylvester's History of Ulster Co. N. Y. 134
Gee — Norton's Fitzwilliam N. H. 581
Whitmore's Copps Hill Epitaphs

Geer — American Ancestry i, 32
Davis Genealogy (1888) 44-6
Eaton's History of Thomaston Me. ii, 235
Geer Genealogy (1856) 84 pages
Hinman's Connecticut Settlers 1st ed. 178
Hurd's History of New London Co. Ct. 525
Paul's History of Wells Vt. 91
Saunderson's Charlestown N. H. 358-60
Savage's Genealogical Dictionary ii, 239
Stiles' History of Windsor Ct. ii, 285-7
Wight Genealogy 47
Gelding — Perkins' Norwich Ct. 462
Gelling — Power's Sangamon Ill. 328
Gelston — Dwight Genealogy 1065-76
Howell's Southampton N. Y. 258-60
New York Gen. and Biog. Record ii, 131-8
Strong Genealogy 354
Gemmill — Claypool Genealogy 161
Gendall — Corliss' North Yarmouth Me.
Gendall, Capt. Walter (188c) 27 pages
Genin — Griffin's Journal L. I. 183
Gentle — Stearns' Ashburnham 714
Gentry — American Ancestry xii
Genung — Gay's Hist. Gaz. of Tioga N. Y.
George — American Ancestry ii, 45
Austin's R. I. Genealogical Dictionary 83
Bangor Hist. Magazine iv, 237; vi, 92
Cochrane's Hist. Francestown N. H. 727
Corliss Genealogy, appendix
Dearborn's Hist. of Salisbury N. H. 595-7
Hayward's History of Hancock N. H. 599
Hoyt's Salisbury Mass. Families 172
Little's History of Weare N. H. 858-60
Paul's History of Wells Vt. 91
Plumb's History of Hanover Pa. 418
Runnel's Hist. Sanbornton N. H. ii, 296-8
Savage's Genealogical Dictionary ii, 242
Slafter Genealogy 6
Thomas Genealogy (1877) 81
Thomas Genealogy (1896) 321-3
Wheeler's History of Newport N. H. 392-4
Wyman's Charlestown Mass. Gens. i, 404
Gerald — Spare Genealogy 35-9
Temple's History of Palmer Mass. 461
Gerard — N. Y. Gen. Biog. Record v, 137
Talcott's N. Y. and N. E. Families 80-5
Gere — Stanton Genealogy 248
Gereardy — Austin's R. I. Dictionary 300
Gereardy Genealogy (1896) 6 pages
New Eng. Hist. and Gen. Reg. lii, 313-18
Gerhard — Kriebel's Schwenkfelders 40
Talcott's N. Y. and N. E. Families 80-5
Germain — American Ancestry i, 32
Eaton's History of Thomaston Me. ii, 236
Germond — Peters Lineage 132-9
Gerould — Am. Ancestry iii, 152; vi, 8
Geroulé Genealogy (1885) 85 pages
Gerould Genealogy Supp. (1890) 15 pages
Gerould Genealogy, Supp. (1895) 17 pages
Hayward's History of Gilsum N. H. 312.
Gerretson — Bergen's Kings Co. 119
Gerrish — Am. Ancestry iv, 103, 124, 223
Ball's History of Lake County Ind. 445-8
Cochrane's Hist. Francestown N. H. 728
Coffin's History of Boscawen N. H. 537-51
Coffin's History of Newbury Mass. 302

Cogswell's Nottingham N. H. 202, 380
Cutts Genealogy 38-40, 48-50, 70-2
Eaton's Annals of Warren Me. 545
Essex Mass. Institute Hist. Colls. v, 27-30
Gerrish Genealogy (1880) 13 pages
Heywood's Hist. of Westminster Mass. 663
Little Genealogy 18, 100
New Eng. Hist. Gen. Reg. vi, 258; li, 67
Savage's Genealogical Dictionary ii, 243
Stackpole's History of Durham Me. 186-91
Gerritsen — Munsell's Albany iv, 126
Gerry — Alden's Am. Epitaphs v, 25, 45
American Ancestry iv, 223
Hudson's Hist. of Sudbury Mass. 442, 614
Vinton's Richardson Genealogy 432
Gesner — Calnek's Annapolis N. S. 515
Gest — American Ancestry v, 48
Getchell — Eaton's Thomaston ii, 236
Hoyt's Salisbury Mass. Families 173
Stackpole's History of Durham Me. 191-3
Wheeler's History of Brunswick Me. 835
Getty — Marshall Genealogy (1884) 219-21
Gheen — Cope Genealogy 66, 146
Palmer and Trimble Gen. 210, 213, 402
Gheer — Egle's Pa. Gens. 2d ed. 690-3
Ghiselin — Bowie Genealogy 131-4
Gholson — American Ancestry xii
Meade's Old Families of Virginia
Richmond Va. Standard ii, 29
Saunders' Alabama Settlers 373-7
Gibb — Hubbard's Stanstead Canada 149
Gibbard—Savage's Gen. Dictionary ii, 244
Gibbes — Gibbes of S. Car. (1899) chart
Gibbins — Folsom's Hist. Saco Me. 112
Gibbon — Meade's Old Churches of Va.
Gibbons — Cope Genealogy 55, 126
Futhey's History of Chester Co. Pa. 564-9
Gibbons Genealogy (1881) 27 pages
Savage's Genealogical Dictionary ii, 245
Sharpless Genealogy 406
Wyman's Charlestown Mass. Gens. i, 406
Gibbs — American Ancestry ix, 192
Ballou's History of Milford Mass. 765-7
Barry's Hist. of Framingham Mass. 252-6
Bemis' History of Marlboro N. H. 506
Benedict's History of Sutton Mass. 649
Bonds' Watertown Mass. Genealogies 236
Daniels' History of Oxford Mass. 577
Davis' Landmarks of Plymouth Mass. 116
Freeman's Hist. Cape Cod ii, 147, 156, 164
Gibbs Family of Boston (1845) 8 pages
Gibbs Assoc. Report (1848) 28 pages
Gibbs Family of Boston (1879) 52 pages
Gibbs Family Legacy (1893) 77 pages
Gibbs Family of Bristol Mass. (1894) 23 p.
Gibbs Family of So. Car. (1899) chart
Gibbs' History of Blandford Mass. 67-71
Heywood's Hist. Westminster Mass. 664-7
Hinman's Connecticut Settlers 1st ed. 213
Jackson's History of Newton Mass. 292
Richmond Va. Standard iii, 28
Savage's Genealogical Dictionary ii, 245-8
Sedgwick's History of Sharon Ct. 88
Smith's Hist. of Peterborough N. H. 91-3
Stearns' History of Ashburnham Mass. 714
Stiles' History of Windsor Ct. ii, 287

Temple's Hist. of N. Brookfield Mass. 595
Whitmore's Heraldic Journal iii, 12-4, 166
Wyman's Charlestown Mass. Gens. i, 406
See also Gibbes
Gibson — Am. Anc. ii, 45; ix, 155; x, 183
Austin's R. I. Genealogical Dict. i, 83
Avon N. Y. Genealogical Record 29
Cochrane's History of Antrim N. H. 505
Cochrane's Hist. Francestown N. H. 729
Cogswell's Hist. of Henniker N. H. 578-86
Densmore's Hartwell Genealogy
Egle's Notes and Queries (1898) 205
Gibson Association (1867) 20 p. (1869) 4 p.
Granite Monthly of Concord N. H. v, 329
Jackson Genealogy 108-16
Joslin's History of Poultney Vt. 265
Lapham's History of Norway Me. 512
New Eng. Hist. Gen. Reg. xxxvii, 388-92
Norton's History of Fitzwilliam N. H. 581
Paige's History of Cambridge Mass. 558
Peyton's History of Augusta Co. Va. 306
Power's Sangamon Co. Ill. Settlers 328-30
Richmond Va. Standard ii, 7
Ridlon's Saco Valley Me. Families 694
Runnels' Sanbornton N. H. ii, 298-301
Salem N. Y. Book of History 33-5
Savage's Genealogical Dictionary ii, 248
Secomb's History of Amherst N. H. 600
Stearns' Hist. Ashburnham Mass. 718-20
Stearns' History of Rindge N. H. 529-32
Temple's History of Palmer Mass. 466
Wyman's Charlestown Mass. Gens. i, 407
Giddinge — Bell's Exeter N. H. 14-6
Giddings — Andrews' New Britain Ct.
Babson's Gloucester Mass. 95
Baldwin Genealogy 1134-6
Giddings Genealogy (1882) 227 pages
Hammatt Papers of Ipswich Mass. 116
Joslin's History of Poultney Vt. 266-8
Orcutt's History of New Milford Ct. 702-7
Savage's Genealogical Dictionary ii, 249
Wight Genealogy 77
Giffen — Paige's Hardwick Mass. 382
Giffin — Temple's N. Brookfield 595
Giffing — Hall's Trenton N. J. Ch. 73
Gifford — American Ancestry ii, 45; x, 193
Austin's R. I. Genealogical Dictionary 84
Austin's Allied Families 103-6
Caulkins' History of Norwich Ct. 175
Freeman's Cape Cod Mass. ii, 164, 426
Gifford's Our Patronymics (1886) 21-3
Gifford Genealogy (1896) 101 pages
Hollister's History of Pawlet Vt. 191
Perkins' Old Houses of Norwich Ct. 461
Thomas Genealogy (1896) 323-7
Walworth's Hyde Genealogy 245
Giger — Power's Sangamon Co. Ill. 330
Gilbert — Adams' Fairhaven Vt. 378-80
Aldrich's History of Walpole N. H. 260-2
American Ancestry vi, 158; vii, 32; xii, 130
Andrews' Hist. of New Britain Ct. 181, 350
Babson's History of Gloucester Mass. 240
Blake's History of Hamden Ct. 246-9
Boyd's History of Conesus N. Y. 155
Caverly's History of Pittsford Vt. 702
Champion Genealogy 295-300, 316-39

Cochrane's Hist. Francest'n N. H. 730-2
Cope Genealogy 90, 192
Cutts Genealogy 214
Davis' Landmarks of Plymouth Mass. 116
Dickerman Genealogy 173
Essex Mass. Inst. Hist. Colls. xvii, 40-50
French's History of Turner Me. 62
Gilbert Narrative (Phila. 1848) 240 pages
Gilbert Genealogy (1850) chart
Gilbert Family of New Eng. (1850) 23 pages
Gilbert Family of Penn. (1864) 2 pages
Gilmer's Georgians 216
Hammatt Papers of Ipswich Mass. 113-5
Kellogg's White Genealogy 24
Lincoln's History of Hingham Mass. ii, 267
Martindale's History of Byberry Pa. 289-99
Middlefield Ct. History
New Eng. Historical and Genealogical
    Register iv, 223-32, 339-49; xlii, 280-2
Orcutt's History of Stratford Ct. 1206
Paige's History of Hardwick Mass. 383
Pompey N. Y. Reunion 311
Savage's Genealogical Dictionary ii, 249-52
Schenck's History of Fairfield Ct. 368
Sharpe's South Britain Ct. Sketches 99
Swain Genealogy 72-4
Swift's Barnstable Mass. Families i, 406
Talcott's N. Y. and N. E. Families 513
Temple's Hist. N. Brookfield Mass. 596-602
Turner Genealogy 57
Wyman's Charlestown Mass. Gens. i, 407
Gilchrist — Chase's Chester N. H. 531
Eaton's History of Thomaston Me. ii, 236
Egle's Notes and Queries 3d ser. i, 213
Hayward's History of Hancock N. H. 600
Holton's Winslow Genealogy i, 337
Leonard's History of Dublin N. H. 340
Saunders' Alabama Settlers 227
Gildersleeve — Champion Genealogy 62
Gildon — Perkins' Norwich Ct. 462
Gile — American Ancestry ii, 46; iv, 224
Cogswell's Hist. of Nottingham N. H. 204
Fullonton's History of Raymond N. H. 228
Guild Genealogy (1887) 221-318
Walker Genealogy (1895) 52-63
Worthen's History of Sutton N. H. 725-9
Giles — Bond's Watertown Mass. 804-7
Crawford Family of Virginia 113
Giles Genealogy (1864) 600 pages
Heywood's Hist. of Westminster Mass. 667
Johnson's History of Bristol Me. 181-4
Runnel's Hist. Sanbornton N. H. ii, 301-4
Savage's Genealogical Dictionary ii, 253
Gilford — Lincoln's Hingham ii, 268
See also under Guilford
Gilkey — Bangor Historical Mag. v, 108-10
Farrow's Hist. of Islesborough Me. 210-5
Walker Genealogy (1895) 64-7
Gill — American Ancestry vii, 74; xi, 84
Coffin's History of Boscawen N. H. 551-3
Clement's Newtown N. J. Settlers
Eiy Genealogy i, 125-7, 255-7
Gill Genealogy (of Canada) (1887-9) 126 p.
Heywood's Hist. Westminster Mass. 667-9
Hoyt's Salisbury Mass. Families 174-6
Hubbard's Hist. of Springfield Vt. 306-11

Lincoln's Hist. Hingham Mass. ii, 268–74
New Eng. Historical and Genealogical
   Register xxxiii, 339–41; xlvi, 212–5
Ripley's Ingersoll Genealogy 85–7
Roome Genealogy 222
Savage's Genealogical Dictionary ii, 254
Smith's Founders of Mass. Bay 347–9
Wentworth's Genealogy i, 345–7
Whitmore's Copps Hill Epitaphs
Wyman's Charlestown Mass. i, 408–10
Gillam — N. E. Hist. Register xix, 344
Savage's Genealogical Dictionary ii, 255
Gillespie — American Ancestry xi, 157
Bartow Genealogy 172
Thomas Genealogy (1896) 556 h–j
Gillet — Gillet Genealogy (1893) 11 pages
Gillet Genealogy (1898) 9 pages, reprint
New Eng. Hist. Register xlvii, 168–77
Gillett — American Ancestry ii, 154; iii,
   19; ix, 117; xii, 50
Barbour's My Wife and Mother 35, 70
Dickinson Genealogy (1896) 54–60
Douglas Genealogy 127–9
Goode Genealogy 259, 291–4
Hine's Lebanon Ct. Hist. Address 156
Judd's History of Hadley Mass. 498
Loomis Genealogy (1880) 420, 584, 633
Orcutt's History of Torrington Ct. 701–4
Orcutt's History of Wolcott Ct. 482–4
Roe's Sketches of Rose N. Y. 129
Savage's Genealogical Dictionary ii, 255
Sedgwick's History of Sharon Ct. 82
Sharp's History of Seymour Ct. 199
Sheldon's History of Deerfield Mass. 172
Sprague's Hist. of Gloversville N. Y. 117
Stiles' History of Windsor Ct. ii, 289–300
Tucker's History of Hartford Vt. 421–5
Gillette — American Ancestry ii, 46, 154;
   iii, 19; viii, 157; xii, 127
Gillette Genealogy (1885) 30 pages
Little's History of Weare N. H. 861
McMath Genealogy 66–75
Gilliam — Jones Genealogy (1891) 157 p.
Richmond Standard ii, 32; iii, 33, 35, 40
Slaughter's Bristol Parish Va. 174
Gilliatt — American Ancestry v, 188
Calnek's History of Annapolis N. S. 516
Gillingham — American Ancestry v, 167
Penn. Magazine of History xxiv, 224–9
Gillson — Deane's Scituate Mass. 275
Jillson Genealogy (1876) 266 pages
Sedgwick's History of Sharon Ct. 83
Gilman — American Ancestry iii, 20
Bangor Me. Historical Magazine iii, 128
Bell's History of Exeter N. H. 16–21
Cochrane's Hist. Francestown N. H. 733
Cogswell's Hist. Nottingham N. H. 283–9
Coit Genealogy 175–81
Corliss' North Yarmouth Me. Magazine
Dickerman Genealogy 519–28
Driver Genealogy 336
Fullonton's Hist. Raymond N. H. 229–32
Gilman Genealogy (1863) 51 pages
Gilman Genealogy (1864) 24 pages
Gilman Genealogy (1869) 324 pages
Gilmans of England, etc. (1895) 231 pages

Hammatt Papers of Ipswich Mass. 115
Hemenway's Vermont Gaz. iv, 154–8
Hubbard's Hist. Stanstead Co. Canada 219
Lancaster's Hist. Gilmanton N. H. 267–72
Little Genealogy 81
New Eng. Hist. and Gen. Reg. xviii, 258
New Hampshire Hist. Soc. Colls. vi, 189
North's History of Augusta Me. 874
Norton's History of Fitzwilliam N. H. 581
Prescott's Paige Genealogy
Runnel's Sanbornton N. H. ii, 304–14
Saunderson's Charlestown N. H. 372
Wentworth Genealogy i, 380–4
Whitmore's Heraldic Journal i, 150
Gilmer — American Ancestry v, 99
Meade's Old Churches of Virginia
Minor's Meriwether Genealogy 65–7
Page Genealogy 200
Peyton's Hist. of Augusta County Va. 288
Richmond Va. Standard i, 46
Gilmore — Bangor Me. Hist. Mag. vi, 102
Cochrane's History of Antrim N. H. 507
Cogswell's History of Henniker N. H. 587
Cutter's History of Jaffrey N. H. 345–9
Gilmore Genealogy (1888) 29 pages
Hatch's History of Industry Me. 623
Merrill's History of Acworth N. H. 218
Montague Genealogy 418
Morrison's Hist. of Windham N. H. 534–7
Parker's Hist. of Londonderry N. H. 273
Secomb's History of Amherst N. H. 601
Sibley's History of Union Me. 452–4
Temple's Hist. of N. Brookfield Mass. 602
Wheeler's History of Newport N. H. 394–6
Williams' History of Danby Vt. 149
Williamson's History of Belfast Me. 95
Gilpatrick — Bangor Hist. Mag. viii, 106
Gilpin — Am. Ancestry iv, 60; ix, 134
Fisher Genealogy (1896) 41–3
Futhey's History of Chester Co. Pa. 570
Gilpin Memorials (1853) 86 pages
Gilpin (Henry D.) Biography (1860) 211 p.
Gilpin Ancestry (1870) 12 pages
Johnson's History of Cecil Co. Md. 511–3
Sharpless Genealogy 232–5, 363–5
Swift's Barnstable Mass. Families i, 406
Thomas Genealogy (1877) 83
Thomas Genealogy (1896) 327
Gilson — Butler's Groton Mass. 402, 471
Green's Groton Mass. Settlers 7
Green's Groton Mass. Epitaphs 241
Gilson Genealogy, see Jillson
Hayward's Hist. of Hancock N. H. 601–4
Hemenway's Vermont Hist. Gaz. v
Heywood's Hist. of Westminster Mass. 669
Norton's History of Fitzwilliam N. H. 582
Randall's Hist. of Chesterfield N. H. 319
Ridlon's Harrison Me. Settlers 64–7
Savage's Genealogical Dictionary ii, 258
Gingrich — Brubacher Genealogy 22
Ginn — Bangor Historical Mag. iv, 238
Gist — Paxton's Marshall Genealogy 297
Penn. Magazine of History v, 457–61
Given — Cushman's Sheepscott Me. 381
Wheeler's Hist. of Brunswick Me. 835
Gladden — Andrews' New Britain Ct.

Gladding — American Ancestry i, 32
Hayes' Wells Genealogy 164
Gladwin — Buckingham Genealogy 282-7
Glascock — Power's Sangamon 331
Glasgow — Thomas Genealogy (1896) 556 i
Glass — Paul's History of Welles Vt. 92
Savage's Genealogical Dictionary ii, 259
Temple's Hist. of N. Brookfield Mass. 602
Winsor's History of Duxbury Mass. 262
Glassell — Hayden's Virg. Gens. 3-44
Slaughter's St. Mark's Parish Va. 136-8
Glazier — American Ancestry xii
Hastings Genealogy 95-101, 164
Hemenway's Vermont Hist. Gaz. v, 525
Herrick's Hist. of Gardner Mass. 351
Keyes' West Boylston Mass. Register 20
Sewall's History of Woburn Mass. 615
Temple's Hist. of No. Brookfield Mass. 603
Ward's History of Shrewsbury Mass. 296
Gleason — American Ancestry vii, 173
Barry's Hist. of Framingham Mass. 256-60
Bond's Watertown Mass. Genealogies 236
Brown's Bedford Mass. Families 13
Clarke Family of Watertown 44, 79-81
Daniels' History of Oxford Mass. 518-22
Davis' Landmarks of Plymouth Mass. 117
Draper's History of Spencer Mass. 205
Eaton's History of Thomaston Me. ii, 237
Hayward's History of Gilsum N. H. 314
Hazen's History of Billerica Mass. 63
Hudson's History of Lexington Mass. 76
Hudson's Hist. Marlborough Mass. 367-9
Hyde's History of Brimfield Mass. 405
Leonard's History of Dublin N. H. 341
Morse's Sherborn Mass. Settlers 90
Norton's Hist. of Fitzwilliam N. H. 583
Old Northwest Gen. Quarterly iii, 23-8, 68-71, 109-17
Paige's History of Cambridge Mass. 559
Paige's History of Hardwick Mass. 384
Savage's Genealogical Dictionary ii, 260
Sibley's History of Union Me. 455-7
Walworth's Hyde Genealogy 445
Washington N. H. History 446
Wight Genealogy 68
Gleim — Egle's Lebanon County Pa. 240
Glen — Bulloch Genealogy
Eldredge Genealogy 29-31
Munsell's Albany Collections iv, 126
Pearson's Schenectady Settlers 76-9
Glendower — Thomas Gen. (1896) 329-32
Gleen — Chase's Chester N. H. 533
Pa. Mag. of Hist. and Biog. xviii, 516
Pearson's Schenectady N. Y. Settlers 304
Glenn — American Ancestry x, 108
Glidden — Amer. Ancestry ix, 231; x, 15
Cushman's Hist. of Sheepscott Me. 382-7
Saunderson's Charlestown N. H. 373
Whitmore's Copps Hill Epitaphs
Glines — Lapham's Hist. Bethel Me. 539
Lapham's History of Rumford Me. 331
Sinclair Genealogy 217
Gloninger — Egle's Penn. Gens. 565
Fahnestock's Wolff Family of Pa. 99
Glossbrenner — Egle's Notes and Queries 3d series iii, 192-3

Glover — American Ancestry ii, 46
Babson's History of Gloucester Mass. 96
Barry's History of Framingham Mass. 260
Cochrane's Hist. of Francestown N. H. 733
Davis Genealogy (1888) 158-75
Eaton's History of Thomaston Me. 238
Essex Inst. Historical Collections v, 130-2
Glover Genealogy (1867) 602 pages
Lapham's History of Rumford Me. 332
New Eng. Hist. and Gen. Reg. xix, 213
Orcutt's History of Stratford Ct. 1207
Paige's History of Cambridge Mass. 559
Savage's Genealogical Dictionary ii, 261-3
Van Rensselaer's New Yorkers
Warren and Clarke Genealogy 71-4
Gloyd — Dyer's Plainfield Mass. 148
Eaton's History of Thomaston Me. ii, 238
Glynn — Hubbard's Springfield Vt. 312
Gobin — American Ancestry vi, 24; x, 68
Goble — Wyman's Charlestown 411
Godbold — Gregg's Old Cheraws 67
Goddard — Am. Ancestry v, 167; vii, 115
Austin's Ancestral Dictionary 20
Barlow Genealogy 229
Barry's Hist. of Framingham Mass. 261-3
Bassett's History of Richmond N. H 397
Benedict's History of Sutton Mass. 649
Bond's Watertown Mass. 237-56, 772
Bulkley's Browne Memorial 104
Davis' Landmarks of Plymouth 119-21
Driver Genealogy 347-52, 513
Goddard Genealogy (1833) 99 pages
Goddard and Frost Families (1899) 5 pages
Hayward's History of Gilsum N. H. 314
Hudson's History of Lexington Mass. 76
Hudson's Marlborough Mass. 397-401
Jackson's History of Newton Mass. 299
Kellogg's White Genealogy 112
Lapham's History of Bethel Me. 540
Lapham's History of Rumford Me. 333
New Eng. Hist. and Gen. Reg. liii, 242-5
Norton's History of Fitzwilliam N. H. 583
Paige's History of Cambridge Mass. 560
Pierce's History of Grafton Mass. 488-90
Read's History of Swanzey N. H. 345
Savage's Genealogical Dictionary ii, 264
Stearns' History of Rindge N. H. 533
Temple's Hist. of N. Brookfield Mass. 603
Updyke's Narragansett Church 153-7
Wall's Reunion of Worcester Mass. 356-9
Ward's Hist. of Shrewsbury Mass. 283-90
Wood's Brookline Mass. Sketches 363-72
Wyman's Charlestown Mass. Gens. i, 412
Goddell — Temple's N. Brookfield 603
Godding — Bond's Watertown 256
Eaton's Thomaston Me. 239
Hudson's History of Lexington Mass. 78
Savage's Genealogical Dictionary ii, 266
Stearns' History of Rindge N. H. 534
Godey — Thomas Genealogy (1877) 84
Thomas Genealogy (1896) 332
Godfrey — Amer. Ancestry iv, 194; vii, 69
Austin's R. I. Genealogical Dictionary 84
Ballou's History of Milford Mass. 768-72
Bangor Me. Historical Magazine ii, 133
Bond's Watertown Mass. Gens. 811

Dow's History of Hampton N. H. 727–35
Freeman's Cape Cod Mass. ii, 375, 609
Gregg's History of Old Cheraws S. C. 103
Pa. Magazine of History iv, 211; xviii, 24
Pierce's Biographical Contributions 52–98
Savage's Genealogical Dictionary ii, 265
Schenck's History of Fairfield Ct. 372–4
Walker Genealogy 25
Godfroy — Hall's Genealogy (1886) 113–8
Hall Genealogy (1892) 23–33
Godolphin — Life of Mrs. Godolphin
Godwin — Lapham's Rumford Me. 334–6
Va. Mag. of History v, 198; vi, 85
Goerg — Heffner Genealogy 45–7
Goes — Munsell's Albany Colls. iv, 126
See also under Hoes
Goewey — American Ancestry i, 32
Munsell's Albany Collections iv, 127
Goff — Morris Genealogy (1887) 47
New Eng. Hist. and Gen. Reg. xviii, 55
Goffe — Bedford N. H. Centennial 306–8
Dwight's Strong Genealogy 178
Paige's History of Cambridge Mass. 561
Savage's Genealogical Dictionary ii, 267
Whitmore's Copps Hill Epitaphs
Going — Chandler's Shirley Mass. 420–6
Gold — American Ancestry vii, 7, 15
Burr Genealogy (1891) 145–9
Gold's History of Cornwall Ct. 284–98
Hinman's Connecticut Settlers 1st ed. 220
Maltby Genealogy 78
Oneida Historical Society Trans. ii, 90–5
Orcutt's History of Stratford Ct. 1207
Pompey N. Y. Reunion 309
Power's Sangamon Co. Ill. Settlers 333
Schenck's History of Fairfield Ct. 370–2
Todd's History of Redding Ct. 193
Walworth's Hyde Genealogy 823
Golden — Morris' Bontecou Genealogy 126
Morse's Sherborn Mass. Settlers 91
Golder — Berger's Kings Co. N. Y. 123
Golding — American Ancestry vii, 6
Savage's Genealogical Dictionary ii, 269
Goldsborough — Amer. Ancestry ix, 87
Hanson's Old Kent Md. 276–96
Smith (Rev. Wm.) Biography
Goldsmith — Ballou's Milford 772
Clement's Newtown N. J. Settlers
Converse Genealogy (1897) 43–52
Livermore's History of Wilton N. H. 381–3
Norton's Hist. of Fitzwilliam N. H. 584
Savage's Genealogical Dictionary ii, 269
Goldstone — Bond's Watertown 774
Goldthwaite — Amer. Ancestry iv, 7
Benedict's History of Sutton Mass. 651
Goldthwaite Genealogy (1899) 411 pages
Longmeadow Mass. Centennial 315
Wheeler's History of Newport N. H. 397
Gonsaulus — Munsell's Albany iv, 127
Gooch — Bass' Hist. of Braintree Vt. 145
Corliss' North Yarmouth Me. 1123, 1195
Machias Me. Centennial 163
Savage's Genealogical Dictionary ii, 270
Goodale — Amer. Ancestry vi, 176; ix, 158
Barry's History of Framingham Mass. 263
Benedict's History of Sutton Mass. 651

Felton Genealogy (1886) 247
Herrick's History of Gardner Mass. 352
Heywood's Hist. Westminster Mass. 670
Howell's Hist. of Southampton N. Y. 260
Hoyt's Salisbury Mass. Families 176
Keyes' West Boylston Mass. Reg. 21–3
Little's History of Weare N. H. 862
Norton's Hist. of Fitzwilliam N. H. 584
Pickering Genealogy
Pierce's History of Grafton Mass. 490
Savage's Genealogical Dictionary ii, 270
Stearns' Hist. of Ashburnham Mass. 721
Ward's History of Shrewsbury Mass. 294
See also under Goodell
Goode — Amer. Ancestry iii, 21; iv, 101
Goode Genealogy(1887) 526 pages
Goodell — Cochrane's Antrim 507–9
Dwight Genealogy 596
Hyde's History of Brimfield Mass. 472
Judd's History of Hadley Mass. 498
Leland Genealogy 102
Power's Sangamon Co. Ill. Settlers 332
Rowell Genealogy 55–9
Saunderson's Charlestown N. H. 373
Goodenough — Lapham's Bethel Me. 541
Goodenow — American Ancestry vi, 39
Bemis' History of Marlboro N. H. 508
Butler's Hist. of Framingham Me. 476
Draper's History of Spencer Mass. 203
Hudson's Hist. of Marlborough Mass. 372
Ridlon's Saco Valley Me. Families 694
Savage's Genealogical Dictionary ii, 271
Ward's History of Shrewsbury Mass. 293
Goodhow — Barry's Framingham 264
Goodhue — American Ancestry xii, 16
Chase's Chester N. H. 533
Cochrane's History of Antrim N. H. 509
Cogswell Genealogy 168
Cogswell's Hist. of New Boston N. H. 407
Driver Genealogy 249
Goodhue Genealogy (1834) 16 pages
Goodhue Genealogy (1891) 394 pages
Hammatt Papers of Ipswich Mass. 119–21
Hayward's Hist. of Hancock N. H. 604–9
Hemenway's Vermont Hist. Gaz. v, 239
Hodgman's Hist. of Westford Mass. 450
Perkins' Old Houses of Norwich Ct. 463
Pickering Genealogy
Runnel's History of Sanbornton N. H.
ii, 314
Savage's Genealogical Dictionary ii, 272
Gooding — Corliss' North Yarmouth Me.
Davis' Landmarks of Plymouth Mass. 118
Walker Genealogy 39
Goodloe — Amer. Ancestry v, 143, xii, 17
Goodman — American Ancestry vi, 6
Judd's History of Hadley Mass. 499
Savage's Genealogical Dictionary ii, 274
Tuttle Genealogy 95–100
Whitman Genealogy 600–4
Goodno — Bass' Hist. Braintree Vt. 146
Goodnow — Bond's Watertown 87
Hudson's History of Sudbury Mass. 34
Norton's Fitzwilliam 585
Rice Genealogy
Sheldon's Hist. of Deerfield Mass. 174

Goodrich — Adams' Fairhaven Vt. 37
American Ancestry ii, 46; iv, 239; x, 144
Andrews' New Britain Ct. 154-9, 214
Boardman Genealogy (1895) 693-5
Bond's Watertown Mass. Genealogies 777
Cogswell's Hist. of Nottingham N. H. 205
Eaton's Annals of Warren Me. 546
Fowler's Chauncey Memorial 167
Glastenbury Ct. Centennial 171
Goodrich's Recollections i, 523-33
Goodrich Genealogy (1883) 109 pages
Goodrich Genealogy (1889) 417 pages
Goodwin's Genealogical Notes 69-85, 308
Guild's Stiles Genealogy 497-9
Kellogg's White Genealogy 78
Leland Genealogy 143-5
N. Eng. Hist. Reg. xvii, 357; xviii, 53-5
Paul's History of Wells Vt. 945
Poor's MerrimackValley Researches 128-30
Randall's Hist. of Chesterfield N. H. 321-3
Savage's Genealogical Dictionary ii, 274
Sedgwick's History of Sharon Ct. 83
Stiles' History of Windsor Ct. ii, 300
Talcott Genealogy 233-5
Talcott's N. Y. and N. Eng. Fams. 515-42
Temple's Hist. of N. Brookfield Mass. 604
Tuttle Genealogy 104-9
Walworth's Hyde Genealogy 263-5.
Whitmore's Heraldic Journal ii, 81
See also Goodridge

Goodridge — Goodridge Gen. (1884) 78 p.
Hatch's Hist. of Industry Me. 624-6
Hemenway's Vermont Hist. Gazetteer v
Heywood's Hist. of Westminster Mass. 671
Marvin's Hist. of Winchenden Mass. 455
Savage's Genealogical Dictionary ii, 275
Stearns' History of Rindge N. H. 535
See also Goodrich

Goodsell — Amer. Ancestry x, 50, 156
Dodd's Hist. of East Haven Ct. 120

Goodspeed — Amer. Ancestry xi, 214; xii
Freeman's Cape Cod 479
Guild's Stiles Genealogy 207
Hadley Genealogy 61-6
Hollister's History of Pawlet Vt. 192
Howland Genealogy 304
New Eng. Hist. and Gen. Reg. iii, 86
Paige's History of Hardwick Mass. 384
Paul's History of Wells Vt. 93-100
Ransom Genealogy 36
Ruggles Genealogy
Savage's Genealogical Dictionary ii, 276
Stone's Hist. of Hubbardston Mass. 274-6
Swift's Barnstable Families i, 391-405

Goodwillie — Amer. Ancestry viii, 9-11

Goodwin — American Ancestry i, 32; iii,
    216; iv, 98; ix, 132, 177; xii, 18, 36
Babson's History of Gloucester Mass. 96
Barbour's My Wife and Mother 33-5
Boyd's Annals of Winchester Ct. 189
Bradbury's Hist. Kennebunkport Me. 246
Brown's Bedford Mass. Families 13
Cogswell's Hist. of Henniker N. H. 588
Crafts Genealogy 205-7
Davis' Landmarks of Plymouth 119-21
Dawson's Historical Mag. (1858) 192-7

Dickerman Genealogy 517-9
Eaton's History of Reading Mass. 80
Freeman's Hist. of Cape Cod Mass. i, 634
Futhey's History of Chester Co. Pa. 570
Goodwin Family of Conn. (1891) 798 pages
Goodwin Family of Va. (1898) 167 p.
Goodwin Family of Maine (1898) 125 p.
Goodwin Family of Penn. (1898) 10 pages
Goodwin's Gen. Notes of Conn. 14-20
Goodwin's Buxton Me. 88, 134, 209, 289
Harvey Genealogy 991-9
Hatch's History of Industry Me. 626-8
Hazen's History of Billerica Mass. 64
Heywood's Hist. of Westminster Mass. 671
Hoyt's Salisbury Mass. Families 177
Hudson's History of Lexington Mass. 78
Litchfield Co. Ct. History (1881) 421
Maine Hist. and Gen. Rec. ix, 154-8; 322-4
Morrison's Hist. of Windham N. H. 537
Old Eliot Me. Monthly ii, (1898) 125-36
Orcutt's History of Torrington Ct. 704
Penney Genealogy 35-9
Porter's Hartford Ct. Settlers 5
Savage's Genealogical Dictionary ii, 277
Sedgwick's History of Sharon Ct. 84
Shourd's Fenwick Colony N. J. 82-4
Stackpole's History of Durham Me. 193
Stearns' Hist. of Ashburnham Mass. 721
Stiles' History of Windsor Ct. ii, 301
Walker Genealogy 23
Walworth's Hyde Genealogy 337
Washington N. H. History 447
Wentworth Genealogy i, 326-8
Wheeler's Hist. of Newport N. H. 398-400
Whitmore Copps Hill Epitaphs
Wyman's Charlestown Mass. i, 414-22

Goodwyn — Meade's Churches of Va.

Goodyear — Blake's Hamden Ct. 449-68
Fiske Genealogy 145-7
Goodyear Genealogy (1899) 250 pages
Savage's Genealogical Dictionary ii, 278

Googins — Bangor. Hist. Mag. viii, 107
Daniel's History of Oxford Mass. 522

Gookin — American Ancestry viii, 206
Atkins Genealogy (1891) 146-51
Dearborn's Hist. Salisbury N. H. 598-600
Dow's History of Hampton N. H. 735
Morse's Sherborn Mass. Settlers 92
N. E. Hist. Reg. i, 345-52; ii, 167-74; iv,
    185-8
Paige's History of Cambridge Mass. 563-6
Richmond Va. Standard iv, 14
Salisbury Family Mems. (1885) 459-73
Savage's Genealogical Dictionary ii, 278-80
Virginia Mag. of History v, (1898) 435

Goold — Amer. Anc. i, 32; ii, 47; ix, 107
Hemenway's Vermont Historical Gaz. v
Lincoln's Hist. of Hingham Mass. ii, 275-7
Whitmore's Copps Hill Epitaphs

Gorbey — Carter Genealogy (1883) 140

Gordan — Richmond Va. Critic (1888)

Gordon — American Ancestry 23, 195;
    iv, 155; vii, 50; viii, 53; x, 56
Bedford N. H. Centennial 308-10
Bell's History of Exeter N. H. 21-4
Chandler's History of Shirley Mass. 426

Cochrane's History of Antrim N. H. 510-2
Cogswell's Hist. of Henniker N. H. 590-4
Cothren's Woodbury Ct. ii, 1498-1501
Dearborn's Hist. of Salisbury N. H. 170
Goode Genealogy 122
Green's Kentucky Families
Hall Genealogy (1892) 66-72
Hayden's Virginia Genealogies 249-53
Hayward's Hist. of Hancock N. H. 610-3
Lincoln's Hist. of Hingham Mass. ii, 277
Morrison's Hist. of Windham N. H. 538-42
Old Northwest Genealogical Quar. ii, 49
Richmond Va. Standard iii, 31, 47
Ridlon's Saco Valley Me. Families 701-5
Robertson's Pocahontas Descendants 236
Slaughter's Bristol Parish Va. 203
Smith's Hist. of Petersborough N. H. 93-5
Walworth's Hyde Genealogy 667-9
Washington N. H. History 448-50
Whitehead's Perth Amboy N. J. 60-8
Gore — Ellis' Hist. of Roxbury Mass. 119
Gore Genealogy (1875) 8 pages, reprint
Mass. Hist. Soc. Pro. (1873) (1875) 423-5
Payne and Gore Genealogy (1875) 30 pages
Plumb's History of Hanover Pa. 415-8
Preble Genealogy 243-5
Savage's Genealogical Dictionary ii, 280
Gorgas — American Ancestry x, 107
Rittenhouse Genealogy 229
Gorges — Gorges Genealogy (1875) 11 p.
N. E. Hist. Gen. Reg. xv, 18-20; xxix, 42-7
Gorham — American Ancestry x, 145
Austin's Allied Families 106-8
Caverly's History of Pittsford Vt. 702
Davis' Landmarks of Plymouth Mass. 121
Freeman's Hist. of Cape Cod Mass. ii, 273
Goodwin's Olcott Genealogy 25
Gorham Fam. of Barnstable (1896) 7 pages
Gorham Fam. of R. I. (1900) 11 pages
Huntington's Stamford Ct. Settlers 38
Joslin's History of Poultney Vt. 268
Lapham's History of Norway Me. 513
New Eng. Hist. and Gen. Register iii, 86;
  x, 293; l, 32-4: lii, 186-92, 357-60, 445;
  liii, 207; liv, 167-74
New York Gen. and Biog. Rec. xxviii,
  133-6; xxix, 45-8, 91
Orcutt's History of Stratford Ct.
Paige's Hardwick Mass. 385, 1208, 1351
Pierce's History of Gorham Me. 169
Savage's Genealogical Dictionary ii, 281
Swift's Barnstable Families i, 407-44
Winsor's History of Duxbury Mass. 263
Wyman's Charlestown Mass. i, 423-5
Gorman — Sharpless Genealogy 163, 238
Gorsline — Peck's Rochester N. Y. 687-90
Riker's Newtown N. Y. 346
Gorton — Austin's R. I. Gen. Dict. 302
Austin's Allied Families 111
Ely Genealogy 183
Narragansett Historical Register vi, 89-91
New Eng. Hist. and Gen. Reg. li, 199-201
Savage's Genealogical Dictionary ii, 282
Goss — American Ancestry v, 121
Cogswell's Hist. of Henniker N. H. 594-7
Dow's History of Hampton N. H. 736

Essex County Mass. Register i, (1894) 128
Goss Family Romance (1886) 24 pages
Hemenway's Vermont Hist. Gaz. v, 188
Lapham's History of Bethel Me. 541
Lapham's History of Paris Me. 610
Lapham's History of Rumford Me. 336-8
Lawrence Genealogy (1881) 33-68
Savage's Genealogical Dictionary ii, 284
Secomb's History of Amherst N. H. 603
Temple's Hist. of N. Brookfield Mass. 604
Gossard — Ely Genealogy 375
Gosseline — Riker's Newtown N. Y. 346
Gossom — Lapham's Bethel Me. 542
Gosweiler — Rupp Genealogy 177-80
Gott — American Ancestry ii, 44
Davis Ancestry (1897) 37-40
Babson's History of Gloucester Mass. 239
Savage's Genealogical Dictionary ii, 284
Temple's Hist. of N. Brookfield Mass. 605
Goucher — Calnek's Annapolis N. S. 517
Goud — Thurston's Winthrop Me. 186
Gould — American Ancestry i, 32; iii, 197;
  iv, 178; vi, 158
Atkins' History of Hawley Mass. 66
Austin's R. I. Genealogical Dictionary 304
Austin's Allied Families 113-5
Ballou's History of Milford Mass. 773-5
Bangor Historical Magazine iv, 238
Bartlett's Wanton Family 127
Binney Genealogy, 24, 88-93
Bradbury's Kennebunkport Me. 247
Burr Genealogy (1891) 142-9
Butler's History of Farmington Me. 477-80
Chandler's History of Shirley Mass. 428
Cleveland's Topfield Mass. Anniversary 52
Cochrane's History of Antrim N. H. 512
Cogswell's Hist. Henniker N. H. 597-603
Cooley's Trenton N. J Settlers 92-5
Daniels' History of Oxford Mass. 523
Dwight Genealogy 976-80
Eaton's History of Reading Mass. 81
Eaton's History of Thomaston Me. ii, 240
Essex Inst. Hist. Collections xi, 115-221
Gould Genealogy (1841) 2 pages
Gould Genealogy (1872) 109 pages
Gould Genealogy (1895) 353 pages
Guild's Stiles Genealogy 24
Hayward's History of Hancock N. H. 613
Heywood's Hist. of Westminster Mass. 672
Hoyt's Salisbury Mass. Families 178
Hudson's History of Lexington Mass. 78
Hyde's Hist. Address at Ware Mass. 51
Kidder's New Ipswich N. H. 379-83
Little's History of Weare N. H. 862-5
Morse's Sherborn Mass. Settlers 93
Munsey's Magazine 1896
Norton's History of Fitzwilliam N. H. 585
Orcutt's History of New Milford Ct. 707
Savage's Geneal gical Dictionary ii, 284-7
Secomb's History of Amherst N. H. 604
Sedgwick's History of Sharon Ct. 85
Stark's History of Dunbarton N. H. 256
Stearns' History of Rindge N. H. 536-8
Temple's Hist. of N. Brookfield Mass. 605
Vinton's Giles Genealogy 169-80
Walworth's Hyde Genealogy 813-6

Wentworth Genealogy i, 306
Wheeler's History of Newport N. H. 401
Wyman's Charlestown Mass. i, 425-9
Goulding — Austin's R. I. Gen. Dict. 84
Morse's Genealogical Register (1859) 73-87
Pierce's History of Grafton Mass. 490-4
Wall's Remin. of Worcester Mass. 48-53
Ward's Rice Genealogy 39
Ward's History of Shrewsbury Mass. 297
Gourley — Miller's Colchester 328-33
Gouveneur — Hoffman Genealogy 516
New York Gen. Record vii, 63
Gove — American Ancestry iv, 122
Bond's Watertown Mass. 257-60, 775
Cochrane's Hist. Francestown N. H. 734
Cogswell's Hist. of Henniker N. H. 603-5
Cogswell's Hist. Nottingham N. H. 206-9
Dow's History of Hampton N. H. 737-9
Hoyt's Salisbury Mass. Families 180
Little's History of Weare N. H. 865-84
Merrill's History of Acworth N. H. 219-21
Paige's History of Cambridge Mass. 566
Potts Genealogy (1895) 277-9
Runnels' Hist. Sanbornton N. H. vii, 314-8
Savage's Genealogical Dictionary ii, 287-9
Washington N. H. History 450
Wyman's Charlestown Mass. Gens. i, 429
Gowdy — Stiles' Windsor Ct. ii, 301
Gowen — American Ancestry ix, 137
Norton's History of Fitzwilliam N. H. 585
Old Eliot Me. Monthly ii, (1898) 37-56; iii
  (1899) 129-37
Wyman's Charlestown Mass. Gens. i, 430
Gower — Butler's Farmington Me. 481-5
Hatch's History of Industry Me. 628-30
Gowey — Am. Ancestry iii, 115; v, 184
Gowing — American Ancestry xii, 16
Benedict's Sutton Mass. 652
Cutter's History of Jaffrey N. H. 352-4
Leonard's History of Dublin N. H. 342-4
Secomb's History of Amherst N. H. 605
Smith's History of Peterborough N. H. 95
Gowinger — Cochrane's Francestown 734
Grace — Welles' Am. Antiquity i, 259-74
Gracey — American Ancestry v, 165
Gracie — N. Y. Gen. Rec. xvi, 81-4
Graeme—Glenn's Colonial Mansions 396-8
Graff — Graff Association (1866) 10 pages
Graff Genealogy (1891) 103 pages
Graffam — Eaton's Thomaston Me. 240
Ridlon's Saco Valley Me. Families 697
Grafton — Eaton's Warren Me. 546
Pierce Genealogy by West (1894)
Savage's Genealogical Dictionary ii, 289
Gragg — Brown's Bedford Families 14
Power's Sangamon Co. Ill. Settlers 333
Graham — American Ancestry i, 33; viii,
  91; ix, 23; x, 101
Baird's History of Rye N. Y. 466
Brown's West Simsbury Ct. Settlers 68-70
Chase's History of Chester N. H. 534
Cleveland's Hist. of Yates Co. N. Y. 291-7
Cothren's Woodbury Ct. 545; ii, 1501
Draper's History of Spencer Mass. 198
Egle's Penn. Genealogies 625
Egle's Notes and Queries 3d ser. iii, 88-90

Fowler's Chauncey Genealogy 229
Hatch's History of Industry Me. 630
Hayden's Virginia Genealogies 163
Hemenway's Vermont Hist. Gaz. v, 190
Hudson's History of Lexington Mass. 78
Huntting's Hist. Pine Plains N. Y. 338-51
Lapham s History of Rumford Me. 338-40
Lewis Genealogy (1893) 233-5, 320-2
Marshall Genealogy (1884) 208-12
Martin's History of Chester Pa. 166-71
Miller's History of Colchester Co. N. S. 239
Morrison's History of Windham N. H. 542
New Eng. Hist. and Gen. Reg. xxi, 189-91
Pelletreau's Westchester N. Y. Wills 411
Power's Sangamon Co. Ill. Settlers 334
Reed's History of Rutland Mass. 124
Richmond Va. Standard iii, 5
Smith's History of Sunderland Mass. 345-8
Temple's History of Whately Mass. 233
Grammer — Slaughter's Bristol Va. 177
Grandy — Johnson Genealogy (1895) 57-60
Sheldon History of Deerfield Mass. 175
Temple's History of Northfield Mass. 454
Granger — American Ancestry iv, 165;
  viii, 86; ix, 119; x, 197
Caverly's History of Pittsford Vt. 703
Deane's History of Scituate Mass. 275
Dodd's History of East Haven Ct. 121
Granger Genealogy (1893) 587 pages
Paige's History of Hardwick Mass. 385
Savage's Genealogical Dictionary ii, 290
Temple's Hist of N. Brookfield Mass. 606
Grannis — Dodd's East Haven Ct. 122
Fletcher's Hatch Genealogy 9-12
Grannis Pedigree (1889) 15x25 inches
Grannis Pedigree (1891) 17x18 inches
Hubbard's Stanstead Co. Canada 147
Hughes Genealogy 161-4
Savage's Genealogical Dictionary ii, 290
Timlow's Southington Ct. Sketches 98-100
Grant — Aldrich's Walpole N. H. 262
Am. Anc. ii, 47; vii 72, 113; viii, 9; xii, 30
Barbour's My Wife and Mother, app. 51
Barrus' History of Goshen Mass. 145
Bond's Hist. of Watertown Mass. 260, 775
Corliss' North Yarmouth Me. Magazine
Driver Genealogy 85
Eaton's History of Thomaston Me. ii, 241
Essex Mass. Inst. Hist. Colls. xxi, 99
Grant Ancestry (1869) 186 pages
Grant Ancestry (1885) 17 pages
Grant Genealogy (1893) 42 pages
Grant Genealogy (1898) 578 pages
Grant Family Reunion (1899) 58 pages
Grant Family Magazine (1900)
Hanson's History of Gardiner Me. 134
Hayward's History of Hancock N. H. 613
Jameson's History of Medway Mass. 487
Little's History of Weare N. H. 884
Missouri Pioneer Families 333
New Eng. Hist. Gen. Register xxi, 173-6
Norton's History of Fitzwilliam N. H. 586
Orcutt's History of Torrington Ct. 704-7
Pierce's History of Grafton Mass. 495
Phoenix's Whitney Genealogy i, 153
Ridlon's Saco Valley Me. Families 698

Savage's Genealogical Dictionary ii, 290-4
Stiles' History of Windsor Ct. ii, 302-44
Tilley's Magazine of N. E. Hist. i,
Waldo's Hist. of Tolland Ct. 122
Wentworth Genealogy i, 132; ii, 21-4
Whitmore's Copps Hill Elitaphs
Wyman's Charlestown Mass. Gens. i, 431
Grantham — Martin's Chester Pa. 290
Granville — Dearborn's Parsonsfield
Grater — Crater Genealogy
Secomb's History of Amherst N. H. 607
Gratiol — Beckwith's Creoles 78-104
Graton — Washburn's Leicester 275
Grattan — Gilmer's Georgians 31
Grave — Young's Wayne Co. Ind. 341
Graves — Adams' Fairhaven Vt. 384-6
Aldrich's History of Walpole N. H. 263-7
American Ancestry i, 33; v, 49; viii, 17,
    136; x, 197; xii, 19
Anderson's Waterbury Ct. i, app. 56
Barbour's My Wife and Mother, app. 42
Barry's History of Framingham Mass. 265
Butler's History of Farmington Me. 485
Conn. Quarterly iii, (1897) 114
Crafts Genealogy 185-7
Craft's History of Whately Mass. 473-97
Dearborn's History of Salisbury N. H. 600
Doolittle's Hist. of Belchertown Mass. 268
Dow's History of Hampton N. H. 739
Eaton's History of Thomaston Me. 242
Ellis' History of Roxbury Mass. 129
Essex Inst. Hist. Collections xxv, 125;
    xxxi, 166-80
Graves Genealogy (1896) 546 pages
Graves Family of Lynn (1898) 3 pages
Hammatt Papers of Ipswich Mass. 123
Hayden's Virginia Genealogies
Heywood's Hist. Westminster Mass. 672-4
Judd's History of Hadley Mass. 501-4
Kellogg's White Genealogy 28, 76
Meade's Old Churches of Virginia
Merrill's History of Acworth N. H. 221
Montague Genealogy 517
Norton's History of Fitzwilliam N. H. 587
Read's History of Swanzey N. H. 346-8
Savage's Genealogical Dictionary ii, 294-8
Sewall's History of Woburn Mass. 68-70
Sheldon's History of Deerfield Mass. 175-9
Smith's Hist. of Sunderland Mass. 348-79
Temple's History of Palmer Mass. 466-8
Temple's History of Whately Mass. 233-40
Washington N. H. History 455-7
Wentworth Genealogy ii, 202
Wheeler's History of Brunswick Me. 835
Wyman's Charlestown Mass. Gens. i, 332
Young's History of Wayne Co. Ind. 341
Gray — Abbott's Andover Mass. 36
Am. Anc. i, 34; ii, 47; iv, 217; vi, 17; xii
American Gen. Record (1897) ii, 190-2
Austin's R. I. Genealogical Dictionary 85
Bangor Me. Historical Magazine v, 192
Barry's History of Hanover Mass. 314
Boyd's History of Conesus N. Y. 155
Bridgeman's Copps Hill Epitaphs 227
Clarke's Kindred Genealogies (1896) 65-100
Corliss' North Yarmouth Me. 346, 1115-7

Cushman's History of Sheepscot Me. 387
Davis' Landmarks of Plymouth Mass. 121
Deane's History of Scituate Mass. 276
Eaton's History of Thomaston Me. ii, 243
Egle's Penn. Genealogies 2d ed. 768-71
Essex Mass. Institute Hist. Colls. i, 188
Freeman's Cape Cod ii, 227, 525, 758
Gray Family of Sauquoit N. Y. (1882) 13 p.
Gray Fam. of Beverly Mass. (1887) 316 p.
Hayward's Hist. of Hancock N. H. 614-30
Huntington's Stamford Ct. Settlers 38
Lapham's History of Paris Me. 611
Livermore's History of Wilton N. H. 383-8
Our Ancestors (1882) 23-30
Pierce Genealogy (1894)
Perry Strong and Gray Memorial (1878)
Pickering Genealogy
Richmond Va. Standard iii, 36
Ridlon's Harrison Me. Settlers 67
Ridlon's Saco Valley Me. Families 699-701
Savage's Genealogical Dictionary ii, 298
Schenck's History of Fairfield Ct. 374
Sedgwick's History of Sharon Ct. 85
Slaughter's St. Mark's Parish Virginia 121
Smith's Hist. of Peterborough N. H. 96-8
Temple's History of Whately Mass. 240
Thomas Genealogy (1896) 333
Todd's History of Redding Ct. 194
Virginia Mag. of History iii, (1896) 402-4
Walworth's Hyde Genealogy 21
Wyman's Charlestown Mass. Gens. i, 434
Graybill — Brubacher Genealogy 214-28
Grayham — Hayward's Hancock N. H.
Graysburg — Clement's Newtown N. J.
Grayson — Balch's Md. Papers 99-105
Cabell Genealogy 452-4
Meade's Old Churches of Virginia
Greaton — Draper's Spencer Mass. 204
Greele — Livermore's Wilton N. H.
Greeley — American Ancestry vii, 90
Butler's History of Farmington Me. 629
Corliss' North Yarmouth Me. Mag. 42-5
Dearborn's Hist. Salisbury N. H. 607-20
Hoyt's Salisbury Mass. Families 180-2
Lancaster's Hist. of Gilmanton N. H. 266
Lincoln's Hist. of Hingham Mass. ii, 279
Livermore's History of Wilton N. H. 388
Poor's Merrimack Valley Researches 89
Savage's Genealogical Dictionary ii, 299
Worthen's History of Sutton N. H. 729-39
Green — American Ancestry ii, 47; iv, 16,
    43, 214; v, 132; vi, 109; vii, 55; x, 39;
    xi, 218; xii, 49
American Annals of Deaf for April 1861
Baker's History of Montville Ct. 234-9
Ballou's History of Milford Mass. 776-80
Bangor Me. Historical Magazine v, 192
Barlow Genealogy 247-9
Bond's History of Watertown Mass. 261
Bouton's History of Concord N. H. 664
Brown's Hist. of Whittingham Vt. 143-54
Butler's History of Farmington Me. 486-8
Butler's History of Groton Mass. 404, 472
Caulkins' History of New London Ct. 471
Cleveland's Yates Co. N. Y. 404, 533
Cogswell Genealogy 221

Cogswell's History of Henniker N. H. 606
Cooley's Trenton N. J. Genealogies 78-92
Cope Genealogy 41, 136
Daniels' History of Oxford Mass. 524
Davis' Landmarks of Plymouth Mass. 121
Dearborn's Hist. of Salisbury N. H. 601-5
Dimond Genealogy 120
Dow's History of Hampton N. H. 739-42
Draper's History of Spencer Mass. 200-2
Eaton's History of Reading Mass. 82-5
Eaton's History of Thomaston Me. ii, 244
Egle's Penn. Genealogies 2d ed. 38-40
Freeman's Cape Cod ii, 219, 290, 332
Goode Genealogy 177, 349
Goss' Melrose Mass. Hist. Address 12
Green Family of Malden Mass. (1858) 80 p.
Green Family of Cambridge (1861) 5 pages
Green Family of Cambridge (1876) 67 pages
Green Family of Warwick R. I. (1877) 71 p.
Green Family of Wales Mass. (1885) 64 p.
Green Fam. of Bethlehem Ct. (1893) 100 p.
Green Fam. of Westerly R. I. (1894) 500 p.
Green's Todd and other Families
Hartwell Genealogy (1887) 27
Hayden's Virginia Genealogies 548
Hemenway's Vermont Gaz. v, 707-10
Heywood's Hist. Westminster Mass. 675-7
Hill's History of Mason N. H. 202
Hollister's History of Pawlet Vt. 193
Howell's Hist. of Southampton N. Y. 261
Hudson's History of Lexington Mass. 79
Huntington's Stamford Ct. Settlers 39
Judd's History of Hadley Mass. 504
Lamborn Genealogy 276
Lapham's History of Paris Me. 612
Little's History of Weare N. H. 885-8
Livermore's History of Wilton N. H. 389
Malden Mass. Bi-Centennial 234-7
Meade's Old Churches of Virginia
New Eng. Hist. and Gen. Register iv, 75;
 xv, 105-9; xvi, 12
North Car. Baptist Hist. Papers iii
Norton's History of Fitzwilliam N. H. 588
Opdyke Genealogy 214-7
Orcutt's History of New Milford Ct. 795
Paige's History of Cambridge Mass. 567-9
Paxton's Marshall Genealogy 121-4
Phœnix's Whitney Genealogy i, 713
Pompey N. Y. Reunion 310
Poor's Merrimack Valley Researches 173
Power's Sangamon Co. Ill. Settlers 340-2
Ransom Genealogy
Richmond Va. Standard ii, 46; iii, 16, 18, 52
Roberts' Old Richland Pa. Fam. 194-204
Runnel's Hist. of Sanbornton N. H. ii, 318
Saunderson's Charlestown N. H. 374
Savage's Genealogical Dict. ii, 299-307
Schenck's History of Fairfield Ct. 375
Secomb's History of Amherst N. H. 608-10
Sewall's History of Woburn Mass. 615
Sharpless Genealogy 307
Slaughter's Fry Genealogy
Slaughter's Life of Wm. Green
Slaughter's St. Mark's Parish Va. 138-42
Spooner Genealogy i, 147-9
Sprague's Hist. of Gloversville N. Y. 118

Stearn's Hist. of Ashburnham Mass. 721-3
Stickney's Minisink Region N. Y. 159
Stiles' History of Windsor Ct. ii, 345
Stone's Hist. of Hubbardston Mass. 276-8
Swift's Barnstable Mass. Families i, 445-8
Temple's Hist. of N. Brookfield Mass. 607
Temple's History of Palmer Mass. 471-3
Vinton Memorial 15, 394-456
Wall's Remin. of Worcester Mass. 341-4
Ward's History of Shrewsbury Mass. 295
Washburn's Hist. Leicester Mass. 366-73
Whitman Genealogy 23-5
Whitmore's Copps Hill Epitaphs
Whitmore's Heraldic Journal iii, 27-31
Wight Genealogy 106
Williams' History of Danby Vt. 152-4
Worden Genealogy 65
Wyman's Charlestown Mass. i, 435-43
Young's History of Wayne Co. Ind. 228
Greenawalt — Egle's Lebanon Co. 240
Egle's Penn. Gens. 2d ed. 303-14
Power's Sangamon Co. Ill. Settlers 339
Greenberry — Dorsey Chart
Greene — American Ancestry iii, 91, 105;
 v, 90, 123, 137, 197; vi, 94, 169, 173;
 vii, 43; viii, 155; ix, 30; xii, 63
Austin's Ancestries 25-7, 79
Austin's Ancestral Dictionary 21
Austin's R. I. Genealogical Dictionary 86-9
Aylsworth Genealogy 279, 481-6
Bailey Ancestry (1892) 24-8
Chandler Genealogy 222-5
Douglas Genealogy, 465-8
Greene Genealogy, see Green
Holton's Winslow Genealogy i, 104-15
Lane Genealogy (1891) 125
Narragansett Historical Register ii, 137-44,
 161-77, 253-65; iii, 20-33; ix, 41-59
New Eng. Hist. Gen. Register iv, 75
New York Gen. and Biog. Rec. xxx, 54-6
Read's History of Swanzey N. H. 348
Rider's Thos. Vernon's Diary 140-50
Shotwell Genealogy 41-6
Strong Genealogy 726-8, 780-2
Thompson's Biog. of John A. Green 13
Updyke's Narragansett Churches 377
Warren's History of Waterford Me. 247
Greenfield — Champion Genealogy 48
Greenhalgh — Eaton's Thomaston 245
Greenhow — Richmond Standard ii, 34
Greening — Power's Sangamon Ill. 338
Greenleaf — American Ancestry xi, 183
Binney Genealogy 61
Bridgeman's Granary Burial Ground 383
Brooks' History of Medford Mass. 515
Coffin's History of Newbury Mass. 303
Dearborn's Hist. of Salisbury N. H. 620-2
Emery's Rem. of Newbury Mass. 24
Freeman's Hist. of Cape Cod Mass. ii, 214
Greenleaf Family Chart (1853)
Greenleaf Genealogy (1854) 116 pages
Greenleaf Genealogy (1896) 553 pages
Hatch's History of Industry Me. 631-5
Hoyt's Salisbury Mass. Families 183-7
Hudson's History of Lexington Mass. 79
Lapham's History of Norway Me. 514

Little's History of Weare N. H. 888
McKeen's History of Bradford Vt. 285-7
New Eng. Hist. and Gen. Register x, 152;
xxi, 88; xxxviii, 299-301; x!i, 210
Perkins' Old Houses of Norwich Ct. 464
Preble Genealogy 246-8
Savage's Genealogical Dictionary ii, 308
Walworth's Hyde Genealogy 715-9
Washington N. H. History 457-60
Whitman Genealogy 145-51
Willis' Law and Lawyers of Me. 522-36
Wyman's Charlestown Mass. Gens. i, 444
Greenlee — Paxton's Marshall Gen. 65
Greenman — Amer. Ancestry xii
Austin's R. I. Genealogical Dictionary 308
Hurd's Hist. New London Co. Ct. 714-20
Greenough — American Ancestry iii, 23;
v, 157; vi, 128
Bridgeman's Granary Burial Ground 366
Chase's History of Chester N. H. 535
Coffin's History of Boscawen N. H. 553
Dearborn's Hist. of Salisbury N. H. 605
Freeman's Hist. of Cape Cod Mass. ii, 674
Greenough Genealogy (1895) 38 pages
Jackson's History of Newton Mass. 295
New Eng. Hist. and Gen. Reg. xvii, 167-9
Poor's Merrimack Valley Researches 79
Savage's Genealogical Dictionary ii, 309
Sheppard's Lewis Memoir (1863)
Sumner Genealogy (1854) 63
Whitmore's Copps Hill Epitaphs
Greenslate — Power's Sangamon 340
Greenway — Meade's Old Fams. of Va.
Greenwood — American Ancestry iii, 80;
v, 121; vii, 86; viii, 8
Barry's Hist. of Framingham Mass. 266
Bemis' History of Marlboro N. H. 510-5
Benedict's History of Sutton Mass. 653
Butler's Hist. of Farmington Me. 488-91
Chapman's Trowbridge Gen. 227-9, 246
Dunster Genealogy 251
Greenwoods in Colonial Service (1899) 11 p.
Hatch's History of Industry Me. 635-7
Herrick's History of Gardner Mass. 352-4
Heywood's Hist. of Westminster Mass. 677
Jackson's Hist. of Newton Mass. 289-91
Lapham's History of Bethel Me. 543
Leonard's History of Dublin N. H. 344-8
Morse's Sherborn Mass. Settlers 94
New Eng. Hist. and Gen. Reg. xiv, 171; xv,
239; xxii, 303
Paige's History of Cambridge Mass. 569
Pierce's History of Grafton Mass. 494
Power's Sangamon Co. Ill. Settlers 335-8
Savage's Genealogical Dictionary ii, 311
Stearns' Hist. of Ashburnham Mass. 723
Stone's Hist. of Hubbardston Mass. 276-81
Ward Genealogy (1851) 29
Whitmore's Copps Hill Epitaphs
Greer — Jackson Genealogy 105
Gregg — American Ancestry xi, 83
Brook's Medford Mass. 517
Cochrane's Hist. of Antrim N. H. 514-20
Cogswell's Hist. of Henniker N. H. 695
Cogswell's Hist. New Boston N. H 353-5
Egle's Penn. Gens. 2d ed. 289-302

Gregg's History of Old Cheraws S. C. 86
Livermore's History of Wilton N. H. 390
Merrill's Hist. of Acworth N. H. 223
Morrison's Hist. of Windham N. H. 543-54
Parker's Hist. of Londonderry N. H. 274-6
Smith's Hist. Peterborough N. H. 98-101
Gregory — American Ancestry i, 33
Bond's Watertown Mass. Genealogies 262
Clarke's Old King Wm. Co. Va. Families
Douglas Genealogy 237
Eaton's History of Thomaston Me. ii, 245
Fillow Genealogy 79-83
Hall's Rec. Norwalk Ct. 186-99, 234-46
New Eng. Hist. Gen. Reg. xxiii, 304-7
Orcutt's History of Stratford Ct. 1208
Power's Sangamon Co. Ill. Settlers 342
Ransom Genealogy
Richmond Va. Standard ii, 4
Savage's Genealogical Dictionary ii, 312
Sedgwick's History of Sharon Ct. 86
Selleck's Norwalk Ct. (1896) 81-5
Slaughter's Fry Genealogy 73
Gregson — Dodd's East Haven Ct. 123
N. E. Hist. and Gen. Reg. xlvi, 151-3
Gresh — Bean's Montgomery Pa. 619-21
Gresham — Goode Genealogy 338
Greter — Crater Genealogy
Grevenradt — N. Y. Gen. Rec. vii, 60
Talcott's N. Y. Families 430-3
Greveraad — Munsell's Albany iv, 128
Grew — Bingham Genealogy 213-28
Gridley — American Ancestry x, 111; xii
Andrews' New Britain 259-63
Kellogg's White Genealogy 84
Putnam's Historical Magazine vi, 46-50
Savage's Genealogical Dictionary ii, 312
Timlow's Southington Ct. Sketches 100-6
Grier — Clyde's Irish Settlers Pa. 49-52
Meginness' West Branch Valley 131-6
Griffin — American Ancestry i, 34; ii, 47;
iv, 165; v, 153; vi, 112; viii, 165, 171
Babson's History of Gloucester Mass. 239
Baird's History of Rye N. Y. 467
Chandler Genealogy 95-8
Chase's History of Chester N. H. 536
Cochrane's Hist. of Antrim N. H. 520-2
Cogswell's Nottingham N. H. 389
Davis' Landmarks of Plymouth Mass. 122
Douglas Genealogy 235
Draper's History of Spencer Mass. 204
Griffin Family Gathering (1863) 7 pages
Griffin Genealogy (1888) 21 pages
Griffin Jour. Long Island (1857) 84-101, 168
Hammatt Papers of Ipswich Mass. 122
Hayden's Virginia Genealogies 110
Herrick Genealogy (1885) 337
Hodgman's History of Westford Mass. 450
Hoyt's Salisbury Mass. Families 187-9
Huntington Genealogy 172
Littell's Passaic Valley Genealogies 158
Meade's Old Churches of Virginia
Morris Genealogy (1898) 505-7, 630-6
Morrison's History of Windham N. H. 554
Nash Genealogy 65
N. E. Hist. Reg. xiii, 108-10; xxxix, 163
N. Y. Gen. and Biog. Rec. xxii, 191-204

Norton's History of Fitzwilliam N. H. 589
Orcutt's History of Stratford Ct. 1209
Queens County N. Y. History 152
Richmond Va. Standard i, 10; iii, 11
Savage's Genealogical Dictionary ii, 313
Stiles' History of Windsor Ct. ii, 346
Temple's Hist. of N. Brookfield Mass. 608
Walworth's Hyde Gen. i, 196; ii, 998-1008
Wyman's Charlestown Mass. i, 445-7
Young's Hist. Chautauqua Co. N. Y. 323
Griffing — Amer. Ancestry viii, 200; x, 33
Griffing Genealogy (1881) 194 pages
Perkins' Old Houses of Norwich Ct. 466
Griffis — American Ancestry vi, 201
Griffith — Amer. Ancestry vi, 120; viii, 121
Daniels' History of Oxford Mass. 525
Dow's History of Hampton N. H. 742
Freeman's Hist. of Cape Cod Mass. ii. 524
Futhey's History of Chester Co. Pa. 573
Read's History of Swanzey N. H. 350
Savage's Genealogical Dictionary ii, 314
Thomas Genealogy (1884) 67
Waldo's History of Tolland Ct. 75-7
Williams' History of Danby Vt. 150-2
Griffiths — Chambers' N. J. Germans
Griffitts — Griffitts Genealogy (1887) 88 p.
Morris Genealogy (1898) 607-11
Griggs — American Ancestry xi, 31
Anderson's Waterbury Ct. i, app. 57
Benedict's History of Sutton Mass. 653
Hyde's History of Brimfield Mass. 405
Thurston Genealogy (1892) 425
Grilley — Anderson's Waterbury 57
Grimball — American Ancestry xii, 101
Wood's Brookline Mass. Sketches 116-22
Grimes — American Ancestry x, 9
Bemis' History of Marlboro N. H. 515
Cochrane's Hist. Francestown N. H. 736
Hartwell Genealogy (1895) 120-6
Hayward's History of Gilsum 316
Hayward's Hist. of Hancock N. H. 622-4
Hudson's History of Lexington Mass. 80
Meade's Old Churches of Virginia ii, 370
Montgomery Genealogy (1897) 35-48
Nealley Chart
Read's History of Swanzey N. H. 350
Smith's Hist. of Peterborough N. H. 101
Stone's Hist. of Hubbardston Mass. 282-4
Grindle — Bangor Hist. Mag. v, 193
Farrow's History of Islesborough Me. 215
Grinnan — Hayden's Virginia Gens. 29
Grinnell — American Ancestry viii, 94
Austin's R. I. Genealogical Dictionary 308
Dwight's Strong Genealogy 1263
Farrow's History of Islesborough Me. 215
Sibley's History of Union Me. 457-9
Walworth's Hyde Genealogy 1018-20
Griscom — Shourd's Fenwick Col. 142
Grist — Perkins' Norwich Ct. 467
Griswold — Aldrich's Walpole 267-9
American Ancestry i, 34; ii, 47; iv, 213;
v, 63; vii, 14, 38; viii, 75
Andrews' History of New Britain Ct. 142
Backus Genealogy 137-41
Boyd's Annals of Winchester Ct. 135
Boyd's History of Conesus N. Y. 156

Caulkins' History of Norwich Ct. 176
Clarke's Old King Wm. Co. Va. Families
Cothren's Hist. of Woodbury Ct. ii, 1497-9
Cregar's White Genealogy
Griffin's Journal of Southold L. I. 203-5
Griswold Family of Conn. (1856) 6 pages
Griswold Ancestry (1872) 1 sheet
Griswold Family of Vermont (1880) 23 p.
Griswold Family of Conn. (1884) 85 pages
Hall's Gen. Notes (1886) 94-8, 104, 170-2
Hibbard's History of Goshen Ct. 455-9
Hollister's History of Pawlet Vt. 195
Hubbard's History of Springfield Vt. 316-8
Humphreys Genealogy 342-4
Huntington Genealogy 72
Kellogg's White Genealogy 43
Lane Genealogy (1899) 17
Magazine of Am. History (1884), 119, 334
Marshall's Grant Ancestry 113
New Eng. Hist. and Gen. Reg. xvii, 355-7
Orcutt's History of New Milford Ct. 708
Orcutt's History of Torrington Ct. 707-9
Perkins' Old Houses of Norwich Ct. 468
Roe's Sketches of Rose N. Y. 183
Salisbury's Fam. Histories (1892) ii, 1-122
Savage's Genealogical Dictionary ii, 316-8
Sedgwick's History of Sharon Ct. 86
Stearns' History of Ashburnham Mass. 724
Stiles' History of Windsor Ct. ii, 346-62
Strong Genealogy 1371-4
Walworth's Hyde Gen. i, 51, 182; ii, 884
Washington N. H. History 460
Young's Hist. Chautauqua Co. N. Y. 539
Groat — American Ancestry i, 34; ii, 48
Groce — Barry's Hanover Mass. 314
Lincoln's Hist. Hingham Mass. ii, 279-82
See also under Gross
Groenendyk — Albany Coll. iv, 128
Groesbeck — American Ancestry i, 34
Munsell's Albany Collections iv, 128
N. Y. Gen. and Biog. Record xxix, 109-12
Talcott's N. Y. and N. E. Families 86-91
Groome — Hanson's Old Kent Md. 180-3
Groot — Munsell's Albany Colls. iv, 129
New York Gen. and Biog. Rec. iv, 8-12
Pearson's Schenectady Settlers 80-6
Grose — Barry's Hanover Mass. 314
See also under Gross.
Gross — American Ancestry x, 67
Barry's History of Hanover Mass. 314
Egle's Penn. Gens. 2d ed. 725, 771-3
Freeman's Cape Cod Mass. ii, 682, 772
New Eng. Hist. and Gen. Reg. xi, 51
Rich's History of Truro Mass. 528-33
Sahler and Gross Genealogy (1895) 38 p.
Savage's Genealogical Dictionary ii, 318
Stearns' Hist. of Ashburnham Mass. 724
Wismer Genealogy 9
See also under Groce and Grose
Grosvenor — Clarke Family (1866) 39
Davis Genealogy 147
Thurston Genealogy (1892) 458-60
Whitman Genealogy 105-7
Grout — American Ancestry ii, 48
Atkins' History of Hawley Mass. 53
Barry's History of Framingham Mass. 267

Bond's Watertown Mass. Genealogies 263
Burnham's History of Brattleboro Vt. 162
Draper's History of Spencer Mass. 202
Grout Genealogy (1858) 86 pages
Hemenway's Vermont Hist. Gaz. v, 162
Merrill's History of Acworth N. H. 224
Morse's Genealogical Register (1859) i, 8–73
Morse's Sherborn Mass. Settlers 95
Pierce's History of Grafton Mass. 495
Saunderson's Charlestown N. H. 375–81
Savage's Genealogical Dictionary ii, 319
Temple's History of Northfield Mass. 454
Wall's Reminis. of Worcester Mass. 108
Warren and Clarke Genealogy 77–84
Grove — Egle's Lebanon Co. Pa. 241
Hammatt Papers of Ipswich Mass. 121
Power's Sangamon Co. Ill. Settlers 343–5
Grover — Babson's Gloucester 273
Clarke's History of Norton Mass. 82
Daniels' History of Oxford Mass. 526
Dimock's Coventry Ct. Records 50–3
Ely Genealogy 319
Farrow's History of Islesborough Me. 216
Hudson's History of Lexington Mass. 81
Lapham's History of Bethel Me. 545–55
Lincoln's History of Hingham Mass. ii, 282
Norton's Hist. of Fitzwilliam N. H. 589–91
Paul's History of Wells Vt. 100
Savage's Genealogical Dictionary ii, 320
Smith's History of Sunderland Mass. 380–2
Temple's History of Palmer Mass. 468
Wakefield Genealogy 191
Wyman's Charlestown Mass. Gens. i, 448
Groves — Hyde's Brimfield Mass. 407
Grow — Daniels' Oxford Mass. 526
Norton's History of Fitzwilliam N. H. 590
Grozier — Rich's Truro Mass. 533
Grubb — American Ancestry iv, 125; ix, 46
Grubb Genealogy (1893) 12 pages
Power's Sangamon Co. Ill. Settlers 345
Smith's History of Delaware Co. Pa. 465
Wyman's Charlestown Mass. Gens. i, 449
Grube — Heinecke Genealogy 33–6
Grumman — Schenck's Fairfield Ct. 375
Grymes — Carter Family Tree
Lee Genealogy (1895) 299
Meade's Old Churches of Virginia i, 370
Page Genealogy 155
Richmond Va. Standard iii, 29, 38
Gubenator—Reily's Life of Cardinal Gibbons ii, 530–7
Gue — American Ancestry ix, 34
Guerard — Bellinger Genealogy 42–9
Guernsey — Anderson's Waterbury 58
Bronson's History of Waterbury Ct. 491
Kasson Genealogy 29–31
Guess — Timlow's Southington Ct. 106
Guest — McPike Genealogy 40–3
Morris Genealogy (1898) 167–78
Penn. Magazine vii, 495; xii, 496
Guffy — Meginnes' W. Branch Val. 551
Guild — Aldrich's Walpole N. H. 269
American Ancestry vi, 39, 56, 152, 155, 187
Austin's Ancestral Dictionary 23
Cochrane's Hist. Francest'n N. H. 737–9
Daniels' History of Oxford Mass. 526

Guild Family of Dedham (1867) 132 pages
Guild Family of W. Dedham (1873) 21 p.
Guild Family of Conn. (1878) 40 pages
Guild Family of Lebanon Ct. (1886) 20 p.
Guild Genealogy (1887) 381 pages
Guild Ancestry (1891) 42 pages
Hill's Dedham Mass. Records i
Middlefield Ct. History
Washington N. H. History 461
Guile — Guild Genealogy 221–318
Guilford — Adams' Fairhaven 381–4
Anderson's Waterbury 58
Draper's History of Spencer Mass. 203
Hayward's History of Hancock N. H. 624
See also under Gilford
Guillow — Hayward's Gilsum 317–9
Guimar — Gumaer's Deerpark N. Y. 53
Guion — American Ancestry xii, 122
Baird's History of Rye N. Y. 467
Bolton's Westchester Co. N. Y. ii, 734
Guiteau — Oneida Hist. Trans. ii, 103–9
Gulch — Ruttenber's Orange Co. 355
Guldner — Boyd's Conesus N. Y. 156
Gulick — Chambers' N. J. Germans
Hayward's Hancock N. H. 624
Salter's Hist. of Monmouth Co. N. J. xxxi
Gulliver — Temple's N. Brookfield
Walker Genealogy 77
Winsor's History of Duxbury Mass. 249
Gumaer — Gumaer's Deerpark N. Y. 53
Stickney's Minisink Region N. Y. 130–3
Gunn — Anderson's Waterbury Ct. i, 59
Baker Genealogy (1867) 52–4
Hayward's History of Gilsum N. H. 319
Johnson Genealogy (1876) 19–21
Montague Genealogy 380–7, 513–7
Orcutt's History of Derby Ct. 723
Orcutt's History of New Milford Ct. 708
Read's History of Swanzey N. H. 352
Savage's Genealogical Dictionary ii, 323
Smith's Hist. of Sunderland Mass. 382–91
Stiles' History of Windsor Ct. ii, 362
Gunnison — American Ancestry vi, 67
Cutts Genealogy 182–4
Gunnison Genealogy (1880) 222 pages
Savage's Genealogical Dictionary ii, 324
Guptill — Eaton's Thomaston Me. 246
Gurley — American Ancestry iii, 24
Goodwin's Genealogical Notes 86–96
Gurley Genealogy (1897) 285 pages
Savage's Genealogical Dictionary ii, 324
Walworth's Hyde Genealogy 886
Gurney — Barry's Hanover Mass. 315
Corliss' North Yarmouth Me. Magazine
Hobart's History of Abington Mass. 383–6
Kingman's No. Bridgewater Mass. 211–5
Lapham's History of Norway Me 515
Mitchell's Hist. of Bridgewater Mass. 168
Poole Genealogy 83
Gusshee — N. E. Hist. and Gen. Reg. i, 344
Gustin—Hubbard's Stanstead Canada 225
Maine Hist. and Gen. Recorder vi, 353–5
Guthrie — Am. Anc. v, 165; x, 120; xi, 32
Buckingham Genealogy 262–5
Cleveland's Hist. of Yates Co. N. Y. 337–9
Guthrie Genealogy (1889) 61 pages

Guthrie Genealogy (1898) 170 pages
Prime's Sands Genealogy 54
Sharpe's South Britain Ct. Sketches 33–9
Gutterson — Cogswell's Henniker 607
Little's History of Weare N. H. 889
Guttredge — Austin's R. I. Dictionary 89
Guy — Goodwin's Foote Genealogy 185
Morse Memorial, appendix 45½
Savage's Genealogical Dictionary ii, 325
Shourd's Fenwick's Colony N. J. 80
Temple's Hist. of N. Crookfield Mass. 609
Guyon — American Ancestry i, 34; viii, 44
Clute's History of Staten Island N. Y. 386
Gwathmey — Richmond Va. Standard ii,
35; iii, 39; iv, 2
Welles' Washington Genealogy 203, 230
Gwynn — Hayden's Virginia Gens. 469
Gyles — Giles Memorial 101–51
Whitmore's Copps Hill Epitaphs
Habersham — American Ancestry v, 129
Bullock Genealogy
Hack — Ball's History of Lake Co. Ind. 417
Hack Circular by C. A. Hack (1881) 4 pages
Hayden's Virginia Genealogies 243
New Eng. Hist. and Gen. Reg. xlviii, 453–6
Hacker — Austin's Allied Families 116–9
Morris Genealogy (1898) 1013
Hackett — Hoyt's Salisbury 190
Lancaster's Gilmanton 273
Paxton's Marshall Genealogy
Runnel's Hist. of Sanbornton N. H. ii, 319
Saunderson's Hist. Charlestown N. H. 381
Savage's Genealogical Dictionary ii, 326
Sinclair Genealogy (1896) 131
Hackleton — Bond's Watertown 264
Hackley — Meade's Old Va. Churches
Walworth's Hyde Genealogy 1059
Haddaway — American Ancestry x, 109
Haddock — Dearborn's Salisbury 622–5
Eaton Grange (1890) 15–7
Haden — Ala. Hist. Soc. Transactions
Hadley — Babson's Gloucester 967
Bolton's Westchester Co. N. Y. ii, 735
Cochrane's Hist. Francestown N. H. 739
Hadley Genealogy (1887) 80 pages
Hayward's Hist. of Hancock N. H. 625–32
Hemenway's Vermont Hist. Gaz. v, 163
Heywood's Hist. Westminster Mass. 678–80
Hodgman's Hist. of Westford Mass. 451
Hoyt's Salisbury Mass. Families 191
Hudson's History of Lexington Mass. 81
Little's History of Weare N. H. 890–3
Machias Me. Centen. 164
Maris Genealogy 101
Smith's Hist. of Peterborough N. H. 102–7
Stearns' Hist. of Ashburnham Mass. 725
Wyman's Charlestown Mass. Gens. i, 451
Hadlock — Babson's Gloucester 97
Herrick Genealogy (1885) 167
Hoyt's Salisbury Mass. Families 192
Little's History of Weare N. H. 893
Savage's Genealogical Dictionary ii, 327
Hadwin — Williams' Danby Vt. 154
Haeffner — See Heffner
Haffield — Hammatt Papers 127
Hagadorn — American Ancestry i, 35

Hagaman — Cope Genealogy 83–7
Hagans — American Ancestry xii
Hagar — Barry's Framingham 268
Bond's Watertown Mass. Genealogy 264–9
Child's Genealogy 560–76
Craft's History of Whately Mass. 503–5
Hudson's Hist. Marlborough Mass. 373–5
Savage's Genealogical Dictionary ii, 328
Ward's History of Shrewsbury Mass. 327
Hagedorn — Pearson's Schenectady 86
Hageman—Am. Anc. ii, 48; vii, 36; ix, 153
Nevius Genealogy
Hagers — American Ancestry ii, 48
Chambers' Early Germans of N. J. 388–92
Heywood's Hist. Westminster Mass. 680–2
Haggard — American Ancestry vii, 7
Haggard Genealogy (1899) 136 pages
Power's Sangamon Co. Ill. Settlers 352
Hahn — Eaton's Thomaston Me. 247
Iowa Illustrated Historical Atlas 275
Haig — Hayward's Hancock N. H. 632
Haige — Pa. Mag. of Hist. xxiv, 81, 97
Haight — American Ancestry i, 35; ii, 48;
v, 73; xi, 116
Strong Genealogy 665–70
Tompkins Genealogy 43
Wetmore Genealogy 220
Haines — American Ancestry iii, 73; iv,
4; v, 197; vi, 151; vii, 169; xii, 83
Baird's History of Rye N. Y. 471
Bangor Me. Historical Magazine viii, 108
Chambers' Early Germans of N. J. 392–4
Chapman's Weeks Genealogy 140–2
Chute Genealogy, appendix 77–82
Cogswell's Nottingham N. H. 390–404
Futhey's History of Chester Co. Pa. 577–84
Haines Fam. of Portsmouth (1869) 29 pages
Haines Family of Penn. (1887) 85 pages
Haines Family, see Haynes
Kirk Genealogy 26, 42–8, 94–104
New Eng. Hist. and Gen. Register xxiii,
148–69, 430–3, xxiv, 422–5; xxv, 185–7
Power's Sangamon Co. Ill. Settlers 346–8
Rhoad's Clover-Croft Chronicles
Ruggles Genealogy by Bailey (1896) 30–6
Runnel's Sanbornton N. H. ii, 321–3
Sharpless Genealogy 224
Hair — Temple's No. Brookfield 609
Hairston — Meade's Old Families of Va.
Hait — Huntington's Stamford 47–54
Hake— American Ancestry vi, 152
Hakes — American Ancestry iii, 86
Hakes Genealogy (1886) 87 pages
Hakes Genealogy 2d ed. (1889) 220 pages
Halbrook — Bassett's Richmond N. H.
Halcott — American Ancestry i, 35
Haldeman — American Ancestry xii, 124
Halderman — American Ancestry xii, 125
Hale — American Ancestry i, 35; iv, 59;
xii, 18, 104
Babson's History of Leicester Mass. 324
Ballou's History of Milford Mass. 780
Barry's History of Framingham Mass. 269
Bassett's History of Richmond N. H. 400
Bridgeman's Granary Epitaphs 343–5
Chute Genealogy, appendix 82–7

Coffin's History of Newbury Mass. 304
Crane's Rawson Genealogy 84–7
Dearborn's History of Salisbury N. H. 625
Driver Genealogy 513
Ely Genealogy 41, 90
Emery Genealogy 60
Emery's Remin. of Newbury Mass. 156–60
Glastenbury Ct. Centennial 166
Hale Genealogy (1877) 19 pages
Hale Ancestry in Eng. (1881) 8 pages
Hale Genealogy (1889) 415 pages
Hale's Lawrence Genealogy 8–11
Hurlbut Genealogy 406
Kellogg's White Genealogy 56
Kilbourne Genealogy 56
Lapham's History of Norway Me. 516
Lawrence and Bartlett Memorial 171
Little Genealogy 574–81
Longmeadow Mass. Centen. app. 64–6
Marvin's History of Winchendon Mass. 457
Middlefield Ct. History
Morse's Grout Genealogy 48–55
New Eng. Hist. and Gen. Register vii, 271;
    xxxi, 83–99; xxxv, 358; xxxvi, 75
Norton's History of Fitzwilliam N. H. 591
Perley's History of Boxford Mass. 99
Power's Sangamon Co. Ill. Settlers 348
Randall's History of Chesterfield N. H. 326
Read's History of Swanzey N. H. 353
Savage's Genealogical Dictionary ii, 329–32
Stearns' History of Rindge N. H. 539–52
Stone's History of Beverly Mass. 38
Stone's History of Hubbardston Mass. 285
Strong Genealogy 331–54
Stuart's Life of Hale 185–202
Temple's Hist. of N. Brookfield Mass. 610
Temple's History of Palmer Mass. 488
Tuttle Genealogy xxxvi
Vinton's Giles Genealogy 99
Warren's History of Waterford Me. 249
Wentworth's Genealogy i, 698
Wheeler's History of Newport N. H. 403–6
Wyman's Charlestown Mass. Gens. 452–5
Halenbeck — Munsell's Albany Collec-
    tions ii, 415; iv, 129
New York Gen. and Biog. Record xxx, 123
Haley — Bradbury's Kennebunkport
Haley Genealogy (1900) 115 pages
Ridlon's Saco Valley Me. Families 706–20
Updyke's Narragansett Churches 160
Wheeler's History of Brunswick Me. 836
Wilson Genealogy (1898) 20–6
Yarmouth N. S. Herald 1896
Hall — Adam's Haven Gen. 2d part 27
Aldrich's History of Walpole N. H. 270–4
Allison Genealogy 88
American Ancestry ii, 78; iii, 24, 68, 88;
    v, 68, 158; vi, 69, 106, 203; vii, 109,
    167,175, 238; ix, 96, 188, 204, 233, 237;
    x, 19, 27, 105, 112, 161; xi, 39; xii,
    10, 26
Anderson's Waterbury Ct. i, app. 60
Atkins' History of Hawley Mass. 47
Austin's R. I. Genealogical Dictionary 90
Austin's Allied Families 119
Baldwin Genealogy 843

Bedford N. H. Centennial 310
Benedict's History of Sutton Mass. 654–7
Blake's Mendon Mass. Association 92–4
Bond's Watertown Mass. Gens. 895
Bouton's History of Concord N. H. 707
Briggs' History of Shipbuilding 355–62
Brooks' History of Medford Mass. 517–27
Buck Genealogy (1894) 53
Calnek's History of Annapolis N. S. 518–20
Carter Family Tree of Virginia
Caverly's History of Pittsford Vt. 704
Chambers' Early Germans of N. J. 394–6
Chandler's History of Shirley Mass. 429
Chapman's Weeks Genealogy 142
Chase's History of Chester N. H. 536–9
Clarke's History of Norton Mass. 82
Cochrane's History of Antrim N. H. 523–6
Cochrane's Hist. Francest'n N. H. 740–4
Cushman's History of Sheepscott Me. 387
Cutter's History of Arlington Mass. 254
Daniels' History of Oxford Mass. 527–9
Davis' History of Wallingford Ct. 750–87
Davis' Landmarks of Plymouth Mass. 123
Dickerman Genealogy 306–27
Draper's History of Spencer Mass. 211
Dwight Genealogy 272
Eaton's Annals of Warren Me. 547
Eaton's Hist. of Thomaston Me. ii, 247–50
Egle's Penn. Genealogies 2d ed. 433–9
Egle's Notes and Queries 1st ser. i. 283–8,
    3d ser. i, 492–4
Ellis Genealogy 394
Farrar Memoir (1853) 31
Foster Genealogy (1889) 74
Freeman's Cape Cod ii, 137, 202, 707–9
Gifford's Our Patronymics 8
Goodwin's Foote Genealogy 107
Greene Genealogy (1894)
Green's Kentucky Families
Hall Family of Medford (1855) **12 pages**
Hall Family of Cleveland (1876) **26 pages**
Hall Family of Conn. (1882) **31 pages**
Halls of New England (1883) **790 pages**
Hall Genealogical Notes (1886) **192 pages**
Hall Family of Detroit (1892) **105 pages**
Hall Family Ancestry (1896) **507 pages**
Hammatt Papers of Ipswich Mass. 129–31
Hanson's Old Kent Md. 87
Hayward's History of Gilsum N. H. 319
Hayward's Hist. of Hancock N. H. 632–6
Hazen's History of Billerica Mass. 65
Heywood's Hist. of Westminster Mass. 682
Hibbard's History of Goshen Ct. 459–62
Hill's History of Mason N. H. 203
Hinman's Conn. Settlers 1st ed. 170–88
Hodgman's History of Westford Mass. 451
Holton's Winslow Genealogy i, 272
Hoyt's Salisbury Mass. Families 193
Hubbard's Hist. of Springfield Vt. 318–20
Hudson's History of Lexington Mass. 83
Humphrey Genealogy 426–31
Jackson's History of Newton Mass. 295–7
Jennings' History of Bennington Vt. 502
Johnson's History of Cecil Co. Md. 480–5
Kellogg's White Genealogy 33
Kingman's No. Bridgewater Mass. 529

Knox Co. Me. Hist. Magazine i, 47 et seq.
Lapham's History of Norway Me. 516-19
Lapham's History of Paris Me. 614-6
Lapham's History of Rumford Me. 341-3
Lincoln's Hist. Hingham Mass. ii, 283-6
Livermore's History of Wilton N. H. 390
Maginness' Biographical Annals 161-3
Maine Hist. Magazine by Porter vii, 117
Mallmann's Shelter Island N. Y. 311
Maltby Genealogy 83
Matthews' History of Cornwall Vt. 286
Middlefield Ct. History
Mitchell's Hist. of Bridgewater Mass. 169
Morrison's History of Windham N. H.
   555-7
New Eng. Historical and Genealogical
   Register vi, 259-60; xiii, 15; xv, 59,
   238; xxiii, 150, 430; xlii 303-7
New Hampshire Hist. Soc. Coll. vii, 381
Norton's History of Fitzwilliam N. H. 591
Orcutt's History of Wolcott Me. 485-7
Orcutt's History of Stratford Ct. 1210
Paige's History of Cambridge Mass. 570
Palmer Genealogy (1886) 53-6
Paul's History of Wells Vt. 102
Pearson's Schenectady N. Y. Settlers 88
Penn. Mag. of Hist. iv, 353-5; xi, 309-17
Pierce's History of Grafton Mass. 496-500
Power's Sangamon Co. Ill. Settlers 348-52
Prentice Genealogy 412
Randall's History of Chesterfield N. H. 327
Read's History of Swanzey N. H. 354
Ridlon's Harrison Me. Settlers 68
Saunderson's Charlestown N. H. 382-5
Savage's Genealogical Dictionary ii, 332-9
Schenck's History of Fairfield Ct. 375
Sewall's History of Woburn Mass. 616
Shourd's Fenwick Colony N. J. 93-104
Stearns' Hist. Ashburnham Mass. 726-28
Stiles' History of Windsor Ct. ii, 363
Swift's Barnstable Mass. Families i, 450-6
Symmes Genealogy 47, 68
Thurston Genealogy
Thurston's History of Winthrop Me. 186
Timlow's Southington Ct. Sketches 106
Tuttle Genealogy xliii
Vinton's Richardson Genealogy 637
Ward's History of Shrewsbury Mass. 304
Washington N. H. History 461-3
Welles' Washington Genealogy 234
Wentworth Genealogy i, ii, 319, 479-81
Wheeler's History of Brunswick Me. 837
Wheeler's Croydon N. H. Centen. 106-12
Wheeler's History of Newport N. H. 406-9
Whipple-Hill Families (1897) 58-60
White Genealogy (1879) 127-9, 132-50
Whitmore's Copps Hill Epitaphs
Whittemore's History Middlesex Co. Ct.
   534
Whittemore's Orange N. J. 439
Winslow Genealogy ii, 922-36
Winsor's History of Duxbury Mass. 263
Wyman's Charlestown Mass. i, 454-60
Young's History of Chautauqua Co. N. Y.
Hallam — Caulkins' New London 358
Savage's Genealogical Dictionary ii, 339

Hallenbeck — Am. Ancestry i, 35; ii, 49
Greene Co. N. Y. History 187, 431
See also Halenbeck
Hallett — Freeman's Hist. of Cape Cod
Howland Genealogy 302-4
New York Gen. and Biog. Rec. vi, 28-9;
   vii, 91
Riker's Annals of Newtown N. Y. 402-6
Savage's Genealogical Dictionary ii, 340
Shotwell Genealogy 264-6
Swift's Barnstable Families i, 473-531
Halley — McPike Genealogy
New York Gen. and Biog. Reg. xxix, 13-6
Halliburton — American Ancestry v, 85
Halliday — American Ancestry xi, 82
Jackson Genealogy 222
Morris' Bontecou Genealogy 192
Hallock — Am. Anc. iii, 25; v, 77; xii, 20
Brown's West Simsbury Ct. Settlers 85
Bunker's Long Island Genealogies 96-102
Dyer's History of Plainfield Mass. 149-55
Hallock Genealogy (1863) 8 pages
Hallock Genealogy 2d ed. (1866) 20 pages
Howell's Hist. of Southampton N. Y. 226
Littell's Passaic Valley Genealogies 165
Mallmann's Shelter Island N. Y. 212
Stickney's Minisink Region N. Y. 165
Halloway — Sullivant Genealogy
Hallowell — Hallowell Gen. (1893) 246
Roberts' Old Richland Pa. Families 190-3
Savage's Genealogical Dictionary ii, 340
Smith's History of Delaware Co. Pa. 466
Halsall — Savage's Gen. Dictionary ii, 341
Halsey — American Ancestry iv, 154, 182,
   226; vii, 36, 132
Halsey Genealogy (1895) 550 pages
Howell's Hist. Southampton N. Y. 262-77
Littell's Passaic Valley Genealogies 156-69
Slaughter's St. Mark's Parish Va. 136
Stiles' History of Windsor Ct. ii, 364
Halstead — American Ancestry xii
Halsted — Amer. Ancestry ii, 49; vi, 13
Baird's History of Rye N. Y. 474
Halsted Genealogy (1896) 34 pages
Savage's Genealogical Dictionary ii, 341
Whittemore's Orange N. J. 406
Ham — American Ancestry ii, 49; iv, 145
Caverno Genealogy 14-6
Eaton's History of Thomaston Me. ii, 250
Herrick Genealogy (1885) 223
Hudson's History of Lexington Mass. 83
Huntting's Hist. of Pine Plains N. Y. 351
Missouri Pioneer Families 265
New Eng. Hist. and Gen. Reg. xxvi, 388-94
Otis Genealogy (1851)
Savage's Genealogical Dictionary ii, 342
Wentworth Genealogy i, 165-8, 483
Wheeler's History of Brunswick Me. 837
Hamant — Temple's No. Brookfield 613
Hamblen — Andrews Gen. (1890) 195-9
Hamlin Genealogy (1894) 70-130
Swift's Barnstable Mass. Fam. i, 522-36
Hamblet — Read's Swanzey N. H. 354
Hambleton — American Ancestry iii, 101
Hambleton Genealogy (1887) 108 pages
Man and Hambleton Families (1876) 124 p.

Hamblin — Andrews' New Britain 273
Cleveland Genealogy 24-6
Freeman's History of Cape Cod ii, 161, 340
Kitchell Genealogy 54
Pierce's History of Gorham Me. 171
Hamel — American Ancestry vii, 202
Hamer — American Ancestry ix, 29
Hamill — Egle's Queries 4th ser. i, 188
Futhey's History of Chester Co. Pa. 584
Hamilton — Adams' Fairhaven Vt. 390
Alexander Genealogy 27-41
American Ancestry xi, 85; xii
Bellinger Genealogy 97-9
Corliss' North Yarmouth Me. Magazine
Eaton Genealogy (1895)
Egle's Penn. Genealogies 2d ed. 315-33
Egle's Notes and Queries 3d ser. iii, 1-15
Freeman's Hist. of Cape Cod Mass. ii, 603
Hamilton Family of N. Y. (1893) 32 p.
Hamilton Family of Worcester (1894) 139 p.
Heywood's Hist. of Westminster Mass. 684
Humphrey Genealogy 285
Leonard's History of Dublin N. H. 348
Little's History of Weare N. H. 894
Locke Genealogy 103
Miller's Hist. Colchester Co. N. S. 353-61
New Eng. Hist. and Gen. Reg. xliv, 361-5
New York Gen. and Biog. Rec. xx, 62-5
Penn. Magazine of History xvii, 175-84
Power's Sangamon Co. Ill. Settlers 353
Randall's History of Chesterfield N. H. 327
Savage's Genealogical Dictionary ii, 343
Sedgwick's History of Sharon Ct. 87
Sheldon's History of Deerfield Mass. 181
Slaughter's St. Mark's Parish Va. 158, 185
Smith (Rev. Wm.) Biography
Stone's History of Hubbardston Mass. 287
Temple's Hist. N. Brookfield Mass. 613-5
Temple's Hist. of Palmer Mass. 476-8, 487
Waddell's Annals of Augusta Co. Va. 51
Hamlen — Dyer's Plainfield Mass. 155-9
Hamlen Genealogy (1881) 12 pages
Hamlet — Hazen's Billerica Mass. 65
Hamlin — Am. Anc. iv, 37; v, 160; viii, 20
Bangor Historical Magazine ii, 192-4
Daniels' History of Oxford Mass. 529
Dwight Genealogy 504-8
Hamlin Gen. (1885) 4 pages
Hamlin Genealogy (1894) 130 pages
Hinman's Conn. Settlers 1st ed. 214-9
Hodgman's History of Westford Mass. 451
Lapham's History of Paris Me. 620-2
Maine Hist. and Gen. Recorder vii, 6
Mitchell's Hist. of Bridgewater Mass. 170
N. E. Hist. Gen. Reg. iii, 133-5; l, 220
North's History of Augusta Me. 875-80
Power's Sangamon Co. Ill. Settlers 353
Ridlon's Saco Valley Me. Families 720-2
Saunderson's Charlestown N. H. 385-8
Sedgwick's History of Sharon Ct. 87
Talcott's N. Y. and N. E. Families 543-51
Warren's History of Waterford Me. 251-3
Hamline — Collin's Hillsdale 59-62
Hamm — American Ancestry ii, 49
Hammaker—Brubacher Genealogy 164-71
Hammatt — Bangor Hist. Mag. vii, 174

Hammell — Roome Genealogy 128
Hammett — Spooner Genealogy i, 421
Hammon — Corliss' North Yarmouth Me.
Hammond — American Ancestry ii, 50;
iii, 183, 212; v, 42, 49; vi, 17; vii, 109,
113; ix, 210; x, 60, 97; xi, 84; xii, 40
American Historical Register i, 867-73
Anderson's Waterbury Ct. i, app. 60
Babson's History of Gloucester Mass. 97
Bangor Historical Magazine i, 211-3
Bond's Watertown Mass. 269-72, 778-86
Caverly's History of Pittsford Vt. 705
Chapman's Trowbridge Genealogy 242
Collins Genealogy 148
Dwight's Strong Genealogy 50
Eaton's History of Thomaston Me. ii, 251
Egle's Notes and Queries (1896) 198
Freeman's History of Cape Cod Mass. ii, 72
Hammond Family of Vermont (1876) 11 p.
Hammond Family of N. H. (1890) 17 pages
Hammond Family of Mass. (1894) 311 p.
Hayward's History of Gilsum N. H. 320
Jackson's Hist. of Newton Mass. 298-305
Lapham's History of Paris Me. 616-20
Lincoln's Hist. of Hingham Mass. ii, 286
N. E. Hist. Gen. Reg. xxx, 28-33; xli, 167
Old Eliot, Me. Monthly i, (1897) 14, 111-15;
iii, (1899) 140
Paige's History of Hardwick Mass. 387
Pierce's History of Grafton Mass. 500
Power's Sangamon Co. Ill. Settlers 354
Prentice Genealogy 410
Raymond's Tarrytown Monument 45-59
Read's History of Swanzey N. H. 355-61
Savage's Genealogical Dictionary ii, 345-8
Stark's History of Dunbarton N. H. 224
Stearns' Hist. of Ashburnham Mass. 728
Swift's Barnstable Mass. Families ii, 67
Washburn's Hist. of Leicester Mass. 375
Wyman's Charleston Mass. Gens. i, 461
Hamor — Neill's Virginia Carolorum 19
Hampton — Power's Sangamon Ill. 396
Richmond Va. Standard ii, 17
Shotwell Genealogy 240
Hanaford — Hall's Norwalk Ct. Records
183-7, 225-8, 250-3, 296-301
Runnels' Hist. of Sanbornton N. H. ii, 323
Hance — American Ancestry xii
Chambers' Early Germans of N. J. 396
Missouri Pioneer Families 270
New York Gen. and Biog. Rec. xxvii, 166
Hanchett — Am. Ancestry iv, 147; viii, 83
Loomis Genealogy (1880) 275-8
Sedgwick's History of Sharon Ct. 88
Hancock — American Ancestry viii, 212
Ballou's History of Milford Mass. 781
Bridgeman's Granary Grounds 384-9
Buxton Me. Centennial 171-3
Daniels' History of Oxford Mass. 530
Goodwin's History of Buxton Me. 169, 278
Cregar's Haines Ancestry 17
Davis Genealogy 61
Dearborn's Hist. of Salisbury N. H. 625-7
Hudson's History of Lexington Mass. 83-8
Johnston Genealogy (1897) 178-84, 205-16
Kelly Genealogy (1892)

Lane Genealogy (1891) 235
Lee Genealogy (1888) 369-75
Longmeadow Mass. Centen., app. 66-8
New Eng. Hist. Reg. ix, 352-4; x, 81; xxxvi, 75-7
Paige's History of Cambridge Mass. 571-4
Penn. Magazine of History x, 100-6
Prentice Genealogy 3, 413
Ridlon's Saco Valley Me. Families 722-4
Runnels' Hist. of Sanbornton N. H. ii, 325
Savage's Genealogical Dictionary ii, 348
Shourd's Fenwick Colony N. J. 85
Whitmore's Heraldic Journal ii, 99
Wyman's Charlestown Mass. Gens. i, 462
Hand — Am. Ancestry i, 35; ii, 50; xii
Crawford Family of Virginia 84-7
Ely Genealogy 182
Hedge's Hist. East Hampton N. Y. 285-90
Howell's Southampton N. Y. 277-82
Kulp's Wyoming Valley Families
Littell's Passaic Valley Genealogies 170-9
Henderson — Henderson Gen. (1885) 80
Handley — Eaton's Thomaston Me. 251
Stearns' Hist. of Ashburnham Mass. 729
Handy — American Ancestry xii
Bassett's Richmond N. H.
Neill Family of Delaware 112-7
Norton's History of Fitzwilliam N. H. 501
Read's History of Swanzey N. H. 361
Thomas Genealogy (1877) 86
Haner — American Ancestry ii, 51
Hanford — Am. Ancestry iv, 176; x, 136
Bolton's Westchester Co. N. Y. ii, 521
Chapman Genealogy 226
Morris' Bontecou Genealogy 102
Savage's Genealogical Dictionary ii, 349
Selleck's Norwalk Ct. (1896) 135-49
Van Hoosear's Norwalk Ct. Epitaphs 14, 22
Wentworth Genealogy ii, 21
Hanger — Peyton's Augusta Co. Va.
Hank — Jenkins' Gwynedd Pa. 328
Hankinson — Chute Genealogy, app. 87-90
Hanks — Hitchcock's Nancy Hanks
Hollister's Pawlet Vt. 196
Walker Genealogy 150
Hanley — Eaton's Thomaston Me. 252
Hanmer — Deane's Scituate Mass. 278
Mitchell's Hist. of Bridgewater Mass. 170
Hann — Chambers' N. J. Germans
Goode Genealogy 300
Lincoln's Hist. of Hingham Mass. ii, 287
Sharpe's South Britain Ct. Sketches 61-4
Hanna — Egle's Hist. Reg. of Pa. i, 81-5
Maine Hist. and Gen. Recorder iii, 124
Hannaford — Dearborn's Parsonsfield
Lapham's History of Norway Me. 519
Smith's Hist. Peterborough N. H. 108-10
Hannah — Austin's R. I. Gen. Dict. 91
Rhode Island Hist. Society Colls. iii, 294
Hannahs — Kilbourn Genealogy 204
Hannay — American Ancestry i, 35
Hannis — Plumb's Hanover Pa. 432
Hannum — Cope's Dutton Genealogy 61
Doolittle's Sketches of Belchertown Mass. 267
Futhey's History of Chester Co. Pa. 605

Jackson Genealogy 241
Lyman's History of E. Hampton Mass. 190
Savage's Genealogical Dictionary ii, 351
Temple's History of Northfield Mass. 456
Hansard — Speed Genealogy 150-2
Hanscom — Old Eliot, Me. Monthly ii, (1898) 8, 11
Machias Me. Centennial 164
Hansen — Munsell's Albany iv, 131
New Eng. Hist. and Gen. Reg. liii, 118-20
Talcott's N. Y. and N. E. Families 434-7
Hanset — Savage's Gen. Dictionary ii, 351
Hansford — Forrest's Norfolk Va. 71
Meade's Old Churches of Virginia
Hanson — Am. Ancestry vi, 64; vii, 148
Austin's Allied Families 120-3
Caverno Genealogy 22-6
Cogswell's Hist. Nottingham N. H. 693-6
Cogswell Genealogy 140
Eaton's History of Thomaston Me. ii, 252
Hanson's Old Kent Md. 99 et seq.
Hubbard's Stanstead Co. Canada 315-17
Lee Genealogy (1895) 157-9
Little's History of Weare N. H. 895
New Eng. Hist. and Gen. Reg. vi, 329-32
Savage's Genealogical Dictionary ii, 352
Wentworth Genealogy ii, 23
Hapgood — Hapgood Genealogy (1859)
Hapgood Genealogy new ed. (1898) 590 p.
Hudson's Marlborough 375
Morse's Grout Genealogy 65-9
Morse's Gen. Register ii, (1859) 111-42
New Eng. Hist. and Gen. Register xvi
Savage's Genealogical Dictionary ii. 352
Stearns' History of Rindge N. H. 553
Vinton's Richardson Genealogy 497
Ward's History of Shrewsbury Mass. 306
Waterford Me. Centennial (1879)
Warren's History of Waterford Me. 253-5
Haraden — Babson's Gloucester 98
Pickering Genealogy
Harback — Bass' Braintree Vt. 147
Benedict's History of Sutton Mass. 657
Jackson's History of Newton Mass. 305
Harbaugh — American Ancestry xii
Harbaugh Genealogy (1856) 148 pages
Harbeson — Green's Kentucky Families
Paxton's Marshall Genealogy 363
Richmond Va. Standard iii, 149
Harbour — Power's Sangamon Ill. 354
Harcourt — Life of Mrs. Godolphin
Hardaway — Meade's Old Families of Va.
Hardcastle — Hardcastle Anniversary (1855) 12 pages
Hardee — American Ancestry v, 127
Harden — American Ancestry vii, 112, 256
Bellinger Genealogy (1895) 9-12
Dow's History of Hampton N. H. 743
Eaton's History of Thomaston Me. 253
Lincoln's Hist. of Hingham Mass. ii, 288
Mitchell's Hist. of Bridgewater Mass. 170
Hardenburgh — Munsell's Albany 131
Clayton's Union Co. N. J. 509, 697-9
Schoonmaker's History of Kingston N. Y.
Sylvester's History of Ulster Co. N. Y. 167
Hardenbrook — Roome Genealogy 205-21

Harder — American Ancestry ii, 51
Hardin — American Ancestry viii, 231
Bangor Me. Historical Magazine v, 194
Collins' History of Kentucky ii, 749
Green's Kentucky Families
Power's Sangamon Co. Ill. Settlers 356
Harding — American Ancestry vi, 38
Austin's R. I. Genealogical Dictionary 92
Barry's History of Hanover Mass. 316
Bradbury's Hist. Kennebunkport Me. 249
Crawford Family of Virginia 112
Daniels' History of Oxford Mass. 531
Eaton's History of Thomaston Me. 253
Freeman's History of Cape Cod ii, 366, 599
Harding Genealogy (1864) 84 pages
Jameson's Hist. of Medway Mass. 488–92
Lapham's History of Bethel Me. 556
Lincoln's Hist. of Hingham Mass. ii, 289
Morse's Genealogical Reg. iv, (1864) 3–85
Morse's Sherborn Mass. Settlers 95–8
New Eng. Hist. and Gen. Reg. xxvi, 382
Pierce's History of Gorham Me. 172
Richmond Va. Standard iii, 7; iv,9
Rich's History of Truro Mass. 535
Savage's Genealogical Dictionary ii, 353
Sheldon's History of Deerfield Mass. 181–3
Wight Genealogy 24
Wyman's Charlestown Mass. Gens. i, 464
Hardwick — Calnek's Annapolis N. S. 520
Hardy — Bangor Hist. Magazine v, 178
Bemis' History of Marlboro N. H. 516–8
Cochrane's History of Antrim N. H. 526
Cochrane's Hist. Francestown N. H. 744
Freeman's Hist. of Cape Cod Mass. ii, 157
Hayward's Hist. of Hancock N. H. 637–9
Leonard's History of Dublin N. H. 349
McKeen's History of Bradford Vt. 318–29
Merrill's History of Acworth N. H. 226
Morrison's History of Windham N. H. 557
Peirce Genealogy by West (1894)
Poor's Merrimack Valley 113, 123-6, 160
Savage's Genealogical Dictionary ii, 355
Temple's Hist. of N. Brookfield Mass. 615
Woodbury's Groveland Mass. Epit. 27–39
Worcester's History of Hollis N. H. 376
Hare — American Ancestry i, 36
Kidder's Hist. of New Ipswich N. H. 383
Stearns' Hist. of Ashburnham Mass. 729
Harford — Cleveland's Yates Co. 287
Harger — Orcutt's Derby Ct. 724–6
Orcutt's History of Stratford Ct. 1211
Hargill — Austin's R. I. Gen. Dict. 92
Hargis — Power's Sangamon Ill. 361
Hargreaves — Bouton Genealogy 204
Haring — American Ancestry iv, 152
Green's Todd Genealogy
Harker — Savage's Gen. Dictionary ii, 536
Harkness — American Ancestry viii, 59
Ballou Genealogy 421–5
Bassett's History of Richmond N. H. 402–6
Southwick Genealogy 364-6, 531–5
Harlakenden — Darling Memorial
Harlakenden chart by Jones (1863) 17x22
New Eng. Historical Register x, 129; xiv,
319; xv, 327–9; xlvi, 368
Paige's History of Cambridge Mass. 574

Prentice Genealogy 415
Walworth's Hyde Genealogy ii, 1162–74
Harlan — American Ancestry vii, 18
Futhey's History of Chester Co. Pa. 587
Jackson Genealogy 125
Power's Sangamon Co. Ill. Settlers 362
Harland — Perkins' Norwich Ct. 470
Harley — Cushman's Sheepscott 388
Harlow — Am. Ancestry iii, 193; vii, 88
Bangor Historical Mag. iii, 199; iv, 98
Davis' Landmarks of Plymouth Mass.
124–9
Hemenway's Vermont Hist. Gaz. v
Hubbard's History of Springfield Vt. 320–4
Lapham's History of Paris Me. 623–5
Lincoln's Hist. of Hingham Mass. ii, 290
New Eng. Hist. and Gen. Reg. xiv, 227–33
Pierce's Biographical Contributions
Saunderson's Charlestown N. H. 388
Ward's History of Shrewsbury Mass. 329
Winsor's History of Duxbury Mass. 264
Harman — American Ancestry ix, 25
New Eng. Hist. and Gen. Reg. xxxi, 165
Savage's Genealogical Dictionary ii, 357
Harmanson — Am. Hist. Mag. of Nash-
ville (1896)
Harmer — Meade's Old Families of Va.
Harmon — American Ancestry ii, 52; xii
Atkin's History of Hawley Mass. 59
Harmon Reunion Souvenir (1896) 18 pages
Harmon chart (1898) 30x36 inches
Hollister's History of Pawlet Vt. 197–9
Machias Me. Centennial 165
Power's Sangamon Co. Ill. Settlers 357
Ridlon's Harrison Me. Settlers 76–81
Smith's History of Sunderland Mass. 391–4
Stackpole's History of Durham Me. 194–7
Temple's Hist. of N. Brookfield Mass. 616
Worden Genealogy 65–8
Harndel — Austin's R. I. Gen. Dict. 93
Harnden — Eaton's Reading Mass. 85
Washington N. H. History 463–5
Harney — Temple's Whately Mass. 241
Harper — Bowie Genealogy 189
Browne Family Notes (1887) 40 pages
Freeman's Hist. of Cape Cod Mass. ii, 68
Futhey's History of Chester Co. Pa. 588
Gould's History of Delaware Co. N. Y. 30–3
Lapham's History of Rumford Me. 343
Power's Sangamon Co. Ill. Settlers 361
Runnel's Hist. Sanbornton N. H. ii, 326–8
Stearns' Hist. of Ashburnham Mass. 729
Stiles' History of Windsor Ct. ii, 365
Harral — American Ancestry xii
Harriman — American Ancestry vi, 164
Bangor Me. Historical Magazine vii, 175
Clayton's Hist. of Union Co. N. J. 198–201
Cogswell's History of Henniker N. H. 610
Davis' History of Wallingford Ct. 787
Dow's History of Hampton N. H. 744
Eaton's Annals of Warren Me. 548
Essex Institute Hist. Collections xxi, 101–6
Fullonton's Hist. Raymond N. H. 234–40
Gage's History of Rowley Mass. 442
Herrick Genealogy (1885) 279–81
Lamb Genealogy (1900) 12–24

Savage's Genealogical Dictionary ii, 358
Washington N. H. History 465
Harrington — American Ancestry v, 120;
ix, 99, 110; xi, 32
Aylsworth Genealogy 64, 456-64
Barry's History of Framingham Mass. 270
Bemis' History of Marlboro N. H. 518-20
Bond's History of Watertown 786, 272-84
Chandler's History of Shirley Mass. 431-3
Cleveland's Hist. of Yates Co. N. Y. 612-4
Cutter's History of Arlington Mass. 256
Draper's History of Spencer Mass. 209
Eaton's History of Thomaston Me. ii, 254
Hayward's History of Hancock N. H. 639
Heywood's Hist. Westminster Mass. 684-7
Hudson's Hist. of Lexington Mass. 89-99
Hudson's Marlborough Mass. 397-401
Leland Genealogy 52
Locke Genealogy 47, 93, etc.
Norton's Hist. of Fitzwilliam N. H. 592-4
Pierce's History of Grafton Mass. 501-4
Savage's Genealogical Dictionary ii, 259
Temple's Hist. of N. Brookfield Mass. 616
Wall's Reminis. of Worcester Mass. 361
Ward's Hist. of Shrewsbury Mass. 317-23
Warren and Clarke Genealogy 87-9
Williams' History of Danby Vt. 157-60
Worcester Mag. and Hist. Journal 327
Wyman's Charlestown Mass. Gens. i, 466
Young's Hist. Chautauqua Co. N. Y. 601
See also Hearnden and Herrington
Harris — American Ancestry i, 36; ii, 52;
iii, 114; iv, 120; v, 118, 149; vi, 94,
146; x, 103
Austin's Ancestral Dictionary 24
Austin's Allied Families 125
Austin's Ancestries 29
Austin's R. I. Gen. Dictionary 310-5
Babson's History of Gloucester Mass. 240
Barry's History of Framingham Mass. 271
Bassett's History of Richmond N. H. 406-9
Bond's Hist. of Watertown Mass. 284, 787
Brown's West Simsbury Ct. Settlers 70
Butler Genealogy (1888) 86-134
Calnek's History of Annapolis N. S. 521 5
Caulkins' History of New London Ct. 269
Chandler's History of Shirley Mass. 432-4
Chute Genealogy, appendix, 90-7
Cochrane's Hist. Francestown N. H. 745
Coe and Ward Memorial 68-70
Coffin's History of Boscawen N. H. 554
Corliss' North Yarmouth Me. 1172-4
Daniels' History of Oxford Mass. 531-4
Davis' History of Bucks County Pa. 235
Eaton's History of Thomaston Me. ii, 255
Egle's Notes and Queries 1st ser. i, 3-5;
3d ser. i, 259-63, 332-5, 351-4, 372-7;
4th ser. i, 197-9
Ely Genealogy 314-6
Essex Mass. Inst. Hist. Colls. xxi, 106-10
Gage's History of Rowley Mass. 443
Hammatt Papers of Ipswich Mass. 124-7
Harris' Biog. Hist. of Lancaster Co. Pa.
Harris Family of Roxbury (1861) 56 pages
Harris Fam. of N. London Ct. (1878) 239 p.
Harris, Memoir of T. W. (1882) 14 pages

Harris Family of Ipswich (1883) 135 pages
Harris Ancestors in N. Eng. (1887) 32 p.
Harris Family of N. J. (1888) 350 pages
Harris Family of Virginia (1893) chart
Howell's Hist. of Southampton N. Y. 282-4
Hudson's History of Lexington Mass. 99
Huntting's Hist. of Pine Plains N. Y. 351-4
Joslin's History of Poultney Vt. 270
Kingsman's No. Bridgewater Mass. 522
Lapham's History of Bethel Me. 557
Maine Historical Magazine viii, 173
Mass. Hist. Society Proceedings (1882)
Miller's Hist. Colchester Co. N. S. 234-7
Mitchell's Hist. Bridgewater Mass. 171-4
Morris (Richard) Genealogy 114
Morrison's Hist. Windham N. H. 558-63
Narragansett Historical Register ii, 292
New Eng. Hist. Gen. Reg. ii, 218; xxv, 185
Norton's Hist. of Fitzwilliam N. H. 594-6
Preble Genealogy 248-50
Randall's Hist. Chesterfield N. H. 329-36
Read's History of Swanzey N. H. 362
Richardson's Woonsocket R. I. 233-8
Richmond Va. Standard ii, 27, 36, 46-9
Robertson's Pocahontas' Descendants
Runnel's Hist. of Sanbornton N. H. ii, 328
Saunder's Alabama Settlers 269, 511
Savage's Genealogical Dictionary ii, 360-6
Stark's History of Dunbarton N. H. 207
Stearns' History of Ashburnham 730-7
Temple's Hist. of N. Brookfield Mass. 617
Thomas Genealogy (1877) 87
Walworth's Hyde Genealogy 126, 546-9
Ward's History of Shrewsbury Mass. 325
Washington N. H. History 466-8
Wheeler's History of Newport N. H. 409
Whitmore's Copps Hill Epitaphs
Wyman's Charlestown Mass. i, 467-75
Young's History of Wayne Co. Ind. 218
Harriss — Goode Genealogy 231-3
Harrison — American Ancestry ii, 52; iii,
172; iv, 159; vi, 28; ix, 90; xii, 107
Anderson's Waterbury Ct. i, app. 61
Balch's Provincial Papers Pa. 131-3
Baldwin's Genealogical Supp. 1060-4
Bronson's History of Waterbury Ct. 495
Cabell Genealogy 515-31
Campbell's History of Virginia 654
Carter Family Tree of Virginia
Condit Genealogy 365-70
Dwight Genealogy 675, 723-5
Egle's Notes and Queries 3d ser. iii, 179-82
Glenn's Colonial Mansions 426-9
Gold's History of Cornwall Ct. 298-303
Goode Genealogy 113, 379, 478, 486
Harrison Ancestry (1893) 96 pages
Hayden's Virginia Genealogies 510-13
Lynchburg Va. Sketches 94-6
Magazine of American History xxi, 403-9
Meade's Old Churches of Virginia i, 311
Missouri Pioneer Families 341
Montague Genealogy 62
Munsey's Magazine 1896
New Jersey Hist. Coll. vi, supp. 119
Orcutt's History of Wolcott Ct. 490-6
Page Genealogy 97, 130, 224, 245

Power's Sangamon Co. Ill. Settlers 358–60
Richmond Va. Critic (1888)
Richmond Va. Standard ii, 24–9, 38, 41
Robertson's Pocahontas' Descendants
Savage's Genealogical Dictionary ii, 366
Slaughter's Bristol 28, 170, 177, 188, 230
Symmes Genealogy 89–92, 118–21
Timlow's Southington Ct. Sketches 130
Waddell's Annals of Augusta Co. Va. 415
White Genealogy (1879) 159–64
Whitehead's Perth Amboy N. J. 86–90
Whittemore's Orange N. J. 70
Wyman's Charlestown Mass. Gens. 475–7
Harry — Bowie Genealogy 421
Harsha — American Ancestry i, 36
Harshberger — Hertzler Gen. 19–24
Harssen — Albany Collections iv, 131
Hart — American Ancestry i, 36; ii, 52;
   v, 131, 140, 176; viii, 112; x, 6, 39
Andrews' New Britain Ct. 149–51, 170–91
Austin's Ancestral Dictionary 26
Austin's R. I. Genealogical Dictionary 314
Bangor Me. Historical Magazine vi, 93
Bolton's Westchester Co. N. Y. ii, 735
Caldwell Genealogy 66
Cooley's Trenton N. J. Gens. 95–119
Davis' History of Wallingford Ct. 787–9
Gold's History of Cornwall Ct. 305–12
Gregg's History of Old Cheraws 67, 105
Hammatt Papers of Ipswich Mass. 131
Hart Family of Bucks Co. Pa. (1867) 159 p.
Hart Family of Conn. (1875) 606 pages
Hart Family of Virginia (1882) 82 pages
Hayward's Hist. of Hancock N. H. 639–41
Lewis' History of Lynn Mass. 227
Littell's Passaic Valley Genealogies 179
Little's History of Weare N. H. 897
Morris Genealogy (1853) 38
New York Gen. and Biog. Rec. xv, 108–11;
   xxi, 36–9; xxvi, 170–7
Orcutt's History of Torrington Ct. 709
Poore Genealogy 131–4
Preston Genealogy (1870) 40–2
Savage's Genealogical Dictionary ii, 367
Sibley's History of Union Me. 459
Timlow's Southington Ct. Sketches 107–30
Tupper's So. Carolina Baptist Ch. 26–32
Tuttle Genealogy 657
Whitmore's Copps Hill Epitaphs
Worthen's History of Sutton N. H. 740–4
Hartford — Wentworth Gen. i, 171–4
Harthorn — Cogswell's Henniker 611
Hudson's Hist. of Marlborough Mass. 378
Washington N. H. History 468
Hartley — American Ancestry iii, 165
Life of R. M. Hartley (1882)
Hartpence — Leach's Morton Ancestry
Hartram — Chambers' N. J. Germans
Hartranft — Kriebel's Schwenkfelders 5
Hartshorn — Anderson's Waterbury i, 61
Cleveland's History of Yates Co. N. Y. 504
Hayward's History of Hancock N. H. 641
Hill's Dedham Mass. Records i
Johnston's History of Cecil Co. Md. 535
Livermore's History of Wilton N. H. 391
Secomb's History of Amherst N. H. 613–9

Sylvester's History of Ulster Co. N. Y. 272
Walworth's Hyde Genealogy 157, 725–9
Whittemore's Hist. Middlesex Co. Ct. 486
Hartshorne — Eaton's Reading 85–7
New York Gen. and Biog. Rec. xiv, 95
Salter's Hist. Monmouth Co. N. Y. xxxiii
Shotwell Genealogy 16, 196
Hartwell — American Ancestry v, 20
Brown's Bedford Mass. Families 14–7
Butler's History of Groton Mass. 405
Chandler's Hist. of Shirley Mass. 435–43
Cleveland's Hist. Yates Co. N. Y. 479–81
Cochrane's History of Antrim N. H. 527
Cutter's History of Arlington Mass. 257
Daniels' History of Oxford Mass. 534–6
Hartwell Family Reunion (1885) 15 pages
Hartwell Family Reunion (1891) 19 pages
Hartwell Genealogy (1887) 197 pages
Hartwell Genealogy (1895) 176 pages
Heywood's Hist. of Westminster Mass. 687
Hudson's History of Lexington Mass. 99
Kingsman's No. Bridgewater Mass. 530
Mitchell's Hist. of Bridgewater Mass. 174
North's History of Augusta Me. 881
Norton's Hist. of Fitzwilliam N. H. 596–8
Potter's Concord Mass. Families 10, 101
Savage's Genealogical Dictionary ii, 369
Stone's Hist. of Hubbardston Mass. 287–9
Winchell Genealogy 251
Wyman's Charlestown Mass. Gens. i, 478
Hartzell — Plumb's Hanover Pa. 423
Harvard — Harvard Genealogy (1885) 46 p.
New Eng. Hist. Register xl, 362–80
Harvell — Secomb's Amherst 619–21
Harvey — Am. Anc. ii, 52; vi, 24; vii, 76
Babson's Hist. of Gloucester Mass. 99–104
Bemis' History of Marlboro N. H. 520–3
Cochrane's Hist. Francestown N. H. 746
Cogswell's Hist. Nottingham 209–13, 696–9
Corliss' North Yarmouth Me. Magazine
Davis' Landmarks of Plymouth Mass. 129
Futhey's History of Chester Co. Pa. 591
Green's Kentucky Families
Harvey Genealogy (1899) 1057 pages
Heywood's Hist. Westminster Mass. 688–90
Hoyt's Salisbury Mass. Families 195
Hyde's History of Brimfield Mass. 473
Mitchell's Hist. of Bridgewater Mass. 174
New Eng. Hist. and Gen. Reg. xii, 313–5
Power's Sangamon Co. Ill. Settlers 363
Randall's Hist. Chesterfield N. H. 336–40
Read's History of Swanzey N. H. 363
Runnel's Hist. of Sanbornton N. H. ii, 329
Savage's Genealogical Dictionary ii, 369
Sedgwick's History of Sharon Ct. 88
Sheldon's History of Deerfield Mass. 184
Smith's History of Sunderland Mass. 394–6
Temple's History of Northfield Mass. 456
Temple's History of Palmer Mass. 488
Worthen's History of Sutton N. H. 745–63
Harvie — Gilmer's Georgians 62, 139
Green's Kentucky Families
Meade's Old Families of Virginia
Paxton's Marshall Genealogy 207
Harwood — Am. Anc. ix, 204, 207; xi, 115
Bass' History of Braintree Vt. 147–9

Benedict's History of Sutton Mass. 658
Craft's History of Whately Mass. 497-9
Daniels' History of Oxford Mass. 536-8
Davis Genealogy 45
Fox's History of Dunstable Mass. 245
Harwood Genealogy (1879) 33 pages
Harwood Genealogy 2d ed. (1896) 104 p.
Holton's Winslow Genealogy i, 295
Jennings' History of Bennington Vt.
Montague Genealogy 341-7
Read Genealogy (1895) 153-7
Richmond Va. Standard ii, 32; iii, 36
Robinson and Harwood Gen. (1837) 96 p.
Savage's Genealogical Dictionary ii, 370
Temple's North Brookfield Mass. 617-20
Temple's History of Whately Mass. 241
Virginia Magazine (1894) ii, 183-5
Washburn's History of Leicester Mass. 374
Worthen's History of Sutton N. H. 764
Harzen — Albany Collections iv, 131
Hasbrouck — American Ancestry vi, 63,
    142; viii, 203; ix, 58; xi, 33
New York Gen. and Biog. Rec. xvii, 261-7
Ruttenber's Newburgh N. Y. 278-81
Ruttenber's Orange County N. Y. 369-71
Schoonmaker's Hist. Kingston N. Y. 480
Sylvester's History of Ulster Co. N. Y. 86
Hascall — Hollister's Pawlet Vt. 199
Strong Genealogy 132-6
Hasell — Am. Ancestry ix, 174; x, 48
New York Gen. and Biog. Rec. xxiii, 147-9
See also under Lazell
Haseltine — Am. Anc. viii, 27; x, 173; xii
Bouton's History of Concord N. H. 709
Chase's History of Chester N. H. 539-42
Essex Inst. Hist. Collections xxi, 110-2
Goodwin's History of Buxton Me. 219
Haseltine Chart (1890) 12 x 18 inches
Livermore's History of Wilton N. H. 400-2
Morrison's Hist. Windham N. H. 568-74
Secomb's History of Amherst N. H. 625-7
Haselton — Lapham's Bethel Me. 558
Hasey — Bangor Historical Mag. iv, 122
Haskell — Am. Ancestry i, 36: vii, 76
Babson's Hist. of Gloucester Mass. 99-104
Bemis' History of Marlboro N. H. 525-7
Chandler's History of Shirley Mass. 443
Corliss' North Yarmouth Me. Magazine
Daniels' History of Oxford Mass. 538
Eaton's Annals of Warren Me. 548
Eaton's History of Thomaston Me. ii, 256
Essex Inst. Hist. Collections xxxii, 133-95
Haskell Fam. Tree by W. O. Haskell 1880
Haskell Genealogy (1896) 63 p. reprint
Haskell Magazine (1898) 100 pages
Hubbard's Hist. of Springfield Vt. 324-7
Norton's History of Fitzwilliam N. H. 598
Ridlon's Harrison Me. Settlers 74-6
Savage's Genealogical Dictionary ii, 371
Spooner Genealogy i, 65, 119-27
Stiles' History of Windsor Ct. ii, 368
Temple's Hist. N. Brookfield Mass. 620-2
Vinton Genealogy 251
White Genealogy (1872) 65-78
Haskett — Austin's Allied Families 127
Driver Genealogy 281

Haskins — American Ancestry ii, 53
Davis' Landmarks of Plymouth Mass. 130
Haskins' Emerson Ancestors 2-27
Paige's History of Hardwick Mass. 391
Temple's Hist. N. Brookfield Mass. 622
Warren's History of Waterford Me. 255
Williams' History of Danby Vt. 159-61
Hasley — Kulp's Wyoming Valley
Hassam — American Ancestry iii, 69-71
Hassam Genealogy (1870) 10 pages
Hassam Genealogy (1880) 12 pages
Hassam Genealogy (1896) 11 pages
New Eng. Hist. Reg. xxiv, 414-22; xliii, 320
Saunderson's Charlestown N. H. 390-2
Hassell — Fox's Dunstable Mass. 245
Paige's History of Cambridge Mass. 574
Savage's Genealogical Dictionary ii, 372
Hassler — American Ancestry xii, 109
Nourse Genealogy 118-22
Hasson — Bouton Genealogy 196-8
Hastings — Adams Genealogy (1880) 56-66
American Ancestry xii, 53
Barry's History of Framingham Mass. 271
Bemis' History of Marlboro N. H. 523-5
Bond's Watertown Mass. 285-95, 789-93
Cochrane's History of Antrim N. H. 528
Cochrane's Hist. Francestown N. H. 748
Corliss Genealogy
Daniels' History of Oxford Mass. 538
Eaton's History of Thomaston Me. ii, 257
Hastings Genealogy (1866) 183 pages
Hudson's Hist. of Lexington Mass. 100-3
Jackson's History of Newton Mass. 305-7
Judd's History of Hadley Mass. 505-9
Kellogg's White Genealogy 100
Lapham's History of Bethel Me. 558-60
Maine Genealogist iii (1877) 33-44
New Eng. Hist. Reg. xiii, 134; xxi, 350-2
Paige's History of Cambridge Mass. 575-9
Paige's History of Hardwick Mass. 392-4
Paul's History of Wells Vt. 102
Poor's Merrimack Valley 130-4, 152-8
Randall's Hist. Chesterfield N. H. 340-3
Saunderson's Charlestown N. H. 392-9
Savage's Genealogical Dictionary ii, 372-5
Secomb's History of Amherst N. H. 622
Sheldon's Hist. Deerfield Mass. 185-8, 401-8
Stearns' Hist. Ashburnham Mass. 737-41
Stearns' History of Rindge N. H. 555
Temple's History of Northfield Mass. 457
Temple's History of Palmer Mass. 480-2
Thurston Genealogy (1892) 421
Ward's History of Shrewsbury Mass. 301-4
Wyman's Charlestown Mass. Gens. i, 480
Hasty — Libby Genealogy 55
Ridlon's Saco Valley Me. Families 725-7
Stackpole's History of Durham Me. 198
Haswell — Peirce Genealogy (1894)
Hatch — Am. Anc. ii, 53; vi, 9, 81, 118
Ballou's History of Milford Mass. 787
Bangor Me. Historical Magazine viii, 37
Boyd's Annals of Winchester Ct. 190
Cochrane's History of Antrim N. H. 529
Corliss' North Yarmouth Me. Magazine
Davis' Landmarks of Plymouth Mass. 130
Deane's History of Scituate Mass. 279

Draper's History of Spencer Mass. 210
Eaton's History of Thomaston Me. ii, 258
Farrow's Hist. Islesborough Me. 217-23
Freeman's Hist. of Cape Cod ii, 438, 473
Hanover Mass. Records (1898)
Hatch Family of Scituate (1874) 23 pages
Hatch Family of Hartford (1879) 36 pages
Hatch Family of Boston (1896) 7 pages
Hatch Genealogy (1879) 36 pages
Hatch's History of Industry Me. 638-42
Hayward's History of Hancock N. H. 1052
Lancaster's History of Lancaster N. H. 272
Lapham's History of Norway Me. 519
Loomis Genealogy (1880) 634
Mitchell's Hist. of Bridgewater Mass. 175
Montague Genealogy 85
N. E. Hist. Gen. Reg. xiv, 197-9; li, 34-8
Paige's History of Hardwick Mass. 394
Pierce's History of Gorham Me. 174
Rich's History of Truro Mass. 535
Savage's Genealogical Dictionary ii, 375
Sedgwick's History of Sharon Ct. 89
Swift's Barnstable Families i, 461-73
Tanner Genealogy 66-70
Waldo's History of Tolland Ct. 89-92
Wheeler's History of Newport N. H. 411
Winslow Genealogy ii, 740-4
Young's History of Warsaw N. Y. 275
Hatcher — Va. Mag. of Hist. v, 98-100
Hatfield — American Ancestry ii, 53
Clute's History of Staten Island N. Y. 387
Hatfield's Elizabeth N. J. 76-8
Strong Genealogy 387
Temple's Hist. of N. Brookfield Mass. 623
Hathaway — Am. Ancestry ii, 53; x, 128
Bangor Me. Historical Magazine iii, 28
Cleveland's Hist. of Yates Co. N. Y. 113-7
Davis' Landmarks of Plymouth Mass. 130
Hathaway Genealogy (1869) 43 pages
Hemenway's Vermont Gaz. iv, 139-42
Holton's Winslow Genealogy i, 243-53
Lapham's History of Norway Me. 519
Lapham's History of Paris Me. 625-7
New Eng. Hist. and Gen. Reg. xxxii, 236
Paige's History of Hardwick Mass. 394-6
Ricketson's Hist. New Bedford Mass. 185
Ruttenber's Hist. of Newburgh N. Y. 313
Ruttenber's Hist. of Orange Co. N. Y. 405
Savage's Genealogical Dictionary ii, 376
Slafter Genealogy 25-7
Spooner Genealogy i, 186-97
Swift's Barnstable Families i, 457-61
Winsor's History of Duxbury Mass. 266
Hatheway — Benedict's Sutton 658
Dwight Genealogy 924-6
Hill's Lawrence-Townley Estate 13-5
Morris Genealogy (1853) 74-80
Hatherly — Deane's Scituate 280-2
Hathorn — Bangor Hist. Mag. vi, 153-5
Hathorne — Eaton's Thomaston 260
Essex Mass. Inst. Hist. Colls. xvii, 153-5
Hathorn Pedigree 9x11 inches
New Eng. Hist. and Gen. Reg. xlii, 363
Hatler — Power's Sangamon Ill. 364
Hatt — Whittemore's Orange N. J. 404
Haugh — Eaton's Reading Mass. 87

Haughton — Baker's Montville Ct. 486-8
Caulkins' New London Ct. 299
Hudson's History of Lexington Mass. 106
Savage's Genealogical Dictionary ii, 378
Haughwout—Alexander Genealogy 162-4
Clute's History of Staten Island N. Y. 388
Haupt — Kratz Genealogy 205-7
Hauxhurst — N. Y. Gen. Rec. xxvi, 19
Havard — Walker Genealogy (1896) 171-9
Haven — Ballou's Milford Mass. 788
Barry's Hist. of Framingham Mass. 272-81
Bemis' History of Marlboro N. H. 527
Benedict's History of Sutton Mass. 659
Haven Genealogy (1843) 104 pages
Haven Family Meeting (1844) 27 pages
Haven Family Meeting (1849) 28 pages
Hemenway's Vermont Hist. Gaz. v, 33
Leland Genealogy 49
Morse's Sherborn Mass. Settlers 99
Norton's History of Fitzwilliam N. H. 599
Savage's Genealogical Dictionary ii, 378
Stearns' Hist. of Ashburnham Mass. 741
Temple's Hist. of N. Brookfield Mass. 623
Wakefield Genealogy 158
Ward's History of Shrewsbury Mass. 330-2
Wheeler's History of Croydon N. H. 112
Wheeler's History of Newport N. H. 412-4
Havener — Eaton's Thomaston 259
Havens — Austin's R. I. Cen. Dict. 93
Cleveland's Yates Co. N. Y. 288-90
Dwight Strong Genealogy 603
Ellis Genealogy 136
Lamb's History of N. Y. City 507
Mallmann's Shelter Island N. Y. 163-76, 239-92
Prime Genealogy (1895) 46
Haviland — American Ancestry ii, 53
Baird's History of Rye N. Y. 475
Pelletreau's Westchester Wills 399-410
Hawes — American Ancestry i, 36; v, 128
Blake's History of Franklin Mass. 529
Cochrane's History of Antrim N. H. 529
Corliss' North Yarmouth Me. 841-4
Daniels' History of Oxford Mass. 539
Dedham Mass. Historical Register i, 60
Farrington Memorial, app. 49
Freeman's History of Cape Cod Mass. ii, 202
Hawes Genealogy (1895) 28 pages
Hill's Dedham Mass. Records i
Joslin's History of Poultney Vt. 272
Leland Genealogy 268
Morse's Sherborn Mass. Settlers 99
Savage's Genealogical Dictionary ii, 379
Sibley's History of Union Me. 459-64
Wentworth Genealogy i, 345-9
Hawk — Eaton's Thomaston Me. 259
Hawke — Hawke, Robt. Memorial (1880)
Lincoln's Hist. of Hingham Mass. ii, 294
Savage's Genealogical Dictionary ii, 380-2
Hawkes — American Ancestry vi, 119
Atkins' History of Hawley Mass. 66
Baker Genealogy (1867) 50-2
Essex Mass. Inst. Hist. Coll. xxiv, 161-80
Hawkes Genealogy (1887) 20 pages, reprint
Judd's History of Hadley Mass. 509

Hawkins — Adams' Fairhaven 391-4
American Ancestry xi, 85, xii
Austin's R. I. Gen. Dictionary 94, 316
Bond's Watertown Mass. Genealogies 295
Dimock's Coventry Ct. Records 55
Garrard Genealogy 77-81
Green's Kentucky Families
Hubbard's History of Springfield Vt. 327
Lapham's History of Norway Me. 520
Leavenworth Genealogy 107
Livermore's History of Wilton N. H. 393-6
Meade's Old Churches of Virginia
Morrison's History of Windham N. H. 574
New York Gen. and Biog. Rec. xvii, 259
Norton's History of Knox Co. Ohio 360
Orcutt's History of Derby Ct. 726
Orcutt's History of New Milford Ct. 709
Savage's Genealogical Dictionary ii, 382-4
Stiles' History of Windsor Ct. ii, 369
Wheeler's Eminent N. Carolinians 450
Wheeler's History of N. Carolina 426
Wyman's Charlestown Mass. Gens. i, 482
Young's Hist. Chautauqua Co. N. Y. 420
Young's History of Wayne Co. Ind. 341
Hawkridge — Cotton Genealogy 11
Hawks — American Ancestry xii
Barrus' Goshen Mass. 147
Sheldon's Hist. of Deerfield Mass. 188-99
White's Discourse Charlemont Mass. 42
Hawksworth — Penn. Mag. x, 100-3
Hawley — Am. Anc. ii, 53; vi, 129; xii
Freeman's Hist. Cape Cod Mass. ii, 69, 139
Futhey's History of Chester Co. Pa. 593
Hawley Family of Marblehead (1887) 8 p.
Hawley Genealogy (1890) 608 pages
Hawley Family of Marblehead (1897) 16 p.
Hughes Genealogy 211-7
Judd's History of Hadley Mass. 509
Middlefield Ct. History
Neill's Virginia Carolorum 142
New York Gen. and Biog. Rec. xvi, 160
Orcutt's History of New Milford Ct. 709
Orcutt's History of Stratford Ct. 1212-8
Power's Sangamon Co. Ill. Settlers 364
Salem N. Y. Book of History 59
Savage's Genealogical Dictionary ii, 384
Strong Genealogy 1435
Temple's History of Whately Mass. 35
Todd's History of Redding Ct. 195
Walworth's Hyde Genealogy 780
Young's Hist. of Chautauqua Co. N. Y. 363
Hawn — Power's Sangamon Co. Ill. 365
Hawthorne — Hathorne Pedigree
Savage's Genealogical Dictionary ii, 377
Hawver — American Ancestry ii, 53
Hawxhurst — Amer. Ancestry x, 73
Haxall — Hayden's Virg. Genealogies 582
Slaughter's Bristol Parish Va. 178-81
Hay — Bond's Watertown Mass. 295
Eaton's History of Reading Mass. 91
Egle's Penn. Genealogies 2d ed. 334-40
Heywood's Hist. Westminster Mass. 690
Richmond Va. Standard ii, 45
Wyman's Charlestown Mass. Gens. 483-7
Hayden — Am. Anc. iv, 135; viii, 156; xii, 57
Anderson's Waterbury Ct. i, app. 62

Bangor Me. Historical Magazine vii, 135
Binney Genealogy 30
Boyd's Annals of Winchester Ct. 273
Crafts Genealogy 271
Eaton's History of Thomaston Me. ii, 260
Faxon Genealogy 52
Hayden Family of Conn. (1859) 15 pages
Hayden Family of Mass. (1877) 46 pages
Hayden Family of Conn. (1885) 20 pages
Hayden Family of Conn. (1888) 329 pages
Hayden's Weitzel Genealogy (1883)
Hayden's Virginia Genealogies 26
Hayes' Wells Genealogy 145-50
Kingman's No. Bridgewater Mass. 521
Lapham's History of Norway Me. 521
Loomis' Genealogy (1880) 591, 736-9
Marshall's Grant Ancestry 114-8
Mitchell's Hist. of Bridgewater Mass. 176
Morris' Bontecou Genealogy 147
Norton's Hist. of Fitzwilliam N. H. 600-2
Orcutt's History of Torrington Ct. 710-2
Pompey N. Y. Reunion 313-8
Savage's Genealogical Dictionary ii, 386
Stearns' Hist. of Ashburnham Mass. 742
Stiles' History of Windsor Ct. ii, 369-83
Thayer Memorial (1835) 72-4
Vinton Genealogy 323-30
Wyman's Charlestown Mass. Gens. i, 488
Hayderschatt — Amer. Ancestry ix, 24
Haydock — Bunker's L. I. Gens. 216
Hayes — American Ancestry ii, 53; iii, 25, 161; ix, 148; xii, 33, 55
Bangor Me. Historical Magazine ii, 11
Burnham's History of Brattleboro Vt. 67
Chapman's Trowbridge Genealogy 42
Corliss' N. Yarmouth Me. Mag. 299-301
Futhey's History of Chester Co. Pa. 593-5
Goode Genealogy 83-5
Hatch's History of Industry Me. 642-7
Hayes Genealogy (1876) 76 pages
Hayes Genealogy 2d ed. (1883) 84 pages
Hayes Genealogy 3d ed. (1884) 354 pages
Hayes' Wells Genealogy 150-8
Hemenway's Vermont Hist. Gaz. v, 67
Hurd's Rockingham Co. N. H. 632-6
Maine Hist. and Gen. Recorder iii, 118-20
New Eng. Hist. and Gen. Reg. vi, 333; xxvii, 79-81; xxxvi, 387-93
Potts Genealogy (1895) 337-40
Richmond Va. Standard iii, 45
Runnel's Sanbornton N. H. ii, 330-3
Savage's Genealogical Dictionary ii, 387
Selleck's Norwalk Ct. (1896) 85-91
Smith's History of Delaware Co. Pa. 467
Stiles' History of Windsor Ct. ii, 383-5
Wentworth Gen. i, 223-36, 429-31, 675-8
Hayford — Faxon Genealogy 60-2
Lawrence and Bartlett Mem. 104-6, 155
Hayhurst — American Ancestry ix, 112
Hayley — See Haley
Haymaker — Olin Gen. by Nye (1892) 123-46
Hayman — American Ancestry iv, 75
Savage's Genealogical Dictionary ii, 388
Wyman's Charlestown Mass. Gens. i, 489
Haymond — Sharpless Genealogy 323

Hayner — American Ancestry ii, 53
Haynes — Am. Anc. i, 36; vi, 138; ix, 28
Bangor Me. Historical Magazine iv, 21
Caulkins History of New London Ct. 309
Chapman's Folsom Genealogy 188
Corliss Genealogy 241
Corliss' North Yarmouth Me. Magazine
Darling Memorial
Farrow's History of Islesborough Me. 223
Frisbie's History of Middlebury Vt. 35-7
Haynes Genealogy (1895) 8 p. reprint
Haynes Genealogy, see Haines
Howell's Hist. of Southampton N. Y. 284-7
Hyde's History of Brimfield Mass. 408
Meade's Old Churches of Virginia
Moore's American Governors i, 311
New Eng. Hist. and Gen. Reg ix, 349-51;
    xxiv, 125, 442; xxxii, 310-2; xlvii,
    71-5; xlix, 304-10
Porter's Hartford Ct. Settlers 6
Roome Genealogy 253
Savage's Genealogical Dictionary ii, 388-91
Smith's History of Dutchess Co. N. Y. 501
Stearns' Hist. of Ashburnham Mass. 755
Temple's History of Palmer Mass. 491-3
Walworth's Hyde Genealogy 1170
Washington N. H. History 468
Hays — American Ancestry xii, 54
Clyde's Irish Settlers 54-9, 387-97
Egle's Hist. Reg. of Interior Pa. i, 208-13
Egle's Penn. Genealogies 2d ed. 334-40
Goode Genealogy 83-5
Humphrey Genealogy 368
McAllister Genealogy 53-7
Hayward — American Ancestry iv, 35;
    v, 148; vi, 37; viii, 86; ix, 136
Austin's Allied Families 127-9
Ballou's History of Milford Mass. 790-815
Brown's Bedford Mass. Families 17
Cochrane's History of Antrim N. H. 530
Cochrane's Hist. Francestown N. H. 748
Daniels' History of Oxford Mass. 539
Davis' Landmarks of Plymouth Mass. 131
Hayward Genealogy (1863) 1 page
Hayward Family Gathering (1879) 35 p.
Hayward's History of Gilsum N. H. 322-5
Hayward's Hist. of Hancock N. H. 641-51
Hyde's History of Brimfield Mass. 474
Kingman's N. Bridgewater Mass. 517-21
Leonard's History of Dublin N. H. 351
Lincoln's Hist. Hingham Mass. ii, 295-7
Loomis Genealogy (1880) 783
Merrill's History of Acworth N. H. 226
Mitchell's Hist. Bridgewater Mass. 176-85
Morse Mem. appendix 51¼
Potter's Concord Mass. Families 11
Savage's Genealogical Dictionary ii, 391-5
Shattuck's History of Concord Mass. 373
Stearns' Hist. of Ashburnham Mass. 742
Whitman's Genealogy 116-9
Wood Genealogy 109-15
Wyman's Charlestown Mass. Gens. i, 489
Haywood — Am. Ancestry ii, 54; xi, 199
Bond's Watertown Mass. Gens. 295
Hubbard's History of Springfield Vt. 328
Wheeler's History of N. Carolina 143

Hazard — Amer. Ancestry iv, 48; v, 201
Andrews' History of New Britain Ct. 311
Austin's Ancestral Dictionary 27
Austin's Ancestries 31
Austin's R. I. Genealogical Dictionary 320
Bartlett's Wanton Family 135
Cleveland's Hist. Yates Co. N. Y. 680-5
Field Genealogy (1895) 119
Hazard's Olden Times in R. I. (1879) 291 p.
Hazard Genealogy (1895) 293 pages
Narragansett Historical Register ii, 45-51
Pell's Howland's Journal (1890) 10, 52
Rhode Island Hist. Society Colls. iii, 312
Riker's Annals of Newtown N. Y. 332
Rodman Genealogy 73
Salisbury Family Memorials (1885) 548-51
Savage's Genealogical Dictionary ii, 395
Updyke's Narragansett Ch. 247-50, 320-2
Hazeltine — American Ancestry vii, 104
Benedict's History of Sutton Mass. 659
Crane's Rawson Family 22-7
Paige's History of Hardwick Mass.
Savage's Genealogical Dictionary ii, 395
Hazelton — Austin's R. I. Dictionary 94
Field's History of Haddam Ct. 46
Hazelton Genealogy (1892) 368 pages
New Hampshire Hist. Soc. Coll. vii, 379
Runnel's Hist. of Sanbornton N. H. ii, 333
Worcester's History of Hollis N. H. 377
Young's Hist. Chautauqua Co. N. Y. 364
Hazen—Am. Anc. ix, 32-4; xi, 213; xii, 128
Chandler's History of Shirley Mass. 445-53
Cope Genealogy 96, 195
Guild's Stiles Genealogy 385
Hemenway's Vermont Hist. Gaz. v, 33
Hazen Genealogy (1879) 7 pages
Hazen's History of Billerica Mass. 67
Hollister Genealogy 203
Little's History of Weare N. H. 898
N. E. Hist. and Gen. Reg. xxxiii, 229-36
Perley's History of Boxford Mass. 78
Slafter Genealogy 66
Tucker's History of Hartford Vt. 425-46
Worthen's History of Sutton N. H. 765
Hazlett — Marshall Genealogy (1884) 222-6
Power's Sangamon Co. Ill. Settlers 366
Heacock — Heacock Genealogy (1869) 28 p.
Robert's Old Richland Pa. Families
Sharpless Genealogy 282, 434
Sprague's Hist. of Gloversville N. Y. 118
Head — American Ancestry ii, 54
Austin's R. I. Genealogical Dictionary 94
Carter's Hist. Pembroke N. H. ii, 138-44
Chase's History of Chester N. H. 542
Eaton's Annals of Warren Me. 549
Poor's Merrimack Valley Researches 144
Runnel's Hist. of Sanbornton N. H. ii, 334
Headly — Bond's Watertown 296
Heald — American Ancestry iii, 178; vii,
    281; ix, 194, 195
Andrews Genealogy (1890) 112-4, 159
Blood's History of Temple N. H. 223-36
Chandler's History of Shirley Mass. 453
Clark's Hist. of Watertown Mass. 95, 162
Dunster Genealogy 245-8
Heald chart by Drury (1880) 11x17 inches

Hodgman's History of Westford Mass. 452
Kidder's Hist. of New Ipswich N. H. 386-8
Locke Genealogy 113
Savage's Genealogical Dictionary ii, 396
Stearns' Hist. of Ashburnham Mass. 743
Stern's Our Kindred (1885) 9-11
Stone's Hist. Hubbardston Mass. 289-91
Washington N. H. History 469-71
Whittemore's Orange N. J. 323
Healey — Barry's Framingham 281
Chase's History of Chester N. H. 543
Dow's History of Hampton N. H. 745
Eaton's Hist. of Thomaston Me. ii, 261-4
Fullonton's Hist. of Raymond N. H. 232-4
Hoyt's Salisbury Mass. Families 197
Jackson's History of Newton Mass. 307
Paige's History of Cambridge Mass. 579
Saunderson's Charlestown N. H. 399
Savage's Genealogical Dictionary ii, 396
Healy — Calnek's Annapolis N. S. 525
Daniels' History of Oxford Mass. 540
Davis Genealogy 65, 69-71
Washington N. H. History 471-6
Wight Genealogy 43
Heard — American Ancestry
Caldwell Genealogy 69
Cochrane's Hist. Francestown N. H. 749
Hammatt Papers of Ipswich Mass. 154-7
Heard Genealogy (1880) 61 pages
Hoyt's Salisbury Mass. Families 198-200
New Eng. Hist. and Gen. Reg. vii, 47-9
Otis Family of N. H. (1851)
Savage's Genealogical Dictionary ii, 397
Wentworth Genealogy i. 160, 258-62
Hearnden — Austin's R. I. Dictionary 95
See also Harrington
Hearne — American Ancestry xii
Hearne Genealogy (1899) 565 pages
Hearsay — Mitchell's Bridgewater 185
Heath — American Ancestry i, 36; ii, 54;
v, 208; xii, 6, 42
Barry's History of Framingham Mass. 233
Bass' History of Braintree Vt. 149
Butler's History of Farmington Me. 492
Chambers' Early Germans of N. J. 398-400
Cogswell's Hist. of Henniker N. H. 614-62
Crafts Genealogy 157-62
Dearborn's History of Salisbury N. H. 627
Dow's History of Hampton N. H. 744
Ellis' History of Roxbury Mass. 121
Hoyt's Salisbury Mass. Families 200-2
Hubbard's Stanstead Co. Canada 184, 311
Littell's Passaic Valley Genealogies 180
Little's History of Weare N. H. 900
Meade's Old Churches of Virginia
Runnel's Hist. of Sanbornton N. H. ii, 335
Savage's Genealogical Dictionary ii, 398
Sedgwick's History of Sharon Ct. 89
Stiles' History of Windsor Ct. ii, 386
Thompson Genealogy (1890) 177
Vinton's Giles Genealogy 122
Wheeler's History of Newport N. H. 415-7
Wood's Brookline Mass. Sketches 322
Heathcote — Heraldic Journal iii, 73
Heathcote — Bolton's Westchester
Lamb's History of New York city 409

Heathcott — Valentine's Manual (1853)
Heaton — American Ancestry ix, 55
Blake's History of Hamden Ct. 256
Childs Genealogy 539
Goodyear Genealogy 85
Hayward's History of Gilsum N. H. 325
Read's History of Swanzey N. H. 365
Savage's Genealogical Dictionary ii, 399
Tuttle Genealogy 657
Wyman's Charlestown Mass. Gens. i, 491
Heatwole—Heatwole Gen. (1882) 24 pages
Hebard — Strong Genealogy 785
Temple's Hist. of N. Brookfield Mass. 624
Hebert — N. E. Hist. Reg. li, 316-21
See also Hebard and Hibbard
Heckler — American Ancestry xii
Hedge — Davis' Landmarks 132
Kellogg's White Genealogy 59
Morris' Bontecou Genealogy 194
Paige's History of Hardwick Mass. 396
Savage's Genealogical Dictionary ii, 400
Schenck's History of Fairfield Ct. 376-8
Sears Genealogy 148
Ward's History of Shrewsbury Mass. 325
Hedges — American Ancestry ii, 54
Chambers' Early Germans of N. J. 400
Cleveland's Hist. of Yates Co. N. Y. 687
Hedges' East Hampton N. Y. 290-301
Howell's Hist. Southampton N. Y. 287-93
Littell's Passaic Valley Genealogies 172
Hedgman — Hayden's Virginia Gens. 303
Hedley — American Ancestry v, 71
Austin's R. I. Genealogical Dictionary 97
Hedrick — Power's Sangamon Ill. 19
Heebner — Kriebel's Schwenkfelders 9-21
Heemstraat—Albany Collections iv, 132
Pearson's Schenectady N. Y. Settlers 91
Heermance — American Ancestry ii, 54
Heermans — N. Y. Gen. Rec. xxi, 58-61
Hefferman — Austin's R. I. Dict. 97
Heffner — American Ancestry xii, 32
Heffner Genealogy (1886) 56 pages
Heffron — Temple's North Brookfield
Hegeman — American Ancestry x, 78
Bergen Genealogy 166
Heilman — Egle's Lebanon Co. Pa. 242
Heinecke — Heinecke Gen. (1869) 241 p.
Heinecke Genealogy 2d ed. (1881) 302 p.
Heiner — Albany Collections iv, 132
Heister — Eyerman Ancestry (1898)
Heller — American Ancestry xii, 54
Eyerman Ancestry (1899) 33
Helme — Austin's R. I. Gen. Dict. 322
Dwight's Strong Genealogy 693
Green's Kentucky Families
Jolliffe Genealogy (1893) 103
Narragansett Historical Register iv, 132
Power's Sangamon Co. Ill. Settlers 367
Sharpless Genealogy 227, 352
Heltribidal — Yates Co. N. Y. 709-11
Hemenway—Adams' Haven Genealogy 25
American Ancestry iii, 182
Bartow Genealogy 196
Bemis' History of Marlboro N. H. 529-31
Haven Genealogy 25
Hayward's History of Gilsum N. H. 327

Hemenway Genealogy (1880) 92 pages
Morse's Sherborn Mass. Settlers 100
Norton's History of Fitzwilliam N. H. 604
Stearns' Hist. of Ashburnham Mass. 743
Ward's Hist. of Shrewsbury Mass. 308-10
Hemingway — Amer. Ancestry ii, 54
Barry's Hist. of Framingham Mass. 282-9
Dodd's History of East Haven Ct. 123-6
Ellis' History of Roxburv Mass. 121
Lapham's History of Rumford Me. 343
Savage's Genealogical Dictionary ii, 401
Tuttle Genealogy 656
Hemming — American Ancestry xi, 95
Hemperley — Parthemore Gen. 29, 79-86
Hemphill — Clyde's Irish Settlers 59-61
Cogswell's History of Henniker N. H. 616
Merrill's History of Acworth N. H. 227
Morrison's Hist. of Windham N. H. 575-84
Hempstead — American Ancestry v, 85
Caulkins' Hist. of New London Ct. 272-4
Iowa Historical Record i, 3-12
Savage's Genealogical Dictionary ii, 401
Walworth's Hyde Genealogy 1014
Hencher — Phelps Purchase N. Y. 410
Henchman — Deane's Scituate Mass. 282
Savage's Genealogical Dictionary ii, 402
Secomb's History of Amherst N. H. 624
Hendee — Caverly's Pittsford Vt. 705
Loomis Genealogy (1880) 532
Hender — Wyman's Charlestown 492
Hendershot — Chambers' N. J. Germans
Plumb's Hanover Pa. 433
Henderson — American Ancestry viii, 149
Barry's History of Hanover Mass. 318
Caldwell Genealogy 72
Cochrane's Hist. Francest'n N. H. 750-3
Driver Genealogy 262
Eaton's History of Thomaston Me. ii, 264
Hayden's Virginia Genealogies 723
Judd's History of Hadley Mass. 510
Lincoln's Hist. of Hingham Mass. ii, 297
Meade's Old Churches of Virginia ii, 233
Richmond Va. Standard ii, 23
Smith's History of Sunderland Mass. 396-9
Wentworth Genealogy i, 387
Wheeler's Hist. N. Carolina i, 116; ii, 102
Wheeler's Eminent N. Carolinians 179-81
Hendley — Hudson's Lexington 103
Hendrie — Barlow Genealogy 234-45
Hendrick — Champion Genealogy 206
Lyman's E. Hampton Mass. Hist. Add. 192
Hendricks — American Ancestry viii, 159
Bergen's Kings Co. N. Y. Settlers 134-42
Power's Sangamon Co. Ill. Settlers 368
Sylvester's History of Ulster Co. N. Y. 335
Hendrickson — American Ancestry i, 36
Cooley's Trenton N. J. Genealogies 119-23
Salter's Hist. of Monmouth Co. N. J. lxviii
Smith's History of Delaware Co. Pa. 467
Hendrixson — American Ancestry xii
Hendry — Am. Cath. Hist. Soc. Rec. ii,
    369-74
American Ancestry xii, 128
Camden Co. N. J. History
Hendy — Caulkins' Norwich Ct. 178
Henery — Eaton's Thomaston Me. 265

Henfield — Pickering Genealogy
Hening — Goode Genealogy 225
Hayden's Virginia Genealogies 255
Henley — Wyman's Charlestown 493
Henly — Richmond Va. Standard iv, 3
Hennion — Roome Genealogy 42-4
Henrahan — Eaton's Thomaston 265
Henry — American Ancestry vi, 48; xii
Cabell Genealogy 324
Campbell's History of Virginia 520
Chambers' Early Germans of N. J. 403
Clarke's Old King Wm. Co. Va. Families
Egle's Notes and Queries 4th ser. i, 2;
    1896, Annual Volume 125
Goode Genealogy 375
Hayden's Virginia Genealogies 438
Hemenway's Vermont Hist. Gaz. iv, 850
Marshall Genealogy (1884) 99-102
Lewis Genealogy (1893) 84
Randall's History of Chesterfield N. H.
    343-5
Richmond Standard i, 37, 46; ii, 39, 42;
    ix, 2. 7
Roome Genealogy 228
Slaughter's St. Mark's Parish 140, 186
Saunderson's Charlestown N. H. 400
Smith's (Rev. Wm.) Biography
Henshaw — Amer. Ancestry x, 181
Bill Genealogy 241
Cleveland Genealogy (1899) 35, 57-60
Denney Genealogy 82
New Eng. Hist. Gen. Reg. xxii, 106-15
Savage's Genealogical Dictionary ii, 404
Sewall's History of Woburn Mass. 616
Ward Genealogy 146
Ward's History of Shrewsbury Mass. 328
Washburn's History of Leicester Mass. 378
Wheeler's History of Brunswick Me. 838
Whitmore's Heraldic Journal 121-4
Wyman's Charlestown Mass. Gens. i, 495
Hensley — Missouri Pioneers 267
Power's Sangamon Ill. 370
Henvis — Penn. Mag. of History vii, 474
Hepbron — Hanson's Old Kent Md.
Hepburn — Egle's Queries (1897) 24
Hepburn Genealogy (1894) 190 pages
Meginness' Hist. Jour. ii, 62-164, etc.
Orcutt's History of Stratford Ct. 1218
Tuttle Genealogy 65
Herbert — American Ancestry vi, 73; xii
Bouton's Hist. of Concord N. H. 665-70
Meade's Old Churches of Virginia
New York Genealogical and Biographical
    Record xxi, 41-3; xxvi, 30
Richmond Va. Standard iii, 30
Savage's Genealogical Dictionary ii, 353
Sheldon's Hist. of Deerfield Mass. 199
Slaughter's Bristol Parish Va. 107, 169
Thomas Genealogy (1877) 87
Thomas Genealogy (1896) 338-43
Hereford — Washington Gen. 204
Herendeen — Narragansett Hist. Reg. iv,
    259
Herkimer — American Ancestry vi, 97
Benton's Herkimer County N. Y. 149-52
Frey Genealogy (1870)

Herman — Mallery's Bohemia Manor
Penn. Mag. of Hist. and Biog. iv, 100-7
Hermance — American Ancestry ii, 54
Sylvester's History of Ulster Co. N. Y. 280
Hermans — Albany Collections iv, 132
New York Gen. and Biog. Record ix, 60-2
Hermon — Power's Sangamon Ill. 371
Herndon — Power's Sangamon Ill. 372
Hero — Ballou's Milford Mass. 816-8
Herr — Harris' Lancaster Co. Pa. 281-4
Herr Memorial Journal (1895) 36 pages
Herreshoff — Browne Mem. 106
Herrick — American Ancestry i, 37; ii, 54;
iii, 26; v, 76; viii, 114
Bassett's History of Richmond N. H. 409
Bemis' History of Marlboro N. H. 531-4
Brockway Genealogy 13-7
Cleveland's Topsfield Mass. Anniv. 64.
Cochrane's History of Antrim N. H. 531
Dodge Ancestry (1896) 17
Driver Genealogy 308-19
Guild's Stiles Genealogy 221
Hemenway's Vermont Gaz. v, 101-3
Herrick Genealogy (1846) 69 pages
Herrick Genealogy 2d ed. (1885) 516 pages
Howell's Hist. Southampton N. Y. 293-7
Hubbard's Hist. of Springfield Vt. 333-5
Joslin's History of Poultney Vt. 273
Lapham's History of Norway Me. 522
Livermore's History Wilton N. H. 396-400
Poor's Merrimack Valley Researches 145
Randall's Hist. of Chesterfield N. H. 345-8
Runnel's Hist. Sanbornton N. H. ii, 336-8
Savage's Genealogical Dictionary ii, 405
Secomb's Hist. of Amherst N. H. 625-7
Stackpole's History of Durham Me. 200
Stearns' History of Ashburnham Mass. 744
Williams' History of Danby Vt. 161-3
Herring — Green's Todd Gen. 109-12
Hill's Dedham Mass. Records i
Lapham's History of Norway Me. 522-4
Herrington — Amer. Anc. v, 64; xii, 119
See also under Harrington
Herrman — Glenn's Col. Mansions 137
Herron — Egle's Queries (1897) 176
Hersey — Barry's Hanover Mass. 317
Butler's History of Farmington Me. 393
Dennysville Me. Centennial 104
Hersey Chart (1895) 27x32 inches
Lapham's History of Paris Me. 627-9
Lincoln's Hist. Hingham Mass. ii, 298-327
Runnel's Hist. of Sanbornton N. H. 337-50
Swift's Barnstable Mass. Families ii, 5-18
Washburn's Hist. of Leicester Mass. 376
Hershey — Brubacher Gen. 38-8, 186-8
Egle's Notes and Queries 3d ser. ii, 18-20;
Annual Volume 1896, 206
Harris' History of Lancaster Co. Pa. 306
Hertzler — Hertzler Gen. (1885) 368 pages
Hervey — Daniel's Oxford Mass. 540
Heseltine — Livermore's Wilton 400-2
Heselton — Washington N. H. 693
Hess — American Ancestry ii, 54
Hess Genealogy (1880) 68 pages
Hess Genealogy 2d ed. (1896) 260 pages
Parthemore Genealogy 198

Hesselton — Livermore's Wilton 400-2
Hesser — Power's Sangamon Ill. 373
Heston — American Ancestry xi, 90
Evans' Fox Genealogy 251-6
Heston Genealogy (1883) 57 pages
Smith (Rev. Wm.) Biography 50-5
Heterick — Chute Genealogy, app. 97-9
Heth — Paxton's Marshall Genealogy
Richmond Va. Standard ii, 26
Hett — Savage's Genealogical Dict. ii, 407
Wyman's Charlestown Mass. Gens. i, 496
Hewes — Bangor Hist. Mag. ii, 120
Bond's Watertown Mass. Genealogies 296
Carter Genealogy (1888) 53-5, 74, 103-5
Farrow's Hist. of Islesborough Me. 224
Hudson's Hist. of Lexington Mass. 103
Martin's History of Chester Pa. 405
Read's History of Swanzey N. H. 367
Savage's Genealogical Dictionary ii, 407
Hewett — Deane's Scituate Mass. 283
Eaton's History of Thomaston Me. ii, 266
Egle's Notes and Queries 4th ser. i, 140
Walworth's Hyde Genealogy 930
See also under Hewitt
Hewey — Hubbard's Springfield Vt. 335.
Hewins — American Ancestry vi, 205
Bangor Me. Historical Magazine v, 194
Morse's Genealogical Reg. ii (1859) 165-76
North's History of Augusta Me. 882
Hewitt — Caverly's Pittsford Vt. 707
Stanton Genealogy 555
Winsor's History of Duxbury Mass. 266
See also under Hewett and Huit
Hewlett — Flint's Peters Lineage 9, 12-4
Queens County N. Y. 432-4
Winslow Genealogy 453
Hext — Bellinger Genealogy 79
Heyden — See Hayden
Heydrick — Amer. Ancestry vi, 117
Kriebel's Schwenkfelders 9-11
Heyl — American Ancestry iii, 71
Heyward — Bellinger Genealogy 64-8
Heywood — Goode Genealogy 171
Herrick's History of Gardner Mass. 355
Heywood's History Westminster Mass.
691-6
Lapham's History of Bethel Me. 560
Marvin's Hist. of Winchendon Mass. 458
Pierce's History of Grafton Mass. 505
Saunderson's Charlestown N. H. 401-9
Stearns' Hist. of Ashburnham Mass. 745
Wall's Reminisc. of Worcester Mass. 30
Ward Genealogy (1851) 40
Ward's History of Shrewsbury Mass. 299
Wheeler's Eminent North Carolinians 63-5
Hiatt — American Ancestry iii, 26
Young's Hist. of Wayne Co. Ind. 328
Hibbard — Amer. Anc. iv, 35; xi, 214; xii
Cleveland Genealogy 142
Hubbard's Hist. of Stanstead Co. Can. 120
Montague Genealogy 124, 439-41
Plumb's History of Hanover Pa. 423
Savage's Genealogical Dictionary ii, 408
Sharpless Genealogy 142-4, 194-8, 310-7
Temple's Hist. of N. Brookfield Mass. 624
See also Hebard and Hebert

Hibberd — Cope's Dutton Genealogy 68
Futhey's History of Chester Pa. 598
Hichborn — Lincoln's Hingham ii, 327
Hickcox — Clarke Gen. (1884) 49-51
Hickes — Benedict's Sutton Mass. 660
Davis' Landmarks of Plymouth Mass. 133
Deane's History of Scituate Mass. 283
Hickey — Goode Genealogy 188
Lincoln's Hist. of Hingham Mass. ii, 328
Richmond Va. Standard ii, 49
Hickman — Futhey's Chester Pa. 600-3
Goode Genealogy 101-3
Jones Genealogy (1891) 189-92
Lewis Genealogy (1893) 131-86
Power's Sangamon Co. Ill. Settlers 374
Hickock — American Ancestry x, 9
Hickok — Adam's Fairhaven Vt. 394-7
Walworth's Hyde Genealogy 304-7
Hickox — Anderson's Waterbury 62-5
Bronson's History of Waterbury Ct. 496-9
Goodwin's Foote Genealogy 202
Hall's Norwalk Ct. Rec. 228-31, 271-7, 290
Heacock Genealogy (1869)
Morris Genealogy (1894) 150
Power's Sangamon Co. Ill. Settlers 376-8
Savage's Genealogical Dictionary ii, 409
Sharpe's History of Seymour Ct. 169
Strong Genealogy 383-6
Hicks — American Ancestry i, 37; ii, 54;
vii, 76; viii, 61; xi, 194
Austin's R. I. Genealogical Dictionary 97
Barton Genealogy, appendix 189
Benedict's History of Sutton Mass. 660
Bunker's Long Island Genealogies 212-5
Calnek's History of Annapolis N. S. 526
Chute Genealogy, appendix 99-105
Corliss' North Yarmouth Me. Magazine
Davis' History of Bucks County Pa. 244
Doty Genealogy 539-41, 543-5
Dwight Genealogy 582-6
Freeman's Hist. of Cape Cod Mass. ii, 357
Gregg's Hist. of Old Cheraws S. C. 81
Hedge's Hist. of East Hampton N. Y. 301
Hicks Lineage (1894) 15 pages
Lamb's Hist. of New York City N. Y. 763
Lamborn Genealogy 282
Leland Genealogy 72
Meade's Old Churches of Virginia
Mott Genealogy 370-81
Paige's History of Cambridge Mass. 580
Savage's Genealogical Dictionary ii, 410
Swift's Barnstable Mass. Families ii, 72
Thompson's Long Island N. Y. ii, 510-2
Valentine's N. Y. Manual (1853) 409
Winsor's History of Duxbury Mass. 266
Hicock — Cothren's Woodbury 564-7
Hidden — Essex Inst. Colls. xxi, 181-4
Hide — Orcutt's Stratford Ct. 1218
Sedgwick's History of Sharon Ct. 89
Hiestand — Cassel Genealogy 69, 129-31
Hiester — Perkiomen Region 18
Higbie — Phœnix's Whitney Gen. i, 370
Prime Genealogy (1895) 46
Higgins — American Ancestry ii, 55
Austin's R. I. Genealogical Dictionary 98
Eaton's History of Thomaston Me. ii, 267

Field's History of Haddam Ct. 46
Freeman's Cape Cod ii, 371, 388, 725
Hatch's History of Industry Me. 647
Hayward's Hist. of Hancock N. H. 652
Hemenway's Vermont Hist. Gaz. v, 104
Jolliffe Genealogy (1893) 95
Leland Genealogy 167-9
Lincoln's Hist. Hingham Mass. ii, 329-31
Orcutt's History of Wolcott Ct. 496-9
Paige's History of Hardwick Mass. 397
Pierce's History of Gorham Me. 175
Power's Sangamon Co. Ill. Settlers 377-9
Pratt's History of Eastham Mass. 120
Randall's Hist. of Chesterfield N. H. 348
Rich's History of Truro Mass. 537
Ridlon's Saco Valley Me. Families 727
Savage's Genealogical Dictionary ii, 411
Walker Genealogy 339
Higginson — Cleveland Gen. (1899) 487-97
Essex Inst. Collections v, 33-42
New Eng. Hist. and Gen. Reg. xlvi, 117
Porter's Hartford Ct. Settlers 13
Savage's Genealogical Dictionary ii, 412-4
Symmes Genealogy 35, 45
Vinton's Giles Genealogy 321-3
High—Keim Family 445
Littell's Passaic Valley 183-5
Wismer Genealogy 53-62
Higley — Amer. Ancestry iv, 143; vi, 190-1
Barbour's My Wife and Mother, app. 59
Brown's West Simsbury Ct. Settlers 76-8
Currier's Castleton Vt. Epitaphs 19-21
Higley Genealogy (1896) 738 pages
Humphrey's Genealogy 160, 443
Stiles' History of Windsor Ct. ii, 387-91
Hildebrant — Chambers' N. J. Germans
Hildreth — Amer. Ancestry x, 61
Cleveland Genealogy 90-2
Eaton's History of Thomaston Me. ii, 267
Hatch's History of Industry Me. 648-50
Hemenway's Vermont Hist. Gag. v, 52
Hildreth Family of Woburn (1857) 8 pages
Hildreth of Woburn, 2d ed. (1879) 9 pages
Hildreth Family of Lowell (1892) 71 pages
Hodgman's Hist. of Westford Mass. 452-5
Howell's Hist. Southampton N. Y. 297-9
Hudson's Hist. of Lexington Mass. 279
New Eng. Hist. and Gen. Reg. xi, 7-12
Randall's Hist. Chesterfield N. H. 349-54
Savage's Genealogical Dictionary ii, 414
Secomb's Hist. of Amherst N. H. 627-30
Sheldon's Hist. of Deerfield Mass. 200
Vinton's Richardson Genealogy 58
Hiler — Chambers' N. J. Germans
Hiles — Ogden Genealogy (1898) 110
Anderson's Waterbury Ct. i, app. 65
Hill — American Ancestry i, 37; vi, 32,
110; vii, 26; viii, 218; ix, 129; x, 186
Austin's R. I. Genealogical Dictionary 98
Babson's History of Gloucester Mass. 104
Baker's History of Montville Ct. 422-9
Ballou's History of Milford Mass. 819
Barry's Hist. of Framingham Mass. 290
Brown's Bedford Mass. Families 17
Brown's W. Simsbury Conn. Settlers 70-2
Buxton Me. Centennial 193-8

Caulkins' Hist. of New London Ct. 307
Chapman Genealogy 223
Clarke's Old King Wm. Co. Va. Families
Cochrane's Hist. of Francestown N. H. 754
Cogswell's Hist. of Henniker N. H. 617
Cogswell's Nottingham N. H. 699, 708
Collin's Hist. of Hillsdale N. Y., app. 62-4
Cooley's Trenton N. J. Genealogies 123
Corliss' North Yarmouth Me. Magazine
Cothren's Woodbury Conn. 567; ii, 1505
Crafts' History of Whately Mass. 501
Cutters' Hist. of Arlington Mass. 257-62
Daniels' History of Oxford Mass. 541
Densmore's Hartwell Genealogy
Draper's History of Spencer Mass. 205-7
Dunstable Mass. Bi-Centennial 162-6
Eaton's History of Candia N. H. 81
Egle's Penn Genealogies 2d ed. 91-3
Eliot Me. Early Settlers 13-5
Emerson's Hist. of Douglas Mass. 153-62
Essex Inst. Collections viii, 118-23; xxi, 184
Evans Genealogy (1893) 83-105
Fogg, Hill and Moody Genealogy (1881)
Hayward's History of Hancock N. H. 652
Hazen's History of Billerica Mass. 68-72
Herrick's History of Gardner Mass. 356
Heywood's Hist. Westminster Mass. 696
Hill Family of Phila. (1854) 511 pages
Hill Family of Maine (1858) 16 pages
Hill Family of Fairfield Ct. (1879) 20 pages
Hill Family of Sunbury Pa. (1887) 13 p.
Hill Family of Dover N. H. (1889) 16 p.
Hill Family of Conn. (1895) 22 pages
Hill Family of Boston (1897) 106 pages
Hill's Old Dunstable Mass. 162
Hine's Lebanon Ct. Hist. Address 157
Holton's Farwell Genealogy 43-5
Hubbard's Stanstead Co. Canada 306
Hurd's History of Fairfield Co. Ct. 583-5
Jameson's History of Medway Mass. 492
Jordan's Leighton Genealogy 101-3
Kilbourn Genealogy 189
Lapham's History of Norway Me. 524-6
Lapham's History of Paris Me. 630
Leland Genealogy 269
Lewis Genealogy (1893) 152-4
Lincoln's Hist. of Hingham Mass. ii, 331
Littell's Passaic Valley Genealogies 186
Locke Genealogy 77
Machias Me. Centennial 179
Maine Hist. and Gen. Rec. v, 158-61, 240
Martin's History of Chester Pa. 173
Meade's Old Churches of Virginia
Mitchell's Hist. Bridgewater Mass. 186-8
Morris Genealogy (1898) 425
Morse's Sherborn Mass. Settlers 100-5
Neally and True Families Chart
N. E. Gen. Reg. xii, 139-45, 261-4; xli, 52
Norton's Hist. of Fitzwilliam N. H. 605
Orcutt's History of New Milford Ct. 710
Paige's History of Cambridge Mass. 581-5
Peck's Rochester N. Y. Centen. 659-61
Penn. Magazine of History xi, 497-9
Phœnix's Whitney Genealogy i, 745
Pompey N. Y. Reunion 322-4
Read's History of Swanzey N. H. 368-71

Richmond Va. Standard iii, 38
Runnel's Sanbornton N. H. ii, 350-4
Savage's Genealogical Dictionary ii, 415-21
Schenck's History of Fairfield Ct. 378
Sewall's History of Woburn (Mass.) 617
Sharpless Genealogy 245
Slaughter's St. Mark's Parish Virg. 193
Smith's Letters of Richard Hill (1854)
Stearns' Hist. Ashburnham Mass. 745-50
Stiles' Hist. of Windsor Ct. ii, 392
Temple's Hist. N. Brookfield Mass. 625-7
Temple's History of Palmer Mass. 478
Temple's Hisory of Whately Mass. 243
Todd's History of Redding Ct. 196
Washington N. H. History 476
Weeler's History of No. Carolina 253
Whipple and Hill Families (1897) 108 pages
Whitmore's Copps Hill Epitaphs
Williams' History of Danby Vt. 163
Winsor's Hist. of Duxbury Mass. 267
Wyman's Charlestown Mass. i, 499-502
Young's History of Wayne Co. Ind. 342
Hillegas — Am. Hist. Reg. (1894) i, 23-8
Hillegas Genealogy (1891) 118 pages
Penn. Magazine of History xviii, 85-9
Hilles — Jackson Genealogy 311-9
Hillhouse — Amer. Ancestry xii, 108
Baker's Montville Ct. 554-62
Tilley's New England Magazine i, 92-7
Updyke's Narragansett Churches 504-6
Walworth's Hyde Genealogy ii, 925-37
Hilliard — Austin's R. I. Gen. Dict. 98
Cleveland Genealogy 200-4
Dow's History of Hampton N. H. 746
Lincoln's Hist. of Hingham Mass. ii, 331
Savage's Genealogical Dictionary ii, 421
Swift's Barnstable Families ii, 69-71
Williams' History of Danby Vt. 164-6
Hillier — Lapham's Norway Me. 526
Savage's Genealogical Dictionary ii, 422
Stiles' History of Windsor Ct. ii, 391
Hillman — Butler's Farmington 494-6
Clement's Newtown N. J. Settlers
Paige's History of Hardwick Mass. 398
Power's Sangamon Co. Ill. Settlers 379
Shourd's Fenwick Colony N. J. 526
Temple's Hist. of No. Brookfield Mass. 627
Hills — Adams Genealogy (1895) 40-2
American Ancestry ii, 55; iii, 177; x, 29,
    33; xi, 36; xii, 98
Bassett's History of Richmond N. H. 410
Blake's History of Franklin Mass. 254
Boyd's Annals of Winchester Ct. 44-7
Chase's History of Chester N. H. 544-7
Cochrane's History of Antrim N. H. 532-6
Eaton's Annals of Warren Me. 550
Eaton's History of Thomaston Me. ii, 268
Green's Gen. of Thos. Greene, appendix
Hayward's Hist. of Hancock N. H. 652-7
Hills Family of Indiana (1878) 23 pages
Hills Family Reunion (1891) 47 pages
Hills Family Assoc. Report (1895-9) 49 p.
Humphrey Genealogy 176
Kidder's Hist. New Ipswich N. H. 388-90
Kimball Family News 229
Lapham's History of Bethel Me. 561

Longmeadow Mass. Centennial, app. 68-70
Malden Mass. Bi-Centennial 231
Morrison's Hist. of Windham N. H. 584-9
New Eng. Hist. Gen. Reg. xxxvi, 77, 165
Orcutt's History of Torrington Ct. 712-5
Poor's Merrimack Valley Researches 152
Read's History of Swanzey N. H. 371-3
Sibley's History of Union Me. 464
Stiles' History of Windsor Ct. ii, 392
Vinton Genealogy 459-61
Wyman's Charlestown Mass. Gens. i, 503
Hillyer — Clute's Staten Island 389
Dorland Genealogy 223-9
Richmond Va. Standard iii, 50
Temple's History of Northfield Mass. 459
Hilt — Eaton s Annals Warren Me. 551
Hilton — Amer. Ancestry i, 37; ii, 55
Chapman's Weeks Genealogy 143
Cleveland's Hist. of Yates Co. N. Y. 213
Coffin's Hist. of Newbury Mass. 305
Cogswell's Hist. Nottingham N. H. 404-6
Davis' Landmarks of Plymouth Mass. 134
Dearborn's Hist. of Parsonsfield Me. 382
Dudley Genealogy 125
Hatch's History of Industry Me. 650
Hilton Genealogy (1896) 24 pages
Johnson's History of Bristol Me. 446-9
Munsell's Albany Collections iv, 132
New Eng. Reg. vii, 50-2, 155; xxxi, 179-94
Richmond Va. Standard i, 38, 40, 48
Savage's Genealogical Dictionary ii, 422-4
Savage's Winthrop's New England i, 116
Stearns' Hist. of Ashburnham Mass. 750
Woodman Genealogy, app. c. 42-8
Wyman's Charlestown Gens. i, 504
Hilts — Chambers' N. J. Germans
Himrod — Cleveland's Yates Co. 426
Davis' Landmarks of Plymouth Mass. 134
McMath Genealogy 26-34
Mellick Genealogy 656-70
Hinchman — Clement's Newtown N. J.
Hinckley — Amer. Ancestry iii, 184
Bangor Me. Historical Mag. v, 194-6
Deane's History of Scituate Mass. 284
Dwight Genealogy 193
Eldredge Genealogy 20-4
Freeman's Cape Cod Mass. i, 343; ii, 574
Glover Genealogy 170, 178
Hinckley Genealogy (1859) 7 pages
Hines' Lebanon Ct. Hist. Address 157
Lincoln's Hist. of Hingham Mass. ii, 332
New Eng. Hist. Gen. Reg. xiii, 208-12
Paige's History of Hardwick Mass. 398
Rich's History of Truro Mass. 533-5
Savage's Genealogical Dictionary ii, 424-6
Strong Genealogy
Swift's Barnstable Families ii, 30-48
Temple's North Brookfield Mass. 627-9
Waldo's History of Tolland Ct. 74
Walworth's Hyde Genealogy 68
Wheeler's Hist. of Brunswick Me. 838
See also under Hinkley
Hinds — American Ancestry xi, 34
Hatfield's Elizabeth N. J. 78
Heywood's Hist. Westminster Mass. 697
Hinds Genealogy (1899) 394 pages

Keyes' W. Boylston Mass. Reg. 24
New Eng. Hist. Reg. xviii, 267
Pierce's Life of Gardner Dean (1883)
Randall's Hist. of Chesterfield N. H. 355
Stearns' Hist. of Ashburnham Mass. 750
Stone's Hist. of Hubbardston Mass. 291-3
Temple's Hist. N. Brookfield Mass. 629-31
Ward's History of Shrewsbury Mass. 305
Hine — Anderson's Waterbury Ct. i, 66
Hine Genealogy (1898) 239 pages
Orcutt's North Milford 711-7
Seymour Ct. Record Aug. 12, 1897, 1 col.
Whittemore's Orange N. J. 459
Hines — Heinecke Genealogy 36
Lincoln's Hist. of Hingham Mass. ii, 333
Salem Press Hist. and Gen. Rec. ii, 47-50
Hinkle — Power's Sangamon Ill. 368
Hinkley — American Ancestry ix, 148
Eaton's Annals of Warren Me. 552
Eaton's History of Thomaston Me. ii, 268
Hatch's History of Industry Me. 651-3
Milliken's Narraguagus Valley Me. 14
Moore's Memoirs of Am. Governors i, 231
New Eng. Hist. and Gen. Reg. iii, 135
See also under Hinckley
Hinkson — Lapham's Rumford Me. 345
Libby Genealogy 27
Sharpless Genealogy 356
Hinman — Am. Ancestry ii, 55; iv, 240;
    x, 125, 191
Brown's West Simsbury Ct. Settlers 72
Cothren's Woodbury Ct. 556-64; ii, 1502-4
Dolbeare Genealogy 21
Hinman Genealogy (1856) 84 pages
Orcutt's History of Stratford Ct. 1218-20
Pompey N. Y. Reunion 327
Power's Sangamon Co. Ill. Settlers 380
Savage's Genealogical Dictionary ii, 426
Seymour Ct. Record June 10, 1897, ⅓ col.
Hinsdale — Am. Anc. ii, 55; iii, 169; xii
Andrews' Hist. of New Britain Ct. 185
Boyd's Annals Winchester Ct. 338-42, 371
Hinsdale Genealogy (1883) 31 pages
Judd's History of Hadley Mass. 511
Kellogg's White Genealogy 32
Leach's Morton Ancestry 124-30
Orcutt's History of Torrington Ct. 715
Savage's Genealogical Dictionary ii, 427
Sheldon's Hist. of Deerfield Mass. 201-7
Hinsdell — Pompey N. Y. Reunion 318-21
Hinsley — Power's Sangamon Ill. 381
Hipsley — Ball's Lake County Ind. 378
Hird — Temple's North Brookfield 631
Hirons — American Ancestry vii, 159
Hiscock — Butler's Farmington 497-9
Hiscox — Austin's R. I. Gen. Dict. 99
Hiserodt — Amer. Ancestry ii, 55
Hitch — Whittemore's Orange N. J. 296-8
Hitchcock — American Ancestry, i 37; ii,
    56; v, 134; vi, 6; viii, 84, 174
Anderson's Waterbury Ct. i, app. 66
Atkins' History of Hawley Mass. 48
Avery Genealogy (1893) 86-8
Boyd's History of Conesus N. Y. 158
Caverly's History of Pittsford Vt. 707
Chapman's Trowbridge Genealogy 51

Corliss' North Yarmouth Me. 1125, 1155
Davis' History of Wallingford Ct. 792-6
Dickerman Genealogy 161-3
Dodd's History of East Haven Ct. 126
Dwight Genealogy 604
Hitchcock Genealogy (1894) 555 pages
Hitchcock Family Excerpts (1897) 4 pages
Hubbard's Stanstead County Canada 257
Hyde's Hist. of Brimfield Mass. 409, 415
Kellogg's White Genealogy 121
New Eng. Hist. and Gen. Reg. xl. 307-9
Orcutt's History of New Milford Ct. 717
Paige's History of Hardwick Mass. 399
Savage's Genealogical Dictionary ii, 428
Sedgwick's History of Sharon Ct. 90
Sharp's History of Seymour Ct. 220
Sheldon's Hist. of Deerfield Mass. 207-11
Stiles' History of Windsor Ct. ii, 393
Temple's History of Palmer Mass. 474-6
Timlow's Sketches Southington Ct. 131-6
Wilbraham Mass. Centennial 298
Hitchings — American Ancestry v, 82; xii, 41
Hite — Paxton's Marshall Genealogy 316
Slaughter's St. Mark's Parish 146, 178
Hitt — Williams' Hist. of Danby Vt. 166
Hix — Bassett's Richmond N. H. 411
Eaton's History of Thomaston Me. ii, 269
Hixon — Aldrich's Walpole N. H. 274
Ballou's History of Milford Mass. 820
Jameson's History of Medway Mass. 493
Hoadley — American Ancestry ix, 192
Anderson's Waterbury Ct. i, app. 67
Boyd's Annals of Winchester Ct. 384
Hoadley Genealogy (1894) 288 pages
Middlefield Ct. History
Hoadly — Savage's Gen. Dict. ii, 429
Hoag — American Ancestry i, 38; ii, 56
Cogswell's Nottingham N. H. 407-9
Little's History of Weare N. H. 900-3
Wight Genealogy 136
See also under Hogg
Hoagland — American Ancestry vi, 35
Hoagland Genealogy (1891) 276 pages
Nevius Genealogy
Hoar — Amer. Ancestry iv, 38; vii, 271
Andrews' History of New Britain Ct. 343-5
Bond's Watertown Mass. Gens. 297-9
Deane's History of Scituate Mass. 285
Farwell Genealogy 22, and Chart
Heywood's Westminster Mass. 697-702
Hoar Family Lineage (1898) 56 pages
Hoar Family Ancestry (1899) 37 pages
Holton's Farwell Genealogy 23
Hyde's History of Brimfield Mass. 415-8
Hudson's History of Lexington Mass. 104
Kidder's Hist. of New Ipswich N. H. 391
New Eng. Hist. Gen. Reg. xvii, 149; liii, 92-101, 186-98, 289-300; liv, 149-52
Paige's History of Cambridge Mass. 585
Parsons Genealogy (1894) 15-8
Parsons Genealogy (1900) 20-6, 69-91
Savage's Genealogical Dictionary ii, 430-2
Shattuck's History of Concord Mass. 374
Temple's Hist. of No. Brookfield Mass. 632
Westminster Mass. Centennial 19

Hobart — American Ancestry xii, 54
Butler's Groton Mass. 406
Claypoole Genealogy 99-101
Deane's History of Scituate Mass. 286
Dennysville Me. Centennial 105
Granite Monthly Concord N. H. (1882) 380
Griffin's Journal Southold N. Y. 201
Hobart Family Groton Mass. (1886) 182 p.
Hobart Fam. Hingham Mass. (1897) Chart
Hobart's Hist. of Abington Mass. 386-401
Hubbard Genealogy 149-56
Jackson's History of Newton Mass. 308
Lincoln's Hist. Hingham Mass. ii, 334-50
Mitchell's Hist. Bridgewater Mass. 374-9
New Eng. Hist. and Gen. Register x, 149
Porter Genealogy 195-7
Savage's Genealogical Dictionary ii, 432-6
Savage's Winthrop's New England ii, 272
Smith (Rev. Wm.) Biography
Stearns' History of Ashburnham Mass. 751
Thayer Memorial (1835) 100-8
Washburn's History of Leicester Mass. 377
Worcester's History of Hollis N. H. 377
Hobbie — Clark Genealogy (1892-7) 171-8
Hobbs — American Ancestry xii
Bond's Watertown Mass. 300
Dearborn's History of Parsonsfield Me. 383
Dow's History of Hampton N. H. 747-55
Hatch's History of Industry Me. 653
Hobbs Genealogy (1855) 16 pages, reprint
Hudson's History of Lexington Mass. 106
Lapham's History of Norway Me. 526-30
New Eng. Hist. and Gen. Reg. ix, 255-63
Ridlon's Harrison Me. Settlers 72-4
Savage's Genealogical Dictionary ii, 436
Stone's History of Hubbardston Mass. 293
Temple's Hist. of N. Brookfield Mass. 632
Topsfield Mass. Hist. Coll. iii (1897)
Hobby — Savage's Gen. Dictionary ii, 437
Whitmore's Copps Hill Epitaphs
Hobson — Austin's R. I. Gen. Dict. 99
Buxton Me. Centennial 243-6
Essex Mass. Inst. Hist. Coll. xxi, 185-8
Futhey's History of Chester Co. Pa. 605
Gage's History of Rowley Mass. 443
Page Genealogy 104
Potts Genealogy (1895) 265-8
Richmond Va. Standard iii, 36
Ridlon's Saco Valley Me. Families 727-37
Savage's Genealogical Dict. ii, 438, 463
Hoch — Keim Genealogy 379-81, 445
Hockenbury — Chambers' N. J. Germans
Hodgdon — Little's Hist. Weare N. H. 903
New Eng. Hist. and Gen. Reg. vii, 155
Sinclair Genealogy 390-7
Hodge — Austin's Allied Families 130
Cochrane's Hist. Francestown N. H. 755
Judd's History of Hadley Mass. 512
Norton's History of Fitzwilliam N. H. 606
Ransom Genealogy 48
Hodges — American Ancestry v, 8; ix, 120
Ammidown Genealogy 36
Bowens of Woodstock Ct. 179
Clarke's History of Norton Mass. 83
Daniels' History of Oxford Mass. 542
Deane's Leonard Genealogy 19

Gregg's History of Old Cheraws S. C. 101
Hodges Genealogy (1837) 22 pages
Hodges Genealogy 2d ed. (1853) 71 pages
Hodges Genealogy 3d ed. (1896) 566 pages
Meade's Old Churches of Virginia
Hanson's Old Kent Md. 309-11
Orcutt's History of Torrington Ct. 717-9
Savage's Genealogical Dictionary ii, 439
Stiles' History of Windsor Ct. ii, 394
Hodgkins — Aldrich's Walpole 274-7
American Ancestry i, 38; xii, 35
Babson's History of Gloucester Mass. 104
Bangor Me. Historical Magazine viii, 108
Bemis' History of Marlboro N. H. 535
Hammatt Papers of Ipswich Mass. 135-51
Savage's Genealogical Dictionary ii, 438
Hodgman — Am. Ancestry iv, 15; vi, 132
Dowse Genealogy 98-100, 198-201
Eaton's Annals of Warren Me. 553
Eaton's History of Reading Mass. 92
Eaton's History of Thomaston Me. ii, 270
Hill's History of Mason N. H. 203
Hodgman Golden Wedding (1865) 14 pages
Savage's Genealogical Dictionary ii, 440
Secomb's History of Amherst N. H. 631
Hodgson — Austin's R. I. Gen. Dict. 100
Futhey's History of Chester Co. Pa. 603
Hodsdon — Bradbury's Kennebunkport
Dearborn's Hist. of Parsonsfield Me. 383
Lapham's History of Bethel Me. 562
Lapham's History of Rumford Me. 345
Old Eliot, Me. Monthly ii (1898) 146
Wentworth Genealogy i, 420-4
Hoes — American Anestry ii, 56
Munsell's Albany Collections iv, 126
New York Gen. and Biog. Rec. xxxi, 52-4, 89-91; 133-5
Hoffman — American Ancestry ii, 56; v, 62; vii, 80; viii, 168; ix, 52; x, 185
Chambers' Early Germans of N. J. 406-16
Egle's Notes and Queries 1st ser. i, 211-5
Hoffman Genealogy (1899) 545 pages
Holgate's American Genealogy 103-8
Huntting's History of Pine Plains N. Y. 357-9
McKean Genealogy 143
Power's Sangamon Co. Ill. Settlers 382
Richmond Va. Standard ii, 32
Ruttenber's Hist. of Newburgh N. Y. 300
Ruttenber's Hist. of Orange Co. N. Y. 386
Schoonmaker's Hist. of Kingston N. Y. 481
Van Rensselaer's New Yorkers
Hoffses — Eaton's Warren Me. 553
Hogan — Albany Collections iv, 133
Hoge — Egle's Penn. Gens. 2d ed. 708-11
Egle's Notes and Queries 1st ser. i, 471-3
Foote's Historical Sketches of Va. ii, 23
Jolliffe Genealogy (1893) 126
Hogeboom — American Ancestry ii, 57
Zabriskie's Claverack N. Y. Church 89-94
Hogeland — Davis' Bucks Co. Pa. 200
Hogg — Bedford N. H. Centennial 311
Cochrane's Hist. Francestown N. H. 756
Cogswell's Hist. New Boston N. H. 423-6
Starks History of Dunbarton N. H. 221
See also under Hoag

Hoisington — American Ancestry xii
Timlow's Southington Ct.
Hoit — American Ancestry v, 54
Bouton's History of Concord N. H. 671, 682
Chase's History of Chester N. H. 548
Cogswell's Nottingham N. H. 708-21
Machias Me. Centennial 167
Holahan — American Ancestry iii, 92
Holbrook — American Anc. i, 38; vii, 6
Austin's Ancestral Dictionary 29
Austin's Allied Families 131-3
Ballou's History of Milford Mass. 820-6
Bangor Me. Historical Magazine vi, 85
Bedford's N. H. Centennial 311
Benedict's History of Sutton Mass. 661
Daniels' History of Oxford Mass. 542
Davis' Landmarks of Plymouth Mass. 135
Deane's History of Scituate Mass. 286
Dodd's History of East Haven Ct. 129
Farrow's History of Islesborough Me. 225
Freeman's Hist. of Cape Cod Mass. ii, 678
Harris (W. C.) Ancestors
Holbrook Genealogy (1851) 19 pages
Hudson's History of Lexington Mass. 279
Hyde's History of Brimfield Mass. 419
Jameson's History of Medway Mass. 494
Kingman's No. Bridgewater Mass. 526
Morse's Sherborn Mass. Settlers 107-54
Orcutt's History of Derby Ct. 729-31
Orcutt's History of Torrington Ct. 719
Pierce's History of Grafton Mass. 505-7
Pompey N. Y. Reunion 324-6
Read's History of Swanzey N. H. 373-80
Savage's Genealogical Dictionary ii, 441-3
Secomb's History of Amherst N. H. 633
Sharp's History of Seymour Ct. 160
Stearns' History of Ashburnham Mass. 752
Temple's History of Palmer Mass. 482-7
Vinton Genealogy 185-8, 330-40
Holcomb — American Ancestry ii, 57; iv, 109; vii, 21; xii
Barbour's My Wife and Mother, app. 60
Lambertville N. J. Record (Aug. 11, 1886)
Loomis Genealogy (1880) 471-4, 517-8, 759-61, 766-8
Marshall's Grant Ancestry 118
Savage's Genealogical Dictionary ii, 443
Stiles' Windsor Ct. ii, 394-7
Holden — Am. Anc. i, 38; iii, 190; iv, 92; vii, 62; viii, 67; xi, 33; xii, 114
Atkins' History of Hawley Mass. 51
Austin's Ancestral Dictionary 30
Austin's R. I. Genealogical Dictionary 100
Barry's History of Framingham Mass. 291
Bond's Watertown Mass. Gen. 309, 794
Butler's History of Groton Mass. 407, 491
Chandler's History of Shirley Mass. 455-82
Clapp's Jones Hill Dorchester Mass. 65-8
Dwight's Strong Genealogy 526
Hartwell Genealogy (1895) 74-83
Hayward's History of Hancock N. H. 657
Hazen's History of Billerica Mass. 73
Heywood's Hist. Westminster Mass. 702-8
Hill's History of Mason N. H. 203
Kidder's Hist. of New Ipswich N. H. 390
Lapham's History of Norway Me. 530

Narragansett Historical Reg. iii, 139–43
Paige's History of Cambridge Mass. 585–7
Saunderson's Charlestown N. H. 410
Savage's Genealogical Dictionary ii, 444
Secomb's History of Amherst N. H. 634
Stearns' Hist. Ashburnham Mass. 753–5
Temple's History of Northfield Mass. 459
Westminster Mass. Centennial 14–7
Wyman's Charlestown Mass. i, 507–12
Holder — Austin's R. I. Gen. Dict. 102
Holdridge — American Ancestry ii, 57
Burleigh's Guild Genealogy 91
Savage's Genealogical Dictionary ii, 446
Hole — American Ancestry xii, 53
Littell's Passaic Valley 187
Holgate — Egle's Queries 4th ser. i, 139
Levering Genealogy (1897) 160–2
Holkins — Stiles' Windsor Ct. ii, 397
Holladay — Hayden's Gens. 357–76
Lewis Genealogy (1893) 147–51
Holland — Aldrich's Walpole N. H. 277
American Ancestry i, 38; iii, 163; xii
Bangor Historical Magazine iii, 84–6
Barry's History of Framingham Mass. 291
Bond's Watertown Mass. Genealogies 302
Holland Chart (1882) by H. W. H.
Holton's Winslow Genealogy i, 509–16
Munsell's Albany Collections iv, 134
New York Gen. and Biog. Rec. ix, 129–31
Pierce Genealogy (1894)
Power's Sangamon Co. Ill. Settlers 382
Savage's Genealogical Dictionary ii, 447
Sharpless Genealogy 437
Temple's Hist. of N. Brookfield Mass. 633
Ward's History of Shrewsbury Mass. 323
Hollaway — Savage's Dict. ii, 450
Worcester Mag. and Hist. Journal ii, 153
Hollenbeck — American Ancestry ii, 57
Loomis Genealogy (1880) 801
Power's Sangamon Co. Ill. Settlers 383
Holley — American Ancestry v, 142
Butler's Hist. of Farmington Me. 499–503
Daniels' History of Oxford Mass. 543
Kitchell Genealogy 80
Orcutt's History of Torrington Ct. 719
Sedgwick's History of Sharon Ct. 90
Holliday — Hanson's Old Kent Md. 246–50
Meade's Old Churches of Va.
Holliman — Austin's R. I. Dictionary 102
Austin's Allied Families 134
Hollinger — Burgner Genealogy 141–50
Egle's Notes and Queries 4th ser. i, 158
Hollingshead — Haine's Ancestry 13–5
Hollingsworth — Hollingsworth Gen. (1884) 144 pages
Jolliffe Genealogy (1893) 145–53
Morris Genealogy (1898) 560–3
Rodman Genealogy 168
Savage's Genealogical Dictionary ii, 448
Smith's History of Delaware Co. Pa. 469
Stern's Our Kindred 6–11, 56–60
Hollinshead — Penn. Mag. xvi, 123–5
Hollis — American Ancestry vii, 25
Barry's History of Hanover Mass. 318
Davis' Landmarks of Plymouth Mass. 135
Lapham's History of Bethel Me. 567

Lincoln's Hist. of Hingham Mass. ii, 351
New Eng. Hist. and Gen. Reg. xlv, 51–61
Hollister — Am. Ancestry ii, 58; iv, 172
Child Genealogy 802
Cothren's Woodbury Ct. 583–7; ii, 1506
Ely Genealogy 261
Glastenbury Ct. Centennial 183
Goodwin's Genealogical Notes 97–106
Hollister Genealogy (1886) 805 pages
Hollister's History of Pawlet Vt. 202–4
Savage's Genealogical Dictionary ii, 449
Sedgwick's History of Sharon Ct. 90
Talcott's N. Y. and N. E. Families 552–67
Holloway — American Ancestry ix, 192
Sullivant Mem. 85–95
Hollowell — American Ancestry vii, 271
Cleveland's Hist. of Yates Co. N. Y. 736–9
Holly — Huntington's Stamford 41–5
Tuttle Genealogy 340–2
Holman — Am. Ancestry iii, 197; viii, 32
Bass' History of Braintree Vt. 194–51
Bemis' History of Marlboro N. H. 537–9
Benedict's History of Sutton Mass. 663–5
Blake's Mendon Mass. Association 144–6
Collin's Hist. Hillsdale N. Y., app. 64–6
Corliss' North Yarmouth Me. Magazine
Daniels' History of Oxford Mass. 543
Driver Genealogy 304
Mitchell's Hist. of Bridgewater Mass. 188
Norton's Hist. of Fitzwilliam N. H. 607–10
Paige's History of Cambridge Mass. 587
Savage's Genealogical Dictionary ii, 450
Stiles' History of Windsor Ct. ii, 398
Temple's Hist. of N. Brookfield Mass. 633
Young's Hist. Wayne Co. Ind. 179, 342–5
Holme — Shourd's Fenwick Colony 91
Holmes — Adams Family of Kingston
Allison Genealogy 67–84
American Ancestry ii, 58; iii, 175; iv, 19, 68; v, 203; x, 10; xi, 96
Anderson's Waterbury Ct. i, app. 68
Austin's Ancestries 71
Austin's R. I. Genealogical Dictionary 103
Avery Genealogy (1893) 282–4
Baker's History of Montville Ct. 327–32
Ballou's History of Milford Mass. 827
Bergen's Kings County N. Y. Settlers 144
Bliss' History of Rehoboth Mass. 207
Bolton's Westchester County N. Y. ii, 736
Bond's Watertown Mass. Gens. 302
Bridgeman's Granary Burial Ground 339
California Register (1900) i
Clark Genealogy (1892) 111
Clute's History of Staten Island N. Y. 390
Cochrane's History of Antrim N. H. 536–8
Cochrane's Hist. Francest'n N. H. 757–60
Corliss' North Yarmouth Me. Magazine
Cushman's History of Sheepscott Me. 391
Daniels' History of Oxford Mass. 544
Davis' Landmarks of Plymouth 136–45
Deane's History of Scituate Mass. 287
Dearborn's History of Salisbury N. H. 628
Dedham Mass. Records i
Eaton's History of Thomaston Me. 271
Essex Mass. Institute Hist. Colls. xxi, 188
Field's History of Haddam Ct. 47

Hammatt Papers of Ipswich Mass. 157
Hayward's Hist. of Hancock N. H. 658–60
Heywood's Hist. of Westminster Mass. 709
Holmes Family of Conn. (1865) 76 pages
Holmes Fam. of So. Carolina (1893) chart
Hubbard's History of Springfield Vt. 338–41
Hudson's History of Lexington Mass. 106
Humphrey Genealogy 373
Huntington's Stamford Ct. Settlers 45
Kingman's N. Bridgewater Mass. 559–71
Lapham's History of Norway Me. 533
Lapham's History of Paris Me. 632–4
Machias Me. Centennial 166
Meade's Old Churches of Virginia
Mitchell's Hist. of Bridgewater Mass. 188
Narragansett Historical Register iv, 294
N. E. Hist. Reg. xix. 362; xxiii, 148, 439
Newport R. I. Historical Mag. (1883) 174
Ogden Genealogy (1898) 107–9
Parker's History of Londonderry N. H. 277
Runnel's Hist. of Sanbornton N. H. ii, 356
Savage's Genealogical Dictionary ii, 451–4
Selleck's Norwalk Ct. (1896) 102
Shourd's Fenwick Colony N. J. 87–90
Smith's History of Dutchess Co. N. Y. 500
Smith's Hist. of Peterborough N. H. 110–7
Stanton Genealogy 556–8
Stark's History of Dunbarton N. H. 241
Taylor Genealogy (1886) 69–85
Temple's Hist. N. Brookfield Mass. 633–5
Tilley's Mag. of New Eng. Hist. ii, 17–41
Vinton's Giles Genealogy 56–9, 76, 181–234
Whitmore's Copps Hill Epitaphs
Winsor's History of Duxbury Mass. 267
Wyman's Charlestown Mass. Gens. i, 513
Holsapple — American Ancestry ii, 58
Holstein — Buck's Montgomery Pa. 25
Holstein Genealogy (1892) 305 pages
Holt — Abbot's Hist. of Andover Mass. 22
American Ancestry i, 38; ii, 59; iv, 217;
v, 24, 118; vii, 31, 101; ix, 121
Bangor Me. Historical Magazine v, 196
Carter's Hist. Pembroke N. H. ii, 146–58
Caulkins' History of New London Ct. 314
Chandler Genealogy 469–73
Cochrane's History of Antrim N. H. 538–41
Cochrane's Hist. Francest'n N. H. 760–2
Coit Genealogy 145–7, 233–6
Davis' History of Wallingford Ct. 796–8
Dawson Genealogy 42
Dodd's History of East Haven Ct. 127
Goode Genealogy 98
Hayward's History of Gilsum N. H. 330
Hayward's History of Hancock N. H. 660
Heywood's Hist. of Westminster Mass. 709
Holt Genealogy (1864) 367 pages
Holt Association (1868) 20 pages
Holt Assoc. Meeting (1871) 7 pages
Holton's Winslow Genealogy i, 133
Hubbard's History of Springfield Vt. 343
Keyes' West Boylston Mass Register 25
Lapham's History of Bethel Me. 563–7
Laphams' History of Norway Me. 531–3
Lapham's History of Paris Me. 634
Lapham's History of Rumford Me. 346
Livermore's Hist. of Wilton N. H. 402–14

Maine Hist. and Gen. Recorder ii, 39
N. E. Hist. and Gen. Reg. xxxviii, 478
Paige's History of Hardwick Mass. 400
Savage's Genealogical Dictionary ii, 454
Secomb's History of Amherst N. H. 635–9
Smiᵗh's History of Peterborough N. H. 117
Stearns' History of Rindge N. H. 556
Stone's History of Hubbardston Mass. 294
Virginia Magazine of History v, 452–4
Washington N. H. History 478
Holtom — Boardman Gen. (1895) 696–9
Holton — Ball's Lake Co. Ind. 405, 414
Benedict's History of Sutton Mass. 665
Cochrane's History of Antrim N. H. 541
Dwight's Strong Genealogy 228
Goodwin's Olcott Genealogy 28
Hemenway's Vt. Hist. Gaz. v, 69, 149–51
Holton Family Chart (1866) 18x24 inches
Holton Family Chart (1872) 18x24 inches
Holton's Farwell Genealogy 93–101, 155–81
Holton's Winslow Memorial i, 327–395
Leach's Morton Ancestry 122–5
Magennis Genealogy 57–9
Savage's Genealogical Dictionary ii, 453–6
Temple's History of Northfield Mass. 460–6
Williams' History of Danby Vt. 167
Holway — Freeman's Cape Cod 161
Holyoke — Bangor Hist. Mag. i, 27–9
Essex Mass. Institute Hist. Colls. iii, 57–61
Lewis' History of Lynn Mass. 121
Pynchon Genealogy
Savage's Genealogical Dictionary ii, 456
Talcott's N. Y. and New Eng. Fams. 568
Tuttle Genealogy xxxii
Homans — American Ancestry v, 107
Homer — American Ancestry v, 107; x, 68
Bridgeman's Kings Chapel Epit. 199–203
Freeman's Hist. of Cape Cod Mass. ii, 713
Homer Genealogy (1889) 27 pages
Hyde's History of Brimfield Mass. 415–8
Savage's Genealogical Dictionary ii, 457
Homes — American Ancestry i, 38
Bowens of Woodstock Ct. 208–10
Morris' Bontecou Genealogy 211
Pierce's My Ancestors (1864)
Tappan Memoir (1834) 119–24
Honeyman — American Ancestry iii, 185
Honness — Chambers' N. J. Germans
Honsberger — Kratz Gen. 14–24, 29–34
Hood — American Ancestry ii, 59
Hood Genealogy (1867) 64 pages
Hood Genealogy (1899) 27 pages
Morris' Bontecou Genealogy 64–6
Savage's Genealogical Dictionary ii, 457
Smith's History of Delaware Co. Pa. 469
Hooe — De Bow's Review xxix, 265
Hayden's Virginia Genealogies 716–9
Hooe Genealogy (1891) 4 pages
Meade's Old Churches of Virginia
Richmond Va. Standard iii, 5
Hoogeboom — Albany Collections iv, 134
Hooghkerke — Albany Collections iv, 134
Hooghteling — Albany Collections iv, 135
Hoogland — Bergen's Kings County 145
Hoogs — Jackson's Newton Mass. 310
Hook — Savage's Gen. Dictionary ii, 457

Hooke — Hoyt's Salisbury Fams. 203-5
Hooker — American Ancestry iv, 129, 230
Cothren's History of Woodbury Ct. 569-77
Dwight Genealogy 844, 1043-50
Hooker Reunion Address (1890) 8 pages
Hooker Reunion (1891) 83 pages
Joslin's History of Poultney Vt. 274-8
Morse's Sherborn Mass. Settlers 105
N. E. Hist. and Gen. Reg. xlvii, 189-92
Paige's History of Cambridge Mass. 589
Porter's Hartford Ct. Settlers 14
Robinson Genealogy (1857)
Savage's Genealogical Dictionary ii, 458-60
Stiles' History of Windsor Ct. ii, 399-403
Temple's Hist. of N. Brookfield Mass. 635
Tuttle Genealogy 88
Hoole — American Ancestry xi, 110
Hooley — Hertzler Genealogy 138-41
Hooper — Aldrich's Walpole 278-82
American Ancestry iv, 138
Bond's Watertown Mass. Genealogies 302
Lapham's History of Paris Me. 635
Mitchell's Hist. Bridgewater Mass. 189-91
New Eng. Hist. and Gen. Reg. xxii, 287
Platt Genealogy (1896) 15-9
Savage's Genealogical Dictionary ii, 460
Wyman's Charlestown Mass. Gens. i, 515
Hoopes — Cope Family 49, 105, 297-9
Jackson Genealogy 235
Painter's Reminiscences (1871) 11
Palmer and Trimble Genealogy 192-5, 198
Hoos — American Ancestry i, 38
Hoover — Plumb's Hanover Pa. 428-30
Young's History of Wayne Co. Ind. 345-50
Hope — Titcomb's N. E. People 102-15
Hopkins — American Ancestry ii, 59; iv, 83, 218, 227, 237; v, 138, 187; ix 82
Anderson's Waterbury Ct. i, app. 69
Austin's Ancestries 33
Austin's Ancestral Dictionary 31
Austin's R. I. Genealogical Dict. 105, 324
Bangor Me. Historical Mag. v, 5; viii, 109
Bronson's History of Waterbury Ct. 502-5
Bunker's Long Island Genealogies 218
Caverly's History of Pittsford Vt. 708
Cochrane's History of Antrim N. H. 542-7
Cochrane's Hist. Francest'n N. H. 762-8
Cushman's History of Sheepscott Me. 391-3
Davis' Landmarks of Plymouth Mass. 145
Durfee's Mem. of Rev. Mark Hopkins
Eaton's History of Thomaston Me. ii, 272
Essex Mass. Institute Hist. Coll. ii, 115-23
Follett Genealogy (1896) 174-9
Freeman's Cape Cod Mass. ii, 384, 508
Goodwin's Genealogical Notes 107-18
Hazen's History of Billerica Mass. 74
Hollister's History of Pawlet Vt. 204
Hopkins Genealogy (1879) 6 pages
Hopkins Genealogy (1881) 82 pages
Judd's History of Hadley Mass. 513
Leach's Morton Ancestry 68-75
Livermore's History of Wilton N. H. 414
Maine Genealogist iii, 1-8
Mallmann's Shelter Island N. Y. 182-97
Meade's Old Churches of Virginia i, 460
Morrison's Hist. Windham N. H. 589-95

Narragansett Historical Reg. vii, 137-55
New Eng. Hist. and Gen. Register v, 43-5
Orcutt's History of Wolcott Ct. 500
Page Genealogy 130
Pompey N. Y. Reunion 321
Randall's Hist. of Chesterfield N. H. 359
Rich's History of Truro Mass. 536
Salem N. Y. Book of History 51-4
Savage's Genealogical Dictionary ii, 461-3
Secomb's History of Amherst N. H. 639
Taylor's Great Barrington Mass. 158
Thomas Genealogy (1877) 89-93
Thomas Genealogy (1896) 346-59
Thompson Genealogy (1854) 103-6
Tuttle Genealogy 350-4
Wyman's Charlestown Mass. Gens. 516-8
Young's Hist. of Chautauqua Co. N. Y. 643
Hopkinson — Guildhall Vt. 242-4
Buxton Me. Centennial 207-10
Essex Mass. Inst. Hist. Colls. xxi, 189-92
McKean Genealogy 149
Penn. Magazine of Hist. and Biog. ii, 314
Poor's Merrimack Vall. Researches 88, 120
Woodbury's Groveland Mass. Epit. 41-8
Hopper — Am. Anc. v, 232; ix, 92, 93; x, 107
Clayton's History of Bergen Co. N. J. 233-6
Hoppin — American Ancestry iv, 45, 87
Power's Sangamon Co. Ill. Settlers 383
Tuttle Genealogy 664-6
Wyman's Charlestown Mass. Gens. i, 518
Hoppock — Chambers' N. J. Germans
Hopson — American Ancestry iv, 167
Hughes Genealogy 108-10
Orcutt's History of Torrington Ct. 720
Paul's History of Wells Vt. 93
Hord — Am. Anc. iii, 27; iv, 45; xi 211
Hord Genealogy (1898) 199 pages
Horn — Barry's Framingham 292
Felton Genealogy (1886) 245
Savage's Genealogical Dictionary ii, 464
Hornbeck — Schoonmaker's Kingston
Sylvester's History of Ulster Co. N. Y. 264
Hornblower — Hornblower Genealogy (1883) 80 pages
New Jersey Hist. Soc. Proc. vii, 237-47
Horne — Clarke Genealogy (1896) 102-36
New Eng. Hist. and Gen. Reg. vii, 156
Ogden Genealogy (1898) 80-2, 120
Sharpless Genealogy 305
Wentworth Genealogy i, 398-400; ii, 206-9
Horner — Am. Ancestry iv, 175; xi, 86
Clyde's Irish Settlement in Pa. 63-71
Egle's Hist. Reg. of Interior Pa. i, 213-5
Hayden's Virginia Genealogies 188-97
Hornsby — Watson's Notable Families 99
Horr — Lapham's Norway Me. 533
Warren's History of Waterford Me. 257
See also under Hoar
Horseley — Goode Gen. 70, 132, 261-3
Horsington — Timlow's Southington Ct.
Horsley — Cabell Genealogy 172-6, 274-81
Hodgman's Westford 456
Horst — Brubacher Genealogy 203
Horswell — Austin's R. I. Dict. 105
Horter — Egle's Queries i, (1894) 347-9

Horton — Am. Anc. i, 38; ii, 59; ix, 11; xii
Baird's History of Rye N. Y. 413-5
Bangor Me. Historical Magazine v, 197
Bolton's Westchester County N. Y. ii, 736
Chambers' Early Germans of N. J. 417-21
Ely Genealogy 25
Horton Family Gathering (1876) 13 pages
Horton Genealogy (1876) 259 pages
Horton Genealogy Supp. (1879) 80 pages
Plumb's History of Hanover Pa. 430-2
Savage's Genealogical Dictionary ii, 465
Williams' History of Danby Vt. 167
Hosford — Joslin's Poultney Vt. 278
Pearson's Schenectady N. Y. Settlers 95
Savage's Genealogical Dictionary ii, 465
Stiles' History of Windsor Ct. ii, 403
Hoskin — Boyd's Winchester Ct. 61.
Hoskins — Barbour's My Wife 74
Martin's History of Chester Pa. 55
Orcutt's History of Torrington Ct. 721
Pierce's Biog. Contributions 139-95
Savage's Genealogical Dictionary ii, 466
Smith's History of Delaware Co. Pa. 470
Stiles' History of Windsor Ct. ii, 404-8
Wakefield Genealogy 108
Hosley — Hayward's Hancock 661-70
Hazen's History of Billerica Mass. 74
Heywood's Hist. of Westminster Mass. 710
Randall's Hist. of Chesterfield N. H. 360
Hosmer — Amer. Ancestry vi, 142; x, 193
Avon N. Y. Genealogical Record 21-6
Brown's Bedford Mass. Families 18
Coffin's History of Boscawen N. H. 555
Guild's Stiles Genealogy 366
Hayward's History of Gilsum N. H. 330
Hill's History of Mason N. H. 203-10
Hosmer Genealogy (1861) 16 pages
Jameson's History of Medway Mass. 495
Potter's Concord Mass. Families 11
Savage's Genealogical Dictionary ii, 466
Shattuck's History of Concord Mass. 375
Stiles' History of Windsor Ct. ii, 408
Temple's History of Northfield Mass. 466
Walworth's Hyde Genealogy 911
Hostetler — Hertzler Genealogy 152-4
Hostetter — American Ancestry viii, 175
Hotaling — Am. Anc. i, 39; ii, 59; xii, 112
Hotchkiss — American Ancestry xii
Andrews' New Britain Ct.
Anderson's Waterbury Ct. i, app. 70-3 ▪
Bronson's History of Waterbury Ct. 505-8
Cothren's History of Woodbury Ct. 579
Davis' History of Wallingford Ct. 798-801
Dodd's History of East Haven Ct. 129
Orcutt's History of Derby Ct. 731
Orcutt's History of New Milford Ct. 718
Orcutt's History of Torrington Ct. 721
Orcutt's History of Wolcott Ct. 502-5
Paul's History of Wells Vt. 105-7
Tuttle Genealogy 652-7
Hottenstein — Keim Fam. 336, 411-3, 432
Hough — American Ancestry vi, 182; vii.
   98, 231, 232; viii, 6
Andrews' History of New Britain Ct. 352
Aylsworth Genealogy 304
Babson's History of Gloucester Mass. 105

Caulkins' History of New London Ct. 302
Caulkins' History of Norwich Ct. 233
Davis' History of Bucks County Pa. 120
Davis' History of Wallingford Ct. 802-6
Lincoln's Hist. of Hingham Mass. ii, 352
N. Y. Gen. and Biog. Record xvii, 97
Orcutt's History of Wolcott Ct. 506
Potts Genealogy (1895) 229-34
Savage's Genealogical Dictionary ii, 468
Tuttle Genealogy 220
Walworth's Hyde Gen. ii, 1100-11, 1152-9
Whitmore's Copps Hill Epitaphs
Young's History of Warsaw N. Y. 280
Young's History of Wayne Co. Ind. 290-9
Houghtaling — Am. Anc. i, 39; vi, 119
Fillow Genealogy 94-6
Greene County N. Y. History 254
Schoonmaker's Hist. Kingston N. Y. 495
Thomas Genealogy (1896) 359-62
Houghton — American Ancestry iii, 175;
   iv, 229; vii, 154; ix, 113; xii, 8
Bemis' History of Marlboro N. H. 539
Douglas Genealogy 163-6
Hale Genealogy 337
Hayward's History of Gilsum N. H. 331
Heywood's Hist. Westminster Mass. 711-3
Houghton Assoc. Report (1848) 27 pages
Houghton Assoc. Report (1869) 60 pages
Hubbard's Hist. of Springfield Vt. 344
Lapham's History of Norway Me. 534
Lapham's History of Paris Me. 635
Lapham's History of Woodstock Me. 225
Power's Sangamon Co. Ill. Settlers 20
Savage's Genealogical Dictionary ii, 469
Sheldon's Hist. of Deerfield Mass. 212
Waterford Me. Centennial 258
Worcester Mag. and Hist. Jour. 281, 342
Houlton — Essex Mass. Inst. Hist. Colls.
   xxix, 149-63, 184-92
Felton Genealogy (1886) 245
House — American Ancestry ii, 59
Barry's History of Hanover Mass. 319
Dean's History of Scituate Mass. 289
French's History of Turner Me. 54
Hanover Mass. Records (1898)
Hubbard's Stanstead Co. Canada 212-4
Mead's History of Greenwich Ct. 370
Housman — Clute's Staten Island 391
Houston — Cooley's Trenton N. J. 124-9
Houston Genealogy (1882) 420 pages
Johnson's History of Bristol Me. 382-4
Merrill's History of Acworth N. H. 228
Power's Sangamon Co. Ill. Settlers 384
Stearns' Hist. of Ashburnham Mass. 755
Williamson's History of Belfast Me. 96-8
Hover — American Ancestry ii, 59
Hovey — Amer. Anc. iv, 152; v, 23, 46, 139
Ammidown Genealogy 35
Andrews Genealogy (1890) 50-3, 61
Benedict's History of Sutton Mass. 666
Bradbury's Hist. Kennebunkport Me. 251
Caldwell Genealogy 71
Cleveland Genealogy 10-20, 96-125 134-55
Cleveland Genealogy 2d ed. 638-46
Cochrane's Hist. of Francestown N. H. 769
Cutter's History of Arlington Mass. 263

Daniel's History of Oxford Mass. 545–8
Davis' Landmarks of Plymouth Mass. 146
Eaton's Annals of Warren Me. 554
Eaton's History of Thomaston Me. ii, 242
Essex County Mass. Register i, (1894) 97–9, 116–8, 133–5, 148–50; ii (1895) 1–3
Hammatt Papers, Ipswich Mass. 158–65
Holton's Farwell Genealogy 49
Hovey Genealogy (1893) 31 pages
Hubbard's Stanstead Co. Canada 246–8
Hudson's History of Lexington Mass. 107
Jackson's History of Newton Mass. 311
Judd's History of Hadley Mass. 514
Little's History of Weare N. H. 905
Paige's Hist. of Cambridge Mass. 589–91
Perley's History of Boxford Mass. 102
Read's History of Swanzey N. H. 380
Savage's Genealogical Dictionary ii, 470
Slafter Genealogy 30
Smith's History of Peterborough N. H. 118
Wyman's Charlestown Mass. Gens. i, 521
Young's History of Warsaw N. Y. 281–3
How — Anderson's Waterbury Ct. i, 73
Bond's Watertown Mass. Genealogies 303
Calnek's Hist. of Annapolis N. S. 527–34
Davis' History of Wallingford Ct. 789–92
Hammatt Papers Ipswich Mass. 133, 152
Huntington's Stamford Ct. Settlers 46
Kidder's History New Ipswich N. H. 391
Morse's Mem. appendix 67¾
New Eng. Hist. and Gen. Reg. xvi, 314
Orcutt's History of Stratford Ct. 1221
Reed's History of Rutland Mass. 113, 125
Temple's North Brookfield Mass. 637–41
Ward Genealogy (1851) 13
Worcester Mag. and Hist. Journal ii, 130
Howard — Adams' Fairhaven Vt. 400–3
American Ancestry iii, 198; xi, 87
Bangor Historical Magazine vi, 3–5
Bass' History of Braintree Vt. 651
Bemis' History of Marlboro N. H. 540
Benedict's History of Sutton Mass. 666
Blood's History of Temple N. H. 227–9
Cochrane's Hist. of Francestown N. H. 770
Daniel's History of Oxford Mass. 548
Davis' Landmarks of Plymouth Mass. 146
Dearborn's Hist. of Salisbury N. H. 629
Eaton's Annals of Warren Me. 555
Eaton's History of Thomaston Me. ii, 273
Hammatt Papers, Ipswich Mass. 166
Hanson's Old Kent Md. 41–8
Hayward's History of Gilsum N. H. 332–4
Heywood's Hist. Westminster Mass. 713–6
Howard Family of Conn. (1884) 238 pages
Howard Family of Mass. (1897) 71 pages
Kingman's N. Bridgewater Mass. 533–46
Lapham's History of Bethel Me. 568, 655
Lapham's History of Rumford Me. 353
Lillie Genealogy (1896) 106–14
Lincoln's Hist. of Hingham Mass. ii, 353–5
Livermore's History of Wilton N. H. 415
Locke Genealogy 111
Malden Mass. Bi-Centennial 246
Meade's Churches of Old Virginia
Mitchell's Hist. Bridgewater Mass. 191–202
North's History of Augusta Me. 882–4

Orford N. H. Centennial 124
Paige's History of Hardwick Mass. 400
Preston Genealogy (1870) 58–63
Proctor Genealogy (1898) 263–8
Read's History of Swanzey N. H. 381
Rhode Island Historical Mag. v, 223–7
Richmond Va. Standard ii, 12; iii, 7
Ridlon's Harrison Me. Settlers 70–2
Ridlon's Saco Valley Me. Families 737–9
Riker's Annals of Newtown N. Y. 398–401
Savage's Genealogical Dictionary ii, 471–3
Secomb's History of Amherst N. H. 640
Sharpless Genealogy 136–8, 183–8, 301–4
Stearns' History of Ashburnham Mass. 756
Stiles' History of Windsor Ct. ii, 409
Saunderson's Charlestown N. H. 415
Temple's Hist. of N. Brookfield Mass. 636
Temple's History of Palmer Mass. 488–91
Thomas Genealogy (1877) 94–6
Thomas Genealogy (1896) 362–9
Washington N. H. History 479
Whitmore's Copps Hill Epitaphs
Worcester Mag. and Hist. Journal ii, 13
Wyman's Charlestown Mass. Gens. 522
Howarth — Daniel's Oxford Mass. 549
Howe — American Ancestry i. 40; iv, 173; v, 86; vi, 148; vii, 135; viii, 36, 38; x, 28; xi, 204; xii, 58
Ballou's History of Milford Mass. 830
Barry's Hist. of Framingham Mass. 292–8
Bassett's Hist. of Richmond N. H. 414–6
Blake Genealogy 42, 50–4
Brook's History of Medford Mass. 528
Chapman's Weeks Genealogy 144
Cochrane's Hist. of Francestown N. H. 771
Cogswell's History Henniker N. H. 618–26
Davis Genealogy 49, 51, 131–3, 148–50
Dedham Mass. Hist. Register x, 2
Dodd's History of East Haven Ct. 130
Dodge Ancestry (1896) 37–41
Draper's History of Spencer Mass. 207–9
Dwight Genealogy 480
Ellis Genealogy 394
Freeman's Cape Cod ii, 189–214, 708–12
Glover Genealogy 356–8
Gregory's History of Northfield Vt. 194–6
Hayward's History of Gilsum N. H. 334
Hayward's History of Hancock N. H. 671
Herrick's History of Gardner Mass. 357–9
Heywood's Hist. Westminster Mass. 716–8
Hill's Dedham Mass. Records i
Hobart's Hist. of Abington Mass. 386–401
Howe (Rev. J. M.) Biog. (1889) 254 pages
Howe Family Gathering (1871) 46 pages
Hubbard's Hist. of Springfield Vt. 345–7
Hubbard's Hist. of Stanstead Co. Can. 321
Hudson's Marlborough Mass. 380–97
Ireland Genealogy 23–7
Joslin's History of Poultney Vt. 280
Lapham's Hist. of Bethel Me. 567, 653–5
Lapham's History of Norway Me. 535
Lapham's History of Paris Me. 637–9
Lapham's History of Rumford Me. 347–53
Little Genealogy 162–5
Livermore's History of Wilton N. H. 415
Merrill's History of Acworth N. H. 229

Morrison's History of Windham N. H. 595
New Eng. Hist. and Gen. Reg. iv, 63-5
Norton's Hist. of Fitzwilliam N. H. 610-4
Paige's History of Hardwick Mass. 401
Paul's History of Wells Vt. 107
Perkins' Old Houses of Norwich Ct. 471
Pierce's History of Grafton Mass. 507-9
Randall's Hist. of Chesterfield N. H. 361
Read's History of Swanzey N. H. 382
Rice Genealogy
Ridlon's Saco Valley Me. Families 130
Runnel's Hist. of Sanbornton N. H. ii, 357
Savage's Genealogical Dictionary 473-6
Smith's Hist. of Peterborough N. H. 120-2
Stearns' Hist. Ashburnham Mass. 757-58
Stearns' History of Rindge N. H. 557-9
Stone's History of Hubbardston Mass. 295
Temple's History of Northfield Mass. 469
Thayer Memorial (1835) 88
Thurston's History of Winthrop Me. 187
Tuttle Genealogy 485
Ward's Hist. of Shrewsbury Mass. 310-7
Washington N. H. History 481-3
Wheeler's History of Newport N. H. 419
Whitmore's Copps Hill Epitaphs
Whittemore's Orange N. J. 434
Wyman's Charlestown Mass. Gens. i, 523
Howell — Am. Ancestry i, 40; v, 191; xii
Am. Hist. Register iii, 56-78; iv, 59-64
Bulkley's Browne Mem. 42, 57-9, 87-9
Chambers' Early Germans of N. J. 421-5
Clement's Newtown N. J. Settlers
Cooley's Trenton N. J. Genealogies 129-41
Hall's Trenton N. J. Presbyterian Ch. 286
Howell's Hist. Southampton N. Y. 300-22
Hughes Genealogy 113-5
Kellogg's White Genealogy 53
Leach's Reading Genealogy 129-88
Missouri Pioneer Families 154
Nevius Genealogy
New York Gen. Rec. xxviii, 49-52, 81-5
Ogden Genealogy (1898) 56
Potts Genealogy (1895) 392
Prime Genealogy (1895) 45
Savage's Genealogical Dictionary ii, 476-8
Sharpless Genealogy 204, 324-7
Stickney's Hist. of Minisink N. Y. 169
Sylvester's Hist. Ulster County N. Y. 136
Howes — American Ancestry ii, 60
Atkins' History of Hawley Mass. 52
Austin's Allied Families 136
Hatch's History of Industry Me. 655-60
Howes Genealogy (1892) 208 pages
Howes Fam. of Madison N. Y. (1893) 16 p.
Orcutt's History of Stratford Ct. 1220
Read's History of Swanzey N. H. 383
Sears Genealogy 56, 147, 159
Swift's Barnstable Families ii, 54-7
Howey — Harris Genealogy (1878) 84
Howland — Aldrich's Walpole 287-9
American Ancestry vi, 178; viii, 63; ix, 100
Austin's Allied Families 137
Bill Genealogy 176-8
Bolton's Westchester Co. N. Y. ii, 549
Davis' Landmarks of Plymouth 147-56
Draper's History of Spencer Mass. 209

Eaton's Annals of Warren Me. 556
Hobart's History of Abington Mass. 403
Howland Genealogy (1885) 463 pages
Howland Genealogy (1887) 12 pages
Mitchell's Hist. of Bridgewater Mass. 379
New Eng. Hist. Gen. Reg. xxxiv, 192-4
Pell's Howland Journal (1890) 5-20
Pierce's Contributions 105-38
Savage's Genealogical Dictionary ii, 478-80
Swift's Barnstable Families ii, 49-53
Thacher Genealogy (1872) 87
Thatcher's Hist. of Plymouth Mass. 129-33
Winsor's Hist. of Duxbury Mass. 269-71
Howlett — American Ancestry iv, 12
Guild's Stiles Genealogy 111
Hammatt Papers, Ipswich Mass. 153
Topsfield Mass. Hist. Collections 1896, ii
Hoxie — Amer. Ancestry ii, 60; ix, 91
Austin's Allied Families 140
Freeman's Hist. of Cape Cod Mass. iv, 163
Savage's Genealogical Dictionary ii, 385
Hoxworth — Jenkins' Gwynedd Pa.
Penn. Mag. of History and Biog. x, 100-3
Hoysradt — American Ancestry ii, 61
Hoyt — American Ancestry i, 40; vi, 136,
    145; xi, 35 219
Baird's History of Rye N. Y. 412
Bouton Genealogy
Calnek's History of Annapolis N. S. 534
Cochrane's Hist. of Francestown N. H. 772
Cogswell's History of Henniker N. H. 626
Davis' Landmarks of Plymouth Mass. 156
Dwight's Strong Genealogy 665
Hall's Records Norwalk Ct. 183-90, 193-9
Hoyt Genealogy (1857) 144 pages
Hoyt Genealogy 2d ed. (1871) 686 pages
Hoyt Family Meeting (1866) 64 pages
Hoyt's Salisbury Mass. Familes 205-9
Hubbard's Stanstead Cc. Canada 276
Huntington Genealogy 77
Huntington's Stamford Ct. Settlers 47-54
Judd's History of Hadley Mass. 514
Kulp's Wyoming Valley Families
Lapham's History of Rumford Me. 354-6
Little's History of Weare N. H. 906-9
Morse Memorial (1896) 81-3
Orcutt's History of Torrington Ct. 722
Runnel's Sanbornton N. H. ii, 358-64
Savage's Genealogical Dictionary ii, 480-2
Selleck's Norwalk Ct. (1896) 353-64
Sheldon's Hist. of Deerfield Mass. 213-8
Stackpole's History of Durham Me. 201
Stark's History of Dunbarton N. H. 247
Stiles' History of Windsor Ct. ii, 410-4
Temple's Hist. of N. Brookfield Mass. 641
Tompkins Genealogy 42
Washington N. H. History 483-5
Wheeler's History of Newport N. H. 421
Worthen's History of Sutton N. H. 769
Hubard — Meade's Old Fams. of Va.
Hubart — Ridlon's Saco Valley 740
See also Hubbard
Hubbard — Aldrich's Walpole 289
American Ancestry iii, 106; iv, 156, **232;**
    v, 135, 224; vi, 29, 122; ix, 89, 90, **94,**
    95, 101, 115, 117, 229, 230, 234

Austin's R. I. Genealogical Dictionary 106
Bemis' History of Marlboro N. H. 541
Benton's History of Guildhall Vt. 237
Bergen Genealogy 127, 156
Blake Genealogy 71
Bond's Watertown Mass.Genealogies 795–9
Champion Genealogy 97–9
Davis' Landmarks of Plymouth Mass. 157
Dickerman Genealogy 494–501
Eaton's History of Candia N. H. 82–6
Ely Genealogy 40, 86–9
Field's History of Haddam Ct. 46
Glastenbury Ct. Centennial 172
Glover Genealogy 123
Goodwin's Olcott Genealogy 20
Guild's Stiles Genealogy 105
Hall's Genealogical Notes (1886) 104
Hammatt Papers, Ipswich Mass. 168–70
Hayward's History of Gilsum N. H. 335
Hayward's Hist. of Hancock N. H. 671–3
Hoyt's Salisbury Mass. Families 209–11
Hubbard Family of Ipswich (1859) 27 p.
Hubbard Fam. of Glastonbury (1872) 34 p.
Hubbard Genealogy (1895) 495 pages
Hubbard's Hist. of Springfield Vt. 347–51
Hubbard Stanstead County Canada 126–8
Huntington's Stamford Ct. Settlers 54
Hyde's History of Brimfield Mass. 419
Judd's History of Hadley Mass. 515–7
Kellogg's White Genealogy 98
Lapham's History of Paris Me. 639
Lincoln's Hist. Hingham Mass. ii, 334–50
Little's History of Weare N. H. 910
Loomis Genealogy (1880) 652–4
Martin's History of Chester Pa. 444
Middlefield Ct. History
Montague Genealogy 310–2
Narrative Historical Register v, 326–8
New Eng. Hist. and Gen. Reg. xlviii, 213
Olin Genealogy by Nye (1892) 242–9
Orcutt's History of Stratford Ct. 1221
Paige's History of Cambridge Mass. 591
Perkins' Old Houses of Norwich Ct. 473
Potter's Concord Mass. Families 12
Randall's Hist. of Chesterfield N. H. 362–6
Reed's History of Rutland Mass. 107–9
Ridlon's Saco Valley Me. Families 740
Saunders' Alabama Settlers 364
Saunderson's Charlestown N. H. 416–30
Savage's Genealogical Dictionary iii, 482–7
Shattuck's History of Concord Mass. 376
Smith's Hist. of Sunderland Mass. 403–24
Stearns' History of Rindge N. H. 559–62
Stiles' History of Windsor Ct. ii, 414
Sullivant Genealogy 275–8
Temple's Hist. of N. Brookfield Mass. 642
Temple's History of Northfield Mass. 470
Vinton's Giles Genealogy 247
Walworth's Hyde Genealogy ii, 824–38
Ward's Rice Genealogy 34
Washburn's History of Leicester Mass. 376
Woman's Charlestown Mass. Gens. i, 525
Hubbell — Amer. Ancestry i, 41; ii, 61; v.
   67; viii, 223
Boyd's Annals of Winchester Ct. 214
Hubbell Genealogy (1881) 463 pages

Jenning's Hist. of Bennington Vt. 278–62
Orcutt's History of Stratford Ct. 1221–4
Ruggles Genealogy
Schenck's History of Fairfield Ct. 379–81
Sears Genealogy 73
Hubbs — Cope Genealogy 96, 194–5
Hubert — Barksdale Genealogy 25–27
Hubert Genealogy (1897) 10 pages
Hubley — Egle's Hist. Reg. Pa. i, 75–7
Egle's Notes and Queries (1897) 200–3;
   (1898) 1–3
Huckel — American Ancestry vi, 145
Huckins — Savage's Gen. Dict. ii, 487
Swift's Barnstable Families ii, 58–66
Huckleberry — Power's Sangamon Ill.
Hudders — Clyde's Irish Settlement Pa.
Hude — Whitehead's Perth Amboy 373
Hudson — Adams Haven Gen. pt. ii, 31
Amer. Ancestry ii, 61; v, 118; ix, 159; xii
Baird's History of Rye N. Y. 415
Bass' History of Braintree Vt. 152
Caverly's History of Pittsford Vt. 709
Daniel's History of Oxford Mass. 549–52
Glenn's Genealogical Notes (1898)
Heywood's Hist. Westminster Mass.719–22
Hudson Genealogy (1892) 28 pages
Hudson's Hist. of Lexington Mass. 107–10
Hudson's Marlborough Mass. 397–401
Hudson's Hist. of Sudbury Mass. 443
Lamb's History of New York City 27
Lincoln's Hist. of Hingham Mass. ii, 356–8
Mallmann's Shelter Island N. Y. 203–39
Middlefield Ct. History
Mitchell's Hist. of Bridgewater Mass. 201
Morris Genealogy (1898) 243
Orcutt's History of Torrington Ct. 722–5
Paige's History of Cambridge Mass. 592
Penn. Magazine of History xvi, 108–10
Power's Sangamon Co. Ill. Settlers 385–7
Savage's Genealogical Dictionary ii, 488–90
Stearns' Hist. of Ashburnham Mass. 758
Whitmore's Copps Hill Epitaphs
Wyman's Charlestown Mass. Gens. i, 525
Huested — American Ancestry ii, 61
Huestis — Bolton's Westchester Co.
Huet — Lincoln's Hingham ii, 358
Savage's Genealogical Dictionary ii, 490
See also under Hewitt and Huit
Huff — Bradbury's Kennebunkport 252
Huffmaster — Hudson's Lexington 110
Power's Sangamon Co. Ill. Settlers 388
Huger — American Ancestry v, 124
South Car. Huguenot Soc. Trans. iv, 11–7
Huggins — Dow's Hampton N. H. 757
Dickerman Genealogy 470
Power's Sangamon Co. Ill. Settlers 390
Hugh — Smith's Delaware Co. Pa. 470
Hughes — American Ancestry iii, 189; iv,
   77, 104; xii
Avery Genealogy (1893) 224–9
California Register (1900) i
Dodd's History of East Haven Ct. 130
Freeman's Hist. of Cape Cod Mass. ii, 576
Gilmer's Georgians 91
Holstein Genealogy 93–227
Hughes Genealogy (1879) 245 pages

Lawrence-Hughes Family of N. J. (1891)
Minor's Meriwether Genealogy 148
Morrison's Hist. Windham N. H. 596–603
Perkins' Old Houses of Norwich Ct. 475
Power's Sangamon Co. Ill. Settlers 389
Richmond Va. Standard i, 42, 45; iii, 14
Virginia Magazine of History v, 208
Hughson — American Ancestry ii, 62
Huhn — American Ancestry x, 27
Huit — Stiles' Windsor Ct. ii, 415
See also under Huet and Hewitt
Hulberd — Hubbard Genealogy 71
Hulbert — Am. Anc. ii, 62; v, 5; ix, 155
Hurlbut Genealogy
Savage's Genealogical Dict. ii 491, 505
Sedgwick's History of Sharon Ct. 92
Hulet — Hollister's Pawlet Vt. 205
Williams' History of Danby Vt. 168–70
Hulett — Johnson Gen. (1895) 83–5
Huling — American Ancestry iii, 153
Austin's Ancestral Dictionary 32
Austin's R. I. Genealogical Dictionary 107
Egle's Notes and Queries 2d ser. ii, 192–7
Hull — American Ancestry ii, 62, 154; iii,
27; v, 110; vii, 50; xi, 87
Am. Antiquarian Soc. Trans. iii, 267–77
Anderson's Waterbury Ct. i, app. 74
Andrews' History of New Britain Ct. 367
Austin's R. I. Genealogical Dictionary 108
Bangor Me. Historical Magazine vi, 129–32
Bouton Genealogy
Cleveland's History Yates Co. N. Y.
194–203
Cothren's Woodbury Ct. 577–9; ii, 1509
Davis' History of Wallingford Ct. 806–21
Dickinson Genealogy (1896) 156–9
Greene Genealogy
Guild's Stiles Genealogy 199
Hull Genealogy (1863) 36 pages
Hull Family of New Haven (1869) 20 pages
Hull Family of New Haven (1894) 78 pages
Jackson's History of Newton Mass. 312
Livermore's Block Island R. I. 330–2
Loomis Genealogy (1880) 59–107
Orcutt's History of Derby Ct. 732–7
Orcutt's History of Stratford Ct. 1225
Phœnix Genealogy iii, 2003
Rhode Island Hist. Society Colls. iii, 292
Richmond Va. Standard iii, 39
Saunderson's Charlestown N. H. 430–2
Savage's Genealogical Dictionary ii, 492–5
Schenck's History of Fairfield Ct. 381
Sharp's History of Seymour Ct. 172
Stiles' History of Windsor Ct. ii, 416
Swift's Barnstable Families ii, 19–29
Todd's History of Redding Ct. 199–204
Tuttle Genealogy 658–64
Wheeler Ancestors (1896) 4–8
Humaston — Anderson's Waterbury 74
Hume — Hume Genealogy (1891) 2 pages
Martin's History of Chester Pa. 294
Morris Genealogy (1887) 62, 95–7
Morris Genealogy (1898) 746–8
Humiston — Davis' Wallingford Ct.
Tuttle Genealogy 64–8
Hummer — Chambers' N. J. Germans

Humphrey — American Ancestry ii, 63,
x, 204; xi, 198
Austin's Allied Families 141
Ballou's History of Milford Mass. 831
Barbour My Wife and Mother, app. 46–9
Brown's W. Simsbury Ct. Settlers 73–85
Corliss' North Yarmouth Me. 695, 833
Daniels' History of Oxford Mass. 552–4
Eaton's History of Thomaston Me. ii, 275
Guild's (Calvin) Ancestry 15
Hibbard's History of Goshen Ct. 462–9
Hubbard's Stanstead Co. Canada 331–3
Humphrey Genealogy (1882) 23 pages
Jenkin's History of Gwynedd Pa. 96
Kingman's N. Bridgewater Mass. 524–6
Lincoln's Hist. of Hingham Mass. ii, 360–9
Morrison's History of Windham N. H. 603
Salem Press Hist. and Gen. Rec. ii, 123–7
Savage's Genealogical Dictionary ii, 495–8
Smith's History of Delaware Co. Pa. 471
Stiles' History of Windsor Ct. 673
Wheeler's Croydon N. H. Centennial 114
Humphreys — Glenn's Merion 241–51
Humphreys Genealogy (1883) 1115 pages
Humphreys Gen. Supplement (1899) 107 p.
Mansfield Genealogy 64–6
Neill Family of Delaware 124–6
New York Gen. and Biog. Record iii, 33
Orcutt's History of Derby Ct. 735
Power's Sangamon Co. Ill. Settlers 391
Preston Genealogy (1870) 23–6
Rhoad's Chronicles, Phila. (1893)
Spooner's Memorial W. Spooner 156–8
Wheeler's History of Brunswick Me. 839
Humphreyville — Stiles Genealogy 29
Hun — American Ancestry i, 41
Munsell's Albany Colls. iv, 135
Talcott's N. Y. and N. E. Fams. 92–112
Hundley — Clarke's King Wm. Fams.
Hungerford — American Ancestry i, 41
Anderson's Waterbury Ct. i, app. 75
Boyd's Annals of Winchester Ct. 173
Caulkins' History of New London Ct. 281
Field's History of Haddam Ct. 47
Orcutt's History of Torrington Ct. 725
Young's Hist. of Chautauqua Co. N. Y. 602
Hunkin — McKeen's Bradford Vt. 201–9
Runnel's Sanbornton N. H. ii, 364–77
Hunking — Wentworth Genealogy i, 180–2
Hunkins — Daniels' Oxford Mass. 554
Hunlock — Kulp's Wyoming Valley
Hunnewell — American Ancestry vi, 77
Fowle Family (1891)
Hunnewell Chart (1892)
Hunnewell Genealogy (1900) 47 pages
Libby Genealogy 44
New Eng. Hist. Gen. Register liv, 140–6
Stackpole's History of Durham Me. 202
Wyman's Charlestown Mass. Gens. 526–8
Hunsberger — Moyer Genealogy 81–99
Hunsicker — Cassel Genealogy 68, 127–9
Hunt — Adams' Haven Genealogy pt. ii, 18
Am. Anc. ii, 63; iv, 57; viii, 213; xii, 110
Atkins' History of Hawley Mass. 55
Austin's R. I. Genealogical Dictionary 109
Baird's History of Rye N. Y. 477

Ballou's History of Milford Mass. 832–41
Bass' History of Braintree Vt. 155
Bemis' History of Marlboro N. H. 542
Bethune and Faneuil Genealogy (1884)
Bolton's Westchester County N. Y. ii, 738
Bond's Watertown Mass. Gens. 304, 972
Bridgeman's Old Granary Burial Gr. 187–9
Chambers' Early Germans of N. J. 425
Chester County Pa. Hist. Soc. Bulletin
   (1898) 21–3
Cleveland's Hist. of Yates Co. N. Y. 651–4
Cooley's Trenton N. J. Genealogies 141–50
Cregar's White Genealogy
Cutter's History of Jaffrey N. H. 373–6
Dodd's History of East Haven Ct. 131
Draper's History of Spencer Mass. 211
Eaton's History of Thomaston Me. ii, 275
Emerson's History of Douglas Mass. 163–72
Gifford's Our Patronymics 19–21
Hall's Trenton N. J. Presbyterian Ch. 195
Hammatt Papers of Ipswich Mass 166
Hayward's History of Hancock N. H. 673–6
Hazen's History of Billerica Mass. 756
Hemenway's Vermont Gaz. v, 289–92
Hine's Lebanon Ct. Address (1880) 157
Hoar Lineage (1898) 21–5
Hobart's History of Abington Mass. 404
Holton's Winslow Genealogy i, 411–22
Hoyt's Salisbury Mass. Families 211–3
Hudson's History of Lexington Mass. 110
Hudson's History of Sudbury Mass. 617
Hunt Genealogy (1862) 414 pages
Jameson's History of Medway Mass. 495
Jessup Genealogy 378–87
Lawrence Genealogy (1858) 40–5
Lincoln's History of Hingham Mass. ii, 369
Loomis Genealogy (1880) 337–50
Morse's Sherborn Mass. Settlers 106
New York Gen. and Biog. Rec. xv, 42
Orcutt's History of New Milford Ct. 719
Paige's History of Hardwick Mass. 401–3
Pierce's History of Gorham Me. 175
Prime's Sands Genealogy 78–86
Read's History of Swanzey N. H. 384
Runnel's Sanbornton N. H. ii, 377–84
Saunderson's Charlestown N. H. 432–44
Savage's Genealogical Dict. ii, 499–502
Sedgwick's History of Sharon Ct. 91
Sharpless Genealogy 280
Sheldon's History of Deerfield Mass. 218
Smith's History of Delaware Co. Pa. 472
Smith's Hist. Peterborough N. H. 123–6
Smith's Hist. of Sunderland Mass. 424–7
Spooner Genealogy i, 228–35
Stearns' Hist. Ashburnham Mass. 758–63
Stearns' History of Rindge N. H. 562–5
Strong Genealogy 331–54, 1175–82
Temple's History of Northfield Mass. 471
Temple's History of Palmer Mass. 479
Wetmore Genealogy 218
Wheeler's History of Brunswick Me. 840
Whitmore's Copps Hill Epitaphs
Winsor's History of Duxbury Mass. 271
Wyman's Charlestown Mass. i, 528–30
Young's Hist. Chautauqua Co. N. Y. 273
Young's History of Wayné Co. Ind. 149

Hunter — American Ancestry i, 41; iv,
   205, 234; xii, 24
Bartlett Wanton Genealogy 129
Bullock Genealogy
Butler's History of Farmington Me. 503–5
Cogswell's History of Henniker N. H. 627
Hudson's Hist. of Marlborough Mass. 401
Hunter Family of Virginia (1895) 50 pages
Hunter Family of Mass. (1896) 5 pages
Miller's Hist. Colchester Co. N. S. 291–4
Power's Sangamon Co. Ill. Settlers 392
Richmond Va. Standard iii, 11, 35, 36
Savage's Genealogical Dictionary ii, 502
Sedgwick's History of Sharon Ct. 92
Slaughter's St. Mark's Parish Virg. 153
Temple's Hist. of N. Brookfield Mass. 642
Temple's History of Palmer Mass. 473
Wheeler's History of Brunswick Me. 840
Wheeler's History of N. Carolina 156
Hunting — Ballou's Milford Mass. 841
Bemis' History of Marlboro N. H. 543
Dedham Historical Register iii, 123–5
Hill's Dedham Mass. Records i
Howell's Hist. of Southampton N. Y. 250
Hunting Genealogy (1888) 83 pages
Jameson's History of Medway Mass. 496
Savage's Genealogical Dictionary ii, 502
Stone's History of Hubbardston Mass.
   206–9
Huntingdon — Stiles' Windsor ii, 417
Huntington — Aldrich's Walpole 291
American Ancestry vi, 41; vii, 141
Bass' History of Braintree Vt. 153
Buckingham Genealogy 153–6
C ulkins' History of Norwich Ct. 179–86
Champion Genealogy
Cochrane's Hist. Francest'n N. H. 774–6
Cogswell's History of Henniker N. H. 628
Coit Genealogy 104, 165–72, 226–33
Cothren's History of Woodbury Ct. 1509
Dolbeare Genealogy 20
Dwight Genealogy 548–56
Hines' Lebanon Ct. Hist. Address 159
Hoyt's Salisbury Mass. Families 213
Huntington's Memories (1857) 119 pages
Huntington Genealogy (1863) 428 pages
Kingman's North Bridgewater Mass. 524
Larned's History of Windham Co. Ct.
Little's History of Weare N. H. 911–3
N. E. Hist. Reg. v, 163; x, 283; xi, 156
Norwich Ct. Jubilee 208
Orcutt's History of Torrington Ct. 725
Perkins' Old Houses Norwich Ct. 476–93
Savage's Genealogical Dictionary ii, 503
Swain Genealogy 107–10
Todd Genealogy (1867)
Waldo's History of Tolland Ct. 72–4
Walworth's Hyde Gen. i, 287–93, 428–35
Huntley — Champion Genealogy 28
Hayward's History of Hancock N. H. 676
Perkins' Old Houses of Norwich Ct. 494
Huntoon — American Ancestry vii, 66
Dearborn's Hist. of Salisbury N. H. 631–40
Dow's Hampton N. H. 757
Huntoon Genealogy (1881) 113 pages
Wheeler's History of Newport N. H. 423

Huntting — Am. Anc. i, 41; iii, 90; ix, 111
Hedges' Hist. East Hampton N. Y. 302–5
Howell's Southampton N. Y. 2d ed. 322–7
Hunting Genealogy (1888) 83 pages
Huntting's History of Pine Plains N. Y. 361
Hurd — American Ancestry ii, 63; vii, 216
Bond's Watertown Mass. Gens. 518
Cochrane's Hist. Francestown N. H. 776
Crafts Genealogy 151–3
Daniels' History of Oxford Mass. 554–6
Freeman's Hist. of Cape Cod Mass. ii, 375
Hayward's History of Gilsum N. H. 337–41
Hazen's History of Billerica Mass. 76
Heywood's Hist. of Westminster Mass. 722
Hurlbut Genealogy 410–2
Kilbourn's Sermon on Mrs. Bowers 17–9
New Eng. Hist. and Gen. Reg. xix, 123–5
Orcutt's History of Stratford Ct. 1222–5
Savage's Genealogical Dictionary ii, 505
Stiles' History of Windsor Ct. ii, 417
Thurston Genealogy (1892) 241–5
Washington N. H. History 485–7
Wyman's Charlestown Mass. Gens. 530–4
Hurlbut — American Ancestry i, 41; iv, 61; v, 98, 179
Boyd's Annals of Winchester Ct. 96–100
Caulkins' History of New London Ct. 358
Cothren's History of Woodbury Ct. 580–2
Gold's History of Cornwall Ct. 245
Hall's Records of Norwalk Ct. 243, 281, 284
Hinman's Connecticut Settlers 1st ed. 170
Hollister's History of Pawlet Vt. 207
Hudson's History of Sudbury Mass. 444
Hurd's History of New London Co. Ct. 534
Hurlbut Family Meeting (1861) 22 pages
Hurlbut Genealogy (1888) 545 pages
Mathew's History of Cornwall Vt. 286
New Eng. Hist. and Gen. Reg. xviii, 58
Plumb's History of Hanover Pa. 425–8
Temple's History of Northfield Mass. 472
Wheeler's History of Newport N. H. 426–31
Hurrin — Littell's Passaic Valley 189
Hurry — Hurry Genealogy (1873) 104 p.
Wyman's Charlestown 534
Hursey — Cogswell's Henniker 630
Hurst — Savage's Gen. Dictionary ii, 506
Husband — American Ancestry viii, 124
Morris Genealogy (1898) 689–91
Power's Sangamon Co. Ill. Settlers 393
Huse — Coffin's Newbury Mass. 305
Cogswell's History of Henniker N. H. 629
Eaton's Annals of Warren Me. 556
Emery Genealogy (1890) 20
Little's History of Weare N. H. 913
Runnel's Sanbornton N. H. ii, 384–9
Savage's Genealogical Dictionary ii, 507
Stark's History of Dunbarton N. H. 217
Huske — Wentworth Genealogy i, 287
Hussey — Austin's Allied Families 142–5
Cushman's History of Sheepscott Me. 393
Dow's History of Hampton N. H. 758–61
Little's History of Weare N. H. 914
New Eng. Hist. and Gen. Reg. vii, 157
Power's Sangamon Co. Ill. Settlers 394–6
Savage's Genealogical Dictionary ii, 507

Husted — American Ancestry i, 41; iii, 175
Huntington's Stamford Ct. Settlers 55
Huntting's Hist. Pine Plains N. Y. 359–61
Huston — Hatch's Industry Me. 660
Pierce's History of Gorham Me. 176
Power's Sangamon Co. Ill. Settlers 394
Hutchins — Amer. Ancestry i, 42; v. 123
Bangor Me. Historical Magazine vii, 175
Bouton's History of Concord N. H. 670
Bradbury's Kennebunkport Me. 252–4
Childs Genealogy 582
Corliss Genealogy 237
Corliss' North Yarmouth Me. Magazine
Dearborn's Hist. Salisbury N. H. 640–2
Farrow's History of Islesborough Me. 226
Forrest's History of Norfolk Va. 55, 71
Hutchins Genealogy (1885) 16 pages
Hutchins (Levi) Autobiography (1865)
Lapham's History of Rumford Me. 356–8
Little's History of Weare N. H. 915
Morris Genealogy (1853) 21–3
Perkins' Old Houses of Norwich Ct. 495–7
Read Genealogy (1895) appendix 4–7
Savage's Genealogical Dictionary ii, 508
Hutchinson — American Ancestry vi, 122; vii, 50; x, 76
Bass' History of Braintree Vt. 153–5
Benedict's History of Sutton Mass. 667
Blake's History of Mendon Association 97
Cochrane's History of Antrim N. H. 551–3
Cochrane's Hist. Francestown N. H. 777–9
Crane's Rawson Genealogy 56–8
Cutter's History of Arlington Mass. 264
Daniels' History of Oxford Mass. 556
Davis' Landmarks of Plymouth Mass. 158
Drake's History of Boston Mass. 227
Essex Inst. Hist. Colls. x, 5–98
Glenn's Genealogical Notes (1898)
Hayward's History of Gilsum N. H. 341
Hayward's Hist. of Hancock N. H. 677–9
Heraldic Journal ii, 171–6; iii, 104–7
Hine's Lebanon Ct. Hist. Address 158
History of Clermont Ohio 548
Hurd's History of New London Co. Ct. 512
Hutchinson Chart (1888) 14x24 inches
Hutchinson Family of Salem (1853) 48 p.
Hutchinson Ancestry (1857) 26 pages
Hutchinson Ancestry (1865) 9 pages
Hutchinson Family of Boston (1865) 38 p.
Hutchinson Ancestry (1866) 24 pages
Hutchinson Family of Salem (1868) 33 p.
Hutchinson Family of Salem (1870) 107 p.
Hutchinson Family of Boston (1888) chart
Hutchinson Family of N. H. (1896) 23 p.
Hutchinsons, Story of the (1896) 2 vols.
Lancaster's Hist. of Gilmanton N. H. 273
Lapham's History of Paris Me. 640–2
Livermore's History of Wilton N. H. 415–21
Narragansett Historical Reg. ii, 177–9
New Eng. Hist. and Gen. Reg. xix, 13–20; xx, 355–67; xxii, 236–54; xxvii, 81
Ridlon's Saco Valley Me. Families 742
Savage's Genealogical Dictionary ii, 508–13
Secomb's History of Amherst N. H. 642–6
Sedgwick's History of Sharon Ct. 92
Temple's History of Northfield Mass. 473

Thompson Genealogy (1890) 238-48
Updyke's Narragansett Churches 106
Walworth's Hyde Genealogy 1126-8
Washington N. H. History 487
Wheeler's History of Newport N. H. 424
Whitmore's Copps Hill Epitaphs
Wyman's Charlestown Mass. Gens. 535-8
Hutton — American Ancestry ix, 139, 181
Jackson Genealogy 229, 246-8
Plumsted Genealogy 63
Huyck — Munsell's Albany Colls. iv, 136
Huycken — Bockee Genealogy 47
Huyler — Nevius Genealogy
Hyatt — Am. Anc. vi, 82, 139, 153; xii, 34
Baird's History of Rye N. Y. 411
Hall's Norwalk Ct. Records 183, 223-90
Hoyt Genealogy 633-6
Young's History of Wayne Co. Ind. 328
Hyde — American Ancestry iii, 176; vii,
110; viii, 154; ix, 215; x, 6, 189; xi,
13; xii, 105, 109
Ammidown's Hist. Collections ii, 68
Bliss' History of Rehoboth Mass. 207
Bond's History of Watertown Mass. 304
Caulkins' History of Norwich Ct. 186-9
Cochrane's History of Antrim N. H. 533
Corliss' North Yarmouth Me. Mag. 618
Douglas Genealogy 178-80
Dwight Genealogy 579
Goodwin's Olcott Genealogy 61
Hayward's History of Gilsum N. H. 337-41
Hine's Lebanon Ct. Hist. Address 157
Huntington Genealogy 81, 90
Hyde Genealogy (1864) 1446 pages
Hyde Family Hubbardston Mass. (1889)
19 pages
Jackson's History of Newton Mass. 313-26
Joslin's History of Poultney Vt. 282-4
Marvin's Hist. of Winchendon Mass. 459
Norwich Ct. Jubilee 203; 206-12
Orcutt's History of Stratford Ct. 1218
Paige's History of Cambridge Mass. 592
Perkins' Old Houses of Norwich Ct. 498
Plumb's History of Hanover Pa. 424
Reed's History of Bath Me. 322
Richmond Va. Standard ii, 27
Savage's Genealogical Dictionary ii, 514-6
Stiles' History of Windsor Ct. ii, 418
Ward's Rice Genealogy 352
Whitney Family of Conn. i, 96
Hyland — Deane's Scituate Mass. 290
Johnston's History of Cecil Co. Md. 522-4
Hyler — Eaton's Thomaston Me. 275
Hynson — Hanson's Old Kent Md.
Hysler — Eaton's Warren Me. 557
Hyslop — Bridgeman's Granary Ep. 95
Sumner Genealogy (1854) 66-8
Iddings — Sharpless Genealogy 274, 410-3
Ide — American Ancestry xi, 88; xii, 66
Daggett's Attleborough 91
Daniels' History of Oxford Mass. 557
Davis' History of Redding Vt. 157
Jameson's History of Medway Mass. 496
Ward's History of Shrewsbury Mass. 333
Iles — Power's Sangamon Ill. 397-401
Iliff — Chambers' N. J. Germans

Ilsley — American Ancestry iv, 190
Hoyt's Salisbury Mass. Families 214-6
Journal of Smith and Dean Portland 128
Little Genealogy 9
Savage's Genealogial Dictionary ii, 517
Immell—Parthemore Gen. 169-71, 191-204
Inches — Sigourney Genealogy 28
Indicott — Indicott Genealogy (1888) 15 p.
Ingalls — Abbott's Andover Mass. 33
American Ancestry ii, 63; iii, 28; xii, 42
Bangor Historical Magazine iv, 149-56
Bassett's History of Richmond N. H. 417
Chase's History of Chester N. H. 549
Emery Genealogy (1890) 19
Hammatt Papers of Ipswich Mass. 170
Lewis' History of Lynn Mass. 111
Livermore's History of Wilton N. H. 421
Merrill's History of Acworth N. H. 231
New Eng. Hist. and Gen. Reg. l, 72
New Hampshire Hist. Soc. Coll. vii, 375
Norton's History of Fitzwilliam N. H. 614
Power's Sangamon Co. Ill. Settlers 401
Ridlon's Harrison Me. Settlers 82
Ridlon's Saco Valley Me. Families 743-61
Runnel's Hist. Sanbornton N. H. ii, 389-92
Savage's Genealogical Dictionary ii, 519
Smith's History of Peterborough N. H. 126
Stearns' History of Rindge N. H. 566-70
Thompson's Hist. Swampscott Mass. 24-7
Washington N. H. History 488
Wyman's Charlestown Mass. Gens. i, 540
Ingell — Norton's Fitzwilliam N. H. 616
Ingersoll — Am. Anc. iv, 218; vi, 6; viii, 4
Babson's History of Gloucester Mass. 106
Corliss' North Yarmouth Me. Magazine
Driver Genealogy 254
Essex Inst. Colls. i, 12, 153; xi, 228-34
Goodwich's Recoll. of a Lifetime i, 516
Goodwin's Genealogical Notes 119-28
Hayes' Wells Genealogy 169
Hudson's History of Lexington Mass. 111
Huntington's Stamford Ct. Settlers 56
Ingersoll Genealogy (1893) 107 pages
Journals of Smith and Dean Portland 54
Maine Hist. Society Collections i, 210
Savage's Genealogical Dictionary ii, 519-22
Smith Genealogy by Wellington Smith
Sweetland Genealogy (1890) 10-22
Taylor's Great Barrington Mass. 105, 123
Wyman's Charlestown Mass. Gens. 540
Ingham — Amer. Ancestry iv, 177; viii, 16
Davis' History of Bucks County Pa. 301
Evans' Fox Genealogy 119-23
Ingham Genealogy (1871) 59 pages
Potts Genealogy (1895) 335
Savage's Genealogical Dictionary ii, 522
Sharpless Genealogy 442
Smith Genealogy (1890) 167-72, 195
Inglis—Cochran-Inglis Family (1899) 18 p.
Penn. Mag. of History v, 335-9
Ingraham — American Anc. iv, 6; xi, 195
Cleveland's Hist. Yates Co. N. Y. 136-8
Eaton's History of Thomaston Me. ii, 276-9
Gladding's Ingraham Estate (1859) 69-75
Goode Genealogy 150
Ingraham Genealogy (1898) 12 pages

Kip's Historical Notes 35-8
North's History of Augusta Me. 885-8
Redfield Genealogy 61
Savage's Genealogical Dictionary ii, 523
Ingram — Judd's Hadley Mass. 519
New Eng. Hist. and Gen. Register xiii, 90
Inman — Austin's R. I. Gen. Dict. 326
Ballou Genealogy 106
Bangor Me. Historical Magazine vi, 30
Daniel's History of Oxford Mass. 558
Mowry Genealogy (Richard) 212, 229-31
Narr. Historical Register vi, 76-9
Plumb's History of Hanover Pa. 434-6
Innes — Green's Kentucky Families
Lindsay Genealogy
Meade's Old Churches of Virginia
Richmond Va. Standard iii, 21
Innis — Innis Association (1870) 20 pages
Ruttenber's Hist. of Newburgh N. Y. 283
Ruttenber's Hist. of Orange Co. N. Y. 375
Irby — Meade's Old Churches of Virginia
Iredell — Bean's Montgomery Pa. 459-61
McRee's Life of Iredell 1-3
Wheeler's History of N. Carolina ii, 93
Ireland — Amer. Ancestry iii, 91; v, 92
Ireland Genealogy (1880) 51 pages
Lawrence Genealogy (1858) 104-6
Wyman's Charlestown Mass. Gens. 541-4
Irish — American Ancestry ii, 63
Austin's R. I. Genealogical Dictionary 110
Davis' Landmarks of Plymouth Mass. 158
Oak's Life of Gen. Jas. Irish (1898)
Pierce's History of Gorham Me. 177
Savage's Genealogical Dictionary ii, 524
Sibley's History of Union Me. 465
Williams' History of Danby Vt. 171-6
Irvin — Meginness' Biographical Annals
of West Branch Valley Pa. 167-9
Irvine — Am. Hist. Reg. iii, 308-12
Bullock Genealogy
Cabell Genealogy 369-76
Egle's Notes and Queries 3 l ser. ii, 186
Green's Kentucky Families
Hall Genealogy by T. P. Hall (1892) 49-58
Sketches of Lynchburgh Va. 84-93
Irving — Bolton's Westchester 739-41
Page Genealogy 97
Irwin — American Ancestry viii, 157
Clyde's Irish Settlement of Pa. 76-8
Irwin Genealogy (1893) 50 pages
Keith's Harrison Ancestry 53-66
Lamborn Genealogy 298
Marshall Gen. (1884) 27-38, 96-9, 150-7
Martin's History of Chester Pa. 274
Power's Sangamon Co. Ill. Settlers 402-6
Wheeler's History of N. Carolina ii, 142
Isaacs — Dwight Genealogy 168-70
Hall's Norwalk Ct. Records 212, 240
Isbell — American Ancestry x, 193
Cregar's White Genealogy
Isbell and Kingman Genealogy (1889) 30 p.
Isham — Amer. Ancestry iii, 28; xi, 213
Bowie Genealogy 426-9
Champion Genealogy 320-5
Goodwin's Foote Genealogy 63-7
Hayward's History of Gilsum N. H. 343

Richmond Va. Standard iii, 38
Sylvester's History of Ulster Co. N. Y. 74
Waldo's History of Tolland Ct. 127
Israel — Greenough Gen. (1895) 38 pages
Isum — Swift's Barnstable Families ii, 73
Ives — Amer. Anc. iv, 36; v, 48; vii, 269
Anderson's Waterbury Ct. i, app. 76
Blake's History of Hamden Ct. 256-61
Bond's Watertown Mass. Gens. 306
Bulkley's Brown Memorial 78-82
Champion Genealogy 61
Cunnabell Genealogy 101
Davis' Hist. of Wallingford Ct. 823-38
Dickerman Genealogy 162-9
Driver Genealogy 320-67
Gold's History of Cornwall Ct. 278-80
Goodyear Genealogy 153
Hibbard's History of Goshen Ct. 469-74
Hollister Genealogy 169-72, 331-3
Hubbard's Stanstead County Canada 271
Savage's Genealogical Dictionary ii, 525
Tuttle Genealogy 463
Vinton's Giles Genealogy 45
Ivins — Salter's Monmouth Co. N. J.
Ivory — Savage's Gen. Dict. ii, 526
Wyman's Charlestown Mass. Gens. i, 545
Izard — Deas' Life of Izard
Goode Genealogy 182
Jack — Gilmer's Georgians 226
Morrison's Genealogy 257
Slaughter's St. Mark's Parish Virg. 160
Jackman — Coffin's Boscawen 556-6
Jackson — American Ancestry i, 42; iii,
88; v, 78, 230; viii, 169; ix, 212; x, 7
Austin's Ancestries 35
Baird's History of Rye N. Y. 415
Balch's Provincial Papers of Pa. 109-21
Barry's Hist. of Framingham Mass. 300
Bond's Watertown Mass. Gens. 306
Brown's Bedford Mass. Families 19
Bunker's Long Island Genealogies 220-6
Cole Genealogy 21
Davis' Landmarks of Plymouth 159-62
Deane's History of Scituate Mass. 291
Dow's History of Hampton N. H. 761
Eaton's History of Thomaston Me. ii, 279
Elderkin Genealogy
Essex Inst. Hist. Colls. xxi, 193-6
Farwell Genealogy 76-8, opposite p. 134
Goode Genealogy 149
Hanson's History of Gardiner Me. 130
Harris Family of New Jersey (1888) 29-35
Herrick's Hist. of Gardner Mass. 359-61
Heywood's Hist. Westminster Mass. 723-6
Hoar Family Lineage (1898) 34-43
Jackson Family of Newton (1839) Chart
Jackson Fam. of Chester Pa. (1878) 371 p.
Jackson Family of Ohio (1890) pamphlet
Jackson Family of Newton (1895) 86 pages
Jackson's Hist. of Newton Mass. 326-53
Kingman's N. Bridgewater Mass. 546-8
Lapham's History of Norway Me. 537
Lapham's History of Paris Me. 642-7
Mitchell's Hist. of Bridgewater Mass. 202
Morrison's Hist. of Windham N. H. 605
New York Gen. and Biog. Rec. xxvi, 79

Norton's Hist. of Fitzwilliam N. H. 616
Orcutt's History of New Milford Ct. 720
Orcutt's History of Stratford Ct. 1226
Paige's History of Cambridge Mass. 592
Queen's County N. Y. History 159, 408
Randall's Hist. of Chesterfield N. H. 366–9
Read's History of Swanzey N. H. 386
Robinson's Items of Ancestry (1894) 17
Roome Genealogy 330-5
Salter's Hist. of Monmouth Co. N. J. lxxiv
Savage's Genealogical Dictionary ii, 526–32
Schenck's History of Fairfield Ct. 382
Sedgwick's History of Sharon Ct. 93
Sharpless Genealogy 386–8
Smith's History of Delaware Co. Pa. 473
Swift's Barnstables Mass. Families ii, 113
Temple's Hist. of N. Brookfield Mass. 643
Thayer Memorial (1835) 109-14
Thompson's Long Island N. Y. ii, 37
Todd's History of Redding Ct. 204
Washburn's History of Leicester Mass. 379
Wyman's Charlestown Mass. Gens. i, 546
Jacob — Austin's Allied Families 149
Barry's History of Hanover Mass. 319–35
Deane's History of Scituate Mass. 291
Hammatt Papers of Ipswich Mass. 171-3
Hobart's Hist. of Abington Mass. 405
Lincoln's Hist. of Hingham Mass. ii, 371–9
Jacobia — American Ancestry ii, 63
Jacobs — American Ancestry viii, 444
Barry's History of Hanover Mass. 319–35
Bergen's Kings Co. N. Y. Settlers 152
Eaton's History of Thomaston Me. ii, 280
Essex Mass. Inst. Hist. Colls. i, 52–5
Palmer and Trimble Genealogy 314, 339–42
Power's Sangamon Co. Ill. Settlers 407
Runnel's Hist. Sanbornton N. H. ii, 392–4
Savage's Genealogical Dictionary ii, 532–4
Jacobson — Clute's Staten Island 392
Jacobus — American Ancestry viii, 183–9
Jacoby — Perkiomen Region Pa. 109
Jacqueline — N. E. Reg. xxxviii, 333
Jacques — Austin R. I. Gen. Dict. 110
Poor's Merrimack Valley Researches 120
Runnel's Hist. Sanbornton N. H. ii, 394–9
Savage's Genealogical Dictionary ii, 538
Jaffrey — Jaffrey's Hist. Jaffrey N. H.
New Eng. Hist. and Gen. Reg. xv, 14
Savage's Genealogical Dictionary ii, 534
Wentworth Genealogy i 303–5
Jaffries — Harris' Bascom Fam. 74-8
Jagger — Howell's Southampton 327
Huntington's Stamford Ct. Families 56
James — American Ancestry vii, 243, 281;
    ix, 95, 143; xi, 216
Austin's R. I. Genealogical Dictionary 111
Babson's History of Gloucester Mass. 107
Barber's Atlee Genealogy 32–8
Barrus' History of Goshen Mass. 212
Briggs' History of Shipbuilding 260–3
Cogswell's Nottingham N. H. 409–11
Davis' History of Bucks County Pa. 386
Deane's History of Scituate Mass. 292–4
Dow's History of Hampton N. H. 762–5
Eaton's Annals of Warren Me. 559
Futhey's History of Chester Co. Pa. 612

James and Stiles Genealogy (1898) 6 pages
Lincoln's Hist. Hingham Mass. ii, 379–81
N. Y. Gen. and Biog. Record xxix, 96-8
Richmond Va. Standard ii, 6
Savage's Genealogical Dictionary ii, 535–7
Sharpless Genealogy 197
Smith's History of Delaware Co. Pa. 474
Willard's Albany Medical Annals 283
Wyman's Charlestown Mass. Gens. i, 547
Jameson — Am. Ancestry iii, 29; iv, 44
Cochrane's Hist. of Antrim N. H. 544–62
Cogswell's History of Henniker N. H. 631
Eaton's Annals of Warren Me. 557–9
Eaton's Hist. of Thomaston Me. ii, 281-4
Harvey Genealogy 513–68
Hoyt's Salisbury Mass. Families 216
Jameson's History of Medway Mass. 496
Kulp's Wyoming Valley Families
Morrison's History of Windham N. H. 605
Plumb's History of Hanover Pa. 437
Ridlon's Saco Valley Me. Families 761–3
Savage's Genealogical Dictionary ii, 537
Stark's History of Dunbarton N. H. 240
Wm. and Mary Coll. Hist. Reg. iii, 199–201
Jamison — Davis' Bucks Co. Pa. 417
New York Gen. and Biog. Record v, 171
Robert's Old Richland Pa. Families 210–2
Wyman's Charlestown Mass. Gens. i, 548
Janes — Amer. Ancestry i, 42; ix, 214
Hyde's History of Brimfield Mass. 421–5
Janes Genealogy (1868) 419 pages
Loomis Genealogy (1880) 394–417
Lyman's History of E. Hampton Mass.
    173–9
Morris and Flynt Genealogies 58
Savage's Genealogical Dictionary ii, 538
Temple's Hist. of Northfield Mass. 473–7
Janeway — Amer. Ancestry vii, 145
Roome Genealogy 100–3
Janney — Amer. Ancestry vi, 137; xi, 117
Janney Family Chart (1868) chart
Jolliffe Genealogy (1893) 169–71
Thomas Genealogy (1877) 97
Janse — Janse (Anneke) Gen. (1870) 31 p.
Munsell's Collections on the History of
    Albany ii, 422–7; iv, 99, 136
Schuyler's Colonial New York ii, 337–66
Jansen — American Ancestry ii, 64; iv,
    133; v, 57; vi, 158
Bergen's Kings Co. N. Y. Settlers 153–66
Munsell's Albany Collections iv, 137
Pearson's Schenectady N. Y. Settlers 97
Prime's History of Long Island N. Y. 360
Schoonmaker's Hist. Kingston N. Y. 482
Sylvester's Hist. of Ulster Co. N. Y. 338
Jaqueline — Meade's Virginia i, 100–6
Jaques — Whitehead's Perth Amboy
Wyman's Charlestown Mass. Gens. i, 548
Jaquett — Jaquett Genealogy (1896) 190 p.
Jaquins — American Ancestry ii, 64
Jaquith — Cutter's Jaffrey N. H. 377–80
Dows Genealogy 79
Hayward's History of Gilsum N. H. 344
Hayward's History of Hancock N. H. 679
Hazen's History of Bellerica Mass. 77
Sewall's History of Woburn Mass. 618

Stearns' History of Ashburnham Mass. 763
Washington N. H. History 489-92
Jarman — Walker Genealogy (1896) 71-3
Jarret — Power's Sangamon Ill. 408
Jarvis — Am. Anc. iii, 166; viii, 3; ix, 228
Bangor Me. Hist. Magazine viii, 227-30
Eaton's Annals of Warren Me. 559
Hall's Norwalk Ct. 211, 234, 257, 269
Huntington's Stamford Ct. Settlers 57
Jarvis Genealogy (1879) 369 pages
Wetmore Genealogy 70
Whitmore's Copps Hill Epitaphs
Jaudon — Jaudon Genealogy (1890) 24 p.
Jauncey — Jauncey Genealogy (1873) 6 p.
Jauncey Genealogy 2d ed. (1876) 24 pages
Jay — Alden's Am. Epitaphs v, 246-50
American Ancestry vi, 151; x, 175
Baird's History of Rye N. Y. 479-85
Bolton's Westchester Co. N. Y. ii, 196
Flanders' Chief Justices of N. Y. i, 11-8
Holgate's American Genealogy 234-44
Lamb's Hist. of New York City i, 602, 697
N. Y. Gen. Biog. Rec. vii, 110-6; x, 114;
xii, 65
Van Rensselaer's New Yorkers
Jayne — Power's Sangamon Co. Ill. Settlers 406
Jaynes — Champion Genealogy 146
Jefferay — Austin's R. I. Dictionary 111
Austin's Allied Families 150 2
Jefferds — Bourne's Wells Me. 761
Jefferies — Darlington Family Gathering 44-52
Jefferis — American Ancestry iii, 197
Jefferis Genealogy (1870) 14 pages
Sharpless Genealogy 293
Jeffers — Hatch's Industry Me. 661
Roe's Sketches of Rose N. Y. 189
Jefferson — Calnek's Annapolis N. S. 535
Campbell's Virginia 604
Goode Genealogy 44
Meade's Old Churches of Virginia
Randall's Life of Jefferson i, 17
Huntington's Stamford Ct. Settlers 57
Slaughter's Fry Genealogy 22
Jeffrey — Salter's Monmouth N. J.
Savage's Genealogical Dictionary ii, 539
Jeffries — Am. Ancestry vi, 143; vii, 24
Baird's History of Rye N. Y. 415
Cope Genealogy 55, 110, 126
Futhey's History of Chester Co. Pa. 613
New Eng. Hist. and Gen. Reg. xv, 14-7
Wentworth Genealogy i, 184
Whitmore's Heraldic Journal ii, 166-8
Jeffry — Essex Inst. Hist. Colls. i, 195
Jefts — Hazen's Hist. Billerica Mass. 78
Hill's History of Mason N. H. 203
Sewall's History of Woburn Mass. 618
Stearns's Hist. of Ashburnham Mass. 763
Washington N. H. History 492-4
Jeggles — Savage's Gen. Dict. ii, 541
Jelliff — Fillow Genealogy 84-6, 150-6
Jelliffe — American Ancestry ix, 132
Jellison — Bangor Hist. Magazine ix, 89
Cochrane's Hist. Francestown N. H. 780
Putnam's Historical Magazine i, 238
12

Jenckes — Bulkley's Browne Mem. 27-9
Capron Genealogy by Holden 200-4
Jencks — Stiles' Windsor Ct. ii, 419
Jenifer — Hanson's Old Kent Md. 124
Jenings — Lee Genealogy (1895) 300
Meade's Old Families of Virginia
Potts Genealogy (1895) 311-3
Richmond Va. Standard iii, 38
Jenkins — American Ancestry i, 42; iv, 174; vi, 171; xii
Deane's History of Scituate Mass. 294-6
Freeman's Hist. of Cape Cod Mass. ii, 87
Harris Genealogy (1878) 43-5, 68-70, 111-9
Harvey Genealogy 920-4
Hayward's Hist. of Hancock N. H. 680
Hobart's Hist. of Abington Mass. 406-9
Hubbard's Hist. of Springfield Vt. 351-3
Jenkins' Hist. Gwynedd Pa. 2d ed. 418-20
Jenkins Genealogy (1887) 16 pages
Kulp's Wyoming Valley Families
Mitchell's Hist. Bridgewater Mass. 203
Narragansett Hist. Reg. iv, 251; v, 151-66
Norton's History of Fitzwilliam N. H. 617
Paige's History of Hardwick Mass. 403
Ridlon's Saco Valley Me. Families 763-5
Rowell Genealogy 65-76
Savage's Genealogical Dictionary ii, 541
Spooner's Genealogy i, 471-83
Swift's Barnstable Families ii, 90-105
Wyman's Charlestown Mass. Gens. i, 550
Jenks — American Ancestry iii, 141
Ammidown Genealogy 45
Austin's R. I. Genealogical Dictionary 112
Capron Genealogy by Holden 20-2
Corliss' North Yarmouth Me.
Davis' Hist. of Bucks Co. Pa. 166-8, 244
Draper's History of Spencer Mass. 213
Driver Genealogy 147
Eaton's History of Thomaston Me. ii, 284
Essex Mass. Inst. Hist. Collections vi, 252-4
Jenks Genealogy (1888) 12 pages
Morris Genealogy (1898) 847
New Eng. Hist. and Gen. Reg. ix, 201
Savage's Genealogical Dictionary ii, 542-4
Smith's Genealogy of Wm. Smith 92-6
Temple's Hist. N. Brookfield Mass. 644-9
Turner's Gen. of Humphrey Turner 55-7
Wheeler's Hist. of Newport N. H. 433-52
Williams' History of Danby Vt. 176
Winslow Genealogy ii, 758-62
Wyman's Hunt Genealogy 114
Jenner — Caverly's Pittsford Vt. 710
Cothren's History of Woodbury Ct. i, 602
Jenner Genealogy (1865) 3 pages, reprint
N. E. Hist. and Gen. Reg. xix, 246-9
Wyman's Charlestown Mass. Gens. 551-3
Jennerson — Chandler's Shirley 483-6
Jenness — Bedford N. H. Centennial 312
Carter's History of Pembroke N. H. ii, 163-7
Cogswell's Hist. Nottingham N. H. 411-9
Dow's History of Hampton N. H. 765-9
Jenness (Richard) Memorial (1872) 6-39
Jenney — Crafts' Whately 505-7
Paige's Hardwick Mass. 403
Spooner Genealogy i, 91, 219-36

Jennings — Aldrich's Walpole N. H. 293
American Ancestry xii, 25, 27
Austin's R. I. Genealogical Dictionary 114
Barry's Hist. of Framingham Mass. 300-3
Burr Genealogy (1891) 146-8
Butler's History of Farmington Me. 505-9
Freeman's Hist. of Cape Cod Mass. ii, 87
Hall's Norwalk Ct. Records 266, 294, 301
Hatch's History of Industry Me. 662
Howell's Hist. Southampton N. Y. 330-2
Jennings Estate Heirs (1852) 14 pages
Jennings Assoc. Report (1863) 34 pages
Jennings Family by Albert Welles (1881)
Jennings Genealogy (1899) 819 pages
Judd's History of Hadley Mass. 519
Littell's Passaic Valley Genealogies 190
Mitchell's Hist. of Bridgewater Mass. 203
Montague Genealogy 653-8
Morse's Sherborn Mass. Settlers 155
Savage's Genealogical Dictionary ii, 544-6
Schenck's Hist. of Fairfield Ct. 383-6
Sedgwick's History of Sharon Ct. 94
Shourd's Fenwick Colony N. J. 119-21
Temple's North Brookfield Mass. 649-50
Jennison — Aldrich's Walpole 293-6
Benedict's History of Sutton Mass. 668
Bond's Watertown Mass. 306-10, 800-14
Daniel's History of Oxford Mass. 558-60
Eaton's History of Thomaston Me. ii, 284
Fiske Genealogy 147
Hemenway Genealogy 12
Hudson's History of Lexington Mass. 111
New Eng. Hist. and Gen. Reg. vii, 71
Savage's Genealogical Dictionary ii, 545
Symmes Genealogy 67
Vinton's Giles Genealogy 235-78
Vinton's Richardson Genealogy 52
Wall's Remin. of Worcester Mass. 56-61
Ward's History of Shrewsbury Mass. 337
Jenny — Temple's Whately Mass. 243
Joeffreys — Austin's R. I. Dict. 330
Jepson — Sigourney Genealogy 25
Jermain — American Ancestry i, 42
Jermyn — Lincoln's Hingham ii, 382
Jernegan — Lincoln's Hingham ii, 383
Jerome — Amer. Ancestry v, 14, 174
Boyd's History of Conesus N. Y. 160
Jessup — Howell's Southampton 332-5
Huntington's Stamford Ct. Settlers 57
Jessup Genealogy (1887) 463 pages
Morris' Bontecou Genealogy
N. Eng. Hist. Gen. Reg. x, 357; xxvi, 403
Prime's Sands Genealogy 87-90
Savage's Genealogical Dictionary ii, 547
Selleck's Norwalk Ct. (1896) 100
Jesup — American Ancestry iii, 135
Schenck's History of Fairfield Ct. 386
Jewell — Am. Anc. i, 42; vii, 202; xii, 59
Cutter's History of Jaffrey N. H. 380-2
Daniel's History of Oxford Mass. 560
Dunster Genealogy 255
Harris Family of New Jersey (1888) 52-80
Hoyt's Salisbury Mass. Families 216
Hudson's Hist. of Marlborough Mass. 403
Jewell Genealogy (1860) 104 pages
Little's History of Weare N. H. 916

Loomis Genealogy (1880) 626-33
New Eng. Hist. and Gen. Reg. xxii, 43-6
Orcutt's History of New Milford Ct. 720
Runnel's Hist. of Sanbornton N. H. ii, 399
Savage's Genealogical Dictionary ii, 547
Waterford Me. Centennial (1879) 261
Jewett — American Ancestry iii. 154; iv,
    139; v, 130; vi, 14
Andrews' History of New Britain Ct. 316
Baker's History of Montville Ct. 563-9
Blood's History of Temple N. H. 229
Bond's History of Watertown Mass. 903-5
Butler's History of Groton Mass. 409, 473
Cregar's White Genealogy
Cutter's History of Jaffrey N. H. 382-4
Daniel's History of Oxford Mass. 560
Davis Genealogy 471, 484-6
Essex Mass. Inst. Hist. Colls. xxii, 1-36
Gage's History of Rowley Mass. 445
Guild's Stiles Genealogy 101-4
Hall's Genealogical Notes (1886) 74, 79-81
Hammatt Papers, Ipswich Mass. 173-5
Hanson's History of Gardiner Me. 137, 158
Hatch's History of Industry Me. 663
Hayes' Wells Family 157
Hayward's History of Hancock N. H. 681
Hodgman's History of Westford Mass. 456
Hudson's History of Lexington Mass. 279
Hyde Genealogy i, 175-80; ii, 858-73
Lapham's History of Bethel Me. 569
Little Genealogy 69
North's History of Augusta Me. 888-94
Orcutt's History of Derby Ct. 737
Parker Ancestry by Ward (1895) 12-6
Pierce's History of Gorham Me. 179
Runnel's Hist. Sanbornton N. H. ii, 400-2
Savage's Genealogical Dictionary ii, 548
Secomb's History of Amherst N. H. 647
Sedgwick's History of Sharon Ct. 93
Sheldon's History of Deerfield Mass. 220
Slafter Genealogy 15-29
Smith's History of Peterborough N. H.
    127-9
Stearns' Hist. of Ashburnham Mass. 763-5
Stearns' Hist. of Rindge N. H. 571-9
Temple's History of Whately Mass. 240
Thurston Genealogy (1892) 19
Wakefield Genealogy 88
Warren's History of Waterford Me. 262-4
Wood Genealogy 154-66
Woodbury's Groveland Mass. Epitaphs 48
Worcester's History of Hollis N. H. 378
Jillson — American Ancestry iii, 94
Ballou Genealogy 148-52
Bassett's History of Richmond N. H. 420-2
Jillson Genealogy (1876) 266 pages
Jipson — Barus' Goshen Mass. 149
Job — Sharpless Genealogy 321
Jocelyn — Dodd's East Haven Ct. 131
Johannes — Bergen's Kings Co. N. Y.
John — Cope Family 48, 101, 199-204
Jenkins' History of Gwynedd Pa. 66-9
Johnes — See Jones
Johns — American Ancestry ii, 64
Sedgwick's History of Sharon Ct. 94
Thomas Genealogy (1896) 370-2

Johnson — Abbott's Andover Mass. 35
Aldrich's History of Walpole N. H. 296–8
American Ancestry i, 42; ii, 64; iii, 154;
iv, 122, 166; vi, 87; vii, 30, 35, 49, 91,
162, 240; viii, 50, 88; x, 39; xi, 64,
88, 206; xii, 31, 106
Anderson's Waterbury Ct. i, app. 76
Austin's R. I. Genealogical Dictionary 114
Austin's Allied Families 154
Ballou's History of Milford Mass. 844–8
Bangor Me. Hist. Mag. v, 198; vii, 135–7
Barry's History of Framingham Mass. 303
Bingham Genealogy 229–34
Bond's Watertown Mass. 310, 539–42
Bowie Genealogy 162–7
Brown's West Simsbury Ct. Settlers 88
Butler's History of Farmington Me. 509–14
Carter Genealogy by Potts (1883) 108
Champion Genealogy
Chase's Hist. of Haverhill Mass. 276, 634–7
Child Genealogy 422
Clarke's Old King Wm. Co. Va. Families
Cleveland Genealogy (1899) 182
Clute's Hist. of Staten Island N. Y. 392–4
Cochrane's Hist. Francestown N. H. 781
Coe and Ward Memorial 60–8
Coffin's History of Boscawen N. H. 560–2
Cogswell's History of Henniker N. H. 632
Cogswell's Nottingham N. H. 726–30
Collin's Hillsdale N. Y. 14, app. 68–74
Cope Genealogy 52, 115
Corliss' North Yarmouth Me. Magazine
Cothren's Woodbury Ct. 600–2; ii, 1510
Cutter's History of Arlington Mass. 265
Daniels' History of Oxford Mass. 561
Davis' Landmarks of Plymouth Mass. 162
Davis' History of Wallingford Ct. 830–6
Deane's History of Scituate Mass. 296
Dearborn's Hist. of Salisbury N. H. 642–4
Densmore's Hartwell Genealogy
Dow's History of Hampton N. H. 770–5
Driver Genealogy 510–2
Eaton's History of Thomaston Me. ii, 284
Ellis' History of Roxbury Mass. 122
Emery's Reminis. Newbury Mass. 201–14
Essex Inst. Hist. Collections xxii, 121–5
Fox's History of Dunstable Mass. 246
Gage's History of Rowley Mass. 446
Gilmer's Georgians 90, 102, 105
Gold's History of Cornwall Ct. 253
Goode Genealogy 174, 321
Guild's Stiles Genealogy 394
Hanson's Old Kent Md. 50–9
Hatch's History of Industry Me. 663–73
Hayward's Hist. of Hancock N. H. 682–6
Holgate's American Genealogy 22–6
Hubbard's History of Springfield Vt. 353–5
Hubbard's Stanstead County Canada 273
Hudson's History of Lexington Mass. 111
Hudson's Hist. Marlborough Mass. 403–6
Johnson's Wonder Working Providence
Poole's ed. Introduction 140
Johnson Family of Boston (1872) 17 pages
Johnson Fam. of Leominster (1876) 85 p.
Johnson Fam. of Charlestown (1878) 12 p.
Johnson Fam. of Charlestown (1879) 16 p.

Johnson Family of New York (1882) 10 p.
Johnson Family of Phila. (1885)
Johnson Family of Reading Vt. (1891) 27 p.
Johnson Family of Ipswich (1892) 200 p.
Johnson Family of Quincy (1895) 154 pages
Kellogg's White Genealogy 37
Kulp's Wyoming Valley Families
Lane Genealogy (1891) 43
Lapham's History of Norway Me. 537
Leland Genealogy 249
Lincoln's Hist. Hingham Mass. ii, 384–6
Littell's Passaic Valley Gens. 193–5
Little's History of Weare N. H. 917–23
McKeen's History of Bradford Vt. 297–305
Martin's History of Chester Pa. 156
Meade's Old Churches of Virginia
Miller's Hist. Colchester Co. N. S. 266–81
Mitchell's Hist. Bridgewater Mass. 204–6
Morris and Flynt Ancestors 16
Morris Genealogy (1894) 24–6
Morse's Sherborn Mass. Settlers 155
Nevius Genealogy
New Eng. Hist. and Gen. Reg. viii, 232,
358–62; xxxiii, 60–6, 81–91, 333–9;
xxxiv, 60–6; xxxviii, 407–10
New Jersey Hist. Soc. Colls. vi, supp. 121
New York Genealogical and Biographical
Record xviii, 150–2; xix, 67–9
North's History of Augusta Me. 894–6
Norton's History of Fitzwilliam N. H. 618
Orcutt's History of Derby Ct. 737–41
Orcutt's History of Stratford Ct. 1226
Orcutt's History of Torrington Ct. 726
Orcutt's History of Wolcott Ct. 588
Paige's History of Cambridge Mass. 593–5
Paige's History of Hardwick Mass. 404–6
Pearson's Schenectady N. Y. Settlers 97
Phœnix's Whitney Genealogy i, 345
Pierce's History of Gorham Me. 180
Poor's Merrimack Valley Researches 107
Power's Sangamon Ill. Settlers 21, 410–4
Queens County N. Y. History 248
Randall's Hist. of Chesterfield N. H. 370–2
Richmond Va. Standard iii, 14, 29
Ridlon's Harrison Me. Settlers 83–6
Roberts' Old Richland Pa. Fams. 128–31
Roseboom and Johnson Genealogy (1897)
35–41, 81–123; (1892) ii, 285–351
Runnel's Hist. Sanbornton N. H. ii, 402–8
Salisbury's Family Histories
Saunderson's Charlestown N. H. 457
Savage's Genealogical Dictionary ii, 549–59
Sewall's Woburn Mass. 73–6, 165–8, 617
Sharp's History of Seymour Ct. 200–3, 222
Sheldon's History of Deerfield Mass. 221
Shourd's Fenwick Colóny N. J. 103–18
Slafter Genealogy 13–5, 50
Slaughter's St. Mark's Parish Virg. 124
Stackpole's History of Durham Me. 203
Stearns' Hist. of Ashburnham Mass. 765
Stearns' History of Rindge N. H. 579
Stiles' History of Windsor Ct. ii, 420
Stone's Johnson Orderly Book (1882)
Temple's Hist. N. Brookfield Mass. 650–4
Temple's History of Northfield Mass. 477
Thomas Genealogy (1877) 98–101

Thomas Genealogy (1896) 372-6
Timlow's Southington Ct. Sketches 137
Tuttle Genealogy 666-8
Vinton's Richardson Genealogy 208
Walworth's Hyde Genealogy 561-4
Ward's Hist. of Shrewsbury Mass. 334-6
Washburn's History of Leicester Mass. 379
Warren's History of Waterford Me. 264
Whitmore's Copps Hill Elitaphs
Whitmore's Heraldic Journal iii, 43-5, 182
Williams' History of Danby Vt. 178
Worthen's History of Sutton N. H. 772-9
Wyman's Charlestown Mass. i, 554-63
Young's History of Wayne Co. Ind. 229
Johnston—Am. Anc. iii, 86; vii, 84; ix, 211
Dickerman Genealogy 265-8
Johnston Genealogy (1897) 216 pages
Magennis Genealogy 164
McRee's Life of Jas. Iredell i, 35-7
Morrison's Hist. of Windham N. H 607-10
New York Gen. and Biog. Rec. v, 172-4
Richmond's Va. Standard ii, 7, 39
Runnel's Sanbornton N. H. ii, 408-10
Slaughter's St. Mark's Parish Virg. 188
Wheeler's Eminent No. Carolinians 120
Whittemore's Orange N. J. 416
Johnstone — American Ancestry iv, 186
Dunster Genealogy 219
Whitehead's Perth Amboy N. J. 68-75
Johonnot — Bridgeman's Granary 181
Hemenway's Vermont Gaz. iv, 917-9
New Eng. Hist. Reg. vi, 357-66; vii, 141-4
Porter's Eddy Genealogy, appendix
Savage's Genealogical Dictionary ii, 559
Joice — Winsor's Duxbury Mass. 273
Joiner — Sheldon's Deerfield 221
Joliffe — American Ancestry xii
Jolliffe Family of Pa. (1878) 40 pages
Jolliffe Family of Va. (1893) 245 pages
Jolls — American Ancestry ii, 66
Jonas — N. E. Gen. Reg. xxxviii, 66
Jones — American Ancestry i, 43; ii, 64;
   iii, 96, 124, 165, 171; iv, 33; v, 55, 140,
   209; vi, 76, 133, 205; vii, 23, 73, 190,
   268; viii, 190; x, 89, 139, 197; xi, 129,
   194; xii
Anderson's Waterbury Ct. i, app. 77
Andrews' History of New Britain Ct. 311
Austin's Ancestral Dictionary 33
Aylsworth Genealogy 487-91
Babson's History of Gloucester Mass. 107
Ballou's History of Milford Mass. 846-60
Bangor Historical Magazine iii, 57; iv,
   55-7; vi, 71; vii, 130-7
Barry's Hist. of Framingham Mass. 304-7
Bemis' History of Marlboro N. H. 544-7
Blake's Hist. of Franklin Mass. 255
Bond's Watertown Mass. 310-22, 814
Bullock Genealogy
Bunker's Long Island Genealogies 227
Butler's History of Farmington Me. 515
Champion Genealogy 332-4
Chapman Genealogy 52, 220
Chapman's Trowbridge Genealogy 52
Clapp's Jones Hill Dorchester Mass. 1-8
Cleveland's History of Yates Co. N. Y. 671

Clute's History of Staten Island N. Y. 395
Cooley's Trenton N. J. Genealogies 150-2
Corliss' North Yarmouth Me. Magazine
Cushman's History of Sheepscott Me. 394
Daniels' History of Oxford Mass. 562
Davis' History of Reading Vt. 139
Davis History of Wallingford Ct. 886-8
Deane's History of Scituate Mass. 297
Dennysville Me. Centennial 106
Densmore's Hartwell Genealogy
Dickerman Genealogy 314-20
Draper's History of Spencer Mass. 214
Dyer's History of Plainfield Mass. 160
Eaton's Annals of Warren Me. 559-69
Eaton's History of Thomaston Me. ii, 285
Foster Pedigree (1897) part iv, 36-48
Freeman's Cape Cod Mass. ii, 208, 476
French's History of Turner Me. 55
Glenn's Welsh Tract 73-86, 294-304, etc.
Goode Genealogy 36. 205, 232, 236
Goodwin's Genealogical Notes 129-36
Green's Kentucky Families
Hammatt Papers of Ipswich Mass. 177-80
Hayward's History of Hancock N. H. 686
Hazen's History of Billerica Mass. 79
Heywood's Hist. Westminster Mass. 727-9
Hill's Hist. Old Dunstable Mass. (1878)
Hinman's Conn. Settlers 1st ed. 179
Hollister's History of Pawlet Vt. 208
Howell's Southampton N. Y. 335-8
Hoyt's Salisbury Mass. Families 218
Hudson's History of Lexington Mass. 280
Hudson's History of Sudbury Mass. 445
Hughes Genealogy 233
Huntington's Stamford Ct. Settlers 38
Jameson's History of Medway Mass. 496-8
Jenkins' History of Gwynedd Pa. 367, 378
Jones Fam. Queens Co. N. Y. (1849) 99 p.
Jones Family of Roxbury (1878) 75 pages
Jones Fam. of Milford Mass. (1884) 182 p.
Jones Family of Southampton (1886) 46 p.
Jones Family of Ipswich (1888) 7 pages
Jones Family of Virginia (1891) 295 pages
Jones' New York in Rev. War i, 58-67
Jones' History of Stockbridge Mass. 148-50
Joslin's History of Poultney Vt. 285-7
Kidder's History of New Ipswich N. H. 393
Kingsman's N. Bridgewater Mass. 549
Lancaster's Hist. of Gilmanton N. H. 273
Lapham's History of Paris Me. 647
Lee Genealogy (1895) 365-7
Leonard's History of Dublin N. H. 355
Lincoln's Hist. Hingham Mass. ii, 386-95
Littell's Passaic Valley Genealogies 196
Little's History of Weare N. H. 924-6
Livermore's History of Wilton N. H. 422
Locke Genealogy 34, 64, 117-22
Maine Hist. and Gen. Recorder v, 54-6
Meade's Old Churches of Virginia
Morris Genealogy (1853) 42-6
Morris Genealogy (1898) 411-3, 448
Morse Memorial, appendix 66
Morse's Sherborn Mass. Settlers 156
New Eng. Hist. and Gen. Reg. vi, 260,
   279-82; xiii, 34; xliv, 158-67; xlvii,
   470-2; xlix, 310-4

New York Genealogical and Biog. Record iii, 195; iv, 40–2; vi, 60–2
N. Y. Hist. Soc. Coll. new series ii, 490
Orcutt's History of Stratford Ct. 1227
Paige Genealogy 100
Paige's History of Cambridge Mass. 595
Palmer and Trimble Genealogy 111–22
Paxton's Marshall Genealogy 145
Penn. Mag. of Hist. and Biog. iv, xiii, 180
Perkins' Old Houses of Norwich Ct. 501
Perry's Jones' Book of Minutes (1894) 15–7
Phœnix's Whitney Genealogy i, 193
Pierce's History of Gorham Me. 179
Potter's Concord Mass. Families 12, 83
Power's Sangamon Co. Ill. Settlers 414–20
Queens County N. Y. History 552–4
Richmond Standard ii, 44, 52; iii, 4, 6, 44
Runnel's Hist. of Sanbornton N. H. ii, 410
Savage's Genealogical Dictionary ii, 560–8
Schenck's History of Fairfield Ct. 387–91
Secomb's History of Amherst N. H. 376
Sedgwick's History of Sharon Ct. 94
Sharpless Genealogy 359
Shattuck's History of Concord Mass. 376
Sheldon's History of Deerfield Mass. 222–5
Sinclair Genealogy 398–400
Slaughter's Bristol Parish Va. 138
Slaughter's St. Mark's Parish Va. 191
Stackpole's History of Durham Me. 204–7
Stearns' Hist. Ashburnham Mass. 767–72
Stearns' History of Rindge N. H. 580
Stiles' History of Windsor Ct. ii, 421
Strong Genealogy 159–62
Swift's Barnstable Families ii. 106–12
Thayer Memorial (1835) 89
Temple's Hist. of N. Brookfield Mass. 654
Thomas Genealogy (1877) 101
Thomas Genealogy (1898) 376
Timlow's Southington Ct. Sketches 138–43
Vinton's Giles Genealogy 278
Waddell's Annals of Augusta Co. Va. 392–5
Walker Genealogy 40
Washington N. H. History 494–507
Wheeler Ancestors (1896) 17
Wheeler's Eminent No. Carolinians 202
Wheeler's History of North Carolina 188
Whitman Genealogy 11–3, 202–8
Whitmore's Copps Hill Epitaphs
Whittemore's Orange N. J. 76
Wilkesbarre Historical Record v, 6
Wyman's Charlestown Mass. Gens. 563–6
Young's Hist. Chautauqua Co. N. Y. 565
Young's History of Wayne Co. Ind. 180
Jop — Daniels' Hist. Oxford Mass. 562
Jordan — American Ancestry ii, 65; v, 122; vi, 36; viii, 48
Bangor Me. Hist. Mag. iv, 71; viii, 110, 220
Collin's History of Hillsdale N. Y. 76
Corliss' North Yarmouth Me. Magazine
Eaton's Annals of Warren Me. 562
Eaton's Hist. of Thomaston Me. ii, 286–8
Gilmer's Georgians 144
Hoar Lineage (1898)
Jordan Genealogy (1882) 488 pages
Lapham's History of Bethel Me. 569
Lapham's History of Norway Me. 538–41

Lincoln's Hist. of Hingham Mass. ii, 395
Maine Hist. Society Collections i, 153–6
Mellick's Story of an Old Farm 675
Neill's Virginia Carolorum 282
Paige's History of Hardwick Mass. 406
Prime Genealogy (1895) 34
Randall's Hist. of Chesterfield N. H. 373
Ridlon's Saco Valley Me. Families 98
Savage's Genealogical Dictionary ii, 568
Scott Genealogy 292–300
Stackpole's History of Durham Me. 207
Walker Genealogy 153
Wheeler's History of Brunswick Me. 841
Joscelyn — Wilder Genealogy 289–96
Jose — Emery Genealogy 379
Ridlon's Saco Valley Me. Families 765
Wentworth Genealogy i, 298
Joslin — Carter Genealogy (1887)
Cochrane's Hist. Francestown N. H. 782
Cogswell's History of Henniker N. H. 634
Cutter's History of Jaffrey N. H. 386–8
Daniels' History of Oxford Mass. 563
Heywood's Hist. of Westminster Mass. 729
Hudson's Hist. of Marlborough Mass. 406
Joslin's History of Poultney Vt. 287–9
Norton's History of Fitzwilliam N. H. 618
Stearns' Hist. Ashburnham Mass. 772–4
Stone's History of Hubbardston Mass. 300
Joslyn — Babson's Gloucester Mass. 108
Mitchell's Hist. of Bridgewater Mass. 206
Josselyn — Barry's Hanover 335–47
Deane's History of Scituate Mass. 299
Hanover Mass. Records (1898)
Lincoln's Hist. of Hingham Mass. ii, 395
Maine Hist. Mag. by Porter vii, 49–54
New Eng. Hist. and Gen. Reg. ii, 306–10; xiv, 15; xl, 290–4
Savage's Genealogical Dictionary ii, 570–2
Spooner Genealogy i, 430–4
Stranahan Genealogy 31–9
Jouet — N. Y. Gen. Record xix, 151–3
Journeay — Clute's Staten Island 396
Joy — Am. Anc. x, 152; xi, 99; xii, 133
Austin's R. I. Genealogical Dictionary 115
Bangor Me. Historical Mag. iv, 74; ix, 88
Dyer's History of Plainfield Mass. 161–3
Hoyt's Salisbury Mass. Families 219
Joy Genealogy (1876) 37 pages
Joy Genealogy (1900) 225 pages
Lincoln's Hist. Hingham Mass. ii, 396–9
Savage's Genealogical Dictionary ii, 572
Schenck's History of Fairfield Ct. 391
Joyce — Savage's Gen. Dictionary ii, 573
Joyner — Stearns' Ashburnham 774
Joynes — Meade's Old Churches of Va.
Richmond Va. Standard ii, 34
Juckett — Sedgwick's Sharon Ct. 94
Judd — American Ancestry xi, 89
Anderson's Waterbury 77–80
Andrews' History of New Britain Ct. 140–8
Bronson's History of Waterbury Ct. 508–13
Edward's Southampton Mass., add. (1841)
Goode Genealogy 290
Hubbard's Stanstead Co. Canada 138, 258
Jones Genealogy 80
Judd Genealogy (1856) 112 pages

Judd's History of Hadley Mass. 520-2
Kellogg's White Genealogy 44, 71
Lee Genealogy (1897) 49-51, 64
Loomis Genealogy (1880) 179-94
Morris and Flynt Genealogy 59-61
New Eng. Hist. and Gen. Reg. xiv, 288
North's History of Augusta Me. 897
Orcutt's History of Torrington Ct. 727
Power's Sangamon Co. Ill. Settlers 420
Savage's Genealogical Dictionary ii, 573-5
Strong Genealogy 275-81
Timlow's Southington Ct. Sketches 115-8
Judevine — American Ancestry ii, 66
Morse's Grout Genealogy 48
Saunderson's Hist. of Charleston N. H. 459
Judkins — Babson's Gloucester Mass. 109
Dearborn's Hist. of Salisbury N. H. 644-6
Lapham's Norway Me. 541
Runnel's Hist. of Sanbornton N. H. 411-3
Savage's Genealogical Dictionary ii, 575
Judson — American Ancestry i 43; ii, 65;
   v, 209; ix, 24; xii, 113
Cothren's Woodbury Ct. 587-600; ii, 1510
Deacon's Stoddard Genealogy
Emery's Taunton Mass. Ministry ii, 35
Goodwin's Genealogical Notes 137-44
Goodwin's Foot Genealogy 275
Goodwin's Olcott Genealogy 32
Huntington's Stamford Ct. Settlers 59
Judson Chart (1860) 15x20 inches
Leavenworth Genealogy 83-5
Orcutt's History of Derby Ct. 741
Orcutt's History of Stratford Ct. 1228-32
Savage's Genealogical Dictionary ii, 575-7
Sprague's History of Gloversville N. Y. 121
Timlow's History of Southington Ct. 143-6
Tuttle Genealogy 115-8
Wayland's Mem. of A. Judson i, 11-3
Julian — American Ancestry vii, 173
Young's History of Wayne Co. Ind. 181-7
Jumel — Temple's N. Brookfield 655-7
Jumper — Eaton's Thomaston Me. 289
June — Huntington's Stamford Ct. 59
Junkin — Thomas Gen. (1896) 556 l
Kaar — Bockee Genealogy 56
Kachlein—Eyerman Ancestry (1899) 17-21
Kaighn — Clement's Newtown N. J.
Kaiser — American Ancestry xi, 89
Kalloch — Eaton's Thomaston 294-7
Eaton's Annals of Warren Me. 563-6
Kame — Ridlon's Saco Valley 550-5
Kane — American Ancestry ii, 66
Dwight's Strong Genealogy 673
Greene's Todd Genealogy
Oneida Historical Society Trans. ii, 90
Pearson's Schenectady N. Y. Settlers 33
Power's Sangamon Co. Ill. Settlers 421
Thomas Genealogy (1877) 103
Thomas Genealogy (1896) 377
Kase — Jerseyman vol. i, 25
Kasson — Am. Anc. iii, 205; vi, 124, 127
Cothren's History of Woodbury Ct. 603
Kasson Genealogy (1882) 51 pages
Sprague's Hist. of Gloversville N. Y. 121
Walworth's Hyde Genealogy 684
Kathan — Vt. Hist. Gaz. v, 13-9

Kauffman — Brubacher Genealogy 164
Kaufman — Harris' Lancaster Pa. 333
Pennypacker's An. Phœnixville Pa. 272
Kaup — Borneman Genealogy 46-57
Kavanagh — Caverno Genealogy
Cushman's History of Sheepscott Me. 395
Kay — Clement's Newtown N. J. Sett.
Kaye — N. Y. Gen. Record xxv, 75-7
Keagy — Keagy Genealogy (1899)
Kean — Page Genealogy 242
Winsor's History of Duxbury Mass. 273
Keane — Savage's Gen. Dict. iii, 1
Kearney — Lamb's N. Y. City 706-756
Morris' Genealogy (1898) 250
Penn. Magazine of Hist. and Biog. v, 100
Whitehead's Perth Amboy N. J. 90-2
Kearny — Plumstead Genealogy 40
Keasbey — Shourd's Fenwick 122-31
Keating — Eaton's Thomaston Me. 289
Keator — American Ancestry viii, 229
Sylvester's History of Ulster Co. N. Y. 247
Kedzie — Kedzie Genealogy (1882) 100 p.
Keeler — American Ancestry i, 43; xii
Bolton's Westchester County N. Y. ii, 742
Bouton Genealogy 34
Caverly's History of Pittsford Vt. 710
Hall's Norwalk Ct. Records 189-91, etc.
Savage's Genealogical Dictionary iii, 2
Selleck's Norwalk Ct. (1896) 120-4
Whitney's Family of Conn. i, 72-84
Young's Hist. Chautauqua Co. N. Y. 642
Keeley — Egle's Notes and Queries (1897)
   181-4, 191-4
Keeling — Richmond Standard iv, 16
Virginia Magazine of History iv, (1896) 200
Keen — Amer. Ancestry v, 22; vii, 168
Briggs' History of Shipbuilding 350-2
Eaton's History of Thomaston Me. 290-2
Mitchell's Hist. of Bridgewater Mass. 206
Penn. Magazine of History and Biog. i, 3;
   ii, 325-35; iii, 334-41; iv, 242-5; 343-
   60, 484-500; v, 85-101, 217-9
Keenan — Eaton's Thomaston Me. 292
Keeney — Cunnabell Genealogy 90
Orcutt's History of Derby Ct. 742-4
Young's History of Warsaw N. Y. 285
Keep — Hodgman's Westford Mass. 456
Keep Genealogy (1899) 263 pages
Longmeadow Mass. Centennial, app. 70-3
New Eng. Hist. and Gen. Reg. xxxvi, 313
Temple's Hist. of N. Brookfield Mass. 657
Keese — American Ancestry x, 170
Austin's R. I. Genealogical Dictionary 115
Hurlbut Genealogy 441
Keeshan — Lincoln's Hingham ii, 401
Kehoe — Lincoln's Hingham ii, 402
Keifer — Harris Family of N. J. 309
Keim — Am. Ancestry viii, 219; ix, 234
Egle's Notes and Queries (1898) 212
Keim Genealogy (1874) 26 pages
Keim Monthly 1898-1900
Keinadt — Keinadt Gen. (1893) 171 pages
Keiser — Keinadt Genealogy 29-32
Keith — Amer. Ancestry vi, 32; ix, 113
Childs Genealogy 475-8
Crane's Rawson Genealogy 176

Eaton's History of Thomaston Me. ii, 292
Green's Kentucky Families
Hemenway's Vermont Gaz. iv, 47–9
Hudson's History of Lexington Mass. 280
Keith Genealogy (1873) 24 pages
Keith Genealogy (1889) 114 pages
Kingman's No. Bridgewater Mass. 551–9
Lapham's History of Paris Me. 649
Leland Genealogy 63–5
Meade's Old Churches of Virginia ii, 212
Mitchell's Hist. Bridgewater Mass. 207–16
Paxton's Marshall Genealogy 27
Pierce's History of Grafton Mass. 509–12
Savage's Genealogical Dictionary iii, 3
Smith Genealogy (1895) 113–5
Spooner Genealogy i, 208–11
Temple's Hist. of N. Brookfield Mass. 658
Temple's History of Palmer Mass. 493
Wheeler's History of Newport N. H. 444
Whitman Genealogy 126, 333–5
Keithley — Missouri Families 162
Keithline — Plumb's Hanover 442–4
Kelker — Egle's Lebanon Co. Pa. 243–5
Kelker Genealogy (1883) 133 pages
Kell — American Ancestry xi, 217
Kelleman — Boyd's Conesus N. Y. 161
Keller — American Ancestry ii, 66
Egle's Penn. Genealogies 2d ed. 341–9
Egle's Notes and Queries (1897) 125–6
Farrow's History of Islesborough Me. 227
Page Genealogy 75
Richmond Va. Standard iv, 3
Kelleran — Eaton's Thomaston Me. 293
Kelley — American Ancestry v, 46; vii,
  284; viii, 228; xii, 105, 134, 135
Ballou's History of Milford Mass. 862
Chapin Genealogy
Cogswell's Hist. Nottingham N. H. 730–2
Dearborn's History of Salisbury N. H. 647
Freeman's Hist. Cape Cod Mass. ii, 709–17
Hadley Genealogy 66–9
Kelley's New Hampton N. H. (1889)
Kelley Fam. Brentwood N. H. (1892) 42 p.
Kelley Family of Norwich Ct. (1897) 137 p.
Lancaster's Hist. of Gilmanton N. H. 274
Little's History of Weare N. H. 927
Morrison's Hist. Windham N. H. 610–2
Norton's History of Fitzwilliam N. H. 619
Temple's Hist. of N. Brookfield Mass. 658
Wheeler's History of Newport N. H. 445–7
Williams' History of Danby Vt. 179–83
Kellogg — American Ancestry iv, 169; vi,
  66, 85; ix, 192; xi, 35
Amer. Geneal. Record (1897) ii, 186–9
Barry's History of Framingham Mass. 307
Camp Genealogy ii, 31
Caverly's History of Pittsford Vt. 711
Chapin Genealogy
Clark and Kellogg Gen. (1877) by A. Clark
Crafts' History of Whately Mass. 507–8
Dwight Genealogy 303
Eaton's Annals of Warren Me. 403
Eaton's History of Thomaston Me. 298
Gold's History of Cornwall Ct. 304
Goodwin's Foote Genealogy 273
Guild's Stiles Genealogy 310

Hall's Norwalk Ct. Records 187–296
Judd's History of Hadley Mass. 523–9
Kellogg Family Meeting (1858) 8 pages
Kellogg Genealogical Items (1860) 8 pages
Kellogg Family of Hadley (1898) 266 pages
Kellogg of Hadley, supp. (1899) 45 pages
Loomis Genealogy (1880) 450
Nash Genealogy 85
New Eng. Hist. and Gen. Reg. xii, 201–6;
  xiv, 125–32; xlviii, 59–64
Prentice Genealogy 412
Savage's Genealogical Dictionary iii, 4–6
Sedgwick's History of Sharon Ct. 94
Selleck's Norwalk Ct. (1896) 371–6
Sheldon's History of Deerfield Mass. 226
Smith's Hist. of Sunderland Mass. 429–31
Temple's Hist. of N. Brookfield Mass. 659
Temple's History of Whately Mass. 244
Thayer Memorial (1835) 61
Kelly — Amer. Ancestry v, 169; xii, 136
Am. Cath. Hist. Soc. Records ii, 369–74
Austin's Allied Families 156–9
Burleigh's Guild Genealogy 100
Chase's History of Chester N. H. 530
Clyde's Irish Settlement in Pa. 79
Egle's Notes and Queries 3d ser. ii, 84–6;
  (1896) 198
Emery Genealogy (1890) 21–3
Guild's Stiles Genealogy 544–6
Hoyt's Salisbury Mass. Families 220–3
Kelly Fam. of Newbury Mass. (1886) 178 p.
Power's Sangamon Co. Ill. Settlers 423
Savage's Genealogical Dictionary iii, 6
Williams' History of Danby Vt. 179–83
Kelsey — Adam's Fairhaven Vt. 406
Anderson's Waterbury Ct. i, app. 81
Buckingham Genealogy 237–9
Chambers' Early Germans of N. J. 427
Chandler's History of Shirley Mass. 487–90
Cogswell's Hist. Nottingham N. H. 213–5
Lincoln's Hist. of Hingham Mass. ii, 402
New Eng. Hist. and Gen. Reg. xix, 242
Stiles' History of Windsor Ct. ii, 421
Stone Genealogy 43
Thompson's Memoir of Eben. Thompson
Wentworth Genealogy i, 645–8
Wheeler's History of Newport N. H. 447–50
Kelso — Cogswell's New Boston 383–5
Kelton — Bassett's Richmond N. H.
Herrick's History of Gardner Mass. 361
Kelton Genealogy (1895) 14 pages
Stearns' Hist. of Ashburnham Mass. 774–6
Kelty — Heywood's Westminster 729
Kemball — Bond's Watertown 323–5
Kemble — Kimball Genealogy (1897)
N. Y. Hist. Soc. Coll. xvii, 7–23
Wyman's Charlestown 568
Kemp — Butler's Hist. Groton Mass. 409
Cochrane's Hist. Francestown N. H. 783
Hazen's History of Billerica Mass. 80
Hodgman's History of Westford Mass. 456
Merrill's History of Acworth N. H. 232
Page Genealogy 75
Savage's Genealogical Dictionary iii, 7
Sheldon's History of Deerfield Mass. 227
Stearns' History of Ashburnham Mass. 776

Worcester's History of Hollis N. H. 379
Kemper — Amer. Ancestry iv, 63; v, 108
Kemper Genealogy (1899) 267 pages
Thayer Memorial (1835) 18
Kemple — Chambers' N. J. Germans
Kempton — Davis' Landmarks 163-5
Rickertson's N. Bedford Mass. 203-5, 209
Wheeler's History of Newport N. H. 450
Kenan — Baillie Genealogy 78-81
Kendall — Am. Ancestry iii, 189; xii, 57
Ballou's History of Milford Mass. 863
Bangor Historical Magazine iii, 198
Barry's Hist. of Framingham Mass. 307-10
Bond's Watertown Mass. Genealogy 325
Cochrane's History of Antrim N. H. 565
Daniels' History of Oxford Mass. 564
Davis' Landmarks of Plymouth Mass. 165
Densmore's Hartwell Genealogy
Douglass Genealogy 265
Ely Genealogy 299-301
Fox's History of Dunstable Mass. 246
Guild's Stiles Genealogy 298-300
Hazen's History of Billerica Mass. 81
Herrick's History of Gardner Mass. 362
Heywood's Hist. Westminster Mass. 730-7
Hill's History of Mason N. H. 203
Hubbard's Stanstead County Canada 295
Hudson's History of Lexington Mass. 113
Kendall Fam. Sterling Mass. (1884) 153 p.
Kendall Fam. of Oneida N. Y. (1888) 21 p.
Lapham's History of Bethel Me. 570
Leonard's History of Dublin N. H. 356
Locke Genealogy 20
Morris Genealogy (1894) 56
Morse's Sherborn Mass. Settlers 157
New Eng. Hist. Gen. Reg. xxxix, 17-23
Norton's Hist. of Fitzwilliam N. H. 619-22
Savage's Genealogical Dictionary iii, 9
Secomb's History of Amherst N. H. 652-5
Sewall's History of Woburn Mass. 619-23
Sheldon's History of Deerfield Mass. 278
Stearns' History of Ashburnham Mass. 776
Temple's History of Northfield Mass. 478
Temple's History of Palmer Mass. 495
Vinton's Richardson Genealogy 255
Wakefield Genealogy 48
Welles' Amer. Family Antiquity ii, 117-28
Wyman's Charlestown Mass. Gens. ii, 569
Kendig — Egle's Pa. Gens. 2d ed. 350-6
Heinecke Genealogy 76-8
Kendrick — Deane's Scituate Mass. 300
Freeman's Hist. of Cape Cod Mass. ii, 732
Joslin's History of Poultney Vt. 289
Little's History of Weare N. H. 927
Paige's History of Cambridge Mass. 595
Savage's Genealogical Dictionary iii, 11
Secomb's History of Amherst N. H. 655-7
Temple's North Brookfield Mass. 659-61
Worcester's History of Hollis N. H. 379
Worthen's History of Sutton N. H. 780-2
Kenea — Orcutt's Hist. of Wolcott Ct. 509
Kenerson — Lincoln's Hingham ii, 403
Keniston — Runnels' Sanbornton 413-6
Kennan—Paxton's Marshall Genealogy 50
Kennard—Old Eliot Me. Monthly i, (1897)
106-9

Kennedy — Cushman's Sheepscott 396
Eaton's Annals of Warren Me. 2d ed. 566
Eaton's History of Thomaston Me. ii, 298
Egle's Notes and Queries 1896 Annual 233
Emery Genealogy (1890) 110
Maxwell Genealogy 58-63
Miller's Hist. of Colchester Co. N. S. 296-9
Missouri Pioneer Families 217
Wentworth Genealogy i, 640-4
Wyoming Commem. Assoc. Proc. (1895)
Kenner — Hayden's Virginia Gens. 83
Kenney — Bass' Hist. of Braintree Vt. 156
Benedict's History of Sutton Mass. 668
Daniels' History of Oxford Mass. 565
Fletcher Genealogy 199
Livermore's History of Wilton N. H. 423
Newfane Vt. Centennial 56-8
Kennicott — Fiskes of Amherst 148
Kenniston — Dow's Hampton N. H. 776
Eaton's History of Thomaston Me. ii, 299
Kennon — Bolling Genealogy 23
Meade's Old Churches of Virginia
Richmond Va. Standard ii, 45
Robertson's Pocahontas' Descendants
Slaughter's Bristol Parish Va. 182-7
Kenny — Jameson's Medway Mass. 498
Kenrick — Jackson's Newton 354-9
Dearborn's Hist. of Salisbury N. H. 481-4
Kensett — Tuttle Genealogy 471-9
Kent — American Ancestry ix, 133
Atkins Genealogy (1891) 151-3
Babson's History of Gloucester Mass. 110
Ballou's History of Milford Mass. 864
Bangor Me. Historical Magazine v, 238
Bouton's History of Concord N. H. 672
Briggs' History of Shipbuilding 369-81
Calnek's History of Annapolis N. S. 536
Capron Genealogy by Holden 188-90
Chase's History of Chester N. H. 551
Coffin's History of Newbury Mass. 307
Deane's History of Scituate Mass. 300
Dwight Genealogy 405, 421-8
Emery's Newbury Mass. Reminisc. 162-5
Futhey's History of Chester Co. Pa. 620
Goodwin's Genealogical Notes 145-9
Hemenway's Vermont Gaz. iv, 158-60
Kent Genealogy (1898) 346 pages
Kent Family of Newbury (1898) 143 pages
Lincoln's Hist. of Hingham Mass. ii, 403-5
Miller's Colchester County N. S. 349-53
Morse's Memorial, appendix No. 101
New Eng. Hist. and Gen. Register xv, 273
New York Gen. Biog. Rec. iv, 83; xvi, 11-5
Poor's Merrimack Vall. Researches 148-50
Power's Sangamon Co. Ill. Settlers 425
Savage's Genealogical Dictionary iii, 11
Secomb's History of Amherst N. H. 658
Tuthill and Kent Chart (1880) 2x2 feet
Waldo's History of Tolland Ct. 126
Wyman's Charlestown Mass. Gens. 570-3
Kentfield — American Ancestry x, 127
Runnels' History of Sanbornton N. H. 416
Kenyon — American Ancestry i, 43; ii, 66;
vi, 70; ix, 21; xii
Austin's R. I. Genealogical Dictionary 116
Blanding Family Chart (1895)

Greene Genealogy (1894)
Thurston Genealogy (1892) 405-7
Kephart — Amer. Ancestry x, 142, 143
Wisner Genealogy 320
Kepler — Young's Wayne Co. Ind. 240
Kerigan — Temple's Palmer Mass. 501
Kerley — Savage's Gen. Dictionary iii, 13
Worcester's Mag. and Hist. Journal ii, 281
Kern — Clyde's Irish Settlement Pa. 80
Chambers' Early Germans of N. J. 429
Kerr — Clyde's Irish Settlement Pa. 81
Egle's Penn. Genealogies 2d ed. 22
Morrison's History of Windham N. H. 375
Richmond Va. Standard iii, 28
Kersey — Cope Genealogy 63, 145
Kershaw — Nevius Genealogy
Kervey — American Ancestry v, 162
Kessler — Power's Sangamon Ill. 425
Kester — Chambers' N. J. Germans
Ketcham — Bunker's L. I. Gens. 230
Huntting's Hist. of Pine Plains N. Y. 365
Savage's Genealogical Dictionary iii, 14
Sedgwick's History of Sharon Ct. 94
Sylvester's History of Ulster Co. N. Y. 101
Ketchum — American Ancestry xi, 233
Cleveland's Yates Co. N. Y. 296-9
Granite Monthly of Concord N. H. iv, 161
Ketelas — Alden's Amer. Epitaphs 181
Ketelhuin — Albany Colls. iv, 137
Keteltas — N. Y. Gen. Rec. xxviii, 172
Kettell — Poore Genealogy 38
Kettelle — Charlestown ii, 574-84
Kettle — Babson's Gloucester Mass. iii
Bond's Watertown Mass. Gens. 325
Munsell's Albany Collections iv, 137
Pearson's Schenectady N. Y. Settlers 99
Savage's Genealogical Dictionary iii, 14-6
Key — Hanson's Old Kent Md. 38
Hayden's Virginia Genealogies 167
Paxton's Marshall Genealogy 28
Richmond Va. Standard iii, 20
Sharpless Genealogy 138
Smith's History of Delaware Co. Pa. 476
Keyes — American Ancestry i, 43
Blake's Lucy Keyes Biog. (1893) 23 ages
Cleveland Genealogy (1899) 91, 190, 409
Cochrane's History of Antrim N. H. 567
Crafts Genealogy 199-202
Davis' History of Reading Vt. 140
Gregory's History of Northfield Vt. 122-9
Hayward's Hist. of Hancock N. H. 688-92
Hemenway's Vermont Hist. Gaz. iv, 627
Heywood's Hist. Westminster Mass. 738
Hodgman's History of Westford Mass. 457
Hudson's Hist. of Marlborough Mass. 409
Hyde's History of Brimfield Mass. 425-8
Keyes Fam. of West Boylston (1857) 15 p.
Keyes Fam. of Newbury (1880) 192 p.
Keyes Family of Watertown (1880) 319 p.
Keyes' West Boylston Mass. Register 26
Lapham's History of Rumford Me. 359-61
Livermore's History of Wilton N. H. 424-6
Merrill's History of Acworth N. H. 233
Power's Sangamon Co. Ill. Settlers 427
Savage's Genealogical Dictionary iii, 16
Seagrave Genealogy, app. 34

Stearns' History of Ashburnham Mass. 777
Stearns' History of Rindge N. H. 582
Swain Genealogy 114-21
Ward's Hist. of Shrewsbury Mass. 339-47
Whitcomb Genealogy 9
Young's Hist. Chautauqua Co. N. Y. 336
Keylor — Magennis Genealogy 73-80
Keyser — American Ancestry v, 29
Cochrane's Hist. Francestown N. H. 784
Keyser Reunion (1889) 161 pages
Plumb's History of Hanover Pa. 438-40
Welles' Washington Genealogy 261
Kezar — Chandler's Shirley 491-5
Dearborn's History of Parsonsfield Me. 383
Hubbard's Stanstead Co. Canada 255
Worthen's History of Sutton N. H. 782-7
Kibbe — Hinman's Settlers 1st ed. 179
Hudson's History of Lexington Mass. 113
Morse's Sherborn Mass. Settlers 158
Stiles' History of Windsor Ct. ii 839
Kibbee — American Ancestry i, 43
Kibby — Cogswell's Henniker N. H. 634
Savage's Genealogical Dictionary iii, 17
Wheeler's History of Newport N. H. 452
Kibling — Ashburnham Mass. 778-82
Kiblinger — Stearns' Ashburnham 779
Kice — Chambers' N. J. Germans
Kidder — Adams' Fairhaven Vt. 406
Aldrich's Hist. of Walpole N. H. 298-300
American Ancestry vi, 161, 181; xii
Bass' History of Braintree Vt. 157
Bemis' History of Marlboro N. H. 548
Benedict's History of Sutton Mass. 669
Brooks' History of Medford Mass. 528
Cleveland's Hist. Yates Co. N. Y. 237-41
Cochrane's History of Antrim N. H. 568
Cochrane's History of Francestown N. H. 785
Daniels' History of Oxford Mass. 566
Guild's Stiles Genealogy 84
Hazen's History of Billerica Mass. 81-4
Hodgman's History of Westford Mass. 459
Kidder Genealogy (1876) 32 pages
Kidder Kenealogy (1886) 175 pages
Kidder's New Ipswich N. H. 394-414
Kidder's New Ipswich N. H. 394-414
Livermore's History of Wilton N. H. 426
Paige's History of Cambridge Mass. 596
Ransom Genealogy
Savage's Genealogical Dictionary iii, 18
Secomb's History of Amherst N. H. 659
Upham Genealogy 38-40
Whittemore's Orange N. J. 292-4
Wyman's Charlestown Mass. 585-8
Kidney — American Ancestry i, 44
Munsell's Albany Collections iv, 138
Kieff — Eaton's Thomaston Me. 299
Kiersen — Riker's Harlem Mass. 512-4
Kierstede — American Ancestry xii
N. Y. Genealogical Rec. xiii, 24-6
Schoonmaker's Hist. Kingston N. Y. 482
Sylvester's History of Ulster Co. N. Y. 73
Kies — Davis Genealogy 80
Kilborn — Andrews' New Britain 198
Hubbard's Stanstead Co. Can. 153-5, 320
Warren's History of Waterford Me. 265
Kilborne — Lapham's Bethel Me. 572

Kilbourn — Amer. Ancestry x, 198, 200
Coffin's History of Boscawen N. H. 562-6
Freeman's Hist. of Cape Cod Mass. ii, 648
Kilbourn Genealogy (1845) 151 pages
Kilbourn Genealogy 2d ed. (1856) 488 p.
Kilbourn's History of Litchfield Co. Ct. 161
N. E. Hist. Gen. Reg. xiii, 372; xviii, 226
Ridlon's Harrison Me. Settlers 90
Savage's Genealogical Dictionary iii, 18-20
Kilbourne — American Ancestry i, 44
Essex Institute Hist. Colls. xxii, 135-9
Kilburn — Aldrich's Walpole 300-2
Ballou's History of Medford Mass. 865-8
Bond's Watertown Mass. Gens. 810
Capron Genealogy by Holden 239-43
Cogswell's History of Henniker N. H. 635
Dearborn's History of Salisbury N. H. 649
Hayward's History of Gilsum N. H. 347
Norton's History of Fitzwilliam N. H. 622
Kilbury — Hemenway's Vt. Gaz. 36
Kilby — Bangor Hist. Magazine vi, 290-2
Dennysville Me. Centennial 107
Lincoln's Hist. of Hingham Mass. ii, 405
New Eng. Hist. and Gen. Reg. xxvi, 43
Savage's Genealogical Dictionary iii, 20
Titcomb's Early New Eng. People 94-101
Whitmore's Heraldic Journal ii, 48
Wilder Genealogy 354
Kilgore — Lapham's Bethel Me. 571
Warren's History of Waterford Me. 266
Kilham — Fiske Family of Amherst 135
Hammatt Papers of Ipswich Mass. 196
Killam — Barry's Hanover Mass. 348
Bass' History of Braintree Vt. 158
Hinman's Connecticut Settlers 1st ed. 170
Killian — Keinadt Genealogy 47-9
Killsa — Eaton's Thomaston Me. 300
Killum — Hayward's Hancock 693
Temple's History of Palmer Mass. 494
Kilmer — Amer. Ancestry ii, 66; viii, 144
Kilmore — American Ancestry ii, 66
Kilpatrick — Cutter's Jaffrey 429
Ridlon's Saco Valley Me. Families 766-87
Kilton — Austin's R. I. Gen. Dict. 116
Kimball — American Ancestry iii, 30, 90;
    iv, 88; vii, 97; viii, 76
Andrews Genealogy (1890) 190-5
Bangor Me. Historical Magazine v, 199
Bells' History of Exeter N. H. 26
Bond's Watertown Mass. Gen. 323-5
Bouton's History of Concord N. H. 673-7
Buxton's Me. Centennial 142-7
Cleveland's History of Yates Co. N. Y. 717
Cochrane's Hist. of Antrim N. H. 569-71
Cochrane's Hist. Francest'n N. H. 786-8
Coffin's History of Boscawen N. H. 566-70
Cogswell's Hist. of Henniker N. H. 636-8
Cogswell's Hist. of Nottingham N. H. 732
Collin's Hist. Hillsdale N. Y., app. 88-90
Crafts Genealogy 214-8
Daniels' History of Oxford Mass. 567
Davis' Landmarks of Plymouth Mass. 166
Driver Genealogy 368-86
Dudley Genealogy 126
Dunster Genealogy 288-99
Eaton's History of Thomaston Me. 300

Eaton Grange (1890)
Essex Inst. Hist. Collections xviii, 148-55
Goodwin's History of Buxton Me. 292
Granite Monthly of Concord N. H. 435-7
Guild's Stiles Genealogy 303
Hammatt Papers Ipswich Mass. 79, 181-6
Hayward's History of Hancock N. H. 694-7
Hoyt's Salisbury Mass. Families 223-8
Kimball Fam. of Salem Mass. (1882) 13 p.
Kimball Family of N. H. (1885) 103 pages
Kimball Genealogy (1897) 1278 p.
Kimball Family News (1898) 298 pages
Lapham's History of Bethel Me. 572-8
Lapham's History of Norway Me. 541
Lapham's History of Rumford Me. 361-4
Lapham's History of Woodstock Me. 230
Lincoln's Hist. of Hingham Mass. ii, 406
Little's History of Weare N. H. 929-31
Livermore's Hist. of Wilton N. H. 427-30
McKeen's History of Bradford Vt. 277-80
New Eng. Hist. and Gen. Reg. xxviii, 241
Norton's History of Fitzwilliam N. H. 622
Orford N. H. Centennial 117
Perley's History of Boxford Mass. 51-3
Pierce's History of Grafton Mass. 512-4
Poor's Merrimack Valley Researches 90
Putnam's Historical Magazine iv, 131
Read's History of Swanzey N. H. 388
Runnel's Sanbornton N. H. ii, 417-22
Saunderson's Hist. Charlestown N. H. 460
Savage's Genealogical Dictionary iii, 21-3
Secomb's History of Amherst N. H. 660
Smith's History of Peterborough N. H. 129
Smith (Rev. Wm.) Biography
Stearns' History of Rindge N. H. 583-9
Temple's Hist. of N. Brookfield Mass. 662
Warren's History of Waterford Me. 268
Wentworth Genealogy i, 162-5
Wheeler's History of Newport N. H. 453-6
Worthen's History of Sutton N. H. 1035-50
Kimber — American Ancestry x, 144
Jackson Genealogy 129
Kimber Genealogy (1894) 82 pages
Kimberly — American Ancestry ix, 222
Kimberly Family Chart (1896) 1x2 feet
Orcutt's History of Stratford Ct. 1232
Orcutt's History of Torrington Ct. 728
Savage's Genealogical Dictionary iii, 23
Kime — Keim and Allied Families 192, 501
Kimmey — American Ancestry i, 44
Kimpton — Bassett's Richmond N. H.
Hollister Genealogy 695-7
Hubbard's Stanstead County Canada 199
Kincard — Windham N. H. 613-5
Kinekel — Page Genealogy 105
Kiner — Keinadt Genealogy 40-5
King — Am. Anc. i, 44; ii, 66; iii, 30; iv,
    160; vi, 10, 107, 166; vii, 186; viii, 76,
    160; ix, 188; x, 13; xi, 91. 233
Atkins' History of Hawley Mass. 44, 97
Austin's R. I. Genealogical Dictionary 117
Ballou's History of Milford Mass. 868
Bangor Me. Historical Magazine viii, 110
Benedict's History of Sutton Mass. 670-81
Bond's Watertown Mass. Gens. 326, 816
Bulloch Genealogy

Chambers' Early Germans of N. J. 430-2
Cincinnati O. Criterion (1888) ii. 369
Clarke's Old King Wm. Co. Va. Families
Corliss' North Yarmouth Me. Magazine
Cutts Genealogy 64
Davis' Landmarks of Plymouth Mass 167
Deane's History of Scituate Mass. 301
Driver Genealogy 236
Dwight Genealogy 119, 550-2, 952-72
Elderkin Genealogy 152-66
Essex Institute Hist. Collections (1880)
Foster Genealogy (1899) 97-108
Goode Genealogy 25 pages
Goodrich's Recoll. of a Lifetime i, 517-9
Goodwin's Olcott Genealogy 30
Griffin's Journal Southold N. Y. 148-52
Hinman's Connecticut Settlers (1846) ed.
Hobart's History of Abington Mass. 410
Holton's Winslow Memorial i, 141, 424-8
Jackson's History of Newton Mass. 359
King Fam. of Raynham Mass. (1866) 28 p.
King Family of Salem Mass. (1880) 8 p.
King Family of Salem Mass. (1857) chart
King Family of Salem Mass. (1891) chart
King Family of Lynn Mass. (1892) chart
King Family of Suffield Ct. (1892) 7 p.
King Family of Monson Mass. (1897) 142 p.
Kings of Marshfield Mass. (1898) 65 pages
Lapham's History of Paris Me. 650-3
Lincoln's History of Hingham Mass. ii, 407
Livermore's History of Wilton N. H. 430-2
Longmeadow Mass. Centennial, app. 73
Loomis Genealogy (1880) 546, 651
Magennis Genealogy 105
Maine Historical and Gen. Recorder i, 1-8,
    33-40, 182-6, 209-11; iii, 118-25
Maine Hist. Society Collections iii, 214
Mallmann's Shelter Island N. V. 293, 315
Meade's Old Churches of Virginia
New Eng. Historical and Gen. Register xi,
    357-9; xvi, 144-50; xlvi, 370-4
New York Gen. and Biog. Record xxxi,
    8-12, 70-4, 135-9
Phœnix Family of Vt. ii, 1275
Power's Sangamon Co. Ill. Settlers 428-31
Randall's Hist. Chesterfield N. H. 373-5
Richmond Va. Standard ii, 9; iii, 13
Roome Genealogy 115 a.
Savage's Genealogical Dictionary iii, 23-7
Sedgwick's History of Sharon Ct. 95
Shotwell Genealogy 16-8, 272-4
Stiles' History of Windsor Ct. ii, 422-6
Strong Genealogy 256, 578, 1256
Taylor's Great Barrington Mass. 117-20
Temple's Hist. of N. Brookfield Mass. 663
Temple's History of Northfield Mass. 479
Temple's History of Palmer Mass. 496-501
Thomas Genealogy (1877) 104
Thomas Genealogy (1896) 379-81
Van Rensselaer's New Yorkers
Wagenseller Genealogy 117-28
Walworth's Hyde Genealogy 285
Welles' Washington Genealogy 229
Wentworth Genealogy i, 299-304
Weygant's Family Record (1897) 51
Wheeler's History of Newport N. H. 456

Whitman Genealogy 28
Whitmore's Copps Hill Epitaphs
Wilson's Address at Palmer Mass. (1852)
Worthen's History of Sutton N. H. 788-90
Wyman's Charleston Mass. Gens. 589
Young's History of Wayne Co. Ind. 187
Kingman — Am. Anc. ii, 66; vi, 75, 85, 116
Briggs' History of Shipbuilding 125
Isbell and Kingman Genealogy (1889) 30 p.
Kingman Genealogy (1896) 4 pages
Kingman's No. Bridgewater Mass. 559-71
Lincoln's History of Hingham Mass. ii, 408
Mitchell's Hist. Bridgewater Mass. 216-20
Savage's Genealogical Dictionary iii, 27
Whitman Genealogy 145
Whittemore's Orange N. J. 370
Kingsbury — Amer. Ancestry iv, 49; xii
Anderson's Waterbury Ct. i, app. 81
Bangor Me. Historical Magazine vii, 236
Blake's History of Franklin Mass. 256
Blood's History of Temple N H. 230
Bond's Watertown Mass. Gens. 849
Caulkins' History of Norwich Ct. 234
Cochrane's Hist. Francest'n N. H. 788-92
Corliss Genealogy 240
Daniels' History of Oxford Mass. 568-73
Dimock's Coventry Ct. Records 67-70
Hayward's History of Gilsum N. H. 348
Hill's Dedham Mass. Records i
Hughes Genealogy 207-11
Kingsbury Genealogy (1857) 4 pages
Locke Genealogy 106
New Eng. Historical and Gen. Register
    xiii, 157-60; xvi, 327, 337-41
Pierce's History of Grafton Mass. 514
Savage's Genealogical Dictionary iii, 28
Stearns' History of Rindge N. H. 589
Stiles' History of Windsor Ct. ii, 426-8
Temple's Hist. of N. Brookfield Mass. 664
Walworth's Hyde Genealogy 39, 677-81
Wight Genealogy 131-3
Wilder Genealogy 184
Kingsland — Hudson Co. N. J. 545-9
Kingsley — American Ancestry v, 173;
    vi, 207; viii, 49
Caverly's History of Pittsford Vt. 712
Coit Genealogy 174
Mitchell's Hist. of Bridgewater Mass. 220
Montague Genealogy 416-8, 621-7, 634-6
Ruggles Genealogy
Savage's Genealogical Dictionary iii, 29
Stanton Genealogy 279
Strong Genealogy 885-90, 1405-13
Warren and Clarke Genealogy 104
Whittemore's Orange N. J. 264
Kinkead — Clarke's King Wm. Fams.
Kinley — Young's Wayne Co. Ind. 241
Kinloch — Spotswood Papers 22
Page Genealogy 162-7
Slaughter's St. Mark's Parish Virg. 166
Kinne—Am. Anc. ii, 67; iv, 97, 140; xii, 78
Kinne Genealogy (1881) 96 pages
Stanton Genealogy 282-4
Kinnecut — American Ancestry ii, 201
Kinney — Am. Anc. v, 93; vii, 125; ix, 192
Cleveland's Hist. Yates Co. N. Y. 510-2

Joslin's History of Poultney Vt. 291
Perkins' Old Houses of Norwich Ct. 502
Pond Genealogy (1875) 19
Power's Sangamon Co. Ill. Settlers 431
Sharpe's History of Seymour Ct. 215
Kinsela — Pearson's Schenectady 100
Kinsley — Lapham's Paris Me. 653
Montague Genealogy 472
Stiles' History of Windsor Ct. ii, 429
Kinsman — Hammatt Papers 192–6
Kinsman Genealogy (1876) 258 pages
Kinson — Little's Hist. Weare N. H. 928
Kip — American Ancestry i, 44
Bergen's Kings County N. Y. Settlers 174
Bolton's Westchester Co. N. Y. ii, 741
Hayes' Wells Genealogy 161–3
Holgate's American Genealogy 109–14
Kip Genealogy (1871) 49 pages
Kip Genealogy (1877) 11 pages, reprint
Munsell's Albany Collections iv, 138
N. Y. Gen. Record viii, 67–73, 124–33; xii, 29–32; xx, 12
Well's Amer. Fam. Antiquity ii, 17–26
Kipp — American Ancestry v, 231; ix, 218
Kirby — American Ancestry ii, 67
Kirby Genealogy (1898) 451 pages
Savage's Genealogical Dictionary iii, 30
Kirk — American Ancestry iii, 170
Cogswell's History of Henniker N. H. 638
Cregar's Haines Ancestry 48–50
Fell Genealogy 62
Futhey's History of Chester Co. Pa. 624
Green's Kentucky Families
Lamborn Genealogy 295
Kirk Genealogy (1872) 252 pages
Potts Genealogy (1895) 261–3
Smith's History of Delaware Co. Pa. 476
Kirkbride — American Ancestry xi, 91
Davis' Bucks Co. 67, 109
Kirkbride Family of Phila. (1878)
Kirkbridge — Rodman Genealogy 213
Kirke — Steele Genealogy (1896)
Kirkland — Brown's Simsbury Ct. 89
Burk and Alvord Genealogy 187–94
Kirkland Genealogy (1894) 5 pages
Muzzey's Reminiscences
New Eng. Hist. and Gen. Reg. xlviii, 66–70
Sanborn Genealogy (1894)
Wetmore Genealogy 584–7
Young's Life of J. T. Kirkland 78–80
Kirkpatrick — Eaton's Warren Me.
Eaton's History of Thomaston Me. ii, 301
How's Kirkpatrick Biography (1870) 75 p.
Kirkpatrick Genealogy (1867) 312 pages
Littell's Passaic Valley Gens. 198–204
Marshall Genealogy (1884) 1c–2, 239
Messler's History of Somerset Co. N. J. 63
Norton's History of Fitzwilliam N. H. 656
Kirtland — Buckingham Gen. 151, 171
Chapman Genealogy 71, 96, 133
Chapman's Pratt Genealogy 260–86
Cothren's History of Woodbury Ct. ii, 1512
Davis' History of Wallingford Ct. 838–40
Doty Genealogy 53
Lewis' History of Lynn Mass. 154
N. E. Gen. Reg. xiv, 241–5; xlviii, 66–70

Savage's Genealogical Dictionary iii, 31
Tuttle Genealogy 542–5
Kissam — American Ancestry iii, 31; v, 186; x, 149; xii, 61
Bartow Genealogy 164–6
Kissam Genealogy (1892) 94 pages
Queens County N. Y. History 437
Kisselbrack — American Ancestry ii, 67
Kitchel — American Ancestry xii
Kitchel Genealogy (1879) 80 pages
Savage's Genealogical Dictionary iii, 32
Stiles of Kentucky (1896) 39–41
Tuttle Genealogy 667
Kite — American Ancestry vi, 82
Sharpless Genealogy 397
Kitteka — Egle's Notes (1898) 96–9
Kittinger — American Ancestry v, 114
Kittle — American Ancestry ii, 67
Kittredge — Aldrich's Walpole 303–5
American Ancestry vi, 32
Chase's History of Chester N. H. 552
Dearborn's History of Salisbury N. H. 399
Draper's History of Spencer Mass. 217
Hayward's Hist. of Hancock N. H. 697–9
Hazen's History of Billerica Mass. 85–8
Savage's Genealogical Dictionary iii, 33
Secomb's History of Amherst N. H. 661
Temple's Hist. N. Brookfield Mass. 664–7
Klein — Albany Collections iv, 138
Kline — Cassel Genealogy 62–4, 109–13
Chambers' Early Germans of N. J. 432–4
Mellick Genealogy 648–56
Knap — Schenck's Fairfield Ct. 391
Knapp — American Ancestry ii, 68; iv, 162; vii, 166, 207
Baird's History of Rye N. Y. 416
Bangor Me. Historical Magazine vi. 94
Benedict's History of Sutton Mass. 682
Bond's Watertown Mass. Gens. 327, 816
Cleveland's Yates Co. N. Y. 149, 711
Cleveland Genealogy 228–31
Draper's History of Spencer Mass. 215
Hemenway's Vermont Hist. Gaz. v. 149
Huntington's Stamford Ct. Settlers 61–4
Jackson's History of Newton Mass. 360
Joslin's History of Poultney Vt. 294–6
Lapham's History of Rumford Me. 365
Paige's History of Hardwick Mass. 408
Runnel's Sanbornton N. H. ii, 422–4
Trubee Genealogy 59–72, 122–7
Young's History of Warsaw N. Y. 287–90
Knappen — American Ancestry ii, 63
Kneale — Savage's Gen. Dict. iii, 35
Kneeland — Amer. Ancestry v, 45; xii, 39
Champion Genealogy 216–8
Herrick's History of Gardner Mass. 364
Hodgman's History of Westford Mass. 459
Kneeland Genealogy (1897) 583 pages
Randall's Hist. of Chesterfield N. H. 375–7
Ridlon's Harrison Me. Settlers 86–9
Knell — Orcutt's Stratford Ct. 1233
Knibloe — Sedgwick's Sharon Ct. 95
Knickerbocker — Am. Anc. i, 45; ii, 68
Hunting's Hist. of Pine Plains N. Y. 366
Munsell's Albany Collections iv, 138
Sedgwick's History of Sharon Ct. 95

Kniffen — Baird's Rye N. Y. 416–20
Knight — Adams Genealogy (1895) 36–8
American Ancestry ii, 68; v, 121; xii, 34
Austin's Ancestries 37
Austin's R. I. Genealogical Dictionary 330
Ballou's History of Milford Mass. 870
Bemis' History of Marlboro N. H. 549
Capron Genealogy by Holden 37–41
Cochrane's History of Antrim N. H. 571
Cochrane's Hist. Francestown N. H. 792
Coffin's History of Newbury Mass. 307
Crafts' History of Whately Mass. 508
Cregar's Haines Ancestry 50–2
Davis Genealogy 155
Davis' History of Bucks County Pa. 120
Draper's History of Spencer Mass. 216
Essex Institute Hist. Collections i, 186
Hammatt Papers of Ipswich Mass. 191
Hayward's History of Gilsum N. H. 350
Hayward's Hist. Hancock N. H. 699–721
Hemenway's Vermont Gaz. v, 137–45
Hinman's Connecticut Settlers i. 320
Hubbard's Hist. of Springfield Vt. 359–61
Hubbard's Stanstead Co. Canada 132–4
Hudson's History of Lexington Mass. 280
Kidder's Hist. of New Ipswich N. H. 415
Knight (Frederick) Biography (1855)
Knight Manu. in Me. Gen. Soc. Lib. 14 p.
Lapham's History of Norway Me. 542
Lapham's History of Paris Me. 654–6
Lapham's History of Rumford Me. 366–8
Livermore's History of Wilton N. H. 432
Lyman's Hist. Easthampton Mass. 181–3
Martindale's Hist. of Byberry Pa. 299–319
New Eng. Hist. and Gen. Register xv, 269
Norton's Hist. of Fitzwilliam N. H. 623–5
Perkins' Old Houses of Norwich Ct. 503
Pierce's History of Gorham Me. 180
Poor's Merrimack Vall. Researches 148–50
Power's Sangamon Co. Ill. Settlers 433
Richmond Va. Standard iii, 8
Robinson's Items of Ancestry (1894) 45
Savage's Genealogical Dictionary iii, 35–40
Secomb's History of Amherst N. H. 662
Sewall's History of Woburn Mass. 624
Stackpole's History of Durham Me. 208–10
Stearns' History of Ashburnham Mass. 782
Temple's Hist. N. Brookfield Mass. 667–9
Temple's History of Northfield Mass. 580
Thomas Genealogy (1877) 104–6
Thomas Genealogy (1896) 383–5
Washington N. H. History 506
Wentworth Genealogy i, 137–9, 467
Wilder Genealogy 160, 172
Wyman's Charlestown Mass. Gens. 590–2
Knights — Low Family Chart (1890)
Kniskern — American Ancestry ii, 68
Knotts — Power's Sangamon Ill. 434
Knower — American Ancestry x, 190
Heywood's Westminster Mass. 739–41
Savage's Genealogical Dictionary iii, 40
Knowles — Austin's R. I. Dict. 332
Austin's Allied Families 160
Bangor Me Historical Magazine v, 199
Chase's History of Chester N. H. 552
Cogswell's Nottingham N. H. 736–43

Cothren's Woodbury Ct. i, 604; ii, 1511
Dow's History of Hampton N. H. 778–81
Freeman's History of Cape Cod ii, 393, 736
Narragansett Historical Register iii, 151
Newport Historical Magazine iv, 248–50
Orcutt's History of New Milford Ct. 721
Penn. Magazine of History xviii, 255
Rich's History of Truro Mass. 538
Savage's Genealogical Dictionary iii, 41
Schenck's History of Fairfield Ct. 392
Thomas Genealogy (1877) 106
Thomas Genealogy (1896) 385
Walker Genealogy 46
Wyman's Charlestown Mass. Gens. 592
Knowlton — American Ancestry i, 45; iii, 208; ix, 244
Barry's History of Framingham Mass. 311
Bemis' History of Marlboro N. H. 550
Butler's History of Farmington Me. 516–24
Caldwell Genealogy 65
Cogswell's History Nottingham N. H. 734–6
Eaton's History of Thomaston Me. ii, 302
Farrow's History of Islesborough Me. 228
Hammatt Papers of Ipswich Mass. 186–91
Hayward's History of Hancock N. H. 721
Hemenway's Vermont Hist. Gaz. v, 463
Hill's History of Mason N. H. 204
Kidder's Hist. of New Ipswich N. H. 415
Knowlton Statue Ceremonies (1895) 53 p.
Knowlton Genealogy (1897) 608 pages
Knowlton Assoc. Prospectus (1897) 88 p.
Leonard's History of Dublin N. H. 457–9
Morse's Sherborn Mass. Settlers 160
New Eng. Hist. and Gen. Register xv, 344–6; xxxiv, 386; l 226
Newfane Vt. Centennial 34–6, 158
Paige's History of Hardwick Mass. 409
Rollo Genealogy 51
Runnel's Hist. of Sanbornton N. H. ii, 424
Savage's Genealogical Dictionary iii, 42
Temple's Hist. of N. Brookfield Mass. 669
Ward's Hist. of Shrewsbury Mass. 348–55
Worthen's History of Sutton N. H. 790–2
Knox — Bangor Me. Hist. Mag. v, 129
Bent's History of Whiteside Co. Ill. 299
Carter's History of Pembroke N. H. ii, 183–9, 332
Chambers' Early Germans of N. J. 123
Chapman's Trowbridge Genealogy 205
Eaton's History of Thomaston Me. ii, 303
Gibb's History of Blandford Mass. 66
Goode Genealogy 122
Hanson's Old Kent Md. 134–6
Knox Family of Hartford (1873) 107 pages
Knox Family of Dover N. H. (1890) 34 p.
Missouri Pioneer Families 274
Richmond Va. Standard ii, 47
Runnel's Hist. of Sanbornton N. H. ii, 425
Slaughter's Bristol Parish Va. 203
Temple's History of Palmer Mass. 496
Wentworth Genealogy i, 252–4
Knypers — American Ancestry vi, 106
Kocher — Plumb's Hanover Pa. 441
Koelliker — Koelliker Genealogy (1883)
Koen — Albany Collections iv, 138

Koiner — American Ancestry x, 142
Keinadt Genealogy 47–55
Kolb — Gregg's Old Cheraws S. C. 83
Kolb Genealogy (1895) 584 pages
Kolloch — N. Y. Gen. Record viii, 184
Phœnix's Whitney Genealogy ii, (1813)
Kollock — Kollock Genealogy (1897) 72 p.
Komer — Peyton's Augusta County Va.
Kool — Cole Genealogy (1876)
Koontz — Spangler Genealogy 223–5
Kortwright — Riker's Harlem 514–9
Sylvester's History of Ulster Co. N. Y. 228
Krause — Egle's Penn. Gens. 567–9
Krantz — Everhart Genealogy 82–4
Kratz — American Ancestry xi, 36
Kratz Genealogy (1892) 315 pages
Krauss — Fahnstock's Wolff Family 108
Kriebel's Schwenkfelders 3–19
Perkiomen Region Pa. iii, 53–6
Kreider — Egle's Lebanon County Pa.
Kreidler — Plumb's Hanover Pa. 440
Kriebel — Kriebel's Schwenkfelders 11–76
Kroesen — Nevius Genealogy
Krum — Collin's Hillsdale N. Y. 75
Kuhn — Kuhn Genealogy (1897) 9 pages
New Eng. Hist. Register li, 441–7
Penn. Mag. of History v, 100
Smith (Rev. Wm.) Biography
Kuhns — American Ancestry x, 42
Kulp — American Ancestry iii, 77
Kolb Genealogy (1895) 584 pages
Kulp's Wyoming Valley Families
Kumler — American Ancestry vii, 85
Kunders — See Conrad Genealogy
Kunkel — American Ancestry xi, 90
Egle's Penn. Genealogies 2d ed. 357–66
Kurtz — Hertzler Genealogy 159–75, 210–2
Egle's Notes and Queries 3d ser. iii, 513
Kuykendall — Gumaer's Deerpark 74
Kuypers — American Ancestry vii, 159
Kyes — Hatch's Hist. of Industry Me. 673
Kyn — Penn. Mag. of History
Kyner — Keinadt Genealogy 32–40
Labaree — Charlestown N. H. 462–8
Labbadie — Beckwith's Creoles 105
Labbertse — Bergen Genealogy 53
Laborie — Orcutt's Stratford Ct. 1233
Lachapelle — Temple's No. Brookfield
Lackey — Benedict's Sutton Mass. 682
La Croix — Jameson's Medway 498
Lacy — Am. Ancestry ii, 68; viii, 115, 143
Cutter's History of Jaffrey N. H. 390–3
Littell's Passaic Valley Genealogies 204–7
Orcutt's History of Stratford Ct. 1353
Power's Sangamon Co. Ill. Settlers 437
Ladd — Am. Ancestry v, 50, 151, 224; x, 17
Austin's R. I. Genealogical Dictionary 118
Bond's Watertown Mass. Gens. 971
Corliss' Genealogy 238
Cutts Genealogy 364
Dearborn's History of Salisbury N. H. 650
Dimock's Coventry Ct. Records 71–3
Farrows' History of Islesborough Me. 228
Hoyt's Salisbury Mass. Families 228–30
Hubbard's Hist. of Stanstead Co. Can. 176
Kitchell Genealogy 58

Ladd Genealogy (1890) 413 pages
Morrison's Hist. of Windham N. H. 616–8
North's History of Augusta Me. 897
Ruggles Genealogy by Bailey (1896) 37–44
Runnel's Sanbornton N. H. ii, 427–31
Savage's Genealogical Dictionary iii, 43
Stark's History of Dunbarton N. H. 241
Stiles' History of Windsor Ct. ii, 429
Walworth's Hyde Genealogy i, 652–65
Waldo's History of Tolland Ct. 123–6
Ladomus — Martin's Chester Pa. 486
La Dow — American Ancestry i, 45
Laflin — American Ancestry xi, 37
Daniels' History of Oxford Mass. 573
Loomis Genealogy (1880) 771
La Forge — Clute's Staten Island 397
La Grange — American Ancestry i, 45
Chambers' Early Germans of N. J. 434
Pearson's Schenectady N. Y. Settlers 59
Laidley — American Ancestry vi, 84, 86
Laighton — Hammatt Papers 197–201
Laird — American Ancestry vii, 140
Lake — Austin's R. I. Gen. Dict. 118
Bergen's Kings Co. N. Y. Settlers 179
Carter's Hist. Pembroke N. H. ii, 190–202
Chambers' Early Germans of N. J. 435
Clute's History of Staten Island N. Y. 398
Crawford Family of Virginia 110–2
Goodyear Genealogy 55–8
Hale Genealogy 315–7
Hammatt Papers of Ipswich Mass. 217–20
Orcutt's History of Stratford Ct. 1234
Power's Sangamon Co. Ill. Settlers 438
Savage's Genealogical Dictionary iii, 44
Sedgwick's History of Sharon Ct. 95
Stearns' History of Rindge N. H. 590–3
Williams' History of Danby Vt. 183
Lakeman — Carter's Pembroke 202–4
Hammatt Papers of Ipswich Mass. 199
Pierce's Gorham Me. 181
Runnel's Hist. of Sanbornton N. H. ii, 431
Lakin — Butler's Groton 410–2, 473
Cochrane's Hist. Francestown N. H. 793
Farnsworth Genealogy (1897) 47–56
Green's Early Groton Mass. Settlers 8
Green's Groton Mass. Epitaphs 242
Hartwell Genealogy (1887) 35
Hayward's Hist. of Hancock N. H. 722–35
N. E. Hist. and Gen. Reg. xlviii, 444–6
Ridlon's Harrison Me. Settlers 91
Runnel's Hist. of Sanbornton N. H. ii, 432
Savage's Genealogical Dictionary iii, 45
Lamar — American Ancestry v, 189
Southern Hist. Assoc. Pubs. i, (1897) 203–10
Worthington Genealogy (1886) 15
Lamb — Am. Anc. v, 125; viii, 124; xi, 211
Barry's Hist. of Framingham Mass. 311–3
Bass' History of Braintree Vt. 158
Caulkins' History of New London Ct. 327
Daniels' History of Oxford Mass. 573–8
Davis Genealogy 29–31, 98
Dickinson Genealogy (1896) 149–51
Draper's History of Spencer Mass. 217–20
Eaton's History of Thomaston Me. 303
Ellis' History of Roxbury Mass.
Heywood's Hist. of Westminster Mass. 741

Lamb's Family Record (1900) 24 pages
Littell's Passaic Valley Genealogies 207
Miller's Hist. of Colchester Co. N. S. 341
Paul's History of Wells Vt. 109–14
Power's Sangamon Co. Ill. Settlers 435–7
Savage's Genealogical Dictionary iii, 46–8
Stearns' History of Rindge N. H. 594
Stone's History of Hubbardston Mass. 302
Temple's Hist. of N. Brookfield Mass. 670
Temple's History of Palmer Mass. 506
Wm. and Mary College Hist. Register iii,
    126–8; vii, 51–4, 109–12
Lambard — North's Augusta Me. 889
Lambert — American Ancestry ii, 69
Blake Genealogy 42
Cothren's Woodbury Ct. 607–12, 1512
Essex Institute Hist. Collections xxii, 133–5
Gage's History of Rowley Mass. 446
Hammatt Papers of Ipswich Mass. 202
Lambert's Hist. of New Haven Ct. 207–16
Lambert Genealogy (1893) 46 pages
Lincoln's Hist. of Hingham Mass. ii, 410
Littell's Passaic Valley Genealogies 208–11
Mellick's Story of an Old Farm N. J. 697
Savage's Genealogical Dictionary iii, 48
Stackpole's History of Durham Me. 210
Strong Genealogy 543
Thurston's History of Winthrop Me. 189
Winsor's History of Duxbury Mass. 274
Lamberton — American Ancestry ix, 135
Hyde's Ware Mass. Address 52
Kulp's Wyoming Valley Families
Savage's Genealogical Dictionary iii, 48
Stiles' History of Windsor Ct. ii, 429
Temple's History of Palmer Mass. 505
Lambertse — Bergen's Kings Co. 180
Lambing — American Ancestry iii, 144
Lamborn — Am. Ancestry vii, 181; ix, 156
Dawson Genealogy 470
Lamborn Genealogy (1894) 487 pages
Maris Genealogy 16, 78
Lamond — Draper's Spencer Mass. 217
La Monte — La Monte Family (1877) 16 p.
Temple's History of Palmer Mass. 502
Lamoreaux — Ransom Genealogy
Lamoure — American Ancestry i, 45
Lamphear — Savage's Gen. Dict. iii, 50
Lamphere — American Ancestry ii, 69
Lampman — Amer. Ancestry i, 46; ii, 69
Lamport — Cleveland's Yates Co. 291
Lamprey — Dow's Hampton 782–97
Lampson — Eaton's Thomaston Me. 303
Hammatt Papers of Ipswich Mass. 201
Lampson Genealogy (1881) 14 pages
Lamreaux — Delamater Genealogy 139–46
Lamson — Amer. Ancestry iv, 131; v, 206
Bell's History of Exeter N. H. 27
Bond's Watertown Mass. Genealogies 329
Burnet's Dod Genealogy 112
Daniels' History of Oxford Mass. 578
Goode Genealogy 291
Leland Genealogy 163
Orcutt's History of Stratford Ct. 1235
Savage's Genealogical Dictionary iii, 49
Secomb's History of Amherst N. H. 644–6
Temple's Hist. No. Brookfield Mass. 670

Temple's History of Whately Mass. 245
Wetmore Genealogy 213–7
Wyman's Charlestown Mass. Gens. 594–7
Lamun — Power's Sangamon Co. Ill. 437
Lancaster — Cogswell's Nottingham
Hoyt's Salisbury Mass. Families 230
Lancaster's Hist. of Gilmanton N. H. 274
Merrill's History of Acworth N. H. 236–8
Perkins' Old Houses of Norwich Ct. 504
Roberts' Old Richland Pa. Families
Runnel's Sanbornton N. H. ii, 433–6
Lance — Chambers' N. J. Germans
Lancey — Livermore's Wilton 432
Lander — American Ancestry xi, 91
Landers — American Ancestry ix 20
Sedgwick's History of Sharon Ct. 95
Landes — Landis Genealogy 68
Landis — American Ancestry iv, 194
Egle's Notes and Queries 3d ser. i, 16–7
Harris' History of Lancaster Co. 357–65
Landis Genealogy (1888) 90 pages
Landon — American Ancestry ii, 69
Burleigh's Guild Genealogy 96–8
Champion Genealogy 390
New York Gen. and Biog. Rec. xxviii, 24–7
Va. Mag. of Hist. and Biog. ii, (1895)
Wyman's Hunt Genealogy 116
Lane — Aldrich's Walpole N. H. 309
American Ancestry ii, 69; iii, 31
Anderson's Waterbury Ct. i, app. 82
Babson's Hist. of Gloucester Mass. 111, 257
Baird's History of Rye N. Y. 420
Bemis' History of Marlboro N. H. 551–3
Brown's Bedford Mass. Families 19–23
Buxton Me. Centennial 198–205
Chapman's Weeks Genealogy 145
Chase's History of Chester N. H. 553–5
Clark's History of Norton Mass. 84
Corliss' North Yarmouth Me. 1085–9
Dow's History of Hampton N. H. 798–808
Eaton's History of Candia N. H. 86
Foster Genealogy (1889) 83
Fullonton's Hist. of Raymond N. H. 240–7
Goodwin's Buxton Me. 260–2, 286, 296
Gregory's History of Northfield Vt. 153–6
Hayward's Joel Lane of N. C. (1900) 23 p.
Hazen's History of Billerica Mass. 88
Hobart's History of Abington Mass. 411–4
Lane Genealogy (1856) 6 pages
Lane Genealogy (1857) 24 pages
Lane Fam. of Hampton N. H. (1885) 35 p.
Lane Families of Mass. Bay (1886) 58 p.
Lane Family of Yarmouth (1888) 12 pages
Lane Genealogies vol. 1 (1891) 296 pages
Lane Genealogies vol. 2 (1897) 299 pages
Lane Family of Wolcott Ct. (1899) 64 pages
Lapham's History of Bethel Me. 578
Lapham's History of Paris Me. 656
Lincoln's Hist. Hingham Mass. ii, 410–22
Livermore's History of Wilton N. H. 433
Morrison's History of Windham N. H. 618
Nevius Genealogy
New Eng. Hist. and Gen. Register ii, 360;
    x, 356; xi, 360; xxvii, 176–81; xlii,
    141–52
Orcutt's History of Stratford Ct. 1235

Orcutt's History of Wolcott Ct. 511
Read's History of Swanzey N. H. 389–94
Richmond Va. Standard iii, 35
Ridlon's Saco Valley Me. Families 873–80
Runnel's Sanbornton N. H. ii, 436–51
Saunderson's Charlestown N. H. 469
Savage's Genealogical Dictionary iii, 50–4
Stearns' Hist. Ashburnham Mass. 783–91
Temple's Hist. of No. Brookfield Mass. 571
Temple's History of Northfield Mass. 480
Timlow's Southington Ct. Sketches 146
Wheeler's History of Newport N. H. 457–9
Whitmore's Copps Hill Epitaphs
Williams History of Danby Vt. 184
Worthen's History of Sutton N. H. 792–801
Wyman's Charlestown Mass. Gens. ii, 597
Lanfair — Sheldon's Deerfield 229
Lang — Coffin's Boscawen N. H. 571
Driver Genealogy 287
Essex Institute Hist. Collections vi, 257
Lapham's History of Rumford Me. 368
Montague Genealogy 302–4
Prescott's Mem. of W. Prescott 430–5
Runnel's History Sanbornton N. H. ii, 452–5
Langdell — Bogswell's New Boston
Livermore's History of Wilton N. H. 434
Secomb's History of Amherst N. H. 666
Langdon — American Ancestry ii, 69; ix, 208; x, 137, 195
Anderson's Waterbury Ct. i, app. 82
Brewster's Portsmouth ii, 53–61, 362–6
Currier's Castleton Vt. Epitaphs 29–31
Green's Todd Genealogy
Jordan's Leighton Genealogy (1885)
Langdon Genealogy (1876) 4 pages
New Eng. Hist. and Gen. Reg. xxx, 33–7
Savage's Genealogical Dictionary iii, 54
Timlow's Southington Ct. Sketches 147–53
Walworth's Hyde Genealogy 446
Wentworth Genealogy i, 329–36
Whitmore's Copps Hill Epitaphs
Wilbraham Mass. Centennial 299–301
Langford — American Ancestry v, 132
Austin's R. I. Genealogical Dictionary 336
Narragansett Historical Register ii, 302–5
Shotwell Genealogy 46
Langhorn — Paige's Cambridge 599
Langhorne — Lynchburg Va. 164–7
Paxton's Marshall Genealogy 296
Langley — Calnek's Annapolis N. S. 536
Cogswell's Nottingham 215
Essex Institute Hist. Collections xxii, 209
New Eng. Hist. and Gen. Register li, 168
R. I. Historical Magazine vi, 304–10
Langmade — Hubbard's Stanstead 178
Langston — Power's Sangamon 439–41
Richmond Va. Standard i, 44, 283
Langstreet — Bergen's Kings Co. 181
Langworthy — Am. Anc. iv, 141; vi, 73
Austin's R. I. Genealogical Dictionary 119
Hurd's History of New London Ct. 727
R. I. Historical Magazine vii, 136
Lanham — Power's Sangamon Ill. 441
Shourd's Fenwick Colony N. J. 535–7

Lanier — Lanier Biography (1877) 87 pages
Meade's Old Genealogies of Virginia
Welles' Washington Genealogy 112 etc.
Laning — Shourd's Fenwick N. J. 535–7
Lankton — Andrews' New Britain 166
Savage's Genealogical Dictionary iii, 56
Lanman — American Ances. iii, 169; x, 44
Chandler Genealogy 503–5
Coit Genealogy 137–9
Davis' Landmarks of Plymouth Mass. 167
Morrison's History of Windham N. H. 619
Talcott's N. Y. and N. E. Families 570–91
Walworth's Hyde Genealogy 892–4
Lanning — Cooley's Trenton N. J. 152–60
Lanphere — Austin's R. I. Dict. 119
Lanphier — Power's Sangamon Ill. 442
Lansing — American Ancestry i, 46
Munsell's Albany N. Y. Coll. iv, 139–42
New York Gen. and Biog. Record iii, 84
Pearson's Schenectady N. Y. Settlers 102
Strong Genealogy 1260–4
Talcott's New York Families 113–66, 417
Lansom — Paige's Cambridge Mass. 597
Lant — American Ancestry ii, 69, 155
Lanterman — Power's Sangamon 442–4
Lantman — Albany Collections iv, 142
Lantz — Egle's Notes and Queries 3d ser. iii, 434–6
Lape — Plumb's Hist. Hanover Pa. 445
Lapham — Amer. Ancestry ii, 70; iii, 63
Austin's Ancestral Dictionary 34
Austin's R. I. Genealogical Dictionary 120
Ballou Genealogy 672–80
Cutts Genealogy 203
Deane's History of Scituate Mass. 302
Hanson's History of Gardiner Me. 138
Lapham Genealogy (1873) 31 pages
Lapham's History of Bethel Me. 578–81
Lapham's History of Paris Me. 657–9
Lapham's Tabular Pedigree 1864
Lapham's History of Woodstock Me. 234
Savage's Genealogical Dictionary iii, 56
Stearns' History of Rindge N. H. 594
Williams' History of Danby Vt. 184–7
Laport — Bass' Hist. of Braintree Vt. 158
Larason — Chambers' Early Germans of N. J. 437–9
Lard — Power's Sangamon Co. Ill. 444
Lardner — American Ancestry v, 38
Large — Fell Genealogy 83
Morris Genealogy (1898) 616
Thomas Genealogy 106
Thomas Genealogy (1896) 386
Larison — American Ancestry vii, 202
Larkin — American Ancestry i, 48; xi, 200
Austin's R. I. Genealogical Dictionary 121
Clermont County Ohio History 357
Daniels' History of Oxford Mass. 580
Morris and Flynt Genealogy 57
Palmer and Trimble Genealogy 200–3
Savage's Genealogical Dictionary iii, 57
Winslow Genealogy ii, 565–70
Wyman's Charlestown Mass. 599–605
Larlazere — Clute's Staten Island 399
Larned — Am. Ancestry iii, 108; vii, 99
Daniels' History of Oxford Mass. 580–6

Larrabee — Chandler's Shirley 496
Corliss' North Yarmouth Me. Magazine
Eaton's History of Thomaston Me. ii, 304
Libby Genealogy 41
Machias Me. Centennial 168
Ridlon's Saco Valley Me. Families 787–873
Savage's Genealogical Dictionary iii, 57
Stackpole's History of Durham Me. 211–3
Stearns' History of Rindge N. H. 595
Wheeler's History of Brunswick Me. 841
Larrey — Pierce's Gotham Me. 181
Larue — Egle's Notes and Queries 3d ser.
iii, 123–5
La Rue — Sharpless Genealogy 416
Larzelere — Cleveland Yates Co. 476
Davis' History of Bucks County Pa. 433
Laselle — American Ancestry xii
See under Lassell
Lash — Eaton's Thomaston Me. 305
Whitmore's Copps Hill Epitaphs
Lashelle — Fisher Genealogy 145
Lasher — American Ancestry ii, 40
Lassell — Bradbury's Kennebunkport
Eaton's History of Thomaston Me. ii, 305
Farrow's History of Islesborough Me. 229
Lapham's History of Norway Me. 543
Lincoln's Hist. Hingham Mass. ii, 423–6
See also under Laselle and Lazell
Latane — Jones Genealogy (1891) 136–40
Meade's Old Churches of Virginia i, 393
Latham — Am. Ancestry ii, 71; iv, 108
Austin's Ancestries 127
Austin's Allied Families 161
Caulkins' History of New London Ct. 312
Lapham's History of Norway Me. 543
Leach's Reading Genealogy 215–36
Mitchell's Hist. Bridgewater Mass. 222–4
Power's Sangamon Co. Ill. Settlers 445
Ripley's Ingersoll Genealogy 96
Savage's Genealogical Dictionary iii, 58
Lathim — Penn. Mag. of History v, 334
Lathrop — Amer. Ancestry i, 48; viii, 150
Bill Genealogy 182
Bridgeman's Granary Epitaphs 391–8
Caulkins' History of Norwich Ct. 217–21
Caverly's History of Pittsford Vt. 712
Dwight Genealogy 772–90
Hall's Genealogical Notes (1886) 106
Lathrop Family Tree (1867)
Lathrop Family of Albany (1882) 13 pages
Lathrop Genealogy (1884) 447 pages
Mitchell's Hist. Bridgewater Mass. 224–7
Morris' Bontecou Genealogy 140
Orcutt's History of Torrington Ct. 729
Paul's History of Welles Vt. 111
Peirce Genealogy (1894)
Perkins' Old Houses of Norwich Ct. 505–13
Savage's Genealogical Dict. iii, 119–22
Waldo's History of Tolland Ct. 94–7
Walworth's Hyde Genealogy i, 246–55
West Springfield Mass. Centennial 118
Winsor's History of Duxbury Mass. 274
Wyman's Charlestown Mass. Gens. 597
Latimer — Am. Anc. i, 48; ii, 71; x, 203
Baker's History of Montville Ct. 314–26
Bartow Genealogy 132–5

Brown's West Simsbury Ct. Settlers 90
Caulkins' History of New London Ct. 288
Clyde's Irish Settlement in Pa. 87–90
Coit Genealogy 280
Freeman's Hist. of Cape Cod Mass. ii, 590
New Eng. Hist. Gen. Reg. xix, 243, 317
Savage's Genealogical Dictionary iii, 59
Stiles' History of Windsor Ct. ii, 430
Thomas Genealogy (1877) 107–17
Walworth's Hyde Genealogy 192, 953
La Tourette — Clute's Staten Island 400
La Trobe — Dotterer's Perkiomen iii, 6–9
Lattin — Orcutt's Stratford Ct. 1236
Smith's History of Dutchess Co. N. Y. 500
Latting — N. Y. Gen. Rec. ii, 8–22, 54–68
Laub — Magennis Genealogy 120–4
Laughton — Hudson's Lexington 114
Vermont Historical Gaz. v, 57–61
Law — American Ancestry ix, 196
Cincinnati Ohio Criterion (1888) ii, 476
Essex Institute Hist. Collections xxii, 210
Hall's Genealogical Notes (1886) 104–12
Hall Genealogy (1892) 11
Kilbourn Genealogy 39–41
Power's Sangamon Co. Ill. Settlers 447
Salem N. Y. Book of History 60
Savage's Genealogical Dictionary iii, 60
Lawler — Temple's No. Brookfield 673
Lawley — Power's Sangamon Ill. 448
Lawrence—Am. Anc. ii, 71; iv, 70; v, 194
American Historical Register iii, 671–6
Ballou's History of Milford Mass. 872
Bassett's History of Richmond N. H. 427
Bemis' History of Marlboro N. H. 554–7
Bergen Genealogy 140
Blake's History of Franklin Mass. 257
Bolton's Westchester Co. N. Y. i, 247
Bond's Watertown Mass. 330–3, 817–50
Brooks' History of Medford Mass. 529
Butler's Hist. of Groton Mass. 413–6, 474
Chambers' Early Germans of N. J. 439–42
Cleveland's Hist. Yates Co. N. Y. 639–42
Cochrane's History of Antrim N. H. 572
Corliss' North Yarmouth Me. Magazine
Cutter's History of Jaffrey N. H. 393–7
Eaton's Annals of Warren Me. 568
Eaton's History of Thomaston Me. ii, 305
Egle's Pa. Genealogies 2d ed. 128–31, 138
Freeman's History of Cape Cod ii, 164, 475
Green's Early Groton Mass. Settlers 9
Green's Groton Mass. Epitaphs 243
Hanson's Hist. of Gardiner Me. 106, 161
Hayward's Hist. of Hancock N. H. 735–7
Heywood's Hist. Westminster Mass. 743
Hill's History of Mason N. H. 196–8, 204
Hinman's Connecticut Settlers 169
Hodgman's History of Westford Mass. 459
Holgate's American Genealogy 201–27
Hudson's Hist. of Lexington Mass. 114–8
Kip's Historical Notes 39–45
Kip's Olden Times in New York 58–61
Lamb's History of New York City i, 231
Lawrence Fam. of Watertown (1847) 64 p.
Lawrence Fam. of Canaan Ct. (1848) 20 p.
Lawrence Fam. of Canaan 2d ed. (1853) 76 p.
Lawrence Ancestry in Eng. (1856) 20 pages

194

Lawrence Fam. of Watertown (1857) 191 p.
Lawrence Fam. of New York (1858) 240 p.
Lawrence Family Wills (1858) 48 pages
Lawrence Fam. of Watertown (1869) 332 p.
Lawrence Estates in Eng. (1871) 24 pages
Lawrence of Watertown, Supp. (1876) 74 p.
Lawrence of Watertown, Supp. (1881) 96 p.
Lawrence Estates in Eng. (1883) 107 pages
Lawrence Estates in Eng. (1888) 94 pages
Lawrence Fam. of New Eng. (1888) 215 p.
Lawrences of Sandwich Mass. (1888) 223 p.
Lawrence Family Cape May N. J. (1891)
  161 pages
Livermore's History of Wilton N. H. 434
Milliken's Narraguagus Valley Me. 3
New Eng. Hist. and Gen. Reg. x, 297–303;
  xl, 208; xlvi, 149–51
New York Gen. and Biog. Record iii, 10,
  26–9, 121–31, 178–83; xvi, 141; xxviii, 55
Paige's History of Hardwick Mass. 410
Potts Genealogy (1895) 303–9
Riker's Annals of Newtown N. Y. 281–90
Ruggles Genealogy
Salter's Hist. of Monmouth Co. N. J. xxxv
Savage's Genealogical Dictionary iii, 60–3
Secomb's History of Amherst N. H. 667–9
Smith's History of Delaware Co. Pa. 476
Stearns' Hist. Ashburnham Mass. 791–98
Temple's Hist. of No. Brookfield Mass. 673
Thomas Genealogy (1877) 197 pages
Thomas Genealogy (1878) 56 pages
Thomas Genealogy (1883) 157 pages
Thomas Genealogy (1896) 387–434
Thompson's Long Island N. Y. ii, 362–7
Tuttle Genealogy, preface 24
Vinton's Richardson Genealogy 686
Wakefield Genealogy 94
Washington N. H. History 506–8
Whitmore's Heraldic Journal iv, 35–8
Winchell Genealogy 251
Worcester's History of Hollis N. H. 380
Wyman's Charlestown Mass. ii, 606–10
Lawrey — Eaton's Warren Me. 569
Laws — Heywood's Westminster 743–5
Smith's History of Peterborough 130
Washington N. H. History 508–10, 696
Lawson — Cogswell's New Boston 419
Forrest's History of Norfolk Va. 71
Hanson's Old Kent Md. 173–5
Mallery's Bohemia Manor
Power's Sangamon Co. Ill. Settlers 449
Savage's Genealogical Dictionary iii, 63
Shourd's Fenwick Colony N. J. 139–41
Lawton — Austin's R. I. Dict. 121–3
Austin's Allied Families 164
Chandler's Hist. of Shirley Mass. 497–501
Paige's Hist. of Hardwick Mass. 411–3
R. I. Historical Magazine iv, 195; v, 236–8
Savage's Genealogical Dictionary iii, 64
Virginia Magazine of History iv (1897) 313
Lawyer — American Ancestry i, 48
Lay — American Ancestry ii, 72; xii, 36
Champion Genealogy 58
Chapman Genealogy 106
Salisbury's Fam. Histories (1892) i, 333–51
Savage's Genealogical Dictionary iii, 64

Walworth's Hyde Genealogy ii, 880–4
Whittemore's Hist. Middlesex Co. Ct. 574
Layton — Allen Genealogy (1883) 6
Eaton Genealogy (1895)
Lazarus — Plumb's Hanover Pa. 449–51
Lazell — American Ancestry xii
Mitchell's Bridgewater 227–9
Savage's Genealogical Dictionary iii, 65
Winsor's History of Duxbury Mass. 275
See also under Hasell
See also under Lassell
Lea — American Ancestry iii, 116
Leach — Am. Anc. i, 48; iv, 17, 113; x, 129
Aylsworth Genealogy 101, 199–201
Caverly's History of Pittsford Vt. 712
Davis' Landmarks of Plymouth Mass. 169
Dow's History of Hampton N. H. 809
Eaton's Annals of Warren Me. 569
Hollister's History of Pawlet Vt. 209
Kingman's No. Bridgewater Mass. 573–5
Leach Genealogy (1898) 42 pages
Mitchell's Hist. Bridgewater Mass. 229–34
Perkins' Old Houses of Norwich Ct. 514
Plumb's History of Hanover Pa. 452
Savage's Genealogical Dictionary iii, 66
Stone's History of Beverly Mass. 29
Temple's History of N. Brookfield Mass.
  674
Walworth's Hyde Genealogy 788
Wyman's Charlestown Mass. Gens. ii, 610
Leadbetter — Barry's Framingham
Savage's Genealogical Dictionary iii, 67
Leader — Savage's Gen. Dict. iii, 67
Leake — American Ancestry x, 25
Valentine's N. Y. Manual (1861) 624–8
Leaming — N. Y. Gen. Rec. xxvi, 150
Learn — Plumb's Hanover Pa. 449
Learned — American Ancestry i, 48; iii,
  32; iv, 175; vii, 81; xi, 38
Ammidown's Historical Collections 254–6
Austin's Allied Families 166
Barry's Hist. Framingham Mass. 314–6
Bond's Watertown Mass. 333–7, 850
Coit Genealogy 183–6
Daniel's History of Oxford Mass. 586–92
Davis Genealogy 15, 33–5, 110–7
Harris' Watertown Mass. Epitaphs 35
Heywood's Hist. Westminster Mass. 746
Learned Genealogy (1882) 346 pages
Learned Genealogy 2d ed. (1898) 505 pages
Leonard's History of Dublin N. H. 359–61
Merrill's History of Acworth N. H. 272
Morse's Sherborn Mass. Settlers 170
Savage's Genealogical Dictionary iii, 68
Sewall's History of Woburn Mass. 624
Washburne's Livermore Me. 24
Leary — Lincoln's Hingham ii, 427
Leathe — Bond's Watertown 337
Pierce's History of Grafton Mass. 530
Leathers — Leathers Genealogy (1891) 8 p.
Stearns' Hist. of Ashburnham Mass. 798
Leathes — Smith's Peterborough 131
Wyman's Charlestown Mass. Gens. 611
Leavens — American Ancestry xii
Leavens Genealogy (1889) 25 pages
Morris Genealogy (1894) 31

Leavenworth — Am. Ancestry viii, 44
Anderson's Waterbury Ct. i, app. 83
Bronson's History of Waterbury Ct. 515-8
Cothren's History of Woodbury Ct. ii, 1513
Leavenworth Genealogy (1873) 376 pages
Orcutt's History of Stratford Ct. 1236
Leaver — Essex Inst. Colls. xxii, 210
Leavit — Buxton Me. Centennial 189-93
Leavitt — American Ancestry x, 201
Bell's History of Exeter N. H. 28
Cogswell Genealogy 180
Cothren's History of Woodbury Ct. 614
Dearborn's History of Parsonsfield Me. 384
Dow's History of Hampton N. H. 809-20
Dwight Genealogy 406-13
French's History of Turner Me. 58-62
Lapham's History of Bethel Me. 581
Leavitt Genealogy (1853) 16 pages
Lincoln's Hist. Hingham Mass. ii, 428-39
Loomis Genealogy (1880) 810
Prescott's Memorial of W. Prescott 514-9
Ridlon's Saco Valley Me. Families 880-4
Runnel's Hist. Sanbornton N. H. 455-61
Sanborn Genealogy (1894)
Savage's Genealogical Dictionary iii, 69-71
Secomb's Hist. of Amherst N. H. 669-71
Tucker's History of Hartford Vt. 447
Le Barnes — American Ancestry ii, 72
Le Baron — Benedict's Sutton Mass. 683
Davis' Landmarks of Plymouth 169-71
Hubbard's Stanstead Co. Canada 248-52
Lapham's History of Paris Me. 659
Lincoln's Hist. of Hingham Mass. ii, 439
New Eng. Hist. Gen. Reg. xxv, 180-2
Lebourneau — Norton's Fitzwilliam
Le Breton — Emery's Newbury 188
Le Broke — Lapham's Paris Me. 660
Lecain — Calnek's Annapolis N. S. 537-93
Lechmere — Heraldic Journal iv, 43
Le Compte — Bolton's Westchester 743
Le Conte — American Ancestry ix, 167
Scudder's J. L. Le Conte Memoir 27 pages
Le Duc — American Ancestry iv, 221
Ledyard — American Ancestry iii, 32
Magazine of American History vi, 191-9
New York Gen. and Biog. Rec. vii, 10-6
Smith Genealogy (1889) 116
Lee — American Ancestry iv, 4, 30, 82, 83,
91, 112, 162, 214, 218, 219, 227, 229;
vii, 22, 197; viii, 120, 148, 231
Andrews' Hist. of New Britain Ct. 141-5
Austin's Ancestral Dictionary 35
Bolton's Westchester Co. N. Y. ii, 734
Camp Genealogy ii, 41-3
Campbell's Spotswood Genealogy 22
Campbell's History of Virginia 659, 745
Carter Family Tree of Virginia
Cleveland's Hist. Yates Co. N. Y. 644-50
Hammatt Papers, Ipswich Mass. 203-6
Hayden's Virginia Genealogies 96
Hayward's History of Hancock N. H. 737
Hemenway's Vermont Hist. Gaz. v. 315-8
Hines' Lebanon Ct. Hist. Address 159
Hubbard's Stanstead Co. Canada 155-9
Kidder's Hist. of New Ipswich N. H. 416
Lee Fam. of Saybrook Ct. (1851) 31 pages

Lee Family of Virginia (1868) 114 pages
Lee Family of Virginia (1872) 11 pages
Lee Family of Farmington Ct. (1874) 8 p.
Lee Family of Delaware (1875) 89 pages
Lee Family of Farmington Ct. (1878) 180 p.
Lee of Farmington, Reunion (1885) 116 p.
Lee Family of Ipswich (1888) 499 pages
Lee Family of Virginia (1890) 11 pages
Lee Family of Virginia (1892) 23 pages
Lee Family of Watertown (1893) 14 pages
Lee Family of Virginia (1895) 586 pages
Lee of Farmington, Reunion (1896) 67 p.
Lee Family Farmington 2d ed. (1897) 527 p.
Lee Fam. of Wayne Co. Pa. (1898) 47 pages
Lee Family Farmington, supp. (1900) 176 p.
Loomis Genealogy (1880) 220-3, 873
Meade's Old Churches Virginia ii, 135-45
Munsey's Magazine xv (1896) 217-30
New Eng. Historical and Genealogical
Register xi, 329; xxvi, 61-9; xxviii,
394-401; xxxviii, 6-7; xliv, 103-11;
xlvi, 64-78; 161-6; xlvii, 21-3; liii, 53-8
Pickering Genealogy
Plumb's History of Hanover Pa. 444
Richmond Va. Critic (1888)
Richmond Va. Standard i, 44, 48; iii, 38,
40; iv, 2, 8, 18, 21
Roe's Sketches of Rose N. Y. 309
Salisbury's Family Histories (1892) iii, 1-76
Savage's Genealogical Dictionary iii, 71-4
Scranton Genealogy 31
Shattuck's History of Concord Mass. 377
Slaughter's Bristol Parish Va. 156
Southern Bivouac (1886) 51
Stiles' History of Windsor Ct. ii, 432
Strong Genealogy 956-64
Taylor's Some Notable Families 54-9
Temple's History of Palmer Mass. 505
Tilley's Mag. of New Eng. Hist. iii, 48-61
Timlow's Southington Ct. Sketches 153-6
Todd's History of Redding Ct. 205
Walworth's Hyde Genealogy 34
Ward Genealogy (1851) 80
Wyman's Charlestown Mass. Gens. 612
Leech — Penn. Mag. of History iv, 244
Leeds — American Ancestry iii, 33
Caulkins' History of New London Ct. 335
Cregar's White Genealogy
Eaton's Annals of Warren Me. 570
Faxon Genealogy 80
Glover Genealogy 350, 383
Huntington's Stamford Ct. Families 65
Leeds Families of New Jersey (1886) chart
Leeds Family of New Jersey (1897) 17 p.
Power's Sangamon Co. Ill. Settlers 449
Savage's Genealogical Dictionary iii, 74
Leek — Blake's History of Hamden Ct. 292
Chambers' Early Germans of N. J. 442
Leeman — Worcester's Hollis N. H. 380
Leeper — American Ancestry x, 96
Leete — Barbour's Wife and Mother 57
Brown's West Simsbury Ct. Settlers 89
Dwight's Strong Genealogy 359
Leete Genealogy (1884) 168 pages
Savage's Genealogical Dictionary iii, **75**
Stone Genealogy 8, 13, 38

Lefavour — American Ancestry v, 59
Le Fever — American Ancestry i, 48
Bolton's Westchester Co. N. Y. ii, 529
Sylvester's History of Ulster Co. N. Y.
Lefferts — Bergen's Kings Co. 185-7
Bergen Genealogy 109
Lefferts Chart (1870) by Wheeler
Lefferts Genealogy (1878) 172 pages
Davis' History of Bucks County Pa. 201
Leffingwell — Am. Ancestry ix, 549
Baker's History of Montville Ct. 306-13
Caulkins' History of Norwich Ct. 189-92
Coit Genealogy 104
Elderkin Genealogy 86-8
Huntington Genealogy 81
Joslin's History of Poultney Vt. 302
Leffingwell Genealogy (1897) 256 pages
New Eng. Hist. and Gen. Reg. xxv, 295
Perkins' Old Houses of Norwich Ct. 515-9
Savage's Genealogical Dictionary iii, 76
Sewall's History of Woburn Mass. 625
Tuttle Genealogy 204
Walworth's Hyde Genealogy 30, 383,1083-7
Legare — Richmond Va. Standard ii, 4
South Car. Huguenot Soc. Trans. iv, 7-9
Writings of Hon. Hugh S. Legare 6
Legg — Ballou's Hist. Milford Mass. 874
Leggett — Amer. Ancestry ii, 72; v, 214
Bolton's Westchester Co. N. Y. ii, 446
Leggett (Maj. Abraham) Narrative 47
Le Grand — Green's Kentucky Families
Lehman — Egle's Notes and Queries 3d
   series ii, 128-31
Wallbridge Genealogy 291-6
Leidy — American Ancestry viii, 216
Mellick's Story of an Old Farm 707
Leigh—Lee Genealogy (1888)
Lincoln's Hist. of Hingham Mass. ii, 439
Richmond Standard ii, 4; iii, 14; iv, 2
Watkins Genealogy 40
Leighton — Am. Ancestry iii, 106; x, 187
Cushman's History of Sheepscott Me. 398
Dennysville Me. Centennial 108
Essex Institute Hist. Collections xxii, 211
Hodgman's History of Westford Mass. 460
Leighton Genealogy (1885) 127 pages
Little's History of Weare N. H. 932
Maine Hist. and Gen. Recorder ix, 221-3
Milliken's Narraguagus Valley Me. 6-8
Old Eliot Me. Monthly (1898) ii, 157-64
Runnel's Hist. of Sanbornton N. H. ii, 461
Savage's Genealogical Dictionary iii, 44
Wentworth Genealogy i, 217-9, 498
Leiper — Spotswood Papers 21
Richmond Va. Standard. v, 4
Robins' Thomas Leiper Biog. (1886) 13 p.
Thomas Genealogy (1887) 117-9, 181, 243
Thomas Genealogy (1898) 435-42
Leisler — Bolton's Westchester 380
Leisler Genealogy (1877) 24 pages
New York Gen. Biog. Record vii, 145-51
Valentine's N. Y. Manual (1860) 594
Leitch — Minor's Meriwether Gen. 51
Leland — Adams' Haven Genealogy 27, 48
American Ancestry xii
Ballou's History of Milford Mass. 875-8

Benedict's History of Sutton Mass. 684-6
Crane's Rawson Genealogy 50
Haven Genealogy 48
Heywood's Hist. of Westminster Mass. 746
Hodgman's History of Westford Mass. 461
Leland Genealogy (1850) 278 pages
Morse's Sherborn Mass. Settlers 160-70
Pierce's History of Grafton Mass. 515-30
Savage's Genealogical Dictionary iii, 76
Stone's History of Hubbardston Mass. 304
Young's Hist. Chautauqua Co. N. Y. 421
Leman — Wyman's Charlestown 614
Lemly — Steele Genealogy (1900)
Lemoine — Goode Genealogy 227
Lemon — Pickering Genealogy
Power's Sangamon Co. Ill. Settlers 450
Temple's History of Palmer Mass. 502
Wyman's Charlestown Mass. Gens. ii, 615
Lennox — Cushman's Sheepscott 399
Lent — Bolton's Westchester Co. 529
Riker's Annals of Newtown N. Y. 315-9
Lentz — American Ancestry x, 164
Leonard — Adams' Fairhaven 426-9
American Ancestry i, 49; ii, 72; iv, 78; vi,
   104; xii, 30
Ammidown Genealogy 46
Austin's Ancestral Dictionary 36
Baldwin Genealogy 1138
Bangor Me. Historical Magazine vi, 87
Blake Genealogy 55
Calnek's History of Annapolis N. S. 539
Caverly's History of Pittsford Vt. 713
Clark's History of Norton Mass. 86
Davis' Landmarks of Plymouth Mass. 171
Freeman's Hist. of Cape Cod Mass. i, 611
Gifford's Our Patronymics 24
Heston Genealogy 37-40, 55
Heywood's Hist. of Westminster **Mass.**
   747
Hough's History of Lewis Co. N. Y. 150
Humphreys Genealogy 392-4
Jennings Genealogy (1899)
Leonard Family of Taunton (1851) 28 pages
Leonard Family of Duxbury (1896) 454 p.
Lincoln Genealogy (1899) 35-44
Mass. Hist. Society Colls. 1st series ii, 173
Mitchell's Hist. Bridgewater Mass. 235-8
Morris and Flint Genealogy 54
N. E. Hist. Reg. v, 403-13; xxxii, 269-71
Paige's History of Hardwick Mass. 413
Parsons and Leonard Gen. (1867) 36 p.
Pompey N. Y. Reunion 329-32
Pond Genealogy (1875) 14
Read's History of Swanzey N. H. 395
Savage's Genealogical Dictionary iii, 78-80
Smith's History of Sunderland Mass. 434-7
Spooner Genealogy (1871) 191-9
Sprague's History of Gloversville N. Y. 122
Temple's History of Whately Mass. 245
Thayer Memorial (1835) 160, 279-310
Vinton's Giles Genealogy 279-310
Walker Genealogy 31
Walworth's Hyde Genealogy 346
Winsor's History of Duxbury Mass. 275
Lepingwell — Sewall's Woburn 625
Lerch — Chambers' N. J. Germans

Lermond — Eaton's Warren Me. 571–4
Eaton's History of Thomaston Me. ii, 306
Le Roux — Bolton's Westchester 529
Leroy — American Ancestry i, 49
Leslie — Johnson's Cecil Co. Md. 520
Washington N. H. History 510–3
Lespenard — N. Y. Gen. Rec. xxiv, 97–116
Lester — American Ancestry ii, 73
Baker's History of Montville Ct. 489–92
Caulkins' History of New London Ct. 286
Hurd's History of New London Co. Ct. 411
Lester Family of Virginia (1897) 13 pages
Roberts' Old Richland Pa. Families 161–3
Southern Hist. Assoc. Pub. i (1897) 127–37
Walworth's Hyde Genealogy 1138
L'Estrange — Baird's Rye N. Y. 44–6
New York Gen. and Biog. Rec. ii, 179 86
Leupp — American Ancestry v, 193
Levally — Aylsworth Genealogy 129
Levensaler — Eaton's Thomaston 307
Leverett — Goodwin's Gen. Notes 188
Leverett Genealogy (1850) 19 pages
Leverett Genealogy 2d ed. (1856) 203 pages
Moore's Mem. Am. Governors i, 374–6
N. E. Hist. Gen. Reg. iv, 121–36; xii, 288
Paige's History of Cambridge Mass. 598
Savage's Genealogical Dictionary iii, 82–4
Leverich — Riker's Newtown N. Y. 350–4
Leveridge — Savage's Gen. Dict. iii, 84
Levering — American Ancestry viii, 153
Levering Genealogy (1858) 193 pages
Levering Family Reunion (1892) 120 pages
Levering Genealogy (1897) 975 pages
Levich — Roberts' Richland Families 213
Levins — Savage's Gen. Dictionary iii, 81
Levis — Ogden Genealogy (1898) 129–31
Smith's Delaware Co. Pa. 477
Levistone — Hazen's Billerica Mass. 90
Lewes — N. E. Hist. and Gen. Reg. iii, 271
Power's Sangamon Co. Ill. Settlers 451–5
Swift's Barnstable Families ii, 115–47
Lewin — Thomas Genealogy (1877) 119
Lewis — Alden's Am. Epitaphs v, 68
American Ancestry iii, 153, 170; v, 35, 97,
    104, 166, 175, 192, 194; vi, 37, 71, 156;
    viii, 64, 117; x, 13, 130, 150; xi, 86,
    101, 209, 233
Anderson's Waterbury Ct. i, app. 83–5
Andrews' History of New Britain Ct. 160–7
Austin's R. I. Genealogical Dictionary 124
Bartow Genealogy 170–2
Bemis' History of Marlboro N. H. 557–9
Bellinger Genealogy 35–8
Bond's Watertown Mass. Gens. 337, 851
Bouton Genealogy
Bradbury's Kennebunkport Me. 257
Briggs' History of Shipbuilding 176
Bronson's History of Waterbury Ct. 518
Bullock Genealogy
Burr Genealogy (1891) 248
Campbell's History of Virginia 588
Carter Family Tree of Virginia
Caulkins' History of New London Ct. 295
Clarke's Old King Wm. Co. Va. Families
Clyde's Irish Settlement in Pa. 91
Cochrane's Hist. Francest'n N. H. 796–9

Corliss' North Yarmouth Me. 1159
Davis' History of Wallingford Ct. 841–5
Davis' Landmarks of Plymouth Mass. 172
Deane's History of Scituate Mass. 303
Dedham Historical Register iv, 137–53; v,
    7–17; vii, 16–9, 39–41
Delafield's Biog. of Francis Lewis (1877)
Dwight Genealogy 552
Field's History of Haddam Ct. 46
Foster Genealogy (1889) 77–82
Freeman's Cape Cod Mass. i, 614; ii, 285
Futhey's History of Chester Co. Pa. 628–36
Gilmer's Georgians 42, 105
Glenn's Merion in Welsh Tract 235–40
Greene Genealogy (1894)
Green's Kentucky Families
Guild's Stiles Genealogy 307
Hayden's Virginia Genealogies 379–94
Hazen's History of Billerica Mass. 91
Heywood's Hist. of Westminster Mass. 748
Hibbard's History of Goshen Ct. 474–80
Hill's Dedham Mass. Records i
Holton's Winslow Genealogy i, 195–205
Howe's Hist. Collections of Va. 181–3
Hubbard's History of Springfield Vt. 363–5
Hudson's History of Lexington Mass. 281
Huntting's History of Pine Plains N. Y. 367
Jackson Genealogy 123, 130, 142
Jenkins' History of Gwynedd Pa. 367
Jones Genealogy (1891) 141, 184–9
Joslin's History of Poultney Vt. 298–302
Judd's History of Hadley Mass. 530
Kulp's Wyoming Valley Families
Lewis' History of Lynn Mass. 180–2
Lewis Family of Virginia (1873) 7 pages
Lewis Letter, Monthly (1887–9) 3 vols.
Lewis Family of Hadley Mass. (1891) 66 p.
Lewisiana, Monthly (1893–1900) 10 vols.
Lewis Family of Va. (1893) 454 pages
Lincoln's Hist. Hingham Mass. ii, 440–8
Livermore's Hist. of Block Island R. I. 336
Livermore's History of Wilton N. H. 434
Marshall Genealogy (1884) 104–6
Mead's History of Greenwich Ct. 216
Meade's Old Churches of Va. ii, 231–3, 325
Mellick's Story of an Old Farm in N. J. 650
Minor's Meriwether Genealogy 10, 44, 52–8
Morris Genealogy (1898) 749, 757–9
Morrison's History of Windham N. H. 620
New Eng. Hist. and Gen. Reg. xvii, 162–6
Orcutt's History of Stratford Ct. 1237–41
Orcutt's History of Wolcott Ct. 513–8
Paul's History of Wells Vt. 114–20
Paxton's Marshall Genealogy 93–9, 162
Pearson's Schenectady N. Y. Settlers 104
Peyton's Hist. of Augusta Co. Va. 285–301
Pierce's History of Gorham Me. 181–3
Platt's Greenough Ancestry 21
Preston Genealogy (1870) 44–8
Randall's History of Chesterfield N. H. 378
Rich's History of Truro Mass. 543
Richmond Va. Standard ii, 32; iii, 23, 24,
    38, 40; iv, 1, 10, 14
Ridlon's Harrison Me. Settlers 93–5
Ridlon's Saco Valley Me. Families 884–8
Robertson's Pocahontas' Descendants

Savage's Genealogical Dictionary iii, 84–90
Sedgwick's History of Sharon Ct. 96
Sharpe's South Britain Ct. Sketches 85–8
Sharpless Genealogy 102–4
Sheppard's Dr. Winslow Lewis (1863) 33 p.
Slaughter's Fry Memoir 74
Slaughter's St. Mark's Parish Va. 184
Smith's History of Delaware Co. Pa. 478–80
Spooner Genealogy (1871) 163–89
Stiles' History of Windsor Ct. ii, 432
Sullivan Genealogy 337–40
Taylor's Some Notable Families 78–81
Timlow's Southington Ct. Sketches 156–66
Virginia Historical Register v, 24
Washington N. H. History 513–5
Welles' Washington Genealogy 164 et seq.
Wheeler's History of Newport N. H. 461
Whitmore's Copps Hill Epitaphs
Winslow Genealogy (1877)
Winslow and Lewis Chart (1877) reprint
Wyman's Charlestown Mass. Gens. 617–9
Young's History of Wayne Co. Ind. 229
Leydich — Dotterer's Hist. Notes of Penn. Ref. Church i, 59
L'Hommedieu — American Ancestry iii, 89; ix, 176
Mallmann's Shelter Island N. Y. 310
New York Gen. and Biog. Record ii, 1–3
Ruggles Genealogy
Vail Genealogy (1894)
Whittemore's Orange N. J. 294
Libbey — Dow's Hampton N. H. 821
Eaton's Annals of Warren Me. 574–7
Eaton's History of Thomaston Me. ii, 308
Hubbard's Stanstead Co. Canada 167
Lapham's History of Paris Me. 651–3
Libbie — Butler Genealogy (1886)
Libby — American Ancestry iv, 207
Cutts Genealogy 144–6, 264–70
Dearborn's Hist. of Parsonsfield Me. 384
Libby Genealogy (1882) 628 pages
Machias Me. Centennial 168
Maine Hist. Society Collections iii, 216
Pierce's History of Gorham Me. 183
Liddle — American Ancestry i, 49
Lide — Gregg's Old Cheraws S. C. 77
Lievense — Albany Collections iv, 143
Liftwich — Meade's Old Families of Va.
Liggett — American Ancestry xii, 26
Light — Egle's Lebanon County Pa. 245
Ransom Genealogy 64
Lightfoot — Meade's Old Fams. of Va.
Power's Sangamon Co. Ill. Settlers 455
Slaughter's Fry Genealogy
Slaughter's St. Mark's Parish Va. 142–4
Wm. and Mary College Hist. Reg. ii, 91–7, 204–7, 259–62
Lighthall — Pearson's Schenectady
Lightfoot — William and Mary College Historical Register iii, 104–11
Lightpipe — Whittemore's Orange N. J. 260
Ligon — Watkins Genealogy 18
Like — American Ancestry i, 49
Lilley — Benedict's Sutton Mass. 686
Daniels' History of Oxford Mass. 593
Eaton's History of Reading Mass. 95
Savage's Genealogical Dictionary iii, 90
Williams' History of Danby Vt. 188
Lillibridge — Irish's Richmond R. I. 91
McIntosh Genealogy 46–50
Stanton Genealogy 348
Lillie — Ellis Genealogy 373
Lillie Genealogy (1896) 122 pages
Morris Genealogy (1894) 105–7, 137
Sedgwick's History of Sharon Ct. 96
Lilly — American Ancestry x, 111, 168, 173
Lilly Genealogy (1881) 4 pages
Reily's Cardinal Gibbons Life ii, 418–23; v, 113–20
Lincoln — Aldrich's Walpole N. H. 312
American Ancestry vi, 56, 141, 163; ix, 157, 176, 191; x, 69, 104, 135, 169
Andrews' History of New Britain Ct. 222
Bangor Me. Historical Magazine v, 38
Cushman's History of Sheepscott Me. 400
Deane's History of Scituate Mass. 304
Dennysville Me. Centennial 108
Eaton's Annals of Warren Me. 577
Eaton's History of Thomaston Me. ii, 308
Ellis Genealogy 107–10
Freeman's Hist. of Cape Cod i, 669; ii, 750
Hemenway's Vermont Hist. Gaz. v, 103
Heywood's Hist. of Westminster Mass. 750
Holland's Life Abraham Lincoln 18–21
Huntington Genealogy 82
Hyde's History of Brimfield Mass. 429
Jenkin's Hist. Gwynedd Pa. 2d ed. 373–5
Kingman's North Bridgewater Mass. 571–3
Lincoln Families of Mass. (1865) 10 pages
Lincoln Family of Wareham (1885) 77 p.
Lincoln Lineage (1887) 7 pages
Lincoln Family of Oakham (1895) 109 p.
Lincolns of Wareham 2d ed. (1899) 124 p.
Lincoln's History of Hingham Mass. ii, 448–8b; iii, 3–21
Livermore's History of Wilton N. H. 435
Mitchell's Hist. of Bridgewater Mass. 238
Muzzy's Reminiscences
New Eng. Historical and Genealogical Reg. xix, 357–61; xli, 153–7; xlviii, 327
New York Gen. and Biog. Rec. iii, 69–71
Norton's History of Fitzwilliam N. H. 628
Perkins' Old Houses of Norwich Ct. 521
Phœnix Whitney Genealogy i, 753
Robbin's Sermon on Noah Lincoln 35–49
Savage's Genealogical Dictionary iii, 91–5
Sheldon's History of Deerfield Mass. 231
Smith's (Rev. Wm.) Biography
Stackpole's History of Durham Me. 214
Temple's Hist. of N. Brookfield Mass. 675
Wall's Reminisc. of Worcester Mass. 345
Washburn's History of Leicester Mass. 384
Washington N. H. History 516–8
Whitmore's Copps Hill Epitaphs
Wyman's Charlestown Mass. Gens. ii, 620
Lind — Bergen's Kings Co. N. Y. 188
Lindabury — Chambers' N. J. Germans
Lindall — N. E. Hist. Reg. vii, 15–24
Savage's Genealogical Dictionary iii, 95
Symmes Genealogy 45, 66–8
Vinton's Giles Genealogy 311–38
Winsor's History of Duxbury Mass. 276

Lindley — Eaton's Warren Me. 577
Herrick Genealogy (1885) 157
Maris Genealogy 199
Power's Sangamon Co. Ill. Settlers 459
Lindsay — American Ancestry i, 49
Lindsay Genealogy (1889) 291 pages
Page Genealogy 202
Power's Sangamon Co. Ill. Settlers 21, 460
Savage's Genealogical Dictionary iii, 96
Lindsey — Eaton's Thomaston Me. 309
Hayward's History of Hancock N. H. 738
Lindsley — Cleveland's Yates Co. 614-8
Condit Genealogy 383-5
Cothren's History of Woodbury Ct. 605
Matthew's History of Cornwall Vt. 287
Orcutt's History of Wolcott Ct. 519
Whittemore's Orange N. J. 78
Line — Plumb's Hanover Pa. 447-9
Lineaweaver — Egle's Lebanon Pa. 246
Lines — American Ancestry v, 82; vii, 206
Bunker's Long Island Genealogies 234-8
Mansfield Genealogy 57-61
Orcutt's History of New Milford Ct. 723
Tuttle Genealogy 207-9
Linfield — Bass' Braintree Vt. 159
Porter Genealogy (1868) 67 pages
Link — American Ancestry ii, 73
Linn — Chase's Hist. of Chester N. H. 555
Egle's Penn. Genealogies 2d ed. 367-82
Linnel — Swift's Barnstable ii, 148-61
Linsey — Barry's Hanover Mass. 348
Lintner — American Ancestry i, 49
Linton — American Ancestry iv, 150
Linton Genealogy (1881) 15 pages
Linzee — Heraldic Journal iv, 38-41
Lippencott — Savage's Gen. Dict. iii, 98
Lippincott — Am. Ancestry iv, 89; v, 147
Clement's Newtown N. J. Settlers
Cole Genealogy 213-6
Lippincott Genealogy (1892) 43 pages
Salter's Hist. Monmouth Co. N. J. xxxix
Shourd's Fenwick Colony N. J. 132-8
Lippitt — Austin's Ancestries 39
Austin's R. I. Genealogical Dictionary
Fuller's History of Warwick R. I. 112-4
New Eng. Hist. and Gen. Reg. xxvii, 70-3
Richmond Va. Standard ii, 147; iii, 37
Updyke's Narragansett Churches 371-4
Lipscomb — Clarke's Old King Wm. Co.
Va. Families
Liscomb — Eaton's Thomaston Me. 310
Merrill's History of Acworth N. H. 238
Lispenard — Bolton's Westchester 744
Lamb's History of New York city i, 723
New York Gen. Biog. Rec. ii, 70; viii, 185
Lister — Babson's Gloucester Mass. 112
Wm. and Mary Coll. Quarterly iii, 245
Litch — Stearns' Ashburnham N. H. 799
Litchfield — American Ancestry xi, 234
Barry's Hanover 349
Daniels' History of Oxford Mass. 594
Deane's History of Scituate Mass. 305
Eaton's History of Thomaston Me. ii, 310
Hubbard's History of Springfield Vt. 366-9
Lincoln's Hist. of Hingham Mass. iii, 22-4
Litchfield Genealogy (1855) 18 pages

Litchfield Chart (1899)
N. E. Hist. Gen. Reg. ix, 181-8, 209-18
Savage's Genealogical Dictionary iii, 98
Lithgow — Bridge Genealogy 79-88
Maine Hist. Society Collections v, 418-23
New York Gen. and Biog. Rec. xxix, 1-13
North's History of Augusta Me. 901
Littell — American Ancestry i, 49
Littell's Passaic Valley Genealogies 213-61
Little — American Ancestry i, 49; iv, 184;
vii, 147; viii, 31, 78
Ball's History of Lake Co. Ind. 448-52
Bangor Historical Magazine v, 34
Chandler's History of Shirly Mass. 501-13
Cochrane's History of Antrim N. H. 573-6
Coffin's History of Boscawen N. H. 572-87
Cushman's History of Sheepscott Me. 401
Davis' Landmarks of Plymouth Mass. 173
Deane's History of Scituate Mass. 306
Dearborn's Hist. of Salisbury N. H. 652-8
Emery's Newbury Mass. Reminisc. 125-34
Harris Family of New Jersey (1888) 149
Hayward's History of Hancock N. H. 739
Hubbard's Stanstead Co. Canada 252-4
Lincoln's History of Hingham Mass. iii, 24
Little Fam. of Newbury Mass. (1877) 16 p.
Little Fam. of Newbury Mass. (1877) 82 p.
Little Fam. of Newbury Mass. (1882) 620 p.
Little Family of Edenton N. C. (1895) 9 p.
Little's History of Weare N. H. 1025
Loomis Genealogy (1880) 719
Perkins' Old Houses of Norwich Ct. 522
Poore Genealogy 109-11
Power's Sangamon Co. Ill. Settlers 461
Savage's Genealogical Dictionary iii, 99
Smith's Hist. of Peterborough N. H. 133-5
Temple's History of Palmer Mass. 507
Upham Genealogy 41-4
Wheeler's History of Newport N. H. 462
Worthen's History of Sutton N. H. 802-11
Littlefield — Am. Ancestry i, 50; iii, 211
Ballou's History of Milford Mass. 880
Bangor Historical Magazine vi, 30
Barry's History of Framingham Mass. 317
Bourne's History of Welles Me.
Bradbury's Hist. Kennebunkport Me. 257
Livermore's Block Island R. I. 333-6
Mitchell's Hist. of Bridgewater Mass. 238
Morse's Sherborn Mass. Settlers 171-3
Savage's Genealogical Dictionary iii, 99
Thayer Memorial (1835) 37
Littlehale — Lapham's Bethel Me. 581
Littlehale Genealogy (1880) 10 pages
Littlehale Genealogy (1889) 128 pages
Worthen's History of Sutton N. H. 812-6
Littlepage — Clarke's Old King Wm.
County Va. Families
Hayden's Virginia Genealogies 397-421
Littleton — Littleton Genealogy (1887) 7 p.
Meade's Old Churches of Virginia
New Eng. Hist. and Gen. Reg. xli. 364-8
Livermore — Barry's Framingham 318
Bond's Watertown Mass. 338-52; 852-4
Brewster's Portsmouth N. H. 11, 145-7
Chandler's History of Shirley Mass. 513-9
Clarke Family of Watertown Mass. 44, 79

Daniels' History of Oxford Mass. 595
Draper's History of Spencer Mass. 214
Dwight Genealogy 642
Harris' Watertown Mass. Epitaphs 36-9
Hudson's History of Lexington Mass. 118
Isbell and Kingman Genealogy 27
Livermore Assoc. Report (1865) 38 pages
Livermore's History of Wilton N. H. 435-9
Savage's Genealogical Dictionary iii, 101
Temple's Hist. of No. Brookneld Mass. 676
Washburn's Notes on Livermore Me. 15-7
Washburn's Hist. of Leicester Mass. 381
Livezey — Davis' Bucks County Pa. 122
Livingston — Alden's Epitaphs v, 265-8
Aldrich's History of Walpole N. H. 312-5
American Ancestry i, 50; ii, 73; iv, 181
American Historical Register i, 650-8
Ball's History of Lake County Ind. 433
Caulkins' History of New London Ct. 364
Clarkson's Hist. Livingston Manor (1869)
Cochrane's History of Antrim N. H. 576
Cogswell's Hist. of Henniker N. H. 640-2
Cogswell's Hist. of New Boston N. H. 439
Glenn's Some Colonial Mansions 327-31
Gunn's Life of J. H. Livingston (1829)
Hoffman Genealogy 490
Holgate's American Genealogy 155-200
Hunt's Life of E. Livingston (1864)
Jones' New York in Rev. War i, 413
Kip's Olden Times in New York (1872)
Kollock Genealogy 41-9
Lamb's History of New York City i, 276
Livingston Family of England (1887-8)
Magazine of American History vi, 276-8
Morris' Bontecou Genealogy 158
Munsell's Albany Collections iv, 143
Munsey's Magazine xv (1896) 585-94
New York Gen. Rec. vi, 276-8; xiv, 113-6;
    xv, 15-7, 105-7, 159-61
O'Callaghan's N. Y. Doc. History iii, 609
Phœnix's Whitney Genealogy i, 913
Schuyler's Colonial New York
Sedgwick's Life Wm. Livingston 17-24
Smith's Hist. of Dutchess Co. N. Y. 396
Smith's Hist. of Petersborough N. H. 135-8
Smith's History of Rhinebeck N. Y.
Strong Genealogy 607-9
Washburn's Hist. of Leicester Mass. 380
Whitmore's Heraldic Journal iii, 76-8
Lloyd — Am. Anc. viii, 211; ix, 200; xi, 102
Glenn's Merion in Welsh Tract 336-80
Glenn's Genealogical Notes (1898)
Gregg's Old Cheraws S. C. 77
Hanson's Old Kent Md. 29-40
Whitmore's Heraldic Journal iii, 76
Hill Genealogy (1854) 27-34
Lloyd Family of Penn. (1870) 88 pages
Lloyd Family of L. I. (1884) 7 pages
McKean Genealogy 180
Meginness' Biographical Annals 183-7
N. E. Hist. and Gen. Reg. xxxviii, 425
Smith's Letter of Richard Hill 27-9
Strong Genealogy 635
Lobaugh — Egle's Pa. Gens. 618-20
Lobdell — American Ancestry viii, 99
Me. Hist. and Gen. Recorder ix. 249-52

Pope Genealogy
Savage's Genealogical Dictionary iii, 102
Williams' History of Danby Vt. 190-4
Lobingier — Egle's Penn. Gens. 499-504
Lockart — Egle's Notes (1898) 66
Locke — Adams' Haven Genealogy 36
Am. Anc. vi, 70, 150; viii, 123; x, 23; xi, 218
Barry's Hist. of Framingham Mass. 318
Chase's History of Chester N. H. 556
Cutter's Hist. of Arlington Mass. 268-74
Daniel's History of Oxford Mass. 595
Dow's Hist. of Hampton N. H. 821-6
Farnsworth Genealogy (1897) 203, 208
Hayward's History of Gilsum N. H. 353
Hazen's History of Billerica Mass. 92
Heywood's Hist. Westminster Mass. 751
Hubbard's Stanstead Co. Canada 179, 312
Hudson's Hist. of Lexington Mass. 119-26
Lapham's History of Bethel Me. 582
Lapham's History of Paris Me. 663
Locke Genealogy (1853) 406 pages
Locke Family of Rye N. H. (1893) chart
Lockes of Rye 2d edition (1897) chart
Lockes of Sullivan N. H. (1900) 24 pages
Morse's Sherborn Mass. Settlers 173
New Eng. Hist. and Gen. Reg. xxxv, 59-66
Norton's Hist. Fitzwilliam N. H. 626-31
Paige's History of Hardwick Mass. 414
Pope Genealogy
Salisbury's Family Histories (1892) 605-16
Saunderson's Charlestown N. H. 470-2
Savage's Genealogical Dictionary iii, 102-4
Sewall's Hist. of Woburn Mass. 177, 625-7
Sheldon's Hist. of Deerfield Mass. 231
Stearns' Hist. of Ashburnham Mass. 800
Stearns' Hist. of Rindge N. H. 596-8
Williams' History of Danby Vt. 194-7
Wyman's Charlestown Mass. Gens. 622-4
Lockerman — N. Y. Gen. Rec. viii, 11-6
Lockett — Watkins Genealogy 24
Lockhart — Amer. Ancestry v, 190-2
Lockman — Clute's Staten Island 401
Lockridge — Power's Sangamon 462-4
Lockwood — Amer. Ancestry iii, 34; vi, 61
Austin's Ancestral Dictionary 37
Austin's R. I. Genealogical Dictionary 125
Austin's Allied Families 167
Barlow Genealogy 396-441
Bolton's Westchester Co. N. Y. ii, 745-8
Hall's Norwalk Ct. Records 184, 265
Hubbard's Hist. of Springfield Vt. 370-81
Huntington's Stamford Ct. Settlers 67-9
Lockwood Genealogy (1889) 910 pages
Mead's History of Greenwich Ct. 313
Paige's History of Cambridge Mass. 599
Savage's Genealogical Dictionary iii, 104
Schenck's History of Fairfield Ct. 392
Sedgwick's History of Sharon Ct. 97
Selleck's Norwalk Ct. (1896) 289-320
Slaughter's St. Mark's Parish Va. 160
Loder — Huntington Stamford Ct. 70
Lodge — American Ancestry viii, 38
Loeck — Albany Collections iv, 144
Loftis — Temple's Palmer Mass. 508
Logan — Am. Ancestry viii, 127; ix, 42
Green's Kentucky Families

Loganian Library Phila. Catalogue (1867)
Miller's Hist. Colchester Co. N. S. 118–26
Missouri Pioneer Families 277
Power's Sangamon Ill. Settlers 465
Richmond Va. Standard iii, 39
Ruttenber's Hist. of Orange Co. N. Y. 407
Sheldon's Hist. of Deerfield Mass. 232
Waddell's Annals Augusta Co. Va. 404–6
Wyman's Charlestown Mass. Gens. ii, 624
Loines — Bunker's L. I. Gens. 234–8
Loman — American Ancestry ii, 74
Lomax — DeBow's Review xxvi, 129
Meade's Old Churches of Virginia i, 405
Southern Bivouac (1886) 649
Lombard — Am. Ancestry vi, 146; viii, 87
Benedict's History of Sutton Mass. 686
Binney Genealogy 30
Cutter Genealogy 124, 327
Deane's History of Scituate Mass. 307
Freeman's History of Cape Cod ii, 330 567
Heywood's Hist.of Westminster Mass. 752
Lombard Genealogy (1883) 71 pages
Lombard Manuscript Me. Gen. Lib. 31 p.
New Eng. Historical and Genealogical
  Register xii, 249–53; xviii, 186–8
Pierce's History of Gorham Me. 184
Reade's History of Swanzey N. H. 396
Rich's History of Truro Mass. 539–43
Savage's Genealogical Dictionary iii 105–7
Swift's Barnstable Mass. Families ii, 217
Vickery and Lombard Genealogy (1864) 5 p.
Lomerson — Chambers' N. J. Germans
Long — Am. Ancestry vi, 75; ix, 21, 58
Austin's R. I. Genealogical Dictionary 126
Brewster's Portsmouth N H. ii, 274–9
Davis' History of Bucks County Pa. 431
Davis' Landmarks of Plymouth Mass. 173
Dimock's Coventry Ct. Records 75
Eaton's History of Thomaston Me. ii, 310
Gilmer's Georgians 227
Goode Genealogy 242
Hoyt's Salisbury Mass. Families 232
Lancaster's History of Gilmanton N. H. 275
Lincoln's History of Hingham Mass. iii, 25
Littell's Passaic Valley Genealogies 262
Long Genealogy (1898) 10 pages
Morris Genealogy (1894) 47
Parthemore Genealogy 72–5, 122–4
Power's Sangamon Co. Ill. Settlers 465
Read's History of Swanzey N. H. 397
Savage's Genealogical Dictionary iii, 107–9
Slaughter's St. Mark's Parish 164, 179
Stiles' History of Windsor Ct. ii, 452
Temple's History of Northfield Mass. 583
Wyman's Charlestown Mass. Gens. 625–8
Longee — Dearborn's Parsonsfield 386
Longenecker — Rupp Genealogy 85–93
Longfellow — Dummer Acad. (1863)
Machias Me. Centennial 169
Maine Hist. Mag. by Porter vii, 101–5
Pierce's History of Gorham Me. 185
Savage's Genealogical Dictionary iii, 110
Titcomb's Early New Eng. People 230–7
Longhorn — Essex Inst. Coll. xxii, 213
Longley — American Ancestry ii, 155
Atkin's History of Hawley Mass. 42–4, 95–7

Butler's History of Groton Mass. 416, 493
Calnek's History of Annapolis N. S. 540
Chandler's History of Shirley Mass. 519–59
Chase's History of Haverhill Mass. 637–9
Cogswell Genealogy 95
Green's Groton Mass. Settlers 10–2
Green's Groton Mass. Epitaphs 244
Longley Genealogy (1884) 50 pages
Savage's Genealogical Dictionary iii, 110
Smith's History of Peterborough N. H. 138
Warren's History of Waterford Me. 270–2
Longstreet — American Ancestry v, 189
Longstreth — Dawson Genealogy 421–39
Hallowell Genealogy 117–41
Rodman Genealogy 162
Longwell — Huntington's Stamford 70
Longworth — Cincinnati, Ohio Criterion
  (1888) ii, 311–3
Longyear — Am. Ancestry iv, 217; vi, 12
Look — Hatch's Hist. of Industry Me. 674
Walworth's Hyde Genealogy 764
Lookermans — Dwight Genealogy 207
N. Y. Gen. and Biog. Rec. v. 69; viii, 11–6
Loomis — American Ancestry i, 50; ii, 74;
  iii, 215; viii, 97, 151; ix, 109; x, 36
Baker's History of Montville Ct. 570–2
Ballou's History of Milford Mass. 882
Barbour's My Wife and Mother, app. 71
Bass' History of Braintree Vt. 159
Boyd's Annals of Winchester Ct. 59, 117–9
Crafts History of Whately Mass. 511–3
Ely Genealogy 154
Guild's Stiles Genealogy 220
Hines' Lebanon Ct. Hist. Address 160–3
Hollister's History of Pawlet Vt. 211
Hurd's History of New London Co. Ct. 513
Kellogg's White Genealogy 30
Loomis Genealogy (1870) 292 pages
Loomis Genealogy 2d ed. (1875) 611 pages
Loomis Female Branches (1880) 1132 pages
Marshall's Grant Ancestry 119–24
Morris and Flynt Genealogy 63
Orcutt's History of Torrington Ct. 730–7
Savage's Genealogical Dictionary iii, 111–5
Stiles' History of Windsor Ct. ii, 432–52
Strong Genealogy 804–7
Temple's History of Palmer Mass. 502–5
Temple's History of Whately Mass. 245
Waldo's History of Tolland Ct. 134
Wentworth Genealogy ii, 290
Wright's Williams Genealogy 26–8, 36–46
Loper — Goode Genealogy 197
Lord — Am. Ancestry ii, 75; x, 143; xii
Bourne's History of Wells Me. 757
Bradbury's Kennebunkport Me. 258–60
Child Genealogy 351–5
Cleveland Genealogy 108–13
Cochrane's Hist. Francest'n N. H. 801–3
Dearborn's History of Parsonsfield Me. 385
Foster Pedigree (1897) vii, 1–36
Freeman's History of Cape Cod ii, 596
Goodwin's Genealogical Notes 347–55
Hammatt Papers of Ipswich Mass. 208–15
Hubbard's Stanstead Co. Canada 279
Kellogg's White Genealogy 22
Lapham's History of Norway Me. 544

Locke Genealogy 109
Lord Ancestry in England (1865) 6 pages
New Eng. Hist. and Gen. Reg. xxxi, 211
Perkins' Old Houses of Norwich Ct. 523-5
Porter's Hartford Ct. Settlers 8-12
Ridlon's Saco Valley Me. Families 889-96
Runnel's Hist. Sanbornton N. H. ii, 462-6
Salisbury's Family Hist. (1892) i, 247-332
Savage's Genealogical Dictionary iii, 115-7
Schenck's History of Fairfield Ct. 393
Secomb's History of Amherst N. H. 671
Sedgwick's History of Sharon Ct. 97
Stanton Genealogy 13
Stiles' History of Windsor Ct. iii, 452-6
Temple's History of Whately Mass. 246
Walworth's Hyde Genealogy ii, 733-43
Wentworth Genealogy i, 242; ii, 408-15
Wyman's Charlestown Mass. ii. 628-31
Lorillard — N. Y. Gen. Rec. viii, 89
Lorimer — Hubbard's Stanstead 243
Loring — Bridgeman's Copps Hill 221
Bridgeman's Granary Epitaphs 350-7
Cochrane's Hist. Francestown N. H. 803
Corliss' N. Yarmouth Me. 875-86, 924-37
Davis' Landmarks of Plymouth Mass. 174
Draper's History of Spencer Mass. 221
Hudson's Hist. of Lexington Mass. 126-8
Hudson's Hist. Marlborough Mass. 410-2
Hudson's History of Sudbury Mass. 353-6
Lincoln's Hist. Hingham Mass. iii, 26-41
Loring Genealogy (1891) 22 pages
Mitchell's Bridgewater Mass. 239, 380-2
New Eng. Hist. Gen. Reg. vii, 163, 326
Orcutt's History of Stratford Ct. 1241
Pickering Genealogy
Savage's Genealogical Dictionary iii, 117-9
Smith's History of Peterborough N. H. 139
Smith Genealogy (1895) 74-7, 128-32
Whitmore's Copps Hill Epitaphs
Winsor's History of Duxbury Mass. 276-80
Wyman's Charlestown Mass. Gens. 631
Losee — American Ancestry ii, 75
Ireland Genealogy 32
Lossing — American Ancestry iii, 182
Lothridge — American Ancestry ii, 75
Lothrop—American Ancestry vii, 51; ix,31
Bass' History of Braintree Vt. 160
Bond's History of Watertown Mass. 453
Davis' Landmarks Plymouth Mass. 175-7
Deane's History of Scituate Mass. 167
Eaton's History of Thomaston Me. ii, 311
Foster Genealogy (1889) 85-90
Freeman's Hist. of Cape Cod i, 139; ii, 243
Holmes' American Annals i, 228-55
Lathrop Genealogy (1884) 457 pages
Lincoln's History of Hingham Mass. iii, 41
Mass. Hist. Society Colls. 2d ser. i, 163
New Eng. Hist. Register ii, 64, 195; iii, 273
Sprague's Annals of Amer. Pulpit i, 49
Stone's History of Bevely Mass. 2408
Swift's Barnstable Fams. ii, 162-211, 215
Lott — Bergen Gen. 121, 131, 137, 158
Bergen's Kings Co. N. Y. Settlers 190-3
Bergen's Van Brunt Genealogy 25, 53
Cooley's Trenton N. J. Settlers 160-2
Hall's Trenton N. J. Presb. Church 71

Sedgwick's History of Sharon Ct. 97
Thompson's Long Island N. Y. ii, 469-72
Loud — Davis' Landmarks 177
Lincoln's History of Hingham Mass. iii, 42
Loud Genealogy (1889) 77 pages
Louden — Winsor's Duxbury 280
Loudon — Perkin's Norwich Ct. 526
Lougee — Lancaster's Gilmanton 275
Runnel's Sanbornton N. H. ii, 466-70
Lounsberry — Baird's Rye N. Y. 421
Huntington's Stamford Ct. Settlers 71
Sharp's History of Seymour Ct. 217-9
Vinton's Giles Genealogy 97
Lounsbury — N. Y. Gen. Rec. xvii, 280
Sylvester's History of Ulster Co. N. Y. 116
Loutrel — Barlow Genealogy 230-4
Lovejoy — Abbott's Andover Mass. 27
American Ancestry ii, 75
Carter's Hist. of Pembroke N. H. ii, 212-5
Eaton's History of Thomaston Me. ii, 312
Hazen's History of Billerica Mass. 92
Lapham's History of Bethel Me. 584
Lapham's History of Norway Me. 545
Livermore's History of Wilton N. H. 439-43
Orcutt's History of Stratford Ct. 1241
Roe's Sketches of Rose N. Y. 237
Runnel's Hist. Sanbornton N. H. ii, 470-4
Savage's Genealogical Dictionary iii, 122
Secomb's History of Amherst N. H. 672-7
Stearns' History of Rindge N. H. 599-601
Worcester's History of Hollis N. H. 380
Loveland — American Ancestry iii, 139
Caverly's History of Pittsford Vt. 714
Hayward's History of Gilsum N. H. 355-7
Loveland Genealogy (1892) 3 vols.
Loveland Genealogy supp. (1897) 38 p.
Lovell — Aldrich's Walpole N. H. 315
American Ancestry ix, 59; xi, 227
Benedict's History of Sutton Mass. 686
Binney Genealogy
Hammatt Papers of Ipswich Mass. 221
Hubbard's History of Springfield Vt. 381-4
Jameson's History of Medway Mass. 499
Keyes' West Boylston Mass. Register 27
Nash's Journal of Sol. Lovell (1881) 109-16
Saunderson's Hist. Charlestown N. H. 471
Savage's Genealogical Dictionary iii, 123
Sedgwick's History of Sharon Ct. 97
Slaughter's St. Mark's Parish Va. 179
Temple's Hist. of N. Brookfield Mass. 676
Wall's Reminisc. of Worcester Mass. 340
Welles' Washington Genealogy 202, 226
See also under Lovewell
Loverain — Crafts Genealogy 59-61
Morse's Sherborn Mass. 173
Loveran — Bond's Watertown 353
Dearborn's History of Salisbury N. H. 658
Loveridge — Loomis Genealogy (1880) 934
Orcutt's History of New Milford Ct. 724
Sheldon's History of Deerfield Mass. 233
Lovering — Dow's Hampton 828-30
Fullonton's History of Raymond N. H. 247
New Eng. Hist. and Gen. Reg. xviii, 336
Norton's History of Fitzwilliam N. H. 631
Lovett — American Ancestry iv, 207
Ballou's History of Milford Mass. 883

Calnek's History of Annapolis N. S. 541
Daniels' History of Oxford Mass. 596
Eaton's History of Thomaston Me. ii, 313
Lincoln's Hist. of Hingham Mass. iii, 43
Livermore's History of Wilton N. H. 439
Milliken's Narraguagus Valley Me. 17
Stone's History of Beverly Mass. 31
Lovewell — Bond's Watertown 353
Fox's History of Dunstable Mass. 246
Heywood's Hist. of Westminster Mass. 753
Stone's History of Hubbardston Mass. 305
See also under Lovell
Loving — Sullivant Memorial 345
Lovis — Lincoln's Hingham iii, 43
Low — American Ancestry vii, 119
Austin's R. I. Genealogical Dictionary 338
Babson's Hist. of Gloucester Mass. 113-5
Cleveland's History of Yates Co. N. Y. 379
Hammatt Papers of Ipswich Mass. 215-7
Hayward's History of Hancock N. H. 740-2
Lincoln's Hist. of Hingham Mass. iii, 44-6
Low Family of Boston (1890) chart
McKeen's History of Bradford Vt. 349-52
Penney Genealogy 61-9
Riker's History of Harlem N. Y. 519
Schoonmaker's Hist. Kingston N. Y. 482
Secomb's History of Amherst N. H. 677-9
See also under Lowe
Lowd — Wentworth Genealogy i, 473-6
Lowden — Mitchell's Bridgewater 240
Savage's Genealogical Dictionary iii, 125
Wyman's Charlestown Mass. Gens. 632-5
Lowder — Bangor Hist. Mag. vi, 298
Lowe — Eaton's Thomaston Me. ii, 313
Hale Genealogy 319-21
Norton's History of Fitzwilliam N. H. 631
Savage's Genealogical Dictionary iii, 125
Stearns' Hist. of Ashburnham Mass. 801-4
Temple's Hist. of N. Brookfield Mass. 677
Lowell — American Ancestry i, 50; x, 134
Bridgeman's Granary Epitaphs 304
Butler's History of Farmington Me. 524-30
Currier's Ould Newbury Mass. 577-9
Cutts Genealogy 359
Eaton's History of Thomaston Me. ii, 313
Hoyt's Salisbury Mass. Families 233-5
Lapham's History of Bethel Me. 584
Lowell Genealogy (1899) 878 pages
New Eng. Hist. and Gen. Reg. liv, 315-9
Ridlon's Harrison Me. Settlers 95-7
Savage's Genealogical Dictionary iii, 126
Stearns' History of Rindge N. H. 601
Washington N. H. History 519-23
Whitmore's Heraldic Journal i, 25-7
Loweree — American Ancestry ix, 39
Lown — American Ancestry ii, 75
Lowndes—Lowndes Genealogy (1876) 84 p.
Martin's History of Chester Pa. 494
New Eng. Hist. Gen. Reg. xxx, 141-64
Lowry — Child Genealogy 799-801
Egle's Penn. Genealogies 2d ed. 18
Goode Genealogy 293
Griffith's Life of Morgan Rhees (1899) 80
Lowrey Genealogy (1892) 16 pages
Timlow's History of Southington Ct. 166
Young's Chautauqua Co. N. Y. 626-9

Loxley — Penn. Mag. xxiii, 265
Rhees Biography (1899) 77-9
Luby — American Ancestry i, 51
Lucas — Chambers' N. J. Germans
Davis' Landmarks 177-9
Emery Genealogy 210
Hibbard's History of Goshen Ct. 480-6
Middletown Ct. History
New Eng. Hist. and Gen. Reg. xxv, 151-3
Luce — American Ancestry i, 51
Bass' History of Braintree Vt. 160
Child Genealogy 244, 779-82
Cleveland Genealogy (1899) 429-31
Davis' Landmarks of Plymouth Mass. 179
Densmore's Hartwell Genealogy
Hatch's History of Industry Me. 675-719
Mallmann's Shelter Island N. Y. 214
Lucken — Penn. Mag. xxiii, 270
Luckenbach — American Ancestry ii, 75
Lucy — Cogswell's Nottingham 216
Ludden — Draper's Spencer Mass. 224
Lyman's Hist. of East Hampton Mass. 191
Thayer Memorial (1835) 47-9
Ludington — Andrews' New Britain
Anderson's Waterbury Ct. i, app. 86
Dodd's History of East Haven Ct. 132-4
Ludington Genealogy (1886) 5 pages
Ludkin — Savage's Gen. Dict. iii, 128
Wyman's Charlestown Mass. Gens. 635
Ludlam — Amer. Ancestry iv, 163; ix, 81
Ludlam Genealogy (1878) 19 pages
Ludlam Genealogy (1896) 52 pages
Ogden Genealogy (1898) 114
Queens County N. Y. History 544
Ludlow — American Ancestry ii, 75; v, 43
Fowler's Our Predecessors 41-52
Howell's Southampton N. Y. 339-41
Littell's Passaic Valley Gens. 264-72
Ludlow Hall Memorial (1866) app.
N. Y. Gen. and Biog. Rec. xxvi, 5
Ruttenber's Orange Co. N. Y. 399-401
Savage's Genealogical Dictionary iii, 129
Thomas Genealogy (1877) 120
Ludwell — Keith's Harrison Ancestry 49
Lee Genealogy (1895) 127-30
Ludwell Genealogy (1879) 3 pages
Meade's Old Churches of Virginia i, 195
N. E. Gen. Reg. xxxiii, 220-2; xxxix, 162
Richmond Va. Standard i, 44
Southern Bivouac (1886) 649
Ludwig — Eaton's Thomaston Me. 314
Keim Genealogy 481-3
Ludwig Genealogy (1866) 223 pages
Rupp Genealogy 158
Lueder — Plumb's Hanover Pa. 451
Lufbery — American Ancestry vi, 9
Lufkin — American Ancestry ix, 206
Babson's History of Gloucester Mass. 112
Chase's History of Chester N. H. 557
Corliss' North Yarmouth Me. 1077-85
Lapham's History of Rumford Me. 369-71
Little's History of Weare N. H. 934
Poor's Merrimack Valley Researches 113
Luke — American Ancestry i, 51
Green's Kentucky Families
Munsell's Albany Collections iv, 144

Lukens — American Ancestry ix, 177
Lull — Caldwell Genealogy (1873) 68
Hammatt Papers of Ipswich Mass. 223
Little's History of Weare N. H. 934
Stanton Genealogy 92
Washington N. H. History 523
Winslow Genealogy ii, 570-2
Lum — Littell's Passaic Valley Gens. 273
Lumbard — Daniels' Oxford Mass. 597
Hllister's History of Pawlet Vt. 212
Hyde's History of Brimfield Mass. 429 32
New Eng. Hist. and Gen. Reg. iii, 272
Lumbert — Bangor Hist. Mag. viii, 38
Lummus — American Ancestry x, 164
Hammatt Papers of Ipswich Mass. 222
Lund — Fox's Dunstable Mass 247
Wheeler's History of Newport N. H. 464
Lundy — Lundy Genealogy (1897) 15 p.
Shotwell Genealogy 249-64
Lunsford — De Bow's Review xxvi
Southern Bivouac (1886) 649
Lunt — Coffin's Newbury Mass. 308
New Eng. Hist. Gen. Reg. xxii, 232-4
Savage's Genealogical Dictionary iii, 131
Wheeler's History of Brunswick Me. 842
Lupton — Howell's Southampton 341
Jolliffe Genealogy (1893) 126
Lurty — American Ancestry iii, 34
Lurvey — Lapham's Paris Me. 664
Lapham's Hist. of Woodstock Me. 238-40
Luscomb — Driver Genealogy 387-93
Lush — Albany Collections iv, 145
Lusk — Andrews' New Britain Ct. 206
Turner's Phelps Purchase N. Y. 422
Luther — American Ancestry v, 5; xi, 103
Cleveland's History of Yates Co. N. Y. 135
Draper's History of Spencer Mass. 221
Lutz — American Ancestry vii, 166
Luxford — Paige's Cambridge 600
Luyhard — Pearson's Schenectady 107
Luyster — American Ancestry x, 75
Bergen's Kings Co. N. Y. Settlers 196-8
Nevius Genealogy 156
Queens Co. N. Y. History 539
Riker's Annals of Newtown N. Y. 358-62
Lyddall — N. E. Hist. Reg. xxxviii, 74
Richmond Va. Standard i, 44
Lydius — Munsell's Albany Colls. iv, 144
Lyell — Whitehead's Perth Amboy 84
Lyford — Cogswell Genealogy 197
Hubbard's Stanstead Co. Canada 182
Lyle — Am. Ancestry vi, 132; vii, 205
Egle's Notes and Queries (1898) 300
Goode Genealogy 118
Green's Kentucky Families
Lyle Genealogy
Richmond Va. Standard iii, 2
Smith (Rev. Wm.) Biography
Lyman — Adams' Fairhaven Vt. 484
American Ancestry i, 51; vi, 45, 116; vii, 24, 185; ix, 106; xi, 104, 231
Austin's Ancestries 41
Barbour's My Wife and Mother, app. 23
Barrus' History of Goshen Mass. 150-2
Bartlett's Wanton Genealogy 131
Doolittle's Belchertown Mass. 253

Dwight Genealogy 124-6, 541, 556-76, 906-8
Hibbard's History of Goshen Ct. 486-93
Hines' Lebanon Ct. Hist. Address 163
Huntington Genealogy 131
Hurd's History of New London Co. Ct. 513
Hyde's History of Brimfield Mass. 532
Judd's History of Hadley Mass. 531
Kellogg's White Genealogy 101
Litchfield County Ct. History (1881) 355
Loomis Genealogy (1880) 333-63, 686-8, 739
Lyman Genealogy (1865) 29 pages
Lyman Family Reunion (1871) 60 pages
Lyman Genealogy (1872) 533 pages
Lyman's Hist. East Hampton Mass. 161-8
Middlefield Ct. History
Montague Genealogy 200-2
Orcutt's History of Derby Ct. 744.
Orcutt's History of Torrington Ct. 744-8
Pickering Genealogy
Power's Sangamon Co. Ill. Settlers 467
Savage's Genealogical Dictionary iii, 134
Smith's History of Sunderland Mass. 438
Strong Genealogy 1203-7
Temple's History of Whately Mass. 844-9
Tucker's History of Hartford Vt. 447
Lynch — Cochrane's Francestown 804
Lynchburg Va. Sketches 9-21
Van Rensselaer's New Yorkers
Lynde — Davis Genealogy 85
Dorr Genealogy
Draper's History of Spencer Mass. 225
Goss' History of Melrose Mass. 10-2
Heywood's Hist. of Westminster Mass.754
Malden Mass. Bi-Centennial 232-4
New Eng. Hist. and Gen. Reg. ix, 323
Oliver's Lynde Diaries (1880), app. 251
Prime's Bowdoin Genealogy 28
Salisbury's Family Histories (1892) 359-425
Savage's Genealogical Dict. iii, 135-70
Sheldon's History of Deerfield Mass. 233-5
Sherburne N. Y. News for Aug. 31 (1889)
Washburn's Hist. of Leicester Mass. 382
Wyman's Charlestown Mass. ii, 637-41
Lyndon — Austin's R. I. Gen. Dict. 340
Lynds — Miller's Colchester N. S. 379-83
Lyne — Clarke's King Wm. Va. Fams.
Richmond Standard iii, 13, 51
Sullivant Memorial 281-94
Lynes — American Ancestry ii, 75
Lynn — Pa. Mag. of History xvii, 376
Power's Sangamon Co. Ill. Settlers 470
Lyon — Am. Anc i, 51: v. 117; x, 104; xii, 33
Baird's History of Rye N. Y. 422-5
Baker's History of Montville Ct. 450-4
Bangor Me. Historical Magazine iii, 209
Barrus' History of Goshen Mass. 150
Bass' History of Braintree Vt. 161
Bolton's Westchester Co. N. Y. ii, 748
Chandler's History of Shirley Mass. 559-61
Egle's Penn. Genealogies 2d ed. 383-407
Ellis Genealogy 238, 376
Goode Genealogy 158
Hyde's History of Brimfield Mass. 433
Littell's Passaic Valley Genealogies 274-6
Mansfield Genealogy 51

Mead's History of Greenwich Ct. 313
Morris Genealogy (1887) 31
New Jersey Historical Colls. vi, supp. 125
NewYork Gen. and Biog. Rec. xxviii, 75-9, 235-7; xxix, 98-100
Norton's History of Fitzwilliam N. H. 631
Power's Sangamon Co. Ill. Settlers 469
Redfield Genealogy 49
Savage's Genealogical Dictionary iii, 137
Schenck's History of Fairfield Ct. 393-5
Stone's History of Hubbardston Mass. 305
Todd's History of Redding Ct. 205
Ward's History of Shrewsbury Mass. 357
Welles' Am. Fam. Antiquity ii, 93-111
Whitman Genealogy 74-6
Wight Genealogy 99
Williams' History of Danby Vt. 189
Woodward's Life of Nath. Lyon 349-56
Lyons — Meade's Old Churches of Va. Richmond Va. Standard ii, 13; iii, 27
Lyster — American Ancestry x, 115
Lytle — American Ancestry vii, 31
Egle's Notes and Queries 1st ser. i, 437-9; 3d ser. iii, 474-9
Rich Genealogy (1892) 31-5
Lyttleton — New Eng. Historical and Gen. Register xxxviii, 67
Maben — Greene Co. N. Y. History 363
Richmond Va. Standard iv, 3
Mabie -- Pearson's Schenectady 118-20
MacArthur—Ridlon's Saco. Valley 896-8
Macarty — Allen's Worcester Mass. 82
Maccarty — Lincoln's Worcester 150
Savage's Genealogical Dictionary iii, 139
MacCurdy — See under McCurdy
MacDonald — American Ancestry vii, 233
MacDonald Fam. of Delaware (1879) 65 p.
MacDonald Family 2d ed. (1879) 123 p.
MacDonald Family supp. (1880) 72 pages
Ridlon's Saco Valley Me. Families 898-901
Mace — Dow's Hampton N. H. 830-4
Macfarlane — Macfarlane Genealogy
Lincoln's Hist. of Hingham Mass. iii, 47
See also under McFarlane
Macgregor — Parker's Londonderry
Mack — American Ancestry i, 51; ii, 76
Bedford N. H. Centennial 313
Hayward's History of Gilsum N. H. 357
Hubbard's Stanstead Co. Canada 226
Lancaster's Hist. of Gilmanton N. H. 278
Livermore's History of Wilton N. H. 443
Mack Genealogy (1879) 81 pages
Olin's Olin Genealogy 45
Parker's Hist. Londonderry N. H. 278-80
Secomb's History of Amherst N. H. 680-3
Sheldon's History of Deerfield Mass. 235
Mackey — Lewis Genealogy (1893) 118-30
Missouri Pioneer Families 173
Mackarness — Goode Genealogy 20, 468
MacKellar — American Ancestry xi, 203
Mackie — Howell's Southampton 342
MacLaren — Kirby Genealogy
Maclay — Egle's Pa. Gens. 2d ed. 408-9
Meginness Biographical Annals 189-92
MacLean — American Ancestry iv, 47
Macmurdo — Slaughter's St. Mark's 183

Macmurphy — Amer. Anc. ix, 128, 241
Macomb — American Ancestry xii
Anthon (Geo. C.) Narrative
Hall Genealogy (1892) 84-6
Navarre Genealogy 239-56
Macomber — American Ancestry xii
Davis Landmarks 180
Pierce's Biographical Contributions 196
Stackpole's History of Durham Me. 215-7
Macon — Richmond Va. Standard iii, 46; iv, 3
Slaughter's St. Mark's Parish Va. 147
Wm. and Mary College Quar. vi, 33-6
Macoone — Austin's R. I. Dictionary 126
Macoy — Jackson's Newton Mass. 363
Macpheadres—Brewster's Portsmouth N. H. Rambles
Macpherson — Cochrane's History of Francestown N. H. 808-21
Penn. Magazine v, 88-92; xxiii, 51
Macy — American Ancestry ii, 76; vi, 49
Hoyt's Salisbury Mass. Families 236
Huntington Genealogy 92
Macy Genealogy (1868) 457 pages
Phœnix's Whitney Genealogy ii, 1281
Savage's Genealogical Dictionary iii, 142
Madden — Ballou's Milford Mass. 887
Campbell's History of Virginia 707
Gilmer's Georgians 70
Meade's Old Churches of Virginia ii, 96
New Eng. Hist. and Gen. Register (1872) 31
Paxton's Marshall Genealogy 146
Slaughter's St. Mark's Parish Va. 144
Maddock — Bond's Watertown 354, 855
Maddocks — Eaton's Thomaston 321
Maddox — Bangor Historical Mag. iii, 220
Savage's Genealogical Dictionary iii, 142
Shourd's Fenwick Colony N. J. 142
Madig — Cushman's Sheepscott Me. 402
Madison — American Ancestry ii, 78
Green's Kentucky Families
Hayden's Virginia Genealogies 256
Lewis Genealogy (1893) 392-402
Meade's Old Churches of Virginia ii, 96-8
Slaughter's St. Ann's Parish Va. 144-7
Magaw — Bergen Genealogy 151
Magee — Boyd's Conesus N. Y. 162
Wyman's Charlestown Mass. Gens. ii, 645
Magennis — Maginness (1891) 248 pages
Magoon — Hubbard's Stanstead 240
Hyde's Hist. Address at Ware Mass. 47
Savage's Genealogical Dictionary iii, 143
Temple's History of Palmer Mass. 511
Winsor's History of Duxbury Mass. 281
Magoun — American Ancestry viii, 96
Barry's History of Hanover Mass. 349
Magoun Genealogy (1891) 33 pages
Magoun Genealogy, supp. (1893) 14 pages
Magruder — American Ancestry v, 164
Mahan — Richmond Standard iii, 14
Mahoney — Temple's No. Brookfield 678
Mailler — Ruttenber's Newburgh 314
Ruttenber's Hist. of Orange Co. N. Y. 397
Main — Tanner Genealogy 26-8
Makepeace—Makepeace Genealogy (1858)
Savage's Genealogical Dictionary iii, 144

Maker — Eaton's Thomaston Me. 321
Malavery — Austin's R. I. Dictionary 340
Malcolm — American Ancestry xii, 36
Malcom — American Ancestry iii, 204
Malcombe — Eaton's Warren Me. 582
Malick — Mellick's Old Farm 627-713
Malin — Cleveland's Yates Co. N. Y. 120
Malins — Austin's R. I. Gen. Dict. 127
Mallary — Joslin's Poultney Vt. 302-4
Mallery — Amer. Ancestry ii, 78; iii, 146
Anderson's Waterbury Ct. i, app. 86
Candee Genealogy 159-65
Schenck's History of Fairfield Ct. 369
Mallett — American Ancestry xii, 30
Austin's R. I. Dictionary 127
Eaton's Annals of Warren Me. 582
Mallett Genealogy (1895) 342 pages
Orcutt's History of Stratford Ct. 1242
Mallory — American Ancestry viii, 161
Boyd's Annals of Winchester Ct. 286
Cothren's Woodbury Ct. 615-8; ii, 1514
Cutter's History of Arlington Mass. 275
Dodd's History of East Haven Ct. 134
New Eng. Hist. Gen. Register liv, 320-5
Orcutt's History of New Milford Ct. 725
Orcutt's History of Stratford Ct. 1242
Paul's History of Wells Vt. 121
Power's Sangamon Co. Ill. Settlers 471
Savage's Genealogical Dictionary iii, 144
Todd's History of Redding Ct. 206
Wyman's Charlestown Mass. Gens. ii, 647
Malone — Power's Sangamon Ill. 472
Maloon — Nottingham N. H. 419-25
Maltby — American Ancestry ix, 201
Davenport Genealogy 207, 218
Davis Genealogy (1888) 97
Dwight's Strong Genealogy 354
Huntington's Stamford Ct. Settlers 73
Leavenworth Genealogy 127
Maltby Genealogy (1895) 157 pages
Paxton's Marshall Genealogy 342
Maltman — Comey Genealogy 38
Man — Bassett's Richmond 428-32
Man and Needles Genealogy (1876) 124 p.
Manahan—Cochrane's Francestown 804-8
Mance — Clute's Staten Island N. Y. 403
Manchester — Austin's R. I. Dict. 127
Mancil — Cope's Dutton Gen. 60, 73, 89
Mandell — American Ancestry xii
Paige's Hardwick 415-7
Spooner Genealogy i, 288
Mandeville — American Ancestry ii, 78;
viii, 190-2; xii, 25
Roome Genealogy 285-7
Whittemore's Orange N. J. 83, 383
Manigault — American Ancestry v 35
South Car. Huguenot Soc. Trans. iv, 48-84
Mank--Eaton's Annals of Warren Me. 583
Manley — Caverly's Pittsford Vt. 714
Hemenway's Vermont Hist. Gaz. v, 105
Kingman's North Bridgewater Mass. 578
Mitchell's Hist. of Bridgewater Mass. 248
Paige's History of Hardwick Mass. 417
Stiles' History of Windsor Ct. ii, 464
Mann — Am. Ancestry iv, 99; vii, 89, 102
Austin's Ancestral Dictionary 38

Austin's R. I. Genealogical Dictionary 129
Ballou's History of Milford Mass. 890
Bangor Me. Historical Magazine vi, 88
Barry's History of Hanover Mass. 350-2
Bass' History of Braintree Vt. 162-4
Bemis' History of Marlboro N. H. 562
Blake's History of Franklin Mass. 258
Corliss' North Yarmouth Me. Magazine
Davis' History of Bucks County Pa. 670
Deane's History of Scituate Mass. 309
Dearborn's History of Salisbury N. H. 659
Dedham Mass. Hist. Register vi, 124-9;
vii, 28-33, 60-5, 140-5
Heywood's Hist. Westminster Mass. 755-7
Hill's History of Mason N. H. 204
Hinman's Connecticut Settlers (1846 ed.)
Hudson's History of Lexington Mass. 128
Jameson's History of Medway Mass. 500
Mann Genealogy (1873) 24 pages
Mann Genealogy (1884) 251 pages
New Eng. Hist. Gen. Reg. xiii, 325-8, 364
Oneida Hist. Society Trans. ii, 120-3
Orcutt's History of Stratford Ct. 1243
Page Genealogy 51
Pierce's History of Gorham Me. 193
Power's Sangamon Co. Ill. Settlers 473
Savage's Genealogical Dictionary iii, 145
Slafter Genealogy 20
Stone's Hist. Hubbardston Mass. 306-8
Temple's History of Palmer Mass. 516
Washington N. H. History 524-6
Manning — Am. Anc. i, 52; iii, 199; xii
Bedford N. H. Centennial 313
Bond's Watertown Mass. 527-9, 945
Daniels' History of Oxford Mass. 598
Eaton's History of Thomaston Me. 322
Emmerton's Gleanings 72
Essex Inst. Hist. Collections xvii, 73-6
Hammatt Papers of Ipswich Mass. 225
Hayward's History of Hancock N. H. 742
Hazen's History of Billerica Mass. 93-5
Lapham's History of Norway Me. 546
Manning Family Chart (1887)
Manning Family Notes (1897) 35 pages
New Eng. Hist. Reg. l, 221; li, 389-406
Paige's History of Cambridge Mass. 601-3
Perkins' Old Houses of Norwich Ct. 527-9
Savage's Genealogical Dictionary iii, 147
Secomb's History of Amherst N. H. 687
Washington N. H. History 526
Wyman's Charlestown Mass. Gens. 650-2
Manrow — Sedgwick's Sharon Ct. 98
Mansell — Bangor Hist. Mag. iv, 9-11
Mansfield — American Ancestry ii, 78;
vii, 204; x, 202; xi, 103
Bond's Watertown Mass. Gens. 355
Daniels' History of Oxford Mass. 599
Davis' History of Wallingford Ct. 847
Hayward's History of Gilsum N. H. 359
Hemenway's Vermont Gaz. v, 198, 211-3
Kidder's Hist. of New Ipswich N. H. 416
Lincoln's Hist. of Hingham Mass. iii, 50-2
Mansfield Genealogy (1885) 198 pages
Orcutt's History of Derby Ct. 745
Savage's Genealogical Dictionary iii, 148
Stiles' History of Windsor Ct. 691

Tuttle Genealogy 667-9
Walworth's Hyde Genealogy 122
Manson — American Ancestry i, 52
Barry's History of Framingham Mass. 319
Hayward's History of Hancock N. H. 742
McKeen's History of Bradford Vt. 370-3
Ridlon's Saco Valley Me. Families 902
Mansur — Blood's Temple N. H. 231
Heywood's Hist. of Westminster Mass. 757
Hubbard's Stanstead Co. Canada 171
Lapham's History of Rumford Me. 372
Livermore's History of Wilton N. H. 444-6
Wyman's Charlestown Mass. Gens. 652
Young's History of Wayne Co. Ind. 188
Manter — Davis' Landmarks 183
Hatch's History of Industry Me. 719-32
Manton — Austin's Ancestral Dict. 39
Austin's R. I. Genealogical Dictionary 342
Narragansett Historical Reg. iv, 296-9
Manuel — Lincoln's Hingham iii, 52
Manwaring—Baker's Montville Ct. 244-50
Caulkins' New London
Walworth's Hyde Gen. ii, 1009-15, 1111-8
Mapes — American Ancestry xi, 103
Weygant's Family Record (1897) 10-2, 23-5, 33-6, 46-8, 58-60, 70-2
Maples — Baker's Montville Ct. 466-70
Morris' Bontecou Genealogy 107
Walworth's Hyde Genealogy 377
Young's Hist. Chautauqua Co. N. Y. 324
Marable — Wyman's Charlestown 653
Maranville — Joslin's Poultney Vt. 305
Marble — Austin's Allied Families 171
Benedict's History of Sutton Mass. 687-9
Daniels' History of Oxford Mass. 599
Lapham's History of Bethel Me. 584
Lapham's History of Paris Me. 667
Lincoln's Hist. Hingham Mass. iii, 53-6
Read's History of Swanzey N. H. 400
Stearns' Hist. Ashburnham Mass. 804-9
Stiles' History of Windsor Ct. ii, 465
See also Marable
Marbury — Bowie Genealogy 458-67
Chester's Hutchinson Ancestry (1866)
New Eng. Hist. and Gen. Reg. xxi, 283
Marcelus — Pearson's Schenectady 115
March — American Ancestry i, 52; iv, 63
Benedict's History of Sutton Mass. 689
Bradbury's Hist. Kennebunkport Me. 261
Brewster's Portsmouth N. H. ii, 129
Chapman's Weeks Genealogy 146
Coffin's History of Newbury Mass. 309
Hoyt's Salisbury Mass. Families 237-9
Lapham's History of Norway Me. 547
March Genealogy (1899) 4 pages
New Eng. Hist. and Gen. Register liii, 121
Runnel's Sanbornton N. H. ii, 474-7
Savage's Genealogical Dictionary iii, 150
Sedgwick's History of Sharon Ct. 99
Marchant — Babson's Gloucester 273
Sedgwick's History of Sharon Ct. 98
Young's History of Warsaw N. Y. 293
Marchbank — Magennis Genealogy 166-8
Marchfield — Hall's Gen. Notes 93
Marcy — Amer. Ancestry vii, 271; viii, 61
Ammidown Genealogy 38

Daniels' History of Oxford Mass. 600
Davis Genealogy 63-5
Davis' Landmarks of Plymouth Mass. 183
Humphreys Genealogy 471
Marcy Genealogy (1897) 15 pages
Morris Genealogy (1887) 53, 183, 190-4
New Eng. Hist. Gen. xxix, 301-14
Plumb's History of Hanover Pa. 457-9
Walker Genealogy 81
Whittemore's Orange N. J. 344
Marden — Chase's Chester N. H. 558
Cochrane's Hist. Francestown N. H. 821
Cogswell's Hist. New Boston N. H. 377-9
Livermore's History of Wilton N. H. 341
Morrison's Hist. of Windham N. H. 621-4
Mardlen — Wyman's Charlestown 635
Marean — Jackson's Newton Mass. 362
Marentette — Navarre Gen. 257-76
Margery — Hayward's Hancock 743
Margeson — Calnek's Annapolis N. S. 542
Margetts — Lincoln's Hingham iii, 56
Mariner — Wheeler's Brunswick 842
Marinus — Pearson's Schenectady 113
Marion — Bridgeman's Kings Chapel Burial Ground 263-9
New Eng. Hist. Gen. Register xlv, 86-8
Savage's Genealogical Dictionary iii, 152
South Car. Huguenot Soc. Trans. iv, 22-6
Maris — Maris Genealogy (1883) 15 pages
Maris Genealogy (1885) 279 pages
Smith's History of Delaware Co. Pa. 482
Marius — Schoonmaker's Kingston 483
Mark — Hayward's Gilsum N. H. 360
Parthemore Genealogy 135
Markham — American Ancestry vi, 114
Hinman's Connecticut Settlers 1st ed. 171
Locke Genealogy 23
Merrill's History of Acworth N. H. 240
Paxton's Marshall Genealogy 16
Savage's Genealogical Dictionary iii, 152
Virginia Magazine of History v, 205-6, 334-6, 439-40; vi, 80-2
Markle — Keim Genealogy 301
See also under Markley
Markley — Markley Gen. (1884) 36 pages
Markley Chart (1886) 1x2 feet
Perkiomen Region Pa. 102
See also under Merkley
Marks — American Ancestry ix, 54
Orcutt's History of Stratford Ct. 1243
Richmond Va. Standard ii, 24
Temple's Hist. of N. Brookfield Mass. 680
Tuttle Genealogy 269
Marquand — Am. Ancestry v, 169; ix, 142
Marquart — American Ancestry ii, 79
Marquis — Durant's Lawrence Co. 182
Marr — American Ancestry vii, 186
Ridlon's Saco Valley Me. Families 903-8
Marrett — Dunster Genealogy 66-9
Hodson's Hist. of Lexington Mass. 128-30
Paige's History of Cambridge Mass. 603-5
Savage's Genealogical Dictionary iii, 153
Marriner — Sedgwick's Sharon Ct. 99
Marseilles — American Ancestry vi, 30
Marselis — Albany Collections iv, 146
Talcott's New York and N. E. Fams. 172-9

Marselisse — Roome Genealogy 203–5
Marsh — Aldrich's Walpole N. H. 319
American Ancestry i, 52; iii, 125, 138, 148; x, 64; xi, 117
Atkin's History of Hawley Mass. 49
Austin's R. I. Genealogical Dictionary 130
Baird's History of Rye N. Y. 486
Bangor Historical Magazine iv, 35–7
Barbour's My Wife and Mother, app. 22
Bass' History of Braintree Vt. 164
Benedict's History of Sutton Mass. 689–91
Cogswell's History of Henniker N. H. 643
Cogswell's Hist. of Nottingham N. H. 230
Craft's History of Whately Mass. 514–6
Dana's History of Woodstock Vt. 614–8
Daniels' History of Oxford Mass. 600
Draper's History of Spencer Mass. 233
Dwight Genealogy 841–4
Eaton's History of Thomaston Me. ii, 323
Gold's History of Cornwall Ct. 282
Hatfield's History of Elizabeth N. J. 81
Heywood's Hist. of Westminster Mass. 758
Hine's Lebanon Ct. Hist. Address 164
Hurd's History of New London Co. Ct. 514
Hyde's Hist. Address at Ware Mass. 50
Judd's History of Hadley Mass. 533–5
Lincoln's Hist. Hingham Mass. iii, 56–64
Marsh Genealogy (1886) 60 pages
Marsh Family of Hingham (1887) 230 p.
Marsh Family of Salem (1888) 283 pages
Marsh Family of Hartford (1895) 584 p.
Morse's Sherborn Mass. Settlers
Orcutt's Hist. of New Milford Ct. 726–30
Paige's History of Hardwick Mass. 418
Perkins' Old Houses of Norwich Ct. 531
Pompey N. Y. Reunion 332–4
Power's Sangamon Co. Ill. Settlers 474
Randall's Hist. Chesterfield N. H. 379–82
Savage's Genealogical Dictionary iii, 154
Sinclair Genealogy (1896) 419–21
Smith's History of Sunderland Mass. 443–7
Stiles' History of Windsor Ct. ii, 465
Temple's History of Whately Mass. 247
Tucker's History of Hartford Vt. 448–52
Wyman's Charlestown Mass. Gens. 654
Marshall — American Ancestry ii, 79; iv, 224, 237; vi, 102, 172
Austin's R. I. Genealogical Dictionary 130
Ballou's History of Milford Mass. 891
Barry's History of Framingham Mass. 320
Bond's Watertown Mass. Gens. 574–8
Calnek's History of Annapolis N. S. 542–5
Carter Family Tree of Virginia
Chute Genealogy, appendix 114–24
Cothren's Woodbury Ct. 631–3; ii, 1575
Davis' Landmarks of Plymouth Mass. 184
Eaton's History of Thomaston Me. ii, 323
Egle's Notes and Queries (1897) 178
Farrow's Hist. of Islesborough Me. 230–2
Freeman's Hist. of Cape Cod Mass. ii, 444
Futhey's History of Chester Co. Pa. 649–52
Goode Genealogy 469
Green's Kentucky Families
Guild's Stiles Genealogy 406
Hatch's History of Industry Me. 732
Haven Genealogy 28

Hayward's History of Hancock N. H. 743
Hazen's History of Billerica Mass. 95–7
Heywood's Hist. of Westminster Mass. 759
Holton's Winslow Mem. i, 103, 118–29
Howell's Hist. of Southampton N. Y. 342
Huntington's Stamford Ct. Settlers 73
Joslin's History of Poultney Vt. 306–8
Kingman's No. Bridgewater Mass. 579
Lamborn Genealogy 272
Lapham's History of Paris Me. 669
Lee Genealogy (1895) 512–4
Leonard's History of Dublin N. H. 361
Littell's Passaic Valley Genealogies 277
Little's History of Weare N. H. 1026–31
Marshall Family of Pa. (1884) 245 pages
Marshall Family of Virginia (1885) 415 p.
Marshall's Grant Ancestry 125
Meade's Old Churches of Va. i, 216, 244
Morris Genealogy (1898) 576
Morse Memorial, appendix 21
Morse's Sherborn Mass. Settlers 175
New York Gen. and Biog. Rec. xxvi, 84
Norton's History of Fitzwilliam N. H. 632
Orcutt's History of Torrington Ct. 737–9
Richmond Standard ii, 7, 32; iii, 4, 14, 16, 39; iv, 1
Savage's Genealogical Dictionary iii, 155–9
Smith's History of Delaware Co. Pa. 482
Stark's History of Dunbarton N. H. 253
Stiles' History of Windsor Ct. ii, 465–72
Sullivant Genealogy 324–34
Symmes Genealogy 131
Thomas Genealogy (1896) 323–7
Vinton's Giles Genealogy 221–3, 345–62
Walworth's Hyde Genealogy 224
Washington N. H. History 527
Wheeler's History of Newport N. H. 446
Wyman's Charlestown Mass. Gens. ii, 657
Marshfield — Morris and Flynt Ancestors (1882) 36
Morton Ancestry 144–6
Savage's Genealogical Dictionary iii, 159
Marsiglia — Baetjer's Carteret Gen. 29
Marsteller — Egle's Hist. Register i, 33
Eyerman Ancestors (1898)
Marston — Am. Anc. i, 52; iii, 158, 159, 200
Cogswell's Nottingham N. H. 425–32
Cutts Genealogy 77
Dearborn's Hist. of Parsonsfield Me. 386
Dow's History of Hampton N. H. 834–53
Eaton's Annals of Warren Me. 583
Freeman's Cape Cod Mass. i, 373; ii, 324
Howland Genealogy 304
Lapham's History of Norway Me. 547
Marston Genealogy (1873) 48 pages
Marston Genealogy (1888) 595 pages
Marston Family Chart (1898) 12x22 inches
New Eng. Hist. and Gen. Register xxvii, 291–307, 390–403; xxxix, 165
Orford N. H. Centennial 118–21
Savage's Genealogical Dictionary iii, 160
Swift's Barnstable Mass. Families ii, 219
Watson's Marston Genealogy (1873) 48 p.
Marten — Potts Genealogy (1895) 135–7
Martense — Bergen Genealogy 123
New York Gen. and Biog. Rec. viii, 62–7

Martin — Aldrich's Walpole N. H. 321
American Ancestry i, 52; ii, 78; iv, 195; vi, 167; xi, 235
Avon N. Y. Genealogical Record 26-9
Babson's History of Gloucester Mass. 115
Bass' History of Braintree Vt. 164
Bassett's History of Richmond N. H. 432
Bedford N. H. Centennial 316
Buckingham Genealogy 107-12
Champion Genealogy 90-4
Chase's History of Chester N. H. 557
Cleveland's History of Yates Co. N. Y. 482
Cochrane's Hist. Francest'n N. H. 822-4
Cothren's Woodbury Ct. 620-31; ii, 1515
Daniels' History of Oxford Mass. 602
Davis' History of Wallingford Ct. 845-7
Eaton Grange 79-82
Eaton's History of Thomaston Me. ii. 324
Egle's Notes and Queries 1896 Annual, volume 130, 234-9
Futhey's History of Chester Co. Pa. 652
Guild's (Calvin) Ancestry 25
Hayward's History of Hancock N. H. 744
Heywood's Hist. Westminster Mass. 760
Hough's History of Lewis Co. N. Y. 172-4
Hoyt's Salisbury Mass. Families 239-42
Hubbard's History of Springfield Vt 385-7
Hubbard's Hist. Stanstead Co. Can. 143
Joslin's History of Poultney Vt. 309
Kitchell Genealogy 59
Lapham's History of Rumford Me. 372-5
Lewis Genealogy (1893) 359-76
Littell's Passaic Valley Gens. 278
Little's History of Weare N. H. 935-7
Livermore's History of Wilton N. H. 447
Martin Genealogy (1880) 358 pages
Martin's Hist. Chester Pa. 102-5, 328-37
McKeen's History of Bradford Vt. 158-62
Meade's Old Churches of Virginia
Minor's Meriwether Genealogy 11-3
Montgomery Genealogy (1897) 62-4
Neill Family of Delaware 94-8
Neill's Virginia Carolorum 20
New Eng. Hist. Gen. Register liv, 27-31
Palmer Genealogy (1886) 65-7
Palmer and Trimble Genealogy 139-42
Power's Sangamon Co. Ill. Settlers 475
Richmond Va. Standard iii, 44
Ridlon's Saco Valley Me. Families 908-12
Salem N. Y. Book of History 61
Savage's Genealogical Dictionary iii, 161-4
Sedgwick's History of Sharon Ct. 99
Sharpless Genealogy 342
Smith Genealogy (1890) 45, 50-2
Smith's History of Dutchess Co. N. Y. 248
Stearns' Hist. of Ashburnham Mass. 809
Temple's Hist. of N. Brookfield Mass. 680
Washington N. H. History 527
Welles' American Family Antiquity iii, 61-107
Wheeler's Hist. of N. Carolina ii, 182, 405
Whitmore's Copps Hill Epitaphs
Wyman's Charlestown Mass. Gens. ii, 658
Young's Hist. Chautauqua Co. N. Y. 451
Young's History of Warsaw N. Y. 294
Young's History of Wayne Co. Ind. 350

Martindale — Davis' Bucks Co. Pa. 231
Martindale's Hist. of Byberry Pa. 319-26
Nash Genealogy 80-4
Martins — Clute's Staten Island 404
Martinus — Chambers' Early Germans of N. J. 447, 584
Martling — Clute's Staten Island 403
Raymond's Tarrytown Monument 162-5
Martyn — Allen's Worcester Mass. 63
Wentworth Genealogy 116
Martz — Heffner Genealogy 37-9
Marvel — See under Marble
Marvin — Am. Anc. i, 52; iii, 311; iv, 25
Barlow Genealogy 223-7
Daniels' History of Oxford Mass. 602
Hall's Norwalk Ct. Records 181-285
Hinman's Connecticut Settlers (1846)
Marvin Genealogy (1848) 36 pages
New Eng. Hist. and Gen. Reg. xvi, 235-54; xxxi, 212; xxxii, 82; li, 330
Porter's Hartford Ct. Settlers 12
Salisbury's Family Hist. (1892) iii, 77, 213
Savage's Genealogical Dictionary, 164
Sedgwick's History of Sharon Ct. 99
Selleck's Norwalk Ct. (1896) 150-3, 371
Talcott's Genealogical Notes 592-609
Walworth's Hyde Genealogy 567, 795
Young's Hist. Chautauqua Co. N. Y. 367
Marye — American Ancestry ix, 173
Meade's Old Churches of Virginia
Richmond Va. Standard ii, 34
Virginia Hist. Society Colls. v, 183-191
Mascarene — Heraldic Journal ii, 125
N. E. Hist. Gen. Reg. ix, 239-47; x, 143-8
Maskell — Ewing Genealogy (1858)
Mason — Adams' Haven Gen. pt. ii, 16
Aldrich's History of Walpole N. H. 322-5
American Ancestry iv, 31, 143, 188; v, 115; vi, 164; ix, 70; x, 62
Ammidown Genealogy 47
Ayer (James) Biography (1892)
Ballou's History of Milford Mass. 892
Bangor Me. Historical Magazine ii, 238
Bemis' History of Marlboro N. H. 564-71
Bond's Watertown Mass. 356-64, 855-7
Bridgeman's Granary Burial Ground 148
Bulkley's Brown Memorial 84
Campbell's History of Virginia 648-50
Carter Family Tree of Virginia
Caulkins' History of Norwalk Ct. 146-8
Chandler Genealogy 41, 140
Corliss' North Yarmouth Me. 1047-52
Dow's History of Hampton N. H. 854-7
Draper's History of Spencer Mass. 230
Dunster Genealogy 300-4
Ely Genealogy 271-3
Goode Genealogy 236
Hanson's Old Kent Md. 269
Harris' Ancestors of W. C. Harris
Hatch's History of Industry Me. 732-4
Hayden's Virginia Genealogies 109
Hayward's History of Hancock N. H. 745
Hill's Dedham Mass. Records i
Hines' Lebanon Ct. Hist. Address 165
Hudson's History of Lexington Mass. 131
Hurd's Hist. New London Co. Ct. 527-9

Jackson's History of Newton Mass. 364
Jameson's History of Medway Mass. 500-2
Lapham's History of Bethel Me. 585-90
Lapham's History of Paris Me. 671
Lee Genealogy (1895) 410-2
Leonard's History of Dublin N. Y. 363-70
Livermore's History of Wilton N. H. 447
Mason (Capt. John) Memoirs 33-43
Mason Family of Roxbury (1891) 39 pages
Mason Family of Pittsburg (1892) 15 pages
Mason Family of Swansea (1897) 122 pages
Mason Family of Pittsburg (1898) 16 pages
Meade's Old Churches of Va. ii, 229
Merrill's History of Acworth N. H. 240
Morse Memorial, appendix 43
Morse's Sherborn Mass. Settlers 175
N. Eng. Hist. and Gen. Reg. xv, 117-22,
  217-24, 318-20; xvii, 39-42, 214-9;
  xviii, 245-57
Norton's History of Fitzwilliam N. H. 633
Page Genealogy 242
Paige's History of Cambridge Mass. 605-8
Paxton's Marshall Genealogy 327
Perkins' Old Houses of Norwich Ct. 533-5
Power's Sangamon Co. Ill. Settlers 476-8
Read's History of Swanzey N. H. 401-3
Runnel's Hist. Sanbornton N. H. 477-81
Savage's Genealogical Dict. iii, 166-70
Schroeder's Boardman Memorial 561-71
Shourd's Fenwick Colony N. J. 150-2
Southern Bivouac (1886) 727
Spark's Am. Biog. 2d series iii, 435-8
Stiles' History of Windsor Ct. ii, 472-5
Symmes Genealogy 69
Temple's History of Northfield Mass. 491
Temple's History of Palmer Mass. 516-8
Virginia Magazine of Hist. iv (1896) 83-5
Ward's History of Shrewsbury Mass. 376
Wyman's Charlestown Mass. Gens. ii, 659
Young's History of Wayne Co. Ind. 286
Masser — Egle's Queries (1897) 190
Massey — Dwight's Strong Genealogy 637
Penn. Mag. of History and Biog. vii, 473
Smith's History of Delaware Co. Pa. 483
Massie — Capell Genealogy 376-9
Goode Genealogy 478
Meade's Old Churches of Virginia ii, 238
Power's Sangamon Co. Ill. Settlers 478
Richmond Va. Standard iii, 8, 27, 31
Watkins Genealogy 29
Mast — Hertzler Genealogy 239
Masten — N. Y. Gen. Rec. xx, 171-5
Master — Kriebel's Schwenkfelders 92-8
Masterman — Dowse Gen. 60-4, 104-20,
  203-32
Masters — Bond's Watertown 364
Paige's History of Cambridge Mass. 609
Mastin — Worthen's Sutton N. H. 817-20
Matheny — Power's Sangamon 476-8
Mather — Alden's Am. Epitaphs i, 120-8
Am. Ancestry i, 53; ii, 79; viii, 4; ix, 103
Andrews' New Britain Ct. 148, 176, 203
Blake's History of Hamden Ct. 263
Crafts' History of Whately Mass. 516-8
Dorr Genealogy
Goodwin's Genealogical Notes 150-6

Hall's Genealogical Notes (1886) 101-3, 106
Hayward's History of Hancock N. H. 745
Huntington's Stamford Ct. Settlers 74
Lamb's History of New York city i, 339
Marshall's Grant Ancestry 125-8
Martin's History of Chester Pa. 171
Marvin Genealogy (1848) 34-6
Mather Genealogy (1848) 76 pages
Mather Genealogy (1890) 540 pages
Mather's Magnalia i, 12
New Eng. Hist. and Gen. Register v. 460;
  vi, 20; xlvii, 171-85; xlix, 29-34
Phœnix's Whitney Genealogy i, 759
Power's Sangamon Co. Ill. Settlers 510-2
Savage's Genealogical Dictionary iii, 171-5
Sheldon's History of Deerfield Mass. 238
Stiles' History of Windsor Ct. ii, 482-92
Temple's History of Whately Mass. 247
Walworth's Hyde Genealogy 173, 585-7
Washington N. H. History 528
Mathes — Folsom Genealogy 168
Mathew — Hemenway's Vt. Gaz. v, 445
Mathews — American Ancestry iv, 74; ix,
  144; xii, 3
Cregar's White Genealogy
Strong Genealogy 654-61
Thomas Genealogy (1884) 41-5
Waddell's Annals of Augusta Co. Va. 190
Wm. and Mary College Quar. vi, 91-3
Mathewson — Austin's R. I. Dict. 131
Merrill's History of Acworth N. H. 241
Ransom Genealogy 60
Mathias — Everhart Genealogy 101
Matlack — Clement's Newtown N. J.
Matson — American Ancestry v, 30; xii, 32
Brown's West Simsbury Ct. Settlers 90
Buck's History of Montgomery Co. Pa. 26
Buck Genealogy (1894) 32-52
Collin's History of Hillsdale N. Y. 94
Savage's Genealogical Dictionary iii, 175
Walworth's Hyde Genealogy 164
Matteson — Austin's R. I. Dict. 132
Cogswell Genealogy 415-7
Williams' History of Danby Vt. 294
Matthews — Am. Anc. vi, 126, 138; vii, 23
Anderson's Waterbury Ct. i, app. 87
Barry's History of Framington Mass. 321
Bemis' History of Marlboro N. H. 571
Clement's Newtown N. J. Settlers
Cogswell's History of Henniker N. H. 644
Eaton's Annals of Warren Me. 584
Eaton's History of Thomaston Me. ii, 326
Freeman's Cape Cod ii, 180-2, 214-6, 225
Gilmer's Georgians 73
Hayward's Hist. of Hancock N. H. 746-56
Herrick's History of Gardner Mass. 367
Hudson's Hist. of Marlborough Mass. 412
Lane Genealogy (1899) 48
Lapham's History of Paris Me. 672
Matthews and Denman Family (1897) 16 p.
Meade's Old Churches of Virginia
N. E. Hist. Gen. Reg. vii, 257; xxxix, 73
Peyton's History of Augusta Co. Va. 317
Power's Sangamon Co. Ill. Settlers 481-3
Read's History of Swanzey N. H. 403
Savage's Genealogical Dictionary iii, 176

Stanton Genealogy 266
Stearns' History of Ashburnham Mass. 809
Temple's Hist. of N. Brookfield Mass. 681
Timlow's Southington Ct. Sketches 167-9
Mattison — Walworth's Hyde Gen. 543
Mattock — Wheeler's North Car. ii, 158
Mattoon — American Ancestry ii, 79
Davis' History of Wallingford Ct. 847
Judd's History of Hadley Mass. 535
Savage's Genealogical Dictionary iii, 177
Temple's History of Northfield Mass. 491-5
Matts — Davis' Hist. of Bucks Co Pa. 463
Mauldin — Johnson's Cecil Co. Md. 510
Maule — Maule Genealogy (1868) 15 pages
Walker Genealogy (1896) 89
Maun — Bass' Hist. of Braintree Vt. 165
Maupin — Richmond Standard i, 24; ii,
   26; iii, 27
Mauran — Mauran Genealogy (1893) 171 p.
Maury — Goode Genealogy 216-8
Lewis Genealogy (1893) 86, 300
Mowry Genealogy
Meade's Old Families of Va. i, 465; ii, 44
Saunders' Alabama Settlers 297-309
Slaughter's Fry Genealogy 68
Taylor's Some Notable Families 94
Virginia Hist. Society Coll. v, (1886) 123-35
Maverick — Maverick Gen. (1894) 8 pages
N. E. Hist. and Gen. Reg. xlviii, 207-9
Savage's Genealogical Dict. iii, 179-82
Sumner's Hist. of E. Boston Mass. 161-77
Titcomb's New Eng. People 244-55
Wyman's Charlestown Mass. Gens. 661
Mavey — Eaton's Warren Me. 414
Eaton's History of Thomaston Me. ii, 326
Mawney — R. I. Hist. Soc. Colls. iii, 314
Mawry — Narr. Hist. Register vi, 81
Slaughter's Fry Memoir 68
Maxam — Sedgwick's Sharon Ct. 100
Maxcy — Daggett's Attleborough 92
Eaton's Annals of Warren Me. 585
Power's Sangamon Co. Ill. Settlers 484
Sibley's History of Union Me. 469
Maxfield — Hoyt's Salisbury 242
Maxim — Davis' Landmarks 185
Lapham's History of Paris Me. 673-6
Sinclair Genealogy 190
Maxson — Austin's R. I. Dictionary 342
Aylsworth Genealogy 477-9
Cope Genealogy 80, 179
Dickinson Genealogy (1896) 152-5
Greene Genealogy (1894)
Narragansett Historical Reg. i, 140-3
Maxwell — American Ancestry xii, 60
Cunnabell Genealogy 51
Littell's Passaic Valley Genealogies 279-81
Maine Hist. and Gen. Rec. iv, 263-6
Maxwell Genealogy (1895) 85 pages
Phœnix Genealogy 17
Power's Sangamon Co. Ill. Settlers 481-3
Smith's History of Sunderland Mass. 447
Temple's History of Palmer Mass. 515
May — American Ancestry iii, 88
Barrus' History of Goshen Mass. 153-5
Child Genealogy 418-21
May's Journey to Ohio in 1788, 7-11

Davis' Landmarks of Plymouth Mass. 184
Draper's History of Spencer Mass. 232
Futhey's History of Chester Co. Pa. 654
Hayward's History of Gilsum N. H. 361
Hayward's History of Hancock N. H. 756-8
Heywood's Hist. of Westminster Mass. 762
May Genealogy (1878) 210 pages
Morris Genealogy (1894) 35
Morris and Flynt Ancestors (1882) 22
Norton's History of Fitzwilliam N. H. 633
Peirce Genealogy (1894)
Savage's Genealogical Dictionary iii, 183
Slaughter's Bristol Parish Va. 187-94
Stearns' Hist. of Ashburnham Mass. 800
Stiles' History of Windsor Ct. ii, 492
Temple's Hist. of N. Brookfield Mass. 682
Walker Genealogy 25
Washington N. H. History 529
Mayberry — Chute Gen., app. 124-7
Mayer — Egle's Notes (1898) 129
Keim Family i, 79, 235
Mayer Family (1878) 179 pages
Mayes — American Ancestry x, 189
Egle's Penn. Genealogies 569-70
Mayhew — American Ancestry x, 106
Ballou's History of Milford Mass. 894-7
Bangor Me. Historical Magazine vii, 176
Barry's History of Framingham Mass. 322
Bond's Watertown Mass. Gens. 364
Caulkin's History of New London Ct. 336
Dennysville Me. Centennial 110
Kellogg's White Genealogy 67
Lincoln's Hist. of Hingham Mass. iii, 66
Savage's Genealogical Dic.ionary iii, 184
See also under Mayo
Maynard — Aldrich's Walpole N. H. 325
American Ancestry ix, 101, 224; xi, 116
Ballou's History of Milford Mass. 897
Barry's Hist. of Framingham Mass. 322-5
Bemis' History of Marlboro N. H. 572
Caulkins' History of New London Ct. 354
Cogswell Genealogy 145
Daniels' History of Oxford Mass. 602
Goode Genealogy 209
Hayward's History of Gilsum N. H. 362-4
Hayward's History of Hancock N. H. 758
Heywood's Hist. Westminster Mass. 762
Hudson's Hist. of Marlboro' Mass. 413-6
Humphreys Genealogy 425
New Eng. Hist. and Gen. Reg. lii, 337-9
Norton's History of Fitzwilliam N. H. 633
Rice Genealogy
Savage's Genealogical Dictionary iii, 185
Stearns' Hist. Ashburnham Mass. 810-4
Temple's Hist. Framingham Mass. 634-6
Ward's Hist. of Shrewsbury Mass. 358-65
Mayo — Am. Anc. v, 28; vi, 47; xi, 109
Daniels' History of Oxford Mass. 603
Davis Genealogy 14, 58
Davis' Landmarks of Plymouth Mass. 185
Foster Genealogy (1889) 61-3
Freeman's Cape Cod Mass. ii, 358-89, 757
Heywood's Hist. of Westminster Mass. 763
Mallmann's Shelter Island N. Y. 316-21
Meade's Old Churches of Virginia
Merrill's History of Acworth N. H. 242

Paige's History of Hardwick Mass. 420
Pratt's History of Eastham Mass. 23
Preble Genealogy 259
Rich's History of Truro Mass. 543
Savage's Genealogical Dictionary iii, 186-9
Swift's Barnstable Families ii, 220-2
See also under Mayhew
McAdams — Morrison's Windham 625-7
Washington N. H. History 530
McAffee — Bedford N. H. Centennial 314
McAllister — American Ancestry viii, 64
Bemis' History of Marlboro N. H. 573-7
Cochrane's History of Antrim N. H. 581-9
Coggswell's Hist. New Boston N. H. 386
Eaton's History of Thomaston Me. ii, 315
Jolliffe Genealogy (1893) 100
McAllister Genealogy (1898) 200 pages
Pierce's History of Gorham Me. 186-8
McAlpine — Green's Kentucky Families
McAlvin — Cochrane's Francestown 824-6
McArthur — American Ancestry ii, 76
McCabe — Jennings Genealogy (1899)
McCaine — Cochrane's Francestown 826-8
McCall — American Ancestry iii, 193
Balch's Provincial Papers of Penn. 80-9
Hurd's Hist. of New London Co. Ct. 526
McCall Family (1884), 4 pages
Pa. Mag. of Hist. and Biography v.339-42,
    451-61; vi, 106-10, 207-16, 329-41
Strong Genealogy 788
Wright's Williams Genealogy 28, 46-8
McCalla — Egle's Notes (1897) 204
McCalley — Stark's Dunbarton 232
McCallom — Coggswell's N. Boston 411
McCallum — Eaton's Warren Me. 578
McCalmont — Egle's Notes and Queries
    (1897) 9-11
McCarty — American Ancestry i, 54
Lincoln's Hist. of Hingham Mass. iii, 66
Meade's Old Churches of Virginia
Richmond Va. Standard iii, 44
Saunders' Alabama Settlers 400-7
McCauley — Cochrane's Antrim 589-91
McCausland — Hanson's Gardiner 69
McClanahan — Paxton's Marshall Gen.
McClanathan — Temple's Palmer 510
McClarty — Green's Kentucky Families
Hayden's Virginia Genealogies 85-91
McClary — Cochrane's Antrim 591
Coggswell's Nottingham N. H. 217-25
Hubbard's History Stanstead Co. Canada
    179
Morrison's Hist. Windham N. H. 627-9
McClaughry — Salem N. Y. Book 62
McClellan — Am. Ancestry ii, 76; iii, 35
Benedict's History of Sutton Mass. 693-7
Chandler Genealogy 272
Morrison Genealogy 403
Pierce's History of Gorham Me. 189-93
Pierce's History of Grafton Mass. 531
Tuttle Genealogy 529
McClelland — Cabell Genealogy 341-54
Marshall Genealogy (1884) 133, 141-9
McClelland Genealogy (1882) 21 pages
Power's Sangamon Co. Ill. Settlers 493
McClento — Chase's Chester N. H. 558

McClintock — Granite Monthly of Con-
    cord N. H. ix, 191-4
Temple's History of Palmer Mass. 511
McClourge — Hayward's Hancock 759
McClung — American Ancestry iv, 56
Green's Kentucky Families
Johnston Genealogy (1897) 143-9, 167-9
Paxton's Marshall Gen. 74-6, 170-8, 280-2
Richmond Va. Standard iii, 5
McClure — American Ancestry vii, 45
Cochrane's History of Antrim N. H. 592-4
Eaton's History of Candia N. H. 89
Egle's Notes and Queries 3d ser. i, 498-500;
    3d ser. ii, 487; (1898) 102, 119
Fullonton's Hist. Raymond N. H. 253-6
Green's Kentucky Families
Merrill's History of Acworth N. H. 242-4
Richmond Va. Standrd iii, 7
Ross and Highland Counties Ohio 415
Secomb's History of Amherst N. H. 683
Stiles' History of Windsor Ct. ii, 475
McCobb — Denny Genealogy 203-5
Hoar Family Lineage (1898) 43-6
Rogers Genealogy (1897) 12-4, 32-7
Thomas Genealogy (1896) 442
McCollum — American Ancestry x, 181
Miller's Colchester 247
Parker's History of Londonderry N. H. 283
Strong Genealogy 932-4
McComas — Power's Sangamon Ill. 494
McComb — Marshall Genealogy (1884) 71-9
McConnell — Am. Anc. iii, 196; xii, 40
Butler Genealogy (1888) 119
Chute Genealogy, Appendix 105-11
Crumline's Washington Co. Pa. 718-20
Egle's Penn. Genealogies 206-8
Hubbard's Stanstead Co. Canada 272
Lewis Genealogy (1893) 75-8
Power's Sangamon Co. Ill. Settlers 490-2
McConihe — Strong Genealogy 1339-42
McCool — Nevius Genealogy
McCord — American Ancestry vi, 183
Egle's Penn. Genealogies 2d ed. 615
Robinson Memorial (1867)
Wakefield Genealogy 79
McCorkell — Howell's Southampton
McCormick — Am. Anc. x, 193; xi, 232
Calnek's History of Annapolis N. S. 545
Egle's Penn. Genealogies 2d ed. 440-7
Hayden's Weitzel Genealogy (1883) 60
McCormick Genealogy (1896) 490 pages
Palmer and Trimble Genealogy
Power's Sangamon Co. Ill. Settlers 486
McCoun — Dwight Genealogy 1101-3
McCoy — American Ancestry xi, 130
Cochrane's Antrim 594-6
Hayward's History of Gilsum N. H. 364
Morrison's Hist. Windham N. H. 629-31
Power's Sangamon Ill. Settlers 487-90
Smith's Hist. Petersborough N. H. 140-2
McCreary — McCreary Genealogy
McCrillis — McCrillis Gen. (1882) 42 p.
Thompson's Memoir of Eben Thompson
McCue — Peyton's Augusta County Va.
McCulloch — Am. Anc. i, 54; viii, 122
Bourne's History of Wells Me. 769

Cabell Genealogy 174, 282–300
McRee's Life of Judge Iredell i, 4–6
McCullough — McCullough Genealogy
McCune — Power's Sangamon Ill. 495
McCurdy — Hyde Genealogy 746–54
Salisbury's Family Histories (1892) i, 1–170
McDaniel — Power's Sangamon 496–8
Williams' History of Danby Vt. 197–203
McDaniels — Andrews Gen. (1890) 125–8
McDonald — Eaton's Thomaston 317
Pearson's Schenectady N. Y. Settlers 108
Pierce's History of Gorham Me. 189
Power's Sangamon Co. Ill. Settlers 498
Richmond Va. Standard iv, 3
Roome Genealogy 290
McDonogh — Wentworth Genealogy i, 517
McDormand — Calnek's Annapolis 547
McDougal — Lindsay Genealogy
McDougall — Navarre Genealogy 280–6
McDowell — American Ancestry vi, 10
Cleveland's History of Yates Co. N. Y.
148
Green's Kentucky Families
Honeyman's Our Home Magazine 257–63
Keith's Harrison Ancestry 67–71
Lewis Genealogy (1893) 306–9
Paxton's Marshall Genealogy 60–8
Peyton's History of Augusta Co. Va. 302
Preston Genealogy (1870) 36–9
Richmond Va. Standard ii, 7; iii, 2
Scott Genealogy (1895) 45
Sullivant Genealogy (1874) 193–7, 295–321
Temple's History of Palmer Mass. 516
Waddell's Annals of Augusta Co. Va. 399
Wheeler's Hist. of N. Carolina 57, 61,
249
McDuffees — McKeen's Bradford 234–7
McDuffie — American Ancestry i, 54
Chase's History of Chester N. H. 560
McElhinney — Wash. Co. Ohio 565
McElroy — McElroy Chart (1900)
McElwane — Temple's Palmer 520–2
McElwee — Clarke's Old King Wm. Co.
Va. Families
Life of Rev. Wm. Smith
McEwen — Boyd's Winchester Ct. 56–8
Orcutt's History of Stratford Ct. 1244–6
Savage's Genealogical Dictionary iii, 189
McFadden — Meginness' Jour. ii, 176–9
McFarland — Allison Genealogy 61
American Ancestry xii, 36
Ballou's History of Milford Mass. 884–6
Bangor Me. Historical Magazine viii, 111
Chase's History of Chester N. H. 562
Daniels' History of Oxford Mass. 605
Rockwood Genealogy 20–2
Salem N. Y. Book of History 63
Winsor's History of Duxbury Mass. 281
McFarlane — McFarlane Gen. (1885) 179
See Macfarlane
McFarren — Cleveland's History of Yates
Co. N. Y. 244–6
McFarren Genealogy (1880)
McGaughey — American Ancestry v, 121
Marshall Genealogy (1884) 5, 80–125
McGaw — Morrison's Windham 632

McGeehee — Gilmer's Georgians 163
Richmond Va. Standard iv, 3
Saunders' Alabama Settlers 448–54, 519–28
McGinness — Magennis Genealogy 3
McGinness Genealogy (1892) 299 pages
Power's Sangamon Co. Ill. Settlers 499
McGlathery — Bangor Hist. Mag. ix, 145
McGlathin — Davis' Landmarks 180–2
McGowan — Harris' Lancaster Pa. 393
Norton's History of Knox Co. Ohio 358
McGraw — Power's Sangamon Ill. 501
McGregor — Newport N. H. 469–71
McGregory — Longmeadow Cent. 74
McGuire — Meade's Old Fams. ii, 149
Richmond Va. Standard iii, 11
McHard — Sheldon's Deerfield 236
McHarg — American Ancestry i, 54
McHenry — Clyde's Irish Set. Pa. 99
Egle's Penn. Genealogies 672
Marshall Genealogy (1884) 138–41
McIlvaine — Carter Genealogy (1883) 105
Cochrane's History of Antrim N. H. 597–9
Cooley's Trenton N. J. Genealogies 162–7
Morrison's History of Windham N. H.
633–8
Washington N. H. History 531
McIntire — Bemis' Marlboro N. H. 577
Daniels' History of Oxford Mass. 605
Hayward's History of Hancock N. H. 759
Heywood's Hist. of Westminster Mass. 764
Stearns' Hist. of Ashburnham Mass. 814–6
McIntosh — Baillie Genealogy (1898) 68–77
Eaton's Thomaston 317
Gregg's History of Old Cheraws S. C. 89
McIntosh Genealogy (1888) 51 pages
Pearson's Schenectady N. Y. Settlers 96
Richmond Va. Standard iii, 50
McIntyre — Bass' Braintree Vt. 165
Cleveland's Hist. of Yates Co. N. Y. 703
Eaton's Annals of Warren Me. 579–81
McIver — Gregg's Old Cheraws 88
McKay — Goode Genealogy 91–3
McKay Genealogy (1895) 76 pages
McKean — Cochrane's Antrim 601–3
Currier's Castleton Vt. Epitaphs 31–3
McKean Genealogy (1890) 286 pages
Merrill's History of Acworth N. H. 244
Morrison's Hist. of Windham N. H. 638–41
Parker's Hist. Londonderry N. H. 284–9
Secomb's History of Amherst N. H. 685–7
McKee — American Ancestry x, 104
Lincoln's Hist. of Hingham Mass. iii, 67
Marshall Genealogy (1884) 9
Waddell's Annals of Augusta Co. Va. 422
McKeen — Poore Genealogy 72–4
McKellem — Richmond Standard iii, 45
McKeller — Eaton's Thomaston 318
McKelvey — American Ancestry xi, 228
Old Northwest Gen. Quarterly i, 20–8
McKenney — Eaton's Thomaston 318
Lapham's History of Paris Me. 666
Ridlon's Saco Valley Me. Families 913–23
McKenzie — Calnek's Annapolis 547
Chute Genealogy, app. 111–14
Dana's History of Woodstock Vt. 610–3
Topsfield Historical Collections (1896) ii

McKinley — Am. Anc. ix, 145, 227; xi, 96
Chase's History of Chester N. H. 563
McKinley Ancestors (1897) 46 pages
McKinney — Libby Genealogy 63
Pearson's Schenectady N. Y. Settlers 111
Power's Sangamon Co. Ill. Settlers 502–4
Ransom Genealogy 74
Sheldon's History of Deerfield Mass. 236
Stiles' History of Windsor Ct. ii, 475
McKinster — Chapman Genealogy 111
McKinstry — American Ancestry ii, 76
Ammidown Genealogy 43–5
Benedict's History of Sutton Mass. 691
New Eng. Historical and Genealogical
    Register xii, 231–7, 321–6; xiii, 39–47
McKinstry Genealogy (1858) 28 pages
McKinstry Genealogy 2d ed. (1866) 46 p.
Stiles' History of Windsor Ct. ii, 476
McKissick — American Ancestry i, 54
McKown — Johnston's Bristol Me. 386
McKnight — Daniels' Oxford Mass. 606
Goode Genealogy 300
Green's Kentucky Families
McKnight Genealogy (1889) 98 pages
Ormsby Genealogy 25
Richmond Va. Standard iii, 7
Stiles' History of Windsor Ct. ii, 477–9
McLane — Cochrane's Francestown 829–32
McLaren — McLaren Reunion (1873) 39
McLaughlin — Bedford N. H. 315
Cochrane's Hist. Francestown N. H. 832
Davis' Landmarks Plymouth Mass. 180–3
Eaton's History of Thomaston Me. ii, 319
Winsor's History of Duxbury Mass. 281
McLean — American Ancestry i, 54
Chambers' Early Germans of N. J. 584
Loomis Genealogy (1880) 596–605
Stiles' History of Windsor Ct. ii, 479–82
McLellan — Eaton's Thomaston 319
Eaton's Annals of Warren Me. 581
McLeod — Joslin's Poultney Vt. 310
McLoon — Eaton's Thomaston Me. 320
McLorinan — Cregar's White Genealogy
McMahon — Bangor Hist. Mag. v, 87
Orcutt's History of New Milford Ct. 730
Saunderson's Charlestown N. H. 474
McMaster — Cleveland's History of Yates
    County N. Y. 342–4
Cochrane's History of Antrim N. H. 603
Cochrane's Hist. Francest'n N. H. 833–8
Hayward's History of Hancock N. H. 760
Humphreys Genealogy 423
Pearson's Schenectady N. Y. Settlers 111
Temple's History of Palmer Mass. 512–5
McMath — American Ancestry xii
McMath Genealogy (1898)
McMillen — Cogswell's N. Boston 362
Saunders' Alabama Settlers 399
McMitchel — Temple's Palmer 515
McMullan — Penn. Magazine vii, 471
McMurphy — American Ancestry ix, 120,
    128, 147, 166, 235, 237, 242
Power's Sangamon Co. Ill. Settlers 504
McMurray — Power's Sangamon 505–7
Salem N. Y. Book of History 42–5
McNab — Power's Sangamon Ill. 507

McNair — American Ancestry xii, 26
Clyde's Irish Settlers of Pa. 102–5
Cushman's History of Sheepscott Me. 404
Davis' History of Bucks County Pa. 475
Egle's Penn. Genealogies 2d ed. 488–94
McNall — Brown's West Simsbury 109
McNeil — Guild's Stiles Genealogy 46–8
Lincoln's History of Hingham Mass. iii, 68
Potts Genealogy (1895) 345–56
McNeill — Cochrane's Antrim 604–6
Cogswell's New Boston N. H. 388–90
Egle's Penn. Genealogies 2d ed. 48–50
Power's Sangamon Ill. Settlers 508–10
Wyman's Charlestown Mass. Gens. 644
McNich — Boyd's Conesus N. Y. 164
McNitt — Temple's Palmer Mass. 511
McPhail — Page Genealogy 106
McPheeters — Green's Kentucky Fam.
McPherson — American Ancestry iv, 141
Welles' Washington Genealogy 248
McPhetres — Bangor Hist. Magazine 31
McPike — McPike Genealogy (1898) 181 p.
McQuesten — Bedford N. H. Centen. 316
Washington N. H. History 532–4
McQuigg — Ransom Genealogy 73
McRae — Meade's Old Churches of Va.
Richmond Va. Standard ii, 36; iii, 37
McSherry — Reily's Life of Cardinal Gib-
    bons ii, 423–33
McVay — American Ancestry ix, 21, 23
McVicar — Boyd's Conesus N. Y. 165
McVickar — Thomas Genealogy (1896) 444
Van Rensselaer's New Yorkers
McWhorter — American Ancestry iii, 219
New Jersey Hist. Soc. Proc. x, 2, 62–4
Young's History of Warsaw N. Y. 298–300
Meach — Walworth's Hyde Genealogy 611
Meacham — Adams' Fairhaven Vt.
Austin's Allied Families 173
Benton's History of Guildhall Vt. 257
Hinman's Connecticut Settlers 1st ed. 171
Humphreys Genealogy 345
Odiorne Genealogy
Power's Sangamon Co. Ill. Settlers 512–4
Savage's Genealogical Dictionary iii, 190
Stiles' History of Windsor Ct. 492
Mead — Aldrich's Walpole N. H. 326–8
American Ancestry ii, 79; v, 98; vi, 64,
    124; viii, 193–4; x, 86
Bolton's Westchester N. Y. ii, 749–52
Bond's Watertown Mass. 364–6, 857
Bouton Genealogy
Buckminster's Hastings Genealogy 30
Caverly's History of Pittsford Vt. 714
Chapman's Weeks Genealogy 147
Coggswell's Hist. Nottingham N. H. 745–7
Converse Genealogy (1897) 24–41
Heywood's Hist. of Westminster Mass. 765
Hodgman's History of Westford Mass. 461
Hudson's Hist. of Lexington Mass. 132–6
Huntington's Stamford Ct. Settlers 74
Hurd's History of Fairfield Co. Ct. 396–9
Lincoln's Hist. of Hingham Mass. iii, 69
Mead Family of Conn. (1882) 107 pages
Mead's History of Greenwich Ct. 277–94
Nevius Genealogy

Orcutt's History of New Milford Ct. 731
Randall's Hist. Chesterfield N. H. 383–91
Stickney's History of Minisink N. Y. 171
Temple's North Brookfield Mass. 683
Vinton's Giles Genealogy 464
Washington N. H. History 534–6
Whittemore's Orange N. J. 374
Wilbur's Life and Genealogy, appendix
Wyman's Charlestown Mass. Gens. ii, 663
Wyoming Historical Record ii, 75
Meade — American Anc. ix, 105; x, 110
Campbell's History of Virginia 690
Goode Genealogy 477
Meade Family of Penn. (1879) 4 pages
Meade's Old Churches of Virginia i, 291–8
N. E. Hist. and Gen. Reg. xxxviii, 107
Page Genealogy 77
Penn. Magazine of History xxiv, 242
Robertson's Pocahontas' Descendants
Savage's Genealogical Dictionary iii, 190
Southern Hist. Assoc. Pubs. under Everard
Meader — American Ancestry vi, 20
Austin's Allied Families 174
Hatch's History of Industry Me. 734–8
Wentworth Genealogy i, 162
Meads — Ridlon's Saco Valley 925
Meane — Paige's Cambridge Mass. 609
Means — American Ancestry vii, 279
Corliss' North Yarmouth Me. Magazine
Egle's Notes and Queries (1897) 42
Hayward's History of Hancock N. H. 761
Livermore's History of Wilton N. H. 449
North's History of Augusta Me. 902
Ridlon's Saco Valley Me. Families 923–5
Mears — Joslin's Hist. of Poultney Vt. 311
Keim Genealogy 400
Mears Genealogy (1873) 31 pages
Savage's Genealogical Dictionary iii, 192
Secomb's History of Amherst N. H. 689
Smith's History of Peterborough N. H. 143
Stiles' History of Windsor Ct. ii, 492
Mebie — Pearson's Schenectady 118–20
Mechem — P lmer Genealogy (1875) 371–3
Meck — Bretz Genealogy 47–51, 91–104
Medary — Jenkins' Gwynedd Pa. 384–6
Meech — Hemenway's Clarke Papers
Wallbridge Genealogy 296–307
Meeker — Hatfield's Elizabeth N. J.
Littell's Passaic Valley Genealogies 282–4
Todd's History of Redding Ct. 207
Whittemore's Orange N. J. 413
Meekins — Crafts' Whately Mass. 628
Judd's Hadley Mass. 536
Savage's Genealogical Dictionary iii, 191
Temple's History of Whately Mass. 248
Meeks — Young's Wayne Co. Ind. 351
Meeter — Palmer and Trimble Gen. 184
Megginson — Cabell Genealogy 446–52
Goode Genealogy 259–61
Robertson's Pocahontas' Descendants
Megredy — Power's Sangamon Ill. 515
Mehan — Eaton's Warren Me. 585
Mehurin — Mitchell's Bridgewater 241
Meigs — Am. Anc. iv, 50; vii, 83; ix, 102
Andrews' History of New Britain Ct. 381
Cothren's History of Woodbury Ct. ii, 1516

Holton's Winslow Genealogy i, 402
Hubbard's Hist. of Stanstead Co. Can. 146
New Eng. Hist. and Gen. Register iv, 91
Savage's Genealogical Dictionary iii, 193
Scranton Genealogy 28
Wilcoxson Genealogy (1893) 26–51
Melcher — Dow's Hampton N. H. 857
Wheeler's History of Brunswick Me. 843
Melendy — Livermore's Wilton 449
Secomb's History of Amherst N. H. 690–7
Melhuish — Bartow Genealogy 178
Melick — Mellick's Old Farm 627–713
Melius — American Ancestry i, 55; ii, 79
Mell — American Ancestry xi, 40
Mellen — Allen's Worcester Mass. 78
American Ancestry ii, 79; x, 132
Ballou's History of Milford Mass. 898–903
Barry's Hist. of Framingham Mass. 325–30
Bassett's History of Richmond N. H. 444
Bond's Watertown Mass. Gens. 857
Daniels' History of Oxford Mass. 607
Heywood's Hist. of Westminster Mass. 765
Lapham's History of Paris Me. 676
Leland Genealogy 182
Morse's Sherborne Mass. Settlers 176
Norton's Hist. of Fitzwilliam N. H. 634–7
Prentice Genealogy 177–9
Rockwood Genealogy 95–101
Savage's Genealogical Dictionary iii, 194
Temple's Hist. of N. Brookfield Mass. 684
Washington N. H. History 536
Wyman's Charlestown Mass. Gens. ii, 644
Mellick — American Ancestry iii, 99
Chambers' Early Germans of N. J. 585
Mellick's Story of An Old Farm 645–7
Mellish — Aldrich's Walpole N. H. 328
Daniels' History of Oxford Mass. 608
Pope Genealogy 314
Mellows — Savage's Gen. Dict. iii, 195
Meloon — Dearborn's Salisbury 662–6
Melory — Dawson Genealogy 67–71
Melvin — Chase's Chester N. H. 564
Densmore's Hartwell Genealogy
Leland Genealogy 75
Little's History of Weare N. H. 938
Stearns' Hist. of Ashburnham Mass. 816
Wyman's Charlestown Mass. Gens. ii, 665
Melward — Austin's Allied Families 175
Melyen — Hatfield's Elizabeth N. J. 82
Mendell — See Mandell
Mendenhall — Am. Anc. vi, 86; viii, 60
Lamborn Genealogy 277
Maris Genealogy 11, 24
Martin's History of Chester Co. Pa. 278
Mendenhall Genealogy (1865) 62 pages
Potts' Carter Genealogy 153
Sharpless Genealogy 168
Smith's History of Delaware Co. Pa. 484
Mendum — American Ancestry xii, 31
Mengel — Power's Sangamon Ill. 516
Menges — American Ancestry iii, 194
Mercer — Amer. Ancestry ii, 80; viii, 168
Carter Family Tree of Virginia
Meade's Old Churches of Virginia 205
Richmond Standard i, 14, 28; ii, 33, 35
Sharpless Genealogy 216, 340

Mercereau — Dawson Genealogy 110
Merchant — Amer. Ancestry i, 55; vi, 175
Todd's History of Redding Ct. 208
Merckly — Rupp Genealogy 175
Meredith — Cabell Genealogy 454–62
Davis' Bucks County Pa. 665
Fell Genealogy 99
Futhey's History of Chester Co. Pa. 655
Goode Genealogy 290
Meade's Old Churches of Virginia
Meredith Genealogy (1879) 7 pages
Power's Sangamon Co. Ill. Settlers 516
Richmond Va. Standard ii, 39
Sharpless Genealogy 372
Slaughter's St. Mark's Parish Va. 188
Smith's History of Delaware Co. Pa. 485
Wayne Co. Pa. Herald for Feb. 6, 1879
Mereness — American Ancestry i, 55
Meriam — Amer. Ancestry iv, 142; ix, 194
Jackson's History of Newton Mass. 367
Locke Genealogy 26, 42, 82–5
Meriam Genealogy (1888) 52 pages
Meriwether — Am. Anc. v, 164; vi, 50, 123
Gilmer's Georgians 188
Jones Genealogy (1891) 149–53
Meade's Old Churches of Virginia
Meriwether Genealogy (1892) 180 pages
Page Genealogy 162
Richmond Standard iii, 5, 24, 27, 32, 39
Taylor's Some Notable Families 82–5
Merkle — Markley Genealogy (1884) 36 p.
Merklin, Merkle and Markley Chart (1886)
Merklin — Markley Genealogy (1884) 36 p.
Merklin, Merkle and Markley Chart (1886)
Mero — Eaton's Annals of Warren Me. 586
Sibley's History of Union Me. 471
Merrell — Am. Ancestry ii, 80; x, 153
Dorland Genealogy 219–31
Poore Genealogy 271–4
Merriam — Aldrich's Walpole N. H. 331
American Ancestry iv, 87
Anderson's Waterbury Ct. i, app. 89
Bemis' History of Marlboro N. H. 578
Brown's Bedford Mass. Families 24
Daniels' History of Oxford Mass. 610–4
Hale's Lawrence Genealogy 11
Harris Genealogy (1883) 32–5, 39
Herrick's History of Gardner Mass. 368
Heywood's Hist. Westminster Mass. 766–75
Hill's History of Mason N. H. 204
Hudson's Hist. of Lexington Mass. 136–40
Lapham's History of Bethel Me. 590
Lapham's History of Norway Me. 549
Merriam Genealogy (1892) 15 pages
New Eng. Hist. and Gen. Reg. xxii, 160
Paige's History of Cambridge Mass. 609
Pierce's History of Grafton Mass. 532–7
Savage's Genealogical Dictionary iii, 197
Shattuck's History of Concord Mass. 378
Stearns' Hist. Ashburnham Mass. 817–25
Washington N. H. History 537
Wyman's Charlestown Mass. Gens. ii, 666
Merrick — American Ancestry xii
Corliss Genealogy, appendix
Eaton's History of Thomaston Me. ii, 228
Foster Genealogy (1889) 60

Freeman's Cape Cod ii, 365, 391, 507, 736
Hyde's History of Brimfield Mass. 433
Merrick Genealogy (1860) 9 pages
Randall's History of Chesterfield N. H. 391
Savage's Genealogical Dictionary iii, 198
Underwood's Pollard Genealogy
Wilbraham Mass. Centennial 301–4
Winsor's History of Duxbury Mass. 282
Merrifield — American Ancestry ii, 80
Ballou's History of Milford Mass. 903
Cleveland's Hist. of Yates Co. N. Y. 315–7
Hemenway's Vermont Gaz. v, 396, 401
Keyes' West Boylston Mass. Register 28
Morse's Sherborn Mass. Settlers 176
Norton's History of Fitzwilliam N. H. 637
Ridlon's Saco Valley Me. Families 926–39
Merrihew — Spooner Genealogy i, 428–24
Merrill — Allison Genealogy 56
American Ancestry iii, 89; x, 55; xi, 104
Anderson's Waterbury Ct. i, app. 89
Andrews' History of New Britain Ct. 226
Bangor Me. Historical Magazine v, 199
Barbour's My Wife and Mother, app. 15–21
Bouton's History of Concord N. H. 679
Bradbury's Kennebunkport Me. 262
Brown's W. Simsbury Ct. Settlers 109–11
Buxton Me. Centennial 163–7
Chase's History of Chester N. H. 565
Chase's History of Haverhill Mass. 276
Clute's Hist. of Staten Island N. Y. 405–7
Coffin's History of Newbury Mass. 309
Corliss' N. Yarmouth Me. 589–92, 1209–14
Dearborn's Hist. of Parsonsfield Me. 387
Douglas Genealogy 125
Dow's History of Hampton N. H. 858
Eaton's History of Thomaston Me. ii, 327
Emery Genealogy (1890) 67–70
French's History of Turner Me. 57
Hatch's History of Industry Me. 738
Hayward's History of Hancock N. H. 762
Heywood's Hist. of Westminster Mass. 775
Hoyt's Salisbury Mass. Families 243–8
Hubbard's Hist. Stamstead Co. Can. 193
Lapham's History of Bethel Me. 390
Lapham's History of Norway Me. 549–53
Lapham's History of Paris Me. 677–9
Little's History of Warren N. H. 555
Little's History of Weare N. H. 939
Me. Hist. and Gen. Rec. i, 192; iii, 178–81
Merrill Genealogy (1899) 20 pages
Montague Genealogy 435–7
Morrison Genealogy 99, 118
Morrison's Hist. of Windham N. H. 641–8
Nash Genealogy 48
New Eng. Hist. and Gen. Register xlv, 304
Orford N. H. Centennial 122
Paul's History of Wells Vt. 123
Phœnix's Whitney Genealogy i, 152
Poore Genealogy 86
Poore's Merrimack Valley 115, 132, 169
Redfield Genealogy 32
Ridlon's Saco Valley Me. Families 939–48
Runnel's Hist. of Sanbornton N. H. ii, 481
Savage's Genealogical Dictionary iii, 99
Secomb's History of Amherst N. H. 698
Sinclair Genealogy 401–4

Slaughter's St. Mark's Parish Va. 160
Stackpole's History of Durham Me. 218-20
Stearns' Hist. of Ashburnham Mass. 825
Thurston Genealogy (1894) 20-2
Washington N. H. History 538
Wheeler's History of Brunswick Me. 843
Winslow Genealogy ii, 830-9
Worcester's History of Hollis N. H. 381
Young's History of Warsaw N. Y. 300
See also under Merrell
Merriman—Adams Genealogy (1894) 72-85
American Ancestry ix, 194, 241
Anderson's Waterbury Ct. i, app. 90
Bontecou Genealogy 67
Davis' History of Wallingford Ct. 848-51
Hubbard's Hist. of Stanstead Co. Can. 269
Power's Sangamon Co. Ill. Settlers 517-9
Temple's History of Northfield Mass. 495-7
Timlow's Southington Ct. Sketches 169-75
Wheeler's History of Brunswick Me. 344
Merrithew — Islesborough Me. 232
Merritt — Adams' Fairhaven Vt. 432
Amer. Ancestry iii, 194; x, 192; xi, 107
Baird's History of Rye N. Y. 426-8
Bunker's Long Island Genealogies 239-48
Cleveland's History of Yates Co. N. Y. 503
Deane's History of Situate Mass. 311
Hubbard's History of Springfield Vt. 388
Paige's History of Hardwick Mass. 421
Ruttenber's Hist. Newburgh N. Y. 272-4
Ruttenber's Hist. of Orange Co. N. Y. 363
Savage's Genealogical Dictionary iii, 200
Stearns' Hist. of Ashburnham Mass. 825
Temple's History of Palmer Mass. 516
Wetmore Genealogy 249
Merriweather — Power's Sangamon
Merrow — Eaton's Reading Mass. 96
Wentworth Genealogy i, 260
Merry — Eaton's Warren Me. 586
Hatch's History of Industry Me. 741-5
Hubbard's Hist. of Stanstead Co. Can. 263
Savage's Genealogical Dictionary iii, 200
Merseilles — Hall's Trenton N. J. 241
Mersereau — American Ancestry xii
N. Y. Gen. and Biog. Record xxvii, 195-8;
xxviii, 17-24, 71-5, 125-9
Mertz — Heffner Genealogy 37-9
Parthemore Genealogy 135
Merwin — American Ancestry ii, 80
Collin's Hist. Hillsdale N. Y., app. 76-88
Hibbard's History of Goshen Ct. 493-5
Orcutt's History of New Milford Ct. 797
Savage's Genealogical Dictionary iii, 201
Merzereau — Clute's Staten Island 408-12
Meschter — Kriebel's Schwenkfelders 12-9
Meserve — American Ancestry iv, 148
Libby Genealogy 37
Machias Me. Centennial 171
Ridlon's Saco Valley Me. Families 948-56
Meservey — Eaton's Thomaston 328
Winslow Genealogy ii, 668-71
Mesick — Amer. Ancestry ii, 80; ix, 150
Mesick Genealogy (1888) 45 pages
Messer — Aldrich's Walpole N. H. 333
American Ancestry iv, 239
Bangor Me. Historical Magazine iv, 162

Corliss Genealogy
Eaton Grange (1890) 31
Sibley's History of Union Me. 472
Worthen's History of Sutton N. H. 821-4
Messerole — Cleveland's Yates Co. 312
Messimore — American Ancestry iii, 35
Messinger — W. Simsbury Ct. 112-4
Calnek's History of Annapolis N. S. 548
Chipman's Hist. of Harrington Mass. 106
Hayward's History of Hancock N. H. 762
Hubbard's History of Springfield Vt. 389
Messinger Genealogy (1863) 14 pages
Messinger Genealogy (1882) 12 p. reprint
Morse's Sherborn Mass. Settlers 177
N. E. Hist. Gen. Reg. ix, 59; xvi, 308-14
Savage's Genealogical Dictionary iii, 201
Stiles' History of Windsor Ct. ii, 493
Messler — American Ancestry iv, 161
Chambers' Early Germans of N. J. 447
Nevius Genealogy 674
Metcalf—Adams' Haven Genealogy 26, 47
Amer. Anc. iii, 181; vi, 77, 103; vii, 136
Ballou's History of Milford Mass. 905-7
Barry's Hist. of Framingham Mass. 331
Bemis' History of Marlboro N. H. 579
Blake's History of Franklin Mass. 259-62
Clarke's Kindred Genealogies (1896) 131-6
Clute's History of Staten Island N. Y. 412
Daniels' History of Oxford Mass. 614
Dedham Hist. Reg. iv, 166-70; v, 22-31
Driver Genealogy 394-432
Eaton's History of Thomaston Me. ii, 329
Freeman's Hist. of Cape Cod Mass. ii, 442
Goodwin's Genealogical Notes 157-62
Green's Kentucky Families
Hammatt Papers of Ipswich Mass. 228
Harris Genealogy (1861) 50-2
Heywood's Hist. of Westminster Mass. 775
Hill's Dedham Mass. Records i
Hyde Genealogy i, 348-54; ii, 1055-63
Jameson's History of Medway Mass. 502
Metcalf Family of Dedham (1867) 12 pages
Metcalf Family of Franklin (1894) 16 pages
N. E. Hist. Gen. Reg. vi, 171-8; xvi, 180
Read's History of Swanzey N. H. 405
Saunderson's Charlestown N. H. 476-81
Savage's Genealogical Dictionary iii, 202-4
Stearns' Hist. of Ashburnham Mass. 826-9
Stearns' History of Rindge N. H. 602-4
Tuttle Genealogy 433
Washington N. H. History 540-2
Wheeler's History of Newport N. H. 471-3
Whipple-Hill Families (1897) 87-9
Wright's Williams Genealogy 34
Metselaer — Munsell's Albany iv, 147
Talcott's N. Y. and N. E. Families 180-3
Mettler — Chambers' N. J. Germans
Mettup — Bond's Watertown 366
Mew — Austin's R. I. Gen. Dict. 133
R. I. Historical Magazine vi, 301-4
Meyer — American Ancestry viii, 37
Cole Genealogy 32-7, 84
Moyer Genealogy
Munsell's Albany Collections iv, 147
New York Gen. and Biog. Rec. ix, 3-16
Michael — American Ancestry ii, 81

Michaux — Meade's Old Fams. of Va.
Michener — Dawson Genealogy 449-51
Michenor — Futhey's Chester Pa. 656-8
Michie — Meade's Old Churches of Va.
Mickle — American Ancestry viii, 238
Clement's Newtown N. J. Settlers
New York Gen. and Biog. Rec. xxviii,
   161-5, 211-4
Mickley — American Ancestry ix, 133
Mickley Genealogy (1893) 182 pages
Micon — Meade's Old Fams. of Va. i, 405
Slaughter's Fry Genealogy 17
Middlebrook — Am. Anc. ii, 81; vii, 283
Orcutt's History of Stratford Ct. 1246-8
Schenck's History of Fairfield Ct. 395
Middlecott — Payne and Gore Gen. 12
Middleton — American Ancestry v, 192
New York Gen. and Biog. Rec. xxviii, 167,
   239-41
Mifflin — American Ancestry viii, 22
Mifflin Fam. of Mass. (1876) 63 pages
Mifflin Family of Penn. (1890) 91 pages
Morris Genealogy (1898) 490-2
Thomas Genealogy (1896) 446-9
Migeon — Orcutt's Torrington Ct. 740
Mighill — Essex Inst. Coll. xxii, 214-9
Gage's History of Rowley Mass. 447
Milburn — American Ancestry vii, 34
Milbury — Calnek's Annapolis N. S. 549
Miles — Allen's Worcester Mass. 165
American Ancestry vi, 15
Anderson's Waterbury Ct. i, app. 90
Chapman's Trowbridge Genealogy 49-51
Davis' History of Wallingford Ct. 852
Heywood's Westminster Mass. 776-82
Hibbard's History of Goshen Ct. 495-502
Hill's History of Mason N. H. 205
McKean Genealogy 126
Miles Family of Mass. (1840) 12 pages
Miles Family of Phila. (1895) 182 pages
Morris' Bontecou Genealogy 109-13
Norton's History of Fitzwilliam N. H. 638
Orcutt's History of New Milford Ct. 731
Pierce's History of Grafton Mass. 537-9
Potts' Carter Genealogy 180
Runnels' Hist. of Sanbornton N. H. ii, 482
Savage's Genealogical Dictionary iii, 206-8
Smith's History of Delaware Co. Pa. 485
Tuttle Genealogy 163
Ward's Hist. of Shrewsbury Mass. 368-70
Westminster Mass. Centennial 30
Milham — American Ancestry ii, 81
Milk — Jour. of Smith and Deane 223
Mill — Plumb's Hist. of Hanover Pa. 453
Millard — American Ancestry i, 55
Loomis Genealogy (188c) 803
Sedgwick's History of Sharon Ct. 100
Milledge — Am. Anc. vii, 242; viii, 122
Millen — Washington N. H. 542-7
Miller — Adams' Fairhaven Vt. 440-2
Am. Anc. ii, 81-6; iii, 225; iv, 63; v, 74,
   135; ix, 21, 150; x, 65, 136, 150; xi, 105
Baird's History of Rye N. Y. 428
Blake's History of Franklin Mass. 262
Blood's History of Temple N. H. 233-7
Bouton Genealogy

Bradbury's Hist. Kennebunkport Me. 263
Brown's West Simsbury Ct. Settlers 108
Calnek's History of Annapolis N. S. 550
Caulkins' History of New London Ct. 327
Chambers' Early Germans of N. J. 155-7,
   448, 590
Chase's History of Chester N. H. 565
Cleveland's History of Yates Co. N. Y. 702
Coe and Ward Memorial 40-6
Daniels' History of Oxford Mass. 614
Douglas Genealogy 96-9
Eaton's Annals of Warren Me. 587
Eaton's History of Thomaston Me. 329
Egle's Penn. Genealogies 2d ed. 495-504
Egle's Notes and Queries (1897) 132
Ely Genealogy 148-50
Essex Institute Hist. Collections xxii, 219
Fahnestock's Wolff Family 96
Foster Genealogy (1889) 122-4
Freeman's Cape Cod i, 250; ii, 182, 210-4
Futhey's History of Chester Co. Pa. 659
Green's Kentucky Families
Greene County N. Y. History 377
Guild's Stiles Genealogy 394, 488
Harris Family of New Jersey (1888) 165-76
Hayward's History of Gilsum N. H. 366
Hayward's History of Hancock N. H. 763-5
Hazen's History of Billerica Mass. 97
Hedge's Hist. East Hampton N. Y. 305-11
Hemenway's Vermont Hist. Gaz. v, 45-51,
   97-9, 129-36, 169-71, 182-4
Heywood's Westminster Mass. 782-91
Hough's History of Lewis Co. N. Y. 230
Hubbard's History of Springfield Vt. 391
Hubbard's Hist. of Stanstead Co. Can. 231
Jackson Genealogy 74-6
Jackson's History of Newton Mass. 365
Kilbourn Genealogy 131
Littell's Passaic Valley Genealogies 285-93
Machias Me. Centennial 170
Maine Hist. and Gen. Recorder viii, 238-42
Merrill's History of Acworth N. H. 246
Middlefield Ct. History
Miller and Morris Genealogy (1876) 300 p.
Miller's Colchester N. S. 15-34, 314-23
Missouri Pioneer Families 358
Munsell's Albany Collections iv, 148
N. Y. Gen. and Biog. Rec. xxvii, 141-4
Norton's History of Fitzwilliam N. H. 639
Orcutt's History of Torrington Ct. 740-2
Paige's History of Cambridge Mass. 610
Painter's Reminiscences (1871) 7
Plumb's History of Hanover Pa. 456
Potts Genealogy (1895) 245-59
Power's Sangamon Co. Ill. Settlers 520-4
Richmond Va. Standard iii, 2
Saunderson's Hist. Charlestown N. H. 482
Savage's Genealogical Dict. iii, 208-12
Sedgwick's History of Sharon Ct. 100
Shourd's Fenwick Colony N. J.
Smith's Hist. Peterborough N. H. 144-61
Stackpole's History of Durham Me. 220-2
Stearns' Hist. Ashburnham Mass. 829-37
Stiles' History of Windsor Ct. ii, 494
Temple's Hist. of No. Brookfield Mass. 68⁀
Temple's History of Northfield Mass. 497

Thurston Genealogy (1892) 419-21, 480-5
Timlow's Sketches of Southington Ct. 175
Westminster Mass. Centennial 20
Whitmore's Heraldic Journal 39, 42
Williamson's History of Belfast Me. 99
Wyman's Charlestown Mass. ii, 668-74
Zabriskie's Claverack N. Y. Church 79-87
Millerd — Loomis Genealogy (1880) 825-8
Millet — American Ancestry iii, 225
Driver Genealogy 142-50
Pickering Genealogy
Washington N. H. History 547
Millett — Am. Ancestry iv, 9, 125; vi, 34
Babson's History of Gloucester Mass. 116
Douglas Genealogy 478-80
Lapham's History of Norway Me. 553-7
Savage's Genealogical Dictionary iii, 212
Wentworth Genealogy i, 385-8
Milligan — American Ancestry x, 113
Milliken — Bangor Hist. Mag. vii, 226-9
Butler's History of Farmington Me. 530-2
Livermore's History of Wilton N. H. 450
Maine Hist. and Gen. Recorder iii, 121
Norton's History of Fitzwilliam N. H. 640
Ridlon's Saco Valley Me. Families 956-1069
Millington — Stiles' Windsor ii, 493
Millis — American Ancestry i, 55
Jameson's History of Medway Mass. 503
Mills — American Ancestry iii, 208; iv,
185; x, 186; xi. 196, 207; xii, 41
Andrews' History of New Britain Ct. 355
Benedict's History of Sutton Mass. 697
Brown's W. Simsbury Ct. Settlers 91-104
Calnek's History of Annapolis N. S. 551
Caverley's History of Pittsford Vt. 715
Chase's History of Chester N. H. 566
Damon Genealogy 127-30
Davis Genealogy (1888) 121-31
Eaton's History of Thomaston Me. ii, 330
Goodwin Family of Maine (1898) 20-4
Goodwin's Foote Genealogy 135
Harris Genealogy (1878) 87-9
Hayward's History of Hancock N. H. 766
Heywood's Hist. of Westminster Mass. 791
Hill's Dedham Mass. Records i
Hudson's History of Lexington Mass. 140
Humphrey Genealogy
Huntington's Stamford Ct. Settlers 75
Lapham's History of Bethel Me. 591
Lapham's History of Woodstock Me. 273
Mills Family of N. H. (1893) 32 pages
Mills Genealogy (1896) 36 pages
Orcutt's History of Stratford Ct. 1248
Orcutt's History of Torrington Ct. 742
Power's Sangamon Co. Ill. Settlers 524
Robinson's Genealogy, appendix (1859
Savage's Genealogical Dictionary iii, 213-5
Secomb's History of Amherst N. H. 698
Sprague's Hist. of Gloversville N. Y. 124
Stark's History of Dunbarton N. H. 212
Stickney's Hist. of Minisink N. Y. 138, 158
Stiles' History of Windsor Ct. ii, 494-500
Titcomb's New Eng. People 92
Turner's Hist. Phelps Purchase N. Y. 351
Vinton Genealogy 341-4
Washington N. H. History 548

Winchell Genealogy 250
Wyman's Charlestown Mass. Gens. ii, 674
Milner — Calnek's Annapolis N. S. 551
Cope Genealogy 58, 135-7
Penn. Mag. of Hist. and Biog. iv, 343-7
Miltimore — Cochrane's Antrim 607
Minard — Leland Genealogy 60
Miner — American Ancestry v, 54, 174
Boyd's Annals of Winchester Ct. 124
Burleigh's Guild Genealogy 93, 95
Douglas Genealogy 172
Frisbie's History of Middlebury Vt. 26-8
Goode Genealogy 173
Hemingway Genealogy 13-8
Matthews' History of Cornwall Vt. 287
Meade's Old Churches of Virginia
Miner Genealogy (1860) 8 pages reprint
New Eng. Hist. and Gen. Reg. xiii, 161-4
Paxton's Marshall Genealogy 222
Perkins' Old Houses of Norwich Ct. 536
Savage's Genealogical Dictionary iii, 215
Stonington Ct. Bi-Centennial 294
Temple's History of Northfield Mass. 498
Whitmore's Heraldic Journal i, 168-76
Mingael — Albany Colls. iv, 148
Ming — Chambers' N. J. Germans 449
Minge — Carter Family Tree
Meade's Old Churches of Virginia
Richmond Va. Standard ii, 32
Minitree — Richmond Va. Stand. iii, 40
Minkler — American Ancestry i, 55; ii, 81
Minnich — American Ancestry x, 106
Minnick — Plumb's Hanover Pa. 453-6
Minor — American Ancestry v, 162; xii
Caulkins' History of New London Ct. 326
Cothren's Woodbury Ct. 642-57; ii, 1533
Hayden's Virginia Genealogies 371
Hollister Genealogy 555-8
Marshall's Grant Ancestry 28
Minor's Meriwether Genealogy 46-51
Orcutt's History of Stratford Ct. 1248
Orcutt's History of Wolcott Ct. 521-4
Minot — Bridgeman's Granary 284-99
Hodgman's History of Westford Mass. 461
Minot Genealogy (1897) 55 pages
N. E. Hist. Gen. Reg. i, 171-8, 256-62
Savage's Genealogical Dictionary iii, 216-8
Shattuck's History of Concord Mass. 379
Wheeler's History of Brunswick Me. 844
Minott — Heywood's Westminster 791-4
Potter's Concord Mass. Families 12
Whittemore's Orange N. J. 372
Minshall — Minshall Genealogy (1867) 8 p.
Painter's Reminiscences (1871) 4-6
Sharpless Genealogy 151
Minton — Young's Chautauqua 605
Minturn — Bartlett's Manton Gen. 143
Updyke's Narragansett Churches 131-3
Mirick — Cogswell's Henniker 646
Jackson's History of Newton Mass. 366
Temple's Hist. N. Brookfield Mass. 685
Trowbridge Genealogy 240
Mish — Egle's Lebanon County Pa. 246
Mitchel — Goode Genealogy 371
Page Genealogy
Richmond Va. Standard ii, 12; iii. 28, 44

Mitchell — Aldrich's Walpole 335
American Ancestry ii, 86; iii, 161; xi, 116, 176; xii, 34
Austin's R. I. Genealogical Dictionary 133
Bradbury's Hist. Kennebunkport Me. 264
Cochrane's Hist. Francestown N. H. 838
Corliss' North Yarmouth Me. 247-56
Cothren's Woodbury 633-42; ii, 1517-32
Cutter Genealogy 175
Davis' Landmarks of Plymouth Mass. 185
Eaton's History of Thomaston Me. ii, 331
Hanson's Old Kent Md. 119
Harris Fam. of New Jersey (1888) 8, 35-45
Hayward's History of Hancock N. H. 766
Hinchman's Nantucket Settlers 83-7
Howell's Hist. of Southampton N. Y. 342
Hubbard's History of Springfield Vt. 392
Hudson's History of Lexington Mass. 140
Johnston's Hist. of Cecil Co. Md. 495-507
Lapham's History of Norway Me. 557
Livermore's Hist. of Block Island R. I. 337
Maltby Genealogy 99
Merrill's History of Acworth N H. 246-8
Mitchell Reunion at Britain Ct. (1859) 28 p.
Mitchell Family Yarmouth Me. (1878) 9 p.
Mitchell Fam. Plymouth Mass. (1894) 32 p.
Mitchell's Hist. Bridgewater Mass. 241-7
Morrison Genealogy 142
New Eng. Hist. and Gen. Register liv, 351
Norton's History of Fitzwilliam N. H. 640
Orcutt's History of Stratford Ct. 1249
Paige's History of Cambridge Mass. 610
Paul's History of Wells Vt. 126
Poor's Merrimack Vall. Researches 85, 155
Potts Genealogy (1895) 269-75
Power's Sangamon Co. Ill. Settlers 526
Ridlon's Saco Valley Me. Families 1069
Rupp Genealogy 126-33
Salisbury's Fam. Histories (1892) i, 171-203
Savage's Genealogical Dict. iii, 219-21
Sharpe's South Britain Ct. Sketches 53-8
Sheldon's History of Deerfield Mass. 240-2
Smith's Hist. Peterborough N. H. 162-4
Stackpole's History of Durham Me. 222-4
Thompson's Long Island N. Y. 508-10
Thurston Genealogy (1892) 90
Whittemore's Orange N. J. 87
Williamson's History of Belfast Me. 100
Winsor's History of Duxbury Mass. 282
Worden Genealogy 53-8, 69-72
Wyman's Charlestown Mass. ii, 678-80
Mitcheson — Paige's Cambridge 610-2
Mitton — Austin's Allied Families 176
Mitts — Power's Sangamon Co. Ill. 526
Mix — Anderson's Waterbury Ct. i, 91
Blake's Jonathan Mix 78-98
Blake's Hamden Ct. History 263-5
Davis' History of Wallingford Ct. 853-7
Savage's Genealogical Dictionary iii, 222
Tuttle Genealogy 669-71
Mixer — Barry's Framingham 331-3
Bond's Watertown Mass. 367-70, 858
Norton's History of Fitzwilliam N. H. 641
Savage's Genealogical Dictionary iii, 223
Stearns' History of Rindge N. H. 605
Ward's History of Shrewsbury Mass. 366

Mixter — Paige's Hardwick 423, 545
Ruggles Genealogy
Spooner Genealogy i, 282
Moak — American Ancestry i, 55; iii, 218
Moelich — Mellick's Old Farm 627-713
Moffat — American Ancestry ii, 86; v, 132
Cutts Genealogy 53, 107
Moffatt — Piper Genealogy (1889) 38-40
Moffett — American Ancestry iv, 41
Green's Kentucky Families
Peyton's History of Augusta Co. Va. 302
Waddell's Annals of Augusta Co. Va. 191, 408-10
Moffitt — Daniels' Oxford Mass. 615-7
Power's Sangamon Co. Ill. Settlers 527
Young's History of Wayne Co. Pa. 352
Moger — Orcutt's Stratford Ct. 1250
Mohler — Heinecke Genealogy 71-5
Rupp Genealogy 149-51
Mol — Munsell's Albany Colls. iv, 148
Molten — American Ancestry ix, 224
Moncure — American Ancestry x, 21
Clarke's Old King Wm. Co. Va. Families
Hayden's Virginia Genealogies 423-58
Meade's Old Churches of Virginia ii, 198
Welles' Washington Genealogy 249
Monell — American Ancestry ii, 86
Monfoort — See under Montfort
Monk — Wentworth Genealogy i, 528
Monohan — Stearns' Ashburnham 831
Monroe — Bond's Watertown 370
Brown's Bedford Mass. Families 25
Green's Kentucky Families
Hollister's History of Pawlet Vt. 216
Hubbard's Hist. of Stanstead Co. Can. 243
Jameson's History of Medway Mass. 503
Norton's History of Fitzwilliam N. H. 641
Paige's History of Hardwick Mass. 424
Ransom Genealogy 68
Secomb's History of Amherst N. H. 701
Warren's History of Waterford Me. 273
Washburn's History of Livermore Me. 33-5
Washington N. H. History 548-50
Wyman's Charlestown Mass. Gens. ii, 681
Montague — American Ancestry xii
Ballou's History of Milford Mass. 908
Hubbard's Hist. of Stanstead Co. Can. 122
Judd's History of Hadley Mass. 537-40
Kellogg's White Genealogy 36, 77
Montague Family Meeting (1882) 107 pages
Montague Family of Mass. (1886) 785 pages
Montague Family of Virginia (1894) 494 p.
New Eng. Hist. and Gen. Reg. xix, 318
Savage's Genealogical Dictionary iii, 224
Smith's Hist. of Sunderland Mass. 449-69
Temple's Hist.. No. Brookfield Mass. 685
Titcomb's Early New Eng. People 268
Montayne — Riker's History of Harlem N. Y. 521-5, 574-80
Montfort — Bergen's Kings Co. 209-11
Nevius Genealogy
New York Gen. Record vii, 152-60
See also Mountfort
Montgomery American Ancestry iii, 35-6; iv, 202; vi, 123; vii, 165; xii, 61
Bass' History of Braintree Vt. 166

Eaton's Annals of Warren Me. 588
Eaton's History of Thomaston Me. ii, 332
Egle's Notes and Queries 4th ser. i, 216
Futhey's History of Chester Co. Pa. 660-2
Green's Kentucky Families
    Meginness' Biographical Annals 210
Montgomery Genealogy (1863) 158 pages
Montgomery Memorables (1866) 7 pages
Montgomery and Somerville Families of
    Ohio (1897) 112 pages
Morris Genealogy (1898) 608
New York Gen. and Biog. Rec. ii, 123-30
Penn. Magazine of Hist. and Biog. iv, 493
Rodenbough's Autumn Leaves 100-22
Strobridge Genealogy 19-22
Thomas Genealogy (1896) 463
Wagenseller Genealogy 149-56
Whitmore's Heraldic Journal ii, 63-6
Young's Hist. Chautauqua Co. N. Y. 606
Montjoy — Dunster Genealogy 169
Montour — Egle's Notes and Queries 3d
    series i, 118-27
Mooar — American Ancestry vi, 118
Cochrane's Hist. Francestown N. H. 840
Worcester's History of Hollis N. H. 382
Moody — Alden's Am. Epitaphs ii, 120
American Ancestry vii, 206; ix, 197
Bangor Me. Historical Magazine ix, 180
Chapman's Weeks Genealogy 147
Cleveland's Dummer Academy, appendix
Coffin's History of Newbury Mass. 310
Eaton's History of Thomaston Me. ii, 332
Eliot Me. Early Settlers 17-23
Emery's Newbury Mass. Reminisc. 160-2
Emery Genealogy (1890) 34, 36
Farrow's History of Islesborough Me. 234
Fogg's Eliot Me. Settlers 13, 19
Fullonton's Hist. Raymond N. H. 250-2
Hatch's History of Industry Me. 745
Hayward's History of Hancock N. H. 767
Hoyt's Salisbury Mass. Families 248-51
Judd's History of Hadley Mass. 540-3
Kimball Genealogy 85-8
Lancaster's Hist. of Gilmanton N. H. 276
Lapham's History of Bethel Me. 592
Lapham's History of Paris Me. 679
Lapham's History of Rumford Me. 376
Lapham's History of Woodstock Me. 240
Montague Genealogy 295
Moody Biographical Sketches (1847) 168 p.
Moody Family of Maine (1851) 22 pages
Moodys of Suffolk Eng. (1899) 9 pages
Nash Genealogy 109
New Eng. Hist. and Gen. Reg. iv, 179
Runnels' Hist. Sanbornton N. H. ii, 483-5
Savage's Genealogical Dictionary iii, 225-7
Temple's History of Northfield Mass. 499
Temple's History of Palmer Mass. 522
Walworth's Hyde Genealogy 180
Wentworth Genealogy i, 531
Mook — Munsell's Albany Colls. iv, 148
Moon — Austin's R. I. Gen. Dict. 133
Walker Genealogy 170
Mooney — Heinecke Genealogy 31-3
Moor — Chandler's Shirley Mass. 562-4
Coggswell's History of New Boston N. H.

Hayward's History of Hancock N. H. 767
Lapham's History of Rumford Me. 377
Miller's Hist. of Colchester Co. N. S. 126-30
Smith's History of Rhinebeck N. Y. 201
Moore — Adam's Fairhaven Vt. 443
Allison Genealogy 67-71
American Ancestry i, 56; ii, 86; iv, 126; v,
    102, 225; vi, 141; ix, 29; xi, 40, 105;
    xii, 60
Bangor Me. Historical Magazine ix, 86
Barbour's My Wife and Mother, app. 67
Barry's History of Framingham Mass. 334
Bedford N. H. Centennial 317-20
Campbell's Spotswood Family of Va. 20-3
Caulkins' History of New London Ct. 321
Chambers' Early Germans of N. J. 449
Chapman's Weeks Genealogy 45-7, 148
Chase's History of Chester N. H. 569
Cleveland's History of Yates Co. N. Y. 517
Cochrane's History of Antrim N. H. 607
Cochrane's Hist. Francest'n N. H. 841-3
Cooley's Trenton N. J Settlers 167
Crafts' History of Whately Mass. 519
Daniels' History of Oxford Mass. 618-23
Davis Genealogy 36, 122-4
Dearborn's History of Salisbury N. H. 667
Dwight Genealogy 587-91
Eaton Grange (1890) 26-8
Eaton's History of Thomaston Me. ii, 333
Egle's Notes and Queries 3d ser. ii, 455-8
Foote's History of Virginia 1st series 506
Fowler Chauncey Memorial 74
Fullonton's History of Raymond N. H. 252
Green's Kentucky Families
Griffin's Journals of Southold N. Y. 215
Hanson's History of Gardiner Me. 157
Harris' History of Lancaster Co. Pa. 399
Heywood's Hist. Westminster Mass. 794-6
Hubbard's Stanstead Co. Canada 291
Hudson's History of Lexington Mass. 140
Irish's History of Richmond R. I. 93
Jackson Genealogy 77-80, 319-22
Keyes' West Boylston Mass. Register 29
Littell's Passaic Valley Genealogies 294
Little's History of Weare N. H. 940
Livermore's History of Wilton N. H. 451
Loomis Genealogy (1880) 754-6
Maine Hist. and Gen. Records viii, 39-43,
    100-4, 146-9
Merrill's History of Acworth N. H. 248
Miller's Hist. Colchester Co. N. S. 333-8
Mitchell's Hist. of Bridgewater Mass. 248
Montague Genealogy 537-9
Moore Family of Easton Pa. (1897) chart
Moore Family of Chester Pa. (1897) 1599 p.
Moore Family of Windsor Ct. (1900) 11 p.
Morrison Genealogy 152
Morrison's Hist. Windham N. H. 649-52
New Eng. Hist. and Gen. Reg. li, 488-94
    lii, 72-5
New York Gen. and Biog. Rec. xv, 57-68
Norton's History of Fitzwilliam N. H. 642
Old Northwest Gen. Quarterly ii, 104-6
Penn. Magazine of History and Biog. i, 473
Piper Genealogy (1889) 46-8
Power's Sangamon Co. Ill. Settlers 528-30

Read's History of Swanzey N. H. 405
Reed's History of Rutland Mass. 121
Richmond Va. Standard ii, 35, 37, 49; iii, 21, 37, 38; iv, 1, 2
Riker's Annals of Newtown N. Y. 327-34
Roberts' Old Richland Pa. Families 171-3
Runnel's Sanbornton N. H. ii, 485-7
Saunders' Alabama Settlers 391-4
Savage's Genealogical Dict. iii, 227-31
Secomb's Hist. of Amherst N. H. 699-701
Sharpless Genealogy 288, 374
Shotwell Genealogy 18-24, 274-6
Slaughter's St. Mark's Parish Va. 140, 165
Smith's Hist. Peterborough N. H. 164-74
Smith, Rev. Wm., Life of (1880) ii, 541-63
Stearns' History of Ashburnham Mass. 831
Stephens Genealogy 139-43, 150-2
Stiles' History of Windsor Ct. ii, 501-6
Strong Genealogy 1077-84
Temple's Hist. N. Brookfield Mass. 686-8
Temple's History of Palmer Mass. 508-10
Temple's History of Whately Mass. 248
Thurston Genealogy (1894) 37-9
Timlow's Southington Ct. Sketches 175-9
Waddell's Annals of Augusta Co. Va. 450
Ward's Rice Genealogy 31
Welles' Washington Genealogy 231
Wheeler's N. Carolina i, 34; ii, 47, 148
Wyman's Charlestown Mass. Gens. ii, 683
Moores — Hayward's Hancock 772
Moorhead — Bean's Montgomery 599-601
Moorman — Goode Genealogy 77
Moors—Bemis' Hist. of Marlboro N. H. 581
Butler's Groton Mass. 418, 493
Hayward's Hist. Hancock N. H. 768-74
Salem Press Hist. and Gen. Rec. i, 15-8
Moran — Navarre Genealogy 298
Morancy — Clarke's King Wm. Fams.
Mordecai — Wheeler's N. Car. ii, 417
More — American Anc. viii, 223; xii, 32
Hatfield's History of Elizabeth N. J. 84
More Family Journal (1892-7) 44 pages
More Family History (1893) 409 pages
Mott Genealogy 302-4
Shourd's Fenwick Colony N. J. 538-40
Morehouse — American Ancestry vii, 7
Collamer's Genealogist 17
Howell's Hist. of Southampton N. Y. 259
Littell's Passaic Valley Genealogies 295
Morehouse Genealogy (1895) 40 pages
Orcutt's History of New Milford Ct. 732-7
Schenck's History of Fairfield Ct. 395
Todd's History of Redding Ct. 208
Morel — Bellinger Genealogy 80-5
Morell — Ellis Roxbury Mass. 124
Morey — American Ancestry ii, 87
Bolton's Westchester County N. Y. i, 238
Davis' Landmarks of Plymouth Mass. 186
Harris Genealogy (1861) 49
Lincoln's Hist. of Hingham Mass. iii, 73
Morey Genealogy (1890) 30 pages
Orford N. H. Centennial 123
Savage's Genealogical Dictionary i i, 232
Worthen's History of Sutton N. H. 824-6
Morgan — Am. Anc. iii, 36; iv, 180; xii, 74
Bolton's Westchester County N. Y. ii, 535

Carter Genealogy by Potts (1883) 34-6
Caulkins' History of New London Ct. 311
Clement's Newtown N. J. Settlers
Clute's History of Staten Island N. Y. 413
Cochrane's Hist. Francestown N. H. 843-6
Coit Genealogy 139-42
Daniels' History of Oxford Mass. 623
Davis' History of Bucks County Pa. 387
Dow's History of Hampton N. H. 859
Draper's History of Spencer Mass. 266
Egle's Notes and Queries (1897) 92
Hall's Norwalk Ct. Records 270-6, 302
Hurd's Hist. New London Co. Ct. 462-6
Hyde's History of Brimfield Mass. 433-7
Jenkins' Hist. of Gwynedd Pa. 2d ed. 410
Lancaster's Hist. of Gilmanton N. H. 277
Livermore's History of Wilton N. H. 451-3
Meade's Old Churches of Virginia ii, 302
Morgan Genealogy (1851) 16 pages
Morgan Genealogy (1869) 280 pages
N. Y. Gen. and Biog. Record xxi, 43, 112
Orcutt's History of New Milford Ct. 737
Paige's History of Hardwick Mass. 424
Paxton's Marshall Genealogy 290
Pennypacker's Phœnixville Pa. 280-2
Perkins' Old Houses of Norwich Ct. 538
Pompey N. Y. Reunion 413
Power's Sangamon Co. Ill. Settlers 530-3
Rittenhouse Genealogy (1897) 93-136
Runnels' Hist. of Sanbornton N. H. ii, 487
Savage's Genealogical Dictionary iii, 232
Temple's Hist. of Northfield Mass. 500-2
Walworth's Hyde Genealogy 520
Webster County Iowa Centennial 68
Worthen's History of Sutton N. H. 826-8
Morison — See Morrison
Morley — American Ancestry ix, 22
Savage's Genealogical Dictionary iii, 233
Morrell — American Ancestry ix, 160
Glover Genealogy 344-6
Hudson's History of Lexington Mass. 141
Riker's Annals of Newtown N. Y. 396
Morrill — Amer. Ancestry iii, 123; x, 172
Bourne's History of Wells Me. 759
Butler's History of Farmington Me. 533
Chase's History of Chester N. H. 571
Cochrane's Hist. Francestown N. H. 846
Coffin's History of Boscawen N. H. 588
Cogswell's Hist. of Henniker N. H. 651-5
Dearborn's Hist. Salisbury N. H. 668-71
Hayward's History of Hancock N. H. 775
Heywood's Hist. Westminster Mass. 796
Hoyt's Salisbury Mass. Families 251-6
Hubbard's Stanstead Co. Canada 155-65
Lancaster's Hist. of Gilmanton N. H. 277
Little's History of Weare N. H. 941
Morrill Fam. Cambridge Mass. (1886) chart
Munsell's Albany Collections iv, 148
Runnels' Sanbornton N. H. ii, 489-93
Savage's Genealogical Dictionary iii, 234
Washington N. H. History 550
Morris— American Ancestry iii, 66; iv, 243; v, 108, 172; vi, 16, 189; viii, 123; x, 5, 105, 155; xii, 33
Ammidown Genealogy 39-41
Anderson's Waterbury Ct. i, app. 92

Bolton's Westchester Co. N. Y. ii, 455
Boyd's History of Conesus N. Y. 165
Cope Genealogy 40
Dodd's History of East Haven Ct. 135-7
Dwight Genealogy 224
Hubbard's History of Springfield Vt. 394-6
Lamb's History of New York city i, 653
Lewis Genealogy (1893) 209-11
Magennis Genealogy 145
Meade's Old Churches of Virginia
Miller and Morris Genealogy (1870) 300 p.
Morris' Bontecou Genealogy 141-3
Morris Family of E. Haven (1853) 103 p.
Morris and Flynt Ancestors (1882) 74 pages
Morris Family of Woodstock (1887) 423 p.
Morris Family Ancestry (1894) 207 pages
Morris Family of Phila. (1898) 1260 pages
N. J. Hist. Society Proc. 2d ser. vii
New York Gen. and Biog. Record vii, 16
Orcutt's History of Torrington Ct. 743
Palmer and Trimble Genealogy 122-5
Paxton's Marshall Genealogy 52
Power's Sangamon Co. Ill. Settlers 533
Roberts' Old Richland Pa. Families
Savage's Genealogical Dictionary iii, 235-7
Schoonmaker's Hist. Kingston N. Y. 484
Shourd's Fenwick Colony N. J. 161-3
Smith's History of Delaware Co. Pa. 486
Stanton Genealogy 265
Thomas Genealogy (1877) 121
Thomas Genealogy (1884) 57-66
Thomas Genealogy (1896) 449-52
Walker Genealogy (1896) 85-7
White Genealogy (1879) 178-94
Whitmore's Heraldic Journal iii, 72
Wilbraham Mass. Centennial 304
Wyman's Charlestown Mass. Gens. ii, 685
Young's History of Warsaw N. Y. 304-7
Morrison — Adams Genealogy (1894) 76-9
Allison Genealogy 44-61
American Ancestry iii, 37, 177; ix, 215
Butler's History of Farmington Me. 534-6
Coffin's History of Boscawen N. H. 590
Coggswell's Hist. Henniker N. H. 655-7
Coggswell's Nottingham N. H. 747-60
Harris' History of Lancaster Co. Pa. 401
Hayward's Hist. Hancock N. H. 776-81
Leonard's Gen. of W. Smith, appendix
Miller's Hist. Colchester Co. N. S. 164-6
Morris Genealogy (1898) 814
Morrison Genealogy (1880) 468 pages
Morrison's Hist. Windham N. H. 653-85
N. E. Hist. and Gen. Reg. xlviii, 413-9
Parker's Hist. of Londonderry N. H. 289
Runnels' Sanbornton N. H. ii, 493, 527
Smith's History of Peterborough N. H. 174-207
Southern Bivouac (1886) 650
Strobridge Genealogy 159-226
Morrow — Alexander Genealogy 80-3
American Ancestry i, 56
Morrison's Hist. of Windham N. H. 685-7
Parthemore Genealogy 30, 87-90
Thurston's History of Winthrop Me. 191
Morse — Aldrich's Walpole N. H. 337-9

American Ancestry iii, 225; vi, 51; vii, 154; xi, 106, 107; xii, 103
Ammidown Genealogy 49-53
Ammidown's Historical Collections i, 377
Ballou's History of Milford Mass. 910
Bangor Me. Historical Magazine v, 200
Barry's Hist. of Framingham Mass. 335-7
Benedict's Hist. of Sutton Mass. 698-700
Blake's History of Franklin Mass. 263
Bond's Watertown Mass. 371-4, 859, 895
Calnek's History of Annapolis N. S. 552-4
Chase's History of Chester N. H. 566-9
Child Genealogy 180-5
Chute Genealogy, appendix 127-36
Cochrane's History of Antrim N. H. 609
Cochrane's Hist. Francest'n N. H. 847-51
Coffin's History of Newbury Mass. 311
Coggswell's Hist. of Henniker N. H. 658
Collin's Hist. of Hillsdale N. Y., app. 93-6
Daniels' History of Oxford Mass. 624
Davis' Landmarks of Plymouth Mass. 187
Dearborn's Hist. of Salisbury N. H. 671-5
Dows Genealogy 87-90, 172-80
Draper's History of Spencer Mass. 234
Eaton's Annals of Warren Me. 590
Eaton's History of Thomaston Me. 333-5
Hale Genealogy 135-42, 147-51
Hayward's History of Gilsum N. H. 367
Hayward's History of Hancock N. H. 781
Heywood's Hist. of Westminster Mass. 797
Hill's Dedham Mass. Records i
Hoyt's Salisbury Mass. Families 256-62
Hudson's Hist. Marlborough Mass. 416-20
Jackson's History of Newton Mass. 368
Jameson's History of Medway Mass. 504-6
Joslin's History of Poultney Vt. 312
Lapham's History of Bethel Me. 592
Lapham's History of Norway Me. 558
Lapham's History of Paris Me. 680-2
Lapham's History of Rumford Me. 378
Larned's History of Windham Co. Ct. i
Leland Genealogy 31, 77
Leonard's History of Dublin N. H. 370-6
Lincoln's Hist. of Hingham Mass. iii, 74
Little's History of Weare N. H. 942
Morris Genealogy (1887) 25, 29
Morse Genealogy (1850) 350 pages
Morse Memorials (1889) 116 pages
Morse Family Meeting (1895) 44 pages
Morse Memorials (1896) 527 pages
Morse's Sherborn Mass. Settlers 178-83
Newfane Vt. Centennial 159-72
New Hampshire Hist. Soc. Coll. vii, 331
Norton's Hist. of Fitzwilliam N. H. 642-6
Parthemore Genealogy 32-4
Pierce's History of Grafton Mass. 539
Poor's Merrimack Valley Researches 147
Preble Genealogy 258
Read's History of Swanzey N. H. 406
Salisbury Family Memorials (1885) 484-96
Savage's Genealogical Dict. iii 237-42
Sibley's History of Union Me. 475-81
Stearns' History of Rindge N. H. 607
Stone's Hist. of Hubbardston Mass. 314-7
Wakefield Genealogy 158
Ward's History of Shrewsbury Mass. 371

Warren's History of Waterford Me. 274
Wheeler's History of Brunswick Me. 844
Whitman Genealogy 750–6
Wilbur's Life and Gen. appendix
Wood Genealogy 254–6
Wyman's Charlestown Mass. Gens. ii, 686
Morson — Hayden's Virginia Gens. 654
Paxton's Marshall Genealogy 326
Wm. and Mary College Hist. Reg. ii, 87
Mortimer — Thomas Genealogy (1896) 452
Welles' Amer. Family Antiquity ii, 241–60
Morton — American Ancestry iv, 234;
 viii, 163; ix, 74, 101
Calnek's History of Annapolis N. S. 554
Clarke Genealogy (1884) 47–9
Collins Genealogy 111–3
Cogswell Genealogy 390–3
Crafts' History of Whately Mass. 521–30
Davis' Landmarks of Plymouth Mass.
 187–92
Eaton's History of Thomaston Me. 335
Hayden's Virginia Genealogies 35
Lapham's History of Paris Me. 682
Lincoln's History of Hingham Mass. iii, 75
Martin's History of Chester Pa. 142-6, 151
Meade's Old Churches of Virginia ii, 31
Mitchell's Hist. of Bridgewater Mass. 382
Morton Fam. of Hatfield Mass. (1881) 61 p.
Morton Family Ancestry (1894) 191 pages
Mourt's Relation (1623) ed. (1865) 26–30
Pierce's History of Gorham Me. 193
Plummer Genealogy (1885) 20–2
Richmond Va. Standard ii, 20; iii, 13
Savage's Genealogical Dictionary iii, 243–5
Slaughter's St. Mark's Parish 136, 173
Stearns' Hist. of Ashburnham Mass. 832
Stiles' History of Windsor Ct. ii, 506–8
Temple's History of Whately Mass. 249–53
Thatcher's History of Plymouth Mass. 147
Thurston's History of Winthrop Me. 191
Van Rensselaer's New Yorkers
Watkins Genealogy 18, 30–4
Wentworth Genealogy i, 521–4
Wyman's Charlestown Mass. Gens. ii, 687
Mosby — Goode Genealogy 219–25, 369
Meade's Old Churches of Virginia
Richmond Va. Standard iii, 14
Slaughter's St. Mark's Parish Va. 136, 173
Moseley — American Ancestry ii, 87; iii,
 152; vi, 7; vii, 53; x, 11; xii, 59
Caulkins' History of Norwich Ct. 235–7
Champion Genealogy 215
Clapp's Jones Hill Dorchester Mass. 53–8
Coggswell's Biog. Rev. S. Moseley (1883)
Cothren's Woodbury Ct. 619; ii, 1516
Meade's Old Churches of Virginia
Montague Genealogy 669–71
Moseley Genealogy (1878) 56 pages
Oneida Hist. Society Trans. ii, 80–3
Robinson Genealogy (1859)
Savage's Genealogical Dictionary iii, 178
Stiles' History of Windsor Ct. ii, 508
Strong Genealogy 1197–1202
Virginia Magazine of History v, 327–34
Walworth's Hyde Genealogy i, 644–52
Wheeler's History of N. Carolina ii, 223

Mosely — N. E. Hist. Gen. Reg. xxv, 71
Ogden Genealogy (1896) 12, 21, 41
Moses — American Ancestry iv, 52; vii,
 104, 142, 174; ix, 82
Ballou Genealogy 296–303
Brewster's Portsmouth N. H. ii, 186–8
Brown's W. Simsbury Ct. Settlers 104–8
Collin's History of Hillsdale N. Y., app. 96
Driver Genealogy 433–7
Moses Genealogy (1890) 138 pages
Peck's Rochester N. Y. Centennial 661–3
Ridlon's Saco Valley Me. Families 1070–4
Runnel's Hist. of Sanbornton N. H. ii, 527
Savage's Genealogical Dictionary iii, 245
Stiles' History of Windsor Ct. ii, 509
Mosher — American Ancestry i, 56; ix,
 215; xi, 41; xii
Austin's R. I. Genealogical Dictionary 135
Crafts' History of Whately Mass. 530
Hubbard's Hist. Stanstead Co. Can. 314
Paul's History of Wells Vt. 124
Pierce's History of Gorham Me. 194
Moshier — Corliss' N. Yarmouth Me.
Mosman — Eaton's Thomaston Me. 336
Heywood's History of Westminster Mass.
 798–803
Moss — Anderson's Waterbury Ct. i, 92
Davis' History of Wallingford Ct. 857–62
Leavenworth Genealogy 68–73
Maltby Genealogy 100
Olin Genealogy by Nye (1892) 36–40
Orcutt's History of Derby Ct. 746
Savage's Genealogical Dictionary iii, 246
Sharpless Genealogy 183
Shourd's Fenwick Colony N. J. 173–5
Tuttle Genealogy 10
See also under Morse
Mosse — Hatfield's Elizabeth N. J. 85
Mossman — Stearns' Ashburnham 833
Mosteller — Power's Sangamon 535
Motley — Driver Genealogy 514
Mott — American Ancestry i, 56; viii, 72;
 ix, 220; x, 87; xi, 195
Austin's Ancestral Dictionary 40
Austin's R. I. Gen. Dictionary 135, 344
Bolton's Westchester County N. Y. ii, 752
Boyd's Annals of Winchester Ct. 37–9
Bunker's Long Island Genealogies 252–60
Deane's History of Scituate Mass. 313
Hinchman's Nantucket Settlers 94–8
Livermore's Hist. Block Island R. I. 338
Mott Genealogy (1890) 418 pages
Mott and Hopper Families (1898) 18 p.
New Eng. Hist. and Gen. Reg. xxi, 216
N. Y. Gen. and Biog. Record xxv, 49–56
Power's Sangamon Co. Ill. Settlers 536
R. I. Hist. Magazine v, 34–6; vii, 289–93
Savage's Genealogical Dictionary iii, 247
Talcott's N. Y. and N. E. Families 610–5
Tompson's Long Island N. Y. ii, 520
Mould — Coit Genealogy 28
Moulson — Penn. Magazine x, 112–4
Moulthrop — American Ancestry viii, 10
Dodd's History of East Haven Ct. 137–9
Orcutt's History of Wolcott Ct. 525–7
Savage's Genealogical Dictionary iii, 247

Sharp's History of Seymour Ct. 224-6
Tuttle Genealogy 46
Moulton—Am. Anc. iii, 209; vi, 74; xi, 43
Bouton's History of Concord N. H. 680
Chase's History of Chester N. H. 571
Currier's Castleton Vt. Epitaphs 35-7
Daniels' History of Oxford Mass. 625
Dearborn's Hist. Parsonsfield Me. 387-9
Dearborn's History of Salisbury N. H. 675
Dow's History of Hampton N. H. 860-78
Draper's History of Spencer Mass. 233
Emery Genealogy (1890) 76, 91
Fullonton's History of Raymond N. H. 257
Hubbard's Stanstead Co. Canada 165-7
King Genealogy (1897) 43-70
Lancaster's Hist. of Gilmanton N. H. 277
Lapham's History of Bethel Me. 593
Maine Hist. and Gen. Recorder v, 1-11,
    81-9, 141-50, 193-201; vi, 263-9,
    323-32, 407-16, 454-68
Moulton Genealogy (1873) 44 pages
Moulton Genealogy (1893) 99 pages
Runnel's Hist. Sanbornton N. H. 528-32
Savage's Genealogical Dictionary iii, 248
Temple's Hist. N. Brookfield Mass. 688
Wales Mass. Centennial 11-4
Wyman's Charlestown Mass. Gens. ii, 680
Mountfort — Bridgeman's Granary Bury-
    ing Ground Boston Epitaphs 112
Savage's Genealogical Dictionary iii. 249
Vinton's Giles Genealogy 148
Whitmore's Copps Hill Epitaphs
Whitmore's Heraldic Journal ii, 80
See also Montfort
Mountjoy — Garrard Genealogy 103-7
Mourt — Mourt's Relation 26-30
Mousall — New Eng. Historical and Gen.
    Register xlvii, 462-7
Savage's Genealogical Dictionary iii, 250
Sewall's History of Woburn Mass. 71, 627
Wyman's Charlestown Mass. ii, 688-92
Mower — Cleveland's Yates Co. 377
Mower Genealogy (1897) 12 pages
Temple's Hist. of N. Brookfield Mass. 688
Wall's Reminisc. of Worcester Mass. 351
Washburn's Hist. of Leicester Mass. 384
Mowry — Am. Anc. v. 119; vi, 121; vii, 19
Austins R. I. Gen. Dictionary 346-9
Ballou's History of Milford Mass. 911
Mowry Family of R. I. (1878) 343 pages
Mowry Family of Mass. (1878) 239 pages
New Eng. Hist. and Gen. Reg. lii, 207-12
Old Northwest Gen. Quarterly ii, 1
Richardson's Woonsocket R. I. 221-4
Moyan — Bergen's Kings Co. N. Y. 211
Moyer — Moyer Genealogy (1896) 739 p.
Mudge — Bangor Historical Mag. iv, 19
Heywood's Hist. of Westminster Mass. 803
Mudge Genealogy (1865) 8 pages
Mudge Genealogy (1868) 443 pages
Phœnix's Whitney Genealogy ii, 1013
Savage's Genealogical Dictionary iii, 252
Sedgwick's History of Sharon Ct. 101
Temple's History of Northfield Mass. 503
Mudgett — Dearborn's Parsonsfield 389
Eaton's Annals of Warren Me. 590

Hoyt's Salisbury Mass. Families 262
Lancaster's History of Gilmanton N. H. 278
Little's History of Weare N. H. 943
Mueller — Egle's Lebanon Pa. 247
Muenscher — Davis Genealogy 189-91
Muhlenberg — Buck's History of Mont-
    gomery County Pa. 118-22
Chamber' Early Germans of N. J. 587-90
Harris' History of Lancaster Co. Pa. 402
Muir — American Ancestry i, 56; xi, 39
Muirhead — Cooley's Trenton 178-81
Muirheid — Guild Genealogy (1887) 48-50
Mulford — Freeman's Cape Cod 375
Hedge's Hist. East Hampton N. Y. 311-6
Kitchell Genealogy 45-7
Mulford Genealogy (1880) 12 pages reprint
New Eng. Hist. Gen. Reg. xxxiv, 171-80
Rich's History of Truro Mass. 544
Southold N Y. Record 172
Suffolk County N. Y. History 30-2
Sutliff Genealogy (1897) 15-26
Tuttle Genealogy 287-91
Mulhannan — Clyde's Irish Sett. Pa. 109
Mullens — Littell's Passaic Valley 297
Savage's Genealogical Dictionary iii, 252
Winsor's History of Duxbury Mass. 283
Muller — Egle's Pa. Gens. 2d ed. 495-504
Mellick Genealogy 683
Munsell's Albany Collections iv, 150
See also Miller
Mullett — Hemenway Genealogy 27
Wyman's Charlestown Mass. Gens. ii, 693
Mulliken — Hudson's Lexington 141-3
Vinton's Giles Genealogy 143
Mullin — Chute Genealogy, app. 105
Mullins — Quisenberry Gen. 123-6
Mullock — Poole Genealogy 140-3
Mulvey — Ridlon's Saco Valley 1075
Mulvihill — Temple's Palmer 522
Mumford — American Ancestry v, 195
Austin's R. I. Genealogical Dictionary 136
Cleveland's Hist. of Yates Co. N. Y. 406-8
Narragansett Historical Register iv, 135
Peck's Rochester N. Y. Centennial 696-8
Savage's Gen. Dictionary iii, 253, 264
Mundell — Stone's Hubbardston 318
Mundy — Mellick's An Old Farm 637
Munford — Bolling Genealogy 32
Meade's Old Churches of Virginia
Richmond Va. Standard i, 44
Slaughter's Bristol Parish Va. 194-9
Munger — Adams' Fairhaven Vt. 435
Hemenway Genealogy 64
New Eng. Hist. Gen. Register liv, 46-50
Savage's Genealogical Dictionary iii, 254
Temple's History of Palmer Mass. 517
Wales Mass. Centennial 10
Young's History of Warsaw N. Y. 307
Munjoy — Heywood's Westminster 804-6
Maine Hist. Society Collections i, 170
Savage's Genealogical Dictionary iii, 255
Munn — Baldwin Gen. Supp. 1122-4
Condit Genealogy 386-9
Cothren's History of Woodbury Ct. 618
Flint's Peters Lineage 58-60
Longmeadow Mass. Centennial 75

Savage's Genealogical Dictionary iii, 254
Shaw's Hist. of Essex Co. N. J. ii, 725-8
Sheldon's History of Deerfield Mass. 243-6
Whittemore's Orange N. J. 92, 329
Munnings — Bond's Watertown 374
Savage's Genealogical Dictionary iii, 255
Munroe — Barry's Hanover Mass. 353
Calnek's History of Annapolis N. S. 555
Cutter's History of Arlington Mass. 277
Draper's History of Spencer Mass. 231
Eaton's History of Thomaston Me. ii, 337
Hazen's History of Billerica Mass. 98
Heywood's Hist. of Westminster Mass. 806
Hudson's Hist. Lexington Mass. 144 61
Lamb's History of New York city i, 602
Locke Genealogy 36, 66-8, 123-8, 302-13
Munroe Genealogy (1853) 15 pages reprint
Muzzey's Reminiscences
New York Gen. and Biog. Rec. iv, 123
Paige's History of Cambridge Mass. 612-4
Ransom Genealogy
Savage's Genealogical Dictionary iii, 256
Spooner's Mem. of W. Spooner 93
Stearns' Hist. Ashburnham Mass. 834-40
Temple's Hist. of N. Brookfield Mass. 689
Ward's History of Shrewsbury Mass. 374
Munsell — Am. Anc. i, 56; iii, 38; x, 20
Loomis Genealogy (1880) 292-9
Munsell Genealogy (1884) 150 pages
New Eng. Hist. Gen. Reg. xxxiv, 246-51
Orcutt's History of Torrington Ct. 748
Roe's Sketches of Rose N. Y. 95
Smith's Hist. of Sunderland Mass. 472-4
Stiles' History of Windsor Ct. ii, 510-5
Strong Genealogy 878
Temple's History of Northfield Mass. 504
Munson — Anderson's Waterbury Ct. 92
Crafts' History of Whately Mass. 531-5
Davis' History of Wallingford Ct. 862-8
Machias Me. Centennial 171
Munson Family (1887) 2 pages
Munson Family Reunion (1887) 88 pages
Munson Family Address (1887) 56 pages
Munson Genealogy (1895) 1235 pages
Munson Family Reunion (1896) 43 pages
Munson Family Traditions (1897) 6 pages
New Eng. Hist. Gen. Reg. xxix, 139-41
Orcutt's History of Torrington Ct. 749
Savage's Genealogical Dictionary iii, 257
Temple's History of Whately Mass. 253
Timlow's Southington Ct. Sketches 179-81
Trowbridge Genealogy 63
Tuttle Genealogy 672
Murch — Bangor Hist. Mag viii, 112
Pierce's History of Gorham Me. 194
Murdock — Am. Anc. viii, 215; ix, 38, 162
Buckingham Genealogy 177-9
Davis' Landmarks of Plymouth Mass. 192
Egle's Notes and Queries 2d ser. ii, 42-5
Hedges' Hist. of East Hampton N. Y. 316
Heywood's Hist. of Westminster Mass. 807
Jackson's Hist. of Newton Mass. 369-71
Keyes' West Boylston Mass. Register 30
Marvin's Hist. of Winchendon Mass. 463
Salisbury's Family Histories (1892) i, 341
Stone's Hist. Hubbardston Mass. 319-21

Temple's History of Palmer Mass. 518-20
Walworth's Hyde Genealogy 168
Ward Genealogy (1851) 55
Whittemore's Hist. Middlesex Co. Ct. 574
Murdough — Washington N. H. 551
Murfee — Gregg's Old Cheraws S. C. 72
Murfree — Wheeler's N. Car. ii, 208
Murphy — Am. Anc. i, 56; iv, 216; vii, 28
Bradbury's Kennebunkport Me. 265
Lincoln's History of Hingham Mass. iii, 76
Murray — Alden's Am. Epitaphs i, 99
American Ancestry ii, 87; ix, 118
Aylsworth Genealogy 491-5
Chase's History of Chester N. H. 571
Cushman's History of Sheepscott Me. 406
Egle's Penn. Genealogies 2d ed. 505-40
Goode Genealogy 122
Green's Kentucky Families
Hanson's Old Kent Md. 267
Judd's History of Hadley Mass. 543
Orcutt's History of Torrington Ct. 744
Pearson's Schenectady N. Y. Settlers 124
Phœnix's Whitney Genealogy ii, 1812
Reed's History of Rutland Mass. 156-8
Robertson's Pocahontas' Descendants
Slaughter's Bristol Parish Va. 199-205
Murrell — Goode Genealogy
Lynchburg Sketches Va. 267-9
Richmond Va. Standard iii, 17
Musgrove — Harris' Lancaster Pa. 404
Musick — Lewis Genealogy (1893) 187-97
Missouri Pioneer Families 405
Musselman — Cassel Genealogy 64, 113-8
Parthemore Genealogy 188-91
Mussey — Savage's Gen. Dict. iii, 258
Secomb's History of Amherst N. H. 702-4
Mutcheler — Fisher Genealogy 105-8
Mutter — Richmond Standard iii, 16
Muzzey — Barry's Framingham 338
Cutter's History of Arlington Mass. 277
Daniels' History of Oxford Mass. 626
Draper's History of Spencer Mass. 227-30
Hoyt's Salisbury Mass. Families 263
Little's History of Weare N. H. 944-6
Washington N. H. History 552
Wheeler's History of Newport N. H. 475
Muzzy — American Ancestry ii, 87
Hudson's Hist. of Lexington Mass. 162-7
Morse's Mem, appendix 52
Paige's History of Cambridge Mass. 614
Stearns' History of Rindge N. H. 608
Ward's History of Shrewsbury Mass. 373
Myer — American Ancestry ii, 88; xi, 42
Banta Genealogy 21
Moyer Genealogy
Riker's History of Harlem N. Y. 525-35
Myers — Amer. Ancestry i, 56; ii, 88
Everhart Genealogy 97-101
Harvey Genealogy 994
Sinclair Genealogy 164-6
Mygate — Savage's Gen. Dict. iii, 259
Mygatt — Baldwin's Gen. supp. 1264-5
Goodwin's Genealogical Notes 163-5
Hinman's Connecticut Settlers 1st ed. 223
Mygatt Genealogy (1853) 116 pages
Orcutt's History of New Milford Ct. 738-40

Myndertse — Albany Collections iv, 149
Pearson's Schenectady Settlers 124-7
Myrick — Bond's Watertown 374, 860
Cushman's History of Sheepscott Me. 407
Savage's Genealogical Dictionary iii, 218
Mytinger — Jennings Genealogy (1899)
Nafe — Nevius Genealogy
Nafew — Nevius Genealogy
Nafle — Nevius Genealogy
Nafls — Nevius Genealogy
Nagel — Riker's Harlem N. Y. 535-9
Nagle — Clyde's Irish Settlers of Pa. 110
Keim Genealogy 401-3
Nahor — Hayward's Hancock N. H. 783
Nalle — Hayden's Virginia Gens. 730
Slaughter's St. Mark's Parish Va. 120
Naney — Savage's Gen. Dict. iii, 260
Nantz — Watkins Genealogy 20
Naphey — Nevius Genealogy
Naphis — Nevius Genealogy
Narramore — Barrus' Goshen Mass. 156
Bassett's History of Richmond N. H. 446
Savage's Genealogical Dictionary iii, 260
Nash — Amer. Ancestry ii, 88; iv, 28
Barrus' History of Goshen Mass. 157
Bliss Genealogy 650
Crafts' History of Whately Mass. 535
Deane's History of Scituate Mass. 313
Dyer's History of Plainfield Mass. 163-5
Farrow's History of Islesborough Me. 235
Hall's Hist. Norwalk Ct. 198 227, 264-73
Hayward's History of Gilsum N. H. 369
Hobart's Hist. of Abington Mass. 414-22
Hubbard's Hist. of Stanstead Co. Can. 121
Hudson's History of Lexington Mass. 167
Jones' History of Stockbridge Mass. 151
Judd's History of Hadley Mass. 543-9
Lincoln's Hist. of Hingham Mass. iii, 78
Maine Hist. Magazine viii, 155-62
Meade's Old Churches of Virginia
Nash Genealogy (1850) 17 pages
Nash Genealogy (1853) 304 pages
Randall's History of Chesterfield N. H. 393
Savage's Genealogical Dictionary iii, 260-3
Schenck's History of Fairfield Ct. 396-8
Selleck's Norwalk Ct. (1896) 104-12
Steele Genealogy (1896)
Stiles' History of Windsor Ct. 515
Temple's History of Whately Mass. 254
Wheeler's History of North Carolina ii, 1
Winsor's History of Duxbury Mass. 284
Wyman's Charlestown Mass. Gens. ii, 695
Nason — Bradbury's Kennebunkport
Bemis' History of Marlboro N. H. 582
Buxton Me. Centennial 206
Dow's History of Hampton N. H. 878
Hazen's History of Billerica Mass. 99
Jordan's Leighton Genealogy (1885)
Little's History of Weare N. H. 946
Nason Genealogy (1859) 8 pages
New Eng. Hist. and Gen. Reg. xvi, 182
North's History of Augusta Me. 902-6
Old Eliot Me. Monthly iii, (1899) 44
Pierce's History of Gorham Me. 195
Ridlon's Saco Valley Me. Families 1075-8
Savage's Genealogical Dictionary iii, 263

Trask's Elias Nason Memoir 36 pages
Nathan — American Ancestry v, 113
Naughtright — Chambers' N. J. 590
Navarre — Hall Genealogy (1892) 75-86
Navarre Genealogy (1897) 418 pages
Nay — Dow's Hampton N. H. 878-80
Fullonton's Hist. Raymond N. H. 258-61
Hayward's History of Hancock N. H. 784
Smith's Hist. Peterborough N. H. 211-6
Naylor — Potts Genealogy (1895) 404
Neafle — Nevius Genealogy
Neal — Andrews' New Britain Ct. 255
Dearborn's Hist. of Parsonsfield Me. 390
Dow's History of Hampton N. H. 880
Driver Genealogy 438-54
Granite Monthly Concord N. H. iv, 266-71
Haley Genealogy (1900) 51-78
Lincoln's History of Hingham Mass. iii, 79
Neal Genealogy (1856) 30 pages
Power's Sangamon Co. Ill. Settlers 538-40
Ridlon's Harrison Me. Settlers 97
Ruggles Genealogy
Savage's Genealogical Dictionary iii, 263-5
Timlow's Southington Ct. Sketches 181-5
Neale — Clarke's King Wm. Va. Families
Pope Genealogy
Richmond Va. Standard iii, 37
Nealley — Nottingham N. H. 231-6
Nealley and True Chart (1878) 21x3
Needham — Am. Anc. iii, 147; iv, 213
Caverly's History of Pittsford Vt. 716
Hazen's History of Billerica Mass. 99
Lapham's History of Bethel Me. 593
Lapham's History of Norway Me. 559-61
Perkins' Old Houses of Norwich Ct. 539
Savage's Genealogical Dictionary iii, 265
Wales Mass. Centennial 8
Needles — Man and Needles Genealogy
Neefus — American Ancestry ii, 88
Nevius Genealogy
Neff — American Ancestry iii, 131
Bass' History of Braintree Vt. 166
Cincinnati Ohio Criterion (1888) ii, 470-4
Corliss Genealogy 237
Egle's Notes Queries 1896 An. vol. 8-10
Neff Genealogy (1886) 352 pages
Negley — American Ancestry iii, 188
Negus — Vermont Hist. Gaz. v, 69
Neidig — Egle's Queries 3d ser. i, 507
Neighbor — Chambers' N. J. Germans 450
Neil — Green's Kentucky Families
Paxton's Marshall Genealogy 276
Neill — American Ancestry iii, 63
Cope Genealogy 99, 101, 196
Jolliffe Genealogy (1893)
Neill Family of Delaware (1875) 127 pages
Neill Family of Delaware (1886) 33 pages
New Eng. Hist. and Gen. Reg. xxv, 296
Sullivant Genealogy (1874) 237
Neilson — Am. Ancestry iv, 41; vii, 127
Clayton's Hist. of Union Co. N. J. 468-70
Neily — Calnek's Annapolis N. S. 556
Neitser — Chambers' N. J. Germans
Nellis — American Ancestry i, 57; xi, 42
Nelson — American Anc. iii, 184; v, 31
Ballou's History of Milford Mass. 914-31

Bassett's History of Richmond N. H. 447
Bolton Genealogy 72
Campbell's History of Virginia 653
Carter Family Tree of Virginia
Chapman's Folsom Genealogy 72
Cushman's History of Sheepscott Me. 407
Davis' Landmarks Plymouth Mass. 193–6
Essex Inst. Hist. Collections xxii, 219–26
Gage's History of Rowley Mass. 448
Goode Genealogy 277
Hudson's History of Lexington Mass. 167
Hyde's History of Brimfield Mass. 475
Lancaster's Hist. of Gilmanton N. H. 279
Lincoln's Hist. Hingham Mass. iii, 79–81
McKeen's History of Bradford Vt. 308
Meade's Old Churches of Virginia i, 205
Miller's Hist. Colchester Co. N. S. 135–42
Nelson Family of Mass. (1867) 25 pages
Nelson Family of New York (1886) 50 p.
Nelson Family of New York (1894) 61 pages
Nelson Family of Virginia
Prescott's Paige Genealogy (1883)
Richmond Va. Critic (1888)
Richmond Va. Standard i, 40; iii, 4, 9, 32
Savage's Genealogical Dictionary iii, 267
Sheldon's History of Deerfield Mass. 247
Strong Genealogy 636
Ward's History of Shrewsbury Mass. 390
Welles' Washington Genealogy 171–93
Whitmore's Heraldic Journal i, 94
Whitmore's Temple Genealogy
Worthen's History of Sutton N. H. 829–42
Nephew — Nevius Genealogy
Nes — Spangler Genealogy 204–8
Nesbit — Harvey Genealogy 247–377
Power's Sangamon Ill. 540
Nesmith — American Ancestry iv, 100
Cochrane's History of Antrim N. H. 613–20
Cochrane's Hist. Francestown N. H. 851
Granite Monthly of Concord N. H. iv, 259
Hayward's History of Hancock N. H. 785
Morrison's Hist. Windham N. H. 687–701
Parker's Hist. Londonderry N. H. 290–2
Nestle — N. Y. Gen. Record viii, 44
Nethaway — American Ancestry i, 57
Nettleton — Anderson's Waterbury 94
Loomis Genealogy (1880) 69–71, 78–81
Humphreys Genealogy 571
Orcutt's History of Derby Ct. 748
Wheeler's Hist. of Newport N. H. 477–80
Neubert — Eaton's Thomaston Me. 338
Neuman — Kriebel's Schwenkfelders 16
Nevens — American Ancestry xii
Bass' History of Braintree Vt. 167
Porter's Eddy Genealogy, appendix
Worcester's History of Hollis N. H. 382
Nevers — Sewall's Woburn Mass. 627
Neville — Egle's Penn. Gens. 541–55
Potter's Amer. Monthly v, 866; vi, 145
Whitehead's Perth Amboy N. J. 120–4
Nevins — Perkins' Norwich Ct. 541
Nevinson — Bond's Watertown 375, 860
Nevitt — Bent's Whiteside Co. Ill. 121
Nevius — Bergen's Kings Co. N. Y. 215
Hoagland Genealogy 266
Honeyman's Our Home Magazine 403–6

Nevius Genealogy (1900) 732 pages
Schureman Genealogy 18, 23, 29–31
New — American Ancestry ii, 88
Jameson's History of Medway Mass. 506
Newbegin — Ridlon's Saco 1078–83
Newberry — Am. Anc. iv, 89; viii, 210
Austin's R. I. Genealogical Dictionary 137
Baker's History of Montville Ct. 471–3
Dwight's Strong Genealogy 97–100
Ely Genealogy 76, 100–2
Loomis Genealogy (1880) 417–9
Newberry Genealogy (1898) 70 pages
New Eng. Hist. and Gen. Reg. xxv, 73
Savage's Genealogical Dict. ii, 268–70
Stiles' History of Windsor Ct. ii, 516–33
Newbie — Clement's Newtown N. J.
Newby — Cregar's White Genealogy
Newcomb — American Ancestry xii
Cunnabell Genealogy 64
Daniels' History of Oxford Mass. 627
Eaton's Annals of Warren Me. 591
Freeman's Cape Cod Mass. ii, 98, 375, 634
Hines' Lebanon Ct. Hist. Address 165
Lincoln's Hist. Hingham Mass. iii, 81–3
Newcomb Genealogy (1874) 600 pages
Orcutt's History of Derby Ct. 747
Paige's History of Hardwick Mass. 425
Putnam's Historical Magazine iii, 131
Wyman's Charlestown Mass. Gens. ii, 697
Wyman's Hunt Genealogy 119
Newcombe — Am. Ancestry i, 57; v, 34
Bond's Hist. of Watertown Mass. 549–51
Eaton's Annals of Warren Me. 416
Marshall Genealogy (1884) 134–8
Newcomb Genealogy (1874) 600 pages
Savage's Genealogical Dictionary iii, 270
Sheldon's History of Deerfield Mass. 248
Newcomer — Brubacher Genealogy 90–2
Newdigate — Salisbury Geneal. (1892) 473
Newell — Adams' Haven Gen. ii, 23
Allen's Worcester Mass. Association 100
Am. Anc. iii, 187; iv, 219; v, 47; viii, 32; xi, 43
Baldwin's Candee Genealogy 167–71
Ballou Genealogy 161–3, 221, 390–5
Bassett's Hist. of Richmond N. H. 448–52
Bemis' History of Marlboro N. H. 503–5
Bulloch Genealogy
Essex Inst. xvii, 79–84; xviii, 1–33; xix, 40
Freeman's Hist. of Cape Cod Mass. ii, 763
Hayward's History of Hancock N. H. 786
Hill's Dedham Mass. Records i
Hyde's History of Brimfield Mass. 438
Kidder's Hist. of New Ipswich N. H. 417
Lapham's History of Bethel Me. 594
Livermore's History of Wilton N. H. 453
Longmeadow Mass. Centennial (1883) 75
Morse's Sherborn Mass. Settlers 184
Newell Genealogy (1878) 266 pages
Orford N. H. Centennial 129
Phœnix's Whitney Genealogy i, 749
Savage's Genealogical Dictionary iii, 270–3
Stackpole's History of Durham Me. 225–8
Stiles' History of Windsor Ct. ii, 533
Temple's Hist. of N. Brookfield Mass. 690
Temple's History of Palmer Mass. 523

Timlow's Southington Ct. Sketches 185–94
Wheeler's History of Newport N. H. 481
Wyman's Charlestown Mass. Gens. ii, 704
Newgate — Prime's Bowdoin Gen. 20-5
Newhall — American Ancestry v, 109
Daniels' History of Oxford Mass. 627
Draper's History of Spencer Mass. 234
Eaton's History of Thomaston Me. ii, 339
Essex Inst. xviii, 1–33, 223–92; xix, 40–60
Lewis and Newhall's Lynn Mass. 484-9
Lincoln's History of Hingham Mass. iii, 83
Newhall Genealogy (1882) 109 pages
Savage's Genealogical Dictionary iii, 273
Washburn's History of Leicester Mass. 385
Wyman's Charlestown Mass. Gens. ii, 705
Newkirk — American Ancestry viii, 230
Winfield's Hist. Hudson Co. N. J. 513-20
Newland — Clarke's Norton Mass. 87
Freeman's History of Cpe Cod Mass. ii, 69
Paige's History of Hardwick Mass. 426
Savage's Genealogical Dictionary iii, 274
Newlin — Futhey's Chester Pa. 669
Platt's Greenough Ancestry 20
Sharpless Genealogy 171, 374
Smith's History of Delaware Co. Pa. 488
Newman — Amer. Ancestry i, 57; viii, 85
Clarke's Old King Wm. Co. Va. Families
Cochrane's History of Antrim N. H. 620
Delamater Genealogy 96–9
Dowse Genealogy 70-7, 137-52
Hammatt Papers of Ipswich Mass. 231
Hayward's History of Gilsum N. H. 371
Huntington's Stamford Ct. Settlers 77
Locke Genealogy 42
McKean Genealogy 183
Newman's Rehoboth Mass. (1860) 62-8
Power's Sangamon Co. Ill. Settlers 542
Reed Genealogy 246
Savage's Genealogical Dictionary iii, 274-6
Slaughter's St. Mark's Paris Va. 120
Washington N. H. History 553-8
Newmarch — Hammatt Papers 233
Newsom — Power's Sangamon Ill. 542
Slaughter's St. Mark's Parish Va. 120
Newton — Am. Anc. i, 57; iv, 78; vi. 16, 24, 170
Anderson's Waterbury Ct. i, app. 94
Ballou's History of Milford Mass. 931
Barbour's My Wife and Mother, app. 28
Barry's History of Framingham Mass. 339
Bemis' History of Marlboro N. H. 585-90
Cochrane's Hist. Francest'n N. H. 852-4
Coggswell's Hist. of Henniker N. H. 660
Daniels' History of Oxford Mass. 628
Draper's History of Spencer Mass. 235
Forrests' History of Norfolk Va. 54
Green's Kentucky Families
Hemenway's Vermont Hist. Gaz v, 469
Heywood's Hist. of Westminster Mass. 808
Hollister Genealogy 210
Hudson's Marlborough Mass. 421-6
Hunt's Biog. of John Newman (1881) 12 p.
Hyde's History of Brimfield Mass. 438
Loomis Genealogy (1880) 725
Meade's Old Churches of Virginia ii, 151
Merrill's History of Acworth N. H. 250

Morris' Bontecou Genealogy 181-4
Morris and Flynt Genealogy 56
Morse's Grout Genealogy 36
Newton Genealogy (1897) 39 pages
New York Gen. and Biog. Record xvi, 131
Norton's History of Fitzwilliam N. H. 646
Otis Family of N. H. (1851)
Page Genealogy 76
Paige's History of Hardwick Mass. 426-8
Paxton's Marshall Genealogy 107
Savage's Genealogical Dictionary iii, 276-8
Sheldon's Hist. Deerfield Mass. ii, 248-50
Smith's History of Sunderland Mass. 475-7
Stiles' History of Windsor Ct. ii, 533
Stone's Hist of Hubbardston Mass. 321-3
Temple's Hist. of N. Brookfield Mass. 692
Tucker's History of Hartford Vt. 452-5
Ward Genealogy (1851) 28
Ward's History of Shrewsbury Mass. 381-7
Washington N. H. History 558-60
Wheeler's History of Newport N. H. 481-3
Worcester Mag. and Hist. Journal ii, 136
Nicholas — Bolling Genealogy 30
Carter Family Tree of Virginia
Chambers' Early Germans of N. J. 454
Meade's Old Churches of Virginia i, 184
Richmond Va. Standard i, 39; iii, 43
Slaughter's Fry Genealogy 59
Nicholls — Lamb's N. Y. City i, 507
Nichols — Aldrich's Walpole 341-3
Am. Anc. ii, 89; iii, 38; v, 77, 159; vi, 90; vii, 25; viii, 42, 117
Anderson's Waterbury Ct. i, app. 94-6
Austin's R. I. Genealogical Dictionary 138
Bangor Me. Historical Magazine ix, 54
Barry's Hist. of Framingham Mass. 340-2
Bass' History of Braintree Vt. 167-9
Benedict's History of Sutton Mass. 700
Bouton Genealogy 22
Briggs' History of Shipbuilding 281-3
Calnek's History of Annapolis N. S. 557
Cleveland's History of Yates Co. N. Y. 658
Cochrane's History of Antrim N. H 622-6
Cothren's History of Woodbury Ct. 657-62
Corliss' North Yarmouth Me. Magazine
Daniels' History of Oxford Mass. 628-33
Deane's History of Scituate Mass. 316
Eaton's History of Reading Mass. 97-9
Eaton's History of Thomaston Me. ii, 339
Essex Inst. Hist. Collection iii, 29-32
Farrow's History of Islesborough Me. 235
Goodwin's Genealogical Notes 312-5
Greene County N. Y. History 193
Gregory's History of Northfield Vt. 90-3
Hemenway's Vermont Hist. Gaz. iv, 621
Herrick's History of Gardner Mass. 369-71
Heywood's Hist. of Westminster Mass. 810
Hodgman's History of Westford Mass. 462
Hoyt's Salisbury Mass. Families 265
Hubbard's History of Springfield Vt. 398
Huntington's Stamford Ct. Settlers 79
Hurlbut Genealogy 439, 453-6
Hyde's History of Brimfield Mass. 438-41
Lincoln's Hist. Hingham Mass. iii, 83-90
Little's History of Weare N. H. 947-9
Maine Hist. and Gen. Recorder viii, 106

Missouri Pioneer Families 363
Morris' Bontecou Genealogy 166
Morrison's History of Windham N. H. 701
New Eng. Hist. and Gen. Reg. xiv, 27
Nichols Genealogy (1882) 17 pages
North's History of Augusta Me. 907
Norton's History of Fitzwilliam N. H. 647
Orcutt's History of Derby Ct. 748
Orcutt's History of Stratford Ct. 1251-8
Orcutt's History of Wolcott Ct. 529
Pickering Genealogy
Resseguie Genealogy 65-7, 73-7
Savage's Genealogical Dict. iii, 278-83
Schenck's History of Fairfield Ct. 398
Secomb's History of Amherst N. H. 705-8
Slafter Genealogy 43-5
Stackpole's History of Durham Me. 229
Stearns' History of Ashburnham Mass. 840
Stone's History of Hubbardston Mass. 324
Temple's Hist. of N. Brookfield Mass. 692
Whitmore's Copps Hill Epitaphs
Williams' History of Danby Vt. 206-10
Worthen's History of Sutton N. H. 842-4
Wyman's Charlestown Mass. Gens. 706-8
Young's Hist. Chautauqua Co. N. Y. 607
Nicholson — Austin's R. I. Dict. 139
Clement's Newtown N. J. Settlers
Eaton's History of Thomaston Me. ii, 339
New Eng. Hist. and Gen. Reg. xxxix, 73
Savage's Genealogical Dictionary iii, 283
Shourd's Fenwick Colony N. J. 164-6
Stanton Genealogy 264
Nickels — Bangor Hist. Mag. ix, 197
Cushman's Sheepscott Me. 408
Hazen's History of Billerica Mass. 100
Milliken's Narraguagus Valley Me. 11
Nickerson — Am. Anc. ii, 89; xi, 108-9
Andrews' History of New Britain Ct. 356
Bangor Historical Magazine iv, 158; v, 7
Davis' Landmarks of Plymouth Mass. 194
Freeman's Hist. Cape Cod Mass. ii, 707-10
Holton's Winslow Genealogy i, 90
Lincoln's History of Hingham Mass. iii, 91
Nicklin — Thomas Genealogy (1896) 454
Nicoll — Nicoll Genealogy (1886) 62 pages
Orcutt's History of Stratford Ct. 1258
Queens County N. Y. History 140-5
Strong Genealogy 600-4
Thompson's Long Island N. Y. ii, 390-7
Nicolls — American Ancestry iii, 136
Wood's Hist. of Long Island N. Y. 147-52
Nightingale — Austin's Anc. Dict. 41
Niles — Am. Anc. i, 57; ii, 89; viii, 15
Austin's R. I. Genealogical Dictionary 139
Savage's Genealogical Dictionary iii, 284
Stiles' History of Windsor Ct. ii, 534-6
Vinton Genealogy 344-51
Walworth's Hyde Genealogy 744-6, 829-32
Whitman Genealogy 181
Wyman's Charlestown Mass. Gens. ii, 708
Nimmo — Wynne's Ellis Genealogy (1849)
Nims — American Ancestry iii, 39
Savage's Genealogical Dictionary iii, 285
Sheldon's History of Deerfield Mass. 250-7
Nipher — American Ancestry vi, 111
Nipper — Power's Sangamon Ill. 543

Nisbet — Bond's Watertown 842
See also under Nesbitt
Nissley — Harris' Lancaster Pa. 425-30
Nissly — Brubacher Gen. 88-113, 137-51
Niver — American Ancestry ii, 89
Nivison — Meade's Old Churches of Va.
Nixon — American Ancestry viii, 207
Barry's History of Framingham Mass. 342
Hudson's History of Sudbury Mass. 410-2
Jennings Genealogy (1899)
Noble — Collin's Hillsdale 6, 740-7
Davis' History of Bucks County Pa. 217
Lapham's History of Norway Me. 562-4
Litchfield County Ct. History (1882) 466
Loomis Genealogy (1880) 474-515, 757-9
Noble Genealogy (1878) 870 pages
Orcutt's History of New Milford Ct. 740-7
Savage's Genealogical Dictionary iii, 285
Stiles' History of Windsor Ct. ii, 536
Taylor's Great Barrington Mass. 112
Noblitt — Martin's Chester Pa. 249
Nock — Lapham's Knox Genealogy
Noe — Littell's Passaic Valley 301-3
Noland — Meade's Old Families of Va.
Nolen — Daniels' Oxford Mass. 633
Nookes — Cope's Will of Wm. Nookes
(1869) 6 pages
Norcross — Bond's Watertown 376-81
Hatch's History of Industry Me. 746-51
Hemenway's Vermont Hist. Gaz. v, 100
Heywood's Hist. of Westminster Mass. 812
Hudson's History of Lexington Mass. 168
Jackson's History of Newton Mass. 372
Randall's History of Cheterfield N. H. 394
Savage's Genealogical Dictionary iii, 286
Stearns' History of Rindge N. H. 609-14
Ward's History of Shrewsbury Mass. 388
Norman — Essex Inst. Hist. Coll. i, 191
Perkins' Old Houses of Norwich Ct. 542
Savage's Genealogical Dictionary iii, 281
Norred — Power's Sangamon Ill. 544
Norris — Am. Anc. iii, 193; vii, 195, 256-63
Cleveland's Hist. of Yates Co. N. Y. 665-7
Coggswell's Nottingham N. H. 236-8
Dow's History of Hampton N. H. 881
Freeman's Hist. of Cape Cod Mass. ii, 82
Fullonton's History of Raymond N. H. 261
Lane Genealogy (1891) 77-80
Martin's History of Chester Pa. 36
Norris Genealogy (1892) 207 pages
Power's Sangamon Co. Ill. Settlers 545
Savage's Genealogical Dictionary iii, 288
Sinclair Genealogy 405-18
North — Am. Anc. i, 57; iii, 110; vi, 3, 4,
18, 186; ix, 65
Andrews' New Britain Ct. 180-2, etc.
Boyd's Annals of Winchester Ct. 126
Eaton's Annals of Warren Me. 592
Hibbard's History of Goshen Ct. 502-7
Huntington Genealogy 175
Kellogg's White Genealogy 80
Loomis Genealogy (1880) 560-5
North Genealogy (1860) 30 pages
North's History of Augusta Me. 908-19
Orcutt's History of Torrington Ct. 749-51
Savage's Genealogical Dictionary iii, 289

Sedgwick's History of Sharon Ct. 101
Northen — Albany Collections iv, 150
Northend — Essex Me. Institute Historical Colls. xii, 71-84; xxii, 226
Gage's History of Rowley Mass. 449
Northend Genealogy (1874) 16 pages reprint
Northrop — American Ancestry i, 58
Baldwin Genealogy 1010
Morris' Bontecou Genealogy 123
Orcutt's History of New Milford Ct. 747-9
Northrup — Am. Anc. iii, 104; x, 200
Bouton Genealogy 456
Currier's Castleton Vt. Epitaphs 37-40
N. E. Hist. and Gen. Reg. xliii, 242-53
Northrup Genealogy (1889) 13 pages
Northup — American Ancestry ix, 130
Austin's R. I. Genealogical Dictionary 140
Norton — Adams' Fairhaven Vt. 444-6
Am. Anc. ii, 89; iv, 190; vi, 190; vii, 249; x, 88, 199; xi, 44, 177
Anderson's Waterbury Ct. i, app. 96
Andrews' History of New Britain Ct. 287
Babson's History of Gloucester Mass. 118
Baldwin Genealogy supp. 1281-3
Baldwin's Candee Genealogy 173-81
Boyd's History of Conesus N. Y. 166
Butler's History of Farmington Me. 536-47
Chase's History of Chester N. H. 572
Dow's History of Hampton N. H. 882
Eaton's Annals of Warren Me. 593
Elderkin Genealogy 133-7
Essex Institute Hist. Collections xvii, 89-98
Fowler's History of Durham Ct. 87
Goode Genealogy 383
Goodwin's Foote Genealogy 239
Hammatt Papers of Ipswich Mass. 233-6
Hatch's History of Industry Me. 751-82
Hibbard's History of Goshen Ct. 507-21
Hoyt's Salisbury Mass. Families 266
Hubbard's Stanstead Co. Canada 333-5
Ireland Genealogy 36-41
Jones' Norton Biography (1848) 26 pages
Joslin's History of Poultney Vt. 315
Lincoln's History of Hingham Mass. 92-4
Litchfield County Ct. History (1881) 371
Munsell's Albany Collections iv, 150
New Eng. Hist. and Gen. Register xiii, 225-31; liii, 87-91; liv, 269-76
New York Gen. and Biog. Record xxix, 91
Norton Family of Guilford (1856) 26 p.
Norton Genealogy (1859) 10 pages reprint
Orcutt's History of Wolcott Ct. 531-5
Paxton's Marshall Genealogy 213
Porter Genealogy (1878) 45-7
Richmond Va. Standard i, 39; ii, 47
Ridlon's Saco Valley Me. Families 1083-5
Robinson Genealogy (1859)
Savage's Genealogical Dictionary iii, 290-4
Slaughter's Fry Genealogy 61
Strong Genealogy 293-8
Temple's History of Northfield Mass. 507
Thayer's Disc. on Thuel Norton (1880) 22-7
Timlow's Sketches of Southington Ct. 194-9
Turner's Phelps Purchase N. Y. 189
Walworth's Hyde Genealogy 328-30
Washburn's History of Livermore Me. 28

Whitmore's Heraldic Journal ii, 105
Worden Genealogy 113-5
Wyman's Charlestown Mass. Gens. ii, 710
Norvell — Lynchburg Va. Record 230-4
Meade's Old Churches of Virginia
Norwood — Babson's Gloucester 118-20
Bassett's History of Richmond N. H. 452
Hallowell Genealogy 193-201
Savage's Genealogical Dictionary iii, 294
Nostrand — Queens Co. N. Y. History 250
Nott — American Ancestry i, 58; vii, 243
Goodwin's Genealogical Notes 165-9
Hubbard's History of Springfield Vt. 400
New Eng. Hist. and Gen. Register xx, 13
Savage's Genealogical Dictionary iii, 294
Nottingham — Power's Sangamon 546
Nourse — Am. Anc. iii, 217; vii, 255; viii, 208
Barry's Hist. of Framingham Mass. 344-7
Fiske Genealogy 136
Hemenway's Vermont Hist. Gaz. v, 106
Merritt's History of Acworth N. H. 251
Nourse Family of Va. (1897) 163 pages
Rittenhouse Genealogy (1897) 58-91
Ward's History of Shrewsbury Mass. 379
Warren's History of Waterford Me. 276
Nowell — Savage's Gen. Dict. iii, 295
Whitmore's Copps Hill Epitaphs
Winchester Mass. Records i, 27
Wyman's Charlestown Mass. Gens. 710-2
Noyes — Adams Genealogy (1895) 34, 43
Am. Anc. iii, 164; iv, 65; v, 17; vii, 131
Carter's Hist. Pembroke N. H. ii, 245-52
Chute Genealogy, appendix 136-8
Coffin's History of Boscawen N. H. 590-2
Coffin's History of Newbury Mass. 312
Cogswell's Hist. of Henniker N. H. 662-4
Corliss' North Yarmouth Me. Magazine
Darling Memorial
Davis' History of Wallingford Ct. 868-71
Dearborn's Hist. of Salisbury N. H. 676-8
Emery Genealogy (1890) 33
Emery's Newbury Mass. Reminisc. 112-6
Hobart's History of Abington Mass. 423-6
Hubbard's Stanstead Co. Canada 137
Joslin's History of Poultney Vt. 316
Journals of Smith and Dean of Me. 158
Kingman's Bridgewater Mass. 582-4
Lapham's History of Norway Me. 564-6
Morrison's Hist. of Windham N. H. 702-9
N. E. Hist. Gen. Reg. xlviii, 18; liii, 35-43
N. Y. Gen. and Biog. Rec. xx, 67
Noyes Genealogy (1861) 13 pages
Noyes Genealogy (1889) 32 pages
Noyes Inscription (1894) 4 pages
Noyes Pedigree (1899) 11 pages
Poore Genealogy 81
Poor's Hist. Researches 119, 129, 136, 168
Savage's Genealogical Dictionary iii, 296-9
Secomb's History of Amherst N. H. 708-10
Sedgwick's History of Sharon Ct. 102
Stanton Genealogy 69-73, 562
Stearns' Hist. of Ashburnham Mass. 840
Walworth's Hyde Genealogy 739-41
Ward's Hist. of Shrewsbury Mass. 288-90
Wheeler's History of Brunswick Me. 844

Wheeler's History of Newport N. H. 485-7
Whitman Genealogy 350-7
Wyman's Hunt Genealogy 119
Nuckolls — Power's Sangamon 547-9
Nuckols — Watkins Genealogy 29
Nudd — Dow's Hampton N. H. 883-8
Nunn — Chambers' N. J. Germans
Nurse — Norton's Fitzwilliam 647-9
Putnam's Historical Magazine iii, 96-102
Reed's History of Rutland Mass. 142
Savage's Genealogical Dictionary iii, 300
Ward's Hist. of Shrewsbury Mass. 379-81
Nute — Dearborn's Parsonsfield Me. 390
Lapham's History of Woodstock Me. 241
Nutt — Cope Genealogy 73, 159
Eaton's History of Thomaston Me. ii, 340
Guild's Stiles Genealogy 316
Secomb's History of Amherst N. H. 710
Nutter — Dearborn's Parsonsfield 391
New Eng. Hist. and Gen. Register vii, 259
Robinson's Items of Ancestry (1894) 26-30
Wentworth Genealogy i, 482; ii, 61
Nutting — American Ancestry xii
Bassett's Richmond 453
Bemis' History of Marlboro N. H. 590
Bond's Watertown Mass. Gens. 381
Butler's Hist. of Groton Mass. 418-20, 475
Cochrane's Hist. Francest'n N. H. 857-9
Cutter's History of Jaffrey N. H. 408-11
Eaton's History of Thomaston Me. ii, 341
Green's Early Groton Mass. Settlers 12
Hayward's History of Hancock N. H. 787
Hodgman's History of Westford Mass. 462
Hudson's History of Lexington Mass. 168
Hyde's History of Brimfield Mass. 441
Lapham's History of Bethel Me. 594
Paige's History of Cambridge Mass. 615
Savage's Genealogical Dictionary iii, 301
Temple's History of Palmer Mass. 524
Wyman's Charlestown Mass. Gens. ii, 712
Nuzum — Sharpless Genealogy 368
Nye — Amer. Ancestry vi, 113; ix, 114, 204
Bangor Me. Historical Magazine v, 6
Bemis' History of Marlboro N. H. 590
Davis' Landmarks of Plymouth Mass. 195
Freeman's Cape Cod Mass. ii, 143, 151-8
Gibb's Blandford Mass. Hist. Address 60
Hemenway's Vermont Hist. Gaz. iv, 59
Lincoln's Hist. of Hingham Mass. iii, 95-7
Olin Genealogy by Nye (1892) 405-25
Paige's History of Hardwick Mass. 429-31
Savage's Genealogical Dictionary iii, 301
Sibley's History of Union Me. 482
Temple's Hist. N. Brookfield Mass. 693-6
Vinton's Giles Genealogy 209-11
Waldo's History of Tolland Ct. 129
Nyssen — Bergen Genealogy 40
Bergen's Kings Co. N. Y. Settlers 92-5
Oak — American Ancestry x, 107
Oakes — Atkin's Hist. of Hawley Mass. 49
Bangor Me. Historical Magazine v, 200
Calnek's History of Annapolis N. S. 558
Corliss' North Yarmouth Me. 635-8
Freeman's Hist. of Cape Cod Mass. ii, 386
Paige's History of Cambridge Mass. 616
Savage's Genealogical Dictionary iii, 302-4

Worcester's Mag. and Hist. Jour. ii, 152
Wyman's Charlestown Mass. Gens. ii, 713
Oakford — Shourd's Fenwick N. J. 173
Oakley — American Ancestry ii, 89
Bockee Genealogy 71-4
Bunker's Long Island Genealogies 261
Flint's Peters Lineage 97-107
Littell's Passaic Valley Genealogies 304-6
Roome Genealogy 170
Ruttenber's Hist. of Orange Co. N. Y. 397
Oakman — Corliss' North Yarmouth Me.
Maine Hist. and Gen. Recorder iii, 151-8
229-37; iv, 127-33, 182-7, 268-77
Read's History of Swanzey N. H. 409
Oaks — American Ancestry x, 157
Smith's History of Sunderland Mass. 477
Oaksmith — Corliss' N. Yarmouth Me.
Oates — N. E. Hist. Gen. Reg. vi, 150-2
See also under Otis
Oatman — Middlebury Vt. 69-73
O'Beirne — Life of Rev. Wm. Smith
Obenchain — American Ancestry vii, 96
Ober — American Ancestry i, 158
Hayward's History of Hancock N. H. 788
Secomb's History of Amherst N. H. 711
Washington N. H. History 560-2
Oberholtzer — Hess Gen. (1896) 175-94
Oblenis — Riker's Harlem N. Y. 539-43
O'Brien — Bangor Hist. Mag. iii, 222-8
Eaton's Annals of Warren Me. 593
Eaton's History of Thomaston Me. ii, 341
Egle's Notes and Queries 3d ser. iii, 42
Pope Genealogy 51-8
Ridlon's Saco Valley Me. Families 1086
O'Daniels — Heywood's Westminster 813
Odell — American Ancestry i, 58
Baird's History of Rye N. Y. 429
Bolton's Westchester Co. N. Y. ii, 653
Greene's Todd Genealogy
Hayward's History of Hancock N. H. 789
Maine Hist. and Gen. Recorder iii, 58-62
New Eng. Hist. and Gen. Reg. xlv
New York Gen. and Biog. Record xvii, 57
Odell Memoranda (1892) 3 pages
Odell Chart (1894) 25x36 inches
Raymond's Tarrytown Monument 79-88
Runnel's Hist. Sanbornton N. H. ii, 532-5
Schenck's History of Fairfield Ct. 399
Secomb's History of Amherst N. H. 712
See also Wodell
Odenheimer — Martin's Chester Pa. 354
Odin — Dorr Genealogy
New Eng. Hist. and Gen. Reg. xii, 223
Odin Genealogy (1858) 4 pages
Wyman's Charlestown Mass. Gens. ii, 713
Odiorne — Brewster's Portsmouth 151
Cutts Genealogy 54-6, 108-10
Odiorne Genealogy (1875) 222 pages
Wentworth Genealogy i, 320
Odlin — Bell's History of Exeter N. H. 34
N. E. Hist. and Gen. Reg. xli, 265-71, 393
Odlin Family (1887) 9 pages reprint
Odlin Genealogy (1893)
Offitt — Savage's Gen. Dictionary iii, 305
Ogden — American Ancestry ii, 90; xii, 118
Baird's History of Rye N. Y. 430

Chambers' Early Germans of N. J. 455-7
Halsted Genealogy (1896) 1
Hatfield's History of Elizabeth N. J. 64-7
Hoffman Genealogy 491-5
Morris Genealogy (1898) 878
New Jersey Hist. Soc. Colls. supp. vi, 148
Ogdens of South Jersey (1894) 35 pages
Ogdens of Elizabeth N. J. (1896) 82 pages
Ogdens of Penn. (1898) 245 pages
Penn. Magazine of Hist. and Biog. xiii, 182
Power's Sangamon Co. Ill. Settlers 549
Salisbury's Fam. Histories (1892) ii, 225-84
Savage's Genealogical Dictionary iii, 306
Schenck's History of Fairfield Ct. 400
Shourd's Fenwick Colony N. J. 167-72
Smith's History of Delaware Co. Va. 489
Timlow's Southington Ct. Sketches 200
Tuttle Genealogy 675
Ogilvie—Selleck's Norw'k Ct. (1896) 252-4
Thayer Memorial (1835) 10
O'Hara — Greene Co. N. Y. History 312
Sullivant Genealogy (1874) 262-72
Olcott — Amer. Ancestry i, 58; iv, 47
Chandler Genealogy 285
Goodwin's Foote Genealogy 49
Kellogg's White Genealogy 41
Olcott Genealogy (1845) 64 pages
Olcott Genealogy 2d ed. (1874) 124 pages
Olcott Lineage (1899) 84 pages
Read's History of Swanzey N. H. 410
Saunderson's Hist. Charlestown N. H. 218
Savage's Genealogical Dictionary iii, 306
Stiles' History of Windsor Ct. ii, 537
Tuttle Genealogy 449-673
Old — Stiles' Hist. Windsor Ct. ii, 537
Temple's Hist. of N. Brookfield Mass. 697
Temple's History of Palmer Mass. 524
Olden — Rodman Genealogy 157
Oldham — Bond's Watertown 382
Brook's History of Medford Mass. 531
Deane's History of Scituate Mass. 317
Livermore's Hist. of Block Is R. I. 338-40
Mallery's Bohemia Manor
Paige's History of Cambridge Mass. 617
Savage's Genealogical Dictionary iii, 307
Smith Genealogy (1895) 91-6
Winsor's History of Duxbury Mass. 285
Olds — Hemenway's Vt. Gaz. v, 446
Loomis Genealogy (1880) 761-3
Olin — Olin (Ezra) Gen. (1892) 441 pages
Olin (John) Genealogy (1893) 324 pages
Oliver — Amer. Ancestry iii, 39-40; v, 53
Drake's History of Boston Mass. 293
Eaton's History of Thomaston Me. ii, 342
Harris' Brattle Genealogy 35-68
Hatch's History of Industry Me. 783
Hutchinson Genealogy (1865) 25-38
Jackson's History of Newton Mass. 373
Lapham's History of Bethel Me. 595-7
Munsell's Albany Collections iv, 150
New Eng. Hist. and Gen. Reg. xix, 100-6
N. Y. Gen. Record xix, 137-46; xx, 1-11
Oliver Ancestry in Eng. (1867) 36 pages
Oliver Family of Boston (1868) 7 pages
Oliver Ancestry in Eng. (1871) 29 pages
Oliver Family of N. Y. (1888) 27 pages

Paige's Hist. of Cambridge Mass. 618-20
Paige's History of Hardwick Mass. 431
Read's History of Swanzey N. H. 411
Richmond Va. Standard iv, 23
Saunders' Alabama Settlers 408-33, 528
Savage's Genealogical Dict. iii, 309-11
Sigourney Genealogy
Wyman's Charlestown Mass. Gens. ii, 714
Olmstead — American Ancestry x, 157
Caulkins' History of Norwich Ct. 192
Caverly's History of Pittsford Vt. 717
Goodwin's Olcott Genealogy 18
Hall's Norwalk 185, 193, 216, 243, 266-8
Harris Genealogy (1878) 91-3
Hyde's Hist. Address at Ware Mass. 46
Kellogg's White Genealogy 41
Olmstead Genealogy (1869) 30 pages
Paige's History of Hardwick Mass. 431
Phœnix's Whitney Genealogy 161
Savage's Genealogical Dictionary iii, 311
Selleck's Norwalk Ct. (1896) 266, 282-5
Temple's Hist. of N. Brookfield Mass. 697
Temple's History of Northfield Mass. 507
Olmsted — Am. Anc. iv, 29; vi, 86; ix, 34, 191
Field's History of Haddam Ct. 47
Loomis Genealogy (1880) 15-58
Norton's History of Fitzwilliam N. H. 650
Paige's History of Cambridge Mass. 620
Stiles' History of Windsor Ct. ii, 538
Olney — Am. Anc. iv, 149; viii, 15, 91
Austin's Ancestries 43, 83, 105
Austin's R. I. Genealogical Dictionary 352
Daniels' History of Oxford Mass. 634-6
Hubbard's History of Springfield Vt. 401
Newport R. I. Hist. Mag. (1883) 188-90
Olney Genealogy (1889) 293 pages
Savage's Genealogical Dictionary iii, 312-4
Onderdonk — Am. Anc. iii, 220; vii, 65
Bergen's Kings County N. Y. Settlers 217
Bunker's Long Island Genealogies 316
New York Gen. and Biog. Record vi, 183
Riker's Annals of Newtown N. Y. 275
O'Neil — Kulp's Wyoming Val. Fams.
Smith (Rev. Wm.) Biography
O'Neill — Eaton's Thomaston Me. 343
Jolliffe Genealogy 175-91
Oney — Olney Genealogy 232-8
Onion — Ballou's Milford Mass. 934
Hill's Dedham Mass. Records i
Oosterhout — Albany Colls. iv, 151
Oothout — Albany Colls. iv, 151
New York Gen. and Biog. Record ii, 69
Pearson's Schenectady Settlers 130-2
Talcott's N. Y. Families 183-92, 418-20
Opdengraeff — Potts Gen. (1895) 37-40
Opdyke — American Ancestry vi, 159
Opdyke Genealogy (1889) 499 pages
Opie — Lindsay Genealogy
Orbeton — Eaton's Thomaston Me. 343
Orcutt — Crafts' Whately Mass. 536-8
Lincoln's Hist. Hingham Mass. iii, 98-101
Merrill's History of Acworth N. H. 251-3
Mitchell's Hist. Bridgewater Mass. 249-52
Paige's History of Hardwick Mass. 432
Savage's Genealogical Dictionary iii, 314

Temple's History of Whately Mass. 255
Ordway — Coffin's Newbury Mass. 312
Cochrane's Hist. Frances't'n N. H. 859–61
Emery Genealogy (1890) 7
Hayward's History of Hancock N. H. 790
Lapham's History of Norway Me. 566–8
Runnel's Hist. Sanbornton N. H. ii, 535–7
Savage's Genealogical Dictionary iii, 315
Organ — Power's Sangamon Ill. 550
Orme — Am. Anc. v, 192; vii, 121; ix, 47
McAllister Genealogy 57–65
Ormes — Bond's Watertown 382
Draper's History of Spencer Mass. 236
Temple's Hist. of N. Brookfield Mass. 698
Ormond — Saunders' Alabama 267
Orms — Adams' Fairhaven Vt. 446–8
Ormsbee — Daniels' Oxford Mass. 636
Ormsby — American Ancestry vii, 117
Bassett's History of Richmond N. H. 453
Hoyt's Salisbury Mass. Families 267
McKeen's History of Bradford Vt. 352–8
Ormsby Genealogy (1892) 48 pages
Savage's Genealogical Dictionary iii, 315
Orne — American Ancestry vii, 89
Clarke's Kindred Genealogies (1896) 102–36
Pickering Genealogy (1897)
Orr — Bedford N. H. Centennial 320–2
Collin's History of Hillsdale N. Y. app. 98
Davis' History of Bucks County Pa. 551–3
Mitchell Genealogy (1894)
Wheeler's History of Brunswick Me. 845
Wyman's Charlestown Mass. Gens. ii, 715
Orrick — Keim Genealogy 316
Missouri Pioneer Families 177
Orris — Savage's Gen. Dictionary iii, 316
Orser — N. Y. Gen. Rec. xxvi, 134–8
Orso — Fowler's Our Predecessors 56
Ort — Chambers' N. J. Germans 458
Orth — Egle's Penn. Gens. 2d ed. 556–78
Egle's History of Lebanon Co. Pa. 248–50
Orton — Am. Anc. vi, 103; ix, 164, 187; x, 16, 92
Cothren's History of Woodbury Ct. ii, 659
Orton Chart (1886) 16x21 inches
Orton Genealogy (1896) 220 pages
Savage's Genealogical Dictionary iii, 316
Sedgwick's History of Sharon Ct. 102
Stiles' History of Windsor Ct. ii, 539
Wyman's Charlestown Mass. Gens. ii, 716
Orvis — Hemenway's Vt. Gaz. v, 89
Savage's Genealogical Dictionary iii, 317
Temple's Hist. of Northfield Mass. 508–10
Orwig — American Ancestry xii, 23
Orwig Genealogy (1898) 28 pages
Wagenseller Genealogy 181–208
Osborn — Am. Anc. i, 58; ii, 90; iv, 26; x, 103
Anderson's Waterbury Ct. i, app. 96–8
Cope Genealogy 74, 164–6
Dimond Genealogy 102
Freeman's Hist. of Cape Cod Mass. ii,89
Hatfield's History of Elizabeth N. J. 87
Hedge's Easthampton N. Y. 317–26
Lincoln's Hist. of Hingham Mass. iii, 101
Littell's Passaic Valley Gens. 306–11
Norton's History of Fitzwilliam N. H. 650

Orcutt's History of New Milford Ct. 804
Orcutt's History of Stratford Ct. 1260
Osborn Genealogy (1891) 11 pages
Phœnix's Whitney Genealogy ii, 1252
Roe's Sketches of Rose N. Y. 58
Savage's Genealogical Dictionary iii, 317–9
Schenck's History of Fairfield Ct. 401
Stiles' History of Windsor Ct. ii, 539–44
Wyman's Charlestown Mass. 716–8
Osborne — American Ancestry iv, 228
Austin's R. I. Genealogical Dictionary 141
Austin's Allied Families 178–80
Coggswell Genealogy 181–3
Hazen's History of Billerica Mass. 101
Herrick Genealogy (1885) 265
Heywood's Hist. of Westminster Mass. 814
Humphreys Genealogy 288–94
Kellogg's White Genealogy 54
Little's History of Weare N. H. 950–2
Mitchell's Hist. of Bridgewater Mass. 252
New Eng. Hist. and Gen. Reg. liv, 283–5
Norton's History of Knox Co. Ohio 298
Wheeler's History of N. Carolina ii, 216
Osburn — American Ancestry vii, 196
Osgood — Abbott's Andover Mass. 19
Andrews' History of New Britain Ct. 324
Bangor Me. Historical Magazine v, 201–4
Binney Genealogy 37–9
Bouton's History of Concord N. H. 681
Carter's Hist. of Pembroke N. H. ii, 252–5
Evans Genealogy (1893) 26–8, 42
Field Genealogy (1895) 123
Fullonton's Hist. of Raymond N. H. 263–8
Hammatt Papers of Ipswich Mass. 237
Hayward's History of Hancock N. H. 791
Hemenway's Vermont Hist. Gaz. v, 397
Herrick Genealogy (1885) 193
Hodgman's History of Westford Mass. 462
Holgate's Am. Genealogies 228–33
Hoyt's Salisbury Mass. Families 268–72
Lancaster's Hist. of Gilmanton N. H. 279
Maine Hist. Society Collections iv, 278
New Eng. Hist. and Gen. Register xiii, 117–21, 200–2; xx, 22–8; xxii, 81
Osgood Genealogy (1894) 478 pages
Read's History of Swanzey N. H. 411
Ridlon's Saco Valley Me. Families 1087–9
Roe's Sketches of Rose N. Y. 11
Runnel's Hist. Sanbornton N. H. 537–40
Saunderson's Charlestown N. H. 495–7
Savage's Genealogical Dictionary iii, 320–2
Stackpole's History of Durham Me. 230–3
Wyman's Charlestown Mass. Gens. ii, 718
Osland — Jackson's Newton Mass. 375
Paige's History of Cambridge Mass. 620
Osmore — Hayward's Hancock 791
Osterhout — American Ancestry ix, 58
Sylvester's History of Ulster Co. N. Y. 336
Ostrander — Amer. Ancestry ii, 90; v, 95
Munsell's Albany Collections iv, 151
Pearson's Schenectady N. Y. Settlers 130
Sylvester's History of Ulster Co. N. Y. 69
Ostrom — American Ancestry ii, 90
Otis — Am. Anc. v, 43; viii, 149, 199; ix, 205; xi, 44
Austin's Allied Families 181–4

Baker's History of Montville Ct. 404-8
Bangor Me. Historical Magazine vii, 233-5
Bond's Biography of Joseph Otis (1855)
Briggs' History of Shipbuilding 251
Cushman's History of Sheepscott Me. 409
Davis' Landmarks of Plymouth Mass. 196
Deane's History of Scituate Mass. 317
Doty Genealogy 47
Ely Genealogy 170
Freeman's Cape Cod Mass. i, 271; ii, 88
Hayward's History of Hancock N. H. 792
Lincoln's Hist. Hingham Mass. iii, 101-3
Mitchell's Hist. of Bridgewater Mass. 252
Muzzey's Reminiscences
New Eng. Hist. and Gen. Register ii,
    281-96; iv, 143-65; v, 171; 177-223;
    xlvi, 211; li, 328-30
Otis Family of Hingham (1850) 39 pages
Otis Family of Dover N. H. (1851) 48 p.
Robinson's Items of Ancestry (1894) 23
Savage's Genealogical Dictionary iii, 323-5
Sigourney Genealogy
Swift's Barnstable Fam. ii, 222-4, 238-40
Thompson's Memoir of Eben Thompson
Wentworth Genealogy i, 397
Williams' History of Danby Vt. 211-5
Ott — Crandell Genealogy (1859)
Eaton's History of Thomaston Me. ii, 344
Ott Genealogy (1882)
Otterson — Chase's Chester N. H. 572
Ottman — American Ancestry i, 59
Ouderkerk — Albany Colls. iv, 152
Pearson's Schenectady N. Y. Settlers 132-4
Oughterson — Miller's Colchester 251
Outman — Orcutt's Stratford Ct. 1261
Outwater — American Ancestry xii
Ovenshire — Cleveland's Yates Co. 142-5
Ransom Genealogy 73
Overbagh — Greene County N. Y. 432-5
Overing — Hudson's Lexington 168
Overstreet — Power's Sangamon 551
Overton — Am Ancestry iii, 40; iv, 17
Chambers' Early Germans of N. J. 458
Hayden's Virginia Genealogies 385
Lincoln's Hist. of Hingham Mass. iii, 104
Oviatt — Humphreys Genealogy 294
Orcutt's History of New Milford Ct. 749
Orcutt's History of Torrington Ct. 752
Owen — American Ancestry ii, 90
Austin's Allied Families 185
Barbour's My Wife and Mother, app. 74-6
Brown's West Simsbury Ct. Settlers 115
Caverly's History of Pittsford Vt. 717
Cleveland's History of Yates Co. N. Y. 745
Glenn's Merion in Welsh Tract 112-53
Humphrey Genealogy 258-60
Lynchburg Va. Sketches 145-8
Minshall Genealogy (1867) 6-8
Nash Genealogy 81
Penn. Magazine of History xiii, 168-83
Power's Sangamon Co. Ill. Settlers 552
Rhoad's Clover-Croft Chronicles (1893)
Richmond Va. Standard iii, 28
Saunders' Alabama Settlers 50
Savage's Genealogical Dictionary iii, 326
Sharpless Genealogy 195

Stiles' History of Windsor Ct. ii, 544-8
Temple's Hist. of N. Brookfield Mass. 698
Wheeler's History of Brunswick Me. 346
Wheeler's History of N. Carolina ii, 42
Oxford — Heywood's Westminster 814
Oxnard — N. E. Hist. Reg. xxvi, 3
Preble Genealogy (1869) 143-50
Oxton — Eaton's Warren Me. 595
Pabodie — Austin's R. I. Gen. Dict. 141
Pace — Chambers' N. J. Germans 459
Packard — Allen's Worcester 146-8
American Ancestry i, 59; iv, 124, 220; xii
Barrus' History of Goshen Mass. 160-2
Bass' History of Braintree Vt. 169
Cushman's History of Sheepscott Me. 410
Draper's History of Spencer Mass. 246
Dyer's History of Plainfield Mass. 165-8
Eaton's Annals of Warren Me. 596
Eaton's History of Thomaston Me. ii, 345
Hudson's Hist. Marlborough Mass. 426-8
Kingman's N. Bridgewater Mass. 585-619
Lapham's History of Norway Me. 568
Lapham's History of Woodstock Me. 242
Lee Genealogy (1895) 369
Mitchell's Hist. Bridgewater Mass. 253-64
Morrison's Hist. Windham N. H. 710-2
Packard Genealogy (1871) 85 pages
Packard Memorial Assoc. (1888) 72 pages
Porter Genealogy by J. W. Porter 43
Ridlon's Harrison Me. Settlers 98
Savage's Genealogical Dictionary iii, 327
Smith's Genealogy (1889) 94
Stearns' Hist. of Ashburnham Mass. 841-3
Thayer's Memorial (1835) 10-2, 19
Packer — Caulkins' New London 324
Lamborn Genealogy 275
Savage's Genealogical Dictionary iii, 327
Wentworth Genealogy i, 182
Packett — Washington Gen. 245
Paddleford — Paige's Cambridge 620
Savage's Genealogical Dictionary iii, 328
Paddock — American Ancestry i, 59
Austin's Allied Families 187-9
Crafts Genealogy 239
Freeman's Hist. Cape Cod Mass. 214, 709
New Eng. Hist. and Gen. Reg. xii, 220-2
Savage's Genealogical Dictionary iii, 328
Sears Genealogy 32, 57
Winsor's History of Duxbury Mass. 286
Paddy — Savage's Gen. Dict. iii, 328-30
Padelford — Deane (John G.) Biog. 32
Padelford Chart (1859) 24x30 inches
Paganel — Thomas Genealogy (1896) 456
Page — Am. Anc. iv, 183; v, 98; vi, 5; vii,
    211; xi, 152
Atkins' History of Hawley Mass. 109
Babson's History of Gloucester Mass. 120
Bakewell Genealogy 70-80
Bangor Me. Historical Magazine ix, 215-8
Bassett's History of Richmond N. Y. 454
Bemis' History of Marlboro N. H. 592
Bond's Watertown Mass. Gens. 383, 865
Brown's Bedford Mass. Families 26
Butler's History of Farmington Me. 632
Butler's History of Groton Mass. 420
Carter Family Tree of Virginia

Chandler's History of Shirley Mass. 565-79
Cogswell's Hist. Henniker N. H. 665-7
Cogswell's Hist. Nottingham N. H. 435-7
Dearborn's History of Salisbury N. H. 679
Dow's History of Hampton N. H. 889-99
Dunster Genealogy 27
Eaton's Annals of Warren Me. 417
Fullonton's Hist. of Raymond N. H. 278
Glenn's Colonial Mansions 195-213
Hazen's History of Billerica Mass. 102
Heywood's Hist. Westminster Mass. 814-6
Hoyt's Salisbury Mass. Families 272-7
Kellogg's White Genealogy 81
Lancaster's Hist. of Gilmanton N. H. 279
Lapham's History of Rumford Me. 379
Lee Genealogy (1895) 482-5
Little Genealogy 146
Loomis Genealogy (1880) 797-9
Macfarlane Genealogy (1893) 134-42
Meade's Churches of Va. i, 147, 195, 331-51
Morris' Bontecou Genealogy 229
New Eng. Hist. and Gen. Reg. xxvi, 75-8
North's History of Augusta Me. 919
Ormsby Genealogy 32-7
Page Genealogy (1883) 250 pages
Page Genealogy (1893) 275 pages
Page Family of Bedford Mass. (1899) chart
Poor's Merrimack Valley Researches 288
Read's History of Swanzey N. H. 412
Richmond Va. Critic 1888
Richmond Va. Standard iii, 4, 29, 37
Robertson's Pocahontas' Descendants
Runnel's Hist. of Sanbornton N. H. 540-3
Savage's Genealogical Dictionary iii, 330
Stark's History of Dunbarton N. H. 186-91
Stearns' History of Rindge N. H. 614-21
Temple's History of Palmer Mass. 526
Welles' Amer. Family Antiquity i, 125-70
Wheeler's History of Newport N. Y. 487-9
Whitmore's Copps Hill Epitaphs
Worthen's History of Sutton N. H. 845-9
Wyman's Charlestown Mass. Gens. ii, 719
Paige — American Ancestry iii, 188
Ammidown Genealogy 27
Cochrane's Hist. of Antrim N. H. 727-32
Cochrane's Hist. Francestown N. H. 863
Davis Genealogy 191
Hayward's History of Hancock N. H. 792-7
Hyde's Hist. Address at Ware Mass. 51
Hyde's History of Brimfield Mass. 442
Little's History of Weare N. H. 952-9
Paige's History of Hardwick Mass. 433-50
Reed Genealogy 114-9
Savage's Genealogical Dictionary iii, 332
Temple's Hist. of N. Brookfield Mass. 698
Welles' Washington Genealogy 263
Winslow Genealogy i, 148-56; ii, 533-8
Paine — Am. Anc. i, 59; iii, 92, 97, 100,
    109; iv, 34, 117; v, 78; vi, 126
Austin's R. I. Genealogical Dictionary 142
Austin's Allied Families 190
Avery Genealogy (1893) 237-9
Bangor Me. Historical Magazine v, 9
Bass' History of Braintree Vt. 170
Brown's West Simsbury Ct. Settlers 117
Chandler Genealogy 236-45

Clark Family of Watertown Mass. 102, 167
Daniels' History of Oxford Mass. 637
Davis' Landmarks of Plymouth Mass. 197
Eaton's History of Thompson Me. ii, 346
Ellis Genealogy 392
Freeman's Cape Cod i, 635; ii, 378, 570-3
Gregory's History of Northfield Vt. 58-72
Griffin's Journal of Southold N. Y. 224
Kellogg's White Genealogy 60
Lapham's History of Bethel Me. 597
Lapham's History of Paris Me. 685
Livermore's Hist. of Block Island R. I. 341
Morris Genealogy (1887) 162, 166
New Eng. Hist. and Gen. Register xv,
    235-7; xxii, 60-4, 187-91, 291-5
Paine Family Register (1857-9) 64 pages
Paine Family of Worcester (1878) 27 pages
Paine Family Records (1878-83) 522 pages
Paine Family of Ipswich (1881) 184 pages
Pierce's History of Gorham Me. 196
Rich's History of Truro Mass. 546-51
Savage's Genealogical Dictionary iii, 332-8
Stiles' History of Windsor Ct. ii, 548
Thayer Memorial (1835) 115-8
Wall's Reminis. of Worcester Mass. 79-90
Washburn's History of Leicester Mass. 389
Whitmore's Heraldic Journal iii, 189
Wyman's Charlestown Mass. Gens. 720-3
Painter — Anderson's Waterbury 98
Austin's R. I. Genealogical Dictionary 143
Cope Genealogy 38, 129
Kirk Genealogy 37
Painter Genealogy (1869) 20 pages
Paiste — Sharpless Genealogy 366 629-32
Palfray — Pickering Genealogy
Palfrey — Essex Inst. Hist. Coll. i 185
Savage's Genealogical Dictionary iii, 339
Palgrave — Prime's Sands Gen. (1886)
Savage's Genealogical Dictionary iii, 339
Pallardie — Missouri Families 181
Palmatier — American Ancestry ii, 90
Palmer — Am. Anc. ii, 90; iii, 101; v, 137,
    211; ix, 68, 217; xi, 152
Austin's R. I. Genealogical Dictionary 143
Baker's History of Montville Ct. 435-42
Baldwin's Denison Genealogy 11-3
Ball's History of Lake County Ind. 386
Barlow Genealogy 395
Bolton's Westchester Co. N. Y. ii, 753
Briggs' History of Shipbuilding 72, 190
Champion Genealogy
Chute Genealogy, appendix 138-44
Clarke' History of Norton Mass. 159-61
Clyde's Irish Settlement in Pa. 113
Cole Genealogy 91-104, 229
Davis Genealogy (1888) 22-32
Dean's History of Scituate Mass. 319-21
Dearborn's History of Parsonsfield Me. 391
Dimock's Coventry Ct. Records 85
Dow's History of Hampton N. H. 899-906
Driver Genealogy 455-9
Eaton's History of Candia N. H. 94
Eaton's History of Thomaston Me. ii, 347
Essex Institute Hist. Colls. xxii, 289-96
Freeman's Cape Cod i, 565; ii, 449, 465
Hanover Mass. Records (1898)

Huntington's Stamford Ct. Settlers 79
Kellogg's White Genealogy 129
Kulp's Wyoming Valley Families
Lawrence and Bartlett Mem. 124
Lincoln's Hist. of Hingham Mass. iii,105
Narragansett Historical Register ii, 300
New Eng. Hist. Gen. Reg. xvi, 171; l, 223
New York Gen. and Biog. Rec. vi, 29-31
Orcutt's History of Torrington Ct. 752
Orford's N. H. Centennial 126, 128
Paige's History of Cambridge Mass. 621
Palmer Family of Penn. (1875) 474 pages
Palmer Family of Conn. (1881) 295 pages
Palmer Family of Conn. supp. (1882) 119 p.
Palmer Reunion Address (1884) 15 pages
Palmer Family of N. H. (1886) 106 pages
Pompey N. Y. Reunion 334
Ransom Genealogy 26-8
Richmond Va. Standard iii, 23
Runnel's Hist. of Sanbornton N. H. ii, 543
Savage's Genealogical Dictionary iii, 340-3
Sharpless Genealogy 182
Stanton Genealogy 67. 558
Stearns' History of Rindge N. H. 621
Stiles' History of Windsor Ct. ii, 548-51
Whittemore's Orange N. J. 447
Williams' History of Danby Vt. 215-7
Worthen's History of Sutton N. H. 849-53
Wyman's Charlestown Mass. Gens. ii, 724
Palmes — Caulkins' N. London Ct. 360
Ogden Genealogy (1898) 84, 131
Pangburn — Albany Colls. iv, 152
Panill — Richmond Stand. ii, 32; iii, 13
Pankey — Watkins Genealogy 37
Pannill — Wm. and Mary College Quarterly vi, 113, 155
Pantry — Porter's Hartford Settlers 15
Tuttle Genealogy 83, 100
Papin — Beckwith's Creoles 124
Goode Genealogy 396
Paragard — Lapham's Norway Me. 569
Pardee — American Ancestry vi, 104
Blake's History of Hamden Ct. 265
Dodd's History of East Haven Ct. 140-2
Orcutt's History of Wolcott Ct. 536
Savage's Genealogical Dictionary iii, 344
Sedgwick's History of Sharon Ct. 103
Timlow's Southington Ct. Sketches 200-2
Pardoe — American Ancestry ix, 95
Paret — American Ancestry iv, 150
Parham — Tyngsboro Mass. Centen. 12
Parish — American Ancestry xii
Baker's Montville Ct. 100
Cleveland's Yates Co. 381
Parish Genealogy (1897) 31 pages
Perkins' Old Houses of Norwich Ct. 544
Savage's Genealogical Dictionary iii, 346
Strong Genealogy 153, 372-4
Thurston Genealogy (1892) 29
Park — Allison Genealogy 53
Amer. Anc. i, 59; ii, 91; iv, 30; xii, 37
Baird's History of Rye N. Y. 431-3
Barry's History of Framingham Mass. 348
Bond's Watertown Mass. 384-8, 865-8
Champney and Park Gen. (1855) 25-36
Cochrane's Hist. Francestown N. H. 863

Collin's Hist. Hillsdale N. Y., app. 99-101
Dickey Genealogy 51-3
Jackson's History of Newton Mass. 382-6
Morrison's Hist. of Windham N. H. 713-31
Morse's Sherborn Mass. Settlers 184
Newfane Vt. Centennial 172
Park Family Sketch (1880)
Pompey N. Y. Reunion 334-6
Ransom Genealogy 71
Sedgwick's History of Sharon Ct. 104
Parke — Amer. Anc. v, 183; viii, 176
Biddle Genealogy (1892) 39-46
Caulkins' History of New London Ct. 282
Glenn's Genealogical Notes (1898)
Meade's Old Churches of Virginia
Potter's American Monthly vi, 85
Savage's Genealogical Dictionary iii, 346-9
Parker — Abbot's Andover Mass. 20
American Ancestry i, 59; ii, 91; iii, 167; v,
202; vi, 22, 179; x, 201; xi, 45
Anderson's Waterbury Ct. i, app. 98
Atkins' History of Hawley Mass. 47
Austin's R. I. Genealogical Dictionary 143
Avery Genealogy (1893) 211-4
Baker's History of Montville Ct. 443-7
Ballou's History of Milford Mass. 936-8
Bangor Hist. Mag. i, 126-31; v, 204-6
Barry's Hist. Framingham Mass. 349-51
Bassett's Hist. of Richmond N. H. 455-7
Bedford N. H. Centennial 323
Bond's Watertown Mass. Gens. 388
Bouton's History of Concord N. H. 682
Brewster's Portsmouth N. H. ii, 120-7
Bridgeman's Granary Burial Gr. 136-44
Butler's History of Farmington Me. 547
Butler's Hist. Groton Mass. 421, 476, 494
Calnek's Hist. of Annapolis N. S. 559-61
Capron Genealogy by Holden 41-3
Carter's Hist. Pembroke N. H. ii, 256-65
Caulkins' History of New London Ct. 306
Chambers' Early Germans of N. J. 460
Chandler's History of Shirley Mass. 580-9
Chute Genealogy, appendix 144-7
Cleveland's Hist. Yates Co. N. Y. 117-9
Cochrane's History of Antrim N. H. 632-5
Corliss's North Yarmouth Me. Magazine
Cothren's Hist. of Woodbury Ct. ii, 1542
Crafts' History of Whately Mass. 538-40
Cutter's History of Jaffrey N. H. 413-8
Cutts Genealogy 242-4
Daniels' History of Oxford Mass. 637
Davis' History of Wallingford Vt. 871-4
Deane's History of Scituate Mass. 320
Dearborn's History of Salisbury N. H. 681
Dickey Genealogy 33-7
Dimock's Coventry Ct. Records 86-8
Eaton's Annals of Warren Me. 597
Eaton's History of Reading Mass. 100-3
Egle's Penn. Genealogies 2d ed. 579-604
Ellis Genealogy 393
Farrow's Hist. Islesborough Me. 236-8 F.
Fitch's Parkers of Wash. Co. N. Y. (1877)
Forrest's History of Norfolk Va. 71
Freeman's Cape Cod ii, 438, 466, 642
Green's Groton Mass. Epitaphs 247
Green's Early Groton Mass. Settlers 13

Green's Kentucky Families
Hartwell Genealogy (1887) 5
Hartwell Genealogy (1895) 34
Hayward's History of Hancock N. H. 797
Hazen's History of Billerica Mass. 104-7
Hemenway's Vermont Hist. Gaz. v, 722
Heywood's Hist. of Westminster Mass. 817
Hill's History of Mason N. H. 205
Hodgman's Hist. of Westford Mass. 463-5
Holton's Farwell Genealogy 80-8
Howell's Hist. of Southampton N. Y. 343
Hoyt's Salisbury Mass. Families 277-9
Hubbard's History of Springfield Vt. 402-8
Hubbard's Hist. Stanstead Co. Can. 304-6
Hudson's Hist. of Lexington Mass. 169-76
Humphrey Genealogy 394-6
Hyde's History of Brimfield Mass. 442-5
Jackson Genealogy 299
Jackson's History of Newton Mass. 375-81
Joslin's History of Poultney Vt. 317
Kidder's Hist. New Ipswich N. H. 417-9
Lamb's History of New York City i, 706
Lincoln's History of Hingham Mass. iii,
    106, 365
Littell's Passaic Valley Genealogies 311
Livermore's History of Wilton N. H. 453-7
Mallmann's Shelter Island N. Y. 305
Martin's History of Chester Pa. 35-7
Meade's Old Churches of Virginia
Milliken's Narraguagus Valley Me. 18
Morrison's Hist. Windham N. H. 713-31
Morse Memorial, appendix 54
Morse's Sherborn Mass. Settlers 185
Muzzey's Reminiscences
N. E. Reg. iv, 139; vi, 375; xvi, 41-4, 91-4
New York Gen. and Biog. Rec. xxix, 190-3,
    xxx, 31-6
Norton's Hist. of Fitzwilliam N. H. 651-5
Orcutt's History of Wolcott Ct. 538
Paige's History of Cambridge Mass. 622
Parker Family of N. Y. (1877) 18 pages
Parker Family of Boston (1888) 10 pages
Parker Family of Roxbury (1890) 10 pages
Parker Family of Saybrook (1892) 51 pages
Parker Family of Lexington (1893) 526 p.
Parker Family of Boston (1894) 51 pages
Parker Family of Ohio (1895) 16 pages
Parker Family of New Jersey (1897)
Paul's History of Wells Vt. 127
Poor's Merrimack Valley 113-5, 124-8
Read's History of Swanzey N. H. 414
Richmond Va. Standard i, 26; iii, 7
Ridlon's Saco Valley Me. Families 1089
Ruggles Genealogy
Salter's Hist. Monmouth Co. N. J. lxxix
Saunderson's Charlestown N. H. 501-5
Savage's Genealogical Dict. iii, 349-58
Secomb's History of Amherst N. H. 714-6
Sewall's History of Woburn Mass. 628
Sharpless Genealogy 457
Shattuck Genealogy 375-7
Sheldon's Hist. of Deerfield Mass. 258-60
Smith's History of Delaware Co. Pa. 490
Stackpole's History of Durham Me. 233-5
Stearns' History of Ashburnham Mass. 843
Stearns' History of Rindge N. H. 622

Stoddard Genealogy (1865) 14, 38, 63-8
Stone's Hist. of Hubbardston Mass. 325-7
Temple's Hist. of N. Brookfield Mass. 699
Temple's History of Whately Mass. 255
Virginia Magazine of History v, 442-7; vi,
    86-8, 195-7, 301-5, 412-8, 420-4
Ward's History of Shrewsbury Mass. 400-4
West Springfield Mass. Centennial (1874)
Whitehead's Perth Amboy N. J. 128-38
Whitman Genealogy 743-50
Whitmore's Copps Hill Epitaphs
Woodbury's Groveland Mass. Epit. 60-71
Worcester's History of Hollis N. H. 383
Worthen's History of Sutton N. H. 853-6
Wyman's Charlestown Mass. Gens. 726-9
Parkhurst — American Anc. i, 60; xii
Ballou's History of Milford Mass. 938-48
Barry's History of Framingham Mass. 351
Bassett's History of Richmond N. H. 457
Bemis' History of Marlboro N. H. 595
Bond's History of Watertown Mass. 388-9
Cochrane's History of Antrim N. H. 635
Hayward's History of Gilsum N. H. 374
Hayward's History of Hancock N. H. 798
Hudson's History of Lexington Mass. 177
Lapham's History of Norway Me. 569
Livermore's Hist. of Wilton N. H. 457-60
Parkhurst Genealogy (1883) 19 pages
Savage's Genealogical Dictionary iii, 358
Secomb's History of Amherst N. H. 716-8
Stone's History of Hubbardston Mass. 328
Temple's History of Palmer Mass. 527
Wyman's Hunt Genealogy 121
Parkinson — Cochrane's Hist. Frances-
    town N. H. 866-9
Cogswell's Hist. New Boston N. H. 404-7
Mills Genealogy (1893) 13-5
Power's Sangamon Co. Ill. Settlers 556
Parkman — Allen's Worcester 56
American Ancestry iii, 196; vi, 57
Ballou's History of Milford Mass. 949-51
Barry's History of Framingham Mass. 352
Bemis' History of Marlboro N. H. 596
Breck Genealogy 20-32
Savage's Genealogical Dictionary iii, 358
Temple's Hist. of N. Brookfield Mass. 699
Whitmore's Copps Hill Epitaphs
Parks — Amer. Ancestry ii, 91; xii, 82
Dearborn's Hist. of Parsonsfield Me. 391
Goode Genealogy 86-8
Montague Genealogy 565-7
New Eng. Hist. and Gen. Register xl, 37
Paige's History of Cambridge Mass. 623
Paul's History of Wells Vt. 129-32
Power's Sangamon Co. Ill. Settlers 552-6
Saunderson's Charlestown N. H. 505
Temple's Hist. of N. Brookfield Mass. 699
Temple's History of Palmer Mass. 525
Welles' Washington Genealogy 212
Parlin — Foster Ancestry 18
Parmelee — Am. Anc. iii, 195; x, 195
Caverly's History of Pittsford Vt. 718
Davis' History of Wallingford Ct. 884
Montague Genealogy 526
New Eng. Hist. Gen. Register liii, 405-11
Salisbury's Fam. Histories (1892) i, 219-33

Wheeler's History of Newport N. H. 490-9
Whittemore's Hist. Middlesex Co. Ct. 211
Parmenter — Barry's Framingham 353
Bemis' History of Marlboro N. H. 596-9
Cochrane's History of Antrim N. H. 636-9
Draper's History of Spencer Mass. 236
Heywood's Hist. Westminster Mass. 818
Ruttenber's Hist. of Newburgh N. Y. 318
Savage's Genealogical Dictionary iii, 359
Temple's History of Northfield Mass. 511
Parmentier — Bergen's Kings Co. 221
Parmly — Bass' Hist. of Braintree Vt. 170
Parrat — Essex Inst. Coll. 296; xxiii, 59
Parris — Bond's Watertown 391
Deane's History of Scituate Mass. 320
Lapham's History of Paris Me. 687
Mitchell's Hist. of Bridgewater Mass. 264
Savage's Genealogical Dictionary iii, 345
Whitman Genealogy 373
Williams' History of Danby Vt. 218-26
Parrish — American Ancestry ii, 91
Power's Sangamon Co. Ill. Settlers 558
Parrott — Austin's R. I. Gen. Dict. 144
Hodgman's History of Westford Mass. 465
Homer Genealogy 18-20
Littell's Passaic Valley Gen. 312-4
Orcutt's History of Stratford Ct. 1354
Parruck — Orcutt's Stratford Ct. 1354
Parry — American Ancestry vi, 67; vii, 20
Battle's History of Bucks Co. Pa. 1099
Davis' History of Bucks Co. Pa. 681-4
Fell Genealogy 88
Futhey's History of Chester Co. Pa. 675
Glenn's Merion in Welsh Tract 291-3
Hotchkin's The York Road 377
Jolliffe Genealogy 211-4
Parry Genealogy (1877) 34 pages
Penn. Magazine and History i, 469
Young's History of Wayne Co. Ind. 353
Parshall — Parshall Gen. (1900) 38 pages
Parsons — Am. Anc. i, 60; ii, 92; iii, 206;
iv, 199; v, 166; vii, 37, 104, 265, 273;
viii, 68; x, 165
Austin's R. I. Genealogical Dictionary 145
Babson's Hist. of Gloucester Mass. 120-5
Barnes' History of Goshen Mass. 162-5
Cochrane's History of Antrim N. H. 639
Coe and Ward Memorials 56-60
Cope Genealogy 148-50
Corliss' North Yarmouth Me. Magazine
Daniels' History of Oxford Mass. 639
Dearborn's Parsonsfield Me. 391, 464-8
Dearborn's History of Salisbury N. H. 683
Dwight Genealogy 468-76
Eaton's Annals of Warren Me. 597
Ely Genealogy 28
Gifford's Our Patronymics 17-9
Hall Genealogy (1892) 14
Hall's Genealogical Notes (1886) 92-105
Hedge's Hist. East Hampton N. Y. 326-30
Hepburn Genealogy 102, 151
Hinman's Connecticut Settlers 1st ed. 171
Holton's Parsons Genealogy
Hough's History of Lewis Co. N. Y. 260
Howell's Southampton N. Y. 2d ed. 343-5
Jordan's Leighton Genealogy

Judd's History of Hadley Mass. 549
Lancaster's History of Gilmanton N. H. 281
Lapham's History of Norway Me. 510
Leach's Morton Ancestry 80-90
Littell's Passaic Valley Genealogies 315-8
Longmeadow Mass. Centennial (1883) 70
Lyman's Hist. Easthampton Mass. 183-5
Middlefield Ct. History
Montgomery County N. Y. History 211
New Eng. Hist. Reg. i, 263-75; xii, 176
Orcutt's History of Torrington Ct. 754
Parsons Family of Springfield (1867) 36 p.
Parsons Family of Hartford (1877) chart
Parsons Family of Alfred Me. (1877) chart
Parsons Fam. of New London (1877) chart
Parsons Family of Clinton Ct. (1878) chart
Parsons Family of Springfield (1878) chart
Parsons Fam. of E. Hampton (1879) 20 p.
Parsons Fam. Parsonsfield Me. (1879) chart
Parsons Family of Enfield Ct. (1880) chart
Parsons Family of Flora Ill. (1894) 8 pages
Parsons Family of Springfield (1900) 109 p.
Peck's Rochester N. Y. Centennial 716-8
Read's History of Swanzey N. H. 415-7
Savage's Genealogical Dictionary iii, 361-4
Sedgwick's History of Sharon Ct. 104
Stiles' History of Windsor Ct. ii, 551-5
Strong Genealogy 1291-1305
Temple's History of Northfield Mass. 511
Temple's History of Palmer Mass. 526
Vinton's Giles Genealogy 136-44
Walworth's Hyde Genealogy 905-19
Washburn's History of Leicester Mass. 387
W. Springfield Mass. Centen. (1874) 119
Whitmore's Copps Hill Epitaphs
Wight Genealogy 134
Winslow Gen. i, 318-23, 345, 354; ii, 710-5
Parthemore — Parthemore Gen. (1885)
Partridge — Am. Anc. v, 52; vii, 250;
ix, 168
Ballou's History of Milford Mass. 951-3
Bass' History of Braintree Vt. 171
Bemis' History of Marlboro N. H. 599
Blake's History of Franklin Mass. 264
Dedham Historical Reg. vii, 51-6, 100-6,
148-51; viii, 14-9
Dickinson's Lyman and Other Fams
Dwight Genealogy 762-72
Eaton's History of Thomaston Me. ii, 348
Herrick's History of Gardner Mass. 371
Heywood's Hist. of Westminster Mass.
818-20
Hoyt's Salisbury Mass. Families 279
Jameson's Hist. of Medway Mass. 506-11
Judd's History of Hadley Mass. 550
Lapham's History of Norway Me. 573
Lapham's History of Paris Me. 689
Loneland Genealogy i, 119-32
Morse's Sherborn Mass. Settlers 186-90
Read's History of Swanzey N. H. 417
Robinson's Items of Ancestry (1894) 63
Savage's Genealogical Dictionary iii, 365-7
Strong Genealogy 1129-31
Vinton's Richardson Mem. 245
Wight Genealogy 21
See also Patridge

Paschall — Morris Gen. (1898) 544–56
Pasco — Stiles' Windsor Ct. ii, 555–7
Paskiel — Eaton's Warren Me. 598
Passmore — American Ancestry v, 15
Sharpless Genealogy 185, 298
Past — American Ancestry xi, 205
Patch — American Ancestry iii, 137
Bassett's History of Richmond N. H. 458
Brooks' History of Medford Mass. 532
Cochrane's Hist. Francest'n N. H. 869–74
Cogswell's Hist. of Henniker N. H. 667
Daniels' History of Oxford Mass. 639
Hodgman's History of Westford Mass. 465
Norton's History of Fitzwilliam N. H. 655
Savage's Genealogical Dictionary 368
Patchen — American Ancestry xii
Sedgwick's History of Sharon Ct. 104
Patchin — Cleveland's Yates Co. 248
Pate — Chappell Genealogy 183–6
Chappell Genealogy 2d ed. (1900) 324–9
Paten — Richmond Va. Standard iii, 33
Patrick — American Ancestry ii, 92
Cutter's History of Jaffrey N. H. 429–37
Lee Genealogy (1888) 370–7
Norton's History of Fitzwilliam N. H. 656
Paige's History of Cambridge Mass. 623
Welles' Washington Genealogy 251
Patridge — Morse Mem., app. 47
Randall's Hist. Chesterfield N. H. 390 6–8
Winsor's History of Duxbury Mass. 287
Pattee — Corliss' Genealogy, appendix
Lapham's History of Bethel Me. 597
Patten — American Ancestry i, 60
Ball's History of Lake County Ind. 396
Bedford N. H. Centennial 324
Blood's History of Temple N. H. 238
Bradbury's Hist. Kennebunkport Me. 267
Brooks' History of Medford Mass. 533
Chase's History of Chester N. H. 573
Cochrane's History of Antrim N. H. 640
Cogswell's History of Henniker N. H. 668
Daniels' History of Oxford Mass. 639
Eaton's History of Candia N. H. 95–100
Hayward's Hist. Hancock N. H. 799–804
Hazen's History of Billerica Mass. 108–10
Hinman's Connecticut Settlers 1st ed. 224
Hodgman's Hist. of Westford Mass. 465
Hurlbut Genealogy 418
Milliken's Narraguagus Valley Me. 12
Paige's History of Cambridge Mass. 624
Patten (Mrs. Ruth) Life of (1834)
Reed's History of Bath Me. 336
Ridlon's Saco Valley Me. Families 1090–2
Savage's Genealogical Dict. iii, 369, 379
Wheeler's History of Brunswick Me. 846
Wyman's Charlestown Mass. Gens. ii, 731
Patterson — Am. Anc. i, 60; v, 9; vi, 36;
vii, 270; x, 144
Andrews' New Britain Ct. 128, 133, 152
Barry's History of Framingham Mass. 356
Bond's Watertown Mass. Genealogies 392
Boyd's History of Conesus N. Y. 167
Chandler's History of Shirley Mass. 589–99
Cleveland's Hist. of Yates Co. N. Y. 225
Cochrane's Hist. Francest'n N. H. 874–6
Cogswell's Hist. Henniker N. H. 668–75

Dickey Genealogy 53–6
Driver Genealogy 460–3
Eaton's Annals of Warren Me. 598
Harris' Hist. of Lancaster Co. Pa. 432–40
Hatch's History of Industry Me. 784–91
Hazen's History of Billerica Mass. 107
Lewis Genealogy (1893) 275–9
Livermore's History of Wilton N. H. 460
Martin's History of Chester Pa. 241
Morrison Genealogy 191
New Eng. Hist. Gen. Reg. xxxvii, 148–55
New York Gen. and Biog. Record xxi, 100
North's History of Augusta Me. 920–2
Orcutt's History of Stratford Ct. 1261
Parker's Hist. Londonderry N. H. 292–4
Patterson Genealogy (1847) 103 pages
Patterson Genealogy (1867) 8 pages
Pearson's Schenectady N. Y. Settlers 135
Phœnix's Whitney Gen. i, 148; ii, 1582
Ridlon's Saco Valley Me. 1092–1102
Roome Genealogy 199
Ruggles Genealogy
Savage's Genealogical Dictionary iii, 370–2
Secomb's History of Amherst N. H. 719
Temple's Hist. of N. Brookfield Mass. 700
Temple's History of Northfield Mass. 513
Walworth's Hyde Gen. 270, 591–3, 1147
Williamson's History of Belfast Me. 102–4
Young's History of Warsaw N. Y. 313–6
Pattison — Young's Chautauqua 543
Patton — American Ancestry x, 41
Green's Kentucky Families
Hubbard's Hist. of Stanstead Co. Can. 120
Power's Sangamon Co. Ill. Settlers 559
Richmond Va. Standard iii, 3
Slaughter's St. Mark's Parish Virg. 178
Whittemore's Orange N. J. 269–74
Pattridge — See Patridge
Paty — Davis' Landmarks 197
Paul — Am. Anc. iii, 123; iv, 231; vi, 173;
vii, 4, 5, 23
Beckwith's Creoles 28–37
Eaton's History of Thomaston Me. ii, 349
Goode Genealogy 143
Guild's Stiles Genealogy 316–8
Hill's Dedham Mass. Records i
Hubbard's Stanstead Co. Canada 167
Paul Family Chart by Geo. H. Paul (179)
Paul Genealogy (1896) 7 pages
Paul's History of Wells Vt. 122–8
Richmond Va. Standard ii, 47
Rodman Genealogy 149–53
Savage's Genealogical Dictionary iii, 372
Strobridge Genealogy 55–8
Wakefield Genealogy 176
Wheeler's History of Newport N. H. 500
Paulen — Power's Sangamon Ill. 561
Paulding — Davis' Landmarks 198
Raymond's Tarrytown Monument 155–61
Paulison — Am. Ancestry iii, 202; iv, 22
Clayton's History of Bergen Co. N. J. 293
Paulk — American Ancestry x, 66
Waldo's History of Tolland Ct. 131–3
Pawley — Gregg's Old Cheraws 100
Pawling — Pennypacker's Phœnixville
Perkiomen Region Pa. iii, 57–60

Paxson — Davis' Bucks County Pa. 276
Paxton — American Ancestry iii, 205
Green's Kentucky Families
Paxton's Marshall Gen. 156-61, 266-72
Richmond Va. Standard iii, 2
Rodman Genealogy 80-2
Payn — Hobart's Abington Mass. 426
Payne — Am. Anc. i, 60; ii, 92; iv, 64; vii, 70
Anderson's Waterbury Ct. i, app. 99
Cleveland Genealogy 173-83, 191-6
Douglas Genealogy 188-91
Hammatt Papers of Ipswich Mass. 240-2
Hayden's Virginia Genealogies 654
Kulp's Wyoming Valley Families
Mass. Histor. Society Proc. (1873) 409-23
New Eng. Hist. and Gen. Register v, 331-3
Payne and Gore Gen. (1875) 30 pages
Preston Genealogy (1870) 58-60
Runnel's Hist. of Sanbornton N. H. ii, 545
Slaughter's St. Mark's Parish Va. 193
Virginia Magazine of History vi, 313-6, 427; vii, 79-82. 200
Walworth's Hyde Genealogy 778-80
Wm. and Mary College His. Reg. ii, 90
Payson — Am. Ancestry vi, 125; xii, 64
Dodge Ancestry (1896) 41-3
Eaton's Annals of Warren Me. 599
Ellis' History of Roxbury Mass. 125
Gage's History of Rowley Mass. 449
Norton's History of Fitzwilliam N. H. 657
Savage's Genealogical Dictionary iii, 372-4
Sinclair Genealogy 230-2
Smith's Hist. of Peterborough N. H. 221
Stearns' History of Rindge N. H. 623-5
Wentworth Genealogy i, 357-60, 683-94
Wyman's Charlestown Mass. Gens. ii, 732
Peabody — Alden Mem. 5
American Ancestry i, 61; iv, 216
Austin's R. I. Genealogical Dictionary 145
Bangor Me. Historical Magazine i, 214
Chandler's History of Shirley Mass. 599
Cochrane's History of Antrim N. H. 641
Cochrane's Hist. Francestown N. H. 877
Cogswell's Hist. of Acworth N. H. 397-9
Cogswell's Hist. of Henniker N. H. 676
Dow's History of Hampton N. H. 906
Dudley Genealogy (1848) 129
Eaton's Annals of Warren Me. 600
Eaton's History of Thomaston Me. ii, 350
Emery's Newbury Mass. Reminisc. 10
Hazen's History of Billerica Mass. 110
Lapham's History of Rumford Me. 380
Livermore's History of Wilton N. H. 461-3
Mitchell's Hist. of Bridgewater Mass. 383
New Eng. Hist. and Gen. Register ii, 153-61, 361-72; iii, 359-74
Peabody Genealogy (1848) 21 pages
Peabody Genealogy 2d ed. (1867) 61 pages
Perley's History of Boxford Mass. 37-9
Pierce's History of Gorham Me. 197
Robinson Genealogy (1859)
Savage's Genealogical Dictionary iii, 374-6
Savage's Life of K. O. Peabody (1855)
Secomb's History of Amherst N. H. 720-4
Smith's History of Peterborough N. H. 223

Wheeler's History of Newport N. H. 501-3
Winsor's History of Duxbury Mass. 285
Peach — N. E. Gen. Reg. liv, 276-9
Peachey — Bitsche Genealogy 7-30, etc.
Meade's Old Families of Virginia
Wm. and Mary College Hist. Reg. iii, 111-5
Peacock — Evans' Fox Genealogy 225-32
Power's Sangamon Co. Ill. Settlers 561
Randall's Hist. of Chesterfield N. H. 398
Savage's Genealogical Dictionary iii, 376
Secomb's History of Amherst N. H. 724
Peake — Hudson's Lexington Mass. 177
Morris Genealogy (1894) 27-30
Morris and Flynt Ancestors (1882) 19-21
Savage's Genealogical Dictionary iii, 377
Peaks — Deane's Scituate Mass. 321
Peale — American Ancestry viii, 133
Hanson's Old Kent Md. 333
Pearce — American Ancestry iv, 97; xii, 11
Austin's Ancestral Dictionary 42
Austin's R. I. Genealogical Dictionary 146
Babson's Gloucester Mass. 125, 266-71
Baird's History of Rye N. Y. 433
Ball's History of Lake County Ind. 401
Bridgeman's Granary Epitaphs 164
Conn. Quarterly iii, (1897) 481
Futhey's History of Chester Co. Pa. 676-8
Hanson's Old Kent Md. 160-2
Homer Genealogy 20-4
Johnston's History of Bristol Me. 240-3
New Eng. Hist. and Gen. Reg. vi, 276-9
Pearce Genealogy (1888) 150 pages
Pearce Genealogy, see Pierce
Pierce's Biog. Contributions 221-32
Rhode Island Historical Magazine v, 40-8
Tilley's Mag. of N. E. History i, 129-49
Pearcy — Walworth's Hyde Gen. 504
See also under Percy and Pearce
Pearl — Cal. Register (1900)
Essex County Mass. Hist. and Gen. Register i, (1894) 65-8
Pearmain — Smith Gen. (1895) 85-90
Pearsall — Bunker's L. I. Gens. 268-71
Mott Genealogy 305-10
N. Y. Gen. and Biog. Record xvi, 1-3
Pearse — Cutts Genealogy 110-2
Pearson — American Ancestry ii, 92; xii
Babson's History of Gloucester Mass. 322
Bangor Me. Historical Magazine vi, 294
Cleveland Genealogy 68-72, 224-6
Coffin's History of Boscawen N. H. 592-4
Dearborn's History of Salisbury N. H. 684
Essex Institute Hist. Coll. xxiii, 69-71
Gage's History of Rowley Mass. 450
Hayden's Virginia Genealogies 354
Hayward's History of Hancock N. H. 805
Heywood's Hist. of Westminster Mass. 820
McKeen's History of Bradford Vt. 268-71
Miller's Hist. of Colchester Co. N. S. 231-3
Munsell's Albany Collections iv, 153
Pearson Genealogy, see Pierson
Potts Genealogy (1895) 287-9
Richmond Va. Standard ii, 47; iii, 35. 37
Runnel's Hist. Sanbornton N. H. ii, 546-8
Savage's Gen. Dictionary iii, 378, 433-5
Smith's Genealogy of Wm. Smith 89

Smith's History of Delaware Co. Pa. 490
Stiles' History of Windsor Ct. ii, 558
Thurston Genealogy (1892) 12-4, 85-8
Thurston Genealogy (1894) 8-11
Walworth's Hyde Genealogy 48, 851-4
Wheeler's History of N. Carolina ii, 385
Whitman Genealogy 96
Pearsons — Hayward's Hancock 804
Worthen's History of Sutton N. H. 856
Peart — Potts Genealogy (1895) 53
Pease — American Ancestry vii, 268
Chandler Genealogy 84
Crafts' History of Whately Mass. 540
Daniels' History of Oxford Mass. 639
Dearborn's Hist. of Parsonsfield He. 392
Dwight Genealogy 314-6, 417-20
Emery Genealogy (1890) 31
Gifford's Our Patronymics 24
Hayward's History of Gilsum N. H. 374
Hinman's Connecticut Settlers 1st ed. 172-5
Humphreys Genealogy 199-202
Huntington Genealogy 153
Longmeadow Mass. Centennial (1883) 76
Montague Genealogy 69
Morris and Flynt Genealogy 41-3
Morris Genealogy (1894) 143-6
New Eng. Hist. and Gen. Reg. iii, 27-30,
  169-75, 233-8, 390-8; ix, 91-3; x, 159
Norton's History of Fitzwilliam N. H. 803
Pease Genealogy (1847) 42 pages
Pease Fam. Early History (1869) 96 pages
Pease Genealogy (1869) 497 pages
Phœnix Family of Maine 16
Plumb's History of Hanover Pa. 465
Power's Sangamon Co. Ill. Settlers 562
Ridlon's Saco Valley Me. Families 1102
Savage's Genealogical Dictionary iii 379
Stiles' History of Windsor Ct. ii, 557
Temple's History of Whately Mass. 256
Ward's Hist. of Shrewsbury Mass. 407-9
Peaslee — Chase's Haverhill 277, 644 ◄─**Peet** — Am. Anc. v, 61; x, 88; xi, 94, 178
Cogswell's Hist. of Henniker N. H. 677
Hoyt's Salisbury Mass. Families 280
Hubbard's Hist. of Stanstead Co. Can. 208
Lancaster's Hist. of Gilmanton N. H. 282
Little's History of Weare N. H. 959-69
Peaslee Pioneers of Kansas (1897) 12 pages
Peaslees of Haverhill Mass. (1899) 72 p.
Washington N. H. History 562
Worthen's History of Sutton N. H. 857-65
Peasley — Washington N. H. History 562
Peat — Orcutt's New Milford Ct. 799
Orcutt's History of Stratford Ct. 1263-6
Peavey — Bass' Hist. of Braintree Vt. 171
Peck — Aldrich's Walpole N. H. 343
Am. Anc. i, 61; ii, 93; iv, 225; v, 123, 196;
  vii, 151; xi, 112
Anderson's Waterbury Ct. i, app. 100
Andrews' Hist. of New Britain Ct. 391, 397
Ballou Genealogy 492-4
Ballou's History of Milford Mass. 954-7
Bouton Genealogy 119
Chapman's Pratt Genealogy 96-8
Cleveland's History of Yates Co. N. Y. 292
Lee Genealogy (1897) 161-5
Lincoln's Hist. of Hingham Mass. iii, 107

Matthew's History of Cornwall Vt. 288
Mead's History of Greenwich Ct. 595-600
Morris' Resseguie Genealogy 116-8
Morse Mem., appendix 67½
N. E. Gen. Reg. xxxii, 83; xxxiii, 438
Orcutt's History of New Milford Ct. 799
Orcutt's History of Stratford Ct. 1266
Orcutt's History of Wolcott Ct. 540
Paige's History of Hardwick Mass. 451
Parker Genealogy (1892) 21-3
Peck Genealogy (1868) 442 pages
Peck Family of New Haven (1877) 253 p.
Perkins' Old Houses of Norwich Ct. 546-8
Phœnix's Whitney Genealogy 1, 464
Resseguie Genealogy 68-71
Savage's Genealogical Dictionary iii, 380-4
Sedgwick's History of Sharon Ct. 104
Stiles' History of Windsor Ct. ii, 558
Timlow's Southington Ct. Sketches 203-5
Tuttle Genealogy 137-9
Walworth's Hyde Gen. 607-11, 729-33, 980
Wentworth Genealogy ii, 470
Whittemore's Orange N. J. 94
Wyman's Charlestown Mass. Gens. ii, 734
Peckett — McKeen's Bradford 292-7
Peckham — American Ancestry xi, 94
Austin's R. I. Genealogical Dictionary 146
Austin's Ancestral Dictionary 43
Austin's Allied Families 191-5
Davis' Landmarks of Plymouth Mass. 139
Hazard Genealogy 94-6
Heywood's Hist. of Westminster Mass. 821
Pecker — Morrison's Windham 734
Peek — Munsell's Albany Colls. iv, 153
Pearson's Schenectady Settlers 135-40
Peele — Driver Genealogy 421
Essex Institute Hist. Colls. xiii, 64-6
Smith's Founders of Mass. Bay 207-11
Peeler — Heywood's Westminster 822
Peers — Temple's North Brookfield 701
Peet — Am. Anc. v, 61; x, 88; xi, 94, 178
California Register i, (1900)
Orcutt's History of Stratford Ct. 1263-6
Pegram — Goode Genealogy 126
Hayden's Virginia Genealogies 314
Meade's Old Churches of Virginia
Richmond Va. Standard ii, 4, 41
Slaughter's Bristol Parish Va. 206-10
Slaughter's St. Mark's Parish Va. 138
Pegues — Gregg's Old Cheraws 94
Peirce — Am. Anc. ii, 93; iv, 212; vi, 156;
  ix, 191
Bangor Me. Historical Magazine v, 8
Benedict's History of Sutton Mass. 700-2
Brooks' History of Medford Mass. 533
Cutter's History of Arlington Mass. 280-2
Essex Institute Hist. Colls. xviii, 170-6
Keyes' West Boylston Mass. Register 32
Leonard's History of Dublin N. H. 381
New Eng. Hist. Gen. Reg. xxi, 61-5, 157-
  62, 257-64, 340-50; xxii, 73-80, 174-85,
  304-10, 428-33; xxix, 273-81
Paige's History of Cambridge Mass. 625
Paige's History of Hardwick Mass. 451
Palmer and Trimble Genealogy 367-9, 401
Peirce Genealogy, see Pierce

Pickering Genealogy
Pierce's History of Grafton Mass. 540-3
Ridlon's Harrison Me. Settlers 102-4
Sewall's History of Woburn Mass. 628
Stearns' Hist. Ashburnham Mass. 844-6
Stearns' History of Rindge N. H. 626-30
Stowe's History of Hubbardston Mass. 329
Wentworth Genealogy i, 321-4
Winsor's History of Duxbury Mass. 288
Peircks — Ward's Shrewsbury 405
Periret — Perkins' Norwich Ct. 549
Pelham — Austin's R. I. Dict. 149
Davis' Landmarks of Plymouth Mass. 199
Heraldic Journal iii, 84-9; iv, 175-82
Jackson's Hist. of Newton Mass. 386-8
New Eng. Hist. Gen. Reg. xxvi, 399;
  xxxiii, 285-95
Paige's History of Cambridge Mass. 625
Pelham Genealogy (1879) 11 pages
Savage's Genealogical Dictionary iii, 385
Pell — American Ancestry ix, 202
Austin's Ancestral Dictionary 45
Bartow Genealogy, appendix 183-7
Bolton's Hist. Westchester Co. N. Y. ii, 40
Pell's Howlands Journal (1890) 17-20
Plumb's History of Hanover Pa. 464
Savage's Genealogical Dictionary iii, 386
Thomas Genealogy (1896) 458-62
Whitmore's Heraldic Journal iii, 75
Pellet — Temple's N. Brookfield 701-3
Pelletreau — Howell's History of South-
  ampton N. Y. 345-8
Suffolk County N. Y. Illus. History 47
Pelletreau Genealogy (1863) 7 pages
Pelouze — Saunderson's Hist. of Charles-
  town N. H. 516-20
Peloubet — Peloubet Gen. (1892) 37 pages
Pels — Albany Collections iv, 153
Pelton — Am. Anc. ii, 93; iv, ii, 153; ix,
  202, 231
Guild's Stiles Genealogy 188-90
Huntington's Stamford Ct. Settlers 80
Pelton Genealogy (1892) 722 pages
Stiles' History of Windsor Ct. ii, 558-61
Peltz — American Ancestry i, 61
Pember — Paul's History of Wells Vt. 138
Walworth's Hyde Genealogy 40, 145
Pemberton — American Ancestry i, 61
Clarke's Old King Wm. Co. Va. Families
Glenn's Genealogical Notes (1898)
Hazen's History of Billerica Mass. 111
Morris Genealogy (1898) 538
New Eng. Hist. and Gen. Register xliii,
  294-8; xlvi, 392-8
Pemberton Genealogy (1890) 26 pages
Pemberton Genealogy (1892) 9 pages
Savage's Genealogical Dictionary iii, 387
Titcomb's Early New Eng. People 38-56
Pendexter — Ridlon's Saco 1107-19
Pendleton — Alden's Epitaphs v, 19
American Ancestry ii, 93
Austin's R. I. Genealogical Dictionary 149
Bangor Me. Historical Magazine i, 92
Cincinnati Ohio Criterion (1888) ii, 372
Dwight Genealogy 554
Eaton's Annals of Warren Me. 602

Eaton's History of Thomaston Me. ii, 351
Farrow's Hist. Islesborough Me. 238-63
Hudson's History of Sudbury Mass. 55
Meade's Old Churches of Virginia ii, 298
Narragansett Historical Reg. i, 183, 191
New Eng. Hist. and Gen. Register xv, 63
Orcutt's History of Stratford Ct. 1266
Prescott's Page Genealogy
Savage's Genealogical Dictionary iii, 388
Slaughter's St. Marks Parish Va. 148-57
Stanton Genealogy 490-2
Penfield — Andrews' New Britain Ct.
Caverly's History of Pittsford Vt. 718
Tattle Genealogy 707
Penfold — Riker's Newtown N. Y. 351
Pengrey — Hammatt Papers 262
See Pingry
Penhallow — Amer. Ancestry ix, 153
Cutts Genealogy 18-20, 57-60, 116-20
New Eng. Hist. Gen. Reg. xxxii, 28-35
Penhallow Genealogy (1878) 22 pages
Penhallow Genealogy 2d ed. (1885) 47 p.
Wentworth Genealogy i, 293-5, 326-8
Penkeville — Goode Genealogy 20
McLean's Trigg Minor
Penley — Lapham's Norway Me. 573
Lapham's History of Paris Me. 689-91
Penn — Am. Hist. Register i, 559-66
Clermont County Ohio History 379
Egle's Notes and Queries (1896) 233
Meade's Old Churches of Virginia
N. E. Hist. and Gen. Reg. xliv, 186-93
Penn Family by Smith (1867) 25 pages
Penn Family by Coleman (1871) 24 pages
Penn Family by Lea (1890) 51 pages
Penn Family by Jenkins (1898) 270 pages
Penn Family by Lea (1900) 46 pages
Penn Mag. of History vols. 14 to 22
Savage's Genealogical Dictionary iii, 389
Wheeler's History of North Carolina ii, 163
Whitmore's Heraldic Journal iii, 135-9
Pennell — Maris Genealogy 147
Ridlon's Saco Valley Me. Families 1103-6
Sharpless Genealogy 87, 231, 360
Smith's History of Delaware Co. Pa. 492
Wheeler's History of Brunswick Me. 847
Penney — Penney Genealogy (1897) 162 p.
See also Penny
Penniman — Ballou's Milford 957-9
Eaton's History of Thomaston Me. ii, 351
Heywood's Hist. Westminster Mass. 823
Jameson's History of Medway Mass. 511
Norton's History of Fitzwilliam N. H. 657-9
Savage's Genealogical Dictionary iii, 389
Vinton Genealogy 76-8, 351-4
Washington N. H. History 563
Pennington — American Ancestry v, 56
Morris Genealogy (1898) 919
N. E. Gen. Reg. xxv, 286-91, 335-8
Pennington Genealogy (1871) 18 pages
Pennock — Cope Genealogy 83, 185
Lamborn Genealogy 285
Maris Genealogy 78
Smith's History of Delaware Co. Pa. 492
Pennoyes — Sedgwick's Sharon Ct. 105
Penny — American Ancestry viii, 230

244

Babson's History of Gloucester Mass. 98
Hudson's History of Lexington Mass. 177
Penny Genealogy, see Penney
Power's Sangamon Co. Ill. Settlers 504
Ruttenber's Hist. of Newburgh N. Y. 281
Ruttenber's Hist. of Orange Co. N. Y. 374
Wyman's Charlestown Mass. Gens. ii, 736
Pennypacker — Futhey's Chester Pa.
Pennypacker's Phœnixville Pa. 276–9
Pennypacker Reunion (1878) 50 pages
Pennypacker Pedigree (1892) 5 pages
Pennypacker Genealogy (1894) 164 pages
Pennypacker Descent (1898) 25 pages
Penoyer — Huntington's Stamford 80
Smith Genealogy (1870)
Penrose — American Ancestry viii, 145
Hallowell Genealogy 145–89
Roberts' Old Richland Pa. Families 205–9
Thomas Genealogy (1896) 462
Pepper — Barry's Framingham 357
Ellis' History of Roxbury Mass. 126
Freeman's Hist. of Cape Cod Mass. ii, 153
Green's Kentucky Families
Hollister's History of Pawlet Vt. 221
Savage's Genealogical Dictionary iii, 391
Pepperrell — Essex Inst. xxxi, 54
Leighton Genealogy 117–20
Maine Gen. and Biog. Recorder (1875) 20
N. E. Hist. Gen. Reg. xiii, 138; xx, 1–6
Parson's Life Sir Wm. Pepperrell 335–41
Pepperrell Gen. (1866) 6 pages, reprint
Savage's Genealogical Dictionary iii, 392
Titcomb's Early New Eng. People 265
Wentworth Genealogy i, 307–9
Perce — American Ancestry v, 144
See also under Percy and Pearce
Perchell — Good Words Feb. (1877)
Percival — American Ancestry xii
Barry's Hanover Mass. 354
Freeman's Cape Cod Mass. ii, 155, 339
Percy — Cothren's Woodbury Ct. 674
Rhode Island Historical Magazine v, 40–8
See also under Pearce
Pereau — Missouri Pioneer Families 178
Perham — American Ancestry iv, 156
Ballou's History of Milford Mass. 959–61
Bangor Me. Historical Magazine ix, 47
Butler's Hist. of Farmington Me. 548–552
Lapham's History of Paris Me. 691
Lapham's History of Woodstock Me. 247
Livermore's History of Wilton N. H. 463
Maine Genealogist i, 33–9
Norton's History of Fitzwilliam N. H. 659
Perine — Mellick Genealogy 634
Perit — Perkins' Norwich Ct. 549
Perkins — Adams Fam. (1861) 22, 25
Adam's History of Fairhaven Vt. 450
Am. Anc. iv. 137; v, 8; ix, 41, 146; x, 166
Anderson's Waterbury Ct. i, app. 101
Ball's History of Lake Co. Ind. 432
Boutell's Burke and Alvord Genealogy 71
Bradbury's Kennebunkport 267–71
Breck Genealogy 139
Butler's History of Farmington Me. 552
Caulkins' Norwich Ct. ed. (1867) 443
Champion Genealogy 349–51

Chapman's Weeks Genealogy 149
Cleveland's Bi-Cen. of Topsfield Mass. 60–2
Cochrane's History of Antrim N. H. 642
Cogswell's History of Henniker N. H. 679
Crawford Family of Virginia 100–3
Crowell's History of Essex Mass. 255
Cushman's Hist. of Sheepscott Me. 411–3
Cutter's History of Jaffrey N. H. 418–20
Davis' Landmarks of Plymouth 199–202
Douglas Genealogy 113–23
Dow's History of Hampton N. H. 907–16
Dudley's Archæolog. Coll. plate 5
Eaton's Annals of Warren Me. 2d ed. 602
Eaton's History of Thomaston Me. ii, 352
Essex Antiquarian iii, (1899) 54
Essex Inst. Hist. Colls. xi, 222–7; xix,
   213–26, 254–69; xx, 19–37, 93–114,
   180–98, 252–73; xxi, 49–63; xxii,
   103–20, 193–208; xxiii, 46–58, 97–112,
   185–200, 281–96
Guild's Stiles Genealogy 124
Hammatt Papers of Ipswich Mass. 243–59
Hanson's Old Kent Md. 189–97
Harford Md. Hist. Soc. Const. (1889) 33
Heywood's Hist. Westminster Mass. 824
Hinman's Connecticut Settlers 1st ed. 180
Hollister's History of Pawlet Vt. 222
Hoyt's Salisbury Mass. Families 281–4
Hubbard's Hist. of Springfield Vt. 406–8
Hubbard's Hist. of Stanstead Co. Can. 293
Kingman's North Bridgewater 619–23
Lapham's History of Norway Me. 574
Lapham's History of Paris Me. 692–4
Lapham's History of Woodstock Me. 247
Little's History of Weare N. H. 969
Livermore's History of Wilton N. H. 464
Loomis Genealogy (1880) 684
Mitchell's Hist. Bridgewater Mass. 265–9
Morrison's Hist. Windham N. H. 734–8
New Eng. Hist. and Gen. Reg. x, 211–6;
   xi, 315; xii, 79–83; xiv, 113–20; xvii,
   63–5; xlvii, 483; l, 34–40
Norton's Hist. of Fitzwilliam N. H. 660–2
Perkins' Old Houses of Norwich Ct. 551–5
Perkins Family of Conn. (1860) 8 pages
Perkins of Ipswich, Records (1872) 16 p.
Parkins Family of Boston (1873) chart
Perkins on Essex, Records (1875) 25 pages
Parkins Family of Ipswich (1882–9) 499 p.
Parkins Family of Boston (1885) 29 pages
Perkins of Ipswich. Letters (1887) 24 p.
Perkins Ancestry (1898) 74 pages
Porter Genealogy 204
Preble Genealogy 261
Putnam Hist. Mag. ii, 189–270; iii, 21–154;
   v, 21–9
Reily's Life of Cardinal Gibbons v, 120–3
Runnel's Sanbornton N. H. ii, 548–53
Savage's Genealogical Dictionary iii, 394–8
Smith's Founders of Mass. Bay 256–67
Stearns' History of Rindge N. H. 630
Temple's History of Palmer Mass. 527
Upham Genealogy 53
Washington N. H. History 564
Whitman Genealogy 611–20
Wyman's Charlestown Mass. Gens. ii, 738

Young's History of Warsaw N. Y. 316-8
Perlee — Nevius Genealogy
Perley — Am. Anc. ii, 94; iii, 96; vi, 177
Gage's History of Rowley Mass. 451
Hammatt Papers of Ipswich Mass. 259
Herrick's History of Gardner Mass. 373
Perley Genealogy (1877) 13 pages
Perley's History of Boxford Mass. 74-8
Ridlon's Harrison Me. Settlers 104-6
Runnel's History of Sanbornton N. H. 553
Savage's Genealogical Dictionary iii, 398
Stark's History of Dunbarton N. H. 254
Perot — Morris Gen. (1898) 666-78
Perrin — Daniels' Oxford Mass. 641
Dearborn's History of Salisbury N. H. 686
Hemenway's Vermont Gaz. iv, 62
Morris Genealogy (1887) 183
N. E. Hist. and Gen. Reg. xxxii, 178-81
Page Genealogy 125
Perrin Genealogy (1885) 224 pages
Savage's Genealogical Dictionary iii, 299
Welles' Washington Genealogy 262
Perrine — American Ancestry vii, 115
Clute's Hist. of Staten Island N. Y. 414-6
May Genealogy 100
N. Y. Gen. and Biog. Record xx, 92
Salter's Hist. of Monmouth Co. N. J. xlv
Perrott — Homer Genealogy 18-20
Richmond Va. Standard iv, 25
Perry — Adams' Haven Genealogy 40
Am. Anc. i, 61; ii, 94; iii, 99, 104, 189; iv,
    10; vii, 138; x, 3, 32, 162; xi, 148, 150
Austin's Ancestral Dictionary 46
Austin's Ancestrics 45
Austin's R. I. Genealogical Dictionary 150
Ballou's History of Milford Mass. 961-5
Bangor Me. Historical Magazine v, 8
Barry's History of Hanover Mass. 354-8
Bassett's Hist. of Richmond N. H. 459-61
Bemis' History of Marlboro N. H. 248-51
Bond's History of Watertown Mass. 402
Briggs' History of Shipbuilding 84
Cleveland's Hist. Yates Co. N. Y. 483, 679
Cochrane's History of Antrim N. H. 643
Cogswell's History of Henniker N. H. 680
Cole Genealogy 43
Conn. Quarterly iii, (1897) 109, 137, 352, 480
Cothren's Woodbury Ct. 660-8; ii, 1543
Cutter's History of Arlington Mass. 282
Daniels' History of Oxford Mass. 641
Davis' Landmarks of Plymouth Mass. 202
Deane's History of Scituate Mass. 322
Dearborn's History of Parsonsfield Me. 393
Eaton's Hist. of Thomaston Me. ii, 352-5
Fiske Genealogy 149
Fox's History of Dunstable Mass. 248
Freeman's Hist. of Cape Cod Mass. ii, 153
Goode Genealogy 353
Hanover Mass. Records (1898)
Hayward's History of Hancock N. H. 806
Hazard Genealogy 103-6
Heywood's Hist. of Westminster Mass. 824
Hudson's History of Lexington Mass. 177
Hudson's History of Sudbury Mass. 446
Hyde's History of Brimfield Mass. 445
Kimball Family News (1898) 201-8

Lapham's History of Norway Me. 575
Lapham's History of Paris Me. 694-6
Lapham's History of Rumford Me. 381
Leavenworth Genealogies 53-64, 73-7
Leland Genealogy 207-10, 212-4, 217, 247
Leonard's History of Dublin N. H. 378-80
Livermore's History of Wilton N. H. 464
Morse's Sherborn Mass. Settlers 190-5
Narragansett Historical Register v, 275-8
Norton's Hist. of Fitzwilliam N. H. 662-6
Orcutt's History of Derby Ct. 750
Orcutt's History of Stratford Ct. 1267
Paige's History of Hardwick Mass. 452
Perry Memoranda (1878) 28 pages
Perry of Prov. Ancestors (1889) 9 pages
Perry Family of Topsham (1890) 13 pages
Read's History of Swanzey N. H. 418
Rhode Island Hist. Mag. v, 29-36, 317-27
Saunderson's Charlestown N. H. 520
Savage's Genealogical Dict. ii, 389-410
Secomb's History of Amherst N. H. 727
Sharpe's History of Seymour Ct. 213-5
Stearns' Hist. of Ashburnham Mass. 846
Stearns' History of Rindge N. H. 631-4
Stiles' History of Windsor Ct. ii, 561
Temple's Hist. of N. Brookfield Mass. 703
Temple's History of Northfield Mass. 514
Todd's History of Redding Ct. 209
Walker Genealogy 141
Wall's Reminisc. of Worcester Mass. 109-11
Wheeler's History of Newport N. H. 503-5
Wight Genealogy 156
Wyman's Charlestown Mass. Gens. ii, 739
Persen — Greene Co. N. Y. Hist. 435-7
Personnet — Young's Wayne Ind. 230
Persons — Humphreys Genealogy 441
Peter — Bangor Historical Mag. v, 205
Bartow Genealogy 131
MacDonald Genealogy supp. (1880) 72 p.
Meade's Old Churches of Virginia
Peters — Abbot's Andover Mass. 37
American Ancestry ii, 94; vii, 249
Bangor Me. Hist. Magazine i, 199-205; iii,
    240; v, 207; vi, 239
Bassett's History of Richmond N. H. 461-3
Bliss Genealogy 683-90
Buckminister's Hastings Genealogy 167
Cogswell's Hist. of Henniker N. H. 681-3
Dearborn's Hist. of Salisbury N. H. 687-9
Eaton's Annals of Warren Me. 602-4
McKeen's History of Bradford Vt. 126-40
New Eng. Hist. and Gen. Reg. ii, 58-64
Palmer and Trimble Genealogy 391-3
Peter's Life of Rev. Hugh Peters 155
Peters Lineage (1896) 175 pages
Peters Family Leaflet
Power's Sangamon Co. Ill. Settlers 564
Saunders' Alabama Settlers 110
Savage's Genealogical Dictionary iii, 401-3
Whitmore's Heraldic Journal i, 190-2
Petersen — Pearson's Schenectady 140
Peterson — Am. Ancestry ii, 94; iii, 182
Bergen's Kings Co. N. Y. Settlers 223-5
Davis' Landmarks of Plymouth Mass. 203
Potts Genealogy (1895) 165-207
Richmond Va. Standard ii, 31

Slaughter's Hist. of Bristol Parish Va. 205
Wheeler's History of Brunswick Me. 847
Winsor's History of Duxbury Mass. 289
Pettee — Cochrane's Francestown 879–82
Hill's Dedham Mass. Records
Morse's Genealogical Reg. (1859) ii, 147–64
Pettibone — Brown's Simsbury Ct. 115
Humphrey Genealogy
Marshall's Grant Ancestry 129
Stiles' History of Windsor Ct. ii, 562
Tuttle Genealogy 710–2
Pettigrew — Wheeler's Eminent N. Carolinians 423–6
Pettingill — Adams Genealogy (1895) 36
Coffin's Newbury 313
Corliss' North Yarmouth Me. 967–9
Dearborn's Hist. Salisbury N. H. 689–706
Kingman's North Bridgewater Mass. 625
Lapham's History of Rumford Me. 381
Lincoln's Hist. of Hingham Mass. iii, 110
Livermore's History of Wilton N. H. 465–7
Mitchell's Hist. of Bridgewater Mass. 269
North's History of Augusta Me. 922–4
Poore Genealogy 89
Poore's Merrimack Valley Researches 131
Savage's Genealogical Dictionary iii, 403
Pettit — American Ancestry ii, 94
Huntington's Stamford Ct. Settlers 82
Littell's Passaic Valley Gens. 319
McKean Genealogy 127, 144–8
Sedgwick's History of Sharon Ct. 105
Petts — Hayward's Gilsum N. H. 375
Heywood's Hist. Westminster Mass. 825
Norton's History of Fitzwilliam N. H. 666
Stearns' History of Ashburnham Mass. 847
Washington N. H. History 565
Petty — Sheldon's Deerfield 261
Temple's Northfield Mass. 514
Pevear — Dickerman Genealogy 119–22
Pevey — Hayward's Hancock N. H. 806
Livermore's History of Wilton N. H. 467–9
Pew — Missouri Pioneer Families 284
Peyton — American Ancestry iii, 128, 220
Clarke's Old King Wm. Co. Va. Families
Hayden's Virginia Genealogies 460–566
Meade's Old Churches of Virginia ii, 466
New Eng. Hist. Gen. Reg. xxxv, 145–7
Peyton's History of Augusta Co. Va. 320–2
Richmond Va. Standard ii, 7; iii, 10
Pfautz — Pfautz Genealogy (1881) 70 p.
Pfeiffer — Pfeiffer Gen. (1899) 67 pages
Pfouts — Plumb's Hanover Pa. 460
Phebus — American Ancestry ix, 141
Phelan — American Ancestry v, 208
Phelps — Abbott's Andover Mass. 38
Am. Anc. i, 61; ii, 94; iv, 32; v, 4, 204; viii, 111; ix, 216; x, 156; xii, 102
Bemis' History of Marlboro N. H. 601
Brown's W. Simsbury Ct. Settlers 116-8
Chandler's History of Shirley Mass. 600–3
Cochrane's Hist. Francestown N. H. 882
Doolittle's Belchert'n Mass. Sketches 263
Foster Pedigree (1897) iv, 1–52
Guild's Stiles Genealogy 175–7, 223
Hall's History of Eastern Vermont 689–94
Hine's Lebanon Ct. Hist. Address 166

Hinman's Connecticut Settlers 1st ed. 175
Hudson's History of Lexington Mass. 178
Hudson's Hist of Marlborough Mass. 428
Huntington Memorial 101
Judd's History of Hadley Mass. 550
Leland Genealogy 269
Livermore's History of Wilton N. H. 469
Loomis Genealogy (1880) 451–6, 713
Lyman's Hist. of Easthampton Mass. 190
Marshall's Grant Ancestry 130–46
Montague Genealogy 195
Nash Genealogy 88
New Eng. Hist. and Gen. Reg. xxv, 190
Orcutt's History of New Milford Ct. 750
Orcutt's History of Torrington Ct. 754
Orford N. H. Centennial 134
Phelps Family of Canada (1862) 44 pages
Phelps Family of Oregon (1870) 54 pages
Phelps Family of Iowa (1878) 23 pages
Phelps Family of Oregon (1880) 1 page
Phelps' History of Simsbury Ct. 172
Phœnix's Whitney Genealogy i, 771
Power's Sangamon Co. Ill. Settlers 565
Rollo Genealogy 52, 55
Savage's Genealogical Dictionary iii, 404–8
Secomb's History of Amherst N. H. 728
Stiles' Hist. of Windsor Ct. ii, 562–606, 841
Stowe's History of Hubbardston Mass. 331
Strong Genealogy 1155–7
Temple's History of Northfield Mass. 515
Turner's Hist. Phelps Purchase N. Y. 150
Wakefield Genealogy 66
Welles Am. Family Antiquity
Worcester's History of Hollis N. H. 383
Worthen's History of Sutton N. H. 866
Phenix — Austin's R. I. Gen. Dict. 151
Phetteplace — R. I. Gen. Dict. 151
Phifer — Wheeler's Eminent North Carolinians 76–9
Philbrick — Bond's Watertown 909
Cochrane's History of Antrim N. H. 644
Dearborn's History of Salisbury N. H. 706
Dow's History of Hampton N. H. 916–26
Hammatt Papers of Ipswich Mass. 109
Jameson's History of Medway Mass. 511
Little's History of Weare N. H. 970–5
N. E. Hist. and Gen. Reg. xxxviii, 279–86
Philbrick Genealogy (1884) 10 pages
Philbrick Genealogy (1886) 202 pages
Runnel's Hist. Sanbornton N. H. ii, 554–7
Savage's Genealogical Dictionary iii, 408
Stearns' History of Rindge N. H. 634
Washington N. H. History 566
Worthen's History of Sutton N. H. 867–70
Philbrook — Eaton's Hist. of Thomaston Me. ii, 356
Farrow's Hist. of Islesborough Me. 263–9
Lapham's History of Bethel Me. 597
Maine Historical Magazine viii, 178
Weeks Genealogy (1889) 150
See Philbrick
Philhower — Chambers' N. J. Germans
Philleo — Am. Ancestry iv, 220; vii, 253
Fillow Genealogy
Philipse — See Phillipse

Phillips — Am. Anc. ii, 94, 95; iii, 40, 213; iv, 205; v, 30; vi, 66, 137; vii, 118; viii, 43, 228; ix, 72, 165
Austin's R. I. Genealogical Dictionary 152
Austin's Allied Families 198
Ballou's History of Milford Mass. 965
Bangor Me. Hist. Mag. v, 170; vi, 97
Barry's History of Framingham Mass. 358
Bass Ancestry 10–3
Bemis' History of Marlboro N. H. 601
Berkshire Co. Mass. Hist. Soc. Coll. i
Binney Genealogy 25
Bond's Watertown Mass. 404, 872–86
Boston Daily Advertiser for Apr. 15 1878
Bouton Genealogy 240–2
Bridgeman's Granary Epitaphs 275–7
Buckingham Genealogy 27
Butler's History of Groton Mass. 426
Cooley's Trenton N. J. Genealogies 181–92
Corliss' North Yarmouth Me.
Daniels' History of Oxford Mass. 642
Davis' Landmarks of Plymouth 204–7
Deane's History of Scituate Mass. 323
Dwight Genealogy 101
Ellis Genealogy 99–104, 377–83
Essex Institute Hist. Colls. xxiii, 134
French's History of Turner Me. 55
Hayward's History of Gilsum N. H. 375
Heywood's Hist. of Westminster Mass. 825
Jackson Genealogy 132 144–7
Jameson's History of Medway Mass. 511
Leonard's History of Dublin N. H. 380
Lillie Genealogy (1896) 97–106
Meade's Old Churches of Virginia ii, 482
Mitchell's Hist. of Bridgewater Mass. 270
Morton's New England Mem. 457
N. E. Hist. Gen. Reg. vi, 273; xv, 270
Norton's Hist. Fitzwilliam N. H. 667–70
Old Northwest Gen. Quar. ii, 100
Ormsby Genealogy 28–32; 37–40
Paige's History of Cambridge Mass. 627
Pearson's Schenectady N. Y. Settlers 141
Phillips Golden Wedding (1867) 45–7
Phillips Genealogy (1885) 233 pages
Phillips Family of Coventry (1887) chart
Phœnix and Phillips Chart (1875) 1x2½ feet
Pierce's History of Grafton Mass. 543–6
Roe's Sketches of Rose N. Y. 163
Salisbury Fam. Memorials (1885) 563–610
Saunders' Alabama Settlers 228
Savage's Genealogical Dict. iii, 409–17
Selleck's Norwalk Ct. (1896) 254
Stearns' Hist. Ashburnham Mass. 848–51
Stow's History of Hubbardston Mass. 332
Taylor's Mem. of Samuel Phillips 345–7
Thomas Genealogy (1896) 463
Thompson's Long Island N. Y. ii, 459–61
Updyke's Narragansett Churches 120
Wentworth Genealogy i, 203
Whitman Genealogy 143
Williams' History of Danby Vt. 224–8
Winsor's History of Duxbury Mass. 291
Wisner's Wm. Phillips Sermon (1827)
Wyman's Charlestown Mass. Gens. 740–8
Phillipse — Bolton's Westchester 515
Lamb's History of New York city 467, 692

New Eng. Hist. Gen. Reg. x, 25–8, 198
New York Gen. Biog. Record ix, 120–4
Whitmore's Heraldic Journal iii, 78–81
Philo — Fillow Genealogy
Philpot — Bond's Watertown Mass. 405
Wentworth Genealogy i, 453
Phinney — Calnek's Annapolis N. S. 561
Freeman's Cape Cod 333
Hudson's Hist. of Lexington Mass. 179–81
Lincoln's History of Hingham iii, 111
Machias Me. Centennial 172
Mitchell's Hist. of Bridgewater Mass. 271
Nash Genealogy 120
New Eng. Hist. and Gen. Register iii, 274
Paige's History of Hardwick Mass. 453
Pierce's History of Gorham Me. 198–200
Ridlon's Harrison Me. Settlers 100–2
Savage's Genealogical Dictionary iii, 417
See also under Finney
Phippen — Driver Genealogy 89
Lincoln's Hist. of Hingham Mass. iii, 112
Phippen Genealogy (1868) 20 pages
Pickering Genealogy
Savage's Genealogical Dictionary iii, 418
Whitmore's Heraldic Journal (1868) iv, 1–20
Phippens — Hemenway's Vt. Gaz. v
Phippeny — Orcutt's Stratford Ct. 1267
Phipps — Ballou's Milford Mass. 966–8
Bangor Me. Historical Magazine v, 9
Blake's Hamden Ct. History 277
Chandler's History of Shirley Mass. 603
Paige's History of Cambridge Mass. 627
Tuttle Genealogy 190–2, 197
Wyman's Charlestown Mass. ii, 749–55
Phips — Daniels' Oxford Mass. 644
Morse's Sherborn Mass. Settlers 195–202
Savage's Genealogical Dict. iii, 419–22
Whitmore's Heraldic Journal i, 152–4
Phœnix — Phœnix Chart (1880)
Phœnix and Phillips Chart (1875) 1x2½ ft.
Phœnix's Whitney Genealogy i, 343
Pibbles — Temple's Palmer Mass. 524
Pickard — American Ancestry xii
Essex Inst. Coll. xxiii, 135–9
Gage's History of Rowley Mass. 451
Hale Genealogy 57–60
Little Genealogy 442–4
Temple's Hist. of N. Brookfield Mass. 705
Pickens — Cleveland's Yates Co. 318
Strobridge Genealogy 17, 58–61
Pickering — Am. Anc. i, 62; iv, 94; vi, 63
Ballou Genealogy 213–5, 524–7
Ballou's History of Milford Mass. 968
Bassett's History of Richmond N. H. 463–7
Brewster's Portsmouth ii, 49–52, 103–6
Chapman's Weeks Genealogy 151
Driver Genealogy 295
Hayward's History of Gilsum N. H. 376
Pickering Family of N. H. (1884) 36 pages
Pickering Fam. supp. (1884) 28 pages
Pickering Family of Salem (1887) 2 vols.
Pickering Family of Salem (1897) 1284 p.
Robinson's Items of Ancestry (1894) 31–3
Savage's Genealogical Dictionary iii, 422
Picket — Boyd's Conesus N. Y. 168

Orcutt's History of New Milford Ct. 751
Orcutt's History of Stratford Ct. 1268
Paxton's Marshall Genealogy (1855) 53-8
Savage's Genealogical Dictionary iii, 423
Stiles' History of Windsor Ct. ii, 607
Pickett — American Ancestry ii, 95
Green's Kentucky Families
Pickle — Chambers' N. J. Germans
Pickman — Heraldic Journal ii, 26
Smith's Founders of Mass. Bay 156-63
Vinton's Giles Genealogy 330
Pickrell — Power's Sangamon 566
Pickup — Calnek's Annapolis N. S. 562
Pickworth — Savage's Dict. iii, 425
Pidgin — Dow's Hampton N. H. 927
Pier — Olin Gen. by Nye (1892) 98-107
Young's Chautauqua 239, 368
Pierce — Adams Gen. (1895) 38-40
Am. Anc. i, 62; ii, 95; iii, 93; ix, 85; xi, 220
Austin's R. I. Genealogical Dictionary 153
Ballou Genealogy 344-6
Ballou's History of Milford Mass. 969-71
Blake Genealogy 46, 62-9
Blood's History of Temple's N. H. 239
Bond's Watertown Mass. 393-402, 869-71
Brewster's Portsmouth N. H. ii, 359-62
Butler's History of Groton Mass. 427, 476
Chandler's History of Shirley Mass. 969-71
Cleveland's History of Yates Co. N. Y. 591
Cochrane's History of Antrim N. H. 645
Cochrane's Hist. Francestown N. H. 883
Cothren's History of Woodbury Ct. 669-72
Cutter's History of Jaffrey N. H. 420-8
Daniels' History of Oxford Mass. 645
Davis' Landmarks of Plymouth 206-8
Deane's History of Scituate Mass. 325
Dow's History of Hampton N. H. 927
Draper's History of Spencer Mass. 246
Eaton's History of Thomaston Me. ii, 358
Gold's History of Cornwall Ct. 244
Hayward's Hist. of Hancock N. H. 807-9
Hemenway's Vermont Gaz. v, 101
Heywood's Hist. Westminster Mass. 825-8
Hubbard's History of Springfield Vt. 409-12
Hubbard's Stanstead Co. Canada 128-31
Hudson's Hist. of Lexington Mass. 181-5
Hyde's History of Brimfield Mass. 446
Judd's History of Hadley Mass. 552
Lapham's History of Norway Me. 576
Livermore's History of Wilton N. H. 469
Locke Genealogy 32, 56, 86-9, 317-20
Loomis Genealogy (1880) 535
Meade's Old Churches of Virginia
Mitchell's Hist. of Bridgewater Mass. 272
New Eng. Hist. and Gen. Register vi,
    276-9; xxi, 61-5, 157-62, 257-64,
    340-50; xxii, 73-9, 174-85; xxix,
    273-81; lii, 52
Norton's History of Fitzwilliam N. H. 670
Pierce Family of Boston (1864) 5 pages
Pierce Ancestors in America (1864) 48 p.
Pierce Family of Old Colony (1870) 490 p.
Peirce Family of Newbury (1875) 11 pages
Peirce Family of Watertown (1880) 278 p.
Peirce Family of Salem (1881) 16 pages
Pierce Family of Charlestown (1882) 376 p.

Pearce Fam. of Rhode Island (1888) 150 p.
Pierce Family of Scituate (1889) 441 pages
Peirce Fam. of Boston new ed. (1894) 97 p.
Pierce's History of Grafton Mass. 540-3
Pope Genealogy 316-8
Power's Sangamon Co. Ill. Settlers 571
Randall's Chesterfield N. H. 399-405
Read's History of Swanzey N. H. 420
Rhode Island Historical Magazine v, 70-8
Ridlon's Saco Valley Me. Families 124
Savage's Genealogical Dict. iii, 426-32
Sewall's History of Woburn Mass. 628
Sharpe's South Britain Ct. Sketches 77-83
Smith's History of Dutchess Co. N. Y. 498
Smith's History of Peterborough N. H. 226
Spooner's Mem. of W. Spooner 109
Stiles' History of Windsor Ct. ii, 607
Stowes' History of Hubbardston Mass. 333
Walker Genealogy 206
Whitcomb and Pierce Gen. (1888) 23 p.
Whitehead's Hist. Perth Amboy N. J. 359
Whitmore's Copps Hill Epitaphs
Worcester's History of Hollis N. H. 384
Wyman's Charlestown Mass. ii, 756-62
Pierpont — Amer. Ancestry v, 89; vii, 249
Anderson's Waterbury Ct. i, app. 102
Blake's History of Hamden Ct. 266
Darling Memorial 40-4
Ellis' History of Roxbury Mass. 126
Pierpont Genealogy (1868) 23 pages
Savage's Genealogical Dictionary iii, 432
Tuttle Genealogy 695-8
Walworth's Hyde Gen. 298-304, 307-9
Pierrepont — Bartow Genealogy 191-5
Dwight Genealogy 1050-65
Kip's Olden Times in New York (1872)
Pierrepont Genealogy (1881) 41 pages
Pierrepoint — Hollister's Conn. i, 459
Piersol — Sewall's Woburn Mass. 629
Sharpless Genealogy 388
Pierson — Am. Anc. i, 62; ii, 95; viii, 104;
    x, 5
Avon N. Y. Genealogical Record 4-16
Clayton's Hist. Union Co. N. J. 330-2, 342
Condit Genealogy 376-80
Howell's Hist. Southampton N. Y. 348-53
Kitchell Genealogy 44
New Jersey Hist. Soc. Colls. vi, supp. 12
Orcutt's History of Derby Ct. 751
Pierson Genealogy (1878) 104 pages
Pierson Fam. of New Haven (1895) 33 p.
Power's Sangamon Co. Ill. Settlers 568
Prime Genealogy (1895) 34
Sewall's History of Woburn Mass. 629
Shaw's Hist. of Essex Co. N. J. ii, 719-21
Stiles' History of Windsor Ct. ii, 607
Whittemore's Orange N. J. 100
Piester — American Ancestry ii, 96
Pigeon — Jackson's Newton Mass. 396
Pike — American Ancestry v, 223
Austin's R. I. Genealogical Dictionary 153
Barry's Hist. Framingham Mass. 350-63
Bell's History of Exeter N. H. 37
Daniels' History of Oxford Mass. 645
Hatch's History of Industry Me. 791
Hoyt's Salisbury Mass. Families 285-90

Lapham's History of Norway Me. 576-9
Morse's Sherborn Mass. Settlers 202
Rich's History of Truro Mass. 551
Ridlon's Saco Valley Me. Families 1119
Runnel's Hist. Sanbornton N. H. ii, 570-2
Savage's Genealogical Dictionary iii, 435-7
Wentworth Genealogy i, 82-4; ii, 406-8
Wheeler's History of Newport N. H. 506-9
Whitehead's Perth Amboy N. J. 360-3
Wyman's Charlestown Mass. Gens. ii, 762
Pilcher — American Ancestry vi, 125
Pillsbury — American Ancestry v, 80, 146
Bangor Me. Historical Magazine v, 208
Caverno Genealogy 35
Coffin's Hist. of Boscawen N. H. 594-600
Coffin's History of Newbury Mass. 314
Cogswell's Hist. of Henniker N. H. 683-90
Cogswell's Hist. of Nottingham N. H. 763
Eaton's History of Thomaston Me. ii, 358
Essex Institute Hist. Coll. xxxi, 181-204
Lane Genealogy (1891) 93
Pillsbury Reunion (1891) 16 pages
Pillsbury Prospectus (1898) 16 pages
Pillsbury Genealogy (1898) 307 pages
Poor's Merrimack Valley Researches 136, 150
Savage's Genealogical Dictionary iii, 437
Smith Genealogy (1895) 78-82
Worthen's History of Sutton N. H. 872-901
Pim — Cope Family of Penn. 48, 104, 204
Futhey's History of Chester Co. Pa. 685
Roberts' Richland Pa. Families 117
Pincin — Deane's Scituate Mass. 324
Pinckney — Bellinger Genealogy 21
Bolton's Westchester 249
Pindar — Herrick Genealogy (1885) 22, 275
Pinder — Austin's R. I. Gen. Dict. 153
Hammatt Papers of Ipswich Mass. 265
Ipswich Mass. Chronicle (1882)
Pine — Thurston Genealogy (1894) 16-20
Pineo — American Ancestry v, 139
Pines — Machias Me. Centennial 173
Pingree — American Ancestry vi, 53, 128
Cogswell's History of Henniker N. H. 690
Dearborn's Hist. Salisbury N. H. 707-13
Hoyt's Salisbury Mass. Families 290
Lapham's History of Norway Me. 579-81
Ridlon's Saco Valley Me. Families 1120
Pingry — Little Genealogy 288-90
Pingry Genealogy (1881) 186 pages
Pinkerton — American Ancestry vii, 63
Barber's Atlee Genealogy 52-4
Coffin's History of Boscawen N. H. 600
Dorland Genealogy 240-3
Hall's Trenton N. J. Presb. Church 237
Parker's Hist. of Londonderry N. H. 295
Pinkham — Bangor Hist. Mag. viii, 235
Cushman's History of Sheepscott Me. 413
Milliken's Narraguagus Valley Me. 18
New Eng. Hist. and Gen. Reg. vii, 353-5
Otis Family of New Hampshire (1851)
Stackpole's History of Durham Me. 237
Pinks — Andrews' New Britain Ct. 377
Pinneo — Porter Genealogy 197-9
Stone Genealogy 34-7
Strong Genealogy 467-9

Tucker's History of Hartford Vt. 455
Pinney — Loomis Genealogy (1880) 549, 666
Savage's Genealogical Dictionary iii, 438
Stiles' Hist. Windsor Ct. ii, 608-19, 842-4
Pinson — Mitchell's Bridgewater 272
Pintard — N. Y. Gen. Record xx, 30
Piper — American Ancestry iv, 69
Blood's History of Temple N. H. 239-41
Cutts Genealogy 156-8
Dearborn's Hist. of Parsonsfield Me. 394-8
Eaton's History of Thomaston Me. ii, 359
Haley Genealogy (1900) 29-50
Hubbard's History of Springfield Vt. 412
Leonard's History of Dublin N. H. 382-4
Locke Genealogy 82
Martin's History of Chester Pa. 269
Piper Genealogy (1819) 20 pages
Piper Genealogy 2d ed. (1889) 121 pages
Runnel's Hist. Sanbornton N. H. ii, 572-8
Savage's Genealogical Dictionary iii, 439
Stearns' History of Ashburnham Mass. 851
Stearns' History of Rindge N. H. 635-7
Pippin — Power's Sangamon Co. Ill. 569
Pirkins — Power's Sangamon Ill. 569-71
Pitcher — American Ancestry ii, 96
Pompey N. Y. Reunion 337-41
Pitkin — Am. Anc. iv, 116; v, 199, 200, 205
Goodwin's East Hartford Ct. 225-30
Huntington's Memoirs 103
Kellogg's White Genealogy 62
Pitkin Genealogy (1887) 418 pages
Salisbury's Fam. Histories (1892) ii, 201-14
Savage's Genealogical Dictionary iii, 440
Stiles' History of Windsor Ct. ii, 619
Pitman — Guild's Stiles Genealogy 342
Missouri Pioneer Families 179
Pitman Genealogy (1868) 48 pages
Savage's Genealogical Dict. iii, 424, 441
Thurston and Pitman Gen. (1865) 80 p.
Pitner — Fisher Genealogy 187-207
Pitson — Corliss' North Yarmouth Me.
Pittee — Morse's Gen. Reg. ii, (1859) 147-9
Porter Genealogy (1878) 15
Pittenger — Harvey Genealogy 852-4
Pittman — Richmond Standard iii, 27
Pitts — American Ancestry x, 204
Daniels' History of Oxford Mass. 646
Pitts Genealogy (1882) 63 pages
Richard Mowry Genealogy 223
Ridlon's Harrison Me. Sett'ers 99
Savage's Genealogical Dictionary iii, 442
Pixlee — Orcutt's Stratford Ct. 1269
Pixley — American Ancestry v, 13
Savage's Genealogical Dictionary iii, 443
Place — Austin's R. I. Gen. Dict. 155
Plaisted — Hanson's Gardiner Me. 136
Maine Historical Magazine viii, 138-43
Ridlon's Harrison Me. Early Settlers 102
Ridlon's Saco Valley Me. Families 1121-3
Ruggles Genealogy
Savage's Genealogical Dictionary iii, 444
Wentworth Genealogy i, 297, 412
Planck — Power's Sangamon Ill. 569-71
Plant — Dickerman Genealogy 488
Orcutt's Stratford Ct. 1270
Plantagenet — Richmond Stand. ii, 48

Plaskitt — Worthington Fam. (1886) 13
Plass — American Ancestry ii, 96; x, 46
Platner — American Ancestry ii, 96
Platt — Am. Anc. vii, 125; viii, 109, 112
Anderson's Waterbury Ct. i, app. 103
Bockee Genealogy 67-9
Boyd's Annals of Winchester Ct. 180
Flint's Peters Lineage 70
Green's Todd Genealogy
Hall's Norwalk Ct. 86-8, 92-7, 200, 249
New York Gen. and Biog. Rec. xvi, 15-20
Oneida Hist. Society Trans. ii, 83-90
Platt Lineage (1891) 398 pages
Platt Fam. of Burlington N. J. (1896) 31 p.
Platt's Old Times Huntington L. I. (1876)
Savage's Genealogical Dictionary iii, 444
Selleck's Norwalk Ct. (1886) 336-40
Sharpe's South Britain Ct. 41-8, 101-3
Stearns' History of Rindge N. H. 637-44
Strong Genealogy 702
Thompson's Long Island N. Y. ii, 472-5
Timlow's Sketches of Southington Ct. 205
Todd's History of Redding Ct. 210
Walworth's Hyde Genealogy 544-6
Platts — Essex Institute Hist. Collections
v, 15; xxiii, 141-5
Hale Genealogy 55-7
Norton's Hist. of Fitzwilliam N. H. 671-4
Poor's Merrimack Vall. Researches 116-30
Stearns' History of Ashburnham Mass. 851
Pleasants — Meade's Old Fams. of Va.
Page Genealogy 245
Richmond Va. Standard ii, 7, 20
Plemly — American Ancestry ii, 97
Plimpton — American Ancestry vi, 34
Ammidown's Hist.Coll. ii, 365-7, 560
Ammidown Genealogy 31
Keyes' West Boylston Mass. Register 33
Norton's History of Fitzwilliam N. H. 674
Plimpton Genealogy (1884) 240 pages
Wight Genealogy 56-8
Plowden — Richmond Standard ii, 48
Plum — Maltby Genealogy 104
Plumb — Am. Anc. iii, 130; v, 178; vii, 148
Ballou's History of Milford Mass. 971
Orcutt's History of Stratford Ct. 1271
Orcutt's History of Wolcott Ct. 541-3
Plumb Genealogy (1890) 57 pages
Plumb Genealogy 2d ed. (1893) 102 pages
Plumb's History of Hanover Pa. 461-4
Young's Hist. of Chautauqua Co. N. Y. 239
Plumbe — Caulkins' N. London Ct. 336
Kellogg's White Genealogy 56
Savage's Genealogical Dictionary iii, 445
Plumer — Albert's History of Westmore-
land County Pa. 658-65
Coffin's History of Newbury Mass. 315
Gage's History of Rowley Mass. 452
Herrick Genealogy (1885) 289
Hudson's History of Lexington Mass. 186
Lane Genealogy (1891) 97
McAllister Genealogy 22-5
Nealley and True Family Chart
Runnel's Sanbornton N. H. ii, 578-85
Thurston Genealogy (1892) 65
Plumley — Hayward's Gilsum N. H. 377

Plummer — American Ancestry xii
Chandler Genealogy 217
Coffin's History of Boscawen N. H. 601-4
Cogswell's Hist. of Henniker N. H. 601-3
Goode Genealogy 233
Lapham's History of Bethel Me. 598
Lee Genealogy (1888) 295-7, 312
New Eng. Hist. and Gen. Reg. xxxviii, 67
Plummer Hall Dedication (1858) 51
Plummer Genealogy (1885) 22 pages
Savage's Genealogical Dictionary iii, 446
Shourd's Fenwick Colony N. J. 176
Stackpole's History of Durham Me. 237-9
Warren's History of Waterford Me. 279
Wentworth Genealogy i, 170
Plumley — American Ancestry v, 26
Plumstead — Penn. Magazine vi, 106-10
Plumstead Family (1887) 168 pages
Plunket — Egle's Notes and Queries 3d
series iii, 210
Hepburn Genealogy 123
Plympton — Plimpton Genealogy (1885)
Cleveland's Hist. of Yates Co. N. Y. 695-7
Savage's Genealogical Dictionary iii, 447
Sheldon's History of Deerfield Mass. 262
Ward's History of Shrewsbury Mass. 410
Poague — Goode Genealogy 163
Waddell's Annals of Augusta Va. 443-6
Pocahontas — Bolling Genealogy
Goode Genealogy 64, et seq. 12
Richmond Va. Standard ii, 10, 12, 32, 36,
38; iv, 4, 20, 21
Robertson's Pocahontas' Descendants
Slaughter's Life of R. Fairfax 72
Pocorny — Barry's Hanover Mass. 359
Poel — Munsell's Albany Colls. iv, 154
Poffenberger — Power's Sangamon
Poindexter — Gilmer's Georgians 103
See also Pendexter
Points — Saunders' Alabama 230-3
Poland — Norton's Fitzwilliam 674
Temple's N. Brookfield Mass. 705-7
Poley — Power's Sangamon Co. Ill. 575
Polhemus — Bergen's Kings Co. 226-8
Honeyman's Our Home Magazine 98, 197
Nevius Genealogy
Riker's Annals of Newtown N. Y. 348-50
Polk — Amer. Historical Magazine of
Nashville i, 154-73, 263-71; ii, 376-95;
iii, 42-73, 155-90, 230-40
Munsey's Magazine for Feb. 1897
Polk Chart (1849)
Pollard — American Ancestry ix, 86
Cabell Genealogy 433-8
Clarke's Old King Wm. Co. Va. Families
Fox's History of Dunstable Mass. 248
Hazen's History of Billerica Mass. 112-4
Kidder's Hist. of New Ipswich N. H. 428
Meade's Old Churches of Va.
Pollard Genealogy (1891) 20 pages
Richmond Va. Standard ii, 45
Savage's Genealogical Dict. iii, 448-50
Stearns' Hist. of Ashburnham Mass. 852
Stowe's History of Hubbardston Mass. 334
Walworth's Hyde Genealogy 469
Polley — Stearns' Ashburnham 853

Pollington — Neill's Va. Carolorum 46
Pollock — American Ancestry vi, 55
Egle's Historical Register of Interior Pa.
   i, 48–63, 95–103, 194–207, 241 -51
Pollock Genealogy (1883) 59 pages
Pollock Genealogy (1884) 26 pages
Tuttle Genealogy 425
See also under Polk
Pollow — Libby Genealogy 28
Polly — Savage's Gen. Dict. iii, 450
Sewall's History of Woburn Mass. 629
Pomeroy — Am. Anc. iv, 168; vii, 67, 72,
   153; x, 195
Chardon, Ohio, Newspaper Aug. 11, Sept.
   22 1886
Collins' Hist. Hillsdale N. Y., app. 101–3
Dickerman Genealogy 327–9
Hubbard's Stanstead Co. Canada 122–5
Judd's History of Hadley Mass. 535
Kellogg's White Genealogy 66
Lawrence Genealogy (1881) 70–81
Lyman's Hist. Easthampton Mass. 188–90
Mack Genealogy 70
N. E. Hist. and Gen. Reg. xliii, 39–43
Rodman's Study in Heredity (1889) 14 p.
Savage's Genealogical Dictionary iii, 450–2
Smith's History of Sunderland Mass. 481–3
Stiles' History of Windsor Ct. ii, 620
Temple's Hist. of Northfield Mass. 517–20
Pomroy — American Ancestry vi, 142
Corliss' North Yarmouth Me. Magazine
Read's History of Swanzey N. H. 421
Sheldon's History of Deerfield Mass. 262
Pond — Adams' Haven Gen. 2d part 10
Am. Anc. vi, 116; ix, 215; xii, 63
Anderson's Waterbury Ct. i, app. 104
Ballou's History of Milford Mass. 972–8
Blake's History of Franklin Mass. 265–73
Caverly's History of Pittsford Vt. 721
Heywood's Hist. of Westminster Mass. 828
Hill's Dedham Mass. Records i
Huntington's Stamford Ct. Settlers 82
Jameson's History of Medway Mass. 513
Joslin's History of Poultney Vt. 319–28
Morse's Sherborn Mass. Settlers 203
Orcutt's History of Torrington Ct. 755
Parker Genealogy (1892) 47–51
Pond Family of Dedham (1873) 210 pages
Pond Family of Windsor (1875) 126 pages
Power's Sangamon Co. Ill. Settlers 576
Savage's Genealogical Dictionary iii, 452
Shotwell Genealogy 6–11
Stiles' History of Windsor Ct. ii, 620
Stowe's Hist. of Hubbardston Mass. 335–8
Wight Genealogy 164
Pontius — Egle's Notes (1898) 30
Pontus — Pope Genealogy
Pool — American Ancestry v, 25
Babson's History of Gloucester Mass. 126–9
Barry's History of Hanover Mass. 359
Fletcher Genealogy 59
Harris Family of New York (1888) 246–58
Hobart's Hist. of Abington Mass. 427–30
Hubbard's Stanstead Co. Canada 292
Lapham's History of Norway Me. 581
Temple's History of Palmer Mass. 527

Poole — American Ancestry iv, 62, 160
Bridgeman's Granary Burial Ground 157
Chambers' Early Germans of N. J. 464
Eaton's History of Reading Mass. 106–9
Mitchell's Hist. of Bridgewater Mass. 273
Morrison's Hist. of Windham N. H. 739
Poole Genealogy (1893) 164 pages
Savage's Genealogical Dictionary iii, 454–6
Sharpless Genealogy 271, 404–6
Vinton's Giles Genealogy 324, 538–40
Poore — Abbot's Hist. Andover Mass. 26
American Ancestry ix, 193; xi, 45
Chase's History of Chester N. H. 574
Cochrane's History of Antrim N. H. 646–8
Currier's Ould Newbury Mass. 81–3
Fullonton's Hist. Raymond N. H. 271–6
Gage's History of Rowley Mass. 452
Hayward's History of Hancock N. H. 809
Poore Genealogy (1881) 332 pages
Poore Family Gathering (1881) 68 pages
Poore Family Gathering (1890) 107 pages
Poore Family Gathering (1893) 52 pages
Poore Family Gathering (1899) 44 pages
Savage's Genealogical Dictionary iii, 456
Thurston Genealogy (1894) 11–3
Titcomb's Early New Eng. People 201–13
Poorman — Parthemore Gen. 176–8
Pope — Am. Anc. iii, 150, 187, 223; v, 147;
   vii, 81
California Register i, (1900)
Cogswell's History of Henniker N. H. 693
Daniels' History of Oxford Mass. 646–8
Davis' Landmarks of Plymouth Mass. 208
Draper's History of Spencer Mass. 245
Eaton's History of Thomaston Me. ii, 360
Egle's Notes and Queries (1897) 185
Essex Institute Hist. Colls. viii, 104–18
Freeman's Hist. of Cape Cod Mass. ii, 152
Glover Genealogy 306–8
Hatfield's History of Elizabeth N. J. 89
Meade's Old Churches of Virginia
Mitchell's Hist. of Bridgewater Mass. 273
New Eng. Hist. and Gen. Reg. xlii, 45–62
Norton's History of Fitzwilliam N. H. 675
Paige's History of Hardwick Mass. 454
Pope Family of Boston (1862) 68 pages
Pope Family of Salem (1869) 14 pages
Pope Family of Kentucky (1879) 15 pages
Pope Family Ancestry (1882) 7 pages
Pope Family of Plymouth (1888) 22 pages
Pope Family of Dorchester (1888) 348 p.
Richmond Va. Standard ii, 34; iii, 35, 36
Ricketson's New Bedford Mass. 205–7
Savage's Genealogical Dictionary iii, 457–9
Spooner Mem. W. Spooner 77–82
Winslow Genealogy ii, 890–917
Popham — Bolton's Westchester Co. 240
Popham Genealogy (1898) 24 pages
Porcher — American Ancestry iv, 109
Pore — Egle's Penn. Genealogies 608–10
Poree — American Ancestry xii, 64
Roberts' Richland Families 113–5
Portage — Prime's Bowdoin Gen. 17
Porter — Aldrich's Walpole N. H. 344
Am. Anc. ii, 97; iv, 74, 84, 103; vii, 210,
   254; viii, 75; xii, 130

Anderson's Waterbury Ct. i, app. 104-7
Andrews' Porter Genealogy (1881)
Austin's R. I. Genealogical Dictionary 155
Bangor Me. Hist. Mag. 59-61; vi, 299
Bemis' History of Marlboro N. H. 604-7
Bronson's History of Waterbury Ct. 519-24
Brooks' History of Medford Mass. 534
Brown's Bedford Mass. Families 28
Butler's History of Farmington Me. 553-7
Cleveland's Topsfield Mass. Bi-Centen. 23
Corliss' North Yarmouth Me. Magazine
Cothren's History of Woodbury Ct. 668
Cuyahoga County Ohio Illus. History 440
Dimock's Coventry Ct. Records 91-3
Dwight Genealogy 241-5, 341-58
Eaton's History of Thomaston Me. ii, 360
Egle's Penn. Genealogies 2d ed. 140-2
Egle's Notes and Queries (1897) 121-2
Goodwin's Genealogical Notes 170-4
Gregory's History of Northfield Vt. 144
Hayward's History of Gilsum N. H. 378
Hemenway's Vermont Hist. Gaz. v, 164
Herrick Genealogy 134-51
Hines' Lebanon Ct. Hist. Address 166
Hollister's History of Pawlet Vt. 224
Hubbard's Hist. of Springfield Vt. 413-7
Huntington Genealogy 200
Judd's History of Hadley Mass. 553-7
Kingman's North Bridgewater Mass. 626
Lapham's History of Norway Me. 582
Lapham's History of Paris Me. 697-9
Leonard's History of Dublin N. H. 384
Loomis Genealogy (1880) 789
Maine Genealogist i, 45-9
Martin's History of Chester N. H. 85-7
Mitchell's History of Bridgewater Ct. 274
Nash Genealogy 72
New Eng. Hist. Gen. Reg. ix, 54; xxx, 460
Osgood's Hist. Sketch of North Danvers 17
Orcit's History of Stratford Ct. 1272
Paul's History of Wells Vt. 140-2
Penn. Magazine of History iv, 292-7
Porter Genealogy (1878) 350 pages
Porter Family of Windsor (1882) 125 pages
Porter Family of Windsor (1893) 888 pages
Porter Family of Farmington (1896) 17 p.
Porter Family of Waterbury Ct. (1896) 8 p.
Richmond Va. Standard iii, 28
Saunderson's Charlestown N. H. 523-5
Savage's Genealogical Dict. iii, 459-64
Smith's History of Peterborough N. H. 226
Stiles' History of Windsor Ct. ii, 620-4
Temple's Hist. N. Brookfield Mass. 707-8
Thayer Memorial (1835) 6-8
Timlow's Southington Sketches 206, 410
Turner Genealogy by H. Turner
Whitman Genealogy 502-14
Worthen's History of Sutton N. H. 901-4
Wyman's Charlestown Mass. Gens. ii, 766
Porterfield — Amer. Ancestry iv, 24
Eaton's History of Thomaston Me. ii, 361
Hall's Trenton N. J. Presby. Church 72
Peyton's History of Augusta Co. Va. 317
Posey — American Ancestry viii, 146
Goode Genealogy 264
Meade's Old Churches of Virginia

Post — Am. Anc. ii, 97; ix, 40; xii
Bolton's Westchester Co. N. Y. ii, 754
Buckingham Genealogy 272-5
Bunker's Long Island Genealogies 263-5
Caulkins' History of Norwich Ct. 194-6
Chapman Genealogy 81
Clute's History of Staten Island N. Y. 417
Eaton's History of Thomaston Me. ii, 361
Howell's Hist Southampton N. Y. 3:3-6
Huron and Erie County Ohio History 123
Hyde's Hist. Address at Ware Mass. 47
Munsell's Albany Collections iv, 154
Nevius Genealogy
Norwich Ct. Jubilee 204-6
Paige's History of Cambridge Mass. 628
Pearson's Schenectady N. Y. Settlers 145
Roome Genealogy 322-9
Savage's Genealogical Dictionary iii, 465
Sewall's History of Woburn Mass. 630
Sharpe's South Britain Ct. Sketches 97
Walworth's Hyde Gen. ii, 4, 11-4, 1033-8
Poster — Maine Genealogist iii, 45-9
Poston — American Ancestry viii, 173
Pote — N. E. Hist. Gen. Reg. xl, 18-20
Pote's Journal 1745-7, 2 vols.
Pott — N. E. Gen. Reg. xxxviii, 199
Richmond Va. Standard iv, 7
Potter — Am. Anc. ii, 97; iii, 220; iv, 179;
v, 178
Anderson's Waterbury Ct. i, app. 107
Austin's Allied Families 200
Austin's Ancestries 47
Austin's R. I. Genealogical Dict. 155, 354
Bailey Ancestry (1892) 19-23
Bangor Historical Magazine viii, 44
Bouton's History of Concord N. H. 683
Calnek's History of Annapolis N. S. 563-5
Chambers' Early Germans of N. J. 464
Champion Genealogy 156
Chute Genealogy, appendix 147-60
Cochrane's History of Antrim N. H. 648
Crafts' History of Whately Mass. 542
Dodd's History of East Haven Ct. 142-4
Driver Genealogy 51-7
Dwight Genealogy 543
Greene Genealogy (1894)
Hammatt Papers of Ipswich Mass. 267-9
Ipswich Mass. Antiq. Papers June (1883)
Littell's Passaic Valley Genealogies 321-35
Montague Genealogy 453-7
New Eng. Hist. Gen. Reg. xviii, 150-3;
liv, 20-6
North's History of Augusta Me. 924-6
Norton's Hist. of Fitzwilliam N. H. 675-9
Orcutt's History of Wolcott Ct. 544
Potter Genealogy (1888) 270 pages
Potter's Concord Mass. Families 13, 127
Rhode Island Hist. Mag. vi, 203
Rhode Island Hist. Soc. Collections iii, 294
Savage's Genealogical Dictionary iii. 466-8
Sprague's History of Gloversville N. Y. 125
Stearns' History of Ashburnham Mass. 853
Temple's Hist. N. Brookfield Mass. 708-13
Timlow's Sketches Southington Ct. 207-10
Washburn's History of Leicester Mass. 388
Wheeler's History of Brunswick Me. 848

Whittemore's Orange N. J. 436
Wyman's Charlestown Mass. Gens. ii, 768
Pottle — Dow's Hampton N. H. 928
Lapham's History of Norway Me. 583
Little Genealogy 45-7
Runnel's Hist. of Sanbornton N. H. ii, 585
Wentworth Genealogy ii, 144
Potts — Am. Anc. i, 62: ii, 97; vii, 120; ix, 171
Cooley's Trenton N. J. Settlers 192-5
Holstein Genealogy
Neill Family of Delaware 99-111
Potts' Carter Genealogy 192
Potts Genealogy (1874) 416 pages
Potts Family Ancestors (1895) 427 pages
Richmond Va. Standard iv, 10
Potwine — Stile's Windsor Ct. ii, 625-9
Poucher — Am. Ancestry ii, 97; xi, 13
Poulter — Hazen's Billerica Mass. 114
Hudson's History of Lexington Mass. 187
Poultney — Thomas Gen. (1877) 122
Thomas Genealogy (1896) 465-9
Pound — Shotwell Gen. 6-11, 266
See also Pond
Povall — Goode Genealogy 68
Powell — Am. Anc. ii, 97; iv, 210; vii, 56; x, 79, 164
Babson's History of Gloucester Mass. 129
Bunker's L. I. Genealogies 29-71
Chase's History of Chester N. H. 575
Corliss' North Yarmouth Me. Magazine
Fowler's Our Predecessors 33-40
Hayden's Virginia Genealogies 508
Kulp's Wyoming Valley Families
Maine Hist. Society Collections vii, 230-8
Meade's Old Churches of Virginia ii, 277
Morris Genealogy (1898) 237-40, 460-86
Nashville Am. Hist. Mag. (1896) Oct.
Ruttenber's Hist. Newburgh N. Y. 304-6
Ruttenber's History of Orange N. Y. 401-3
Savage's Genealogical Dictionary iii, 469
Sharpless Genealogy 162
Slaughter's St. Mark's Parish Va. 193
Smith's History of Delaware Co. Pa. 493
Van Kleeck's Thos. Powell Biog. (1857)
Power — American Ancestry ii, 98
Austin's R. I. Genealogical Dictionary 356
Austin's Ancestral Dictionary 47
Narragansett Historical Register vii, 17-24
Power's Sangamon Co. Ill. Settlers 578
Savage's Genealogical Dictionary iii, 470
Powers — Am. Anc. iii, 112; v, 233; vi, 20
Bass' History of Braintree Vt. 172
Bassett's History of Richmond N. H. 467
Blood's History of Temple N. H. 241
Caverly's History of Pittsford Vt. 720
Chandler's History of Shirley Mass. 605
Cleveland Genealogy (1899) 145
Fox's History of Dunstable Mass. 249
Hale Genealogy 238-43
Hayward's History of Gilsum N. H. 379
Hayward's History of Hancock N. H. 810
Hemenway's Vermont Gaz. v, 370-3
Hubbard's History of Springfield Vt. 417
Hyde's History of Brimfield Mass. 446
Lapham's History of Bethel Me. 599-602

Leland Genealogy 104-7, 111-5, 117
Livermore's History of Wilton N. H. 471
Mitchell's Hist. of Bridgewater Mass. 275
Paige's History of Hardwick Mass. 455
Powers Genealogy (1884) 199 pages
Randall's Hist. of Chesterfield N. H. 406
Saunderson's Charlestown N. H. 525
Smith's Hist. of Peterborough N. H. 227
Washington N. H. History 567-70
Wheeler's Croyden N. H. Centennial 130-8
Worcester's History of Hollis N. H. 384
Wyman's Charlestown Mass. Gens. 768
Pownal — Heraldic Journal iii, 56-8
Pownall — Harris' Lancaster Pa. 450
Wyman's Charlestown Mass. Gens. 770
Poyllon — Clute's Staten Island 416
Poythress — Goode Genealogy 55
Meade's Old Churches of Virginia
Richmond Va. Standard i, 48; ii, 34, 46
Robertson's Pocahontas' Descendants 30
Slaughter's Bristol Parish Va. 173
Virginia Magazine vii, (1899) 71
Praa — Riker's Newtown N. Y. 382
Prall — American Ancestry viii, 131
Clute's History of Staten Island N. Y. 418
Pratt — Am. Anc. i, 62; ii, 98; iv, 229; v, 3, 229; ix, 125
Andrews' Hist. of New Britain Ct. 242-287
Austin's R. I. Genealogical Dictionary 157
Barbour's My Wife and Mother, app. 25
Barry's Hist. of Framingham Mass. 363-9
Barry's History of Hanover Mass. 359
Bass' History of Braintree Vt. 172-5
Bemis' History of Marlboro N. H. 607
Blood's History of Temple N. H. 242-5
Bond's Watertown Mass. Genealogies 551
Buckingham Genealogy 211-3
Chandler's History of Shirley Mass. 605
Chapman Genealogy 256-62
Clark's History of Norton Mass. 88
Claypoole Genealogy 78, 159
Corliss' North Yarmouth Me. Magazine
Daniels' History of Oxford Mass. 648-54
Davis Genealogy 159
Davis' Landmarks of Plymouth Mass. 809
Deane's History of Scituate Mass. 326
Eaton's History of Reading Mass. 109
Futhey's History of Chester Co. Pa. 689
Gold's History of Cornwall Ct. 267-72
Hayward's History of Hancock N. H. 811
Heywood's Hist. of Westminster Mass. 829
Hollister's History of Pawlet Vt. 226
Hudson's History of Sudbury Mass. 447
Ketchum's History of Buffalo N. Y. ii, 174
Kidder's Hist. of New Ipswich N. H. 419
Kingman's N. Bridgewater Mass. 623-5
Lapham's History of Paris Me. 700-2
Letchworth's Life S. F. Pratt (1874) 211 p.
Lincoln's Hist. Hingham Mass. iii, 115-9
Loomis Genealogy (1880) 668
Mitchell's Hist. Bridgewater Mass. 275-9
Morse's Sherburn Mass. Settlers 203
Norton's Hist. of Fitzwilliam N. H. 679-84
Olin Genealogy by Nye (1892) 177-84
Orford N. H. Centennial 130-3
Paige's History of Cambridge Mass. 628

Paige's History of Hardwick Mass. 456
Paul's History of Wells Vt. 142
Pierce's History of Grafton Mass. 546
Pompey N. Y. Reunion 341-7
Porter's Hartford Ct. Settlers 17-9
Pratt Family of Dorchester (1860) 8 pages
Pratt Family of Conn. (1864) 420 pages
Pratt Family of Weymouth (1889) 226 p.
Pratt Family of Weymouth (1897) 164 p.
Pratt Family of Hartford (1900) 204 pages
Pratt Manuscript in Me. Gen. Soc. 48 p.
Savage's Genealogical Dictionary iii, 471-6
Sedgwick's History of Sharon Ct. 106
Sheldon's History of Deerfield Mass. 263
Spooner Genealogy i, 762
Stearns' Hist. of Ashburnham Mass. 853
Timlow's Southington Ct. Sketches 211-3
Wakefield Genealogy 43
Walker Genealogy 54
Walworth's Hyde Genealogy 407-9
Ward's Hist. of Shrewsbury Mass. 392-9
Worcester's History of Hollis N. H. 385
Wyman's Charlestown Mass. Gens. 770-3
Pratte — Beckwith's Creoles 105-9
Pray — Austin's R. I. Gen. Dict. 358
Daniels' History of Oxford Mass. 654
Dearborn's History of Parsonsfield Me. 398
Paul's History of Wells Vt. 143
Pope Genealogy
Wentworth Genealogy i, 468-70
Preble — Am. Anc. v, 143; vii, 100; xi, 111
Corliss' North Yarmouth Me. Magazine
Journals of Smith and Deane 251
New Eng. Hist. Reg. xxii, 311-7, 404-19;
  xxiv, 253-64
Preble Genealogy (1850) 28 pages
Preble Genealogy (1868) 336 pages
Ruggles Genealogy
Savage's Genealogical Dictionary iii, 477
Prence — Savage's Gen. Dict. iii, 447
Winsor's History of Duxbury Mass. 293
See also under Prince
Prendergast — Young's Chautauqua Co.
  N. Y. 278-81, 526
Prentice — Allen's Worcester Mass. 55
American Ancestry i, 63; ii, 155
Bond's Watertown Mass. Genealogies 407
Caulkins' Hist. of New London Ct. 328-30
Cogswell's Hist. of Nottingham N. H. 765
Cothren's History of Woodbury Ct. 672
Cutter's History of Arlington Mass. 284-6
Daniels' History of Oxford Mass. 655
Fox's History of Dunstable Mass. 248
Hayward's Hist. of Hancock N. H. 812-4
Jackson's History of Newton Mass. 389-95
Kidder's Hist. of New Ipswich N. H. 420
Leland Genealogy 98-100
Morse's Sherborn Mass. Settlers 204
New Eng. Hist. Gen. Reg. vii, 74; viii, 333
Paige's Hist. of Cambridge Mass. 628-36
Pierce's History of Grafton Mass. 547-52
Power's Sangamon Co. Ill. Settlers 579
Prentice Genealogy (1852) 280 pages
Prentice Fam. of N. London Ct. (1875) 14 p.
Prentice Genealogy 2d ed. (1883) 446 pages
Randall's Hist. of Chesterfield N. H. 408

Savage's Genealogical Dict. iii, 478-80
Stanton Genealogy 74-7
Temple's History of Northfield Mass. 520-2
Wyman's Charlestown Mass. ii, 773-6
Prentis — Meade's Old Families of Va.
Prentiss — Baldwin Genealogy 884-6
Lapham's History of Paris Me. 703
Morse's Richards Genealogy 99
Pierce's History of Gorham Me. 200
Prentiss Genealogy, see Prentice
Stone's History of Hubbardston Mass. 339
Presby — American Ancestry xi, 113
Prescott — Alden's Am. Epitaphs ii, 59
American Ancestry iii, 219; iv, 111
Butler's History of Groton Mass. 428
Butler's Hist. of Farmington Me. 557-60
Chase's History of Chester N. H. 575
Cogswell's Nottingham N. H. 437-44
Cutter's History of Jaffrey N. H. 441-6
Dow's History of Hampton N. H. 928-30
Eaton's History of Thomaston Me. ii, 363
Farnsworth Genealogy (1897) 125-52
Fullonton's Hist. Raymond N. H. 277-80
Green's Early Groton Mass. Settlers 15-7
Green's Groton Mass. Epitaphs 249-51
Hale Genealogy 231-6
Hayward's History of Hancock N. H. 814
Heywood's Hist. of Westminster Mass. 829
Hodgeman's Hist. of Westford Mass. 466-9
Keyes' West Boylston Mass. Reg. 34
Lancaster's Hist. of Gilmanton N. H. 283
Lane Genealogy (1891) 44-8
Morris Genealogy (1894) 51
Morrison's History of Windham N. H. 740
N. E. Hist. Reg. vi, 274; x, 297; xxii, 225
Norton's Hist. of Fitzwilliam N. H. 684-6
Palmer Genealogy (1886) 41
Potter's Concord Mass. Families 13, 94
Prescott Genealogy (1870) 653 pages
Runnel's Sanbornton N. H. ii, 586-96
Savage's Genealogical Dictionary iii, 480-2
Shattuck's History of Concord Mass. 381
Thurston's History of Winthrop Me. 191
Titcomb's Early New Eng. People 133-43
Tuttle Genealogy xxvii
Presho — Randall's Chesterfield 409
Pressey — Hoyt's Salisbury 291
Presson — Chase's Chester N. H. 576
Hemenway's Vermont Hist. Gaz. v, 61
Temple's History of Northfield Mass. 522
See also under Preston
Pressy — Cogswell's Henniker 694-6
Dearborn's History of Salisbury N. H. 713
Worthen's History of Sutton N. H. 904-12
Prest — American Ancestry i, 63
Preston — Abbot's Andover Mass. 36
Adams' Haven Genealogy part ii, 32
American Ancestry ii, 98; iv, 190; x, 158
Blake's Hist. of Mendon Association 262-4
Boyd's Annals of Winchester Ct. 35-7
Cochrane's Hist. Francestn N. H. 885-7
Cothren's History of Woodbury Ct. 662-6
Davis' History of Bucks County Pa. 269
Davis' History of Wallingford Ct. 885-8
Dennysville Me. Centennial 110
Draper Silver Wedding (1871) 4-6

Driver Genealogy 129, 450
Futhey's History of Chester Co. Pa. 689
Green's Kentucky Families
Guild's Stiles Genealogy 27-30
Hanson's Old Kent Md. 169-71
Hayward's History of Hancock N. H. 814
Hemenway's Vermont Hist. Gaz. v, 718
Hudson's History of Lexington Mass. 187
Johnston Genealogy (1897) 207-13
Joslin's History of Poultney Vt. 328
Kidder's Hist. New Ipswich N. H. 421-3
New Eng. Hist. and Gen. Register xiv, 26
Orcutt's History of Stratford Ct. 1272
Paxton's Marshall Genealogy 71
Peyton's History of Augusta Co. Va. 303-7
Plumb's History of Hanover Pa. 465
Power's Sangamon Co. Ill. Settlers 580
Preston Family of Virginia (1842) 10 pages
Preston Genealogy 2d ed. (1864) 16 pages
Preston Genealogy 3d ed. (1864) 26 pages
Preston Genealogy 4th ed. (1870) 64 pages
Richmond Va. Standard i, 12; ii, 7, 44; iii,
 20, 27
Ruggles Genealogy by Bailey (1896) 27-9
Savage's Genealogical Dictionary iii, 482
Sharpless Genealogy 214
Slaughter's St. Mark's Parish Va. 188
Waddell's Annals of Augusta Co. Va. 117
Prevoost — Bartow Genealogy 158
New York Gen. and Biog. Rec. xiii, 27-9
Price — Alexander Genealogy (1898)
American Ancestry xi, 128; xii
Ballou's History of Milford Mass. 979
Bond and Price Genealogy (1872) 35 pages
Bond's Watertown Mass. Gens. 407, 911
Cope Genealogy 82, 181
Embree and Price Biography (1881) 67 p.
Glenn's Merion in Welsh Tract 92-7
Green's Kentucky Families
Hatfield's History of Elizabeth N. J. 90
Hibbard's History of Goshen Ct. 521
Lancaster's Hist. of Gilmanton N. H. 284
Meade's Old Churches of Virginia
Mitchell's Hist. of Bridgewater Mass. 279
Penn. Magazine of History xv, 125
Price Genealogy (1864) 86 pages
Price Golden Wedding (1870) 48 pages
Richmond Va. Standard iii, 12
Rodman Genealogy 163-6
Saunders' Alabama Settlers 119-22
Savage's Genealogical Dictionary iii, 484
Sharpless Genealogy 358
Sullivant Genealogy 221
Virginia Magazine of History vi, 78-80
Prichard — Bedford N. H. Centennial 326
Bronson's History of Waterbury Ct. 524-6
Hoyt's Salisbury Mass. Families 292
Kidder's Hist. New Ipswich N. H. 424-8
Lincoln's Hist. of Hingham Mass. iii, 119
McKeen's History of Bradford Vt. 339-49
See also under Pritchard
Prickett — Pa. Mag. of Hist. xviii, 512
Priest — Adams' Fairhaven Vt. 449
Bemis' History of Marlboro N. H. 608-10
Bond's Watertown Mass. Genealogies 408
Brown's West Simsbury Ct. Settlers 118

Guild's Stiles Genealogy 306
Hayward's Hist. of Hancock N. H. 815-21
Little's History of Weare N. H. 975-7
Savage's Genealogical Dictionary iii, 486
Stearns' History of Rindge N. H. 645
Wood Genealogy 137-43
Wyman's Charlestown Mass. Gens. 777
Prime — American Ancestry x, 131
Cothren's History of Woodbury Ct. 674
Dowd Genealogy
Essex Inst. Hist. Colls. xxiii, 145-7
N. Y. Gen. and Biog. Rec. xvii, 197-208
Orcutt's History of New Milford Ct. 753
Prime Family of Rowley (1887) 40 pages
Prime Family Notes (1888) 118 pages
Prime Family of Milford Ct. (1895) 45 p.
Prime's Autobiography (1873) 293 pages
Queens County N. Y. History (1882)
Randall's History of Chesterfield N. H. 409
Read's History of Swanzey N. H. 423
Resseguie Genealogy 71-3
Wetmore Genealogy 62
Primm — Power's Sangamon Ill. 581-4
Prince — Am. Anc. v, 141, 229; x, 158;
 xi, 113
Babson's History of Gloucester Mass. 129
Baker's History of Montville Ct. 712
Benedict's History of Sutton Mass. 702
Calnek's History of Annapolis N. S. 565
Corliss' North Yarmouth Me. 51-5, 78-9,
 563-73, 726-30, 760-4, 789-94, 844-52
Daniels' History of Oxford Mass. 655-7
Davis' Landmarks of Plymouth Mass. 209
Deane's History of Scituate Mass. 327
Denny Genealogy 215-7
Drake's Rev. Thos. Prince (1851) 12 pages
Dudley's Archæological Coll. plate 4
Eaton's Annals of Warren Me. 604
Eaton's History of Thomaston Me. ii, 364
Ely Genealogy 194
Essex Inst. Coll. xiv, 249-57; xxvii, 171-82
Foster Genealogy (1889) 55-7
Freeman's Cape Cod Mass i, 357; ii, 363
Gage's History of Rowley Mass. 453
Guild's Stiles Genealogy 44-6
Hemenway's Vermont Hist. Gaz. v
Knox Co. Me. Hist. Mag. i, 53 et seq.
Lincoln's Hist. of Hingham Mass. iii, 120
Maine Genealogist iii, 103
Mitchell's Hist. Bridgewater Mass. 384-6
Nealley and True Family Chart
New Eng. Hist. and Gen. Reg vi, 375-83
Orcutt's History of Stratford Ct. 1273
Pickering Genealogy
Poore Genealogy 57-61
Pratt's History of Eastham Mass. 12-4
Prince Family of Hull (1888) 32 pages
Prince Family Meeting (1891) 10 pages
Prince Family of Salem (1891) 11 pages
Prince Family of Williamsburg (1898) 11 p.
Prince's War Records (1898) 88 pages
Prince Genealogy (1899) 153 pages
Queens County N. Y. History 124
Savage's Genealogical Dictionary iii, 487
Secomb's History of Amherst N. H. 731-7
Sullivant Genealogy 223-8

Walworth's Hyde Genealogy 936
Winsor's History of Duxbury Mass. 293
Prindle — Anderson's Waterbury 111
Joslin's History of Poultney Vt. 329
Orcutt's History of New Milford Ct. 753
Temple's Hist. of Northfield Mass. 523
Prioleau — South Car. Huguenot Society
  Transactions vi, (1899) 5–37
Prior — Bunker's Long Island Gens. 272
Coe and Ward Memorial 70
Littell's Passaic Valley Genealogies 338
Perkins' Old Houses of Norwich Ct. 556
Savage's Genealogical Dictionary iii 488
Stiles' History of Windsor Ct. ii, 630–2
Temple's History of Northfield Mass. 524
Winsor's History of Duxbury Mass 294
Pritchard — Anderson's Waterbury Ct. i,
  app. 108–11
Bontecou Genealogy 152–5
Orcutt's History of Derby Ct. 753
Savage's Genealogical Dictionary iii, 485
Wyman's Charlestown Mass. Gens. ii, 777
See also under Prichard
Pritner — Conrad Genealogy 55–7
Priuli — Priuli Gen. (1894) 23 pages
Proctor — Amer. Ancestry iii, 208; xi, 46
Bemis' History of Marlboro N. H. 610
Bridgeman's Kings Chapel Epitaphs 270
Cochrane's Hist. Francestown N. H. 887
Cogswell Genealogy 170
Cogswell's Hist. Henniker N. H. 696, 700
Dearborn's Hist. of Salisbury N. H. 714–6
Felton Genealogy 246
Hammatt Papers of Ipswich Mass. 271
Heywood's Hist. Westminster Mass. 830
Hodgeman's History of Westford Mass. 469
Journals of Smith and Dean 204
Livermore's History of Wilton N. H. 471
Locke Genealogy 106
Morrison's Hist. of Windham N. H. 741–4
New Eng. Hist. and Gen. Register li, 409
Power's Sangamon Co. Ill. Settlers 584
Preble Genealogy 250–2
Proctor Genealogy (1868) 46 pages
Proctor Genealogy (1873) 19 pages
Proctor Genealogy (1898) 307 pages
Savage's Genealogical Dictionary iii, 489
Smith's Founders of Mass. Bay 171–99
Stackpole's History of Durham Me. 239
Stearns' Hist. of Ashburnham Mass. 855
Warren's History of Waterford Me. 281–3
Washington N. H. History 570–8
Whitmore's Copps Hill Epitaphs
Worcester's History of Hollis N. H. 385
Proper — American Ancestry ii, 98
Prosser — Meade's Old Fams. of Va.
Poore Genealogy 269–71
Proud — Howell's Southampton 356
Proudfit — N. Y. Rec. xxix, 121–3
Prout — Bond's Watertown Mass. 409
Savage's Genealogical Dictionary iii, 490
Wyman's Charlestown Mass. Gens. ii, 779
Prouty — American Ancestry viii, 135
Deane's History of Scituate Mass. 328
Draper's History of Spencer Mass. 237–45
Hemenway's Vermont Hist. Gaz. v, 451

Hyde's History of Brimfield Mass. 447
Lincoln's Hist. of Hingham Mass. iii, 120
Temple's Hist. of N. Brookfield Mass. 714
Provender — Corliss' N. Yarmouth Me.
Daniels' History of Oxford Mass. 657
Provoost — Baird's Rye N. Y. 488
Hoffman Genealogy 509–11
New York Gen. and Biog. Rec. vi, 1–24
Provoost Genealogy (1875) 29 pages
See also under Prevoost
Provost — American Ancestry v, 206
Huntington's Stamford Ct. Families 83
Provost Genealogy (1895) 148 pages
Pruyn — Am. Anc. i, 63; ii, 99; x, 16
Munsell's Albany Collections iv, 155
New York Gen. and Biog. Rec. xiii, 11–15,
  71–7, 156–64; xiv, 23–31, 53–65, 101–10;
  xv, 17–22, 97–103; xvii, 208–14; xxi,
  8–26, 124–9, 172–7; xxii, 15–21; xxvii,
  159; xxviii, 206–8; xxix, 69–74, 128–37,
  224–37
Pryor — Goode Genealogy 124
Mitchell's Hist. of Bridgewater Mass. 280
Virginia Mag of Hist. vii, 75–9, 206–8, 325
Puffer — Barry's Framingham 369
Heywood's Hist. Westminster Mass. 830–3
Hudson's History of Lexington Mass. 188
Hudson's History of Sudbury Mass. 448
Hyde's History of Brimfield Mass. 447
Lapham's History of Rumford Me. 383
Lincoln's Hist. of Hingham Mass. iii, 121
Morse Genealogy, app. 41
New Eng. Hist. Gen. Reg. xxii, 288–90
Puffer Genealogy (1882) 9 pages
Savage's Genealogical Dictionary iii, 492
Smith's Hist. of Peterborough N. H. 229
Smith's History of Sunderland Mass. 486–8
Stearns' History of Ashburnham Mass. 855
Purdy — Futhey's Chester Co. Pa. 699
Jackson Genealogy 128
Pugsley — Bockee Genealogy 107–12
Huntting's Hist. of Pine Plains N. Y. 374
Pulciver — Babson's Gloucester 130
Pulford — Orcutt's Stratford Ct. 1274
Pullen — Thurston's Winthrop Me. 192
Whitmore's Copps Hill Epitaphs
Pulliam — Power's Sangamon 584–6
Pulman — American Ancestry i, 64
Pulsifer — American Ancestry ix, 69
Leland Genealogy 97
Montague Genealogy 497–9
Savage's Genealogical Dictionary iii, 493
Pultz — Smith's Rhinebeck N. Y. 195
Pulver — American Ancestry ii, 99–100
Orcutt's History of Torrington Ct. 756
Pumpelly — Am. Anc. i, 64; v, 12
New York Gen. and Biog. Rec. xxvii, 65
Pope Genealogy 315
Pumpelly Genealogy (1893) 25 pages
Punchard — Punchard Gen. (1857) 68 p.
Punderson — Am. Anc. ii, 100; viii, 123
Chapman's Trowbridge Genealogy 46–8
Perkins' Old Houses of Norwich Ct. 557
Savage's Genealogical Dictionary iii, 493
Purchas — Savage's Gen. Dict. iii, 494
Purdie — Richmond Standard iii, 30

Purdy — American Ancestry xi, 111
Baird's Rye N. Y. 434-40
Bolton's Westchester Co. N. Y. ii, 754-6
Calnek's History of Annapolis N. S. 566
Cleveland's History of Yates Co. N. Y. 499
Davis' History of Bucks County Pa. 202
Huron and Erie Counties Ohio History 288
Huntington's Stamford Ct. Setlers 83
Ruttenber's Hist. of Newburgh N. Y. 277
Ruttenber's Hist. Orange Co. N. Y. 367
Walworth's Hyde Genealogy 1024
Purington — Corliss' N. Yarmouth Me.
Hoyt's Salisbury Mass. Families 294
Lapham's History of Norway Me. 583
Little's History of Weare N. H. 977-9
Purmort — Bell's Hist. Exeter N. H. 38
Purnell — Richmond Standard iii, 4
Purple — Temple's Northfield Mass. 525
Purrington — Cogswell's Henniker 700
Lapham's History of Bethel Me. 598
Otis Family of N. H. (1851)
Rich's History of Truro Mass. 552
See also under Purington
Purvines — Power's Sangamon 587-90
Pusey — Morris Genealogy (1898) 691
Greenough Ancestry 22
Pusey Genealogy (1883) 14 pages
Pushee — Hodgman's Westford 470
Norton's History of Fitzwilliam N. H. 686
Pushor — Emery Genealogy (1890) 117
Putman — American Ancestry xi, 113; xii
Pearson's Schenectady Settlers 142-5
Putnam — Adams' Fairhaven Vt. 453
Am. Anc. iii, 113; vi, 162; vii, 188; viii, 91, 93, 132, 215; ix, 225
Austin's Allied Families 202
Barber's Atlee Genealogy 25
Benedict's History of Sutton Mass. 702-13
Blake's Hamden Ct. History 267-76
Brown's Bedford Mass. Families 28
Cochrane's Hist. Francestown N. H. 888
Converse Genealogy (1897) 33-82
Cutter's History of Arlington Mass. 287
Daniels' History of Oxford Mass. 658
Dickerman Genealogy 56-60
Hayward's Hist. of Hancock N. H. 821-30
Hazen's History of Billerica Mass. 115
Hubbard's History of Springfield Vt. 419-21
Lapham's History of Rumford Me. 383-8
Leland Genealogy 156
Livermore's Hist. of Wilton N. H. 472-87
McKeen's History of Bradford Vt. 265-7
Morrison's History of Windham N. H. 744
Pierce's History of Grafton Mass. 552-5
Porter Genealogy 264
Prime Genealogy (1895) 51
Putnam Family Address (1855) 37 pages
Putnam Genealogy (1891-5) 400 pages
Randall's Hist. of Chesterfield N. H. 410
Ross County Ohio Pioneer Records
Saunderson's Charlestown N. H. 526-33
Savage's Genealogical Dictionary iii, 495-7
Secomb's History of Amherst N. H. 737-9
Stearns' History of Ashburnham Mass. 856
Temple's Hist. of N. Brookfield Mass. 715
Vinton Genealogy 477-80
17

Vinton's Upton Genealogy 485-91
Wall's Reminisc. Worcester Mass. 90-100
Wheeler's Croydon N. H. Centen. 126-9
Wyman's Charlestown Mass. Gens. ii, 779
Young's Chautauqua Co. N. Y. 566-8
Putney — Barrus' Goshen Mass. 166
Bassett's History of Richmond N. H. 469
Cochrane's History of Antrim N. H. 651
Coffin's History of Boscawen N. H. 605-7
Cogswell's History of Henniker N. H. 701
Hubbard's History of Stanstead Co. Ill. 281
Norton's History of Fitzwilliam N. H. 687
Stark's History of Dunbarton N. H. 217
Washington N. H. History 578
Wheeler's History of Newport N. H. 511
Worthen's History of Sutton N. H. 912-9
Puysley — American Ancestry ii, 100
Pygan — Caulkins' New London Ct. 341
Redfield Genealogy 11
Pyle — Cope Genealogy 70, 151
Darlington Family Gathering 24, 27
Futhey's History of Chester Co. Pa. 702
Lamborn Genealogy 287
Palmer-Trimble Gen. 83-5, 153-6, 220-3
Power's Sangamon Co. Ill. Settlers 590
Sharpless Gen. 166, 176-8, 281-6, 427-44
Pynchon — Candee Genealogy 183-204
Clarke's Kindred Genealogies (1896) 137-41
Dwight Genealogies 628-34
Ellis' History of Roxbury Mass. 128
Longmeadow Mass. Centennial, app. 77-80
New Eng. Historical and Genealogical
    Register xx, 243; xxxvii, 361; xxxviii, 46-8; xlviii, 249-63
Old Northwest Gen. Quarterly iii, 15
Pynchon Genealogy (1898) 24 pages
Savage's Genealogical Dictionary iii, 497
Talcott's N. Y. and N. E. Families 616-8
Whitmore's Heraldic Journal ii, 49-53
Pyne — Lincoln's Hingham iii, 122
Qua — Salem N. Y. Book of History 63
Quackenbos — American Ancestry vii, 67
Munsell's Albany Collections iv, 155
New York Gen. and Biog. Record xxiv, 174-9; xxv, 17-23, 77-9, 133-7
Pearson's Schenectady Settlers 146-9
Talcott's N. Y. Families 193-215, 420-2
Quackenbush — American Ancestry xii
Quaintance — Lamborn Genealogy 275
Quarles — Clarke's King Wm. Fams.
Quarrier — Quarrier Gen. (1890) 44 pages
Quick — Plumb's Hist. of Hanover Pa. 466
Quicke — N. E. Hist. Reg. xxxviii, 60
Quigley — Cochrane's Francestown 889-92
Egle's Notes and Queries (1898) 264-6
Morrison's Windham 745
Temple's Hist. of N. Brookfield Mass. 716
Quimby — Bolton's Westchester 706
Chase's History of Chester N. H. 577
Coffin's History of Boscawen N. H. 607
Corliss' North Yarmouth Me. Magazine
Dearborn's History of Salisbury N. H. 716
Hubbard's Hist. of Stanstead Co. Can. 168
Little's History of Weare N. H. 979

Runnel's Hist. Sanbornton N. H. ii, 596–8
Whittemore's Orange N. J. 105
Quin — Hayward's Hancock N. H. 830
Sheldon's History of Deerfield Mass. 265
Quinby — American Ancestry ix, 63
Fell Genealogy 82
Hoyt's Salisbury Mass. Families 295
Quincy — American Ancestry iv, 159
Bond's Watertown Mass. Genealogies 909
Collin's Hist. of Hillsdale N. Y., app. 103
Cutts Genealogy
Jackson's Tab. Ped. Quincy Family
Muzzey's Reminiscences
N. E. Hist. and Gen. Reg. xi, 71–3, 157
Quincy Genealogy (1841) 9 pages
Quincy Genealogy (1857) 8 pages
Salisbury Family Mems. (1885) 295–372
Vinton's Giles Genealogy 147
Whitmore's Heraldic Journal iii, 178–82
Quinn — Preble Co. Ohio History 157–9
Quintard — Huntington's Stamford 83
Selleck's Norwalk Ct. (1896) 420–5
Quinton — Adam's Fairhaven Vt. 455
Temple's History of Palmer Mass. 527
Quisenberry — Amer. Ancestry ix, 216
Quisenberry Genealogy (1897) 204 pages
Quitterfield — Sedgwick's Sharon 106
Race — Cleveland's Yates Co. 486–91
Chambers' Early Germans of N. J. 465
Collin's Hist. of Hillsdale N. Y., app. 104
Rackliff — Eaton's Thomaston ii, 365
Hatch's History of Industry Me. 792–7
Racket — Griffin's Journal 128–30
Rackley — Corliss' N. Yarmouth Me.
Radcliff — Albany Collections iv, 156
Young's History of Wayne Co. Ind. 355
Raddin — Littell's Passaic Valley 339
Railey — Richmond Va. Standard ii, 46
Railsback — Young's Wayne Ind. 150
Rainborowe — Rainborowe Gen. (1886)
Raines — Peck's Rochester N. Y. 718–23
Rainsford — Savage's Gen. Dict. iii, 502
Raitt — Old Eliot Me. Monthly i, (1897) 105
Rakestraw — Morris Genealogy (1898) 640
Raleigh — Cochrane's Antrim 653–5
N. E. Hist. and Gen. Reg. xvi, 107
Ralph — Austin's R. I. Gen. Dict. 360
Ralston — Clyde's Irish Settlers of Pa.
117–24
Egle's Penn. Genealogies 458
Egle's Notes and Queries 2d ser. ii, 316–8
Power's Sangamon Co. Ill. Settlers 591
Rambo — Buck's Montgomery Co. Pa. 24
Ramillie — Hubbell Genealogy 301
Ramsay — American Ancestry i, 64
Forrest's History of Norfolk Va. 71
Ramsdell — Ballou's Milford Mass. 982
Barry's History of Hanover Mass. 361
Bassett's History of Richmond N. H. 469
Butler's History of Farmington Me. 560–2
Cutts Genealogy 453–9
Daniels' History of Oxford Mass. 659
Hanover Mass. Records (1898)

Mitchell's Hist. of Bridgewater Mass. 280
Read's History of Swanzey N. H. 424–6
Ruttenber's Hist. of Orange Co. N. Y. 403
Spooner Genealogy i, 483–7
Stearns' History of Rindge N. H. 646
Ramsey — Davis' Bucks County Pa. 420
Hayward's Hist. of Hancock N. H. 830–2
Johnston's History of Cecil Co. Md. 537–48
Keith's Harrison Ancestry 72–82
Preble County Ohio History 222
Scott Genealogy 300–3
Slaughter's Bristol Parish Va. 210–2
Rand — American Ancestry vi, 35; viii, 84
Bedford N. H. Centennial 326
Bond's Watertown Mass. Gens. 409
Cochrane's History of Antrim N. H. 655
Cochrane's Hist. Francest'n N. H. 892–4
Cogswell's Hist. of Nottingham N. H. 444
Dearborn's Hist. of Parsonsfield Me. 398
Dow's History of Hampton N. H. 930
Hayward's History of Hancock N. H. 832
Hemenway Genealogy 42–8
Heywood's Hist. Westminster Mass. 833–6
Paige's History of Hardwick Mass. 458
Rand Genealogy (1898) 269 pages
Saunderson's Charlestown N. H. 533
Savage's Genealogical Dict. iii, 503, 505
Stearns' History of Rindge N. H. 647–53
Ward's History of Shrewsbury Mass. 412–4
Wentworth Genealogy i, 257
Wyman's Charlestown Mass. ii, 782–98
Randall — Am. Anc. iii, 137, 213; xii
Austin's Ancestries 49
Austin's R. I. Genealogical Dictionary 157
Bass' History of Braintree Vt. 175
Bassett's Hist. of Richmond N. H. 470–4
Bond's Watertown Mass. Genealogies 409
Calnek's History of Annapolis N. S. 567
Chute Genealogy, appendix 160–7
Cleveland's Hist. Yates Co. N. Y. 293–296
Davis Genealogy (1888) 56–8
Davis' Landmarks of Plymouth Mass. 210
Deane's History of Scituate Mass. 329
Dearborn's Hist. of Parsonsfield Me. 399
Eaton's History of Thomaston Me. ii, 368
Hayward's History of Gilsum N. H. 380
Hinman's Connecticut Settlers (1846) 226
Hubbard's History of Springfield Vt. 421–3
Lapham's History of Norway Me. 583
Norton's History of Fitzwilliam N. H. 688
Orcutt's History of New Milford Ct. 753–5
Randall Genealogy (1868) 34 pages
Randall Genealogy (1879) 289 pages
Randall's Hist. Chesterfield N. H. 412–5
Read's History of Swanzey N. H. 426
Runnel's Hist. Sanbornton N. H. ii, 598
Savage's Genealogical Dictionary iii, 505–7
Sedgwick's History of Sharon Ct. 106
Stackpole's History of Durham Me. 240
Stearns' Hist. Ashburnham Mass. 857–62
Stiles' History of Windsor Ct. ii, 632
Temple's History of Palmer Mass. 527
Wentworth Genealogy i, 483
Wheeler's History of Brunswick Me. 848
Whittemore's Orange N. J. 418
Williams' History of Danby Vt. **229**

Winsor's History of Duxbury Mass. 295
Randel — Hubbard's Springfield Vt. 421–3
Randolph — Am. Anc. v, 32; viii, 8; xi, 176
Bartlett's Wanton Family 133
Bolling Mem.
Campbell's History of Virginia 629
Carter Family Tree
Cleveland's History of Yates Co. N. Y. 733
Glenn's Colonial Mansions 456–9
Goode Genealogy 111–5
Green's Kentucky Families
Hayden's Virginia Genealogies 133
Jolliffe Genealogy 217–21
Keim Gen. (1899) 321, 368, 392–4, 407, 434, 526
Lee Genealogy (1895) 406–8
Littell's Passaic Valley Genealogies 340
Lynchburg Va. Sketches 190–4
Meade's Old Churches of Va. i, 138–40
Paxton's Marshall Genealogy 26
Prescott's Page Genealogy
Randall's Life of Jefferson i, 7–10
Richmond Va. Critic (1888)
Richmond Va. Standard i, 3, 23; ii, 36; iii, 6, 16, 26, 38
Robertson's Pocahontas' Descendants 33
Slaughter's Bristol Parish Va. 212–22
Southern Bivouac (1886) 730
Wm. and Mary College Hist. Reg. iv, 125–7; vi, 122–4, 195–7
Ranger — Maltby Genealogy 107
Temple's Hist. of N. Brookfield Mass. 716
Rankin — Amer. Ancestry i, 64; vi, 195
Dearborn's History of Salisbury N. H. 166
Eaton's History of Thomaston Me. ii, 366
Parker's History of Londonderry N. H. 296
Ridlon's Saco Valley Me. Families 1123–5
Speed Genealogy 142–7
Ranlett — American Ancestry vii, 63
Eaton's History of Thomaston Me. ii, 367
Rann — Joslin's Hist. of Poultney Vt. 330
Ranney — Adams' Fairhaven Vt. 459
Ellis Genealogy 383–92
Hemenway's Vermont Hist. Gaz. v
Kellogg's White Genealogy 91
Ranney Reunion (1866) 48 pages
Ransom — Joslin's Poultney Vt. 331–3
Ketchum's History of Buffalo N. Y. ii, 136
Loomis Genealogy (1880) 595
Power's Sangamon Co. Ill. Settlers 592
Ransom Genealogy (1882) 234 pages
Welles' Washington Genealogy 265
Rantoul — American Ancestry iii, 210
Essex Inst. Colls. v, 130–2; xxi, 241–68
Rantoul Genealogy (1885) 28 pages
Rapalje — Holgate's Am. Gen. 16–21
New York Gen. and Biog. Rec. xxvii, 35–7
See Rapelye
Rape — Power's Sangamon Co. Ill. 593
Rapelye — Almy Genealogy (1897) 91–132
American Ancestry iv, 91
Bergen Genealogy 15
Bergen's Kings Co. N. Y. Settlers 231–5
Prime's History of Long Island 358–60
Riker's Annals of Newtown N. Y 267–80
Rarick — Chambers' N. J. Germans 466

Rasin — Morris Genealogy (1898) 621
Rasor — Eberhardt Genealogy 67
Rathbone — American Ancestry i, 64
Austin's R. I. Genealogical Dictionary 159
Livermore's Block Island R. I. 306–10
Narragansett Historical Register
Ruggles Genealogy
Talcott's N. Y. and N. E. Families 619–53
Rathbun — American Ancestry vi, 13
Rathvon — Life of S. S. Rathvon 6–8
Ratliff — Young's Wayne Co. Ind. 355
Rattoone — American Ancestry i, 65
Raub — Chambers' N. J. Germans 467
Rauch — Power's Sangamon Ill. 595–7
Raught — American Ancestry ii, 100
Rauss — Rauss Mem. (1878) 60–8
Ravenel — Ravenel Records (1898) 279 p.
South Carolina Huguenot Society vi, 38–45
Ravenscroft — Meade's Va. i, 488
Rawle — American Ancestry iv, 130
Rawle Family of England (1898)
Rawlins — Deane's Scituate Mass. 330
N. E. Hist. Gen. Reg. viii, 255–8; x, 306
Rawlins Genealogy (1870) 84 pages
Rawlins Genealogy (1874) 348 pages
Savage's Genealogical Dictionary iii, 509
Rawson — Amer. Ancestry i, 65; vi, 139
Andrews' History of New Britain Ct. 81
Ballou's History of Milford Mass. 983–7
Bassett's History of Richmond N. H. 474
Benedict's History of Sutton Mass. 714
Daniels' History of Oxford Mass. 660
Emerson's Hist. of Douglass Mass. 208–11
Freeman's Hist. of Cape Cod Mass. ii, 218
Glover Genealogy 212, 254–7, 293–9
Hayward's History of Gilsum N. H. 381
Lapham's History of Paris Me. 704–8
Lapham's History of Rumford Me. 388
New Eng. Hist. and Gen. Reg. iii, 297–330
Paige's History of Hardwick Mass. 458
Pierce's History of Grafton Mass. 555
Rawson Genealogy (1849) 148 pages
Rawson Genealogy 2d ed. (1875) 334 pages
Rawson Ancestry in Eng. (1887) 54 pages
Savage's Genealogical Dictionary iii, 510–2
Temple's History N. Brookfield Mass. 719
Washburn's History of Leicester Mass. 389
Ray — Amer. Ancestry ii, 100; iv, 131
Austin's R. I. Genealogical Dictionary 160
Calnek's History of Annapolis N. S. 567
Cogswell's History of Henniker N. H. 703–6
Davis Genealogy (1888) 107–11
Essex Institute Hist. Collections xviii, 81–7
Field's History of Haddam Ct. 46
Heywood's Hist. Westminster Mass. 836
Holden's Life of David Ray (1881) 24 p.
Lapham's History of Rumford Me. 388
Lincoln's Hist. of Hingham Mass. iii, 123
Livermore's Block Island R. I. 286–93
Power's Sangamon Ill. Settlers 597–9
Prime's Sands Genealogy 41–9
Savage's Genealogical Dictionary iii, 512
Secomb's History of Amherst N. H. 739
Sheldon's History of Deerfield Mass. 266
Raymond—Am. Anc. i, 66; iii, 160; iv, 215; vi, 183; vii, 18, 21–2, 32, 74, 273; ix, 28

Bailey Ancestry (1892) 29-31
Baker's History of Montville Ct. 573-90
Bemis' History of Marlboro N. H. 610
Bolton's Westchester Co. N. Y. ii, 756
Brooks' History of Medford Mass. 535
Caulkins' History of New London Ct. 292
Davis' Landmarks of Plymouth Mass. 210
Hall's Norwalk Ct. Records 184, 93, 205
Hayward's History of Gilsum N. H. 382
Hayward's History of Hancock N. H. 833
Heywood's Hist Westminster Mass. 837-42
Hodgman's History of Westford Mass. 470
Hudson's Hist. of Lexington Mass. 188-90
Little's History of Weare N. H. 980
Marvin's Hist. of Winchendon Mass. 467
Paige's History of Hardwick Mass. 459
Raymond Genealogy (1886) 298 pages
Savage's Genealogical Dictionary iii, 512
Sedgwick's History of Sharon Ct. 107
Selleck's Norwalk Ct. (1896) 24-33
Stearns' Hist. of Ashburnham Mass. 862
Stearns' History of Rindge N. H. 653-5
Stone's History of Beverly Mass. 33
Temple's Hist. of N. Brookfield Mass. 718
Van Hoosen's Norwalk Ct. Epitaphs 33
Walworth's Hyde Genealogy 875-80, 951-3
Wyman's Charlestown Mass. Gens. ii, 800
Young's History of Warsaw N. Y. 320-2
Raynor — Howell's Southampton 356-8
Morris' Bontecou Genealogy 80-3, 138
Savage's Genealogical Dictionary iii, 513
Wyman's Charlestown Mass. Gens. ii, 801
Rayves — Cutts Genealogy 40-2, 76-8
Razee — Ballou Genealogy 520-4
Hayward's History of Hancock N. H. 833
Rea — See Ray
Read — Am. Anc. i, 66; iii, 41; vii, 130;
   ix, 24
Am. Historical Register ii, 1126
Appleton's Baker Ancestry 103-31
Ballou's History of Milford Mass. 987-9
Bassett's History of Norwich Ct. 197
Caulkins' History of Arlington Mass. 288
Chambers' Early Germans of N. J. 467
Corliss' North Yarmouth Me. Magazine
Cutler's History of Richmond N. H. 475
Daggett's History of Attleboro Mass. 98
Daniels' History of Oxford Mass. 661
Draper's History of Spencer Mass. 248
Foote's Hist. of Virginia 2d series i, 573-5
Goode Genealogy 195
Hodgeman's Hist. Westford Mass. 470-3
Hudson's History of Sudbury Mass. 49-51
Meade's Old Churches of Virginia ii, 28
Mitchell's Hist. of Bridgewater Mass. 280
Morris and Flynt Genealogy 53
New Eng. Hist. and Gen. Register xxxvii,
   238; xxxviii, 67
Orcutt's History of Stratford Ct. 1355
Paige's History of Cambridge Mass. 636-9
Perkins' Old Houses of Norwich Ct. 559
Read Family of Rehoboth (1859) chart
Read Family of Geneva N. Y. (1895) 116 p.
Read Genealogy, see Reed Genealogy
Read's History of Swanzey N. H. 427-32
Richmond Va. Standard iv, 25

Sanderson's Signers 544-60
Savage's Genealogical Dict. iii, 515-20
Schenck's History of Fairfield Ct. 402
Secomb's History of Amherst N. H. 741
Sharp's History of Delaware i, 186-202
Todd's History of Redding Ct. 210-4
Tuttle Genealogy 76-81
Whipple-Hill Families (1897) 80-2
Whitmore's Copps Hill Epitaphs
Williams' History of Danby Vt. 230-3
Wyman's Charlestown Mass. ii, 802-6
Reade — American Ancestry x, 105
Green's Kentucky Families
Hildreth Genealogy 57
Taylor's Some Notable Families 73-7
Virginia Magazine of Hist. iv, (1896) 204-7
Reading — American Ancestry ix, 154
Cooley's Trenton N. J. Gens. 195-203
Reading Genealogy (1898) 286 pages
Reagh — Calnek's Annapolis N. S. 568
Reamy — Sullivant Genealogy 201-19
Reape — Austin's R. I. Gen. Dict. 160
Reaume — Navarre Genealogy 319-28
Reckard — Jennings Genealogy (1899)
Recor — Andrews' New Britain Ct. 281
Rector — Cleveland's Yates Co. 352-6
Redding — Corliss' N. Yarmouth Me.
Daniels' History of Oxford Mass. 661
Hayward's History of Gilsum N. H. 383
Savage's Genealogical Dictionary iii, 520
Reddinge — Cregar's White Genealogy
Redfield — Am. Anc. iii, 107; iv, 158; v,
   113; vi, 112
Caulkins' History of New London Ct. 279
Redfield Genealogy (1819) 1 page
Redfield Genealogy (1839) 11 pages
Redfield Genealogy (1860) 337 pages
Saunderson's Charlestown N. H. 534-9
Savage's Genealogical Dictionary iii, 521
Redington — Aldrich's Walpole 345
American Ancestry vii, 213
Bond's Watertown Mass. Gens. 543-5
Cleveland's Topsfield Mass. Bi-Centen. 65
Perley's History of Boxford Mass. 22
Redliff — Albany Collections iv, 156
Redlon — Buxton Me. Mem. 152-6
Ridlon's Saco Valley Me. Families 112-6
Ridlon's Ancient Ryedales (1884)
Redman — Ames' Redman Farm 12
Dearborn's Hist. of Parsonsfield Me. 399
Dow's History of Hampton N. H. 931-4
Redmond — Whittemore's Orange N. J. 364
Redwood — Newport Hist. Mag. i, 7-16
Reed — Am. Anc. ii, 101; iii, 145, 168; iv,
   230; v, 12, 135; vi, 149; vii, 275, 282;
   viii, 166; ix, 97; xii, 66
Barry's History of Hanover Mass. 363
Bolton's Westchester Co. N. Y. ii, 756
Bouton Genealogy
Brown's Bedford Mass. Families 28
Chardon Ohio Newspaper Mar. 29, 1882
Cleveland's History of Yates Co. N. Y. 413
Cochrane's History of Antrim N. H. 657-9
Cooley's Trenton N. J. Genealogies 203-6
Corliss' North Yarmouth Me. Magazine
Crafts' History of Whately Mass. 543

Dickerman Genealogy 411–6
Eaton's History of Thomaston Me. ii, 268
Egle's Notes and Queries (1896) 115
Freeman's Hist. of Cape Cod Mass. ii, 234
Green's Kentucky Families
Hall's Trenton N. J. Presb. Church 74, 196
Heywood's Hist. Westminster Mass. 842
Hobart's History of Abington Mass. 431–8
Hodgeman's Hist. of Westford Mass. 473
Hollister's History of Pawlet Vt. 228–30
Hudson's Hist. of Lexington Mass. 190–8
Huntington's Stamford Ct. Settlers 84
Lapham's History of Norway Me. 584
Lincoln's Hist. of Hingham Mass. iii, 125
Loomis Genealogy (1880) 540–4
Maine Hist. and Gen. Recorder v, 129–34
Mellick's Story of An Old Farm 676
Merrill's History of Acworth N. H. 258–60
Morris Genealogy (1894) 55
Norton's Hist. of Fitzwilliam N. H. 688–94
Orcutt's History of Torrington Ct. 756
Pierce's History of Grafton Mass. 556
Poole Genealogy 82
Proctor Genealogy (1898) 249–61
Reed Genealogy (1861) 588 pages
Reed and Winn Genealogy (1883) 49 pages
Reed Family of Taunton (1895) 8 pages
Reed Genealogy, see Read
Reed's Life of Esther Reed (1853)
Reed's History of Rutland Mass. 129–31
Sedgwick's History of Sharon Ct. 107
Sewall's History of Woburn Mass. 630–2
Sheldon's History of Deerfield Mass. 266
Slafter Genealogy 42
Spooner Genealogy i, 473–5
Spooner's Mem of W. Spooner 135
Stearns' Hist. of Ashburnham Mass. 863
Stiles' History of Windsor Ct. ii, 633–9
Talcott's N. Y. and N. E. Fams. 654–69
Temple's Hist. of N. Brookfield Mass. 720
Temple's History of Whately Mass. 256
Walker Genealogy 147
Washington N. H. History 579–82
Welles' Washington Genealogy 232
Wheeler's History of Brunswick Me. 849
Wheeler's History of Newport N. H. 513–5
Williams' History of Danby Vt. 230–3
Worcester's History of Hollis N. H. 386
Reeder — Cooley's Trenton N. J. 206–11
Fisher Genealogy 109–20
Reehm — Egle's Queries 3d ser. iii, 266
Reel — American Ancestry vii, 212
Rees — Rees Family (1899) 6 pages
Reese — American Ancestry i, 66; xii
Munsell's Albany Collections iv, 156
Pearson's Schenectady N. Y. Settlers 149
Thomas Genealogy (1877) 124
Thomas Genealogy (1896) 469
Reeve — Amer. Ancestry viii, 18; xii
Griffin's Journal of Southold N. Y. 195–7
Howell's Southampton N. Y. 2d ed. 359
Keim Genealogy 460–2
New Eng. Hist. and Gen. Reg. liii, 74–6
Ruttenber's Hist. Orange Co. N. Y. 375–7
Ruttenber's Hist. Newburgh N. Y. 286–6
Shourd's Fenwick Colony N. J. 179–84

Reeves — American Ancestry vi, 205
Brooks' History of Medford Mass. 535–7
Chambers' Early Germans of N. J. 468
Howell's Hist. of Southampton N. Y. 358
Pennypacker's Phœnixville Pa. 270–2
Savage's Genealogical Dictionary iii, 522
Reger — Chambers' N. J. Germans
Reid — American Ancestry i, 66
Bartow Genealogy 167, 182
Cabell Genealogy 597–601
Crane's Rawson Genealogy 154
Green's Kentucky Families
Morrison's History of Windham N. H. 746
Parker's Hist. of Londonderry N. H. 297
Power's Sangamon Co. Ill. Settlers 599–602
Stone's History of Hubbardston Mass. 340
Young's History of Wayne Co. Ind. 433
Reighard — Parthemore Gen. 166–9, 186–8
Reily — Reily's Life of Gibbons v, 130
Reimer — Perkiomen Region Pa. 102
Reinewald — Schwenkfelders 12–5
Reist — Harris' Lancaster Co. Pa. 480
Relyea — Sylvester's Ulster Co. 143
Remer — Cleveland's Yates Co. 274–82
Remick — American Ancestry ix, 165
Eliot, Me. Miscellany (1897) 14–6
Freeman's Hist. of Cape Cod Mass. ii, 375
Hatch's History of Industry Me. 797–800
Hubbard's Hist. of Stanstead Co. Can. 267
N. Eng. Hist. and Gen. Reg. xlvii, 473–7
Old Eliot Me. Monthly iii, (1899) 113, 116
Piper Genealogy (1889) 31
Remington — American Ancestry iii, 75
Austin's R. I. Genealogical Dictionary 161
Ely Genealogy 253
Essex Institute Hist. Colls. xxiii, 147–9
Fuller's History of Warwick R. I. 166–8
Lincoln's Hist. Hingham Mass. iii, 126–9
Paige's History of Cambridge Mass. 639
Savage's Genealogical Dictionary iii, 523
Remsen — Bergen's Kings Co. 236–40
Riker's Annals of Newtown N. Y. 385–93
Renaud — Bolton's Westchester ii, 757
Renaudet — Bartow Gen. App. 200–2
Rendall — Ridlon's Saco Valley 1128
Renick — Egle's Notes and Queries 3d
    series ii, 469–71
Southern History Assoc. Pubs. iii, 221–8
Renninger — Rupp Genealogy 241–6
Rentoul — Essex Inst. Colls. xxi, 241
See Rantoul
Renwick — Greene's Todd Genealogy
Van Rensselaer's New Yorkers
Requa — Bolton's Westchester ii, 757
Raymond's Tarrytown Monument 133–54
Resseguie — Resseguie Gen. (1888) 99 p.
Revell — Cregar's White Genealogy
Savage's Genealogical Dictionary iii, 524
Revere — American Ancestry v, 41
Rexford — American Ancestry vii, 33
Hubbard's Stanstead Co. Canada 264–6
Rexford Genealogy (1891) 77 pages
Sedgwick's History of Sharon Ct. 107
Tuttle Genealogy 235
Reyner — Hanson's Old Kent Md. 190
Lane and Reyner Gen. (1857) 24 pages

Leach's Morton Ancestry 154-6
N. E. Hist. and Gen. Reg. xi, 237-40, 360
Reynolds — Am. Anc. i, 66, ii, 101; iv, 13; v, 171; ix, 139, 236; x, 191; xi, 46
Austin's Ancestral Dictionary 48
Austin's R. I. Genealogical Dictionary 162
Aylsworth Genealogy 153, 302
Ballou's History of Milford Mass. 989
Caulkins' History of Norwich Ct. 197
Chapman Genealogy 110
Cleveland's History of Yates Co. N. Y. 608
Cregar's Haines Ancestry 54
Davis' History of Wallingford Ct. 888-90
Dennysville Me. Centennial 110
Futhey's History of Chester Co. Pa. 710
Greene Genealogy
Hurd's History of Fairfield Co. Ct. 404
Kingman's N. Bridgewater Mass. 629-35
Mitchell's Hist. of Bridgewater Mass. 282
Paul's History of Wells Vt. 144
Perkins' Old Houses of Norwich Ct. 560
Poor's Merrimack Valley Researches 116
Rawson Genealogy 17
Reynolds Genealogy, see Runnels
Savage's Genealogical Dictionary iii, 525
Sharpless Genealogy 221
Smith Genealogy (1889) 106
Strong Genealogy 1364
Reynor — Essex Inst. Colls. xxiii, 149
Hammatt Papers of Ipswich Mass. 275
Rhea — Power's Sangamon Ill. 611
Rhees — Griffith's Life of Morgan John Rhees (1899) 74-6
Rhinehart — Sylvester's Ulster N. Y.
Chambers' Early Germans of N. J. 470
Rhinelander — Am. Anc. ix, 226; x, 188
Bolton's Westchester Co. N. Y. ii, 757
Rhinelander Chart (1896) 27x40 inches
Rhoades — Eaton's Thomaston ii, 369
Hill's Dedham Mass. Records i
Parthemore Genealogy 210-3
Rhoad's Clover-Croft Chronicles (1893)
Secomb's History of Amherst N. H. 742
Rhodes — American Ancestry iv, 203
Austin's Ancestral Dictionary 49
Austin's Ancestries 97
Austin's R. I. Genealogical Dictionary 364
Bemis' History of Marlboro N. H. 611-3
Bradbury's Kennebunkport Me. 271
Cothren's History of Antrim N. H. 659
Harris Genealogy (1883) 116-20
Howell's Southampton 2d ed. 360, 420
Hudson's History of Lexington Mass. 281
Savage's Genealogical Dictionary iii, 526
Wyman's Charlestown Mass. Gens. ii, 807
Rhone — Kulp's Wyoming Valley Fams.
Riant — Butler's Farmington Me. 562
Rice — American Ancestry i, 67; ii, 102; iii, 79, 204; v, 205; vi, 46, 157; vii, 8, 113; viii, 7; x, 142
Atkins' History of Hawley Mass. 54
Austin's R. I. Genealogical Dictionary 162
Bangor Me. Historical Magazine iv, 165-7
Barry's Hist. of Framingham Mass. 371-82
Bassett's History of Richmond N. H. 476
Benedict's History of Sutton Mass. 714

Calnek's History of Annapolis N. S. 568-72
Chute Genealogy, appendix 168-74
Cogswell's Hist. Henniker N. H. 707-16
Corliss' North Yarmouth Me. Magazine
Daniels' History of Oxford Mass. 661
Draper's History of Spencer Mass. 246-8
Hartwell Genealogy (1895) 170-4
Hayward's History of Hancock N. H. 834
Hemenway's Vermont Gaz. v, 40, 97
Heywood's Hist. Westminster Mass. 843-6
Hubbard's History of Springfield Vt. 423-6
Hudson's Hist. of Marlboro Mass. 431-41
Jameson's History of Medway Mass. 513
Joslin's History of Poultney Vt. 336
Kellogg's White Genealogy 131
Leland Genealogy 88, 98, 100, 103
Middlefield Ct. History
Missouri Pioneer Families 288
Morris' Bontecou Genealogy 96, 165
New Eng. Hist. and Gen. Reg. x, 171
North's History of Augusta Me. 926-30
Norton's Hist. of Fitzwilliam N. H. 694-7
Old Northwest Gen. Quarterly iii, 112-4
Paige's History of Cambridge Mass. 640
Paige's History of Hardwick Mass. 460-3
Pierce's History of Grafton Mass. 557
Pompey N. Y. Reunion 304-9
Randall's Hist. of Chesterfield N. H. 415
Reed's History of Rutland Mass. 111
Rice Genealogy (1858) 379 pages
Rice Meeting Address (1851) 14 pages
Rice Tabular Pedigree
Richmond Va. Standard iii, 15
Savage's Gen. Dictionary iii, 527-32
Sedgwick's History of Sharon Ct. 107
Sheldon's History of Deerfield Mass. 267
Smith's Hist. of Sunderland Mass. 489-92
Stearns' Hist. Ashburnham Mass. 864-70
Stearns' History of Rindge N. H. 656
Stone's History of Hubbardston Mass. 341
Temple's Hist. of N. Brookfield Mass. 721
Thomas Genealogy (1877) 125-8
Thomas Genealogy (1898) 471-7
Wall's Rem. of Worcester Mass. 40-3, 354
Ward's Hist. of Shrewsbury Mass. 415-20
Westminster Mass. Centennial 36-8
White's Discourse at Charlemont Mass. 45
Wight Genealogy 183, 185-7
Wyman's Charlestown Mass. Gens. ii, 808
Young's Hist. Chautauqua Co. N. Y. 301
Rich — Am. Ancestry iv, 170; x, 147; xii
Andrews' History of New Britain Ct. 231
Bangor Me. Historical Magazine v, 12
Benedict's History of Sutton Mass. 715
Corliss' North Yarmouth Me. Magazine
Daniels' History of Oxford Mass. 662-4
Davis' History of Bucks County Pa. 304
Davis Genealogy 36-45
Farrow's History of Islesborough Me. 270
Freeman's Hist. of Cape Cod Mass. ii, 375
Heywood's Hist. of Westminster Mass. 846
Machias Me. Centennial 174
Pierce's History of Gorham Me. 201
Rich Genealogy (1892) 39 pages
Rich's Townsend Genealogy (1877)
Rich's History of Truro Mass. 552-60

Stearns' Hist. of Ashburnham Mass. 870
Temple's Hist. of N. Brookfield Mass. 723
Wheeler's History of Brunswick Me. 850
Richards — American Ancestry i, 67; iii,
　117; v, 116; vi, 38; vii, 131, 191; ix,
　151; x, 46, 97; xi, 47
Anderson's Waterbury Ct. i, app. 112
Andrews' New Britain Ct. 134-7, 163. 286
Barry's History of Framingham Mass. 382
Brown's West Simsbury Ct. Families 120
Butler's History of Groton Mass. 495
Caulkins' History of New London Ct. 318
Chandler's History of Shirley Mass. 607
Cochrane's Hist. Francestown N. H. 895
Cogswell's Hist. of New Boston N. H. 395
Corliss' North Yarmouth Me. Magazine
Davis' Landmarks of Plymouth Mass. 212
Dolbeare Genealogy 19
Dudley Genealogy 131
Dyer's History of Plainfield Mass. 168-72
Eaton's History of Thomaston Me. ii, 370
Hall's Norwalk Ct. 210, 242, 245, 252, 259
Hayward's History of Hancock N. H. 835
Hibbard's History of Goshen Ct. 522-5
Hill's Dedham Mass. Records i
Hinman's Connecticut Settlers 1st ed. 226-9
Jackson's History of Newton Mass. 399
Joslin's History of Poultney Ot. 333-6
Kulp's Wyoming Valley Families
Lapham's History of Paris Me. 709
Locke Genealogy 107
Martin's History of Chester Pa. 289
Mitchell's Hist. of Bridgewater Mass. 283
Morse's Genealogical Reg. (1861) iii, 1-236
Olin Genealogy by Nye (1892) 323-57
Orcutt's History of Wolcott Ct. 548
Paige's History of Hardwick Mass. 463
Penn. Mag. of History vi, 69-86; xxii, 254
Prime Genealogy (1895) 48
Richards Genealogy (1861) 243 pages
Richards Family of Penn. (1882) 20 pages
Savage's Gen. Dictionary iii, 532, 535
Sedgwick's History of Sharon Ct. 107
Selleck's Norwalk Ct. (1896) 265
Sharpless Genealogy 351
Spooner Genealogy i, 393
Temple's Hist. of N. Brookfield Mass. 723
Thayer Memorial (1835) 85-7
Thurston's History of Winthrop Me. 194
Tucker's History of Hartford Vt. 456-8
Walker Genealogy (1896) 90-3, 142-8
Walworth's Hyde Genealogy 225-7
Washington N. H. History 582-4
Wentworth Genealogy i, 652-6
Wheeler's Hist. of Newport N. H. 516-9
Whitmore's Copps Hill Epitaphs
Worthen's History of Sutton N. H. 920-4
Richardson — Adams Gen. (1894) 39, 46
Amer. Anc. ii, 102; iv, 85; v, 25, 125, 234;
　vi, 187; vii, 142, 165; x, 72; xii, 100
Anderson's Waterbury Ct. i. app. 113
Austin's R. I. Genealogical Dictionary 163
Barry's Hist. of Framingham Mass. 383
Bass' History of Braintree Vt. 176
Bemis' History of Marlboro N. H. 613-9
Blake's History of Franklin Mass. 273-6

Bond's Watertown Mass. Gens. 411
Boyd's Hitory of Conesus N. Y. 169
Bronson's History of Waterbury Ct. 526
Cabell Genealogy 515-9
Clarke's History of Chester N. H. 577-9
Cochrane's History of Antrim N. H.
Cochrane's Hist. Francest'n N. H. 896-9
Coffin's History of Newbury Mass. 316
Cutter's History of Arlington Mass. 289
Dimock's Coventry Ct. Records 94-6
Eaton's History of Thomaston Me. ii, 371
Essex Inst. Hist. Colls. xvi, 110-26, 171-91
Fletcher Genealogy 241
Fox's History of Dunstable Mass. 249
Haven Genealogy part ii, 11-21
Hayward's History of Gilsum N. H. 385
Hayward's History of Hancock N. H. 835
Hazen's History of Billerica Mass. 117-22
Herrick's History of Gardner Mass. 377
Hodgman's History of Westford Mass. 474
Hubbard's Stanstead Co. Canada 139
Hudson's Hist. of Lexington Mass. 198
Hudson's History of Sudbury Mass. 449
Jackson's History of Newton Mass. 397-9
Jameson's Hist. of Medway Mass. 514-20
Joslin's History of Poultney Vt. 336
Kulp's Wyoming Valley Families
Lapham's History of Bethel Me. 602
Lapham's History of Norway Me. 585
Lapham's History of Paris Me. 710
Lapham's History of Rumford Me. 389
Leonard's History of Dublin N. H. 387
Livermore's History of Wilton N. H. 487
Locke Genealogy 32, 56, 69, 129, 132
Morris Genealogy (1894) 52-4
Morris Genealogy (1898) 311
Morrison's Hist. of Windham N. H. 748-51
Morse's Sherborn Mass. Settlers 206-10
New Eng. Hist. and Gen. Register ix, 68
Morton's Hist. of Fitzwilliam N. H. 697-702
Paige's History of Cambridge Mass. 640
Paige's History of Hardwick Mass. 464
Randall's Hist. of Chesterfield N. H. 416
Read's History of Swanzey N. H. 433-7
Richardson Genealogy (1876) 944 pages
Richardson Family of Del. (1878) 60 pages
Richardson Fam. of Cambridge (1880) 39 p.
Richardson Family of Woburn (1896) 22 p.
Savage's Genealogical Dict. iii, 535, 539
Secomb's History of Amherst N. H. 743-5
Sewall's History of Woburn Mass. 71, 633-6
Smith's History of Peterborough N. H. 231
Spare Genealogy 39-41
Stearns' Hist. of Ashburnham Mass. 871
Stiles' History of Windsor Ct. ii, 640
Temple's Hist. of N. Brookfield Mass. 723
Thomas Genealogy (1877) 128
Thomas Genealogy (1896) 477-80
Vinton Genealogy 375-93
Wakefield Genealogy v 86
Ward's History of Shrewsbury Mass. 420
Washburn's History of Leicester Mass. 390
Wheeler's History of Newport N. H. 519
Whitmore's Copps Hill Epitaphs
Wight Genealogy 105
Willey's Nutfield N. H. History 131-3

Winchester Mass. Record ii, 199–203
Wyman's Charlestown Mass. ii, 809-15
Richbell — Bolton's Westchester ii, 757
Mott Genealogy 311–9
Richey — Morrison's Windham 751
Richmond — Amer. Ancestry ii, 102; iv, 189; viii, 146; xii
Austin's R. I. Genealogical Dictionary 163
Brownell Genealogy (1892) part iii, 1–9
Dawson Genealogy 108
Eaton's Annals of Warren Me. 604
Guild's Stiles Genealogy 116–20
Orcutt's History of New Milford Ct. 799
Paige's History of Hardwick Mass. 465
Pierce's Biographical Contributions 233–42
Richmond Genealogy (1897) 614 pages
Savage's Genealogical Dictionary iii, 539
Sedgwick's History of Sharon Ct. 107
Temple's Hist. of N. Brookfield Mass. 724
Thurston's History of Winthrop Me. 194
Walker Genealogy 33
Waters Genealogy (1882) 28–31
Rickard — Bass' Hist. of Braintree Vt. 176
Davis' Landmarks Plymouth Mass. 212–4
Hubbard's Hist. Stanstead Co. Canada 191
Jennings Genealogy ii, (1899)
Mitchell's Hist. of Bridgewater Mass. 284
Power's Sangamon Co. Ill. Settlers 613
Savage's Genealogical Dictionary iii, 539
Ricker — Butler Genealogy (1886)
Clermont County Ohio History 430, 439
Corliss' North Yarmouth Me. Magazine
Dearborn's Hist. of Parsonsfield Me. 400-2
Haley Genealogy (1900) 79–100
Lapham's History of Woodstock Me. 250
Maine Genealogist ii, 106–12; iii, 9–17, 45–9
New Eng. Hist. Gen. Reg. v, 308–10, 464
Poland Spring Me. Souvenir (1895) 9–21
Ricker Genealogy (1877) 20 pages
Ruggles Genealogy
Wentworth Gen. i, 124–35, 420; ii, 137–46
Ricketson — Calnek's Annapolis 572
Ricks — American Ancestry x, 137
Savage's Genealogical Dictionary iii, 544
Riddell — Richmond Va. Standard i, 9
Riddell Genealogy (1852) 44 pages
Ridlon's Ancient Ryedales (1884) 786 pages
Riddick — Meade's Old Families of Va.
Riddle — Bedford N. H. Centen. 327–34
Nourse Family of Virginia 93–9
Power's Sangamon Co. Ill. Settlers 614-6
Ridlon's Ancient Ryedales (1884)
Rideout — Corliss' North Yarmouth Me.
Livermore's History of Wilton N. H. 488
Worcester's History of Hollis N. H. 386
Rider — American Ancestry ii, 102
Bangor Me. Historical Magazine vi, 98
Barry's History of Framingham Mass. 383
Child Genealogy 580
Davis' Landmarks Plymouth Mass. 214–6
Eaton's History of Thomaston Me. ii, 372
Hubbard's Stanstead Co. Canada 239
Montague Genealogy 86–9
Morse's Sherborn Mass. Settlers 210
Morse Genealogy, appendix 37½
Norton's History of Fitzwilliam N. H. 702

Paul's History of Wells Vt. 145
Rich's History of Truro Mass. 560
Savage's Genealogical Dictionary iii, 540
Sheldon's History of Deerfield Mass. 269
Spooner Genealogy i, 428–34
Ward's History of Shrewsbury Mass. 421
Wyman's Charlestown Mass. Gens. ii, 815
Ridgeley — Power's Sangamon 26, 616
Ridgely — American Ancestry x, 139
Dorsey Family Chart
Life of Rev. Wm. Smith
Ridgeway — Pa. Magazine of History and Biography xii, 495; xvii, 381–3
Power's Sangamon Co. Ill. Settlers 617
Ridgway — American Ancestry v, 101
Ridlands — Ridlon's Ancient Ryedales
Ridley — Rich's Hist. of Truro Mass. 561
Ridlon's Ancient Ryedales (1884)
Ridlon — American Ancestry iii, 98
Dearborn's History of Parsonsfield Me. 402
Ridlon's Ancient Ryedales (1884)
Rifenburgh — Amer. Ancestry ii, 102
Riford — Bass' Hist. of Braintree Vt. 176
Rigby — Tuttle Genealogy 566
Rigg — Barber's Atlee Genealogy 38–42
Quisenberry Genealogy 26–8
Rigglesworth — Jolliffe Genealogy 139–41
Riggs — American Ancestry i, 67
Babson's History of Gloucester Mass. 131
Baldwin Genealogy 88–90
Bemis' History of Marlboro N. H. 619
Cleveland's Hist. of Yates Co. N. Y. 220–3
Humphreys Genealogy 128
Littell's Passaic Valley Genealogies 341–3
Orcutt's History of Derby Ct. 753–6
Resseguie Genealogy 36–9
Savage's Genealogical Dictionary iii, 541
Sharpe's History of Seymour Ct. 197
Wentworth Genealogy i, 467
Wheeler Ancestors (1896) 13
Righter — American Ancestry i, 68
Riker — American Ancestry iii, 209
Riker's Annals of Newtown N. Y. 299–315
Riker Genealogy (1851) 19 pages
Riley — Andrews' New Britain Ct. 267
Leland Genealogy 157
Montague Genealogy 101–5
New Eng. Hist. and Gen. Register xx, 18
Pearson's Schenectady N. Y. Settlers 155
Rindge — Am. Ancestry iii, 226; v, 222
Caldwell Genealogy 67
Hammatt Papers of Ipswich Mass. 277–87
Hoyt's Salisbury Mass. Families 299
New Eng. Hist. and Gen. Register xlv, 3
Wentworth Genealogy i, 320
Rinehart — Goode Genealogy 171
Rinehimer — Plumb's Hanover 472–4
Riner — Johnson Genealogy (1895) 85
Ring — American Ancestry ii, 103
Babson's History of Gloucester Mass. 132
Corliss' North Yarmouth Me. 913–24
Davis' Landmarks of Plymouth Mass. 216
Hoyt's Salisbury Mass. Families 296–9
Livermore's History of Wilton N. H. 489
Savage's Genealogical Dictionary iii, 542
Ringgold — Old Kent Md. 60–70

Thomas Genealogy (1896) 480
Ringo — Hall's Trenton N. J. Ch. 71
Ringwold — Harris' Lancaster 493-6
Rintoul — Essex Inst. Collections xxi, 241
Ripley — Am. Anc. iv, 57; x, 58; xi, 118
Barry's History of Hanover Mass. 364
Boyd's History of Conesus N. Y. 169
Bradford Genealogy (1895)
Bradford Genealogy (1898) 6-8
Davis' Landmarks of Plymouth Mass. 217
Dwight Genealogy 429-34
Lapham's History of Bethel Me. 604
Lapham's History of Paris Me. 711-4
Lapham's History of Rumford Me. 390
Lincoln's Hist of Hingham Mass. iii, 131-8
Mitchell's Hist. of Bridgewater Mass. 285
Montague Genealogy 353-5
Morrison's History of Windham N. H. 752
N. E. Hist. and Gen. Reg. xlviii, 198
Ripley Genealogy (1866) 7 pages
Ripley Genealogy (1867) 48 pages
Ripley's Ingersoll Genealogy 98
Savage's Genealogical Dictionary iii, 543
Winsor's History of Duxbury Mass. 296.
Risedorph — American Ancestry ii, 103
Rishworth — Bangor Hist. Mag. viii, 58
Rising — Bass' History of Braintree Vt. 177
Risley — Guild's Stiles Genealogy 213
Stiles' History of Windsor Ct. ii, 641
Young's Hist. Chautauqua Co. N. Y 490.
Ristine — Humphrey Genealogy 445
Ritchie — Calnek's Annapolis 573-80
Cochrane's Antrim N. H. 661
Smith's Hist. of Peterborough N. H. 232-5
Rittenhouse — Holstein Genealogy
Rittenhouse Genealogy (1893) 322 pages
Rittenhouse Genealogy vol. 2 (1894-5) 128 p.
Rittenhouse (Joseph) Family (1896) 10 p.
Rittenhouse Genealogy, supp. (1897) 139 p.
Ritter — American Ancestry x, 131; xi, 97
Dwight's Strong Genealogy 1391
Washington N. H. History 584
Ritzema — N. Y. Gen. Rec. ix, 192
Rivenburgh — Amer. Ancestry ii, 103
Rivers — Eaton's Thomaston Me. 373
Rives — American Ancestry v, 163
Cabell Genealogy 401-46
Cincinnati Ohio Criterion (1888) ii, 370
Prescott's Page Genealogy
Slaughter's Fry Genealogy 66
Rix — Hubbard's Stanstead Canada 170
Roach — Calnek's Annapolis 580-2
Hatch's History of Industry Me. 800
Roades — Smith's Delaware Pa. 496
Roak — Stackpole's Durham Me. 242
Roakes — Eaton's Warren Me. 610
Roan — Egle's Pa. Gens. 2d ed. 605-10
Roane — Meade's Old Families of Va.
Virginia Magazine of History v, (1897) 89
Robard — Va. Mag. of History vii, 312
Robb — Cochrane's Antrim N. H. 662
Merrill's History of Acworth N. H. 260
Sinclair Genealogy 360-2
Smith's Hist. Peterborough N. H. 235-42
Robbe — Hayward's Hancock 836-9

Robbins — Amer. Anc. i, 68; v, 80, 100; vii, 184; viii, 208; ix, 102, 193; x, 200
Barry's History of Hanover Mass. 364
Bemis' History of Marlboro N. H. 619-21
Bunker's Long Island Genealogies 275-7
Chandler's History of Shirley Mass. 609-12
Cochrane's History of Antrim N. H. 663
Corliss' North Yarmouth Me. Magazine
Cutter's History of Arlington Mass. 289-92
Daniels' History of Oxford Mass. 664-6
Davis' Landmarks of Plymouth 217-20
Deane's History of Scituate Mass. 333
Dedham Historical Register viii, 106-22
Dickerman Genealogy 509-60
Dows Genealogy 194-7
Dunster Genealogy 163
Eaton's Annals of Warren Me. 605
Eaton's History of Thomaston Me. ii, 373-6
Fox's History of Dunstable Mass. 249
Goodwin's Foote Genealogy 186
Greene's Todd Family
Hall's Genealogical Notes (1886) 88-90
Heywood's Hist. of Westminster Mass. 847
Hinman's Connecticut Settlers (1846)
Hodgeman's Hist. of Westford Mass. 475
Hudson's Hist. of Lexington Mass. 199-202
Mack Genealogy 20-9
Mitchell's Hist. of Bridgewater Mass. 286
New Eng. Hist. and Gen. Reg. xx, 15-7
Paige's History of Cambridge Mass. 641-4
Pierce's History of Grafton Mass. 558
Power's Sangamon Co. Ill. Settlers 619
Robbins Chart (1843) 13x16 inches
Robbins Chart (1881) 2x3 feet
Savage's Genealogical Dictionary iii, 545
Sheldon's Hist. of Deerfield Mass. 269-71
Sibley's History of Union Me. 486-94
Stearns' History of Ashburnham Mass. 871
Stearns' History of Rindge N. H. 659-62
Temple's History of Northfield Mass. 527
Thurston's History of Winthrop Me. 194
Whitman Genealogy 409-16
Winsor's History of Duxbury Mass. 297
Wyman's Charlestown Mass. ii, 816-9
Robblee — Calnek's Annapolis 582
Roberdeau — McKean Genealogy 160
Roberdeau Genealogy (1876) 196 pages
Roberson — Am. Ancestry iv, 135; ix, 159
Robert — American Ancestry ix, 207
Roberts—Am. Ancestry ii, 103; vi, 21, 137, 169, 213; vii, 17, 248; ix, 209; xii, 76
Anderson's Waterbury Ct. i, app. 114
Austin's R. I. Genealogical Dictionary 164
Babson's History of Gloucester Mass. 133
Brown's History of Whitingham Vt. 183-8
Brown's West Simsbury Ct. Settlers 119
Buxton Me. Centennial 180
Carter Genealogy by Potts (1883) 109-11
Chambers' Early Germans of N. J. 471
Cleveland's Hist. of Yates Co. N. Y. 740
Cooley's Trenton N. J. Genealogies 211
Davis' History of Bucks County Pa. 459
Davis' Landmarks of Plymouth Mass. 220
Dearborn's Hist. of Parsonsfield Me. 403
Dodd's History of East Haven Ct. 144
Farrow's History of Islesborough Me. 271

Futhey's History of Chester Co. Pa. 714
Glenn's Welsh Tract 98–110, 280–6, etc.
Guild's Stiles Genealogy 101
Hemenway's Vermont Hist. Gaz v, 720
Huntington's Stamford Ct. Families 86
Jameson's History of Medway Mass. 520
Jenkin's Hist. Gwynedd Pa. 2d ed. 196–232
Kewaunee Wis. Owl for April 1899
Lapham's History of Bethel Me. 656
Lapham's History of Rumford Me. 391
Leland Genealogy 69, 121
Lincoln's Hist. of Hingham Mass. iii, 139
Loomis Genealogy (1880) 625, 807
New Eng. Hist. Reg. vii, 63; xlii, 242–8
Orcutt's History of New Milford Ct. 755
Orcutt's History of Torrington Ct. 757
Pierce's History of Gorham Me. 202
Pierce's History of Grafton Mass. 558
Potts' Carter Genealogy 109
Power's Sangamon Co. Ill. Settlers 620
Richmond Va. Standard iii, 3
Roberts Family of N. J. (1852) chart
Roberts Family of Simsbury Ct. (1888) 7 p.
Roberts Family of Simsbury Ct. (1896) 54 p.
Roberts' Old Richland Pa. Families 106–41
Runnel's Hist. of Sanbornton N. H. ii, 599
Savage's Genealogical Dictionary iii, 546–8
Sedgwick's History of Sharon Ct. 107
Sharpless Genealogy 190, 306, 424
Slaughter's St. Marks Parish Va. 144
Stackpole's History of Durham Me. 243–5
Stiles' History of Windsor Ct. ii, 641–7
Temple's Hist. of N. Brookfield Mass. 724
Wentworth Genealogy i, 248, 503–6
Whitmore's Copps Hill Epitaphs
Williams' History of Danby Vt. 234
Wyman's Charlestown Mass. Gens. ii, 819
Robertson — Am. Ancestry iii, 103; ix, 158
Am. Hist. Mag. Nashville i, 174–88, 271–9,
  375–89; ii, 45–59; iii, 21–32, 190–2
Barlow Genealogy 203–23
Chamber's Early Germans of N. J. 472
Darling Genealogy 112
Dearborn's Hist. of Salisbury N. H. 717–9
Dimock's Coventry Ct. Records 97
Greene County N. Y. History 411–3
Johnston Genealogy (1897) 164
Lapham's History of Bethel Me. 605
Lindsay Genealogy
Meade's Old Churches of Virginia
New York Gen. and Biog. Rec. xxiv, 104–8
Randall's Hist. Chesterfield N. H. 417–22
Richmond Va. Standard ii, 36
Robertson's Pocahontas' Descendants
Runnel's History of Sanbornton N. H. 478
Saunderson's Hist. Charlestown N. H. 540
Slaughter's Bristol Parish Va. 222
Slaughter's St. Mark's Parish Va. 159
Tiernan Genealogy 197–202
Waddell's Annals of Augusta Co. Va. 420
Robeson — American Ancestry v, 171
Norton's History of Fitzwilliam N. H. 702
Robie — American Ancestry ix, 172
Chase's History of Chester N. H. 579–82
Corliss Genealogy 9, 240
Dow's History of Hampton N. H. 934–7

Eaton's History of Candia N. H. 100–2
Fullonton's Hist. of Raymond N. H. 280–4
Little's History of Weare N. H. 982
Pierce's History of Gorham Me. 203
Robie Genealogy (1892) 24 pages
Whitmore's Copps Hill Epitaphs
Robins — Clarke's King Wm. Va. Fams.
Crafts Genealogy 191–3
Neill's Virginia Carolorum 158
Plumb's History of Hanover Pa. 469–72
Richmond Va. Standard ii, 43; iii, 1
Virginia Magazine of Hist. ii, (1894) 186–9
Whitmore's Copps Hill Epitaphs
Robinson — Am. Anc. i, 68; ii, 103; iii, 102;
  iv, 5, 84, 207; v, 154; vi, 18, 59, 155,
  186; vii, 48; xi, 100; xii, 82, 85
Am. Gen. Record (1897) ii, 175–7
Austin's R. I. Genealogical Dictionary 165
Babson's Hist. of Gloucester Mass. 134–43
Ball's History of Lake County Ind. 402
Ballou's History of Milford Mass. 994–6
Bangor Me. Historical Mag. v, 11; vi, 96
Barry's Hist. of Framingham Mass. 383
Bartlett's Wanton Genealogy 145–B
Bell's History of Exeter N. H. 39
Bond's Watertown Mass. Genealogies 412
Brown's Bedford Mass. Families 29
Campbell's History of Virginia 546
Carter Family Tree of Virginia
Clarke's Old King Wm. Co. Va. Families
Cochrane's History of Antrim N. H. 665–7
Coe and Ward Memorial 50–2
Cogswell Genealogy 138
Cogswell's Hist. Nottingham N. H. 446–50
Collin's Hist. Hillsdale N. Y., app. 105–15
Cushman's History of Sheepscott Me. 414
Daggett's History of Attleboro Mass. 94
Daniels' History of Oxford Mass. 666–8
Davis' Landmarks of Plymouth Mass. 221
Deane's History of Scituate Mass. 332
Dearborn's History of Salisbury N. H. 719
Dodd's History of East Haven Ct. 144
Eaton's Annals of Warren Me. 605–9
Eaton's History of Thomaston Me. 376–83
Egle's Penn. Gens. 2d ed. 611–26
Follett Genealogy (1896) 179–84
Freeman's Cape Cod Mass. ii, 438, 482
Hayden's Virginia Genealogies 569–84
Hayward's Hist. of Hancock N. H. 840–5
Hazard Genealogy 157–9
Hazard's Olden Times (1879) 291 pages
Hemenway's Vermont Gaz. iv, 168; v, 471
Herrick Genealogy (1885) 295
Hollister's History of Pawlet Vt. 230–2
Hooker's Life of Gen. David Robinson
Hudson's History of Lexington Mass. 202–6
Hudson's History of Sudbury Mass. 450
Hyde's History of Brimfield Mass. 448
Jackson's History of Newton Mass. 401
Johnston Genealogy (1897) 128
Kelley Genealogy (1892)
Lamb's History of New York City i, 604
Lane Genealogy (1891) 93–5
Lapham's History of Bethel Me. 602
Lapham's History of Paris Me. 714–6
Lawrence and Bartlett Mem. 111–30

Lincoln's Hist. of Hingham Mass. iii, 139
Littell's Passaic Valley Genealogies 344
Loomis Genealogy (1880) 921
Marshall Genealogy (1884) 24–6
Meade's Old Churches of Virginia i, 378
Mitchell's Hist. Bridgewater Mass. 386–8
Morrison's History of Windham N. H. 753
N. E. Hist. Gen. Reg. xiv, 17–21; xxxix, 313; xliv, 285; xlviii, 204–7; liii, 198–200
Norton's History of Fitzwilliam N. H. 702
Paige's Hist. of Cambridge Mass. 644
Paige's History of Hardwick Mass. 466–77
Power's Sangamon Co. Ill. Settlers 621–3
R. I. Hist. Society Collections iii, 308
Richmond Va. Standard i, 46; ii, 2; iii, 7, 29, 30, 33, 48; iv, 1, 25
Robinson Fam. of Attleboro (1831) 36 p.
Robinson Family of Vermont (1837) 96 p.
Robinson Fam. of Southington (1859) 214 p.
Robinson Family of Penn. (1867) 142 pages
Robinson Fam. of Dorchester (1890) 60 pp.
Robinson's Items of Ancestry 3–7
Ruggles Genealogy.
Runnel's Sanbornton N. H. ii, 600–9
Savage's Genealogical Dict. iii, 549–56
Schenck's History of Fairfield Ct. 403
Sharpless Genealogy 238, 368
Sinclair Genealogy 193–5
Smith's Hist. of Sunderland Mass. 493–6
Spooner Memorial of W. Spooner 63
Stackpole's History of Durham Me. 245
Strong Genealogy 289–93
Swift's Barnstable Families ii, 228–32
Temple's History of Palmer Mass. 528–30
Timlow's Southington Ct. Sketches 221–3
Turner's Hist. Phelps Purchase N. Y. 387
Updyke's Narragansett Churches R. I. 280
Vinton's Giles Genealogy 363–72
Walworth's Hyde Genealogy 294–7
Robson — Cleveland's Yates County 386
Roby — Savage's Genealogical Dict. iii, 548
Secomb's History of Amherst N. H. 747–9
Worthen's History of Sutton N. H. 931–6
Rochester — Amer. Ancestry iii, 42; xi, 47
Peck's Rochester N. Y. Centennial 669–72
Rochester Genealogy (1882) 25 pages
Rockefeller — Amer. Ancestry ii, 103
Chambers' Early Germans of N. J. 472
Rockett — Lincoln's Hingham iii, 140
Savage's Genealogical Dictionary iii, 556
Rockwell — American Ancestry ix, 193
Baird's History of Rye N. Y. 440
Boyd's Annals of Winchester Ct. 364–71
Eldridge's Rockwell Sermon (1852) 27 p.
Hayward's History of Hancock N. H. 845
Loomis Gen. (1880) 327–33, 447–9, 536–8
Mathew's History of Cornwall Vt. 288
New York Gen. and Biog. Rec. ii, 99–102
Phœnix Whitney Genealogy ii, 1259
Rockwell Genealogy (1873) 224 pages
Savage's Genealogical Dictionary iii, 557
Sedgwick's History of Sharon Ct. 107
Stiles' History of Windsor Ct. ii, 647–60
Tuttle Genealogy 677–9
Walworth's Hyde Genealogy 292
Whittemore's Orange N. J. 424

Rockwood — American Ancestry vi, 79
Ballou's History of Milford Mass. 996–1000
Blake's History of Franklin Mass. 276
Butler's History of Groton Mass. 431
Daniel's History of Oxford Mass. 668
Hemenway Genealogy 58
Jameson's History of Medway Mass. 520
Livermore's Hist. of Wilton N. H. 490–2
Morse's Sherborn Mass. Settlers 211–31
Norton's Hist. of Fitzwilliam N. H. 703–5
Randall's Hist. of Chesterfield N. H. 422
Reade's History of Swanzey N. H. 438
Rockwood Genealogy (1856) 146 pages
Savage's Genealogical Dictionary iii, 558
Stearns' Hist. Ashburnham Mass. 871–74
Thurston Genealogy (1892) 423
Wright Genealogy 19
Rodenbough — Rodenbough's Autumn Leaves (1892) 146–58
Rodes — Va. Mag. of History vi, 418–20; vii, 82–7, 203–5, 324
Rodgers — Egle's Notes and Queries 3d ser. iii, 222–8
Hubbard's Stanstead 201
N. E. Hist. Gen. Reg. x, 352: xvii, 43–50
Power's Sangamon Co. Ill. Settlers 625
Sullivant Genealogy 243–6
Walworth's Hyde Genealogy 527–9
Rodman — American Ancestry vi, 165
Austin's Ancestral Dictionary 50
Austin's R. I. Genealogical Dictionary 166
Bolton's History of Westchester Co. ii, 541
Bunker's Long Island Genealogies 282–4
Daniel's History of Oxford Mass. 669
Davis' History of Bucks County Pa. 146
Newport Historical Magazine iv, 218–20
Pell's Howland's Journal (1890) 9
Rodman Family of Penn. (1886) 287 pages
Rodman Fam. of Newport (1887) 27 pages
Ruggles Genealogy
Rodney — Fisher Genealogy (1896) 60
Jaquett Genealogy 182–5
Morris Genealogy (1898) 821
Roe — Am. Anc. iv, 178, 183; vi, 8; xii, 87
Roe Genealogy (1890) 16 pages
Roe's Sketches of Rose N. Y. 19
Ruttenber's Hist. Orange Co. N. Y. 371–3
Savage's Genealogical Dictionary iii, 559
Stiles' History of Windsor Ct. ii, 660–2
Strong Genealogy 610–3
Roel — Hemenway's Vt. Gaz. v, 185
Roeloffson — Chambers' Germans
Roff — Littell's Passaic Valley 345–8
Rogers — Alden's Am. Epitaphs ii, 70–4
American Ancestry ii, 104; iv, 21, 149; vi, 127; vii, 203; viii, 151, 216; x, 34, 37
Anderson's Waterbury Ct. i, app. 115
Austin's Ancestral Dictionary 51
Austin's R. I. Genealogical Dictionary 167
Babson's History of Gloucester Mass. 314
Baker's History of Montville Ct. 176–222
Ballou Genealogy 574–8
Bangor Me. Hist. Magazine v, 10; vi, 96
Barlow Genealogy 175–203
Barry's History of Hanover Mass. 366
Bond's Watertown Mass. Genealogies 412

Briggs' History of Shipbuilding 202–13
Burleigh's Guild Genealogy 54
Caulkins' New London Ct. 201–3, 337
Champion Genealogy 128
Child Genealogy 650
Cochrane's Hist. Fracestown N. H. 902
Cogswell's History of Henniker N. H. 717
Corliss' North Yarmouth Me. Magazine
Davis' Landmarks of Plymouth Mass. 221
Deane's History of Scituate Mass. 331
Dearborn's Hist. of Salisbury N. H. 721
Dudley's Roger Genealogy 131
Egle's Notes and Queries 3d ser., iii, 226–8
Essex Institute Hist. Collections xxiii, 231
Freeman's Cape Cod ii, 92, 361, 369, 733
Gernerd's Now and Then (1892) iii, 221–39
Gold's History of Cornwall Ct. 261–7
Greene Genealogy (1899)
Hammatt Papers, Ipswich Mass. 290–315
Hayes' Wells Genealogy 157
Hayward's History of Hancock N. H. 846
Hazen's History of Billerica Mass. 122–6
Hodgeman's Hist. of Westford Mass. 425
Howell's Hist. Southampton N. Y. 360–7
Hubbard's Hist. of Stanstead Canada 186
Hudson's Hist. of Sudbury Mass. 450
Hurd's Hist. of New London Co. Ct. 383–5
Jackson's History of Newton Mass. 402
Joslin's History of Poultney Vt. 33
Lincoln's Hist. of Hingham Mass. iii, 140
Litchfield County Ct. History (1881) 318–21
Maine Hist. and Gen. Rec. iv, 83–7; ix, 51–3
McKeen's History of Bradford Vt. 365–7
Merrill's History of Acworth N. H. 261
Mitchell's Hist. of Bridgewater Mass. 288
N. E. Hist. Gen. Reg. iv, 179; v, 106–52,
    224, 311–30; xii, 337–42; xiii, 61–9;
    xvii, 43–51; xxiii, 273; xxxix, 225–30;
    xli, 158–88
New Jersey Hist. Soc. Coll. vi, Supp. 132
New York Genealogical and Biographical
    Record, viii, 97–107, 145–64; xv, 150–
    9; xvi, 10–25, 72–86, 157–71
Old Eliot Me. Monthly iii (1899) 92
Orcutt's History of Wolcott Ct. 550
Orford N. H. Centennial 135–7
Paige's History of Hardwick Mass. 477
Pierce's Biographical Contributions 243–50
Ridlon's Saco Valley Me. Families 96
Rogers' (N. P.) Writings (1849)
Rogers Family —— (1851) 48 pages
Rogers Fam. of Littleton (1885) 6 pages
Rogers Fam. of N. Jersey (1888) 18 pages
Rogers Fam. of Plymouth (1896) 26 pages
Rogers Fam. of Georgetown (1897) 37 pages
Rogers Fam. of Londonderry (1897) 12 p.
Rogers Fam. of Marshfield (1898) 194 p.
Rogers Fam. of Georgetown (1898) 5 pages
Rogers of Plymouth 2d ed. (1898) 27 pages
Runnel's Hist. of Sanbornton N. H. ii, 609
Savage's Genealogical Dict. iii. 559–69
Selleck's Norwalk Ct. (1896) 161–92
Stanton Genealogy 66
Stebbins Genealogy 13
Stiles' History of Windsor Ct. ii, 662
Temple's History of Palmer Mass. 530

Todd's History of Redding Ct. 214
Walworth's Hyde Gen. i, 374–84, 566–80
West Springfield Mass. Centennial 120
Wheeler's History of Brunswick Me. 850
William's History of Danby Vt. 234
Winsor's History of Duxbury Mass. 297
Worthen's History of Sutton N. H. 936
Roggen — Schoonmaker's Kingston N. Y.
    485
Rohrer — Farthemore Genealogy 38, 111–3
Rokes — Locke Genealogy 81
Rolfe — American Ancestry v, 148; ix, 39
Bolling Memorial
Bouton's History of Concord N. H. 685–7
Coffin's History of Boscawen N. H. 668
Hale Genealogy 33–43
Hartwell Genealogy (1895) 66–74
Hoyt's Salisbury Mass. Families 300–3
Lapham's History of Rumford Me. 391–3
Neill's Virginia Carolorum 194
N. E. Gen. Reg. iii, 149–52; xxxviii, 69
Paige's History of Cambridge Mass. 645
Paxton's Marshall Genealogy 35
Richmond Va. Standard iv, 21
Rolfe Genealogy (Descendants of Poca-
    hontas) by Robertson and Brock (1887)
    84 pages
Savage's Genealogical Dictionary iii, 570
Roll — Littell's Passaic Valley 349–55
Power's Sangamon Co. Ill. Settlers 627
Rollins — Amer. Ancestry iii, 203; x, 175
Chapman's Weeks Genealogy 152
Cochrane's History of Antrim N. H. 668
Dow's History of Hampton N. H. 937
Eaton's Annals of Warren Me. 610
Granite Monthly of Concord N. H. v, 73–9
Hayward's History of Gilsum N. H. 385
Leonard's History of Dublin N. H. 389
New Eng. Hist. and Gen. Reg. viii, 253–9
Rollins Chart (1881) by E. A. Rollins
Rollins Genealogy
Runnel's Sanbornton Mass. N. H. ii, 610–6
Wentworth Gen. i, 388–90; ii, 68–81, 99
See Rawlins Genealogy
Rollo — American Ancestry x, 205
Rollo Genealogy (1896) 56 pages
Stiles' History of Windsor Ct. ii, 662
Rolph — Shourd's Fenwick Colony 185
Winchester Mass. Record ii, 501–3
Romer — Raymond's Tarrytown 176
Romeyn — American Ancestry ix, 182
Bergen's Kings Co. N. Y. Settlers 243–5
Stickney's History of Minisink N. Y. 43
Rood — Adam's Hist. of Fairhaven Vt. 458
Loomis Genealogy (1880) 700–2
Orcutt's History of Torrington Ct. 759
Tanner Genealogy 56–8
Roof — American Ancestry iii, 43; v, 160
Rooker — American Ancestry i, 68
Walworth's Hyde Genealogy 639
Rooks — Bangor Hist. Magazine v, 14
Roome — American Ancestry xii
Roome Genealogy (1883) 410 pages
Roop — Egle's Notes and Queries (1895)
    512–3
Roos — Hoffman Genealogy 489

Munsell's Albany Collections iv, 158
Pearson's Schenectady N. Y. Settlers 153
Roosa — N. Y. Gen. Rec. xxxi, 163-6
Roosevelt — Am. Ancestry iv, 96; vi, 19
Green's Todd Genealogy
Holgate's Amer. Genealogy 136-43
Root — American Ancestry ii, 105; vii, 183; ix, 238; xii
Anderson's Waterbury Ct. i, app. 115
Andrew's History of New Britain Ct. 274
Austin's Ancestral Dictionary 52
Boltwood's Noble Genealogy 262, 267
Cochrane's Hist. Francestown N. H. 902
Cothren's History of Woodbury Ct. 674-6
Dimock's Coventry Ct. Records 98-102
Doolittle's Hist. of Belchertown Mass. 100
Hayward's History of Gilsum N. H. 386
Kilbourn Family 42
Loomis Genealogy (1880) 456-65, 658
Mack Genealogy 75-81
Root Genealogy (1870) 533 pages
Savage's Genealogical Dictionary iii, 572-4
Sheldon's Hist. of Deerfield Mass. 271-3
Smith's Hist. of Sunderland Mass. 496-501
Strong Genealogy 80-3, 310-3, 953-6
Taylor's Hist. Great Barrington Mass. 115
Temple's History of Northfield Mass. 529
Timlow's Southington Ct. Sketches 213-21
Rootes — Virginia Magazine of History iv, 204-11, 332
Roots — American Ancestry viii, 201
Schenck's History of Fairfield Ct. 403
Roper — Caldwell Genealogy (1873) 63
Hammatt Papers, Ipswich Mass. 315-7
Holton's Winslow Memorial i, 238-42
Savage's Genealogical Dictionary iii, 574
Ropes — American Ancestry vii, 12
Driver Genealogy 226, 441
Essex Institute Historical Collections vii, 25-34, 91-4, 133-40, 150-67, 198-205, 248-55; viii, 49-62; ix, 112-27; xxvi, 56-8
Pickering Genealogy 5-11
Whittemore's Orange N. J. 274-6
Rorick — American Ancestry vii, 279
Rosborough — Marshall Gen. (1884) 234-6
Pierce's History of Grafton Mass. 559
Rosbough — Clyde's Irish Sett. 126-8
Clyde's Revolution and Gen. 74-93
Rose — American Ancestry x, 20; xii
Austin's R. I. Genealogical Dictionary 167
Barry's History of Hanover Mass. 367
Bond's Watertown Mass. Gens. 413
Cleveland's Hist. Yates Co. N. Y. 524-6
Cooley's Trenton N. J. Genealogies 212-4
Cregar's White Genealogy
Deane's History of Scituate Mass. 332
Dimock's Coventry Ct. Records 102
Eaton's History of Thomaston Me. ii, 383
Farrow's History of Islesborough Me. 272
Fowler Genealogy (1867) 9
Howell's Hist. Southampton N. Y. 367-71
Hubbard's Hist. of Stanstead Canada 135
Livermore's Hist. of Block Island R. I. 342
Meade's Old Churches of Virginia i, 398
New Eng. Historical Gen. Register xx, 18

Orcutt's History of Stratford Ct. 1275
Orcutt's History of Torrington Ct. 759
Orcutt's History of Wolcott Ct. 553
Richmond Va. Standard i, 24; ii, 30; iii, 10; iv, 1
Rose Family of Virginia (1895) chart
Savage's Genealogical Dictionary iii, 575
Slaughter's St. Mark's Parish Va. 147-184
Temple's History of Northfield Mass. 530
Thrall Genealogical Appendix
Turner's Hist. Phelps Purchase N. Y. 236
Walker Genealogy 43
Wyman's Charlestown Mass. Gens. ii, 822
Roseboom — American Ancestry x, 163
Munsell's Albany Collections iv, 148
Roseboom Genealogy (1897) 140 pages
Talcott's N. Y. and N. E. Families 449
Rosebrook — Benton's Guildhall Vt. 209
Daniel's History of Oxford Mass. 670
Rosenberger — Rosenberger Gen. (1892)
Rosewell — Bond's Watertown Mass. 924
Chapman's Trowbridge Genealogy 34-6
Ross — Austin's R. I. Gen. Dict. 168
Clark and Ross Genealogy (1870) 11 pages
Cochrane's Hist. Francestown N. H. 905
Cogswell's History of Henniker N. H. 718
Corliss' North Yarmouth Me. Magazine
Driver Genealogy 408
Egle's Notes and Queries (1897) 23; (1898) 60
Hammatt Papers 317
Hanson's Old Kent Md. 55
Harris Family of New Jersey (1888) 228-44
Hazen's History of Billerica Mass. 126
Joslin's History of Poultney Vt. 338
Littell's Passaic Valley Genealogies 356-61
Paige's History of Hardwick Mass. 478
Pierce's History of Gorham Me. 203
Power's Sangamon Ill. Settlers 328-30
Ridlon's Harrison Me. Settlers 106
Ruggles Genealogy
Savage's Genealogical Dictionary iii, 577
Sheldon's Hist. of Deerfield Mass. 274
Temple's Hist. of N. Brookfield Mass. 725
Walker Genealogy (1896) 110-2
Washington N. H. History 585
Wheeler's History of Brunswick Me. 851
Rossell — Sims' Rosellana (1859) 8 pages
Rosseter — Savage's Dictionary iii, 577-9
Rossiter — N. E. Hist. Gen. Reg. ix, 337
Walworth's Hyde Genealogy 571
Rossman — American Ancestry ii, 105
Rotch — Freeman's Cape Cod ii, 630
Hinchman's Nantucket Settlers 104-9
Ricketson's Hist. New Bedford Mass. 108
Rodman Genealogy 72, 124-6, 199
Secomb's History of Amherst N. H. 750-2
Rothrock — Pa. Mag. of Hist. xxi, 499
Roudebush — Clermont Co. O. 512-5
Roulhac — Roulhac Gen. (1894) 109 pages
Rounds — Ballou Genealogy 346-8
Goodwin's History of Buxton Me. 241-3
Roundy — Bangor Hist. Magazine v, 208
Norton's Hist. of Fitzwilliam N. H. 705
Rounsevel — Washington N. H. 585-7
Rounseville — N. E. Reg. xix, 47-52
Pierce's Biog. Gen. Contributions 251-86

Rouse — Amer. Anc. i, 68; ii, 105; x, 166
Greene County N. Y. History 227
Rauss Memorabilia 60-8
Savage's Genealogical Dictionary iii, 579
Winsor's History of Duxbury Mass. 299
Wyman's Charlestown Mass. Gens. ii, 824
Rowan — Egle's Queries 3d ser. iii, 231-4
Jackson Genealogy 226
Rowe — American Ancestry ii, 106
Babson's Hist. of Gloucester Mass. 143-6
Bangor Me. Historical Magazine ix, 55
Corliss' North Yarmouth Me. Magazine
Dodd's History of East Haven Ct. 145
Dow's History of Hampton N. H. 938
Hayes' Wells Genealogy 194
Hughes Genealogy 62-5
Lamborn Genealogy 122, 293
Lapham's History of Bethel Me. 602
Lapham's History of Norway Me. 587
Lapham's Hist. of Woodstock Me. 252-4
Morrison's History of Windham N. H. 754
Paul's History of Wells Vt. 145
Savage's Genealogical Dictionary iii, 580
Smith's Hist. of Sunderland Mass. 501-6
Tuttle Genealogy 101, 679
Wentworth Genealogy i, 326
Wyman's Charlestown Mass. Gens. ii, 825
Rowell — American Ancestry ix, 139
Bangor Me. Historical Magazine ix, 55
Chase's History of Chester N. H. 583
Cochrane's Hist. Francestown N. H. 906
Eaton's History of Thomaston Me. ii, 384
Hoyt's Salisbury Mass. Families 303-6
Knox Co. Me. Hist. Mag. i 45, etc.
Little's History of Weare N. H. 983
Rowell Genealogy (1898) 216 pages
Runnel's Hist. of Sanbornton N. H. ii, 616
Stiles' History of Windsor Ct. 767
Wheeler's History of Newport N. H. 523
Worthen's History of Sutton N. H. 937-9
Rowland — American Ancestry xii, 86
Daniels' Oxford Mass. 670-2
Davis' Hist. Bucks Co. Pa. 384
Lewis Genealogy (1893) 239-56
Orcutt's History of Stratford Ct. 1357
Richmond Va. Standard ii, 34
Rowland Genealogy (1893) 33 pages
Savage's Genealogical Dictionary iii, 581
Schenck's History of Fairfield Ct. 403
Stiles' History of Windsor Ct. ii, 664-7
Wight Genealogy 115
Rowlandson — Hoyt's Salisbury Mass.
 Families 306-8
Savage's Genealogical Dictionary iii, 581
Rowlee — Sedgwick's Sharon Ct. 108
Rowley — Amer. Ancestry ii, 106; iii, 190
Andrew's History of New Britain Ct. 378
Boyd's Annals of Winchester Ct. 276-9
Loomis Genealogy (1880) 749-51
Savage's Genealogical Dictionary iii, 582
Stiles' History of Windsor Ct. ii, 667-9
Roy — Meade's Old Churches Va. i, 405
Richmond Va. Standard ii, 47
Royall — Brook's Medford Mass. 538
Corliss' North Yarmouth Me. Mag. 573-80
Lapham's History of Paris Me. 717

Lynchburg Va. Sketches 254-7
Maine Hist. Soc. Collections i, 195
Meade's Old Churches of Virginia
New Eng. Hist. Gen. Reg. xxxix, 348-58
Paxton's Marshall Genealogy 293-5
Power's Sangamon Co. Ill. Settlers 630
Royall Genealogy (1885) 27 pages reprint
Savage's Genealogical Dictionary iii, 583
Wyman's Charlestown Mass. Gens. ii, 826
Royce — Aldrich's Walpole N. H. 346-8
American Ancestry ii, 106; v, 63
Anderson's Waterbury Ct. i, app. 116
Andrews' History of New Britain Ct. 190
Caulkins' History of New London Ct. 199
Davis' History of Wallingford Ct. 896-900
Guild's Stiles Genealogy 322
Saunderson's Charlestown N. H. 541
Savage's Genealogical Dictionary iii, 569
Royer — Harris' Lancaster Pa. 508-10
Hertzler Genealogy 327-9
Wagenseller Genealogy 169-71
Roys — American Ancestry ii, 107
Royster — Watkins Genealogy 38
Rozell — American Ancestry v, 169
Cooley's Trenton N. J. Genealogies 214-6
Ruby — Rupp Genealogy 169-74
Ruck — Savage's Genealogical Dict. iii, 584
Ruckel — Power's Sangamon Ill. 631
Rucker — American Ancestry v, 75
Power's Sangamon Co. Ill. Settlers 630
Ruckes — Richmond Standard iii, 28
Ruckman — Littell's Passaic Valley 362
Rudd — American Ancestry i, 68; xii, 87
Baker's History of Montville Ct. 343-5
Caulkins' Hist. of Norwich Ct. 239, 251
Savage's Genealogical Dictionary iii, 584
Walworth's Hyde Gen. ii, 717-25, 1122-6
Ruddell — Ridlon's Ancient Ryedales
Rudderow — N. Y. Record xxix, 112-4
Ruddock — N. Y. Gen. Rec. xxvi, 119
Rudulph — Johnston's Cecil Co. 513-9
Ruffin — Meade's Old Families of Va.
Page Genealogy 242
Richmond Va. Standard ii, 31
Slaughter's Bristol Parish Va. 230
Rugg — Adams' Haven Genealogy 27
American Ancestry vi, 133; vii, 19; ix, 223
Andrews' History of New Britain Ct. 179
Barry's Hist. of Framingham Mass. 384-6
Heywood's Hist. Westminster Mass. 848
Judd's History of Hadley Mass. 558
Norton's History of Fitzwilliam N. H. 705.
Paige's Hist. of Cambridge Mass. 646
Savage's Genealogical Dictionary iii, 585
Stearn's History of Rindge N. H. 662-7
Temple's Hist. of Framingham Mass. 691
Ruggles — Am. Anc. iii, 157; v, 19; ix, 152
Bangor Me. Historical Magazine v, 104
Barbour's My wife and Mother, app. 54
Bond's Watertown Mass. Gens. S 107
Calnek's Hist. of Annapolis N. S. 583-94
Chute Genealogy, appendix 174-80
Deane's History of Scituate Mass. 334
Dudley Genealogy 903, 1016, 1086
Eaton's History of Thomaston Me. ii, 385
Ellis' History of Roxbury Mass. 129

Freeman's History of Cape Cod Mass. 99
Holton's Winslow Mem. 395-401
Joslin's History of Poultney Vt. 340-3
N. Y. Gen. and Biog. Rec. xxv, 164; xxviii, 214-7
Old Northwest Gen. Quarterly i, 59-61
Orcutt's Hist. of New Milford Ct. 756-9
Paige's History of Hardwick Mass. 479-90
Plumb's History of Hanover Pa. 467
Ruggles Genealogy (1892) 232 pages
Ruggles Family Chart 20x32
Ruggles of England (1894) 4 pages
Ruggles Lineage (1896) 14 pages
Savage's Genealogical Dictionary iii, 586-8
Spooner Mem. of W. Spooner 86
Spooner Genealogy i, 236-99
Strong Genealogy 637-9
Suffield Mass. Celebration (1859) 105-7
Temple's History of Palmer Mass. 530-2
Tucker Genealogy (1895) 271-5
Winslow Genealogy ii, app. 23-9
Rumbaugh — Rumbaugh Gen. (1888) 104
Rummage — Plumb's Hanover Pa. 474
Rumery — Ridlon's Saco 1129-33
Rumrill — Bass' Hist. Braintree Vt. 178
Chandler Genealogy 82
Longmeadow Mass. Centennial, app. 80
New Eng. Hist. and Gen. Reg. xxxviii, 48
Saunderson's Hist. Charlestown N. H. 543
Rumsey — Calnek's Annapolis N. S. 594
Fowler's Our Predecessors 61-74
Johnston's History of Cecil Co. Md. 508-10
Todd's History of Redding Ct. 214
Young's History of Warsaw N. Y. 323-5
Rundell — Amer. Ancestry ii, 107; vii, 62
Rundlet — Bell's Hist. of Exeter N. H. 40
Runnel's Hist. Sanbornton N. H. ii, 618-20
Runey — Wyman's Charlestown ii, 829
Runk — American Ancestry iv. 168
Runkle — Chambers' N. J. Germans 591-4
Runkle Genealogy (1899) 366 pages
Runnels — Morrison's Windham 748
Runnels' Hist. Sanbornton N. H. i, 479-81
Runnels Genealogy (1873) 355 pages
Worcester's History of Hollis N. H. 386
Runyan — Runyan Genealogy (1891) 8 p.
Runyon — Goode Genealogy 157
Chambers' Early Germans of N. J. 474-6
Littell's Passaic Valley Genealogies 364-6
Rupley — Rupp Genealogy 77-86
Rupp — Rupp Genealogy (1875) 292 pages
Rusco — Bouton Genealogy 389
Selleck's Norwalk Ct. (1896) 113-20
Rush — Alden's Amer. Epitaphs v, 163
American Ancestry xii
Penn. Magazine of History xvii, 325-35
Potts Genealogy (1895) 43-51
Rushmore — Bunker's L. I. Gens. 279
Rusk — Temple's North Brookfield 725
Rusling — American Ancestry iv, 36
Ruso — American Ancestry i, 68
Russ — Me. Hist. and Gen. Rec. iii, 246
Russell — Abbot's Andover Mass. 36
Aldrich's Hist. of Walpole N. H. 349-52
American Ancestry v, 233; vi, 198; ix, 86
Ammidown Genealogy 13

Anderson's Waterbury Ct. i, app. 116
Bemis' History of Marlboro N. H. 623-5
Bond's Watertown Mass. Gens. 413
Boyd's Annals of Winchester Co. Ct. 290-4
Bridgeman's Granary Epitaphs 244-51
Buddington's Charlestown Mass. Church 252-5
Butler's History of Farmington Me. 563-7
Chapman's Trowbridge Genealogy 41-5
Chase's History of Chester N. H. 583
Cochrane's Hist. Francestown N. H. 907
Corliss' North Yarmouth Me. 355-8
Cutter Genealogy 393
Cutter's Hist. of Arlington Mass. 292-9
Daniels' History of Oxford Mass. 672-4
Davis' Landmarks Plymouth Mass. 222-4
Deane's History of Scituate Mass. 334
Densmore's Hartwell Genealogy
Dodd's History of East Haven Ct. 146
Driver Genealogy 243
Dunster Genealogy 308
Eaton's Annals of Warren Me. 611
Eaton's History of Thomaston Me. ii, 385
Essex Inst. Coll. xvi, 171-91; xxv, 290-2
Freeman's Cape Cod i, 345; ii, 285, 300
Goodwin's Foote Genealogy 285
Hall's Lawrence Genealogy 13
Hayward's History of Gilsum N. H. 387
Hayward's Hist. of Hancock N. H. 847-54
Herrick Genealogy (1885) 253
Heywood's Hist. Westminster Mass. 849
Hill's History of Mason N. H. 205
Hinchman's Nantucket Settlers 87-9
Hudson's Hist. of Lexington Mass. 206-10
Hyde's History of Brimfield Mass. 448
Kilbourne Family 114
Kimball's Richardson Gen. (1880) 19-39
Lapham's Hist. of Bethel Me. 606-11, 657
Leonard's History of Dublin N. H. 390
Lewis Genealogy (1893) 259
Livermore's History of Wilton N. H. 492-5
Locke Genealogy 28, 50, 78, 96
Meade's Old Families of Virginia
Morse's Sherborn Mass. Settlers 231
N. E. Hist. and Gen. Reg. vi, 274; xx, 19; xxvii, 289-91
Olin Genealogy by Nye (1892) 186-93
Orcutt's History of Stratford Ct. 1276
Paige's Hist. of Cambridge Mass. 646-51
Pierce Genealogy (1894)
Potter's Concord Mass. Families 87
Richmond Va. Standard iii, 40
Rickerson's New Bedford Mass. 153-6
Ridlon's Harrison Me. Settlers 106
Runnels' Hist. Sanbornton N. H. 11, 621
Russell Family of Woburn (1879) 212 pages
Russell Family of Kentucky (1884) 124 p.
Savage's Genealogical Dict. iii, 589-95
Secomb's History of Amherst N. H. 752
Sewall's Hist. Woburn Mass. 157, 161, 636
Sharpe's South Britain Ct. Sketches 95
Sheldon's History of Deerfield Mass. 275-7
Sim's Stemmata Rosellana 8
Smith's Hist. of Sunderland Mass. 506-16
Stearns' Hist. of Ashburnham Mass. 874-8
Stearns' History of Rindge N. H. 667-70

Stiles' History of Windsor Ct. ii, 670
Sylvester's History of Ulster Co. N. Y. 70
Talcott's N. Y. and N. E. Families 670-8
Thomas Genealogy (1877) 129
Thomas Genealogy (1896) 482
Walker Genealogy 185
Walworth's Hyde Genealogy 1171-3
Washington N. H. History 587-9
Whitmore's Copps Hill Epitaphs
Whitmore's Heraldic Journal iv, 32, 102-9
Whittemore's Hist. Middlesex Co. Ct. 169
Wilbraham Mass. Centennial 305
Winsor's History of Duxbury Mass. 299
Worthen's History of Sutton N. H. 940-3
Wyman's Charlestown Mass. ii, 829-41
Russworm — Corliss' N. Yarmouth Me.
Rust — American Ancestry iv, 18, 55, 58, 155; v, 115
Cutts Genealogy 63, 124
Dimock's Coventry Ct. Records 103-5
Hammatt Papers of Ipswich 319
Lapham's History of Norway Me. 588-90
Rust Genealogy (1891) 528 pages
Stanton Genealogy 280
Strong Genealogy 1139-42
Rutan — Littell's Passaic Valley 366
Rutenburg — Austin's R. I. Dict. 168
Rutgers — Lamb's N. Y. City i, 723
Munsell's Albany Collections iv, 158
N. Y. Gen. and Biog. Record ii, 22-4; xvii, 82-93; xxx, 75, 253
Rutgers Genealogy (1886) 27 pages, reprint
Rutherford — Bingham Gen. 193-202
Egle's Pa. Genealogies 627-44
Egle's Notes and Queries i, (1894) 121-3
Miller's Hist. of Colchester Co. N. S. 133-5
New York Gen. and Biog. Record xi, 156-8
Richmond Va. Standard ii, 22, 25, 26, 40
Rutherford Genealogy (1894) 355 pages
Temple's History of Palmer Mass. 532
Thomas Genealogy (1877) 130-2
Thomas Genealogy (1896) 483-5
Trowbridge Genealogy 25
Van Rensselaer's New Yorkers
Rutland — Thomas Family (1877) 132
Thomas Genealogy (1896) 485
Rutter — James Potts Gen. (1874) 369
Neill Family of Delaware 118-21
Rutty — American Ancestry xii
Ruyter — American Ancestry i, 69
Munsell's Albany Collections iv, 159
Ryan — Mellick Genealogy 659-61
Ryckman — Albany Collections iv, 159
Pearson's Schenectady N. Y. Settlers 154
Ryder — Bangor Historical Mag. v, 11
Bartow Genealogy, appendix 190
Daniels' History of Oxford Mass. 674
Farrow's Hist. of Islesborough Me. 273-6
Freeman's Hist. of Cape Cod Mass. ii, 630
Jessup Genealogy 122-5
Ryder (Mrs. A. F.) Life of (1888) 44 pages
Stark's History of Dunbarton N. H. 242
Rye — Davis' Hist. of Bucks Co. Pa. 275
Ryers — Clute's Staten Island N. Y. 419
Ryerson — Am. Ancestry iii, 196; xi, 118
Bergen's Kings Co. N. Y. Settlers 240

Calnek's History of Annapolis N. S. 595
Iowa Illustrated Atlas 265
Lapham's History of Paris Me. 718-21
Roome Genealogy 7-12, 19-23
Ryland — Am. Ancestry vii, 206, 226, 279
Ryman — American Ancestry iii, 221
Rymes—Rymes Genealogy (1897) 13 pages
Wentworth Genealogy i, 183
Ryno — American Ancestry iv, 95
Ryther — Cunnabell Genealogy 61
See Rider
Sabeere — Austin's R. I. Gen. Dict. 169
Saben — Bassett's Richmond 478-80
Mowry (Richard) Genealogy 207, 210
Sabin — American Ancestry ix, 37, 209
Ammidown Family 17-9
Chandler Genealogy 140
Chapman's Trowbridge Genealogy 52
Dwight Genealogy 505-9
Hobart's Life of Rev. A. Sabin 126-9
May Genealogy 52
New Eng. Hist. and Gen. Reg. xxxvi, 5208
Norton's Hist. of Fitzwilliam N. H. 706-8
Paige's History of Hardwick Mass. 490
Sabin Genealogy (1882) 11 pages, reprint
Savage's Genealogical Dictionary iv, 1
Whipple-Hill Families (1897) 64
Sacia — American Ancestry ii, 107
Sackett — American Ancestry ii, 107
Power's Sangamon Co. Ill. Settlers 633
Riker's Annals of Newtown N. Y. 344-8
Sackett Ancestors (1899) 31 pages
Savage's Genealogical Dictionary iv, 2
Weygant's Family Record (1897) 2-6, 14-8, 26-9, 38-42, 50-4, 61-5
Young's Chautauqua Co. N. Y. 423
Sadd — Stiles' Windsor Ct. ii, 671-4
Sadler — Babson's Gloucester Mass. 146
Lewis Genealogy (1893) 245
Savage's Genealogical Dictionary iv, 3
Saffarrens — Amer. Ancestry x, 91
Saffin — Deane's Scituate Mass. 355
New Eng. Hist. and Gen. Reg. xlv, 41
Savage's Genealogical Dictionary iv, 3
Safford — Adams' Fairhaven Vt. 464
American Ancestry iv 196
Corliss' North Yarmouth Me. Magazine
Dana's History of Woodstock Vt. 52
Driver Genealogy 120
Essex Institute Hist. Colls. (1883) xx, 89-93
Follett Genealogy (1896) 160-74
Hammatt Papers 321
Hubbard's Hist. of Springfield Vt. 427-30
Kidder's Hist. of New Ipswich N. H. 429
Montague Genealogy 420-2
Paige's History of Hardwick Mass. 491
Pompey N. Y. Reunion 350
Randall's Hist. of Chesterfield N. H. 424
Richmond Va. Standard iii, 36
Robinson and Safford Gen. (1837) 36 p.
Vinton Genealogy 477
Wallbridge Genealogy 307-21
Washington N. H. History 589-94
Sage — American Ancestry ix, 29
Brown's Bedford Mass. Families 30
Hurlbut Genealogy 406, 426-8

Kellogg's White Genealogy 52
Montague Genealogy 109-12
Sage Genealogy (1878) 82 pages
Sagendorf — American Ancestry ii, 107-8
Sager — American Ancestry i, 69
Sahler — American Ancestry ix, 56
Sahler Genealogy (1895) 38 pages
Sailes — Narragansett Hist. Reg. ii, 293
Saint — See St. Clair, St. John
Salisbury — Bridgeman's Granary 291
Cleveland's History of Yates Co. N. Y. 609
Greene County N. Y. History 436-8
Munsell's Albany Collections iv, 159
Salisbury's Fam. Memorials (1885) 696 p.
Salisbury's Family Histories (1892) 1536 p.
Schoonmaker's Kingston N. Y. 483-7
Talcott's N. Y. and N. E. Families 216-23
Salkeld — Bockee Genealogy 98-106
Salkeld Genealogy (1867) 8 pages
Salley — American Ancestry xii
Salmon — Cleveland's Southold 109-23
Chambers' Early Germans of N. J. 476
Morrison's History of Windham N. H. 755
Orcutt's History of Stratford Ct. 1276
Savage's Genealogical Dictionary iv, 6
Salmond — Barry's Hanover Mass. 368
Salter — Allen and Salter Families (1883)
Austin's R. I. Genealogical Dictionary 170
Chambers' Early Germans of N. J. 477
Corliss' North Yarmouth Me.
Salter Genealogy (1882) 11 pages
Savage's Genealogical Dictionary iv, 6
Stearns' History of Ashburnham Mass. 878
Wyman's Charlestown Mass. Gens. ii, 842
Saltmarsh — Bond's Watertown 414, 913
Cochrane's History of Antrim N. H. 669
Saltonstall — American Ancestry iii, 214;
iv, 233; viii, 237; x, 203
Bartlett's Wanton Genealogy 149
Bond's Watertown Mass. Gens. 415, 914-30
Chase's History of Haverhill Mass. 645-7
Coit Genealogy 187
Drake's History of Boston Mass. 68
Dudley Genealogy 132
New Eng. Hist. and Gen. Reg. xxv, 78-81
Phippen's Saltonstall Family Chart
Saltonstall Genealogy (1897) 277 pages
Savage's Genealogical Dictionary iv, 7-9
Whitmore's Heraldic Journal i, 161-4
Saltsman — Hughes Genealogy 139-41
Samborne — See Sanborn
Sammis — Doty Genealogy 565
Sammons — N. Y. Gen. Record vii, 121
Sammons' Montgomery Co. N. Y. 144-6
Sampson — American Ancestry i, 69
Babson's History of Gloucester Mass. 255
Bests' History of Whiteside Co. Ill. 251
Bradbury's Hist. Kennebunkport Me. 272
Briggs' History of Shipbuilding 69-71
Davis' Landmarks of Plymouth 224-9
Freeman's Hist. of Cape Cod Mass. ii, 763
Heywood's Hist. of Westminster Mass. 849
Lapham's History of Norway Me. 591
Norton's History of Fitzwilliam N. H. 707
Richmond Va. Standard ii, 35
Ridlon's Harrison Me. Settlers 114-7

Sampson Genealogy (1864) 136 p., reprint
Savage's Genealogical Dictionary iv, 9
Spooner Genealogy i, 428
Stearns' History of Ashburnham Mass. 884
Temple's Hist. of N. Brookfield Mass. 726
Vinton's Giles Genealogy 373-496
Warren's History of Waterford Me. 286
Washington N. H. History 594
Winsor's History of Duxbury Mass. 300-4
Wyman's Charlestown Mass. Gens. ii, 842
Samson — American Ancestry xi, 119
Littell's Passaic Valley 368
Matthews' History of Cornwall Vt. 289
Samson Genealogy (1900) pamphlet
Stearns' Hist. Ashburnham Mass. 879-83
Samuels — Wakefield Genealogy 217
Sanborn — American Ancestry iii 43;
viii, 160, 164; x, 44
Chapman's Weeks Genealogy 153
Child Genealogy 375-8
Cogswell's Hist. of Henniker N. H. 719-22
Cogswell's Hist. Nottingham N. H. 450-3
Dearborn's Hist. of Parsonsfield Me. 403-5
Dearborn's Hist. of Salisbury N. H. 722-7
Dow's History of Hampton N. H. 939-61
Lancaster's Hist. of Gilmanton N. H. 284-7
Lapham's History of Bethel Me. 612
Lapham's History of Norway Me. 591
Machias Me. Centennial 174
N. E. Hist. Gen. Reg. x, 271-80, 313-22;
xii, 271; xxxix, 245-55; li, 57-64
Reed Genealogy 135
Ridlon's Saco Valley Me. Families 125
Runnels' Hist. Sanbornton N. H. ii, 621-95
Sanborn Genealogy (1856) 21 pages
Samborn of England (1885) 11 pages
Sanborn Genealogy (1887) 75 pages
Sambornes of England (1894) 16 pages
Sambornes of England (1895) 30 pages
Samborne Ancestry (1897) 8 pages
Samborne Ancestry (1897) 10 pages
Sanborn Genealogy (1899) 692 pages
Savage's Genealogical Dictionary iv, 11-3
Worthen's History of Sutton N. H. 944
Sandborn — Smith Geneal. (1890) 196-204
Sandelands — Penn. Magazine of History
ii, 443-50; iii, 331-4; iv, 240-2
Sanders — Babson's Gloucester 241-4
Bergen's Kings County N. Y. Settlers 247
Bulkley's Browne Mem. 102, 118-21
Calnek's History of Annapolis N. S. 595-9
Hazen's History of Billerica Mass. 128
Heywood's Hist. of Westminster Mass. 850
Hoyt's Salisbury Mass. Families 309
Munsell's Albany Collections iv, 160
Pearson's Schenectady Settlers 155-7
Power's Sangamon Ill. Settlers 634-40
Rich Genealogy (1892) 27-31
Runnels' Hist. Sanbornton N. H. ii, 695-8
Saunderson's Charlestown N. H. 543
Stiles' History of Windsor Ct. ii, 675
Wentworth Genealogy i, 441
Sanderson — Barry's Framingham 386
Bond's Watertown Mass. Gens. 416-21, 930
Burke and Alvord Genealogy 37
Butler's History of Groton Mass. 431, 477

Cleveland Genealogy 124-33
Heywood's Hist. of Westminster Mass. 850
Montague Genealogy 496
Randall's Hist. of Chesterfield N. H. 425-9
Sheldon's History of Deerfield Mass. 278
Smith's Hist. of Sunderland Mass. 517-24
Stearns' History of Ashburnham Mass. 884
Temple's History of Whately Mass. 257-9
Worcester's History of Hollis N. H. 386
Sandford — Schenck's Fairfield Ct. 404
Sandles — Marshall Genealogy (1884) 47
Sands — American Ancestry iii, 43
Austin's R. I. Genealogical Dictionary 170
Bolton's Westchester Co. N. Y. i, 716
Bunker's Long Island Genealogies 285-7
Buxton Me. Centennial 217-20
Livermore's Hist. Block Island R. I. 275-84
Ridlon's Saco Valley Me. Families 1133-7
Sands Genealogy (1886) 91 pages
Savage's Genealogical Dictionary iv, 13
Sullivant Genealogy 348-51
Thompson's Long Island N. Y. ii, 463-9
Sandys — Essex Inst. Colls. xxiii, 232
Neill's Virginia Carolorum 159
Sanford — Am. Anc. i, 69; ii, 108; iv 154,
     177; vi, 204; ix, 50; x, 98, 99, 141
Anderson's Waterbury Ct. i, app. 117
Austin's R. I. Genealogical Dictionary 171
Chapman Genealogy 211
Chute Genealogy, appendix 180-94
Currier's Castleton Vt. Epitaphs 42
Daniels' History of Oxford Mass. 674
Dwight Genealogy 477-9
Eaton's Annals of Warren Me. 612
Hinman's Connecticut Settlers 1st ed. 231
Howell's Hist. of Southampton N. Y. 371-4
Hurd's History of Fairfield Co. Ct. 478-80
Jameson's History of Medway Mass. 521
Journals of Smith and Dean 230
Matthews' History of Cornwall Vt. 289
Morris' Bontecou Genealogy 104-6, 175
New Eng. Hist. and Gen. Reg. xxvii, 81
Orcutt's History of New Milford Ct. 759-63
R. I. Historical Magazine vii, 293-304
R. I. Hist. Society Collections iii, 298
Sanford Genealogy (1894) 70 pages
Savage's Genealogical Dictionary iv, 13-6
Sedgwick's History of Sharon Ct. 109
Seneca Co. N. Y. Illus. History (1876) 68,
Todd's History of Redding Ct. 215-21
Whitmore's Heraldic Journal iii, 62
Wight Genealogy 107
Sanger — Am. Anc ii, 108; vi, 102; ix, 104
Barry's History of Framingham Mass. 387
Bond's Watertown Mass. Gens. 421-3, 931
Hayward's History of Gilsum N. H. 388
Leland Genealogy 20
Morse's Sherborn Mass. Settlers 232-9
Morse Memorial, appendix
Oneida Hist. Society Trans. (1889) 85-7
Sanger Genealogy (1851) 12 pages
Savage's Genealogical Dictionary iv, 16
Sankey — American Ancestry iv, 136
Durant's Hist. of Lawrence Co. Pa. 165-8
New Eng. Hist. and Gen. Register xl, 109
Sharpless Genealogy 367

Santvoort — N. Y. Gen. Rec. vii, 117
Sapp — Norton's Knox County Ohio 385
Sares — See Sears
Sargeant — Caverly's Pittsford Vt. 723
Chase's History of Chester N. H. 584-6
Eaton's History of Candia N. H. 102
Freeman's Hist. of Cape Cod Mass. ii, 263
Hemenway's Vermont Hist. Gaz. v, 21-4
New Eng. Hist. and Gen. Reg. x, 184
Randall's Hist. of Chesterfield N. H. 427-9
Sargeant Genealogy, see Sargent
Savage's Genealogical Dictionary iv, 17-20
Sargent — American Ancestry ii, 108; iii,
     44, 216; iv, 108; vii, 91, 195
Babson's Hist. of Gloucester Mass. 148-57
Bangor Me. Hist. Mag. ii, 125-31; vi, 98
Bartow Genealogy 137-40
Bass' History of Braintree Vt. 179
Bemis' History of Marlboro N. H. 625-8
Binney Genealogy 109
Boston Journal for Sept. 1, 1876
Cochrane's Hist. Francestown N. H. 908
Cogswell's Hist. of Henniker N. H. 722
Corliss' North Yarmouth Me.
Davis' Landmarks of Plymouth Mass. 229
Denny Genealogy 94-6
Dow's History of Hampton N. H. 961-3
Hollister's History of Pawlet Vt. 234
Hoyt's Salisbury Mass. Families 310-4
Little's History of Weare N. H. 984
Malden Mass. Bi-Centennial 230
Morrison's History of Windham N. H. 755
New Eng. Hist. and Gen. Reg. xxv, 209
Norton's Hist. of Fitzwilliam N. H. 708
Sanborn Genealogy 44-50
Sargent Family of Malden (1858) 108 pages
Sargent Family of Gloucester (1871) 51 p.
Sargent Family of Sullivan Me. (1887) 8 p.
Sargent Family of Amesbury (1893) 21 p.
Sargent Family of Malden (1895) 218 pages
Sargent Family of Amesbury (1899) 331 p.
Stowe's Hist. Hubbardston Mass. 344-7
Temple's Hist. of N. Brookfield Mass. 726
Walworth's Hyde Genealogy 548
Washburn's Hist. of Leicester Mass. 391-6
Whitehead's Perth Amboy N. J. 141-3
Worthen's History of Sutton N. H. 945-54
Wyman's Charlestown Mass. Gens. ii, 845
Sartell — Green's Groton Settlers 17
Green's Groton Mass. Epitaphs 251
New Eng. Hist. and Gen. Reg. vi, 274
Prentice Genealogy 402
Sartelle — Eaton's Thomaston 386
Sartwell — Saunderson's Charlestown
Sasse — Ball's Lake County Ind. 418-20
Sater — Levering Gen. (1897) 275-7
Satterlee — Am. Ancestry iv, 198; viii, 80
Pearson's Schenectady N. Y. Settlers 169
Sattley — Power's Sangamon Ill. 640
Saulsbury — William' Danby Vt. 253
Saum — Plumb's Hist. Hanover Pa. 483
Saunders — Austin's R. I. Dict. 173
Ballou's History of Milford Mass. 1001-3
Davis' Landmarks of Plymouth Mass. 230
Driver Genealogy 271, 464-8
Eaton's History of Thomaston Me. ii, 386

Farrow's History of Islesborough Me. 276
Glover Genealogy 140–8
Greene Genealogy
Hall's Norwalk Ct. 226, 236, 242, 251
Herrick's History of Gardner Mass. 378
Hubbard's Stanstead Co. Canada 136
Lapham's History of Bethel Me. 658
Lapham's History of Norway Me. 592–4
Little Genealogy 84–6
Little's History of Weare N. H. 985
Meade's Old Families of Virginia
Norton's Hist. of Fitzwilliam N. H. 708–10
Page Genealogy 73
Paige's History of Cambridge Mass. 651
Richmond Va. Standard ii, 46
Saunders Genealogy (1872) 39 pages
Saunders' Alabama Settlers 318–31, 339–64, 459–69
Smith's Founders of Mass. Bay 26–156
Savage's Genealogical Dictionary iv, 20–2
Warren's History of Waterford Me. 288
Wheeler's Eminent N. Carolinians 450–2
Saunderson — Crafts' Whately 546–56
Savage's Genealogical Dictionary iv, 22
Washburn's History of Leicester Mass. 400
Saur — Penn. Mag. of History vi, 127
Savage — American Ancestry ix, 55
Bangor Me. Hist. Mag. v, 209; viii, 87
Bridgeman's Kings Chapel Epitaphs 296
Clarke Genealogy (1885) 50
Cochrane's Hist. Francestown N. H. 909
Eaton's History of Thomaston Me. ii, 387
Freeman's Hist. of Cape Cod Mass. ii, 332
Meade's Old Families of Virginia
Merrill's History of Acworth N. H. 262
Neill Family of Delaware 122
N. E. Hist. and Gen. Reg. xlviii, 311–6
North's History of Augusta Me. 931
Rich's History of Truro Mass. 566
Salem N. Y. Book of History 65
Savage Genealogy (1894) 26 pages
Savage's Genealogical Dictionary iv, 23–7
Stowe's Hist. of Hubbardston Mass. 347
Symmes Genealogy 24, 35
Timlow's Southington Ct. Sketches 224
Tucker's Hist. of Hartford Vt. 458–60
Virginia Mag. of History i, 443–5
Wyman's Charlestown Mass. Gens. ii, 847
Savary — American Ancestry iii, 111; iv, 73, 228; xii, 122
Davis' Landmarks Plymouth Mass. 230–2
Harriman's History of Warner N. H.
Rawlins Genealogy 28
Savage's Genealogical Dictionary iv, 28
See also Savery
Savery — N. E. Hist. Reg. xli, 369–88
Savery Genealogy (1887) 20 pages
Savery Genealogy (1893) 286 pages
See also Savary, Savory, Severy
Savil — Savage's Gen. Dict. iv, 27
Saville — Babson's Gloucester 284
Hudson's History of Lexington Mass. 211
Savory — Lamb Genealogy 6–11
Woodbury's Bradford 86–90
Woodbury's Groveland Mass. Epit. 80–5
Sawin — Bond's Watertown Mass. 423

Dunster Genealogy 310
Herrick's History of Gardner Mass. 397
Heywood's Hist. Westminster Mass. 851–9
Hudson's Hist. of Marlborough Mass. 442
Hyde Family of Hubbardston 8–12
Mitchell's Hist. of Bridgewater Mass. 289
Morse Mem., appendix 16
Morse's Sherborn Mass Settlers 239
Savage's Genealogical Dictionary iv, 29
Sawin Family (1866) 48 pages
Slafter Genealogy 11
Stearns' Hist. of Ashburnham Mass. 885–7
Thayer's Memorial (1835) 42
Warren's History of Waterford Me. 289
Sawtell — Bond's Watertown Mass. 424
Butler's History of Groton Mass. 432, 495
Chandler's History of Shirley Mass. 613–9
Green's Early Groton Mass. Settlers
Green's Groton Mass. Epitaphs 252
Heywood's Hist. of Westminster Mass. 859
Savage's Genealogical Dictionary iv, 29
Smith's Hist. of Sunderland Mass. 525
Stearns' Hist. of Ashburnham Mass. 887
Stearns' History of Rindge N. H. 679–86
Temple's History of Northfield Mass. 531
Sawyer — Am. Ancestry i, 69; ii, 108; iv, 81; xii
Babson's Hist. of Gloucester Mass. 146–8
Ballou's History of Milford Mass. 1003
Bangor Me. Hist. Mag. vi, 274–6; viii, 235
Bemis' History of Marlboro N. H. 628
Carter Genealogy (1887)
Cleveland's Hist. of Yates Co. N. Y. 593–6
Cochrane's Hist. of Antrim N. H. 670–5
Cochrane's Hist. Francest'n N. H. 910–2
Cogswell's Hist. of Henniker N. H. 723–9
Cogswell's Hist. of Nottingham N. H. 453
Corliss' North Yarmouth Me.
Dearborn's Hist. of Salisbury N. H. 728–70
Eaton's History of Reading Mass. 111
Eaton's History of Thomaston Me. ii, 387
Egle's Notes and Queries 1st ser. i, 88–90; 3d ser. iii, 176–8
Emery Genealogy (1890) 10
Essex Institute Hist. Colls. xxiii, 232–4
Farrow's Hist. of Islesborough Me. 277
Hayward's History of Gilsum N. H. 389
Hayward's History of Hancock N. H. 854–7
Heywood's Hist. Westminster Mass. 860–3
Little Genealogy 72–7, 132–5
Little's History of Weare N. H. 986–8
Livermore's History of Wilton N. H. 495
McKeen's History of Bradford Vt. 271–6
Milliken's Narraguagus Valley Me. 16
Morris Genealogy (1894) 49
New Eng. Hist. Gen. Reg. xxviii, 194–8
Orford N. H. Centennial 142
Pierce's History of Gorham Me. 204
Poore Genealogy 114, 118–20
Poor's Merrimack Valley Researches 80
Rawlins Genealogy 110
Read's History of Swanzey N. H. 440–2
Ridlon's Saco Valley Me. Families 1137–46
Savage's Genealogical Dictionary iv, 30
Sawyer Golden Wedding (1869) 12 pages
Sawyer Immigrants (1883) 120 pages

Sawyer Family of Newbury (1889) 59 pages
Sawyer Family of Newbury (1891) 11 pages
Stearns' History of Ashburnham Mass. 888
Temple's History of Northfield Mass. 532
Wakefield Genealogy 58
Walker Genealogy (1895) 36-51
Ward's History of Shrewsbury Mass. 442
Wheeler's History of Newport N. H. 526-8
Wyman's Charlestown Mass. Gens. ii, 848
Saxe — Slafter Genealogy 17
Saxton — Anderson's Waterbury 118
Chute Genealogy, appendix 194-6
Faxon Genealogy 86-92
Savage's Genealogical Dictionary iv, 31
Sheldon's Hist. of Deerfield Mass. 279-84
Stiles' History of Windsor Ct. 770
See also Sexton
Sayer — Bourne's Hist. Wells Me. 489-92
Homer Genealogy 14
Lincoln's Hist. of Hingham Mass. iii, 143
Savage's Genealogical Dictionary iv, 32
Sayler — Amer. Anc. viii, 48, 71, 73, 81
Sayler Genealogy (1898) 164 pages
Sayles — American Ancestry i, 69
Austin's Ancestries 71-3
Austin's R. I. Genealogical Dict. 370
Ballou Genealogy 353-6, 371-8
Savage's Genealogical Dictionary iv, 33
Sayre — Hill's Lawrence-Townley Estate 69-71
Howell's Hist. Southampton N. Y. 374-84
Kitchell Genealogy 47-50
Littell's Passaic Valley Genealogies 360-2
Power's Sangamon Co. Ill. Settlers 641
Sayres — Martin's Chester Pa. 288
Shourd's Fenwick Colony N. J. 227-32
Sayward — American Ancestry x, 114
Babson's History of Gloucester 157
Dow's History of Hampton N. H. 963
Eaton's History of Thomaston Me. ii, 387
Sayward Genealogy (1890) 177 pages
Scales — American Ancestry v, 67
Cogswell's Nottingham N. H. 238-42
Corliss' North Yarmouth Me. Magazine 163
Crawford Families of Virginia 104
Essex Institute Hist. Colls. xxiii, 234-6
Journals of Smith and Dean 56
Nealley Chart
Scammel — Ballou's Milford 1004-10
Scammon — Putnam's Historical Magazine iii, 119-23, 187-9, 214-20
Savage's Genealogical Dictionary iv, 34
Scammon Genealogy (1892) 21 pages
Weeks Genealogy (1889) 23, 154
Scarborough — Amer. Ancestry iii, 218
Cincinnati Ohio Criterion (1888) ii, 371
Hayden's Virginia Genealogies 439
Meade's Old Families of Virginia
Savage's Genealogical Dictionary iv, 34
Virginia Magazine of Hist. iv (1897) 316-8
Scarlet—Savage's Genealogical Dict. iv, 35
Scarlett — Dutton Gen. 53, 62, 74-7
Palmer and Trimble Genealogy
Schafner — Calnek's Annapolis 599
Scharp — Albany Collections iv, 165
Schauer — See Shower

Schell — Schell Genealogy (1896) 94 pages
Schellenger — Hedge's History of East Hampton N. Y. 320-3
Schellinx — See Schellenger
Schenck — Amer. Ancestry iv, 162, 182
Bergen's Kings Co. N. Y. Settlers 249-55
Honeyman's Our Home Magazine 551-4
Schenck Memoir (1876) 83 pages
Schenck Genealogy (1883) 163 pages
Schenck Genealogy, supp. (1885) 26 pages
Schenkel — Chambers N. J. Germans
Schepmoes — Schoonmaker's Kingston
Schermerhorn — Am. Anc. ii, 108; vi, 57
Munsell's Albany Collections iv, 161
New York Gen. and Biog. Rec. ii, 22-4
Pearson's Schenectady N. Y. Sett. 158-65
Talcott's N. Y. and N. E. Fams. 224-7
Schieffelin — N. E. Hist. Reg. li, 449-53
Schieffelin Genealogy (1897) 7 pages
Thomas Family 134-7
Thomas Genealogy (1896) 487-95
Schilling — Am. Cath. Collections ii, 341
Schmidt — Smith's Rhinebeck N. Y. 187
Schneider — Perkiomen Region 142, 161, 172-6, 190-2; iii, 28-30, 39
Schoenheit — Chambers' N. J. 594
Schoffe — Stearns' Ashburnham 889
Scholfield — Baker's Montville Ct. 267-77
Schollay — Page Genealogy 100
Schooley — Chambers' N. J. Germans
Schoonhoven — Amer. Ancestry ii, 108
Schoonmaker — American Ancestry iv, 199; v, 172, 193
Bergen Genealogy 112
Munsell's Albany Collections iv, 161
New York Gen. and Biog. Rec. xix, 22-6
Schoonmaker's Hist. Kingston N. Y. 487-9
Sylvester's History of Ulster Co. N. Y. 103
Schott — Egle's Notes and Queries 4th ser. i, 23
Schrach — Perkiomen Region Pa. 58
Schrick — N. Y. Gen. Rec. ix, 115, 124
Schroeder — Washington Genealogy 235
Schropp — Egle's Notes and Queries 3d ser. iii, 158-60
Schubert — Schwenkfelders 14
Schultz — American Ancestry ii, 108
Kriebel's Schwenkfelders 3-54
Ruttenber's History of Newburg N. Y. 315
Ruttenber's Hist. of Orange Co. N. Y. 393
Smith's History of Rhinebeck N. Y.
Schureman — Amer. Ancestry vii, 40-1, 179; viii, 18
Greene County N. Y. History 438
New York Gen. and Biog. Rec. xxi, 61-4; xxiii, 201-12; xxiv, 132-42; xxv, 82-9
Schureman Genealogy (1889) 55 pages
Schuyler — Amer. Anc. iv, 137; vi, 92, 154
Baxter's Colony of New York (1898)
Chambers' Early Germans of N. J. 482
Heraldic Journal iii, 145-8; iv, 22
Hoffman Genealogy 508
Lamb's History of New York City i, 672
Munsell's Albany Collections iv, 162
New Eng. Hist. and Gen. Register li, 336

New York Genealogical and Biog. Record
i, 3, 28; ii, 190; v, 4–6, 60–8, 75; viii,
164–7; ix, 158, 164–7
Pearson's Schenectady N. Y. Settlers 166
Schuyler Genealogy (1874) 11 pages
Schuyler's Colonial New York (1885) 1048 p.
Van Rensselaer's New Yorkers
Winfield's Hist. Hudson Co. N. J. 531–44
Schwartz — American Ancestry i, 69
Schweinitz — American Ancestry iv, 186
Schwenk — Perkiomen Region iii, 51
Scoby — Cochrane's Francestown 912
Scofield — American Ancestry xi, 47
Caverly's Pittsford Vt. 724
Davis' History of Bucks County Pa. 303
Fell Genealogy 104
Huntington's Stamford Settlers 87–93
Savage's Genealogical Dictionary iv, 35
Tuttle Genealogy 344
Scollay — Harris Gen. (1883) 73–87
Stearns' Hist. of Ashburnham Mass. 889
Scoresby — Sylvester's Ulster County 129
Scott — American Ancestry i, 70; iii, 95,
126, 173; ix, 163, 193; xi, 48, 95; xii
Am. Monthly Magazine (1894) iv, 183–5
Anderson's Waterbury Ct. i, app. 118–22
Atkins' History of Hawley Mass. 42
Austin's Ancestral Dictionary 53
Austin's R. I. Genealogical Dictionary 372
Ballou Genealogy 381–9
Ballou's History of Milford Mass. 1011–3
Barbour's My Wife and Mother, app. 72
Bass' History of Braintree Vt. 179
Bass' History of Richmond N. H. 480
Boyd's Hist. of Conesus N. Y. 177
Bronson's Hist. of Waterbury Ct. 527–32
Capron Genealogy by Holden 17–20
Cleveland's History of Yates Co. N. Y. 387
Cleveland Genealogy 221–34
Craft's History of Whately Mass. 557–64
Craft's Genealogy 179–81
Clyde's Irish Settlement in Pennsylvania
Daniel's History of Oxford Mass. 675
Egle's Notes and Queries 3d ser. ii, 438–41;
iii, 131–4, 136–9; 4th series, i, 138–40
(1897) 9
Essex Institute Hist. Colls. xxiii, 237–40
Gage's History of Rowley Mass. 454
Goode Genealogy 357
Hall Genealogy (1892) 59–66
Hammatt Papers, Ipswich Mass. 327
Hayden's Virginia Genealogies 587–668
Heraldic Journal i, 103–6
Howell's Hist. of Southampton N. Y. 384
Judd's History of Hadley Mass. 559
Kulp's Wyoming Valley Families
Longmeadow Mass. Centennial 81
Machias Me. Centennial 174
Maine Hist. and Gen. Recorder ii, 24–8
Matthew's History of Cornwall Vt. 289
McGinness and Scott Genealogy (1892)
Meade's Old Churches of Virginia ii, 208
Miller's Hist. of Colchester Co. N. S. 131
Montague Genealogy 465–7
New Eng. Hist. Reg. xxii, 14–8; xxiii, 121
New York Gen. and Biog. Rec. ii, 174–9

Norton's History of Fitzwilliam N. H. 710
Paige's History of Cambridge Mass. 652
Porter's Hartford Ct. Settlers 19
Power's Sangamon Co. Ill. Settlers 641–4
Putnam's Historical Magazine vi, 293–301
Randall's Hist. Chesterfield N. H. 429–32
Read's History of Swanzey N. H. 442
Richmond Va. Standard ii, 39, 47
Saunders' Alabama Settlers 442
Savage's Genealogical Dictionary iv, 36–9
Scott Family Antiquity (1869) 15 pages
Scott Family of Penn. (1895) 323 pages
Slaughter's St. Mark's Parish Va. 121, 190
Smith's Hist. Peterborough N. H. 244–52
Smith's Hist. of Sunderland Mass. 526–30
Stiles' History of Windsor Ct. ii, 675
Temple's History of Palmer Mass. 545
Temple's History of Whately Mass. 260–3
Tilley's New Eng. Notes and Queries i, 2
Wallbridge Genealogy 321–3
Washburn's History of Leicester Mass. 400
Wm. and Mary College Hist. Reg. ii, 88
Williams' History of Danby Vt. 254
Wyman's Charlestown Mass. Gens. ii, 850
Scotton — Wyman's Charlestown 851
Scottow — Savage's Gen. Dict. iv, 39
Scouller — American Ancestry xii
Scovill — American Ancestry vii, 109
Anderson's Waterbury Ct. i, app. 123–5
Scoville — American Ancestry ii, 230
Bronson's History of Waterbury Ct. 532–4
Gold's History of Cornwall Ct. 258–60
Loomis Genealogy (1880) 617
Orcutt's History of Torrington Ct. 760–2
Scranton — Austin's R. I. Dictionary 171
Savage's Genealogical Dictionary iv, 41
Scranton Genealogy (1855) 104 pages
Screven — American Ancestry ix, 149
Cutt's Genealogy 27, 51, 103–6, 208–13
Hayden's Virginia Genealogies 212
Tupper's S. Carolina Baptist Church 20–6
Scribner — Chase's Chester N. H. 587
Dearborn's Hist. Salisbury N. H. 774–80
Fullonton's Hist. of Raymond N. H. 284–7
Hall's Hist. Norwalk Ct. 189, 200, 233, 301
Hayward's History of Gilsum N. H. 390
Ridlon's Harrison Me. Settlers 107–10
Schuyler's Colonial New York ii, 439–55
Selleck's Norwalk Ct. (1896) 425–30
Scripps — American Ancestry viii, 89
Scripps Genealogy (1882) 28 pages
Scripture — Hill's Mason N. H. 205
Scriven — American Ancestry i, 70
Scrivens — Tupper's Baptist Ch. in S. C.
Scudamore — Thomas Gen. (1896) 495–7
Scudder — Amer. Ancestry iv, 93; v, 50
Bouton Genealogy
Cooley's Trenton N. J. Genealogies 216–61
Freeman's Hist. Cape Cod Mass. ii, 336–40
Hall's Trenton N. J. Presbyt. Church 73
Littell's Passaic Valley Genealogies 373–5
Savage's Genealogical Dictionary iv, 43
Suffolk Co. N. Y. History (1882) 77–84
Swift's Barnstable Families ii, 233–5
Scull — American Ancestry viii, 94
Shourd's Fenwick Colony N. J. 218–23

Thomas Genealogy (1896) 498–501
Seabury — American Ancestry i, 70
Caulkins' Hist. of New London Ct. 443–5
Corliss' North Yarmouth Me. 373–8, 403–9
Flint's Peters Lineage 26–30
Harris Genealogy (1878) 61, 93–6
Savage's Genealogical Dictionary iv, 43
Updyke's Narragansett Churches 139–44
Winsor's History of Duxbury Mass. 305
Seager — Draper's Spencer Mass. 250
Paige's History of Cambridge Mass. 652
Seagrave — American Ancestry iv, 47
Seagrave Genealogy (1881) 93 pages
Sealey — Sinclair Genealogy 371–3
Seals — Barksdale Genealogy 31–4
Chambers' N. J. Germans 484
Seaman — American Ancestry x, 83
Bolton's History of Westchester N. Y. 758
Bunker's Long Island Genealogies 134–63
Mott Genealogy 296–9
New York Gen. and Biog. Rec. xi, 149–55
Queen's County N. Y. History 158
Seaman Genealogy (1860) 6 pages
Searight — American Ancestry xi, 49
Searight Genealogy (1893) 228 pages
Searing — Bunker's Long Island Gens. 289–91
Searle — American Ancestry viii, 66
Atkins Genealogy (1891) 72–4
Austin's R. I. Genealogical Dictionary 374
Blood's History of Temple N. H. 245–9
Cochrane's Hist. Francestown N. H. 913
Cogswell Genealogy 95–6
Cogswell's History of Henniker N. H. 733
Dearborn's Hist. of Salisbury N. H. 771
Gage's History of Rowley Mass. 454
Hill's History of Mason N. H. 206
Potts Genealogy (1895) 315–7
Savage's Genealogical Dictionary iv, 45
Searles — Fox's Dunstable Mass. 249
Chambers' Early Germans of N. J. 484
Cochrane's Hist. Francestown N. H. 913
Searls — American Ancestry vii, 141
Sears — Adams' Haven Genealogy 28
American Ancestry iii, 163; ix, 67
Atkins' History of Hawley Mass. 50
Bouton Genealogy 386
Crane's Rawson Genealogy 126
Daniel's History of Oxford Mass. 676–9
Davis' Landmarks of Plymouth Mass. 126
Deane's History of Scituate Mass. 336
Eaton's History of Thomaston Me. ii, 388
Ellis Genealogy 393
Freeman's Cape Cod Mass. ii, 706–14
Homer Genealogy 14
Lincoln's Hist. of Hingham Mass. iii, 14
Mitchell's Hist. of Bridgewater Mass. 289
New Eng. Hist. and Gen. Reg. xl, 261–8
Orcutt's History of Stratford Ct. 1277
Paige's History of Hardwick Mass. 492
Ransom Genealogy
Savage's Genealogical Dictionary iv, 46
Sears Family Notices (1855) 14 pages
Sears' Olden Time (1857)
Sears Genealogy (1890) 665 pages
Sedgwick's History of Sharon Ct. 109

Thurston's History of Winthrop Me. 195
Walker Genealogy 40
Whitmore's Heraldic Journal ii, 137
Whittemore's Hist. Middlesex Co. Ct. 212
Seaton — Hayward's Hancock 857–9
Richmond Va. Standard iii, 30
Seaton (W. W.) Biography
Secomb's History of Amherst N. H. 755–7
Washington N. H. History 595
Seaver — Barry's Framingham 389
Davis' Landmarks of Plymouth Mass. 234
Heywood's Hist. Westminster Mass. 863–9
New Eng. Hist. Gen. Reg. xxvi, 303–23
Read's History of Swanzey N. H. 442–4
Savage's Genealogical Dictionary iv, 46
Seaver's Genealogy (1872) 52 pages
Slafter Genealogy 47–9
Ward's History of Shrewsbury Mass. 441
Seaverns — American Ancestry ix, 193
Binney Genealogy 53
Bond's Watertown Mass. Gens. 425
Savage's Genealogical Dictionary iv, 47
Seavey — Lane Gen. (1894) 125–7
Seavy — Bradbury's Kennebunkport
Dow's History of Hampton N. H. 964
Lapham's History of Bethel Me. 612
Spooner Genealogy i, 290
Sebastian — Read's Swanzey N. H. 444
Sebring — Bergen's Kings Co. N. Y. 258
Fowler's Our Predecessors 17–28
Roome Genealogy 160–5
Secomb — Brooks' Medford Mass. 540
Secomb's History of Amherst N. H. 757–61
Secor — Bolton's Westchester Co. 758
Seddon — Richmond Standard ii, 47, 49
Sedgwick — Cothren's Woodbury 1557
Dewey's Life of Catharine Sedgwick
Dwight Genealogy 735–50
Gold's History of Cornwall Ct. 315–8
Goodwin's Genealogical Notes 175–89
Greene's Todd Family
Hinman's Connecticut Settlers 1st ed. 232
King Genealogy (1897) 73–82
New Eng. Hist. and Gen. Reg. xx, 236
Savage's Genealogical Dictionary iv, 48
Sedgwick Statue Dedication (1868)
Stiles' History of Windsor Ct. ii, 676
Temple's History of Palmer Mass. 539–41
Tuttle Genealogy 679–81
Walworth's Hyde Genealogy 271–3
Wyman's Charlestown Mass. Gens. ii, 852
See — Raymond's Tarrytown 171
Seebolt — Egle's Notes (1898) 43
Seeley — Litchfield Ct. (1881) 658
Savage's Genealogical Dictionary iv, 49
Schenck's History of Fairfield Ct. 405
Taylor Genealogy (1886) 65–9
Williams' History of Danby Vt. 255
Seely — Cilley Genealogy 2–4
Huntington's Stamford 93–6
Mitchell's Hist. of Bridgewater Mass. 289
Orcutt's History of New Milford Ct. 763
Orcutt's History of Stratford Ct. 1277
Strong Genealogy 653
Seelye — Amer. Ancestry v, 90; ix, 150
Roe's Sketches of Rose N. Y. 145

Segar — American Ancestry iii, 118
Austin's R. I. Genealogical Dictionary 174
Jackson's History of Newtown Mass. 403-5
Lapham's History of Bethel Me. 613
Lapham's History of Rumford Me. 393
Pearson's Schenectady N. Y. Settlers 166
Savage's Genealogical Dictionary iv, 44
Stiles' History of Windsor Ct. ii, 676
Segers — Albany Collections iv, 164
Seguine — Clute's Staten Island 420
Segur — Brown's West Simsbury Ct. 122
Sehner — Am. Cath. Hist. Coll. ii, 367-9
Seibert — Schwenkfelders 63
Seidenberger — Eaton's Warren 614
Seiders — Eaton's Warren Me. 613
Seidlinger — Eaton's Warren Me. 613
Seifers — Chambers' N. J. Germans
Seipt — Kriebel's Schwenkfelders 35
Seirs — Sewall's Woburn Mass. 637
Selby — Orcutt's Stratford Ct. 1278
Selden — Field's Hist. of Haddam Ct. 46
Goode Genealogy 284, 485
Hayden's Virginia Genealogies 62
Judd's History of Hadley Mass. 560
May Genealogy 89, 99, 115-7
Meade's Old Churches of Virginia i, 140
Montague Genealogy 66
Richmond Va. Stand. ii, 34; iii, 23, 35, 37
Savage's Genealogical Dictionary iv, 50
Selden Reunion Address (1877) 15 pages
Sheldon's Hist. of Deerfield Mass. 285
Strong Genealogy 944-6
Walworth's Hyde Genealogy i, 581-7
Selfridge — Ward's Shrewsbury 440
Selkirk — American Ancestry i, 70
Selkrigg — Anderson's Waterbury 125
Selleck — Amer. Ancestry ii, 109; xi, 94
Hall's Norwalk Ct. 249, 265, 280, 301
Huntington's Stamford Ct. Settlers 96-8
Morris' Bontecou Genealogy 198
Savage's Genealogical Dictionary iv, 50
Selleck's Norwalk Ct. (1896) 436-48
Sellham — Stearns' Ashburnham 893
Semple — Alexander Genealogy 125-7
Semple Family Tree (1888) 36x40 inches
Semple Genealogy (1888) 60 pages
Senchion — Stiles' Windsor Ct. ii, 676
Sensendorfer — Egle's Notes (1898) 218-20
Sener — American Ancestry x, 117
Sension — See St. John
Senter — Morrison's Windham 757-61
Sention — See St. John
Sergeant — American Ancestry iv, 225
Dwight Genealogy 627
Penn. Magazine of History ii, 438-42
Temple's History of Northfield Mass. 532
Serven — Cole Genealogy (1876) 42-53
Sessions — American Ancestry v, 19; ix,
181, 243; x, 40, 100
Hyde's History of Brimfield Mass. 449
Sessions Genealogy (1890) 252 pages
Seton — Seton Genealogy (1890) 28 pages
Settle — Wheeler's Eminent North Caro-
linians 391-3
Sever—America Ancestry v, 133
Wentworth Genealogy i, 236

Severance — Austin's Allied Families 206
Bangor Historical Magazine v, 13
Dearborn's Hist. of Salisbury N. H. 772-4
Hoyt's Salisbury Mass. Families 314
North's History of Augusta Me. 932
Savage's Genealogical Dictionary iv, 52
Severance Genealogy (1893) 155 pages
Sheldon's Hist. of Deerfield Mass. 285-90
Temple's History of Northfield Mass. 533
Washington N. H. History 596-605
Severit — Savery Genealogy
Severn — New Eng. Hist. Reg. xxxviii, 67
Severy — Benedict's Sutton Mass. 716
Savery Genealogy
Sevey — Machias Me. Centennial 175
Sevier — Wheeler's North Car. ii, 19, 23
Wheeler's Eminent North Carolinians 462
Sewall — Alden's Epitaphs ii, 116-8
Am. Ancestry iv, 179, 202; vii, 44; viii, 82
Amer. Antiquarian Society Trans. iii, 144
Bridgeman's Granary Epitaphs 128-32
Butler's History of Farmington Me. 567
Dudley Genealogy (1848) 133
Dummer Academy and History (1863)
Dunster Genealogy 97
North's History of Augusta Me. 933-8
Salisbury's Family Mem. (1885) i, 145-212
Savage's Genealogical Dictionary iv, 53-7
Titcomb's Early New Eng. People 214-30
Whitmore's Heraldic Journal i, 68-70
Whitmore's Payne and Gore Genealogy 17
Wood's Brookline Mass. Sketches 109-12
Seward — American Ancestry i, 70
Andrews' History of New Britain Ct. 383
Chambers' Early Germans of N. J. 485
Dwight's Strong Genealogy 254
New Eng. Hist. and Gen. Reg. lii, 323-9
Orcutt's History of Wolcott Ct. 556
Savage's Genealogical Dictionary iv, 57
Sewitz — Eyerman Ancestors (1898)
Sexton — Amer. Ancestry i, 70; ix, 203
Douglas Genealogy 73-5
Hinman's Connecticut Settlers 1st ed. 180
Richmond Va. Standard ii, 19, 23
Sheldon's History of Deerfield Mass. 279-84
Stiles' History of Windsor Ct. ii, 677-9
See also Saxton
Seymour — American Ancestry ii, 109; iv,
131; v, 70; vi, 61; xi, 10
Anderson's Waterbury Ct. i, app. 125
Andrews' Hist. of New Britain Ct. 139, 257
Barbour's My Wife and Mother, app. 22
Bass' History of Braintree Vt. 179
Hall's Records of Norwalk Ct. 181
Hollister Genealogy 52
Howell's Southampton N. Y. 2d ed. 385-7
Hubbard's Hist. of Springfield Vt. 432
Huntington's Stamford Ct. Settlers 98
Judd's History of Hadley Mass. 561
Kilbourn's History of Litchfield Ct. 304-6
Lane Genealogy (1899) 42
Lincoln's Hist. of Hingham Mass. iii, 144
Morris Genealogy (1894) 147-54, 180
New York Gen. and Biog. Rec. xi, 116-20
Orcutt's History of Torrington Ct. 762
Pompey N. Y. Reunion 302-4

Ruttenber's History of Newburg N. Y. 292
Ruttenber's Hist. of Orange N. Y. 377
Savage's Genealogical Dictionary iv, 58
Selleck's Norwalk Ct. (1896) 153–60
Seymour Pedigree (1880) 12x17 inches
Sheldon's History of Deerfield Mass. 290
Strong Genealogy 1037–40
Tuttle Genealogy 86–8
Watson Genealogy (1865) 8–11
Whitman Genealogy 569–74
Seyssen — Pearson's Schenectady 237
Shackelford — Cabell Gen. 288–91
Richmond Va. Standard iii, 32
Slaughter's St. Mark's Parish Va. 156
Shackford — American Ancestry vi, 154
Chase's History of Chester N. H. 583
Kilby's History of Eastport Me. 444
Portsmouth N. H. Journal of Mar. 29, 1890
Shackford Genealogy (1888) 8 pages
Shackley — Lapham's Norway Me. 594
Shaddinger — Wismer Gen. 71–86
Shadic — American Ancestry ii, 109
Shaeffer — Egle's Lebanon Co. Pa. 250
Shafer — Chambers' N. J. Germans
Shaffner — Egle's Notes and Queries 3d
series, i, 500–2
Shafter — Vt. Hist. Gaz. v 363–8
Slafter Genealogy 133–5
Shailer — Field's Hist. of Haddam Ct. 45
Shakespear — Shakespear Chart (1882)
Shanahan — Montgomery Co. N. Y. 147
Shane — Fisher Genealogy 122–6
Shanefelter — Reily's Life of Cardinal
Gibbons ii, 547, 551–5
Shannon — Cutts Genealogy 40, 67–70,
131–6 253–9
Meginness' Historical Journal ii, 275
New Eng. Hist. and Gen. Register v, 245
Pearson's Schenectady N. Y. Settlers 167
Smith Genealogy by Wellington Smith
Shapleigh — N. E. Hist. Reg. v, 345
Old Eliot, Me. Monthly ii, (1898) 173–200
Savage's Genealogical Dictionary iv, 59
Wentworth Genealogy ii, 33–40
Shapley — Caulkins' N. London Ct. 350
Wyman's Charlestown Mass. Gens. ii, 854
Sharp—Adams' Hist. of Fairhaven Vt. 463
American Ancestry ii, 109
Bass' History of Braintree Vt. 180
Clement's Newtown N. J. Settlers
Clyde's Irish Settlement in Pa. 131
Cope Genealogy 79, 173–5
Davis Genealogy 51, 144
Egle's Notes and Queries (1896) 73, 143
Missouri Pioneer Families 289
Munsell's Albany Collections iv, 164
Orcutt's History of Derby Ct. 757
Richmond Va. Standard iii, 6
Savage's Genealogical Dictionary iv, 60
Sharp Genealogy (1874) 34 pages
Sharp Genealogy (1880) 178 pages
Sharp Family Monthly (1893–6) 212 pages
Sharpe's History of Seymour Ct. 207–10
Shourd's Fenwick Colony N. J. 244–8
Smith's Hist. of Rhinebeck N. Y. 211–3
Wood's History of Brookline Mass. 106–9

Sharpenstine — See Sharps
Sharpless — Futhey's Chester 722–4
Sharpless Genealogy (1816) 123 pages
Sharpless Genealogy (1888) 1333 pages
Smith's History of Delaware Co. Pa. 500
Sharps — Chambers Early Germans of
New Jersey 486–92
Sharrott — Clute's Staten Island 421
Sharswood — Caulkins' N. London 347
Shattuck — Barry's Farmingham 390
Bemis' History of Marlboro N. H. 629
Bond's Hist. Watertown Mass. 426–9, 933
Butler's Hist. of Groton Mass. 434, 477–9
Clark Genealogy (1898) 16
Cleveland's Hist. of Yates Co N. Y. 547–9
Cochrane's Hist. Francest'n N. H. 914–9
Cunnabell Genealogy 62
Cushman's History of Sheepscott Me. 416
Green's Early Groton Mass. Settlers 19
Green's Groton Mass. Epitaphs 253
Hayward's Hist. of Hancock N. H. 860
Hubbard's Hist. of Springfield Vt. 446
Hudson's Hist. of Marlborough Mass. 444
Keyes' West Boylston Mass. Gen. Reg. 34
Kidder's Hist. of New Ipswich N. H. 429
Livermore's History of Wilton N. H. 496
Loomis Genealogy (1880) 733–6
Pompey's N. Y. Reunion 350–2
Savage's Genealogical Dictionary iv, 61
Secomb's History of Amherst N. H. 761–3
Shattuck Genealogy (1855) 414 pages
Sheldon's History of Deerfield Mass. 290
Smith's Founders of Mass. Bay
Temple's History of Whately Mass. 263
Temple's History of Northfield Mass. 534
Wheeler's History of Newport N. H. 526–8
Worcester's History of Hollis N. H. 387
Wyman's Charlestown Mass. Gens. ii, 855
Shatzel — Cole Genealogy 71–3
Shaurman — American Ancestry ii, 110
Shaw — Alden's Epitaphs ii, 56, 217
Am. Anc. i, 70; ii, 110; v, 7; x, 112; xii, 100
Austin's R. I. Genealogical Dictionary 174
Bangor Me. Hist. Mag. vii, 89–95; ix, 211
Breck Genealogy 33–9
Calnek's History of Annapolis N. S. 600
Cleveland's Hist. of Yates Co. N. Y. 223–5
Davis' Landmarks Plymouth Mass. 235–7
Davis Genealogy 474
Dearborn's Hist. of Salisbury N. H. 780–5
Dow's History of Hampton N. H. 964–75
Dyer's History of Plainfield Mass. 172–5
Eaton's History of Thomaston Me. ii 388
Foster Genealogy (1889) 114–6
Freeman's Cape Cod Mass. i, 587; ii, 327
Hanson's History of Gardner Me. 138
Hatch's History of Industry Me. 801–8
Hyde's History of Brimfield Mass. 449–51
King Genealogy (1897) 101–11
Kingman's N. Bridgewater Mass. 641–3
Lapham's History of Bethel Me. 613
Lapham's History of Paris Me. 721–3
Lawrence and Bartlett Mem. 166–70
Little's History of Weare N. H. 988
McKeen's History of Bradford Vt. 329–38
Mitchell's Hist. Bridgewater Mass. 290–2

New Eng. Hist. Gen. Reg. xxxiv; li, 191-5
Ridlon's Saco Valley Me. Families 124
Runnels' Sanbornton N. H. ii, 699-704
Ruttenber's Hist. of Orange Co. N. Y. 409
Savage's Genealogical Dictionary iv, 63-6
Shaw Biog. of R. S. Shaw (1880) 34 pages
Sinclair Genealogy 268-72
Stiles' History of Windsor Ct. ii, 679
Temple's History of Palmer Mass. 547-52
Thurston's History of Winthrop Me. 195
Wales Mass. Centennial 15
Whitmore's Copps Hill Epitaphs
William's Life of W. Shaw (1851)
Winsor's History of Duxbury Mass. 306
Shays — Humphrey Genealogy 368-70
Shea — Hayward's Hancock N. H. 861
Temple's Hist. of N. Brookfield Mass. 727
Sheafe — Adams' Haven Genealogy 35
Thomas Genealogy (1896) 501-3
Wentworth Genealogy ii, 307-16
Wyman's Charlestown Mass. Gens. ii, 856
Sheaff — Brewster's Rambles About Portsmouth N. H. 2d series 126-31
Kitchell Genealogy 62
New Eng. Hist. and Gen. Reg. iv, 310-5
Savage's Genealogical Dictionary iv, 66
Whitmore's Heraldic Journal iv, 81-9
Shearer — Martindale's Byberry 374-7
Temple's History of Palmer Mass. 543
Shearman — Cleveland's Yates Co. 454
Talcott's N. Y. and N. E. Fams. 679-720
Shears — American Ancestry ii, 110
Hughes Genealogy 110
Savage's Genealogical Dictionary iv, 67
Shed — Bangor Hist. Mag. vi, 90
Brook's Hist. of Medford Mass. 540
Butler's History of Groton Mass. 436, 479
Hazen's History of Billerica Mass. 130-3
Hill's History of Mason N. H. 206
Savage's Genealogical Dictionary iv, 67
Wyman's Charlestown Mass. ii, 857-9
Shedd — Cutter's Jaffrey N. H. 456-61
Lapham's History of Norway Me. 596
Smith's Hist. of Peterborough N. H. 254
Stearns' History of Rindge N. H. 687
Temple's Hist. of N. Brookfield Mass. 727
Washington N. H. History 605
Shee — Egle's Notes and Queries 3d series iii, 372-4
Sheeleigh — American Ancestry x, 71
Sheffer — American Ancestry ii, 110
Sheffield — Amer. Ancestry v, 188; vi, 33
Austin's R. I. Genealogical Dictionary 175
Ballou's History of Milford Mass. 1013
Barry's Hist. of Framingham Mass. 391
Livermore's Hist. Block Island R. I. 344-7
Morse's Sherborn Mass. Settlers 240
Pierce's Biog. Contributions 287-94
Savage's Genealogical Dictionary iv, 68
Vinton's Giles Genealogy 349-51
Sheilds — See Shields
Shekell — Turner's Phelps Purchase
Shelby — American Ancestry viii, 51
Sheldon — Adams' Fairhaven 468-72
American Ancestry ii, 100; iii, 192; iv, 62, 86, 171; vi, 100; vii, 114; ix, 98

Austin's R. I. Genealogical Dictionary 176
Bartow Genealogy 141
Caverly's History of Pittsford Vt. 725
Cushman's History of Sheepscott Me. 418
Gifford's Our Patronymics 19
Greene Genealogy (1894)
Hayward's History of Hancock N. H. 862
Hazen's History of Billerica Mass. 133
Hollister's History of Pawlet Vt. 235
Kellogg Family Notes (1898) 19
Leach's Morton Ancestry 108-11
Livermore's History of Wilton N. H. 496-9
Loomis Genealogy (1880) 585-90
Orcutt's History of Torrington Ct. 762
Savage's Genealogical Dictionary iv. 69-71
Sheldon Genealogy (1855) 112 pages
Sheldon of Vermont (1877) chart
Sheldon's Hist. of Deerfield Mass. 291-301
Stiles' History of Windsor Ct. ii, 680
Strong Genealogy 882-4, 1124
Walworth's Hyde Genealogy 171, 847-51
Whittemore's Orange N. J. 408-10
Williams' History of Danby Vt. 256
Young's History of Warsaw N. Y. 328-30
Shell — Parthemore Gen. 157-65, 178-81
See also under Schell
Shelley — Orcutt's Stratford Ct. 1278
Pierce's Biog. Contributions 295
Shelton — American Ancestry i, 70
Hurd's Hist. of Fairfield Co. Ct. 417-9, 588
New Eng. Hist. and Gen. Reg. xi, 272
Orcutt's Hist. of Stratford Ct. 1279-81
Orcutt's History of Torrington Ct. 763
Power's Sangamon Co. Ill. Settlers 645
Richmond Va. Standard iii, 6
Saunders' Alabama Settlers 457
Shelton Genealogy (1857) 5 pages
Strong Genealogy 640-8
Wynne's Ellis Genealogy (1849) 11 pages
Shepard — Alden's Am. Epitaphs i, 62
Allison Genealogy 72
American Ancestry i, 70; ii, 111; v, 20, 33, 106; vii, 273; ix, 170, 185; x, 194
Barbour's My Wife and Mother, 25-7
Bedford Mass. Centennial 335-7
Clarke's History of Norton Mass. 88
Cleveland Genealogy 166-8
Corliss' North Yarmouth Me.
Dodd's History of East Haven Ct. 148
Dodge Ancestry (1896) 32-7
Driver Genealogy 477
Ellis Genealogy 397
Gibbs' History of Blandford Mass. 64
Gold's History of Cornwall Ct. 319
Hinman's Connecticut Settlers 1st ed. 235
Jackson's History of Newton Mass. 489
Lancaster's Hist. of Gilmanton N. H. 287
Leland Genealogy 149
New Eng. Hist. and Gen. Reg. xxxii, 322-37
Paige's History of Cambridge Mass. 653
Parson's Dodge Ancestry (1896)
Power's Sangamon Co. Ill. Settlers 647-9
Prentice Genealogy 415
Savage's Genealogical Dictionary iv, 71-7
Secomb's History of Amherst N. H. 763-7
Shepard Family of Cambridge (1878) 18 p.

Shepard Family of Cambridge (1886) 63 p.
Shepard Family of Malden (1893) 50 pages
Shepard Family of Vermont (1894) 16 pages
Shourd's Fenwick Colony N. J. 202-17
Sibley's History of Union Me. 494
Stiles' History of Windsor Ct. ii, 681-3
Strong Genealogy 1387-1404
Waldo's History of Tolland Ct. 103
Whittemore's Orange N. J. 422
Wyman's Charlestown Mass. ii, 859-61
Shepardson — Amer. Ancestry x, 146
Daniels' History of Oxford Mass. 680
Shepherd — Lee Genealogy (1895) 470
Meade's Old Families of Virginia
Sedgwick's History of Sharon Ct. 109
Timlow's Southington Ct. Sketches 225-7
Sheple — Butler's Groton Mass. 437
Farnsworth Genealogy (1891) 54, 57
Shepley — Corliss' N. Yarmouth Me.
Green's Early Groton Mass. Settlers 20
Green's Groton Mass. Epitaphs 186
Sheppard — Am. Ancestry vii, 41; viii, 74
Hoyt's Salisbury Mass. Families 316
Sharpless Genealogy 329
Sheppard Genealogy (1891) 39 pages
Sheppy — Savage's Gen. Dict. iv, 87
Sherburne — Brewster's Rambles About
    Portsmouth N. H. 2d series 44-52
Cogswell's Nottingham N. H. 767-70
Cutts Genealogy
Dow's History of Hampton N. H. 975
Knox Genealogy 31-4
N. E. Hist. and Gen. Reg. ix, 180; xvii, 352
Robinson's Items of Ancestry (1894) 43
Savage's Genealogical Dictionary iv, 77
Tuttle Genealogy 45
Wentworth Genealogy i, 189-92, 328-38
Sherer — Eaton's Thomaston Me. 389
Sheriff — Austin's R. I. Gen. Dict. 177
Sherman — Aldrich's Walpole N. H. 354
Amer. Ances. ii, 111; iii, 44; iv, 229; v, 62;
    viii, 126, 158; ix, 131, 221, 222; xi, 177
Austin's R. I. Genealogical Dictionary 178
Ball's History of Lake Co. Ind. 413
Bond's Watertown Mass. 429-33, 934
Chapman's Trowbridge Genealogy 53
Cothren's Hist. of Woodbury Ct. 679-88;
    ii, 1544-9, 1543a p. —.
Cushman's History of Sheepscott Me. 417
Davis' Landmarks of Plymouth 237-44
Damon Genealogy 115, 131
Deacon's Stoddard Genealogy
Dwight Genealogy 1105-8
→ Eaton's History of Thomaston Me. ii, 390
Farrow's Hist. of Islesborough Me. 278-80
Gifford's Our Patronymics 27
Hinman's Connecticut Settlers 1st ed. 235
Hollister's History of Connecticut ii, 450
Hudson's Hist. Marlborough Mass. 444-6
Hurd's History of Fairfield Co. Ct. 147
Hyde's Hist. Address at Ware Mass. 50
Hyde's Hist. of Brimfield Mass. 451-4
Jackson's History of Newton Mass. 409
Mitchell's Hist. of Bridgewater Mass. 293
Narragansett Historical Register ii, 226-33,
    245-53; iii, 7-20, 92-4

New Eng. Hist. and Gen. Register xxiv,
    63-73, 155-64; xxvii, 73-6; li, 309-15,
    357; liv, 152-62
Orcutt's History of New Milford Ct. 763-6
Orcutt's History of Stratford Ct. 1282-90
Pierce's History of Grafton Mass. 560-2
Prescott Mem. 89-91
Roe's Sketches of Rose N. Y. 11, etc.
Savage's Genealogical Dictionary iv, 78-86
Selleck's Norwalk Ct. (1896) 128, 133
Sewall's History of Woburn Mass. 355-7
Sherman Genealogy (1887) 94 pages
Sherman Family of Stratford (1895) chart
Sherman Ancestry (1897) 9 pages
Sherman Family of Stratford (1900) 12 p.
Spooner Genealogy i, 28, 43-9
Stiles' History of Windsor Ct. ii, 680
Stoddard Genealogy (1865) 15, 46, 68-72
Talcott's N. Y. and N. E. Fams. 679-720
Temple's Hist. of N. Brookfield Mass. 728
Temple's History of Palmer Mass. 555
Tuttle Genealogy 681-3
Wakefield Genealogy 110
Ward's History of Shrewsbury Mass. 438
Williams' History of Danby Vt. 257
Winslow Genealogy ii, 561-5
Wyman's Charlestown Mass. Gens. ii, 862
Sherrard — American Ancestry xii
Sherrard Genealogy (1890) 409 pages
Sherrett — Guild's Stiles Genealogy 226
Sherrill — American Ancestry xii
Hedge's Easthampton 333
Sherrill Genealogy (1894) 132 pages
Sherrod — Goode Genealogy 186
Saunders' Alabama Settlers 233-5
Sherry — Temple's No. Brookfield 729
Shertzer — American Ancestry iii, 132
Sherwin — Blood's Temple N. H. 249
Hayward's History of Hancock N. H. 863
Marvin's Hist. of Winchendon Mass. 469
Stearns' History of Rindge N. H. 688-95
Sherwood — American Ancestry i, 71; ii,
    111; iv, 219; v, 11; ix, 108
Baird's History of Rye N. Y.
Bolton's History of Westchester Co. N. Y.
Burr Genealogy
Fairfield County Ct. History
Fillow Genealogy 74
Hinman's Connecticut Settlers part 6
Hubbell Genealogy
Huntington's Stamford Ct. Settlers
Litchfield County Ct. History
New England Hist. and Gen. Reg.
Orcutt's History of Stratford Ct. 1290-3
Orcutt's History of New Milford Ct.
Savage's Genealogical Dictionary iii, 180;
    iv, 86, 195, 298, 478
Schenck's History of Fairfield Ct. 408-11
Smith's History of Dutchess Co. N. Y.
Tuttle Genealogy
Whitney Genealogy
Sheward — Sharpless Genealogy 197
Shewell — Keim Genealogy 311
Rodenbough's Autumn Leaves (1892)
    174-203
Shibles — Eaton's Thomaston Me. 391

Shields — American Ancestry v, 69
Richmond Va. Standard iii, 27
Wm. and Mary College Hist. Reg. iii, 268–71; iv, 59; v, 22–4
Shillaber — American Ancestry vii, 48
Cutts Genealogy
Shillaber Family Gathering (1877) 48 pages
Smith's Founders of Mass. Bay 211–43
Shimer — Rittenhouse Genealogy 243–8
Shindel — Egle's Lebanon Co. Pa. 251
Shinkle -- Power's Sangamon Ill. 650
Shinn — American Ancestry v, 42
Shipley — American Ancestry iv, 23
Thomas Genealogy (1877) 137
Thomas Genealogy (1896) 503–6
Worcester's History of Hollis N. H. 387
Shipman — Andrews' New Britain Ct.
Chambers' Early Germans of N. J. 492
Champion Genealogy
Cothren's History of Woodbury Ct. ii, 1551
Fisher Genealogy 21–51
Hurd's History of New London Co. Ct. 410
Littell's Passaic Valley Genealogies 376
Penn. Mag. of Hist. and Biog. i, 109–11
Savage's Genealogical Dictionary iv, 87
Young's History of Warsaw N. Y. 332
Shippee — Austin's R. I. Gen. Dict. 179
Wyman's Charlestown Mass. Gens. ii, 863
Shippen — American Ancestry xii
Balch's Prov. Papers 5–138
Carter Family Tree
Egle's Notes and Queries (1896) 181–6
Hanson's Old Kent Md.
Heraldic Journal iii, 16–8; iv, 1–20
Lee Genealogy (1895) 130
Penn. Mag. i, 109–11, 212–6; xxiv, 257–9
Savage's Genealogical Dictionary iv, 87
Shippen Genealogy (1877) 16 pages, reprint
Shipway — Cutts Genealogy 18
Shirley — Chase's Chester N. H. 589–91
Morrison Genealogy 279
New Eng. Hist. and Gen. Register x, 47
Norton's History of Fitzwilliam N. H. 711
Runnels' Hist. Sanbornton N. H. ii, 704–7
Whitmore's Heraldic Journal ii, 117
Shiverick — Freeman's Cape Cod 475
Shivers — Clements' Newtown N. J. Settlers
Shober — Morris Gen. (1898) 584, 727–9
Shoemaker — Conrad Genealogy 38
Kulp's Wyoming Valley Families
Levering Genealogy (1897) 128, 152–4
Morris Genealogy (1898) 277–80, 499–501
Penn. Magazine of History vi, 497
Plumb's History of Hanover Pa. 478
Potts Genealogy (1895) 31–6
Shoemaker Genealogy (1893) 112 pages
Walworth's Hyde Genealogy 812
Shoop — Parthemore Genealogy 160–2
Shorey — Hatch's Industry Me. 808
Hubbard's Stanstead County Canada 337
Old Eliot, Me. Monthly iii, (1899) 55–60
Wentworth Genealogy i, 440
Short — Meade's Old Families of Va.
Poor's Merrimack Valley Researches 123
Power's Sangamon Co. Ill. Settlers 651–4

Savage's Genealogical Dictionary iv, 88
Symmes Genealogy 117
Shorter — Saunders' Alabama 245–50
Shotswell — Savage's Gen. Dict. iv, 61
Shotten — Austin's R. I. Gen. Dict. 180
Shotwell — American Ancestry iv, 240
Hatfield's History of Elizabeth N. J. 92
Littell's Passaic Valley Gens. 377–81
Shotwell Genealogy (1897) 300 pages
Shoup — Power's Sangamon Ill. 654
Shourds — Shourds' Fenwick 233–8
Shove — Baylies' New Plymouth iv, 78
Corliss' North Yarmouth Me.
Emery's Taunton Mass. Ministry i, 172–5
Savage's Genealogical Dictionary iv, 89
Shower — Everhart and Shower Lineage (1883) 107–33
Showers — Champion Genealogy 62
Showham — Clarke's Old King Wm. County Va. Families
Shrewsbury — Washington Gen. 213
Shrimpton — Savage's Gen. Dict. iv, 90
Sumner Genealogy (1854) 61–3
Sumner's Hist. of East Boston Mass. 254
Shrom — Egle's Pa. Gens. 2d ed. 86
Shuerman — See Schureman
Shuey — American Ancestry vi, 19
Shuey Family (1876) 279 pages
Shufelt — American Ancestry ii, 111–12
Shuff — Power's Sangamon Ill. 656
Shugart — Young's Wayne Ind. 300
Shull — Montgomery Co. N. Y. 153
Shult — American Ancestry ii, 112
Shulter — American Ancestry i, 71
Shultis — American Ancestry ii, 112
Shultz — American Ancestry ii, 112
Shumway — American Ancestry ii, 112
Ammidown Genealogy 37
Daniels' History of Oxford Mass. 681–90
Davis' Landmarks of Plymouth Mass. 241
Heywood's History of Westminster Mass. 869
Jameson's History of Medway Mass. 522
Shuphelt — American Ancestry ii, 113
Shurtleff — Brockway Genealogy 17
Davis' Landmarks Plymouth Mass. 241–3
Hubbard's Hist. of Stanstead Co. Can. 287
Lapham's History of Norway Me. 597
Lapham's History of Paris Me. 723–5
Little Genealogy 299–301
Maine Genealogist i, 6, 97–113
Norton's Hist. of Fitzwilliam N. H. 712
Paige's History of Hardwick Mass. 494
Randall's Hist. of Chesterfield N. H. 433
Spooner's Mem. W. Spooner 118–22
Stearns' History of Rindge N. H. 695–7
Savage's Genealogical Dictionary iv, 92
Shuster — Egle's Notes and Queries 3d series ii, 1–5
Shute — Bouton's Concord N. H. 687
Chase's History of Haverhill Mass. 278
Kelley Genealogy (1892)
Lincoln's Hist. Hingham Mass. iii, 146–9
Runnels' Sanbornton N. H. ii, 707–10
Savage's Genealogical Dictionary iv, 92
Sumner's History of E. Boston Mass. 234

Whitmore's Copps Hill Epitaphs
Whitmore's Heraldic Journal ii, 32-4
Shutt — Power's Sangamon Ill. 657
Shuttleworth—Blake's History of Franklin Mass. 277
Shutts — American Ancestry ii, 112
Sibley — Am. Anc. 11, 113; iii, 45; viii, 36
Benedict's History of Sutton Mass. 717-26
Daniels' History of Oxford Mass. 690-2
Davis Genealogy 170-3
Draper's History of Spencer Mass. 253
Hayes' Wells Genealogy 159
Leland Genealogy 80
Morse Mem., appendix
Peck's Rochester N. Y. Centennial 708-13
Pierce's History of Grafton Mass. 562
Savage's Genealogical Dictionary iv, 93
Sibley's History of Union Me. 495-7
Temple's Hist. of N. Brookfield Mass. 728
West's Life of H. H. Sibley (1889)
Siboutsen — Riker's Newtown N. Y. 316
Sickels — American Ancestry i, 71; ii, 113; xi, 62; xii
Davis Genealogy (1888) 112-5
Munsell's Albany Collections iv, 165
Sickle — Davis' Hist. of Bucks Co. Pa. 150
Siders — Lincoln's Hingham iii, 149
Sigourney — Ammidown's Colls. i, 145
Butler Genealogy (1888) 135-49
Daniels' History of Oxford Mass. 692
Hinman's Connecticut Settlers (1896) 171
Savage's Genealogical Dictionary iv, 94
Sigourney Genealogy (1857) 31 pages
Whitmore's Copps Hill Epitaphs
Sikes — Champion Genealogy 206-9
Dwight Genealogy 329-34
Montague Genealogy 162, 176-9
Silcock — Longmeadow Mass. Centen. 81
Sill — American Ancestry i, 71; iv, 66
Hyde Gen. i, 163-70; ii, 768-824, 984-8
Loomis Genealogy (1880) 365-7
Oneida Historical Society Trans. ii, 100-3
Paige's Hist. of Cambridge Mass. 655
Savage's Genealogical Dictionary iv, 96
Sill Genealogy (1855) 12 pages
Sill Genealogy (1859) 108 pages
Sill Family of Ct. (1897) 32 pages
Stiles' History of Windsor Ct. ii, 684-6
Silliman — American Ancestry x, 202
Huntington Genealogy 181
Savage's Genealogical Dictionary iv, 97
Schenck's History of Fairfield Ct. 406-8
Silloway — American Ancestry vii, 94
Silsbee — Chase's Chester N. H. 591
Driver Genealogy 469-74
Essex Institute Hist. Colls. xvii, 257-328
Hayward's History of Gilsum N. H. 391
Merrill's History of Acworth N. H. 263-6
Saunderson's Charlestown N. H. 546-8
Savage's Genealogical Dictionary iv, 98
Silsbee Genealogy (1880) 71 pages, reprint
Sims — American Ancestry xii
Silver — Lapham's Rumford Me. 394-6
Runnels' Hist. Sanbornton N. H. ii, 710-3
Silvernail — American Ancestry ii, 114
Silvester — American Ancestry ii, 114

Simcock — Smith's Delaware Co. 501
Simmons — Amer. Ancestry i, 72; ii, 114
Barry's History of Hanover Mass. 371-4
Cleveland's Hist. of Yates Co. N. Y. 330-2
Davis' Landmarks of Plymouth Mass. 244
Eaton's Annals of Warren Me. 615
Eaton's History of Thomaston Me. ii, 392
Egle's Notes and Queries (1897) 187
Hinman's Connecticut Settlers 1st ed. 176
Lincoln's History of Hingham Mass. iii, 150
Meginness' Hepburn Genealogy 122-5
Mitchell's Hist. of Bridgewater Mass. 386
Savage's Genealogical Dictionary iv, 100
Sylvester's History of Ulster Co. N. Y. 58
Winsor's History of Duxbury Mass. 307-9
Simms — Essex Inst. Hist. Coll. vi, 160
Kellogg's White Genealogy 97
Richmond Va. Standard iii, 37
Simonds — Brown's Bedford Families 31
Cochrane's History of Antrim N. H. 678-80
Deane's History of Scituate Mass. 338
Hollister's History of Pawlet Vt. 237
Hudson's Hist. of Lexington Mass. 212
Norton's Hist. of Fitzwilliam N. H. 713-5
Saunderson's Charlestown N. H. 548-50
Secomb's History of Amherst N. H. 767
Sewall's History of Woburn Mass. 637-40
Simonds Chart (1869) 17x22 inches
Temple's History of Northfield Mass. 535
Washington N. H. History 606, 693
Wyman's Charlestown Mass. Gens. ii, 866
Simons — Bergen's Kings Co. N. Y. 261
Little's History of Weare N. H. 989-91
Worthen's History of Sutton N. H. 956-9
Simonson — American Ancestry xi, 5
Clute's Staten Island 422-4
Dawson Genealogy 81
Nevius Genealogy
Richmond Va. Standard iii, 7
Simonton — Eaton's Thomaston ii, 393
Egle's Penn. Gens. 2d ed. 735-7
Simonton Manuscript in Me. Gen. Library
Simpkins — Freeman's Cape Cod ii, 760
Thacher's Biography of S. G. Simpkins
Simpson — Bangor Hist. Mag. vi, 185-220, 229-35
Barry's History of Framingham Mass. 391
Cogswell's Nottingham N. H. 243-6, 455-63
Daniels' History of Oxford Mass. 694
Egle's Penn. Genealogies 2d ed. 536-8
Egle's Notes and Queries 3d ser. iii, 209
Kelly's N. Hampton N. H. Reminisc. (1889)
Lapham's History of Rumford Me. 396
Littell's Passaic Valley Genealogies 384-6
McKeen's History of Bradford Vt. 280-2
Morrison's Hist. of Windham N. H. 761-71
Pope Genealogy 320
Power's Sangamon Ill. Settlers 657-60
Savage's Genealogical Dictionary iv, 101
Simpson Genealogy (1891) 51 pages
Wyman's Charlestown Mass. Gens. ii, 867
Sims — N. E. Hist. and Gen. Reg. l, 426
Symmes Genealogy 162-5
Walworth's Hyde Genealogy 155, 713
Sinclair — American Ancestry ix, 154
Bangor Me. Historical Magazine v, 210

285

Cope Genealogy 98-195
Draper's History of Spencer Mass. 255
New York Gen. and Biog. Record x, 170
Sinclair Genealogy (1896) 453 pages
Young's Hist. Chautauqua Co. N. Y. 269
Singer — Eaton's Thomaston Me. ii, 394
Singleterry— Barry's Framingham
Benedict's History of Sutton Mass. 726-8
Daniel's History of Oxford Mass. 694
Hoyt's Salisbury Mass. Families 317
Savage's Genealogical Dictionary iv, 102
Sinkler — Sinclair Genealogy 57-9
Sinnett — Wheeler's Brunswick 851
Sinnickson — Shourd's Fenwick 188-201
Sip — Winfield's Hudson Co. N. J. 524-6
Sipperly — American Ancestry ii, 114
Smith's History of Rhinebeck N. Y. 188
Sisson — American Ancestry xii, 9
Austin's Allied Families 208-10
Austin's Ancestral Dictionary 54
Austin's R. I. Genealogical Dictionary 181
Cleveland's Hist. of Yates Co. N. Y. 505
Nourse Family of Va. 81-7
Wilder Genealogy 217, 225
Sitgreaves — Penn. Mag. xiii, 254
Sitzer — American Ancestry ii, 114
Sively — Plumb's Hanover Pa. 479
Siverly — Elderkin Genealogy
Sixberry — Albany Collections iv, 165
Sizer — Hayes' Wells Genealogy 117
Skatts — American Ancestry iv, 51
Skeel — Am. Anc. iv, 174; vi, 135; ix, 206
Cothren's History of Woodbury Ct. 709
Skeels — Sharpe's So. Britain 65-9
Skelding — Huntington's Stamford 99
Skellenger — Chambers' Early Germans
of New Jersey 494-6
Skellin — Babson's Gloucester 158
Brown's Bedford Mass. Families 31
Skelton — Campbell's Virginia 606
Dedham Mass. Historical Register 10-4
Durrie's Steele Genealogy 69
Jones Genealogy (1891) 183-8
Maris Genealogy 98
Meade's Old Families of Virginia
Richmond Va. Standard iii, 4, 5
Savage's Genealogical Dictionary iv, 103
Skies — Temple's North Brookfield 729
Skiff — American Ancestry ii, 115
Freeman's Hist. of Cape Cod Mass. ii, 86
Sedgwick's History of Sharon Ct. 110
Skiff Genealogy (1895) 24 pages
Tilley's Magazine of N. E. History, ii,
185-7
Skillin — Corliss' North Yarmouth Me.
Skillings — Lapham's Paris Me. 725
Maine Historical and Gen. Recorder ii,
45-9, 100-7, 169-80, 250-2; iii, 40
Pierce's History of Gorham Me. 206
Preble Genealogy 138
Skillings Genealogy (1885) 22 pages
Skillings Reunion (1894) 4 pages
Skillman — American Ancestry iv, 111
Nevius Genealogy
Skilton — American Ancestry x, 201
Cothren's History of Woodbury Ct. 711-3

Hazen's History of Billerica Mass. 134
Wyman's Charlestown Mass. Gens., ii, 868
Skinkle — American Ancestry ii, 115
Skinner — Am. Anc. ii, 115; iv, 190; ix, 193
Andrew's History of New Britain Ct. 256
Chambers' Early Germans of N. J. 496
Clark's History of Norton Mass. 88
Daniel's History of Oxford Mass. 694
Eaton's Annals of Warren Me. 615
Field's History of Haddam Ct. 46
Humphrey Genealogy 455
Lamb's History of New York City 606, 706
Loomis Genealogy (1880) 108-28, 859-65
New Eng. Hist. Gen. Register liii, 401-5
Savage's Genealogical Dictionary iv, 105
Sedgwick's History of Sharon Ct. 110
Stiles' History of Windsor. Ct. ii, 687-92
Whitehead's Perth Amboy N. J. 99-120
Wyman's Charlestown Mass. Gens. ii, 869
Skipton — Power's Sangamon Ill. 661
Skipwith — Meade's Old Families of Va.
Robertson's Pocahontas' Descendants
Slaughter's Bristol Parish Va. 225-31
Southern Bivouac (1886) 729
Skolfield — Wheeler's Brunswick 852
Skyrem — Meade's Va. Churches i, 381
Skyrme — Richmond Va. Standard iv, 2
Slaughter's Fry Genealogy 22
Slack — Cooley's Trenton N. J. 261
Davis' History of Bucks County Pa. 123
Hubbard's Hist. of Springfield Vt. 435-7
Narragansett Historical Register i. 314
Slade — Gifford's Our Patronymics 25-7
Stiles' History of Windsor Ct. ii, 692
Slader — Merrill's Acworth N. H. 226-8
Slafter — Amer. Ancestry iv, 204; vi, 182
Slafter Genealogy (1869) 155 pages
Thomas Genealogy (1877) 145-8
Slaght — Chambers' N. J. Germans 497
Slagle — Keinadt Genealogy 95-101
Wolff Family of Pennsylvania 97-9
Slason — Barry's Hanover Mass. 374
Huntington's Stamford Ct. Sett. 99-101
Slater — Ammidown's Hist. Coll. i, 496
Power's Sangamon Co. Ill. Settlers 661-4
Slaughter's St. Ann's Parish Va. 137-65
Slaughter — Meade's Old Fams. of Va.
Richmond Va. Standard iii, 19
Slaughter's St. Mark's Parish Va. 156, 185
Slauson — Tuttle Genealogy 337-9
Slawson — Amer. Ancestry i, 72; x, 203
Savage's Genealogical Dictionary iv, 106
Young's Hist. of Chautauqua Co. N. Y. 424
Slaymaker — Egle's Notes and Queries
(1893) 127
Harris' Lancaster 536-48
Slayton — Amer. Anc. viii, 127; xii, 89
Hemenway's Vermont Gazetter iv, 137-9
Slayton Genealogy (1879) 12 pages
Slayton Genealogy (1898) 332 pages
Sleeper — American Ancestry ix, 127
Chase's History of Chester N. H. 592
Cochrane's Hist. Francestown N. H. 921-6
Dow's History of Hampton N. H. 976
Eaton's History of Thomaston Me. ii, 395
Hubbard's Stanstead County Canada 343

Little's History of Weare N. H. 991
Sleight — Schoonmaker's Kingston 489
Sylvester's Hist. of Ulster Co. N. Y. 112
Slick — Barber's Atlee Genealogy 75-7
Sliker — Boyd's Hist. Conesus N. Y. 170
Slimmer — Parthemore Genealogy 193-5
Slingerland — American Ancestry i, 72
Munsell's Albany Collections iv, 166
Pearson's Schenectaday N. Y. Settlers 171
Roome Genealogy 261-76
Slingluff — Bean's Montgomery Pa. 474-7
Slingsby — Slingsby Genealogy (1879)
Sliter — American Ancestry i, 72
Dickerman Genealogy 261
Sloan — Chandler's Shirley Mass. 619
Douglas Genealogy 138
Egle's Notes and Queries 2d ser. ii, 174-6
Paige's History of Hardwick Mass. 495
Sigourney Genealogy 25
Strong Genealogy 463-5
Temple's History of Palmer Mass. 555
Sloane — Cogswell Genealogy 399-401
Slocomb — Adams' Haven Gen. ii, 9-13
Benedict's History of Sutton Mass. 728
Calnek's History Annapolis N. S. 601-3
Pierce's History of Grafton Mass. 563
Vinton's Richardson Genealogy 764-70
Ward's History of Shrewsbury Mass. 442
Whipple-Hill Families (1897) 83-6
Slocum — Am. Anc. ii, 115; iii, 45, 113, 150
Austin's R. I. Genealogical Dict. 181-3
New Eng. Hist. Gen. Reg. xxxiv, 391-5
Savage's Genealogical Dictionary iv, 107
Slocum Preliminary Gen. (1880) 7 pages
Slocum Genealogy (1882) 644 pages
Wheeler's Eminent North Carolinians 464
Sloper — Timlow's Southington 227-9
Slosson — New York Gen. and Biog.
  Record iii, 107-16, 165-75
Slosson Genealogy (1872) 20 pages
Sluman — Bliss Genealogy 665
Perkins' Old Houses of Norwich Ct. 562
Sluyter — Mallory's Bohemia Manor
Schureman Genealogy 26
Smack -- Bergen's Kings Co. N. Y. 264
Small — American Ancestry xi, 137
Corliss' North Yarmouth Me.
Eaton's History of Thomaston Me. ii, 396
Bolton's Winslow Genealogy i, 89-91
Lapham's History of Rumford Me. 397
Libby Genealogy 32
Milliken's Narraguagus Valley Me. 3
Rich's History of Truro Mass. 561
Ridlon's Saco Valley Me. Families 135
Savage's Genealogical Dictionary iv, 108
Secomb's History of Amherst N. H. 769
Small Genealogy (1893) 59 pages
Stearns' History of Ashburnham Mass. 893
Wheeler's History of Brunswick Me. 853
Smalley — American Ancestry iv, 99
Andrews' History of New Britain Ct. 133
Freeman's History of Cape Cod Mass. ii,
  359
Littell's Passaic Valley Gens. 387-91
Penn. Magazine of History xxiv, 396
Walworth's Hyde Genealogy 513

Smart — Bangor Hist. Mag. viii, 37
Dearborn's Hist. of Parsonsfield Me. 405
Hubbard's Hist. of Springfield Vt. 452
Runnels' Hist. of Sanbornton N. H. ii, 713
Washington N. H. History 606
Smead — Collord Ancestors 10-3
Hayward's Gilsum N. H. 391
Read's History of Swanzey N. H. 446
Savage's Genealogical Dictionary iv, 108
Sheldon's Hist. of Deerfield Mass. ii, 301-8
Smedley — American Ancestry iii, 207
Cope Genealogy 49, 106-9
Dawson Genealogy 441
Sharpless Genealogy 135, 276, 417-22
Smith's Hist. of Delaware County Pa. 502
Smelt — Mead's Old Fams. of Va. i, 401
Smiley — Cochrane's Francestown 926
Hubbard's Hist. of Springfield Vt. 453-6
Morrison's Windham N. H. 771
Plumb's History of Hanover Pa. 475-7
Smith's Hist. Peterborough 255-8
Smith — Adams' Fairhaven Vt. 468-72
Alden's American Epitaphs i, 203-5
Allen Genealogy (1896) 69
American Ancestry i, 72, ii, 115-7; iii, 46,
  183; iv, 113, 209; v, 3, 10, 58, 153; vi,
  27, 108, 127, 177; vii, 77, 107, 132; viii,
  35, 70, 101, 235; ix, 46, 93, 125, 132,
  210; x, 53, 84, 128, 145, 151, 171, 177,
  197; xi, 48, 121, 221; xii, 91, 92, 112
Anderson's Waterbury Ct. i, app. 126-8
Andrews' Hist. of New Britain Ct. 129, 135
Austin's Ancestral Dictionary 55
Austin's R. I. Gen. Dict. 183-5, 376-85
Babson's Hist. of Gloucester Mass. 158-60
Baird's History of Rye N. Y. 433, 490
Baker's History of Montville Ct. 293-305
Ballou's History of Milford Mass. 1016-9
Bangor Me. Historical Magazine v, 14-6;
  viii, 233; ix, 178
Barrus' History of Goshen Mass. 170
Barry's History of Hanover Mass. 374-7
Bass' History of Braintree Vt. 180
Beckwith's Creoles 44
Bedford N. H. Centennial 337
Bell's History of Exeter N. H. 43
Bemis' History of Marlboro N. H. 631-4
Bergen's Kings Co. N. Y. Settlers 265
Blake's History of Hamden Ct. 276
Bockee Genealogy 53-67
Bolton's Westchester Co. N. Y. ii, 759
Bond's Watertown Mass. 433-41, 935
Bouton Genealogy 283-7
Bradbury's Kennebunkport Me. 274
Briggs' History of Shipbuilding 85-92
Brown's Bedford Mass. Families 32
Brown's West Simsbury Ct. Settlers 124
Bulkley's Browne Memorial 155-7
Bunker's Long Island Genealogies 293-6
Butler's Hist. of Farmington Me. 568-70
Caulkins' Hist. of New London Ct. 321-4
Caulkins' History of Norwich Ct. 199
Caverly's History of Pittsford Vt. 725
Chambers' Germans of N. J. 498-502
Chandler's History of Shirley Mass. 620-3
Chase's History of Chester N. H. 593-7

Chute Genealogy, appendix 196–200
Clark Genealogy (1898) 19
Clark's History of Norton Mass. 89
Clarke Genealogy (1885) 41–3
Cleveland's Yates Co. N. Y. 125–8, 273
Cochrane's History of Antrim N. H. 680–6
Cochrane's Hist. Francestown N. H.927–30
Cogswell's Hist. of Henniker N. H. 734–41
Cogswell's Nottingham 463–9, 770–2
Cogswell's New Boston N. H. 349–52
Cole Genealogy 226–8
Collin's History of Hillsdale N. Y. app. 116
Condit Genealogy 381
Cooley's Trenton N. J. Gens. 262–6
Corliss' North Yarmouth Me.
Cothren's History of Woodbury Ct. 677–9
Crafts Genealogy 284–90
Crafts' History of Whately Mass. 564–83
Cregar's White Genealogy
Cutter's History of Arlington Mass. 300
Daniels' History of Oxford Mass. 695–7
Davis' History of Bucks County Pa. 273
Davis' Landmarks of Plymouth Mass. 245
Dearborn's Hist. of Parsonsfield Me. 406
Dearborn's Hist. of Salisbury N. H. 786–96
Dedham Mass. Historical Register vi,135–9
Dodd's History of East Haven Ct. 149–52
Doolittle's Belchertown Mass. 251–3
Douglas Genealogy 232–4
Dow's History of Hampton N. H. 977–82
Draper's History of Spencer Mass. 256
Eager's History of Orange Co. N. Y. 544
Eaton's Annals of Warren Me. 616
Eaton's History of Candia N. H. 103–5
Eaton's History of Reading Mass. 111–4
Eaton's Hist. of Thomaston Me. ii, 397–9
Ellis Genealogy 96–9, 398–407
Emery's Newbury Mass. Rem. 118–24
Essex Institute Hist. Collections xxiii, 305
Field's History of Haddam Ct. 45
Flint's Peters Lineage 48–56
Foster Pedigree (1897) vii, 37–40
Freeman's Cape Cod Mass. 80, 217, 372
French's History of Turner Me. 55, 63–6
Gage's History of Rowley Mass. 455
Glover Genealogy 104–140
Goode Genealogy 89, 164–9
Goodwin's Foote Genealogy 276–81
Goodwin's Genealogical Notes 190–6
Goodyear Genealogy 186–8
Green's Kentucky Families
Guild's Stiles Genealogy 109
Hall's Norwalk Ct. Records 208, 220, 250
Hammatt Papers, Ipswich Mass. 333–7
Hanson's History of Gardner Me. 77
Harvey Genealogy 886–927
Hatch's History of Industry Me. 811–4
Hayden's Virginia Genealogies 19–21
Hayward's History of Gilsum N. H. 393
Hayward's Hist. of Hancock N. H. 864–6
Hemenway Genealogy 54
Heywood's Hist. Westminster Mass. 870–5
Hill's Dedham Mass. Records i
Hine's Lebanon Ct. Historical Address 168
Hinman's Connecticut Settlers 1st ed. 236
Hobart Genealogy 159

Hollister Genealogy 697–9
Hollister's History of Pawlet Vt. 238–42
Hoyt's Salisbury Mass. Families 318
Hubbard's Stanstead Canada 132, 223
Hubbard's Hist. Springfield Vt. 437, 456–9
Hudson's Hist. of Lexington Mass. 218–29
Huntington's Stamford Ct. Settlers 102–8
Huntting's Hist. of Pine Plains, N. Y. 379
Joslin's History of Poultney Vt. 345–9
Journals of Smith and Dean 22–5
Judd's History of Hadley Mass. 562–81
Keith's Harrison Ancestry 62–4
Kellogg Family Notes (1898) 20–5
Kellogg's White Genealogy 70–2
Kidder's Hist. of New Ipswich N. H. 430
Kulp's Wyoming Valley Families
Lancaster's Hist. of Gilmanton N. H. 288
Lapham's History of Bethel Me. 614
Lapham's History of Norway Me. 598–601
Lapham's History of Paris Me. 726–8
Leland Genealogy 68, 100
Leonard's History of Dublin N. H. 392–4
Lincoln's Hist. Hingham Mass. iii, 152–5
Littell's Passaic Valley Genealogies 392
Little's History of Weare N. H. 992
Livermore's Histtory of Wilton N. H.
    499–503
Loomis Genealogy (1880) 279–89, 746–8
Machias Me. Centennial 176
Mack Genealogy 58–64
Magazine of American History vi, 276–8
Martin's History of Chester Pa. 456
Merrill's History of Acworth N. H. 268–70
Miller's Colchester Co. N. S. 215–25, 261
Montague Genealogy 89
Morrison Genealogy 143–8, 167–74
Morrison's Hist. of Windham N. H. 772–6
Morse's Sherborn Mass. Settlers 241
Munsell's Albany Collections iv, 166
Neill's Virginia Carolorum 18
Nevius Genealogy
New Eng. Hist. and Gen. Reg. vii, 132,
    279; viii, 66; xii, 185; xiv, 28–30; xx,
    125; xxvi, 190–7; xlv, 222–8
N. Y. Gen. and Biog. Rec. i, 4, 20–2; x,
    32–5; xxvii, 100; xxx, 200–3
North's History of Augusta Me. 938–40
Norton's Hist. of Fitzwilliam N. H. 715–20
Opdyke Genealogy 69–84
Orcutt's History of Derby Ct. 759–61
Orcutt's History of New Milford Ct. 767
Orcutt's History of Torrington Ct. 763
Otis Genealogy (1851)
Page Genealogy 71
Paige's History of Hardwick Mass. 496–8
Pearson's Schenectady Settlers 171–3
Penn. Magazine of Hist. iv, 373; xiv, 218
Perley's History of Boxford Mass. 33
Pierce's History of Gorham N. H. 205
Pierce's History of Grafton Mass. 564
Power's Sangamon Ill. Settlers 24, 664–71
Preston Genealogy (1870) 54–8
Randall's Hist. Chesterfield N. H. 434–42
Ransom Genealogy 43
Reed's History of Rutland Mass. 119
Resseguie Genealogy 67

Richmond Va. Standard iii, 2, 7, 47; iii, 16, 24, 36
Ridlon's Saco Valley Me. Families 1147–9
Ruggles Genealogy by Bailey (1896) 26
Runnels' Sanbornton N. H. ii, 715–41
Ruttenber's Hist. of Orange Co. N. Y. 356
Saunderson's Charlestown N. H. 550–2
Savage's Genealogical Dict. iv, 109–37
Sedgwick's History of Sharon Ct. 110–3
Secomb's History of Amherst N. H. 770–5
Selleck's Norwalk Ct. (1896) 431–6
Sheldon's Hist. of Deerfield Mass. 308–14
Shourds' Fenwick's Colony N. J. 250–4
Slafter Genealogy 81
Slaughter's St. Mark's Parish 136, 178
Smith Family of New York (1849) 49 pages
Smith Fam. Peterborough N. H. (1852) 24 p.
Smith Fam. of Stonington Ct. (1870) 53 p.
Smith Family of Conn. (1871) 7 pages
Smith Fam. Burlington N. J. (1877) 296 p.
Smith Fam. of St. Albans Vt. (1878) 16 p.
Smith Fam. Wrightstown Pa. (1883) 113 p.
Smith Fam. Buckingham Pa. (1885) 52 p.
Smith Fam. of Hingham Mass. (1889) 28 p.
Smith Fam. New London Ct. (1889) 318 p.
Smith Fam. E. Haddam Ct. (1890) 269 p.
Smith Fam. Pembroke Mass. (1895) 146 p.
Smith Fam. Long Island (1898) 151 pages
Smith's Founders of Mass. Bay 331–47
Smith's History of Delaware Co. Pa. 502
Smith's Hist. Peterborough N. H. 258–87
Smith's Hist. of Sunderland Mass. 532–51
Speed Genealogy 88
Sprague Hist. of Gloversville N. Y. 128
Stearn's Hist. Ashburnham Mass. 894–96
Stearns' History of Rindge N. H. 697–701
Stiles' History of Windsor Ct. ii, 692–4
Stone's History of Hubbardston Mass. 349
Strong Genealogy 648
Sullivant Genealogy 229–33
Swift's Barnstable Mass. Families ii, 236
Tanner Genealogy 58–60
Temple's Hist. N. Brookfield Mass. 730–4
Temple's Hist. of Northfield Mass. 536–9
Temple's History of Palmer Mass. 532–9
Temple's History of Whately Mass. 263–8
Thompson's Long Island N. Y. ii, 442–8
Thurston's History of Winthrop Me. 196
Timlow's Southington Ct. Sketches 230–6
Todd's History of Redding Ct. 221
Torrey Genealogy 39–43
Underwood's Pollard Genealogy
Waddell's Annals of Augusta Co. Va. 413
Ward's Hist. of Shrewsbury Mass. 430–7
Washington N. H. History 607–14
West Springfield Mass. Centennial 120–2
Whitmore's Copps Hill Epitaphs
Whitney Genealogy (1860) 74–6
Whittemore's Orange N. J. 106
Williams' History of Danby Vt. 258–62
Wm. and Mary College Hist. Register, iv, 46–52, 95–103, 183–7; vi, 41–52
Winsor's History of Duxbury Mass. 309
Wood's History Long Island N. Y. 142–7
Worcester's History of Hollis N. H. 388
Worthen's Hist. of Sutton N. H. 959–61

Wyman's Hunt Genealogy 126
Wyman's Charlestown Mass. ii, 871–81
Smithey — American Ancestry v, 87
Smiton — Austin's R. I. Gen. Dict. 186
Smock — American Ancestry i, 73
Smyser — Egle's Reg. Int. Pa. i, 154–6
Smyser Family (1852) 28 pages
Smyth — American Hist. Reg. i, 233–8
New Eng. Hist. and Gen. Reg. xxvi, 190–7
Snavely — Brubacker Genealogy 151–4
Egle's History of Lebanon Co. Pa. 251
Egle's Notes and Queries 3d ser. iii, 558
Snedeker — American Ancestry xii, 4
Snediker — Bergen's Van Brunt Gen. 15
Bergen's Kings Co. N. Y. Settlers 266–8
Queen's County N. Y. History 249
Sneeringer — Reily's Life of Cardinal Gibbons ii, 440–2
Sneider — Davis' Bucks County Pa. 464
Snell — Amer. Anc. iii, 46; v, 180; vi, 72
Corliss' North Yarmouth Me.
Kingman's North Bridgewater 624–39
Lincoln's Hist. of Hingham Mass. iii, 155
Mitchell's Hist. of Bridgewater Mass. 295–9
Strong Genealogy 60–3
Temple's Hist. of N. Brookfield Mass. 734
Tuttle Genealogy 683
Snelling — Heraldic Journal ii, 10
New Eng. Hist. and Gen. Reg. lii, 342–6
Savage's Genealogical Dictionary iv, 137
Strong Genealogy 631
Symmes Genealogy 106
Whitmore's Copps Hill Epitaphs
Snethen — Missouri Pioneers 292
Snicker — Washington Gen. 188, 219
Snively — Egle's Notes and Queries 3d series iii, 218
Snively Genealogy (1883) 77 pages
Snoddy — American Ancestry viii, 74
Snodgrass — Davis' Bucks Co. Pa. 665
Egle's Penn. Genealogies 2d ed. 737
Power's Sangamon Co. Ill. Settlers 671
Snook — Chambers' N. J. Germans
Snow — American Ancestry ii, 117; iv, 132 238; x, 102, 194; xi, 65
Bangor Hist. Mag. iv, 19; v, 12; vi, 89
Bemis' History of Marlboro N. H. 634
Calnek's History of Annapolis N. S. 603
Daniels' Hist. of Oxford Mass. 697
Davis' Landmarks of Plymouth Mass. 245
Draper's History of Spencer Mass. 252
Eaton's History of Thomaston Me. 400–4
Foster Genealogy (1889) 109–13
Freeman's Cape Cod ii, 365, 371, 373, 386
Hazen's History of Billerica Mass. 134
Hodgman's History of Westford Mass. 476
Jameson's History of Medway Mass. 523
Judd's History of Hadley Mass. 581
Kingman's N. Bridgewater Mass. 637–41
Knox Co. Me. Hist. Magazine i, 23–31
Lapham's History of Rumford Me. 398
Leland Genealogy 108–11
Leonard's History of Dublin N. H. 394
Locke Genealogy 27, 46–51, 91
Mitchell's History Bridgewater Mass. 300–4

New Eng. Hist. and Gen. Register xlvii, 81–6, 186–9, 341; xlviii, 71–3, 188–90; xlix, 71–3, 202, 451–3; li, 204–9
Paige's History of Hardwick Mass. 498
Pratt's History of Eastham Mass. 20
Randall's Hist. of Chesterfield N. H. 442–6
Read's History of Swanzey N. H. 447–9
Rich's History of Truro Mass. 563
Savage's Genealogical Dictionary iv, 138
Sears Genealogy 81
Sewall's History of Woburn Mass. 640–2
Snow Genealogy (1899) 18 pages
Temple's Hist. of N. Brookfield Mass. 735
Washburn's Hist. of Leicester Mass. 401
Washington N. H. History 614
Welles' Amer. Family Antiquity iii, 17–40
Wheeler's History of Brunswick Me. 853
Whitman Genealogy 296
Winsor's History of Duxbury Mass. 309
Wyman's Charlestown Mass. Gens. ii, 881
Snowdeal — Eaton's Thomaston 404
Snowden — Carter Genealogy (1883) 235
Salisbury Family Memorials (1885) 520–8
Thomas Family of Maryland 138–45
Thomas Genealogy (1896) 507–19
Snyder — American Ancestry ii, 117–18
Chambers' Early Germans of N. J. 503
Greene County N. Y. History 317
Harbaugh Genealogy 119–22
Keim and Allied Families 173–5
Kriebel's Schwenkfelders 38
Munsell's Albany Collections iv, 167
Smith's History of Rhinebeck N. Y. 193
Soames — Runnels' Sanbornton 741
Soden — Bond's Watertown 441
Sohier — Sigourney Genealogy 27
Sohner — Gibbons (Cardinal) ii, 706
Solander — Hyde's Brimfield Mass. 455
Soley — Wyman's Charlestown 882
Solley — Wentworth Genealogy i, 287
Somerby — Savage's Gen. Dict. iv, 139
Somerby Chart (1853)
Wentworth Genealogy i, 384
Somers — American Ancestry viii, 45
Orcutt's History of Wolcott Ct. 558
Somerville — Hayden's Va. Gens. 16
Montgomery and Somerville Families of Ohio (1897) 112 pages
Tiernan Genealogy 118–23
Somes — American Ancestry v, 14
Bangor Hist. Magazine vi, 147; viii, 219
Cushman's History of Sheepscott Me. 419
Hoyt's Salisbury Mass. Families 320
Savage's Genealogical Dictionary iv, 140
Whitmore's Copps Hill Epitaphs
Sommes — Babson's Gloucester 160–2
Sonmans — Whitehead's History of Perth Amboy N. J. 75–80
Sonn — American Ancestry ii, 118
Soper — Barry's Hanover Mass. 377
Freeman's Hist. of Cape Cod Mass. ii, 647
Hanson's History of Gardiner Me. 128
Roe's Sketches of Rose N. Y. 258
Stiles' History of Windsor Ct. ii, 694
Vinton's Giles Genealogy 351–3
Sorber — Plumb's Hanover Pa. 477

Sornborger — Amer. Ancestry ii, 118
Collin's Hist. of Hillsdale N. Y., app. 116
Soule — American Ancestry x, 152
Barry's History of Hanover Mass. 377
Butler's History of Farmington Me. 570
Corliss' North Yarmouth Me. 813–8 etc.
Mitchell's Bridgewater Mass. 304, 386
Orcutt's History of New Milford Ct. 768
Savage's Genealogical Dictionary iv, 140
Soule Genealogy (1882) 31 pages
Temple's Hist. of N. Brookfield Mass. 736
Williams' History of Danby Vt. 265
Soulice — Bolton's Westchester 759
Sour — American Ancestry ii, 118
Southall — American Ancestry vii, 157
Goode Genealogy 333
Richmond Va. Standard ii, 29, 42; iii, 6, 8
Southard — American Ancestry ii, 118
Souther — American Ancestry iii, 115
Avery Genealogy (1893) 333–5
Dow's History of Hampton N. H. 982
Lincoln's Hist. Hingham Mass. iii, 156–61
Souther Genealogy (1886) 41 pages
Whitmore's Heraldic Journal ii, 139
Wyman's Charlestown Mass. Gens. ii, 884
Southerne — N. E. Reg. xxxviii, 199
Southey — N. E. Hist. Reg. xxxviii, 67
Southgate — N. E. Hist. Reg. xix, 252
Temple's History of Palmer Mass. 546
Washburn's Hist. of Leicester Mass. 396–8
Worcester's Mag. and Hist. Jour. ii, 100
Southland — Young's Chautauqua 239
Southmayd — Anderson's Waterbury 129
Babson's History of Gloucester Mass. 162
Dwight Genealogy 522, 534
Savage's Genealogical Dictionary iv, 141
Southward — Essex Inst. xiv, 77–81
Southwick — Amer. Ancestry i, 73; iii, 101
Bemis' History of Marlboro N. H. 635
Eaton's History of Reading Mass. 114
Pierce's History of Grafton Mass. 566
Power's Sangamon Co. Ill. Settlers 672–4
Southwick Genealogy (1881) 609 pages
Williams' History of Danby Vt. 263–5
Southworth — Am. Ancestry viii, 28, 30
Brownell Genealogy (1892) 10–4
Corliss' North Yarmouth Me.
Davis' Landmarks of Plymouth 246–8
Eaton's History of Thomaston Me. ii, 404
Holton's Winslow Genealogy i, 242
Kingman's Hist. of N. Bridgewater Mass.
Mitchell's Hist. of Bridgewater Mass. 305
Montague Genealogy 533
Orcutt's Hist. of Stratford Ct. 1294
Paige's History of Hardwick Mass. 499
Savage's Genealogical Dictionary iv, 143
Southworth Genealogy (1892) 11 pages
Southworth Genealogy 2d ed. (1897) 32 p.
Strong Genealogy 1330–2
Temple's Hist. of N. Brookfield Mass. 737
Thatcher's Hist. of Plymouth Mass. 127
Thayer Memorial (1835) 49
Upham Genealogy 59–62
Walworth's Hyde Genealogy 691
Winsor's History of Duxbury Mass. 314–7
Soutter — Richmond Standard ii, 47

Sovereen — Chambers' N. J. Germans
Soward — Paxton's Marshall Gen. 187
Sower — Penn. Mag. of History vi, 127
Sower Family of Phila. (1888) chart
Spackman — Cope Gen. 42, 68
Spafford — Essex Inst. Coll. xx, 89-92
Hubbard's Hist. of Springfield Vt. 447-9
Saunderson's Charlestown N. H. 552
Sedgwick's History of Sharon Ct. 113
Spafford Genealogy, see Spofford Geneal.
Spaford — Hurd's New London Ct. 527
Spaíahour — American Ancestry ix, 227
Spalding — Am. Anc. vi, 65; x, 11; xii, 95
Butler's History of Groton Mass. 437, 479
Eaton's History of Thomaston Me. ii, 405
Emery Genealogy 469
Hemenway's Vermont Hist. Gaz. v, 24-7
Heywood's Hist. Westminster Mass. 875-9
Hodgman's Hist. of Westford Mass. 476
Larned's History of Windham Co. Ct.
Livermore's Hist. of Wilton N. H. 503-6
Loomis Genealogy (1880) 780
Perkins' Old Houses of Norwich Ct. 563
Ransom Genealogy
Secomb's History of Amherst N. H. 776-8
Spalding Genealogy (1872) 619 pages
Spalding Memorial (1887) 323 pages
Spalding Genealogy 2d ed. (1897) 1276 pages
Stearns' Hist. Ashburnham Mass. 896-99
Spalter — Guild's Stiles Genealogy 294
Spangler — American Ancestry xi, 227
Egle's Lebanon Pa. 252-4
Spangler Genealogy (1883) 13 pages
Spangler Genealogy (1896) 605 pages
Spann — Hayden's Virginia Gens. 245
Spare — Spare Genealogy (1884) 67 pages
Sparhawk — Aldrich's Walpole 356-9
Bangor Me. Historical Magazine v, 29
Bond's Watertown Mass.Genealogies 545-7
Brewster's Portsmouth N. H. ii, 185
Cutts Genealogy 125
Daniels' History of Oxford Mass. 697-9
Essex Institute Hist. Collections xxv, 30-
  43, 119-36, 280-94; xxvi, 51-8, 123-9;
  xxvii, 149-71; xxviii, 151-79
Leland Genealogy 22
Morse's Sherborn Mass. Settlers 242
New Eng. Hist. and Gen. Reg xix, 125-7
Paige's History of Cambridge Mass. 656-9
Savage's Genealogical Dictionary iv, 144
Sparhawk Genealogy (1865) 3 pages, reprint
Sparks — Cope Genealogy 80, 177-9
Greggs' History of Old Cheraws S. C. 98
Temple's Hist. of N. Brookfield Mass. 738
Sparrow — Dudley's Arch Coll. pl. 4
Freeman's Cape Cod Mass. ii, 361, 733
Savage's Genealogical Dictionary iv, 145
Spaulding — American Ancestry ii, 119;
  vi, 107; viii, 174
Ballou's History of Milford Mass. 1021
Brown's Bedford Mass. Families 32
Chandler's History of Shirley Mass. 624
Cochrane's Hist. Francest'n N. H. 930-4
Cutter's History of Jaffrey N. H. 466-76
Daniels' History of Oxford Mass. 699
Douglas Genealogy 473

Farwell Genealogy 64-72
Hayward's Hist. of Hancock N. H. 867-79
Hazen's History of Billerica Mass. 135-7
Hill's History of Mason N. H. 206
Holton's Farwell Genealogy 63-72
Hudson's Hist. of Lexington Mass. 229
Hyde's History of Brimfield Mass. 455
Kidder's Hist. of New Ipswich N. H. 430-2
Norton's Hist. of Fitzwilliam N. H. 721
Phœnix's Whitney Genealogy 571
Randall's Hist. of Chesterfield N. H. 446
Savage's Genealogical Dictionary iv, 145
Spaulding Genealogy, see Spalding
Washington N. H. History 615-24
Worthen's History of Sutton N. H. 961
Spayd — Egle's Notes and Queries 3d series
  ii, 494-5
Spear — Bass' Hist. of Braintree Vt. 181-4
Binney Genealogy 28
Bridgeman's Copps Hill Epitaphs 225-7
Corliss' North Yarmouth Me.
Davis' Landmarks of Plymouth Mass. 248
Eaton's Annals of Warren Me. 618-23
Eaton's Hist. of Thomaston Me. ii, 406-10
Freeman's Hist. of Cape Cod Mass. ii, 628
New Eng. Hist. and Gen. Reg. xviii, 158-61
Savage's Genealogical Dictionary iv, 146
Smith's History of Sunderland Mass. 551
Temple's History of Palmer Mass. 544
Speed — American Ancestry i, 73; ii, 119
Cushman's History of Sheepscott Me. 419
Richmond Va. Standard iii, 16
Slaughter's Fry Genealogy
Speed Genealogy (1892) 206 pages
Speed Genealogy (1894) 35 pages
Speer — Harrison Ancestry 74-7
Speke — Hayden's Virginia Gens. 489
Spelman — Amer. Ancestry i, 73; ii, 119
N. E. Hist. Gen. Reg. xxxviii, 323, 428
Spence — Cutts Genealogy 215-7
Hanson's Old Kent Md. 151-4
Spencer — American Ancestry i, 74; ii,
  119; xi, 49, 138, 202; xii, 104
Anderson's Waterbury Ct. i, app. 129
Austin's R. I. Genealogical Dict. 186-8
Bangor Me. Hist. Magazine vi, 132-5
Boyd's Annals of Winchester Ct. 93-6
Brown's West Simsbury Ct. Settlers 126
Cleveland's Hist. of Yates Co. N. Y. 250-62
Field's History of Haddam Ct. 45
Goodwin's Gen. Notes 197-210, 310-23
Greene Genealogy (1894)
Hanson's Old Kent Md. 187-9
Hinman's Connecticut Settlers 1st ed. 237
Hollister Genealogy 314-22
Hubbard's Hist. of Springfield Vt. 450
Hughes Genealogy 116
Hurlbut Genealogy 409
Jameson's Hist. of Medway Mass. 523
Jenkin's Hist. Gwynedd Pa. 2d ed. 416-8
Littell's Passaic Valley Genealogies 394
Mack Genealogy 65-9
Meade's Old Families of Virginia
Ogden Genealogy (1896) 21-4
Orcutt's History of Torrington Ct. 764
Paige's Hist. of Cambridge Mass. 659

Roberts' Old Richland Pa. Fam. 120, 223
Saunderson's Charlestown N. H. 553
Savage's Genealogical Dict. iv, 147-50
Sedgwick's History of Sharon Ct. 113
Spencer Family History (1889) 26 pages
Spencer Family of Talbot Md. (1892) 26 p.
Spencer Fam. of Cromwell Ct. (1896) 44 p.
Spencer Family of Cambridge (1898) chart
Spencer Family of Maine (1898) 247 pages
Townsend Genealogy (1895) not paged
Watkins Genealogy 34-7
Whittemore's History of Middlesex Ct.
Wyman's Charlestown Mass. Gens. ii, 886
Young's Hist. Chautauqua Co. N. Y. 611
Spengler — Spengler Geneal. (1896) 605 p.
Sperry — American Ancestry x, 173
Anderson's Waterbury Ct. i, app. 130
Dickerman Genealogy 180-93, 407, 416-20
Matthew's Hist. of Cornwall Ct. 290
Stiles' History of Windsor Ct. ii, 695-8
Turner's Phelps and Gorham Purchase 190
Tuttle Genealogy 684
Spicer — Bergen's Kings Co. N. Y. 269
Caulkins' History of New London Ct. 335
Clement's Newtown N. J. Settlers
Stanton Genealogy 103
Spickler — Burgner Genealogy 121-31
Spier — American Ancestry ii, 119
Stiles' History of Windsor Ct. ii, 698
Spink — Austin's R. I. Gen. Dict. 188
Spining — Collord Ancestors 14-7
Spinner — Davis' Bucks Co. Pa. 449
Spinney — Calnek's Annapolis N. S. 604
Hatch's History of Industry Me. 814
Wentworth Genealogy i, 267
Spinning — Littell's Passaic Valley 396
Spofford — American Ancestry iv, 55; v,
    171; vii, 35; viii, 88
Bedford N. H. Centennial 334-6
Blood's History of Temple N. H. 251
Eaton's History of Thomaston Me. ii, 410
Gage's History of Rowley Mass. 455
N. E. Reg. viii, 335-44; ix, 61-7, 273-8
Norton's Hist. of Fitzwilliam N. H. 722
Perley's History of Boxford Mass. 45
Savage's Genealogical Dictionary iv, 151
Smith's Hist. of Peterborough N. H. 288
Spofford Genealogy (1851) 64 pages
Spofford Genealogy (1870) 128 pages
Spofford Ancestry (1886) 10 pages
Spofford Genealogy (1888) 502 pages
Titcomb's Early New Eng. People 270-3
Woodbury's Sketch of Bradford Mass. 90-2
Spohn — Heffner Genealogy 43-5
Spooner — American Ancestry iv, 203
Austin's Allied Families 215-7
Bond's Watertown Mass. Genealogies 905
Cleveland's Hist. of Yates Co. N. Y. 742-4
Davis' Landmarks of Plymouth Mass. 248
Douglas Genealogy 94-6
Holton's Winslow Genealogy i, 515
New Eng. Hist. and Gen. Reg. xxiii, 407-10
Perkins' Old Houses of Norwich Ct. 565
Savage's Genealogical Dictionary iv, 151
Spooner Genealogy (1871) 242 pages
Spooner Genealogy (1883) 694 pages

Temple's Hist. of N. Brookfield Mass. 738
Wetmore Family 126
Spoor — American Ancestry ii, 119
Munsell's Albany Collections iv, 167
New Eng. Hist. and Gen. Register li, 345
Spotswood — Campbell's Virginia 409
Goode Genealogy 115-8, 226-8
Lindsay Genealogy
Meade's Old Churches of Virginia i, 165
Richmond Va. Stand. ii, 12; iii, 38; iv, 18
Siaughter's St. George's Parish Va. 54-7
Slaughter's St. Mark's Parish 1-6, 165-8
Spotswood Genealogy (1868) 44 pages
Welles' Washington Genealogy 259
Whittemore's Orange N. J. 284
Sprague — Amer. Ancestry i, 74; iii, 218
Austin's Ancestries 51
Austin's R. I. Genealogical Dictionary 189
Ballou's History of Milford Mass. 1023-4
Bangor Me. Historical Magazine iv, 90
Bass Ancestry 7
Bassett's History of Richmond N. H. 484-6
Binney Genealogy 54-6
Bond's Watertown Mass. Gens. 944
Buckingham Genealogy (1872) 249-52
Buckingham Genealogy (1892) 70-6
Butler's History of Farmington Me. 571-4
Clute's History of Staten Island N. Y. 426
Dennysville Me. Centennial 111
Draper's History of Spencer Mass. 250
Dwight Genealogy 782-4
Eaton's History of Thomaston Me. ii, 411
Farrow's Hist. of Islesborough Me. 281-4
Goss' Hist. Address at Melrose Mass. 13-6
Hines' Lebanon Ct. Hist. Address 168
Hurd's History of New London Ct. 515
Joslin's History of Poultney Vt. 350-2
Lapham's History of Bethel Me. 659
Lincoln's Hist. Hingham Mass. iii, 163-83
Malden Mass. Bi-Centennial 237
Mitchell's Hist. of Bridgewater Mass. 306
Paige's Hist. of Cambridge Mass. 545
Paul's History of Wells Vt. 147
Savage's Genealogical Dictionary iv, 153-6
Schenck's History of Fairfield Ct. 411
Spooner's Mem. of W. Spooner 98
Sprague Genealogy (1828) 68 pages
Sprague Genealogy (1847) 191 pages
Sprague Family of R. I. (1881) 74 pages
Sprague Family Items (1894) 6 pages
Tucker's History of Hartford Vt. 460-2
Washburn's Hist. of Leicester Mass. 403
Wheeler's Hist. of Brunswick Me. 854
Winsor's Hist. of Duxbury Mass. 317-20
Wyman's Charlestown Mass. ii, 887-93
Woonsocket R. I. History 203
Young's Hist. Chautauqua Co. N. Y. 491
Sprake — American Ancestry xii
Hazen's History of Billerica Mass. 137
Spraker — Montgomery Co. 159-62
Sprat — N. Y. Gen. Rec. xii, 174
Spring — Bond's Watertown 441-9, 936
Evans Genealogy (1893) 43
Hyde's History of Brimfield Mass. 455
Jackson's History of Newton Mass. 415-8
Livermore's History of Wilton N. H. 506

Old Eliot, Me. Magazine iii, (1899) 145, 153
Ridlon's Saco Valley Me. Families 1150-2
Savage's Genealogical Dictionary iv, 156
Tuttle Genealogy 352
Wyman's Charlestown Mass. Gens. ii, 893
Springer — American Ancestry i, 74
Geauga Republican, Chardon Ohio March 29, 1882
Hanson's History of Gardiner Me. 151
Munsell's Albany Collections iv, 167
Power's Sangamon Co. Ill. Settlers 675
Springer Genealogy (1831) 144 pages
Springsteen — Munsell's Albany iv, 168
Springstein — American Ancestry ii, 119
Sproat — American Ancestry viii, 212
Deane's History of Scituate Mass. 340
Johnston's History of Bristol Me. 334-6
Sprogell — American Ancestry iv, 5
Sproul — Calnek's Annapolis N. S. 605
Sprout — Paige's Hardwick Mass. 505
Sprung — Bergen's Kings Co. N. Y. 271
Spurr — Ames' Redman Farm
Calnek's History of Annapolis N. S. 606
Chute Genealogy, appendix 200
Davis Genealogy 252
Savage's Genealogical Dictionary iv, 158
Wight Genealogy 86
Spyker — Egle's Notes (1897) 184
Squier — American Ancestry ii, 120
Cleveland's Hist. of Yates Co. N. Y. 430-2
Hodgman's Hist. of Westford Mass. 478
Littell's Passaic Valley Gens. 397-402
Savage's Genealogical Dictionary iv, 158
Squiers — American Ancestry xii
Squire — Cothren's Woodbury Ct. 709
Paige's History of Cambridge Mass. 659
Schenck's History of Fairfield Ct. 411
Sharpe's South Britain Ct. Sketches 163
Squires — Hedges' East Hampton 335
Howell's Southampton 387-9
Livermore's History of Wilton N. H. 507
Staats — American Ancestry i, 74; ii, 120
Bergen's Kings County N. Y. Settlers 272
McPike Genealogy
Munsell's Albany Collections iv, 168
New Jersey Hist. Society Colls. vii, (1882)
New York Gen. and Biog. Rec. ii, 140
Schuyler's Colonial New York ii. 396-8
Smith's History of Rhinebeck N. Y. 202
Stabler — Thomas Gen. (1896) 519-23
Stackhouse — Potts Genealogy (1895) 281-6
Stackpole — Baker Genealogy (1867) 18-20
Eaton's History of Thomaston Me. 412
Hanson's History of Gardiner Me. 109
Otis Genealogy (1851)
Ridlon's Saco Valley Me. Families 1152
Stackpole Genealogy (1899) 252 pages
Stackpole's History of Durham Me. 249-52
Stacey — Stearns' Ashburnham 899
Stacy — Babson's Gloucester Mass. 285
Ballou's History of Milford Mass. 1025-7
Barry's Hist. of Framingham Mass. 393
Bulloch's Stewart Genealogy 22
Caldwell Genealogy 74
Clement's Newtown N. J. Settlers
Cochrane's History of Antrim N. H. 686

Collins Genealogy 149
Dearborn's Hist. of Parsonsfield Me. 407
Hammatt Papers, Ipswich Mass. 343-6
Martin's History of Chester Pa. 41-7
Paige's History of Cambridge Mass. 660
Savage's Genealogical Dictionary iv, 159
Tanner Genealogy 42-5
Stacye — Cregar's White Genealogy
Stafford — Amer. Ancestry i, 74; ii, 120
Austin's Allied Families 218
Austin's R. I. Genealogical Dictionary 384
Daniels' History of Oxford Mass. 699
Munsell's Albany Collections iii, 440-50
Power's Sangamon Co. Ill. Settlers 675
Savage's Genealogical Dictionary iv, 160
Slafter Genealogy 76-8
Stafford Genealogy (1870) 27 pages
Updyke's Narragansett Churches 375
Vinton Genealogy
William's History of Danby Vt. 266
Stagg — N. E. Hist. Reg. xxxix, 161
New York Gen. Biog. Rec. ix, 85-91, 131
Stahl — Eaton's Warren Me. 623
Stahnaker — American Ancestry xii
Stainwood — Babson's Gloucester 163
Staley — Pearson's Schenectady 175
Power's Sangamon Co. Ill. Settlers 682
Stall — American Ancestry ii, 120
Stallion — Cauklins' New London 346
Stallworth — Goode Genealogy 546
Stanard — Meade's Old Families of Va.
Thomas Genealogy (1896) 524-6
Wheeler's History of Newport N. H. 535
Stanbrough — Southampton 389
Stanbury — Robinson's Ancestry 53-5
Stancliffe — Savage's Dict. iv, 161
Standish — Davis' Landmarks 250
Eaton's Annals of Warren Me. 623
Mitchell's Hist. of Bridgewater Mass. 307-9
Savage's Genealogical Dictionary iv, 161-3
Standish Genealogy (1895) 149 pages
Wetmore Genealogy 607-10
Winsor's History of Duxbury Mass. 320-2
Standlake — Deane's Scituate 344
Standley — Andrews' New Britain Ct.
Porter's Hartford Ct. Settlers 20
See also Stanley
Stanfield — Potts Genealogy (1895) 365-7
Stanford — Morse's Sherborne Mass. 242
Stanford Genealogy (1898) 45 pages
Winsor's History of Duxbury Mass. 322
Staniford — Hammatt Papers 339-42
Ipswich Mass. Antiq. Papers (May 1882)
Stanley — Anderson's Waterbury 137
Andrews' Hist. of New Britain Ct. 168, etc.
Butler's Hist. of Farmington Me. 574
Cochrane's Hist. Francest'n N. H. 934-6
Cutter's History of Jaffrey N. H. 479-82
Daggert's Hist. of Attleborough Mass. 94
Davis' History of Wallingford Ct. 900-3
Joslin's History of Poultney Vt. 352
Judd's History of Hadley Mass. 582
Leonard's History of Dublin N. H. 396
Livermore's History of Wilton N. H. 507
Morse's Mem., appendix 55
Read's History of Swanzey N. H. 450

Ridlon's Saco Valley Me. Families 1153–9
Savage's Genealogical Dictionary iv, 163–6
Slaughter's Bristol Parish Va. 131
Stanley Genealogy (1887) 352 pages
Stearns' History of Rindge N. H. 701–4
Stiles' History of Windsor Ct. ii, 698
Thurston's History of Winthrop Me. 196
Walworth's Hyde Genealogy 335–7
Stannard — Adams' Fairhaven Vt. 467
American Ancestry ii, 120
Boyd's Annals of Winchester Ct. 73
Stansbrough — Howell's Southampton
Stansbury — American Ancestry xii
Stanton — Am. Anc. i, 75; iv, 23, 222; v,
   9; vii, 217–275; viii, 13; ix, 49; xi, 230
Austin's R. I. Genealogical Dictionary 388
Caulkins' History of New London Ct. 296
Davis Genealogy (1888) 32–42
Leland Genealogy 65
Prentice Genealogy 407
Savage's Genealogical Dictionary iv, 166
Stanton Genealogy (1891) 613 pages
Stonington Ct. Bi-Centennial 293
Wentworth Genealogy i, 459
Wyman's Charlestown Mass. Gens. ii, 895
Stanwood — American Ancestry xi, 137
Bangor Hist. Magazine viii, 24
Hoyt's Salisbury Mass. Families 321
New Eng. Hist. and Gen. Reg. l, 540–3
North's History of Augusta Me. 940
Savage's Genealogical Dictionary iv, 167
Stanwood Genealogy (1899) 317 pages
See also under Stainwood
Stanyan — Dow's Hampton N. H. 983
Staples — Amer. Ancestry iv, 8; ix, 124
Ballou's History of Milford Mass. 1028
Corliss' North Yarwouth Me.
Eaton's Hist. of Thomaston Me. ii, 414
Holton's Winslow Genealogy i, 460
Hudson's Hist. of Lexington Mass. 230
Lapham's History of Bethel Me. 659
Miller's History of Colchester Co. N. S.
   11–4
Ridlon's Saco Valley Me. Families 1159
Savage's Genealogical Dictionary iv, 168
Staples Genealogy (1880) 55 pages
Schenck's History of Fairfield Ct. 412
Trubee Genealogy 90, 140–3
Wheeler's History of Brunswick Me. 854
Williams' History of Danby Vt. 267
Stapleton — American Ancestry ix, 76
Austin's R. I. Genealogical Dictionary 190
Keim and Allied Families 153
Perkiomen Region iii, 19–21
Starbird — Lapham's Paris Me. 728
Starbuck — Amer. Gen. Rec. ii, 196–9
Austin's Allied Families 220
New Eng. Hist. and Gen. Register viii, 129
Savage's Genealogical Dictionary iv, 171
Starin — Amer. Ancestry v, 215; ix, 175
Montgomery and Fulton Co. N. Y. 124
Starin Genealogy (1892) 233 pages
Welles' Amer. Fam. Antiquity ii, 171–87
Stark — Amer. Ancestry x, 204; xi, 50, 120
Chamber's Early Germans of N. J. 505
Champion Genealogy 372

Stark's History of Dunbarton N. H. 176
Walworth's Hyde Geneal. i, 248–53, 514–22
Starke — Richmond Standard iii, 3, 6
Wm. and Mary College Quarterly iv,
   270–2; v, 56
Starkey — Bassett's Richmond 486–9
Bemis' History of Marlboro N. H. 635
New Eng. Hist. and Gen. Reg. xlvi, 144–9
Norton's History of Fitzwilliam N. H. 723
Read's History of Swanzey N. H. 451–5
Richmond Va. Standard ii, 32; iii, 33
Starkey Genealogy (1892) 10 pages, reprint
Starks — American Ancestry i, 75; ii, 120
Atkin's History of Hawley Mass. 64
Orcutt's History of Torrington Ct. 765
Starkweather — Aldrich's Walpole
American Ancestry ix, 108
Stanton Genealogy 327–33
Stiles' History of Windsor Ct. ii, 699
Wetmore Genealogy 71
Starling — Amer. Ancestry viii, 113, 150
Butler's History of Farmington Me. 576
Green's Kentucky Families
Paxton's Marshall Genealogy 165
Sullivant Genealogy 7–78
Starr — American Ancestry vii, 54
Caulkins' Hist. of New London Ct. 318–20
Dickerman Genealogy 557–60
Eaton Genealogy (1895)
Eaton's History of Thomaston Me. ii, 414
Ely Genealogy 228
Freeman's Hist. of Cape Cod Mass. ii, 187
Hinman's Connecticut Settlers 1st ed. 238
Jackson Genealogy 72, 77
Mitchell's Hist. of Bridgewater Mass. 309
Orcutt's History of Milford Ct. 769
Power's Sangamon Co. Ill. Settlers 683
Savage's Genealogical Dict. iv, 169–71
Sharpless Genealogy 188
Sheldon's Hist. of Deerfield Mass. 315
Starr Genealogy (1879) 577 pages
Strong Genealogy 285–8
Winsor's History of Duxbury Mass. 323
Starrett — Calnek's Annapolis 607–9
Cochrane's History of Antrim 686–8
Cochrane's Hist. Francestown N. H. 936–41
Cogswell's Hist. New Boston N. H. 427–9
Eaton's Annals of Warren Me. 624–8
Eaton's History of Thomaston Me. ii, 415
Eaton's History of Warren Me. 428–30
Knox Co. Me. Hist. Mag. i, 99–110, 157–88
Start — American Ancestry x, 153
Kidder's Hist. of New Ipswich N. H. 432
Start Genealogy (1894) 30 pages
Stauffer — Brubacher Genealogy 156–86
Egle's Notes and Queries 4th ser. i, 305
Harris' Hist. of Lancaster Pa. 555
Stauffer Genealogy (1899) 371 pages
Staunton — American Ancestry v, 173
Stavast — Potts Genealogy (1895) 75
Stavely — Hanson's Old Kent Md. 190
St. Clair — American Ancestry x, 22
Eaton's History of Thomaston Me. 385
Egle's Notes and Queries (1897) 55–85
Power's Sangamon Co. Ill. Settlers 677
Sinclair Genealogy

Steadman — American Ancestry v, 188
Bond's Watertown Mass. Gens. 450
Chute Genealogy, appendix 201-6
Stearns — Aldrich's Walpole 361-4
American Ancestry iii, 118; iv, 197; vii,
  29, 108; viii, 80
Andrews Gen. (1890) 114-6, 147-58, 184-90
Ballou's History of Milford Mass. 1029-31
Barrus' History of Goshen Mass. 167-70
Barry's History of Framingham Mass. 394
Bass' History of Braintree Vt. 184
Bond's Watertown 450-582, 937-49, 552-82
Brown's Bedford Mass. Families 32-41
Cogswell's Nottingham N. H. 469-72
Craft's History of Whately Mass. 584
Cutter's History of Arlington Mass. 301-3
Davis' History of Reading Vt. 153-6
Eaton's History of Thomaston Me. ii, 415
Hayward's History of Gilsum N. H. 394
Hayward's History of Hancock N. H. 880
Hazen's History of Billerica Mass. 139-44
Heywood's Hist. Westminster Mass. 879-8
Hudson's History Lexington Mass. 230-3
Hyde Family of Hubbardston 3-5
Kidder's Hist. of New Ipswich N. H. 433
Lane Genealogy (1891) 90-2
Lapham's History of Bethel Me. 616-9
Lapham's History of Paris Me. 730-2
Lincoln's Hist. of Hingham Mass. iii, 184
Livermore's History of Wilton N. H. 508
Norton's Hist. of Fitzwilliam N. H. 724
Paige's History of Cambridge Mass. 660
Pierce's History of Grafton Mass. 567
Randall's Hist. of Chesterfield N. H. 447-9
Read's History of Swanzey N. H. 455-7
Savage's Genealogical Dictionary iv, 173-5
Secomb's History of Amherst N. H. 779-81
Stearns Genealogy (1891) 68 pages
Stearns Genealogy (1894) 7 pages
Stearns' Hist. Ashburnham Mass. 899-903
Stearns' History of Rindge N. H. 704-10
Temple's History of Northfield Mass. 539
Thayer's Memorial (1835) 65
Waldo's History of Tolland Ct. 111-4
Wilder Genealogy 165, 308
Wyman's Charlestown Mass. Gens. ii, 896
Stebbings — Draper's Spencer 255
Stebbins — Amer. Ancestry i, 75; iv, 242
Baker's History of Montville Ct. 419-21
Caulkins' History of New London Ct. 314
Doolittle's Hist. of Belchertown Mass. 256
Dwight's Strong Genealogy 230, 770, 1143
Ely Genealogy 28
Hemenway's Gaz. v, 288, 323, 394-6
Hyde's History of Brimfield Mass. 456-8
Leach's Morton Ancestry 102-6
Longmeadow Mass. Centennial, app. 82-7
McKeen's History of Bradford Vt. 394-7
Morris and Flynt Genealogy 38
New Eng. Hist. and Gen. Reg. v, 71-8,
  351-4; xxxviii, 157-9
Orcutt's History of New Milford Ct. 770
Porter's Hartford Ct. Settlers 21, 25
Savage's Genealogical Dictionary iv, 175-8
Sheldon's Hist. of Deerfield Mass. 315-28
Stebbins Genealogy (1771) 24 pages

Stebbins Genealogy (1879) 31 pages
Stebbins of N. Y. Heirs (1880) 20 pages
Stebbins Fam. of Wilbraham (1886) 16 p.
Temple's Hist. of Northfield Mass. 540-5
Temple's Hist. of No. Brookfield Mass. 740
Temple's History of Palmer Mass 552-5
West Springfield Mass. Centennial 122
Wilbraham Mass. Centennial 305-9
Stedman — Andrews' New Britain Ct.
Bass' History of Braintree Vt. 185
Caulkins' Hist. of New London Ct. 342
Heywood's Hist. Westminster Mass. 882
N. E. Hist. Gen. Reg. xiv, 69-74; xx, 126
Newfame Vt. Centennial 173
Odiorne Genealogy
Paige's History of Cambridge Mass. 661-3
Savage's Genealogical Dictionary iv, 178
Sedgwick's History of Sharon Ct. 114
Stearns' History Ashburnham Mass. 905
Stiles' History of Windsor Ct. ii, 699
Steel — Livermore's Wilton 508-10
Steele — American Ancestry i, 75; vi, 182;
  vii, 78; x, 26; xi, 51; xii, 125
Anderson's Waterbury Ct. i, app. 131
Andrews' Hist. of New Britain Ct. 179, etc.
Baldwin Genealogy 814
Cochrane's History Antrim N. H. 688-93
Cothren's Woodbury 688-93; ii, 1559-61
Egle's Notes and Queries 3d ser. ii, 28
Hanson's Old Kent Md. 37
Harris' Hist. of Lancaster Co. Pa. 561-5
Hayward's Hist. of Hancock N. H. 881
Hubbard's Hist. of Springfield Vt. 459
Hubbard's Stanstead Co. Canada 218
Huntington Genealogy
Longmeadow Mass. Centennial, app. 87
Marvin's Hist. of Winchenden Mass. 471
Morris and Flynt Genealogy 62
Morrison's History of Windham N. H. 777
Morrison Genealogy 241
New York Gen. and Biog. Rec. xxi, 41
Orcutt's History of Derby Ct. 761-4
Orcutt's History of Torrington Ct. 765
Paige's History of Cambridge Mass. 663
Phœnix's Whitney Genealogy i, 148
Plumb's History of Hanover Pa. 482
Power's Sangamon Co. Ill. Settlers 684
Ransom Genealogy 42
Ridlon's Saco Valley Me. Families 1160
Robinson's Items of Ancestry (1894) 59
Runnels' Hist. of Sanbornton N. H. ii, 743
Savage's Genealogical Dictionary iv, 179
Secomb's History of Amherst N. H. 781
Sharpe's History of Seymour Ct. 203-5
Smith's Hist. of Peterborough N. H. 290-7
Smith (Rev. Wm.) Biography
Sprague's Hist. of Gloversville N. Y. 128
Stearns' Ashburnham Mass. 905
Stearns' History of Rindge N. H. 710
Steele Genealogy (1859) 145 pages
Steele Fam. of Chester Pa. (1896) 40 pages
Steele Family of S. Car. (1900) 143 pages
Strong Genealogy 1249-54 1428-35
Waldo's History of Tolland Ct. 31-5
Washington N. H. History 624-6
Welles' Washington Genealogy 203, **227**

Steelman — Penn. Mag. of Hist. v, 219
Steere — Austin's R. I. Gen. Dict. 191
Narrati7e Historical Register vi, 86–8
Pearson's Schenectady N. Y. Settlers 176
Steger — Perkiomen Region Pa. 46
Steiner — American Ancestry vii, 65
Steiner Genealogy (1880) 21 pages
Steiner Genealogy (1896) 103 pages
Stelle — Littell's Passaic Valley 403
Stephens — Amer. Anc. viii, 80, 90; ix, 79
Chambers' Early Germans of N. J. 505–7
Davis' Landmarks of Plymouth Mass. 506
Garrard Genealogy 95–101
Goode Genealogy 312
Hill's Lawrence-Townley Estate
Hough's History of Lewis Co. N. Y. 139
Howell's Hist. of Southampton N. Y. 390–2
Lapham's History of Paris Me, 732
Lawrence and Bartlett Mem. 120
Paige's History of Hardwick Mass. 506
Pope Genealogy
Ransom Genealogy 29–31, 56, 59
Stephens Genealogy (1892) 185 pages
Walker Genealogy (1896) 186–93
Whitmore's Heraldic Journal i, 111
Stephenson — Lincoln's Hist. of Hingham Mass. iii, 185–9
Pierce's Gorham Me. 207
Power's Sangamon Co. Ill. Settlers 684
Read's History of Swanzey N. H. 457–9
Savage's Genealogical Dictionary iv, 182
Turner Genealogy 40–3
Steptoe — Meade's Old Families of Va.
Richmond Va. Standard iii, 29
Sterling — American Ancestry xi, 114
Balch's Provincial Papers
Jerseyman ii, 6
Orcutt's History of New Milford Ct. 770
Orcutt's History of Stratford Ct. 1294–6
Plumb's History of Hanover Pa. 479
Strong Genealogy 720–4
Walworth's Hyde Genealogy 797–805
Stern — McFarlan and Stern Gen. (1885) 92–126
Sternbergh — American Ancestry vi, 81
Sterne — American Ancestry ii, 120
Sterns — American Ancestry ix, 231
Sterry — Perkins' Norwich Ct. 566
Stetson — Adams' Fairhaven Vt. 472–5
Adams' Family of Kingston Mass. 58–62
American Ancestry ix, 97
Bangor Me. Hist. Mag. iii, 184–6; v, 210
Barry's History of Hanover Mass. 378–83
Briggs' History of Shipbuilding 219–23
Davis' Landmarks of Plymouth Mass. 253
Deane's History of Scituate Mass. 340–2
Eaton's Annals of Warren Me. 2d ed. 628
Eaton's History of Thomaston Me. ii, 416
Hanover Mass. Records (1898)
Hobart's History of Abington Mass. 437–40
Hudson's History of Lexington Mass. 234
Lawrence and Bartlett Memorial 132–7
Leach's Morton Ancestry 76–9
Lincoln's Hist. of Hingham Mass. iii, 189
.itchell's Hist. of Bridgewater Mass. 310
Savage's Genealogical Dictionary iv, 183

Stackpole's Hist. of Durham Me. 253–5
Stetson Genealogy (1847) 116 pages
Whittemore's Oranges N. J. 262–4
Wyman's Charlestown Mass. Gens. ii, 898
Wyman's Hunt Genealogy 141
Stevens — Abbot's Andover Mass. 21
American Ancestry ii, 120; iv, 18, 125; v, 214; vi, 40, 117; x, 145
Anderson's Waterbury Ct. i, app. 132
Babson's Hist. of Gloucester Mass. 164–9
Bangor Me. Hist. Mag. v, 211; viii, 233
Barry's Hist. of Framingham Mass. 395
Bedford N. H. Centennial 338
Bouton Genealogy 320
Bradbury's Kennebunkport Me. 276
Caverly's History of Pittsford Vt. 726
Chapman Genealogy 96
Cochrane's Hist. Francestown N. H. 941–3
Cogswell's Nottingham N. H. 246–8, 472–4
Corliss' North Yarmouth Me.
Crafts Genealogy 223–5
Cunnabell Genealogy 97
Daniels' History of Oxford Mass. 700
Dearborn's Hist. Salisbury N. H. 797–802
Dickinson Genealogy (1897) 56–60
Eaton's Annals of Warren Me. 629
Eaton's History of Thomaston Me. ii, 417
Freeman's Cape Cod Mass. ii, 683, 773
Fullonton's Hist. of Raymond N. H. 287
Greene County N. Y. History 313
Guild's Stiles Genealogy 77
Hatch's History of Industry Me. 815–7
Hayward's Hist. of Hancock N. H. 881–3
Heywood's Hist. Westminster Mass. 882
Hill's Lawrence-Townley Estate
Hodgman's History of Westford Mass. 478
Hollister's History of Pawlet Vt. 243–5
Hoyt's Salisbury Mass. Families 322–8
Hubbard's Hist. of Springfield Vt. 440
Hudson's History of Lexington Mass. 234
Hudson's Hist. Marlborough Mass. 447–50
Hudson's Hist. of Sudbury Mass. 171, 315
Huntington's Stamford Ct. Settlers 108
Lapham's History of Bethel Me. 619
Lapham's History of Norway Me. 602–5
Lapham's History of Paris Me. 733–5
Lapham's History of Rumford Me. 399–401
Littell's Passaic Valley Genealogies 404
Livermore's History of Wilton N. H. 510–2
McKeen's History of Bradford Vt. 381
Milliken's Narraguagus Valley Me. 9
Montague Genealogy (1894) 126
Neill's Virginia Carolorum 417
N. Y. Gen. Biog. Rec. xv, 145–50; xxvi, 7
Paul's History of Wells Vt. 148
Pearson's Schenectady N. Y. Settlers 177
Pierce's History of Gorham Me. 207
Pompey N. Y. Reunion 417
Reed's History of Rutland Mass. 101–5
Rich's History of Truro Mass. 564–6
Saunderson's Charlestown N. H. 570–4
Savage's Genealogical Dict. iv, 184–90
Secomb's History of Amherst N. H. 783–7
Slaughter's St. Mark's Parish Va. 128
Smith's Founders of Mass. Bay 354–9
Smith's Hist. of Peterborough N. H. 297

Stearns' Hist. of Ashburnham Mass. 906-8
Stevens Genealogy (1891) 12 pages
Temple's Hist. No. Brookfield Mass. 740-3
Thurston's Hist. of Winthrop Me. 197-9
Wheeler's Hist. of Newport N. H. 537-40
Whitehead's Perth Amboy N. J. 143-5
Whitmore's Copps Hill Epitaphs
Willard Genealogy 387-9
Worthen's Hist. of Sutton N. H. 962-4
Wyman's Charlestown Mass. ii, 899-901
Stevenson — American Ancestry iv, 155; v, 150; x, 81
Bartow Genealogical Appendix 187
Hanson's Old Kent Md. 84
Jerseyman (1898) iv, 17-9
Meade's Old Families of Virginia
Mott Genealogy 363
New York Gen. and Biog. Rec. xiii, 117-24
Paige's History of Cambridge Mass. 663
Potts Genealogy (1895) 291-302
Read's History of Swanzey N. H. 457
Salem N. Y. Book of History 45-8
Scott Genealogy 167-82
Slaughter's St. Mark's Parish Va. 168
Stever — American Ancestry ii, 120
Champion Genealogy 100
Steward — Young's Chautauqua 441
Stewart — Adams' Haven Gen. pt. ii, 8
Am. Anc. i, 76; ii, 120; ix, 93; x, 137; xi, 121
Aylsworth Genealogy 468-71
Bullock Genealogy
Burleigh's Guild Genealogy 55
Butler's Hist. of Farmington Me. 576-82
Cassel Genealogy 33-5
Cleveland's Yates County N. Y. 502, 558
Clyde's Irish Settlement in Pa. 131
Davis' History of Bucks Co. Pa. 70
Egle's Penn. Genealogies 2d ed. 645-67
Egle's Notes and Queries 1st ser. i, 31-3; 3d ser. i, 492-4; iii, 442, 467-72, 489; (1898) 185
Gernard's Now and Then iii, 1-5
Freeman's Hist. of Cape Cod Mass. 93, 597
Hanson's Old Kent Md. 263-75
Hubbard's Stanstead County Canada 214
Johnson Genealogy (1895) 121-3
Littell's Passaic Valley Genealogies 406
Meginness' Biographical Annals 234-7
Narragansett Historical Register i, 247
N. Y. Gen. and Biog. Record xxiv, 114-6
Pierce's History of Gorham Me. 209
Plumb's History of Hanover Pa. 479-82
Power's Sangamon Co. Ill. Settlers 686
Ridlon's Harrison Me. Settlers 111-4
Roseboom Genealogy 88-95
Roe's Sketches of Rose N. Y. 53
Savage's Genealogical Dictionary iv, 190
Smith's Hist. Peterborough N. H. 298-300
Stewart Genealogy (1895) 23 pages
Tanner Genealogy 6-9
Updyke's Narragansett Churches 253
Walworth's Hyde Genealogy 750
Watson's Johnson Family (1872)
Wentworth Genealogy i, 243
Wilkesbarre Pa. Hist. Record i, 17
Wyman's Charlestown Mass. Gens. ii, 901

Stichter — Keim Family 424-7
Stickle — American Ancestry ii, 121
Stickler — Whittemore's Orange 276-80
Stickles — American Ancestry ii, 121
Stickney — Amer. Ancestry i, 76; ix, 42
Bouton's History of Concord N. H. 687-9
Brown's History of Whitingham Vt. 165-8
Cochrane's History of Antrim N. H. 693-5
Cutter's History of Jaffrey N. H. 484-90
Driver Genealogy 413-5
Evans Genealogy (1893) 29-32
Gage's History of Rowley Mass. 456-8
Granite Monthly Concord N. H. v, 328-39
Guild's Stiles Genealogy 294
Hayward's History of Hancock N. H. 883
Hazen's History of Billerica Mass. 144-6
Hemenway's Vermont Gaz. v, 145, 713-5
Morrison's History of Windham N. H. 777
Poore Genealogy 37-41, 44-8
Poor's Merrimack Valley Researches 294
Preble Genealogy 254
Savage's Genealogical Dictionary iv, 191
Stearns' Hist. of Ashburnham Mass. 908
Stearns' History of Rindge N. Y. 711-3
Stickney Genealogy (1869) 526 pages
Stickney Family Longevity (1886) 5 pages
Stickney's Hist. of Minnisink N. Y. 171
Washburn's Hist. of Leicester Mass. 404
Woodbury's Sketch of Bradford Mass. 92-5
Stiff — Va. Mag. of History iii, 317-9
Stiger — Chambers' N. J. Germans
Stileman — Savage's Gen. Dict. iv, 192
Stiles — Atkins' Hist. of Hawley Mass. 53
Bulloch Genealogy
Cothren's Woodbury 693-701; ii, 1549-51
Densmore's Hartwell Genealogy
Hubbard Genealogy (1859)
Livermore's Hist. of Wilton N. H. 512-4
Loomis Genealogy (1880) 660-5
Orcutt's History of Stratford Ct. 1296-1301
Perley's History of Boxford Mass. 27
Ridlon's Harrison Me. Settlers 117
Savage's Genealogical Dictionary iv, 193-6
Secomb's History of Amherst N. H. 788
Stiles Family of Mass. (1863) 48 pages
Stiles Family of Mass. (1892) 683 pages
Stiles Family of Conn. (1895) 782 pages
Stiles Family of Kentucky (1896) 46 p.
Stiles' History of Windsor Ct. ii, 700-21
Temple's History of Whately Mass. 269
Stille — American Ancestry iv, 177
N. Y. Gen. and Biog. Record vii, 49-53
Penn. Magazine of Hist. and Biog. iv, 484
Stillman — Alfred Centre N. Y. Sabbath Recorder for March 20, 1890
American Ancestry i, 76; iv, 158
Bangor Me. Historical Magazine v, 27
Goodwin's Foote Genealogy 281-8
Greene Genealogy (1894)
Hinman's Conn. Settlers 1st ed. 239-42
Judd's History of Hadley Mass. 582
New Eng. Hist. and Gen. Register xx, 128
Power's Sangamon Co. Ill. Settlers 687
Savage's Genealogical Dictionary iv, 196
Stillman, Wm., Works (1852) 188 pages

Stillwell — Bergen's Kings Co. 275-82
Clute's History of Staten Island N. Y. 424-6
Stillwell Early Memoirs (1878) 289 pages
Stillwell Genealogy (1883) 62 pages
Stilson — Dwight Genealogy 701-3
Orcutt's History of New Milford Ct. 771
Stimpson — Ballou's Milford 1031-3
Barry's History of Framingham Mass. 396
Bond's Watertown Mass. Genealogies 583
Chandler's History of Shirley Mass. 625
Eton's History of Reading Mass. 114
Eaton's History of Thomaston Me. ii, 418
Pond Genealogy (1875) 22
Savage's Genealogical Dictionary iv, 196
Waldo's History of Tolland Ct. 87
Wyman's Charlestown Mass. ii, 903-5
Stimson — Amer. Anc. v, 10; vi, 99-100
Hubbard's Hist. of Springfield Vt. 442
Norton's Hist. of Fitzwilliam N. H. 725
Stearns' Hist. Ashburnham Mass. 300
Temple's History of Palmer Mass. 541-3
Stinson — Allison Genealogy 94-6
Stark's History of Dunbarton N. H. 196
Stirk — Potter Genealogy (1895) 87
Stirling — Balch's Provincial Pa. 124-8
Stites — American Ancestry xi, 215
Clayton's History of Union Co. N. J. 373-5
Littell's Passaic Valley 407-10
New York Gen. and Biog. Rec. xxviii, 165-7, 237-9; xxix, 93-8
Stith — Goode Genealogy 210-2
Meade's Old Churches of Virginia i, 137
Richmond Va. Standard i, 10
Stitt — Power's Sangamon Co. Ill. 688
St. John — American Ancestry v, 226
Bouton Genealogy 9
Clark Genealogy (1892-7) 161
Cochrane's Hist. Francestown N. H. 944
Hall's Norwalk Ct. 185, 190-5, 204, 223
Ketchum's History of Buffalo N. Y. ii, 234
New Eng. Hist. Gen. Register xiv, 59-61
Phœnix's Whitney Genealogy i, 147
Sedgwick's History of Sharon Ct. 108
Selleck's Norwalk Ct. (1896) 93-6, 324-36
St. John of Bridgeport Biog. (1864) 19 p.
St. John Fam. N. Y. and Ohio (1887) 31 p.
St. John Genealogy (1890) 4 pages
St. John, Will of Samuel of New Haven
Thomas Genealogy (1877) 133
Van Hoosear's Norwalk Ct. Epitaph 9-11
Stoakham — Baird's Rye N. Y. 433
Stobo — Bellinger Genealogy 101
Bullock Genealogy
Stockbridge — American Ancestry iii, 47
Barry's History of Hanover Mass. 384-92
Corliss' North Yarmouth Me. 806-9
Crafts' History of Whately Mass. 585-8
Deane's History of Scituate Mass. 342-4
Hanover Mass. Records (1898)
Savage's Genealogical Dictionary iv, 197
Temple's History of Whately Mass. 269
Winsor's History of Duxbury Mass. 323
Stockett — American Ancestry iii, 120
Stockett Chart by Boogher (1884)
Stockett Gen. by F. Stocket (1892) pamphlet

Stocking — Amer. Anc. i, 76; ix, 23; xii
Goodwin's Olcott Genealogy 53
New Eng. Hist. and Gen. Reg. l, 171-6
Orcutt's History of Torrington Ct. 766
Savage's Genealogical Dictionary iv, 198
Stockman — Dow's Hampton N. H. 985
Spooner Genealogy i, 390
Stockton — Am. Anc. v, 110 vi, 134; xii
Cregar's White Genealogy
Glenn's Colonial Mansions 91-3
Stockton T. J. Life Sketches (1898) 120
Stockton Genealogy (1889) by Cregar, 39 p.
Stockton Genealogy (1881) 70 pages
Stockton Fam. in Eng. U. S. (1888) 39 p.
Stockwell — American Ancestry ix, 217
Benedict's History of Sutton Mass. 729-33
Chandler Genealogy 303
Daniels' History of Oxford Mass. 701-3
Davis Genealogy 175
Hemenway's Vermont Hist. Gaz. v, 190
Lincoln's Hist. of Hingham Mass. iii, 191
Morse's Grout Genealogy 47
Sheldon's Hist. of Deerfield Mass. 328
Tuttle Genealogy 247
Stoddard — Am. Anc. v, 47, 79, 166; ix, 98
Anderson's Waterbury Ct. i, app. 132
Ballou's History of Milford Mass. 1033
Barry's History of Hanover Mass. 392
Cleveland's Hist. of Yates Co. N. Y. 534
Cothren's Woodbury Ct. 713-21; ii, 1553-7
Davis' Landmarks of Plymouth Mass. 253
Draper's History of Spencer Mass. 249
Dwight Genealogy 1030-5
Dwight's Strong Genealogy 308, 534
Gold's History of Cornwall Ct. 283
Goodwin's Foote Genealogy 269
Goodwin's Genealogical Notes 15
Kilbourne Genealogy 172
Kingman's N. Bridgewater Mass. 658
Lincoln's Hist. Hingham Mass. iii, 191-216
New Eng. Hist. Reg. v, 21-6; x, 81; xx, 124
Orcutt's History of Derby Ct. 764-7
Randall's Hist. of Chesterfield N. H. 450-5
Savage's Genealogical Dict. iv, 199-201
Sharpe's History of Seymour Ct. 165-9
Sharpe's South Britain Ct. Sketches 155
Stearns' Hist. of Ashburnham Mass. 912
Stoddard Fam. of Boston (1849) 23 pages
Stoddard Fam. of Boston (1865) 95 pages
Stoddard Fam. of N. London (1872) 36 p.
Stoddard of Wethersfield (1873) 96 pages
Stoddard of Woodbury Ct. (1893) 86 p.
Sumner Genealogy 63
Sumner's History of East Boston Mass. 226
Temple's North Brookfield Mass. 743-6
Tuttle Genealogy 685
Wetmore Genealogy 289-92
Whitmore's Copps Hill Epitaphs
Wyman's Charlestown Mass. Gens. ii, 905
Stodder — Barbour's Low Chart (1890)
Breck Genealogy 43
Deane's History of Scituate 345
Lincoln's Hist. Hingham Mass. iii, 191-216
Savage's Genealogical Dictionary iv, 201
Stokes — Clement's Newtown N. J.
Clement's Report of Collins Heirs 33-46

Davis' History of Bucks County Pa. 611
Meade's Old Families of Virginia
Power's Hist. of Sangamon Co. Ill. 690-2
Virginia Magazine of History vi, 95-9
Warner's Stokes Memories (1892)
Welles' Am. Family Antiquity i, 195-262
Stoliker — American Ancestry ii, 122
Stone — American Ancestry i, 76; iii, 47;
    iv, 103; v, 5, 196, 210; vi, 5, 35, 120,
    131; vii, 11, 266; viii, 33, 64; ix, 166;
    x, 40; xi, 123, 202
Austin's Allied Families 223
Austin's Ancestral Dictionary 57
Austin's R. I. Genealogical Dictionary 192
Aylsworth Genealogy 97, 181, 339-43
Barrus' History of Goshen Mass. 171-6
Barry's Hist. Framingham Mass. 396-413
Bemis' Hist. of Marlboro N. H. 637-42
Bond's Watertown 521-7, 584-91, 950-5
Bradbury's Hist. Kennebunkport Me. 277
Bretz Genealogy 77-81
Butler's History of Groton Mass. 438-40
Chapman's Trowbridge Genealogy 224-6
Cleveland's Hist. of Yates Co. N. Y. 124
Coffin's History of Boscawen N. H. 612-5
Cogswell's Hist. of Henniker N. H. 742
Cutter's History of Arlington Mass. 303
Daniels' History of Oxford Mass. 703-10
Driver Genealogy 237
Eaton's History of Thomaston Me. ii, 418
Emerson's History of Douglas Mass. 205-7
Farnsworth Genealogy (1897) 288-93
Farrow's History of Islesborough Me. 284
Farwell Genealogy 29-34
Fowler's History of Durham Ct. 88
Freeman's Hist. of Cape Cod i, 390; ii, 220
Goodwin's Genealogical Notes 211-4
Green's Early Groton Mass. Settlers 21
Hammatt Papers, Ipswich Mass. 347-51
Hanson's History of Gardiner Me. 169
Hanson's Old Kent Md. 114-8
Harris' Watertown Mass. Epitaphs 50-6
Haven Genealogy 29
Hayden's Weitzel Genealogy (1883)
Hayden's Virginia Genealogies 175
Hayward's Hist. of Hancock N. H. 884-6
Herrick's History of Gardner Mass. 3 1
Heywood's Hist. Westminster Mass. 883
Hodgman's Hist. of Westford Mass. 478
Hudson's Hist. of Lexington Mass. 235-9
Hurlbut Genealogy 429-31
Jackson's History of Newton Mass. 411-5
Kellogg's White Genealogy 37
Lapham's History of Paris Me. 735
Leonard's History of Dublin N. H. 397
Little's History of Weare N. H. 993
Locke Genealogy 51-97
Morse's Sherborn Mass. Settlers 242-4
Nash Genealogy 149
New Eng. Hist. and Gen. Register x, 229;
    xxxvi, 366-8; xlix, 314-6; liii, 345-50
New York Gen. and Biog. Rec. xxvii, 90-4
North's History of Augusta Me. 941
Norton's Hist. of Fitzwilliam N. H. 725-40
Old Northwest Gen. Quarterly ii, 51-3, 103
Orcutt's Hist. of New Milford Ct. 800

Paige's History of Cambridge Mass. 663-6
Paige's History of Hardwick Mass. 508
Pickering Genealogy
Pierce's History of Grafton Mass. 567-9
Power's Sangamon Co. Ill. Settlers 689
Randall's Hist. of Chesterfield N. H. 455-9
Read's History of Swanzey N. H. 459-61
Reed Genealogy 108
Reed's History of Rutland Mass. 145-9
Rice Genealogy
Savage's Genealogical Dictionary iv, 203-10
Sheldon's History of Deerfield Mass. 329
Smith Genealogy (1870)
Stearns' History of Ashburnham 913-6
Stearns' History of Rindge N. H. 713-5
Steele Genealogy (1896)
Stone Family of R. I. (1866) 193 pages
Stone Family Poem (1869) 12 pages
Stone Family of Dorchester (1882) 4 pages
Stone Family of Guilford (1888) 192 pages
Stone Family of Watertown (1892) 78 pages
Stone Ancestry in England (1897) 12 pages
Stone Family of Watertown (1899) 8 pages
Stowe's Hist. of Hubbardston Mass. 350-3
Temple's Hist. N. Brookfield Mass. 746-9
Virginia Magazine of History iii, (1896) 272
Vinton's Upton Genealogy 493-503
Ward's Hist. of Shrewsbury Mass. 423-30
Warren and Clarke Genealogy 143
Warren's History of Waterford Me. 292-5
Washburn's History of Leicester Mass. 398
Wheeler's History of Brunswick Me. 855
Whitmore's Copps Hill Epitaphs
Wyman's Charlestown Mass. ii, 906-10
Stoner — Steiner Gen. (1896) 43-9
Stoning — Little's Weare N. H. 995
Stoors — Walworth's Hyde Gen. 360
Stoothoof — Bergen Gen. 99-101, 145
Nevius Genealogy 158
Storer — American Ancestry x, 154
Bourne's History of Wells Me. 768
Cincinnati Ohio Criterion (1888) ii, 315
Corliss' North Yarmouth Me. 1099-1102
Davis' History of Bucks County Pa. 540
Dows Genealogy 131-7
Eaton's Annals of Warren Me. 629
Morris' Bontecou Genealogy 68-70, 115
New Eng. Hist. and Gen. Reg. vi, 275
Savage's Genealogical Dictionary iv, 210
Wyman's Charlestown Mass. Gens. ii, 910
Storey — American Ancestry v, 136
Storm — American Ancestry ii, 122; iv,
    160; viii, 179
Delamater Genealogy 214-6
Hoffman Genealogy 511-6
Raymond's Tarrytown Monument 166-8
Smith Genealogy (1890) 70
Storrow — Slaughter's St. Marks 122
Wentworth Genealogy i, 513-5
Storrs — American Ancestry v, 97; vi, 27
Champion Genealogy
Cleveland Genealogy (1899) 396-8
Goodwin's Genealogical Notes 215-20
Longmeadow Mass. Centen., 318 app. 88
Oneida Hist. Society Trans. ii, 111-5
Savage's Genealogical Dictionary iv. 211

Storrs Genealogy (1886) 580 pages
Strong Genealogy 1029-31
Story — Cochrane's Antrim N. H. 695
Hammatt Papers, Ipswich Mass. 351-3
Ruttenber's Hist. of Orange Co. N. Y. 392
Savage's Genealogical Dictionary iv, 211-3
Stark's History of Dunbarton N. H. 229
Washington N. H. History 627
Wetmore Genealogy 455-60
Stoughton — Austin's Allied Fams. 225
Clapp's Jones Hill Dorchester Mass. 9-18
Hinman's Connecticut Settlers 1st ed. 242
New Eng. Hist. Gen. Reg. v, 350; xv, 350
Prime's Nelson Genealogy (1886)
Savage's Genealogical Dictionary iv, 213-6
Stiles' Hist. of Windsor Ct. ii, 721-42, 846
Tuttle Genealogy 438
Stout — Cregar's White Genealogy
Hayes' Wells Genealogy 106-10
Penn. Magazine of History v, 88-92
Power's Sangamon Co. Ill. Settlers 692
Salter's Hist. of Monmouth Co. N. J. lvi
Stout Genealogy (1878) pamphlet
Street's Penelope Stout (1897) 8
Stover — American Ancestry xii
Babson's Gloucester Mass. 170
Bangor Me. Historical Magazine v, 210
Eaton's History of Thomaston Me. ii, 419
Stauffer Genealogy (2899) 371 pages
Wheeler's History of Brunswick Me. 855
See also under Staufher
Stow — American Ancestry ix, 230; x, 199
Anderson's Waterbury Ct. i, app. 133
Daniel's History of Oxford Mass. 710
Hartwell Genealogy (1895) 104-27
Hough's Hist. of Lewis County N. Y. 139
Hudson's Hist. Marlborough Mass. 450-4
Kelley Genealogy (1897) 24-8
Kellogg's White Genealogy 39
Middlefield Ct. History
Pierce's History of Grafton Mass. 569-73
Savage's Genealogical Dictionary iv, 216-9
Sears Genealogy 122
Timlow's Southington Ct. Sketches 236
Stowe — American Ancestry v, 76
Baldwin Genealogy 332-4
Eaton's History of Thomaston Me. ii, 419
Ellis' History of Roxbury Mass. 130
Hudson's History of Lexington Mass. 239
Stearns' Hist. of Ashburnham Mass. 916
Stearns' History of Rindge N. H. 715
Stowe's Hist. of Hubbardston Mass. 353-5
Temple's Hist. of N. Brookfield Mass. 749
Temple's History of Palmer Mass. 555
Todd's History of Redding Ct. 222
Tuttle Genealogy 686-95
Wheeler's History of Newport N. H. 540
Stowel — Hill's Dedham Mass. Rec. i
Stowell — Bond's Watertown 591
Jackson's History of Newton Mass. 405-9
Lapham's History of Paris Me. 736-9
Lincoln's Hingham Mass. ii, 16-23
Norton's History of Fitzwilliam N. H. 740
Stearns' Hist. of Ashburnham Mass. 917
Wall's Remin. Worcester Mass. 53-6, 362
Washington N. H. History 628-30

Stower — Washburn's Leicester 399
Wyman's Charlestown Mass. Gens. ii, 911
Stowers — Denny Genealogy
Hoyt's Salisbury Mass. Families 328
Lincoln's Hist. of Hingham Mass. iii, 224
Savage's Genealogical Dictionary iv, 219
Stoyell — Butler's Farmington Me. 582
Strachan — Richmond Standard iii, 23
Straight — Austin's R. I. Gen. Dict. 193
Bailey Genealogy (1895) 41-4
Bond's Watertown Mass. Gens. 592
Stranahan — Stranahan Genealogy (1868)
Strang — American Ancestry vii, 64
Austin's Rhode Island Gen. Dictionary 390
Baird's History of Rye N. Y. 444-6
Bartow Genealogy, part 2
Bolton's Westchester Co. N. Y. ii, 673
New Eng. Hist. and Gen. Reg. xix, 325-9
N. Y. Gen. and Biog. Rec. xxi, 130-9
Robertson's Pocahontas' Descendants
Strassburger — Dotterer's Notes 92-5
Perkiomen Region 90-4
Stratford — Daniel's Oxford Mass. 710
Stratton — America Ancestry xii
Bond's Watertown 592-6
Cregar's Haines Ancestry 15-7
Cutter's History of Jaffrey N. H. 419
Foster Ancestry 21
Hedges' Hist. of East Hampton 335
Hemenway's Vermont Gaz. v, 329-31
Hudson's Hist. of Marlborough Mass. 454
Morse's Sherborn Mass. Settlers 244
Olin Genealogy by Nye (1892) 280-322
Orcutt's History of Stratford Ct. 1301
Paige's History of Cambridge Mass. 666
Penn. Magazine of History xiv, 212
Read's History of Swanzey N. H. 461-3
Reed's History of Rutland Mass. 116
Savage's Genealogical Dictionary iv, 220-2
Stearns' History of Rindge N. H. 717-9
Temple's Hist. of Northfield Mass. 545-50
Whitmore's Copps Hill Epitaphs
Wyman's Charlestown Mass. Gens. ii, 913
Straw — Fiske Family of Amherst 176-8
Little's History of Weare N. H. 996
Strawbridge — Egle's Queries (1897) 47
Power's Sangamon Co. Ill. Settlers 693
Strobridge Genealogy 227-80
Strawn — Roberts' Richland Fams. 164-9
Streator — American Ancestry vii, 35
Street — Amer. Anc. v, 96, 103; ix, 179
Davis' History of Wallingford Ct. 903-5
Dodd's History of East Haven Ct. 153
Emery's Hist. Taunton Ministry i, 155-8
Morris Genealogy (1853) 30-6
New Eng. Hist. and Gen. Reg. xliv, 183-6;
xlvi, 256-67; xlvii, 548-55
Ogden Genealogy (1898) 104-7
Savage's Genealogical Dictionary iv, 222
Smith's History of Rhinebeck N. Y. 197
Street Genealogy (1890) 3 pages
Street Genealogy (1895) 542 pages
Streeter — Adams' Haven Gen. part ii, 7
American Ancestry v, 88
Ballou Genealogy 273
Barry's History of Framingham Mass. 414

Bassett's History of Richmond N. H. 489
Daniels' History of Oxford Mass. 711-3
Dyer's History of Plainfield Mass. 125-7
Hubbard's Hist. of Springfield Vt. 444-6
New Eng. Hist. Gen. Reg. xxxvi, 161-4
Norton's Hist. of Fitzwilliam N. H. 741-3
Paige's History of Cambridge Mass. 666
Randall's Hist. of Chesterfield N. H. 460-4
Read's History of Swanzey N. H. 463
Savage's Genealogical Dictionary iv. 223
Stearns' History of Rindge N. H. 719
Streeter Genealogy (1882) 4 pages, reprint
Streeter Genealogy (1896) 323 pages
Wakefield Genealogy 185-91
Wyman's Charlestown Mass. Gens. ii, 913
Stretch — Shourds' Fenwick 255-67
Stretcher — Kollock Genealogy 25-9
Strettell — Penn. Magazine i, 241; ii, 114
Morris Genealogy (1898) 454
Strever — American Ancestry ii, 122
Huntting's Hist. of Pine Plains N. Y. 382
Stribling — Paxton's Marshall Gen. 55
Strickland — Bangor Magazine iii, 8-11
Power's Sangamon Co. Ill. Settlers 694
Ridlon's Harrison Me. Settlers 110
Savage's Genealogical Dictionary iv, 224
Washburn's Notes on Livermore Me. 37
Washington N. H. History 694
Stringfellow — Slaughter's St. Mark's
Parish, Virginia 158, 171
Stringham — American Ancestry x, 3
Strobridge — Strobridge Genealogy (1891)
Strode — Power's Sangamon Co. Ill.
Settlers 695
Stroh — Rupp Genealogy 156-8
Strong — American Ancestry v, 131; x,
73, 95, 97; xi, 122
Andrews' History of New Britain Ct. 345
Baker Genealogy (1867) 46-8
Cothren's Hist. of Woodbury Ct. ii, 1552
Dwight Genealogy 1085-9
Edwards' Southampton Mass. Add. (1841)
Fowler's Chauncey Mem. 91
Heywood's Hist. Westminster Mass. 884
Hines' Lebanon Ct. Hist. Address 169
Hinman's Connecticut Settlers 1st ed. 243
Hollister's History of Pawlet Vt. 246-8
Huntington Genealogy 167
Judd's History of Hadley Mass. 583
Kellogg's White Genealogy 83
Kulp's Wyoming Valley Families
Leach's Morton Ancestry 92-100
Lee Genealogy (1897) 467-75
Loomis Gen. (1880) 421-47, 538, 791-3,
889-906
N. E. Hist. Reg. viii, 181-3; xxiii, 294-7
Orcutt's History of Torrington Ct. 767
Orford N. H. Centennial 142
Perkins' Old Houses of Norwich Ct. 568
Perry and Strong Memoranda (1878)
Robinson Genealogy, appendix (1859)
Savage's Genealogical Dictionary iv, 224-8
Sedgwick's History of Sharon Ct. 114
Stiles' History of Windsor Ct. ii, 743-8
Strong Genealogy (1871) 1586 pages
Temple's History of Palmer Mass. 556-9

Thompson's Long Island N. Y. ii, 448-58
Tucker's History of Hartford Vt. 462-5
Strother — Gilmer's Georgians 60
Johnston Genealogy (1897) 185-9, 202-4
Meade's Old Families of Virginia
Paxton's Marshall Genealogy 146
Slaughter's St. Mark's Parish Va. 169-71
Southern Hist. Assoc. ii (1898) 149-73
Strother Genealogy (1898) 23 pages
Taylor's Some Notable Families 61-8
Wm. and Mary College Quar. vi, 113, 155
Strothers — Green's Kentucky Families
Stroud — American Ancestry v, 107
Broadhead's Delaware Water Gap 250-4
Strout — Freeman's Cape Cod ii, 630
Milliken's Narraguagus Valley Me. 4
Stackpole's History of Durham Me. 255-9
Strowbridge — Strobridge Gen. 250-8
Temple's Northfield
Struble — Cleveland's Yates Co. 723-5
Chambers' Early Germans of N. J. 508
Strycker — Strycker Gen. (1887) 112 pages
Stryker — American Ancestry iii, 48
Bergen Genealogy 49, 79, 185
Bergen's Kings Co. N. Y. Settlers 287-90
Chambers' Early Germans of N. J. 510
Nevius Genealogy
Oneida Historical Society Trans. ii, 134-6
Stuart — American Ancestry viii, 39
American Historical Register i, 441-5
Austin's Ancestries 53
Cogswell's History of Henniker N. H. 744
Cochrane's History of Antrim N. H. 696-8
De Bow's Review xxvi, 131
Gilmer's Georgians 50
Green's Kentucky Families
Morrison's History of Windham N. H.
778-82
Pearson's Schenectady N. Y. Settlers 179
Peyton's Hist. of Augusta Co. Va. 308-11
Power's Sangamon Co. Ill. Settlers 696
Richmond Va. Standard i, 12
Selleck's Norwalk Ct. (1896) 321-4
Stuart Fam. of Essex Mass. (1894) 180 p.
Stuart Fam. of Penn. (1894) 8 pages
Waddell's Annals of Augusta Co. Va. 192
Wm. and Mary Coll. Quar. vi, 113-6, 155-8
Stubbs — Amer. Ancestry vi, 89; xi, 122
Corliss' North Yarmouth Me. 499, 1026-9
Cregar's Haines Ancestry 52
Pope Genealogy
Power's Sangamon Co. Ill. Settlers 697
Studley — Barry's Hanover 392-9
Deane's History of Scituate Mass. 339
Eaton's Annals of Warren Me. 630
Hanover Mass. Records (1898)
Hobart's Hist. of Abington Mass. 441-3
Lincoln's Hist. Hingham Mass. iii, 225-7
Sedgwick's History of Sharon Ct. 115
Studly — American Ancestry ii, 122
Studwell — Baird's Rye N. Y. 446
Stump — Reily's Life of Cardinal Gibbons
v, 123-8
Stupplebeen — American Ancestry ii, 122
Sturdevant — Corliss' North Yarmouth
Richmond Va. Standard iii, 33

Sturges — Amer. Ancestry i, 77; viii, 205
Dimond Genealogy 32
Freeman's Hist. of Cape Cod Mass. ii, 203, 216, 299
Huntington's Stamford Ct. Families 111
Pierce's History of Gorham Me. 209
Savage's Genealogical Dictionary iv, 229
Schenck's History of Fairfield Ct. 412-4
Sturges Genealogy (1898) 16 pages
Sturges Genealogy 2d ed. (1900) 46 pages
Sturgis — American Ancestry x, 114
Dudley's Archæological Coll. plate 5
Heraldic Journal (1868) iv, 133-6
Olin Genealogy by Nye (1892) 326-34
Sturtevant — Davis' Landmarks 254
Hayward's History of Gilsum N. H. 395
Lapham's History of Paris Me. 740-2
Mitchell's Hist. of Bridgewater Mass. 311
Paige's History of Hardwick Mass. 509
Porter Genealogy (1878) 97
Stutzman — Hertzler Genealogy 217-31
Stuyvesant — New York Historical Society Collections, new series i, 455
Valentine's N Y. Manual (1852) 413
Van Rensselaer's New Yorkers
Styler — Conrad Genealogy 42
Sublett — Page Genealogy 124
Sudam — American Ancestry ii, 123
Sugden — Brown's West Simsbury 121
Sullivan — Bangor Hist. Mag. vi, 277-89
Eaton's History of Thomaston Me. 420
New. Eng. Hist. Gen. Reg. xix, 289-306
Sullivan Family of Berwick Me. (1891) 22 pages
Sullivan Fam. Berwick Me. (1893) 170 p.
Thomas Genealogy (1896) 526
Whitmore's Copps Hill Epitaphs
Wyman's Charlestown Mass. Gens, ii, 914
Sullivant — Paxton's Marshall Gen. 164
Sullivant Biography (1874) 99-184
Summer — Hertzler Genealogy 305-10
Summerill — Shourd's Fenwick 239-43
Summers — American Ancestry xii, 92
Orcutt's Stratford Ct. 1302
Sumner — Allen Genealogy (1896) 69
American Ancestry v, 56, 156; vi, 188
Ammidown Genealogy 41-3
Ballou's History of Milford Mass. 1035-45
Bass' History of Braintree Vt. 185
Bridgeman's Granary Epitaphs 90-4, 96
Draper's History of Spencer Mass. 251
Eaton's Annals of Warren Me. 630
Hill's Dedham Mass. Records
Hudson's History of Lexington Mass. 240
Keim and Allied Families 275
N. E. Hist. and Gen. Reg. viii, 128 d-v; ix, 297-306
Paige's History of Hardwick Mass. 510
Read's History of Swanzey N. H. 465
Ruggles Genealogy
Savage's Genealogical Dictionary iv, 230-2
Slafter Genealogy 73
Sumner Memoirs (1854) 70 pages
Sumner Genealogy (1879) 204 pages
Sumner (Rev. Joseph) Memorial (1888)
Sumner's Hist. of East Boston Mass. 291

Ward's History of Shrewsbury Mass. 439
Wyman's Charlestown Mass. Gens. ii, 915
Sunderland — Freeman's Cape Cod
Savage's Genealogical Dictionary iv, 232
Sunderlin — Cleveland's Yates Co. 151
Frisbie's History of Middletown Vt. 30
Sutherland — Amer. Anc. i, 77; ii, 123
Cleveland's Hist. Yates Co. N. Y. 693, 750
Cleveland Genealogy 215-22
Sutliff — Anderson's Waterbury 133
Orcutt's History of Wolcott Ct. 561
Sheldon's Hist. of Deerfield Mass. 330
Sutliff Genealogy (1897) 50 pages
Sutphen — American Ancestry v, 124
Chambers' Early Germans of N. J. 511
Bergen's Kings County N. Y. Settlers 291
Nevius Genealogy
Sutton — Bolton's Westchester 759
Caldwell Genealogy 73
Chambers' Early Germans of N. J. 512-6
Cleveland's Hist. of Yates Co. N. Y. 507
Deane's History of Scituate Mass. 346
Hubbard's Hist. of Stanstead Co. Can. 335
Kulp's Wyoming Valley Families
Lincoln's Hist. of Hingham Mass. iii, 227
Savage's Genealogical Dictionary iv, 233
Wyman's Charlestown Mass. Gens. ii, 916
Suydam — Bergen Genealogy 111
Bergen's Kings Co. N. Y. Settlers 287-90
Phœnix's Whitney Genealogy i, 120
Riker's Annals of Newtown N. Y. 319-26
Taylor's Great Barrington Mass. 111
Swackhamer — Chambers' Early Germans of New Jersey 517-9
Swaddle — Baker's Montville Ct. 592
Swaffer — Sharpless Genealogy 1239
Smith's History of Delaware Pa. 504
Swain — American Ancestry ii, 123
Austin's Allied Families 227
Cochrane's History of Antrim N. H. 699
Davis' History of Reading Vt. 158-60
Dow's History of Hampton N. H. 985
Eaton's History of Reading Mass. 115-7
Fullonton's Hist. of Raymond N. H. 289
Hinchman's Nantucket Settlers 93
Lapham's History of Rumford Me. 401-3
Runnells' Hist. Sanbornton N. H. ii, 743-8
Savage's Genealogical Dictionary iv, 234-6
Sedgwick's History of Sharon Ct. 115
Swain Tabular Pedigree (1895) 11x17 inches
Swain Genealogy (1896) 137 pages
Wyman's Charlestown Mass. Gens. ii, 917
Swaine — Goode Genealogy 155
Swallow — Dunster Genealogy 225-32
Guild's Stiles Genealogy 295-300
Swaltzlander — Davis' Bucks Co. Pa. 667
Swan — Amer. Ancestry i, 77; ii, 123; xii
Ballou Genealogy 426-9
Bangor Historical Magazine iii, 24; v, 63
Bassett's History of Richmond N. H.
Brook's History of Medford Mass. 541
Cutter's History of Arlington Mass. 304-7
Eaton's Annals of Warren Me. 631
Egle's Penn. Genealogies 2d ed. 668-73
Egle's Notes and Queries 1st ser. i, 154-7
Essex Institute Hist. Collections xxiii, 308

Evans Genealogy (1893) 17–23
Hanson's History of Gardiner Me. 164
Humphrey Genealogy 257–9
Jones Genealogy (1891) 39
Lapham's History of Bethel Me. 620–3
Lapham's History of Paris Me. 742–5
Meade's Old Families of Virginia
New Eng. Hist. and Gen. Reg. x, 44; xxxiii, 403–6
New York Gen. and Biog. Rec. xxix, 213–5 xxx, 10–4, 118–20
North's History of Augusta Me. 941
Paige's History of Cambridge Mass. 667
Richmond Va. Standard iii, 36
Runnells' Hist. Sanbornton N. H. ii, 748
Savage's Genealogical Dictionary iv, 236
Sedgwick's History of Sharon Ct. 115
Sheldon's Hist. of Deerfield Mass. 331
Smith Genealogy (1889) 130
Smith's History of Peterborough N. H. 300–6
Temple's History of Northfield Mass. 551
Tyngsborough Mass. Centennial 15
Washburn's Hist. of Leicester Mass. 401
Winchester Mass. Record ii, 438–59
Wyman's Charlestown Mass. ii, 917–20
Swart — American Ancestry i, 77
Bergen's Kings Co. N. Y. Settlers 294–6
Munsell's Albany Collections iv, 170
Pearson's Schenectady Settlers 179–84
Swartout — Stickney's Minisink 134
Swarts — Chambers' N. J. Germans
Swartwout — Amer. Anc. iii, 49; viii, 27
Gumaer's History of Deerpark N. Y. 50–3
Schoonmaker's Hist. Kingston N. Y. 489
Sylvester's Hist. of Ulster Co. N. Y. 46
Swayne — Appleton's Baker Ancestry 131
Salisbury's Family Hist. (1892) ii, 355–61
Sharpless Genealogy 189, 305
Swazey — Chambers' N.J. Germans 519–24
Swearingen — Swearingen Gen. (1884)
Swearingen Genealogy 2d ed. (1894) 80 p.
Tiernan Genealogy 12–28
Sweat — Lapham's Bethel Me. 623
Lapham's History of Rumford Me. 403
Sweatt — Little Genealogy 235–7
Sweeney — Eaton's Thomaston ii, 420
Sweet — Amer. Ancestry ii, 123; viii, 28
Austin's R. I. Genealogical Dictionary 194
Bassett's History of Richmond N. H. 494
Butler's History of Farmington Me. 634
Champion Genealogy 63
Coffin's History of Newbury Mass. 319
Greene Genealogy
Hazard's Old Times in R. I. (1879) 291 p.
Pompey N. Y. Reunion 352–60
Power's Sangamon Co. Ill. Settlers 698
Savage's Genealogical Dictionary iv, 238
Sheldon's Hist. of Deerfield Mass. 332
Sweet Family of Vermont (1898) 21 pages
Thurston's History of Winthrop Me. 199
Walworth's Hyde Genealogy 502–6
Washington N. H. History 630–3
Sweetland — Eaton's Thomaston 421
Sweetland Genealogy (1890) 30 pages

Sweetser — Bemis' History of Marlboro N. H. 642
Corliss' N. Yarmouth Me. 1092–5, 1138–42
Johnson Genealogy (1876) 5–9
Norton's Hist. of Fitzwilliam N. H. 742–4
Poor's Merrimack Valley Researches 112
Savage's Genealogical Dictionary iv, 239
Whitmore's Copps Hill Epitaphs
Wyman's Charlestown Mass. Gens. ii, 921
Sweezey — Dickerman Genealogy 408–11
Sweitzer — Hayden's Sweitzer Memorial
Kratz Genealogy 195–208
Swell — Thomas Genealogy (1896) 482
Swetland — Longmeadow Centennial 89
Sedgwick's History of Sharon Ct. 115
Swetland Narrative and Gen. (1875) 42 p.
Swett — Bangor Historical Magazine v, 16
Bedford N. H. Centennial 339
Cochrane's History of Antrim N. H. 701
Corliss' North Yarmouth Me.
Dearborn's Hist. of Salisbury N. H. 803
Dow's History of Hampton N. H. 987–9
Eaton's History of Thomaston Me. ii, 421
Lapham's History of Paris Me. 745
Maine Hist. and Gen. Recorder vi, 313
New Eng. Hist. and Gen. Reg. vi, 49–62
Pierce's History of Gorham Me. 210
Savage's Genealogical Dictionary iv, 239
Swett Genealogy (1851) 26 pages
Wheeler's History of Brunswick Me. 855
Swift — Allen's Worcester Mass. 41
American Ancestry ii, 123; iii, 6, 225; v, 156; vi, 180; viii, 197; xi, 156
Balch's Provincial Papers 90–3
Barry's History of Framingham Mass 414
Crafts' History of Whately Mass. 588–90
Davis' Landmarks of Plymouth Mass. 255
Eatons' Annals of Warren Me. 631
Eaton's History of Thomaston Me. ii, 421
Freeman's Cape Cod ii, 150–4, 478–83
Hatch's History of Industry Me. 817–9
Hinchman's Nantucket Settlers 100–4
Jessup Genealogy 139–42
Kellogg's White Genealogy 98
Kollock Genealogy 38–41, 51–9
Lapham's History of Norway Me. 606
Lapham's History of Paris Me. 746–9
Mitchell's Hist. Bridgewater Mass. 311
Orcutt's History of Derby Ct. 767
Penn. Magazine of History vi, 329–33
Ransom Genealogy 56–8
Savage's Genealogical Dictionary iv, 241
Swift (Joseph G.) Memoirs (1890) 370 p.
Temple's History of Whately Mass. 270
Walworth's Hyde Genealogy 940–3
Whitmore's Copps Hill Epitaphs
Swinington — Cochrane's Francestown 944
Swinney — Sharpless Genealogy 540
Swisher — Mageniss Genealogy 70–2
Swits — American Ancestry vii, 130
Munsell's Albany Collections iv, 170
Pearson's Schenectady Settlers 184–7
Swoope — Saunders' Alabama 203
Swope Genealogy (1896) 400 pages
Swords — American Ancestry xi, 38
New York Gen. Biog. Rec. i, 10–2

Sykes — Saunders' Alabama Sett. 257–60
Savage's Gen. Dict. iv, 95
Sylvester — Barry's Hanover 400–8
Briggs' History of Shipbuilding 66–8
Davis' Landmarks of Plymouth Mass. 256
Deane's History of Scituate Mass. 347–50
Eaton's History of Thomaston Me. ii, 421
Hanover Mass. Records (1898)
Kingman's No. Bridgewater Mass. 649
Magazine of American History xvii, 361
Mallman's Shelter Island N. Y. 177
Mitchell's Hist. of Bridgewater Mass. 293
Savage's Genealogical Dict. iv, 98–100
Stackpole's History of Durham Me. 259–61
Washburn's History of Leicester Mass. 402
Wheeler's History of Brunswick Me. 854
Winsor's Hist. of Duxbury Mass. 324
Wood's Hist. of Long Island N. Y. 192–4
Syme — Meade's Old Families of Va.
Richmond Va. Standard ii, 39, 40; iii, 40
Slaughter's Bristol Parish Va. 40
Slaughter's St. Mark's Parish Va. 187
Symes — N. Y. Gen. Biog. Rec. v, 1–4
Symmes — Brook's Medford Mass. 542
Cleveland's Southold L. I. Records 193
Cogswell Genealogy 86–8
Cutter's History of Arlington Mass. 307
Davis' Landmarks of Plymouth Mass. 257
Hodgman's History of Westford Mass. 478
Keith's Harrison Ancestry 83–5
Locke Genealogy 39, 71
N. E. Hist. Reg. xiii, 135–7; xxxviii, 199
Savage's Genealogical Dictionary iv, 242–4
Symmes Genealogy (1873) 184 pages
Whitman Genealogy 298–301
Wyman's Charlestown Mass. ii, 927–31
Symonds — Babson's Gloucester 169
Baker Ancestry by Appleton 19–102
Goodwin's Olcott Genealogy 32
Hammatt Papers, Ipswich Mass. 355–66
Hayward's Hist. of Hancock N. H. 886–95
Perley's History of Boxford Mass. 39
Pickering Genealogy
Savage's Genealogical Dictionary iv, 244–7
Stearns' History of Rindge N. H. 720–3
Whitmore's Heraldic Journal i, 42–5
Tabb — American Ancestry vi, 125
Goode Genealogy 195
Hayden's Virginia Genealogies 477
Lee Genealogy (1895) 382
Meade's Old Families of Virginia
Richmond Va. Standard iii, 31, 43
Wm. and Mary College Quarterly vii, 45–9
Taber — Austin's R. I. Gen. Dict. 195
Freeman's Hist. of Cape Cod Mass. 180
Griffin's Journal Southold N. Y. 143–7
Spooner Genealogy i, 77–81
Spooner's Memorial of W. Spooner 65–8
Tabor — McKeen's Bradford Vt. 260–3
Savage's Genealogical Dictionary iv, 247
Washington N. H. History 633–6
Williams' History of Danby Vt. 269
Tackler — Temple's Palmer Mass. 562
Taft — Am. Ancestry v, 26; vi, 121, 167
Austin's Allied Families 229–31
Ballou's History of Milford Mass. 1047–9

Bassett's Hist. of Richmond N. H. 496–9
Capron Genealogy by Holden 232–4
Caverly's History of Pittsford Vt. 727
Chapin Genealogy
Chapin's Uxbridge Mass. Address 170–4
Crane's Rawson Genealogy 40–3
Daniels' History of Oxford Mass. 714
Guild's Stiles Genealogy 399
Guild's (Calvin) Ancestry 9
Hayward's Hancock N. H. 706, 896–7
Heywood's Hist. Westminster Mass. 884
Norton's History of Fitzwilliam N. H.
744–6
Power's Sangamon Co. Ill. Settlers 699
Read's History of Swanzey N. H. 465–8
Smith's Hist. of Sunderland Mass. 554
Taft Family Meeting (1874) 103 pages
Taft Family Meeting (1891) 28 pages
Temple's History of Palmer Mass. 559–61
Taggard — Hartwell Gen. (1895) 161–4
Taggart — Smith's Peterborough 306
Tailer — Clapp's Jones Hill 19–45
Prime's Nelson Genealogy 50
Tainter — Bond's Watertown 596–8, 956
Brown's History of Whitingham Vt. 181–3
Hemenway's Vermont Hist. Gaz. v, 719
Hudson's Hist. of Marlborough Mass. 450
Pierce's History of Grafton Mass. 573
Taintor — Am. Ancestry iii, 49; vii, 47
Goodwin's Foote Genealogy 52, 178, 196
Loomis Genealogy (1880) 195–220
New Eng. Hist. and Gen. Reg. iii, 155
Savage's Genealogical Dictionary iv, 248
Sheldon's Hist. of Deerfield Mass. 333
Taintor Fam. of Fairfield Ct. (1847) 82 p.
Taintor Fam. Watertown Mass.(1859) 100 p.
Tait — Goode Genealogy 254
Talbot — American Ancestry xi, 229
Bangor Historical Mag. i, 73–9; viii, 180
Bond's Hist. of Watertown Mass. 529–32
Cochrane's Hist. Francestown N. H. 945
Davis' Landmarks of Plymouth Mass. 258
Garrard Genealogy 82–6
Hill's Dedham Mass. Records i
Meade's Old Families of Virginia
Missouri Pioneer Families 295
N. E. Hist. and Gen. Register ix, 129–31
Pompey N. Y. Reunion 360
Pope Genealogy 315
Power's Sangamon Co. Ill. Settlers 700-2
Read's History of Swanzey N. H. 468
Sharpless Genealogy 275, 413–6
Thomas Genealogy (1877)
Thomas Genealogy (1896) 527
Talcott — Am. Anc. i, 77; iii, 50; iv, 104
Glastenbury Ct. Centennial 168
Hollister Genealogy 43–8
Middlefield Ct. History
New Eng. Hist. Reg. xx, 129; xxi, 215–7
Root Genealogy 263
Savage's Genealogical Dictionary iv, 250–2
Talcott Genealogy (1876) 316 pages
Taliaferro — Amer. Ancestry ix, 88
Clarke's Old King Wm. Co. Va. Families
Marshall Genealogy 83–6, 195–200, 313–5
Meade's Old Families of Virginia

Richmond Va. Standard ii, 47; iii, 31, 32, 35, 44, 50; iv, 19, 23
Saunders' Alabama Settlers 250, 512
Tallett — Tuttle Genealogy 245-9
Tallmadge — American Ancestry i, 77
Dwight Genealogy 1111
Huntington Stamford Ct. Settlers 111
Huntting's Hist. of Pine Plains N. Y. 384
Nash Genealogy 23
Orcutt's History of Torrington Ct. 768
Ransom Genealogy 58
Thompson's Long Island N. Y. ii, 461-3
Talman — William and Mary College Historical Register iii, 101-4
Tallman — Austin's Allied Fams. 232-4
Austin's R. I. Genealogical Dictionary 196
Savage's Genealogical Dictionary iv, 252
Talmadge — Hedge's History of Easthampton N. Y. 336-42
Howell's Southampton N. Y. 2d ed. 392-4
Savage's Genealogical Dictionary iv, 252
Talmage — Amer. Ancestry x, 106
Tambling — Matthews' Cornwall 290
Tandy — Dearborn's Salisbury N. H. 804
Hayward's Hancock N. H. 897
Anisenberry Genealogy
Washington N. H. History 636
Tannehill — Ashland County Ohio 275
Tanner — Am. Ancestry ii, 124; ix, 41
Tanner Genealogy (1893) 110 pages
Young's History of Warsaw N. Y. 337-9
Tapley — Amer. Ancestry x, 133
Livermore's History of Wilton N. H. 514
Savage's Genealogical Dictionary iv, 253
Wyman's Charlestown Mass. Gens. ii, 931
Wyman's Hunt Genealogy 299
Taplin — Hubbard's Stanstead 190
Tappan — American Ancestry v, 212
Bridgeman's Granary Epitaphs 371-7
Hoyt's Salisbury Mass. Families 330-2
North's History of Augusta Me. 943
Salisbury Family Memorials (1885) 67
Savage's Genealogical Dictionary iv, 253-6
Tappan (Mrs. Sarah) Memoir (1834) 124-32
Tappan Genealogy (1884) 126 pages
Tappan (Rev. D. D.) Biog. (1890) 28 pages
See also under Toppen
Tappen — Schoonmaker's Kingston 489
Tarbell — Bass' Braintree Vt. 186
Bond's Watertown Mass. Gens. 598-601
Butler's History of Groton Mass. 440, 480
Cochrane's Hist. Francestown N. H. 946
Dunster Genealogy 173
Farnsworth Genealogy (1897) 158, 173-5
Green's Early Groton Mass. Settlers 21-4
Green's Groton Mass. Epitaphs 255-8
Hayward's Hist. Hancock N. H. 898-901
Hazen's History of Billerica Mass. 147
Heywood's Hist. Westminster Mass. 885
Hill's History of Mason N. H. 206
Hyde's Hist. of Brimfield Mass. 458-60
Livermore's History of Wilton N. H. 515
Stearns' History of Rindge N. H. 723-5
Tarbox — American Ancestry xii
Bemis' Hist. of Marlboro 644
Eaton's Thomaston Me. 423

Hanson's History of Gardiner Me. 108
New Eng. Hist. and Gen. Reg. xlii, 27-39
Savage's Genealogical Dictionary iv, 256
Stiles' History of Windsor Ct. ii, 748
Tarlton — Savage's Gen. Dict. iv, 256
Tarr — Babson's Gloucester Mass. 170
Eaton's History of Thomaston Me. ii, 423
Savage's Genealogical Dictionary iv, 257
Vinton's Giles Genealogy 536
Wheeler's History of Brunswick Me. 854
Tasker — American Ancestry viii, 170
Cogswell's Hist. Nottington N. H. 772-8
Tate — Eaton's Thomaston Me. ii, 423
Goode Genealogy 77
Peyton's History of Augusta Co. Va. 312
Waddell's Annals of Augusta Co. Va. 192
Wentworth Genealogy ii, 473
Tatman — American Ancestry ix, 172
Totman Genealogy (1895) 32 pages
Tatnall — Rodman Genealogy 144-9, 221
Tator — American Ancestry ii, 124
Tatum — Clarke's King Wm. Va. Fams.
Goode Genealogy 478
Tayer — Austin's R. I. Gen. Dict. 197
Tayloe — Meade's Va. Churches ii, 181
Taylor — Alden Genealogy 54
Alexander Genealogy 180-8
American Ancestry i, 78; ii, 124; iii, 218; v, 16, 66; vi, 3, 136; vii, 135, 208; ix, 51, 116, 186, 219; x, 117, 172; xi, 123-4; xii
Anderson's Waterbury Ct. i, app. 134
Andrew's History of New Britain Ct. 236
Atkins' History of Hawley Mass. 64
Atlantic Monthly for July 1878
Austin's R. I. Genealogical Dictionary 197
Ball's History of Lake County Ind. 379-84
Bangor Me. Historical Magazine iv, 16
Bassett's Hist. of Richmond N. H. 499-501
Benedict's History of Sutton Mass. 733
Brown's West Simsbury Ct. Settlers 124
Carter Family Tree of Virginia
Chatham Mass. Monitor June 6 and Sept. 19, 1882
Chute Genealogy, appendix 206-13
Cleveland's Yates Co. N. Y. 319-21, 559
Clute's History of Staten Island N. Y. 427
Cochrane's History of Antrim N. H. 702-5
Cochrane's Hist. Francestown N. H. 947-9
Cushman's Hist. of Sheepscott Me. 420-6
Daniels' History of Oxford Mass. 715
Darlington Gathering 25
Davis' History of Bucks County Pa. 136
Davis' Landmarks of Plymouth Mass. 258
Dow's History of Hampton N. H. 989-93
Dwight Genealogy 366-84
Eaton's History of Reading Mass. 117
Eaton's History of Thomaston Me. ii, 423
Ellis Genealogy 392
Ely Genealogy 140
Fox's History of Dunstable Mass. 250
Freeman's Hist. of Cape Cod Mass. ii, 207
Futhey's History of Chester Co. Pa. 737-9
Gilmer's Georgians 217
Goodwin's Foote Genealogy
Green's Kentucky Families

Hall's Norwalk Ct. 117, 120, 128, 177, 184
Harris' History of Lancaster Co. Pa. 608
Hayden's Virginia Genealogies 671–84
Hayward's History of Gilsum N. H. 397
Hayward's Hist. of Hancock N. H. 901–10
Hemenway's Vermont Hist. Gaz. v, 186
Heywood's Hist. Westminster Mass. 885–7
Hubbard's Hist. of Springfield Vt. 460–4
Hubbard's Stanstead Co. Canada 173, 282
Hudson's Hist. of Marlborough Mass. 455
Hudson's Hist. of Sudbury Mass. 450
Judd's History of Hadley Mass. 583–5
Kidder's Hist. of New Ipswich N. H. 434
Lee Genealogy (1895) 530
Leland Genealogy 75
Lewis Genealogy (1893) 376–8
Little's History of Weare N. H. 997
Longmeadow Mass. Centennial, app. 89
Maris Genealogy 87
Martin's History of Chester Pa. 162
Meade's Old Churches of Virginia ii, 98
Miller's Hist. Colchester Co. N. S. 108–11
Morrison Genealogy 272
Morrison's History of Windham N. H. 782
Newfane Vt. Centennial 174–6
N. E. Hist. Gen. Reg. ii, 395; xx, 128, 237
Newport R. I. Historical Mag. ii, 243–9
North's History of Augusta Me. 944–6
Norton's Hist. of Fitzwilliam N. H. 746–8
Orcutt's History of New Milford Ct. 773–6
Orcutt's History of Torrington Ct. 769
Page Genealogy 241
Paige's History of Hardwick Mass. 511
Painter's Reminiscence (1871) 1–4
Palmer and Trimble Genealogy
Parker's Hist. Londonderry N. H. 298–300
Paxton's Marshall Genealogy 183
Pott's Carter Genealogy 113
Power's Sangamon Ill. Settlers 702–10
Randall's Hist. of Chesterfield N. H. 465
Richmond Va. Standard ii, 7; iii, 16, 17,
23; iv, 1, 25
Runnells' Sanbornton N. H. ii, 748–73
Savage's Genealogical Dict. iv, 259–65
Secomb's History of Amherst N. H. 789
Sedgwick's History of Sharon Ct. 115
Sharpless Genealogy 156, 163, 451
Sheldon's Hist. Deerfield Mass. ii, 333–45
Slaughter's St. Mark's Parish Va. 172
Smith's Hist. of Delaware Co. Pa. 505–7
Smith's Hist. of Sunderland Mass. 555–8
Stearns' Hist. Ashburnham Mass. 918–22
Stiles' Hist. of Windsor Ct. ii, 749
Taylor Fam. Deerfield Mass. (1859) chart
Taylor Family of New Jersey (1861) 9 p.
Taylor Family of Saratoga (1886) 88 pages
Taylor Fam. of Kennet Pa. (1891) chart
Taylor, Life of Henry B. Taylor (1892)
Taylor Family of Virginia (1898) 110 pages
Temple's Hist. of Northfield Mass. 553–6
Temple's History of Palmer Mass. 564
Temple's History of Whately Mass. 270
Ward's History Shrewsbury Mass. 445–8
Washburn's History of Leicester Mass. 405
Washington N. H. History 637–9
White's Hist. Disc. Charlemont Mass. 41

Whittemore's Orange N. J. 411
Worcester's History of Hollis N. H. 389
Wyman's Charlestown Mass. ii, 932–4
Young's Chautauqua Co. N. Y. 509, 569
Tazewell — Grigsby's Life of Tazewell
Meade's Old Churches of Virginia i, 480
Richmond Va. Standard ii, 34
Robertson's Pocahontas' Descendants
Teackle — Clarke's King Wm. Families
Hanson's Old Kent Md. 311–3
Teague — Eaton's Hist. of Warren Me. 632
Lincoln's Hist. of Hingham Mass. iii, 229
Teal — Cutter's Arlington Mass. 307–9
Wyman's Charlestown Mass. ii, 934–7
Teall — Teall Genealogy (1889) 7 pages
Teaton — Amer. Ancestry i, 78; ii, 124
Teats — Chambers' N. J. Germans 322–5
Tebbetts — American Ancestry ii, 124
Tebbitts — N. E. Hist. Reg. viii, 130–2
Tebbs — Paxton's Marshall Genealogy 367
Teed — Tuttle Genealogy 256
Teel — Chambers' N. J. Germans 524
Teeple — Chambers' N. J. Germans
Teetor — American Ancestry vii, 253
Cincinnati Ohio Criterion (1888) iii, 752
Tefft — Austin's R. I. Gen. Dict. 392
Tifft Genealogy (1896) 9–38
Teller — Bergen's Kings Co. N. Y. 297
Bolton's Westchester Co. N. Y. ii, 760
Munsell's Albany Collections iv, 170
New York Gen. Rec. ii, 139; ix, 153–60
Pearson's Schenectady N. Y. Sett. 188–90
Temple — American Ancestry i, 78; ii, 124;
xi, 51, 124
Barry's History of Framingham Mass. 416
Bemis' History of Marlboro N. H. 645
Blood's History of Temple N. H. 268–79
Cochrane's History of Antrim N. H. 705
Coffin's History of Boscawen N. H. 617
Cogswell's History of Henniker N. H. 746
Cooley's Trenton N. J. Gens. 266–9
Eaton's History of Reading Mass. 117–9
Fox's History of Dunstable Mass. 250
Hayward's History of Gilsum N. H. 398
Hemenway Genealogy 10
Hemenway's Vt. Historical Gazette v, 90
Heraldic Journal i, 92–4; ii, 185–90; iii, 43
Herrick's History of Gardner Mass. 382–4
Heywood's Hist. Westminster Mass. 887
Hudson's History of Marlborough Mass.
457
Keyes' West Boylston Mass. Register 35
New Eng. Hist. and Gen. Reg x, 73–7
Richmond Va. Standard iv, 2
Savage's Genealogical Dictionary iv, 266
Sheldon's Hist. of Deerfield Mass. 345
Temple Genealogy (1856) 15 pages
Temple Genealogy (1871) 22 pages
Temple Genealogy (1887) 100 pages
Temple Genealogy (1894) 111 pages
Temple Genealogy (1896) 146 pages
Temple Genealogy (1899) 239 pages
Temple Genealogy (1900) 316 pages
Temple's History of Whately Mass. 271
Ward's Hist. of Shrewsbury Mass. 448–51
Wyman's Charlestown Mass. Gens. ii, 937

Templeton — Chase's Chester N. H. 597
Cochrane's History of Antrim N. H. 705-7
Morrison's Hist. of Windham N. H. 783-5
Smith's Hist. Peterborough N. H. 307-10
Strong Genealogy 636
Ten Broeck — American Ancestry i, 78; ii, 124; iii, 50
Munsell's Albany Collections iv, 171
New York Genealogical and Biographical Record xvi, 153-7; xix, 69-76; xx, 122-31, 150-60; xxv, 80-2; xxx, 124
Schoonmaker's Hist. Kingston N. Y. 489
Talcott's N. Y. and N. E. Families 450
Ten Broeck Gen. by Jackson (1886) 12 p.
Ten Broeck Genealogy (1897) 277 pages
Ten Eyck — American Ancestry i, 78-9
Bergen's Kings County N. Y. Settlers 297
Munsell's Albany Collections iv, 171
New York Gen. and Biog. Rec. i, 31
Pearson's Schenectday N. Y. Settlers 191
Roome Genealogy 96
Schoonmaker's Hist. Kingston N. Y. 490
Talcott's N. Y. and N. E. Families 228-52
Tennant — Austin's R. I. Gen. Dict. 198
Loomis Genealogy (1880) 927-33
Tenney — Amer. Ancestry i, 80; iii, 148
Atwood Genealogy (1889)
Ballou's History of Milford Mass. 1049-51
Bangor Me. Historical Magazine v, 212
Bemis' History of Marlboro N. H. 646-54
Benedict's History of Sutton Mass. 734
Chandler's Genealogy 210
Chase's History of Chester N. H. 598
Cochrane's History of Antrim N. H. 708-9
Essex Institute Hist. Collections xxiv, 43
Gage's History of Rowley Mass. 458
Hayward's History of Hancock N. H. 910-22
Little's History of Weare N. H. 998
Mills Genealogy (1893) 5-7
Poor's Merrimack Valley Researches 79
Runnells' Hist. Sanbornton N. H. ii, 773
Savage's Genealogical Dictionary iv, 267
Spooner Genealogy i, 199-201
Stark's History of Dunbarton N. H. 250
Stearns' Hist. of Ashburnham Mass. 921
Stone's Hist. of Hubbardston Mass. 356
Temple's History of Palmer Mass. 561
Tenney Genealogy (1875) 76 pages
Tenney Genealogy (1891) 369 pages
Wheeler's Hist. of Newport N. H. 544-6
Woodbury's Sketches Bradford Mass. 95-7
Woodbury's Groveland Mass. Epitaphs 92-8
Worcester's History of Hollis N. H. 389
Terbell — Howell's Southampton 394
Terhune — Bergen Genealogy 106
Bergen's Kings County N. Y. Settlers 298
Clayton's Bergen Co. N. J. 254
N. Y. Gen. and Biog. Record xi, 159-67
Terpening — Sylvester's Ulster Co. 142
Terrell — Anderson's Waterbury 134-6
Humphrey Genealogy 207
Lewis Genealogy (1893) 344-58
Slaughter's St. Mark's Parish Va. 124
Terren — Cochrane's Francestown 950

Terrill — Cothren's Woodbury Ct. 721
Hubbard's Stanstead Co. Canada 139-41
Littell's Passaic Valley Gens. 411
Orcutt's Hist. of New Milford Ct. 779-82
Terry — Am. Anc. ii, 125; vi, 20; vii, 138
Chambers' Early Germans of N. J. 525
Davis Genealogy (1888) 135-57
Dwight Genealogy 292-9, 365
Goodwin's Genealogical Notes 221-3
Griffin's Journal Southold 116-23; 213-5
Hinman's Connecticut Settlers 1st ed. 176
Kellogg Genealogy, supp. (1899) 3-9
Livermore's Block Island R. I. 296-301
Meade's Old Families of Virginia
Savage's Genealogical Dict. iv, 268-70
Stiles' History of Windsor Ct. ii, 750-2
Strong Genealogy 596
Terry Genealogy (1887) 349 pages
Terryberry — Chambers' N. J. Germans
Terwilliger — Pearson's Schenectady
Tetherly — American Ancestry ii, 125
Teunis — Bergen's Kings Co. N. Y. 300
Tew — Austin's R. I. Gen. Dict. 394
Austin's Allied Families 236
Tewksbury — Cogswell's New Boston
Little's History of Weare N. H. 998
Stark's History of Dunbarton N. H. 255
Thacher — American Ancestry i, 80; xii
Eaton's History of Thomaston Me. ii, 424
Hall's Norwalk Ct. Records 224, 243, 261
N. E. Magazine (1834) vii, 1-16 reprint
N. E. Hist. and Gen. Reg. clxx, 171; xliii
Pierce's History of Gorham Me. 210
Richmond Va. Standard iii, 43
Roseboom Genealogy 82-7
Selleck's Norwalk Ct. (1896) 449-69
Robinson's Items of Ancestry (1894) 6
Thacher Genealogy (1872) 92 pages
Thacher Ancestry in Eng. (1885) 6 pages
Waldo's Thacher Sermon (1869) 36 pages
Winsor's History of Duxbury Mass. 325
Thackara — Clement's Newtown N. J.
Thacker — Hayden's Virginia Gens. 236
Thatcher — Bangor Hist. Mag. ii, 220
Bemis' Hist. of Marlboro N. H. 655-8
Bond's Watertown Mass. Genealogies 601
Brigg's Thatcher Memoir (1883) 8 pages
Davis' Landmarks of Plymouth Mass. 258
Eaton's Annals of Warren Me. 632
Eaton's History of Thomaston Me. ii, 425
Farnsworth Genealogy (1897) 284-7
Freeman's Hist. of Cape Cod i, 142; ii, 194
Whitmore's Heraldic Journal iv, 75-80
Hines' Lebanon Ct. Hist. Address 170
Hughes Genealogy 111-3
New Eng. Hist. and Gen. Register xiii, 245-7; xiv, 11; xxxvii, 12-4
Orcutt's History of New Milford Ct. 812
Paige's History of Cambridge Mass. 669
Palmer and Trimble Genealogy 177-81
Savage's Genealogical Dictionary iv, 270-4
Sharpless Genealogy 344
Slafter Genealogy 45
Wheeler's History of Newport N. H. 546
Thaxter — American Ancestry vii, 38
Hobart's History of Abington Mass. 444

Lincoln's Hist. Hingham Mass. iii, 229-39
Machias Me. Centennial 177
Pope Genealogy 328
Savage's Genealogical Dictionary iv, 274
Wheeler and Thaxter Gen. (1898) 74 pages
Thayer — Allen's Worcester Mass. 181
American Ancestry i, 81; ii, 125; v, 80; vi, 171; vii, 9; viii, 16
Austin's Allied Families 241
Austin's Ancestral Dictionary 58
Ballou Genealogy 234-7, 407-11
Ballou's History of Milford Mass. 1051-93
Bass' History of Braintree Vt. 186-9
Bassett's Hist. of Richmond N. H. 502-7
Blake's History of Franklin Mass. 278
Capron Genealogy by Holden 211-4
Cleveland's Hist. of Yates Co. N. Y. 704-6
Davis' Landmarks of Plymouth Mass. 259
Eaton's History of Thomaston Me. ii, 423
Emmerson's Hist. Douglas Mass. 173-84
Hayward's History of Hancock N. H. 922
Jameson's History of Medway Mass. 524
Kingman's North Bridgewater Mass. 665
Lapham's History of Paris Me. 749-52
Lincoln's Hist. Hingham Mass. iii, 239-41
Mitchell's Hist. of Bridgewater Mass. 312
Montague Genealogy 480
Morrison's Hist. of Windham N. H. 785-7
New Eng. Hist. and Gen. Reg. xiii, 335
Paige's History of Hardwick Mass. 512
Power's Sangamon Co. Ill. Settlers 710
Savage's Genealogical Dictionary iv, 275-8
Smith's Hist. of Peterborough N. H. 310-6
Thayer Memorial (1835) 280 pages
Thayer Genealogy (1874) 708 pages
Thayer Ancestry (1890) 58 pages
Thayer Ancestors (1894) 180 pages
Thayer Fam. of Taunton (1896) 69 pages
Vinton Genealogy 355-65
Wyman's Charlestown Mass. Gens. ii, 939
Theall — Baird's Hist. of Rye N. Y. 447
Thing — Bell's Exeter N. H. 45-7
Dudly Genealogy 135
Hatch's History of Industry Me. 819
Wentworth Genealogy i, 201
Thissell — Washington N. H. Hist. 639.
Thoburn — Amer. Ancestry viii, 133
Thoits — Corliss' North Yarmouth Me.
Thom — Allison Genealogy 48-50
Morrison Genealogy 91
Morrison's Hist. of Windham N. H. 787-99
Thomas — American Ancestry ii, 125; v, 121-207; vii, 149; viii, 101; xi, 180, 189; vii, 85; viii, 39, 47, 57, 181; x, 26, 37, 103; xii
Anderson's Waterbury Ct. i, app. 136
Austin's R. I. Genealogical Dictionary 198
Aylsworth Genealogy 84, 136, 278
Baird's History of Rye N. Y. 492
Bolton's Westchester Co. N. Y. ii, 760
Boyd's History of Conesus N. Y. 172
Brigg's History of Shipbuilding 147-75
Brown's West Simsbury Ct. Settlers 124
Butler's Hist. of Farmington Me. 583
Chambers' Early Germans of N. J. 527
Claverly's History of Pittsford Vt. 727
Clermont County Ohio History 330
Cleveland's Hist. of Yates Co. N. Y. 519

Cothren's Woodbury Ct. 722; ii, 1561
Cunnabell Genealogy 87-9
Daniels' History of Oxford Mass. 715
Davis' Landmarks of Plymouth 259-62
Dow's History of Hampton N. H. 993
Eaton's Annals of Warren Me. 633
Eaton's Hist. of Thomaston Me. ii, 425-7
Egle's History of Lebanon Co. Pa. 254-6
Egle's Penn. Genealogies 2d ed. 674-93
Farrow's History Islesborough Me. 284-7
Futhey's History Chester Co. Pa. 739-43
Glenn's Welsh Tract 111, 294-304
Gregg's History of Old Cheraws S. C. 94
Hanson's Old Kent Md. 130-6
Hines' Lebanon Ct. Historical Address 171
Holton's Winslow Genealogy i, 168-78
Jackson Genealogy 127
Keyes West Boylston Mass. Register 36
Lapham's History of Rumford Me. 404
Lincoln's Hist. Hingham Mass. iii, 241-3
Lincoln's History of Worcester Mass. 246
Littell's Passaic Valley Gens. 412-23
Mitchell's Hist. of Bridgewater Mass. 313
Orcutt's History of Wolcott Ct. 563
Paige's History of Hardwick Mass. 513-5
Pierce's History of Gorham Me. 211
Power's Sangamon Co. Ill. Settlers 713
Prime's Sands Genealogy 50-3
Randall's Hist. of Chesterfield N. H. 466
Richmond Va. Standard iii, 44
Roe's Sketches of Rose N. Y. 258
Runnells' Hist. Sanbornton N. H. ii, 775-8
Savage's Genealogical Dict. iv, 279-83
Sharpless Genealogy 201
Slaughter's St. Mark's Parish Va. 148
Smith's History of Delaware Co. Pa. 507
Stackpole's History of Durham Me. 262-5
Stearns' History of Rindge N. H. 726-8
Strong Genealogy 786
Sullivant Genealogy 259-62
Thatcher's History of Plymouth Mass. 90
Thomas Fam. of Maine (1850) chart
Thomas Fam. of Boston (1869) chart
Thomas Fam. of Maryland (1877) 197 pages
Thomas Fam. of Md. vol. 2 (1878) 56 pages
Thomas Fam. of Maryland (1883) 157 pages
Thomas Fam. of Hilltown Pa. (1884) 69 p.
Thomas Family of Ohio (1885) 39 pages
Thomas Fam. of Hardwick (1891) 221 pages
Thomas Fam. of Braintree (1895) 6 pages
Thomas Family of Maryland (1896) 648 p.
Thomas Fam. of Pa. (1896) 17 pages
Walker Genealogy (1896) 69, 114-21
Walworth's Hyde Gen. 29, 110-2, 470-3
Whitman Genealogy 21
Whitmore's Copps Hill Epitaphs
Winsor's History of Duxbury Mass. 325
Wyman's Charlestown Mass. Gens. ii, 939
Young's Hist. of Wayne Co. Ind. 301-4
Thomes — Pierce's Gorham Me. 211
Thompson—Allison Genealogy 221
American Ancestry i, 81; ii, 126; iii, 50, 51, 108, 120, 122; iv, 127; v, 207; vi, 180, 189; vii, 85; viii, 39, 47, 57, 181; x, 26, 37, 103; xii
American Historical Register iii, 481-4

Anderson's Waterbury Ct. i, app. 136
Andrews' Hist. of New Britain Ct. 163, 232
Austin's Allied Families 243
Baker's History of Montville Ct. 594-7
Ballou Genealogy 389
Ballou's History of Milford Mass. 1063-5
Barry's History of Hanover Mass. 409
Bassett's History of Richmond N. H. 507
Bemis' History of Marlboro N. H. 658
Bradbury's Hist. Kennebunkport Me. 279
Capron Genealogy by Holden 205-7, 222-6
Chapman's Weeks Genealogy 155
Cochrane's Hist. of Antrim N. H. 709-11
Cochrane's Hist. Francestown N. H. 950-2
Cogswell's Hist. Nottingham N. H. 474-6
Corliss' North Yarmouth Me.
Cothren's Woodbury Ct. 727-37; ii, 1562-5
Daniels' History of Oxford Mass. 716
Davis' History of Wallingford Ct. 905
Davis' Landmarks Plymouth Mass. 262
Dearborn's Hist. of Salisbury N. H. 805-8
Dodd's History of East Haven Ct. 154-6
Eaton's Hist. of Thomaston Me. ii, 427-9
Egle's Penn. Genealogies 460
Egle's Notes and Queries 3d ser. iii, 482-7
Hammatt Papers, Ipswich Mass. 369
Hatch's History of Industry Me. 820-5
Hayden's Virginia Genealogies 131
Hayward's Hist. of Gilsum N. H. 399-401
Hayward's History of Hancock N. H. 923
Hibbard's History of Goshen Ct. 526-48
Hubbard's Hist. of Springfield Vt. 464-6
Hudson's Hist. of Sudbury Mass. 451
Huntting's Hist. Pine Plains N. Y. 385-8
Hyde's History of Brimfield Mass. 460
Joslin's History of Poultney Vt. 354-6
Journals of Smith and Dean 68
Kingman's No. Bridgewater Mass. 668-72
Lapham's History of Rumford Me. 405-8
Leavenworth Genealogy 110-2
Lincoln's Hist. of Hingham Mass. iii, 243
Maginness' West Branch Valley 512-37
Mallery's Bohemia Manor
Mitchell's Hist. of Bridgewater Mass. 314
Morrison's Hist. of Windham N. H. 799
Nevius Genealogy
New Eng. Hist. and Gen. Register iv, 180; xiii, 112-6, 318-20
New York Genealogical and Biographical Record xxi, 33-51; xxii, 66-74; 132-40; xxvii, 1-26
Norton's Hist. of Fitzwilliam N. H. 747-9
Orcutt's History of Stratford Ct. 1304-7
Paige's History of Cambridge Mass. 670
Power's Sangamon Co. Ill. Settlers 711-3
Prescott's Memoirs 435-7
Randall's Hist. of Chesterfield N. H. 467-9
Read's History of Swanzey N. H. 470-5
Ridlon's Saco Valley Me. Families 1174-7
Runnells' Sanbornton N. H. ii, 778, 91
Salem N. Y. Book of History 66
Saunders' Alabama Settlers 469-81
Saunderson's Hist. Charlestown N. H. 580
Savage's Genealogical Dict. iv, 283-90
Schenck's History of Fairfield Ct. 414
Schureman Genealogy 11, 20

Sears Genealogy 229-31
Sewall's Woburn Mass. 390-402, 643-5
Shourd's Fenwick Colony N. J. 283
Slaughter's St. Mark's Parish Va. 174-7
Stiles' History of Windsor Ct. ii, 753-61
Stowe's Hist. of Hubbardston Mass. 357-9
Temple's Hist. No. Brookfield Mass. 751
Thompson Fam. of Plymouth (1841) 84 p.
Thompson Fam. of Goshen (1854) 106 p.
Thompson Fam. of Durham (1886) 86 p.
Thompson Fam. Charlestown (1887) 246 p.
Thompson Fam. of Penn. (1887) 20 pages
Thompson Fam. of N. J. (1889) 29 pages
Thompson Fam. of Plymouth (1890) 272 p.
Thompson's Long Island N. Y. ii, 425-31
Tuttle Genealogy 703
Vinton's Richardson Genealogy 343
Washington N. H. History 640
Wheeler's History of Brunswick Me. 857
Whitman Genealogy 94-6
Williams' History of Danby Vt. 269-72
Winchester Mass. Record ii, 34-40
Wyman's Charlestown Mass. ii, 940-4
See also under Thomson
Thoms — Ridlon's Harrison Me. Sett. 118
Thomson — American Ancestry iv, 6; vii, 223; x, 138
Lane Genealogy (1891) 65
Richmond Va. Standard iii, 68
Roberts' Old Richland Pa. Families 188
Temple's History of Palmer Mass. 563-5
Thomson Genealogy See Thompson
Thorburn — American Ancestry vii, 146
Thorley — Essex Inst. Collections xxiv, 47
Savage's Genealogical Dictionary iv, 295
Thorn — American Ancestry ii, 126
Cope Genealogy 71-155
Eaton Genealogy (1895)
Lincoln's Hist. of Hingham Mass. iii, 245
Ridlon's Saco Valley Me. Families 123
Runnels' Hist. Sanbornton N. H. ii, 791-5
Savage's Genealogical Dictionary iv, 289
Sylvester's Hist. of Ulster Co. N. Y. 174
Tompkins Genealogy 22-39
Thorndyke — Eaton's Thomaston 429
Little's History of Weare N. H. 999
Savage's Genealogical Dictionary iv, 290
Smith's Founders of Mass. Bay 165-71
Whitmore's Heraldic Journal 1865, 54-6
Thorne — Bunker's Long Island Gens. 105
Calnek's Annapolis N. S. 610-2
Mott Genealogy 362
N. Y. Gen. and Big. Records xix, 153-60; xx, 77-88; xxii, 174-82
Shotwell Genealogy 132-4
Thornhill — Heraldic Journal i, 52-4
Thorning — Hayward's Hancock 924
Hudson's History of Lexington Mass. 240
Thornton — American Ancestry iv, 10
Austin's R. I. Genealogical Dictionary 199
Bassett's History of Richmond N. H. 508
Boltwood's Noble Genealogy 361-4
Bond's Watertown Mass. 601-4, 957
Cabell Genealogy 282-4
Clarke's Old King Wm. Co. Va. Families
Cutts Genealogy 168-70

De Bow's Review xxxi, 128
Freeman's Hist. of Cape Cod Mass. ii, 200
Green's Kentucky Families
Goode Genealogy 212–6
Hayden's Virginia Genealogies 279
Martindale's Hist. of Byberry Pa. 334-6
Meade's Old Families of Virginia
Merrill's History of Acworth N. H. 273
Minor's Meriwether Genealogy 62
Morrison Genealogy 258
Pearson's Schenectady N. Y. Settlers 194
Power's Sangamon Co. Ill. Settlers 714
Prescott's Page Geneaolgy
Richmond Va. Standard ii, 29, 31; iii, 5, 21
Savage's Genealogical Dictionary iv, 291-3
Slaughter's St. Mark's Parish Va. 174
Taylor's Some Notable Families 96-8
Thornton Chart (1845) by J. W. T.
William and Mary College Historical
    Register iv, 89–93, 157–64; v, 58–60,
    197–200; vi, 53–7, 109–13, 238–44
Thoroughgood — Richmond Va. Stand-
    ard iv, 13-6
Virginia Magazine of Hist. and Biog. ii
    (1895) 414-8; iii (1896) 321
Thorp — Child Genealogy 803-7
Davis' History of Wallingford Ct. 907
Hill's Dedham Mass. Records i
Huntington's Stamford Ct. Settlers 112
Meade's Old Churches of Virginia i, 198
Thorpe — American Ancestry xii
Boyd's Conesus N. Y. 173
Little's History of Weare N. H. 1001
Savage's Genealogical Dictionary iv, 293
Thrall — Amer. Ancestry xi, 125; xii, 93
Orcutt's Torrington Ct. 770-2
Roy's Thrall Sermon (1894) 17–35
Stiles' History of Windsor Ct. ii, 761-4
Thrall Genealogy (1862)
Thrall Genealogy 2d ed. (1890)
Thrasher — Davis' Landmarks 263
Jameson's History of Medway Mass. 524
Poore Genealogy 66
Threlkeld — Hayden's Va. Gens. 161
Thresher — Bass' Braintree Vt. 189
Throckmorton — Amer. Ancestry x, 61
Austin's R. I. Genealogical Dictionary 200
Browning's Magna Charta Barons 189–204
Salter's History of Monmouth Co. N. J. 58
Savage's Genealogical Dictionary iv, 294
Slaughter's St. Mark's Parish Va. 31
Watkins Genealogy 33
Welles' Washington Genealogy 170–92
William and MaryCollege Historical Regis-
    ter iii, 46–52, 192–5, 240–2; iv, 128–30
Throop — American Ancestry i, 82
Hine's Lebanon Ct. Hist. Address 171
Huntington Genealogical Notes 99–101
Litchfield County Ct. History (1881) 391
Walker Genealogy 44
Walworth's Hyde Genealogy 73, 255–9
Thurber — Ballou's Milford 1065-8
Bass' History of Richmond N. H. 509
Savage's Genealogical Dictionary iv, 295
Thurber Genealogy (1867) 10 pages
Thurston Genealogy (1892) 559–61

Thurlow — Lapham's Norway Me. 606
Lapham's History of Woodstock Me. 260
Martin's History of Chester Pa. 506
Thurman — American Ancestry iii, 51
Thurstin — Bass' Braintree Vt. 190
Sedgwick's History of Sharon Ct. 116
Thurston — Aldrich's Walpole 368
American Ancestry vi, 77
Austin's R. I. Genealogical Dictionary 201
Bemis' History of Marlboro N. H. 659
Blake's History of Franklin Mass. 280
Blake's Mendon Mass. Association 91
Bolton Genealogy 35
Chute Genealogy, appendix 213–6
Daniels' History of Oxford Mass. 716
Hayward's History of Gilsum N. H. 402
Heywood's Hist. Westminster Mass. 888
Paige's History of Hardwick Mass. 515
Pierce's History of Grafton N. H. 573-5
Savage's Genealogical Dictionary iv, 296
Temple's Hist. of N. Brookfield Mass. 753
Thurston Fam. of Newport (1865) 80 pages
Thurston Fam. of Newport (1868) 70 pages
Thurston Genealogies (1880) 598 pages
Thurston Family Gathering (1885) 75 pages
Thurston Genealogies 2d ed. (1892) 744 p.
Thurston Ancestry (1894) 95 pages
Wm. and Mary College Hist. Register iv,
    23–7, 116–8, 180–3
Thweatt — Richmond Standard iii, 16
Thwing — American Ancestry iii, 106
Ballou's History of Milford Mass. 1068–71
Jackson's History of Newton Mass. 427
Savage's Genealogical Dictionary iv, 298
Thwing Genealogy (1883) 214 pages
Tibbals — Savage's Gen. Dict. iv, 298
Tibbets — American Ancestry i, 82
Bangor Me. Historical Mag. vi, 91, 294
Cushman's History of Sheepscott Me. 426
New Eng. Hist. and Gen. Register viii, 130
Savage's Genealogical Dictionary iv, 300
Tibbetts — Bangor Historical Mag. iv, 21
Eaton's History of Thomaston Me. ii, 433
Hanson's History of Gardiner Me. 74
Ridlon's Saco Valley Me. Families 1162-8
Thurston Genealogy (1894) 35-7, 83-5
Wentworth Genealogy i, 446; ii, 4–6
Tibbitts — Austin's R. I. Gen. Dict. 202
Tibout — Bergen's Kings Co. N. Y. 302
Tice — Locke Genealogy 82
Roome Genealogy 336
Tichenor — N. J. Hist. Soc. Coll. vi, 134
Shaw's History of Essex Co. N. J. ii, 724
Tichnor — American Ancestry iv, 50
Tickner — Deane's Scituate Mass. 351-3
Sedgwick's History of Sharon Ct. 116
Ticknor — N. E. Hist. Reg. xviii, 381
Tidd — Hodgman's Westford Mass. 478
Hudson's Hist. of Lexington Mass. 240–5
Paige's History of Cambridge Mass. 670
Sewall's History of Woburn Mass. 645
Vinton's Richardson Genealogy 252
Wyman's Charlestown Mass. Gens. ii, 945
Tidy — Libby Genealogy 30
Tiebout — Green's Todd Genealogy
Tiernan — Tiernan Gen. (1899) 222 pages

Tiff— Brown's West Simsbury Ct. 124
Tiffany — Aldrich's Walpole N. H. 368
Capron Genealogy by Holden 165-70
Champion Genealogy 52
Daniels' History of Oxford Mass. 717
Hine's Lebanon Ct. Hist. Address 169
Wales Mass. Centennial 27
Tifft — American Ancestry ii, 126
Tifft Genealogy (1896) 159 pages
Tiger— Chambers' N. J. Germans
Tilden — Am. Anc. ii, 126; vi, 49; viii, 229
Bass' History of Braintree Vt. 190
Bemis' History of Marlboro N. H. 660
Briggs' History of Shipbuilding, 36, 264-8
Deane's History of Scituate Mass. 353-5
Farrow's History of Islesborough Me. 287
Hanson's Old Kent Md. 302-9
Hines' Lebanon Ct. Hist. Address 170
Hurd's Hist. of New London Co. Ct. 515
Maine Genealogist ii, 47-51
Savage's Genealogical Dictionary iv, 301
Tucker's History of Hartford Vt. 465-7
Tileston — American Ancestry vii, 26
Locke Genealogy 95
New Eng. Hist. and Gen. Reg. xiii, 121-3
Savage's Genealogical Dictionary iv, 302
Washington N. H. History 641
Tilghman — Old Kent Md. 230, 245-62
Thomas Genealogy (1877) 148
Thomas Genealogy (1896) 528-30
Tilley — American Ancestry iv, 152
Austin's Ancestral Dictionary 59
Tilley Genealogy (1878) 79 pages
Tillinghast — Amer. Anc. v, 111; vi, 195
Austin's Ancestral Dictionary 60
Austin's Ancestries 77
Austin's R. I. Genealogical Dictionary 203
Bartlett's Wanton Genealogy 139
Bond's Watertown Mass. Gens. 906-8
Narragansett Historical Register iv, 140
New Eng. Hist. and Gen. Reg. xiii, 282
Newport R. I. Historical Mag. i, 156-62
Savage's Genealogical Dictionary iv, 303
Tillotson — Clark Ancestry (1891) 14-8
Hughes Genealogy 133-5
Orford N. H. Centennial 138-41
Savage's Genealogical Dictionary iv, 304
Tillson — American Ancestry xii
Davis' Landmarks 263
Eaton's History of Thomaston Me. ii, 433
Sylvester's History of Ulster Co. N. Y. 133
Thurston Genealogy (1892) 129-31
Whitman Genealogy 74-7
Tilly — Temple's No. Brookfield 753
Tilney — Whittemore's Orange N. J. 298
Tilson — Bass' Hist. of Braintree Vt. 190
Tilton — Barrus' Goshen Mass. 177
Bergen's Kings Co. N. Y. Settlers 303
Cogswell's Nottingham N. H. 476-80
Dow's History of Hampton N. H. 994-6
Fullonton's Hist. of Raymond N. H. 290-3
Lancaster's Hist. of Gilmanton N. H. 289
Poore Genealogy 39
Runnells' Hist. Sanbornton N. H. ii, 795-8
Savage's Genealogcal Dictionary iv, 304
Tilyou — Littell's Passaic Valley 424

Timberlake—Austin's R. I. Gen. Dict. 204
Timlow — Timlow's Souhington 237
Tindall — Cooley's Trenton N. J. 269
Shourd's Fenwick Colony N. J. 282
Tinker — American Ancestry ix, 154
Champion Genealogy 132
Coit Genealogy 259-62, 265-7
Eaton's History of Thomaston Me. ii, 434
Guild's Stiles Genealogy 198
Hayward's History of Gilsum N. H. 402-5
Huntington Genealogy 125
Tinker Genealogy (1889) 11 pages
Tinkham — Amer. Ancestry i, 82; x, 103
Davis' Landmarks of Plymouth Mass. 264
Tinklepaugh — American Ancestry ii, 727
Tinsley — Goode Genealogy 212
Lincoln's Hist. of Hingham Mass. iii, 247
Tirrell — Dyer's Plainfield Mass. 179
Lincoln's Hist. of Hingham Mass. iii, 247
Mitchell's Hist. of Bridgewater Mass. 315
Porter Genealogy (1878) 49
Tirrell Manuscript in Me. Gen. Lib. 79 p.
Tisdall — Hyde's Hist. of Ware Mass. 52
Walker Genealogy 18-20
Tisdel — Ely Genealogy 404
Tisdell — Hines' Lebanon Ct. Add. 172
Winsor's History of Duxbury Mass. 326
Tise — American Ancestry xii
Tison — Bingham Genealogy 203-8
Titcomb — American Ancestry vi, 72; xii
Bourne's History of Wells Me. 764
Butler's Hist. of Farmington Me. 584-92
Coffin's History of Newbury Mass. 319
Corliss' North Yarmouth Me.
Lapham's History of Norway Me. 607
Morrison's History of Windham N. H. 801
North's History of Augusta Me. 947
Runnells' Hist. Sanbornton N. H. ii, 810
Titcomb's Early New Eng. People 144-84
Titcomb Manuscript Me. Gen. Lib. 270 p.
Titcombe— Savage's Gen. Dict. iv, 307
Titharton — Orcutt's Stratford Ct. 1307
Titman — Chambers' N. J. Germans
Titus — Amer. Anc. iv, 174; ix, 85; x, 84
Bunker's Long Island Genealogies 103-16
Cooley's Trenton N. J. Genealogies 270-7
Eaton's History of Thomaston Me. ii, 434
Flint's Peters Lineage 20-4
Hayward's History of Hancock N. H. 924
Heywood's Hist. Westminster Mass. 889
Ireland Genealogy 39
Littell's Passaic Valley Genealogies 426
Mott Genealogy 288-95
New York Gen. and Biog. Record xii 92-9
Randall's Hist. of Chesterfield N. H. 470-2
Riker's Annals of Newtown N. Y. 327
Silbey's History of Union Me. 510
Titus Genealogy (1881) 8 pages, reprint
Titzel — Rupp Genealogy 187-91
Tobey — American Ancestry ii, 127
Eliot Me. Miscellany (1897) 2-4
Freeman's Hist. of Cape Cod Mass. ii, 147
Hemenway's Vermont Hist. Gaz. iv, 169
Sedgwick's History of Sharon Ct. 116
Spooner Genealogy i, 64
Tobias — American Ancestry ii, **127**

Tobie — Cochrane's Francestown 953
Toby — Hollister's Hist. of Pawlet Vt. 249
Todd — Am. Anc. iv, 164; vii, 174; xii, 94
Anderson's Waterbury Ct. i, app. 137
Blake's History of Hamden Ct. 276
Chambers' Early Germans of N. J. 530-2
Chase's History of Chester N. H. 598
Cochrane's Hist. of Antrim N. H. 712-4
Cochrane's Hist. Francestown N. H. 954-7
Dickerman Genealogy 217-9, 221-4
Edwards Genealogy (1894)
Egle's Notes and Queries 1896 An. 221-5
Essex Institute Hist. Colls. xxiv, 47-55
Gage's History of Rowley Mass. 460
Green's Kentucky Families
Hayward's History Hancock N. H. 925-8
Lane Genealogy (1899) 49-51
Lincoln's Hist. Hingham Mass. iii, 247-9
Littell's Passaic Valley Gens. 427
Meade's Old Families of Virginia
Mellick's Story of an Old Farm 636
Orcutt's History of Wolcott Ct. 564-9
Parker's History Londonderry N. H. 301
Power's Sangamon Co. Ill. Settlers 715-7
Richmond Va. Standard iii, 44
Savage's Genealogical Dictionary iv, 309
Scott Genealogy 283-92
Slaughter's St. Mark's Parish Va. 186
Stearns' History of Rindge N. H. 728-33
Todd Genealogy (1867) 143 pages
Tuttle Genealogy 251-337
Virginia Mag. of History iii, 79-83
Todhunter — Thomas Gen. (1877) 149
Toler — American Ancestry viii, 134
Richmond Va. Standard iii, 16
Toles — Aylsworth Genealogy 103, 207-9
Roe's Rose N. Y. Sketches 86
Tolford — American Ancestry x, 182
Chase's History of Chester N. H. 598
Toll — American Ancestry vii, 3; ix, 143
Pearson's Schenectady Settlers 195-7
Tolles — Doty Genealogy 117
Tolley — Power's Sangamon Co. Ill. 717
Tollman — Deane's Scituate Mass. 356
Tolman — Bemis' Marlboro 661-4
Daniels' Oxford Mass. 718
Dedham Mass. Historical Register v, 42-4,
  67-76, 109-17, 174-7; vi, 27-34; xi,
  45-8, 104
Eaton's Thomaston Me. 435-8
Hatch's History of Industry Me. 825-7
Locke Genealogy 321-3
Mitchell's Hist. of Bridgewater Mass. 312
N. E. Hist. and Gen. Register xiv, 247-60
Savage's Genealogical Dictionary iv, 310
Tolman Genealogy (1894) 29 pages
Tomblen — Temple's N. Brookfield 754
Tomkyns — Bolten's Westchester 232
Tomlin — Hayden's Virginia Gens. 127
Power's Sangamon Ill. Settlers 720
Ward's Hist. of Shrewsbury Mass. 453
Tomlins — Savage's Gen. Dict. iv, 210
Tomlinson — American Ancestry ii, 127
Bassett's History of Richmond N. H. 501
Clement's Newtown N. J. Settlers
Cooley's Trenton N. J. Genealogies 277

Cothren's Hist. of Woodbury Ct. ii, 1570-6
Cushman's Hist. of Sheepscott, Me. 427
Hinman's Connecticut Settlers 1st ed. 245
Martindale's Hist. of Byberry Pa. 369-74
Orcutt's History of Derby Ct. 769-72
Orcutt's History of Stratford Ct. 1307-18
Savage's Genealogical Dictionary iv, 310
Sharpe's History of Seymour Ct. 210-3
Tomlinson Genealogy (1891) 228 pages
Tompkins — American Ancestry ii, 127;
  iv, 132; xi, 115
Anderson's Waterbury Ct. i, app. 138
Austin's R. I. Genealogical Dictionary 205
Carter Family Tree of Virginia
Chase's History of Haverhill Mass 582
Felton Genealogy (1886) 244
Garnett's Tompkins Sketches (1870) 140 p.
Littell's Passaic Valley Genealogies 428
Mitchell's Hist. of Bridgewater Mass. 316
Savage's Genealogical Dictionary iv, 311
Tompkins Genealogy (1893) 65 pages
Tompson — Hazen's Billerica Mass. 148
New Eng. Hist. and Gen. Reg. xv, 112-7
Ridlon's Saco Valley Me. Families 1174-7
Tonkin — Cregar's White Genealogy
Toogood — Wentworth Genealogy i, 156
Tooker — Stickney's Minisink N. Y. 172
Toot — Egle's Notes and Quer. (1895) 29-31
Toothaker — Farrow's Islesborough 287
Hazen's History of Billerica Mass. 149
Wheeler's History of Brunswick Me. 857
Topliff — American Ancestry viii, 17
Topliffe — Savage's Gen. Dict. iv, 312
Topp — American Ancestry x, 167
Toppan — American Ancestry iv, 100
Bowens of Woodstock Ct. 197-202
Dow's History of Hampton N. H. 996-8
Little Genealogy 86-8
New Eng. Hist. Gen. Reg. xxxiii, 66-8;
  xxxiv, 48-58
New England Magazine iv, 60-3
Spaulding Genealogy 513-21
Toppan Genealogy (1862) 30 pages
Toppan; see Tappan
Topping — Howell's Southampton 394-8
Chambers' Early Germans of N. J. 532
Torr — Thompson Ebenezer Memoir
Torrence — Power's Sangamon Ill. 719
Torrey — American Ancestry v, 173
Austin's R. I. Genealogical Dictionary 206
Ballou's History of Milford Mass. 1071-4
Barry's History of Hanover Mass. 410
Benedict's History of Sutton Mass. 735
Briggs' History of Shipbuilding 247-9
Daniels' History of Oxford Mass. 719
Davis' Landmarks of Plymouth Mass. 265
Deane's History of Scituate Mass. 358-60
Dyer's History of Plainfield Mass. 177-9
Eaton's History of Thomaston Me. ii, 438
Hobart's History of Abington Mass. 446-8
Holton's Winslow Genealogy i, 218-31
Lincoln's Hist. of Hingham Mass. iii, 249
Mitchell's Hist. of Bridgewater Mass. 316
Narr. Historical Register vii, 294-7
New Eng. Hist. and Gen. Reg. xlv, 301
Power's Sangamon Co. Ill. Settlers 720

Randall's Hist. of Chesterfield N. H. 472
Savage's Genealogical Dictionary iv, 313
Temple's Hist. No. Brookfield Mass. 755
Torrey (Jason) Memoir (1885) 131 pages
Torrey Genealogy (1885) 50 pages
Torrey Genealogy (1890) 206 pages
Tosh — Austin's R. I. Gen. Dict. 207
Livermore's Hist. Block Island R. I. 347
Totman — Corliss' North Yarmouth Me.
Davis' Landmarks of Plymouth Mass. 266
Lincoln's Hist. of Hingham Mass. iii, 250
Tolman Genealogy (1895) 3 pages
Whitman Genealogy 318-25
Totten — Clute's Staten Island 427
Littell's Passaic Valley Genealogies 429-32
Mansfield Genealogy 46-8
Tottenham — See Tottingham
Tottingham — Caverly's Pittsford 728
Gale Genealogy (1866) 173-81
Heywood's Hist. Westminster Mass. 890
Sewall's History of Woburn Mass. 646
Stearns' Hist. of Ashburnham Mass. 921-3
Tourneur — Riker's Harlem N. Y. 543-6
Tourtellot — Austin's R. I. Dict. 207
Tourtellotte — American Ancestry ix, 24
Tourtillot — Bangor Mag. vi, 32-4
Tower — Amer. Ancestry vii, 95; ix, 104
Barry's Hist. of Framingham Mass. 418
Barry's History of Hanover Mass. 410
Binney Genealogy 84-7
Deane's History of Scituate Mass. 357
Hubbard's Hist. of Springfield Vt. 466-9
Hudson's History of Lexington Mass. 245
Lincoln's Hist. Hingham Mass. iii, 251-67
Norton's History of Fitzwilliam N. H. 749
Porter Genealogy (1878) 113
Thayer Memorial 33
Tower Genealogy (1891) 887 pages
Whipple-Hill Families (1897) 62
Towle — Amer. Ancestry v, 154; vi, 168
Chase's History of Chester N. H. 599
Cochrane's Hist. Francestown N. H. 957
Dearborn's Hist. of Parsonsfield Me. 407
Dow's History of Hampton N. H. 998-1016
Maine Historical Recorder i, 179-81
N. E. Hist. and Gen. Reg. xliii, 364-70
Ridlon's Saco Valley Me. Fams. 1177-84
Towle Genealogy (1889) 8 pages
Worthen's History of Sutton N. H. 965
Towles — Lynchburg Va. 311-20
Town — Daniels' Oxford Mass. 720-6
Lapham's History of Bethel Me. 624
Lapham's History of Norway Me. 608-9
Towne — American Ancestry v, 45
Barry's Hist. Framingham Mass. 418-20
Bemis' History of Marlboro N. H. 664
Bradbury's Kennebunkport Me. 280
Cleveland's Topsfield Bi-Centen. app. 26
Doolittle's Belchertown Mass. 258-60
Dunstable Mass. Bi-Centennial (1875) 142-4
Hayward's History of Gilsum N H. 403
Hayward's History of Hancock N. H. 928
Kidder's Hist, New Ipswich N. H. 435-7
Livermore's History of Wilton N. H. 516
Locke Genealogy 72, 145
Loring's Hist. of Piscatauqua Co. Me. 39

Morrison's Hist. of Windham N. H. 801-3
N. E. Reg. xx, 367-71; xxi, 12-22, 217-22
Paige's History of Cambridge Mass. 670
Savage's Genealogical Dictionary iv, 316-8
Secomb's History of Amherst N. H. 792-6
Towne Genealogy (1878) 16 pages
Towne Genealogy (1880) 130 pages
Towne Fam. Warwick Mass. (1891) 12 p.
Washington N. H. History 642
Towner — Hibbard's Goshen 548-53
Townes — Little's Hist. Weare N. H. 1003
Slaughter's St. Mark's Parish 191
Townley — Hill's Lawrence-Townley Estate (1888)
Littell's Passaic Valley Genealogies 433-43
Richmond Va. Standard iii, 38
Usher's Lawrence-Townley Estate (1883)
Towns — Norton's Fitzwilliam N. H. 750
Townsend — American Ancestry i, 82; iii, 52; iv, 133-243; vii, 71; viii, 106; ix, 78, 112; x, 13, 85; xi, 52
Barry's History of Framingham Mass. 420
Bolton's Westchester Co. N. Y. ii, 543
Bond's Watertown Mass. Genealogies 604
Bunker's L. I. Genealogies 118-25
Chase's History of Chester N. H. 601
Cleveland's Yates Co. 270, 344, 508-10
Dearborn's Hist. Salisbury N. H. 808-15
Eager's History of Orange Co. N. Y. 567
Eaton's History of Reading Mass. 119
Essex Inst. Colls. xix, 269-96; xx, 37-52
Hayward's History of Gilsum N. H. 404
Hills' History of Mason N. H. 207
Kellogg's White Genealogy 90
Leonard's History of Dublin N. H. 401
Lincoln's Hist. of Hingham Mass. iii, 267
Maris Genealogy 59
Martindale's History of Byberry Pa. 330-4
Morris' Bontecou Genealogy 118
New E. Hist. and Gen. Reg. xxix, 97-107
New York Gen. and Biog. Record iv. 189
Norton's History of Fitzwilliam N. H. 750
Ogden Genealogy (1898) 73, 101-4, 159-66
Perkins' Old Houses of Norwich Ct. 569
Queen's County N. Y. History 490-2
Ridlon's Saco Valley Me. Fams. 1168-74
Savage's Genealogical Dict. iv 318-20
Sharpless Genealogy 174-6, 461
Smith's Genealogy of Wm. Smith 55-7
Stearns' Hist. of Ashburnham Mass. 923-6
Stearns' History of Rindge N. H. 736
Thompson's Long Island N. Y. ii, 343-53
Townsend Fam. of New York (1865) 233 p.
Townsend Fam. of Lynn (1875) 15 pages
Townsend Fam. of Buffalo (1877) 37 pages
Townsend Fam. of New Salem (1879) 33 p.
Townsend Fam. of Lynn (1881) 27 pages
Townsend Fam. of Boston (1883) 43 pages
Townsend Fam. of Lynn (1884) 138 pages
Townsends of Eng. and Am. (1895) 110 p.
Townsends of Buffalo (1897) 62 pages
Walker Genealogy (1896) 149-53
Ward's History of Shrewsbury Mass. 452
Whitmore's Copps Hill Epitaphs
Wyman's Charlestown Mass. ii, 948-50
Townsley — Hyde's Brimfield Mass. 462

Tozer — Barry's Framingham Mass. 420
Bemis' Hist. of Marlboro N. H. 666
New Eng. Hist. and Gen. Reg. xvi, 133
Wentworth Genealogy i, 142-8
Tozier — Bangor Hist. Mag. vi, 293
Trabue — Virginia Hist. Soc. Colls. v, 167
Virginia Magazine of History iv
Tracy — American Ancestry ii, 128; iv,
44; xi, 52; xii, 93
Andrews' Hist. New Britain Ct. 357, 375
Caulkins' History of Norwich Ct. 200-5
Eaton's History of Thomaston Me. ii, 438
Huntington Genealogy 107, 135, 144-6
Oneida Hist. Society Trans. ii, 95-7
Perkins' Old Houses of Norwich Ct. 570-6
Robinson's Items of Ancestry (1894) 49
Savage's Genealogical Dictionary iv, 320
Stackpole's History of Durham Me. 265-8
Tracy Genealogy (1888) 136 pages
Tracy Ancestry in Eng. (1895) 100 pages
Tracy Family Lineage (1895) 32 pages
Tracy Genealogy (1898) 294 pages
Tracys of Maine (1900) 32 pages
Tucker's History of Hartford Vt. 467-70
Walworth's Hyde Gen. i, 435-61, 1076-91
Winsor's History of Duxbury Mass. 326
Trafford — American Ancestry ii, 128
Trafton — Ridlon's Harrison Me. 120
Trail — Heraldic Journal (1866) ii, 18
Traill — Hist. Reg. of Penn. ii, 256-60
Train—Crafts' Whately Mass. 590-2
Savage's Genealogical Dictionary iv, 321
Temple's History of Whately Mass. 271
Washington N. H. History 643-5
Traine — Barry's Framingham 421
Bond's Watertown Mass. Gens. 605-7
Trask — Babson's Gloucester Mass. 283
Bass' History of Braintree Vt. 191
Benedict's History of Sutton Mass. 735
Bond's Watertown Mass. Gens. 83-86
Hatch's History of Industry Me. 827-32
Hudson's History of Lexington Mass. 245
Hyde's History of Brimfield Mass. 463
N. E. Hist. and Gen. Register liv, 279-83
Savage's Genealogical Dictionary iv, 322
Sheldon's Hist. of Deerfield Mass. 346
Trask Genealogy (1877) 36 pages
Washburn's Hist. of Leicester Mass. 405
Wyman's Charlestown Mass. Gens. ii, 950
Traugh — Mellick Genealogy 706
Traver — American Ancestry ii, 128; xii
Travers — Hayden's Virginia Gens. 297
Meade's Old Churches of Virginia ii, 204
Richmond Va. Standard iii, 18
Travis — Barry's Framingham 422
Bond's Watertown Mass. Gens. 607
Meade's Old Families of Virginia
Richmond Va. Standard ii, 34
Savage's Genealogical Dictionary iv, 323
Treadway — Bond's Watertown 607
Sill Genealogy (1897) 28
Wyman's Charlestown Mass. Gens.
Treadwell — Am. Ancestry i, 83; iv, 123
Hammatt Papers, Ipswich Mass. 370-5
Herrick Genealogy (1885) 258
Orcutt's History of New Milford Ct. 779

Savage's Genealogical Dictionary iv, 325
Smith's Hist. of Peterborough N. H. 319
Warren's History of Waterford Me. 296
Wetmore Genealogy 582
Treat — Am. Anc. iii, 52; v, 181; ix, 198
Bangor Historical Magazine ii, 85-7, 104;
iv, 169-76, 200
Freeman's Cape Cod Mass. i, 350; ii, 381
Glastenbury Ct. Centennial 185
Goodwin's Gen. Notes 224, 36, 328
Hollister's History of Connecticut i, 371
New Eng. Hist. and Gen. Reg. xx, 129
Orcutt's Hist. of New Milford Ct. 779-82
Portor's Eddy Genealogy, appendix
Rich's History of Truro Mass. 566
Savage's Genealogical Dictionary iv, 325-8
Stanton Genealogy 438, 451-3
Stiles' History of Windsor Ct. ii, 765
Talcott's N. Y. and N. Eng. Fams. 721-3
Treat Genealogy (1893) 637 pages
Vinton's Giles Genealogy 133, 149
Trecothick — Heraldic Jour. iv, 90-4
Tredway — Barry's Framingham 423
Bond's Watertown Mass. Genealogies 607
Savage's Genealogical Dictionary iv, 324
Walworth's Hyde Genealogy 564-6
Tredwell — American Ancestry iii, 69
Brewster's Portsmouth N. H. ii, 135-40
Flint's Peters Lineage 56-8
Trego — Futhey's Chester Co. Pa. 748
Smith's Genealogy of Wm. Smith 23-6
Trego Family (1884) 138 pages
Tremain — American Ancestry ii, 129
Collin's Hist. of Hillsdale N. Y., app. 117
Lee Genealogy (1888) 333
Tremblay — Navarre Genealogy 354-64
Tremper — American Ancestry xi, 61
Collord Ancestors 31-3
Trenchard — Amer. Anc. vi, 92; vii, 283
Trent — Cooley's Trenton N. J. 278-92
Meade's Old Families of Virginia
Penn. Magazine of History iv, 100-8
Peyton's History of Augusta Co. Va. 291
Trerice — N. E. Hist. Reg. xlvi, 173
Trescott — Boyd's Conesus N. Y. 173
Savage's Genealogical Dictionary iv, 329
Trevett — Alden's Epitaphs iii, 190
Trevilian — Richmond Standard ii, 46
Treworgy — Bangor Hist. Mag. v, 212-4
Trezevant — Richmond Stand. ii, 31, 33
Tribble — Davis' Landmarks 266
Trim — Farrow's Islesborough Me. 287-9
Trimble — Clarke's King Wm. Va. Fams.
Claypoole Genealogy 91-9, 155
Futhey's Chester Pa. 748
Palmer and Trimble Gen. (1875) 474 pages
Waddell's Annals Augusta Co. Va. 411-3
Trimmer — Cleveland's Yates Co. 300-2
Chambers' Early Germans of N. J.
151-5, 533-9
Trimnal — Stearns' Ashburnham 926
Trimper — American Ancestry ii, 129
Triplett — Lindsay Genealogy
Tripp — Amer. Ancestry ii, 129; iv, 173
Austin's Allied Families 246
Austin's R. I. Genealogical Dictionary 208

Newport Historical Magazine iv, 50–7
Ricker's Poland Me. Centennial 107
Spooner Genealogy i, 42
Trist — Page Genealogy 240
Tristram — Folsom's Saco Me. 180
Troop — Calnek's Annapolis N. S. 612–4
Trott — N. E. Hist. Reg. xliii, 79–81
Perkins' Old Houses of Norwich Ct. 577
Savage's Genealogical Dictionary iv, 331
Trott Genealogy (1889) 4 pages and chart
Trotter — Albany Collections iv, 172
Power's Sangamon Co. Ill. Settlers 724–7
Trow — Daniels' Hist. Oxford Mass. 726
Mitchell's Hist. of Bridgewater Mass. 317
Paige's History of Hardwick Mass. 516
Smith's Hist. of Sunderland Mass. 558
Washington N. H. History 646
Wyman's Charlestown Mass. Gens. ii, 953
Trowbridge — Amer. Anc. i, 83; xi, 177
Barry's Hist. of Framingham Mass. 423–5
Bond's Watertown Mass. Gens. 608, 958
Butler's History of Groton Mass. 441
Cothren's Woodbury Ct 737–44; ii, 1565
Jackson's History of Newton Mass. 419–26
Lincoln's Hist. of Hingham Mass. iii, 268
Morris' Bontecou Genealogy 74, 119
Norton's Hist. of Fitzwilliam N. H. 751
Orcutt's History of Stratford Ct. 1318
Paige's History of Cambridge Mass. 671
Phœnix's Whitney Genealogy i, 727
Read's History of Swanzey N. H. 476
Savage's Genealogical Dictionary iv, 322–4
Strong Genealogy 544–6
Trowbridge Fam. Dorchester (1854) 32 p.
Trowbridge Fam. N. Haven (1872) 461 p.
Tuttle Genealogy 550–61
Wall's Reminiscences Worcester Mass. 362
Troxell — Power's Sangamon Ill. 727
Truant — Davis' Landmarks 267
Truax — American Ancestry i, 83
New York Gen. and Biog. Rec. xxvi, 80
Pearson's Schenectady Settlers 197–203
Trubee — Trubee Gen. (1894) 151 pages
True — American Ancestry ix, 160; x, 152
Butler's History of Farmington Me. 592
Chase's History of Chester N. H. 601
Cochrane's History of Antrim N. H. 715
Cochrane's Hist. Francestown N. H.958–61
Cogswell's Hist. Nottingham N. H. 481–5
Corliss' North Yarmouth Me. 27–32
Dearborn's History of Salisbury N. H.
815–8
French's History of Turner Me. 53
Hatch's History of Industry Me. 832–4
Hayward's Hist. of Hancock N. H. 929–31
Hoyt's Salisbury Mass. Families 334–6
Lapham's History of Bethel Me. 624
Nealley and True chart (1878)
Power's Sangamon Co. Ill. Settlers 728
Runnells' Hist. of Sanbornton N. H. ii, 811
Savage's Genealogical Dictionary iv, 334
Smith's Founders of Mass. Bay 267–331
Stackpole's Hist. of Durham Me. 268
True chart by H. A. True (1894)
Truehart — Goode Genealogy 220
Truell — Secomb's Amherst N. H. 796

Truesdale — Jackson's Newton 426
Paige's History of Cambridge Mass. 672
Truesdell — Am. Anc. ii, 129; ix, 171, 233
Collin's Hist. Hillsdale N. Y., app. 118–21
Daniels' History of Oxford Mass. 727
Savage's Genealogical Dictionary iv, 335
Young's History of Warsaw N. Y. 341
Trueworthy — Amer. Ancestry iv, 99
Truex — Munsell's Albany Colls. iv, 173
Trull — Hazen's Billerica Mass. 150–2
Lapham's History of Norway Me. 609–10
Truman — Sharpless Genealogy 243
Young's History of Wrsaw N. Y. 291
Trumble— American Ancestry i, 83
Essex Institute Hist. Collections xxiv, 55–7
Trumbo — Power's Sangamon Ill. 729
Trumbull — Amer. Anc. v, 33; viii, 196
Barry's History of Framingham Mass. 425
Champion Genealogy
Daniels' History of Oxford Mass. 727
Hines' Lebanon Ct. Hist. Address 84–109
Hurd's Hist. of New London Co. Ct. 490–7
N. E. Hist. and Gen. Reg. xlix, 148–52,
322–32, 417–26
Paige's History of Cambridge Mass. 672
Perkins' Old Houses of Norwich Ct. 578
Rollo Genealogy 52–4
Savage's Genealogical Dictionary iv, 336
Stiles' History of Windsor Ct. ii, 765–9
Trumbull Genealogy (1886) 46 pages
Trumbull Genealogy (1895) 27 pages
Tucker's Hist. of Hartford Vt. 470
Tuttle Genealogy 704
Walworth's Hyde Genealogy 586
Wyman's Charlestown Mass. ii, 954–6
Trussell — Eaton's Thomaston 439
Tryon — Huntington's Stamford 113
New Eng. Hist. and Gen. Reg. xx, 130
Sheldon's Hist. of Deerfield Mass. 347
Tubbs — American Ancestry vi, 147
Barry's History of Hanover Mass. 411
Bemis' History of Marlboro N. H. 667
Cleveland's Yates Co. N. Y. 286, 288
Hayward's Hist. of Hancock N. H. 931–3
Lapham's History of Norway Me. 610
Smith's Hist. Peterborough N. H. 321–3
Washington N. H. History 646
Winsor's History of Duxbury Mass. 327
Tuck — Butler's Farmington Me. 593
Corliss' North Yarmouth Me.
Dearborn's Hist. of Parsonsfield Me. 407–9
Dow's History of Hampton N. H. 1016–23
Hurd's Hist. of Rockingham Co. Ct. 364
Richmond Va. Standard iii, 33
Savage's Genealogical Dictionary iv, 337
Tuck Genealogy (1877) 138 pages
Tucke — N. E. Hist. Gen. Reg. x, 197
Tucker — American Ancestry i, 83; iv, 70;
vi, 175; ix, 148
Babson's History of Gloucester Mass. 171
Bartow Genealogy 159–63
Bemis' Hist. of Marlboro N. H. 668–70
Bolling Genealogy 25
Chandler Genealogy 295–7
Cogswell's Hist. of Henniker N. H. 748–51
Cogswell's Nottingham N. H. 778–80

Daniels' History of Oxford Mass. 727-9
Dearborn's Hist. Salisbury N. H. 818-20
Densmore's Hartwell Genealogy
Dickerman Genealogy 122, 568-73
Draper's History of Spencer Mass. 257
Emmet Memoir (1898)
Forrest's History of Norfolk Va. 56
Freeman's Hist. of Cape Cod Mass. ii, 507
Goode Genealogy 125
Hall's Trenton N. J. Presbyt. Church 233
Herrick Genealogy (1885) 113-5, 120
Hoyt's Salisbury Mass. Families 337
Hudson's History of Lexington Mass. 246
Greene Genealogy
Journals of Smith and Dean 225
Kidder's Hist. of New Ipswich N. H. 437
Lapham's History of Norway Me. 611
Lincoln's Hist. of Hingham Mass. iii, 268
Littell's Passaic Valley Genealogies 444-52
Lynchburg Va. Sketches 305
Meade's Old Families of Virginia
Milliken's Narraguagus Valley Me. 6
Morris Genealogy (1894) 108
Morse's Sherborn Mass. Settlers 246
New Eng. Hist. and Gen. Register xxv,
   32, 440; liii, 86
Orcutt's History of Derby Ct. 772
Paige's History of Hardwick Mass. 517
Putnam's Historical Magazine v, 1-6
Savage's Genealogical Dict. iv, 338-40
Sharpe's History of Seymour Ct. 219
Sheppard's Life of Tucker
Slaughter's Bristol Parish Va. 159
Temple's No. Brookfield Mass. 756-9
Tucker Fam. of N. Jersey (1851) 37 pages
Tucker Fam. of Mass. (1895) 414 pages
Tucker's History of Hartford Vt. 471-5
Wall's Reminiscence Worcester Mass. 359
Ward's Hist. of Shrewsbury Mass. 453-5
Washburn's History of Leicester Mass. 405
Welles' Washington Genealogy 200
Wyman's Charlestown Mass. Gens. ii, 956
Wynne's Ellis Genealogy (1849) 11 pages
Tuckerman — American Ancestry iv, 76
Stearns' Hist. of Ashburnham Mass. 926
Tudor — American Ancestry v, 75
Goodwin's Foote Genealogy 286
Loomis Genealogy (1880) 129-48
Savage's Genealogical Dictionary iv, 340
Stiles' History of Windsor Ct. ii, 767-9
Tudor's Diary (1896) 20-37
Tuell — Lapham's Paris Me. 754-6
Tuffs — American Ancestry i, 84
Tufts — American Ancestry iv, 32; vii, 168
Ammidown's Hist. Collections i, 453-5
Brook's History of Medford Mass. 543-5
Butler's Hist. of Farmington Me. 595-601
Calnek's Hist. of Annapolis N. S. 614
Cutter's Hist. of Arlington Mass. 310-2
Guild's Stiles Genealogy 97
Hudson's Hist. of Lexington Mass. 247
Malden Mass. Bi-Centennial 249-51
Morrison's Hist. of Windham N. H. 803
New Eng. Hist. and Gen. Reg. ix, 223; li,
   299-305
Savage's Genealogical Dictionary iv, 341

Symmes Genealogy 114
Wyman's Charlestown Mass. ii, 957-92
Tukey — Cushman's Sheepscott 427
Tullar — Collin's Hillsdale N. Y. 121-3
Tuller — Humphrey Genealogy
Phelps' West Simsbury Ct. Settlers 125
Tulley — Richmond Standard iii, 59
Tully — Essex Institute Hist. Colls. i, 188
New Eng. Hist. and Gen. Reg. iii, 157-63
Savage's Genealogical Dictionary iv, 342
Tupper — Am. Ancestry iv, 193, 234; v, 7
Calnek's Hist. of Annapolis N. S. 616
Freeman's Cape Cod Mass. i, 697; ii, 71
Magazine of American History xxii, 324-7
Miller's Hist. Colchester Co. N. S. 225-31
Paige's History of Hardwick Mass. 518
Tupper Genealogy (1890) 3 pages
Turberville — Lee Genealogy (1895) 93-6
Meade's Old Churches of Virginia iii, 146
Turell — Brook's Medford Mass. 555
New E. Hist. and Gen. Register xliv, 139
Savage's Genealogical Dictionary iv, 343
Turk — Albany Collections iv, 173
Roome Genealogy 232
Turley — Power's Sangamon Ill. 731
Turnbull — Cushman's Sheepscott 428
Turner — American Ancestry i, 84; iv,
   143, 198; ix, 66
Anderson's Waterbury Ct. i, app. 139
Austin's R. I. Genealogical Dictionary 209
Austin's Ancestral Dictionary 61
Baker's Hist. of Montville Ct. 251-60
Ball's History of Lake Co. Ind. 376
Bangor Me. Historical Magazine ix, 55
Barry's History of Hanover Mass. 411-5
Briggs' Hist. of Shipbuilding 80-2, 190-3
Bulloch Genealogy
Butler's Hist. of Farmington Me. 601
Caulkins' History of New London Ct. 346
Chase's History of Chester N. H. 602
Clement's Newtown N. J. Settlers
Cleveland's Hist. of Yates Co. N. Y. 538
Crafts' History of Whately Mass. 592
Cutter's Hist. of Jaffrey N. H. 498-500
Daniels' History of Oxford Mass. 729
Davis Genealogy 105
Davis' Landmarks of Plymouth 267-9
Deane's History of Scituate Mass. 360-3
Eaton's History of Thomaston Me. ii, 440
Farrow's Hist. of Islesborough Me. 289
French's Hist. of Turner Me. 49-51
Hanover Mass. Records (1898)
Hayward's Hist. of Hancock N. H. 939
Hubbard's Stanstead Co. Canada 279
Hudson's History of Lexington Mass. 248
Johnson Genealogy (1895) 124
Lincoln's Hist. of Hingham Mass. iii, 270
Meade's Old Churches of Va. ii, 181-6
Merrill's History of Acworth N. H. 275
Middlefield Ct. History
Mitchell's Hist. of Bridgewater Mass. 317
New Eng. Hist. and Gen. Register xxxvii,
   52; xli, 215-8
New York Gen. and Biog. Record xiii,
   124-30; xxiv, 148
Perkins' Old Houses of Norwich Ct. 580

Pierce's History of Grafton Mass. 575
Power's Sangamon Co. Ill. Settlers 729
Richmond Va. Standard iii, 5; iv, 1
Salem N. Y. Book of History 67
Savage's Genealogical Dictionary iv, 344-9
Slaughter's St. Mark's Parish Va. 179
Smith's Hist. of Peterborough N. H. 320
Stackpole's Hist. of Durham Me. 269-71
Stearns' History of Rindge N. H. 737
Turner Family of Scituate (1852) 63 pages
Turner Family of N. Haven (1894) 6 pages
Tuttle Genealogy 705
Vinton Genealogy 55, 100, 179
Wheeler's Eminent N. Carolinians 454
Wheeler's History of North Carolina ii, 438
Winsor's History of Duxbury Mass. 327
Wyman's Charlestown Mass. 972-5
Turney — Savage's Gen. Dict. iv, 349
Schenck's History of Fairfield Ct. 414
Trubee Genealogy 130-2
Turpin — Austin's R. I. Gen. Dict. 209
Goode Genealogy 42
Power's Sangamon Co. Ill. Settlers 730
Turpin Chart (1879) by Bancroft
Turrill — American Ancestry vi, 50
Buck Genealogy 215-9
Whittemore's Orange N. J. 367
Tuthill — American Ancestry v, 228
Griffin's Journal Southold N. Y. 58-67
Keith's Harrison Ancestry 85-7
Mallmann's Shelter Island 206, 292-300
New E. Hist. and Gen. Reg. xxii, 317-35
New York Gen. and Biog. Rec. xxix,
    123-7, 215-20
Stickney's History of Minisink N. Y. 121
Tuthill Family Meeting (1867) 60 pages
Tuthill Meeting Address (1868) 23 pages
Tuthill and Kent Chart (1880) 2x2 feet
Tuthill Genealogy (1898) 12 pages. reprint
Whitmore's Heraldic Journal (1866)
Tuttle — Amer. Ancestry iii, 223; vii, 79
Anderson's Waterbury Ct. i, app. 139
Austin's Allied Families 247-9
Baker's History of Montville Ct. 598
Cochrane's History of Antrim N. H.
    717-22
Cogswell Genealogy 18
Cogswell's Nottingham N. H. 248-51
Corliss' North Yarmouth Me.
Cothren's Woodbury Ct. 723-7; ii, 1556-70
Davis' Hist. of Wallingford Ct. 908-24
Dickerman Genealogy 398-401
Dodd's History of E. Haven Ct. 156-8
Hall's Norwalk Ct. 203, 241, 267, 281, 290
Hamden Ct. History 277-9
Hammatt Papers, Ipswich Mass. 375
Hayward's Hist. of Hancock N. H. 933-9
Hudson's History of Lexington Mass. 248
Hughes Genealogy (1879) 1-8
Lapham's History of Norway Me. 612
Lapham's History of Paris Me. 757
Litchfield County Ct. History (1881) 508
Little's History of Weare N. H. 1004
N. E. Hist. Reg. viii, 132-4; xxi, 132-42
Orcutt's History of Torrington Ct. 773
Orcutt's History of Wolcott Ct. 570-4

Otis Genealogy (1851)
Robinson's Items of Ancestry (1894) 18-22
Runnells' Hist. Sanbornton N. H. ii, 812-4
Savage's Genealogical Dictionary iv, 350-2
Temple's Hist. of N. Brookfield Mass. 760
Tuttle Fam. of N. Hampshire (1842) chart
Tuttle Fam. of N. Haven (1873) 22 pages
Tuttle Fam. of N. Haven (1883) 814 pages
Tuttle Fam. of Ipswich (1885) 46 pages
Wentworth Genealogy i, 542, 545
Winslow Genealogy ii, 580-9
Wyman's Charlestown Mass. Gen. ii, 975
Wyman's Hunt Genealogy 129
Tweed — Tweed Genealogy (1887) 30 p.
Twiggs — Goode Genealogy 192
Twining — American Ancestry vii, 143
Freeman's Hist. of Cape Cod Mass. ii, 359
Hayward's History of Gilsum N. H. 406
Savage's Genealogical Dictionary iv, 353
Twining Genealogy (1890) 172 pages
Twiss — Cochrane's Antrim N. H. 722-4
Little's History of Weare N. H. 1005
Secomb's Hist. of Amherst N. H. 798-801
Twist — Power's Sangamon Co. Ill. 732
Twitchell — Am. Ancestry i, 83; iv, 115
Ballou's History of Milford Mass. 1076
Bassett's Hist. of Richmond N. H. 510-2
Child Genealogy 560-76
Daniels' History of Oxford Mass. 729-31
Heywood's Hist. Westminster Mass. 891
Lapham's History of Bethel Me. 626-35
Lapham's History of Paris Me. 758
Leland Genealogy 255
Leonard's History of Dublin N. H. 402-8
Morse's Sherborn Mass. Settlers 246-51
Norton's History of Fitzwilliam N. H. 752
Orcutt's History of Derby Ct. 773
Orcutt's History of Wolcott Ct. 575-7
Read's History of Swanzey N. H. 477
Sawin Genealogy 19-21
Timlow's Southington Ct. Sketches 238
Twitty — Lewis Genealogy (1893) 320-5
Twombly — Caverno Genealogy 8
Lapham's History of Norway Me. 613
New Eng. Hist. and Gen. Reg. viii, 263
Wentworth Genealogy i, 485-91
Tybbot — Babson's Gloucester 173
Tyler — American Ancestry ii, 126; iii,
    144; iv, 170; v, 21; xii
Anderson's Waterbury Ct. i, app. 140
Austin's R. I. Genealogical Dictionary 210
Ballou's History of Milford Mass. 1077
Bassett's Hist. of Richmond N. H. 512-4
Bradbury's Hist. Kennebunkport Me. 281
Bridgeman's Kings Chap. Bur. Gr. 289-91
Burnham's History of Brattleboro Vt. 83
Campbell's Hist. of Virginia 723
Chase's History of Chester N. H. 602
Cogswell's History of Henniker N. H. 751
Coit Genealogy 220, 288-91
Daggett's Hist. of Attleborough Mass. 95
Daniels' History of Oxford Mass. 731
Davis Genealogy 145-7
Davis' History of Wallingford Ct. 923-8
Eaton's History of Thomaston Me. ii, 440
Field's History of Haddam Ct. 46

Goode Genealogy 121
Heraldic Journal iii
Holden's Capron Genealogy 191
Hudson's History of Lexington Mass. 281
Lapham's History of Bethel Me. 625
Livermore's Hist. of Wilton N. H. 516-8
Meade's Old Families of Virginia
Mitchell's Biog. of Daniel Tyler (1883)
Paul's History of Wells Vt. 151
Perley's History of Boxford Mass. 50
Randall's Hist. of Chesterfield N. H. 473-6
Richmond Va. Critic (1888)
Richmond Va. Standard i, 49
Ridlon's Saco Valley Me. Families 1184-7
Savage's Genealogical Dictionary iv, 354-6
Sedgwick's History of Sharon Ct. 116
Sheldon's Hist. of Deerfield Mass. 349
Shourd's Fenwick Colony N. J. 268-80
Stearns' Hist. of Rindge N. H. 737
Temple's Hist. No. Brookfield Mass. 760
Tyler Family Reunion (1897) 47 pages
Tyler Family Reunion (1898) 43 pages
Tyler Family Reunion (1899) 47 pages
Tyler Life and Times
Walworth's Hyde Genealogy 578-80
Wyman's Charlestown Mass. Gens. ii, 976
Tymens — N. Y. Gen. Biog. Rec. vii, 123
Tymensen — Albany Collections iv, 173
Tyndale — New Eng. Hist. and Gen. Reg.
    viii, 263; xviii, 185
Tyng — Alden's Am. Epitaphs ii, 97-102
Atkins Genealogy (1891) 87-115, 136-44
Dunstable Mass. Bi-Centen. 80-8, 167-81
Emery's Newbury Mass. Remin. 167-9
Fox's History of Dunstable Mass. 250
Goold's Portland in the Past
Maine Historical Society Collections i, 214
Pierce's History of Gorham Me. 212
Savage's Genealogical Dict. iv, 356-8
Tyngsborough Mass. Centennial 3
Wyman's Charlestown Mass. Gens. ii, 946
Tyrell — Savage's Gen. Dict. iv, 306
Tyrrel — Hayward's Hancock 940-3
Tyson — Evans' Fox Genealogy 42-7, 73
New York Gen. and Biog. Rec. xxi, 40
Thomas Genealogy (1877) 152
Thomas Genealogy (1896) 531-7
Ufford — Orcutt's Stratford Ct. 1319
Uline — American Ancestry i, 84
Ulmer — Eaton's Thomaston Me. 440-4
Ulrich — Martin's Chester Pa. 279
Umholtz — Egle's Queries i (1894) 209
Umsted — Eyerman Ancestor (1899) 22
Uncas — Narrative Hist. Reg. v, 328-30
New Eng. Hist. and Gen. Reg. xxv, 190
Underhill — American Ancestry i, 84; iv,
    8, 174; ix, 84; xi, 6; xii
Baird's History of Rye N. Y. 448
Bartow Genealogy 174-6
Bockee Genealogy 57-9
Bolton's Westchester Co. N. Y. ii, 404
Bunker's Long Island Genealogies 297-307
Chase's History of Chester N. H. 602-8
Field Genealogy (1895) 107-11
Huron and Erie Counties Ohio History 254
Mott Genealogy 257-68

Savage's Genealogical Dictionary iv, 358
Sullivant Genealogy 355-69
Underwood — American Ancestry iii, 133
Austin's R. I. Genealogical Dictionary 210
Ball's History of Lake County Ind. 391
Ballou's History of Milford Mass. 1078-81
Barry's Hist. of Framingham Mass. 426
Bond's Watertown Mass. Genealogies 610
Cutter's History of Jaffrey N. H. 501-3
Daniels' History of Oxford Mass. 732
Draper's History of Spencer Mass. 258
Freeman's Hist. of Cape Cod Mass. i, 642
Hodgman's Hist. Westford Mass. 478-80
Hudson's History of Lexington Mass. 250
Lewis Genealogy (1893) 258
McKeen's History of Bradford Vt. 209-23
Morse's Sherborn Mass. Settlers 251
New Eng. Hist. Gen. Reg. xxxviii, 400-5
Power's Sangamon Co. Ill. Settlers 733
Read's History of Swanzey N. H. 478
Savage's Genealogical Dictionary iv, 359
Sharpless Genealogy 435
Stowe's Hist. of Hubbardston Mass. 360-2
Underwood Genealogy (1884) 8 pages
Wentworth Genealogies i, 182
Wyman's Charlestown Mass. Gens. ii, 977
Unthank — Austin's R. I. Gen. Dict. 211
Updike — American Ancestry vi
Austin's Ancestries 55
Updyke — Austin's R. I. Gen. Dict. 396
Rhode Island Hist. Society Colls iii, 311
Updyke Genealogy, see Opdyke Genealogy
Updyke's Narragansett Churches 281-3
Upham — American Ancestry ii, 129; ii,
    53-4, 64, 71; iv, 6; vii, 50, 194
Barry's Hist. of Framingham Mass. 427
Bond's Watertown Mass. Gens. 611-6
Buckingham Genealogy 276
Cogswell Genealogy 183-7
Cogswell's Nottingham N. H. 274-80
Daniels' History of Oxford Mass. 732
Draper's History of Spencer Mass. 258
Freeman's History of Cape Cod Mass. ii,
    569
Heywood's Hist. Westminster Mass. 892
Hyde's History of Brimfield Mass. 463
Livermore's History of Wilton N. H. 518
Malden Mass. Bi-Centennial 247
New Eng. Hist. and Gen. Reg. xxiii, 33-8,
    130-5; xxxiii, 41-4
Norton's Hist. of Fitzwilliam N. H. 753
Savage's Genealogical Dictionary iv, 360
Secomb's History of Amherst N. H. 802-6
Stearns' Hist. of Ashburnham Mass. 926
Upham Genealogy (1845) 92 pages
Upham Family of Cal. (1884) 18 pages
Upham Family of Salem (1885) 80 pages
Upham Family of Castine (1887) 68 pages
Upham Genealogy (1892) 573 pages
Upham Fam. of Amherst (1897) 66 pages
Wall's Rem. Worcester Mass. 101-5, 352
Washburn's History of Leicester Mass. 406
Wyman's Charlestown Mass. Gens. ii, 978
Upsall — Upsall Genealogy (1880) 12 p.
Upshaw — Meade's Old Fams. of Va.
Upshear — Power's Sangamon Ill. 675

Upson — American Ancestry vi, 11
Anderson's Waterbury Ct. i. app 140-2
Bronson's History of Waterbury Ct. 534-6
Lee Genealogy (1897) 145-65
Orcutt's History of Wolcott Ct. 578-91
Savage's Genealogical Dictionary iv, 362
Sharpe's History of Seymour Ct. 164
Timlow's Sketches Southington Ct. 239-48
Upton — American Ancestry iii, 54-6; xii
Bangor Me. Historical Magazine iii, 192
Bouton Genealogy 309-17
Crane's Rawson Genealogy 19-21
Eaton's History of Reading Mass. 120
Essex Institute Hist. Collections vii, 247
Hayward's History of Gilsum N. H. 406
Heywood's Hist. Westminster Mass. 893
Lapham's History of Norway Me. 613-6
New Eng. Hist. and Gen. Reg. xl. 147-55
Prime Genealogy (1895) 50
Smith's Hist. of Peterborough N. H. 324-7
Upton Genealogy (1874) 547 pages
Upton Fam. of Charlemont (1886) 11 pages
Upton Family Records (1893) 532 pages
Virginia Magazine of History iii (1895) 60
Urffer — Kriebel's Schwenkfelders 51
Urie — Egle's Penn. Genealogies 459
Urner — American Ancestry x, 58
Urner Genealogy (1893) 175 pages
Urquhart — Goode Genealogy 181
Harvey Genealogy 846-52
Saunders' Alabama Settlers 454
Usher — Brook's Medford Mass. 556-8
Fox's History of Dunstable Mass. 251
New Eng. Hist. and Gen. Register xxiii,
410-4; liv, 76-80
Paige's History of Cambridge Mass. 673
Ridlon's Saco Valley Me. Families 1187-92
Savage's Genealogical Dictionary iv, 362
Usher Genealogy (1869) 11 pages
Usher Genealogy (1895) 160 pages
Wyman's Charlestown Mass. Gens. ii, 979
Ussell — Winsor's Duxbury Mass. 327
Ustick — American Ancestry xii
Ustick Genealogy (1891) 26 pages
Ustick Genealogy, part 2 (1894) 74 pages
Utie — Wm. and Mary Coll. Reg. iv, 52-8
Utley — Morris' Bontecou Genealogy 162
Paige's History of Hardwick Mass. 519
Utter — Austin's Allied Families 251
Utz — Garr Genealogy 91
Vail — American Ancestry ii, 129; iii, 114;
vi, 21-2, 89; x, 195
Aylsworth Genealogy 223
Griffin's Journal Southold N. Y. 220-2
Hyde's History of Brimfield Mass. 465
Littell's Passaic Valley Genealogy 453
New York Gen. and Biog. Record ii, 151-3
Phœnix's Whitney Genealogy i, 392
Redfield Genealogy 67
Shotwell Genealogy 243-8
Vail Genealogy (1857-63) 31 pages
Vail Family of Southold (1894) 57 pages
Walworth's Hyde Genealogy 580
Williams' History of Danby Vt. 272-80
Valentine — Amer. Ancestry ii, 129; xi. 7
Bolton's Westchester Co. N. Y. ii, 761

Bunker's Long Island Genealogies 307-12
Dows Genealogy 191
Littell's Passaic Valley Genealogy 455-8
New Eng. Hist. and Gen. Reg. xx, 221-6
Queens County N. Y. History 89, 507
Slaughter's St. Mark's Parish Va. 192
Valentine Genealogy (1874) 248 pages
Vales — Hill's Dedham Mass. Records
Vallet — Baker's Montville Ct. 261-6
Van Aernam — American Ancestry i, 84
Van Aken — American Ancestry i, 84
Sylvester's History of Ulster Co. N. Y. 98
Van Allen — American Ancestry i, 84; ii,
130; iii. 56, 220; vi, 168
Munsell's Albany Collections iv, 174
Van Alst — Riker's Newtown 380-3
Van Alstyne — American Ancestry i, 84;
ii, 130; iv, 133; ix, 118
Huntting's Hist. of Pine Plains N. Y. 389
Munsell's Albany Collections iv, 174
New York Gen. and Biog. Record x, 50
Pearson's Schenectady N. Y. Settlers 205
Van Alstyne Genealogy (1897) 142 pages
Van Antwerp — American Ancestry i, 84
Munsell's Albany Collections iv, 175
Pearson's Schenectady Settlers 205-10
Roome Genealogy 118-21
Van Arnhem — Albany Collections iv, 175
Pearson's Schenectady N. Y. Settlers 210
Van Arsdale — Amer. Ancestry vi, 113
Nevius Genealogy
Riker Genealogy
Riker's Annals of Newtown N. Y. 307
Van Artsdalen — Davis' Bucks Co. Pa.
Van Atta — Chambers' N. J. Germans
Van Auken — Gumaer's Deerpark 69-72
McMath Genealogy 48-64
Van Baal — N. Y. Gen. Record ix, 155
Van Bebber — Potts Genealogy (1895) 41
Van Benschoten — American Ancestry ii,
131; iv, 12
Van Benthuysen — Am. Ancestry i, 85
Munsell's Albany Collections iv, 176
Pearson's Schenectady N. Y. Settlers 210
Van Bergen — Greene Co. N. Y. 438-41
Munsell's Albany Collections iv, 176-8
Talcott's N. Y. and N. E. Fams. 292-304
Van Blarcom — Amer. Ancestry iv, 7
Calnek's Hist. of Annapolis N. S. 616
Van Boerum — Bergen's Kings Co. N. Y.
Settlers 39-42
Van Borsum — N. Y. Gen. and Biog. Rec.
xxvi, 192-201; xxvii, 50-2, 101-3
Van Brakel — Albany Collections iv, 177
Van Brocklin — Pompey N. Y. 387-90
Van Brugh — N. Y. Rec. xiv, 142-4
Van Brunt — American Ancestry iv, 183
Bergen Genealogy 117-9, 148
Bergen's Kings Co. N. Y. Settlers 310-3
Van Brunt Genealogy (1867) 79 pages
Van Buren — Amer. Anc. ii, 131; x, 161
Munsell's Albany Collections iv, 177-9
New York Gen. and Biog. Rec. ix, 9; xvii,
58-60; xxviii, 121-5, 207-11
Schoonmaker's Kingston N. Y. 490
Strong Genealogy 1185-7

Van Buskirk — Calnek's Annapolis 617
Chambers' Early Germans of N. J. 541
Chute Genealogy, appendix 217–22
Clute's History of Staten Island 428
Winfield's Hist. Hudson Co. N. J. 487–96
Van Campen — Brodhead's Delaware
  Water Gap 238–40
Vance — Alexander Gen. (1878) 189–92
American Ancestry x, 171
Bass' History of Braintree Vt. 192
Hayden's Virginia Genealogies 457
Miller's Hist. Colchester Co. N. S. 190–2
Sinclair Genealogy 357
Vancil — Power's Sangamon Ill. 735–7
Van Cleef — Bergen's Kings Co. 314
Cooley's Trenton N. J. Settlers 292–9
Nevius Genealogy
Van Cortlandt — Bolton's Hist. of West-
  chester Co. N. Y. i, 99
Hoffman Genealogy 506–8
Lamb's History of New York City i, 607
New York Gen. Rec. v, 70–2; viii, 12
Schuyler's Colonial New York
Valentine's N. Y. City Common Council
  Manual (1853) 385, (1854) 402
Whitmore's Heraldic Journal iv, 20–2
Van Dam — Lamb's N. Y. City i, 496
New York Gen. and Biog. Record ii, 24
Valentine's N. Y. Manual (1865) 714–25
Van De Boe — American Ancestry ii, 132
Van De Carr — American Ancestry ii, 132
Vandegriff — American Ancestry xii
Van Demark — Schoonmaker's History of
  Kingston N. Y.
Vandenberg — Greene Co. N. Y. 460
Munsell's Albany Collections iv, 178–80
Pearson's Schenectady N. Y. Settlers 213
Smith's Hist. of Dutchess Co. N. Y. 499
Talcott's New York and N. E. Fams. 305
Vanderbeck — Amer. Ancestry viii, 195
Bergen's Kings Co. N. Y. Settlers 317–9
Vanderbilt — Bergen Genealogy 130
Bergen's Kings Co. N. Y. Settlers 319–21
Clute's History of Staten Island N. Y.
  429–31
Crawford Family of Virginia 90–9
Vanderbogart—Albany Collections iv, 180
Pearson's Schenectady N. Y. Settlers 215
Talcott's N. Y. and N. E. Fams. 307–11
Van Derburgh — Am. Ancestry ii, 132
Vandercook — American Ancestry ix, 57
Van Deren — Power's Sangamon 737
Vandergrift — Bergen's Kings Co. 316
Vanderheyden—Albany Collections iv, 181
Pearson's Schenectady N. Y. Settlers 216
Thomas Genealogy (1877) 153
Weise's History of Troy N. Y. 14
Woodworth's Reminiscence Troy N. Y.
  70–4
Van Der Kar — Albany Collections 181
Van Derlyn — Schoonmaker's History of
  Kingston N. Y.
Vanderpoel — American Ancestry i, 85;
  ii, 132; vii, 90
Aylsworth Genealogy 144, 287
Munsell's Albany Collections iv, 182

New York Gen. and Biog. Rec. ii, 192
Talcott's N. Y. and N. E. Fams. 323–42
Vandersaal — Heinecke and Vandersaal
  Genealogy (1869) 37–80
Vandersluys — Pennypacker's Annals of
  Phœnixville Pa. 269
Vanderveer — Am. Anc. i, 85; iv, 118, 157
Bergen Genealogy 110
Bergen's Kings Co. N. Y. Settlers 323–5
Vandervliet — Bergen's Kings Co. 325
Van Der Volgen — Pearson's Schenectady
  N. Y. Settlers 217
Vandervort — Bergen's Kings Co. 326
Pearson's Schenectady N. Y. Settlers 72
Vanderwerken — Albany Colls. iv, 183
Vanderzee — American Ancestry i, 85
Munsell's Albany Collections iv, 183
Van Deusen — American Ancestry ii, 133;
  ix, 58, 180; xi, 61
Collord Ancestors 27–30
Munsell's Albany Collections iv, 183
New York Gen. and Biog. Record xxix,
  42–4; xxx, 46–9, 101–5, 152–8, 205–8;
  xxxi, 55
Talcott's N. Y. and N. E. Families 312–7
Taylor's Great Barrington Mass. 128–30
Van Deusen Genealogy (1893) 36 pages
Van Deventer — American Ancestry iii, 57
Bergen's Kings Co. N. Y. Settlers 327
Cole Genealogy 208
Vandever — Power's Sangamon 738
Vandewater — Bergen's Kings Co. 328
Van Doorn — Norton's Fitwilliam 753
Van Doren — Honeyman's Our Home
  Magazine 53–5, 337–42, 571–3
Nevius Genealogy
Power's Sangamon Co. Ill. Settlers 739
Van Driessen — Talcott's New York and
  New England Families 318–22
van Driest — Van Brunt Genealogy 29
Van Dusen — Collins Hist. of Hillsdale
  N. Y., appendix 123–5
Van Duzen — N. Y. Gen. Record xx, 3
Van Duyn—Allen Gen. (1883) 16–8
Bergen's Kings County 330–3
N. Y. Gen. and Biog. Record x, 155–61
Riker's Annals of Newtown N. Y. 393–5
Van Dyck — American Ancestry ii, 134;
  iv, 147; ix, 207
Bergen's Van Brunt Genealogy 11–3
Bergen's Kings Co. N. Y. Settlers 333–8
Munsell's Albany Collections iv, 184
New York Gen. and Biog. Record ix, 52;
  xxx, 57–9
Pearson's Schenectady Settlers 219–21
Van Dyke — American Ancestry xii, 96
Mellick Genealogy 637
Nevius Genealogy
Smith (Rev. Wm) Biography
Vane — N. E. Hist. and Gen. Reg. ii, 142
Van Eman — Scott Genealogy 249–54
Van Epps — American Ancestry i, 86
Eldredge Genealogy 28
Harvey Genealogy 977–9
Munsell's Albany Collections iv, 184a
Pearson's Schenectady Settlers 221–6

Van Etten — Am. Ancestry vii, 168, 170
Gumaer's History of Deerpark N. Y. 133
N. Y. Gen. Biog. Rec. xxxi, 52-4, 183, 229
Pearson's Schenectady N. Y. Settlers 226
Schoonmaker's Hist. Kingston N. Y. 491
Smith's Hist. of Rhinebeck N. Y. 200
Sylvester's History of Ulster Co. N. Y. 116
Van Fleet — Chambers' Early Germans
of New Jersey 541-4
Van Gaasbeek — American Ancestry i, 86
N. Y. Gen. Biog. Rec. xxv, 28-35, 56-66
Schoonmaker's Hist. Kingston N. Y. 492
Van Gelder — Amer. Ancestry viii, 194
Van Guyseling — Pearson's Schenectady
N. Y. Settlers 226
Van Guysling — American Ancestry i, 86
Van Hoesen — Amer. Anc. ii, 134; iv, 30
Munsell's Albany Collections iv, 184
Van Hook — N. Y. Gen. Rec. x, 47
Van Hoosear — Amer. Ancestry iii, 143
Fillow Genealogy 130, 214-9
Van Horn — Nevius Genealogy
Smith's Genealogy of William Smith 69-71
Winfield's Hist. Hudson Co. N. J. 507-13
Van Horn Association Report (1879) 20 p.
Van Horn's Our Ancestors i (1882) 30-6
Van Horne — Opdyke Genealogy 432
Chambers' Early Germans of N. J. 544
Van Houten — Cole Genealogy 45, 77-80
New York Gen. and Biog. Rec. xxvii, 183-90; xxviii, 9-12
Roome Genealogy 48-54
Van Imboch — Sylvester's Ulster Co. 48
Van Ingen — Pearson's Schenectady 228
Van Inwegen — Deerpark 59-61
Van Kerk — Bergen's Van Brunt Gen. 8
Bergen's Kings C. N. Y. Settlers 369-71
Van Keuren — Smith's Rhinebeck 186
Sylvester's History of Ulster C. N. Y. 164
Van Laer — Plumsted Genealogy 64
Van Leer — Smith's Delaware Pa. 588
Van Loon — American Ancestry i, 86
Greene County N. Y. History 194
Munsell's Albany Collections iv, 184
Van Meter — Power's Sangamon 740
Shourd's Fenwick Colony N. J. 301-7
Vann — American Ancestry xi, 53
Van Name — Clute's Staten Island 431
Van Natten — American Ancestry i, 86
Power's Sangamon County Ill. Settlers 742
Van Ness — Amer. Anc. ii, 135; viii, 195
Bergen's Kings Co. N. Y. Settlers 346
Munsell's Albany Collections iv, 184
Pearson's Schenectady N. Y. Settlers 226
Roome Genealogy 36-41, 279-82
Talcott's N. Y. and N. E. Families 343-9
Van Nest — Am. Ancestry iii, 110; vi, 176
Chambers' Early Germans of N. J. 545
Nevius Genealogy
Van Norstrand — Bergen's Kings Co. N.
Y. Settlers 349-51
Munsell's Albany Collections iv, 184
Power's Sangamon Co. Ill. Settlers 743
Van Nuyse — Bergen Genealogy 157
Bergen's Kings Co. N. Y. Sett. Gen. 351-3
Van Nydeck — Van Nydeck Gen. (1885)

Van Oblenis — Amer. Ancestry vii, 175
Van O'Linda — Albany Collections iv, 184
Pearson's Schenectady Settlers 229
Van Orden — Greene Co. N. Y. 441-3
Van Pelt — Bergen's Kings Co. 353-9
Chambers' Early Germans of N. J. 546
Clute's Hist. of Staten Island N. Y. 432-4
Van Petten — Amer. Anc. ii, 135; iii, 57
Munsell's Albany Collections iv, 184
Pearson's Schenectady Settlers 230-5
Power's Sangamon Co. Ill. Settlers 742
Van Ranst — Huntting's Pine Plains
Van Reed — Egle's Historical Register
Interior Penn, ii, 38-42
Van Rensselaer — Am. Anc. i, 86; ii, 136
Glenn's Some Colonial Mansions 165-8
Holgate's American Genealogy 33-55
Kip's Historical Notes 46-9
Lamb's Hist. of New York City, i, 62, 140
Munsell's Albany Collections iv, 184
New York Gen. and Biog. Record v, 72-5
Schuyler's Colonial New York
Van Rensselaer Genealogy (1888) 240 p.
Van Rensselaer Fam. Letters (1875) 2 vols.
Van Rensselaer's New Yorkers
Whitmore's Heraldic Journal i, 33
Van Ripen — Winfield's History of Hudson Co. N. J. 497-507
Van Salsbergen — Albany Collections. iv
Van Santvoord — American Ancestry i,
87; ii, 137
Munsell's Albany N. Y. Collections iv, 184
Pearson's Schenectady N. Y. Settlers 236
Van Schaick — Amer. Ancestry ii, 137
Hedge's Hist. East Hampton N. Y. 342-4
Holgate's American Genealogy 143-54
Munsell's Albany N. Y. Collections iv, 184
N. Y. Gen. Biog. Rec. ii, 19; vii, 53-6
Pearson's Schenectady N. Y. Settlers 237
Smith Genealogy (1890) 57
Talcott's N. Y. and New Eng. Fams. 350-2
Van Schelluyne — Munsell's Albany N.
Y. Collections iv, 184
Van Schlichtenhorst — Schuyler's Colonial New York
Van Schoonhoven — Amer. Ances. i, 87
Munsell's Albany N. Y. Collections iv, 184
Van Scoy — Hedge's History of East
Hampton N. Y. 342-4
Van Sickle — American Ancestry x, 31
Chambers' Early Germans of N. J. 547
Littell's Passaic Valley 382
Mellick's Story of an Old Farm 687
Van Sickle Genealogy (1880) 236 pages
Van Siclen — American Ancestry iii, 57-8
Van Slyck — American Ancestry x, 101
Munsell's Albany Collections iv, 184
Pearson's Schenectady N. Y. Sett. 239-43
Van Slyke — American Ancestry i, 87;
ii, 137; iii, 58; ix, 111
Greene Co. N. Y. History 378
Van Stone — Eaton's Thomaston 444
Van Sweringen — See Swearingen
Van Sycklen — Bergen's Kings Co. 361
Vansyoc — Cope Family of Pa. 84, 188
Vant — Ballou's Milford Mass. 1081

Van Tassel — American Ancestry ii, 138
Bolton's Hist. Westchester Co. N. Y. ii, 545
Raymond's Tarrytown Monument 110-24
Van Tienhoven — Potts Gen. (1895) 77-80
Van Tuyl — Roome Genealogy 146-9
Van Valkenburgh — American Ancestry i, 87; ii, 138; xii, 108
Munsell's Albany N. Y. Collections iv, 184
Pearson's Schenectady N. Y. Settlers 243
Van Vechten — American Ancestry i, 88; iii, 200: vi, 78; vii, 13
Bergen's Kings Co. N. Y. Settlers 363
Chambers' Early Germans of N. J. 548-50
Greene Co. N. Y. History 443-7
Munsell's Albany N. Y. Collections iv, 184
Talcott's N. Y. and N. E. Families 352-72
Van Vlack — American Ancestry i, 88
Van Vleck — American Ancestry ii, 139
Bergen's Kings Co. N. Y. Settlers 364
Pearson's Schenectady N. Y. Settlers 244
Van Voorhees — Van Voorhees Genealogy (1888) 725 pages
Van Voorhis — American Ancestry i, 88; iii, 58, 176; iv, 14; v, 207
Bergen Genealogy 144, 172
Bergen's Van Brunt Genealogy 10, 17
Van Voorhis Ancestry (1881) 239 pages
Van Voorhees Genealogy (1888) 725 pages
Van Vorst — American Ancestry iii, 59
Pearson's Schenectady Settlers 245-8
Winfield Hist. of Hudson Co. N. J. 425-39
Van Vranken — Amer. Ancestry i, 88
Munsell's Albany Collections iv, 184
Pearson's Schenectady Settlers 248-53
Van Wagenen — N. Y. Gen. and Biog. Record x, 86-9, 107-10; xxi, 118-24; xxii, 151-4; xxiii, 64-72
Sylvester's History of Ulster Co. N. Y. 227
Van Wagenen Genealogy (1884) 69 pages
Van Wart — American Ancestry v, 230
Bolton's Westchester Co. N. Y. ii, 762
Raymond's Tarrytown Monument 125-32
Van Wie — Albany Collections iv, 184
Van Winkle — American Ancestry iv, 60
Roome Genealogy 176
Winfield's Hist. Hudson Co. N. J. 469-87
Van Woert — American Ancestry iv, 72
Munsell's Albany Collections iv, 184
Van Wormer — American Ancestry i, 88
Pearson's Schenectady Settlers 253
Van Wyck — American Ancestry xi, 8
Bergen's Kings Co. 367
Queens County N. Y. History 206
Van Zandt — Albany Collections iv, 184
Richmond Va. Standard iii, 16
Roome Genealogy 98-100
Varian — Barber's Atlee Genealogy 45
Varian Genealogy (1881) 102 pages
Varick — N. Y. Gen. Rec. viii, 16-20
Valentine's N. Y. City Manual (1853) 413
Varleth — New York Gen. and Biog. Record ix, 54-60, 113, 153; x, 35, 145
Varney — American Ancestry ii, 139
Babson's History of Gloucester Mass. 173
New Eng. Hist. and Gen. Reg. ix, 55
Otis Genealogy (1851)

Runnells' Hist. Sanbornton N. H. ii, 814
Savage's Genealogical Dictionary iv, 366
Spalding's Varney Discourse (1882) 17-9
Stackpole's History of Durham Me. 271-3
Wentworth Genealogy i, 425-7, 705
Varnum — American Ancestry iii, 59-60
Chase's History of Chester N. H. 608
Farmer and Moore's Hist. Colls. ii, 271
New E. Hist. and Gen. Reg. v, 79-82, 250
Vars — American Ancestry iv, 228
Narragansett Hist. Reg. ii, 125; iii, 298-300
Vars Genealogy (1883-7) 500 pages
Vassall — Bridgeman's Kings Chapel Epitaphs 228-31
Daniels' History of Oxford Mass. 732
Deane's History of Scituate Mass. 366-70
Ellis History of Roxbury Mass. 132
N. E. Reg. xvii, 56-61, 113-28; xxv, 39-44
Paige's History of Cambridge Mass. 674
Ruggles Genealogy
Savage's Genealogical Dictionary iv, 367
Vassall Genealogy (1862) 26 pages
Whitmore's Heraldic Journal ii, 17
Vaughan — Amer. Anc. ii, 139; xi, 142
Austin's R. I. Genealogical Dictionary 400
Cutts Genealogy 21-3, 36-8, 66, 128-30
Eaton's Annals of Warren Me. 634
Eaton's History of Thomaston Me. ii, 445
Eaton's History of Warren Me. 432
Furness' Vaughan Discourse
Goode Genealogy 247-9
Meade's Old Families of Virginia
N. E. Hist. Gen. Reg. v, 245; xix, 343-56
Ridlon's Saco Valley Me. Families 1192-6
Savage's Genealogical Dictionary iv, 368
Vaughan Genealogy (1865) 40 pages
Vaughan Family Chart by Watkins
Wentworth Genealogy i, 296
Williams' History of Danby Vt. 280
Vaux — American Ancestry vi, 115
Morris Genealogy (1898) 832-4
Veach — Power's Sangamon Ill. 743
Veazie — Bangor Hist. Mag. ii, 70-5
Cogswell's Hist. of Nottingham N. H. 486
Eaton's History of Thomaston Me. ii, 445
Farrow's Hist. of Islesborough Me. 290-3
Hanson's Old Kent Md. 176-80
Savage's Genealogical Dictionary iv, 369
Wheeler's History of Brunswick Me. 858
Vedder — American Ancestry ii, 139; iv, 8
Veeder — Am. Ancestry i, 88; ix, 35, 205
Munsell's Albany Collections iv, 184
Pearson's Schenectady Settlers 254-71
Veghte — Messler's Somerset N. J. 61
N. Y. Gen. and Biog. Record ix, 180
Veits — Andrews' New Britain Ct. 394
Venable — American Ancestry viii, 110
Cabell Genealogy 268-71
Goode Genealogy 75
Meade's Old Families of Virginia
Green's Kentucky Families
Richmond Va. Standard iii, 13, 16, 21, 26
Watkins Genealogy 20, 22
Wheeler's History of N. Carolina ii, 165
Venner — N. E. Historical Reg. xlvii, 444
Ventres — Field's Haddam Ct. 45

Ventris — N. E. Historical Reg. xlvii, 88
Verbrugge — Albany Colls. iv, 184
Verdenberg — N. Y. Rec. ix, 62-4
Verdon — Thomas Gen. (1896) 538-40
Veren — Savage's Gen. Dict. iv, 370
Vermilye — American Ancestry v, 108
Bolton's Westchester Co. N. Y. ii, 762
Riker's History of Harlem N. Y. 546-50
Wentworth Genealogy ii, 594-6
Verneelen — Riker's Harlem, 551-4
Vernier — Navarre Genealogy 366-90
Vernon — Austin's R. I. Gen. Dict. 402
Martin's History of Chester Pa. 293
New E. Hist. and Gen. Reg. xxxiii, 312-9
Rider's Diary of Thos. Vernon 117-40
Sharpless Genealogy 153
Smith's History of Delaware Co. Pa. 509
Vernon Genealogy (1879) 8 pages
Vernooy — Chambers' N. J. Germans
Schoonmaker's Kingston N. Y. 493
Sylvester's History of Ulster Co. N. Y. 166
Verplanck — American Ancestry i, 88; vi,
 87; x, 129
Hoffman Genealogy 497-502
Lamb's History of New York City i, 260
Munsell's Albany Collections iv, 184
New York Gen. and Biog. Record i, 35-9;
 xxiv, 39-44, 60-7
Schuyler's Colonial New York
Verplanck Ancestry (1870) 62 pages
Ver Planck Genealogy (1892) 306 pages
Verrill — American Ancestry iv, 109
Eaton's History of Thomaston Me. ii, 445
Lapham's History of Norway Me. 616
Verry — Capron Genealogy 207-11
Read's History of Swanzey N. H. 478
Verstille — Stiles' Windsor Ct. ii, 770-3
Very — Babson's Gloucester Mass. 173
Driver Genealogy 221, 328
Essex Inst. Hist. Collections i, 116; ii, 33-8
Savage's Genealogical Dictionary iv, 372
Vinton's Giles Genealogy 47, 533-6
Vescelius — American Ancestry i, 89
Chambers' Early Germans of N. J. 551
Vesey — Bass' History of Braintree Vt. 192
Viall — Daniels' Oxford Mass. 733
Jillson's Viall Genealogy (1885)
Narragansett Hist. Reg. iii, 97-113, 177-99
Viall Genealogy (1885) 37 pages, reprint
Vibber — Baker's Montville Ct. 231-4
Vickers — Old Kent Md. 334-7
New Eng. Hist. and Gen. Reg. xviii, 186-8
Vickers Genealogy (1864) 5 pages
Vickery — Freeman's Cape Cod ii, 590
Mitchell's Hist. of Bridgewater Mass. 319
New Eng. Hist. and Gen. Reg. xviii, 186-8
Rich's History of Truro Mass. 566
Washington N. H. History 647-9
Vickroy — Barber's Atlee Genealogy 70-80
Videtto — Corliss' N. Yarmouth Me.
Vidito — Calnek's Annapolis 618
Viele — American Ancestry i, 89; iv, 16
Munsell's Albany Collections iv, 184
Pearson's Schenectady Settlers 271-4
Viele Chart by E. L. Viele
Viets — Hollister's Hist. Pawlett Vt. 251

Vigal — Power's Sangamon Co. Ill. 744
Vilas — Chandler Genealogy 379
Hudson's History of Lexington Mass. 252
Vilas Genealogy (1875) 221 pages
Viles—Bond's Watertown Mass. Gens. 616
Hatch's History of Industry Me. 834-8
Vinal — Barry's Hanover Mass. 415
Deane's History of Scituate Mass. 364-6
Vincent — American Ancestry ii, 140; viii,
 25; x, 105; xii
Atkins' History of Hawley Mass. 52
Austin's R. I. Genealogical Dictionary 213
Baker's History of Montville Ct. 448
Meginness' North Branch Val. Pa. 428-31
Mellick's Story of an Old Farm 662
Vine — American Ancestry i, 89
Viner — Heywood's Westminster 894
Viney — Power's Sangamon Ill. 744
Vinge — Potts Genealogy (1895) 81-3
Vinhagen — Albany Collections iv, 184
Talcott's N. Y. and N. E. Families 373-5
Vining — Barry's Hanover Mass. 415
Boogher's Miscellaneous Americana 20-5
Fisher Genealogy (1896) 37
Porter Genealogy 208 d.-208 h.
Stackpole's History of Durham Me. 273-6
Stanton Genealogy 384-7
Stiles' History of Windsor Ct. ii, 773
Vinson — Babson's Gloucester 174
Vinton — American Ancestry v, 6
Barrus' History of Goshen Mass. 178
Bass' History of Braintree Vt. 193
Eaton's History of Reading Mass. 121
Judd's History of Hadley Mass. 585
Savage's Genealogical Dictionary iv, 375
Thayer Memorial (1835) 8-10
Vinton Genealogy (1858) 538 pages
Vinton's Giles Genealogy 71-3
Washburn's Hist. of Leicester Mass. 406
Wyman's Charlestown Mass. Gens. ii, 982
Virgin — American Ancestry ix, 64
Bouton's History of Concord N. H. 715
Davis' Landmarks of Plymouth Mass. 269
Lapham's History of Norway Me. 617
Lapham's History of Rumford Me. 409-16
Visscher — American Ancestry i, 89
Montgomery and Fulton Co. N. Y. 148
Munsell's Albany Collections iv, 184
Pearson's Schenectady Settlers 274
Talcott's N. Y. and N. E. Fams. 253-91
Vittum — Dow's Hampton N. H. 1023
Vivian — Hayden's Virginia Gens. 294
Vliet — Mellick Genealogy 685
Vodges — American Ancestry ii, 75
Vokes — Paige's Hardwick Mass. 519
Vollintine — American Ancestry iv, 174
Voorhees — American Ancestry i, 90
Honeyman's Our Home, 289-92, 467-9
Munsell's Albany Collections iv, 184
Nevius Genealogy
Voorhees Lineage (1896) 6 pages
See also Van Voorhees
Voorhies — Bergen's Kings Co. 374-81
Vorback — Stearns' Ashburnham 927
Vorse — Cleveland's Yates Co. N. Y. 701
Vos — Munsell's Albany Collections iv, 184

Vosburgh — American Ancestry i, 90; ii, 140; vi, 83; x, 100
Munsell's Albany Collections iv, 184
Vose — Amer. Anc. i, 90; iv, 79; v, 136
Bangor Me. Historical Magazine vi, 148
Bass' History of Braintree Vt. 193
Bedford N. H. Centennial 340
Cochrane's History of Antrim N. H. 725–9
Cochrane's Hist. Francestown N. H. 962–8
Eaton's Annals of Warren Me. 636
Eaton's Hist. of Thomaston Me. ii, 445–7
Eaton's Annals of Warren Me. 432
Little Genealogy 60–2
North's History of Augusta Me. 948–52
Savage's Genealogical Dictionary iv, 376
Stearns' Hist. of Ashburnham Mass. 928
Washington N. H. History, 650–3
Wyman's Charlestown Mass. Gens. ii, 983
Vosler — Chambers' N. J. Germans.
Votaw — American Ancestry xi, 53
Voter — Butler's Farmington Me. 602–4
Vowles — Baird's Hist. of Rye N. Y. 449
Vredenberg — Powers' Sangamon Co. Ill. Settlers 745
Vredenburgh — Amer. Ancestry vii. 180
Hoffman Genealogy 496
N. Y. Gen. Biog. Rec. ix, 62–4; xxi, 164–8
Schureman Genealogy 17, 28
Vreeland — N. Y. Gen. Rec. ix, 7
Winfield's Hudson County N. J. 439–69
Vroom — Bergen's Kings Co. N. Y. 382
Calnek's Hist. of Annapolis N. S. 618–20
McPike Genealogy
Vrooman — American Ancestry i, 90; iv, 19; vii, 19; ix, 206
Munsell's Albany Collections iv, 184
Pearson's Schenectady Settlers 276–85
Wack — Chambers' N. J. Early Germans 109–14, 553
Waddams — Litchfield County Ct. History (1881) 358–65
Waddell — Miller's Colchester 160–4
Montgomery Genealogy (1897) 37
Peyton's History of Augusta Co. Va. 318
Savage's Genealogical Dictionary iv, 377
Waddell's Annals of Augusta Co. Va. 210
Waddington — Shourd's Fenwick 347
Wade — American Ancestry i, 91; xii
Boyd's Annals of Winchester Ct. 115–7
Brook's History of Medford Mass. 558–60
Calnek's Hist. of Annapolis N. S. 620–2
Caulkins' History of Norwich Ct. 205
Chappell Genealogy (1895) 102–6
Cogswell Genealogy 20
Davis' Landmarks of Plymouth Mass. 270
Deane's History of Scituate Mass. 370
Eaton's Annals of Warren Me. 637
Eaton's History of Thomaston Me. ii, 447
Hammatt Papers, Ipswich Mass. 379–84
McKean Genealogy 186
Meade's Old Families of Virginia
Mitchell's Hist. of Bridgewater Mass. 319
N. E. Hist. Reg. xi, 163, 210; xxvii, 309
Plumb's History of Hanover Pa. 485
Roe's Sketches of Rose N. Y. 162
Savage's Genealogical Dictionary iv, 377–9

Shourd's Fenwick Colony N. J. 342–6
Sutliff Genealogy (1897) 22
Wade Genealogy (1900) 96 pages
West Springfield Mass. Centenn. (1874) 123
Wyman's Charlestown Mass. Gens. ii, 984
Wadhams — Hyde Gen. 317–22, 324–7
Hibbard's History of Goshen Ct. 553–9
Kulp's Wyoming Valley Families
Wadleigh — Dearborn's Parsonsfield
Hubbard's Stanstead Co. Canada 259–61
Runnells' Hist. Sanborn N. H. ii, 815–21
Worthen's History of Sutton N. H. 967–92
Wadley — American Ancestry viii, 73
Wadsworth — American Ancestry i, 91; ii, 141; v, 73; vi, 187; ix, 38
Andrews' History of New Britain Ct. 227
Baldwin's Candee Genealogy 205–15
Cogswell's Hist. of Herkimer N. H. 752–6
Corliss' North Yarmouth Me.
Davis' Landmarks of Plymouth Mass. 270
Douglas Genealogy 130–2
Fowler's History of Durham Ct. 124–6, 682
Gold's History of Cornwall Ct. 243
Hinman Connecticut Settlers (1846) ed.
Kellogg's White Genealogy 85
Lawrence and Bartlett Mem. 77–88
Leland Genealogy 54–6
Paige's History of Cambridge Mass. 675
Pierce's History of Grafton Mass. 575–7
Power's Sangamon Co. Ill. Settlers 745
Savage's Genealogical Dict. iv, 379–81
Stiles' History of Windsor Ct. ii, 774
Thurston's History of Winthrop Me. 200
Timlow's Southington Ct. Sketches 248–50
Vinton's Giles Genealogy 315–8
Wadsworth Genealogy (1883) 257 pages
West Springfield Mass. Centen. (1874) 123
Winsor's History of Duxbury Mass. 328–32
Wagener — Eyerman Ancestry (1899) 24–7
Schwenkfelders 36
Wagenseller — American Ancestry xi, 141
Wagenseller Chart (1897)
Wagenseller Genealogy (1898) 225 pages
Wager — American Ancestry ii, 142
Roe's Sketches of Rose N. Y. 243
Whipple-Hill Families (1897) 47–9
Waggaman — American Ancestry viii, 60
Wm. and Mary Coll. Hist. Reg. ii, 98–135
Waggener — Richmond Standard iii, 28
Waggoner — Am. Anc. i, 91; ii, 142 v, 198
Wagner — American Ancestry ix, 157
Montgomery and Fulton Co. N. Y. 157
Sharpe's South Britain Ct. Sketches 49–52
Wainwright — Amer. Ancestry vii, 102
Davis Ancestry (1897) 48
Hammatt Papers, Ipswich Mass. 384–7
Savage's Genealogical Dictionary iv, 381
Stiles' History of Windsor Ct. ii, 847
Wait — American Ancestry ii, 142; iii, 60; iv, 117; v, 51
Austin's R. I. Genealogical Dictionary 404
Daniels' History of Oxford Mass. 734
Davis' Landmarks of Plymouth Mass. 271
Judd's History of Hadley Mass. 586
Norton's History of Fitzwilliam N. H. 754
Savage's Genealogical Dictionary iv, 382–5

Sheldon's Hist. of Deerfield Mass. 350
Temple's History of Whately Mass. 272-7
Waite — Barry's Framingham 428
Bass' History of Braintree Vt. 194
Benedict's History of Sutton Mass. 736
Bond's Watertown Mass. Genealogy 617
Cleveland's Hist. of Yates Co. II. Y. 518
Crafts' History of Whately Mass. 593-611
New Eng. Hist. and Gen. Register xxiv,
    103; xxxi, 421-5; xxxii, 188-96
New England Magazine iv, 48-59
Potter's Concord Mass. Families 77
Stowe's Hist. of Hubbardston Mass. 362-5
Temple's Hist. N. Brookfield Mass. 762-7
Waite Fam. of Madden (1878) 11 pages
Waite Fam. of Boston (1878) 4 pages
Waite Fam. Portsmouth R. I. (1893) 22 p.
Walworth's Hyde Genealogy 896-901
Washburn's History of Leicester Mass. 410
Wyman's Charlestown Mass. Gens. 986-9
Waitt — Hayward's Hancock N. H. 943
Wakefield — Adams' Haven Gen. ii, 34
Alexander Genealogy 133-47
American Ancestry vi, 58, 188; x, 190
Bangor Me. Historical Magazine viii, 234
Bass' History of Braintree Vt. 194
Bemis' History of Marlboro N. H. 671
Benedict's History of Sutton Mass. 737
Daniels' History of Oxford Mass. 735
Eaton's History of Reading Mass. 121
Hanson's History of Gardiner Me. 158
Hemenway's Vermont Hist. Gaz. v, 161
Leonard's History of Dublin N. H. 409
Milliken's Narraguagus Valley Me. 15
Savage's Genealogical Dictionary iv, 385
Secomb's History of Amherst N. H. 807-9
Sharpless Genealogy 299
Wakefield Genealogy (1897) 352 pages
Wheeler's History of Newport N. H. 553-6
Wight Genealogy 66-8
Wakely — Babson's Gloucester 174
Cothren's History of Woodbury Ct. 754
Orcutt's History of Stratford Ct. 1320-2
Orcutt's History of Wolcott Ct. 592
Porter's Hartford Ct. Settlers 22
Savage's Genealogical Dictionary iv, 386
Schenck's History of Fairfield Ct. 415-7
Sharpe's South Britain Ct. Sketches 71
Wakeman — Dimond Genealogy 68-71
Jessup Genealogy 94-6
Redfield Genealogy 49
Savage's Genealogical Dictionary iv, 387
Schenck's History of Fairfield Ct. 417
Wakeman Genealogy (1900) 400 pages
Walbridge — Amer. Anc. vii, 147; xi, 54
Jenning's History of Bennington Vt. 275-7
Temple's History of Northfield Mass. 558
See also under Wallbridge
Walcott — American Ancestry xv, 142
Savage's Genealogical Dictionary iv, 338
Walker Genealogy 148
Wheeler's History of Newport N. H. 557-9
Walden — Baker's Montville Ct. 709
N. E. Hist. Reg. clxix, 62-4
Waldo — American Ancestry ii, 142
Bridgeman's Kings Chapel Epitaphs 292

Cogswell Genealogy 15-8
Dwight Genealogy 837-9
Essex Institute Hist. Collections iv, 136
Fox's History of Dunstable Mass. 251
Greene's Todd Genealogy
Kingman's No. Bridgewater Mass. 676
Maine Hist. and Gen. Recorder iv, 223-5
Mitchell's Hist. of Bridgewater Mass. 320
New Eng. Hist. and Gen. Reg. xviii, 176;
    lii, 213-28
Randall's Hist. of Chesterfield N. H. 476-8
Salisbury Family Memorials (1885) 21
Savage's Genealogical Dictionary iv, 389
Sedgwick's History of Sharon Ct. 116
Waldo Genealogy (1883) 145 pages
Waldo Genealogy (1898) 21 pages, reprint
Waldo's History of Tolland Ct. 93.
Wetmore Genealogy 448-50
Williams' History of Belfast Me. 44
Waldorph — American Ancestry ii, 142
Chambers' Early Germans of N. J. 554
Waldron — Amer. Ancestry ii, 142; xi, 57
Collord Ancestors 21-3
Cutts Genealogy 34-6, 121-3
Gale Genealogy (1866) 184
Greene County N. Y. History 308
Hayward's History of Gilsum N. H. 407
Munsell's Albany Collections iv, 184
N. E. Hist. Reg. viii, 78; ix, 55; xix, 223
Otis Genealogy (1851)
Riker's History of Harlem N. Y. 554-67
Savage's Genealogical Dict. iv, 389-91
Waldron Genealogy (1879) 10 pages
Walker Genealogy 45
Wentworth Genealogy i, 400-4
Waldruf — Richmond Standard ii, 32
Wales — Ballou's Milford Mass. 1084-6
Carey's Hist. of Bridgewater Mass.
Faxon Genealogy 45
Hyde's History of Brimfield Mass. 464
Savage's Genealogical Dictionary iv, 391
Thayer Memorial (1835) 155-62
Wales Mass. Centennial 23
Wales Genealogy (1875) 56 pages
Walford — Cleveland's Yates Co. 590
Walgamot — Power's Sangamon 782-4
Walke — Richmond Stand. iii, 50, 52
Robertson's Pocahontas' Descendants
Virginia Mag. Hist. v (1897) 88 a. 139-53
Walker — American Ancestry iv, 27, 69,
    235; ix, 206; x, 14, 54, 123, 149, 171; xii
Ammidown's Historical Collections ii, 65-8
Austin's R. I. Genealogical Dictionary 214
Ballou's History of Milford Mass. 1086-95
Barry's Hist. of Framingham Mass. 430
Bassett's Hist. of Richmond N. H. 514
Bedford N. H. Centennial 344-7
Benedict's History of Sutton Mass. 737
Bond's Watertown Mass. Genealogies 618
Bolton's History of Concord N. H. 689
Bradbury's Hist. Kennebunkport Me. 281
Burleigh's Guild Genealogy 241-3
Calnek's History of Annapolis N. S. 622
Chandler's History of Shirley Mass. 627-60
Child Genealogy 266-79
Clarke's Old King Wm. Co. Va. Families

Cochrane's History of Antrim N. H. 729
Cothren's Woodbury Ct. 744-7; ii, 1576
Daniels' History of Oxford Mass. 735
Deacon's Stoddard Genealogy
Eaton's History of Reading Mass. 123
Egle's Penn. Genealogies 2d ed. 711-3
Egle's Notes and Queries 4th ser. i, 130
Elderkin Genealogy 138-51
Evans Genealogy (1893) 21
Goode Genealogy 124
Guild's Stiles Genealogy 194, 367
Harris's History of Lancaster Co. Pa. 610
Hayward's Hist. of Hancock N. H. 944-6
Hazen's Hist. of Billerica Mass. 152-4
Hemenway's Vermont Gaz. v, 94, 402
Heywood's Hist. Westminster Mass. 894-6
Hubbard's Hist. Springfield Vt. 471-80
Hudson Hist. of Sudbury Mass. 451
Hurlbut Genealogy 407
Jameson's History of Medway Mass. 525-7
Kulp's Wyoming Valley Families
Lapham's History of Bethel Me. 636
Lapham's History of Paris Me. 760
Lapham's History of Rumford Me. 416-8
Meade's Old Churches of Virginia ii, 42
Morse's Sherborn Mass. Settlers 253
New Eng. Hist. and Gen. Reg. xxxix 166
Orcutt's History of Stratford Ct. 1322
Page Genealogy 179
Paige's History of Hardwick Mass. 519
Power's Sangamon Co. Ill. Settlers 747-9
Randalls' Hist. of Chesterfield N. H. 478
Richmond Va. Standard ii, 47; iii, 6, 29,
35; iv, 2
Ridlon's Harrison Me. Settlers 121-5
Ridlon's Saco Valley Me. Families 1196-9
Robertson's Pocahontas' Descendants
Saunderson's Charlestown N. H. 582-92
Savage's Genealogical Dictionary iv, 392-8
Sewall's Hist. Woburn Mass. 169-74, 647
Sibley's History of Union Me. 514
Slaughter's Bristol Parish Va. 232
Slaughter's Fry Genealogy 62
Slaughter's St. Mark's Parish Va. 166
Smith's Hist. of Peterborough N. H. 328
Stearns' Hist. of Ashburnham Mass. 928
Stearns' History of Rindge N. H. 741
Swift Genealogy 32
Taylor's Some Notable Families 86-93
Temple's Hist. N. Brookfield Mass. 767-72
Temple's History of Palmer Mass. 567
Thomas Family of Md. (1877) 154
Thomas Genealogy (1896) 541-3
Walker Fam. of Plymouth (1861) 451 pages
Walker Fam. of Shirley (1887) 60 pages
Walker Fam. of Rehoboth (1895) 72 pages
Walker Fam. of Chester Pa. (1896) 443 p.
Walker Manuscript in Me. Gen. Soc. Lib.
155 pages
Washington N. H. History 653-5
Wetmore Genealogy 117-21
Wheeler's History of Brunswick Me. 858
Whipple-Hill Families (1897) 49-57
Winchester Mass. Record ii, 226-31
Winsor's History of Duxbury Mass. 322
Worthen's History of Sutton N. H. 992-4

Wyman's Charlestown Mass. Gens. 990-2
Young's History of Warsaw N. Y. 342-4
Walkley — American Ancestry ix, 213
Field's History of Haddam Ct. 45
Timlow's Sketches of Southington Ct. 193
Walkup — Barry's Framingham 431-3
Wall — Eaton's Thomaston Me. 449
Lamborn Genealogy 299
Power's Sangamon Co. Ill. Settlers 749
Wallace — Am. Anc. i, 91; vi, 139; ix, 199
Ball's History of Lake County Ind. 423
Bemis' History of Marlboro N. H. 672
Bolton's Westchester County N. Y. ii, 763
Cochrane's History of Antrim N. H. 730-4
Cogswell's Hist. of Henniker N. H. 756-65
Daniels' History of Oxford Mass. 736
Eaton's Annals of Warren Me. 638
Eaton's History of Thomaston Me. ii, 449
Egle's Penn. Gens. 2d ed. 429-33, 694-7, 718
Egle's Notes and Queries 2d ser. ii, 316-8
Fullonton's History of Raymond N. H. 294
Green's Kentucky Families
Hayden's Virginia Genealogies 687-735
Hayward's History of Hancock N. H. 946
Heraldic Journal iii, 186
Lamb's Hist. of New York City i, 743, 756
Little's History of Weare N. H. 1007
Maine Historical Mag by Porter vii, 36
Merrill's History of Acworth N. H. 276
Milliken's Narraguagus Valley Me. 5
Norton's History of Fitzwilliam N. H. 755
Parker's Hist. of Londonderry N. H. 302-7
Power's Sangamon Co. Ill. Settlers 747-9
Scott Genealogy 303-8
Secomb's History of Amherst N. H. 801
Slaughter's St. Mark's Parish Va. 137
Smith's Hist. of Peterborough N. H. 330
Stearns' Hist. of Ashburnham Mass. 929-35
Wallace Family of Virginia (1870) chart
Whitsett's Life of Judge Caleb Wallace
Wallbridge — Newton Gen. (1897) 31-9
Wallbridge Genealogy (1898) 369 p.
See also under Walbridge
Waller — American Ancestry xi, 143
Bolling Genealogy 38
Caulkins' History of Norwich Ct. 206
Clarke's Old King Wm. Co. Va. Families
Cothren's History of Woodbury Ct. 754
Grigsby's Tazewell Genealogy 9
Hayden's Virginia Genealogies 382
Meade's Old Families of Virginia
New Eng. Hist. and Gen. Reg. xii, 74
Orcutt's History of New Milford Ct. 782
Paxton Marshall Genealogy 242
Richmond Va. Standard ii, 34, 40; iii, 6
Savage's Genealogical Dictionary iv, 399
Walley — Bridgeman's Granary 33-6
Freeman's Cape Cod i. 290-2; ii, 274, 774
Salisbury Family Memoirs (1885) 283-92
Savage's Genealogical Dict. iv, 399-401
Steele Genealogy (1896)
Willard Genealogy 400
Walling — Austin's R. I. Dictionary 214
Wallingford — Bemis' Marlboro 672
Hubbard's Stanstead Co. Canada 182
Hurd's Hist. of Rockingham Co. N. H. 869

New Eng. Hist. and Gen. Rec. xx, 335
Otis Genealogy (1851)
Wentworth Gen. i, 390-3; ii, 81-3, 91-102
Worcester's History of Hollis N. H. 389
Wallis — Babson's Gloucester 175
Emerson's Hist. of Douglas Mass. 185-99
Hammatt Papers, Ipswich Mass. 389-91
Maine Historical Soc. Collections i, 214
Ransom Genealogy 65
Runnells' Sanbornton N. H. ii, 821-7
Savage's Genealogical Dictionary iv, 401
Stearns' Hist. of Ashburnham Mass. 930
Walmsley — Martindale's History of By-
berry Pa. 336-47
Rodman Genealogy 141, 217
Waln — Morris Genealogy (1898) 510-5
Walsh — Eaton's Thomaston Me. 449
Ruttenber's Hist. of Newburgh N. Y. 296
Ruttenber's Hist. of Orange Co. N. Y. 408
Smith's Hist. of Sunderland Mass. 561
Walsworth—Brown Gen. (1879) 11-3, 22-6
Williams Genealogy (1887)
Walter — American Ancestry x, 205
Dorr Genealogy
Lamborn Genealogy 286
New Eng. Hist. and Gen. Reg. viii, 209-14
Savage's Genealogical Dictionary iv, 403
Sharpless Genealogy 341
Waltermire — American Ancestry ii, 143
Walters — Chambers' N. J. Germans
Walther — Stearns' Ashburnham 935
Walton — American Ancestry iv, 84; xii
Blood's History of Temple N. H. 252
Davis' History of Bucks County Pa. 87
Eaton's History of Reading Mass. 123-5
Guild's Stiles Genealogy 93-5
Kidder's History New Ipswich N. H. 438
Lamb's History of New York City i, 685
Lapham's History of Norway Me. 618
Martindale's Hist. of Byberry Pa. 347-62
Meade's Old Families of Virginia
New Eng. Hist. and Gen. Register ix, 57
Randalls' Hist. Chesterfield N. H. 479-81
Richmond Va. Standard i, 45; ii, 2, 6; iii, 27
Savage's Genealogical Dictionary iv, 405
Stearns' History of Rindge N. H. 743
Walton Ancestral Chart (1897) by Hasell
Wentworth Genealogy i, 186-8
Walworth — American Ancestry i, 91; iii,
221; viii, 132
Amer. Monthly Magazine (1894) iv, 199
Caulkins' History of New London Ct. 345
Guild's Stiles Genealogy 492
Walworth Genealogy (1897) 196 pages
Walworth's Hyde Genealogy i, 530-46
Wandel — Clute's Staten Island 434
Wandell — American Ancestry xi, 141
Wands — American Ancestry i, 92
Wanton — Austin's R. I. Gen. Dict. 215
Bartlett's R. I. Hist. Tracts iii, 7-114
Briggs' Hist. of Shipbuilding 204-9
Deane's History of Scituate Mass. 371-7
Savage's Genealogical Dictionary iv, 406
Updyke's Narragansett Churches 305
Wanton Genealogy (1878) 152 pages
Wanzer — Orcutt's New Milford 782-4

Ward — American Ancestry i, 92; iv, 173;
v, 40, 124, 177, 232; vi, 43; ix, 109; x,
204; xi, 53
Austin's Ancestries 57
Austin's R. I. Genealogical Dict. 216, 406
Ballou's History of Milford Mass. 1095
Barry's Hist. of Framingham Mass. 433
Bemis' Hist. of Marlboro N. H. 673-6
Bolton's Westchester Co. N. Y. i, 254
Bond's Watertown Mass. Gens. 619
Chambers' Early Germans of N. J. 556
Chapman's Trowbridge Genealogy 244-6
Cleveland Genealogy (1899) 126, 256, 593
Coe and Ward Memorial (1898) 31-40
Cogswell's Hist. of Henniker N. H. 765-70
Corliss' North Yarmouth Me.
Cothren's History of Woodbury Ct. 755
Cutts Genealogy 114-6
Daniels' History of Oxford Mass. 737
Davis' Landmarks of Plymouth Mass. 271
Dean's Memoir of N. Ward (1868) (1871)
Denny Genealogy
Douthett and Ward Genealogy 15-9
Dow's History of Hampton N. H. 1024
Driver Genealogy 240, 284-6, 486
Essex Inst. Colls. v, 207-19; xvii, 180-90
Goode Genealogy 109
Goodwin's Genealogical Notes 237-41
Green's Todd Genealogy
Hammatt Papers of Ipswich 391
Hayward's Hist. of Hancock N. H. 947-9
Heywood's Hist. Westminster Mass. 897
Hudson's Hist. Marlborough Mass. 450-62
Hyde's History of Brimfield Mass. 465
Jackson's History of Newton Mass. 428-37
Joslin's History of Poultney Vt. 356-9
Judd's History of Hadley Mass. 587
Kellogg's White Genealogy 57
Kitchel Genealogy 29-33
Lincoln's Hist. Hingham Mass. iii, 274-7
Littell's Passaic Valley Genealogies 462-5
Meade's Old Families of Virginia
Middlefield Ct. History
Morrison's History of Windham N. H. 805
New Eng. Hist. and Gen. Reg. xvii, 334-
42; xviii, 154-6; xli, 282-4
New Jersey Hist. Soc. Colls. vi, supp. 136
New York Gen. and Biog. Rec. vi, 123-8
Norton's Hist. of Fitzwilliam N. H. 755
Norton's Hist. of Knox County Ohio 362
Old Northwest Gen. Quarterly ii, 129
Orcutt's History of Stratford Ct. 1323
Paige's History of Cambridge Mass. 676
Paige's History of Hardwick Mass. 520
Pearson's Schenectady N. Y. Settlers 286
Pickering Genealogy
Pierce's History of Grafton Mass. 577
Pope Genealogy
Read's History of Swanzey N. H. 479
Rhode Island Hist. Soc. Collections iii, 310
Robertson's Pocahontas' Descendants
Runnells' Sanbornton N. H. ii, 827-31
Savage's Genealogical Dict. iv, 406-15
Schenck's History of Fairfield Ct. 418-20
Secomb's History of Amherst N. H. 811
Sharpe's So. Britain Ct. Sketches 159, 165

Sheldon's Hist. of Deerfield Mass. 351
Sprague's Hist. of Gloversville N. Y. 130
Stearns' Hist. Ashburnham Mass. 935-42
Temple's Hist. of N. Brookfield Mass. 773
Temple's History of Palmer Mass. 565
Turner's Phelp's Purchase in N. Y. 558
Wall's Reminisc. Worcester Mass. 30-2
Ward Fam. of Sudbury (1851) 265 pages
Ward Fam. of Newport (1875) 20 pages
Ward's Hist. of Shrewsbury Mass. 457-65
Whittemore's Orange N. J. 108
Wyman's Charlestown Mass. Gens. 993-5
Wardell — Wardell Chart (1897)
Warden — Foster Genealogy (1889) 73
Warder — Morris Genealogy (1898) 398
Wardle — Savage's Gen. Dict. iv, 415
Wardrobe — Barry's Hanover 416
Dearborn's Hist. of Salisbury N. H. 820
Wardwell — Hammatt Papers 393
Haven Genealogy, part ii, 21
Huntington's Stamford Ct. Settlers 114
Lapham's History of Rumford Me. 418-20
Worcester's History of Hollis N. H. 389
Ware — Amer. Anc. iii, 116; x 165; xii
Bangor Me. Historical Magazine v, 17
Bemis' History of Marlboro N. H. 676
Blake's History of Franklin Mass. 281-3
Clark Fam. of Watertown 85, 140-4
Deacon's Stoddard Genealogy
Hayden's Virginia Genealogies 23, 39
Hayward's Hist. of Hancock N. H. 949-58
Hayward's History of Gilsum N. H. 408-10
Jameson's Hist. of Medway Mass. add. 3
Leland Genealogy 22-4, 252
Lincoln's Hist. of Hingham Mass. iii, 277
Meade's Old Families of Virginia
Morse's Sherborn Mass. Settlers 253-5
New Eng. Hist. and Gen. Reg. vi, 145-50;
  xli, 21-52, 394-402
Norton's Hist. of Fitzwilliam N. H. 756
Paul's History of Wells Vt. 152
Porter's Eddy Genealogy, appendix
Prentice Genealogy 22-4
Read's History of Swanzey N. H. 480
Richmond Va. Standard iii, 28
Savage's Genealogical Dictionary iv, 416
Sheldon's Hist. of Deerfield Mass. 352
Shourd's Fenwick Colony N. J. 329-41
Sibley's History of Union Me. 515
Trask's Ware Genealogy
Upham Genealogy 54-6
Ware Journal (1852) 24 pages
Ware Family of Dedham (1887) 47 pages
Ware Fam. of New Jersey (1891) 31 pages
Ware Fam. of Wrentham (1896) 8 pages
Wight Genealogy 30-2
Warfield — Amer. Ancestry vi, 21; xii
Ballou's History of Milford Mass. 1100
Capron Genealogy by Holden 214-6
Thomas Genealogy (1877) 155-7
Thomas Genealogy (1896) 543-7
Warfield Genealogy (1898)
Warham — Stiles' Windsor Ct. ii, 775
Waring — American Ancestry v, 137
Bowie Genealogy 471-96
Clarke's Old King Wm. Co. Va. Families

Hall's Hist. of Norwalk Ct. 194, 223, etc.
Huntington's Stamford Ct. Settlers 114
Jones Genealogy (1891) 135
Waring Genealogy (1898) 60 pages
Warland — Paige's Cambridge 677
Warley — American Ancestry iv, 172
Warner — American Ancestry i, 92; ii,
  143; iii, 162; iv, 150, 151; viii, 47, 62;
  ix, 22, 136; x, 124
Anderson's Waterbury Ct. i, app. 143-7
Austin's Allied Families 253
Austin's R. I. Genealogical Dictionary 408
Babson's History of Gloucester Mass. 258
Bass' History of Braintree Vt. 194
Blake's History of Hamden Ct. 280
Bronson's Hist. of Waterbury Ct. 536-41
Caverly's History of Pittsford Vt. 728
Cothren's Hist. of Woodbury Ct. i, 752-4
Crafts' History of Whately Mass. 611
Crowell's Mem. of A. Warner (1884) 90 p.
Daniels' History of Oxford Mass. 738
Doolittle's Belchertown Mass. 264
Douglas Genealogy 219
Dyer's History of Plainfield Mass. 181-3
Ely Genealogy 24
Evan's Fox Genealogy 91-102
Field's History of Haddam Ct. 48
Fox's History of Dunstable Mass. 252
Glenn's Merion in Welsh Tract 381-3
Goodwin's Foote Genealogy 201
Green's Kentucky Families
Hammatt Papers, Ipswich Mass. 394-9
Heywood's Hist. Westminster Mass. 898
Hollister's History of Pawlet Vt. 253
Hoyt's Salisbury Mass. Families 340
Hurlbut Genealogy 405
Judd's History of Hadley Mass. 588-91
Loomis Genealogy (1880) 721-3
Merrill's History of Acworth N. H. 278
Montague Genealogy 63, 155-8, 441-3
Morris' Bontecou Genealogy 139
Nash Genealogy 36
New Eng. Hist. and Gen. Register xiv,
  125-32; xv, 135; xx, 64-8, 318
Norton's History of Fitzwilliam N. H. 757
Orcutt's History of New Milford Ct. 792
Orcutt's History of Wolcott Ct. 594-7
Paige's History of Cambridge Mass. 678
Paige's History of Hardwick Mass. 521-7
Peck's Rochester N. Y. Centen. 681-5
Richmond Standard iii, 23, 38, 52; iv, 23
Savage's Genealogical Dict. iv, 418-22
Secomb's History of Amherst N. H. 812
Sharpe's South Britain Ct. Sketches 98
Sheldon's Hist. of Deerfield Mass. 353
Sherburne N. Y. News for Aug. 31, 1889
Smith's Hist. of Sunderland Mass. 563-9
Spooner's Memorial of W. Spooner 92
Stiles' History of Windsor Ct. ii, 775
Taylor's Some Notable Families 69-72
Temple's History of Northfield Mass. 559
Tuttle Genealogy xliv
Virginia Magazine of History ii (1895) 423
Walworth's Hyde Gen. 597-600, 943-5
Warner Genealogy (1866) 4 pages, reprint
Warner Genealogy (1872) 13 pages

Wentworth Genealogy i, 329
Wilbraham Mass. Centennial 310
Young's Hist. Chautauqua Co. N. Y. 583
Warren — American Ancestry i, 92; iv, 3, 41, 121, 172; vi, 29; vii, 161; viii, 43; ix, 45, 70, 220; x, 203; xi, 54–5
Ballou's History of Milford Mass. 1100–2
Barry's History of Framingham Mass. 433
Bond's Watertown Mass. 619–26, 960–3
Bouton Genealogy 11–4
Bridgeman's Granary Epitaphs 223–7
Buckminster's Hastings Genealogy 56–62
Chandler's History of Shirley Mass. 661–6
Cochrane's History of Antrim N. H. 735
Cochrane's Hist. Francestown N. H. 968–70
Cogswell Genealogy 96
Cutter's History of Arlington Mass. 313
Davis Genealogy 130
Davis' Landmarks of Plymouth Mass. 272
Doty Genealogy 40
Farrow's Hist. of Islesborough Me. 293–8
Hanson's History of Gardiner Me. 84
Hayward's Hist. of Hancock N. H. 958–65
Heywood's Hist. Westminster Mass. 899
Hudson's Hist. of Marlborough Mass. 462
Hyde's History of Brimfield Mass. 466
Kellogg's White Genealogy 76
Kingman's N. Bridgewater Mass. 677–80
Lapham's History of Paris Me. 762
Leland Genealogy 53
Leonard's History of Dublin N. H. 410
Loring's One Hundred Boston Orators 45
Merrill's History of Acworth N. H. 279
Mitchell's Hist. of Bridgewater Mass. 321
N. Y. Gen. and Biog. Record xviii, 150–2
Norton's History of Fitzwilliam N. H. 758
Odiorne Genealogy
Pierce's History of Grafton Mass. 578–84
Pierce's Biog. Contributions 297–311
Richmond Va. Standard ii, 47
Ridlon's Saco Valley Me. 1199–1207
Ruttenber's Hist. Newburgh N. Y. 284–6
Ruttenber's Hist. of Orange Co. N. Y. 378
Savage's Genealogical Dictionary iv, 423–8
Sedgwick's History of Sharon Ct. 117
Selleck's Norwalk Ct. (1896) 268–81
Sheldon's Hist. of Deerfield Mass. 354
Stackpole's History of Durham Me. 277–80
Stowe's Hist. of Hubbardston Mass. 365–7
Upham Genealogy 56–9
Virginia Magazine of History vi, 200–3
Warren Genealogy (1854) 113 pages
Warren Lineage (1874) 7 pages
Warren Autobiography (1884) 59 pages
Warren Ancestry (1886) 120 pages
Warrens of Chelmsford (1890) 128 pages
Warrens of Williamsburg (1894) chart
Warren and Clarke Gen. (1894) 238 pages
Warren's History of Waterford Me. 298
Washburn's Hist. of Leicester Mass. 408
Wyman's Charlestown Mass. Gens. 995–7
Young's Hist. Chautauqua Co. N. Y. 570
Warriner — Amer. Ancestry xi, 114; xii
Ely Genealogy 99
Montague Genealogy 61
Savage's Genealogical Dictionary iv, 428

Temple's History of Northfield Mass. 560
Temple's History of Palmer Mass. 569
Warriner Genealogy (1899) 287 pages
Wilbraham Mass. Centennial 311–3
Warrington — Hawley Mass. 94
Warwick — Lynchburg Va. 235–8
Savage's Genealogical Dictionary iv, 429
See also under Worrick
Warying — Meade's Old Families of Va.
Washburn — American Ancestry ii, 144; iv, 240; v, 38
Barrus' History of Goshen Mass. 179
Davis' Genealogy 78, 182–9
Davis' Landmarks of Plymouth 273–6
Eaton's Hist. of Thomaston Me. ii, 450
Faxon Genealogy 97–106
Hayward's Hist. of Hancock N. H. 965–78
Huron and Erie Cos. Ohio History 348
Lapham's History of Paris Me. 763–5
Mitchell's Hist. of Bridgewater Mass. 322
Orcutt's History of Derby Ct. 774
Orcutt's History of New Milford Ct. 784
Orcutt's History of Stratford Ct. 1324
Paige's Hist. of Hardwick Mass. 527
Power's Sangamon Co. Ill. Settlers 751
Savage's Genealogical Dictionary iv, 429
Seymour Ct. Record for Feb. 26, 1891
Smith's Washburn Sermon (1867) 15 pages
Smith's Hist. Peterborough N. H. 330–3
Stanton Genealogy 281
Temple's Hist. of N. Brookfield Mass. 773
Temple's History of Palmer Mass. 569
Washburn Genealogy (1892) 16 pages
Washburn Genealogy (1899) 104 pages
Washburn's Hist. of Leicester Mass. 412–5
Washburn's Notes Livermore Me. 77–9
Washburn MSS. in Me. Gen. Lib. 24 pages
Washington — Alden's Epitaphs v, 71–3
American Ancestry iv, 243; v, 35; viii, 162
Bolling Genealogy 64
Campbell's History of Virginia 456
Ford's Washington Wills (1891)
Green's Kentucky Families
Hayden's Virginia Genealogies 81, 517
Heraldic Journal (1866) ii, 66–74, 145–65
Irving's Life of George Washington i, 1–7
Lee Genealogy (1895) 209–15
Meade's Old Churches Virginia ii, 166–71
Munsey's Magazine 1896
New Eng. Hist. and Gen. Register vi, 384; xvii, 248–51; xxi, 25–35; xliv, 195–200, 301–8; xlv, 199–218
Paxton's Marshall Genealogy 98
Pennsylvania Magazine of History and Biography xvi, 261–98; xvii, 208–10
Prescott's Page Genealogy
Richmond Va. Standard iii, 37, 52
Simpkinson's The Washingtons (1860)
Slaughter's St. Mark's Parish Va. 186
Southern Bivouac (1886) 726
Spark's Life of Washington i, 539–54
Washington Facsimiles (1862) 15 pages
Washington Ancestry (1866) 23 pages
Washington Pedigree (1879) 370 pages
Washington Maternal Anc. (1885) 28 pages
Washington Ancestry (1889) 53 pages

Washington Pedigree (1890) 18 pages
Washington Pedigree (1891) 6 pages
Washington Genealogy (1891) 71 pages
Washington Family (1893) 115 pages
Welles' American Fam. Antiquity i, 17–20
Wason — Chase's Chester N. H. 611
Cogswell's Hist. of New Boston N. H. 390
Fullonton's Hist. of Raymond N. H. 295
Hayward's Hist. of Hancock N. H. 978–82
Wass — Maine Hist. Rec. ix, 301
Wasson — Young's Wayne Co. Ind. 357
Waste — Brown's Whitingham Vt. 162–5
Hemenway's Vermont Gazetteer v, 713
Watcher — N. E. Hist. Gen. Reg. xiv, 11
Waterbury — American Ancestry xi, 139
Huntington's Stamford Ct. Settlers 116–9
Orcutt's History of New Milford Ct. 784
Strong Genealogy 909
Welles' Amer. Fam. Antiquities iii, 167–93
Waterhouse — Brewster's Rambles About
Portsmouth N. H. 2d series 98
Machias Me. Centennial 178
Savage's Genealogical Dictionary iv, 431
Stackpole's Hist. of Durham Me. 280
Waterman — Am. Anc. i, 92; ii, 144; iv, 24
Austin's Ancestries 91–7
Austin's R. I. Genealogical Dict. 408–13
Briggs' History of Shipbuilding 138
Caulkins' History of Norwich Ct. 206–8
Davis' Landmarks of Plymouth Mass. 276
Deane's History of Scituate Mass. 377–9
Freeman's Hist. of Cape Cod Mass. ii, 328
Hurd's Hist. of New London Ct. 520–2
Lincoln's Hist. Hingham Mass. iii, 278–80
Mitchell's History Bridgewater Mass. 333
Narragansett Historical Reg. ii, 291
New Eng. Hist. Gen. Reg. xxiii, 104. 472
Perkins' Old Houses of Norwich Ct. 582
R. I. Hist. Mag. v, 85–91, 191–204, 342–4
Savage's Genealogical Dictionary iv, 431–3
Tanner Genealogy 81–6
Walworth's Hyde Genealogy 464–71
Winsor's History of Duxbury Mass. 323
Waters — Am. Ancestry vi, 129–31, 189;
xii, 5, 38
Baird's History of Rye N. Y. 449
Benedict's History of Sutton Mass. 738–46
Bond's Watertown Mass. Gens. 626
Chapman's Weeks Genealogy 58
Cushman's History of Sheepscott Me. 429
Driver Genealogy 155–7, 267
Felton Genealogy (1886) 247
Lincoln's Hist. Hingham Mass. iii, 280–3
New Eng. Hist. and Gen. Reg. li, 406–9
Savage's Genealogical Dictionary iv, 433–6
Wakefield Genealogy 76
Waters Genealogy (1882) 31 pages
Wyman's Charlestown Mass. Gens. 997–9
Watkins — Aldrich's Walpole 374–8
American Ancestry i, 92; v, 72
Cleveland Genealogy (1899) 2136–42
Meade's Old Churches of Virginia i, 450
Morse Memorial, appendix No. 37 3-4
Morse's Sherborn Mass. Settlers 255
Orcutt's History of Stratford Ct. 1324
Richmond Standard ii, 40; iii, 14, 26, 27, 32

Saunders' Alabama Settlers 235–45, 251–4,
485–511
Stearns' Hist. of Ashburnham Mass. 942
Watkins Genealogy (1849) 50 pages
Watkins Genealogy 2d ed. (1888) 42 pages
Watkinson — Champion Genealogy 314–6
Pelletreau's Westchester N. Y. Wills
Watmough — Titcomb's Early New Eng-
land People 116–22
Watros — Strong Genealoy 871–6
Watrous — American Ancestry ii, 144
Avon N. Y. Genealogical Record 17–21
Chapman's Pratt Genealogy 267
Caulkins' Hist. of New London Ct. 295
Temple's History of Northfield Mass. 561
Walworth's Hyde Genealogy 46
Watson — American Ancestry i, 93; ii,
144; iii, 121; iv, 53, 175, vii, 26
Austin's Ancestral Dictionary 62
Austin's R. I. Genealogical Dictionary 217
Barbour's My Wife and Mother, app. 21
Bass' History of Braintree Vt. 195
Bradbury's Kennebunkport Me. 283
Cleveland's Hist. of Yates Co. N. Y. 343
Cogswell's Hist. of Nottingham N. H. 251
Daniels' History of Oxford Mass. 738
Davis' History of Bucks County Pa. 277
Davis' Landmarks Plymouth Mass. 277–9
Deane's Life of E. Watson (1864) 16 pages
Dearborn's Hist. of Salisbury N. H. 821–8
Dorr's Life of John Fanning Watson 12–4
Draper's History of Spencer Mass. 264–8
Eaton's Annals of Warren Me. 639
Eaton's History Thomaston Me. ii, 454–6
Gibbs' History of Blandford Mass. 63
Lapham's History of Norway Me. 618
Little's History of Weare N. H. 1008
Locke Genealogy 79
Maine Hist. and Gen. Recorder vi, 384;
ix, 259–62, 316, 341, 370–6
Meade's Old Families of Virginia
Missouri Pioneer Families 190
New Eng. Hist. and Gen. Reg. xviii, 363–8
Orcutt's History of Torrington Ct. 774
Otis Genealogy (1851)
Paige's History of Cambridge Mass. 681
Pearson's Schenectady N. Y. Settlers 287
Pierce's History of Gorham Me. 214
Power's Sangamon Ill. Settlers 752–4
Preble Genealogy 252
Ransom Genealogy 69–71
Rhode Island Hist. Soc. Collections iii, 315
Ridlon's Harrison Me. Settlers 125–7
Savage's Genealogical Dictionary iv, 436–8
Shotwell Genealogy 35
Stiles' Hist. of Windsor Ct. ii, 776–81
Temple's History of N. Brookfield Mass.
774
Temple's History of Palmer Mass. 568
Warren's History of Waterford Me. 299
Washburn's History of Leicester Mass. 411
Watson Fam. of Hartford (1865) 47 pages
Watson Fam. of Leicester (1894) 163 pages
Watson's Some Notable Families 1–37
Wetmore Genealogy 64
Wheeler's History of Newport N. H. 560

Whitehead's Perth Amboy N. J. 125-8
Wyman's Charlestown Mass. 1000-2
Wattles — Gould's Delaware Co. 143-8
Watton — Eaton's Warren Me. 642
Watts — Davis' Bucks County Pa. 203
De Peyster and Watts Gen. (1854) 249 p.
Eaton's Annals of Warren Me. 639, 642
Eaton's Hist. Thomaston Me. ii, 451, 454
Egle's Notes and Queries 1st ser. i, 42-5
Lamb's Hist. of N. Y. City i, 507, 568, 756
Leach's Reading Genealogy 203-14
Morrison's History of Windham N. H. 806
Power's Sangamon Co. Ill. Sett. 754, 756
Savage's Genealogical Dictionary iv, 438
Wyman's Charlestown Mass. Gens. 1002
Waugh — Egle's Penn. Gens. 2d ed. 95
Way — Amer. Ancestry iv, 72; ix, 145
Anderson's Waterbury Ct. i, app. 147
Caulkins' History of New London Ct. 362
Cleveland's Hist. of Yates Co. N. Y. 643
Dodd's History of East Haven Ct. 159
Douglas Genealogy 204-6
Palmer and Trimble Genealogy 218-20
Power's Sangamon Co. Ill. Settlers 756
Riker's Annals of Newtown N. Y. 378-80
Saunderson's Charlestown N. H. 593
Savage's Genealogical Dict. iv, 439-41
Sedgwick's History of Sharon Ct. 117
Washington N. H. History 655
Way Genealogy (1887) 23 pages
Whitmore's Copps Hill Epitaphs
Wayne — American Ancestry iv, 75
Bellinger Genealogy 85
Neff Genealogy 248-50
N. E. Hist. and Gen. Reg. xxxviii, 199
Richmond Va. Standard i, 40
Wayt — Peyton's Augusta Co. Va. 318
Weare — Chute Gen., app. 222-30
Cogswell's History of Nottingham N. H.
    487-92
Corliss' North Yarmouth Me. 475-82
Dow's History of Hampton N. H. 1026-32
Hubbard's Stanstead Co. Canada 171
Lane Genealogy (1891) 37
Maine Hist. and Gen. Recorder vii, 90-9
New Haven Hist. Soc. Collections viii, 380
Savage's Genealogical Dictionary iv, 441
Upham Genealogy 54-6
Weare Genealogy (1879) 8 pages
Wears — Heywood's Westminster 90-2
Weatherbee — Hill's Dedham Records
Weathern — Butler's Farmington 605-7
Weaver — American Ancestry ii, 144;
    vii, 30
Austin's R. I. Genealogical Dictionary 412
Bailey Ancestry (1892) 40-2
Cleveland's Hist. of Yates Co. N. Y. 526-8
Everhart Genealogy (1883) 90-6
Jennings Genealogy ii (1899)
New Eng. Historical and Gen. Register
    xviii, 256; xlvii, 48-60
Paige's History of Hardwick Mass. 528
Pearson's Schenectady N. Y. Settlers 294
Pierce's Biog. Gen. Contributions 312-400
Sharpless Genealogy 229-31, 355-9
Spooner Genealogy i, 401-4

Walworth's Hyde Genealogy 557
Weaver Genealogy (1893) 13 pages
Webb — American Ancestry x, 199; xii
Anderson's Waterbury Ct. i, app. 147
Bangor Historical Magazine iii, 29-35
Bass' History of Braintree Vt. 195
Cushman's History Sheepscott Me. 430-2
Driver Genealogy 75-90
Eaton's Annals of Warren Me. 643
Essex Institute Hist. Colls. xvi, 213-35
Freeman's Hist. of Cape Cod Mass. ii, 393
Hayden's Virginia Genealogies 43
Holton's Winslow Memorial i, 305-17
Huntington's Stamford Ct. Settlers 119-24
Jessup Genealogy 294-7
Lamborn Genealogy 273
New York Gen. and Biog. Rec. xxvi, 190-2
Paige's History of Hardwick Mass. 529
Pierce's History of Gorham Me. 215-7
Power's Sangamon Co. Ill. Settlers 757-9
Savage's Genealogical Dictionary iv, 443-6
Schenck's History of Fairfield Ct. 420
Selleck's Norwalk Ct. (1896) 149, 398-402,
    470
Vinton's Giles Genealogy 497-532
Virginia Magazine of History iii, (1895) 57
Webb Genealogy (1880) 24 pages, reprint
Wilcoxson Genealogy (1893) 52-75
Wyman's Charlestown Mass. Gens. 1003
Webber — Aldrich's Walpole N. H. 379
American Ancestry xi, 140
Babson's Hist. of Gloucester Mass. 176-8
Brown's Bedford Mass. Families 42
Corliss' North Yarmouth Me.
Hyde's History of Brimfield Mass. 466
Maine Historical Society Collections 215
Savage's Genealogical Dictionary iv, 446
Stackpole's History of Durham Me. 281
Temple's History N. Brookfield Mass. 774
Temple's History of Palmer Mass. 569
Walker Genealogy 341
Webber Early History (1878) 42 pages
Webber Genealogy (1897) 54 pages
Wheeler's History of Brunswick Me. 859
Wyman's Charlestown Mass. Gens. 1004
Weber — Brook's Medford Mass. 560
Power's Sangamon Co. Ill. Sett. 759, 762
Rupp Genealogy 100-5
Webster — American Ancestry iv, 149; vi,
    22; viii, 205; ix, 51, 172; x 38; xi, 55,
    140
Andrews' Hist. of New Britain Ct. 188, 235
Bangor Me. Hist. Mag. iv, 121-5; vii, 172
Barbour's My Wife and Mother, app. 23
Bass' History of Braintree Vt. 195
Bouton's History of Concord N. H. 699
Boyd's History of Conesus N. H. 174
Chase's History of Chester N. H. 610-2
Chester's History of Haverhill Mass. 79
Coffin's Hist. of Boscawen N. H. 617
Cochrane's History of Antrim N. H. 736
Cogswell's Hist. of Henniker N. H. 771
Dearborn's Hist. Salisbury N. H. 828-48
Dickinson Genealogy (1896) 69-71
Dow's History of Hampton N. H. 1032-7
Dowse Genealogy 113-5

Eaton's History of Thomaston Me. ii, 456
Ely Genealogy 221-3
Foster Pedigree (1897) viii, 1-40
Goodwin's Genealogical Notes 242-9
Hammatt Papers 401
Hayward's History of Gilsum N. H. 410
Hoyt's Salisbury Mass. Families 342-5
Huntington's Stamford Ct. Settlers 124
Judd's History of Hadley Mass. 592
Kilbourne's Kilbourne Genealogy 111
Lancaster's Hist. of Gilmanton N. H. 288
Little's History of Weare N. H. 1008
Longmeadow Mass. Centennial, app. 97
Meade's Old Families of Virginia
Morrison's Hist. of Windham N. H. 807-9
Morse Memorial (1896) 79-81
N. E. Hist. Reg. vii, 102; ix, 159-61; li, 360
New Hamp. Hist. Soc. Coll vii, 382, 398
Poor's Researches 107-13, 146, 170, 296
Poore Genealogy 91-6
Runnells' Sanbornton N. H. ii, 831
Savage's Genealogical Dict. iv, 447-50
Shotwell Genealogy 11-5, 269-72
Stackpole's History of Durham Me. 282
Stiles' Hist. of Windsor Ct. ii, 781-3
Tanner Genealogy 54-6
Temple's History of Northfield Mass. 562
Thurston Genealogy (1892) 176-9
Timlow's Southington Ct. Sketches 250-4
Webster Family of Conn. (1836) 8 pages
Webster Family of Conn. (1876) 9 pages
Webster Fam. of Ipswich (1884) 14 pages
Webster Fam. of Hampton (1894) 45 pages
Worden Genealogy 49-52
Young's History of Warsaw N. Y. 347-50
Wedge — Ballou's Milford Mass. 1102
Breck Genealogy 131
Temple's Hist. of N. Brookfield Mass. 774
Wedgwood — Dearborn's Parsonsfield
Dow's History of Hampton N. H. 1037
Weed — American Ancestry ii, 145
Anderson's Waterbury Ct. i, app. 148
Cleveland's Hist. Yates Co. N. Y. 229-30
Eaton's History of Thomaston Me. ii, 456
Hall's Norwalk Ct. Records 225, 263, 296
Hoyt's Salisbury Mass. Families 345-8
Huntington's Stamford Ct. Fams. 124-33
Knox Co. Me. Hist. Mag. i, 37-9
Paige's History of Cambridge Mass. 682
Savage's Genealogical Dictionary iv, 451
Sinclair Genealogy 174
Weeden — American Ancestry 43
Austin's Allied Families 255-7
Austin's Ancestries 59
Austin's R. I. Genealogical Dict. 414
Narragansett Hist. Reg. vii, 298-302
Savage's Genealogical Dictionary iv, 452
Weeks — American Ancestry ii, 145; vii,
    139; viii, 239; ix, 84, 155; x, 90, 101;
    xii, 135
Barrus' History of Goshen Mass. 180-4
Bassett's Hist. of Richmond N. H. 517-9
Bunker's Long Island Genealogies 323-5
Dearborn's History of Parsonsfield Me. 411
Driver Genealogy 220
Eaton's Hist. of Thomaston Me. ii, 457

Freeman's Cape Cod Mass. ii, 512, 527
Hollister's History of Pawlet Vt. 253
Hudson's Hist. Marlborough Mass. 463-5
Jenning's History of Bennington Vt. 308
Journals of Smith and Dean Me. 90
Lancaster's Hist. of Gilmanton N. H. 289
New Eng. Hist. Gen. Reg. xxxix, 234-41
Paige's History of Hardwick Mass. 529
Plumb's History of Hanover Pa. 484
Roe's Sketches of Rose N. Y. 310
Runnells' Sanbornton N. H. ii, 832-41
Savage's Genealogical Dictionary iv, 452-4
Walworth's Hyde Genealogy 959
Weeks Family of Dorchester (1885) 468 p.
Weeks Fam. of Salisbury Vt. (1888) 20 p.
Weeks Fam. of N. Hampshire (1889) 202 p.
Weeks' Ancient History (1892) 174 pages
Week's History of Salisbury Vt. 199-201
Weeman — Stackpole's Durham Me. 284
Weems — Hayden's Virginia Gens. 352
Richmond Va. Standard iii, 36
Weiant — See Weygant
Weiderwax — American Ancestry ii, 145
Weidman — American Ancestry i, 93
Egle's History of Lebanon Co. Pa. 256
Weigand — See Weygant
Weighley — Egle's Lebanon Pa. 353
Weightman — American Ancestry v, 81
Aylsworth Genealogy 98, 183, 344
Weir — Egle's Penn. Gens. 2d ed. 705-7
New Eng. Hist. and Gen. Reg. xxv, 246-8
Richmond Va. Standard iii, 26
Weirman — Egle's Notes and Queries,
    Annual Volume (1896) 139-41
Weise — Chambers' N. J. Germans
Egle's Notes and Queries 1st ser. i, 288-91
Weiser — American Ancestry ix, 162
American Historical Register iv, 176-83
Penn. Hist. Society Collections i (1851) 1-6
Weiser Biog. (1876) 9-15, 100-15
Weisiger — Goode Genealogy 134
Weitzel — American Ancestry xii
Weitzel Genealogy (1881) 9 pages
Weitzel Genealogy (1883) 81 pages
Weizel — Davis' Bucks County Pa. 432
Welch — American Ancestry ii, 145; v, 99
Buckingham Genealogy 13
Corliss' North Yarmouth Me.
Eaton's History of Thomaston Me. ii, 457
Hayward's History of Hancock N. H. 982
Lincoln's Hist. of Hingham Mass. iii, 283
New E. Hist. and Gen. Reg. xxiii, 417-23
Orcutt's History of New Milford Ct. 785
Savage's Genealogical Dictionary iv, 454
Smith's History of Rhinebeck N. Y. 192
Stiles' History of Windsor Ct. ii, 783
Walworth's Hyde Genealogy 1135-8
Wyman's Charlestown Mass. 1006-9
Weld — Alden's Epitaphs i, 112; iii, 41
Am. Anc. v, 176, 208; vii, 212, 251; viii, 32
Bass' History of Braintree Vt. 196
Cogswell Genealogy 402
Dunstable Mass. Bi-Centennial 51, 182
Ellis' History of Roxbury Mass. 133-5
Faxon Genealogy 43-5
Fox's History of Dunstable Mass. 252

Hyde's History of Brimfield Mass. 467
Lee Genealogy of Ipswich 360-2
New Eng. Historical and Gen. Register
   vii, 309; viii, 207; ix, 42
Savage's Genealogical Dict. iv, 456-73
Sheldon's Hist. of Deerfield Mass. 355
Temple's Hist. of No. Brookfield Mass. 776
Weldon — Andrew's N. Britain Ct. 293
Weller — Orcutt's N. Milford Ct. 785
Savage's Genealogical Dictionary iv, 474
Sheldon's Hist. of Deerfield Mass. 356
Welles — Amer. Ancestry vii, 156; ix, 127
Glastenbury Ct. Centennial 164
Goodwin's Genealogical Notes 250-63
Huntington's Stamford Ct. Settlers 133
Kulp's Wyoming Valley Families
New York Gen. and Biog. Rec. v, 80-3;
   xxvii, 172-6
Orcutt's History of Stratford Ct. 1325-30
Prentice Genealogy 196-8
Raymond's Burritt Sketch
Talcott's N. Y. and N. E. Families 724-8
Tuttle Genealogy 130-5
Walworth's Hyde Genealogy 767, 1005
Welles Genealogy, see Wells
Wellesley — Cowley Genealogy
Wellford — American Ancestry x, 23
Paige Genealogy 161
Paxton's Marshall Genealogy 247
Richmond Va. Standard ii, 29, 47
Welling — Cooley's Trenton 299-304
Guild Genealogy by Burleigh 47
Wellington — Aldrich's Walpole 379
Bemis' History of Marlboro N. H. 676
Bond's Watertown Mass. 627-37, 963
Buckminster's Hastings Genealogy 41-3
Cutter's History of Arlington Mass. 314
Daniels' History of Oxford Mass. 739
Heywood's Hist. Westminster Mass. 903
Hudson's Hist. of Lexington Mass. 253-9
Paige's History of Cambridge Mass. 682-4
Pickering Genealogy
Savage's Genealogical Dictionary iv, 480
Stearns' History of Rindge N. H. 744-6
Temple's Hist. of N. Brookfield Mass. 776
Wellington Genealogy (1892) 26 pages
Wellman — American Ancestry vii, 140
Driver Genealogy 491-6
Goodwin's Genealogical Notes 322-7
Hayward's History of Hancock N. H. 983
Savage's Genealogical Dictionary iv, 481
Slafter Genealogy 4-7
Washington N. H. History 656-8
Wellman Genealogy (1867) 68 pages
Wells — Adams' Haven Gen. pt. ii, 22
American Ancestry i, 93, vi, 44; vii, 20,
   215; ix, 225; x, 205; xi, 56, 96
Andrews' History of New Britain Ct. 229
Austin's R. I. Genealogical Dictionary 217
Barbour's My Wife and Mother, App. 30
Bass' History of Braintree Vt. 196
Camp Genealogy ii, 32-8
Caulkins' History of New London Ct. 355
Chase's History of Chester N. H. 613
Cochrane's Hist. Francestown N. H. 970
Crafts' Genealogy 183-5

Crafts' History of Whately Mass. 612-20
Dearborn's Hist. of Salisbury N. H. 851
Field's History of Haddam Ct. 45
Goodwin's Olcott Genealogy 35
Hammatt Papers 402-4
Hollister Genealogy 704
Hoyt's Salisbury Mass. Families 348-53
Hubbard's Hist. of Stanstead Co. Can. 181
Joslin's History of Poultney Vt. 360
Judd's History of Hadley Mass. 592-4
Kellogg's White Genealogy 99
Kilbourne Genealogy 215
Missouri Pioneer Families 192
Morris Genealogy (1898) 523-5
New Eng. Hist. and Gen. Reg. xii, 157-60;
   xx, 131-3; xliii, 359; xliv, 208
Orcutt's Hist. of New Milford Ct. 786-8
Orcutt's History of Stratford Ct. 1330
Paige's History of Hardwick Mass. 530
Pompey N. Y. Reunion 390
Potts Genealogy (1895) 101-4
Prentice Genealogy 28
Roome Genealogy 180
Saunders' Alabama Settlers 481-5
Savage's Genealogical Dict. iv, 474-80
Sheldon's Hist. of Deerfield Mass. ii, 356-71
Smith Genealogy (1890) 45-8
Stiles' Hist. of Windsor Ct. ii, 784-8
Temple's History of Whately Mass. 278-81
Trufee Genealogy 144-6
Walworth's Hyde Genealogy 412-4
Wells Fam. of Hartford (1848) 27 pages
Wells Fam. of Maine (1874) 81 pages
Wells Fam. of Mass. (1874) 127 pages
Welles Family of Eng. (1876) 312 pages
Wells Fam. of Southold (1878) 300 pages
Welles Family of Hartford (1892) chart
Wells Family of Hebron Ct. (1898) chart
Whitmore's Copps Hill Epitaphs
Worthen's Hist. of Sutton N. H. 996-1002
Welsh — Chambers' N. J. Germans 558
Jaquett Genealogy 187-90
Martin's History of Chester Pa. 32-4
Welton — Anderson's Waterbury Ct. i,
   app. 148-53
Bronson's Hist. of Waterbury Ct. 541-51
Calnek's History of Annapolis N. S. 622
Orcutt's History of Wolcott Ct. 598-606
Welton Family Chart
Wemp — Albany Collections iv, 184
Wemple — American Ancestry iv, 53
Pearson's Schenectady Settlers 289-93
Roome Genealogy 232-5
Wendell — American Ancestry i, 93; v,
   136, 233; ix, 92
Bridgman's Kings Chapel Epitaphs 234-8
Butler's Hist. of Farmington Me. 607-13
Camp Genealogy ii, 44
Harris' Bascom Genealogy 37-42
Hodgman's History of Westford Mass. 480
Journals of Smith and Dean of Me. 28
Munsell's Albany Collections iv, 184
New Eng. Hist. and Gen. Reg. xxii, 420;
   xxxvi, 242-55
Pearson's Schenectady N. Y. Settlers 293
Salisbury's Memorial (1885) 459-72

Talcott's N. Y. and N. E. Fams. 376–416
Wendell Genealogy (1882) 49 pages
Whitmore's Heraldic Journal i, 49
Wendover — Am. Anc. ii, 145; ix, 181, 209
N. Y. Gen. and Biog. Record xxvi, 178–85
Wenning — Stearns' Ashburnham 942
Wensley — See Winslow
Wentworth — American Ancestry ii, 145; vii, 80; viii, 100
Bangor Historical Magazine iv, 240
Brewster's Portsmouth N. H. ii, 116–8
Butler's History of Farmington Me. 613
Buxton Me. Centennial 229–31
Caulkins' History of Norwich Ct. 222
Cogswell Genealogy 193–5
Corliss' North Yarmouth Me.
Dearborn's Hist. of Parsonsfield Me. 412
Eaton's History of Thomaston Me. ii, 458
Hayward's Hist. of Hancock N. H. 984–6
Holton's Winslow Memorial i, 404–20
Jordan's Leighton Genealogy (1885)
New Eng. Hist. and Gen. Register iv, 321–38; vi, 212–4, 291; vii, 265, 304; viii, 48, 246; xviii, 49–53; xix, 65–9; xxii, 120–39; xxxvi, 315–8; xlii, 170–2
New Hampshire Hist. Soc. Coll. v, 238–43
Otis Genealogy (1851)
Savage's Genealogical Dictionary iv, 484–6
Vinton's Giles Genealogy 168
Wentworth Genealogy (1850) 20 pages
Wentworth Genealogy (1870) 1426 pages
Wentworth Genealogy (1878) 2279 pages
Whitmore's Heraldic Journal iii, 170–2
Wentz — Stanton Genealogy 340
Wersler — Anderson, Davies and Wersler Genealogy (1880) 80 pages
Wertmiller — Alden's Epitaphs v, 156
Werts — Chambers' N. J. Germans 561–7
Wescott — Pierce's Gorham Me. 217
Savage's Genealogical Dictionary iv, 486
Wesley — Mitchell's Bridgewater 333
Wessell — Potts Gen. (1895) 55–74
Wesson — Adams' Haven Gen. pt. ii, 6
Norton's History of Fitzwilliam N. H. 758
West — Amer. Anc. vi, 57; vii, 230; x, 53
Austin's R. I. Genealogical Dictionary 218
Bouton's History of Concord N. H. 700
Bowie Genealogy 195
Chase's History of Chester N. H. 413
Child Genealogy 378–82
Clarke's Old King Wm. Co. Va. Families
Cochrane's Hist. Francestown N. H. 970
Davis' Landmarks of Plymouth Mass. 279
Dearborn's Hist. of Salisbury N. H. 851–3
Essex Institute Hist. Collections xvi, 213
Freeman's Hist. of Cape Cod Mass. ii, 229
Gilpin Genealogy (1870) 10–2
Goode Genealogy 477
Hatch's History of Industry Me. 838–40
Hemenway's Vermont Hist. Gaz. iv, 167
Hines' Lebanon Ct. Hist. Address 173
Hurd's Hist. of New London Co. Ct. 516
Machias Me. Centennial 178
Meade's Old Families of Virginia
Nashville Am. Hist. Mag. (1896)
Neill's Virginia Carolorum 15

Norton's History of Knox Co. Ohio 367
Peirce Genealogy (1894)
Power's Sangamon Co. Ill. Settlers 762
Richmond Va. Standard i, 49; ii, 47; iii, 37
Saunderson's Charlestown N. H. 607
Savage's Genealogical Dictionary iv, 487
Southern Bivouac (1886) 648
Stanton Genealogy 220
Stern's Our Kindred (1885) 82–9
Stiles' History of Windsor Ct. ii, 789
Waldo's History of Tolland Ct. 116–22
Walworth' Hyde Genealogy 246–8
Winsor's History of Dusenbury Mass. 334
Westbrook — N. Y. Record xviii, 41–4
Schoonmaker's Hist. Kingston N. Y. 494
Sylvester's History of Ulster Co. N. Y. 110
Westcott — American Ancestry iv, 34; vii, 105; viii, 207
Austin's Allied Families 259
Austin's R. I. Genealogical Dictionary 416
Ballou's History of Milford Mass. 1103
Bolton's Westchester Co. N. Y. ii, 546
Hudson's History of Lexington Mass. 260
Tanner Genealogy 15–20
Westcott Genealogy (1886) 161 pages
Westcott Genealogy (1890) 200 pages
Westervelt — American Ancestry i, 93; iii, 60; vii, 39; xii
Westfall — American Ancestry ii, 146
Gumaer's Hist. of Deerpark N. Y. 67, 72
Westgate — Austin's R. I. Dict. 219
Davis' Landmarks of Plymouth Mass. 279
Jennings Genealogy ii (1899)
Walworth's Hyde Genealogy 512
Westlake — Boyd's Winchester Ct. 327
Orcutt's History of Torrington Ct. 775
Westland — Stiles' Windsor Ct. ii, 789
Orcutt's History of Torrington Ct. 775
Weston — Am. Anc. iv, 148; ix, 197; x, 30
Cochrane's History of Antrim N. H. 739
Cochrane's Hist. Francestown N. H. 971
Davis' Landmarks of Plymouth 280–2
Drisco's Life of Hannah Weston (1857)
Eaton's History of Reading Mass. 125
Eaton's Annals of Warren Me. 644
Hayward's Hist. of Hancock N. H. 986–95
Hill's History of Mason N. H. 207
Hubbard's Hist. of Springfield Vt. 481
Hubbard's Stanstead Co. Canada 285
Jewett's Ball and Weston Genealogy (1867)
Lapham's History of Norway Me. 619
Maine Hist. and Gen. Recorder iii, 215
Morris Genealogy (1894) 119–24, 139
Morrison's History of Windham N. H. 810
New Eng. Historical and Genealogical Register xli, 285–96; l, 201–6
North's History of Augusta Me. 952–6
Pierce's History of Gorham Me. 217
Savage's Genealogical Dictionary iv, 489
Smith's Hist. of Peterborough N. H. 333
Stackpole's History of Durham Me. 284
Stearns' Ashburnham Mass. 942–44
Temple's History of N. Brookfield Mass. 777
Washington N. H. History 658
Weston Genealogy (1887) 23 pages

Willis Law and Lawyers of Me. 510-7
Winsor's History of Duxbury Mass. 334-6
Westover — American Ancestry ii, 146
Andrews' History of New Britain Ct. 334
Kilbourne Genealogy 195
Walworth's Hyde Genealogy 500-2
Westwood — Meade's Old Churches of Virginia ii, 230
Porter's Hartford Connecticut Settlers 22
Wetherbee — American Ancestry x, 104
Hayward's History of Gilsum N. H. 412
Heywood's Hist. Westminster Mass. 904-6
Randalls' Hist. of Chesterfield N. H. 482
Read's History of Swanzey N. H. 482
Saunderson's Charlestown N. H. 609-12
Stearns' Hist. of Ashburnham Mass. 944-6
Stearns' History of Rindge N. H. 747-54
Temple's Hist. N. Brookfield Mass. 778-80
Wetherby — Norton's Fitzwilliam 758
Ward's Hist. of Shrewsbury Mass. 475-81
Wethered — Old Kent Md. 318-20
Thomas Genealogy (1877) 158-61
Thomas Genealogy (1896) 547-50
Wetherell — Caulkins' N. London 363
Clark's History of Norton Mass. 90
Daniels' History of Oxford Mass. 740
Sheldon's Hist. of Deerfield Mass. 406
Temple's Hist. of N. Brookfield Mass. 780
Wakefield Genealogy 193
Wetherill — Savage's Dict. iv, 491
Wetherwax — American Ancestry i, 94
Wetmore — Amer. Ancestry i, 94; iv, 197
Anderson's Waterbury Ct. i, app. 153
Andrews' History of New Britain Ct. 379
Baird's History of Rye N. Y. 495
Boyd's Annals of Winchester Ct. 66-70
Dwight Genealogy 499-503
Huntington Genealogy 97
Kellogg's White Genealogy 88
Middlefield Ct. History
New Eng. Hist. and Gen. Register xiv, 136
Orcutt's History of Stratford Ct. 1330-2
Phœnix's Whitney Genealogy ii, 1663
Tuttle Genealogy 434-8
Wetmore Genealogy (1861) 670 pages
Wetsell — American Ancestry ii, 146
Wetzel — Egle's Notes and Queries 3d ser. ii, 403
Weyborn — Deane's Scituate 383
Weygant — Weygant's Family Record (1897) 6-9, 19-22, 30-2, 43-5, 55-8, 66-70
Weyant Genealogy (1899) 37 pages
Weymouth — Savage's Dict. iv, 492
Whaley — Austin's R. I. Gen. Dict. 221
Baker's History of Montville Ct. 501-4
Whalley — Penn. Mag. of History ii, 351
Whaples — American Ancestry vii, 26
Andrews' History of New Britain Ct. 178
Wharff — Babson's Gloucester 178
Maine Historical Society Collections i, 135
Penney Genealogy 71-3, 87-122
Wharton — American Ancestry vii, 93
Corliss' North Yarmouth Me.
Fisher Genealogy (1896) 66, 103-8
Goode Genealogy 126, 245
Morris Genealogy (1898) 899

Ormsby Genealogy 40-2
Penn. Mag of Hist. i, 324-9; ii, 50-8, 211
Rodman Genealogy 97, 129-31
Savage's Genealogical Dictionary iv, 494
Wharton Genealogy (1880) 134 pages
Wheat — Bond's Watertown Mass. 637
Draper's History of Spencer Mass. 272
Hollister Genealogy 295-7
Jackson's History of Newtown Mass. 460
Savage's Genealogical Dictionary iv, 495
Worcester's History of Hollis N. H. 390
Wheatley — Loveland Genealogy i, 163-74
Perkins' Old Houses of Norwich Ct. 584
Wheaton — Ballou Genealogy 315-21
Bliss' Rehoboth Mass. 268
Caverly's History of Pittsford Vt. 729
Converse Genealogy
Lincoln's Hist. of Hingham Mass. iii, 284
Morse's Sherborn Mass. Settlers 255
Orcutt's History of New Milford Ct. 789
Pompey N. Y. Reunion 367-72
Savage's Genealogical Dictionary iv, 495
Whedon — Hollister's Pawlet Vt. 255
Wheelden — Bangor Hist. Magazine v, 17
Wheeler — Adams' Haven Gen. ii, 33
American Ancestry i, 94; ii, 146; iii, 112, 167; iv, 13; v, 227, 234; vi, 162; vii, 7, 30, 37, 246, 278; viii, 25, 241; ix, 199; x, 56; xi, 55
Ball's History of Lake Co. Ind. 408-12
Bangor Historical Magazine vi, 247
Barry's Hist. of Framingham Mass. 435
Bassett's History of Richmond N. H. 521
Bemis' History of Marlboro N. H. 251-3
Bond's Watertown Mass. Gens. 721
Burr Genealogy (1891) 236-40
Cleveland's Yates Co. N. Y. 197, 214-6
Collin's Hist. of Hillsdale N. Y., app. 128
Cothren's Woodbury Ct. 747-52; ii, 1576
Cunnabell Genealogy 117
Eaton's History of Thomaston Me. ii, 458
Gage's History of Rowley Mass. 461
Hayward's Hist. of Hancock N. H. 995-8
Hemenway's Genealogy 66
Hemenway's Vermont Hist. Gaz. v, 476
Herrick's History of Gardiner Me. 385
Heywood's Hist. Westminster Mass.906-10
Hill's History of Mason N. H. 207
Hobart's History of Abington Ct. 449
Hoyt's Salisbury Mass. Families 353-6
Hubbard's Hist. of Stanstead Canada 323
Hudson's Hist. of Marlborough Mass. 465
Hudson's Hist. of Sudbury Mass. 452
Hughes Genealogy 197-201
Jameson's History of Medway Mass. 527
Joslin's History of Poultney Vt. 361
Kidder's Hist. of New Ipswich N. H. 440
Lapham's History of Bethel Me. 637-41
Lapham's History of Rumford Me. 420
Leland Genealogy 120
Morrison's History of Windham N. H. 811
Morse Memorial, appendix No. 45½
Morse's Richards Genealogy 148
Munsell's Albany Collections iv, 184
North's History of Augusta Me. 956
Norton's Hist. of Fitzwilliam N. H. 759

Orcutt's History of Derby Ct. 775-7
Orcutt's History of Stratford Ct. 1333-44
Orford N. H. Centennial 141
Paige's History of Hardwick Mass. 531-4
Pierce's History of Grafton Mass. 584-92
Poor's Merrimack Valley Researches 297
Potter's Concord Mass. Families 14
Randalls' Hist. of Chesterfield N. H. 483-9
Saunderson's Charlestown N. H. 612-4
Savage's Genealogical Dict. iv, 496-502
Schenck's History of Fairfield Ct. 421
Secomb's History of Amherst N. H. 822-6
Sharpe's History of Seymour Ct. 161-3
Shattuck's History of Concord Mass. 385
Stearns' Hist. of Ashburnham Mass. 946
Stowe's Hist. Hubbardston Mass. 367-70
Temple's Hist. of N. Brookfield Mass. 780
Wakefield Genealogy 152-5
Ward's Hist. of Shrewsbury Mass. 471-4
Washington N. H. History 659
Welles' Amer. Family Antiquity iii, 41-55
Wheeler and Warren Gen. (1892) 121 pages
Wheeler Ancestors (1896) 24 pages
Wheeler and Thaxter Gen. (1898) 74 pages
Wheeler's Croydon N. H. Centen. 149-54
Wheeler's Hist. of Newport N. H. 564-70
Worcester's History of Hollis N. H. 290
Worthen's History of Sutton N. H. 1002-5
Wyman's Charlestown Mass. Gens. 1012-4
Wheelock — Alden's Epitaphs ii, 77
American Ancestry vi, 134; xi, 56
Ballou's History of Milford Mass. 1105-8
Calnek's Hist. of Annapolis N. S. 623
Chute Genealogy, appendix 230-41
Cochrane's Hist. Francestown N. H. 972
Daniels' History of Oxford Mass. 741
Harris' Ancestors of W. C. Harris
Hick's Life of Ralph Wheelock (1899) 51 p.
Huntington Genealogy 78
Pierce's History of Grafton Mass. 592-6
Read's History of Swanzey N. H. 483
Runnells' Hist. Sanbornton N. H. ii, 842
Savage's Genealogical Dictionary iv, 502
Temple's Hist. of N. Brookfield Mass. 780
Ward's Rice Genealogy 14
Ward's Hist. of Shrewsbury Mass. 465-71
Wight Genealogy 36
Wheelwright — Bangor Me. Hist. Mag.
ix, 76-80, 182
Currier's Ould Newbury Mass. 645
Dow's History of Hampton N. H. 1039
New Eng. Hist. and Gen. Register xv, 270
Prime Genealogy (1895) 33
Savage's Genealogical Dictionary iv, 502-4
Wentworth Genealogy i, 72-4, 659
Wheelwright Genealogy (1894) 35 pages
Whelen — Life of Rev. Wm. Smith
Whelpley — Schenck's Fairfield Ct. 492
Wherry — American Ancestry xi, 204
Whetten — Todd Genealogy
Whipple — Adams' Fairhaven 485-8
Aldrich's History of Walpole N. H. 381
Amer. Anc. iii, 213; iv, 26, 100; xi, 125
Andrews' Hist. of New Britain Ct. 295, 350
Austin's Allied Families 262
Austin's Ancestries 61

Austin's R. I. Genealogical Dictionary 221
Ballou Genealogy 415-9
Ballou's History of Milford Mass. 1108-10
Bassett's Hist. of Richmond N. H. 523-31
Benedict's History of Sutton Mass. 746
Cogswell Genealogy 67-9
Cogswell's Hist. New Boston N. H. 432-4
Cutts Genealogy
Emerson's Hist. of Douglas Mass. 199-205
Hammatt Papers, Ipswich Mass. 405-10
Hayes' Wells Genealogy 165
Hill's History of Mason N. H. 207
Hubbard's Hist. of Springfield Vt. 483-6
Lane and Whipple Gen. (1857) 24 pages
Leland Genealogy 44-6, 50, 116, 148
New E. Hist. and Gen. Reg. xxxii, 403-7
Norton's Hist. of Fitzwilliam N. H. 760-2
Paige's History of Hardwick Mass. 534
Pierce's History of Grafton Mass. 596-600
Putnam's Historical Magazine iv, 5-14,
62-6; v, 183-5
Runnells' Sanbornton N. H. ii, 843-5
Saunderson's Charlestown N. H. 614-6
Savage's Genealogical Dictionary iv, 505-7
Stearns' Hist. of Ashburnham Mass. 947
Stiles' History of Windsor Ct. ii, 789
Vinton's Giles Genealogy 259-61
Wheeler's Croydon N. H. Centennial 154-6
Wheeler's History of Newport N. H. 575-7
Whipple Fam. of Ipswich (1857) 36 pages
Whipple Fam. of R. I. (1873) 63 pages
Whipple Fam. of R. I. (1881) 46 pages
Whipple and Hill Fams. (1897) 108 pages
Whiston — Deane's Scituate Mass. 380
Whitaker — Amer. Ancestry vii, 101
Austin's Allied Families 263-6
Austin's Ancestral Dictionary 63
Cogswell's History of Henniker N. H. 785
Dickey Genealogy 61
Hayward's History of Hancock N. H. 998
Howell's Southampton 2d edition 398
Littell's Passaic Valley Gens. 466-77
New Eng. Hist. and Gen. Reg. xxxix, 165
Richmond Va. Standard iii, 9
Shourd's Fenwick Colony N. J. 349-58
Whitbeck — American Ancestry ii, 146
Whitcher — Eaton's Thomaston 459
Hubbard's Stanstead Co. Canada 119
Runnells' Hist. of Sanbornton N. H. 844-6
Whitcomb — Amer. Anc. viii, 148; xii, 37
Bassett's History of Richmond N. H. 531
Bemis' History of Marlboro N. H. 680-3
Cogswell's Hist. of Henniker N. H. 773-9
Corliss' North Yarmouth Me.
Deane's History of Scituate Mass. 380-2
Hayward's Hist. Hancock N. H. 999-1013
Herrick Genealogy (1885) 199
Hubbard's Hist. of Springfield Vt. 492-9
Hubbard's Hist. of Stanstead Co. Can. 289
Lincoln's Hist. Hingham Mass. iii, 285-7
Norton's Hist. of Fitzwilliam N. H. 762-5
Paige's History of Hardwick Mass. 535-7
Read's History of Swanzey N. H. 483-94
Savage's Genealogical Dictionary iv, 507
Warren's History of Waterford Me. 301-3
Whitcomb Genealogy (1888) 23 pages

Whitcomb Genealogy (1893) 32 pages
Worthen's History of Sutton N. H. 1006
Whitcombe — Lapham's Norway Me.
Reed Genealogy 112
Stearns' Hist. of Ashburnham Mass. 948
White — Adams Genealogy (1894) 41–70
American Ancestry ii, 146; iii, 149; iv, 56,
   73, 118, 130, 132, 227; v, 46, 116, 170;
   vi, 150; vii, 155, 236, 245; viii, 37, 39,
   130; ix, 59, 128, 200; x, 206; xi, 56;
   xii, 121
Austin's Allied Families 269
Avery Genealogy (1893) 62–75
Babson's History of Gloucester Mass. 229
Ballou's History of Milford Mass. 1110–2
Barber's Atlee Genealogy 24–32
Barbour's My Wife and Mother, app. 31
Barrus' History of Goshen Mass. 194–9
Barry's Hist. of Framingham Mass. 435
Barry's History of Hanover Mass. 416–8
Bartow Genealogy 144–52
Bass' History of Braintree Vt. 197
Bassett's History of Richmond N. H. 522
Bemis' Hist. of Marlboro N. H. 683–92
Benedict's History of Sutton Mass. 747
Blake's Blake Genealogy 60
Bolton's Westchester Co. N. Y. ii, 546
Bond's Watertown 638–41, 886–900, 964
Breck Genealogy 49
Briggs' History of Shipbuilding 353
Capron Genealogy by Holden 27, 41–5
Chase's History of Chester N. H. 614
Chase's History of Haverhill Mass. 53, 277
Clarke Family of Waterford 77, 129
Clarke's History of Norton Mass. 97
Cleveland Genealogy 32–8
Cochrane's History of Antrim N. H. 745–8
Cochrane's Hist. Francestown N. H. 973–5
Cogswell's Hist. Nottingham N. H. 504–7
Coit Genealogy 40–8, 73–95
Collin's Hist. of Hillsdale N. Y., app. 126
Cooley's Trenton N. J. Genealogies 304–7
Corliss' North Yarmouth Me.
Crafts' History of Whately Mass. 620–4
Crafts Genealogy 67–9
Daniels' History of Oxford Mass. 741
Davis' Landmarks of Plymouth 282–4
Deane's History of Scituate Mass. 382
Dearborn's Hist. of Salisbury N. H. 854
Dickerman Genealogy 489–94
Draper's History of Spencer Mass. 261–4
Dyer's History of Plainfield Mass. 183–5
Eaton's History of Thomaston Me. ii, 459
Elderkin Genealogy 26–32
Ely Genealogy 35, 69–71
Freeman's Hist. of Cape Cod Mass. ii, 227
Granite Monthly of Concord N. H. iv, 49
Hall's Records of Norwalk Ct. 231, 279
Hayden's Weitzel Gen. (1883) 29–32, 35–48
Hayward's History of Gilsum N. H. 414–6
Hayward's History of Hancock N. H. 1013
Herrick's History of Gardiner Mass. 385
Heywood's Hist. Westminster Mass. 911–4
Hill's Dedham Mass. Records i
Hodgman's History of Westford Mass. 480
Howell's Southampton N. Y. 399–405

Hubbard's Hist. of Springfield Vt. 486–91
Hubbard's Stanstead Co. Canada 221, 336
Hudson's History of Lexington Mass. 260
Hughes Genealogy 125–8
Huntington Stamford Ct. Settlers 133
Hurlburt Genealogy 407
Jackson's History of Newton Mass. 461
Johnson Genealogy (1895) 29, 44–56
Judd's History of Hadley Mass. 594–602
Kellogg Genealogy, supp. (1899) 9–11
Kirby Genealogy
Little's History of Weare N. H. 1009
Longmeadow Mass. Centennial, app. 90
Loomis Genealogy (1880) 527–33
Lyman's Hist. of East Hampton Mass. 186
Magazine of American History (1877)
Maine Hist. and Gen. Recorder ix, 377–9
Maltby Genealogy 123
Meginness Biographical Annals 258–61
New Eng. Hist. and Gen. Register xiv,
   137; lii, 421–6; liii, 392–6
New Hampshire Hist. Soc. Colls. vii, 376
New Jersey Hist. Soc. Colls. vii, (1882)
Norton's Hist. of Fitzwilliam N. H. 765–9
Oneida Hist. Soc. Trans. ii, 25–33, 73–6
Paige's History of Cambridge Mass. 684
Paige's History of Hardwick Mass. 537
Palmer and Trimble Genealogy 397–9
Penn. Magazine of History and Biography
   i, 63–75, 420–39; ii, 157
Pierce's History of Grafton Mass. 600–2
Pope Genealogy 321
Randalls' Hist. Chesterfield N. H. 489–91
Reed Genealogy 130
Rice Genealogy
Richmond Va. Standard iii, 29
Roseboom Genealogy 74–7
Saunders' Alabama Settlers 458
Saunderson's Hist. Charlestown N. H. 617
Savage's Genealogical Dict. iv, 508–16
Sedgwick's History of Sharon Ct. 117
Shourd's Fenwick Colony N. J. 308–28
Smith's Hist. Peterborough N. H. 334–43
Stearns' Hist. Ashburnham Mass. 949–52
Stile's History of Windsor Ct. ii, 790
Strong Genealogy 429–32, 1312–5
Taylor's Great Barrington Mass. 110
Temple's Hist. of N. Brookfield Mass. 780
Temple's History of Northfield Mass. 563
Temple's History of Palmer Mass. 566
Temple's History of Whately Mass. 281–3
Thatcher's Hist. of Plymouth Mass. 23
Thayer Memorial (1835) 163–73
Thurston's Hist. of Winthrop Me. 201
Vinton Genealogy 365–74
Walker Genealogy 25
Washington N. H. History 660–5
West Springfield Mass. Centennial 123
Wetmore Genealogy 326
Wheeler's History of Brunswick Me. 859
Wheeler's History of Newport N. H. 575–7
Wheeler's History of North Carolina 215
White's Discourse Charlemont Mass. 42
White Fam. of Hartford (1860) 322 pages
White Fam. of Haverhill (1863) 47 pages
White Fam. of Marblehead (1872) 81 pages

White Fam. of Douglass (1878) 44 pages
White Fam. of Maryland (1879) 211 pages
White Fam. of New Jersey (1882) 11 pages
White Fam. of Philadelphia (1888) 194 p.
White Fam. of Haverhill (1889) 80 pages
White Fam. of Paris Hill N. Y. (1892) 32 p.
White Fam. of Plymouth (1895) 393 pages
White Reunion at Salem (1898) 22 pages
White Fam. of Watertown (1898) 8 pages
Whitmore's Copps Hill Epitaphs
Williams' History of Danby Vt. 286
Wood Genealogy 91–108
Wyman's Charlestown Mass. 1015–8
Wyman's Hunt Genealogy 131
Young's History of Wayne Co. Ind. 220
Whiteford — American Ancestry vi, 23
Whitehall — Atlee Genealogy 102–8
Whitehead — Condit Genealogy 390–2
Hatfield's Elizabeth N. J. 99
Lapham's History of Paris Me. 767
Opdyck Genealogy 95
Riker's Annals of Newton N. Y. 374
Savage's Genealogical Dictionary iv, 516
Whitehill — Egle's Hist. Reg. ii, 270–8
Egle's Notes and Queries 3d ser. iii, 201
Goode Genealogy 169
Whitehouse — Lapham's Norway Me.
Whiteman — American Ancestry ii, 147
Narragansett Historical Reg. iii, 267–75
Stearns' Hist. of Ashburnham Mass. 952
Whitesides — Power's Sangamon 674
Whitfield — Cochrane's Francestown N. H. 975–8
New Eng. Register li, 410–2
Savage's Genealogical Dictionary iv, 517
Whitford — Austin's R. I. Gen. Dict. 223
Aylsworth Genealogy 479–81
Bailey Genealogy (1895) 58–61
Greene Genealogy (1894)
Whitgift — N. E. Hist. Reg. xxiii, 262–6
Whithed — Vt. Hist. Gaz. v, 332–6
Whiting — Adams' Haven Genealogy 26
American Ancestry ii, 147; vii. 124
Andrews' Hist. of New Britain Ct. 340
Bass' History of Braintree Vt. 198
Benedict's History of Sutton Mass. 747
Bingham Genealogy 249
Blake's History of Franklin Mass. 283
Blake's History of Hamden Ct. 311
Blood's History of Temple N. H. 255
Boyd's Annals of Winchester Ct. 137
Chapman's Trowbridge Genealogy 36–9
Cochrane's Hist. Francestown N. H. 980–2
Collins' Hist. of Hillsdale N. Y., app. 126
Davis' Landmarks Plymouth Mass. 284–6
Dedham Historical Register iv, 41–3
Drake's History of Boston Mass. 363
Dwight Genealogy 100
Eaton's Annals of Warren Me. 545
Fox's History of Dunstable Mass. 252
Goodwin's Genealogical Notes 329–46
Guild's Stiles Genealogy 85 Hanover Mass. Records (1898)
Hayden's Virginia Genealogies 194, 479
Hayward's Hist. of Hancock N. H. 1013–5
Hazen's History of Billerica Mass. 155–61

Hill's Dedham Mass. Records i
Hodgman's History of Westford Mass. 480
Huntington Genealogy
Huntington's Stamford Ct. Settlers 134
Jameson's History of Medway Mass. 528
Leland Genealogy 180
Lewis' History of Lynn Mass. 274
Livermore's Hist. of Wilton N. H. 519–22
Meade's Old Families of Virginia
Mitchell's Hist. of Bridgewater Mass. 334
Morse' Sherborn Mass. Settlers 257
New Eng. Historical and Genealogical Register xvii, 214–6; xxiv, 86
Old Northwest Gen. Quarterly ii, 105
Orcutt's History of Stratford Ct. 1345
Orcutt's History of Torrington Ct. 778–85
Perkins' Old Houses of Norwich Ct. 585–8
Robie Genealogy by R. E. Robie 17–24
Savage's Genealogical Dict. iv, 518–22
Schroeder's Boardman Memorial 372–80
Secomb's History of Amherst N. H. 826–8
Stickney Genealogy 506
Temple's Hist. N. Brookfield Mass. 782–5
Temple's History of Palmer Mass. 571
Washington N. H. History 665
Welles' Washington Genealogy 170, 192
Whiting Genealogy (1871) 334 pages
Whiting Fam. of Hartford (1888) 8 pages
Whitmore's Heraldic Journal i, 59–61
Worcester's History of Hollis N. H. 391
Wyman's Charlestown Mass. Gens. 1018
Young's History of Warsaw N. Y. 350–2
See also under Whiton
Whitlock —Currier's Castleton Vt. Epitaphs 48
Whitlock Genealogy (1880)
Whitman —Austin's R. I. Gen. Dict. 224
Barrus' History of Goshen Mass. 193
Calnek's Hist. of Annapolis N. S. 624–7
Chute Genealogy, appendix 241–5
Cogswell's History of Henniker N. H. 778–80
Davis' Landmarks of Plymouth Mass. 286
Dickerman Genealogy 227–9
Freeman's Hist. of Cape Cod Mass. ii, 680
Guild's Stiles Genealogy 376
Hazen's History of Billerica Mass. 161
Heywood's Hist. Westminster Mass. 915–7
Hobart's History of Abington Mass. 451–3
Hudson's History of Lexington Mass. 261
Kilbourn Genealogy 105
Lapham's History of Bethel Me. 641
Lapham's History of Norway Me. 622
Lapham's History of Paris Me. 767–9
Mitchell's Bridgewater Mass. 335–43
Narragansett Hist. Register iii, 267–75
Parthemore Genealogy 140–3
Savage's Genealogical Dictionary iv, 523–5
Tuttle Genealogy 84–90
Whitman Genealogy (1832) 44 pages
Whitman Genealogy (1889) 1261 pages
Wood Genealogy 185–8
Wyman's Charlestown Mass. Gens. 1020
Whitmarsh — Dyer's Plainfield Mass. 186
Faxon Genealogy 50–2
Lapham's History of Norway Me. 622

Mitchell's Hist. of Bridgewater Mass. 343
Savage's Genealogical Dictionary iv, 525
Whitmore — American Ancestry i, 94
Brook's History of Medford Mass. 561-5
Cutter's History of Arlington Mass. 316
Daniels' History of Oxford Mass. 742
Dearborn's Hist. of Salisbury N. H. 855
Holton's Farwell Genealogy 102, 182-4
Hudson's Hist. of Lexington Mass. 262-4
N. E. Hist. and Gen. Reg. x, 356; xiii, 301
Norton's Hist. of Fitzwilliam N. H. 769
Orcutt's History of Torrington Ct. 775-8
Paige's History of Cambridge Mass. 684-6
Pierce's History of Gorham Me. 218
Savage's Genealogical Dictionary iv, 526-8
Smith's Hist. of Sunderland Mass. 570-3
Stearns' Hist. Ashburnham Mass. 953-57
Wetmore Genealogy (1861) 27-36
Whitmore Genealogy (1855) 24 pages
Whitmore Family Tracts (1875) 79 pages
Wyman's Charlestown Mass. Gens. 1020
Whitney — Allen's Worcester 90-2
American Ancestry v, 118, 120, 161; viii, 129; ix, 40, 107
Aylsworth Genealogy 241
Ballou's History of Milford Mass. 1112-21
Barry's Hist. of Framingham Mass. 426
Bemis' History of Marlboro N. H. 693
Blake's Hist. of Hamden Ct. 281-311
Bolton Genealogy 39-42
Bond's Watertown 348, 598, 642-52. 964-6
Browning's Magna Charta Barons 251
Butler's Hist. Groton Mass. 444, 481, 497
Chandler's History of Shirley Mass. 667-75
Cochrane's Hist. Francestown N. H. 979
Cogswell's Hist. of Henniker N. H. 780-4
Daniels' History of Oxford Mass. 743
Draper's History of Spencer Mass. 264
Dwight Genealogy 832
Eaton's History of Thomaston Me. ii, 460
Hall's Norwalk Ct. Records 189, 192-9
Hayward's History of Gilsum N. H. 416
Hemenway's Vermont Gaz. v, 162, 444
Heywood's Hist. Westminster Mass. 917-31
Herrick's History of Gardiner Mass. 387-9
Hubbard's Hist. of Springfield Vt. 501-5
Hudson's History of Lexington Mass. 264
Hudson's Hist. Marlborough Mass. 466-8
Huntington's Stamford Ct. Settlers 135
Jackson's History of Newton Mass. 463
Joslin's History of Poultney Vt. 364
Lapham's History of Norway Me. 623
Leland Genealogy 59, 196, 261-4
Lincoln's Hist. of Hingham Mass. iii, 288
Livermore's History of Wilton N. H. 522
Locke Genealogy 75
Marvin's Hist. of Winchendon Mass. 473-5
Montague Genealogy 483-5
Morse's Sherborn Mass. Settlers 257-60
N. E. Reg. xi, 113-21, 225-30; xii, 215-9
Norton's Hist. of Fitzwilliam N. H. 770-2
Orcutt's History of Derby Ct. 777-80
Orcutt's History of Stratford Ct. 1345
Peck's Rochester N. Y. Centennial 675
Petersham Mass. Centennial 107
Phelps West Simsbury Ct. Settlers 136

Pierce's History of Gorham Me. 219
Pierce's History of Grafton Mass. 602
Ridlon's Harrison Me. Settlers 134-8
Savage's Genealogical Dict. iv, 528-32
Sawtell's Hist. of Townsend Mass. 448-55
Sheldon's Hist. of Deerfield Mass. 371
Sinclair Genealogy 245-7
Stearns' Hist. Ashburnham Mass. 957-71
Stearns' History of Rindge N. H. 756-62
Temple's Hist. of Northfield Mass. 564
Thurston's Hist. of Winthrop Me. 201
Tucker's History of Hartford Vt. 475
Tuttle Genealogy 113
Ward's History of Shrewsbury Mass. 474-7
Westminster Mass. Centennial 23, 34
Wheeler's History of Brunswick Me. 860
Wheeler's History of Newport N. H. 571-3
Whitney Fam. of Watertown (1857) 26 p.
Whitney Fam. of Boston (1858) 7 pages
Whitney Fam. in England (1859) 11 pages
Whitney Fam. of Conn. (1860) 142 pages
Whitney Fam. of Conn. (1878) 2762 pages
Whitney Fam. of Watertown (1890) 101 p.
Whitney Fam. of Watertown (1895) 692 p.
Whitney Ancestry in Eng. (1896) 295 pages
Whitney Fam. of Watertown (1898) 156 p.
Whiton — American Ancestry v, 70
Barry's History of Hanover Mass. 419-41
Cochrane's Hist. of Antrim N. H. 749-61
Dyer's History of Plainfield Mass. 185
Lincoln's Hist. Hingham Mass. iii, 288-310
Marvin's Hist. of Winchendon Mass. 475
Perkins' Old Houses of Norwich Ct. 588
Savage's Genealogical Dictionary iv, 532
Whiting Genealogy (1871)
See also under Whiting
Whitsitt — American Ancestry viii, 77
Whitson — Bunker's L. I. Gens. 318-22
Jackson Genealogy 82, 86-8
Whittaker — Austin and Whittaker Chart (1881)
Cleveland's Hist. of Yates Co. N. Y. 283-6
Dearborn's Hist. of Salisbury N. H. 853
Little's History of Weare N. H. 1010
Pennypacker's Hist. Phœnixville Pa. 273
Whittan — Shourd's Fenwick's Colony 365-7
Whittemore — American Ancestry iv, 61, 156; vii, 143
Bond's Hist. of Watertown Mass. 652, 966
Cochrane's History of Antrim N. H. 761-5
Cochrane's Hist. Francestown N. H. 982
Cutter's History of Arlington Mass. 317-21
Daniels' History of Oxford Mass. 743
Dearborn's Hist.. Salisbury N. H. 855-60
Draper's History of Spencer Mass. 270-2
Dustin Genealogy 46-8
Hayward's History of Gilsum N. H. 416
Hayward's Hist. Hancock N. H. 1015-23
Hudson's Hist. of Lexington Mass. 264-6
Kidder's History New Ipswich N. H. 441
Lapham's History of Paris Me. 769
Locke Genealogy 34, 116
Malden Mass. Bi-Centennial 240-4
New Eng. Hist. and Gen Reg. xxi, 169-72
Norton's Hist. of Fitzwilliam N. H. 772-83

Olin's Olin Genealogy 89-99
Paige's Hist. of Cambridge Mass. 686-91
Ridlon's Harrison Me. Settlers 130
Savage's Genealogical Dictionary iv, 533-5
Sewall's History of Woburn Mass. 648
Smith's Hist. of Peterborough N. H. 344-8
Stearns' History of Rindge N. H. 762-4
Stowe's Hist. of Hubbardston Mass. 370
Ward's History of Shrewsbury Mass. 484
Washburn's History of Leicester Mass. 407
Whittemore Genealogy (1880) 48 pages
Whittemore Genealogy 2d ed. (1890) 106 p.
Whittemore Genealogy 3d ed. (1893) 132 p.
Whittemore's Orange N. J. 432
Wyman's Charlestown Mass. ii, 1021-9
Whitten — Dearborn's Parsonsfield
Wheeler's History of Brunswick Me. 860
Whittiam — Daniels' Oxford Mass. 744
Whittier — Amer. Ancestry vii, 111, 159
Butler's Hist. of Farmington Me. 614-6
Chase's History of Chester N. H. 615
Cogswell's Nottingham N. H. 492-504
Granite Monthly Concord N. H. iv, 336-46
Hoyt's Salisbury Mass. Families 357-60
Poor's Merrimack Valley Researches 141
Savage's Genealogical Dictionary iv, 535
Thurston's History of Winthrop Me. 201
Wheeler's History of Newport N. H. 570
Whittier Chart (1882) 30x43 inches
Whittier Genealogy (1873) 22 pages
Whittingham — N. E. Reg. xxvii, 427-34,
    xxxiv, 34-6
Savage's Genealogical Dictionary iv, 536
Whittingham Gen. (1873) 7 p. (1880) 3 p.
Worthen's Hist. of Sutton N. H. 1008-11
Whittle—Little's Hist. Weare N. H. 1011
Robertson's Pocahontas' Descendants
Slaughter's Bristol Parish Va. 186, 204
Whittlesey — American Ancestry ix, 199
Andrews' New Britain Ct. 235, 317, 355
Bartow Genealogy 2d part
Chapman's Trowbridge Genealogy 37
Cothren's History of Woodbury Ct. 756-65
Davis' History of Wallingford Ct. 928-35
Fowler's Chauncey Genealogy 203
New Eng. Hist. and Gen. Register xx, 321
Orcutt's History of Wolcott Ct. 607
Savage's Genealogical Dictionary iv, 537
Scranton Genealogy 43
Strong Genealogy 423-7
Whittlesey Genealogy (1855) 125 pages
Whittlesey Meeting Address (1855) 22 p.
Whittlesey Fam. of Ohio (1872) 14 pages
Whittlesey Military Record (1874) 14 pages
Whittlesey Genealogy (1898) 414 pages
Whittredge — Babson's Gloucester 178
Dodge Ancestry (1896) 14-6
Whitwell — Barry's Hanover Mass. 418
Wiatt — Lynchburg Va. 242-4
Wibird — Wentworth Genealogy i, 292
Wickenden — Austin's R. I. Gen. Dict. 224
Wicker — Paige's Hardwick Mass. 538
Wickes — American Ancestry i, 94
Austin's R. I. Genealogical Dictionary 420
Hanson's Old Kent Md. 89-99
Howell's Hist. Southampton N. Y. 405-7

Pompey N. Y. Reunion 365
Updyke's Narragansett Churches 381
Wickham — Amer. Ancestry ii, 148; xii
Austin's R. I. Genealogical Dictionary 225
Carter Family Tree of Virginia
Davis Genealogy (1888) 142-58, 175-80
Meade's Old Fams. of Virginia
Richmond Va. Standard iv, 2
Savage's Genealogical Dictionary iv, 538
Wickham Genealogy (1899) 12 pages
Wickwire — Baker's Montville Ct. 360-4
Gold's History of Cornwall Ct. 261
Perkins' Old Houses of Norwich Ct. 589
Wicom — Essex Inst. Coll. xxiv, 58-60
Wiegner — Schwenkfelders 15-7
Wier — Aldrich's Walpole N. H. 382-7
Cochrane's History of Antrim N. H. 765
Wierman — Egle's Notes (1898) 22
Literary Era (1899)
Wiestling—Egle's Pa. Genealogies 719-32
Wiggin — Amer. Ancestry vii, 18; xii
Chapman's Weeks Genealogy 156
Cogswell's History of Henniker N. H. 785
Cogswell's Hist. Nottingham N. H. 781-3
Dearborn's Hist. of Parsonsfield Me. 413
Dow's History of Hampton N. H. 1042
Eaton's History of Thomaston Me. ii, 460
Hurds' History of Rockingham Co. 548-50
New Eng. Hist. and Gen. Reg. ix, 143
Runnells' Hist. Sanbornton N. H. ii, 847
Savage's Genealogical Dictionary iv, 539
Wentworth Genealogy i, 175
Wiggin (Chas. E.) Memoir (1888) 148 pages
Wiggin Genealogy (1896) 14 pages
Young's History of Wayne Co. Ind. 438
Wiggins — American Ancestry iv, 84
Egle's Penn. Genealogies 2d ed. 733-9
Egle's Notes and Queries 2d ser. ii, 418
Griffin's Journal Southold N. Y. 130-2
Plumb's History of Hanover Pa. 486
Wigglesworth — Amer. Ancestry vi, 66
Bond's Watertown Mass. Gens. 176
Deane's Wigglesworth Biog. (1863) (1871)
Essex Institute Hist. Collections xxv, 125
Little Genealogy 129-32
Malden Mass. Bi-Centennial 155
New Eng. Hist. and Gen. Reg. xv, 334-6
Paige's History of Cambridge Mass. 691
Savage's Genealogical Dictionary iv, 540-2
Wight — American Ancestry iii, 67; v, 4;
    vi, 45; vii, 11
Ballou's History of Milford Mass. 1121
Bemis' History of Marlboro N. H. 695
Daniels' History of Oxford Mass. 744
Eaton's History of Thomaston Me. ii, 461
Hill's Dedham Mass. Records i
Hyde's History of Brimfield Mass. 467
Lancaster's Hist. of Gilmanton N. H. 290
Lapham's History of Bethel Me. 642-4
Leonard's History of Dublin N. H. 412
Morris Genealogy (1898) 762
New Eng. Hist. and Gen. Reg. xlii, 91-3
Savage's Genealogical Dictionary iv, 542
Wakefield Genealogy 184
Wight Genealogy (1848) 119 pages
Wight Genealogy (1890) 357 pages

Wightman — Austin's R. I. Dict. 226
Narragansett Historical Register iii, 267–75
Opdyck Genealogy 84
Timlow's Southington Ct. Sketches 254–6
Walworth's Hyde Genealogy 559–61
Wilbor — American Ancestry i, 94; ii, 148
Wilbour — Austin's Ancestries 63
Wilbur — Austin's R. I. Dictionary 227–9
Huntting's Hist. of Pine Plains N. Y. 390
Mitchell's Hist. of Bridgewater Mass. 343
Savage's Genealogical Dictionary iv, 544
Stowe's History of Hubbardston Mass. 371
Wilbur Genealogy (1871) 89 pages
Wilbur (L. F.) Life with Genealogy (1881)
Williams' History of Danby Vt. 284
Wilcocks — Thomas Gen. (1896) 551–3
Wilcott — Lincoln's Hingham iii, 310
Stearn's Hist. of Ashburnham 971
Wilcox — Amer. Ancestry ii, 148; v, 86,
    120, 225; vii, 134; viii, 43; x, 199, 202
Austin's R. I. Genealogical Dictionary 422
Brown's W. Simsbury Ct. Settlers 13, 126
Davis' Hist. of Wallingford Ct. 935–9
Fowler Genealogy 41
Greene Genealogy
Guild Genealogy by Burleigh 54–6
Hayward's History of Gilsum N. H. 417
Hayward's History of Hancock N. H. 1023
Hollister's History of Pawlet Vt. 256
Kellogg's White Genealogy 50
Lewis Genealogy (1893) 241–5
Littell's Passaic Valley Genealogies 480–8
Meade's Old Families of Virginia
Morris Genealogy (1898) 241–3
Narragansett Hist. Register vii, 281–93;
    ix, 60–70
New Eng. Hist. Reg. xiv, 37; xxix, 25–29
Orcutt's History of Torrington Ct. 785
Paige's History of Cambridge Mass. 694
Power's Sangamon Co. Ill. Settlers 766
Savage's Genealogical Dictionary iv, 546
Scranton Genealogy 29
Stanton Genealogy 289, 468–70
Sullivant Genealogy 255
Timlow's Sketches of Southington Ct. 256
Walworth's Hyde Genealogy 1141
Wheeler and Thaxter Gen. (1898) 37
Wheeler's Hist. of Newport N. H. 578–82
Wilcox Genealogy (1875) 8 pages
Wilcox Ancestry (1887) 11 pages
Wilcoxson Genealogy (1893) 11–25
Wilcoxson — Orcutt's Stratford 1346–8
Savage's Genealogical Dictionary vi, 547
Wilcoxson Genealogy (1893) 82 pages
Wild — Bemis' Marlboro N. H. 695
Brook's Medford Mass. 566
Faxon Genealogy 128
Kingman's North Bridgewater Mass. 682
Randalls' Hist. of Chesterfield N. H. 491–4
Thayer Memorial (1835) 83
Wilde — American Ancestry v, 168
Bradbury's Kennebunkport Me. 285
Smith's Hist. of Sunderland Mass. 573
Whittemore's Orange N. J. 452
Wilder — Am. Anc. vii, 282; ix, 218; x, 4
Barry's History of Hanover Mass. 442

Blake's Hist. of Mendon Association 139
Cochrane's Hist. Francestown N. H. 983
Dennysville Me. Centennial 111
Dunster Genealogy 186–94
Hayward's History of Gilsum N. H. 418
Hayward's History of Hancock N. H. 1023
Hemenway's Vermont Gaz. v, 147, 166
Herrick's History of Gardner Mass. 288–90
Heywood's Hist. Westminster Mass. 932
Leonard's History of Dublin N. H. 413
Lincoln's Hist. Hingham Mass. iii, 311–29
Locke Genealogy 52, 97–100, etc.
Marvin's Hist. of Winchendon Mass. 475
New Eng. Hist. and Gen. Reg. xxi, 120
Norton's History of Fitzwilliam N. H. 783
Roseboom Genealogy 96–114
Savage's Genealogical Dictionary iv, 549
Smith's Hist. Peterborough N. H. 348–50
Stearns' Hist. of Ashburnham Mass. 972–6
Stearns' History of Rindge N. H. 764–8
Temple's History N. Brookfield Mass. 786
Vinton's Richardson Genealogy 776
Wilder Genealogy (1878) 394 pages
Worcester Mag. and Hist. Journal ii, 340–2
Wyman's Charlestown Mass. Gens. 1030
Wyman's Hunt Genealogy 132
Wildes — Hancock N. H. 1024
Wildman — American Ancestry i, 95
Conn. Quarterly iii. (1897) 137
Wildrick — Chambers' N. J. Germans.
Wilds — Chandler's Shirley Mass. 675–9
Wildy — Eaton's Warren Me. 646
Eaton's History of Reading Mass. 125–7
Pearson's Schenectady N. Y. Settlers 298
Power's Sangamon Co. Ill. Settlers 767–9
Raymond's Tarrytown Monument 175
Wiley — Daniels' History Oxford Mass.
    744–6
Herrick Genealogy (1885) 87
Lamborn Genealogy 282
Lapham's History of Bethel Me. 644
Smith's Hist. of Sunderland Mass. 575–7
Washington N. H. History 666
Wyman's Charlestown Mass. Gens. 1030
Wilford — Corliss' Genealogy 237
Wilhoit — Garr Genealogy 82–4, 519
Wilker — Stearns' Ashburnham 976–8
Wilkerson — Goode Genealogy 162, 295–7
Missouri Pioneer Families 382
Wilkes — Greene's Todd Genealogy
Wilkie — American Ancestry i, 95
Wilkins — American Ancestry xii, 89
Bolton's Westchester 274
Calnek's History of Annapolis N. S. 627
Cochrane's History of Antrim N. H. 767
Cogswell's History of Henniker N. H. 786
Hayward's History of Hancock N. H.
    1025–7
Hazen's History of Billerica Mass. 162
Hudson's Hist. of Marlborough Mass. 468
Lapham's History of Norway Me. 623
Meade's Old Families of Virginia
Savage's Genealogical Dictionary iv, 550
Secomb's History of Amherst N. H. 829–37
Stearns' Hist. of Ashburnham Mass. 978
Washington N. H. History 667

Wilkinson — American Ancestry i, 95;
ii, 148; vi, 189; viii, 155; ix, 67, 236
Ammidown's Historical Collections i, 491
Austin's Ancestries 65
Austin's R. I. Genealogical Dictionary 424
Ballou Genealogy 446–50
Ballou's History of Milford Mass. 1123–6
Barlow Genealogy 159–75
Bemis' Hist. of Marlboro N. H. 695–8
Crane's Rawson Genealogy 152
Cushman's History of Sheepscott Me. 432
Davis Genealogy 150–2
Flint's Peters Lineage 125–31
Lamborn Genealogy 273
Orcutt's History of New Milford Ct. 791
Savage's Genealogical Dictionary iv, 551
Sharpless Genealogy 229
Updyke's Narragansett Churches 237
Whitmore's Heraldic Journal i, 85–7
Wilkinson Genealogy (1869) 585 pages
Wyman's Charlestown Mass. Gens. 1031
Will — American Ancestry ix, 219
Willard — Adam's Fairhaven 503–6
Allen's Worcester Mass. Association 93
American Ancestry i, 95; iv, 85; ix, 135;
xi, 232; xii, 96
Barry's Hist. Framingham Mass. 439–41
Bemis' Hist. of Marlboro N. H. 698
Bond's Watertown Mass. Gens. 808
Chandler's History of Shirley Mass. 682–8
Cochrane's Hist. of Francestown N. H. 983
Dwight Genealogy 680–9
Farmer and Moore's Hist. Coll. i, 178–80
Hemenway's Vermont Gaz. v, 179–81
Hollister's History of Pawlet Vt. 258–63
Holton's Winslow Memorial i, 205
Jackson's History of Newton Mass. 444
Leonard's History of Dublin N. H. 414
Lincoln's Hist. of Hingham Mass. iii, 329
Little's History of Weare N. H. 1012
Lowell Mass. Old Residents Coll. i, 337–52
McKeene's History of Bradford Vt. 305–7
New Eng. Historical and Genealogical
Register iv, 305; xx, 320; xxiv, 84
Norton's History of Fitzwilliam N. H.
784–6
Pierce's History of Grafton Mass. 603–6
Potter's Concord Mass. Families 15
Randalls' Hist. of Chesterfield N. H. 494
Read's History of Swanzey N. H. 495
Ridlon's Harrison Me. Settlers 133
Saunderson's Charlestown N. H. 618–29
Savage's Genealogical Dictionary iv, 552–5
Sheldon's Hist. of Deerfield Mass. 372
Smith's Founders of Mass. Bay 199–207
Stearns' Hist. Ashburnham Mass. 979–88
Titcomb's Early New Eng. People 57–81
Vinton's Giles Genealogy 252–4
Warren's History of Waterford Me. 305
Washington N. H. History 668
Willard Memoir (1858) 471 pages
Willard Genealogy (1879) 10 pages
Wyman's Charlestown Mass. Gens. 1032
Willemsen — Abeel Genealogy 12–4
N. Y. Gen. and Biog. Record xxvi, 134–9
Willes — Walworth's Hyde Genealogy 454

Willets — American Ancestry ii, 149
Bunker's Long Island Genealogies 72–95
Mott Genealogy 238–40
Willett — Am. Hist. Reg. iv, 378–88
Austin's R. I. Genealogical Dict. 426–31
Bartow Genealogy, appendix 195
Bolton's Westchester Co. N. Y. ii, 765
Calnek's History of Annapolis N. S. 627
Chambers' Early Germans of N. J. 568
Daggett's Hist. of Attleborough Mass. 130
Mott Genealogy 236–51, 343
Munsell's Albany Collections iv, 184 a
New Eng. Hist. and Gen. Register ii, 376
New York Gen. and Biog. Record xix, 76,
174; xxvii, 171
Rhode Island Hist. Society Colls. iii, 313
Savage's Genealogical Dictionary iv, 555–7
Updyke's Narragansett Churches 266–80
Willey — Am. Anc. vi, 50, 91; vii, 160
Ball's History of Lake County Ind. 433
Bangor Me Historical Magazine vii, 181
Caulkins' History of New London Ct. 310
Cogswell's Hist. of Nottingham N. H. 784
Harvey Genealogy 593–8
Hayward's Hist. of Hancock N. H. 1027
Hollister's History of Pawlet Vt. 263
Loomis Genealogy (1880) 785
Milliken's Narraguagus Valley Me. 2
Ridlon's Saco Valley Me. Families 169
Savage's Genealogical Dictionary iv, 557
Waldo's History of Tolland Ct. 107
Willey Genealogy (1868) 141 pages
Willey Family Outline (1886) 15 pages
Willey Genealogy (1888) 183 pages
Willguss — Hyde Genealogy 1035
Williams — American Ancestry i, 95; ii,
149; iii, 171; iv, 11, 52, 154; v, 139,
236; vi, 143, 183; vii, 32, 243; viii, 14;
ix, 24, 194, 201; x, 182, 205; xi, 126,
128; xii
Anderson's Waterbury Ct. i, app. 154
Andrews' History of New Britain Ct. 332
Austin's Ancestries 69–121
Austin's Ancestral Dictionary 64
Austin's R. I. Genealogical Dictionary 430
Baker's Hist. of Montville Ct. 458–65
Ballou's History of Milford Mass. 1126
Bangor Me. Historical Magazine iv, 114–6
Barrus' History of Goshen Mass. 184–91
Bass' History of Braintree Vt. 198
Bassett's History of Richmond N. H. 543
Bergen's Kings Co. N. Y. Settlers 388–90
Blake Genealogy 60
Bond's Watertown Mass. Genealogies 654
Bulloch Genealogy
Bunker's Long Island Genealogies 326–30
Butler's History of Groton Mass. 444, 482
Calnek's Hist. of Annapolis N. S. 629
Caulkins' Hist. of New London Ct. 348–50
Caulkins' History of Norwich Ct. 252
Claremont County Ohio History 308
Cleveland's Hist. of Yates Co. N. Y. 596–9
Coit Genealogy 210–3
Condit Genealogy 371–5
Corliss' North Yarmouth Me.
Cutter's History of Arlington Mass. 321–4

Dana's History of Woodstock Vt. 619–23
Daniels' History of Oxford Mass. 746-8
Davenport Genealogy 202–6
Deane's Leonard Genealogy 11–8
Deane's History of Scituate Mass. 385
Densmore's Hartwell Genealogy
Dickerman Genealogy 330–41
Dodd and Burnet's Dodd Genealogy 51
Dow's History of Hampton N. H. 1043
Dwight Genealogy 824–8
Eaton's Annals of Warren Me. 647
Eaton's Hist. of Thomaston Me. ii, 462–4
Ellis Genealogy 101–6, 234, 395–7
Emery's Taunton Ministry i, 43–6
Farrow's History of Islesborough Me. 298
Freeman's Cape Cod Mass. i, 565, etc.
Futhey's History of Chester Co. Pa. 764
Glenn's Merion in Welsh Tract 89–91
Goodwin's Genealogical Notes 14
Greene Genealogy (1894)
Hancock County Illus. History 781–8
Harris' History of Lancaster Co. Pa. 620
Hayward's Hist. of Hancock N. H. 1027
Heywood's Hist. Westminster Mass. 933
Hill's History of Mason N. H. 207
Hines' Lebanon Ct. Hist. Address 175
Hoyt's Salisbury Mass. Families 360–2
Hubbard's Stanstead Co. Canada 218
Hudson's Hist. of Lexington Mass. 266
Hudson's Marlborough Mass. 469–72
Hurd's New London County Ct. 694–700
Hyde's History of Brimfield Mass. 468
Jackson's History of Newton Mass. 438–43
Jones' History of Stockbridge Mass. 141–8
Joslin's History of Poultney Vt. 363
Judd's History of Hadley Mass. 602
Kellogg's White Genealogy 106
Larned's History of Windham Co. Ct.
Littell's Passaic Valley Genealogy 478–80
Longmeadow Mass. Centennial, app. 91–5
Loomis Genealogy (1880) 605–7, 621–5,
    774–9, 845–8
Maine Hist. and Gen. Recorder vi, 255–62
Meade's Old Families of Virginia
Mellick's Story of an Old Farm 687
Mitchell's Hist. of Bridgewater Mass. 344
Morrison's Hist. of Windham N. H. 813–8
Morse Memorial, appendix No. 68
Munsell's Albany Collections iv, 184
New E. Hist. and Gen. Register x, 154–6;
    xii, 297; xx, 205–7; xxxiv, 69-77;
    xxxvi, 277–91
Newport Historical Magazine iii, 115–30
North's History of Augusta Me. 957–64
Norton's History of Knox Co. Ohio, 341
Orcutt's History of New Milford Ct. 791
Orcutt's History of Torrington Ct. 785
Pearson's Schenectady N. Y. Settlers 296
Penn. Magazine x, 107–14; xviii, 239–44
Pierce's Biog. Gen. Contributions 401–11
Pierce's History of Gorham Me. 220
Power's Sangamon Co. Ill. Settlers 769–73
Preble Genealogy 255
Read's History of Swanzey N. H. 496
Richmond Va. Standard iii, 37
Salem N. Y. Book of History 28–31

Savage's Genealogical Dict. iv, 558–72
Sedgwick's History of Sharon Ct. 117
Sheldon's Hist. Deerfield Mass. ii, 374–88
Slaughter's St. Mark's Parish Va. 177
Smith's Hist. of Sunderland Mass. 577–9
Stackpole's Hist. of Durham Me. 286-8
Stanton Genealogy 272–5, 361–3
Stiles' History of Windsor Ct. ii, 791–3
Stoddard Genealogy (1865) 14, 41–3
Stowe's Hist. of Hubbardston Mass. 372–5
Strong's Funeral Discourse 1803
Tanner Genealogy 71–8
Tilley's Mag. of New Eng. Hist. i, 65–91
Underwood's Pollard Genealogy
Waldo's History of Tolland Ct. 36
Walworth's Hyde Genealogy 27
Ward Genealogy (1851) 10
Wheeler's Eminent N. Carolinians 418–21
Wheeler's Hist. of North Carolina ii, 409
Wheeler's History of Newport N. H. 582.
Whitman Genealogy 81–4
Whitmore's Copps Hill Epitaphs
Whittemore's Orange N. J. 113
Williams' History of Danby Vt. 282–4
Williams Fam. of Roxbury (1847) 424 pages
Williams Fam. of Roxbury (1880) 15 pages
Williams Fam. of Roxbury (1882) 17 pages
Williams Fam. of Roxbury (1886) 28 pages
Williams Fam. of Lebanon (1887) 187 pages
Williams Fam. of Ireland (1889) 68 pages
Williams Fam. of R. I. (1889) 139 pages
Williams Fam. of Roxbury (1891) 29 pages
Williams Fam. Grafton N. H. (1899) 20 p.
Worthen's History of Sutton N. H. 1011
Wyman's Charlestown Mass. Gens. 1033
Williamson — Abeel Genealogy 12–4
American Ancestry iii, 176; iv, 110; xii
Bangor Me. Historical Magazine i, 124
Futhey's History of Chester Co. Pa. 765
Matthew's History of Cornwall Vt. 290
Nevius Genealogy
Page Genealogy 99
Richmond Va. Standard iii, 14, 51; iv, 3
Savage's Genealogical Dictionary iv, 572
Smith's History of Delaware Co. Pa. 511
Wheeler's History of North Carolina ii, 409
Virginia Magazine of History vi (1898) 76–8
Williamson Family of Pa. (1884) 8 pages
Williamson Fam. of Mass. (1896) 66 pages
Williamson Family of N. Y. (1896) 23 pages
Winsor's History of Duxbury Mass. 337
Willicutt — Barrus' Goshen Mass. 191
Willing — Balch's Provincial Pa. 100–9
Morris Genealogy (1898) 486
Penn. Magazine of History v, 452–5
Smith (Rev. Wm.) Biography
Willington — Bass' Braintree Vt. 199
Willis — American Ancestry ii, 150; iii,
    61; viii, 30; x, 87, 170
Brook's History of Medford Mass. 566–9
Bunker's Long Island Genealogies 126–33
Cole's Cole Genealogy 132–49
Daniels' History of Oxford Mass. 748
Davis' Landmarks of Plymouth Mass. 287
Deacon's Stoddard Genealogy
Douglas Genealogy 224–6

Eaton's Hist. of Thomaston Me. ii, 464
Freeman's Hist. of Cape Cod Mass. ii, 55
Hatch's History of Industry Me. 840-4
Hazen's History of Billerica Mass. 162
Hudson's History of Lexington Mass. 277
Hudson's Hist. of Sudbury Mass. 453
Kingman's N. Bridgewater Mass. 684-6
Lapham's History of Bethel Me. 644
Lapham's History of Paris Me. 770
Maine Hist. and Gen. Recorder iii, 217-28
Meade's Old Families of Virginia
Mitchell's Hist. Bridgewater Mass. 345-52
Morse's Gen. Reg. ii (1859) 181-228
Mott Genealogy 269-87
New Eng. Historical and Gen. Reg. xx, 6;
   xxii, 186; xxxviii, 74; liii, 217-24
New York Genealogical and Biographical
   Record xv, 170-6; xvi, 171-3
Paige's History of Hardwick Mass. 539
Power's Sangamon Co. Ill. Settlers 773-5
Read's History of Swanzey N. H. 496
Richmond Va. Standard iii, 52, 136
Ricketson's New Bedford Mass. 187-9, 193
Savage's Genealogical Dictionary iv, 573-8
Slaughter's Fry Genealogy 74
Spooner Genealogy i, 197-211, 462-9
Whitman Genealogy 34-6
Willis Genealogy (1863) 8 pages
Willis Family of Virginia (1898) 156 pages
Winsor's History of Duxbury Mass. 337
Wyman's Charlestown Mass. Gens. 1035
See also under Wyllis
Williston — American Ancestry xii
Little Genealogy 237
Lyman's Easthampton 179
Stiles' History of Windsor Ct. ii, 793
Strong Genealogy 1150-3
Whitmore's Copps Hill Epitaphs
Willitt — Mott Genealogy
Willits — American Ancestry x, 90
Willman — Howell's Southampton 407
Willocks — Whitehead's History of Perth
   Amboy N. J. 80-4
Willoughby — American Ancestry iv, 177
Eaton Genealogy 117
Hazen's History of Billerica Mass. 183
Hibbard's History of Goshen Ct. 560
Neill's Virginia Carolorum 157
New Eng. Historical and Genealogical
   Register xxx, 67-78; xl, 50-6
Salisbury's Family Histories (1892) 507-604
Savage's Genealogical Dictionary iv, 578
Virginia Mag. of History i, 447-50; iv, 82
Watson's Some Notable Families 44-6
Willoughby N. London Rep. (1864) 28 p.
Willoughby N. London Report (1866) 13 p.
Willoughby Family of N. Eng. (1876) 15 p.
Willoughby Family of N. Eng. (1881) 7 p.
Willoughby Ancestry in Eng. (1885) 11 p.
Worcester's History of Hollis N. H. 391
Wyman's Charlestown Mass. Gens. 1036
Wills — American Ancestry x, 5
Chambers' Early Germans of N. J. 569
Deane's History of Scituate Mass. 384
Egle's Penn. Genealogies 2d ed. 696-702
Futhey's History of Chester Co. Pa. 767

Richmond Va. Standard iii, 27
Waldo's History of Tolland Ct. 70-2
Willson — American Ancestry iv, 9; vii,
   167; ix, 125
Baird's History of Rye N. Y. 497-9
Cogswell's Hist. of Henniker N. H. 787-9
Cogswell's Hist. of New Boston N. H. 387
Daniels' History of Oxford Mass. 748
Shotwell Genealogy 241-3
Young's Hist. Chautauqua Co. N. Y. 371
Wilmarth — Ballou's Milford 1128-30
Daggett's Hist. of Attleborough Mass. 95
Daniels' History of Oxford Mass. 749
Wheeler's History of Newport N. H. 583-5
Wilmer — American Ancestry v, 173
Hanson's Old Kent Md. 325-31
Morris Genealogy (1898) 625
Slaughter's Bristol Parish Va. 228
Wilmot — Anderson's Waterbury Ct. i,
   app. 155
Huntington's Stamford 136
Savage's Genealogical Dictionary iv, 580
Wilsey — American Ancestry ii, 150
Wilson — Abbott's Andover Mass. 37
American Ancestry i, 95; ii, 150; v, 90; vi,
   186; viii, 34, 92
Bangor Me. Historical Magazine vii, 229
Barry's Hist. of Framingham Mass. 441
Blake's History of Franklin Mass. 285
Bond's Watertown Mass. Gens. 895
Boyd's Annals of Winchester Ct. 317-9
Brown's Bedford Mass. Families 44
Butler's History of Groton Mass. 445
Chandler's History of Shirley Mass. 688
Chapman's Trowbridge Genealogy 229
Chase's History of Chester N. H. 615-9
Clyde's Irish Settlement in Pa. 138-45
Cochran's History of Antrim N. H. 770-2
Cochrane's Hist. Francestown N. H. 984-6
Crafts Genealogy 27-9
Cunnabell Genealogy 23
Cushman's History of Sheepscott Me. 435
Dearborn's Hist. of Salisbury N. H. 860-2
Dennysville Me. Centennial 113
Draper's Hist. Spencer Mass. 258, 268-70
Durant's Hist. of Lawrence Co. Pa. 174-8
Eaton's Annals of Warren Me. 648
Eaton's History of Thomaston Me. ii, 464
Egle's Penn. Genealogies 2d ed. 740-55
Egle's Notes and Queries 1896, Annual
   Volume, 126, 210-2
Ellis' History of Roxbury Mass. 135
Fell Genealogy 73
Gibbs' Hist. Address Blandford Mass. 65
Granite Monthly Concord N. H. vii, 339-52
Gregg's History of Old Cheraws S. C. 102
Guild's Stiles Genealogy 120
Hanson's Old Kent Md. 184-7
Hayward's History Gilsum N. H. 419-21
Hayward s History of Hancock N. H. 1028
Hazen's History of Billerica Mass. 163-5
Hemenway's Vermont Hist. Gaz. v, 210
Hepburn Genealogy 104-14
Heywood's Hist. Westminster Mass. 934
Hill's History of Mason N. H. 209
Hudson's History of Lexington Mass. 266

Jackson's History of Newton Mass. 445-7
Jameson's History of Medway Mass. 528
Kidder's Hist. of New Ipswich N. H. 442
Lapham's History of Paris Me. 772
Lancaster's Hist. of Gilmanton N. H. 287
Little's History of Weare N. H. 1013
Livermore's History of Wilton N. H. 523-6
McKeen's History of Bradford Vt. 248-59
Merrill's History of Acworth N. H. 282-5
Milliken's Narraguagus Valley Me. 6
Morris Genealogy (1898) 502
Morrison's Hist. of Windham N. H. 818-29
Morse Memorial, appendix No. 42
Nevius Genealogy
Norton's Hist. of Fitzwilliam N. H. 786-90
Orcutt's History of Torrington Ct. 786
Poore Genealogy 71-8
Power's Sangamon Co. Ill. Settlers 775-9
Read's History of Swanzey N. H. 497-9
Rhode Island Hist. Society Colls. iii, 293
Roe's Sketches of Rose N. Y. 267
Runnells' Hist. of Sanbornton N. H. ii, 848
Savage's Genealogical Dict. iv, 581-90
Schenck's History of Fairfield Ct. 422
Sewall's History of Woburn Mass. 648
Sheldon's Hist. of Deerfield Mass. 389
Smith's Hist. Peterborough N. H. 350-61
Smith's History of Rhinebeck N. Y. 204-6
Stark's History of Dunbarton N. H. 240
Stearns' History Ashburnham Mass. 988
Stiles' History of Windsor Ct. ii, 794-6
Waddell's Annals of Augusta Co. Va. 417
Washburn's Hist. of Leicester Mass. 409
Washington N. H. History 668
Watson's Johnson Families (1872)
Wheeler's History of Brunswick Me. 860
Wilson Association Report (1866) 28 pages
Wilson Genealogy (1894) 63 pages
Wilson Genealogy 2d ed. (1898) 98 pages
Wyman's Charlestown Mass. ii, 1037-40
Wilton — Stiles' Windsor Ct. ii, 793
Wiltse — American Ancestry xii
Wiltsie — Amer. Ancestry ii, 150; ix, 51
Riker's Annals of Newton N. Y. 373
Wimble — Bass Ancestry 6
Egle's Notes and Queries 3d ser. i, 112-4
Winagle — Parthemore Genealogy 21-4
Winans — American Ancestry ii, 151
Cleveland's Hist. of Yates Co. N. Y. 310-2
Clute's History of Staten Island N. Y. 435
Humphrey Genealogy 370-2
Winch — Barry's Framingham 442-7
Bemis' History of Marlboro N. H. 700
Hayward's Hist. of Hancock N. H. 1029
Norton's Hist. of Fitzwilliam N. H. 790-2
Old Northwest Gen. Quarterly iii, 109-17
Winchell — Am. Ancestry i, 96; iv, 98
Andrews' Hist. New Britain Ct. 269, 304
Densmore's Hartwell Genealogy
Ely Genealogy 264-6
Loomis Genealogy (1880) 465-71
Orcutt's History of Torrington Ct. 785
Power's Sangamon Co. Ill. Settlers 779
Roe's Sketches of Rose N. Y. 169
Savage's Genealogical Dictionary iv, 591
Stile's Hist. of Windsor Ct. ii, 796

Temple's History of Whately Mass. 283
Wheeler's History of Brunswick Me. 861
Winchell Genealogy (1869) 271 pages
Winchenbauch — Eaton's Warren Me.
Winchester — American Ancestry xii
Bangor Historical Magazine iii, 76
Barry's Hist. of Framingham Mass. 447
Bond's Watertown Mass. Gens. 655
Bowens of Woodstock Ct. (1897) 167, 172
Calnek's History of Annapolis N. S. 630
Crafts' Genealogy 135-7
Hayward's History of Gilsum N. H. 421
Hollister's History of Pawlet Vt.
Jackson's History Newton Mass. 447-51
Savage's Genealogical Dictionary iv, 591
Stearns' Hist. Ashburnham Mass. 989-98
Winchester Genealogy (1897) 45 pages
Wood's Brookline Mass. Sketches 115
Wincoll — Bond's Watertown 655
Winder — Winder Pedigree (1896) chart
Windle — Jackson Genealogy 75, 186, 214
Windnagle — Egle's Notes and Queries
    4th series i, 24
Window — Babson's Gloucester 179
Windship — Leland Genealogy 177
Windsor — Savage's Gen. Dict. iv, 603
Thomas Genealogy (1895) 553
Wine — Temple's North Brookfield 786
Winegar — Doty Genealogy 662-6
Winegar Genealogy (1859)
Wines — Blake's Mendon Assoc. 255-7
Wheeler's History of Newport N. H. 586
Winfield — American Ancestry iii, 143
Bross' Legend of the Delaware 117
Winfield Genealogy (1882) 16 pages
Wing — American Ancestry i, 96; iii, 119
Austin's Allied Families 271-4
Barrus' History of Goshen Mass. 192
Bassett's History of Richmond N. H. 533
Boyd's History of Conesus N. Y. 176
Cleveland's Hist. of Yates Co. N. Y. 409
Freeman's Cape Cod ii, 100, 159-64, 200-5
Kewaunee, Wis., Owl (1900) i
Paige's History of Hardwick Mass. 540
Pierce's History of Grafton Mass. 606
Savage's Genealogical Dictionary iv, 593-5
Spooner Genealogy i, 56-63, 375-83
Stiles' History of Windsor Ct. ii, 797
Williams' History of Danby Vt. 285
Wing Genealogy (1881) 334 pages
Wing Family Deed (1884) 4 pages
Wing Genealogy 2d ed. (1888) 581 pages
Wingate — Alden's Epitaphs iii, 205
American Ancestry vii, 72
Chapman's Weeks Genealogy 158
Cogswell's Hist. of Nottingham N. H. 785
Dow's History of Hampton N. H. 1044
New Eng. Hist. and Gen. Reg. xiii; ix, 143
North's History of Augusta Me.
Runnells' Hist. of Sanbornton N. H. ii, 850
Savage's Genealogical Dictionary iv, 595
Wentworth Genealogy ii, 58-61, 469-71
Wingate Genealogy (1886) 293 pages
Winger — American Ancestry iv, 129
Wingfield — Claypoole Genealogy 151
Goode Genealogy 90

Winkley — American Ancestry v, 60
Winn — American Ancestry ii, 151
Cleveland Genealogy (1879) 77
Cleveland Genealogy (1899) 2415-50
Cochrane's Hist. Francestown N. H. 986
Nourse Fam. of Virginia 47-52
Reed Genealogy (1883) 49 page
Savage's Genealogical Dictionary iv, 596
Sewall's Hist. of Woburn Mass. 649-51
Virginia Magazine of History vi, 203-5
Winne — Amer. Ancestry i, 96; v, 202
Munsell's Albany Collections iv, 184
Pearson's Schenectady N. Y. Settlers 297
Winniett — Calnek's Annapolis 631-3
Winning — Hazen's Billerica 165
Winship — American Ancestry i, 96; x, 168, 174, 177
Cogswell's Hist. of Henniker N. H. 789
Cutter's History of Arlington Mass. 324-30
Hayward's Hist. of Hancock N. H. 1030
Heywood's Hist. Westminster Mass. 935-7
Hill's History of Mason N. H. 208
Hudson's Hist. of Lexington Mass. 267-74
Paige's Hist. of Cambridge Mass. 690-700
Perkins' Old Houses of Norwich Ct. 591
Savage's Genealogical Dictionary iv, 597
Wyman's Charlestown Mass. Gens. ii, 1041
Winslow — American Ancestry v, 84, 133; vi, 56, 145; vii, 10
Barry's History of Hanover Mass. 443
Caverly's History of Pittsford Vt. 730
Cogswell's Hist. of Nottingham N. H. 252
Corliss' North Yarmouth Me. 1102-4
Davis' Landmarks of Plymouth 288-92
Deane's History of Scituate Mass. 388-90
Dudley's Archæological Coll., plate 4
Eaton's History of Thomaston Me. ii, 465
Foster Genealogy (1889) 64-72
Freeman's Cape Cod Mass. i, 302; ii, 764
Hanson's History of Gardiner Me. 65
Hatch's History of Industry Me. 844-6
Holton's Farwall Genealogy 96
Hoyt's Salisbury Mass.
Lapham's History of Paris Me. 772
Mitchell's Bridgewater Mass. 352, 387-90
Moore's American Governors i, 131-8
New Eng. Hist. and Gen. Register iv, 297-303; xvii, 159-62; xxi, 209-11; xxv, 355-8; xxvi, 69-75
Paige's History of Hardwick Mass. 541-3
Savage's Genealogical Dict. iv, 598-603
Spooner's Genealogy i, 427
Spooner's Memorial of W. Spooner 88
Temple's Hist. No. Brookfield Mass. 787
Thacher's Plymouth Mass. 90, 94-7, 143
Timlow's Sketches of Southington Ct. 257
Whitmore's Copps Hill Epitaphs
Winslow Family of Maine (1877) chart
Winslows of Swanzey (1877) chart
Winslows of Foxboro (1879) chart
Winslow Gen (1877-88) 1496 pages, 2 vols.
Winsor's History of Duxbury Mass. 338
Worden Genealogy 117
Winsor — Austin's Ancestries 99-103
Austin's R. I. Genealogical Dictionary 434
Holton's Winslow Memorial i, 180-5

Winsor Genealogy (1847) 12 pages
Winsor's Hist. of Duxbury Mass. 339-46
Winston — Amer. Anc. viii, 147; ix, 130
Bartholomew and Winston Rec. (1899) 6-38
Cogswell Genealogy 248
Hayden's Virginia Genealogies 729
Lynchburg Va. Sketches 220-9
Meade's Old Families of Virginia
Richmond Va. Standard i, 41; ii, 26, 39
Savage's Genealogical Dictionary iv, 605
Slaughter's St. Mark's Parish Va. 183-92
Timlow's Sketches of Southington Ct. 257
Tuttle Genealogy 140
Virginia Magazine of History v
Winter — American Ancestry xii
Bond's Watertown 656
Hazen's History of Billerica Mass. 165
Savage's Genealogical Dictionary iv, 605
Stearns' Hist. of Ashburnham Mass. 998
Temple's Hist. of No. Brookfield Mass. 788
Winterbottom — Paige's Hardwick 543
Wintermute — Chambers' Early Germans of New Jersey 570
Winthrop — American Ancestry iii, 61
Deacon's Stoddard Genealogy
Drake's History of Boston Mass. 72
Dudley Genealogy 138
Hollister's History of Connecticut i, 296
Moore's American Governors i, 268-72
New Eng. Hist. and Gen. Reg. xviii, 182-6
Paige's History of Cambridge Mass. 700
Savage's Genealogical Dict. iv, 606-14
Savage's Hist. of New England i, 76-82
Shotwell Genealogy 136-8
Thomas Genealogy (1896) 554-6
Vinton's Giles Genealogy 336-8
Winthrop Family Notes (1864) 10 pages
Winthrop Family Pedigree (1874) 38 pages
Winthrop Family in Ireland (1883) 29 p.
Winthrop Genealogy (1887) 16 pages
Winthrop's Life of Novernor Winthrop
Wyman's Charlestown Mass. Gens. 1043
Wire — Chambers' N. J. Germans 571
Wires — Temple's No. Brookfield 788
Wirt — Bretz Genealogy 5-8, 24-44
Egle's Notes and Queries 4th ser. i, 163-7
Wise — Ball's Lake County Ind. 393-6
Bourne's History of Wells Me. 763
Cleveland's Hist. of Yates Co. N. Y. 336
Cutts Genealogy 56, 113
Hambleton Genealogy
Hammatt Papers 413
Meade's Old Families of Virginia
Power's Sangamon Co. Ill. Settlers 780
Richmond Va. Critic (1888)
Richmond Va. Standard iv, 3
Savage's Genealogical Dictionary iv, 614
Sheldon's Hist. of Deerfield Mass. 389
Wismer — Wismer Gen. (1893) 372 pages
Wistar — Morris Genealogy (1898) 356-66
Wister — Rodman Genealogy 195
Wiswall — Ballou's Milford 1130-3
Bemis' History of Marlboro N. H. 701-4
Bradbury's Kennebunkport Me. 286
Calnek's Hist. of Annapolis N. S. 633-6
Clapp's Jones Hill Dorchester Mass. 46-52

Clark Fam. of Watertown Mass. 105, 169
Crafts Genealogy 250–4
Davis' Landmarks of Plymouth Mass. 292
Heywood's Hist. Westminster Mass. 937
Jackson's History of Newton Mass. 451–60
Morse's Richards Genealogy 149
Morse's Sherborn Mass. Settlers 260
New E. Hist. and Gen. Register xl, 58–62
Paige's History of Cambridge Mass. 701
Robinson's Genealogy (1859)
Savage's Genealogical Dictionary iv, 615
Wiswall Genealogy (1886) 4 pages
Wiswell — Bangor Hist. Magazine v, 18
Corliss' North Yarmouth Me.
Witbeck — American Ancestry ii, 151
Greene County N. Y. History
Munsell's Albany Collections iv, 184
Witham — Babson's Gloucester 179–81
Bangor Me. Historical Magazine v, 214
Eaton's History of Thomaston Me. ii, 466
Ridlon's Harrison Me. Settlers 131
Withee — Hatch's Industry Me. 846
Hill's History of Mason N. H. 208
Witherbee — Amer. Ancestry iii, 175
Hemenway Genealogy 18–22
Hudson's Hist. of Marlborough Mass. 472
Witherby — Ward's Shrewsbury 478–81
Witherell — American Ancestry x, 148
Davis' Landmarks of Plymouth 293
Paige's History of Cambridge Mass. 701
Withers — Meade's Old Fams. of Va.
Richmond Va. Standard ii, 32; iii, 33
Saunders' Alabama Settlers 515–7
Slaughter's Bristol Parish Va. 234–6
Virgina Magazine of History vi, 309–13,
425; vii, 87–91
Witherspoon — Calnek's Annapolis N. S.
636
Chase's History of Chester 619
Cochrane's Hist. Francestown N. H. 987
Lamb's History of New York City i, 752
Withington — Cogswell's Henniker
Hill's History of Mason N. H..208
Locke Genealogy 40, 63, 79
Norton's Hist. of Fitzwilliam N. H. 792
Pope Genealogy 322
Savage's Genealogical Dictionary iv, 618
Withrow — Power's Sangamon Ill. 781
Richmond Va. Standard iii, 40
Witman — Egle's Historical Register ii, 76
Witmer — Egle's Lebanon Co. Pa. 256
Witt — Hudson's Marlborough 473–5
Lapham's History of Norway Me. 624
Lewis' History of Lynn Mass. 190
Montague Genealogy 185–8
Randall's Hist. of Chesterfield N. H. 496
Stowe's Hist. of Hubbardston Mass. 376
Temple's North Brookfield Mass. 788–90
Witter — Allen and Witter Gen. (1872)
American Ancestry iv, 12; v, 68; vi, 131
Austin's Allied Families 276
Greene Genealogy (1894)
Wixam — Freeman's Cape Cod 370
Wodell — Austin's R. I. Gen. Dict. 434
Wodell Genealogy (1880) 100 pages
Woertman — Bergen's Kings Co. 392

Woglom — Clute's Staten Island 437
Wolcott — Ammidown Genealogy
Ammidown's Historical Collection
Barry's History of Hanover Mass. 445
Cleveland's Hist. of Yates Co. N. Y. 200
Daniels' History of Oxford Mass. 750
Hollister's History of Conn. i, 190; ii, 268
Huntington Genealogy 247
Kellogg's White Genealogy 44
Lamb's History of New York City 608, 664
Longmeadow Mass. Centennial 95
N. E. Hist. Reg. i, 251–5; ix, 338; xx, 204
Orcutt's History of Torrington Ct. 787–90
Prime Genealogy (1895) 48
Robinson Genealogy (1859) appendix
Savage's Genealogical Dictionary iv, 620–4
Salisbury's Fam. Hists. (1892) ii, 169–200
Stiles' History of Windsor Ct. ii, 798–826
Walworth's Hyde Genealogy 1120–2
Wolcott Genealogy (1881) 439 pages
Wolf — Chambers' N. J. Germans 572
Egle's Notes and Queries (1897) 189
Walworth's Hyde Genealogy 995–8
Wolff — American Ancestry ix, 182
Lincoln's Hist. of Hingham Mass. iii, 331
Wolff Genealogy (1863) 113 pages
Wollaston — Maris Genealogy 79, 169
Womack — American Ancestry iv, 71
Wonson — Babson's Gloucester 274
Wood — American Ancestry i, 97; ii,
151; iii, 157, 223; iv, 48, 171; v, 100,
234; vi, 98; ix, 110; xii, 111
Atkin's History of Hawley Mass. 67
Austin's R. I. Genealogical Dictionary 230
Ballou's History of Milford Mass. 1136–43
Ball's History of Lake County Ind. 435–8
Bangor Me. Historical Magazine v, 214–7
Barry's History of Framingham Mass. 447
Barry's History of Hanover Mass. 445
Bolton's Westchester Co. N. Y. ii, 765
Bouton Genealogy
Canfield Genealogy, chart 5
Champion Genealogy 130
Chapin's Uxbridge Mass. Address 126–8
Chase's History of Chester N. H. 619
Clement's Newtown N. J. Settlers
Clute's Hist. of Staten Island N. Y. 437
Cochrane's History of Antrim N. H. 773
Cochrane's Francestown N. H. 988, 1007
Cogswell's Hist. of Henniker N. H. 793–8
Cole Genealogy 67–73, 244–51
Crane's Rawson Genealogy 27
Daniels' History of Oxford Mass. 751
Davis' Landmarks of Plymouth Mass. 293
Dennysville Me. Centennial 113
Densmore's Hartwell Genealogy
Draper's History of Spencer Mass. 260
Dunster Genealogy 171
Eaton's History of Thomaston Me. ii, 467
Essex Inst. Hist. Coll. xix, 61–4; xxiv, 61
Freeman's Hist. of Cape Cod Mass. ii, 465
Gage's History of Rowley Mass. 461
Guild's Stiles Genealogy 348
Hayden's Virginia Genealogies 436
Hayward's Hist. of Gilsum N. H. 422
Hayward's Hist. of Hancock N. H. 1032–43

Hemenway's Vermont Hist. Gaz. iv, 519
Herrick's History of Gardner Mass. 390-2
Heywood's Hist. Westminster Mass. 938-47
Hollister's History of Pawlet Vt. 265
Howell's Hist. Southampton N. Y. 441-4
Hubbard's Hist. of Stanstead Canada 116
Hudson's Hist. Marlborough Mass. 476
Joslin's History of Poultney Vt. 364
Lapham's History of Rumford Me. 44
Littell's Passaic Valley Genealogies 488
Little's History of Weare N. H. 1014
Loomis Genealogy (1880) 772-4
Lyman's Hist. of Easthampton Mass. 192
Meade's Old Families of Virginia
Miner's Meriweather Genealogy 13
Mitchell's Hist. of Bridgewater Mass. 353
Morse's Sherborn Mass. Settlers 261-4
New York Gen. and Biog. Record xxi, 23
Olin Genealogy by Nye (1892) 95-115
Paige's History of Hardwick Mass. 543
Perley's History of Boxford Mass. 71-3
Pierce's History of Grafton Mass. 607-12
Poor's Merrimack Valley Researches 95
Potter's Concord Mass. Families 16, 38
Powers' Sangamon Co. Ill. Settlers 784
Randalls' Hist. Chesterfield N. H. 496-502
Richmond Va. Standard ii, 39, 42; iii, 6
Saunderson's Charlestown N. H. 631
Sedgwick's History of Sharon Ct. 118
Selleck's Norwalk Ct. (1896) 471-82
Sharpless Genealogy 272, 545
Smith's History of Delaware Co. Pa. 511
Stearns' Hist. Ashburnham Mass. 999-1005
Stearns' History of Rindge N. H. 770-4
Stiles' History of Windsor Ct. ii, 826
Tanner Genealogy 50-2
Temple's Hist. No. Brookfield Mass. 790
Temple's History of Palmer Mass. 569-71
Thurston's History of Winthrop Me. 202
Walworth's Hyde Genealogy 228-30
Washington N. H. History 669-74
Watkins Genealogy 24
Westminster Mass. Centennial 31
Wood Family of Concord (1871) 26 pages
Wood Family of Chicopee (1883) 3 pages
Wood Family of Rowley (1884) 34 pages
Wood Family of Littleton (1885) 292 pages
Worcester's History of Hollis N. H. 392
Wyman's Charlestown Mass. Gens. 1044-8
Woodard — Temple's N. Brookfield 795
Woodbridge — American Ancestry ii, 151
Barbour's My Wife and Mother, app. 55
Bulloch Genealogy
Cochrane's Hist. Francestown N. H. 989
Cushman's Hist. of Sheepscott Me. 433-5
Dudley Genealogy 138-40
Dwight Genealogy 1076-89
Jones' Stockbridge Mass. 128-41
Judd's History of Hadley Mass. 603
Lapham's History of Norway Me. 625
New E. Hist. and Gen. Reg. xxxii, 292-6
Perkins' Old Houses of Norwich Ct. 593-5
Pilgrim Record Society Bulletin i, 3-5
Savage's Genealogical Dictionary iv, 630-4
Stiles' History of Windsor Ct. ii, 827
Strong Genealogy 358-61, 470, 1017-9

Walworth's Hyde Genealogy 573, 922-5
Woodbridge Genealogy (1878) 7 pages
Woodbridge Genealogy (1883) 272 pages
Woodburn — Morrison's Windham 829
Parker's Hist. Londonderry N. H. 307-11
Woodbury — Am. Anc. i, 97; vii, 61; x, 47
Babson's Hist. Gloucester Mass. 181, 286
Ballou's History of Milford Mass. 1134
Bedford N. H. Centennial 348-53
Benedict's History of Sutton Mass. 748-57
Calnek's Hist. of Annapolis N. S. 637-9
Chandler's History of Shirley Mass. 688
Cochrane's Hist. of Antrim N. H. 775-80
Cochrane's Hist. Francestown N. H. 990-9
Cogswell's Hist. of New Boston N. H. 441
Davis Genealogy 475
Dodge Ancestry (1896) 20-3
Driver Genealogy 391
Dwight Genealogy 973-5
Essex Inst. Hist. Coll. i, 150; xxiv, 1-42;
    xxxv, 257-72; xxxvi, 31-8
Fiskes of Amherst N. H. 161
Hartwell Genealogy (1895) 82-4
Hubbard's Hist. of Springfield Vt. 507-10
Kellogg Genealogy, supp. (1899) 12-8
Lapham's History of Bethel Me. 646
Lapham's History of Paris Me. 773-5
Little's History of Weare N. H. 1015
Merrill's History of Acworth N. H. 286-8
Poore Genealogy 61-5
Savage's Genealogical Dictionary iv, 634
Secomb's History of Amherst N. H. 835-41
Stackpole's History of Durham Me. 288
Stark's History of Dunbarton N. H. 218
Stone's History of Beverly Mass. 21-3
Temple's Hist. No. Brookfield Mass. 795-7
Wheeler's History of Newport N. H. 587
Woodbury Genealogy (1887) 42 pages
Woodbury's Old Planters in N. E. (1885)
Woodcock — Daggett's Attleborough 35
Dedham Historical Register iv, 172-9
Eaton's History of Thomaston Me. ii, 467
Hayward's History of Gilsum N. H. 423
Hill's Dedham Mass. Records i
Read's History of Swanzey N. H. 499
Savage's Genealogical Dictionary iv, 636
Thurston's History of Winthrop Me. 203
Woodford — American Ancestry viii, 209
Boyd's Annals of Winchester Ct. 388-91
Humphreys Genealogy
Jones Genealogy (1891) 132-5
Richmond Va. Standard iii, 22
Savage's Genealogical Dictionary iv, 638
Stanton Genealogy 382
Woodhouse — Greene's Todd Genealogy
Lee Genealogy of Ipswich 401-16
New Eng. Hist. and Gen. Reg. xxxviii, 67
Savage's Genealogical Dictionary iv, 639
Wm. and Mary College Hist. Reg. i, 227-32
Woodhull — Amer. Anc. v, 164; vii, 156
Bolton and Woodhull Genealogy (1862)
Chambers' Early Germans of N. J. 573
Cooley's Trenton N. J. Genealogies 306-12
Eager's Hist. of Orange Co. N. Y. 542-4
Eaton's History of Thomaston Me. ii, 468
Kilbourne Genealogy 181

New York Genealogical Recorder i, 25; iii, 10-20; iv, 54-61, 124-7; xxvii, 52-5, 95-7
Spooner Genealogy i, 260-2
Thompson's Hist. Long Island ii, 397-402
Wetmore Genealogy 58-60, etc.
Whitmore's Heraldic Journal ii, 113-5
Woodis — Lee Gen. of Ipswich 401-16
Temple's Hist. No. Brookfield Mass. 797
Woodman — Am. Anc. v, 211; vii, 216
Austin's R. I. Genealogical Dictionary 230
Buxton Me. Centennial 147
Coffin's History of Newbury Mass. 322
Cogswell's Hist. of Nottingham N. H. 506
Fullonton's Hist. of Raymond N. H. 296
Hayward's History of Hancock N. H. 1043
Hoyt's Salisbury Mass. Families 364-8
Hubbard's Hist. of Stanstead Co. Can. 295
Ridlon's Saco Valley Me. Fams. 108, 118
Runnells' Sanbornton N. H. ii, 850-65
Savage's Genealogical Dictionary iv, 640
Woodman Fam. of Newbury (1855) 16 p.
Woodman Fam. of Kingston (1856) 54 p.
Woodman Fam. of Buxton (1874) 125 pages
Woodmansey — Savage's Dict. iv, 641
Woodnutt — Shourd's Fenwick Colony N. J. 368-73
Woodruff — American Ancestry i, 97; iii, 174, 226; viii, 154; x, 169
Anderson's Waterbury Ct. i, app. 1155
Andrews' Hist. New Britain Ct. 138, etc.
Baldwin Genealogy 51-3
Baldwin Genealogy, supp. 1012-4
Clayton's History of Union Co. N. J. 291-3
Cooley's Trenton N. J. Gens. 306-12
Hatfield's Elizabeth N. J. 105
Hinman's Connecticut Settlers 1st ed. 246
Howell's Hist. of Southampton N. Y. 407
Kilbourn Genealogy 113
Roome Genealogy 115 q—s
Savage's Genealogical Dictionary iv, 642
Sedgwick's History of Sharon Ct. 119
Shourd's Fenwick Colony N. J. 374
Timlow's Southington Ct. Sketches 257-73
Walworth's Hyde Genealogy 274-6
Woods — Andrews' New Britain 160
Butler's Hist. of Farmington Me. 617
Butler's Hist. of Groton Mass. 406-8, 482
Chandler's Hist. of Shirley Mass. 689-91
Cochrane's Hist. Francestown N. H. 1000-2
Cogswell's Hist. Henniker N. H. 798-801
Corliss' North Yarmouth Me.
Crafts' History of Whately Mass. 625-7
Ely Genealogy 142-6, 301-11
Hayward's History of Gilsum N. H. 423
Hayward's Hist. of Hancock N. H. 1043-5
Hill's History of Mason N. H. 208
Hudson's Hist. Marlborough Mass. 477-80
Norton's Hist. of Fitzwilliam N. H. 793-5
Paul's History of Wells Vt. 153
Richmond Va. Standard iii, 32
Stowe's Hist. of Hubbardston Mass. 377
Temple's History of Whately Mass. 284
Washington N. H. History 674
Wheeler's Hist. of Newport N. H. 589
Woodside — Wheeler's Brunswick 862

Woodson — Green's Kentucky Families
Meade's Old Churches of Virginia ii, 3
Richmond Va. Standard ii, 20, 27
Woodsum — Ridlon's Harrison Me. 127
Ridlon's Saco Valley Me. Families 208-18
Woodville — Mead's Old Families ii, 82
Slaughter's St. Mark's Parish Va. 192
Woodward — American Ancestry i, 97; ii, 151; iv, 219; vii, 196, 203; x, 50
Anderson's Waterbury Ct. i, app. 156
Austin's R. I. Genealogical Dictionary 232
Babson's History of Gloucester Mass. 244
Bass' History of Braintree Vt. 199
Bassett's History of Richmond N. H. 535
Bemis' Hist. of Marlboro N. H. 704-9
Blake's History of Franklin Mass. 284
Bond's Watertown Mass. 657-68, 968-75
Bronson's History of Waterbury Ct. 551
Cochrane's History Francestown N. H. 1002-5
Daniels' History of Oxford Mass. 751
Dodd's History of East Haven Ct. 159
Eaton's History of Reading Mass. 127
Farrow's History of Islesborough Me. 301
Hayward's History of Hancock N. H. 1045
Heywood's History Westminster Mass. 947-9
Hines' Lebanon Ct. Hist. Address 174
Hubbard's Hist. of Springfield Vt. 511
Hubbard's Hist. of Stanstead Canada 281
Hudson's Hist. of Sudbury Mass. 55
Hurd's Hist. of New London Co. Ct. 516
Jackson Genealogy 227
Jackson's History of Newton Mass. 464
Johnson Genealogy (1876) 30-2
Kirk Genealogy 16-8, 38-42
Lincoln's Hist. Hingham Mass. iii, 332-4
Maine Historical and Genealogical Recorder iii, 244-7; iv, 15-22; vii, 23-31; viii, 90-4, etc.; ix, 178-282
Morris Genealogy (1853) 52-8
New England Historical and Genealogical Register xviii, 265; l, 300-4; li, 169-81
Orcutt's History of Torrington Ct. 790-2
Paige's History of Cambridge Mass. 702
Perkins' Old Houses of Norwich Ct. 596
Potts Genealogy (1895) 331
Read's History of Swanzey N. H. 501
Riker's Annals of Newtown N. Y. 383
Runnells' Hist. Sanbornton N. H. ii, 865
Savage's Genealogical Dictionary iv, 643-7
Sharpless Genealogy 160
Stearns' Hist. of Ashburnham Mass. 1006
Stickney's History of Minisink N. Y. 157
Stiles' History of Windsor Ct. ii, 827
Stoddard Genealogy (1865) 11, 18
Stowe's Hist. Hubbardston Mass. 378-80
Temple's History of Northfield Mass. 566
Tyngsborough Mass. Centennial 17
Washington N. H. History 675-80
Wheeler's History of Brunswick Me. 862
Woodward Fam of Penn. (1879) 114 pages
Woodwards of Bristol Me. (1887) 14 pages
Woodwards of Lisbon Me. (1899) 23 pages
Worthen's Hist. of Sutton N. H. 1013-8
Wyman's Charlestown Mass. Gens. 1049

Woodworth — American Ancestry ii, 152; viii, 116, 147
Chute Genealogy, appendix 245-71
Cleveland's Hist. of Yates Co. N. Y. 226-9
Deane's History of Scituate Mass· 391-5
Montague Genealogy 121-3
Paul's History of Wells Vt. 154
Peck's Rochester N. Y. Centennial 674
Savage's Genealogical Dictionary iv, 647
Woodworth Genealogy (1898) 142 pages
Woolcott — Temple's History of North Brookfield Mass. 790-4
Wooley — Austin's R. I. Gen. Dict. 212
Bassett's History of Richmond N. H. 536
Woolfolk — Paxton's Marshall Genealogy
Woollen — American Ancestry iv, 214
Woolley — Howell's Southampton 408
Woolsey — Bolton's Westchester 765
Cooley's Trenton N. J. Genealogies 315-7
Dwight Genealogy 248-56, 1089-1105
Dwight's Strong Genealogy 367
Greene Co. N. Y. History 191
Mott Genealogy 359
New York Gen. and Biog. Record iv, 143-55; v, 12-25, 76-83, 139-47; vi, 24-8
Thompson's Hist. of Long Island ii, 437-42
Woolson — Barry's Framingham 448
Bond's Hist. of Watertown Mass. 668, 975
Crosby Genealogy 24
Kidder's Hist. of New Ipswich N. H. 444
Secomb's History of Amherst N. H. 841
Woolworth — Amer. Ancestry ix, 142
Longmeadow Mass. Centennial. app. 95-7
Woolworth Genealogy (1893) 209 pages
Wooster—Anderson's Waterbury 156
Child Genealogy 110-2
Eaton's History of Thomaston Me. ii, 468
Freeman's Hist. of Cape Cod Mass. ii, 98
Hollister's History of Pawlet Vt. 266
Huntington's Stamford Ct. Settlers 136
New York Gen. and Biog. Rec. xxx, 242-7; xxxi, 39-47
Orcutt's History of Derby Ct. 780-4
Orcutt's History of New Milford Ct. 801
Orcutt's History of Stratford Ct. 1348
Savage's Genealogical Dictionary iv, 649
Sharpe's History of Seymour Ct. 223
See Worcester
Wootton — Bowie Genealogy 113
Worcester — Amer. Anc. iv, 222; v, 166
Blake's Hist. Mendon Association 268-70
Chandler's History of Shirley Mass. 691-3
Chute Genealogy, appendix 271-4
Ely Genealogy 258
Hoyt's Salisbury Mass. Families 368
Norton's Hist. of Fitzwilliam N. H. 795
Read's History of Swanzey N. H. 502
Ruggles Genealogy
Savage's Genealogical Dictionary iv, 650
Stearns' Hist. of Ashburnham Mass. 1006
Worcester Genealogy (1856) 111 pages
Worden — American Ancestry vii, 211
Hemenway's Vermont Hist. Gaz. v, 165
Randalls' Hist. of Chesterfield N. H. 502
Worden Genealogy (1868) 164 pages
Wordin — Orcutt's Stratford Ct. 1358

Workman — American Ancestry viii, 217
Orcutt's Hist. of Torrington Ct. 792
Power's Sangamon Co. Ill. Settlers 785-8
Worley — American Ancestry xii
Wormall — Futhey's Chester Pa. 772
Winsor's History of Duxbury Mass. 347
Wormely — Preble Genealogy 155-9
Wormell — Eaton's Thomaston 469
Wormley — Carter Family Tree
De Bow's Review xxvi, 129
Hayden's Virginia Genealogies 230
Lee Genealogy (1895) 144-7
Meade's Old Churches of Virginia i, 371
Page Genealogy 47
Southern Bivouac (1886) 649
Wormsted — Alden's Epitaphs iii, 122
Worrall — Maris Genealogy 121
Sharpless Genealogy 355
Smith's History of Delaware Co. Pa. 515
Worrell — Martin's Chester Pa. 324
Worrick — Lincoln's Hingham iii, 334
Worsham — Slaughter's Bristol Va. 237
Worsley — Daniels' Oxford Mass. 752
Bemis' Hist. of Marlboro N. H. 709
Worster — Draper's Spencer Mass. 264
Worth — Amer. Ancestry ii, 152; iv, 40
Emery's Newbury Mass. Reminisc. 126
Futhey's Hist. of Chester Co. Pa. 774-7
Hubbard's Hist. of Stanstead Co. Can. 141
Savage's Genealogical Dictionary iv, 652
Worthen — Hayward's Hancock 1046
Hoyt's Salisbury Mass. Families 370-2
Worthern — Chase's Chester N. H. 620
Worthington — Amer. Ancestry iv, 120; v, 64; vii. 56, 170; viii, 23; x, 17
Barbour's My Wife and Mother, app. 39
Bowie Genealogy 497-511
Dorsey Family Chart
Ely Genealogy 320
Fiske Family of Amherst N. H. 24a, 24c
Futhey's History of Chester Co. Pa. 777
Goodwin's Foote Genealogy 87
Goodwin's Genealogical Notes 264-74
Goodwin's Recoll. of a Lifetime 537-9
Loomis Genealogy (1880) 367-82
Martindale's Hist. of Byberry Pa. 362-9
New Eng. Hist. and Gen. Reg. xliii, 361
Ross and Highland Counties Ohio 405
Savage's Genealogical Dictionary iv, 653
Stoddard Genealogy 19
Whitmore's Heraldic Journal iv, 69-75
Worthington Family of Md. (1886) 20 pages
Worthington Genealogy (1894) 489 pages
Worthley — Cochrane's Antrim 761-5
Corliss' North Yarmouth Me.
Little's History of Weare N. H. 1018
McKeen's History of Bradford Vt. 307
Wortman — American Ancestry ix, 184
Chambers' Early Germans of N. J. 574-6
Cleveland's Hist. Yates Co. N. Y. 747-50
Wright — Adams Genealogy (1894) 41, 49
American Ancestry i, 98; ii, 152; iv, 71, 90, 107, 169; v, 140; vii, 61; ix, 79; xi, 127. 184; xii, 94
Andrews' New Britain Ct. 175-8, etc.
Bangor Me. Historical Magazine v, 216

350

Barlow Genealogy 460–72
Barry's Hist. of Framingham Mass. 449
Bassett's History of Richmond N. H. 537
Bemis' Hist. of Marlboro N. H. 710–2
Boyd's Annals of Winchester Ct. 263–5
Brown's Bedford Mass. Families 45
Bunker's Long Island Genealogies 331–4
Burleigh's Guild Genealogy 28, 62
Cleveland's Yates Co. N. Y. 152, 537
Cochrane's History of Antrim N. H. 782
Collins' Hist. of Hillsdale N. Y., app. 129
Crafts Genealogy 63
Cunnabell Genealogy 71
Cushman's History of Sheepscott Me. 436
Davis' Landmarks of Plymouth Mass. 294
Deane's History of Scituate Mass. 393
Draper's History of Spencer Mass. 270
Dunster Genealogy 233, 249
Freeman's Hist. of Cape Cod Mass. ii, 44
Harvey Genealogy 782–91
Hayward's History of Gilsum N. H. 424
Hazen's History of Billerica Mass. 160
Hemenway's Vermont Hist. Gaz. v
Heywood's Hist. Westminster Mass. 949
Hibbard's History of Goshen Ct. 560–72
Hines' Lebanon Ct. Hist. Address 175
Hodgman's History of Westford Mass. 481
Hollister's History of Pawlet Vt. 267
Howell's Southampton 2d ed. 409
Hudson's History of Lexington Mass. 275
Kellogg's White Genealogy 109
Lancaster Hist. of Gilmanton N. H. 290
Little's History of Weare N. H. 1020
Livermore's Hist. of Block Island R. I. 348
Locke Genealogy 56, 69
Loomis Genealogy (1880) 592–5
Lyman's Hist. Easthampton Mass. 168–73
Miller's Hist. Colchester Co. N. S. 143–6
Montague Genealogy 194
Morris and Flynt Ancestors (1882) 34
Morris Genealogy (1894) 52
New Eng. Historical and Genealogical
    Register iv, 355–8; xx, 208–10; xxxv,
    74–82; xxxvii, 76–83; xl, 280–4
New York Gen. Biog. and Record iii, 35–45
Norton's Hist. of Fitzwilliam N. H. 796–9
Olin's Olin Genealogy 46
Power's Sangamon Co. Ill. Settlers 788
Putnam's Hist. Mag. v, 230–4; vi, 91–5
Read's History of Swanzey N. H. 503
Reed's History of Rutland Mass. 105
Savage's Genealogical Dict. iv, 654–61
Sewall's History of Woburn Mass. 175, 650
Sheldon's Hist. of Deerfield Mass. 390–5
Slafter Genealogy 20–3
Spooner's Memorial of W. Spooner 94
Stearns' Hist. of Ashburnham Mass. 1006
Stiles' History of Windsor Ct. ii, 829
Stowe's Hist. of Hubbardston Mass. 380–2
Talcott's N. Y. and N. E. Fams. 729–47
Temple's Hist. of N. Brookfield Mass. 798
Temple's Hist. of Northfield Mass. 567–74
Timlow's Southington Ct. Sketches 273–5
Washington N. H. History 680–9
Wheeler's History of Newport N. H. 590
Willimantic Ct. Journal for June 24, 1864

Worcester's History of Hollis N. H. 393
Worthen's Hist. of Sutton N. H. 1019
Wright Fam. of Springfield (1881) 8 pages
Wright Fam. of Long Island (1899) 24 p.
Wyman's Charlestown Mass. Gens. 1051
Wroth — Hanson's Old Kent Md. 199–202
Wurts — Sylvester's Ulster Co. N. Y. 125
Wyatt — Meade's Old Families of Virginia
Morris and Flynt Ancestors (1882) 30
Neill's Virgiina Carolorum 13, 155
Paige's History of Hardwick Mass. 544
Richmond Va. Standard ii, 32, 33
Runnells' Hist. Sanbornton N. H. ii, 865–8
Savage's Genealogical Dictionary iv, 661
Secomb's History of Amherst N. H. 842
Shourd's Fenwick Colony N. J. 359–64
Virginia Magazine of Hist. iii (1895) 177–9
Wyatt Ancestry in Eng. (1898) chart
Wyborne — Savage's Gen. Dict. iv, 662
Wyckoff — Bergen Genealogy 120
Bergen's Van Brunt Genealogy 35
Bergen's Kings Co. N. Y. Settlers 394–8
Cole Genealogy 208
Honeyman's Our Home, 148, 193–5
Meginnes' West Branch Valley 537–44
Mellick's Story of an Old Farm 685
Nevius Genealogy 161–3
New York Gen. and Biog. Record x, 153
Power's Sangamon Co. Ill. Settlers 765
Riker's Annals of Newtown N. Y. 407
Wycoff — American Ancestry iv, 108
Wyer — Austin's Allied Families 277
New Eng. Hist. and Gen. Reg. xxv, 246–8
Washburn's Notes on Livermore Me. 17
Wheeler's History of Brunswick Me. 362
Wyman's Charlestown Mass. Gens. 1052–6
Wyeth — Cutter's Arlington 331–3
Egle's Penn. Genealogies 2d ed. 756–64
Morse's Sherborn Mass. Settlers 264
Paige's History of Cambridge Mass. 702–6
Savage's Genealogical Dictionary iv, 663
Wygant — Amer. Anc. x, 105; xi, 140
Weygant's Family Record (1897) 30–2
Wyles — Hyde's Brimfield Mass. 468
Wyley — Hayward's Hancock N. H.
Wylie — American Ancestry xi, 139
Wylie Chart (1899) 13x16 inches
Wylie Genealogy (1900) 32 pages
Wyllie — Eaton's Warren Me. 649
Wyllis — Glastenbury Ct. Centennial 162
New Eng. Hist. and Gen. Reg xxxvii, 33–7
Porter's Hartford Ct. Settlers 23
Walworth's Hyde Genealogy 1171–4
See also under Willis
Wylly — Bullock Genealogy
Wyman — Aldrich's Walpole N. H. 388
American Ancestry v, 203
Bond's Watertown Mass. Gens. 670–2
Brook's History of Medford Mass. 569
Corliss' North Yarmouth Me. 161–3, 661–3
Cutter's Hist. of Arlington Mass. 334
Daniels' History of Oxford Mass. 752
Farrow's Hist. of Islesborough Me. 302
Glover Genealogy 403
Hartwell Genealogy (1895) 85–9
Hayward's History of Gilsum N. H. 425

Hayward's History of Hancock N. H. 1047
Hazen's History of Billerica Mass. 166
Heywood's Hist. Westminster Mass. 950
Hoar Lineage (1898) 26-62
Hudson's Hist. of Lexington Mass. 275-7
Lapham's History of Rumford Me. 423
Little's History of Weare N. H. 1021
Locke Genealogy 42, 49, 94
Marvin's Hist. of Winchendon Mass. 476
New Eng. Hist. and Gen. Reg. iii, 33-8,
    84; l, 45
Pierce Genealogy (1894)
Reed Genealogy 66, 98
Savage's Genealogical Dictionary iv, 663-6
Sewall's Hist. of Woburn Mass. 207, 651-7
Stowe's Hist. of Hubbardston Mass. 382
Thurston's Hist. of Winthrop Me. 203
Vinton's Richardson Genealogy 189, 400
Ward's Hist. of Shrewsbury Mass. 482-4
Wheeler's History of Newport N. H. 591
Wyman Genealogy (1849) 6 pages, reprint
Wyman Genealogy (1880) 22 pages
Wyman Family in Eng. (1897) 39 pages
Wyman's Charleston Mass. 1057-9
Wyngart — Albany Colls. iv, 184y.
Wynkoop — American Ancestry i, 98; ii,
    153; vii, 39; xi, 203
Davis' Hist. of Bucks Co. Pa. 358
Munsell's Albany Collections iv, 184y.
Schoonmaker's Hist. Kingston N. Y. 494
Sylvester's Hist. of Ulster Co. N. Y. 101
Wynkoop Genealogy (1866) 34 pages
Wynkoop Genealogy 2d ed. (1878) 130 p.
Wynne — Glenn's Merion Pa. 261-79
Wynnstay - · Glenn's Merion 387
Wythe — Campbell's Hist. of Virginia 657
Meade's Old Families of Virginia
Wm. and Mary College Hist. Reg. ii, 69
Yager — Garr Genealogy 519-22
Yale — American Ancestry i, 98; x, 201
Davis' Hist. of Wallingford Ct. 939-41
New Eng. Hist. and Gen. Register liii, 80
Poore's Merrimack Valley Researches 106
Savage's Genealogical Dictionary iv, 666
Smith Genealogy by Wellington Smith
Tuttle Genealogy 4
Yale Family Chart (1850) 27x40 inches
Yale Genealogy (1850) 201 pages
Yancey — Peyton's Augusta Co. Va. 288
Wheeler's History of North Carolina ii, 78
Yanney — Spooner Genealogy i, 354-6
Yard — American Ancestry iv, 211
Cregar's Haines Ancestry 25-7
Hall's Trenton N. J. Presb. Churches 157
Ormsby Genealogy 42
Yardley — N. E. Hist. Reg. xxxviii, 69
Yardley Genealogy (1881) 257 pages
See also Yeardley
Yarnall — Futhey's Chester Pa. 778
Sharpless Genealogy 196, 255, 263
Joliffe Genealogy (1893) 93
Smith's History of Delaware Co. Pa. 517
Yates — American Ancestry i, 98; vii, 209;
    viii, 90; xi, 139
Farrow's Hist. of Islesborough Me. 303
Hayden's Virginia Genealogies 121

Lapham's History of Paris Me. 775
Meade's Old Churches of Virginia i, 360
Munsell's Albany Collections iv, 184
Pearson's Schenectady Settlers 298-302
Peck's Rochester N. Y. Centennial 695
Power's Sangamon Co. Ill. Settlers 789-91
Richmond Va. Standard ii, 29
Robertson's Pocahontas' Descendants
Saunders' Alabama Settlers 368-73
Terrill's Yates Memorials (1887)
Virginia Magazine of Hist. vii, 91-4, 330
Wm. and Mary College Hist. Reg. iv, 66
Yaw — Bouton Genealogy 407
Yeager — Fisher Genealogy 57-61
Yeager Genealogy (1889) 221 pages
Yeakel — Kriebel's Schwenkfelders 9-48
Yeamans — Sumner Genealogy (1854) 64-6
Sumner's History of E. Boston Mass. 231
Yeardley — Nashville Tenn. Hist. Mag.
    (1896) i, 339-74
Neill's Virginia Carolorum 16
Yeardley Genealogy (1896) 36 pages.
See also Yardley
Yeates — Life of (Rev. Wm.) Smith
Penn. Mag. of Hist. v, 219-22; vii, 200-5
Yeatman — Lamborn Genealogy 284
Yeaton — Milliken's Narraguagus 18
Yelverton — Eager's Orange Co. 487
Meade's Old Families of Virginia
Yeomans — Daniels' Oxford Mass. 752
Waldo's History of Tolland Ct. 92
Yerks — Davis' Hist. Bucks Co. Pa. 219
Leach's Reading Genealogy 189-202
Raymond's Tarrytown Monument 168-70
Yerrington — Bill Genealogy 219-22
Yessler — Heinecke Genealogy 78-80
Yoakum — Power's Sangamon Ill. 791
Yocom — Buck's Montgomery Pa. 26
Power's Sangamon Co. Ill. Settlers 792-5
Yoder — Hertzler Gen. 111, 132, 189, 256-75
Keim and Allied Families 176-8
York — Babson's Gloucester Mass. 182
Corliss' North Yarmouth Me.
Harvey Genealogy 909-14
Lapham's History of Bethel Me. 646-9
Maine Hist. and Gen. Rec. ii, 217-30; iii,
    17-25
Shourd's Fenwick Colony N. J. 376-84
Stackpole's History of Durham Me. 289
Stanton Genealogy 427
York Genealogy (1885) 22 pages
Yost — American Ancestry vii, 103
Yosti — Missouri Pioneer Families 193
Young — American Ancestry iv, 25; v, 59;
    viii, 196; xi, 202; xii, 123
Bangor Historical Magazine v, 19
Bass' History of Braintree Vt. 199
Calnek's Hist. of Annapolis N. S. 639
Chapman's Folsom Genealogy 52
Corliss' North Yarmouth Me.
Daniels' History of Oxford Mass. 752
Deane's Hist. of Scituate Mass. 393
Dow's History of Hampton N. H. 1046
Dudley Genealogy 140
Eaton's Annals of Warren Me. 650
Eaton's Hist. of Thomaston Me. ii, 470-2

Egle's Notes and Queries 3d ser. iii, 500
Freeman's Cape Cod Mass. ii, 971, 378
Futhey's History of Chester Co. Pa. 780
Gale Family 184
Griffin's Jour. Southold N. Y. 90–5, 221–3
Hanson's History of Gardiner Me. 132
Harris Family of New Jersey (1888) 9–29
Heinecke Genealogy 38
Heywood's Hist. Westminster Mass. 953
Hubbard's Hist. of Stanstead Canada 134
Jameson's History of Medway Mass. 529
Kellogg's White Genealogy 88
Lapham's History of Bethel Me. 649
Lapham's History of Norway Me. 625–7
Lapham's History of Paris Me. 776–8
Lincoln's Hist. of Hingham Mass. iii, 335
Loomis Genealogy (1880) 516
Missouri Pioneer Families 225
Mitchell's History of Bridgewater Mass. 254
Munsell's Albany Collections iv, 184
New Eng. Hist. and Gen Reg. liii, 217
Orcott's History of New Milford Ct. 801
Power's Sangamon Co. Ill. Settlers 795
Ridlon's Saco Valley Me. Families 1218
Savage's Genealogical Dict. iv, 669–71
Smith's History of Peterborough N. H. 361–3
Washington N. H. History 689
Whitmore's Copps Hill Epitaphs
Young's Hist. Chautauqua Co. N. Y. 529
Young's Hist. of Warsaw N. Y. 357–61
Youngs of Penn. (1869) 110 pages
Youngs of Nottingham N. H. (1897) chart
Young Family of Virginia (1895) chart
Younghause — American Ancestry ii, 152
Younglove — American Ancestry iv, 123
Hoyt's Salisbury Mass. Families 373–5
Savage's Genealogical Dictionary iv, 671

Youngman — New Eng. Hist. and Gen.
Register xxxiv, 401–4; xxxv, 45–7
Smith's Hist. of Peterborough N. Y. 363–5
Youngman Genealogy (1882) 26 pages
Youngs — American Ancestry ix, 79
Chambers' Early Germans of N. J. 576–80
Cleveland's Hist. of Yates Co. N. Y. 692
Huntington's Stamford Ct. Families 137
Mott Genealogy 302
New York Gen. Biog. Record xiv, 65–70
Raymond's Tarrytown Monument 174
Savage's Genealogical Dictionary iv, 672
Thomson's Hist. of Long Island ii, 382–5
Youngs Genealogy (1890) 142 pages
Youring — Worthen's Sutton N. H. 1020–3
Yuill — Miller's Colchester Co. 281–90
Yulen — Norton's Fitzwilliam N. H.
Zabriskie — American Ancestry vii, 68
N. Y. Gen. Record xxiii, 26–33, 139–47
Roome Genealogy 156
Zaliffe — Poole Genealogy 146–50
Zane — Clement's Newton N. J. Settlers
Penn. Magazine of History xii, 123–5
Power's Sangamon Co. Ill. Settlers 796
Zearing — Amer. Ancestry ix, 204; xi, 81
Rupp Genealogy 105–56, 252, 274
Zeh — American Ancestry i, 98
Zehring — Egle's Lebanon Pa. 258–60
Rupp Genealogy 133–9, 252–9, 274
Zeilin — Martin's Chester Pa. 269
Zeliffe — Poole Genealogy 146–50
Zimmerman — Borneman Gen. 33–46
Dimond Genealogy 64–6
Power's Sangamon Co. Ill. Settlers 797
Zinn — Egle's Penn. Genealogies 261–3
Zook — Hertzler Genealogy 283–316
Zububuhla — Goode Genealogy 169
Zug — Hertzler Genealogy 276–330
Zumwalt — Missouri Families 195

SUPPLEMENT
1900 to 1908

TO THE

Index to Genealogies

PUBLISHED IN 1900

ALBANY, N. Y.
JOEL MUNSELL'S SONS, PUBLISHERS
1908

INDEX.

Abbe
Allen's History of Enfield, Ct., 23
Abbott
Abbott Family of Ohio (1905), 41 pages
Abbott Family of Rowley (1906), 2 vols.
Greene's Hist. Boothbay Me. 486
Ramsdell's Hist. of Milford N.H. 559-62
Sanford's Hist. Hopkinton N.Y. 427-35
Stackpole's History Kittery Me. 270-2
Temple's Hist. Framingham Mass. 453
Treman Genealogy
Well's History of Newbury Vt. 420-5
Abercrombie
Gulf States Hist. Mag. i, 350
Abernathy
Walker Family of Virginia, 86
Abney
Richmond Va. Times, Sept. 18, 1904
Aborn
Quinby's New Eng. Fam. H'st. i 45
Ache
Boehm Genealogy (1902), 133-54
Achenbach
Achenbach Family (1896), 39 pages
Acheson
Crumrine's Hist. Wash. Co., Va., 479-81
Achey
Egle's Dauphin County, Pa., 1883, 233-5
Acker
New Jersey Hist. Soc. Proc., iii (1898), 95
Ackerman
Harvey's Hud. and Berg. Co., N. J., 53-5
Labaw's Preakness, N. J., History, 21-4
Ackley
Hall Memoranda, 1902, 217-23
Treman Genealogy
Acres
Essex Antiquarian, i, 9
Acton
Warfield's Maryland, 145
Adams
Adams Family (1886), 31 pages
Greene's Hist. Boothbay, Me., 487-90
Thornton Family (1905), 12-4
Adams Fam. of Newbury, Mass. (1900), 564 pages
Adams Fam. of Braintree (1901), 19 p.
Adams Fam. of Hartford (1905), 8 p.
Burlington Co., N. J., Democrat, Mar. 20 to July 3, 1903
Carter's Hist. of Pembroke, N. H., ii, 5
Chappell Genealogy (1900), 342-69

Dodge's Sketch of Phinehas Adams (1880), 24 pages
Habersham, Gen.
Hanna's Ohio Valley Genealogies, 1-2
Hill Genealogy, 1904, 43
Jameson Genealogy
Lawrence Genealogy (1904)
Litchfield, Me., History, 1897, 23-5
Lundy Genealogy, 323, 408
Muzzey's Reminiscences, 48-76
New Eng. Hist. Reg., lix, 315-22
Peoria County, Ill., History, 723
Putnam's Hist. Mag. (1899), 247-50
Ramsdell's History, Milford, N. H., 563
Richmond, Va., Times, Dec. 17, 1905
Seymour, Conn., History, 362-3
Shourds' Fenwick's Colony, N. J., 12
Stackpole's History, Kittery, Me., 272-5
Stiles, Wethersfield, Ct., ii, 11-27
Temple's History Framingham, 454-6
Treman Genealogy
Va. Magazine of History, viii, 312-4, 420, ix, 200, 313, 432
Vorce Genealogy, 85-7
Well's History of Newbury, Vt., 425
Woodruff's Litchfield, Conn., Gen. Reg., 5
Addis
Downing Genealogy (1902), 133 pages
Addison
Baltimore Sun, Nov. 27, 1904
Addoms
Manning Genealogy, 268
Adgate
Woolsey Genealogy
Agin
Agin Family of N. J. (1889), 28 pages
Agnew
Agnew, D. H., Life of (1892)
Aiken
Peoria County, Ill., History, 621
Treman Genealogy
Aitkin
Well's History of Newbury, Vt., 425
Albertson
Bean's Hist. Montgomery Co., Pa., 477
Hall's Hist. Atlantic City, N. J., 369-72
Albright
Small Fam. of Penn. (1905), 99-123
Stockard's History of Alamance, N. C.
Stockard's Hist. Lawrence, Ark., 192-204
Albro
Kewaunee, Wis., Owl, Oct., Nov., 1901

Alcock
Stackpole's History, Kittery, Me., 275–6
Alcott
Alcott Genealogy (1899), 48 pages
Alden
Alden Autobiography (1890), 404–19
Alden Fam. of Penn. (1903), 101 pages
Alden and Smith Ancestors (1903),144 p.
Alden Fam. of Cairo, N. Y. (1905), 55 p.
Ames Genealogy (1898)
Ames Genealogical Notes (1900), 26–7
Dedham Historical Reg., xii, 74–94
Edson Ancestry (1901), 27–30
Hallock Pedigree (1906), 50
Jennings Genealogy (1899), ii, 532–4
Tucker Genealogy (1903)
Aldis
Aldis Genealogy (1905), 28 pages
Dedham Hist. Register, xiv, 18–24, 60–5, 87–94, 119–21
Aldrich
Kellogg's Hist.,Bernardston,Mass.,285–8
Thayer Ancestors (1894), 11–4
Treman Genealogy
Aldus
See Aldis.
Alexander
Baltimore Sun, Nov. 5, 1905
Colby Family of N. H., 61–8
Crumrine's Washington, Pa., 596, 627
Litchfield, Me., History, 1897, 25–8
Peoria County, Ill., History, 723
William and Mary Coll. Quar., viii, 262; ix, 54, 252–4; x, 63, 132–4, 137–40, 178–85; xi, 60–7, 115–21, 247
Allard
Litchfield, Me., History, 1897, 28
Allbee
Bellows Falls Times, Jan. 17, 1904
Allen
Allen Family of Watertown (1900), 35 p.
Allen Fam. of Portsmouth, N. H. (1902), 5 pages
Allen Family of Va. (1905)
Allen Family of Nantucket (1905), 123 p.
Barnett and Allen Families of Va. (1874), 24 pages
Berkshire Hist. Soc. Coll. (1895), 53–77
Clarke's King Wm. Co., Va., Fams., 171
Converse Genealogy (1905), 671–802
Cornell Genealogy, 394
Crayon's Rockaway, N. J., Rec., 193–7
Dennison Genealogy (1906), 29
Hall Memoranda, 1902, 53
Hallock Pedigree (1906), 50–7
Harvey's Hud. and Berg. Co., N. J., 107
Jameson Genealogy
Jennings Genealogy, ii, 535–43
Keith's Pa. Prov. Councillors, pt. ii, 140–54
Kellogg's Bernardston, Mass., 289–99
Lefferts Ancestral Chart (1905)
Litchfield, Me., History, 1897, 28–31
Moore Family of Chester, Pa., 116
New Eng. Hist. and Gen. Reg., liv, 396–401; lvi, 26–30

Richmond, Va., Times, Dec. 11, 1904
Stackpole's History Kittery, Me., 276–80
Treman Genealogy
Wells Genealogy (1903), 61
Wells Hist. of Newbury, Vt., 426
William and Mary Coll. Quar., viii, 110–2
Woodruff's Litchfield, Ct., Gen. Reg., 7
Alley
Essex Antiquarian, iv (1900), 68, 79, 85
Greene's History Boothbay, Me., 490
Allibone
Treman Genealogy
Allis
Hodge Genealogy (1900)
Allison
Bronsdon Genealogy, 177–84
Crumrine's Hist. Washington, Pa., 720
Allston
See Allston.
Allyn
Allen's History of Enfield, Ct., 23
Almy
Cornell Genealogy, 33
Tilley's Mag. of N. E. Hist. (1892), 182–4
Alsop
Treman Genealogy
Alston
Alston Family of Carolina (1901), 554 p.
Southern History Assoc., v, (1901), 546
Alvord
Wells Family of Greenfield (1905), 19–26
Ambler
Bean's Hist. Montgomery Co., Pa., 1101
McIlhany's Virginian Families (1903)
Richmond, Va., Times, Jan. 28, 1906
Willis Family of Va., 128
Ambrose
Carter's Hist. Pembroke, N. H., ii, 6, 330
Amee
Stackpole's Hist. Kittery, Me., 809–10
Ames
Ames Genealogical Notes (1900), 31 p.
Benjamin Genealogy, 75–7
Essex Antiquarian, iv (1900), 93–5
Ramsdell's Hist. Milford, N. H., 564–6
Stiles' Wethersfield, Ct., ii, 29
Treman Genealogy
Amidon
Amidon Genealogy (1904), 165 pages
Ammonet
Ammonet Genealogy (1899), 8 pages
Amory
Amory's English Ancestors (1872), 34 p.
Amory Family of Boston (1901), 373 p.
Lawrence Genealogy (1904)
Amos
Wallbridge Genealogy, 25–7
Amsden
Ramsdell's Hist. Milford, N. H., 566
Anderson
Anderson and Perrine Family of N. J. (1902), 1–13
Andersons of Kentucky (1902), chart
Baltimore Sun, April 1, 8, 1906
Boogher's Virg. Gleanings (1903), 308–23

Essex Antiquarian, iv (1900), 156
Genung Family of L. I.
Landrum's History Spartanburg, S. C.
Amer. Hist. Mag., ii (1898), 240–59
Landrum's Hist. Spartanburg, S. C.,
  253–65
New Eng. Hist. and Gen. Reg., xliv,
  121–3
Peoria County, Ill., History, 707
Ramsdell's Hist. Milford, N. H., 567
Robertson Family of Va., 62, 126–8
Symme's Tennent, N. J., Church, 458
William and Mary Quarterly, xii, 116,
  196; xiv, 32
Woods' Hist. of Albemarle Co., Va., 138

Anderton
Essex Antiquarian, iv (1900), 157

Andrew
Andrew, Life of Gov. J. A. (1889), 30 p.
Kittochtinny Magazine, i, 241–52
Prindle Genealogy, 263–6
Seymour, Conn. History, 364–6

Andrews
Andrews Fam. of Boston (1886), 8 p.
Andrews of Woburn, Ancestry (1900),
  13 pages
Andrews Fam. Lineage (1906), 8 pages
Duncan Fam. of Penn. (1905), 25
Edson Ancestry (1901), 25–7
Essex Antiquarian, iv (1900), 118, 157–
  9, 197
Greene Fam. of R. I. (1905), 103–11
Hall Memoranda, 1902, 223–8
Kellogg's Hist. Bernardston, Mass., 299
Le Baron Genealogy, 230
Nash's Fifty Puritan Ancestors, 101
Old Northwest Gen. Quarterly, 179
Phenix, R. I., Gleaner
Stackpole's History Kittery, Me., 281–2
Treman Genealogy

Andrus
Stiles' Wethersfield, Ct., ii, 30–38

Angell
Deer Island, Me., Press for 1900
Thayer Ancestors (1894),15–7

Angier
Temple's History Framingham, 458

Annable
Essex Antiquarian, v (1901), 63

Annetts
Temple's History Framingham, 459

Antes
Bean's Hist. Montgomery Co., Pa., 851–3
Dotterer Genealogy, 96–9
MacMinn's On the Frontier, 19, 409

Anthony
Anthony Genealogy (1904), 379 pages
Tilley's Mag. of N. E. History (1902),
  118–27
Va. Mag. of History, ix (1902), 328–31

Antis
Dotterer Genealogy

Apple
Bean's Hist. Montgomery Co., Pa., 959

Appleby
Clayton's Hist. Union Co., N. J., 782

Appleton
Appleton's Fuller Diary, 1894
Carter's Hist. of Pembroke, N. H., ii, 11
Felt's History of Ipswich, Mass.
Harris Ancestry (1898)
Lawrence Genealogy (1904)

Applewhite
Evans Family of S. C. (1905)

Archdale
New Eng. Hist. and Gen. Reg., xliv,
  157–60

Archer
Landrum's Hist. Spartanburg, S. C., 428

Armistead
Baltimore Sun, Sept. 16, 23, 30; Oct. 7
  1906
Richmond, Va., Times, May 27, 1906
Tyler Letters, iii (1896), 217
William and Mary Quarterly, vii, 17–
  181; viii, 63–70; xi, 144, 253; xiv,
  282–5

Armstrong
Armstrong Chronicles (1902), 407 pages
Armstrong (Francis) Fam. N. J. (1727),
  Manuscript in N. J. Hist. Soc. Lib.
Lundy Genealogy, 409–17
Mass. Magazine, i (1885), 149–58
McGarock Family of Va.
Penn. Mag. of History, xxix, 483–6

Arno
Litchfield, Me., History, 1897, 31

Arnold
Arnold Family of Braintree (1902), 48 p.
Hanna's Ohio Valley Genealogies, 3
Hull Genealogy (1904), 37–9
Southern History Assoc., ix, 42–5
Thayer Ancestors (1894), 18–21
Temple's History Framingham, 460

Arthur
Strong Genealogy, 130–2

Ash
Peoria County, Ill., History, 623

Ashbridge
Smedley Genealogy, 295, 305–7

Ashburner
Treman Genealogy

Ashby
Baltimore Sun, Dec. 3, 10, 1905
Essex Antiquarian, iv (1900), 56–8
Green's Culpeper County, Virg.

Ashford
Litchfield, Me., History, 1897, 32

Ashman
Baltimore Sun, Aug. 11, 18, 1907

Ashton
Baltimore Sun, Dec. 8, 15, 1907; Jan. 19
  1908
Essex Antiquarian, v (1901), 184–7
See also under Assheton.

Ashurst
Treman Genealogy

Aspinwall
Aspinwall Genealogy (1901), 262 pages

Assheton
Keith's Pa. Prov. Councillors, pt. ii,
  281–307

Astor
McClure's Magazine, xxiv (Apr., 1905), 563–78
Athearn
Hallock Pedigree (1906), 59
Atherton
Alston Genealogy, 532, 536
Kellogg's Bernardston, Mass., 301–4
Putnam's Mag. (1899), 98–104, 181–3
Warren Genealogy (1903), 180–5
Atkins
Essex Antiquarian, iv (1900), 75–7
Hall Memoranda, 1902, 79–83
Mayer Genealogy, 145–7
New Eng. Hist. Gen. Reg., lx, 154
Atkinson
Baltimore Sun, May 14, 1905
Burlington Co., N. J., Democrat, Mt. Holly, July —, Oct. 17, 1902
Essex Antiquarian, iv (1900), 81–4; v, (1901), 188–90
Hanna's Ohio Valley Genealogies, 4
Penn. Mag. Hist., xxx (1906), 57–79, 220 –37, 332–47, 479–502; xxxi, 157–75
Richmond, Va., Times, Jan. 14, 1906
Well's History of Newbury, Vt., 427–30
Atlee
Penn. Mag. of History (1878), 74
Atwater
Abbott, Jas. S., Memorial (1905), 41 p.
Atwater Genealogy (1901), 492 pages
Seymour, Conn., History, 366–9
Atwell
Essex Antiquarian, v (1901), 190
Atwood
Essex Antiquarian, iv (1900), 106–8; vi (1902), 44
Hinman's Puritan Settlers, 77–80
Noyes' Hampstead, N. H., ii, 768–72
Peoria County, Ill., History, 623
Stiles' Wethersfield, Ct., ii, 38–42
Well's History of Newbury, Vt., 430
Wright's Manuscript Genealogy of Atwood Fam. in Boston Pub. Lib. (1895)
Auchmoody
Le Fevre's Hist. of New Paltz, N. Y., 451
Augur
Augur Genealogy (1904), 260 pages
Auld
Greene's History Boothbay, Me., 492–4
Aull
See under Awl.
Aumack
Beekman's Monmouth, N. J., Settlers, 94–7
Austin
Carter's History Pembroke, N. H., ii, 11
Dover, N. H., Enquirer for May 19, 1859
Essex Antiquarian, iv (1900), 120–2; vi (1902), 46–8
Averill
Essex Antiquarian, iv (1900), 129–34
Ramsdell's Hist. Milford, N. H., 569–72
Avery
Avery Ancestry (1899), 11 pages

Chesebrough Genealogy, 21–4, 41–4, 96–9
Essex Inst. Hist. Coll., xl, 89–95
Hall Memoranda, 1902, 189–92
New York Prominent Families (1897)
Peoria County, Ill., History, 623
Well's History of Newbury, Vt., 431–3
Wheeler's Stonington, Ct., 199–210
Axtell
American Ancestry, xii, 165
Ayars
Treman Genealogy, 1546–65, 1800–20 1820k–al
Ayer
Carter's Hist. of Pembroke, N. H., ii, 12
Essex Antiquarian, iv (1900), 145–50, 172–5, 182; vi (1902), 88–93
Litchfield, Me., History, 1897, 33
Treman Gen., 973–1031, 1169–1901
Wood Fam. of Sackville, N. B., 27
Ayers
Clayton's History of Union Co., N. J.,285
Crayon's Rockaway, N. J., Rec., 81, 125
Aylett
Clarke's King Wm. Co., Va., Fams., 26–8
Aymar
Aymar Fam. of N. Y. (1903), 65 pages
Ayrault
Stiles' Wethersfield, Ct., ii, 42–44
Ayres
Green Genealogy (1904), 102–9
Treman Genealogy, 973–1031, 1169–1901
Wells Genealogy (1903), 63–5

Babb
Litchfield, Me., History, 1897, 33–5
Babbidge
Deer Island, Me., Press for 1900
Essex Antiquarian, iv (1900), 188–90
Hosmer's Hist. Deer Isle, Me., 94, 113–5
Babbitt
Babbitt Genealogy (1898), 4 pages
Strong Genealogy, 259
Babcock
Babcock Genealogy (1903), 889 pages
Babcock Family (1903), 119 pages
Chesebrough Genealogy, 100–2, 210–8
Clarke and Pendleton Ancestors, 32–9
Clayton's Hist. of Union Co., N. J., 530
Essex Antiquarian, v (1901), 37–9
Hall's Hist. of Atlantic City, N. J., 373
Wheeler's Hist. Stonington, Ct., 211–222
Babson
Essex Antiquarian, v (1901), 1–6
Bache
Barclay Genealogy, 119–22, 135–9
Phila. North American, Dec. 1, 1907
Bachelder
Litchfield, Me., History, 1897, 35
Bacheller
Essex Antiquarian, vii, 134–6
Bachman
Egle's Dauphin Co. Pa., 1883, 235–6

Backus
Chappell Genealogy (1900), 247–50
Nash's Fifty Puritan Ancestors, 110
Bacon
Bacon Fam. of Va. (1883), 10 pages
Bacon Family of Dedham (1902), 13 p.
Bent Progenitors (1903), 25–7
Essex Antiquarian, v (1901), 24–6; vi (1902), 94
Gosnold Ancestry (1904), 19–26
Hall Memoranda, 1902, 56–63
New Eng. Hist. Gen. Register, lvi, 364–74; lvii, 329–11
Richmond, Va., Times, Sept. 17; Oct. 8, 1905
Shourd's Fenwick's Colony, N. J., 252–4
Temple's History, Framingham, 461
Vir. Mag. of History, xiv, 411–9
William and Mary Coll. Quar., x, 267–71
Bacot
Alston Genealogy, 90a
Badger
Essex Antiquarian, v (1901), 49–52
Ramsdell's History of Milford, N. H., 572
Badgley
Clayton's Hist. of Union Co., N. J., 389
Newark, N. J., Ev. News, June 23, 1906
Baer
Penn. German, vii, 333–7
Bagg
Bagg Family (1896), 16 pages
Kellogg's Hist. Bernardston, Mass., 304–7
Baggs
Jackson Genealogy (1890), 22–6
Bagley
Essex Antiquarian, v (1901), 65–70; vi (1902), 128
Bailey
Bailey Fam. of Penn. and Ohio (1879), 24 pages
Bailey Paternal Pedigree (1906), chart
Clapp Ancestors (1902), 14–8
Crumrine's Hist. Washington, Pa., 901
Dean Genealogy (1903), 57–60
Essex Antiquarian, v (1901), 81–6, 110–20, 123–32
Hoyt's Salisbury, Mass., Families, 612–4
Litchfield, Me., History, 1897, 36–8
New Eng. Hist. and Gen. Register, lv, 276–8; xli, 60–4
Peoria County, Ill., History, 624
Temple's History, Framingham, 462
Waterhouse Family of Me., 15
Well's History of Newbury, Vt., 433–58
Bainbridge
Buford Fam. of Va. (1903), 112
Baird
Crumrine's Hist. Washington, Pa., 541
Kittochtinny Magazine, i, 95–104
Lawson Genealogy (1903), 225–7
Symme's Tennent, N. J., Church, 436
Baker
Baker Fam. Bucks Co., Pa. (1901), 32 pp.
Baltimore Sun, Aug. 27, 1905
Bronsdon Genealogy, 266–8
Clayton's Union Co., N. J., 342, 384, 387

Cleveland's Yates County, N. Y., 677–9
Crumrine's Hist. Washington, Pa., 671
Essex Antiquarian, v (1901), 158–69; vi, 155, 170, 181
Evans Family of S. C. (1905)
Genung Family of L. I.
Litchfield, Me., History, 1897, 38–46
Penn. Mag. of History, xxx, 491–3
Peoria County, Ill., History, 624
Smedley Genealogy, 42–6
Southern Hist. Assoc. Pubs, v, 388–400, 477–96
Stacy's Midway Church Gd., 273–6
Treman Genealogy
Twining Genealogy (1905), 7–12
Balch
Balch Family of Salem (1905), chart
Balch Reunion (1905), 52 pages
Balch Divines (1905), 7 pages
Balch Genealogy (1907)
Essex Antiquarian, vi (1902), 1–14
Stiles' Wethersfield, Ct., ii, 45
Balding
Russell Genealogy, 185
Baldwin
Baldwins of England (1884), 28 pages
Baldwin Ancestry (1904), 102 pages
Baldwin MSS. in N. J. Hist. Soc. Lib.
Bean's Hist. Montgomery Co., Pa., 965
Brush-Bowers Genealogy (1904), 106–9
Maulsby Genealogy, 47, 85–9
Peoria County, Ill., History, 753
Prindle Genealogy, 6–11
Sanford's Hist. Hopkinton, N. Y., 440–4
Seymour, Conn., History, 369–76
Smedley Genealogy, 160
Warfield's Maryland, 158–60
Well's History of Newbury, Vt., 458
Wheeler's Hist. of Stonington, Ct., 223–8
Woodruff's Litchfield, Ct., Gen. Reg., 10–3
Ball
Ball Family of Newark (1888), chart
Ball Family of Springfield (1902), 80 p.
Baltimore Sun, Jan. 8, 1905; July 15, 22, 1906
Essex Antiquarian, vi, 185
Green's Culpeper County, Virg.
Hull Genealogy (1904), 21
Keuka College Union Record, i, ii
New Eng. Hist. Gen. Reg., lxi, 118
Ramsdell's History Milford, N. H., 574
Stackpole's History Kittery, Me., 282–3
Temple's History, Framingham, 462
Treman Genealogy
Va. Magazine Hist., vii, 440; viii, 80–3
William and Mary Quarterly, xi, 137
Ballance
Green Family of Virginia
Peoria County, Ill., History, 625
Ballanger
Landrum's Hist. Spartansburg, S. C.
Ballard
Ballard Family History (1903), 71 pages
Baltimore Sun, Jan. 5, 1908
Essex Antiquarian, vi (1902), 35–40, 186
Peoria County, Ill., History, 625

Temple's History, Framingham, 463-5
Thayer Ancestors (1894), 22
Treman Genealogy
Wood's Hist. Albemarle Co., Va., 140
Ballenger
Landrum's Spartansburg, S. C., 378-86
Ballou
Ballou Statue Dedication (1901), 77 p.
Bancroft
Bancroft Family (1869), 1 page
Bancroft Family (1872), 2 pages
Bancroft Family (1876), chart
Bancroft Fam. of Windsor (1900), chart
Bancroft Fam. Lynnfield, Mass., Manuscript L. I. Hist. Soc., Brooklyn, 69 pp.
Brush-Bowers Genealogy (1904), 113
Essex Antiquarian, vi (1902), 57-9, 187
Gamble's Family Data (1906), 156
New Eng. Hist. and Gen. Reg., lvi, 197
Old Northwest Gen. Quar., x, 67-75
Bangs
Bangs Family (1854), chart
Gray Genealogy (1889), 148-55
Banister
Temple's History, Framingham, 465
Virginia Mag. of History, xi, 164
Banks
Alston Genealogy, 252-71
Baltimore Sun, June 4, 11, 1905
Treman Genealogy
Bant
Bronsdon Genealogy, 254-66
Banta
Treman Genealogy
Barber
Anderson-Perrine Family, 81-6
Buell Genealogy, 40
Essex Antiquarian, vi, 189
Green Family of Virginia
Temple's History, Framingham, 466
Barbour
Anderson and Perrine Family, 81-6
Baltimore Sun, Jan. 14, 21, 1906
Green's Culpeper County, Virg.
Barclay
Barclay Genealogy (1904), 474 pages
Roosavelt Genealogy, 24, 43
Symme's Tennent, N. J., Church, 459
Bard
Habersham Genealogy, 29
Kittochtinny Magazine, i, 95-104, 308-13, 327-56
Swope Genealogy, 180
Bardwell
Pocumtuck Valley, Mass., Hist., 493-5
Whaley Genealogy, 180-3
Barkalow
Beckman's Monmouth, N. J., Settlers, 100-13
Barkelew
Clayton's Hist. of Union Co., N. J., 758
Barker
Barker Colonial Fam. (1900), 4 pages
Barker Family Address (1900), 17 pages
Barker Fam. of Plymouth (1901), 102 p.
Barker Pedigree, by E. T. Barker

Essex Antiquarian, vi (1902), 60-72, 101-3, 106-7, 116-8, 190; vii, 36-8
Hinchman's Nantucket Sett., ii, 155, 246
Ramsdell's Hist. Milford, N. H., 575-7
Well's Hist. of Newbury, Vt., 461
Barksdale
Wood's Hist. Albemarle Co., Va., 141-3
Barnard
Crumrine's Hist. Washington, Pa., 978
Essex Antiquarian, vi (1902), 120-31; vii, 38-40
Hinchman's Nantucket Settlers, ii, 245
Hoyt's Salisbury, Mass., Families, 614
Lowell Genealogy, 36-9
Newhall Ancestry, 68
Wood Genealogy (1901), 46
Barnes
Baltimore Sun, Dec. 31, 1905
Barnes Genealogy (1903), 221 pages
Evans' Scioto Co., Ohio, History, 1220
Essex Antiquarian, vii, 40
Green Family of R. I. (1905), 226-32
Le Baron Genealogy, 69, 164
New York Gen. Biog. Record, xxxvii, 140-5, 213-8, 261-5; xxxviii, 34-8
Stiles' Wethersfield, Ct., ii, 46-9
Barnett
Barnett and Allen Fam. (1874), 24 pages
Well's Hist. of Newbury, Vt., 460
Barney
Essex Antiquarian, vii, 41-3
Barnhill
Roosavelt Genealogy, 50
Barnitz
Swope Genealogy, 96-102
Barns
West Virginia Hist. Mag., iii, No. iii
Woodruff's Litchfield,Ct.,Gen. Reg.,14-7
Barnwell
South Car. Hist. and Gen. Mag., ii, 46-88
Barr
Baltimore Sun, Dec. 11, 1904
Barr Genealogy (1901), 216 pages
Essex Antiquarian, vi, 156
McKinney Family of Pa., 114-8
Old Northwest Gen. Quar. (1906), 83-5
Woolsey Genealogy
Barrell
Hayford Genealogy, 177-83
Barrett
Barrett of Virginia (1901), 3 charts
Essex Antiquarian, vii, 43
Hanna's Ohio Valley Genealogies, 5
Hoyt's Salisbury, Mass., Families, 565
William and Mary Coll. Quar., vii, 201
Barricklow
Hanna's Ohio Valley Genealogies, 5
Barrington
Habersham Genealogy, 35
Barron
Britton Ancestry (1901)
Tucker Genealogy (1901), 63
Barry
Landrum's Spartansburg, S. C., 200-4
Barstow
Litchfield, Me., History, 1897, 46

Barter
Greene's Hist. Boothbay, Me., 495–7
Hosmer's Hist. of Deer Isle, Me., 195–7
Stackpole's History Kittery, Me., 283–4
Bartlett
Carter's Hist. of Pembroke, N. H, ii, 20–2
Essex Antiquarian, vii, 1–17, 59–61, 63–4, 91–4
Hall's Hist. of Atlantic City, N. J., 375
Hoyt's Salisbury, Mass., Families, 615–8
Litchfield, Me., History, 1897, 47–9
Nash's Fifty Puritan Ancestors, 148
New Eng. Hist. and Gen. Reg., lvi, 155–61
Old Eliot, Me., Mag. (1901), iv, 5–9
Putnam's Hist. Mag. (1896), 105
Ramsdell's Hist. Milford, N. H., 577–81
Richmond, Va., Times, April 2, 1905
Stackpole's Hist. Kittery, Me., 284–91
Treman Genealogy
Well's History of Newbury, Vt., 462
Bartoll
Essex Antiquarian, vii, 64
Barton
Baltimore Sun, Oct. 8, 1905
Barton Genealogy (1898), 8 pages
Barton Genealogy (1900), 148 pages
Charleston, S. C., News, Oct. 15, 1905
Essex Antiquarian, vii, 75
Kellogg'sHist.Bernardston,Mass.,309–11
Stokes Genealogy, 56, 304
Bartow
Clayton's Hist. of Union Co., N. J., 613
Small Fam. of Penn. (1905), 173–81
Stevenson Family of N. Y., 95–8
Bass
Bass Family of Roxbury (1904), chart
Bass Manuscript in N. J. Hist. Soc. Lib.
Hill Genealogy, 1904, 36
Newhall Ancestry, 180
Vinton Genealogy, 290, 374
Bassett
Baltimore Sun, July 14,21,28,Aug.4,1907
Bassett Family Reunion (1902), 33 pages
Essex Antiquarian, vii, 77–9
Hall Memoranda, 1902, 73–5
Litchfield, Me., History, 1897, 50–2
Seymour, Conn., History, 376–90
Va. Magazine of History, vii, 437
Willis Family of Va., 125–7
Batchelder
Carter's Hist. of Pembroke, N. H., ii, 23
Hill Genealogy, 1904, 85
Essex Antiquarian, vii, 105–15, 141–3
Batcheller
Britton Ancestry (1901)
Dalton and Batcheller Ped. (1873), 6 pp.
Jenkins Family of Pa., 1904, 141–4
Bateman
McGarock Family of Va.
Strong Genealogy, 643–5
Bates
Bates Family of Hingham (1904), 28 p.
Bean's Hist. Montgomery Co., Pa., 594
Carter's Hist. of Pembroke, N. H., ii, 23
Essex Antiquarian, vii, 182, 187
Lamb Fam. of N. J. (1904), 11–7

Topliff Genealogy (1906)
Treman Genealogy
Walker Family of Virginia, 115–9
Bath
Bent Progenitors (1903), 52–4
Bathurst
Meriwether Genealogy (1899), 39–44
Batt
Batt Fam. Ancestry (1897), 26 pages
Essex Antiquarian, vii, 188
Battell
Crissey's Hist. of Norfolk, Ct., 445–66
LeBaron Genealogy, 151–3
Batter
Essex Antiquarian, viii, 42
Battin
Essex Antiquarian, vii, 189; viii, 37
Strong Genealogy, 989
Bauer
Stauffer and Bauer Genealogy, 65–154
Baxter
New York Gen. and Biog. Record, xxxi, 204–8; xxxviii, 84–6
Stiles' Wethersfield, Ct., ii, 50
Bayard
Cornell Genealogy, 379–81
New Jersey Soc. Proc., ii (1900), 101–5
Bayles
Bayles Genealogy (1900), 41 pages
Clayton's Hist. of Union Co., N. J., 793
Baylor
Richmond, Va., Times, June 24, 1906
Bayly
Green Family of Virginia
Bayne
William and Mary Coll. Quar., xiii, 284–7
Baytop
Stubbs Genealogy, 95
Beach
Crayon's Rockaway, N. J., Rec., 160–4
Seymour, Conn., History, 390–3
Woodruff's Litchfield, Conn., Gen. Reg., 20–5
Beacham
Essex Antiquarian, viii, 44
Beadle
Essex Antiquarian, vii, 172–5, 183
Stiles' Wethersfield, Ct., ii, 52
Beaker
Sabine Genealogy
Beakes
Penn. Magazine of Hist., xxx, 500–2
Beal
Essex Antiquarian, vii, 184; viii, 45
Treman Genealogy
Beale
Richmond, Va., Times, Oct. 9, 1904; Nov. 26, 1905
Warfield's Maryland, 101–4
Beall
Baltimore Sun, Jan. 31, 1904
Hanna's Ohio Valley Genealogies, 6
Beals
Ramsdell's Hist. Milford, N. H., 582
Beaman
Crayon's Rockaway, N. J., Records, 198

Bean
Bean Family (1903), chart
Bean Gen. (1903), 112 pages
Essex Antiquarian, vii, 185; viii, 46
Bear
Bear Family of Pa. (1906)
Essex Antiquarian, viii, 14
Beard
Kittochtinny Magazine, i, 95-104
Warfield's Maryland, 106
Beardsley
Sayre Genealogy, 235-7
Beath
Greene's History Boothbay, Me., 497-9
Beatty
Crall Ancestry
Old Northwest Gen. Quar., viii, 141-3
Beauchamp
Pound and Kester Gen., 561, 568
Beauford
See Buford.
Beauman
Beauman Memoirs (1900), 137 pages
Beaver
Bean's Hist. Montgomery Co., Pa., 666
Bechtel
Stauffer and Bauer Genealogy, 55-61
Beck
Essex Antiquarian, viii, 14
New Eng. Hist. Gen. Reg., lx, 299
N. Y. Gen. Biog. Rec., xxxviii, 98-103
Becker
Becker Ped. MSS. in N. Y. Gen. Biog.
  Soc. Lib.
Becket
Essex Antiquarian, viii, 15-7, 92
Beckford
Essex Antiquarian, viii, 60-4, 93
Beckley
Beckley Genealogy (1905), 23 pages
Stiles' Wethersfield, Ct., ii, 53-75
Beckwith
Beckwith Notes, No. 3 (1901), 64 pages
Beckwith Notes, No. 4 (1903), 58 pages
Bedell
American Ancestry, xii, 191
Bedinger
Bittinger and Bedinger Fam.(1904),63 p.
Beebe
Beebe Genealogy (1905), 126 pages
Treman Genealogy
Woodruff's Litchfield, Ct., Gen. Reg., 25
Beecher
Amity, Conn., Records, pt. 1
Humphreyville Genealogy, 28-30
Prindle Genealogy, 3-19
Seymour, Conn., History, 393-7
Beekman
New Amsterdam Year Book, i, 3-6
N. Y. Gen. and Biog. Rec., xxxiii, 42-5
Behymer
Manning Genealogy, 383
Beidler
Beidler Fam. of Pa. (1903), 549 pages
Beitler
Beidler Family of Pa.

Belcher
Belcher Fam. of New Eng. (1906), 32 p.
Clayton's Hist. of Union Co., N. J., 183
Dedham, Mass., Hist. Reg., xiii, 1-5
Essex Antiquarian, viii (1904), 140
New Eng. Hist. and Gen. Reg., lviii,
  335; lx, 125-36, 243-56, 358-64
Peoria County, Ill., History, 714
Temple's History, Framingham, 468
Belden
Converse Genealogy (1905), 703-16
N. Y. Gen. Biog. Record, xxxvii, 87
Stiles' Wethersfield, Ct., ii, 75-92
Belding Fam., Wethersfield (1896), 22 p.
Belfield
Meriwether Genealogy (1899), 60
Richmond, Va., Times, Oct. 2, 1904
Belknap
Belknap Genealogy (1889), 78 pages
Essex Antiquarian, viii (1904), 141
Temple's History, Framingham, 469
Bell
Bell Family of Md. (1894), 45 pages
Bell Fam. of Md. Supp. (1897), 19 pages
Buford Family of Va. (1903)
Essex Antiquarian, viii (1904), 142
Jameson Genealogy
Moore Family of Chester, Pa., 124
Peoria County, Ill., History, 724
Warden Genealogy, 33-5
Bellamy
New Eng. Hist. Gen. Reg., lxi, 338-40
Stackpole's Hist. Kittery, Me., 291-2
Bellanger
Shourds' Fenwick's Col., N. J., 218-20
Bellingham
New Eng. Hist. Gen. Reg., xxxvi, 381-6
Bellows
Bellows Fam., Springfield, Vt. (1901),
  14 pages
Bellows Parentage (1902), 8 pages
Putnam's Gen. Mag., ii (1901), 73-84
Belt
Baltimore Sun, Oct. 16, 30; Nov. 13, 1904
Balt. Sun, Oct. 16, 30; Nov. 13, 1904
Bement
Allen's History of Enfield, Ct., 23
Bemis
Bemis Genealogy (1900), 287 pages
Newhall Ancestry, 64-7
Tower's Hist. Sketch of Spencer, Mass.
Benedict
Lancaster Genealogy, 180-9
Seymour, Conn., History, 397-9
Benezet
Keith's Pa. Prov. Coun., pt. ii, 209-12
Small Fam. of Pa. (1905), 190-212
Benjamin
Benjamin Genealogy (1900), 112 pages
Rix Genealogy, 190-4
Bennett
Baltimore Sun, Oct. 9, 1904
Dennison Genealogy (1906), 19-59
Emory's Col. Fam. of Md., 226-8
Essex Antiquarian, viii, 88-92
Greene's Hist. Boothbay, Me., 499-510

New Eng. Hist. Gen. Reg., lvi, 241–7
Temple's History, Framingham, 471
Treman Genealogy
Wheeler's Hist. Stonington, Ct., 229–32
Bensen
Labaw's Preakness, N. J., Hist., 98, 317
Benson
Lancaster Genealogy, 41–4
Landrum's Spartanburg, S. C., 386–9
Temple's History, Framingham, 472
Van Deusen Genealogy (1901), 9–11
Bent
Bent Progenitors (1903), 78 pages
Temple's History, Framingham, 472
Bentley
Bentley Gleanings (1905), 128 pages
Crumrine's Hist. Washington, Pa., 969
Wheeler's Hist. Stonington, Ct., 233–5
Benton
Benton Genealogy (1901), 354 pages
Benton Fam. of Leedsville, N. Y. (1904), chart
Benton Fam. of Leedsville (1906), 92 p.
Benton Family (1906), 95 pages
New Eng. Gen. Reg., lx, 300–5, 340–6
Stiles' Wethersfield, Ct., ii, 94–97
Woodruff's Litchfield, Ct., Gen. Reg., 27
Berdan
Harvey's Hud. and Berg. Co., N. J., 195
Labaw's Preakness, N. J., Hist., 11–4, 80
Bergen
Crall Ancestry
Treman Genealogy
Bergey
American Ancestry, xii, 150
Penn. German, vii, 331
Berkeley
Baltimore Sun, May 6, 13, 20, 1906
Page Genealogy, 2d ed., 1893, 158, 175
Richmond, Va., Times, Oct. 29; Nov. 12; Dec. 3, 1905
William and Mary Coll. Quar., vi, 135–52; vii, 83–93
Berkhimer
Bean's Hist. Montgomery Co., Pa., 866
Bernard
Tiernan Genealogy (1901), 415–36
Walker Family of Virginia, 607–10
William and Mary Quar., vi, 62–4, 181–7
Berry
Clayton's Hist. of Union Co., N. J., 582
Essex Antiquarian, viii, 102–5; ix, 46, 86
Evans Family of S. C. (1905)
Glenn's Colonial Mansions, ii, 389–94
Hall's Hist. of Greenland, N. H., 156–61
Harvey's Hud. and Berg. Co., N. J., 100
Labaw's Preakness, N. J., History, 77
Litchfield, Me., History, 1897, 52–5
Parson's Hist. of Rye, N. H. 296–306
Rich's Gen. Record (1896), 3
Stackpole's Hist. Kittery, Me., 293–4
Bertholf
Harvey's Hud. and Berg. Co., N. J., 107
Bessom
Essex Antiquarian, ix, 89

Bestor
Peoria County, Ill., History, 627
Bethea
Evans Family of S. C. (1905)
Bethel
Hanna's Ohio Valley Genealogies, 6–7
Bethune
New Eng. Hist. Gen. Reg., lx, 238
Betts
Genung Family of L. I.
Seymour, Conn., History, 399–400
Stevenson Family of Long Island, 48–50
Beverley
Baltimore Sun, Aug. 21, 1904
Bevier
New Paltz Independent, Apr. 7, 14; June 30; July 7, 14, 21, 1899
LeFevre's Hist. New Paltz, N. Y., 223–52, 521–3
Bickford
See Beckford.
Bickley
William and Mary Quarterly, x, 126–31
Bidwell
Merrick Genealogy, 427–9
Stiles' Wethersfield, Ct., ii, 99–101
Bigelow
Bellows Falls Times (1905)
Boylston, Mass., Centennial (1887)
Britton Ancestry (1901)
Converse Genealogy (1905), 27
Lawrence Genealogy (1904)
Temple's History, Framingham, 474
Well's Genealogy (1903), 67–72
White Genealogy (1900), 111–82
Bigod
Palmer's Hist. Lanesborough, Mass., 49
Bigsbee
See Bixby.
Biles
Essex Antiquarian, viii (1904), 120–2
Penn. Mag. of History, xxvi (1902), 58–61, 206, 348–59
Biley
Batt and Biley Ancestry (1897), 26 p.
Bill
Woolsey Genealogy
Billing
Stackpole's Hist. Kittery, Me., 294–7
Chesebrough Genealogy, 87
Hosmer's Hist. of Deer Isle, Me., 44
Litchfield, Me., History (1897), 55
Temple's History, Framingham, 476
Wheeler's Hist. Stonington, Ct., 236–43
Binder
Bean's Montgomery Co., Pa., 465, 954–6
Bingham
Benton (David) Ancestors (1906)
Hanna's Ohio Valley Genealogies, 7–9
Bininger
N. Y. Gen. and Biog. Rec., xxxiii, 135–7
Bird
Baltimore Sun, Nov. 17, 1907
Bird Family of Virg. (1903), 13 pages
Temple's History, Framingham, 476
Topliff Genealogy (1906)

Woodruff's Litchfield, Ct., Gen. Reg.,
29
Birge
Woodruff's Litchfield, Ct.,Gen.Reg.,30–2
Birney
Hanna's Ohio Valley Genealogies, 9–10
Bisbee
Handy's Sumner, Me., 111–36, 196–202
Bishop
Benton-Bishop Ancestry (1906), 48–50
Converse Genealogy (1905), 827–36
Essex Antiquarian,viii (1906) ,122–6; ix,
141
Nash's Fifty Puritan Ancestors, 170
N. Y. Gen. Rec., xxviii, 89–92, 129–31
Woodruff's Litchfield, Ct., Gen. Reg., 32
Wood's Hist. Albemarle Co., Va., 143
Bissell
Edson Ancestry (1901), 5–7
Nash's Fifty Puritan Ancestors, 42–4
Woodruff's Litchfield,Ct.,Gen. Reg.,33–7
Bisson
Bean's Hist. Montgomery Co., Pa., 865
Essex Antiquarian, viii (1904), 132
Bitting
Dotterer Genealogy, 85
Bittinger
Bittinger Genealogy (1904), 63 pages
Bixby
Converse Genealogy (1905), 805–23
Essex Antiquarian, viii, 145–9
Temple's History, Framingham, 477
Blachley
Hinman's Conn. Settlers, 241
Woodruff Genealogy (1903), 121–3
Blackford
Swift's Barnstable Families, i, 99–103
See also Blatchford, Blackford.
Black
Deer Island, Me., Press for 1900
Essex Antiquarian, viii, 174
Stackpole's Hist., Kittery, Me., 297
Wood's History Albemarle Co., Va.
Blackburn
Baltimore Sun, Jan. 5, 1908
Buford Family of Va. (1903), 132
William and Mary Coll.Quar. (1896), 266
Blackiston
Treman Genealogy
Blackleach
Hinman's Puritan Settlers, 241–3
Blackledge
Harvey's Hud. and Berg. Co., N. J., 126
Blackly
Crumrine's Washington, Pa., 848–50
Blackman
Watkins Blackman Heirs (1900), 16 p.
Blague
Hamlin Genealogy (1900), 79
Blaine
McKinney Family of Pa., 124–34
Robinson Family of Pa. (1902), 54–8
Blair
Blair Genealogy (1900), 198 pages
Blair Fam. MSS. in Virg. Hist. Soc. Lib.
Greene's Hist. Boothbay, Me., 501

Harvey's Hud. and Berg. Co., N. J., 84–6
Lawson Genealogy (1903)
William and Mary Quar., vii, 133
Blaisdell
Hoyt's Salisbury, Mass., Fams., 618–42
Rowell Genealogy
Blake
Baltimore Sun, July, 1904
Bates Gen. Notes, No. 2 (1903), 18 pages
Bean's Hist. Montgomery Co., Pa., 699
Bellows Falls Times (1905)
Charleston, S. C., News, Sept. 17, 1905
Greene's History Boothbay, Me., 502
Litchfield, Me., History, 1897, 56
Tucker Genealogy (1901), 134–6
Tucker Genealogy (1903)
Blakeman
Nash's Fifty Puritan Ancestors, 88–90
Blakesley
Blakesley Genealogy (1902), 15 pages
New Eng. Hist. Gen. Reg., lvi, 277–89
Blakison
Baltimore Sun, Dec. 4, 1904
Blanch
Harvey's Hud. and Berg. Co., N. J., 127
Blanchard
Crayon's Rockaway, N. J., Records, 272
Essex Antiquarian, ix, 26–32
Medford Hist. Register, vi, 20, 47–9
Litchfield, Me., History, 1897, 57
New. Eng. Hist. Gen. Reg., lx, 373–6
Ramsdell's Hist. Milford, N. H., 586–
94
Sanford's Hist. Hopkinton, N. Y., 437–9
Treman Genealogy
Bland
Baltimore Sun, Oct. 30, 1904
Page Genealogy, 2d ed (1893), 252
Richmond, Va., Times, Feb. 12, 1905
Blanding
Dary Genealogy, 19
Blaney
Essex Antiquarian, ix, 32–6
Blasdell
Essex Antiquarian, ix, 49–59
Blashfield
Essex Antiquarian, x, 131
Blatchley
New Eng. Hist. Gen. Reg., lviii, 357–9
Blawvelt
Harvey's Hud. and Berg. Co., N. J., 68
Bleeker
N. Y. Gen. Biog. Rec., xxxiv, 231–4
Blennerhassett
Richmond, Va., Times, June 25, 1905
Blinman
New Eng. Hist. Gen. Reg. (1900), 39–43
Blinn
Stiles' Wethersfield, Ct., ii, 104–8
Blish
Blish Genealogy (1905), 366 pages
Bliss
Bliss Genealogy (1904), 39 pages
Seymour, Conn., History, 400–1
Treman Genealogy
Well's History of Newbury, Vt., 466

Blodgett
Blodgett Genealogy (1906), 144 pages
Manchester Hist. Soc. Coll., i, 121, 172
Blood
New Eng. Hist. Gen. Reg., liii, 322–4
Treman Genealogy
Bloomfield
Brush-Bowers Genealogy (1904), 68–91
Bloss
White Genealogy (1900), 492–6
Blosse
Richmond, Va., Times, June 11, 1905
Blosser
Kagy Genealogy, 364–81
Blossom
Blossom Pedigree (1870), Broadside
Blount
Blount and Blunt Family (1904), chart
Virginia Mag. of History, v (1897), 202–4
Blue
Evans Family of S. C. (1905)
Old Northwest Gen. Quar., vii, 48
Blunt
Blount and Blunt Family (1904), chart
Essex Antiquarian, ix, 110
Blush
Blish and Blush Gen. (1905), 366 pages
Blyth
Essex Antiquarian, ix, 112
Board
Treman Genealogy, 890–972, 1168
Boardman
Boardman Fam. in Topsfield(1902), 27 p.
Essex Antiquarian, ix, 145–52
Stiles' Wethersfield, Ct., ii, 108–23
Topsfield, Mass., Hist. Coll., viii, 102–28
Boarman
Baltimore Sun, Sept. 23, 1906
Bodine
Sinnott Genealogy
Treman Genealogy
Bodle
Treman Genealogy
Bodwell
Essex Antiquarian, ix, 171–6
Bodswell
Reed Genealogy (1901), 452
Boehm
Boehm Reminiscences by Wakely (1875)
Boehm Genealogy (1902), 154 pages
Kagy Genealogy, 35–7
Penn. German, viii, 248
Boerum
Burdge's Life Simon Boerum (1876), 14
See Booream, Boorem
Bogart
New Amsterdam Year Book, ii, 10–2
Treman Genealogy
Bogert
Harvey's Hud. and Berg. Co., N. J., 57–61, 132
Boggs
Hanna's Ohio Valley Genealogies, 10
Boice
Clayton's Hist. Union Co.,N. J., 116, 319

Hall's Hist. of Atlantic City, N. J., 376–8
N. Y. Gen. and Biog. Rec., xxxiii, 56
Boies
Boies (1901), chart, blue print
Bolden
Litchfield, Me., History, 1897, 58
Bolles
Bolles Family of Mass. (1890), 3 pages
Quimby's New Eng. Fam. Hist., i, 40
Bolling
Baltimore Sun, Nov. 12, 19, 1905
Keith's Pa. Prov. Councillors, pt. ii, 24–5
Meriwether Genealogy (1899), 57
Richmond, Va., Times, Oct. 4, 1903
Tiernan Genealogy (1901), 398–414
Va. Magazine of History, vii, 352–4
Bolton
Chesebrough Genealogy, 30
Habersham Gen.
Well's History of Newbury, Vt., 467
Boltwood
New Eng. Hist. Gen. Reg., lix, 342
Strong Genealogy, 1317, 1329, 1333
Bomar
Landrum's Spartanburg, S. C., 354–63
Bond
Baltimore Sun, April 28, May 5, 1907
Essex Antiquarian, ix, 177
Newburgh, N. Y., Hist. Papers, x, 20
Smedley Genealogy, 185
Bonney
Hayford Genealogy, 240–4
Bonsall
Dunwoody Genealogy (1899), 145
Bontecoe
New Paltz, N. Y., Independent (1901)
Booker
Va. Magazine of History, vii, 429–32
William and Mary Coll. Quar., vii, 49
Bookwalter
Stauffer and Bauer Gen., 70–84, 146–8
Boone
Boone Family (1902), 4 pages
Missouri Historical Review, i, 72–84
Penn. German, iii (Jan., 1902), 41–3; vii, 327
Walker Family of Virginia, 523
Booraem
Booraem Fam. (1905), chart
See Boerum, Van Boerum
Booream
Clayton's Hist. of Union Co., N. J., 755
Boorse
Bean's Montgomery Co., Pa., 1090–2
Booth
Allen's History of Enfield, Ct.
Forman Genealogy, 30, 145
N. Y. Gen. Biog. Rec., xxxii, 235–41
Peoria County, Ill., History, 725
Seymour, Conn., History, 408–9
Stubbs Family of Virginia, 96–8
Borden
Borden Pedigree (1901), 15 pages
Jennings Genealogy, ii, 544–59
Tilley's Mag. N. E. Hist. (1892), 247–52

Bordley
Emory's Col. Fam. of Md., 191–5, 228–37
Boreman
Baltimore Sun, Sept. 9, 16, 1906
Borland
Gray Genealogy (1889), 54–69
Borton
Haines Family of N. J., 394–6
Stokes Family of N. J.
Bortz
Pennsylvania German, vii, 279
Bosler
Bean's Hist. Montgomery Co., Pa., 634–6
Boss
Flemington, N. J., Advertiser, Dec. 27, 1906
Bostwick
Bostwick Genealogy (1901), 1172 pages
Boswell
Stubbs Family of Virginia, 105–9
Bosworth
Litchfield, Me., History, 1897, 59
Botsford
Botsford Act of Incorporation (1905), 8 pp.
LeBaron Genealogy, 250, 395
Prindle Genealogy, 23–7
Seymour, Conn., History, 401–7
Bouchelle
Mallery's Bohemia, 43–5
Boude
American Historical Reg., i, 367–70
Bringhurst Genealogy, 129–33
Boulton
Lewis Family of Va. (1906)
Bound
Clayton's Hist. of Union Co., N. J., 815
Bourland
Peoria County, Ill., History, 628
Bourn
DeWolf Genealogy, 285–7
New Eng. Hist. and Gen. Reg., lv, 276
Bourne
Tucker Genealogy (1901), 96–8
Tucker Genealogy, 1903
Boutelle
Brush-Bowers Genealogy (1904), 102–5
Muzzey's Reminiscences, 300–7
Ramsdell's Hist. Milford, N. H., 595
Boutwell
Temple's History, Framingham, 478
Bowden
Essex Antiquarian, x, 38–46; xi, 43–7
Landrum's Spartanburg, S. C., 390–3
Bowditch
Essex Antiquarian, x, 55
Bowdoin
Bowdoin Genealogy, 3d ed. (1900), 18 p.
Bowen
Baltimore Sun, Sept. 25, 1904
Essex Antiquarian, x, 57
Reynolds Fam. of R. I. (1903), 25–7
Bower
Stauffer and Bauer Genealogy, 38, 87–97
Bowerman
Kewaunee, Wis., Owl, Sept., 1904, 324

Bowers
Brush-Bowers Genealogy (1904), 92–6
Dunwoody Genealogy (1899), 146–50
Habersham Gen.
Stauffer and Bauer Gen., 149–55
Treman Genealogy
Bowie
Baltimore Sun, Jan. 28; Feb. 4, 1906; Jan. 6, 13, 1907
Bowker
See Buker
Bowler
Bowler Genealogy (1905), 293 pages
Bowles
Stern's Our Kindred, 94, 100–2
Bowman
American Ancestry, xii, 40
Litchfield, Me., History (1897), 60
Bowne
Bowne Family of N. J. (1903), 47 pages
Glenn's Colonial Mansions, ii, 93–121
Jerseyman, vii, 1–8, 12–6, 20–4; viii, 13–6, 24–33
Symmes' Tennent, N. J., Church, 409
Bowyer
Richmond, Va., Times, Aug. 6, 13, 1905
Box
Bronsden and Box Genealogy, 203–53
Boyce
Essex Antiquarian, x, 58
Well's Hist. of Newbury, Vt., 469–71
Boyd
Baltimore Sun, Oct. 27, Nov. 3, 1907
Boyd Family History (1905), 112 pages
Greene's History Boothbay, Me., 504–6
Richmond, Va., Times, Dec. 10, 1905
Treman Genealogy
Boyden
Boyden Genealogy (1901), 267 pages
Boykin
Boykin Family of Va. (1876)
Boynton
Essex Antiquarian, x, 97–108
Bracken
Bracken Genealogy (1901), 79 pages
Brackett
Hall's Hist. of Greenland, N. H., 151–2
Stackpole's Hist. Kittery, Me., 298–301
Temple's History Framingham, 480
Bradbury
Essex Antiquarian, x, 145–50
Rich's Gen. Record (1896), 12
Braddy
Evans Family of S. C. (1905)
Bradfield
Bean's Hist. Montgomery Co., Pa., 704–6
Bradford
Ames Genealogy (1898), 15 pages
Ames Genealogical Notes (1900), 13–7
Bradford Family Line (1897), 8 pages
DeWolf Genealogy, 276–8
Ellis Genealogy (1900), 7–12
Essex Antiquarian, x, 180
LeBaron Genealogy, 53–6, 128–32, 273
Ramsdell's Hist. Milford, N. H., 596–8
Rich's Gen. Record (1896), 6

Robertson Family of Va.
Tucker Genealogy (1901),,137–51
Tucker Genealogy (1903)
Whittemore's New England Ancestors
  (1900), 100 pages
Bradish
Bradish Family (1888), chart
Temple's History Framingham, 480
Bradley
Essex Antiquarian, xi, 1–6
Greene Family (1905), 233–5
Nash's Fifty Puritan Ancestors, 69
New Eng. Hist. Gen. Reg., lvii, 134–41
Seymour, Conn., History, 409–11
Treman Genealogy
Woodruff's Litchfield, Ct., Gen. Reg., 18-
  20
Bradstreet
Bradstreet Family of Ipswich, MSS. in
  Boston Public Library, 11 pages
Essex Antiquarian, xi, 52–60, 136–8
Gamble's Family Data (1906), 56
Brady
McKinney Family of Pa., 140–227
Bragg
Essex Antiquarian, xi, 62–4
Brainard
Treman Genealogy
Brandegee
Stiles' Wethersfield, Ct., ii, 128–33
Branham
Vawter Family of Va., 172–214
Branin
Bean's Hist. Montgomery Co., Pa., 813
Branson
Hanna's Ohio Valley Genealogies, 12
Brant
Clayton's Hist. of Union Co., N. J., 376
Bras
Bras MSS. in N. J. Hist. Soc. Lib., 5 p.
Brassfield
Peoria County, Ill., History, 630
Brattle
Stiles' Wethersfield, Ct., ii, 133
Bray
Essex Antiquarian, xi, 101–7
Hosmer's Hist. of Deer Isle, Me., 86
Quinby's New Eng. Fam. Hist., i, 59
William and Mary Coll. Quar., xiii, 266–9;
  xiv, 51
Breadish
See Bradish
Breakenridge
Breakenridge Gen. (1903), 49 p., type-
  written
Breck
Breck Family of Sherborn (1902), 16 p.
Hill Genealogy, 1904, 42
New Eng. His. Gen. Register, lvi, 380–4
Treman Genealogy
Breckenridge
Breckenridge Centennial (1895), 101 p.
Breckenridge Fam. Reunion (1898), 98 p.
Breckenridge Family (1904), chart
Breed
Breed Family of Stonington (1900), 15 p.

Essex Antiquarian, xi, 145–57
Wheeler's Hist. Stonington, Ct., 244–8
Breeden
Stackpole's Hist. Kittery, Me., 302–3
Brengle
Shriver Genealogy, 84–8
Brent
Baltimore Sun, March 27, 1904
Old Northwest Gen. Quar. (1900), 64–7
Virginia Mag. of Hist., xii, 439–45; xiii,
  105–12, 219–22, 318–24, 435–41; xiv,
  95–101, 209–15, 314–9, 425–31
Brett
Forman Genealogy, 31
Hayford Genealogy, 146–50
Brewer
Baltimore Sun, Dec. 25, 1904
Dennison Genealogy (1906), 27–30
Greene's History Boothbay, Me., 507
Quinby's New Eng. Fam. Hist., i, 30–4
Temple's History, Framingham, 481–3
Treman Genealogy
Whitmore Genealogy (1875), 39, 44–6
Brewster
Haxtun's Mayflower Compact Signers
Treman Genealogy
Wheeler's Hist. Stonington, Ct., 249–50
Brewton
South Car. Hist. Gen. Mag., ii, 128–52
Breyandt
N. J. Hist. Soc. Proc., ii (1900), 148–50
Briar
Stackpole's Hist. Kittery, Me., 303–4
Brice
Baltimore Sun, Jan. 6, 13, 20, 1907
Brickett
Carter's Hist. of Pembroke, N. H., ii, 24
Cochrane's Hist. Francestown, N. H.,
  543
Essex Antiquarian, xi, 178–81
Well's Hist. of Newbury, Vt., 472
Bridge
Temple's History Framingham, 483
Warden Genealogy, 82–4
Bridges
Essex Antiquarian, xii, 26–8
Temple's History Framingham, 483
Treman Genealogy
Brice
Warfield's Maryland, 156–8
Brigden
Stiles' Wethersfield, Ct., ii, 134
Brigham
Brigham Fam. Meetings (1900), 64 pages
Brigham Genealogy (1907)
Bright
New Eng. Hist. Gen. Reg., xxxv, 117–21
William and Mary Quarterly, xii, 29
Brimblecome
Essex Antiquarian, xii, 34–8
Bringhurst
Beidler Family of Pa., 216–24
Bringhurst Genealogy (1901), 153 pages
Phila. North American, Oct. 20, 1907
Brinley
Temple's History Framingham, 484

Brinser
Penn. German, ii (1901), 23–5
Brinton
Smedley Genealogy, 123, 218–20
Briscoe
Baltimore Sun, July 5, 1903
Richmond, Va., Times, June 5, 1904
Bristol
Humphreyville Genealogy, 31
New Eng. Hist. Gen. Reg., lix, 167–72
Old Northwest Gen. Quar., vi, 179
See under Bristow
Bristow
New Eng. Hist. Gen. Reg., lvii, 263–6
Virg. Histor. Mag. (1905), 59–62
See under Bristol
Britton
Britton Ancestry (1901), 50 pages
Broaddus
Green's Culpeper County, Virg.
Broadish
See Bradish
Broadwell
Crayon's Rockaway, N. J., Records, 274
Brock
Well's Hist. of Newbury, Vt., 473–8
Brockett
Abbott, Jas. S. Memorial (1905), 41 p.
Brockett Genealogy (1905), 266 pages
Brockman
Brockman Family So. Car. (1905), 104 p.
Clark Family of So. Car. (1905)
Brodhead
Ellenville, N. Y., Journal, Jan. 16, 1903
Harris Ancestry (1898)
New Paltz, N. Y., Independent, Jan. 30, 1903
Brodie
Hill, Rodger and Brodie Families of Scotland and New York, (1888) 81 p.
Brodnax
William and Mary Quar.,xiv, 52–8; 135–8
Bronsdon
Bronsdon and Box Gen. (1902), 311 p.
Bronson
Peoria County, Ill., History, 707
Brooke
Baltimore Sun, Nov. 29, 1903; Sept. 25; Oct. 9, 1904
Bean's Hist. Montgomery Co., Pa., 1043
Keith's Pa. Prov. Councillors, ii, 155–7
Maryland Hist. Mag., i (1906)
Page Genealogy, 2d ed., 1893, 142
Stackpole's Hist. Kittery, Me., 304–8
Va. Mag. of History, ix, 314–8, 435–8; x, 87–90, 197–9, 301–4; 443–5; xi, 93–5, 200–3, 336–8, 444–7; xii, 102–8, 216–9, 321–5; xiii, 100–4, 223, 445–7; xiv, 106, 220, 325, 436
William and Mary Quarterly, xi, 210–3
Brooks
Brooks C. T. Mem. (1884), 29–37, reprint
Brooks Fam. of Stratford, Ct. (1897), 7 p.
Brooks Family of Woburn (1904), 20 p.
Brush-Bowers Genealogy (1904), 98–101
Kellogg's Hist.Bernardston,Mass.,314–7

Lawrence Genealogy (1904)
Merrick Genealogy, 430–3
New Eng. Hist. Gen. Reg., lviii, 48–54, 125–36
Old Eliot, Me., Mag. (1901), iv, 12–4
Old Northwest Gen. Quar., vii, 89–92
Ramsdell's Hist. Milford, N. H., 599
Southworth Genealogy (1905), 62–6
Broun
Broun Family of Va. (1906), 4 pages
Richmond, Va., Times, Feb. 12, July 30, 1905
William and Mary Quarterly, xiii, 25
Brower
Harvey's Hud. and Berg. Co., N. J., 130
Brown
Abbott, Jas. S. Memorial (1905), 41 p.
Am. Hist. Mag., vii (1902), 148, 219, 362
Bent Progenitors (1903), 13
Blair Family of Virg. (1898), 209–57
Boogher's Virg. Gleanings (1903), 380–2
Britton Ancestry (1901)
Brown Fam. Concord, Mass. (1901), 11 p.
Brown Fam. Reading, Mass. (1897), 32 p.
Clayton's Hist. Union Co., N. J., 581, 821
Crayon's Rockaway, N. J., Records, 127
Forrest Genealogy, 36–55
Green's Culpeper County, Virg.
Green's Hist. Boothbay, Me., 508
Hopkins, Goodwin and Brown (1895), 19 pages
Humphreyville Genealogy, 32–4
Jameson Genealogy
Lancaster Genealogy, 82–8
Litchfield, Me., History, 1897, 62–7
Muzzey's Reminiscences, 138–42
Parson's Hist. of Rye, N. H., 308–20
Patterson Memoir (1902), 424–6
Ramsdell's Hist. Milford, N. H., 600–2
Richmond, Va., Times, Jan. 17, 1904
Russell Genealogy (1879), 56–8
Stackpole's Hist. Kittery, Me., 301–2
Temple's History Framingham, 485–8
Walker Family of Virginia, 154
Wells Family of Md. (1892), 39–47
Well's Hist. of Newbury, Vt., 479
West Virg. Hist. Mag., i, pt. iv, 21
Wheeler's Hist. Stonington, Ct., 251–72
White Genealogy (1900), 51
Wilcox Genealogy (1902), 17–9
Wood's Hist. Albemarle Co., Va., 151–4
Browne
Chesebrough Genealogy, 516
Gamble's Family Data (1906), 97–112
Gustin Ancestry, 15
Meriwether Genealogy (1899), 31–7
New Eng. Hist. Gen. Reg., lxi, 116–8
Warfield's Maryland, 164–70, 490–3
Brownell
Brownell Fam. Danbury, Ct.(1903),52 p.
Brownell Fam. Souvenir (1906), 20 p.
Browning
Green's Culpeper County, Virg.
Wheeler's Hist. Stonington, Ct., 273–5
Bruce
Baltimore Sun, Sept. 24, Oct. 1, 1905

Moohead Family of Penn., 47–58
Temple's History Framingham, 488
Va. Mag. of History, xi, 197–200, 328–32, 441–3; xii, 93–6, 446–53
White Genealogy (1900), 207
Bruen
Crayon's Rockaway, N. J., Records, 83
Bruer
See Brewer
Bruff
Glenn's Colonial Mansions, ii, 391–4
Brummett
Temple's History Framingham, 489
Brush
Brush Genealogy (1891), 9 pages
Brush Family of Phila. (1900), 20 pages
Brush-Bowers Genealogy (1904), 118 p.
Sanford's Hopkinton, N. Y., 435–7, 440
Bruyn
N. Y. Gen. Biog. Rec., xxviii, 1–8
Bryan
Green's Culpeper County, Virg.
Mayer Genealogy, 75–9
Walker Family of Virginia, 122–6
Bryant
Hall's Hist. Atlantic City, N. J., 378
N. J. Hist. Soc. Proc., ii (1900), 148–50
Whittemore's L. I. Homes, 20–3
Bryden
Peoria County, Ill., History, 754
Bryer
Greene's Hist. Boothbay, Me., 509
Buchanan
Hanna's Ohio Valley Genealogies, 13
McKean Genealogy (1902), 120–4, 130–9, 150–7
Well's History of Newbury, Vt., 480–2
Bucher
Egle's Dauphin Co., Pa., 1883, 236–7
Penn.-German, iv (1903), 291–308
Buchtel
Penn.-German (1907), viii, 589–94
Buck
Stiles' Wethersfield, Ct., ii, 137–47
Buckelew
Clayton's Hist. Union Co., N. J., 812, 816
Buckingham
Southworth Ancestry (1903), 36
Buckley
Seymour, Conn., History, 411
Smedley Genealogy, 131
Buckman
Bean's Hist Montgomery Co., Pa., 702
Buckmaster
See Buckminster
Buckminster
Temple's History Framingham, 490
Buckner
Buckner Family of Va. (1906), 44 pages
William and Mary Coll. Quar., vi, 196–8; vii, 57–9
Buckwalter
Stauffer and Bauer Genealogy, 70–84, 146–8
Budd
Budd Genealogy (1881), 68 pages

Le Fevre's Hist. New Paltz, N. Y., 453
New Paltz, N. Y., Independent, Feb. 13, 1903
Buell
American Ancestry, xii, 163
Nash's Fifty Puritan Ancestors, 129–34
Well's Hist. of Newbury, Vt., 480
Woodruff's Litchfield, Ct., Gen. Reg., 38–45
Buffington
West Va. Hist. Mag., i, pt. iv, 18–20
Buffum
Kewaunee, Wis., Owl for June, 1901
Buford
Buford Family of Va. (1903), 409 pages
McGarock Family of Va.
Bugg
William and Mary Coll. Quar., x, 271
Buker
Bronsdon Genealogy, 156–8
Litchfield, Me., History, 1897, 68–70
See Bowker
Bulfinch
Our Work, Boston, May 1, 1906
Bulkeley
Stiles' Wethersfield, Ct., ii, 147–63
Bull
Ontario Hist. Society Papers, v (1904)
Woodruff's Litchfield, Ct., Gen. Reg., 45
Woodruff's Litchfield, Ct., Gen.Reg.,45–7
Bullard
Jabez Bullard (1903), leaflet
Temple's History Framingham, 492
Bullitt
West Va. Hist. Mag., iv, 214–7
Bulloch
Roosevelt Genealogy, 69–72
Bean's Hist. Montgomery Co., Pa., 601
Britton Ancestry (1901)
New Eng. Hist. Gen. Reg., lxi, 275
Bunce
Stiles' Wethersfield, Ct., ii, 164
Bunker
Hinchman's Nantucket Settlers, ii, 237–42, 248
Litchfield, Me., History (1897), 70
Bunting
Lundy Genealogy, 259–61
Burbank
New Eng. Hist. Gen. Reg., lxi, 139–42
Well's Hist. of Newbury, Vt., 482–4
Burch
Wheeler's Hist. Stonington, Ct., 276–8
Wood's History Albemarle Co., Va., 155
Burd
Keith's Pa. Prov. Councillors, pt.i, 67–77
Burdick
Treman Genealogy
Burem
See Boerum
See Van Boerum
Burges
Alston Genealogy, 328–31
Burgess
Baltimore Sun, Nov. 1, 1903
Kewaunee, Wis., Owl, Dec., 1904, 350

2

Warfield's Maryland, 49–55, 370, 438
Woodruff's Litchfield, Ct., Gen. Reg., 47
Burgis
New Eng. Hist. Gen. Reg., lvii, 404–6
Burgoyne
Richmond, Va., Times, Nov. 22, 1903
Burk
Kellogg's Hist. Bernardston, Mass., 318
Burke
Clarke's King Wm. Co., Va., Fams., 116
Emory's Colonial Fams. of Md., 174–83
Litchfield, Me., History (1897), 71–3
William and Mary Quarterly, xi, 143
Burlingame
Stevens Genealogy (1906), 30–2
Burnet
Burnet Genealogy (1894), 8 pages
Burnet MSS. in N. J. Hist. Soc. Lib.
Clayton's Hist. Union Co., N. J., 121, 378
N. J. Hist. Soc. Proc., ii (1902), 88–91
Burnham
Carter's Hist. of Pembroke, N. H., ii, 26
Greene's Hist. Boothbay, Me., 511
Ramsdell's Hist. Milford, N. H., 605–8
Stiles' Wethersfield, Ct., ii, 166
Burnley
Wood's History Albemarle Co., Va.,156–8
Burns
Dunwoody Genealogy (1899), 55–9
Ramsdell's Hist. Milford, N. H., 608–20
Tucker Genealogy, 1903
Burr
Burr Genealogy, 4th ed. (1902), 628 p.
Burr Ancestors (1903), chart
Litchfield, Me., History, 1897, 74
Old Northwest Gen. Quar., vi, 174–6
Burritt
Burritt Family (1898), 54 pages
Burrough
Stokes Genealogy, 292
Burroughs
Well's Hist. of Newbury, Vt., 484
Burrows
Chesebrough Genealogy, 71–3
Kellogg's Hist.Bernardston,Mass., 321–7
Stiles' Wethersfield, Ct., ii, 168–70
Wheeler's Hist. Stonington, Ct., 279–84
Burt
Guthrie Genealogy (1898), 86–90
Old Colony Hist. Soc. (1899), 82–96
Ramsdell's Hist. Milford, N. H., 620–2
Woolsey Genealogy
Burton
Burton Reunion (1906), 32 pages
New Eng. Hist. Gen. Reg., lx, 28–30
Thayer Ancestors (1894), 30–4
Well's Hist. of Newbury, Vt., 486
White Genealogy (1900), 625
Burum
See Boerum
Burwell
Baltimore Sun, May 12, 19, 26, June 2, 1907
Burwell
Page Genealogy, 2d ed., 1893, 69–71

William and Mary Quar., ii, 230–3; xiv, 258–60
Willis Family of Va., 123
Bush
Allen's History of Enfield, Ct., 24
Boylston, Mass., Centennial (1887)
Peoria County, Ill., History, 633
Bushnell
Barton Genealogy, 99–113
Hyde and Dana Genealogy (1904), 32
Old Northwest Gen. Quar., vii, 137–45
Buster
Wood's Hist. Albemarle Co., Va., 158
Buswell
Tucker Genealogy (1901), 33–5
Butler
Baltimore Sun, Nov. 27, 1904
Genung Family of L. I.
Hallock Pedigree (1906), 58, 71
Jameson Genealogy
Jones Genealogical History (1900), 60
Lawson Genealogy (1903)
South Car. Hist. Gen. Mag., iv, 296–311
Stackpole's Hist. Kittery, Me., 308–10
Stiles' Wethersfield, Ct., ii, 170–91
Temple's History Framingham, 494
Butt
Preston Genealogy, 1899
Butterfield
Butterfield, Gen.D. Biog., 1–7
Warren Genealogy (1903), 76–9
Well's History of Newbury, Vt., 487
Buttles
Old Northwest Gen. Quar., vi, 191; vii
Buttolph
Old Northwest Gen. Quar., vi, 191; vii
Stiles' Wethersfield, Ct., ii, 192–200
Button
Button Genealogy, 2d ed. (1903), 18 p.
Buttrick
Temple's History Framingham, 495
Butts
Butts Genealogy (1898), 153 pages
Buxton
Ramsdell's Hist. of Milford, N. H., 623
Well's History of Newbury, Vt., 487
Byley
Batt and Biley Families (1897)
Byrd
Baltimore Sun, Aug. 7, 1904
Bassett's Writings of Col. Byrd (1901), 444–51
Glenn's Colonial Mansions, i, 17–58
Page Genealogy, 2d ed., 1893, 97–8
Richmond, Va., Times, March 11, 1906
Willis Family of Va., 108–14
Byrne
Robertson Family of Va., 60, 118

Cabell
Baltimore Sun, June 25, 1905
Cadwalader
Keith's Pa. Prov.Councillors,pt.ii,371–97
Cadwell
Belden Genealogy, 224–7

Cady
Allen Family of Nantucket (1905), 107
Treman Genealogy
Cagey
Kagy Genealogy, 241–3
Cahoone
Fernald's Genealogical Exchange, i, 25
Caine
Caine Family (1902), 10 portraits
Caldwell
Baltimore Sun, Sept. 3, 10, 1905
Byram Genealogy (1898), 24–32
Caldwell Chronicle (1899), 50 pages
Caldwell Family of Ipswich (1904), 317 p.
Caldwell Family of Prov. (1906), 18 p.
Jackson Genealogy (1890), 63–72
Landrum's Hist. Spartanburg,S.C.,303–6
New Eng. Hist. Gen. Reg., lxiii, 36–8
Peoria County, Ill., History, 725
Richmond, Va., Times, Dec. 3, 1905
Sayre Genealogy, 99–102
Caleff
Acadiensis, Canada, Quar., vii, 261–73
Calhoun
Calhoun Family of S. C. (1907), 42 pages
So. Car. Hist. Mag., ii, 162; vii, 81, 152
Calkins
Hyde and Dana Genealogy (1904), 42–4
Mayflower Descendants, iv (1902), 17–9
Call
Buell Genealogy, 159, 161
Callahan
Greene Family (1902)
Callard
Clayton's Hist. Union Co., N. J., 851
Calvert
Baltimore Sun, May 17, Dec. 13, 1903
Morris' The Lords Baltimore (1874),61 p.
Smedley Genealogy, 121–3
Calvin
McAllister Family of N. C.
Cameron
Greene's Hist. Boothbay, Me., 511
West Va. Hist. Mag., ii, 57–65
Camm
William and Mary Coll. Quar., xiv, 130,
  261
Camp
Amer. Hist. Mag., iv (1899), 31–40
Clayton's Hist. Union Co., N. J., 123
Landrum's Hist. Spartanburg, S. C., 505
Seymour, Conn., History, 415–6
Stiles' Wethersfield, Ct., ii, 201–3
Campbell
Bellows Falls Times, April 7, 1904
Dennison Genealogy (1906), 19, 91–3
Greene's Hist. Boothbay, Me., 512
Hanna's Ohio Valley Genealogies, 14
Harvey's Hud. and Berg. Co., N. J., 203
Hosmer's History of Deer Isle, Me., 52–4
Litchfield, Me., History, 1897, 76
McAllister Family of N. C. (1900), ii,
  supp., 1–5; iii, 181
Penn. Mag. of History, xxviii, 62–70
Symmes' Tennent, N. J., Church, 412
Treman Genealogy

Walker Family of Va. (1902)
Canaga
Hanna's Ohio Valley Genealogies, 15
Candler
Candler Genealogy (1890), 35 pages
Candler Genealogy, 2d ed. (1902), 189 p.
Canfield
Seymour, Conn., History, 412–5
Cannon
Amer. Hist. Mag., iv (1898), 9–22
Virg. Mag. of History, x, 99
Cantine
Cantine Genealogy (1903), 14 pages
Capen
Temple's History Framingham, 496
Capers
So. Car. Hist. Mag., ii (1901), 273–98
Carbee
Well's Hist. of Newbury, Vt., 489
Carleton
New Eng. Hist. and Gen. Reg., lv, 52–5
Well's History of Newbury, Vt., 493–5
Carlisle
Greene's Hist. Boothbay, Me., 513
Old Northwest Gen. Quar., viii, 1–12
Carlton
Carter's Hist. of Pembroke, N. H., ii, 26
Carman
Brusch-Bowers Genealogy (1904), 62–7
Hosmer's History of Deer Isle, Me., 76
Carnegie
Keith's Pa. Prov. Councillors, pt. ii,
  180–82
Carney
Carney Genealogy (1904), 221 pages
Shourd's Fenwick's Col., N. J., 108–10
Carpenter
Carpenter and Lloyd Family of Phila.
  (1870), 88 pages
Carpenter Family of R. I. (1901), 370 p.
Ferrier Genealogy, 12–4
Glenn's Colonial Mansions, ii, 376–88
Keith's Pa.Prov.Councillors,pt.ii,95–110
Kellogg's Bernardston, Mass., 329–34
Penn. Magazine of History, xxxi, 371
Shourd's Fenwick's Col., N. J., 338–9
Warden Genealogy, 51–8
Carr
Carr Family Lineage (1902), 64 pages
Carter's Hist. of Pembroke, N. H., ii, 27
William and Mary Coll. Quar., viii, 106–
  8, 130–2
Wood's Hist. Albemarle Co., Va., 159–63
Carrigan
Jenkins Family of Pa., 1904, 124
Carrington
Seymour, Conn., History, 417
Southern Hist. Assoc. Pubs., v, 228–31
Carroll
Baltimore Sun, May 1, 1904; Feb. 19,
  1905
Keith's Pa.Prov.Councillors,pt.ii,357–61
Peoria County, Ill., History, 634
Warfield's Maryland, 501–18
Carson
Hanna's Ohio Valley Genealogies, 16

Moore Family of Chester, Pa. (1897), 38,
56, 93, 1437–9
Peoria County, Ill., History, 634
Carter
Carter Family of Woburn (1884), 8 p.
Glenn's Colonial Mansions, i, 217–94
Green's Culpeper County, Virg.
Keith's Pa. Prov.Councillors, pt. ii, 24–6
New Eng. Hist. and Gen. Reg., lv, 223
Richmond, Va., Times, May 1, 1904
Robie Genealogy (1900), 131 pages
Well's History of Newbury, Vt., 495–8
William and Mary Coll. Quar., ix, 34–7
Willis Family of Va., 103–7
Wood's Hist. Albemarle Co., Va., 163–5
Cartwright
Hinchman's Nantucket Settlers, ii, 249
Nashville Am. Hist. Mag. for July, 1900
New England Magazine of History
Carver
New Eng. Hist. and Gen. Reg., lv, 221
Cary
Baltimore Sun, Nov. 25; Dec. 2, 9, 1906
Cary Family Ancestors (1902), chart
Cary Fam.Association Bull.(1903),10 pp.
Cary Family in England (1906), 105 p.
Hull Genealogy (1904), 27
New Eng. Hist. Reg. (1895), 396–403
Page Genealogy, 2d ed.,1893,105–8,258–9
Richmond, Va., Times, May 29, 1904
Virginia Magazine of Hist., ix, 104–11
Cascaden
Bean's Hist. Montgomery Co., Pa., 576
Case
Crissey's History of Norfolk, Ct., 554
Old Northwest Gen. Quar., vii, 49–55
Cason
Baltimore Sun, Aug. 6, 1905
Cass
New Eng. Hist. and Gen. Reg., lvi, 305–8
Casselberry
Bean's Hist. Montgomery Co., Pa., 481
Cassidy
Wintermute Gen., 246
Casterline
Crayon's Rockaway, N. J., Records, 85
Castle
Strong Genealogy, 519
Caswell
Parson's History of Rye, N. H., 321–4
Stackpole's History Kittery, Me., 311
Cates
Cates Genealogy (1904), 52 pages
Roberts Family of Maine, 66–71
Cathcart
Sherrard Genealogy, 380–2
See also Kithcart
Catlett
Stubbs Family of Virginia, 100
Catlin
Stiles' Wethersfield, Ct., ii, 204
Woodruff's Litchfield, Ct., Gen.Reg.,50–7
Caulkins
Hodge Genealogy (1900)
Cave
Green's Culpeper County, Virg.

Caywood
Baltimore Sun, Sept. 3, 1905
Chabot
Chabot Genealogy (1906), 24 pages
Chace
Chace Family of Ohio (1900), 42 pages
Ford's History of Clinton, Mass., 130–5
Chadbourne
Chadbourne Genealogy (1904), 61 pages
Old Eliot, Me., Mag. (1901), iv, 16–8
Stackpole's Hist. Kittery, Me., 311–5
Chadsey
N. Y. Gen. Record, xxxii, 67–71, 153–6,
217–21
Chadwick
Bean's Hist. Montgomery Co., Pa.,615–7
Seymour, Conn., History, 422–3
Chalker
New Eng. Hist. Gen. Reg., lix, 133
Challis
Robinson's Symon, Indian (1903), 7–10
Chalmers
Richmond, Va., Times, Jan. 8, 1905
Well's History of Newbury, Vt., 490–3
Chamberlain
Carter's Hist. of Pembroke, N. H., ii, 28
Chamberlain Gen. Bureau(1901), 7 pages
Maine Hist. Soc. Coll. (1894), 309
Well's History of Newbury, Vt., 498–515
Chamberlin
Chamberlin Fam. Union Co.,Pa.(1901), 1
Guthrie Genealogy (1898), 56–8, 86
Chambers
Chambers Fam. of Pa. (1904), 28 pages
Jennings Genealogy, ii, 610–5
Kittochtinny Magazine, i, 136–58, 279–
96, 407–19
Champe
Willis Family of Va., 118–20
Champion
Treman Genealogy
Champlin
Chesebrough Genealogy, 479
Clarke and Pendleton Ancestors, 59–62
Chancellor
Baltimore Sun, Jan. 8, 1905
Chandler
Allen's History of Enfield, Ct., 26
Chandler Family (1903), 31 pages
Chandler Fam. of Worcester (1903), 37 p.
Chandler Ancestry (1904), 11 pages
Clayton's Hist. Union Co., N. J., 221–3
Dedham Historical Register, xii, 101–7,
132–5; xiii, 27–31, 53–7, 83–8, 114–20;
xiv, 36
Handy's Hist. of Sumner, Me., 103–9, 178
Le Baron Genealogy, 194–5
Sanford's Hist. Hopkinton, N. Y., 444–
57
Stackpole's Hist. Kittery, Me., 315–7
Treman Genealogy
Chapin
Allen's History of Enfield, Ct., 26
Bellows Falls Times, April, 1905
Hinman's Puritan Settlers, 534
Kellogg's Bernardston, Mass., 335–48

Palmer's Annals of Chicopee St., Mass., 5–8, 17

Chaplin
Hinman's Puritan Settlers, 536

Chapline
Baltimore Sun, July 24, 31, 1904

Chapman
Clayton's Hist. Union Co., N. J., 824
Hall's History of Greenland, N. H., 162
Hinman's Puritan Settlers, 538–45
Landrum's Spartanburg, S. C., 411–3
Penn. Mag. of History, xxvii, 112–4
Stackpole's History Kittery, Me., 317–8
Treman Genealogy
Wheeler's Hist. Stonington, Ct., 287–7
William and Mary Quarterly, x, 134

Charles
Carter's History of Pembroke, N.H., ii, 29

Chase
Chandler Ancestry (1904), 7–11
Chase Fam. of Newbury (1871), chart
Chase Fam. of Yarmouth (1872), chart
Chase Fam. Shirley, Mass. (1888), 32 p.
Chace Fam. of Ohio (1900), 42 pages
Chase Reunion (1901), 48 pages
Chase Fam. of Haverhill (1904), chart
Genung Family of L. I.
Hoyt's Salisbury, Mass., Families, 645–9
Litchfield, Me., History, 1897, 77
New Eng. Hist. Gen. Reg., lviii, 38
Ramsdell's Hist. Milford, N. H., 627
Stackpole's History Kittery, Me., 318
Towle Genealogy, 139–48
Warfield's Maryland, 187–9

Chastain
Baltimore Sun, July 7, 1907

Chatfield
Seymour, Conn., History, 418–22

Chauncey
Old Eliot, Me., Mag. (1901), iv, 49
New Eng. Hist. and Gen. Reg., lv, 432–9
Treman Genealogy

Checkley
Whitmore's Heraldic Journal, ii, 131–2

Cheever
Peoria County, Ill., History, 635
Woolsey Genealogy

Cheney
Carter's Hist. of Pembroke, N. H., ii, 30
Ramsdell's Hist. Milford, N. H., 628–30
Tucker Genealogy (1901), 55–7

Chesebrough
Chesebrough Genealogy (1903), 686 p.
Mumford Memoirs (1900), 119–21
Wheeler's Hist. Stonington, Ct., 288–309

Chester
Chester Family of Boston (1896), 11 p.
Old Northwest Gen. Quar., x, 154–66
Stiles' Wethersfield, Ct., ii, 208–19

Chevalier
Keith's Pa.Prov.Councillors,pt.ii,117–9

Chew
Baltimore Sun, 1903
Keith's Pa. Prov. Councillors, pt.ii,324–61
Richmond, Va., Times, July 16, 1905
Warfield's Maryland, 109–12

Cheyney
Smedley Genealogy, 225–7

Chick
Litchfield, Me., History (1897), 78
Stackpole's Hist. Kittery, Me., 319–20

Chickering
Carter's Hist. Pembroke, N. H., ii, 30
Chickering Genealogy (1902), 15 pages
Hayford Genealogy, 170–7

Chidester
Vorce Genealogy, 35

Chidsey
New Eng. Hist. Gen. Reg., lx, 268–70

Child
Stackpole's History Kittery, Me., 320
Temple's History Framingham, 499

Childs
Lawson Genealogy (1903)

Chiles
William and Mary Coll. Quar., viii, 105

Chipman
Chipman Genealogy (1904), 232 pages

Chisman
William and Mary Quarterly, xiii, 70

Chittenden
Sanford's Hist. Hopkinton, N. Y., 462–6

Choice
Landrum's Hist. Spartanburg, S. C., 467

Christian
Evans Family of S. C. (1905)
Richmond, Va., Times, Aug. 21, 1904
Va. Magazine of History, viii, 104
William and Mary Quar., viii, 70–4, 122–8, 265–71; ix, 47–52, 243–5

Christie
Harvey's Hud. and Berg. Co., N. J., 106

Christopher
Clayton's Hist. of Union Co., N. J., 291
Perkins' Conn., Farm (1905)
Strong Genealogy, 658–60

Chubbuck
Edson Ancestry (1901), 20

Church
Bent Progenitors (1903), 62–5
Dover, N. H., Enquirer, May–June, 1879
Fernald's Genealogical Exchange, i, 12–4
Seymour, Conn., History, 423–4
Treman Genealogy
Wells Family (1905), 42–4

Churchill
Churchill Fam. in America (1904), 722 p.
Hodge Genealogy (1900)
Stiles' Wethersfield, Ct., ii, 219–34
William and Mary Coll. Quar., vii, 186–90; viii, 48–50, 200–2; ix, 40, 246–9; x, 39–44

Cilley
Carter's Hist. of Pembroke, N. H., ii, 31
Hoyt's Salisbury, Mass., Families, 567

Cissel
Warfield's Maryland, 430

Claflin
Claflin Genealogy (1903), 473 pages
New Eng. Hist. Gen. Reg., lxi, 111
Temple's History Framingham, 501

Clagett
Baltimore Sun, March 13, 1904
Claghorn
Strong Genealogy, 861–5
Claiborne
Claiborne Pedigree (1900)
Clarke's King Wm. Co., Va., Fams., 33–6
Richmond, Va., Times, Feb. 26, 1905
Clapp
Clapp Family Ancestors (1902), 68 pages
Stiles' Wethersfield, Ct., ii, 234–6
Clark
Beckwith Family (1899)
Bronson Genealogy, 48–67
Clark Fam. Hunterdon, N. J. (1892), 8 p.
Clark Fam. of Hunterdon, N. J. (1898),
  9 pages
Clark Fam. of Rowley (1905), 93 pages
Clark Family (1905), 77 pages
Clark Fam. of So. Car. (1905), 634 pages
Clark Ancestors (1906), 215 pages
Clayton's Hist. Union Co., N. J., 97, etc.
Crayon's Rockaway, N. J., Records, 165
Crumrine's Hist. Washington, Pa., 545
Edson Ancestry (1901), 16
Genung Family of L. I.
Green Genealogy (1904), 111–34
Hall's Hist. Atlantic City, N. J., 379–84
Hanna's Ohio Valley Genealogies, 18–9
Hastings Genealogy (1899), 165–70
Heath Genealogy (1905), 25–7
Humphreyville Genealogy, 34–6
Jameson Genealogy
Kingsbury Family (1904), 43–58
Lawson's Genealogy (1903), 285
Le Baron Genealogy, 258–59
Litchfield, Me., History, 1897, 79
New Eng. Hist. and Gen. Reg., liv, 384–
  7; lix, 132
Old Eliot, Me., Magazine (1901), iv, 51
Ramsdell's Hist. Milford, N. H., 630–6
Reed Genealogy (1901), 702–7
Seymour, Conn., History, 424–5
Stackpole's History Kittery, Me., 320–3
Stiles' Wethersfield, Ct., ii, 236–8
Temple's History Framingham, 502
Treman Genealogy
Well's History of Newbury, Vt., 516–9
Wood's Hist. Albemarle Co., Va., 165
Clarke
Anderson-Perrine-Clarke Family of N.
  J., 128–40
Clarke Family of Madison, N, Y. (1902),
  128 pages
Clarke Family of Newbury (1902), 468 p.
Clarke Family of R. I. (1902), 337 pages
Hall Memoranda, 1902, 174–6
New Eng. Hist. Gen. Reg., lviii, 267–74
Clarkson
Bringhurst Genealogy, 115–20
Wood's Hist. Albemarle Co., Va., 166–8
Claud
McGavock Family of Va.
Clay
Clay Family of S. C. (1897), chart
Habersham Genealogy, 37

Rix Genealogy, 216
Robertson Family of Va.
Van Meter's Va. and Ky. Families, 22–8
Clayes
Old Northwest Gen. Quar., iii, 163–6
Clayton
Clayton Genealogy (1904), 41 pages
Green's Culpeper County, Virg.
Slaughter's Life of Wm. Green, 66
Symme's Tennent, N. J., Church, 410
Clearwater
La Fevre's Hist. New Paltz, N.Y., 470–3
Cleaveland
Lawrence Genealogy (1904)
Cleaver
Bean's Hist. Montgomery Co., Pa., 1156
Cleaves
Litchfield, Me., History, 1897, 81
Clemens
Hanna's Ohio Valley Genealogies, 19
Clement
Carter's Hist. of Pembroke, N. H., ii, 32
Lamb Family of N. J. (1904), 7–10
Shourds' Fenwick's Colony, N. J., 185–7
Clements
Dover, N. H., Enquirer, April 26, May
  3, 1855
Meriwether Genealogy (1899), 29
Clemons
Seymour, Conn., History, 425–6
Clendenan
American Ancestry, xii, 150
Stockard's Hist. of Alamance, N. C.
Clendenin
Clendenin Family (1900), 20 pages
West Virg. Hist. Mag., iv, 189–213
Clendinen
Clendinen Fam. W.Va. (1905), blue print
Cleveland
Cleveland Genealogy (1871), 11 pages
Cleveland Ancestry (1892), 25 pages
Clifford
Carer's Hist. of Pembroke, N. H., ii, 33
Clift
Merrill Ancestors (1903), 17–20
Wheeler's Hist. of Stonington, Ct., 310–2
Cloise|
Temple's History Framingham, 506–10
See Cloyes
Clopper
N. Y. Gen. Biog. Rec., xxxvi, 138–40
Clopton
Richmond, Va., Times, Nov. 13, 1904;
  July 23, 1905
William and Mary Quar., x, 54–8; xi,
  67–74
Closson
Deer Island, Me., Press for 1900
Hosmer's Hist. of Deer Isle, Me., 45
Clough
Hoyt's Salisbury, Mass., Families, 650
Litchfield, Me., History, 1897, 83
Cloutman
Dover, N. H., Enquirer for Nov. 18, 1869
Clowes
Penn. Mag. of History, xxix, 489–93

Cloyd
McGavock Fam. of Va., 17, 40–2, 153–6
Cloyes
Temple's History Framingham, 506–10
Clyde
Thornton Family (1905), 16–9
Coale
Keith's Pa.Prov.Councillors,pt.ii,278–80
Coalter
Walker Family of Virginia, 110, 120
Coates
Glenn's Colonial Mansions, i, 97–120
Wheeler's Hist. Stonington, Ct., 313–4
Cobb
Crayon's Rockaway, N. J., Rec., 276–80
Habersham Gen.
Jones Genealogical History (1900), 5
Reed Genealogy (1901), 446–8
Wheeler's Hist. Stonington, Ct., 315–8
Cobbs
Baltimore Sun, Nov. 10, 17, 24; Dec. 1, 8, 1907
Lewis Family of Va. (1906)
Coburn
Ramsdell's Hist. Milford, N. H., 636
Well's History of Newbury, Vt., 519
Cochran
Clayton's Hist. of Union Co., N. J., 512
Hanna's Ohio Valley Genealogies, 20
Cochrane
Cochrane Ancestry (1904), 10 pages
Well's History of Newbury, Vt., 520
Cocke
Alston Genealogy, 334–7
Amer. Hist. Mag., iv (1899), 110
Va. Mag. of History, x, xi, 102
Wood's Hist. Albemarle Co., Va., 169–71
See also under Cockey
Cockey
Baltimore Sun, June 24, July 1, Oct. 28, 1906
Codd
Virginia Mag. of History, x, 374
Coddington
Coddington Family of N. J. (1907), 37 p.
Cody Genealogy (1902), 23 pages
Coe
Coe Family (1885), 16 pages
Connet Genealogy, 44
Duncan Family (1905), 42–4
Guthrie Genealogy (1898), 4–6
Newburgh, N.Y.,Telegram, July 28, 1895
Coeymans
Coemans MSS. N. J. Hist. Soc. Lib., 4 p.
Coffin
Allen Family of Nantucket (1905), 101–4
Hallock Pedigree (1906), 64–6
Hinchman's Nantucket Set., ii, 251–5
Le Baron Genealogy, 253–54, 398–400
Scales' History of Dover, N. H., 280–92
Sinnott Genealogy
Stackpole's History Kittery, Me., 324
Coggeshall
Cornell Genealogy, 371–4
Greene Family of R. I. (1905), 281 pages
Hinchman's Nantucket Set., ii, 216–20

Coggin
Coggin Genealogy (1897), 11 pages
Ramsdell's History Milford, N. H., 639
Cogswell
Dover, N. H., Enquirer for April, 1880
Forrest Genealogy, 86–94
Prindle Genealogy, 256–9
Tucker Genealogy (1901), 94
Tucker Genealogy, 1903
Coke
William and Mary Coll. Quar., vii, 127–9
Colburn
Colburn, Rufus C., Life (1899), 15 pages
Ramsdell's Hist. Milford, N. H., 640–4
Well's History of Newbury, Vt., 521
Colby
Carter's Hist. of Pembroke, N. H., ii, 49
Colby Family of N. H. (1895), 152 pages
Colby Family (1902), 15 pages
Handy's Hist. of Sumner, Me., 109–11
Hosmer's Hist. Deer Isle, Me., 85, 118–20
Hoyt's Salisbury, Mass., Fams., 651–98
Litchfield, Me., History (1897), 84–6
Sewall Genealogy (1904), 13, 20
Colcock
So. Car. Hist. Mag., iii (1902), 216–41
Cole
Clarke's King Wm. Co., Va,. Fams., 36
Crayon's Rockaway, N. J., Records, 129
Green's Culpeper County, Virg.
Harvey's Hud. and Berg. Co., N. J., 157
Lawson Genealogy (1903)
Old Eliot, Me., Magazine (1901), iv, 53
Old Northwest Gen. Quar., ix, 65–76
Stokes Genealogy, 284
Stuart Genealogy (1894), 73–6
Stackpole's History Kittery, Me., 324–8
Warfield's Maryland, 133
William and Mary Quar. (1897), 177–81
Colegrove
Treman Genealogy
Coleman
Allen Family of Nantucket (1905)
Coleman Fam. Gloucester (1906), 240 p.
Egle's Dauphin Co., Pa. (1883), 237–8
Green's Culpeper County, Virg.
Habersham Genealogy, 26
Stiles' Wethersfield, Ct., ii, 241–5
Stubbs Family of Virginia, 110–2
Coles
Baltimore Sun, Sept. 4, Dec. 4, 18, 1904
N. Y. Gen. Biog. Rec., xxxvi, 58–63
Va. Magazine of History, vii, 428
Wood's History Albemarle Co., Va., 172
Colfax
N. J. Hist. Soc. Proc., ser. 2, v, 4, 145–52
Colket
Hinchman's Nantucket Set., ii, 231–3
Collamore
Collamore Family (1887), 44 pages
Collamore Union Bull. (1902), 5 sheets
Coller
Temple's History Framingham, 511
Colleton
So. Car. Hist. and Gen. Mag., i (1900), 325–41, ii (1901), 244–8

Collier
Southworth Ancestry (1903), 37–9
William and Mary Coll. Quar., viii, 202,
  255–7; ix, 183–5
Collins
Buell Genealogy, 228
Byram Genealogy (1898), 33–46
Haines Family of N. J., 253–75
Hall's Hist. of Atlantic City, N. J., 384–9
Jenkins Family of Pa. (1904), 175–7
Lamb Family of N. J. (1904), 1–6
Landrum's Hist. Spartanburg, S. C., 416
Le Baron Genealogy, 134
Litchfield, Me., History (1897), 86
New Eng. Hist. Gen. Reg., lxi, 281–8
Stiles' Wethersfield, Ct., ii, 246
Stokes Family of N. J.
Wheeler's Hist. Stonington, Ct., 319–21
Woodruff's Litchfield, Ct.,Gen.Reg.,61–3
Colson
Putnam's Hist. Mag. (1898), 121–4
Colston
Baltimore Sun, Apr. 8, 1906; Nov. 10,
  17, 1907
Meriwether Genealogy (1899), 60
Colton
Salter Memorial (1900), 41–5
Colvin
McAllister Fam. of N. C. (1900), 149–55
Colwell
Downing Genealogy
Comee
Warren Genealogy (1903), 152–4
Comins
Cummings Genealogy (1904)
Compton
Chappel Genealogy (1900), 295–303
Comstock
Comstock Genealogy (1905), 249 pages
Treman Genealogy
Conant
Ramsdell's Hist. Milford, N. H., 645–7
Warren Genealogy (1903), 162–8
Conard
Bean's Hist. Montgomery Co., Pa., 1181
Roberts' Plymouth, Pa., Meeting, 211
Conary
Hosmer's History of Deer Isle, Me., 57
Cone
Cone Genealogy (1903), 547 pages
Hall Memoranda (1902), 196–206
Hamlin Genealogy (1900), 144–6, 214–9
Heath Genealogy (1905), 28–38
Lancaster Genealogy, 145–54
Treman Genealogy
Coney
Coney Progenitors (1906), 13 pages
New Eng. Hist. Gen. Reg., lxi, 47–56
Conger
Fernald's Genealogical Exchange, iii, 43
Wash., D. C., Hist. Bulletin, iv, 20, 43,
  65, 87, 123, 141; vi, 42–4; vii, 43
Conklin
Harvey's Hud. and Berg. Co., N. J., 157
Conkling
Conkling Family (1895), 11 pages

Connable
Kellogg's History Bernardston, Mass.,
  352–8
Connet
Connet Genealogy (1905), 53 pages
Connor
Carter's Hist. of Pembroke, N. H., ii, 49
Sayre Genealogy, 370–3
Conover
Beekman's Monmouth, N. J., Set., 19–35
Clayton's Hist. of Union Co., N. J., 738
Gustin Ancestry, 65–7
Symmes' Tennent, N.J., Church, 413, 437
Treman Genealogy
Conrad
West Virginia Hist. Mag., v, 140–51
Constantine
Stearns' Hist. Ashburnham, Mass., 645–8
Contee
Baltimore Sun, Nov. 20, 1904
Converse
Converse Genealogy (1905), 961 pages
Putnam's Gen. Mag., ii (1901), 95–100
Conway
Conway Family of Virginia (1904), 8 p.
Green's Culpeper County, Virg.
Richmond, Va., Times, Jan. 10; Sept. 25,
  1904
William and Mary Quarterly, xii, 264–7
Cook
Baltimore Sun, Aug. 11, 18, 25; Sept. 1,
  8, 1907
Cook Family of Long Is. (1886), 21 pages
Hill Genealogy (1904), 53
Lawson's Genealogy (1903), 191–205
Litchfield, Me., History (1897), 87
Mayflower Descendant, iii, 95–105
Stockard's History of Alamance, N. C.
Treman Genealogy
Tucker Genealogy (1901), 217
Cooke
Green's Culpeper County, Virg.
Hall Memoranda (1902), 109
Mayflower Descendant, iii (1901, 95–105
Newport, R. I., Mercury
Cooley
Jenkins Family of Pa. (1904), 180
New Eng. Hist. and Gen. Reg., xxxiv,
  266, 386–9; xxxv, 25–7, 159–63
Coolidge
Britton Ancestry (1901), 46
Temple's History Framingham, 513–5
Coon
See Kuhn
Cooper
Alston Genealogy, 170
Cooper Fam.Rockaway, N.J.(1894),13 p.
Cooper Fam.Woodbury,N.J.(1896),21 p.
Cooper Family of Piscataway Co., N. J.,
  Manuscript in N. J. Hist. Soc.
Crayon's Rockaway, N. J., Rec., 211–6
Harvey's Hud. and Berg. Co., N. J., 160
Litchfield, Me., History (1897), 88
Moore Family of Chester, Pa., 82–4, 106
Sayre Genealogy, 219–21
Seymour, Conn., History, 426–7

Shourd's Fenwick's Colony, N. J., 41
Stackpole's History Kittery, Me., 328–9
Treman Genealogy
Woodruff Genealogy (1902), 124–8
Cope
Hanna's Ohio Valley Genealogies, 22
Copeland
Clark and Copeland Ancestors (1906), 215 pages
Hanna's Ohio Valley Genealogies, 22–3
Copp
Chesebrough Genealogy, 329
Wheeler's Hist. Stonington, Ct., 322–4
Corbett
Kellogg's History Bernardston, Mass., 359–61
Corbin
Baltimore Sun, Nov. 6, 20, 1904
Corbin Family of Conn. (1905), 378 p.
Richmond, Va., Times, July 2, 1905
Corey
Corey Genealogy (1900), 12 pages
N. Y. Gen. and Biog. Record, xxxi, 225–9; xxxii, 30–5
Coriell
Clayton's Hist. Union Co., N. J., 321, 325
Corlies
N. Y. Gen. Biog. Rec., xxxv, 187, 249
Sinnott Genealogy
Tucker Genealogy (1901), 43
Well's History of Newbury, Vt., 522–5
Cornell
Cornell Genealogy (1902), 468 pages
Hinchman's Nantucket Set., ii, 211–5
Hull Genealogy (1904), 23
Cornhill
Cornell Genealogy (1902)
Cornwall
Cornell Genealogy (1902)
Cornwall Genealogy (1901), 178 pages
Mayer Genealogy, 136
Nash's Fifty Puritan Ancestors, 123
Cornwell
Cornell Genealogy, 415–7, 419
Corsen
Corson Genealogy
Corser
Corser Genealogy (1902), 336 pages
Corson
Bean's Hist. Montgomery Co., Pa., 643–7, 1033–8, 1152
Corson Genealogy (1902?), 192 pages
Evans' Scioto Co., Ohio, History, 1223
Robert's Plymouth, Pa., Meeting, 221–4
Cortelyou
Clayton's Hist. of Union Co., N. J., 794
Cornell Genealogy, 381
Corwin
Hallock Pedigree (1906), 62
Cory
Clayton's Hist. of Union Co., N. J., 342
Sayre Genealogy, 248–50
Cotton
Carter's Hist. of Pembroke, N. H., ii, 50
Cotton Family of Portsmouth, N. H. (1905), 26 pages

New Eng. Hist. Gen. Reg., lviii, 294–9; 337–42; lix, 34–40, 186–92
Cottrell
Clarke and Pendleton Ancestors, 42–5
Mayer Genealogy, 84–6
Wheeler's Hist. Stonington, Ct., 325–7
Couch
Nash's Fifty Puritan Ancestors, 99
Richardson Family of Va., 35–41
Stackpole's History Kittery, Me., 329
Stiles' Wethersfield, Ct., ii, 251
Coulston
Bean's Hist. Montgomery Co., Pa., 1158
Coursen
Woodruff Genealogy (1902), 128–35
See Corson
Covert
Covert Ancestry (1906), 15 pages
N. Y. Gen. Record, xxxvii, 117–22, 197–201, 267–71
Covey
Sandford's Hopkinton, N. Y., 457–62
Cowden
Fitchburg, Mass., Soc. Proc., iii, 19–38
Jenkins Family of Pa. (1904), 209
Cowell
Maine Hist. Society Colls. (1894), 306
Cowing
Treman Genealogy
Cowles
Cowles Family of Va. (1903), 2 charts
Crissey's Hist. of Norfolk, Ct., 514–7
Cowperthwaite
Burlington, N. J., Democrat, March 20 to July 3, 1903
Stokes Genealogy, 281–3
Cox
Emory's Colonial Families of Md., 184–7
Potts Genealogy (1901), 257–60
Smedley Genealogy, 92, 172
Coy
Putnam's Hist. Mag., ii (1894), 177
Cozad
Cozad Family MSS. chart by H. S. Clark, of Newburgh, N. Y., in N. Y. Hist. Soc. Lib., 1904
Crady
Peoria County, Ill., History, 755
Crafts
Quinabang Hist. Soc. Leaflets, i, 183–90
Craig
Boogher's Virg. Gleanings (1903), 292–307
Crumrine's Hist. Washington, Pa., 740
New Paltz Independent, Aug. 16, 1895
Richmond, Va., Times, May 22, 1904
Symmes' Tennent, N. J., Church, 462–5
William and Mary Quarterly, x, 124
Craighead
Crumrine's Hist. Washington, Pa., 706
Craighill
Blair Family of Virg. (1898), 199–202
Crall
Crall Ancestry (1905)
See Croll

Cram
Carter's Hist. of Pembroke, N. H., ii, 51
Litchfield, Me., History (1897), 89
Cranch
Clark's Jas. Greenleaf (1901)
New Eng. Hist. Reg., i, 77–80; xxvii, 40
Crane
Carter's Hist. of Pembroke, N. H., ii, 52
Clayton's Union Co., N. J., 383, 385, 402
Crane Family of Chilton (1868), 89 pages
Crane Family of N. J. (1899), 24 pages
Crayon's Rockaway, N. J., Rec., 200–10
Lawson Genealogy (1903)
Nash's Fifty Puritan Ancestors, 93–8
Stiles' Wethersfield, Ct., ii, 254–60
Treman Genealogy
Cranmer
Lamb Family of N. J. (1904), app. 5–9
Crapster
Cumming Family of Md. (1905), chart
Warfield's Maryland, 449
Crary
New Eng. Hist. Gen. Reg., lx, 350–4; lxi, 79–82
Cravens
Boogher's Virg. Gleanings (1903), 379
Crawford
Alston Genealogy, Supp. 300 a-d
Bean's Hist. Montgomery Co.,Pa.,936–8
Crawford Memorial (1904), 299 pages
Litchfield, Me., History (1897), 91
Richmond, Va., Times, Oct. 22, 1905
Vawter Family of Virginia, 336–49
Crawley
Chappell Genealogy (1900), 162–8
William and Mary Coll. Quar., viii, 108
Creed
Richmond, Va., Times, Nov. 27, 1904
Creighton
Larimer Family of Penn., 63
Cresap
Baltimore Sun, Dec. 9, 16, 23, 30, 1906
Cresap Family chart
Cresse
Hall's Hist. of Atlantic City, N. J., 461
Cressey
Old Northwest Gen. Quar., vii, 255–7
Cripps
Shourd's Fenwick's Col., N. J., 237, 366
Crispe
Crispe Genealogy (1901), 409 pages
Crispell
Le Fevre's Hist. New Paltz, N. Y., 524–7
New Paltz, N. Y., Independent, Jan. 17, 1902
Crist
Pound and Kester Genealogy, 126–8,134
Crockett
Hosmer's Hist. of Deer Isle, Me., 107–9
McGavock Family of Va.
Stackpole's History Kittery, Me., 329–31
Crofoot
Kewaunee, Wis., Owl for 1900 and 1901
Croll
Penn. German, ii (1901), 32–42; v, 31-42

Cromwelin
Small Fam. of Pa. (1905), 213–8
Cromwell
Waylen's House Cromwell (1897), 286 p.
Whaley Genealogy, 156
Crook
Landrum's Hist. Spartanburg, S. C., 328
Crooker
Burlington Co., N. J., Democrat, March 27, 1903
Crosby
N. Y. Gen. Record, xxxii, 111–6, 161–3, 225–8
Ramsdell's Hist. Milford, N. H., 650–60
Croshaw
William and Mary Quarterly, ii, 270–2
Crowder
Richmond, Va., Times, Nov. 5, 1905
Crowe
Crowell Genealogy (1903), 109 pages
Crowel
Crowel Genealogy (1899), 55 pages
Crowel Genealogy, supp. (1904), 64 pages
Crowell
American Ancestry, xii, 151
Crowell MSS., in N. J., Hist. Soc. Lib.
Crowell Genealogy (1903), 109 pages
Kellogg's Hist.Bernardston,Mass., 361-3
Crowfoot
Stiles' Wethersfield, Ct., ii, 260
Crown
New Eng. Hist. Gen. Reg., lvii, 406–10
Cruger
Cruger Genealogy (1875), 8 p. reprint
West Va. Hist. Magazine, iii, 204
Crumrine
Crumrine's Hist. Washington, Pa., 978
Cruser
Clayton's Hist. Union Co., N. J., 796
Cruttenden
Griffing Genealogy, 71
Nash's Fifty Puritan Ancestors, 150
Cudworth
New Eng. Hist. Gen. Reg., xxi, 249
Culver
Sandford's Hist. Hopkinton, N. Y., 467
Seymour, Conn., History, 427–8
Woodruff's Litchfield,Ct.,Gen.Reg.,65–8
Cumming
Cumming Family of Md. (1905), chart
Habersham Gen.
Cummings
Cummings Fam., Topsfield (1903), 532 p.
Cummings Fam., Ipswich (1904), 643 p.
Handy's History of Sumner, Me., 53–9
Ramsdell's Hist. Milford, N. H., 660
Cummins
Hunt Genealogy (1906), 129–36
Cunnabell
Warden Genealogy, 31–3
Cunningham
American Ancestry, xii, 204
Crumrine's Hist. Washington, Pa., 483
Cunningham Genealogy (1901), 16 pages
Hanna's Ohio Valley Genealogies, 26
Lawrence Genealogy (1904)

Litchfield, Me., History (1897), 92
New Eng. Hist. and Gen. Reg., lv, 304–9, 416–24
Van Meter's Va. and Ky. Fams., 166–71
White Genealogy (1900), 323–7
Cuppage
William and Mary Quarterly, xi, 137
Currier
Hoyt's Salisbury, Mass., Fams., 699–704
Stuart Genealogy (1894), 174–8
Well's History of Newbury, Vt., 525
Curtis
Dennison Genealogy (1906), 29, 35
Le Baron Genealogy, 102, 226–8
New Eng. Hist. and Gen. Reg., liv, 447–9; lxi, 258–65
Old Eliot, Me., Magazine (1901), iv, 61
Stackpole's History Kittery, Me., 331–2
Stiles' Wethersfield, Ct., ii, 262–7
Curtiss
Curtiss Fam. Stratford, Ct. (1903), 252 p.
Woodruff's Litchfield, Ct., Gen. Reg., 68
Curwen
Putnam's Hist. Mag. (1898), 97–101
Cushing
Cushing Genealogy, 2d ed. (1906), 668 p.
Scales' History of Dover, N. H., 296–8
Treman Genealogy
Cushman
Kellogg's Bernardston, Mass., 363–74
Custer
Bean's Montgomery Co., Pa., 1056, 1070, 1191
Hanna's Ohio Valley Genealogies, 27
See Kester
Custis
Baltimore Sun, Dec. 15, 22, 29, 1907; June 5, 12, 19, 1908
Boogher's Virg. Genealogies (1903), 328
Cuthbert
Clay Family of S. C. (1897), chart
Habersham Genealogy, 47–9
Cutler
Kellogg's Hist. Bernardston,Mass., 374–6
Newhall Ancestry, 187–91
Temple's History Framingham, 517
Cutter
Clayton's Hist. Union Co., N. J., 581
Peoria County, Ill., History, 638
Cutting
Beste-Cutting chart
Temple's History Framingham, 517
Cutright
Peoria Co., Ill., History, 638
Cutts
Old Eliot, Me., Mag. (1901), iv, 56–61
Stackpole's History Kittery, Me., 333–7

Dabney
Richmond, Va., Times, Jan. 17, 1904
Dade
William and Mary Quarterly, xii, 245–9
Dadmun
Temple's History Framingham, 519

Daggett
Butler Ancestry (1895), 9–23
Hallock Pedigree (1906), 57
Daily
Well's History of Newbury, Vt., 526
Daingerfield
William and Mary Coll. Quar., viii, 96–100; ix, 188
See also Dangerfield
Willis Family of Va., 121
Dakin
Tucker Genealogy, 1903
Dallas
Phila. North American, Dec. 22, 1907
Dalliber
New Eng. Hist. Gen. Reg., xxxi, 312
Dally
Clayton's Hist. Union Co., N. J., 583
Dalton
Parson's Hist. of Rye, N. H., 328–32
Daly
New Amsterdam Year Book, i, 10–3
Dam
Stackpole's History Kittery, Me., 337
Dameron
William and Mary Quarterly, xi, 137
Damon
Damon Family of Vt. (1897), 60 pages
Hyde Park Hist. Rec., v (1905), 29–37
Dana
American Historical Mag. (1906)
Hyde and Dana Genealogy (1904), 114 p.
Lawrence Genealogy (1904)
Newhall Ancestry, 137–41
Dandridge
Clarke's King Wm. Co., Va., Fams., 39
Richmond, Va., Times, Aug. 13, 1905
William and Mary Coll. Quar., v, 81; vi, 254; xii, 126–8; xiv, 267
Dane
Essex Co., Mass., Reg., i (1894), 123–6
White Genealogy (1900), 205
Danford
Sabine Genealogy
Danforth
Danforth Genealogy (1902), 476 pages
Litchfield, Me. History (1897), 94–6
Ramsdell's History, Milford, N. H., 662
Stiles' Wethersfield, Ct., ii, 267–70
Daniel
Evans Family of S. C. (1905)
Hill Genealogy (1904), 40–2
Daniell
New Eng. Hist. Gen. Reg., lv, 317–21
Daniels
Claflin Genealogy, 419–26
Ramsdell's History of Milford, N. H.,663
Temple's History, Framingham, 520
Darby
Clayton's Hist. Union Co., N. J., 415
Warren Genealogy (1903), 142–5
See Derby
Darden
Richmond, Va., Times, May 6, 1906
Darling
Russell Gen. (1900), 10, 16–9, 29–36

Temple's History Framingham, 521

Darlington
Darlington Genealogy (1900), 680 pages

Darnall
Baltimore Sun, March 20, Nov. 1904

Darracott
Ramsdell's Hist. Milford, N. H., 664–6

Darrow
Blackman Genealogy, 10, 16

Darwin
New Eng. Hist. Gen. Reg., lx, 20

Dary
Dary Genealogy (1903), 25 pages

Davenport
Bronsdon Genealogy, 150–2
Crayon's Rockaway, N. J., Records, 131
Well's History of Newbury, Vt., 532

Davey
Colburn, Rufus C., Life of (1899), 15 p.

Davidson
Emory's Colonial Families of Md., 195–9
Evans' Scioto Co., Ohio, History, 1224–6
Hanna's Ohio Valley Genealogies, 27

Davies
Baltimore Sun, Oct. 21, 28; Nov. 4, 1906

Davis
Baltimore Sun, July 17, 31, 1904
Bean's Montgomery Co., Pa., 739–41,801
Boogher's Virg. Gleanings (1903), 324–8
Carter's Hist. of Pembroke, N. H., ii, 58
Clark Family of S. Car. (1905)
Colby Family of N. H., 112–5
Crumrine's Hist. Washington, Pa., 957
Davis, Capt. Eben, Life of (1873), 17 p.
Davis, Capt. Joseph, sketch (1897), 17 p.
Davis, John, Doylestown, Pa., Life (1886)
Davis Family of Georgia (1905), 122 p.
Davis Ancestral chart (1905)
Deer Island, Me., Press, March and Oct., 1900
Evans Family of S. C. (1905)
Greenlaw's Genealogical Advertiser, iv (1901), 42
Habersham Gen.
Hoyt's Salisbury, Mass., Families, 704–42
Jameson Genealogy
Jones Genealogical Hist. (1900), 26–8
Le Baron Genealogy, 109
Litchfield, Me., History (1897), 96
Maulsby Genealogy, 137
Peoria County, Ill., History, 640
Scales' History of Dover, N. H., 298–305
Seller's Delaware Families, 76–98
Seymour, Conn., History, 428–38
Temple's History Framingham, 522
Treman Genealogy
Virg. Mag. of History, xii, 325–8
Warden Genealogy, 167–221
Warfield's Maryland, 113–6
Wheeler's Hist. Stonington, Ct., 328–30

Davison
Baltimore Sun, March 4, 11, 1906

Dawson
Alston Genealogy, 517–31
Smedley Genealogy, 76
Wood's Hist. Albemarle Co., Va., 176–9

Day
Crayon's Rockaway, N. J., Rec., 281–5
Day Genealogy (1902), 11 pages
Greene's History Boothbay, Me., 516
Seymour, Conn., History, 438–40
Wells Genealogy (1903), 73

Dayton
Clayton's Hist. Union Co., N. J., 240

Deadman
See Dadmun

Dean
Dean Fam. Grafton, N. H. (1902), 35 p.
Dean Fam. of Ohio (1903), 69 pages
Dean Fam. of Penn. (1903), 149 pages
Landrum's Spartanburg, S. C., 334–49
Seymour, Conn., History, 440–1
Stiles' Wethersfield, Ct., ii, 271–83
Temple's History Framingham, 522
Treman Genealogy
Wheeler's Hist. Stonington, Ct., 331–3

Deane
New Eng. Hist. Gen. Reg., lix, 32–4

Dearborn
New Eng. Hist. Gen. Reg., lx, 308–10

Dearing
Old Eliot, Me., Magazine (1901), iv, 62

Dearth
See Death

Death
Temple's History Framingham, 523

De Baun
Harvey's Hud. and Berg. Co., N. J., 138

De Bow
Clayton's History Union Co., N. J., 865
Harvey's Hud. and Berg. Co., N. J., 160

De Camp
De Camp Fam. of Ohio (1896), 177 pages
De Camp Genealogy (1900), 77 pages

Decker
Greene's History Boothbay, Me., 517

DeClark
Harvey's Hud. and Berg. Co., N. J., 130

De Costa
De Costa Pedigree (1876)

Dedman
See Dadmun

Deering
Jameson Genealogy
Stackpole's History Kittery, Me., 337–48

De Forest
De Forest Genealogy (1900), 288 pages

Deforrest
Seymour, Conn., History, 441–2

De Foussat
So. Car. Huguenot Soc. Trans., xii (1905)

De Groot
Harvey's Hud. and Berg. Co., N. J., 162

DeGrove
N. Y. Gen. Biog. Rec., xxxvii, 224–8
See De Groot

De Hart
Clayton's Hist. Union Co, N.J., 125–741

De Kay
Deckertown, N. Y., Independent, Sept. 10–7, 1897

De Kruyft
Lawson Genealogy (1903)
Delaplain
Shoemaker Genealogy, 94
De Long
Bingham Genealogy, 84, 125–8
Penn.-German, iv (1903), 375–83; v, 22
Demarest
Harvey's Hud. and Berg. Co., N. J., 64–7, 93–6
Labaw's Preakness, N. J., History, 67–9
Demere
Habersham Gen.
Deming
Deming Genealogy (1904), 694 pages
Hall Memoranda (1902), 133–6
Well's History of Newbury, Vt., 528
De Mont
Crayon's Rockaway, N. J., Records, 87
Dench
Lea Genealogy (1906), 409–12, 519–21
Denise
Symmes' Tennent, N. J., Church, 411
Denison
Chesebrough Gen., 37–41, 79–86, 518
Denison Genealogy (1880), 8 pages
Denison-Sheldon Family (1905), chart
Wheeler's Hist. Stonington, Ct., 334–61
See also under Dennison
Denman
Clayton's Hist. Union Co., N. J., 290
Dennett
Litchfield, Me., History (1897), 98
Old Eliot, Me., Mag. (1901), iv, 64–7
Stackpole's History Kittery, Me., 348–52
Dennis
Lundy Genealogy, 193–6, 418
Litchfield, Me., History (1897), 99–101
White Genealogy (1900), 54
Dennison
Dennison Genealogy (1906), 148 pages
Denniston
Crumrine's Hist. Washington, Pa., 968
De Normandie
De Normandie Gen. (1901), 308 pages
Denslow
Hodge Genealogy (1900), 339–45
Dent
Wash., D. C., Hist. Bull., v, vi, 34, 60
Denton
Stevenson Fam. of Long Island, 133–9
Depew
N. Y. Gen. and Biog. Record, xxxii, 53–6, 77–80, 141–4, 231–5
DePeyster
Acadiensis, Canada, Quarterly, vii, 287
Bringhurst Genealogy, 123–6
Roosevelt Genealogy, 19, 34–6
De Priset
Richardson Family of Va., 3
Depue
Treman Genealogy
De Puy
N. Y. Gen. and Biog. Record, xxxii, 53–6, 77–80, 141–4, 231–5

Derby
Derby Genealogy (1904), 22 pages
Derby Family of Stow (1905), 141 pages
Lawrence Genealogy (1904)
De Rie
Gustin Ancestry
De Riemer
De Riemer Fam. of N. Y. (1905), 47 p.
N. Y. Gen. Biog. Rec., xxxvi, 5–14
De Rosset
Meares' Ancestral Dames (1901), 17 p.
Derr
Luzerne Register (1887), 139–4
Derry
Dary Family of Norton, Mass.
De Sille
N. Y. Gen. and Biog. Rec., xxxiv, 24–8
Despard
Huguenot Soc. of Am., Proc. iii (1903)
de Treville
Habersham Gen.
Detweiler
Funk Genealogy
Peoria County, Ill., History, 641
Deuch
Temple's History Framingham, 524
Devinney
Lamb Family of N. J., app., 18
De Voe
Clayton's Hist. Union Co., N. J., 781
Dewees
Dewees Family of Pa. (1905), 294 pages
Dotterer Genealogy
Holstein Genealogy, 148–52
Penn. Mag. of History, xxviii, 251
Dewell
Cressey's Hist. of Norfolk, Ct., 566
Dewey
Hanna's Ohio Valley Genealogies, 28
Hodge Genealogy (1900)
Sanford's History Hopkinton, N. Y., 468
Dewing
Dewing Genealogy (1904)
New Eng. Hist. Gen. Reg., lvii, 101–8
De Witt
N. Y. Gen. and Biog. Rec., xxxiv, 200–6
Dewitt
Treman Genealogy
De Wolf
De Wolf Genealogy (1902), 325 pages
Le Baron Genealogy, 132–4, 275–82
Dexter
Dexter Family of Malden (1904), 279 p.
Dexter Fam. of Worcester (1905), 353 p.
Dey
Labaw's Preakness, N. J., History, 24–42
Treman Genealogy, 741–889, 1159–68
Deyo
New Paltz Independent, 1894; Oct. 11, 1895; Jan. 8, 1897
Le Fevre's Hist. New Paltz, N. Y., 253–79, 515–7
Diamond
Stackpole's History Kittery, Me., 352
Dibble
Seymour, Conn., History, 442–4

Dibrell
Lewis Family of Va. (1906)
Dickerson
Anderson-Perrine Family, 98–106
Crayon's Rockaway, N. J., Rec., 217–25
Hanna's Ohio Valley Genealogies, 29–30
Old Northwest Gen. Quar., x, 55–8
Woodruff Genealogy (1902), 135–7
Dickie
Chappell Genealogy (1900), 266–80
Dickinson
Carpenter's Hist. of Amherst, Mass., 22
Dickenson MSS., in N. J., Hist. Soc. Lib.,
20 pages
Keith's Pa. Prov. Councillors, pt. ii, 53–64, 390–4
McGavock Family of Va.
Moore Family of Chester, Pa., 102
Pocumtuck Valley, Mass., Hist., 491–3
Stiles' Wethersfield, Ct., ii, 284–91
Woodruff's Litchfield, Ct., Gen. Reg., 70
Dicks
Barber Genealogy (1890), 108–15
Dickson
Crumrine's Hist. Washington, Pa., 626
Downing Genealogy
Tucker Genealogy (1901), 231
Dietrich
Dietrich Family Reunion (1906), 20 p.
Penn.-German, viii (1907), 428–34
Swope Genealogy, 254–8
Digges
Baltimore Sun, May 8, 1904; Oct. 9, 1904
Richmond, Va., Times, March 12, 1905
Diggins
New Eng. Hist. Gen. Register, lxi, 142–5
See also under Dickens
Dikeman
Kewaunee, Wis., Owl for Sept., Oct.,
Nov., 1901; March, 1902
Dildine
Dotterer Genealogy
Dillwyn
Penn. Mag. of History, xxviii, 248
Dilts
Dilts Genealogy (1890), 20 pages
Lundy Genealogy, 418
Dimock
Stiles' Wethersfield, Ct., ii, 291–302
Dinkel
Small Family of Penn. (1905), 124–37
Dinkle
Mayer Genealogy, 79–83
Dinsmore
Dinsmore Fam. of Conway, Mass. (1896),
16 pages
Robinson Genealogy (1901), 27
Dinwiddie
Dinwiddie Genealogy (1902), 120 pages
Disbrow
Clayton's Hist. Union Co., N. J., 527,
783
Disbrowe
New Eng. Hist. Gen. Reg., xli, 353–63
Dismant
Bean's Hist. Montgomery Co., Pa., 673

Divoll
Bellows Falls Times, March, 1904
White Genealogy (1900), 45, 84–7
Dix
Stiles' Wethersfield, Ct., ii, 302–10
Dixey
Warren Genealogy (1903), 118–20
Dixon
Evans Family of S. C. (1905)
Glenn's Colonial Mansions, ii, 390–4
Old Eliot, Me., Magazine (1901), iv, 68
Stackpole's History Kittery, Me., 353–61
William and Mary Coll. Quar., x, 272
Doan
Brooke's Annals of Revolution (1843)
Dunwoody Genealogy (1899), 160–2
Doane
Acadiensis, vii (1907), 58–61
Doane Genealogy (1902), 533 pages
New Eng. Hist. Gen. Reg., lix, 160
Dobbins
Baltimore Sun, Aug. 19, 1906
McKean Genealogy (1902), 66–72
Dodderer
Wintermute Gen., 136–141
See Dotterer
Doddridge
Wells Fam. of Ohio (1892), 54–61
West Virg. Hist. Mag., ii, Jan., 54, 58
Dodge
Carter's Hist. Pembroke, N. H., ii, 67–9
Dodge Fam. of Essex, Mass. (1886), 8 p.
Dodge Family of R. I. (1904), 233 pages
Greene's History Boothbay, Me., 519
Harris Ancestry (1898)
White Genealogy (1900), 49–58, 216–74,
285–92
Doe
Carter's Hist. of Pembroke, N. H., ii, 69
Well's Hist. of Newbury, Vt., 529–32
Doggett
Merrell Family Ancestors (1903)
Dolbeare
Dolbeares of Boston (1893), 4 pages
Dolbee
Parson's History of Rye, N. H., 333
Dole
Deer Island, Me., Press for 1900
Deering, Me., News, March 21, 1900
Doll
Beauman Family of N. Y., 39, 133–7
Dolloff
Greene's History Boothbay, Me., 519
Morse's Sketches of Perkins and Dolloff
(1898), 31–66
Dolson
New Paltz, N. Y., Independent, Jan. 30,
1903
Riker's Hist. of Harlem, N. Y., 103, 532
Dominick
New Amsterdam Year Book, i, 7–9
Donaldson
Crumrine's Hist. Washington, Pa., 902
Done
Doane Genealogy

Doolittle
Allen Family of Nantucket (1905)
Hall Memoranda (1902), 49–52
Seymour, Conn., History, 444–5
Door
Maine Hist. Soc. Coll. (1894), 307–9
Dore
Dover, N. H., Enquirer for June 4, 1868
Doremus
Labaw's Preakness, N. J., History, 14–8
Dorman
Seymour, Conn., History, 445
Dorr
See also under Door
Dorrance
Dorrance Genealogy (1901), 24 pages
Dorset
Jerseyman, ix (1903), 6, 9–13
Dorsey
Baltimore Sun, June 26; July 3, 1904;
   Jan. 12, 19, 1908
Cumming Family of Md. (1905), chart
Meriwether Genealogy (1899), 134
Warfield's Maryland, 55, 337, 390, etc.
Doten
Le Baron Genealogy, 81–4, 191, 195
Dotterer
Dotterer Genealogy (1903), 164 pages
See Dodderer
Doty
Clayton's Hist. Union Co., N. J., 390
Dougherty
Crayon's Rockaway, N. J., Records, 167
Doughty
Hall's Hist. Atlantic City, N. J., 389–91
Douglas
Jenkins Family of Pa. (1904), 125–9
Keim and Allied Families, 625
Douglass
Litchfield, Me., History (1897), 102–6
New Eng. Hist. Gen. Reg., xxxi, 166
Dow
Deer Island, Me., Press for 1900
Gray Genealogy (1889), 21–4
Hosmer's History of Deer Isle, Me., 73
Hoyt's Salisbury, Mass., Families, 742–4
Parson's History of Rye, N. H., 334–6
Tucker Genealogy (1901), 40
Tucker Genealogy (1903)
Downing
Beidler Family of Pa., 260–3
Downing Genealogy (1902), 133 pages
Smedley Genealogy, 95–7, 178–84
Stackpole's Hist. Kittery, Me., 361–2
Downman
Baltimore Sun, May 7, 1905
Downs
Dover, N. H., Enquirer for Aug. 2, 1877
Parson's History of Rye, N. H., 337–9
Peoria County, Ill., History, 643
Dowrst
Parson's History of Rye, N. H., 339
Drake
Parson's History of Rye, N. H., 340–2
Pound and Kester Genealogy, 291–300
Richmond, Va., Times, June 19, 1904

Treman Genealogy
Woodruff Genealogy (1902), 137–9
Draper
Sellers Delaware Families, 99–128
Tucker Genealogy, 1903
Dresser
Whaley Genealogy, 184–7
Drinker
Keith's Pa. Prov. Councillors, pt. ii, 29–31
Drinkwater
Drinkwater Genealogy (1901), 15 pages
Drowne
N. Y. Gen. Biog. Rec., xxxv, 171
Old Eliot, Me., Magazine (1901), iv, 70
Stackpole's Hist. Kittery, Me., 362–3
Drummond
Landrum's Spartanburg, S. C., 423–7
New Eng. Hist. Gen. Reg. (1903), 241
Dryden
Thayer Ancestors (1894), 36
Duane
Phila. North American, Dec. 8, 1907
Du Bois
Burhans Genealogy, 16–8
Newburgh, N. Y., Hist. Papers, xiii,
   191–8
New Paltz, Independent, March 27,
   1896; Jan. to April, 1898
Le Fevre's Hist. New Paltz, N. Y., 280–
   347, 510–4
Dubois
Richmond, Va., Times, July 31, 1904
Symmes' Tennent, N. J., Church, 405–8
Dudley
Carter's Hist. Pembroke, N. H., ii, 77–9
Dudley Genealogy, supp. (1901), 22 p.
Gamble's Family Data (1906), 28
Jenkins Family of Pa. (1904), 162
Treman Genealogy
Tucker Genealogy (1901), 85–92
Tucker Genealogy (1903)
Duke
Buford Fam. of Va. (1903), 123–5
Page Genealogy, 2d ed. (1893), 229–30
Richmond, Va., Times, Mar. 6, 1904
Wood's Hist. Albemarle Co., Va., 181
Dulany
Baltimore Sun, March 26, 1905
Warfield's Maryland, 184–7
Dummer
Stuart Genealogy (1894), 148–51
Dumont
N. Y. Gen. Biog. Rec., xxxiv, 191
Dunbar
American Ancestry, xii, 193
Well's Hist. of Newbury, Vt., 534–7
Duncan
Clayton's Hist. Union Co., N. J., 865
Duncan Family of Penn. (1905), 44 p.
Landrum's Hist. Spartanburg, S. C.
Williamson Family of York, Pa., 14–20
Dunckel
Small Family of Penn. (1905), 124–37
Duncklee
Colby Family of N. H., 9–14
Ramsdell's Hist. Milford, N. H., 670–5

Dunham
Clayton's Union Co., N. J., 253, 513, 602
Dunlap
Hanna's Ohio Valley Genealogies, 30–2
Litchfield, Me., History (1897), 107–9
West Virg. Hist. Mag., iii, 255–9
Dunlevy
Dunlevy Genealogy (1901), 335 pages
Dunn
Guthrie Genealogy (1898), 76–9
Treman Genealogy
Dunning
Gray Genealogy (1889), 42–53
Dunster
Dunwoody Genealogy (1899), 151–5
New Eng. Hist. Gen. Reg., lxi, 186–9
Dunton
Greene's History Boothbay, Me., 520
Dunwoody
Dunwoody Genealogy (1899), 172 pages
Du Pre
Alston Genealogy, 47–9
Dupuis
N. Y. Gen. Biog. Rec., xxxii, 53–6, 77–
80, 141–4, 231–5
Dupuy
Baltimore Sun, Dec. 11, 1904
Durand
Seymour, Conn., History, 445–6
Durfee
Durfee Genealogy (1902), 2 vols.
Jennings Genealogy, ii, 560–2
Warden Genealogy, 44–50
Durfey
Sandford's Hist. Hopkinton,N.Y.,469–74
Durham
Evans Family of S. C. (1905)
Durrett
Wood's Hist. Albemarle Co., Va., 183–5
Durstine
Beidler Family of Pa., 138–45
Dutcher
Dutcher Genealogy (1906)
Dutrow
See Dotterer
Dutton
Ramsdell's Hist. Milford, N. H., 675–7
Duvall
Warfield's Maryland, 104–6
Duyckinck
Cornell Genealogy, 383
Dwight
Alston Genealogy, supp., 68a–c
Hamlin Genealogy (1900), 80
Humphreyville Genealogy, 36–8
N. Y. Gen. Biog. Rec., xxxiii, 14–6
Well's Genealogy (1903), 75
Dyer
Dyer Family of Virg. (1906), chart
Thayer Ancestors (1894), 38–42

Eachus
Smedley Genealogy, 257
Eades
Wood's History Albemarle Co., Va., 186

Eager
White Genealogy (1900), 421–4
Eames
Claflin Genealogy, 411–4
Temple's Framingham, Mass., 531–6
Ean
Le Fevre's Hist. New Paltz, N. Y., 474–8
New Paltz, N. Y., Independent, Feb. 6,
1903
Earl
Treman Genealogy
Earle
Harvey's Hud. and Berg. Co., N. J., 232
Jennings Genealogy (1899), ii, 563–7
Landrum's Spartanburg, S. C., 266–77
Litchfield, Me., History (1897), 110–3
Early
Egle's Dauphin Co., Pa. (1883), 238–40
Earnest
Peoria County, Ill., History, 644
Eastlack
Stokes Genealogy, 56, 304–6
Eastman
Carter's Hist. of Pembroke, N. H., ii, 79
Colby Family of N. H., 86–101
Eastman Genealogy (1901), 1000 pages
Forrest Genealogy, 112–7
Sandford's Hopkinton, N. Y., 474–83
Treman Genealogy
Well's Hist. of Newbury, Vt., 537–40
Easton
Peoria County, Ill., History, 755
Eaton
Berkshire Hist. Soc. Coll. (1897), 260–5
Clark Family of Vermont (1905), 28–36
Dedham Hist. Reg., xi, 111–26; xii, 10–
20; 43–53
Deer Island, Me., Press for 1899, article
20–8
Eaton Family Assoc. (1898), 8 pages
Eaton Family of Dedham (1900), 67 p.
Eaton Genealogy (1900), 69 pages
Hosmer's Hist. Deer Isle, Me., 41–3,68,75
Hoyt's Salisbury, Mass., Fams., 745–8
Peoria County, Ill., History, 644
Preston Genealogy (1899)
Temple's History Framingham, 536–9
Eberle
Peoria County, Ill., History, 644
Eckhard
Peoria County, Ill., History, 645
Ecoff
Lancaster Genealogy, 130–2
Eddy
Bronsdon Genealogy, 84–91
Edgar
Clayton's Hist. Union Co., N. J., 851
Edge
Harvey's Hud. and Berg. Co., N. J.,
151–3
Smedley Geneal.,46–50,89, 160,177,276
Edgecomb
Converse Genealogy (1905), 754, 769
Litchfield, Me., History (1897), 113
Edgehill
Temple's History Framingham, 539

Edgell
Temple's History Framingham, 539
Edgerly
Dover, N. H., Enquirer, Dec. 8, 22, 1864
Edmands
Temple's History Framingham, 540
Edmonstone
Baltimore Sun, Feb. 23, 1904
Edmunds
Parson's History of Rye, N. H., 342
Temple's History Framingham, 540
Edsall
Edsall Genealogy (1899), 72 pages
Ferrier Genealogy, 15
Harvey's Hud. and Berg. Co., N. J., 163
Edson
Edson Ancestry (1901), 98 pages
Edson Genealogy (1904), 630 pages
Edwards
Ames Genealogy (1898)
Baltimore Sun, Oct. 30; Nov. 6, 1904
Bronsdon Genealogy, 42–7
Clarke's King Wm. Co., Va., Fams., 41–7, 112–94
Edwards' Autobiography (1897), 133 p.
Edwards Family of Mass. (1903), 167 p.
Edwards Family of Concord, Mass., (1907), 28 pages
Hull Genealogy (1904), 18
Jones Genealogical History (1900), 11
Kellogg's Hist. Bernardston, Mass., 383
Lawson's Genealogy (1903), 288–92
New Eng. Hist. Gen. Reg., lvi, 60–3
Richardson Genealogy (1906)
Stiles' Wethersfield, Ct., ii, 314–17
Temple's History Framingham, 541
Eells
Eells Genealogy (1903), 218 pages
Hamlin Genealogy (1900), 175–6
Wheeler's Hist. Stonington, Ct., 362–4
Efford
Virg. Hist. Mag. (1895), 195
Egbert
Bean's Hist. Montgomery Co., Pa., 939
Egerton
American Ancestry, xii, 188
Eggleston
Richmond, Va., Times, Oct. 1, 1905
Nash's Fifty Puritan Ancestors, 41
Elcock
Munson Genealogy, 88
Elder
Treman Genealogy
Eldredge
Ramsdell's Hist. Milford, N. H., 678
Eldridge
Hoyt's Salisbury, Mass., Families, 568
Elgan
Pound and Kester Genealogy, 194–200
Eliot
Eliot Family of England (1885), 7 pages
Eliot Reunion (1901), 114 pages
Eliot Genealogy (1905), 344 pages
Stackpole's Hist. Kittery, Me., 363–4
Treman Genealogy
Virg. Mag. of History, xiii, 95–9
3

Elkins
Parson's History of Rye, N. H., 343
Ellerbe
Evans Family of S. C., 1905
Ellery
White Genealogy (1900), 325
Ellet
Keith's Pa.Prov.Councillors,pt.ii,96–101
Ellett
Clarke's King Wm. Co.,Va.,Fams., 47–51
Ellicott
Baltimore Sun, March 12, 1905
Warfield's Maryland, 496–500
Elliott
Carter's Hist. Pembroke, N. H., ii, 80–2
Colby Family of N. H., 125–8
Habersham Genealogy, 15–8
Keith's Pa. Prov. Councillors, pt. ii, 176–80
McAllister Family of N. C.
Peoria County, Ill., History, 646
Pound and Kester Genealogy, 100
Ellis
Ellis Family of Sandwich (1900), 54 p.
Goodrich's Hist. Dryden, N. Y., 191–4
Habersham Gen.
Jerseyman, vii, 14–5
Lamb Family of N. J. (1904), 20–4
Richmond, Va., Times, May 21, 1905
Ellison
Ellison Family of Boston (1903), 19 p.
Elmendorf
Chesebrough Genealogy, 122, 124
Clayton's Hist. Union Co., N. J., 510
Elmer
Clayton's Hist. of Union Co., N. J., 131
Eltinge
Le Fevre's Hist. New Paltz, N. Y., 481–98
Shriver Genealogy, 18
West Virg. Hist. Magazine, iii, pt. ii
Elwell
Elwell Family of Dorchester (1899), 30 p.
Elwell Fam. of Hardwick (1900), 10 p.
Elwell Family of Goshen (1900), 4 pages
Elwell Fam., Westhampton (1902), 24 p.
Ely
Bean's Hist. Montgomery Co., Pa., 911
Ely Ancestry (1902), 700 pages
Metcalf Genealogy (1898), 61
Treman Genealogy
Emerson
Emerson Genealogy Criticisms, 15 pages
Gamble's Family Data (1906), 187–91
Greene's History Boothbay, Me., 521–4
Litchfield, Me., History (1897), 114–6
Ramsdell's Hist. Milford, N. H., 679–81
Emery
Cox's Biog. of Matthew G. Emery, 1904
Stackpole's Hist. Kittery, Me., 365–71
Willis' Old Eliot, Me. (1901), iv, 101–9
Emes
See Eames
Emmons
Emmons Genealogy (1905), 300 pages
Treman Genealogy
Woodruff's Litchfield, Ct.,Gen.Reg.,72–5

Emms
See Eames
Emory
Emory's Colonial Fams. of Md., 187–91
Endecott
Putnam's Hist. Mag. (1899), 111–4, 176–80, 251–4
Hall's Hist. Atlantic City, N. J., 391–9
Endle
Stackpole's Hist. Kittery, Me., 371–2
Engle
Bean's Hist. Montgomery Co., Pa., 814
Haines Family of N. J., 396–400
Stokes Family of N. J.
West Virg. Hist. Mag., v, 153–6
English
Genung Family of L. I.
Hodge Genealogy, 1900
Strong Genealogy, 854–6
Symmes' Tennent, N. J., Church, 440–6
Ennalls
Baltimore Sun, May 6, 1906
Eno
Treman Genealogy
Enos
Edson Ancestry (1901), 14–6
Ensign
Woodruff's Litchfield, Ct., Gen. Reg., 75
Eppes
Baltimore Sun, June 3, 10, 1906
Ernst
Mayer Genealogy, 86–8
Erskine
Keith's Pa. Prov. Councillors, pt.ii,384–7
Erving
Bowdoin Genealogy (1894), 41–51
Bowdoin Genealogy (1900), 15
Eskridge
Va. Mag. of Hist. and Biog., vii, 434–6; viii, 89–91, 211–3, 318–20; ix, 201–3
Espy
Espy Genealogy (1905), 126 pages
Estabrook
Treman Genealogy
Estep
Hanna's Ohio Valley Genealogies, 33
Estes
Lewis Family of Va. (1906)
Esty
Esty Genealogy (1900), 2 pages
Temple's History Framingham, 542
Topsfield, Mass., Hist. Coll., v (1899), 105–16
Eubank
Woods' Hist. Albemarle Co., Va., 188
Eustace
William and Mary Quarterly, xi, 209
Euston
Mayer Genealogy, 147–9
Evans
Bean's Hist. Montgomery Co.,Pa.,919–21
Beidler Family of Pa., 267–72
Bronsdon Genealogy, 41
Dunwoody Genealogy (1899), 60–4
Evans Family of So. Car. (1905), 98 p.
Haines Family of N. J., 337–56

McAllister Family of N. C.
Peoria County, Ill., History, 646
Pound and Kester Genealogy, 326–36
Scales' History of Dover, N. H., 293–5
Stokes Family of N. J.
Treman Genealogy
Evarts
New Eng. Hist. Gen. Reg., lxi., 25–30
Eve
Penn. Mag. of History (1881), 19
Evelyn
Evelyn Genealogy (1881), 392 pages
Everett
Everett Genealogy (1902), 389 pages
Woods' History Albemarle Co., Va., 189
Eversfield
Baltimore Sun, April 9, 1905
Eves
Haines Family of N. J., 320–36
Stokes Family of N. J.
Ewer
Kewaunee, Wis., Owl for Sept., 1902
Ewing
Crumrine's Washington, Pa., 556–8, 730
McGavock Family of Va., 30, 68, 157
Eyerman
Eyerman Ancestry (1902), 92 pages
Eyre
Penn. Mag. of History (1879), 296
Treman Genealogy, 1494–1545, 1680–1799

Fairbanks
Fairbanks Family Quar. (1903), 54 pages
Hall Memoranda (1902), 184–7
Hill Genealogy (1904), 39
New Eng. Hist. Gen. Reg., lx, 152–4
Temple's History Framingham, 543
White Genealogy (1900), 462–6
Fairchild
Crayon's Rockaway, N. J., Records, 286
Seymour Conn,., History, 447–9
Fairfax
Baltimore Sun, Jan. 15, 1905
Richmond, Va., Times, Nov. 29, 1903
William and Mary Coll. Quar., xiii, 260
Fairfield
Allen's Hist. of Wenham, Mass., 136
Falconer
New Eng. Hist. Gen. Reg., lx, 21–3
Fanning
Fanning Genealogy (1905), 2 vols.
Wheeler's Hist. Stonington, Ct., 365–6
Farber
Crayon's Rockaway, N. J., Records, 133
Farley
Caldwell's Ipswich Soldiers (1902), 8 p.
Farley Genealogy (1897), 63 pages
Gulf States Hist. Mag., i, 428–31
Farman
Forman Genealogy, 60
Well's History of Newbury, Vt., 546–8
See Forman
Farnam
Woodruff's Litchfield, Ct.,Gen.Reg.,76–8

Farnham
Greene's Hist. Boothbay, Me., 524–6
Farnsworth
Tucker Genealogy (1901), 44–7
Tucker Genealogy, (1903)
Farnum
Carter's Hist. of Pembroke, N. H., ii, 90
Farr
Litchfield, Me., History (1897), 117
Tucker Genealogy (1901), 47
Farrand
Well's History of Newbury, Vt., 542
Farrar
Bronsdon Genealogy, 270
Crumrine's Hist. Washington, Pa., 929
McIlhany's Virginia Families (1903)
Va. Mag. of History, vii, 432–4; viii, 97,
    206–9, 424–7; ix, 203–5, 322–4; x, 89,
    206, 308–10
Whitmore Genealogy (1875), 37–42
Farrin
Litchfield, Me., History (1897), 118
Farrington
Humphreyville Genealogy, 39
Treman Genealogy
Farwell
Ramsdell's Hist. Milford, N. H., 682–4
Fatteral
Treman Genealogy
Fauntleroy
Baltimore Sun, Nov. 11, 1906
Richmond, Va., Times, April 29, 1906
Fauquier
William and Mary Coll. Quar., viii, 171–7
See Farquhar
Fawcett
Lea Genealogy (1906)
Fay
Temple's History Framingham, 545
Feake
Hull Genealogy (1904), 48, 56
Fearn
Lewis Family of Va., 1906
Fearne
Lea Genealogy (1906)
Feeter
Feeter Family of U. S. (1901), 125 pages
Fegeley
Bean's Hist. Montgomery Co., Pa., 603–5
Felch
Bent Progenitors (1903), 21–3
Felder
Felder Genealogy (1900), 12 pages
Fell
Robinson Family (1906), 129–32
Fellows
Carter's Hist. of Pembroke, N. H., ii,
    91
Chesebrough Genealogy, 335
Wheeler's Hist. Stonington, Ct., 367–8
Felrath
Peoria County, Ill., History, 647
Fenn
Strong Genealogy, 732
Fenno
Page Platter (1902), 3–7

Fenton
Bean's Hist. Montgomery Co., Pa., 814
Moore Family of Chester, Pa., 112
Temple's History Framingham, 546
Fenwick
Baltimore Sun, Oct. 30; Nov. 20, 1904;
    Dec. 16, 1906
Seller's Delaware Families, 23–75
Shourd's Fenwick's Colony, N. J., 9–13
Ferdon
Harvey's Hud. and Berg.Co.,N.J.,184–6
Ferguson
Benton (David) Ancestors, 1906
Deer Island, Me., Press for 1900
Stackpole's Hist. Kittery, Me., 372–5
Thornton Family (1905), 32–4
Willis' Old Eliot, Me. (1901), iv, 161
Fernald
Stackpole's Hist. Kittery, Me., 375–401
Willis' Old Eliot, Me., ii (1898), 89–91;
    iv (1901), 137–47
Ferrar
See under Farrar
Ferree
Shriver Genealogy, 15–7, 37–43
Swope Genealogy, 376–80
Ferrier
Ferrier Family of N. Y. (1906), 56 pages
Ferris
Peck Genealogy (1877), app. ix–xiii
Prindle Genealogy, 11
Ferry
Strong Genealogy, 1507–10
Ferson
Old Northwest Gen. Quar., viii, 27–30
Fessenden
Preble's Life of W. P. Fessenden (1871),
    24 pages
Fetters
Shourds' Fenwick's Colony, N. J., 303
Feurt
Evans' Scioto Co., Ohio, History, 1226–8
Fichter
Crayon's Rockaway, N. J., Rec., 226–31
Ficklin
Woods' Hist. Albemarle Co., Va., 192
Field
Field Family of N. J. (1876), 4 pages
Field Ancestors (1904), chart
Green's Culpeper County, Virg.
Jerseyman, x (1904), 7–9
Kellogg's Hist. Bernardston, Mass., 386–8
N. Y. Gen. and Biog. Record, xxxii, 6–11
Stackpole's Hist. Kittery, Me., 401
Stevenson Family of New Jersey, 145–7
Treman Genealogy
Fielder
Landrum's Spartanburg, S. C., 439–43
Fielding
Virg. Mag. of History, xi, 453–6; xii, 9–9
    102, 214
Filkin
N. Y. Gen. Biog. Rec., xxxiv, 109–11
Finley
Hanna's Ohio Valley Genealogies, 34–6
Pound and Kester Genealogy, 30–2

Finney
Finney Family of Mass. (1906), 13 pages
Lawson's Genealogy (1903), 247–68
McKean Genealogy (1902), 106
New Eng. Hist. Reg., lx, 67–73, 155–9
Firebaugh
Hanna's Ohio Valley Genealogies, 37
Fish
Fish Golden Wedding (1867), 104 pages
Wheeler's Hist. Stonington, Ct., 369–75
Fisher
Dedham, Mass., Hist. Reg., xiii, 5–7
Dotterer Genealogy
Gulf States Hist. Mag., i (1902), 134–8
Fisher Family of N. J. (1890), 159 pages
Greene's Hist. Boothbay, Me., 526
Keith's Pa. Prov. Councillors, pt. ii, 17–9
McIlhany's Virginia Families, 1903
Needham, Mass., Gazette, Mar. 26, 1864
Peoria County, Ill., History, 648
Phila. North American, Nov. 3, 1907
Ramsdell's Hist. Milford, N. H., 686–8
Treman Genealogy
Fisk
Allen's Hist. of Wenham, Mass., 133
Well's History of Newbury, Vt., 543
Fiske
Britton Ancestry (1901)
Temple's History Framingham, 547–50
Tucker Genealogy (1901), 59–62
Tucker Genealogy (1903)
White Genealogy (1900), 24–7
Fitch
Coddington Genealogy, 26–8
Fitch Fam., Reading, Mass. (1902), 23 p.
Harris Ancestry, 1898
New Eng. Hist. Gen. Reg., lv, 288–94, 400–7; lvi, 41–7
N. Y. Gen. and Biog. Rec., xxxiv, 155–8
Fite
Fite Family of Pa. (1907), 175 pages
Fitts
Alston Genealogy, 347–57
Stackpole's History of Kittery, Me., 402
Fitz
Richmond, Va., Times, Feb. 25, 1906
Fitz Hugh
Baltimore Sun, June 18, Dec. 17, 24 ,1905
Fitzhugh
Richmond, Va., Times, Aug. 23, 1903
Va. Mag. of History, vii, 425–7; viii, 91–5, 209–11, 314–7, 430–2; ix, 99–104
Fitz Randolph
Fitz Randolph MSS. in N. J. Hist. Soc. Lib.
Fladger
Evans Family of S. C., 1905
Flagg
Flagg Genealogy (1903), 228 pages
Temple's History Framingham, 550
Well's Genealogy (1903), 77
Flanders
Stuart Genealogy (1894), 70–3
Flanningham
Jennings Genealogy, ii, 367–71

Flatt
Clayton's Hist. Union Co., N. J., 286
Flegg
Temple's History Framingham, 550
Fleming
Lawson's Genealogy (1903), 1–114
Richmond, Va., Times, March 27, 1904
William and Mary Quarterly, xii, 45–7
Flemming
Newhall Ancestry, 150
Fletcher
Britton Ancestry, 1901
Bronsdon Genealogy, 110–4
Clayton's Hist. Union Co., N. J., 197
Warren and Jackson Genealogy (1903), 51–4
Flierboom
Harvey's Hud. and Berg. Co., N. J., 164
Flinn
Ramsdell's Hist. Milford, N. H., 689
Flint
Flint Family of Me. (1882), 29 pages
Flournoy
Habersham Gen.
Henry Family of Va. (1900), 41–51
Flower
Stiles' Wethersfield, Ct., ii, 323–26
Floyd
Richmond, Va., Times, Sept. 10, 1905
Fluck
Beidler Family of Pa., 278–83
Fly
Waterhouse Family of Me., 13–5
Foard
Lancaster Genealogy, 57–66
Fogelman
Gernhardt Genealogy, 201–27
Fogg
Fogg Family (1903), 49 pages
Stackpole's History Kittery, Me., 402–7
Willis' Old Eliot, Me. (1901), iv, 149–60; vi, 99–103
Folger
Hinchman's Nantucket Settlers, ii, 257
Follansbee
Hoyt's Salisbury, Mass., Families, 567
Follett
Stackpole's Hist. Kittery, Me., 409–10
Willis' Old Eliot, Me. (1901), iv, 147–9
Folsom
Eastman Genealogy (1901), 115–7
Folts
Herkimer Genealogy, 145
Folwell
Treman Genealogy
Fones
Glenn's Colonial Mansions, ii, 116
Hull Genealogy (1904), 25
Fontaine
Clarke's King Wm. Co., Va., Fams., 51–4
Fontaine Family of Va. (1899), 3 pages
Green's Culpeper County, Virg.
Maury's Huguenot Memoirs, 2d ed.(1872)
Maury's Huguenot Memoirs, 3d ed.,(1900)
Richmond, Va., Times, Aug. 9, 1903

Foote
Buell Genealogy, 100
Hodge Genealogy (1900), 354–6
Stiles' Wethersfield, Ct., ii, 326–29
Treman Genealogy
Footman
Habersham Gen.
Forbes
Stiles' Wethersfield, Ct., ii, 330–32
Ford
Carter's Hist. of Pembroke, N. H., ii, 98
Crayon's Rockaway, N. J., Rec., 89–93
Gray Genealogy (1889), 125–9
Lancaster Genealogy, 57–66
Stackpole's Hist. Kittery, Me., 407–9
Well's Hist. of Newbury, Vt., 545
Fordham
Le Baron Genealogy, 109
Fordyce
Crayon's Rockaway, N. J., Records, 169
Jennings Genealogy, ii, 42–5, 89–92
Foreman
Well's Hist. of Newbury, Vt., 546–8
See Farman
Forest
De Forest Genealogy (1900)
Forman
Forman Genealogy (1905)
Symmes' Tennent, N. J., Church, 427–31
Forney
Shriver Genealogy, 102–9
Swope Genealogy, 209–14, 376
Forrest
Baltimore Sun, July 24, 1904
Forrester
Temple's History Framingham, 551
Forster
Landrum's Hist. Spartanburg, S. C.
Forsyth
Forsyth Genealogy (1903), 90 pages
Mass. Magazine, i (1885), 147
Richmond, Va., Times, Sept. 29, 1903
Forward
Moore Genealogy (1903), 8, 15–7, 33, 64
Fosdick
Newhall Ancestry, 60–2
Foss
Dover, N. H., Enquirer for Dec. 5, 19, 1854, Jan. 4, 1855
Lundy Genealogy, 419
Parson's History of Rye, N. H., 344–52
Rice's New Hampshire Lake Region
Foster
Carter's Hist. of Pembroke, N. H., ii, 98
Hosmer's History of Deer Isle, Me., 51
Kellogg's Bernardston, Mass., 389–92
Landrum's Hist. Spartanburg, S. C., 285–94, etc.
Lawrence Genealogy, 1904
N. Y. Gen. Biog. Rec., xxxiv, 282–4
Peoria County, Ill., History, 649
Ramsdell's Hist. Milford, N. H., 691-6
Stackpole's Hist. Kittery, Me., 410–2
Stiles' Wethersfield, Ct., ii, 334
Temple's History Framingham, 552
Topliff Genealogy, 1906

Foulke
Lancaster Genealogy, 30, 115, 225–40
Foust
Stockard's History of Alamance, N. C.
Fowke
Baltimore Sun, Sept. 17, 1905; July 14, 1907
Richmond, Va., Times, Dec. 20, 1903
Fowle
Carter's Hist. of Pembroke, N. H., ii, 99
New Eng. Hist. Gen. Reg., xxiii, 109
Fowler
Fowler Family of Va. (1901), 327 pages
Fowlers of Eng. and Amer. (1904), 65 p.
Nash's Fifty Puritan Ancestors, 159–65
Old Northwest Gen. Quar., v, 133–48
Seymour, Conn., History, 455–6
Treman Genealogy
Fox
Kellogg's Bernardston, Mass., 392–5
Richmond, Va., Times, Nov. 5, 1905
Stiles' Wethersfield, Ct., ii, 335–7
William and Mary Coll. Quar., viii, 108
Foxworth
Evans Family of S. C. (1905), 30, 33
Foy
Stackpole's Hist. of Kittery, Me., 412–3
Foye
Parson's History of Rye, N. H., 352–4
Frambes
Hall's Hist. Atlantic City, N. J., 400–6
Francis
Francis' Genealogy (1900), 19 pages
Rich's Gen. Record (1896), 2, 7
Stiles' Wethersfield, Ct., ii, 337–49
Francisco
William and Mary Quar., xiv. 107–12
Frankland
S. C. Hist. Mag., iv, 39, 43, 52, 110
Franklin
Cornell Genealogy, 385–7
Richmond, Va., Times, Oct. 30, 1904
Frary
Blair Genealogy (1900), 163–5
Fraser
So. Car. Hist. Gen. Mag., v, 56–8
Frazer
Frazer's Persifor Frazer (1907), 410–5
Harris Ancestry, 1898
Frazier
Crumrine's Hist. Washington, Pa., 759
Peoria County, Ill., History, 649
Freas
Bean's Hist. Montgomery Co., Pa., 1153-5
Freeborne
Freeborne Family chart
Freeman
Clarke's King Wm. Co.,Va., Fams., 55–7
Clayton's Hist. Union Co., N. J., 255
Freeman Genealogy (1901), 54 pages
Freer
New Paltz Independent, Aug. 18, 1899, Dec. 26, 1902
Le Fevre's New Paltz, N. Y., 349–66, 527

N. Y. Gen. and Biog. Rec., xxxiii, 31–7;
xxxiv, 11–6, 132–8, 171–7, 273–7;
xxxv, 24–8, 123–7, 172–8, 241–4
Freese
Freese Family (1906), 78 pages
French
Britton Ancestry, 1901
Clayton's Hist. Union Co., N. J., 341
Connet Genealogy, 45–8
French Rec. in England (1896), 608 p.
Pound and Kester Genealogy, 170–7
Ramsdell's Hist. Milford, N. H., 696–701
Richmond, Va., Times, Jan. 22, 1905
Seymour, Conn., History, 449–55
Tucker Genealogy (1901), 263–8
Tucker Genealogy (1903)
White Genealogy (1900), 509
Frere
See Freer
Fretts
Beidler Family of Pa., 75–90
Fretwell
Woods' Hist. Albemarle Co., Va., 195–7
Fretz
Doylestown, Pa., Intelligencer, Sept. 12, 1903
Fretz Family Reunion (1900), 125 pages
Frey
Shriver Genealogy, 142–4
Frink
Putnam's Hist. Mag., iv (1894), 158
Stackpole's Hist. Kittery, Me., 437
Wheeler's Hist. Stonington, Ct., 376–380
Frisbie
New Eng. Hist. Gen. Reg., lviii, 178–84
Frissell
Temple's History Framingham, 553
Frizell
Temple's History Framingham, 553
Frizzell
Kellogg's Hist. Bernardston, Mass., 395–7
Frost
Essex Inst. Hist. Coll., xxxvii, 277–80;
xxxviii, 153–60
Gray Genealogy (1889), 144–7
Litchfield, Me., History (1897), 120–2
New Eng. Hist. and Gen. Reg., lv, 442;
lxi, 222–4
Quinby's New Eng. Fam. History Quar., i, 3–28
Salter Memorial (1900), 33–40
Sanford's Hist. Hopkinton, N. Y., 483–5
Stackpole's Hist. of Kittery, Me., 413–32
Temple's History Framingham, 554
Willis' Old Eliot, Me. (1901), iv, 168–76
Fry
Bird Family of Va. (1903), 13
Green's Culpeper County, Virg.
Willis' Old Eliot, Me. (1901), iv, 165
Woods' Hist. Albemarle Co., Va., 197
Frye
Stackpole's Hist. Kittery, Me., 432–7
Treman Genealogy
Fulford
Well's Ancestry (1900), 109–48

Fuller
Appleton's Diary of S. Fuller, 1894
Blish Genealogy, 294–307
Ellis Genealogy (1900), 13–6
Fuller Family (1902), 30 pages
Greene's Hist. Boothbay, Me., 527
Hayford Genealogy, 139–41
Jennings Genealogy, ii, 634
New Eng. Gen. Reg., lv, 192–6, 410–6
N. Y. Gen. and Biog. Rec., xxxiii, 171–9,
211–3, 227–35; xxxiv, 17–23, 124–32,
182–90, 267–71; xxxv, 48–56, 112–9,
159–64, 244–7; xxxvi, 33–8
Ramsdell's Hist. Milford, N. H., 702
Temple's History Framingham, 555
Well's Hist. of Newbury, Vt., 549
Fullerton
Greene's Hist. Boothbay, Me., 472–4
Newburgh, N. Y., Papers, xiii, 199–209
Fulton
Fulton Family of Pa. (1900), 246 pages
Hanna's Ohio Valley Genealogies, 39J
Well's Hist. of Newbury, Vt., 550
Funk
Funk Genealogy (1899), 874 pages
Furbish
Stackpole's Hist. Kittery, Me., 437–43
Furman
Furmans of So. Car. (1897), 3 pages
Fyfe
New Eng. Hist. Gen. Reg., lvi, 167–72

Gable
Gable Family (1906), 9 pages
Gabler
Peoria County, Ill., History, 651
Gage
Dover, N. H., Enquirer for Nov. 26, 1863
Gager
Henry Family (1905), 54
Woolsey Genealogy
Gaines
Richmond, Va., Times, Sept. 11, 1905
Gaither
Warfield's Maryland, 107–9, 419–28
Gale
Carter's Hist. Pembroke, N. H., ii, 115–7
Temple's History Framingham, 557
Well's Genealogy (1903), 79
Gallaher
Baltimore Sun, Jan. 29; Feb. 12, 1905;
Oct. 28; Nov. 4, 1906
West Va. Hist. Mag., i, pt. iv, 29
Gallot
Temple's History Framingham, 557
Galloway
Keith's Pa. Prov. Councillors, pt. ii, 227–34
Gallup
Stevens Family of Boston (1906), 25
Temple's History Framingham, 557
Wheeler's Hist. Stonington, Ct., 381–96
Galpin
Stiles' Wethersfield, Ct., ii, 351

Galt
William and Mary Coll. Quar., viii, 259–62

Gamage
Gamage Genealogy (1906), 78 pages

Gamble
Gambles Family Data (1906), 202–21
Sherrard Genealogy, 372–80

Gambrill
Warfield's Maryland, 373

Gano
Gano Pedigree (1900), 2 leaves

Gantt
Baltimore Sun, Oct. 1, 8, 15, 29, 1905

Gard
Crayon's Rockaway, N. J., Records, 289

Gardiner
Baltimore Sun, Mar. 18, 25; May 6, 1906
Genung Family of L. I.
Haines Family of N. J., 375–9
N. J. Hist. Soc. Proc., Ser. 2, vii, 255–67
Keith's Pa.Prov.Councillors,pt.ii,289–94
New Eng. Hist. Gen. Reg., lx, 270
Stokes Family of N. J.

Gardner
Essex Inst. Hist. Collections, xxxvii, 81–104, 201–48, 369–92; xxxviii, 73–96, 209–24, 289–312, 369–89; xxxix, 33–56, 169–84, 349–64; xl, 33–48, 161–76, 257–72, 353–74
Hinchman's Nantucket Settlers, ii, 260
Lowell Genealogy, 60–3
Newhall Ancestry, 100
Small Family of Penn., 233

Garfield
Well's Genealogy (1903), 81–3

Garland
Parson's History of Rye, N. H., 356–67
Woods' Hist. Albemarle Co.,Va., 198–201

Garlington
Chappell Genealogy (1900), 330–41

Garner
Beidler Family of Penn., 238–45
Robertson Family of Va.

Garnet
Gernhardt Genealogy, 97–138

Garnett
Green's Culpeper County, Virg.

Garnhart
Gernhardt Genealogy

Garrabrant
Harvey's Hud. and Berg. Co., N. J., 164

Garratt
Smedley Genealogy, 171–3, 282

Garrett
Woods' Hist. Albemarle Co., Va., 201–3

Garrigus
Crayon's Rockaway, N. J., Rec., 94–6, 289

Garth
Woods' Hist. Albemarle Co., Va., 203–5

Gary
Evans Family of S. C. (1905)

Gaskel
Allen Family of Nantucket, 1905

Gaskell
Glenn's Colonial Mansions, ii, 307

Gaskins
Baltimore Sun, Dec. 18, 1904
William and Mary Quarterly, xi, 276–9

Gassaway
Baltimore Sun, July 3, 1904
Warfield's Maryland, 170–4, 380–5

Gast
Morr Genealogy, 119–22

Gaston
Hanna's Ohio Valley Genealogies, 40–8

Gatchell
Litchfield, Me., History (1897), 123–8

Gates
Gates Fam. of Stow, Mass. (1907), 147 p.
Temple's History Framingham, 558
Treman Genealogy

Gause
Evans Family of S. C. (1905)

Gautier
Harvey's Hud. and Berg. Co., N. J., 166

Gaylord
Crissey's Hist. of Norfolk, Ct., 544

Gayman
See Gehman

Geatrell
Bean's Hist. Montgomery Co., Pa., 914

Geddes
Small Family of Penn., 1905

Gedney
Newburgh, N. Y., Papers (1905), 121–30

Gehman
Pennsylvania-German, vii, 301

Geisinger
Beidler Family of Pa., 49–52

Gentry
Woods' Hist. Albemarle Co., Va., 205

Genung
Genung Genealogy (1906), 711 pages

George
McGinness and Scott Genealogy, 271–81
Well's Hist. of Newbury, Vt., 552–5

Gerard
Seymour, Conn., History, 456

German
Carter's Hist. of Pembroke, N. H., ii, 122

Gernerd
See Gernhart

Gernhart
Gernhart Genealogy (1904), 315 pages

Gerould
Gerould Gen. (1900), 10 pages
Old Northwest Quarterly, ix, 255

Gerrish
Gerrish Genealogy, 2d ed. (1901), 14 p.
Lowell Genealogy, 9–11
Scales' Hist. of Dover, N. H., 310–4
Stackpole's Hist. Kittery, Me., 443–9
Willis' Old Eliot, Me., v (1902), 2–4

Gibbes
Alston Genealogy, 57

Gibbon
Shourd's Fenwick's Colony, N. J., 107

Gibbs
Lundy Genealogy, 261–4, 420
Temple's History Framingham, 559–62

Woodruff's Litchfield, Ct.Gen.Reg.,85–91

Gibson
Duncan and Gibson Families of Pa. (1905), 44 pages
Gibson Genealogy (1900), 542 pages
Lea Genealogy, 1906
Sanford's Hopkinton, N. Y., 489–92
Well's His. of Newbury, Vt., 556

Giffin
Giffin's Report and Gen. (1881), 12 p.

Gilbert
Carter's Hist. Pembroke, N. H., ii, 123
Converse Genealogy (1905), 739–43
Gilbert Family of Hartford, Ct. (1902), 17 pages
Hamlin Genealogy (1900), 172–5
Le Baron Genealogy, 103–6, 228
Litchfield, Me., History (1897), 129
Richardson Genealogy, 1906
Seymour, Conn., History, 459–60
Stiles' Wethersfield, Ct., ii, 353–5
Swope Genealogy, 380
Tucker Genealogy (1901), 126–34
Tucker Genealogy (1903)
White Genealogy (1900), 195–204, 214–6

Gile
Carter's Hist. of Pembroke, N. H., ii, 123
Forrest Genealogy, 95–111
Greene's Hist. Boothbay, Me., 529–32
Ramsdell's Hist. Milford, N. H., 704–6

Gill
Peoria County, Ill., History, 652
Tucker Genealogy (1901), 30–3
Warfield's Maryland, 130

Gillett
Moore Genealogy (1903), 41
Treman Genealogy

Gillette
Seymour, Conn., History, 457–9

Gilliam
Richmond, Va.,Times, Dec. 18, 1904

Gillingham
Burlington, N. J., Democrat, Jan. 2, 1903
Gillingham Genealogy (1901), 117 pages

Gillpatrick
New Eng. Hist. and Gen. Reg., liv, 100

Gilman
Carter's Hist. Pembroke, N. H., ii, 124–8

Gilmer
Page Genealogy, 2d ed. (1893), 221
Richmond, Va., Times, June 18, 1905
Woods' Hist. Albemarle Co., Va., 206–8

Gilmore
Hanna's Ohio Valley Genealogies, 48
McKinney Family of Pa., 39–47

Gilpatrick
Shepardson Genealogy (1907), 8

Gilpin
Baltimore Sun, March 19, 1905
Stern's Our Kindred, 75, 126–31

Gilyard
Seymour, Conn., History, 456–7

Girty
Butterfield's Hist. Girtys (1890), 426 pp.

Gissage
William and Mary Quarterly, x, 126–8

Givens
Boogher's Virg. Gleanings (1903), 224–6

Gladding
Bristol County R. I. Records
Gladding Family (1865), chart
Gladding Genealogy

Glass
Litchfield, Me., History (1897), 130–2

Glassell
Green's Culpeper County, Virg., i, 60

Glattfelder
Glattfelder Genealogy (1901), 124 pages

Gleason
Old Northwest Quarterly, iii (1900), 161–7; iv (1901), 7; v (1902), 82–4, 130–2
Temple's History Framingham, 563–5

Gleim
Egle's Dauphin County, Pa. (1883), 240

Gleison
Temple's History Framingham, 563–5
See also Gleason

Glendening
See under Clendenin

Glesing
Temple's History Framingham, 563–5
See also under Gleason

Glezen
Temple's History Framingham, 563–5
See also under Gleason

Glidden
Carter's Hist. of Pembroke, N. H., ii, 129

Gloninger
Swope Genealogy, 45–67

Glover
Temple's History Framingham, 565
Vawter Family of Virginia, 352–61

Goble
Crayon's Rockaway, N. J., Records, 135
Goble Family MSS. in N. J. Hist. Soc.
Newhall Ancestry, 135
Pound and Kester Genealogy, 125–36

Godbold
Evans Family of S. C., 1905

Goddard
Britton Ancestry, 1901
Flagg Genealogy, 1903
Pickering's Nathaniel Goddard (1906), 272 pages
Temple's History Framingham, 565–7

Goding
Goding Genealogy (1906), 175 pages

Godsoe
Stackpole's Hist. Kittery, Me., 449

Goetschins
Harvey's Hud. and Berg. Co., N. J., 166

Goff
Stiles' Wethersfield, Ct., ii, 356–68

Goffe
Dexter's Life of Whalley and Goffe (1876), 32 pages

Going
Old Northwest Gen. Quar., vii, 244

Gold
Burr Genealogy, 1901

Goldin
Ferrier Genealogy, 47
Goldsborough
Keith's Pa. Prov. Councillors, pt. ii, 92–4, 403–6
Goldsmith
Litchfield, Me., History (1897), 132
Goldstone
Newhall Ancestry, 157
Goldthwaite
Salem Hist. and Gen. Magazine, 124–8
Gooch
Hoyt's Salisbury, Mass., Families, 573
Virg. Mag. of History, iii, 113
William and Mary Quar. (1896), 110–2
Woods' Hist. Albemarle Co., Va., 208–10
Goodale
Britton Ancestry (1901)
Well's Genealogy (1903), 85
Goodell
Sanford's Hist. Hopkinton, N. Y., 485–9
Goodenow
See under Goodnow
Goodman
Woods' Hist. Albemarle Co., Va., 210
Goodno
Clark Fam. of Vermont (1905), 25, 43–6, 50
Goodnow
Temple's History Framingham, 567–9
Goodrich
Old Northwest Quarterly, ix, 259
Stackpole's Hist. Kittery, Me., 452–3
Stiles' Wethersfield, Ct., ii, 369–90
Treman Genealogy
Goodridge
Gamble's Family Data (1906), 136–8
Goodrich Gen. (1889), 356–65
Goodwill
Strong Genealogy, 43
Goodwin
Hopkins, Goodwin and Brown Families (1895), 19 pages
Le Baron Genealogy, 49, 56, 116–39, 251–88
Litchfield, Me., History (1897), 133–8
Ramsdell's Hist. Milford, N. H., 706–9
Richmond, Va., Times, March 25, 1906
Stackpole's Hist. Kittery, Me., 453–61
Treman Genealogy
Well's Hist. of Newbury, Vt., 557–9
William and Mary Coll. Mag., 1897, 1899
Willis' Old Eliot, Me., v (1902), 7–9
Woodruff's Litchfield, Ct., Gen. Reg., 96–9
Goold
Stackpole's Hist. Kittery, Me., 461–6
Willis' Old Eliot, Me., v (1902), 12
Goolsby
Woods' Hist. Albemarle Co., Va., 211
Gordon
Baltimore Sun, May 7, 1905
Carter's Hist. of Pembroke, N. H., ii, 130
Crayon's Rockaway, N. J., Rec., 232–8
Litchfield, Me., Hist. (1897), 138
Richmond, Va., Times, Dec. 13, 27, 1903

Symmes' Tennent, N. J., Church, 424–7
William and Mary Quarterly, xi, 11
Gore
Warden Genealogy, 35
Wheeler's Hist. Stonington, Ct., 397–9
Gorham
Gorham Family of Hardwick (1902), 8 p.
Gorham Fam. of Ct. and Vt. (1903), 6 p.
Gorham Family of Plymouth (1904), 7 p.
Hinchman's Nantucket Set., ii, 262–9
New Eng. Hist. Gen. Reg., lvi, 75–80; lvii, 325–7; lix, 91–5
Gorton
Reynolds Genealogy (1903), 28
Gosnold
Gosnold Ancestry (1904), 34 pages
Goss
Clark Family of Virginia (1905)
Goss Family of Virginia (1905), 141 p.
Towle Family of N. H., 129–36
Parson's History of Rye, N. H., 367–73
Ramsdell's Hist. Milford, N. H., 710
White Genealogy (1900), 274–8
Woods' Hist. Albemarle Co., Va., 212
Gottschall
Pennsylvania-German, vii, 281–3
Gotwals
Funk Genealogy
Gould
Burr Genealogy, 1901
Essex Antiquarian, iv (1900), 92
Ford's History of Clinton, Mass., 110–2
Gamble's Family Data (1906), 119–29
Gould Family of Ontario (1902), 15 pages
N. Y. Gen. Biog. Record, xxxvii, 90
Pierce's Indian History
White Genealogy (1900), 196–344
Gourdin
Charleston, S. C., Sunday News, 1904
Gowell
Handy's Hist. of Sumner, Me., 74–8
Litchfield, Me., History (1897), 140
Stackpole's Hist. Kittery, Me., 466–8
Willis' Old Eliot, Me., v (1902), 11
Gowen
Stackpole's Hist. Kittery, Me., 468–71
Willis' Old Eliot, Me., v (1902), 5–7
Gower
Litchfield, Me., History (1897), 142
Graeme
Keith's Pa. Prov. Councillors, pt. ii, 157–66
Gragg
Peoria County, Ill., History, 653
Graham
Graham Papers of No. Car. (1904)
McAllister Family of N. C.
McGavock Family of Va.
Treman Genealogy
Grandine
Lawson Genealogy (1903)
Grannis
Grannis Genealogy (1906), 55 pages
Grant
Buell Genealogy, app., iii–xvi, etc.
Crissey's History of Norfolk, Ct., 556
Grant Revolutionary Ancestors, 8 pages

Litchfield, Me., History (1897), 143
Stackpole's Hist. Kittery, Me., 471-4
Strong Genealogy
Treman Genealogy
Well's History of Newbury, Vt., 560
Wheeler's Hist. Stonington, Ct., 400-4
Willis' Old Eliot, Me., v (1902), 15
Woodruff's Litchfield, Ct., Gen.Reg.,83-5
Graves
Graves Ancestry (1895), 17 pages
Lawson's Genealogy (1903), 283
Litchfield, Me., Hist. (1897), 144
New Eng. Hist. Gen. Reg., lvi, 260-4
Pocumtuck Valley, Mass., Hist., 495-7
William and Mary Quarterly, xii, 116
Wood Genealogy (1901), 57
Gray
Deer Island, Me., Press for 1899, Art. 22
Gray Genealogy (1889), 195 pages
Gray Reunion at Sedgwick, Me. (1903),
  52 pages
Greene's History Boothbay, Me., 532
Kellogg's Bernardston, Mass., 400-2
Litchfield, Me., History (1897), 145-7
Moore Family of Chester, Pa., 135
Virg. Mag. of History, xi, 210
Walker Family of Virginia, 295
William and Mary Quar., xii, 267-71
Greeley
Greeley Fam. of Salisbury (1905), 911 p.
Green
Alston Genealogy, 506
Baltimore Sun, Dec. 31, 1905
Bellows Falls Times, 1905
Colby Family of N. H., 69-77
Deer Island, Me., Press for 1900
Gray Genealogy (1889), 14-20
Green Family of Virginia, 1900
Greene
Greene Fam. of Lowell (1904), 227 pages
Green Family of R. I. (1907), 14 pages
Greenlaw's Genealogical Advertiser, iv
  (1901), 51
Hosmer's Hist. of Deer Isle, Me., 65
Jones Genealogical Hist. (1900), 28-33
Kellogg's Bernardston, Mass., 402-6
Lawrence Genealogy, 1904
New Eng. Hist. Gen. Reg., lvii, 328
Peoria County, Ill., History, 653
Ramsdell's Hist. Milford, N. H., 712-4
Richmond, Va., Times, March 26, 1905
Robertson Family of Va.
Smedley Genealogy, 129, 228-33
Stackpole's Hist. Kittery, Me., 474-5
Treman Genealogy
Va. Mag. of History, viii, 77-80, 213-6,
  317, 421-4
Willis' Old Eliot, Me., v (1902), 13
Greenawalt
Egle's Dauphin Co., Pa. (1883), 240-1
Greene
Chesebrough Genealogy, 52
Green's Culpeper County, Virg.
Greene Fam. of Boston (1901), 148 p.
Greene Fam. of Plymouth (1903), 11 p.
Greene Family of R. I. (1903), 892 pages

Greene's History Boothbay, Me., 533
New Eng. Hist. Gen. Reg., lvii, 17-21
Newhall Ancestry, 54-9
Reynolds Family (1903), 24
Sanford's Hist. Hopkinton, N. Y., 492
Greenlaw
Deer Island, Me., Press for Feb. 15, 1900
Hosmer's Hist. of Deer Isle, Me., 43, 62
Greenleaf
Clark's James Greenleaf (1901), 355 p.
Greene's Hist. Boothbay, Me., 534-7
Lunt's Sermon on Thos. Greenleaf
Treman Genealogy
Greenman
Wheeler's Hist. Stonington, Ct., 405-7
Greenough
Bronsdon Genealogy, 59-64
Shannon Genealogy, 528-37
Greenwood
Bronsdon Genealogy, 37-40
Greenwood Col. Services (1899), 11 p.
Peoria County, Ill., History, 654
Temple's History Framingham, 570
Warren Genealogy (1903), 148-50
Greer
Byram Genealogy (1898), 46-55, 58
Gregg
Evans Family of S. C., 1905
Gregg Family Origin (1897), 9 pages
Gregory
Baltimore Sun, Jan. 15, 1905
Clarke's King Wm. Co., Va., Fam. 58-61
New Eng. Hist. and Gen. Reg., lv, 343
Richmond, Va., Times, Nov. 20, Dec. 4,
  1904
Temple's History Framingham, 571
William and Mary Quarterly, xi, 266
Greig
Well's History of Newbury, Vt., 561
See Gregg
Grenaway
New Eng. Hist. Gen. Reg. (1878), 55
Gresham
Richmond, Va., Times
Grey
Stackpole's Hist. Kittery, Me., 475-7
Gridley
Benton Genealogy (1901), 101
Canton, Mass., Memorial (1877), 6
Griffin
Griffin Fam. Fishkill, N. Y. (1900), chart
Griffin Fam. of Del. (1905), 235 pages
N. Y. Gen. Biog. Rec., xxxvi, 197-9;
  xxxvii, 54
Rees Family of Del. (1904), 38
Treman Genealogy
Griffis
Treman Genealogy
Griffith
Baltimore Sun, Feb. 12, 1905
Griffith Family of Md.
Griffith Fam. of Chester, Pa. (1905), 85 p.
Jenkins Family of Pa. (1904), 119
Meriwether Genealogy (1899), 151-62
Powell and Griffith Gen. (1866), 119 pp.
Smedley Genealogy, 216

Warfield's Maryland, 347–51

Griffitts
Keith's Pa. Prov. Councillors, ii, 184

Griggs
Clayton's Hist. Union Co., N. J., 780

Grigsby
Baltimore Sun, May 21, 1905; Oct. 6, 1907
Grigsby Genealogy (1905), 8 pages
Grigsby Genealogy, 2d ed. (1905), 8 p.
McCormick Genealogy

Grimes
Cumming Family of Md. (1905), chart
Stiles' Wethersfield, Ct., ii, 392

Grimmesey
Hunt Family of N. J. (1906), 99–104

Grinnan
Green's Culpeper County, Virg.

Grinnell
Whittemore's New England Ancestors (1900), 100 pages

Griswold
Buell Genealogy, 27
Clarke's King Wm. Co., Va., Fams., 61–3
Edson Ancestry (1901), 8
Hall Memoranda (1902), 149–59
Hyde and Dana Genealogy (1904), 8–11
Nash's 50 Puritan Ancestors, 102–5, 124
Old Northwest Gen. Quarterly, vi, 171–3; x, 127–9, 149–53
Stiles' Wethersfield, Ct., ii, 394–404
Woodruff's Litchfield,Ct.,Gen.Reg.,93–6

Groden
Martindale's Hist. of Byberry, Pa., 250

Gross
Deer Island, Me., Press for 1900

Grosscup
Penn. German (1907), 74

Grosvenor
Evan's Scioto Co., Ohio, History, 1230

Grout
Temple's History Framingham, 572
Treman Genealogy

Grove
Egle's Dauphin Co., Pa. (1883), 241–2

Grover
Greene's Hist. Boothbay, Me., 537
Litchfield, Me., History (1897), 147
Noyes' Hampstead, N. H., ii, 762–7

Groves
Alston Genealogy, 389–402
Litchfield, Me., History (1897), 148

Grow
Well's History of Newbury, Vt., 562–4

Growdon
Keith's Pa.Prov.Councillors,pt.ii,223–35

Grubb
Pennsylvania-German, vii, 283–6
White Genealogy (1900), 351–5

Grymes
Baltimore Sun, Oct. 22, 29, 1905

Gubtail
Stackpole's Hist. Kittery, Me., 481–2

Guiford
Coddington Family of N. J.

Guerard
Guerard Family (1901), chart

Guerrant
William and Mary Quarterly, xi, 206

Guiford
Coddington Genealogy, 21

Guild
Seymour, Conn., Hist., 460–2

Guisbert
Dotterer Genealogy

Gunnison
Stackpole's Hist. Kittery, Me., 477–81
Willis' Old Eliot, Me., v (1902), 15–7

Gunton
Gunton, Dr. Wm., Life of (1878), 46 p.

Gustin
Gustin Ancestry (1900), 136 pages

Gutterson
Ramsdell's Hist. Milford, N. H., 715–22

Gwynn
Baltimore Sun, Nov. 12, 19, 26, 1905

Haas
Penn.-German, vii, 350–2

Habersham
Habersham Genealogy (1901), 222 pages

Hack
Hack Genealogy (1894), 4 pages

Hackett
New Eng. Hist. Gen. Reg. (1879), 9–11

Hadley
American Ancestry, xii, 201
Colby Family of N. H., 77–9

Hadlock
Ramsdell's Hist. Milford, N. H., 722

Haff
Bunker's Long Island, N. Y., Gens.
Crall Ancestry

Hafford
Hayford Genealogy, 51–70

Hagaman
Fisher Family of New Jersey, 43–91

Hagar
Temple's History Framingham, 573

Hager
Temple's History Framingham, 573

Haggett
Carter's Hist. of Pembroke, N. H., ii, 131

Haight
Genung Family of L. I.
Haight Family of Canada (1899), 71 p.
Hoyt Genealogy (1871), 286–617
See Hoyt

Haines
Haines Genealogy (1902), 400 pages
Hall's Hist. of Greenland, N. H., 175–6
Stokes Family of N. J.

Hait
Hoyt Genealogy (1871), 292–604
See Hoyt

Hakes
Peoria County, Ill., History, 757

Haldeman
Barber Genealogy (1890), 91–4
Penn.-German, vi (July, 1905), 291

Hale
Bellows Falls Times, 1905

44

Dover, N. H., Enquirer, March 22, May 10, 1877
Hale Family of Newburyport (1902), 117 pages
Hale Family of Conn. (1907), 13 pages
Johnston's Biog. of Nathan Hale, 1901
Kellogg's Bernardston, Mass., 407–21
Litchfield, Me., History (1897), 149
New Eng. Hist. Gen. Reg., lxi, 177–85
Stiles' Wethersfield, Ct., ii, 405–8
Well's History of Newbury, Vt., 564–8
Haley
McPike's British Archive Extracts (1906), 37 pages
Peoria County, Ill., History, 655
Stackpole's Hist. Kittery, Me., 483–7
Wheeler's Hist. Stonington, Ct., 408–10
Hall
Baltimore Sun, Oct. 7, 14, Dec. 23, 1906
Carter's Hist. of Pembroke, N. H., ii, 132
Crayon's Rockaway, N. J., Records, 290
Clayton's Hist. Union Co., N. J., 638–40
Converse Genealogy (1905), 100–5
Dunwoody Genealogy (1899), 142–4
Emory's Col. Families of Md., 223–6
Forrest Genealogy, 54–74
Hall Fam. of Wallingford (1902), 60 p.
Hall Genealogy (1902), 244 pages
Hall Family Ancestors (1904), 29 pages
Hamlin Genealogy (1900), 79, 111
Hanna's Ohio Valley Genealogies, 49
Litchfield, Me., History (1897), 150–4
McGinness and Scott Genealogy, 146–56
Parson's History of Rye, N. H., 376
Peoria County, Ill., History, 656
Prindle Genealogy, 21–3
Ramsdell's Hist. Milford, N. H., 723–6
Roberts Family of Maine, 24–8
Scales' History of Dover, N. H., 255–66
Smedley Genealogy, 142
So. Car. Hist. Mag., iii (1902), 31–4
Treman Genealogy
Warfield's Maryland, 99
Woodruff's Litchfield, Conn., Gen. Reg., 100–3
Hallam
Wheeler's Hist. Stonington, Ct., 411–3
Halley
McPike's British Archive Extracts (1906), 37 pages
N. Y. Gen. and Biog. Rec., xxxiv, 52–6, 106–8
Well's History of Newbury, Vt., 569
Halliday
Thompson Genealogy (1907), 280
Halligan
Seymour, Conn., History, 462–3
Hallock
Hallock Genealogy (1906), 83 pages
N. Y. Gen. Biog. Rec., xxxvii, 55–7
Treman Genealogy
Hallowell
Bean's Hist. of Montgomery Co. Pa., 688–93, 909, 988
Halsey
Sayre Genealogy, 217–9

Halsted
Halsted Genealogy (1896), 69 pages
Ham
Dover, N. H., Enquirer for Sept. 22, 1859
Hamblett
Ramsdell's Hist. Milford, N. H., 727–9
Hamel
Bean's Hist. Montgomery Co., Pa., 696
Hamer
Bean's Hist. Montgomery Co., Pa., 649
Robinson Family (1906), 132–8
Hamill
Kittochtinny Mag. (1905), i, 378–83
Hamilton
Crayon's Rockaway, N. J., Records, 291
Hanna's Ohio Valley Genealogies, 50–2
Jenkins Fam. Pa. (1904), 120–4, 156–61
Keith's Pa.Prov.Councillors,pt.ii,120–54
McCormick Genealogy
Penn. Magazine of History, xxv, 134–6
Roberts Family of Maine, 89–100
Stackpole's Hist. Kittery, Me., 488–91
Hamlin
Abbott, Jas. S. Memorial (1905), 41 p.
Hamlin Fam. of Middletown (1900), 479 pages
Hamlin Fam. of Barnstable (1902), 1411 pages
William and Mary Quarterly, xi, 59
Hammans
Smedley Genealogy, 53
Hammatt
Le Baron Genealogy, 68, 161–4
Hammond
American Ancestry, xii, 183
Baltimore Sun, Oct. 4, 1903; Aug. 13, 1905
Colby Family of N. H., 86–95
Hammond Genealogy (1902), 685 pages
Keith's Pa.Prov.Councillors,pt.ii,149–51
Le Baron Genealogy, 141–3
Old Eliot, Me., Magazine, i, No. 1
Sinnott Genealogy
Stackpole's Hist. Kittery, Me., 492–9
Tucker Genealogy (1901), 57–9
Tucker Genealogy (1903)
Warfield's Maryland, 178–84
Wells Family of Ohio (1892), 62–4
White Genealogy (1900), 336–9
Willis' Old Eliot, Me., v (1902), 17–29
Hammons
Stackpole's Hist. Kittery, Me., 491–2
Hamner
Woods' Hist. Albemarle Co., Va., 214–6
Hampton
Landrum's Hist. Spartanburg, S. C., 240–52
Smedley Genealogy, 109, 200–2
Hance
N. Y. Gen. and Biog. Rec., xxxv, 6–15, 127–35, 184–90, 249–56; xxxvi, 17–22, 102–4
Hancock
Ferrier Genealogy, 23–6
Lamb Family of N. J. (1904), 61
Richmond, Va., Times, May 6, 1906

Stokes Genealogy, 283
Hancox
Chesebrough Genealogy, 68
Wheeler's Hist. Stonington, Ct., 414-5
Hand
De Camp Genealogy (1896), 23-45
Nash's Fifty Puritan Ancestors, 112-21
New Eng. Hist. Gen. Reg., lv, 31-4
Haney
Lawson Genealogy, 1903
Hankinson
Wintermute Gen., 44-8
Hanks
Missouri Historical Review, i, 72-84
Hanmer
Stiles' Wethersfield, Ct., ii, 410-2
Hanna
American Ancestry, xii, 178
Hanna's Ohio Valley Genealogies, 52-8
Hanscom
Litchfield, Me., History (1897), 154
Stackpole's Hist. Kittery, Me., 499-509
Willis' Old Eliot, Me., v (1902), 39-50
Hanson
Baltimore Sun, July 29; Aug. 5, 12, 1906
Dover, N. H., Enquirer for Feb. 3, 1876
Narragansett Sun of Windham, Me.,
  March to May (1900), 9 numbers
Waterhouse Family of Me., 8
Hardaway
Cody Genealogy, 10-5
Hardaway Family (1906), 55 pages
Hardenbergh
Le Fevre's Hist. of New Paltz, N. Y.,
  455-63
Hardin
Woods' Hist. Albemarle Co., Va., 217
Harding
Bean's Hist. Montgomery Co., Pa., 1014
Le Baron Genealogy, 192
McGavock Family of Va., 74
Hardison
Stackpole's Hist. Kittery, Me., 510
Hardon
Field-Hardon Family (1904), Broadside
Hardy
American Ancestry, xii, 193
Deer Island, Me., Press for 1899, Art. 12,
  13, 14
Hosmer's History of Deer Isle, Me., 66-8
Temple's History Framingham, 575
Hardyman
Va. Magazine of History, vii, 354
William and Mary Quarterly, v, 272; xi,
  47-50
Hare
Keith's Pa.Prov.Councillors,pt.ii,129-35
Harger
Anderson and Perrine Family, 100-3
Seymour, Conn., History. 463-4
Haring
Harvey's Hud. and Berg. Co., N. J., 61-3
Labaw's Preakness, N. J., History, 65-7
Harlan
Lea Genealogy, 1906
Small Family of Penn., 220

Harleston
So. Car. Hist. Mag., iii (1902), 150-73
Harley
Bean's Hist. Montgomery Co.,Pa.,782-4
Harmanson
Yeardley Genealogy, 10-3
Harmon
Harmon MSS., in Suffield, Conn., town
  clerk's office
Walker Family of Virginia, 364
Harness
Van Meter's Va. and Ky. Fams., 171-3
Harper
Bean's Hist.Montgomery Co.,Pa.,629-31
Woods' Hist. Albemarle Co., Va., 218
Harriman
Crayon's Rockaway, N. J., Rec., 239-42
Litchfield, Me., History (1897), 155-8
Harrington
Britton Ancestry, 1901
Bronsdon Genealogy, 273
Newhall Ancestry, 151
Temple's History Framingham, 570
White Genealogy (1900), 478-85
Harris
Amer. Hist. Mag., iv (1899), 43
Greene's History Boothbay, Me., 538
Harris Ancestry (1898), 69 pages
Harris Family of Penn. (1903), 135 p.
Harris Fam. of Machias, Me. (1903),19 p.
Harris Fam. of N. H. (1907), 31 pages
Stiles' Wethersfield, Ct., ii, 412-6
Stuart Genealogy (1894), 89-107
Topliff Genealogy, 1906
Treman Genealogy
Virg. Mag. of History, iv (1897), 248
Woods' Hist. Albemarle Co., Va., 219-22
Harrison
Amer. Monthly Magazine, xix, 139-45
Baltimore Sun, April 30, 1905; Sept. 2;
  Dec. 16, 23, 30, 1906
Bougher's Virg. Gleanings (1903), 373-9
Evans Family of S. C., 1905
Glenn's Colonial Mansions, i, 401-29
Hanna's Ohio Valley Genealogies, 58
Keith's Pa.Prov.Councillors,pt.ii, 44-6
Page Genealogy, 2d ed. (1893), 143, 263-
  4, 266-9
Richmond, Va., Times, June 24, July 29,
  1906
Treman Genealogy
Va. Magazine of History, vii, 357
Woodruff's Litchfield, Ct., Gen. Reg.,
  103-7
Harry
Bean's Hist. Montgomery Co., Pa., 717
Roberts' Plymouth, Pa., Meeting,218-21
Harshman
Winters Genealogy, 32-5, 42, 59
Hart
Hamlin Genealogy(1900), 112-3, 149-53
Hart Fam. of Ipswich (1900), 8 pages
Harts' Life of W. A. Hart, 5-9
Hart Genealogy (1904), 631 pages
Stiles' Wethersfield, Ct., ii, 417
Wheeler's Hist. Stonington, Ct., 416-7

Woods' Hist. Albemarle Co., Va., 223

Hartman
Penn.-German, vii, 344–50; viii, 160–9, 259–67

Hartshorn
Genung Genealogy, 36–41
Ramsdell's Hist. Milford, N. H., 730–2
Treman Genealogy

Hartshorne
Gamble's Family Data (1906), 158

Harvey
Caldwell Family of Prov. (1906)
Harvey's Hud. and Berg. Co., N. J., 73–8

Harvie
Richmond, Va., Times, July 8, 1906
Woods' Hist. Albemarle Co., Va., 224
West Virg. Hist. Mag., ii, 44

Harwood
Warfield's Maryland, 96–9
William and Mary Coll. Quar., x, 198; xi, 264

Hasbrouck
Le Fevre's Hist. New Paltz, N. Y., 369–406, 517–21
New Paltz Independent, Sept. 16, 23, 30; Nov. 18, 25; Dec. 23, 1898

Haseldon
Evans Family of S. C., 1905

Haseltine
Carter's Hist. Pembroke, N. H., ii, 133–7
Well's History of Newbury, Vt., 569–71

Haskell
Hosmer's Hist. Deer Isle, Me., 72, 78–84

Hassam
Hassam Genealogy (1902), 11 pages

Hasselbach
McCreary's First Baltimore Book

Hassell
Keith's Pa.Prov.Councillors,pt.ii,208–18

Hastings
Hastings Fam. of Clinton, N. Y. (1899), 202 pages
Kellogg's History Bernardston, Mass., 423–5
New Eng. Hist. Gen. Reg., liv, 406–8
Temple's History Framingham, 577
Tucker Genealogy (1901), 53–5
Tucker Genealogy (1903)

Hatch
Hall's Hist. of Greenland, N. H., 177–83
Litchfield, Me., History (1897), 160
Ramsdell's Hist. Milford, N. H., 732
Stiles' Wethersfield, Ct., ii, 419

Hathaway
Chace and Hathaway Gen. (1900), 42 p.
Crayon's Rockaway, N. J., Records, 171
Hinchman's Nantucket Settlers, ii,183–8
Old Colony Hist. Soc. (1899), 76–81
Tucker Genealogy (1901), 104–15
Tucker Genealogy (1903)

Hathorn
American Ancestry, xii, 174

Hathorne
Essex Inst. Hist. Coll., xli, 77–92

Hatton
Baltimore Sun, July 31, 1904

Haughwout
Lefferts Genealogy, 1878
Lefferts-Haughwout Fam. (1903), 24 p.
N. Y. Gen. and Biog. Rec., xxxiii, 49–52, 167–70, 235–41

Haven
American Ancestry, xii, 191
Temple's History Framingham, 578–84

Havens
Stiles' Wethersfield, Ct., ii, 420–25

Haverfield
Hanna's Ohio Valley Genealogies, 58

Haverstick
Kagy Genealogy, 196–205

Haviland
Haviland Genealogy (1895), 122 pages

Hawke
Hill Genealogy (1904), 60

Hawkins
Alston Genealogy, 272
Gray Genealogy (1889), 125, 129–31, 167–9, 171–82
Hawkins Plymouth Heroes, 1888
Pound and Kester Genealogy, 424–9
Seymour, Conn., History, 464–6
Tuttle Genealogy (1871), 19–21
Warfield's Maryland, 43

Hawks
Converse Genealogy (1905), 697
Hallock Pedigree (1906), 71–4

Hawxhurst
N. Y. Gen. and Biog. Rec., xxxii, 172–6, 221–4; xxxiii, 24–7

Haxall
William and Mary Quarterly, xii, 47

Hay
William and Mary Coll. Quar., vii, 53

Hayden
Flagg Genealogy (1903), 36

Hayes
Dover, N. H., Enquirer for Jan. 20–7, 1876
Hayes Family of Lyme,Ct. (1904), 192 p.

Hayford
Hayford Genealogy (1901), 253 pages

Hayman
Glenn's Colonial Mansions, ii, 312–3, 330

Haymond
West Virg. Hist. Mag., iv, 232–41

Hayne
So. Car. Hist. Mag., v (1904), 168–88

Haynes
Jones Genealogical History (1900), 9–11
Temple's History Framingham, 584
Wells Genealogy (1903), 87–90

Hays
Crumrine's Hist. Washington, Pa., 712
Swope Genealogy, 380
Walker Family of Va., 496–511

Hayt
Hoyt Genealogy (1871), 292–604
See Hoyt

Hayward
Gates Fam. of Stow, Mass. (1907), 134–7

Hazen
Le Baron Genealogy, 114–6, 248, 393

New Eng. Hist. Gen. Reg., lv, 241
Treman Genealogy
Well's History of Newbury, Vt., 572
Wintermute Gen., 40–3
Hazlewood
Penn. Mag. of Hist., xxvi, 6
Headley
Clayton's Hist. Union Co., N. J., 380
Crayon's Rockaway, N. J., Records, 292
Headley Fam, of N. J. (1905), 223 pages
Heald
Handy's Hist. of Sumner, Me., 165–74
Ramsdell's Hist. Milford, N. H., 735–9
Healey
Seymour, Conn., History, 466–7
Healy
Warden Genealogy, 3, 6, 36–44
Heard
Dover, N. H., Enquirer for March, 1879
Hoyt's Salisbury, Mass., Families, ii
Temple's History Framingham, 604
Willis' Old Eliot, Me., v (1902), 53–5
Stackpole's History Kittery, Me., 511–2
See also under Hurd
Hearl
Stackpole's History Kittery, Me., 512–3
Hearne
Hearne Gen., 2d ed. (1907), 750 pages
Hearsey
New Eng. Hist. Gen. Reg., lviii, 115–7
Heath
Baltimore Sun, Nov. 27; Dec. 4, 1904
Glenn's Colonial Mansions, ii, 306–7
Greenwich, N. Y., Journal, Sept. 4, 1901
Heath Association (1904), 19 pages
Heath Fam. of Roxbury (1905), 42 pages
Morse's Sketches of Perkins and Heath (1898), 25–30
Pearl Genealogy (1900), 11–33
Richmond, Va., Times, Jan. 29, 1905; Aug. 5, 1906
Temple's History Framingham, 585
Well's History of Newbury, Vt., 573
William and Mary Quarterly, xi, 206
Heaton
Burlington Co., N. J., Democrat, March 13, 1903
Heberling
Hanna's Ohio Valley Genealogies, 60
Hecker
Funk Genealogy
Hedge
Shourd's Fenwick's Colony of N. J., 13–6
Hedges
Sayre Genealogy, 228–30
Heebner
Bean's Hist. Montgomery Co., Pa., 588
Dotterer Genealogy, 64
Heilman
Egle's Dauphin Co., Pa. (1883), 242–3
Heist
Bean's Hist. Montgomery Co., Pa., 813
Heller
Bean's Hist. Montgomery Co., Pa., 820
Helling
Collord Ancestors, 44

Hemenway
Lawrence Genealogy, 1904
Temple's History Framingham, 585–92
Hemsley
Keith's Pa.Prov.Councillors,pt.ii,406–9
Henderson
Henderson Family of Va. (1902), 37 p.
Jackson Genealogy (1890), 45–61
Sanford's Hist. Hopkinton, N. Y., 498
Symmes' Tennent, N. J., Church, 439
Treman Genealogy
Well's History of Newbury, Vt., 574–6
West Virg. Hist. Mag., v, 108–14
Wood's Hist. Albemarle Co., Va., 226–8
Hendricks
Beekman's Monmouth, N. J., Settlers, 113–42
Hendrickson
Beekman's Monmouth, N. J., Settlers, 113–42
Symmes' Tennent, N. J., Church, 452–4
Hendryx
Seymour, Conn., History, 467–8
Henkel
Penn.-German, iv (Apr., 1903), 247–51; vii (Dec., 1906), 397–400
Henkle
Swope Genealogy, 381
Henneway
See under Hemenway
Hennion
Labaw's Preakness, N. J., Hist., 18–21
Henry
Baltimore Sun, July 10, 1904; March 18, 25, 1906
Clarke's King Wm. Co., Va., Fams., 63
Green's Culpeper County, Virg.
Henry Fam. of Kentucky (1900), 125 p.
Henry Family of Mass. (1905), 65 pages
Hunt Family (1906), 127
Henshaw
West Virg. Hist. Mag., iv, 149–71
Herbert
Clayton's Hist. Union Co., N. J., 761
Symmes' Tennent, N. J., Church, 461
Richmond, Va., Times, July 29, 1906
William and Mary Coll. Quar., viii, 147
Herd
Temple's History Framingham, 604
Herde
Temple's History Framingham, 604
See also under Hurd
Hereford
American Ancestry, xii, 36
West Virg. Hist. Mag., v, 114–8
Heritage
Stokes Genealogy, 290
Herkimer
Herkimer Genealogy (1903), 147 pages
Herndon
Va. Mag. of History, ix, 318–22, 439–41; x, 90–92, 200, 304–6, 430, 441–3; xi, 98–101,203–5,332–5,448–51; xii, 109–11, 212–4
Herr
Swope Genealogy, 370

Herrick
White Genealogy (1900), 389–99
Herrington
Herrington Family of Md. (1902), chart
Herrman
Glenn's Colonial Mansions, i, 123–38
Herschman
Winter's Genealogy, 32–5, 42, 59
Hersey
Edson Ancestry (1901), 20–3
Handy's History of Sumner, Me., 91
Hesselius
Penn. Mag. of History, xxix, 129–33
Hewins
Tapley Genealogy, 22
Hewitt
Wheeler's Hist. Stonington, Ct., 418–28
Hewlett
Acadiensis, vii (1907), 62–8
Hext
So. Car. Hist. Gen. Mag., vi, 29–40, 126
Heyward
Heyward Fam. of So. Car. (1896), chart
Hibbard
Hibbard Gen. (1901), 428 pages
Smedley Genealogy, 238–40
Tucker Genealogy (1901), 249–54
Tucker Genealogy (1903)
Well's History of Newbury, Vt., 576–8
Hibberd
Dunwoody Genealogy (1899), 118
Hickling
Ames' Genealogical Notes (1900), 28
Hickman
Buford Family of Va. (1903)
William and Mary Quarterly, x, 204
Hicks
Cornell Genealogy, 382
Keith's Pa. Prov. Councillors, pt. ii, 456
Richmond, Va., Times, Aug. 20, 1905;
   July 1, 1906
Stackpole's History Kittery, Me., 513–4
Stevenson Family of Long Island, 58
William and Mary Quarterly, xi, 130–2
Higgins
Clayton's Hist. Union Co., N. J., 385,785
Deer Island, Me., Press for March to July,
   1901
Le Baron Genealogy, 110–3, 239–44
Higginson
Higginsons in England (1903), 38 pages
Putnam's Hist. Mag. (1896), 191; (1897)
   1, 66–72, 157–60; (1898), 85, 117–20;
   (1899), 157–61
High
Landrum's Hist. Spartanburg, S. C.,
   408–11
Hight
Hoyt Genealogy (1871), 117–9, 623
See Hoyt
Hildreth
Hildreths of New Eng. (1894), 60 pages
Hill
American Ancestry, xii, 25, 30, 116, 120
Bellows Falls Times, 1905
Clarke's King Wm. Co., Va., Fams., 64–7

Clayton's Hist. Union Co., N. J., 673
Crayon's Rockaway, N. J., Rec., 243–7
Forrest Genealogy, 120–8
Green's Culpeper County, Virg.
Hill, Rodger and Brodie Families of
   Scotland and New York (1888), 81 p.
Hill Family of Dorchester (1904), 22 p.
Hill Family of Dorchester (1904), 97 p.
Hill Family of Va. (1905)
Keith's Pa. Prov. Councillors, pt.ii,30–3
New Eng. Hist. Gen. Reg., lvii, 87–93;
   lviii, 157–67, 237–46
Stackpole's Hist. Kittery, Me., 514–29
Temple's History Framingham, 593
Virg. Mag. of History, iii (1895), 156–9
Willis' Old Eliot, Me., v (1902), 59–76
Hillary
Baltimore Sun, May 20, 1906
Hillegas
Bean's Hist. Montgomery Co., Pa., 654–6
Hillen
Baltimore Sun, Aug. 6, 13, 1905
Hillman
Hillman Genealogy (1905), 203 pages
Hills
Hills Genealogy (1902), 148 pages
Hills Genealogy (1906), 713 pages
Newhall Ancestry, 46–50
Hilton
Hilton Genealogy (1877), 18 pages
Hilton Genealogy (1879), 24 pages
Hilton Genealogy (1882), 9 pages
Hilton Fam., Dover, N. H. (1905), 12 p.
New Eng. Hist. Gen. Reg., xxxvi, 40–6
Scales' Hist. of Dover, N. H., 176–80
Hilyard
Haines Family of N. J., 80
See Hilliard
Hinchman
Labaw's Preakness, N. J., History, 88
Stokes Genealogy, 279
Hinckley
Wheeler's Hist. Stonington, Ct., 429–32
Hindman
Sherrard Genealogy, 392–4
Walker Family of Va. (1902)
Hinds
Preston Genealogy (1899)
Ramsdell's Hist. Milford, N. H., 741–3
Sheppard's Life of S. Tucker, 199
Hine
Seymour, Conn., History, 468–70
Hines
Hanna's Ohio Valley Genealogies, 61
Hinkson
Smedley Genealogy, 209
Hinman
Bingham's Life of Tim. Hinman, 35 p.
Hinningway
See under Hemenway
Hinsdale
Hall Memoranda (1902), 111–20
Hinsdale Genealogy (1906), 507 pages
Old Northwest Gen. Quar., iv, 109–17
Hinton
Alston Genealogy, 304

Hitchcock
Jenkins Family of Pa. (1904), 150–2
Lawson Genealogy (1903), 244–6
Peoria County, Ill., History, 660
Seymour, Conn., History, 471–2
Hitchings
Moore's Loyalist Families (1898), 100 p.
Wells Genealogy (1903), 91–7
Hite
Baltimore Sun, July 16, 23, 1905
Richmond, Va., Times, June 26, 1904
West Va. Hist. Mag., i, pt. iv, 23; iii, pt.i
William and Mary Quarterly, x, 120–2
Hoadley
Buell Genealogy, 124
Seymour, Conn., History, 472
Hoagland
Crayon's Rockaway, N. J., Rec., 97–100
Hoar
Hoar Will and Notes (1891), 7 pages
Wood Genealogy (1901), 57–9
Hoard
See Hoar
Hobart
Bean's Hist. Montgomery Co., Pa., 547
Bent Progenitors (1903), 46
Wheeler's Hist. Stonington, Ct., 433–4
Hobbs
Carter's Hist. of Pembroke, N. H., ii, 145
Cumming Family of Md. (1905), chart
Parson's History of Rye, N. H., 378
Warfield's Maryland, 470–9
Hobby
New Eng. Hist. Gen. Reg., lix, 253
Whitmore's Heraldic Journal, iv, 116–9
Hobson
Bean's Hist. Montgomery Co., Pa., 1066
Gamble's Family Data (1906), 222–31
New Eng. Hist. Gen. Reg., lix, 46
Page Genealogy, 2d ed. (1893), 116
William and Mary Quarterly, xi, 74
Hochstetler
See Hostetler
Hockaday
Van Meter's Va. and Ky. Families, 73
Hodgdon
Greene's Hist. Boothbay, Me., 540–6
Hodge
Hodge Genealogy (1900), 455 pages
Peoria County, Ill., History, 660
Hodges
Dunwoody Genealogy (1899), 159
Hodgkin
New Eng. Hist. Gen. Reg., lviii, 281–3
Hodgkins
New Eng. Hist. Gen. Reg., lviii, 283–5
Hodsdon
Hodsdon Genealogy (1904), 164 pages
Hodson
Stackpole's Hist. Kittery, Me., 529–35
Hoffer
Hoffer Family of Pa. (1868), 31 pages
Hoffman
Bean's Hist. Montgomery Co., Pa., 1018
Hoge
Baltimore Sun, May 28, 1905

4

Hoge's Life of Moses D. Hoge
Hogg
Noyes' Hist. of Hampstead, N. H., ii, 780
Hogue
Jackson Genealogy (1890), 18–35
Hoit
Hoyt Genealogy, 1871
See Hoyt
Hoke
Swope Genealogy, 185–247
Holbrook
New Eng. Hist. Gen. Reg., lviii, 305
Sanborn's Four Boston Fams. (1904), 7 p.
Seymour, Conn., History, 472–8
Holcomb
Buell Genealogy, 66
Fisher Family of New Jersey, 126–9
Nash's Fifty Puritan Ancestors, 45
Edson Ancestry (1901), 5
Holden
Deer Island, Me., Press for Dec. 28, 1899
   to Jan. 11, 1900
Holder
Holder Genealogy (1902), 348 pages
Holderly
West Virg. Hist. Mag., i, pt. iv, 28
Holdrum
Harvey's Hud. and Berg. Co., N. J.,
   237–9
Hole
Hole Genealogy (1904), 134 pages
Holland
Baltimore Sun, Dec. 18, 1904
Chappell Genealogy (1900), 231–3
Ramsdell's Hist. Milford, N. H., 744–6
Hollenbeck
Wyoming Hist. Society, iii
See Hallenbeck
Hollingshead
Stokes Genealogy, 290
Hollingsworth
Baltimore Sun, Feb. 26, 1905; March 25,
   1906
Phila. North American, Dec. 15, 1907
Hollister
Stiles' Wethersfield, Ct., ii, 428–32
Holloway
McIlhany's Virginia Families (1903)
Holmes
Beekman's Monmouth, N. J., Settlers,
   116–20
California Register (1900), 3–5
Chesebrough Genealogy, 314–6, 512
Hall's Hist. of Greenland, N. H., 173–4
Hanna's Ohio Valley Genealogies, 63–5
Jerseyman, ix (1903), 25–32
New Eng. Hist. Gen. Reg., lviii, 21–8,
   143–50, 254–60
Parson's History of Rye, N. H., 379
Stackpole's History Kittery, Me., 536
Stiles' Wethersfield, Ct., ii, 433
Tucker Genealogy (1903)
Wheeler's Hist. Stonington, Ct., 435–41
Holt
Crissey's History of Norfolk, Ct., 560
Ramsdell's Hist. Milford, N. H., 746–50

Stockard's History of Alamance, N. C.
Tucker Genealogy (1901), 219-22
Tucker Genealogy (1903)
Holton
Greene's Hist. Boothbay, Me., 547-9
Holton Family of Conn. (1866), chart
Holton Family of Vermont (1872), chart
Holton Family of Mass. (1879), chart
Homes
Hallock Pedigree (1906), 67-70
Hood
Dunwoody and Hood Genealogy, 74-117
Ramsdell's Hist. Milford, N. H., 751-5
Hooe
Virg. Mag. of History, xii, 319
Hoogland
New Eng. Hist. Gen. Reg. (1893), 59
Hooker
Abbott, Jas. S., Memorial (1905), 41 p.
Hamlin Genealogy (1900), 63-5, 91-3
Hooker Ancestors' Homes (1900), 26 p.
Newhall Ancestry, 164-6
Old Northwest Gen. Quarterly, vii, 12-4
Stiles' Wethersfield, Ct., ii, 434-8
Hooper
Ames' Genealogical Notes (1900), 18-20
Baltimore Sun, Nov. 13, 1904
Hooper (1904), chart
Hooper Biog. Sketch (1906), 42 pages
No. Car. Booklet, v, July, 1905, 64-71
Stackpole's History Kittery, Me., 537-8
Tucker Genealogy (1901), 192-7
Tucker Genealogy (1903)
Smedley Genealogy, 117-21, 212-8
Hooven
Bean's Hist. Montgomery Co., Pa., 478
Hoover
Bean's Hist. Montgomery Co., Pa., 1006
Hope
Richmond, Va., Times, Feb. 18, 1906
William and Mary Coll. Quar., viii, 257
Hopkins
Crumrine's Hist. Washington, Pa., 560-3
Green Family of R. I. (1905), 191-4
Hopkins Family of R. I. (1889), 28 pages
Hopkins, Goodwin and Brown (1895), 19 pages
Hopkins Family of R. I. (1899), chart
Keith's Pa. Prov.Councillors,pt.ii,265-80
Nicholson Family of N. J. (1897), 56-80, 144-8
Peoria County, Ill., History, 661
Ramsdell's Hist. Milford, N. H., 755-60
Richmond, Va., Times, May 15; June 19, 1904
Rochester, N. Y., Hist. Soc. Pubs., ii, 52-7
Sanford's Hist. Hopkinton, N. Y., 493-8
Southern Hist. Assoc. Pubs., iv, 395-442
Wallace Family of Md., 1902
Woodruff's Litchfield, Ct., Gen. Reg., 109
Wood's Hist. Albemarle Co., Va., 229
Hopkinson
Phila. North American, Jan. 12, 1908
Keith's Pa. Prov. Councillors, ii, 265-80

Hopper
Harvey's Hud. and Bergen Co., N. J., 71
Mott and Hopper Family (1898), 18 p.
Putnam's Hist. Mag. (1896), 1-4
Hoppin
Treman Genealogy
Hopton
Lea Genealogy, 1906
Hord
Hord Genealogy Supp. (1903), 30 pages
Horne
Temple's History Framingham, 596
Horner
Blair Family of Virg. (1898), 209-57
Moore Family of Chester, Pa., 96
Horsey
Baltimore Sun, July 23, 30, 1905
Horsford
Woodruff's Litchfield, Ct. Gen. Reg., 110-2
See Hosford
Horton
N. Y. Gen. Biog. Rec., xxxvi, 38-46, 104-14
Rich's Gen. Record (1896), 10
Horwitz
Baltimore Sun, April 30, 1905
Hosie
Treman Genealogy
Hoskins
Bronsdon Genealogy, 224-53, 285-99
Hosmer
Hosmer Family (1902), 101 pages
Nash's Fifty Puritan Ancestors, 147
Temple's History Framingham, 597
White Genealogy (1900), 30, 61, 436-56
Hotchkiss
New Eng. Hist. Gen. Reg., lviii, 283-5
Hottenstein
Keim and Allied Families, 663
Houchin
Wells Genealogy (1903), 99
Hough
Clayton's Hist. Union Co., N. J., 132
Penn. Magazine of History, xxx, 489
Houghton
Wadsworth Family (1904), 15 pages
White Genealogy (1900), 78, 545-53
Houreal
Mayer Genealogy, 122-40
Houston
Barber Genealogy (1890), 24-33
Habersham Genealogy
Peoria County, Ill., History, 709
Richmond, Va., Times, April 24, 1904
Walker Family of Virginia, 570, 588-99
West. Virg. Hist. Mag., iii, No. 3
Hovey
Hovey, Daniel, Memoir (1900), 11 pages
How
Clayton's Hist. Union Co., N. J., 756
Temple's History Framingham, 598-603
Howard
Baltimore Sun, Jan. 17, 1904; March 5, May 28, June 11, 18, July 30, 1905
Bellows Falls Times (1905)

Deer Island, Me., Press for 1899, Art. 21
Greene Family of R. I. (1905), 183–90
Hosmer's Hist. of Deer Isle, Me., 69–72
Howard Family of R. I. (1901), 168 p.
Howard Family of Bridgewater (1903), 330 pages
Keith's Pa.Prov.Councillors,pt.ii,343–50
Litchfield, Me., History (1897), 168–70
Palmer's Hist. Lanesborough, Mass.
Ramsdell's Hist. Milford, N. H., 760–3
Warfield's Maryland, 67–77, 385–9
William and Mary Quar., ix, 189–91; xi, 264

Howe
Ramsdell's Hist. Milford, N. H., 763–6
Temple's History Framingham, 599–603
White Genealogy (1900), 52–4, 59, 102–110, 191–5, 314–21

Howell
Anderson - Perrine - Howell Family of N. J., 125–8
Sayre Genealogy, 173
Treman Genealogy

Howes
Howes Family Tree (1859), chart
Metcalf Genealogy (1898), 59–61

Howland
Stone's Life of John Howland (1857), 5
Tucker Genealogy, 1903
Woolsey, Newton and Howland Ancestry (1901), 256 pages

Hoxie
Kewaunee, Wis., Owl for April, 1901
Wheeler's Hist. Stonington, Ct., 442

Hoyt
Genung Family of L. I.
Hoyt's Salisbury, Mass., Families, pt. x
Jenkins Family of Pa. (1904), 152
Kellogg's Hist. Bernardston, Mass., 428
Noyes' Hist. of Hampstead, N. H., ii, 745–8
Treman Genealogy
See Haight, Hayt, Hoit

Hubard
William and Mary Coll. Quar., vi, 244

Hubbard
Clarke and Pendleton Ancestors, 26–31
Gustin Ancestry, 75
Hall Memoranda (1902), 84–7
Hamlin Genealogy (1900), 162–5
Nash's Fifty Puritan Ancestors, 166–8
New Amsterdam Year Book, i, 15–6
Richmond, Va., Times, Dec. 25, 1904
Stackpole's Hist. Kittery, Me., 538–41
Stiles' Wethersfield, Ct., ii, 440

Hudson
Baltimore Sun, Jan. 21, 1906
New Eng. Hist. Gen. Reg. (1901), 135
Temple's History Framingham, 603
Treman Genealogy
Woods' History Albemarle Co., Va., 230

Huff
Haines Family of N. J., 243

Huger
Huger Family of S. C. (1899), 2 pages
Richmond, Va., Times, March 11, 1906

Hugg
Stokes' Genealogy, 286

Hughes
Bean's Hist. Montgomery Co., Pa., 713
California Register (1900), 5–10
Peoria County, Ill., History, 661
Stevenson Family of New Jersey, 36, 67
West Virg. Hist. Mag., iv, July, 1904

Hughey
Larimer Family of Penn., 75–8

Hulburt
Stiles' Wethersfield, Ct., ii, 442–53

Hulings
Holstein Genealogy, 18

Hull
Blish Genealogy, 307–18
Buell Genealogy, 144
California Gen. Soc. (1902), 66–72
Hull Family of Fairfield (1902), 8 p.
Hull Family Memoranda (1903), 7 pages
Hull Fam. of Gt. Barrington (1903), 8 p.
Hull Family of Hingham (1904), 64 p.
Hull Family Review (1904), 10 pages
Hull Family Association (1905), 16 p.
N. Y. Gen. Biog. Rec., xi, 101–3
Prindle Genealogy, 137
Seymour, Conn., History, 478–9
Van Meter's Va. and Ky. Families, 81
Wheeler's Hist. Stonington, Ct., 443–4

Hulse
Beekman's Monmouth, N. J., Set., 91–3

Hulshart
Beekman's Monmouth, N. J., Set., 91–3

Humaston
Woodruff's Litchfield, Ct., Gen. Reg., 112

Hume
American Ancestry, xii, 9
Hume Family of Virginia (1903), 287 p.
William and Mary Coll. Quar., viii, 251–6; viii, 84

Humes
Moore Family of Chester, Pa., 137

Hummel
Dotterer Genealogy

Humphrey
Bean's Hist. Montgomery Co., Pa., 618
Crissey's Hist. of Norfolk, Ct., 564–6
Humphrey Genealogy (1881), 14 pages
Jenkins Family of Pa. (1904), 188–91
Keith's Pa.Prov.Councillors,pt.ii,287–94
Seymour, Conn., History, 479–80

Humphreyville
Humphrey Genealogy
Humphreyville Ancestral Record (1903), 56 pages
Mayer Genealogy, 110–4

Hungerford
Hall Memoranda (1902), 213–7

Hunn
Stiles' Wethersfield, Ct., ii, 453–5

Hunnewell
Hunnewell Family Notes (1900), 6 pages
Stiles' Wethersfield, Ct., ii, 455–7

Hunsicker
Bean's Hist. Montgomery Co., Pa., 407, 552, 1027, 1067–9

Funk Genealogy
Hunt
Hunt Family of N. J. (1906), 202 pages
Treman Genealogy
Vinton Genealogy, 332
Wintermute Gen., 232
Hunter
Baltimore Sun, Nov. 11, 18, 1906
Bean's Hist. Montgomery Co., Pa., 738
Dunwoody Genealogy (1899), 121–4
Old Northwest Gen. Quar., viii, 73–9
West Va. Hist. Magazine, v, 151–3
William and Mary Coll. Quar., vii, 154
Huntington
Crayon's Rockaway, N. J., Records, 137
Hyde and Dana Genealogy (1904), 12–20
Litchfield, Me., History (1897), 171–5
Woolsey Genealogy
Hurd
Buell Genealogy, 104
Evans' Scioto Co., Ohio, History, 1230
Seymour, Conn., History, 480–3
Temple's History Framingham, 604
See also under Heard
Hurlbut
Hall Memoranda (1902), 127–32
Hodge Genealogy (1900)
Hurlburt
Seymour, Conn., History, 483–6
Hurry
N. Y. Gen. Biog. Rec., xxxv, 198
Husband
Baltimore Sun, Dec. 24, 1905
Hussey
Hinchman's Nantucket Set., ii, 270–5
Hutchings
Greene's Hist. Boothbay, Me., 549
Hutchins
Stackpole's Hist. Kittery, Me., 542–7
Tucker Genealogy (1901), 42
Tucker Genealogy (1903)
Willis' Old Eliot, Me., v (1902), 57
Hutchinson
Carter's Hist. Pembroke, N.H. ii,, 158–62
Fulton Genealogy, 31, 38, 89–97, 149
Hutchinson Family (1876), 73 pages
Hutchinson Genealogy (1885), 23 pages
Hutchinson Farm in Winchester, Mass. (1901), 7 pages
Jenkins Family of Pa. (1904), 172–4
Litchfield, Me., History (1897), 175–81
Ramsdell's Hist. Milford, N. H., 767–96
Wells Genealogy (1903), 101
Hutson
Temple's History Framingham, 603
See also under Hudson
Huxley
Huxley Genealogy (1901), 85 pages
Huyett
Penn.-German, viii (1907), 160–2
Huyler
Harvey's Hud. and Berg. Co., N. J., 86
Hyatt
Treman Genealogy
Hyde
Blackman Genealogy, 19–21

Hyde and Dana Genealogy (1904), 114 p.
Seymour, Conn., History, 486–7
Wheeler's Hist. Stonington, Ct., 445–6
Hyer
Clayton's Hist. Union Co., N. J., 141
Hynson
Baltimore Sun, Nov. 6, 1904
Emory's Colonial Families of Md., 218

Ingalls
Ingalls Genealogy (1903), 324 pages
Well's History of Newbury, Vt., 580–2
Ingersoll
Seymour, Conn., History, 487
Stackpole's History Kittery, Me., 547
Willis' Old Eliot, Me. (1902), v, 87
Ingham
Treman Genealogy
Inglis
Cochran-Inglis Family (1899), 10–3
Ingraham
Chesebrough Genealogy, 34
Ingram
Potts Genealogy (1895), 335
Sharpless Genealogy, 442
Inman
Amer. Hist. Mag., vii (1902), 300
Walker Family of Virginia, 183–99
Innes
Willis Family of Va., 139
Inskeep
Penn. Mag. of History, xxviii, 129
Iredell
Jones Genealogical History (1900), 61–5
Ireland
Penn. Magazine of History, xxv, 417
Irish
Irish, General James, Life (1898), 70 p.
Irons
Thayer Ancestors (1894), 56–8
Irvine
Walker Family of Virginia, 80
Irving
Treman Genealogy
Irwin
Baltimore Sun, Nov. 26, 1905
Crumrine's Hist. Washington, Pa., 685
Larimer Family of Penn. (1903)
Woods' Hist. Albemarle Co., Va., 232
Isham
Forman Genealogy, 31
Ivers
Heraldic Journal, i (1865), 92–4
Ives
Abbott, Jas. S., Memorial (1905), 41 p.
Izard
S. C. Hist. Gen. Mag., ii (1901), 205–40

Jack
Litchfield, Me., History (1897), 182–5
Peoria County, Ill., History, 662
Jackson
Crayon's Rockaway, N. J., Rec., 101–3

Crayon's The Evergreen (1903), 20–5
Jackson Family of Pa. (1890), 124 pages
Jackson Family of Cambridge, Mass.
(1905), 456 pages
Keith's Pa. Prov. Councillors, pt. ii, 78–82
Le Baron Genealogy, 257–58
Litchfield, Me., History (1897), 185–7
N. Y. Gen. Biog. Record, xxxvii, 81–91
Quinby's New Eng. Family Hist., i, 22,
28–30
Warren and Jackson Families (1903)aaa
Warren and Jackson Fams. (1903), 121–
32
William and Mary Quarterly, xii, 196
Willis' Old Eliot, Me. (1902), v, 93
Jacob
Hill Genealogy (1904), 61
Robertson Genealogy, 53–5, 88–99
Jacoby
Beidler Family of Pa., 19–24
Jacques
Clayton's Hist. Union Co., N. J., 556
Jaggard
Jennings Gen., ii, 371, 375–7, 381–9
James
Keith's Pa.Prov.Councillors,pt.ii,216–20
Seymour, Conn., History, 487–8
Smedley Genealogy, 81
Jameson
Jameson Genealogy (1901), 599 pages
Woods' Hist. Albemarle Co., Va., 234
Jamison
Hanna's Ohio Valley Genealogies, 66–8
Janes
Stiles' Wethersfield, Ct., ii, 459
Janney
Janney Genealogy (1904), 37 pages
Penn. Mag. of History, xxvii, 212–37
So. Hist. Assoc., viii, 119–28, 196–211,
275–86
Jaquelin
Baltimore Sun, Feb. 25, 1906
William and Mary Coll. Quar., v, 50–3
Jaquett
Jaquett Genealogy, 2d ed. (1907), 226 p.
Jaquith
Litchfield, Me., History (1897), 187
Jarrett
Bean'sHist.MontgomeryCo.,Pa.,908–10
1017
Jaudon
Glenn's Colonial Mansions, ii, 323–8
Jefferds
Wells Genealogy (1903), 103
Jefferie
Newhall Ancestry, 159
Jefferis
Darlington Genealogy, 112–5
Jefferson
Glenn's Colonial Mansions, ii, 201–41
Page Genealogy, 2d ed. (1893), 263
Woods' Hist. Albemarle Co., Va., 235–8
Jeffries
Treman Genealogy
Jellison
Stackpole's Hist. Kittery, Me., 548–9

Jenckes
Thayer Ancestors (1894), 59–61
Jenings
Jennings Genealogy, ii, 338–47
Stevenson Family of New Jersey, 23–30
Jenkins
Baltimore Sun, Feb. 25, March 4, 11,
1906
Bean's Hist. Montgomery Co., Pa., 964
Jenkins Family of Penn. (1904), 244 p.
Lancaster Genealogy, 27–30
Litchfield, Me., History (1897), 406
Stackpole's Hist. Kittery, Me., 549–54
Willis' Old Eliot, Me. (1901), iv, 85–9; v,
(1902), 94
Jenks
Treman Genealogy
Jenness
Parson's History of Rye, N. H., 380–98
Jennie
Sanford's Hist. Hopkinton, N. Y., 500
Jennings
Richmond, Va., Times, May 8, 1904
Temple's History Framingham, 607
Welles' Amer. Fam. Antiquity (1881),
133–208
Jennison
Temple's History Framingham, 607
Jerdone
William and Mary Quarterly, xii, 29
Jervey
S. C. Hist. Mag., vii, 31–46, 109–13
Jess
Sinnott Genealogy
Jesson
New Eng. Hist. Gen. Reg. (1893), 104
Jessup
Jessup Golden Wedding (1903), 32 pages
Jewell
Litchfield, Me., History (1897), 188–91
Symmes' Tennent, N. J., Church, 447–9
Jewett
Prime Genealogy (1897), 72–9
Ramsdell's Hist. Milford, N. H., 797–9
Treman Genealogy
Well's Hist. of Newbury, Vt., 584–6
Jillson
Jillson Ancestry (1879), 28 pages
Jobs
Clayton's Hist. Union Co., N. J., 133
John
Maulsby Genealogy, 36–43
Johns
Southern Hist. Assoc. Pubs., iv, 416–26
Johnson
Bean's Hist. Montgomery, Co. Pa., 663
Buford Family of Va., 1903
Deer Island, Me., Press for Jan. 12 to
July, 1901
Greenlaw's Genealogical Advertiser, iv
(1901), 50
Hamlin Genealogy (1900), 107
Hanna's Ohio Valley Genealogies, 68
Jameson Genealogy
Johnson Family of New Haven (1902),
11 pages

Johnsons of Wallingford (1901), 4 pages
Johnsons of Wallingford (1904), 32 p.
Johnson Fam. of Woburn (1905), 53 p.
Lancaster Genealogy, 117–20
Litchfield, Me., History (1897), 191–3
Lowell Genealogy, 43–5
New Eng. Hist. and Gen. Reg., lv, 369–72; lvi, 132–40, 297; lix, 79–86, 143, 275–82
Newhall Ancestry, 77–98
Parson's History of Rye, N. H., 398
Peoria County, Ill., History, 663
Sayre Genealogy, 270–6
Seymour, Conn., History, 489–502
Sherrard Genealogy, 386–92
Stackpole's Hist. Kittery, Me., 554–8
Temple's History Framingham, 608–10
Thayer Ancestors (1894), 62–5
Treman Genealogy
Wells Genealogy (1903), 105
Well's Hist. of Newbury, Vt., 586–97
White Genealogy (1900), 54
Willis' Old Eliot, Me. (1902), v, 88–92
Woodruff's Litchfield, Ct., Gen. Reg., 113–5

Johnston
Conover's Col. John Johnston Memoir, 1902
Hamlin Genealogy (1900), 235–40
Johnston Fam. of Wilton, N. Y. (1900), 118 pages
N. Y. Gen. and Biog. Rec., xxxiii, 240–9; xxxiv, 33–6
Richmond, Va., Times, May 13, 1906
Sherrard Genealogy, 386–92
Well's History Newbury, Vt., 597–9
Alston Genealogy, 70–2

Johnstone
Johnstone Fam. N. J. (1905), blue print
Jones Genealogical Hist. (1900), 65–73
Tucker Genealogy (1901), 179–85
Tucker Genealogy (1903)

Jolliffe
New Eng. Hist. Gen. Reg. (1888), 71

Jones
Alden Genealogy (1903)
Alston Genealogy, 282–91
Baltimore Sun, July 16, 1905; Jan. 7, 1906
Bascom's Fort Edward, N. Y., 74–9
Bean's Montgomery Co., Pa., 718, etc.
Blish Genealogy, 328–31
Gray Genealogy (1889), 54–9
Green's Culpeper County, Virg.
Jameson Genealogy
Jones Fam. of So. Car. (1900), 73 pages
Jones Fam. of Nova Scotia (1905), 38 p.
Jones Fam. of Fort Neck, N. Y. (1906), 183 pages
Jones Family of L. I. (1907), 435 pages
New Eng. Hist. Gen. Reg., lix, 386; lx, 164–8; lxi, 149–57, 244–54, 354–9
Parson's History of Rye, N. H., 400
Penn. Mag. of History, xxx, 366–71
Ramsdell's Hist. Milford, N. H., 800–3
Roberts' Plymouth, Pa., Meeting, 217

Southern History Assoc., viii, 147–56, 219–32
Stackpole's Hist. Kittery, Me., 558–9
Temple's History Framingham, 610–2
Treman Genealogy
Woodruff's Litchfield, Ct., Gen. Reg., 116
Woods' Hist. Albemarle Co., Va., 238–40

Jordan
Evans Family of S. C. (1905)
Hosmer's Hist. of Deer Isle, Me., 109–11
Nash's Fifty Puritan Ancestors, 169

Jordine
Clayton's Hist. Union Co., N. J., 254

Joslin
Bangor, Me., Hist. Magazine, vii, 107

Jouett
Woods' Hist. Albemarle Co., Va., 240–2

Joy
Edson Ancestry (1901), 31–5
Joy Genealogy (1900), 225 pages
Stackpole's Hist. Kittery, Me., 559–60

Joyce
Deer Island, Me., Press for Feb. 15, 1900

Judd
Hastings Genealogy (1899), 97–106

Judkins
Litchfield, Me., History (1897), 194

Jund
Dotterer Genealogy

Kagay
Kagy Genealogy

Kagy
Kagy Genealogy (1899), 675 pages
See Keagy

Kasson
Well's History of Newbury, Vt., 600

Kathan
Mansfield's Capt. John Kathan (1902), 159 pages

Kay
Jennings Genealogy, ii, 372, 379–80

Keach
Peoria County, Ill., History, 758

Keagy
Kagy Genealogy

Kearney
Alston Genealogy, 489–505
Clayton's Hist. Union Co., N. J., 497

Keeley
Bean's Hist. Montgomery Co., Pa., 798

Keen
Stackpole's Hist. Kittery, Me., 560–4

Keener
Swope Genealogy, 322, 340, 355

Keep
New Eng. Hist. Gen. Reg., xxxvi, 165–7

Keim
Mayer Genealogy, 107–9

Keir
Seymour, Conn., History, 502–5

Keith
Baltimore Sun, Nov. 18, 25; Dec. 2, 1906
Bean's Montgomery Co., Pa., 883–8

Peoria County, Ill., History, 664
Kelker
Egle's Dauphin Co., Pa. (1883), 243–5
Keller
Keller Genealogy (1905), 192 pages
Kelley
Carter's Hist. Pembroke, N. H., ii, 167–9
Greene's Hist. Boothbay, Me., 550–2
Kelley's New Hampshire, 91–122
Kellogg
Jenkins Family of Pa. (1904), 148–50
Kellogg Genealogy (1903), 3 vols.
Nash's Fifty Puritan Ancestors, 24
Reynolds and Kellogg Gen. (1897), 20 pp.
Stiles' Wethersfield, Ct., ii, 463–5
Temple's History Framingham, 613
Treman Genealogy
Wheeler's Hist. Stonington, Ct., 447
Kelly
Kelly Family of So. Car. (1900), 7 pages
Woods' Hist. Albemarle Co.,Va., 242–4
Kelsey
Buell Genealogy, 137, 147, 164
Stiles' Wethersfield, Ct., ii, 465
Kelso
Walker Family of Virginia, 75
Kemp
Baltimore Sun, July 9, 16, 1905
Gamble's Family Data (1906), 159–77
N. Y. Gen. Biog. Rec., xxxv, 101–7
Kemper
Beauman Family Memoirs, 41–50
Kendall
Bean's Hist. Montgomery Co., Pa., 922
Boylston, Mass., Centennial, 1887
Gamble's Family Data (1906), 154
Hill Genealogy (1904), 82
Litchfield, Me., History (1897), 195
Ramsdell's Hist. Milford, N. H., 805–7
Temple's History Framingham, 613–6
Kenderdine
Bean's Hist. Montgomery Co., Pa., 1104
Kendrick
Well's History of Newbury, Vt., 601
Kennan
American Ancestry, xii, 189
Kennard
Stackpole's Hist. Kittery, Me., 565–8
Willis' Old Eliot, Me., (1902), v, 96–9
Kennedy
Bean's Montgomery Co., Pa., 1015, 1129
Greene's Hist. Boothbay, Me., 476
Kennedy Family of Penn. (1881), 87 p.
Wyoming Commem. Assoc. Proc., 1895
Kenner
William and Mary Coll. Quar., viii, 108;
ix, 185–9; xiv, 173–81
Kennerson
Forrest Genealogy, 118
Kenney
Greene's Hist. Boothbay, Me., 553
Kenniston
Greene's Hist. Boothbay, Me., 554
Kennon
Baltimore Sun, June 18, 25, 1905; Oct.
20, 1907

Richmond, Va., Critic, Oct. 29, 1888
Virg. Mag. of History, xiii, 91
William and Mary Coll. Quar., xiv, 132–
5, 268–75; xv, 45
Kenricke
Hall Memoranda (1902), 187
Kent
Bent Progenitors (1903), 41
Gray Genealogy (1889), 132–45
McGavock Family of Va., 15, 35–9, 156
Sanford's Hist. Hopkinton, N. Y., 501–8
Well's History of Newbury, Vt., 602–7
Kenworthy
Bean's Hist. Montgomery Co., Pa., 586
Kerby
William and Mary Coll. Quar., xiv, 154–8
See also under Kirby
Kercheval
Pound and Kester Gen., 82, 92–106
Kerley
White Genealogy (1900), 27
Kerr
Fulton Genealogy, 131, 138, 141–6
Hanna's Ohio Valley Genealogies, 70
Symmes' Tennent, N. J., Church, 390–
2, 441
Woods' Hist. Albemarle Co., Va., 244
Kerwin
Lawson's Genealogy (1903), 228–34
Kester
Pound and Kester Gen. (1904), 628 pp.
Ketcham
Crayon's Rockaway, N. J., Records, 173
Key
Baltimore Sun, Sept. 11, 1904
Stackpole's Hist. Kittery, Me., 568–9
Woods' Hist. Albemarle Co., Va., 245
Keyes
Keyes Family (1875), 10 pages
Well's History of Newbury, Vt., 607–10
White Genealogy (1900), 83
Keyser
Hoyt's Salisbury, Mass., Families, 572
Kibbe
Allen's History of Enfield, Ct., 30
Kilborn
Woodruff's Litchfield, Ct., Gen. Reg.,
119–25
Kilbourne
Old Northwest Gen. Quar., vi, 182–6;
x, 81
Stiles' Wethersfield, Ct., ii, 467–71
Kilgore
Landrum's Hist. Spartanburg, S. C., 446
Kilgour
McIlhany's Virg. Fams. (1903), 176
Kilham
New Eng. Hist. Gen. Reg., lvi, 344–6
Allen's Hist. of Wenham, Mass., 144
Killam
Allen's History of Enfield, Ct., 30
Preston Genealogy, 1899
Killough
Small Family of Penn., 227–9
Kilmer
Kilmer Family (1897), 214 pages

Kilton
Dary Genealogy, 20
Kimball
Carter's Hist. Pembroke, N. H., ii, 169–82
Dover, N. H., Enquirer for Aug., 1880
Kimball (1901), chart
Kimball-Weston Ancestry (1902), 103 p.
Treman Genealogy
White Genealogy (1900), 89–94
Kimberley
Stiles' Wethersfield, Ct., ii, 471
Kimberly
Prindle Genealogy, 239–42
Kimble
Crayon's Rockaway, N. J., Records, 139
Kimbrough
Alston Genealogy, 292–7
Kimmel
Hanna's Ohio Valley Genealogies, 71
Kinch
Clayton's Hist. Union Co., N. J., 126
Kincheloe
Baltimore Sun, Dec. 29, 1907
King
Clarke's King Wm. Co., Va., Fams., 68
Genung Family of L. I.
Greene Family of R. I. (1905), 143–8,
   178–82, 195–204, 220–5
Habersham Gen.
Hoffman's Memorial of J. A. King
   (1901), 26 pages
King Family of Troy (1897), 56 pages
Larimer Family of Penn., 81–90
New Eng. Hist. Gen. Reg., lviii, 347
N. Y. Gen. and Biog. Rec., xxxi, 198–
   204; xxxii, 89–93; xxxiii, 71–5, 149–9;
   xxxvi, 222–7, 263–7
Peoria County, Ill., History, 665
Smedley Genealogy, 262
Stackpole's Hist. Kittery, Me., 569–70
Treman Genealogy
Willis' Old Eliot, Me. (1902), v, 100
Kingsbury
Benton Genealogy (1901), 147–52
Kingsbury Family of Dedham (1901),
   258 pages
Kingsbury Fam. of Keene, N. H. (1904),
   63 pages
Kingsbury Directory (1904), 31 pages
Kingsbury Family of Ipswich (1905),
   732 pages
Temple's History Framingham, 617
Treman Genealogy
Kingsley
Kingsley Family (1890), 1 page
Kinkead
Clarke's King Wm. Co., Va., Fams., 69–73
Woods' Hist. Albemarle Co., Va., 246
Kinney
Hall Genealogy (1904), 4
McIlhany's Virg. Fams. (1903), 1–26
Kinsey
Hanna's Ohio Valley Genealogies, 72
Peoria County, Ill., History, 665
Southern Hist. Assoc. Pubs., iv, 427,
   431–3; v, 300–3

Kinsolving
Woods' Hist. Albemarle Co., Va., 247
Kinzie
Bean's Hist. Montgomery Co., Pa., 1130
Kip
Kip Genealogy (1894), 3 vols.
Kipp
Harvey's Hud. and Berg. Co., N. J., 96–9
Labaw's Preakness, N. J., History, 43–9
Kipshaven
Seller's Delaware Families, 129–37
Kirby
Cornell Genealogy, 392
Hall Memoranda (1902), 229–31
N. Y., Gen. Biog. Rec., xxxiii, 129–34
Stiles' Wethersfield, Ct., ii, 473
Warfield's Maryland, 143–5
Woodruff's Litchfield, Ct., Gen. Reg., 125
See Kerby
Kirk
Bean's Montgomery Co., Pa., 700, 912
Kirkam
Stiles' Wethersfield, Ct., ii, 474
Kirkham
New Eng. Hist. Gen. Reg., lix, 254–7
Kirkland
Muzzey's Reminiscences, 143–56
Kirkner
Clayton's Hist. Union Co., N. J., 324
Kirkpatrick
Clayton's Hist. Union Co., N. J., 503
Kirkpatrick Memorial (1867), 17–29
Kirtland
Southworth Ancestry (1903), 39–42
Kirtley
Buford Family of Va., 1903
Kistler
Penn.-German, vii (May, 1906), 124–31
Kitchel
Crayon's Rockaway, N. J., Rec., 248–53
Kithcart
Sherrard Genealogy, 383–5
Kittelle
Green Family of R. I. (1905), 175–7
Kittredge
Carter's Hist. of Pembroke, N. H., ii,
   182
Klaarwater
See Clearwater
Knaggs
Detroit Evening News, Nov., 1901
Knaggs Family (1902), 56 pages
Knapp
Old Northwest Quarterly, ix, 258
Knauss
Pennsylvania-German, vii, 287–92
Kneale
Bean's Hist. Montgomery Co., Pa., 463
Knickerbocker
Dutcher and Knickerbocker Gen., 1906
Knight
Bean's Hist. Montgomery Co., Pa., 1015
Bellows Falls Times, 1905
Deer Island, Me., Press for 1900
Downing Genealogy (1902), 133 pages
Greene's Hist. Boothbay, Me., 556–8

Hoyt's Salisbury, Mass., Families, pt. 10
Keith's Pa.Prov.Councillors,pt.ii,419–21
Ramsdell's History, Milford, N. H., 813
Stackpole's History, Kittery, Me., 570–2
Well's History of Newbury, Vt., 611
Willis' Old Eliot, Me., (1902), v. 101
Knipe
Bean's Montgomery Co., Pa., 642, 664
Knowles
Parson's History of Rye, N. H., 402–4
Knowlton
Litchfield, Me., History (1897), 197
Preston Genealogy (1899)
Ramsdell's Hist, Milford, N. H., 814–6
Rand Genealogy, 232
Temple's History Framingham, 618
Knox
Starrett's Gen. Henry Knox (1902), 34 p.
Koster
See Kester
Koues
Treman Genealogy
Krall
See Croll
Kramer
Small Family of Penn. (1905)
Krater
Wintermute Gen., 26–9
See also Crater
Kratz
Bean's Hist. Montgomery Co., Pa., 1069
Krause
Dotterer Genealogy
Pennsylvania-German, vii, 298–301
Kreider
Egle's Dauphin Co., Pa. (1883), 245
Krey
Perkiomen Region, iii, 82
Krieble
Bean's Hist. Montgomery Co., Pa., 1182
Kuhlthan
Clayton's Hist. of Union Co., N. J., 757
Kuhn
Morris and Kuhn Ancestry (1905), 294 p.
Phila. North American, Nov. 10, 1907
Kulp
Bean's Hist. Montgomery Co., Pa., 698
Kunze
Penn.-German, iii (1902), 108
Kurr
Dotterer Genealogy, 58, 117
Kuster
See Kester
Kyle
Jackson Genealogy (1890), 84–95

La Bar
Burrell's Reminiscences of Geo. La Bar
(1870), 12, 31
Lacey
Gulf States Hist. Mag., i, 41–4
Lacey Family of So. Car. (1900), 4 pages
Lacy
Baltimore Sun, May 28, 1905
Goodrich's Hist. of Dryden, N. Y., 218

Ladd
Carter's Hist. Pembroke, N. H., ii, 189
Treman Genealogy
Well's History of Newbury, Vt., 612
Laforge
Clayton's Hist. Union Co., N. J., 294
Laidley
West Virg. Hist. Mag., i, pt. iv, 20
Laine
Hall Memoranda, 1902, 193
Laing
Lundy Genealogy, 308–14, 317, 420
Laird
Symmes' Tennent, N. J., Church, 402–5
Lake
Bellows Falls Times, Dec., 1904
Gallup Genealogy, 23, 266, 274
Hall's Hist. Atlantic City, N. J., 406
Lakin
Gambles' Bancroft Data (1906), 113
Lamar
Baltimore Sun, Oct. 22, 29; Dec. 3,
1905
Lamar Genealogy (1897), 10 pages
Lamb
Bronsdon Genealogy, 193–5
Lamb Fam. of New Jersey (1904), 100 p.
Lamb Family of Conn. (1903), 7 pages
Newhall Ancestry, 102–9
Temple's History, Framingham, 619
White Genealogy (1900), 697–9
Lambard
Litchfield, Me., History (1897), 198
Lambert
Britton Ancestry (1901), 32
Clayton's Hist. Union Co., N. J., 416
Lambert MSS. in N. J. Hist. Soc. Lib.,
19 pages
McIlhaney's Virginia Families, 132
Lamberton
Converse Genealogy (1905), 681
Lamprey
Parson's History of Rye, N. H., 404
Lamson
Crayon's Rockaway,N.J.,Records,107–9
Greene Family of R. I. (1905), 237–42
Lamson Genealogy (1876), 73 pages
Lancaster
Brown Fam. of Pa. (1885), pt. ii, 31–5
Lancaster Genealogy (1902), 302 pages
Lancey
Carter's Hist. of Pembroke, N. H., ii, 204
Landis
Beidler Genealogy, 19–28, 224–33
Pound and Kester Genealogy, 37–40, 44
Landon
Woodruff's Litchfield, Ct., Gen. Reg.,
127–30
Landsley
McGavock Family of Va.
Lane
Ferrier Genealogy, 44–7
Lane Fam. of No. Car. (1900), 23 pages
Smith and Lane Family of Rockport
(1905), 4 pages
Topliff Genealogy, 1906

Usher, Hannah L., Biography (1903), relating to Lanes of Buxton, Me.
West Virg. Hist. Mag., i, pt. iv, 26

Lanesborough
Palmer's Hist. Lanesborough, Mass., 40–4

Lanford
Landrum's Hist. Spartanburg, S. C., 422

Lang
Parson's History of Rye, N. H., 405–9
Well's History of Newbury, Vt., 614

Langdon
Parson's History of Rye, N. H., 410–2
Treman Genealogy

Langhorne
Baltimore Sun, Dec. 25, 1904

Langley
Crumrine's Hist. Washington, Pa., 485

Langworthy
Chesebrough Genealogy, 102–4

Lanier
Glenn's Colonial Mansions, ii, 74–7

Lansing
Van Deusen Genealogy (1901), 96–8

Lapp
Beidler Family of Pa., 258–60

Larcom
Essex Inst. Hist. Coll., xliii. 190–2

Lardner
Keith's Pa.Prov.Councillors,pt.ii,316–24

Large
Lundy Genealogy, 421

Larimer
Larimer Genealogy (1903), 196 pages

Larison
Larison Family of N. J. (1888), 472 p,

Larkin
Warren Genealogy (1903), 96–8

Larnett
See under Learned

Laroe
Harvey's Hud. and Berg. Co., N. J., 169

La Rue
See Rue

Larzelere
Bean's Montgomery Co., Pa., 557, 986–8

La Serre
Old Northwest Gen. Quar., viii, 40–2; ix, 86

Lasher
Lasher Genealogy (1904), 270 pages

Latane
Virg. Mag. of History, xi, 103

Lathrop
Converse Genealogy (1905), 834
Lathrop Review, De Costa (1884), 8 p.
Rich's Gen. Record (1896), 1
Woolsey Genealogy

Latimer
Small Family of Penn. (1905), 138–71

Latour
Acadiensis Quarterly (1904), 12–35
Jack's Hist. of St. John, N. B., 156–8
Latours of Mass. Bay (1904), 24 pages

Latshaw
Stauffer and Bauer Genealogy, 97–9

Lattimer
Stiles' Wethersfield, Ct., ii, 478–81

Laughlin
Sanford's Hist. Hopkinton, N. Y., 508

La Valley
Greene Family of R. I. (1905), 148, 151

Law
Clark's, Jas., Greenleaf and Thos., Law, 1901
Hanna's Ohio Valley Genealogies, 74

Lawrence
Cornell Genealogy, 374–6
Crissey's History of Norfolk, Ct., 509–11
Crumrine's Hist. Washington, Pa., 597
Cumming Family of Md. (1905), chart
Gustin Ancestry, 109–16
Keith's Pa.Prov.Councillors,pt.ii,431–55
Lawrence Fam. of Groton (1904), 344 p.
Le Baron Genealogy, 149–51
New England Hist. Gen. Reg., lxi, 276
Sanford's Hist. Hopkinton, N. Y., 509
Temple's History, Framingham, 621
Warfield's Maryland, 434

Lawson
Baltimore Sun, Aug. 20, 1905
Evans Family of S. C., 1905
Lawson's Genealogy (1903), 115–190

Lawton
Clarke and Pendleton Ancestors, 40

Layport
Hanna's Ohio Valley Genealogies, 75

Layton
Treman Genealogy

Lea
Lea Family of Penn., 1906

Leach
Stackpole's History Kittery, Me., 572–4
Willis' Old Eliot, Me. (1902), v, 111

Leake
McGavock Family of Pa.
Richmond, Va., Times, Feb. 14, 1904
Woods' Hist. Albemarle Co., Va., 248–50

Lear
Parson's History of Rye, N. H., 412

Learned
Temple's History Framingham, 622

Leason
Temple's History Framingham, 563–5
See also under Gleason

Leavens
Leavens Genealogy (1903), 152 pages

Leavenworth
Seymour, Conn. History, 506–7

Leavitt
Carter's Hist. of Pembroke, N. H., ii, 205

Le Baron
De Wolf Genealogy, 279
Le Baron Genealogy (1904), 521 pages

Leddell
Woodruff Genealogy (1902), 147–50

Lee
Clayton's Hist. of Union Co., N, J., 415
Crayon's Rockaway, N. J., Rec., 141–8
Crumrine's Washington, Pa., 732, 741
Evans Family of S. C., 1905
Lee Family of Watertown (1893), 16 p.

Lewis Family of Va., 1906
New Eng. Hist. Gen. Reg., lxi, 116–8
Pound and Kester Genealogy, 83–92
Richmond, Va., Times, Nov. 8, 1903;
  Jan. 21, 1906
Treman Genealogy
William and Mary Quar., ix, 197–9; xi,
  206
Leech
Mayer Genealogy, 91–3
Shoemaker Genealogy, 82–6
Yerkes Genealogy (1904), 205–23
Leedom
Bean's Hist. Montgomery Co., Pa., 647
Leeds
Hall's Hist. Atlantic City, N. J., 407–15
Leet
Well's History of Newbury, Vt., 616
Leete
Leete Family of England, London, 1906
Lefevre
Le Fevre's Hist.,New Paltz, N. Y., 407–
  50, 529
New Paltz Independent, June 25, 1897;
  May 6, 13, 1898; Mar. 16, 23, 30;
  April 6, 1900
Swope Genealogy, 381
Leffert
Downing Genealogy (1902), 133 pages
Lefferts
Bean's Hist. Montgomery Co., Pa., 989–
  91
Lefferts-Haughwout Fam. (1903), 24 p.
Lefferts Ancestral chart, 1905
New York Gen. and Biog. Rec., xxxiii,
  49–52, 167–70, 235–41
Leffingwell
Hyde and Dana Genealogy (1904), 34–7
Leforge
Pound and Kester Genealogy, 145–8
Leftwick
Baltimore Sun, Aug. 13, 20, 1905
Leggett
Evans Family of S. C., 1905
Gustin Ancestry, 81–94
Mayer Genealogy, 132–6
Leidy
Reed Family of Pa. (1905), 87–111
Leighton
Stackpole's Hist. Kittery, Me., 574–81
Treman Genealogy
Well's History of Newbury, Vt., 616
Willis' Old Eliot, Me. (1902), v, 104–11
Leishman
Greene's History, Boothbay, Me., 478
Leland
Hill Genealogy (1904), 44
Lemont
Litchfield, Me., History (1897), 200
Le Moyne
Crumrine's Hist. Washington, Pa., 543
Lenhart
Bean's Hist. Montgomery Co., Pa., 817
Lundy Genealogy, 422–44
Lenher
Lundy Genealogy, 422–44

Lent
Lent Genealogy (1903), 171 pages
Lenthall
Eells Genealogy
Leonard
Britton Ancestry, 1901
Caldwell Family of Prov., 1906
Jennings Genealogy ,ii, 568–75
Leonard Family of N. J. (1883), 5 pages
Reed Genealogy (1901), 425–8
Le Roy
New Paltz Independent, 1901
Le Seur
Lasher Genealogy
Leslie
Peoria County, Ill., History, 686
Well's History of Newbury, Vt., 617–9
Letcher
Buford Family of Va. (1903), 116–8
Levering
Baltimore Sun, Jan. 8, 1905
Levings
Leavens Genealogy (1903), 152 pages
Lewis
Baltimore Sun, Jan. 22, Aug. 27, 1905
Beidler Family of Pa., 252–8
Buford Family of Va., 1903
Carter's Hist. Pembroke, N. H., ii, 205–7
Clarke's King Wm. Co., Va., Fams., 73–9
Essex Inst. Hist. Coll., xliii, 65–88, 121–
  44, 233–56, 321–44; xliv, 65
Greene's Hist. Boothbay, Me., 559–64
Habersham Gen.
Hill Genealogy (1904), 57–9
Lewis Fam., Wellfleet, Me. (1877), chart
Lewis Family of Va., 1906
N. Y. Gen. and Biog. Rec., xxxiv, 111
Ramsdell's Hist. Milford, N. H., 819–21
Richmond, Va., Times, Oct. 11, 1903
Smedley Genealogy, 237
Stackpole's Hist. Kittery, Me., 581–4
Van Meter's Va. and Ky. Fams., 5–44
Vawter Family of Virginia, 350–1
Watson's A Royal Lineage
West Virg. Hist. Mag., iv, 81–149
William and Mary Quar., ix, 191, 259–
  65; x, 48–54; xi, 39–47
Willis Family of Va., 95–102
Woodruff's Litchfield, Ct., Gen. Reg.,
  131–3
Woods' Hist. Albemarle Co., Va., 251–7
Libbey
Willis' Old Eliot, Me. (1902), v, 112–21
Libby
Litchfield, Me., History (1897), 201–4
Parson's History of Rye, N. H., 413–9
Stackpole's History Kittery, Me., 584–7
Tarleton Genealogy, 47–9
Light
Egle's Dauphin Co., Pa. (1883), 245
Well's Genealogy (1903), 107
Lightfoot
Smedley Genealogy, 194–6
Willis Family of Va., 131–3
Lillard
Green's, Culpeper County, Virg.

Lillington
Alston Genealogy, 362–9
Lincoln
Edson Ancestry (1901), 23–5
Litchfield, Me., History (1897), 204
Missouri Historical Review, i, 72–84
Muzzey's Reminiscences, 101–13
Lindley
Stockard's Hist. of Alamance, N. C.
Lindsay
Baltimore Sun, April 14, 21, 28, May 5, 1907
Kittochtinny Magazine, i, 241–52
Lindsay Family Assoc. (1904), 16 pages
Page Genealogy, 2d ed. (1893), 223
Richmond, Va., Times, Jan. 3, 1904
Virg. Mag. of History, x, 96, 203, 310; xi, 101
Lindsey
Well's History of Newbury, Vt., 619–21
Lindsley
Crayon's Rockaway, N. J., Records, 183
N. Y. Mail and Express for Dec. 20, 1902, Jan. 2, 1903
Lineaweaver
Egle's Dauphin Co., Pa. (1883), 246–7
Linekin
Greene's History Boothbay, Me., 564
Lines
Conn. Magazine, ix, April, 1905
Lines Gen. (1905), 15 pages, reprint
Seymour, Conn., History, 507–8
Linfield
Thayer Ancestors (1894), 68
Lingan
Baltimore Sun, June 18, 1905
Linn
McKinney Family of Pa., 102–7
Linsley
Woodruff's Litchfield, Ct., Gen. Reg., 133
Lippincott
Haines Family of N. J., 78
Sinnott Genealogy
Stokes Genealogies, 294–6
Lipscomb
Clarke's King Wm. Co., Va., Fams., 80
Landrum's Hist. Spartanburg, S. C., 371–7
Lispenard
Lispenard Genealogy (1893), 20 pages
N. Y. Gen. Biog. Rec., xxiv, 97–116
Liston
Pound and Kester Genealogy, 395–482, 588
Litchard
Gernhardt Genealogy, 225–60
Litchfield
Clapp Ancestors (1901), 48–51
Litchfield Genealogy (1901–5), 304 p.
Littell
Bedell Family, 11–5
Clayton's Hist. Union Co., N. J., 350, 392
Little
Amer. Hist. Mag., vii (1902), 154
Blair Family of Va. (1898), 171–6, 192
Carter's Hist. Pembroke, N. H., ii, 207–9

Kittochtinny Mag. (1905), i, 358–63
Noyes' History of Hampstead, N. H., ii, 748–53
Treman Genealogy
Well's History of Newbury, Vt., 621
Littlefield
Hoyt's Salisbury, Mass., Fams., 575–83
Temple's History Framingham, 625
Thayer Ancestors (1894), 71
Wells Genealogy (1903), 109–11
Littlejohn
Littlejohn Family (1850), chart
North Car. Hist. and Gen. Reg., i
Littlepage
Clarke's King Wm. Co., Va., Fams., 81–3
Livermore
Benjamin Genealogy, 39–44
Livermore Genealogy (1902), 479 pages
Temple's History Framingham, 625
Livezey
Bean's Hist. Montgomery Co., Pa., 1038
Robert's Plymouth, Pa., Meeting, 212–7
Shoemaker Genealogy, 95–7
Livingston
Glenn's Colonial Mansions, i, 297–331
Stuart Genealogy (1894), 84
Livingstone
Moore's Loyalist Fams. (1898), 100 p.
Lloyd
Baltimore Sun, July 19, 1903
Bean's Hist. Montgomery Co., Pa., 876, 991
Dunwoody Genealogy (1899), 125
Keith's Pa. Prov. Councillors, pt. i, 7–45
Temple's History Framingham, 625
Lobach
Keim and Allied Families, 684–6
Lobaugh
Peoria County, Ill., History, 745
Lobb
Dunwoody Genealogy (1899), 119
Lobengier
Egle's Dauphin Co., Pa. (1883), 247–8
Lock
Le Baron Genealogy, 254–55, 400–2
Locke
Carter's History of Pembroke, N. H., ii, 209–12
Parson's History of Rye, N. H., 419–43
Lockwood
Jenkins Family of Pa. (1904), 153
Stiles' Wethersfield, Ct., ii, 484
Treman Genealogy
Lodge
Bean's Hist. Montgomery Co., Pa., 940
Treman Genealogy
Logan
Jenkins Family of Pa. (1904), 199–213
Keith's Pa. Prov. Councillors, pt. ii, 1–40
Walker Family of Virginia, 82–90
Loker
Well's Genealogy, 1903
Long
Jones Genealogical Hist. (1900), 14–9
Longacre
Beidler Family of Pa., 224–8

Longaker
Bean's Hist. Montgomery Co., Pa., 794
Longley
Boylston, Mass., Centennial, 1887
Bent Progenitors (1903), 29–35
Longstreet
Jerseyman, x (1904), 29
Longstreth
Smedley Genealogy, 143–5
Loomis
Conn. Magazine, x, No. 2, 361–71
Treman Genealogy
Lord
Litchfield, Me., History (1897), 204–8
Lord Genealogy (1898), 40 pages
Lord Family of Vt. (1903), 116 pages
Rowell Genealogy
Stackpole's Hist. Kittery, Me., 587–601
Treman Genealogy
Well's Genealogy (1903), 115–8
Willis' Old Eliot, Me. (1902), v, 122
Woodruff's Litchfield, Ct., Gen. Reg., 134
Loring
Bronsdon Genealogy, 274
Lawrence Genealogy (1904)
Lothrop
Blish Genealogy, 318–27
Clapp Ancestors (1902), 51–3
Hall Memoranda (1902), 35–46
Lothrop Ancestors (1901), 37 pages
Lott
Clayton's Hist. of Union Co., N. J., 519
N. Y. Gen. Biog. Rec., xxxvi, 205
Loucks
Beidler Family of Pa., 108–124
Peoria County, Ill., History, 669
Lounsbury
Seymour, Conn., History, 508–11
Love
Greene's History Boothbay, Me., 565
Hanna's Ohio Valley Genealogies, 76
Love Family of Virginia (1905), 4 pages
Moore Fam. of Chester, Pa.,39, 57, 94, 99
Lovejoy
Benjamin Genealogy, 101–3
Ramsdell's Hist. Milford, N. H., 822–30
Treman Genealogy
Loveland
Seymour, Conn., History, 512–3
Stiles' Wethersfield, Ct., ii, 486–9
Lovell
Bellows Falls, Vt., Times, Mar. 9, 16, 1905
Lovewell
Well's History of Newbury, Vt., 622
Low
Le Fevre's Hist. New Paltz, N. Y., 468
New Paltz, N. Y., Independent, 1895;
    Sept. 19, 1902
Lowe
Deer Island, Me., Press for 1899, Art. 20
Lowe Family of Ipswich (1901), 189 p.
Peoria County, Ill., History, 719
Lowell
Jackson Genealogy, 1905
Lawrence Genealogy, 1904
Litchfield, Me., History (1897), 208

Lowndes
Baltimore Sun, Sept. 15, 22, 29; Oct. 6,
    1907
Lownes
Dunwoody Family (1899), 127
Smedley Genealogy, 124–6, 220–4
Lowry
Lawson Genealogy, 1903
Ludden
Strong Genealogy, 339–41, 890–2
Thayer Ancestors (1894), 73
Luddington
Luddington Genealogy (1904), 13 pages
New Eng. Hist. Gen. Reg., lviii, 72–82
Ludlow
Clayton's Hist. Union Co., N. J., 351
N. J. Hist. Soc. Proc., iii (1898), 43–50
Ludlum
Keith's Pa. Prov. Councillors, pt. ii, 437–9
See Ludlam
Luffbery
Clayton's Hist. Union Co., N. J., 293
Lukens
Bean's Hist. Montgomery Co., Pa.,
    595, 780–2, 875, 904
Hanna's Ohio Valley Genealogies, 77
Lukens Family (1900), chart
Lum
Crayon's Rockaway, N. J., Rec., 254–6
Seymour, Conn., History, 513–5
Lummus
White Genealogy (1900), 87
Lumpkin
Cody Genealogy, 4–6
Lund
Ramsdell's Hist. of Milford, N. H., 831
Lundy
Lundy Genealogy (1902), 485 pages
Lunt
Litchfield, Me., History (1897), 209–11
Tapley Genealogy, 24–6
Lusk
Stiles' Wethersfield, Ct., ii, 490–3
Lydecker
Harvey's Hud. and Berg. Co., N. J.,
    145
Lydston
Litchfield, Me., History (1897), 211
Stackpole's History Kittery, Me., 601–3
Willis' Old Eliot, Me. (1902), v, 123
Lyell
Jerseyman, x (1904), 2
Lyford
Essex Inst. Hist. Coll., xxxvii, 305–20,
    393–408; xxxviii, 57–72, 184–208
Lyford Genealogy (1902), 88 pages
Lyle
Hanna's Ohio Valley Genealogies, 77
Lyman
Lyman Family (1872), chart
Treman Genealogy
Lynch
Alston Genealogy, 72–4
Ramsdell's Hist. Milford, N. H., 832
Richmond, Va., Times, June 11, 1905
Woods' Hist. Albemarle Co., Va., 258

Lyne
Clarke's King Wm. Co., Va., Fams., 83, 120

Lyon
Crayon's Rockaway, N. J., Rec., 174–82
Genung Family of L. I.
Kittochtinny Mag. (1905), i, 413–5
Lyon Genealogy (1905), 491 pages
Hanna's Ohio Valley Genealogies, 78

Lytle
Peoria County, Ill., History, 719

Mabie
Harvey's Hud. and Berg. Co., N. J., 171
N. Y. Gen. Biog. Rec., xxxviii, 98–103

Macauley
William and Mary Quarterly, xii, 29

Macbeth
Macbeth Genealogical Abstract (1907), 50 pages

Mac Clafelin
Temple's History Framingham, 501

Mac Clintock
Hall's History Greenland, N. H., 214–9

Maccubin
Baltimore Sun, June 10, 17, 1906
Warfield's Maryland, 177

Macdonough
Macdonough Ancestry (1901), 526 pages

Mace
Parson's History of Rye, N. H., 444–6

MacGregor
Baltimore Sun, Oct. 2, 1904

Mack
Treman Genealogy, 343–740, 1097–1159
Mack Genealogy (1905), 1788 pages

Mackenzie
Baltimore Sun, June 25, July 2, 1905
Old Northwest Gen. Quar., viii, 33; x, 167–74

MacKinlay
MacKinlay Family Gathering (1893), 13 pages
MacKinlay Fam. Gathering (1894), 22 p.

Mackoy
Evan's Scioto Co., Ohio, History, 1235

MacLaren
MacLaren Genealogy (1899), 14 pages

MacLaughlin
MacLaughlin of Clan Owen (1879), 87 p.

MacLean
MacLean Genealogy (1889), 480 pages

Maclin
William and Mary Coll. Quar., vii, 108

Macomb
Gustin Ancestry, 119–28

Macomber
Macomber Fam. of Taunton (1907), 8 p.
Temple's History Framingham, 627

Macon
Alston Genealogy, 507–15
William and Mary Quarterly, xii, 29

Macpherson
Glenn's Colonial Mansions, ii, 445–83

Macy
Hinchman's Nantucket Set., ii, 195, 275

Maulsby Family of Pa., 71–7

Maddocks
Greene's Hist. Boothbay, Me., 581–3

Maddox
Baltimore Sun, Dec. 3, 1905

Madison
Baltimore Sun, March 19; July 9, 1905
Green's Culpeper County, Virg.
Watson's Some Notable Families, 52
William and Mary Coll. Quar., ix., 37, 40; x, 271–8
Willis Family of Va., 150

Magee
Clayton's Hist. Union Co., N. J., 811

Magie
Clayton's Hist. Union Co., N. J., 385

Magoon
Litchfield, Me., History (1897), 211–3

Magruder
Baltimore Sun, Dec. 25, 1904
Woods' Hist. Albemarle Co., Va., 260–2

Mahon
Temple's History Framingham, 630

Main
Wheeler's Hist. Stonington, Ct., 448–54

Makepeace
Gustin Ancestry, 7–12

Malbone
Tilley's Mag. of N. E. Hist. (1891), 170

Malcolm
Litchfield, Me., History (1897), 214

Maling
See under Mellen

Mallonee
Warfield's Maryland, 142

Mallory
Virginia Mag. of Hist., xii, 398–401; xiii, 216–9, 324–9, 441–5; xiv, 101–6, 215–20, 320–5, 431–6
Wheeler's Hist. Stonington, Ct., 455–6

Maltby
Old Northwest Gen. Quar., ix, 314–25

Mandeville
Gustin Ancestry

Manigault
Habersham Genealogy, 36

Mann
Carter's Hist. Pembroke, N. H., ii, 216–9
Treman Genealogy

Manning
Manning Genealogy (1902), 857 pages
Wheeler's Hist. Stonington, Ct., 457–8

Mansfield
Deer Island, Me., Press for 1900
Seymour, Conn., History, 515–7
Warren Genealogy (1903), 188–90

Manson
Temple's History Framingham, 630

Mansur
Mansur Genealogy (1889), pamphlet
Mansur Genealogy (1901), 59 pages
Putnam's Gen. Mag., ii (1901), 29–43, 105–28, 185–203

Mapes
N. Y. Gen. and Biog. Rec., xxxiii, 52
Marbury
Thayer Ancestors (1894), 76–9
Marcelis
Marcelis MSS. in N. J. Hist. Soc. Lib.
March
Bean's Hist. Montgomery Co., Pa., 610
Hall's Hist. of Greenland, N. H., 197–8
Marcy
Hill Genealogy (1904), 71
Marcy Family of Roxbury (1875), 14 p.
Marcy Family (1902), 16 pages
Quinabaug Hist. Soc. Leaflet, i, 131–46
Marden
Parson's History of Rye, N. H., 446–58
Maris
Dunwoody Genealogy (1899), 133–7
Markhain
Keith's Pa. Prov. Councillors, pt. i, 1–6
Markley
Bean's Hist. Montgomery Co., Pa., 661
Dotterer Genealogy, 44–8, 87–99
Marks
Woods' Hist. Albemarle Co., Va., 262
Markwell
Pound and Kester Genealogy, 49–60
Marot
Tyler Letters, iii (1896), 220
Marquand
Jennings Genealogy, ii, 414, 424–6
Marques
Crumrine's Hist. Washington, Pa., 723
Marr
Greene's Hist. Boothbay, Me., 583–5
Litchfield, Me., History (1897), 215
Stackpole's Hist. Kittery, Me., 604–5
Marriott
Warfield's Maryland, 132
Marrit
Temple's History Framingham, 631
Marsh
Bronsdon Genealogy, 120–35
Buell Genealogy, 193
Moore Family of Chester, Pa., 104
Stiles' Wethersfield, Ct., ii, 496–8
Tucker Genealogy (1901), 39
Woodruff Genealogy (1902), 140–2
Woodruff's Litchfield, Ct., Gen. Reg., 139–46
Marshall
Baltimore Sun, Oct. 13, 1907
Deer Island, Me., Press for 1899, Art. 14, 17, 18
Hosmer's Hist. of Deer Isle, Me., 79, 81
Lea Genealogy, 1906
Maulsby Genealogy, 131–3
New Eng. Hist. Gen. Reg., lix, 291–7
Noyes' History of Hampstead, N. H., ii, 780–6
Penn. Mag. of History, xxix, 331–3
Richmond, Va., Times, July 24, 1904; July 8, 1906
Temple's History Framingham, 632
Treman Genealogy
Virg. Mag. of History, xii, 328–31

Marston
Keith's Pa. Prov. Councillors, pt.ii,442–5
Litchfield, Me., History (1897), 216
Parson's History of Rye, N. H., 458
Towle Genealogy, 75–80
Martin
Baltimore Sun, April 15, 22, 29, 1906
Bean's Hist. Montgomery Co., Pa., 638
Carter's Hist. Pembroke, N. H., ii, 220–3
Clark Family of Vermont (1905), 55–8
Dary Genealogy, 18
Hanna's Ohio Valley Genealogies, 88
Hoyt's Salisbury, Mass., Families, pt. x
Pound and Kester Genealogy, 204–12
Richmond, Va., Times, April 23, 1905
Well's History of Newbury, Vt., 624
William and Mary Quar., x, 116; xi, 206
Woods' Hist. Albemarle Co., Va., 263–5
Marts
Pound and Kester Genealogy, 268–78
Marvell
Ramsdell's Hist. Milford, N. H., 837–40
Marvin
Marvin Ancestry in Eng. (1900), 184 p.
Marvin Genealogy (1904), 658 pages
Maryott
Smith Genealogy (1889), 167
Mason
Baltimore Sun, April 9; Sept. 3, 10, 1905
Green's Culpeper County, Virg.
Lawrence Genealogy, 1904
Mason Genealogy (1902), 144 pages
Parson's History of Rye, N. H., 459
Quinabaug Hist. Soc. Leaflets, i, 205–14
Wheeler's Hist. Stonington, Ct., 460–5
Woodruff's Litchfield, Ct., Gen. Reg., 146–8
Massey
Smedley Genealogy, 187
Massie
Old Northwest Gen. Quar. (1900), 63
William and Mary Quar., xiii, 196–203
Woods' Hist. Albemarle Co., Va., 266
Masters
Jenkins Family of Pa. (1904), 183–97
Mather
Bean's Hist. Montgomery Co., Pa., 821
Drake's Memoir of Cotton Mather (1851), 16 pages
Mathes
Temple's History Framingham, 633
See also under Matthews
Mathew
Wheeler's Hist. Stonington, Ct., 459
Mathews
Peoria County, Ill., History, 729
Mathis
Temple's History Framingham, 633
Matlack
Lamb Family of N. J. (1904), 50–60
Smedley Genealogy, 157–9, 272–6
Stokes Genealogy, 293
Matteson
Greene Family of N. J. (1905), 120–2, 185, 265–75

Matthews
Baltimore Sun, June 9, 16, 23, 1907
Greene's Hist. Boothbay, Me., 586–8
McGavock Family of Va.
Parson's History of Rye, N. H., 460
Temple's History Framingham, 633
Wells Genealogy (1903), 119–22
Mauldin
Baltimore Sun, Dec. 11, 1904
Maule
Penn. Mag. of History, xxvi, 479
Maulsby
Maulsby Genealogy (1902), 200 pages
Maultsby
See Maulsby
Maupin
Virg. Mag. of History, viii, 216–8
Woods' History Albemarle Co., Va., 267
Mauran
Rhodes Ancestral (1901) chart
Mauray
Mauray's Huguenot Memoirs, 1853
Richmond, Va., Times, Jan. 24, 1904;
  Oct. 15, 1905
William and Mary Quarterly, x, 122–4
Woods' History Albemarle Co., Va., 268
Maxwell
Crumrine's Hist. Washington, Pa., 824
Habersham Genealogy, 10–4
Hanna's Ohio Valley Genealogies, 88
May
Bean's Hist. Montgomery Co., Pa., 770
Crumrine's Hist. Washington, Pa., 702
Keim and Allied Families, 622–3, 638
Stiles' Wethersfield, Ct., ii, 500
Mayes
Crumrine's Hist. Washington, Pa., 762
Mayfield
Boone Family (1902), 4 pages
Mayhew
Greenlaw's Gen. Advertiser, iv, 1–8
Hallock Pedigree (1906), 45–9
Kewaunee, Wis., Owl for May, Oct., 1901
Mayhew Ancestry in Eng. (1901), 10 p.
Sinnott Genealogy
Temple's History Framingham, 633
Maynard
Baltimore Sun, Sept. 18, 1904
Old Northwest Gen. Quarterly, iii, 166
Temple's History Framingham, 634–6
Mayo
Baltimore Sun, June 11; Aug. 6, 1905
Deer Island, Me., Press for April 29 to
  May 25, 1901
Richmond, Va., Standard, 1876 to 1880
Richmond, Va., Times, Jan. 15, 1905
Temple's History Framingham, 633
Woods' History Albemarle Co., Va., 269
McAdam
William and Mary Quarterly, xiii, 25
McAfee
Woods-McAfee Fam., Va. (1905), 503 p.
McAlister
Handy's History of Sumner, Me., 97–100
McAllister
Lewis Family of Va., 1906

McAllister Family of N. C. (1900), 244 p.
Well's Hist. of Newbury, Vt., 625–7
McAlpin
Lawson's Genealogy (1903), 280–2
McBride
Kittochtinny Magazine, i, 426
McCabe
Jennings Genealogy, ii, 576–83
McCall
Wells Family of Ohio (1892), 20–4
McCarter
McCarter Family of N. J. (1900), 132 p.
McCarty
Baltimore Sun, April 16, 1905
Chappell Genealogy (1900), 260–2
Hayden's Virginia Genealogies, 84a–91
Lancaster Genealogy, 206–66, 289
McCaughey
Jackson Genealogy (1890), 7–10
McClanahan
Buford Family of Va., 1903
McClanahan Genealogy (1894), 43 pages
McCleary
Crumrine's Hist. Washington, Pa., 780
McClenachan
Keith's Pa. Prov. Councillors, pt. ii, 46–8
McClintock
Greene's Hist. Boothbay, Me., 567–9
McKee Family of Ky. (1900), chart
New Eng. Hist. Gen. Reg. (1856), 99
Old Northwest Gen. Quar., vii, 73–80
McClung
Buford Family of Va. (1903), 81
McClung Genealogy (1904), 296 pages
Walker Family of Virginia, 75
McClurg
William and Mary Coll. Quarterly,
  (1892), 164
McCobb
Greene's Hist. Boothbay, Me., 570–3
McCollum
Evans Family of S. C., 1905
McComb
Gustin Ancestry
Jenkins Family of Pa. (1904), 206–8
McConnel
Crumrine's Hist. Washington, Pa., 718
McConnell
Carter's Hist. of Pembroke, N. H., ii,
  224
Hanna's Ohio Valley Genealogies, 79
McCord
McKinney Family of Pa., 85–139
Robinson Family of Pa. (1902), 95
McCormick
Hanna's Ohio Valley Genealogies, 80
McIlhany's Virginia Fams. (1903), 221–7
McCoskey
Pound and Kester Genealogy, 375–83
McCoy
Hanna's Ohio Valley Genealogies, 80
Pound and Kester Gen., 200, 214–23
McCrea
Bascom's Fort Edward, N. Y., 56–60
McCrillis
Rice's New Hampshire Lake Region

McCrosky
Walker Family of Va., 1902
McCue
Glenn's Col. Mansions, ii, 321-3, 331-3
McCullough
Hanna's Ohio Valley Genealogies, 81
McCurda
Hilton-McCurda Family (1905), 12 p.
McCurdy
Larimer Family of Penn., 55-60
McCutcheon
Carter's Hist. Pembroke, N. H., ii, 225-8
McDaniel
Carter's Hist. Pembroke, N. H., ii, 228
McDonald
Old Northwest Gen. Quar., viii, 24-6
McDonough
Manning Genealogy, 384
McDougall
Greene's Hist. Boothbay, Me., 573
McDowell
Buford Family of Va. (1903), 78-81
Clayton's Hist. Union Co., N. J., 784
Landrum's Hist. Spartanburg, S. C., 393-8
McEachern
Evans Family of S. C., 1905
McElfresh
Cumming Family of Md. (1905), chart
McElroy
Cumming Family of Md. (1905), chart
McEwen
Seymour, Conn., History, 520-1
McFadden
Hanna's Ohio Valley Genealogies, 82-4
McFarland
Bean's Hist. Montgomery Co., Pa., 611
Crumrine's Hist. Washington, Pa., 564
McFarlane
McKinney Family of Pa., 54-8
McFarland
Greene's Hist. Boothbay, Me., 574-7
McFarren
McFarren Genealogy (1880), 54 pages
McFarren Genealogy Supp. (1905), 9 p.
McGavock
McGavock Family of Va. (1903), 175 p.
McGaw
Thornton Family of N. H. (1905), 11, 14
McGehee
Woods' History Albemarle Co., Va., 259
McGraw
Goodrich's Hist. Dryden, N. Y., 199-202
McGregor
Temple's History Framingham, 571
See also under Gregory
Lawrence Genealogy, 1904
McGregory
Temple's History Framingham, 571
See also under Gregory
McIlhany
McIlhany's Virginia Fams. (1903), 133-75
McIndoe
Well's History of Newbury, Vt., 627-9

McIntire
McIntire's Address at Charlton, Mass., (1906), 64-75
McIntosh
Buford Family of Va. (1903), 109-12
Stacy's Midway Church, Ga., 280
McKean
McKean Genealogy (1902), 213 pages
McKean Historical Notes (1906), 250 p.
Phila. North American, Oct. 13, 1907
McKee
McKee Family of Ky. (1900), chart
McKeith
Well's History of Newbury, Vt., 629
McKennan
Crumrine's Hist. Washington, Pa., 485
McKethan
McAllister Family of N. C. (1900), 26
McKibben
Jennings Genealogy, ii, 39, 83-9
McKinley
Washington Historical Bulletin, viii, 5-7
McKinney
McKinney Genealogy (1905), 325 pages
McKown
Greene's Hist. Boothbay, Me., 577-80
McLain
Crumrine's Hist. Washington, Pa., 760
McLaughlin
Larimer Family of Penn., 1903
McLean
McLean Fam., Hartford, Ct. (1900), 30
McLellan
Litchfield, Me., History (1897), 218
McMasters
Larimer Family of Pa., 67-72
McMillan
Moore Family of Chester, Pa., 119
McMillen
Landrum's Hist. Spartanburg, S. C., 420-2
McNary
Crumrine's Hist. Washington, Pa., 717
McNeil
Treman Genealogy
Woodruff's Litchfield, Ct., Gen. Reg., 136-8
McNeill
McAllister Family of N. C. (1900), 165
McNutt
McGavock Family of Va., 23, 56-8
McCormick Genealogy
McPheeters
Walker Family of Virginia, 65-75, 94
McPherson
See Ferson
McPike
Old Northwest Gen. Quar., vii, 267-70
McVickar
McVikar Genealogy (1906), 25 pages
McWhorter
West Va. Hist. Mag., ii, Jan., 68-73
Meacham
Allen's History of Enfield, Ct., 31
Mead
Genung Family of L. I.

Lowe Genealogy, 113–43
Mead Genealogy (1901), 471 pages
Mead Family Christmas (1902), 307 p.
Richmond, Va., Times, Nov. 1, 1903
Treman Genealogy
Tucker Genealogy (1903)
William and Mary Coll. Quar., x, 191–7, 242–5
Meade
Baltimore Sun, Aug. 21, 1904; March 24, 31, April 7, 1907
Richmond, Va., Times, Feb. 4, 1906
William and Mary Quar., xiii, 36–45, 73–102
Meader
Litchfield, Me., History (1897), 219–21
Well's History of Newbury, Vt., 632
Means
Lawrence Genealogy, 1904
So. Carolina Hist. Mag., vii, 204–16
Mears
Hanna's Ohio Valley Genealogies, 89
Mebane
Stockard's History of Alamance, N. C.
Medbery
Wilcox Genealogy (1902), 20, 29
Meech
Treman Genealogy
Meedinger
Jennings Genealogy, ii, 584
Meet
Crall Ancestry
Megaw
Hanna's Ohio Valley Genealogies, 89
Meigs
Conn. Mag., x, No. 2, 372–80
Hamlin Gen. (1900), 108–10, 147–9
Meigs Genealogy (1901), 374 pages
Meigs (1902), chart
Meigs Family (1905), chart
Nash's Fifty Puritan Ancestors, 136–41
Melendy
Ramsdell's Hist. Milford, N. H., 842–4
Mell
Mell Genealogy (1897), 89 pages
Mellen
Temple's History Framingham, 636–8
Well's Hist. of Newbury, Vt., 633–5
Melling
See under Mellen
Melvin
Palmer and Melvin Gen. (1905), 450 p.
Melzar
Ramsdell's Hist. Milford, N. H., 844
Mendenhall
Lundy Genealogy, 233
Smedley Genealogy, 126, 224
Mendum
Stackpole's Hist. Kittery, Me., 605–9
Willis' Old Eliot, Me. (1902), v, 127
Mengel
Penn.-German, viii (1907), 167–9
Mercer
Baltimore Sun, Sept. 17, 24, 1905
Fernald's Genealogical Exchange, i, 6, 11, 20, 51, 58

Goodrich's Life Gen. Hugh Mercer, 1906
Smedley Genealogy, 83
Merchant
Evans Family of S. C., 1905
Hosmer's Hist. Deer Isle, Me., 190–2
Meredith
Keith's Pa. Prov.Councillors,pt.ii,394–7
Meres
Meres Family of England (1891), 21 p.
Meriwether
Lewis Family of Va., 1906
Meriwether Genealogy, 1890
Meriwether and Minor Lineage, 1895
Meriwether Genealogy, 1899
Page Genealogy, 2d ed. (1893), 178–80
Woods' Hist. Albemarle Co., Va., 270–4
Merriam
Merriam Genealogy (1906), 500 pages
Newhall Ancestry, 153–6
Temple's History Framingham, 638
Merrick
Merrick Genealogy (1902), 494 pages
Noyes' Hist. Hampstead, N. H., ii, 756–9
Seymour, Conn., History, 517–20
Treman Genealogy
Merrill
Buell Genealogy, 195
Fernald's Genealogical Ex., iii, 42
Hoyt's Salisbury, Mass., Families, pt. x
Le Baron Genealogy, 217
Merrill Family of Ipswich (1886), 4 p.
Merrill Family of N. H. (1899), 64 pages
Merrill Family Ancestors (1903), 25 p.
Nash's Fifty Puritan Ancestors, 28–30
Ramsdell's Hist. Milford, N. H., 845–8
Sanford's Hist. Hopkinton, N. Y., 513
Washington Bulletin (1906), 52, 118
Well's Hist. of Newbury, Vt., 635–7
Merriman
See Merryman
Merritt
Clapp Ancestors (1902), 53–6
Temple's History Framingham, 631
Merrow
Dover, N. H., Enquirer July 2–9, 1868
Merry
Greene's Hist. Boothbay, Me., 588
Merryman
Merryman Genealogy (1905), 123 pages
Merseles
Harvey's Hud. and Berg. Co., N. J., 172
Merselis
Labaw's Preakness, N. J., Hist., 49–53
See Marselis
Meschter
Bean's Hist. Montgomery Co., Pa., 672
Meserve
Dover, N. H., Enquirer for Dec. 19, 1867
Well's History of Newbury, Vt., 637
Mesick
Mesick Genealogy (1883), 45 pages
Messinger
Lowe Genealogy, 107–9
Messler
Clayton's Hist. Union Co., N. J., 761

Metcalf
Fairbanks Family Quar. (1903), No. 1
Gamble's Family Data (1906), 139–42
Hall Memoranda (1902), 176–82
Litchfield, Me., History (1897), 221–3
Metcalf Genealogy (1898), 62 pages
William and Mary Coll. Mag., i, 6–15; v, 10
Meyer
Clayton's Hist. Union Co., N. J., 663
Harvey's Hud. and Berg. Co., N. J., 168
Meyer Family of Penn. (1890), 131 pages
Morr Genealogy, 71–133, 243–71
Pennsylvania-German, vii, 275–9
Roosavelt Genealogy, 5, 7
Meylen
See under Mellen
Michal
Swope Genealogy, 204–6
Micheau
Clayton's Hist. Union Co., N. J., 126
Jerseyman, x (1904), 3
Michie
Woods' Hist. Albemarle Co., Va , 274–6
Middagh
Crall Ancestry
Middleton
So. Car. Hist. Mag., i (1900), 228–62
Mifflin
Keith's Pa.Prov.Councillors,pt.ii,362–70
Mifflin Life and Ancestry (1905), 240 p.
Phila. North American, Oct. 6, 1907
Miles
Evans Family of S. C., 1905
Seymour, Conn., History, 521–4
Miley
Mayer Genealogy, 160–5
Milledge
Habersham Gen., 6–8
Miller
Clayton's Hist. Union Co., N. J., 340
Crayon's Rockaway, N. J., Records, 110
Fulton Genealogy, 191–5
Hall Memoranda (1902), 64–8
Hanna's Ohio Valley Genealogies, 91
Henderson Family of Va., 19–21
Jameson Genealogy
Kip's Memoir of C. Miller (1848), 309 p.
Le Baron Genealogy, 214
Peoria County, Ill., History, 759
Smedley Genealogy, 300
Stiles' Wethersfield, Ct., ii, 502–4
Treman Genealogy
West Va. Hist. Mag., ii, April, 38–53
William and Mary Quarterly, xi, 206
Wood Genealogy (1901), 44
Millett
Scales' History of Dover, N. H., 309–10
Millikan
Cal. Hist. Gen. Soc. Pub., iii
Milliken
White Genealogy (1900), 411–3
Milling
See under Mellen
Millins
See under Mellen

Mills
Baltimore Sun, Oct. 16, Dec. 4, 1904
Buell Genealogy, 28
Crayon's Rockaway, N. J., Records, 185
Crissey's History of Norfolk, Ct., 545
Hanna's Ohio Valley Genealogies, 91
Maulsby Genealogy, 56–60, 99
McKee Family of Ky. (1900), chart
McKinney Family of Pa., 124–8
Old Northwest Gen. Quar., vii, 93
Ramsdell's Hist. Milford, N. H., 848–51
Well's History of Newbury, Vt., 639
Woods' History Albemarle Co., Va., 276
Milton
McIlhany's Virginia Families, 177–214
Miner
Chesebrough Genealogy, 514, 523
Treman Genealogy
Tuttle Genealogy (1871), 6–9
Wheeler's Hist. Stonington, Ct., 466–78
Minge
Va. Mag. of History, iii (1895), 159
Minor
Baltimore Sun, April 23, 1905
Meriwether and Minor Lineage, 1895
Richmond, Va., Times, Feb. 5, 1905
Virg. Mag. of History, x, 97, 436–40; xi, 207–9, 335, 443
William and Mary Quar., viii, 196–8, 247–51; ix, 52–60, 179–82
Woods' Hist. Albemarle Co., Va., 277–9
Minshall
Barber Genealogy (1890), 103
Smedley Genealogy, 78, 143–7
Mintier
Hanna's Ohio Valley Genealogies, 92
Mintzer
Bean's Hist. Montgomery Co., Pa., 480
Misener
De Camp Genealogy (1896), 95–101
Mish
Egle's Dauphin County, Pa. (1883), 246
Missimer
Bean's Hist. Montgomery Co., Pa., 796
Mitchell
Bean's Hist. Montgomery Co., Pa., 969–71
Hanna's Ohio Valley Genealogies, 92
Hinchman's Nantucket Set., ii, 141, 295
Litchfield, Me., History (1897), 223–6
Stackpole's Hist. Kittery, Me., 609–16
Stiles' Wethersfield, Ct., ii, 504–8
Willis' Old Eliot, Me. (1902), v, 128–31
Mixer
Temple's History Framingham, 640
Mixser
See under Mixer
Mixter
See under Mixer
Moffitt
Peoria County, Ill., History, 730
Moir
Bean's Hist. Montgomery Co., Pa., 602
Moland
Egle's Penn. Genealogies, 417–24
Keith's Pa. Prov. Councillors, pt. ii, 417

Moler
Tucker Genealogy (1901), 226–8
Tucker Genealogy (1903)
Molineux
Molyneux Genealogy
Molone
New Eng. Hist. Gen. Reg. (1857), 307
See Meloon
Molyneux
Molyneux Genealogy (1904), 370 pages
Moncrief
Vawter Family of Virg., 248–54
Monroe
Gray Genealogy (1889), 48–51
Woods' Hist. Albemarle Co., Va., 279–81
Montague
Richmond, Va., Times, April 30, 1905
Stiles' Wethersfield, Ct., ii, 509
Montgomery
Greene's Hist. Boothbay, Me., 589–92
Keith's Pa. Prov. Councillors,pt.ii,355–7
Landrum's Hist. Spartanburg, S. C.,
    319–28
Penn. Mag. of History, xxx, 453–8
Stockard's History of Alamance, N. C.
Mooar
Mooar Genealogy (1901), 97 pages
Ramsdell's Hist. Milford, N. H., 853–5
Moody
Green Genealogy (1904), 187–206
Moody, G., Autobiography (1890), 24
Moon
Sanford's Hist. Hopkinton, N. Y., 510–3
Woods' Hist. Albemarle Co., Va., 281–3
Mooney
Peoria County, Ill., History, 676, 759
Moore
Baltimore Sun, Feb. 19, 1905; May 27,
    1906
Bean's Hist. Montgomery Co., Pa., 631
Carter's Hist. Pembroke, N. H., ii, 230–6
Haines Family of N. J., 380–91
Hanna's Ohio Valley Genealogies, 93
Jameson Genealogy
Keith's Pa.Prov.Councillors,pt.ii,74–94
Landrum's Hist. Spartanburg, S. C.,
    189–99
Litchfield, Me., History (1897), 226–8
McGavock Family of Va.
Moores of New Brunswick (1898), 100 p.
Moore Family of Newtown, N. Y. (1903),
    541 pages
Moore Family of Sudbury (1904), 22 p.
Moore Family of Windsor (1903), 308 p.
New Eng. Hist. Gen. Reg., lvii, 300–9,
    362–70; lviii, 176–8
Quinby's New Eng. Fam. Hist., i, 38–40
Ramsdell's Hist. Milford, N. H., 855–7
Richmond, Va., Times, April 29, 1906
Sayre Genealogy, 118–21, 223–38
Smedley Genealogy, 110, 202–6
Smith Genealogy (1889), 109
So. Carolina Hist. Mag., iv, 38–42
Stackpole's Hist. Kittery, Me., 616–18
Stokes Family of N. J.
Stokes Genealogy, 16

Temple's History Framingham, 641
Treman Genealogy
Walker Family of Virginia, 68, 130, 148
Wells Genealogy (1903), 123–6
White Genealogy (1900), 208
Willis' Old Eliot, Me. (1902), v, 133
Woods' Hist. Albemarle Co., Pa., 283–5
Moorhead
McKinney Family of Pa., 93–6
Moorhead Genealogy (1901), 65 pages
Robinson Family of Pa. (1902), 162–71
Moorman
Woods' History Albemarle Co., Va., 285
Moors
Warren and Jackson Fams. (1903), 47–8
Morancy
Clarke's King Wm. Co., Va., Fams.,85–7
More
N. Y. Gen. Biog. Rec., xxxvi, 213–20,
    291–301
Morehouse
Jennings Genealogy, ii, 417
Treman Genealogy
Morey
Hosmer's History of Deer Isle, Me., 93
Morford
Jerseyman, x (1904), 18–20
Morgan
Bean's History Montgomery Co., Pa.,
    1192–4
Carter's Hist. Pembroke, N., H., ii, 236–8
Colby Family of N. H., 79–83
Morgan Genealogy (1900), 297 pages
Richmond, Va., Times, Aug. 28, 1904
Stiles' Wethersfield, Ct., ii, 511
Warren Genealogy (1903), 100–3
Wheeler's Hist. Stonington, Ct., 479–81
Yates Family of Me. (1906), 1–5
Morgrage
Stackpole's Hist. Kittery, Me., 618–9
Morgridge
Litchfield, Me., History (1897), 228
Morison
Bean's Hist. Montgomery Co., Pa., 693
Morr
Morr Genealogy (1896), 295 pages
Morrell
Litchfield, Me., History (1897), 229
Stackpole's Hist. Kittery, Me., 619–23
Willis' Old Eliot Me., (1902), v, 131
Morrill
Hoyt's Salisbury, Mass., Fams., 765–95
Morrill Genealogy (1903), 21 pages
Morris
Amer. Hist. Magazine of N. Y., i (1906),
    25–44
Baltimore Sun, Dec. 10, 17, 1905
Bean's Hist. Montgomery Co., Pa.,870–2
Clark's James Greenleaf, 1901
Converse Genealogy (1905), 195–8
Crayon's The Evergreen (1903), 28–30
Glenn's Colonial Mansions, i, 118–20
Hanna's Ohio Valley Genealogies, 94
Jenkins Family of Pa. (1904), 115–7
Keith's Pa. Prov. Councillors, pt. i, 33–
    6, pt. ii, 246–7

McGavock Family of Va.
Morris Ancestry (1905), 294 pages
Morrison's Among Ourselves (1901), 2 v.
Morris MSS. in N. J. Hist. Soc. Lib.,
  chart
Penn. Magazine of History, ii
Phila. North American, Jan. 19, 1908
Tucker Genealogy (1901), 233-7
Tucker Genealogy (1903)
West Virginia Hist. Mag., v, 65-92
Woods' Hist. Albemarle Co., Va., 286-8
Morrison
Benjamin Genealogy, 68-74
Carter's History Pembroke, N. H., ii, 238
Jennings Genealogy, ii, 46-9, 93-6
Old Northwest Gen. Quarterly, ii, 58-60
Walker Family of Va., 1902
Morrow
Old Northwest Gen. Quarterly, ix, 1-6
West Virg. Hist. Mag., iii, 188
Morse
Bent Progenitors (1903), 56
Carter's Hist. Pembroke, N. H., ii, 239
Genung Family of L. I.
Hill Genealogy (1904), 46
Lamb Family of N. J., app., 17
Morse Genealogy (1903-5), 2 vols
Temple's History Framingham, 643-5
Well's History of Newbury, Vt., 640
Morton
Morton Family of Virginia (1901), 22 p.
So. Carolina Hist. Gen. Mag., v, 108-16
Virg. Mag. of History, xi, 205-7, 339,
  451-3; xii, 96-9
Mosby
Amer. Hist. Mag., iii (1898), 317-31
Richmond, Va., Times, April 3, 1904
Moses
Forman Genealogy, 133
Moss
Hall Memoranda (1902), 28-34
Morse Genealogy, 1903
Temple's History Framingham, 643-5
Van Meter's Va. and Ky. Families, 45
Wheeler's Hist. Stonington, Ct., 482-3
Woodruff's Litchfield, Ct., Gen. Reg.,
  151-3
Mossom
William and Mary Quarterly, v, 66
Mosteller
Gernhardt Family of Pa., 300
Mott
Fernald's Genealogical Exchange, iii, 33
Gustin Ancestry
Hinchman's Nantucket Set., ii, 160-8
Jerseyman, x (1904), 13
Mott Genealogy (1899), 8 pages
Mott Genealogy (1906), 8 pages
N. Y. Gen. Biog. Rec., xxxvi, 58-63,
  135-8, 279-85
Motz
Morr Genealogy, 81-4
Moulthroup
Seymour, Conn., History, 525-6
Moulton
Essex Antiquarian (1898), 46

Moulton Family Annals (1906), 454 p.
Parson's History of Rye, N. H., 463-5
Temple's History Framingham, 645
Moultrie
So. Car. Hist. Gen. Mag., v, 229-60
Mount
Symmes' Tennent, N. J., Church, 443,
  450
Mouring
William and Mary Quarterly, xii, 116
Mousall
Newhall Ancestry, 162
Mow
Parson's History of Rye, N. H., 465
Mowbray
Palmer's History Lanesborough, Mass.,
  47-60
Mowday
Bean's Hist. Montgomery Co., Pa., 771
Mower
Mower Genealogy (1904), 16 pages
Mowry
Thayer Ancestors (1894), 81-4
Moyer
Stauffer and Bauer Gen., 62-4, 131-45
Mudridge
Willis' Old Eliot, Me. (1902), v, 134
Mueller
Peoria County, Ill., History, 677
Muhlenberg
Muhlenberg Genealogy (1900), 89 pages
Penn.-German Society Pub., x
Penn.-German, i (1900), 3-11; iii (1902),
  17, 59, 147
Muirson
Woolsey Genealogy
Mulford
Shourds' Fenwick's Colony, N. J., 231,
  294-8
Mulkey
Mulkey Genealogy (1899), 35 pages
Muller
Egle's Dauphin County, Pa. (1883), 247
Mulloy
Litchfield, Me., History (1897), 231-3
Shepardson Genealogy (1907), 6
Thompson Fam. of Me. (1907), 190-247
Mumford
Chesebrough Genealogy, 55-7, 194-203
Mumford Genealogy (1900), 248 pages
Perkins' Conn. Family, 1905
William and Mary Quarterly, xi, 76,
  260
Munford
Richmond, Va., Times, March 19, 1905
Munning
Manning Genealogy, 797-801
Munroe
Lexington, Mass., Hist. Soc., ii, 131
Mackenzie's Hist. of the Munroes, 1898
Munroe Clan (1900), 80 pages
Muzzey's Reminiscences, 130-7
Newhall Ancestry, 185-6
Munsell
Munson Genealogy, 1133
Well's History of Newbury, Vt., 642

Munson
Seymour, Conn., History, 526–8
Murdock
Crumrine's Hist. Washington, Pa., 487
Murphy
Lancaster Genealogy, 154–70
Murray
Baltimore Sun, April 7, 14, 21, 1907
Greene's Hist. Boothbay, Me., 592–4
New Eng. Hist. and Gen. Reg., lv, 255–8
Muscoe
William and Mary Coll. Quar., xiii, 262
Muse
Baltimore Sun, July 15, 1906
Myers
Bean's Hist. Montgomery Co., Pa., 632–4
Treman Genealogy
Myrick
Gray Genealogy (1889), 77–9
Mytinger
Jennings Genealogy, ii, 584–604

Nabor
Neighbour Genealogy
Nachbar
Neighbour Genealogy
Nance
Nance Genealogy (1904), 372 pages
Nash
Nash's Fifty Puritan Ancestors, 1–17
Nash Family of Penn. (1903), 94 pages
New Eng. Hist. and Gen. Reg., liv, 404–6
Oberholtzer Family (1903)
Converse Genealogy (1905), 706–11
Treman Genealogy
Nason
Hosmer's History of Deer Isle, Me., 86
Stackpole's Hist. Kittery, Me., 624–39
Willis' Old Eliot, Me. (1902), v, 136–8
Naylor
Baltimore Sun, March 12, 1905
Neafie
Labaw's Preakness, N. J., History, 70–7
Neal
Litchfield, Me., History (1897), 233–8
Stackpole's Hist. Kittery, Me., 639–40
Neale
Baltimore Sun, Aug. 6, 1905
Clarke's King Wm. Co., Va., Fams., 87–92, 136–8
Emory's Colonial Families of Md., 221–3
Needham
Ramsdell's Hist. Milford, N. H., 858
Strong Genealogy, 1107
Neighbor
Neighbor Family (1906), 48 pages
Neilson
Nelson Genealogy, 1904
Nelson
Baltimore Sun, May 6, 13, 1906
Britton Genealogy, 29–31
Kellogg's Hist. Bernardston, Mass., 437
Lowell Genealogy, 14–7
Nelson Genealogy (1904), 57 pages
Page Genealogy, 2d ed. (1893), 155–194

Richmond, Va., Times, Dec. 13, 1903
Roebling's Journal S. Constant, 410–23
Well's History of Newbury, Vt., 642–4
Woods' History Albemarle Co., Va., 288
Nephew
Habersham Gen.
Nesbitt
Tucker Genealogy (1901), 223–6
Tucker Genealogy (1903)
Nettleton
Buell Genealogy, 149, 151
Hall Memoranda (1902), 72
Le Baron Genealogy, 107–9
Nevins
Schureman Genealogy, 1902
New
Stubbs Family of Virginia, 113
Newberry
Bean's Hist. Montgomery Co., Pa., 659
Edson Ancestry (1901), 13
Newbold
Stevenson Family of New Jersey, 76–8
Newcomb
Hodge Genealogy (1900)
Kellogg's Hist. Bernardston, Mass., 438–49
Newcomer
Beidler Family of Pa., 15–72
Newell
Carter's Hist. of Pembroke, N. H., ii, 241
Habersham Gen.
Temple's History Framingham, 648
Newhall
Hinchman's Nantucket Set., ii, 189–94
Newhall Ancestry (1899), 222 p.
Newkirk
Harvey's Hud. and Berg. Co., N. J., 131
Newlin
Dunwoody Genealogy (1899), 129–32
Stockard's History of Alamance, N. C.
Newman
Boogher's Va. Gleanings (1903), 237–82
Clarke's King Wm. Co., Va., Fams., 92–4
Newmarch
Stackpole's History Kittery, Me., 641
Willis' Old Eliot, Me. (1902), v, 139
Newmarsh
Andrews Family (1890)
Newport
Bean's Hist. Montgomery Co., Pa., 694
Newton
Temple's History Framingham, 649
Woolsey and Newton Ancestry (1901), 256 pages
Nicholas
Baltimore Sun, Sept. 25, 1904; April 2, 1905
Van Meter's Va. and Ky. Fams., 69–72
Woods' Hist. Albemarle Co., Va., 289–91
Nicholls
Landrum's Hist. Spartanburg, S. C., 328–33
Nichols
Gamble's Family Data, 1906
Greene Fam. of R. I. (1905), 207–58, 280
Temple's History Framingham, 650

Treman Genealogy
Nicholson
Baltimore Sun, Sept. 25, 1904
Nicholson Ancestors (1897), 148 pages
See under Nickerson
Nichson
See under Nickerson
Nickerson
Greene's Hist. Boothbay, Me., 595
Litchfield, Me., History (1897), 239–43
Temple's History Framingham, 651
Nickson
See under Nickerson
Nicol
Peoria County, Ill., History, 678
Niles
Stokes Family of N. J.
Well's History of Newbury, Vt., 644
Nisbet
Patterson Memoir (1902), 428
Nixon
Baltimore Sun, Nov. 24, Dec. 1, 1907
Jennings Genealogy, ii, 55–8, 98–108, 605–25
See under Nickerson
Nixson
See under Nickerson
Noble
Bean's Hist. Montgomery Co., Pa., 484
Crumrine's Hist. Washington, Pa., 758
Noblit
Noblit Genealogy (1906), 401 pages
Noe
Clayton's Hist. Union Co., N. J., 391
Norcross
Kewaunee, Wis., Owl for Sept., 1902, 93
Norman
Stacy's Medway Church, Ga., 278
Norris
Carter's Hist. Pembroke, N. H., ii, 242–5
Keith's Pa. Prov. Councillors, pt.ii,41–72
Norris Family of Maine (1906), 62 pages
North
Nash's Fifty Puritan Ancestors, 62
Stiles' Wethersfield, Ct., ii, 517–20
Northrup
Peck Genealogy (1877), app. xiv
Norton
Benton (David) Ancestors (1906)
Buell Genealogy, 93, 241
Fernald's Genealogical Exchange, i, 33–5, 44–6, 66, 84; iii, 72
Hallock Pedigree (1906), 60–1
Nash's Fifty Puritan Ancestors, 64–7, 158
Parson's History of Rye, N. H., 466
Norwood
Warfield's Maryland, 161
Nott
Stiles' Wethersfield, Ct., ii, 521–3
Nourse
Temple's History Framingham, 653–5
Well's History of Newbury, Vt., 645
See under Nurse
Nowell
Ramsdell's Hist. Milford, N. H., 862–4

Nowland
Peoria County, Ill., History, 679
Noyes
Chesebrough Genealogy, 317, 525
Deer Island, Me., Press for 1900
Handy's History of Sumner, Me., 72–4
New Eng. Hist. and Gen. Reg., lv, 196–9
Noyes Genealogy (1904), 2 vols.
Wells Genealogy (1903), 127
Wheeler's Hist. Stonington, Ct., 484–501
Nurse
Essex Inst. Hist. Coll. (1875), 151
See under Nourse
Nusbueckle
Doylestown, Pa., Democrat, July 17, 1902
Nute
Dover, N. H., Enquirer, April 30, 1868
Nutt
Cochrane's Francestown, N. H., 855
Nutter
Scales' History of Dover, N. H., 122–6
Treman Genealogy
Nutting
Litchfield, Me., History (1897), 243
Nyce
Dotterer Genealogy
Nye
Nye Family chart, 2 editions
Nye Reunion (1903), 78 pages; (1904), 117 pages; (1905), 101 pages; (1906), 109 pages

Oak
Oak Genealogy (1906), 90 pages
Oatman
Prindle Genealogy, 260–2
Ober
Warren Family (1903), 82–4
Oberholtzer
Beidler Family of Pa., 73–182
Oberholtzer (1903), 370 pages
O'Brien
Bean's Hist. Montgomery Co., Pa., 598
O'Briens of Machias, Me. (1904), 87 p.
Ochs
Boehm Genealogy (1902), 133–54
Ochterloney
Ochterloney Family (1902), 16 pages
Odell
Peoria County, Ill., History, 680
Odiorne
Parson's History of Rye, N. H., 467–71
Temple's History Framingham, 655
Oeland
Landrum's Hist. Spartanburg, S. C., 495
Offley
Baltimore Sun, July 28, Aug. 4, 1907
Virg. Mag. of History, xii, 201
Ogden
Clayton's Hist. Union Co., N. J., 195
Halsted and Ogden Gen. (1890), 69 pages
Ogier
Bangor Historical Magazine, vol. iii

Ogle
Baltimore Sun, Dec. 25, 1904
Warfield's Maryland, 248–50
Oglevee
Hanna's Ohio Valley Genealogies, 94
See also under Ogilvie
Okerson
Symmes' Tennent, N. J., Church, 414
Old
Woods' History Albemarle Co., Va., 291
Oldfield
Peoria County, Ill., History, 746
Oliver
Clayton's Hist. Union Co., N. J.. 241
Lawrence Genealogy (1904)
Lowell Genealogy, 8
Treman Genealogy
Olmstead
New Eng. Hist. Gen. Reg., lix, 355–60
Treman Genealogy
Well's Hist. of Newbury, Vt., 646–8
Olney
Thayer Ancestors (1894), 86–8
Oothout
Van Deusen Genealogy (1901), 107
Ordway
Hoyt's Salisbury, Mass., Families, 583–5
Orem
Baltimore Sun, Dec. 22, 1907
Orne
Greene's Hist. Boothbay, Me., 596–8
Orr
Evans Family of S. C., 1905
Orrock
Baltimore Sun, Feb. 10, 17, 24, 1907
Orth
Egle's Dauphin County, Pa.(1883), 248–9
Orton
Woodruff's Litchfield, Ct. Gen. Reg., 158–62
Orvis
Orvis Genealogy (1895), 13 pages
Orvis Genealogy (1896), 15 pages
Osborn
Clayton's Hist. Union Co., N. J., 130, 293
Old Northwest Gen. Quar., ix, 150–61
Woodruff's Litchfield, Ct., Gen. Reg., 162–4
Osgood
Quinby's New Eng. Fam. Hist., i, 74–7
Ramsdell's Hist. Milford, N. H., 866–70
Stacy's Medway Church, Ga., 279
Tapley Genealogy, 18–22
Treman Genealogy
Ostrander
Ostrander Genealogy (1902), Broadside
Sackett Ancestry (1899), 30
Otey
Buford Family of Va., 1903
Otis
Muzzey's Reminiscences, 21–47
Oulton
New Eng. Hist. and Gen. Reg., liii, 391
Outcalt
Clayton's Hist. Union Co., N. J., 740

Outwater
Harvey's Hud. and Berg. Co., N. J., 169
Overholt
Beidler Family of Pa., 73–182
See also Oberholtzer
Overmeyer
Overmeyer Genealogy (1905), 344 pages
Overton
Strong Genealogy, 157
Owen
Boone Family (1902), 4 pages
Dunwoody Genealogy (1899), 65–9
Gustin Ancestry, 43–5
Litchfield, Me., History (1897), 245
Owen Family of R. I. (1857), chart
Treman Genealogy
William and Mary Quarterly, ix, 156–60
Owens
Habersham Gen.
Owings
Warfield's Maryland, 389

Pabodie
Tucker Genealogy (1901), 155–7
Tucker Genealogy (1903)
Paca
Baltimore Sun, July 3, 24, 1904
Warfield's Maryland, 235–7
Packer
Chesebrough Genealogy, 35–7, 69–77
Fish Golden Wedding (1867), 104 pages
Hall's History of Greenland, N. H., 213
Paddlefoot
See under Paddleford
Paddleford
Temple's History Framingham, 657
Paddock
Gray Genealogy (1889), 184
Hinchman's Nantucket Settlers, ii, 299
Page
Baltimore Sun, July 31, 1904; Jan. 20, 27, Feb. 3, 10, 1907
Glenn's Colonial Mansions, i, 171–213
Gray Genealogy (1889), 45–8
Thorne's Page Platter (1902), 31 pages
Tucker Genealogy (1901), 36–9
Tucker Genealogy (1903)
Welles' Amer. Family Antiquity, 125–70
Well's History of Newbury, Vt., 648
Wheeler's Hist. Stonington, Ct., 502–3
Paine
Carter's Hist. of Pembroke, N. H., ii, 255
Litchfield, Me., History (1897), 246
N. Y. Gen. and Biog. Rec., xxxii, 135–7
Old Northwest Gen. Quar., vii, 270
Sturgis' Paine Children (1905), 16 pages
West Virg. Hist. Mag., i, pt. iv, 25
Worcester Society of Antiquity, Proc.
Painter
Converse Genealogy (1905), 679–81
Hunt Family of N. J. (1906), 74–126
Palmer
Buell Genealogy, 30, 68
Chesebrough Genealogy, 53–5, 526–30
Crayon's Rockaway, N. J., Records, 112

Keith's Pa.Prov.Councillors,pt.ii,114–9
Litchfield, Me., History (1897), 247–9
New Eng. Hist. Gen. Reg., xliv, 83–9
Palmer Family (1890), 50 pages
Palmer Family of Conn. (1901), 240 p.
Palmer Family of Conn. (1905), 450 p.
Temple's History Framingham, 657
Treman Genealogy
Wheeler's Hist. Stonington, Ct., 504–26
Woodruff's Litchfield, Ct., Gen. Reg.,
  164–6

Pancoast
Hunt Family of N. J. (1906), 27

Pannebecker
Dotterer Genealogy

Paris
Paris, Col. Isaac, Life of (1880), 32 pages

Park
Kellogg's Hist. Bernardston, Mass.,453–7
Park Fam., Stonington, Ct. (1876), 14 p.
Park Genealogy (1902), 88 pages
Temple's History Framingham, 658
Wheeler's Hist. Stonington, Ct., 527–8

Parke
Parke Family (1906), 333 pages

Parker
Baltimore Sun, Nov. 13; Dec. 4, 1904
Bent Progenitors (1903), 38
Britton Ancestry, 1901
Bronsdon Genealogy, 275
Farwell Family (1878), chart
Gamble's Bancroft Data (1906), 146
Litchfield, Me., History (1897), 249–51
Lundy Genealogy, 211–9, 448
Muzzey's Reminiscences, 114–29
New Eng. Hist. Gen. Reg., liv, 387–9
Newhall Ancestry, 167–9, add. 12–4
Parker Fam. of Kittery, Me. (1900), 3 p.
Ramsdell's Hist. Milford, N. H., 870–3
Richmond, Va., Times, Aug. 14, 1904
Stackpole's Hist. Kittery, Me., 642–3
Temple's History Framingham, 658–62
Thompson Genealogy (1907), 275–9
Treman Genealogy
Va. Magazine of History, viii, 106
Warren Genealogy (1903), 65–7
Willis' Old Eliot, Me. (1902), v, 145

Parkhurst
Parkhurst Family (1897), 51 pages
Parkhurst Family of Framingham,
  (1897), 21 pages
Temple's History Framingham, 662

Parkinson
Crumrine's Hist. Washington, Pa., 834
Hanna's Ohio Valley Genealogies, 96

Parkis
Temple's History Framingham, 662
See also under Parkhurst

Parks
Clarke Family of So. Car. (1905), 634 p.
Litchfield, Me., History (1897), 251
Parks Family of So. Car. (1905), 145 p.
Strong Genealogy, 1223–6

Parmele
Hastings Genealogy (1899), 173–5
Buell Genealogy, 149

Parmele, Rev. S., Memorial, 1882
Woodruff's Litchfield, Ct., Gen. Reg.,
  167–70

Parmenter
Kellogg's Hist. Bernardston, Mass.,
  458–62
Temple's History Framingham, 664

Parmly
Harvey's Hudson and Bergen Co., N. J.,
  79–82

Parrott
Buford Fam. of Va. (1903), 19–21

Parry
Eliot, Me., Miscellany (1897), 1
Haines Family of N. J., 149a

Parshall
Parshall Genealogy, 2d ed. (1903), 301 p.

Parsons
Allen's History of Enfield, Ct., 32
Ellis Genealogy (1900), 49–51
Henry Family of Topsfield (1905), 50–3
Litchfield, Me., History (1897), 252
Parsons of Somers, Ct. (1878), chart
Parsons Fam., Springfield (1901), 187 p.
Parson's History of Rye, N. H., 473–83
Treman Genealogy
Whaley Genealogy, 202
Woodruff's Litchfield,Ct.,Gen.Reg.,170

Partridge
New Eng. Hist. Gen. Reg., lvii, 50–8,
  184–92, 281–8, 389–97
Partridge Genealogy (1904), 46 pages
Waterhouse Family of Me., 16

Pascall
Lea Genealogy, 1906

Paschall
Glenn's Colonial Mansions, i, 110–20

Passmore
Moore Family of Chester, Pa., 152–6

Pastorius
Shoemaker Genealogy, 73

Patch
New Eng. Hist. and Gen. Reg., lvi, 198

Pate
Buford Family of Va., 1903
William and Mary Quarterly, v, 279; xii,
  116, 196

Patrick
West Virg. Hist. Mag., ii, 43

Patten
Litchfield, Me., History (1897), 252

Patterson
Bean's Hist. Montgomery Co., Pa., 470
Conover's Col. Robt. Patterson Memoir
  (1902), 452 pages
Crumrine's Washington, Pa., 727, 739
Hanna's Ohio Valley Genealogies, 96
Lundy Genealogy, 299–301, 448
Patterson Family of Conn. (1892), 55 p.
Shourd's Fenwick's Colony, N. J., 295
Temple's History Framingham, 666
Walker Family of Va., 1902

Patton
Hanna's Ohio Valley Genealogies, 97

Patty
Maulsby Genealogy, 133–6

Paul
Bean's Hist. Montgomery Co., Pa., 915
Stackpole's Hist. Kittery, Me., 643–8
Willis' Old Eliot, Me. (1902), v, 142–5
Paulding
Treman Genealogy, 834–54, 877
Pawling
Bean's Hist. Montgomery Co., Pa., 652
Burhans Genealogy, 320–36
Pawling Genealogy (1905), 84 pages
Perkiomen Region, Pa., iii, 72–6
Paxson
Bean's Hist. Montgomery Co., Pa., 1099
Paxton
Clayton's Hist. Union Co., N. J., 811
Crumrine's Hist. Washington, Pa., 713
Paxton Genealogy (1904), 56 pages
Walker Family of Virginia, 587
William and Mary Quarterly, x, 207–9
Payne
Pound and Kester Genealogy, 32–7
Treman Genealogy
Whittemore's L. I. Homes, 10–4
Payson
Carter's Hist. of Pembroke, N. H., ii, 266
Peabody
Lawrence Genealogy, 1904
Peabody Family (1904), 47 pages
Ramsdell's Hist. Milford, N. H., 874–9
Wheeler's Hist. Stonington, Ct., 529–30
Peach
Well's Hist. of Newbury, Vt., 650–7
Peacock
Haines Family of N. J., 215, 222
Ramsdell's Hist. Milford, N. H., 879
Peak
Harvey's Hud. and Bergen Co., N. J., 174
Pearl
California Register (1900), 10–2
Pearl Genealogy (1900), 33 pages
Pearson
William and Mary Quarterly, x, 64
Pearsons
Ramsdell's Hist. Milford, N. H., 880–2
Pease
Allen's History Enfield, Ct., 33
Crissey's Hist. of Norfolk, Ct., 507–9
Peaslee
Hodsdon Genealogy, 1904
Peck
Hall Memoranda (1902), 47–9, 54–6
Humphreyville Genealogy, 40–2
Sanford's Hist. Hopkinton, N. Y., 515
Treman Genealogy
Woodruff's Litchfield, Ct., Gen. Reg., 171–6
Pecker
Hoyt's Salisbury, Mass., Fams., 585–8
Morrill Ancestry (1903), 17–21
Peckham
New Eng. Hist. Gen. Reg., lvii, 31–9, 154–63
Newport, R. I., Mercury
Pees
Crumrine's Hist. Washington, Pa., 881

Peet
California Register (1900), i, 15–8
Pegram
Buford Family of Va., 278–82
Peirce
Baltimore Sun, May 27; June 3, 1906
Warren Genealogy (1903), 134–7
Pemberton
Clarke's King Wm. Co., Va., Fams., 151–3
Glenn's Colonial Mansions, ii, 191–4
Pendleton
Baltimore Sun, March 12, 1905
Britton Genealogy, 18–20
Clarke and Pendleton Ancestors (1902), 9, 46–54
Crissey's History of Norfolk, Ct., 567–9
Green's Culpeper County, Virginia
Page Genealogy, 2d ed. (1893), 239–46
Richmond, Va., Times, Feb. 7, 1904
Slaughter's Life of Wm. Green, 67–9
Van Rensselaer's New Yorkers, 3
Wheeler's Hist. Stonington, Ct., 531–6
William and Mary Quarterly, x, 201
Penick
Richmond, Va., Times, Aug. 19, 1906
Penington
Shoemaker Genealogy, 103
Penn
Baltimore Sun, June 9, 16, 1907
Keith's Pa. Prov. Councillors, pt. ii, 424–9
Pennell
Lamb Family of N. J., app. 19
Smedley Genealogy, 90
Penniman
Robinson Family (1902), 38–47
Pennington
Hall's Hist of Atlantic City, N. J., 417–21
Keith's Pa. Prov. Councillors, pt. ii, 251–5
See Penington
Penrose
Bean's Hist. Montgomery Co., Pa., 905–8
Dunwoody Genealogy (1899), 53–5
Penn. Magazine of History, xxv, 285
Penrose Genealogy (1903), 163 pages
Peper
Lawson's Genealogy (1903), 206–24
Pepper
Temple's History Framingham, 667
Pepperell
Willis' Old Eliot, Me. (1902), v, 147
Pepperrell
Essex Inst. Coll., xxxvii, 265–80, 409–16; xxxviii, 153–60, 315–20; xxxix, 81–96; xl, 73–88; xli, 229–36; xlii, 169
Maine Hist. Soc. Coll. (1893), 426–30
Quinby's New Eng. Fam. Hist., i, 51–9
Salter Memorial (1900), 27–32
Stackpole's Hist. Kittery, Me., 649–50
Percy
Crayon's Rockaway, N. J., Records, 187
Perham
Britton Ancestry, 1901
Ramsdell's Hist. Milford, N. H., 883
Perkins
Conn. Magazine, Jan. (1905), 196–203
Converse Genealogy (1905), 832

Ferrier Genealogy, 17–27
Parson's History of Rye, N. H., 483–7
Peoria County, Ill., History, 681, 760
Perkins Family (1905), 8 pages
Seymour, Conn., History, 529–30
White Gen. (1900), 47–9, 94–102
Woolsey Genealogy
Perley
Perley Genealogy (1906), 770 pages
Permenter
See under Parmenter
Perrine
Anderson and Perrine Fam. (1902), 17–79
Clayton's Hist. Union Co., N. J., 864
Crayon's Rockaway, N. J., Rec., 257–9
Crumrine's Hist. Washington, Pa., 842
Symmes' Tennent, N. J., Church, 392–9
Treman Genealogy
Seymour, Conn., History, 530–1
Perrott
Buford Family of Va. (1903)
Virginia Mag. of Hist., v (1897), 165–7
Perry
Coddington Family of N. J.
De Wolf Genealogy, 281–4
Hanna's Ohio Valley Genealogies, 98
Litchfield, Me., History (1897), 255
Warden Genealogy, 222
Pescud
William and Mary Quar., xiv, 113–7
Peter
Essex Inst. Coll., xxxviii, 1, 12
Penn.-German, vii, 352–4
Peterman
Perkiomen Region, Pa., iii (1900), 120, 135–7, 160, 167
Peters
Keith's Pa. Prov. Councillors, ii, 235–41
Peters Fam. of New Eng. (1903), 444 p.
Pettibone
Crissey's Hist. of Norfolk, Ct., 538–9
Nash's Fifty Puritan Ancestors, 40
Pettigrew
Stackpole's Hist. Kittery, Me., 649–55
Willis' Old Eliot, Me. (1902), v, 149
Pettingell
Pettingell Genealogy (1906), 582 pages
Pettingill
Carter's History Pembroke, N. H., ii, 267
Pettit
McKean Genealogy (1902), 119, 128, 147
Pettus
Richmond, Va., Times, Oct. 8, 1905
Petty
Jennings Gen., ii, 30, 58–62, 111–114
Peyton
Baltimore Sun, June 17, 24; July 1, 1906
Evans Family of S. C. (1905)
Richmond, Va., Times, July 3, 1904
Phelps
Carter's History Pembroke, N. H., ii, 268
Edson Ancestry (1901), 9–13
Harris Ancestry (1898)
Nash's Fifty Puritan Ancestors, 31–8

Old Northwest Gen. Quar., vii, 104; x 127–48
Peoria County, Ill., History, 746–8
Phelps Ancestry (1885), 2 pages
Phelps Genealogy (1897), 52 pages
Phelps Genealogy (1899), 1865 pages
Sanford's Hist. Hopkinton, N. Y., 516–20
Treman Genealogy
Wheeler's Hist. Stonington, Ct., 537–9
Woodruff's Litchfield, Ct., Gen. Reg., 177–9
Philbrick
Parson's History of Rye, N. H., 487–97
Stackpole's Hist. Kittery, Me., 655–7
Treman Genealogy
Philipse
Glenn's Colonial Mansions, ii, 245–78
Phillips
Berkshire Hist. Soc. Papers (1890), 213–30
Carter's History Pembroke, N. H., ii, 269
Hanna's Ohio Valley Genealogies, 98–100
Lowe Genealogy, 111
Peoria County, Ill., History, 683
Phillips Family of Duxbury (1903), 39 p.
Richmond Times, April 1, 1906
Stackpole's Hist. Kittery, Me., 657–60
Stuart Genealogy (1894), 43–7
Treman Genealogy
Van Meter's Va. and Ky. Families, 44
Wells Genealogy (1903), 129
William and Mary Quarterly, xiii, 66
Phinney
Hayford Family, 110, 191–5
Phipps
Temple's History Framingham, 668
Phips
Gamage Genealogy, 42, 50
Phoenix
Stackpole's Hist. Kittery, Me., 661–2
Piatt
McKinney Family of Pa., 187, 198–203, 213–5
Pickering
Deer Island, Me., Press for 1900
Hall's History of Greenland, N. H., 204
Pickernell
Stackpole's Hist. Kittery, Me., 662–3
Pickett
Treman Genealogy
Pickman
Essex Inst. Hist. Coll., xxxix, 97, 104–6, 120
Pidgin
Litchfield, Me., History (1897), 257
Pierce
Greene Family of R. I. (1905), 160–74
Greene's Hist. Boothbay, Me., 599–602
Jameson Genealogy
Newhall Ancestry, 169–72
Ramsdell's Hist. Milford, N. H., 884–6
Stackpole's Hist. Kittery, Me., 664
Stiles' Wethersfield, Ct., ii, 530
Temple's History Framingham, 669

Pierpont
Abbott, Jas. S., Memorial (1905), 41 p.
Woodruff's Litchfield, Ct., Gen. Reg., 177
Pierson
Pound and Kester Genealogy, 397–402
Pike
Litchfield, Me., History (1897), 257–9
McPike's British Archive Ex., 1906
Temple's History Framingham, 670
Wells Genealogy (1903), 131–4
Pillsbury
Carter's Hist. of Pembroke, N. H., ii, 270
Pilsbury
Stackpole's Hist. Kittery, Me., 664–5
Willis' Old Eliot, Me. (1902), v, 151
Pilson
Woods' History Albemarle Co., Va., 296
Pim
Smedley Genealogy, 161–4
Pinckney
Warfield's Maryland, 127
Pinkard
William and Mary Quarterly, xii, 262–4
Pinkham
Greene's Hist. Boothbay, Me., 602–7
Litchfield, Me., History (1897), 259–61
Scales' History Dover, N. H., 134–7
Pinney
Edson Ancestry (1901), 17–9
Old Northwest Gen. Quar., vi, 186–90;
vii, 165–73
Piper
Guthrie Genealogy (1898), 53
Pitfield
Brown Family of Pa. (1885), pt. iii, 1–13
Pitman
Dover, N. H., Enquirer for Mar. 28, 1854
Pittenger
Hanna's Ohio Valley Genealogies, 100
Pitti
Ford's History of Clinton, Mass., 159
Pitts
Warfield's Maryland, 142, 160
Pixley
New York Gen. Biog. Rec., xxvii, 65
Pixley Genealogy (1900), 95 pages
Strong Genealogy
Place
Lancaster Genealogy, 170–2
Rix Genealogy, 211–3
Plaisted
Plaisted Genealogy (1904), 66 pages
Stackpole's Hist. Kittery, Me., 665–8
Willis' Old Eliot, Me. (1902), v, 153
Plant
Ford's History of Clinton, Mass., 141, 157
Plants
Crumrine's Hist. Washington, Pa., 781
Plater
Warfield's Maryland, 243–5
Platts
Prime Genealogy (1897), 68–71
Pleas
Lancaster Genealogy, 170–9
Plimpton
Litchfield, Me., History (1897), 261

Ploeg
Burhans Genealogy, 317–9
Plumb
Chesebrough Genealogy, 336–8
Woodruff's Litchfield, Ct. Gen. Reg., 180
Plummer
Plummer Family of Phila. (1874), 25 pp.
Plummer Family of Newbury, Mass.,
(1904), 63 pages
Plumstead
Keith's Pa. Prov. Councillors, pt. ii,
167–83
Podge
McClanahan Genealogy, 38–40
Poe
Gulf States Hist. Mag., i, 281–3
Kittochtinny Magazine, i, 192–205
New York Gen. Biog. Rec., xxxviii, 55–69
Poellnitz
McAllister Family of N. C.
Polhemus
Stevenson Genealogy (1903), 8–10,
Jerseyman, ix (1903), 21, 23
Polk
Amer. Hist. Mag., iv, 46, 124
Baltimore Sun, Sept. 4, 1904
Jones Genealogical Hist. (1900), 20–6
Walker Family of Va., 511, 632–8
Pollard
Clarke's King Wm. Co., Va., Fams., 184–
94
Pollard Family of Billerica (1902), 8 p.
Richmond, Va., Times, Jan. 1, Feb. 5,
Apr. 16, 1905
Wheeler's Hist. Stonington, Ct., 540
William and Mary Quarterly, x, 202; xv,
64–9
Pollison
Crayon's Rockaway, N. J., Records, 152
Pollock
Jackson Genealogy (1890), 73–5
Pomeroy
New Eng. Hist. and Gen. Reg., lvii, 208–
13, 268–73
Pomeroy Family (1903), 15 pages
Treman Genealogy
Wheeler's Hist. Stonington, Ct., 541–2
Pomfret
Richmond, Va., Times, Sept. 18, 1904
Pond
Conn. Magazine, x, No. 1 (1906), 161–76
Ramsdell's Hist. Milford, N. H., 887–9
Treman Genealogy
Poole
Gamble's Bancroft Data (1906), 144
Pope
California Register (1900), 12–5
Cal. Hist. Gen. Soc. Pub., iii
Clayton's Hist. of Union Co., N. J., 322
Stackpole's Hist. Kittery, Me., 668
William and Mary Quarterly, xii, 192–6,
250–3; xiii, 280–4
Poppino
Sayre Genealogy, 266–8
Pordage
Bowdoin Genealogy (1887)

Bowdoin Genealogy (1894), 30

Porter
Allen's Hist. of Wenham, Mass., 142
Anderson-Perrine Family, 149–61
Buell Genealogy, 33, 36, 48, 55, etc.
Essex Institute Hist. Coll., xxxix, 311–4
Grigsby Family of Va. (1905), 8
Hanna's Ohio Valley Genealogies, 101
Kittochtinny Magazine, i, 313
McCormick Genealogy
Penn. Mag. of History, xxvi, (1902), 156
Porter Leaflets (1896)
Temple's History Framingham, 672
Treman Genealogy
Well's Hist. of Newbury, Vt., 657–9

Porterfield
McIlhany's Virginian Families (1903), 30
Norris' Shenandoah Valley

Post
Harvey's Hud. and Bergen Co., N. J., 72
Labaw's Preakness, N. J., History, 85–7
Post Genealogy (1905), 351 pages
Sanford's Hist. Hopkinton, N. Y., 513–5
Treman Genealogy

Pottenger
Baltimore Sun, Mar. 25, 1906; Mar.
10, 17, 24, 31, 1907
Bowie Genealogy

Potter
Clayton's Hist. Union Co., N. J., 320, etc.
Litchfield, Me., History (1897), 262–72
Newhall Ancestry, 51–3
Peoria County, Ill., History, 760
Potter Family of R. I. (1885), 13 pages
Potters of New Haven (1902) 9 pages
Sayre Genealogy, 250–2
Temple's History Framingham, 672

Potts
Bean's Hist. Montgomery Co., Pa., 605,
1100
Potts Genealogy (1901), 792 pages

Poultney
Baltimore Sun, Feb. 5, 1905

Pound
Pound Genealogy (1904), 628 pages

Powell
Baltimore Sun, March 3, 1907
Evans Family of S. C. (1905)
Powell and Griffith Gen. (1866), 119 p.

Power
Power Family (1870), chart
William and Mary Coll. Quar., i, 55, 144,
210; vii, 129

Powers
Deer Island, Me., Press for 1899, Art.
21–4; also 1900, 1901
Kellogg's Hist. Bernardston, Mass., 463
Ramsdell's History Milford, N. H., 889
Well's History of Newbury, Vt., 659–63

Powless
Harvey's Hud. and Berg. Co., N. J.,
175

Poythress
Va. Mag. of Hist., vii, 71, 190, 438–40

Prall
Fisher Family of New Jersey, 136–48

Pratt
Habersham Gen.
Hall Memoranda (1902), 144–8, 170–3
Southworth Ancestry (1903), 42–5
Mayflower Descendant, iii (1901), 1–8
Smedley Genealogy, 234–6
Temple's History Framingham, 673–7
Treman Genealogy

Pray
New Eng. Hist. and Gen. Reg., lv, 280
Stackpole's Hist. Kittery, Me., 669–72
Willis' Old Eliot, Me., (1902) v, 154

Prendergast
Kewaunee, Wis., Owl, vii, 436
Hazeltine's Hist. Ellicott, N. Y., 1–19

Prentice
Converse Genealogy (1905), 726–73
Wheeler's Hist. Stonington, Ct., 543–5

Prescott
Acadiensis, v, 95–101
Bent Progenitors (1903), 35–8
Carter's Hist. Pembroke, N. H., ii, 271
Ford's History of Clinton, Mass., 33–72
Lawrence Genealogy (1904)
Lowe Genealogy, 88–105
Prescott Family of Lancaster, Mass.
(1906), 6 pages
Sandwich, N. H., Reporter, ii
Well's History of Newbury, Vt., 663

Pressy
Hosmer's History Deer Isle, Me., 88,
91

Preston
Baltimore Sun, July 8, 15, 22, 1906
Bean's Hist. Montgomery Co., Pa., 665
Glenn's Colonial Mansions, ii, 343–88
Humphreyville Genealogy, 42–8
Keith's Pa. Prov. Councillors, pt. ii,
73–113
Preston Family of Conn. (1899), 67 pages
Prestons of New Haven and Va. (1900),
368 pages
Shourds' Fenwick's Colony, N. J., 178
Warfield's Maryland, 112
Wells Family Greenland (1905), 57–61

Prewitt
Van Meter's Va. and Ky. Families, 74–6

Price
Clayton's History Union Co., N. J., 853
Green Family of Virginia
Gustin Ancestry, 49–51
Hanna's Ohio Valley Genealogies, 102
Shoemaker Genealogy, 40–4, 65, 106
Woods' History Albemarle Co., Va., 298

Prichard
Seymour Conn., History, 531–3

Prickitt
Haines Family of N. J., 357–74
Stokes Family of N. J.

Priest
Priest Genealogy (1900), 538 pages

Prime
Prime Genealogy (1897), 79 pages

Prince
Baltimore Sun, Sept. 30, 1906
Kewaunee, Wis., Owl for Oct., 1901

Prindle
Prindle Genealogy (1906), 354 pages
Seymour Conn., History, 533
Pring
New Eng. Hist. Gen. Reg. (1887), 86
Prior
Allen's History of Enfield, Ct., 37
Pritchard
Hanna's Ohio Valley Genealogies, 102
Proudfit
Crumrine's Hist. Washington, Pa., 930
Prout
New Eng· Hist. and Gen. Reg., lv, 95–106
Prout Ancestry (1901), 14 pages, reprint
Provoost
New York Gen. and Biog. Rec., xviii, 1
Roosevelt Genealogy, 33
Prowell
American Ancestry, xii, 202
Prudden
Prudden Genealogy (1901)l 169 pages
Pulford
Seymour Conn., History, 533–4
Pulsifer
Handy's History of Sumner, Me., 60–71
Purchase
Essex Antiquarian, x, 167
Purington
Litchfield, Me., History (1897), 273
Purple
Kellogg's Hist. Bernardston, Mass., 465
Purrington
Putnam's Hist. Mag. (1899), 47–53, 140–4, 191–8
Puryear
Stockard's History Alamance, N. C.
Putnam
Le Baron Genealogy, 246–48, 392–93
Jenkins Fam., Pa. (1904), 166–72, 192–7
Metcalf Genealogy (1898), 57–9
Putnam Leaflets (1895–1896)
Ramsdell's History Milford, N. H., 891–4
Sanford's Hist. Hopkinton, N. Y., 516
Well's History of Newbury, Vt., 665–7
Pyle
Darlington Genealogy, 80–4, 95, 98, 121
Moore Family of Chester, Pa., 131
Pynchon
Treman Genealogy

Quackenbush
Labaw's Preakness, N. J., History, 89–91
Symmes' Tennent, N. J., Church, 456
Quarles
Clarke's King Wm. Co., Va., Fams., 96, 156–77
Woods' History Albemarle Co., Va., 299
Quarterman
Stacy's Midway Church, Ga., 265–72
Quigley
McKinney Family of Pa., 140, 227–89
Quinby
Quinby Family chart (1907)
Quinby's New Eng. Fam. Hist., i, 61–74
Waterhouse Family of Me., 18–22

Quincy
Muzzey's Reminiscences, 77–100
Quinton
Shourds' Fenwick's Colony, N. J., 122–3
Quisenberry
Quisenberry Genealogy (1900), 137 pp.

Race
Greene's Hist. Boothbay, Me., 608
Rackliff
Stackpole's Hist. Kittery, Me., 672–3
Penn. Magazine of History, xxx, 493–8
Raitt
Stackpole's Hist. Kittery, Me., 673–6
Willis' Old Eliot, Me., v (1902), 160
Ralston
Hanna's Ohio Valley Genealogies, 102
Ramage
Hanna's Ohio Valley Genealogies, 103
Rambo
Jenkins Family of Pa. (1904), 101–8
Ramsay
Woods' History Albemarle Co., Va., 300
Ramsdell
Ramsdell's Hist. Milford, N. H., 895–8
Ramsey
Crumrine's Hist. Washington, Pa., 958
Fulton Genealogy, 169–90
Hanna's Ohio Valley Genealogies, 103
Peoria County, Ill., History, 732
Ranck
Swope Genealogy, 251–4, 260
Rand
Parson's History of Rye, N. H., 499–514
Randall
Abbott's Poems of J. W. Randall, 39–45
Dover, N. H., Enquirer, Sept.-Oct., 1859
Dunwoody Genealogy (1899), 163
Litchfield, Me., History (1897), 274–6
Parson's History of Rye, N. H., 514–8
Randall Family of Mass. (1889), 35 pp.
Randall Family (1906), 64 pages
Warfield's Maryland, 116–21, 129
Well's History Newbury, Vt., 668–70
Wheeler's Hist. Stonington, Ct., 546–53
Randolph
Baltimore Sun, March 19, 1905
Clayton's Hist. Union Co., N. J., 602
Glenn's Colonial Mansions, i, 433–59
Mayer Genealogy, 97–103
Page Genealogy, 2d ed. (1893), 251–72
Treman Genealogy
William and Mary Quar., vii, 122–4, 145 –7; viii, 119–22, 263–5; ix, 182, 250–2
Woods' Hist. Albemarle Co.. Va., 301–3
Rank
Egle's Dauphin Co., Pa., (1883), 249–50
Rankin
Hanna's Ohio Valley Genealogies, 104
Ranney
Eaton Ancestry (1900), 9
Ranney Memorial Assoc. (1903), 23 p.
Ransom
Ransom Genealogy (1903), 408 pages
Treman Genealogy

William and Mary Coll. Quar., xiv, 129
Ransone
Richmond, Va., Times, Feb. 25, March
4, 1906
William and Mary Coll. Quar., x, 264–7
Rapalje
Crall Ancestry
Rathbone
Chesebrough Genealogy, 530–4
Rathbone Genealogy (1898), 837 pages
Rathbun
Alden and Smith Ancestors (1903), 30–4,
59–66
Rathvon
Swope Genealogy, 117, 142
Rawle
Glenn's Colonial Mansions, ii, 125–97
Keith's Pa.Prov.Councillors,pt.ii,255–63
Rawlings
Baltimore Sun, May 14, June 11, 1905
Warfield's Maryland, 134
Rawson
Treman Genealogy
Ray
Benton (David) Ancestors, 1906
Le Baron Genealogy, 209–11
Raymond
Jenkins Family of Pa. (1904), 137–41
Preston Genealogy, 1899
Rayner
Topliff Genealogy (1906)
Raynes
Hosmer's History Deer Isle, Me., 98–102
Raynor
N. Y. Gen. Biog. Rec., xxxvii, 187
Rea
Hanna's Ohio Valley Genealogies, 105
Woods' History Albemarle Co., Va., 303
Read
Bean's Hist. Montgomery Co., Pa., 657
Keith's Pa.Prov.Councillors,pt.ii,185–94
Le Baron Genealogy, 125, 268
Reade
Baltimore Sun, Sept. 15, 22, 29; Oct. 6,
1907
Lewis Family of Va., 1906
Richmond, Va., Times, Dec. 24, 1905
Watson's A Royal Lineage
William and Mary Coll. Quar., xii, 65;
xiv, 117–26, 281
Willis Family of Va., 155
Reading
Bean's Hist. Montgomery Co., Pa., 658
Jerseyman, vii, 12–6
Reaugh
Pound and Kester Genealogy, 40–3
Reber
Reber Family of Pa. (1901), 40 pages
Reckard
Jennings Gen., ii, 32–4, 63–74, 626–58
Redington
New Eng. Hist. Gen. Reg., lxi, 225–35
Reed
Bean's Hist.Montgomery Co.,Pa.,1010–2
Crumrine's Hist. Washington, Pa., 481,
822

Greene's Hist. Boothbay, Me., 610–20
Hall's Hist. of Atlantic City, N. J., 421–3
Peoria County, Ill., History, 761
Reed Family of Weymouth (1901), 785 p.
Reed, Lt.-Col. Jacob, Memoir (1905),
198 pages
Pound and Kester Genealogy, 112–25,
227
Temple's History Framingham, 680
Reen
Peoria County, Ill., History, 685
Rees
Dunwoody Genealogy (1899), 70
Rees
Maulsby Genealogy
Rees Genealogy (1899), 11 pages
Rees Family of Delaware (1906), 80 pp.
Smedley Genealogy, 93
Reese
Bean's Hist. Montgomery Co., Pa., 1013
Reese Genealogy (1903), 322 pages
Reesor
Pound and Kester Genealogy, 484, 492
Reeve
Sanford's Hist. Hopkinton, N. Y.,536–40
Reeves
Sinnott Genealogy
Regester
Smedley Genealogy, 127, 227
Reichel
N. Y. Gen. Biog. Record (1899), 177–80
Reid
Bean's Hist. Montgomery Co., Pa., 656
Small Family of Penn. (1905), 182–9
Symmes' Tennent, N. J., Church, 431–6
Well's History of Newbury, Vt., 671
Reiff
Dotterer Genealogy
Funk Genealogy
Stauffer and Bauer Genealogy, 114–29
Reinhold
Pennsylvania-German, vii, 295–8
Reiss
Rice Family of Pa. (1900), 16 pages
Relyea
Le Fevre's Hist. New Paltz, N. Y., 502
New Paltz Independent, 1901
Remick
Remick Genealogy, 3
Parson's History of Rye, N. H., 518–20
Remick Genealogy (1893), 7 pages
Stackpole's Hist. Kittery, Me., 677–99
Willis' Old Eliot, Me., v (1902), 161–70
Remington
Mumford Memoirs (1900), 103
Sanford's Hist. Hopkinton, N. Y., 525–8
Strong Genealogy, 1348–55
Renfrew
Well's History of Newbury, Vt., 672–4
Renick
Virg. Mag. of History, x, 92
Renshaw
Shriver Genealogy, 64–8
Reton
Fernald's Genealogical Exchange, i, 6,
51

Reyner
New Eng. Hist. and Gen. Reg., xi, 360
Reyners
Scales' History of Dover, N. H., 357–61
Reynolds
Eaton Ancestry (1900), 52–64
Kulp's Wyoming Families, 777–87
Newport, R. I., Mercury, Aug. 13, 1904
Reynolds Family of R. I. (1897), 20 pp.
Reynolds Fam. 8th Reunion (1900), 15 p.
Reynolds Fam. 9th Reunion (1901), 20 p.
Reynolds Family of Kingston, R. I. (1903), 42 pages
Reynolds Family of Conn. (1905), 38 pp.
Seymour Conn., History, 534–5
Stiles' Wethersfield, Ct., ii, 539
William and Mary Quarterly, xii, 128
Wyoming Pa., Society Proc. iv, 20–32
Reynor
Britton Ancestry (1901)
Scales' History of Dover, N. H., 116–20
Reys
Rice Family of Pa. (1900), 16 pages
Rhea
Symmes' Tennent, N.J.,Church, 399–402
Rhett
South Car. Hist. Gen. Mag., iv, 36–74, 108–89
Rhodes
Bean's Hist. Montgomery Co., Pa., 864
Rhodes Ancestral chart, 1901
Richmond, Va., Times, Sept. 10, 1905
Stiles' Wethersfield, Ct., ii, 540
Wheeler's Hist. Stonington. Ct., 554–6
Wintermute Gen., 34–9, 204–19
Rice
Bean's Hist. Montgomery Co., Pa., 703
Bent Progenitors (1903), 17
Clark and Rice Ancestors (1906), 215 p.
Ford's History of Clinton, Mass., 116
Green Genealogy (1904), 181–6
Green's Culpeper County Virg.
Hill Genealogy (1904), 45
Penn. Magazine of History, xxiv, 524
Quinby's New Eng. Fam. Hist., i, 35–7
Rice Family of Pa. (1900), 16 pages
Rice Fam. of Conway, Mass. (1904), 47 p.
Stackpole's Hist. Kittery, Me., 700–1
Temple's History Framingham, 680–7
Wells Genealogy (1903), 135–8
Willis' Old Eliot, Me., v (1902), 171
Rich
Rich's Gen. Record (1896), 3–5
Richard
Treman Genealogy
Richards
Clayton's Hist. Union Co., N. J., 261, 375
Hall's History Atlantic City, N. J., 424–7
Lawrence Genealogy (1904)
Sayre Genealogy, 322–6
Smedley Genealogy, 173–5
Stiles' Wethersfield, Ct., ii, 542
Temple's History Framingham, 687
Richardson
Bean's Hist. Montgomery Co., Pa., 746
Carter's Hist. Pembroke, N. H., ii, 274–8

Chesebrough Genealogy, 536
Deer Island, Me., Press for 1899, Art. 18
Landrum's Spartanburg, S. C.,413–5
Lawson Genealogy (1903)
Litchfield, Me., History (1897), 276–83
Ramsdell's Hist. Milford, N. H., 899
Richardson Family, Woburn (1903), 6 p.
Richardson Family of Va. (1905), 50 p.
Richardsons of Stonington, Ct. (1906), 147 pages
Richmond, Va., Times, April 9; Sept. 3, 1905
Small Family of Penn. (1905), 219–35
Temple's History Framingham, 687
Warfield's Maryland, 174–7
Warren Genealogy (1903), 90–4
White Genealogy (1900), 539–45
Richmond
Putnam's Hist. Mag. (1896), 260–3
Rickard
Jennings Genealogy, ii, 626–31
Ricker
Dover, N. H., Enquirer, Dec. 7–Feb. 8, 1877
Well's History of Newbury, Vt., 674
Ricks
See Rix
Riddick
Alston Genealogy, supp., 146a–d
Rideout
Ramsdell's Hist. Milford, N. H., 901
Rider
Gray Genealogy (1889), 25–36
Temple's History Framingham, 688
Ridgely
Baltimore Sun, May 24, 1904
Warfield's Maryland, 77–83, 351, 379, 416
Ridgway
Phila. North American, Nov. 24, 1907
Old Northwest Gen. Quar., v, 5, 39–42
Ridley
Litchfield, Me., History (1897), 283–5
Ridout
Warfield's Maryland, 100
Rieth
Penn.-German, iv, 253–7; v (1904), 90–2
Riggs
Crumrine's Hist. Washington, Pa., 644
Riggs Gen. (1901), 147 pages
Seymour, Conn., History, 535–44
Symmes' Tennent, N. J., Church, 411
Warfield's Maryland, 354–61
Rightmire
Jennings Genealogy, ii, 617–20
Riley
Stiles' Wethersfield, Ct., ii, 543–8
Ring
Litchfield, Me., History (1897), 285–8
Risdon
Sanford's Hist. Hopkinton, N. Y., 520–5
Risley
Risley Family Assoc. (1906), 8 pages
Ritchey
Hanna's Ohio Valley Genealogies, 150

Ritchie
Crumrine's Washington, Pa., 604, 624
Riter
Beidler Family of Pa., 263–6
See Ritter
Rittenhouse
Bean's Hist. Montgomery Co., Pa., 577
Lawson Genealogy (1903)
Ritter
Pennsylvania-German, vii, 292–5
See Riter
Rives
Page Genealogy, 2d ed. (1893), 231–3
Woods' Hist. Albemarle Co., Va., 304–6
Rix
Rix Genealogy (1906), 240 pages
Robards
Va. Magazine of History, viii, 418–20;
  ix, 195–8; x, 98, 205, 307; xi, 96–8
Robarts
Crayon's Rockaway, N. J., Records, 114
Robbins
Crissey's Hist. Norfolk, Ct., 392–404
Le Baron Genealogy, 62–4, 153–7, 256
Stiles' Wethersfield, Ct., ii, 549–84
Treman Genealogy
Robert
Treman Genealogy
Roberts
Bean's Hist. Montgomery Co., Pa., 966,
  1012, 1183
Crayon's The Evergreen (1903), 15–9
Kewaunee, Wis., Owl, Sept.–Oct. 1900
Lancaster Genealogy, 105–14
Peoria County, Ill., History, 680
Potts Genealogy (1901), 261
Roberts Family of Me. (1903), 143 pages
Sanford's History Hopkinton, N. Y.,
  528–36
Scales' History of Dover, N. H., 91–4
Shoemaker Genealogy, 58, 91–3
Robertson
Bellows Falls Times, April, (1905)
Buford Family of Va. (1903), 92–116
Carter's History Pembroke, N.H., ii, 278
Robertson Family of Va. (1900), 289 p.
Stiles' Wethersfield, Ct., ii, 585
Tiernan Genealogy (1901), 383–90
Robeson
Bean's Hist. Montgomery Co., Pa., 944
Robie
Robie Genealogy, 2d ed. (1900), 131 p.
Robins
Clarke's King Wm. Co., Va., Fams., 97,
  147–51
Smedley Genealogy, 214
Robinson
Baltimore Sun, Aug. 26, 1906
Barclay Genealogy, 117
Burton and Robinson Reunion (1906),
  32 pages
Carter's Hist. Pembroke, N, H., ii, 279–
Carter's Hist. Pembroke, N.H., ii, 279–86
Clarke's King Wm. Co., Va., Fams., 98
Coddington Family of N. J.
Clayton's Hist. Union Co., N. J., 388

Handy's History of Sumner, Me., 81–3
Jameson Genealogy
Jenkins Family of Pa. (1904), 163
Litchfield, Me., History (1897), 288–96
McKinney Family of Pa., 89, 110–24
New Eng. Hist. Gen. Reg., lvi, 57–9
Richmond, Va., Times, May 20, Sept. 16,
  1906
Robinson Family of Va. (1895), 125 p.
Robinson Fam. Rehoboth (1901), 27 p.
Robinson Family Assoc. (1902), 104 p.
Robinson Family of Pa. (1902), 233 p.
Robinson Fam. of Reading, Vt. (1903),
  68 pages
Robinson Family Ancestry (1903), 28 p.
Robinson and Kinsfolk (1906), 159 p.
Stern's Our Kindred, 85
Temple's History Framingham, 689
Treman Genealogy
Van Rensselaer's New Yorkers, 7, 18
Well's History Newbury, Vt., 675
Roby
New Eng. Hist. Gen. Reg., lx, 92
Rockhill
Jerseyman, Flemington, N. J., ii (1893),
  14–6
Rockwell
Habersham Genealogy, 22–4
Rockwood
Hill Genealogy (1904), 54
Rockwood Fam. of Grafton (1905), 36 p.
Rodes
Amer. Hist., Mag. iv (1899), 43; ix
  (1904), 183–6
Woods' Hist. Albemarle Co., Va., 306–8
Rodger
Hill, Rodger and Brodie Fams. of Scot-
  land and New York (1888), 81 pages
McKinney Family of Pa., 234, 256–72
Rodgers
Rodgers Family of Pa. (1876), 4 pages
Roe
Jennings Genealogy, ii, 377, 389–94
Roe Diary (1904), 5–13
Treman Genealogy
Rogers
Bean's Hist. Montgomery Co., Pa., 550
Brush-Bowers Genealogy (1904), 42–4
Converse Genealogy (1905), 734–8
Eliot, Me., Miscellany (1897), 5–8
Habersham Genealogy, 28
Eliot, Me., Miscellany (1897), 5–8
Hanna's Ohio Valley Genealogies, 106
Litchfield, Me., History (1897), 296
McIlhany's Virg. Fams. (1903), 228–63
Old Northwest Gen. Quarterly, iv, 85
Richmond, Va., Times, March 13, 1904
Robertson Genealogy, 205–24
Rogers Family (1887) chart
Rogers Fam., Mansfield, Ct. (1901), 7 p.
Rogers Family of Conn. (1902), 520 p.
Rogers of New Hampshire (1902), 15 p.
Rogers Estate, Kittery, Me. (1906), 7 p.
Shourds' Fenwick's Colony, N. J., 73
Sinnott Genealogy
Stackpole's Hist. Kittery, Me., 701–9

6

Tucker Genealogy (1901), 153–5
Tucker Genealogy (1903)
Well's Hist. Newbury, Vt., 676–81
White Genealogy (1900), 88
William and Mary Quarterly, xii, 128
Willis' Old Eliot, Me., v (1902), 173–80
Woods' Hist. Albemarle Co., Va., 308–10
Rolfe
Baltimore Sun, Nov. 5, 1905
Keim and Allied Families, 616–9
Roller
Richmond, Va., Times, Feb. 19, 1905
Rollins
Litchfield, Me., History (1897), 297
Well's History of Newbury, Vt., 681
Romaine
Harvey's Hud. and Berg. Co., N. J., 78
Romeyn
Harvey's Hudson and Bergen Co., N. J.,
   139–44
Ronk
LeFevre's Hist. New Paltz, N. Y., 500–2
New Paltz Independent, Aug. 16, 1895
Roos
Gustin Ancestry
Roosa
N. Y. Gen. Record, xxxi, 235–7
Roosavelt
Whittemore's L. I. Homes, 38–44
Roosevelt
New Amsterdam Year Book, ii, 7–9
Roosevelt Genealogy (1902), 121 pages
Washington Hist. Bulletin (1906), 50
Root
Kellogg's Bernardston, Mass., 467–9
Treman Genealogy
Rootes
Rootes Family of Va. (1906)
Roots
Eaton Ancestry (1900), 65
Ropes
Essex Inst. Hist. Coll., xl, 5-8
Wells Genealogy (1903), 139–41
Well's History of Newbury, Vt., 682–4
Rorer
Bean's Hist. Montgomery Co., Pa 902–4
See Rohrer
Rosbrugh
Clyde's Life J. Rosbrugh (1880), 75–101
Rose
Lamb Family, N. J. (1904), pp., 12–6
Penn. Mag. of History, xxviii, 102–4
Stiles' Wethersfield, Ct., ii, 589–91
Rosebrooks
Strong Genealogy, 1105
Rosenberger
Bean's Hist. Montgomery Co., Pa., 872
Ross
American Ancestry, xii, 193
Gulf States Hist. Mag., i (1902), 207–11
Hanna's Ohio Valley Genealogies ,107
Ross Memorial (1884), 17 pages
Stackpole's Hist. Kittery, Me., 709–10
Rossiter
New Eng. Hist. Gen. Reg., lv, 149–54
Wheeler's Hist. Stonington, Ct., 557–8

Woodruff's Litchfield, Ct., Gen. Reg.,185
Rotch
Hinchman's Nantucket, ii, 176–82, 301
Lawrence Genealogy (1904), 143–52
Roush
Morr Genealogy, 35–70
Rowan
Baltimore Sun, Sept. 25, 1904
Rowe
Seymour, Conn., History, 534–5
Rowell
American Ancestry, xii, 197
Rowland
Bean's Hist. Montgomery Co., Pa., 636
Clayton's Hist. Union Co., N. J., 796
Hanna's Ohio Valley Genealogies, 107
Rowlandson
Putnam's Hist. Mag. (1899), 123
Stiles' Wethersfield, Ct., ii, 591–3
White Genealogy (1900), 413–5
Rowley
N. Y. Gen. Biog. Rec., xxxvii, 57–66,
   97–103, 203–8, 251–6; xxxviii, 136–9
Roy
Va. Magazine of History, viii, 331
Royal
Bean's Hist. Montgomery Co., Pa., 521
Royall
Va. Magazine of History, viii, 75, 296
Royer
Bean's Hist. Montgomery Co., Pa., 653
Rue
Clayton's History Union Co., N. J., 865
Symmes' Tennent, N. J., Church, 455
See La Rue
Ruffner
West Virg. Hist. Mag., i, pt. ii, 31–8, pt.
   iii, 33–41, pt. iv, 46–54; ii, pt. i, 45–53,
   pt. ii, 60–74, pt. iii, 36–44
Rugg
Seymour, Conn., History, 535–6
Temple's History Framingham, 691
Ruggles
Carter's Hist. Pembroke, N. H., ii, 286
Treman Genealogy
Tucker Genealogy (1901), 64–82
Tucker Genealogy (1903)
Well's History of Newbury, Vt., 684
Rumph
Rumph Family of So. Car. (1903), 10 p.
Rumsey
Baltimore Sun, June 5, 1904
West Virg. Hist. Mag., iii (1903), 185–7
Rundell
Strong Genealogy, 260
Runyon
Clayton's Hist. of Union Co., N. J., 673
Leonard's Piscataway, N. J., Planters,
   21–31
Rush
Phila. North American, Nov. 17, 1907
Jenkins Family of Pa. (1904), 129–33
Rusk
Pound and Kester Genealogy, 431–7
Russell
Abbott, Jas. S., Memorial (1905), 41 p.

Cornell Genealogy, 393
Hamlin Genealogy (1900), 61–3, 85–91, 118–20
Hinchman's Nantucket Set., ii, 149–51
Le Baron Genealogy, 147, 263, 296
New Eng. Hist. Gen. Reg., lviii, 364–71; lix, 22–32; lx, 383–6
Russell Fam. of Cambridge (1900), 52 p.
Russell, Charles H., Memoir (1903)
Russell Fam. of Dartmouth (1904), 20 p.
Seymour, Conn., History, 546
Stiles Wethersfield, Ct., ii, 593–614
Treman Genealogy
Well's History of Newbury, Vt., 686
West Virg. Hist. Mag., i, pt. ii, 26
Wheeler's Hist. Stonington, Ct., 559–61
William and Mary Quarterly, xi, 264
Woodruff's Litchfield, Ct. Gen. Reg., 186
Rust
Richardson Genealogy (1906)
Rutgers
Roosavelt Genealogy, 9, 15–7
Rutherford
Baltimore Sun, Sept. 11, 18, 1904
Richmond, Va., Times, Nov. 6, 1904
Walker Family of Va. (1902)
West Virg. Hist. Mag., i, pt. iv, 54–61
Rutter
Yerkes Genealogy (1904), 225–32
Ryan
Crissey's History of Norfolk, Ct., 573–5
Ryder
Clayton's Hist. of Union Co., N. J., 740
Ryerson
Harvey's Hud. and Berg. Co., N. J., 179
Labaw's Preakness, N. J., History, 82
Ryerson MSS. N. J. Hist. Soc. Lib., 83 p.
Ryerson Genealogy (1902), 89 pages
Treman Genealogy
Ryno
Clayton's Hist. of Union Co., N. J., 295
Ryther
Kellogg's Bernardston, Mass., 469–75

Sabin
Hamlin Genealogy (1900), 154–7
Sabine
Sabine Family of Boston (1904), 15 p.
Temple's History Framingham, 693
Sackett
Tucker Genealogy (1901), 174–7
Tucker Genealogy (1903)
Safford
Stackpole's Hist. Kittery, Me, 710-1
Sage
Hamlin Genealogy (1900), 115–8
Salisbury
Treman Genealogy
Sallee
Pound and Kester Genealogy, 200–4
Sally
Litchfield, Me., History (1897), 299
Salter
Jerseyman, x (1904), 22–4

Parson's History of Rye, N. H., 521
Salter's John Salter (1900), 58 pages
Saltonstall
Lawrence Genealogy (1904)
Mumford Memoirs (1900), 196–209
Sampson
Cambridge Genealogical Advertiser, iv, 83–7
Le Baron Genealogy, 201–2
Litchfield, Me., History (1897), 299
Sanborn
Litchfield, Me., History (1897), 300
Treman Genealogy
Sandee
Santee Genealogy
Sanders
Wells Genealogy (1903)
Sanderson
Kellogg's Bernardston, Mass., 475–7
Temple's History Framingham, 693
Sandi
Santee Genealogy
Sands
Cornwell Genealogy, 387–9
Gulf States Hist. Mag., i, 352–4
Sandy
Santee Genealogy
Sanford
Chesebrough Genealogy, 534
New Eng. Hist. and Gen. Reg., lvi, 294–7; lviii, 200
Sanford's Hist. Hopkinton, N. Y., 558–66, 571–4
Tuttle Genealogy (1871), 11–6
Woodruff's Litchfield, Ct. Gen. Reg., 187–90
Sanger
Claflin Genealogy, 414–9
Temple's History Framingham, 694
Santee
Santee Genealogy (1899), 106 pages
Santee Fam. Quar. (1899–1900), 24 p.
Sappington
Warfield's Maryland, 378
Sarchet
Sarchet Family of Ohio (1902), 11 pages
Sargeant
Bellows Falls Times, Mar. 2, 1905
Sargeant MSS. in N. J. Hist. Soc. Lib.
Sargent
Carter's Pembroke, N. H., ii, 287–91
Greene's Hist. Boothbay, Me., 621
Lawrence Genealogy (1904)
New Eng. Hist. Gen. Reg., lviii, 377–86
Ramsdell's Hist. Milford, N. H., 906–10
Rowell Genealogy
Sargent Genealogy (1904), 12 pages
Sater
Baltimore Sun, Jan. 14, 21, May 20, 1906
Satterlee
Chesebrough Genealogy, 44–7, 105–10
Saunders
Hosmer's Hist. Deer Isle, Me., 88
Parson's History of Rye, N. H., 523–5
William and Mary Coll. Quar., xiv, 145–50

Saurman
Martindale's Hist. Byberry, Pa., 343–7
Savage
Baltimore Sun, Dec. 18, 1904
Clayton's Hist. of Union Co., N. J. 286
Nash's Fifty Puritan Ancestors, 61
Ramsdell's Hist. Milford, N. H., 910–2
Richmond, Va., Times, May 28, 1905
Savery
Anderson-Perrine Family, 167–80
Savory
Savory Genealogy (1904), 16 pages
Savil
Vinton Genealogy, 298
Sawin
Hill Genealogy (1904), 48
Sawtell
Gamble's Family Data (1906), 178–85
Sawyer
Carter's Hist. Pembroke, N. H., ii, 291–3
Ford's History Clinton, Mass., 75, 113
Greene's Hist. Boothbay, Me., 622
Hoyt's Salisbury, Mass., Fams., 589–97
Litchfield, Me., History (1897), 300–3
Lowe Genealogy, 84–7
Ramsdell's Hist. Milford, N. H., 912
Well's Hist. of Newbury, Vt., 686–8
White Genealogy (1900), 79–81
Saxton
Chesebrough Genealogy, 513–5
Say
Penn. Mag. of History, xxix, 216–23
Sayer
Hoyt's Salisbury, Mass., Families, 596
Sayers
Sayre Genealogy, 254–60
Sayles
Thayer Ancestors (1894), 97–101
Saylor
Bean's Hist. Montgomery Co., Pa., 1195
Saylor
Stauffer and Bauer Genealogy, 156–64
Sayre
Clayton's History of Union Co., N. J., 388
Scales
West Virg. Hist. Mag., i, pt. iv, 22
Scammon
Stackpole's Hist. Kittery, Me., 711–3
Willis' Old Eliot, Me., v (1902), 182
Scarborough
Baltimore Sun, Mar. 26, 1905, pages 8, 9
Scarburgh
William and Mary Quar., vii, 189
See Scarborough
Scarlett
William and Mary Quarterly, xi, 145
Schaeffer
Penn.-German, vii (Dec., 1906), 389
Schamp
Jerseyman, vii (1901), 25
Scheetz
Bean's Hist. Montgomery, Co. Pa., 662
Schell
Penn.-German, ii (1901), 133–9
Schenck
American Ancestry, xii, 88

Beekman's Monmouth, N. J., Set., 1–16
Gustin Ancestry, 71
Jerseyman, x (1904), 28
Symmes' Tennent, N. J., Church, 441–3
Schermerhorn
N. Y. Gen. Biog. Rec., xxxvi, 141–7,
  200–5, 254–60
Schermerhorn Genealogy (1903), 19 p.
Schley
Shriver Genealogy, 123–7
Schmuck
Lundy Genealogy, 177–9, 449
Stevenson Family of New Jersey, 74
Schofield
Seymour, Conn., History, 546
Scholfield
Merryman Family of Maine, 65–8
Scholl
Bean's Hist. Montgomery Co., Pa., 744–6
Schooley
N. J. Hist. Soc. Proc., ser. 2, ix, 245–9
Lundy Genealogy, 189–209, 449–55
Schoolfield
Baltimore Sun, July 8, 1906
Schoonmaker
Burhan's Genealogy, 22–5
Le Fevre's Hist. New Paltz, N. Y., 499
Schryver
Schriver Genealogy, 158
Schuler
Mayer Genealogy, 141, 151–60
Schumacher
See Shoemaker
Schureman
Schuremans of New Jersey (1902), 142 p.
Schuremans of New York (1903), 41 p.
Schuyler
Glenn's Colonial Mansions, ii, 397–441
Herkimer and Schuyler Genealogy
  (1903), 147 pages
Treman Genealogy
Tucker Genealogy (1901)
Schwenck
Dotterer Genealogy
Schwenk
Dotterer's Perkiomen, Pa., iii, 51, 188–91
Stauffer and Bauer Genealogy, 106–30
Scott
Clayton's Hist. of Union Co., N. J., 505
Hanna's Ohio Valley Gen., 109–11
Hosmer's History of Deer Isle, Me., 63
Kellogg's Bernardston, Mass., 477–82
Maulsby Family of Pa.
McGavock Family of Va.
McGinness and Scott Genealogy (1892),
  143–286
New Eng. Hist. Gen. Reg., lx, 168–75
Phila. North American, Jan. 5, 1908
Richmond, Va., Times, Oct. 16, 1904
Scott Family of R. I. (1868), 9 pages
Scott Family of Providence (1906), 10 p.
Scott Family of Hatfield, Mass. (1906),
  220 pages
Stockard's History of Alamance, N. C.
Temple's History Framingham, 696
Thayer Ancestors (1894), 102–5

Walker Family of Virginia, 296
Well's History of Newbury, Vt., 688
Woods' History Albemarle Co., Va., 312
Scranton
Nash's Fifty Puritan Ancestors, 151-5
Screven
Maine Hist. Soc. Coll. (1894), 275-84
Habersham Gen.
Scudder
Clayton's Hist. of Union Co., N. J., 340
Scull
Hall's Hist. Atlantic City, N. J., 428-33
Lamb Family of N. J. (1904), 18
Seabury
Peoria County, Ill., History, 689
Putnam's Hist. Mag. (1899), 165, vii,
225-9
Searight
Searight Memorial, 66 pages
Searle
Putnam's Hist. Mag. (1896), 263-5
Strong Genealogy, 271, 558, 1208-10
Wheeler's Hist. Stonington, Ct., 562-5
Searles
Ramsdell's Hist. Milford, N. H., 913
Sears
Sayre Genealogy, 260-5
Seaton
Pound and Kester Genealogy, 18-21
Seaver
Temple's History Framingham, 696
Seavey
Greene's Hist. Boothbay, Me., 623
Parson's History of Rye, N. H., 526-37
Seawell
William and Mary Coll. Quar., vii, 194;
viii, 54-62
Sedgwick
Berkshire Hist. Soc. Coll. (1900), 91-106
Seeley
Hoyt's Salisbury, Mass., Families, 567
Sehner
Sehner Ancestry (1896), 6 pages
Sehren Ancestry (1896), 16 pages
Selden
William and Mary Coll. Quar., vi; vii,
50; xii, 259
Sellers
Hosmer's History Deer Isle, Me., 105-7
Sellers and Wemple Gen. (1903), 139 p.
Selser
Bean's Hist. Montgomery Co., Pa., 968
Semple
Robertson Gen., 34-8, 43-53, 65-80
Sendee
Santee Genealogy
Sendie
Santee Genealogy
Sendy
Santee Genealogy
Seneca
Shourd's Fenwick's Colony, N. J., 188
Sentie
Santee Genealogy
Sergeant
Wardell Family, chart

Seton
Seton Genealogy (1899), 438 pages
Sever
Temple's History Framingham, 696
Severance
Carter's Hist. Pembroke, N. H., ii, 294
Kellogg's Bernardston, Mass., 482-4
Rich's Gen. Record (1896), 7-9
Severns
Collord Ancestors, 7-9, 44
Sewall
Drake's History of Boston (1856)
New Eng. Hist. Gen. Reg., i, 111-3
Sewall Genealogy (1904), 20 pages
Seward
Nash's Fifty Puritan Ancestors, 156
Sewell
Baltimore Sun, May 7, 1905
Warfield's Maryland, 135-40
Seymour
Blair Genealogy (1900), 175-80
Buell Genealogy, 195
Conn. Mag., x, No. 1 (1906), 156-9
Seymour Pedigree (1900), 10 pages
Seymour Progenitor (1906), 5 pages
Seymour Arms (1906), 31 pages
Stiles' Wethersfield, Ct., ii, 618-24
Tucker Genealogy (1901), 237-42
Tucker Genealogy (1903)
Woodruff's Litchfield, Ct. Gen. Reg.,
192-5
Shackford
Carter's Hist. Pembroke, N. H., ii, 295
Shackleford
Richmond, Va., Times, May 7, 1905
Shackelton
Wintermute Gen., 248-50
Shackley
Stackpole's Hist. Kittery, Me., 713-5
Shaeffer
Egle's Dauphin Co., Pa. (1883), 250-1
Shafer
Gernhardt Genealogy, 89-97
Shambaugh
Hanna's Ohio Valley Genealogies, 111
Shannon
Bean's Hist. Montgomery Co., Pa., 479
Noyes' Hist. Hampstead, N. H., ii,
753
Shannon Genealogy (1905), 578 pages
Shapleigh
Newhall Ancestry, 63
Stackpole's Hist. Kittery, Me., 716-28
Treman Genealogy
Willis' Old Eliot, Me., v (1902), 184-96;
vi, 1-13, 60
Shapley
Parson's History of Rye, N. H., 537-9
Sharp
Haines Family of N. J., 208-52
Hanna's Ohio Valley Genealogies, 111
Sharp Family, Chester, Pa. (1903), 36 p.
Stokes Family of N. J.
Sharpe
Reese Genealogy, 73-6, 105, 112
Seymour, Conn., 546-8

Shatswell
Hammatt Papers of Ipswich, 330–2
Shattuck
Carter's Hist. Pembroke, N. H., ii, 296
Ramsdell's Hist. Milford, N. H., 916
Shaw
Bean's Hist. Montgomery Co., Pa., 969
Litchfield, Me., History (1897), 303
Ramsdell's Hist. Milford, N, H.. 917–9
Shaw Genealogy (1904), 435 pages
Tucker Genealogy (1901), 117–25
Tucker Genealogy (1903)
Shawban
Clarke's King Wm. Co., Va., Fams., 99
Sheafe
New Eng. Hist. Gen. Reg., lv, 208–20
Parson's History of Rye, N. H., 539
Sheafe Genealogy (1901), 14 pages
Sheafe chart (1902)
Sheakley
Larimer Family of Penn. (1903), 45–52
Sheals
Sanford's Hist. Hopkinton, N. Y., 576
Shearer
Bean's Hist. Montgomery Co., Pa., 779
Sheather
New Eng. Hist. Gen. Reg., lix, 45
Shedd
Hodge Genealogy (1900)
Ramsdell's Hist. Milford, N. H., 919–21
Well's History of Newbury, Vt., 689
Shee
Keith's Pa. Prov. Councillors, pt. ii, 434–5
Sheffield
Chesebrough Genealogy, 537
Wheeler's Hist. Stonington, Ct., 566–7
Sheldon
Denison-Sheldon Family (1905) chart
Holton-Sheldon Family (1879) chart
Kellogg's Hist. Bernardston, Mass.,
  485–92
Sanford's Hist. Hopkinton, N. Y., 540–
  2, 546–52, 567–70
Smedley Genealogy, 149
Shelley
New Eng. Hist. Gen. Reg., lx, 332–5
Shelly
Beidler Family of Pa., 52–61
Shelton
Shelton Reunion (1877), 104 pages
Woods' Hist. Albemarle Co., Va., 313–5
Shenck
Kagy Genealogy, 104
Shepard
Bean's Hist. Montgomery Co., Pa., 1040
Dedham Hist. Register, xiv, 27–31
Old Northwest Gen. Quar., ix, 51–8
Ramsdell's Hist. Milford, N. H., 921–3
Shepard Family (1891), 39 pages
Shepard Family of Worcester (1903), 4 p.
Temple's History Framingham, 699
Woolsey Genealogy
Shepardson
Old Northwest Gen. Quar., ix, 59–64
Shepardson Fam., Salem, Mass. (1906),
  6 pages

Shepardson Family of Salem (1907), 8 p.
Shepardson Family of Salem (1907), 7 p.
Shepardson Family of Salem (1907), 8 p.
Shepherd
Gustin Ancestry, 55–8
Stackpole's Hist. Kittery, Me., 715–6
West Virg. Hist. Mag., iii, 31, 190
Shepley
Britton Ancestry (1901), 39
Sheppard
Shoemaker Genealogy, 47
Treman Genealogy
Sherburne
New Eng. Hist. Gen. Reg., lviii, 227–35,
  391–6; lix, 56–61; lxi, 82
Parson's History of Rye, N. H., 541
Sherburne Genealogy (1904), 22 pages
Sherman
Greene's Hist. Boothbay, Me., 624–6
Mumford Memoirs (1900), 27–9
Nash's Fifty Puritan Ancestors, 78
New Eng. Hist. Gen. Reg., lix, 397–400;
  lxi, 271–4
Newhall Ancestry, 72–6, 192–7
Robinson Genealogy (1901), 12–5
Thayer Ancestors (1894), 106–8
Tucker Genealogy (1901), 255–63
Tucker Genealogy (1903)
Sherwin
Gray Genealogy (1889), 36–41
Sherwood
N. Y. Mail and Express, Dec. 13, 1902
Shields
Tyler Letters, iii (1896), 218–20
Shindell
Egle's Dauphin Co., Pa. (1883), 251
Shinn
Shinn Genealogy (1903), 334 pages
Shipman
American Ancestry, xii, 157
Clark Family of Vermont (1905), 29, 52–5
Southworth Ancestry (1903), 45–50
Shippen
Keith's Pa. Prov. Councillors, pt. i, 46–141
Shippen Ancestors in Eng. (1904), 20 p.
Penn. Mag. of History, xxiv, 402; xxviii,
  385–402
Shoemaker
Bean's Hist. Montgomery Co., Pa., 741,
  1083, 1177–80
Brown Family of Pa. (1885), pt. ii, 21–3
Funk Genealogy
Keith's Pa. Prov. Councillors, pt. ii,
  242–64
Phila. North American, Oct. 27, 1907
Shoemaker Family, Phila. (1903), 524 p.
Shores
Treman Genealogy
Shorey
Litchfield, Me., History (1897), 304
Stackpole's Hist. Kittery, Me., 728–30
Short
Boone Family (1902), 4 pages
Seymour, Conn., History, 548–9
William and Mary Coll. Quar. (1895),
  246, 261

Shotwell
Hanna's Ohio Valley Genealogies, 112
Lundy Genealogy, 159, 455–7
Shreve
Shreve Genealogy (1901), 672 pages
Shriver
Shriver Genealogy (1888), 160 pages
Swope Genealogy, 371–5
Shurtleff
Le Baron Gen., 42, 94–7, 213, 215–7
Litchfield, Me., History (1897), 305
Shurtleff Lineage (1895) chart
Sias
Well's History of Newbury, Vt., 691
Sibley
Bean's Hist. Montgomery Co., Pa., 943
Hastings Genealogy (1899), 77–80
Sickles
Harvey's Hud. and Berg. Co., N. J., 179
Sikes
Buell Genealogy, 163
Silliman
Harris Ancestry (1898)
Peoria County, Ill., History, 762
Simeral
Hanna's Ohio Valley Genealogies, 113
Simmons
Hoyt's Salisbury, Mass., Families, 601
Putnam's Hist. Mag. vi, 212–7; 313, vii,
3–6, 77–85
Simms
Woods' History Albemarle Co., Va., 315
Simonds
Hoyt's Salisbury, Mass., Families, 600
Jenkins Family of Pa. (1904), 144–8
Sanford's Hist. Hopkinton, N. Y.,554–8
Simpson
Carter's Hist. Pembroke, N. H., ii, 296
Hanna's Ohio Valley Genealogies, 114
Kelley's New Hampshire, 122–43
Stackpole's Hist. Kittery, Me., 730–1
Treman Genealogy
Sims
Richmond, Va., Times, June 3, 1906
Sims Family (1874) chart
Sinclair
See St. Clair
Siner
Pound and Kester Genealogy, 108–11
Singletary
Temple's History Framingham, 700
Sinnett
Merryman Family of Maine, 52–9
Sinnott
Sinnott Genealogy (1905), 254 pages
Sisson
Kewaunee, Wis., Owl, June, 1904, 283
Wheeler's Hist. Stonington, Ct., 568–9
Sitgreaves
Jones Genealogical History (1900), 33
Skaats
Stiles' Wethersfield, Ct., ii, 627
Skeel
Strong Genealogy, 1007–10
Skeels
Seymour, Conn., History, 549–51

Skelton
Meriwether Genealogy, (1899), 59
New Eng. Hist. Gen. Reg., lii, 347–9; liii,
64–71
Skiff
Allen Family of Nantucket (1905)
Kewaunee, Wis., The Owl (1901), 32
Skiles
West Virginia Hist. Mag., iii, 188
Skilling
Willis' Old Eliot, Me., vi (1903), 15
Skillman
N.Y. Gen. Biog. Rec., xxxvii, 22–6, 91–6,
167–73, 277–82; xxxviii, 29–34, 103–12
Skinner
Baltimore Sun, Oct. 13, Nov. 24, 1907
Fernald's Genealogical Exchange, i, 7,
17–20, 26–9, 35, 42, 52, 59, 67–9, 74, 82
New Eng. Hist. Gen. Reg., liv, 413–22
Skinner Fam., Marblehead (1900), 10 p.
Skipworth
Richmond, Va., Times, Nov. 15, 1903
Slack
Chesebrough Gnealogy, 66–8
Slate
Kellogg's Bernardston, Mass., 492–504
Slater
McGinness and Scott Genealogy, 212–6
Slaughter
Baltimore Sun, Feb. 11, 18, 1906
Green's Culpeper County, Va.
Slaughter Family of Va. (1906), chart
Slauson
Kewaunee, Wis., Owl for Feb.-Mar., 1901
Sleeper
Musgrove's Hist. Bristol, N. H.
Parson's History of Rye, N. H., 541–3
Slemmons
Hanna's Ohio Valley Genealogies, 115
Slemons
Quinby's New Eng. Fam. History Quar.,
i, 20–2
Slingluff
Penn.-German, vii, 341–4
Sloan
Crumrine's Hist. Washington, Pa., 599
Ramsdell's Hist. Milford, N. H., 923
Slocum
Old Northwest Gen. Quar., x, 76–9
Slosson
Slosson Genealogy (1896), 37 pages
Slote
Harvey's Hud. and Berg. Co., N. J., 182
Sluyter
Schureman Fam. of New Jersey, 58, 94–9
Small
Deer Island, Me., Press for 1900
Dennison Family of Maine (1906), 26–94
Hosmer's Deer Isle, Me., 102–5, 111, 121
Litchfield, Me., History (1897), 306
Maine Hist. Soc. Colls. (1893), 359–404
Small Family of Penn. (1905), 393 pages
Stackpole's Hist. Kittery, Me., 733–4
Willis' Old Eliot, Me., vi (1903), 16
Smart
Shepardson Genealogy (1907), 5

Smead
Converse Genealogy (1905), 698–701
Gray Genealogy (1889), 172–4
Smedley
Smedley Genealogy (1901), 1,000 pages
Woodruff's Litchfield, Ct., Gen. Reg.,
    197–9
Smelt
Richmond, Va., Times, June 17, 1906
Smith
Alden and Smith Ancestors (1903), 129
Anderson, Perrine, Smith Fam., 87–117
Baltimore Sun, Feb. 25; Mar. 4. 1906;
    Jan. 27, Feb. 3, 1907
Bavis and Smith Ancestors (1880), 4 p.
Bean's Montgomery Co., Pa., 522, etc.
Boogher's Va. Gleanings (1903), 330–72
Carpenter's Hist. of Amherst, Mass., 23
Cornell Genealogy, 394–8
Carter's Hist. Pembroke, N. H., ii, 298
Clayton's Hist. of Union Co., N. J., 375
Connet Genealogy, 49–53
Crayon's Rockaway, N. J., Rec., 267–9
Crumrine's Washington, Pa., 948–50
Greene's Hist. Boothbay, Me., 626–8
Hanna's Ohio Valley Genealogies, 115
Harris Ancestry (1898)
Hill Genealogy (1904), 49–51
Keith's Pa. Prov. Councillors, pt. ii, 27–
    40, 272–4
Lamb Family of N. J. (1904), opp. 10
Landrum's Hist. Spartanburg, S. C.,
    205–19, 278–84
Le Fevre's Hist. New Paltz, N. Y., 503
Litchfield, Me., History (1897), 307–27
McAllister Family (1900), 190–210
McGavock Family of Va.
Meriwether Genealogy (1899), 62
Merrick Genealogy, 424-6
Nash's Fifty Puritan Ancestors, 71
New Eng. Hist Gen. Reg., lv, 267–71
Page Genealogy, 2d ed. (1893), 79
Ramsdell's Hist. Milford, N. H., 925–31
Reed Genealogy (1901), 416–23
Richmond, Va., Times, Feb. 4, April 22,
    1906
Sanford's Hopkinton, N. Y., 570, 574–6
Sayre Genealogy, 65, 221–3
Scales' History of Dover, N. H., 87–90
Seymour, Conn., History, 551–554
Smith Fam., Woodbridge, N. J., MSS. in
    N. J. Hist. Soc. Lib.
Smith Family of New York (1879), 4 p.
Smith of Ipswich (1900), 79 pages
Smith of Peterboro, N. H. (1900), 202 p.
Smith Fam. Topsfield, Mass. (1902), 15 p.
Smith Family of Rowley (1905), 4 pages
Smith Family of Phila. (1906)
So. Car. Hist. Gen. Mag., iv, 46, 239–57
Stackpole's Hist. Kittery, Me., 734–6
Stiles' Wethersfield, Ct., ii, 628–57
Temple's History Framingham, 701
Topsfield, Mass., Hist. Coll., viii, 87–101
Treman Genealogy
Tucker Genealogy (1903)
Virg. Mag. of History, ii, 391; iii, 194–8

Warren Genealogy (1903), 170–2
Well's History of Newbury, Vt., 692–5
Wheeler's Hist. Stonington, Ct., 570–5
Willis Family of Va., 152–4
Wintermute, Gen., 229–31
Woodruff's Litchfield, Ct., Gen. Reg.,
    201–7
Woods' History Albemarle Co., Va., 316
Woolsey Genealogy
Smock
Beekman's Monmouth, N. J., Settlers
Gustin Ancestry, 61
Smyth
Neff Genealogy, Addenda, 17–35
Seymour, Conn., History, 554–5
Snaverly
Egle's Dauphin Co., Pa. (1883), 251–2
Snead
William and Mary Quarterly, x, 125
Snedeker
Clayton's Hist. of Union Co., N. J. 795
Sneden
Harvey's Hud. and Berg. Co., N. J., 183
Snell
Carter's Hist. Pembroke, N. H., ii, 299
Wells Genealogy (1903)
Snickers
McIlhany's Virg. Fams. (1903), 107–11
Snoddy
Landrum's Spartanburg, S. C., 295–303
Snook
Wintermute Gen., 29
Snow
Kellogg's Bernardston, Mass., 505–8
Stackpole's Hist. Kittery, Me., 736
Snowden
Baltimore Sun, Jan. 29, 1905
Warfield's Maryland, 361–4
Snyder
Goodrich's Hist. Dryden, N. Y., 194–9
Hanna's Ohio Valley Genealogies, 116
Tucker Genealogy (1901), 165–71
Tucker Genealogy (1903)
Soblet
Sublett Genealogy (1896), 32 pages
Solendine
New Eng. Hist. Gen. Reg., lx, 366–9
Somerby
Temple's History Framingham, 702
Somers
Hall's Hist. Atlantic City, N. J., 433–8
Somerville
Baltimore Sun, July 26, 1903; Aug. 25;
    Sept. 1, 8, 1907
Green's Culpeper County, Virg.
Tiernan Genealogy (1901), 83, 270
Somes
Deer Island, Me., Press for 1900
Topliff Genealogy (1906)
Sonmans
Clayton's Hist. of Union Co., N. J., 610
Souder
Funk Genealogy, 600–8
Soule
Dennison Genealogy (1906), 89–97
Southworth Genealogy (1905), 38

Stevens Genealogy (1906), 44
Southall
McGavock Family of Va.
Richmond, Va., Times, March 4, 1906
William and Mary Quarterly, xii, 29–31
Southard
Crayon's Rockaway, N. J., Records, 115
Southworth Genealogy (1905), 443–7
Southmayd
Hamlin Genealogy (1900), 41, 75
Southwood
Lawson Genealogy (1903)
Southworth
American Ancestry, xii, 198
Putnam's Hist. Mag. (1896), 209–12, (1907), 102–5, 309–12
Southworth Ancestry (1900), 27 pages
Southworth Ancestry (1903), 50 pages
Southworth Genealogy (1905)
Woolsey Genealogy
Sower
Penn.-German, ii (1901), 64
Sower's Montgomery, Pa., Men (1879)
Spalding
Ramsdell's Hist. Milford, N. H., 932–5
Warren Genealogy (1903), 70–3
Spangler
Egle's Dauphin Co., Pa. (1883), 252–4
Shriver Genealogy, 69–72
Sparhawk
Sparhawk Genealogy (1892), 113 pages
Stackpole's History Kittery, Me., 737
Sparks
Pound and Kester Genealogy, 375–8
Sparrow
Southern Hist. Assoc. Pubs., iv, 427–431
Spaulding
Carter's Hist. Pembroke, N. H., ii, 300
Treman Genealogy
Spear
Litchfield, Me., History (1897), 327–32
Specht
Perkiomen Region, Pa., iii, 66
Speer
Harvey's Hud. and Berg. Co., N. J., 209
Speers
Crumrine's Washington, Pa., 643, 649
Spencer
Buell Genealogy, 215
Clayton's Hist. of Union Co., N. J., 209
Emory's Colonial Fams. of Md., 164–73
Hall Memoranda (1902), 207–13
Huxley Genealogy, 18–22
Lancaster Genealogy, 46
Polwer Genealogy (1905)
Seymour, Conn, History, 555–6
Spencer Family of Haddam Co.
Stackpole's Hist. Kittery, Me., 737–40
Treman Genealogy
Whittelsey's Joseph Spencer (1904), 11 p.
Whittemore's New England Ancestors (1900), 100 pages
Woodruff's Litchfield, Ct. Gen. Reg., 199
Sperry
Humphreyville Genealogy, 48–50
Seymour, Conn., History, 556–7

Sphar
Crumrine's Hist. Washington, Pa., 651
Spicer
Brown Fam., Pa. (1885), pt. iii, 14–24
Spike
Temple's History Framingham, 670
See also under Pike
Spillin
Stackpole's Hist. Kittery, Me., 731–2
Spinney
Dover, N. H., Enquirer for Feb. 19, 1863
Greene's History Boothbay, Me., 628
Stackpole's Hist. Kittery, Me., 740–7
Willis' Old Eliot, Me., vi (1903), 18–22
Spinning
Clayton's Hist. of Union Co., N. J., 390
New Eng. Hist. Gen. Reg., lix, 267–9
Spofford
Deer Island, Me., Press for 1900
Spoor
Spoor Genealogy (1901), 173 pages
Spore
Spoor Genealogy
Spottswood
Baltimore Sun, Jan. 28; Feb. 4, 1906
Whitmore's Heraldic Journal, iv, 114
Richmond, Va., Times, Jan. 31, 1904
Spottswoode
Green's Culpeper County Virg.
Sprague
Hill Genealogy (1904), 62
Lawrence Genealogy (1904)
Old Northwest Gen. Quar., ix, 77–85
Sanford's Hist. Hopkinton, N. Y., 552–4
Sprague Fam. of R. I. (1902), 32 pages
Sprague Family of R. I., 2d ed. (1905), 49 pages
Sprigg
Baltimore Sun, Feb. 11, 18; June 3,1906; July 7, 1907
Spriggins
Stackpole's History Kittery, Me., 732
Spring
Converse Genealogy (1905), 27
Springer
Litchfield, Me., History (1897), 332–38
Springers of Europe (1897), chart
Sprong
New York Gen. Biog. Rec., xxxvii, 270
Sproul
Cambridge Genealogical Advertiser, iv, 78–81
Sprowls
Crumrine's Hist. Washington, Pa., 763
Spurr
Spoor Genealogy
Squiers
Ramsdell's Hist. Milford, N. H., 935
Squire
Clayton's Hist. of Union Co., N. J., 289
Sanford's Hist. Hopkinton, N. Y., 542–6
Stacey
Willis' Old Eliot, Me., vi, 69
Stackhouse
Stackhouse Genealogy (1906), 47 pages

Stackpole
American Ancestry, xii, 117
Stackpole's Hist. Kittery, Me., 748–9
Welch Genealogy (1906), 41–69
Stacy
New Eng. Hist. Gen. Reg., lviii, 91
Penn. Magazine of History, xxx, 498
Stackpole's Hist. Kittery, Me., 749–51
Temple's History Framingham, 703
Stafford
Stockard's History of Alamance, N. C.
Stagg
Labaw's Preakness, N. J., History, 93–6
Stahl
Hanna's Ohio Valley Genealogies, 117
Stahler
Bean's Hist. Montgomery Co., Pa., 773
Stahr
Beidler Family of Pa., 274–86
Stalnaker
American Ancestry, xii, 198
Standish
Jenks' Life of Myles Standish (1905)
Stiles' Wethersfield, Ct., ii, 658–62
Stanford
American Ancestry, xii, 97
Stanford Genealogy, 2d ed. (1906),
149 p.
Stanley
Buell Genealogy, 227
Richmond, Va., Times, July 8, 1906
Stackpole's History Kittery, Me., 751
Stiles' Wethersfield, Ct., ii, 662
Stannard
Buell Genealogy, 140
Whittemore's New England Ancestors
(1900), 100 pages
Stansel
Stansel Family of S. C. (1900), 7 pages
Stanton
Chesebrough Genealogy, 61, 535
Converse Genealogy (1905), 743–54
Hinchman's Nantucket Set., ii, 221–3
Stanton Genealogy (1882), 52 pages
Wheeler's Stonington, Ct., 576–604
Stanwood
Shannon Genealogy, 516–27
Stanyan
Carter's Hist. Pembroke, N. H., ii, 301
Staples
Hosmer's History of Deer Isle, Me., 47
Litchfield, Me., History (1897), 338
Smedley Genealogy, 54
Stackpole's Hist. Kittery, Me., 752–8
Willis' Old Eliot, Me., vi (1903), 29–43
Starbird
Litchfield, Me., History (1897), 339
Starbuck
Hinchman's Nantucket Set., ii, 302–4
Hallock Pedigree (1906), 77–9
Scales' History of Dover, N. H., 128–31
Stark
Pound and Kester Genealogy, 354–9
Rowell's Gen. Stark's Farm (1904), 22 p.
Stark Genealogy (1887), 13 pages
Stark Family Association (1905), 34 p.

Starkweather
Starkweather Genealogy (1904), 356 p.
Starns
See under Stearns
Starr
Smedley Genealogy, 254–7
Stauffer
Beidler Family of Pa., 145–55
Stauffer Genealogy (1897), 203 pages
St. Clair
Old Northwest Gen. Quar., ix, 43,
166–8
St. Clair Fam. of Penn. (1897), 30 pages
See Sinclair
Stearns
Stearns Genealogy (1897), 16 pages
Stearns Geneaogy (1901), 1275 pages
Stearns Memoranda (1901), 173 pages
Temple's History Framingham, 704
Stebbins
Stebbins Genealogy (1904), 1386 pages
Well's History of Newbury, Vt., 695
Steadman
Stiles' Wethersfield, Ct., ii, 664
Steele
Dunwoody Genealogy (1899), 164–72
Love Family of Va. (1905), 1, 2
Patterson Memoir (1902), 428
Seymour, Conn., History, 557–61
Steele Fam. of So. Car. (1900), 143 pages
Steele Fam. of Chester, Pa. (1902), 100 p.
Steele Fam. of Boston (1905), 54 pages
Stiles' Wethersfield, Ct., ii, 665
Steelman
Hall's Hist. Atlantic City, N. J., 438–40
Steere
Steere Genealogy (1890), 216 pages
Stees
Morr Genealogy, 273–95
Steevens
Steevens Family of Guilford, Ct. (1906),
162 pages
Stephens
Virg. Mag. of History, xi, 217
Steiger
Shriver Genealogy, 94–7
Steinman
Mayer Genealogy, 73–5, 89–91
Stelle
Leonard's Piscataway, N. J., Planters,
13–20
Stephens
Crumrine's Hist. Washington, Pa., 949
New Eng. Hist. Gen. Reg., lvi, 356–61
Willis' Old Eliot, Me., vi, 71
Steptoe
Baltimore Sun, Oct. 15, 1905
Richmond, Va., Times, May 14; Nov.
19, 26, 1905
Sterling
Buell Genealogy, 217
Sterling Fam. of N. J. (1893), 29 pages
Sterne
See under Stearns
Sterrett
See Starrett

Stetson
Dennison Family of Me. (1906), 42–100
Handy's History of Sumner, Me., 88
Steuart
Hanson's Old Kent, Md., 263–75
Stevens
Buell Genealogy, 42, 127
Carter's Hist. Pembroke, N. H., ii, 301–3
Gamble's Family Data (1906), 134
Jameson Genealogy
Litchfield, Me., History (1897), 340–6
Metcalf Genealogy (1898), 50–4
Nash's Fifty Puritan Ancestors, 135
Noyes' Hist. Hampstead, N. H., ii, 772–5
Stevens Fam. of Conn. (1891), 59 pages
Stevens Family of Eng., 1904
Stevens Family of Boston (1906), 48 p.
Temple's History Framingham, 705
Well's Hist. of Newbury, Vt., 696–701
See Steevens
Stevenson
Crumrine's Hist. Washington, Pa., 934
Jennings Genealogy, ii, 341–56
Jerseyman, Flemington, N. J., iv (1898),
  1–5, 9–12, 17–9, 25–7; v (1899), 33–5,
  41–3, 49–52; vi (1900), 1–4, 9–14, 17–
  22, 25–33; ix, 15–24
McIlhany's Virginia Families (1903)
Stevenson Family of L. I. and N. J.
  (1902), 181 pages
Steward
Wheeler's Hist. Stonington, Ct., 605–8
Stewart
Amer. Hist. Mag., vii (1902), 148
Benton (David) Ancestors (1906)
Crumrine's Hist. Washington, Pa., 842
Hanna's Ohio Valley Genealogies, 118
McAllister Family of N. C. (1900), 176
McKee Family of Ky. (1900), chart
McKinney Family of Pa., 47–54
Shourds' Fenwick's Colony, N. J., 345
Shriver Genealogy, 112–4
Stewart, A. T., Relatives (1876), 294 p.
Stewart Family of N. H. (1905), 215 p.
Treman Genealogy
Tuttle Genealogy (1871), 23–6
Wheeler's Hist. Stonington, Ct., 605–8
See Steuart
Stickle
Crayon's Rockaway, N. J., Rec., 260–6
Stickney
Carter's Hist. Pembroke, N. H., ii, 304–6
Ramsdell's Hist. Milford, N. H., 938
Treman Genealogy
Stidham
Sellers' Delaware Families, 138–60
Stiegel
Lancaster Co., Pa., Soc. Papers, ii, 63–5
Stileman
Tarleton Genealogy, 27–9
Stiles
Clay Family of S. C. (1897), chart
Clayton's Hist. of Union Co., N. J., 517
Habersham Genealogy, 50–4
Humphreyville Genealogy, 50–6
Sayre Genealogy, 300–2

Seymour, Conn., History, 561–2
Stiles Genealogy (1859), 31 pages
Stillman
Clayton's Hist. of Union Co., N. J., 128
Stiles' Wethersfield, Ct., ii, 667–84
Stillman Genealogy (1903), 42 pages
Stillwell
Treman Genealogy
Stimpson
N. E. Hist. Gen. Reg., lix, 242–52, 365–77
Ramsdell's Hist. Milford, N. H., 939–41
Stimpson Genealogy (1907), 206 pages
Stinson
Hosmer's Hist. Deer Isle, Me., 54–7, 120
Litchfield, Me., History (1897), 346
Stipp
McKee Family of Ky. (1900), chart
Stirling
Alston Genealogy, 210–30
Keith's Pa. Prov. Councillors, pt. i, 110–4
Stites
Woodruff Genealogy (1902), 143
Stith
Richmond, Va., Times, April 17, 1904
Va. Magazine of History, viii, 95
Stivers
Jennings Genealogy, ii, 540–2
St. John
St. John Genealogy (1907), 624 pages
Stockbridge
Reed Genealogy (1901), 401–11
Stockdale
Crumrine's Hist. Washington, Pa., 651
Stockett
Warfield's Maryland, 93–6
Stocking
Benton (David) Ancestors (1906)
Stocking Ancestry (1903), 202 pages
Stockton
Glenn's Colonial Mansions, i, 61–93
Lawrence Genealogy (1904)
Lundy Genealogy, 457
Richmond, Va., Times, Sept. 6, 1903
Woods' Hist. Albemarle Co., Va., 319–21
Stoddard
Seymour, Conn., History, 562–5
Stiles' Wethersfield, Ct., ii, 684–90
Woodruff's Litchfield, Ct. Gen. Reg.,
  207–11
Stodder
Hill Genealogy (1904), 64
Stokes
Lancaster Genealogy, 91–102
Stokes Genealogy (1903), 339 pages
Stolp
Lawson Genealogy (1903)
Stone
Britton Ancestry (1901)
Ford's History of Clinton, Mass., 118
Lowe Genealogy, 150–9
Nash's Fifty Puritan Ancestors, 23
Newhall Ancestry, 173–9
Old Northwest Quarterly, iv, 45–7, 124
Stackpole's Hist. Kittery, Me., 758–9
Stone of Guilford, vol. 2 (1898), 349 p.
Stone Family Association (1901), 92 p.

Stone Fam. of Cambridge (1904), 55 p.
Stone Fam. of Columbus, Ohio (1907)
Temple's History Framingham, 706–16
Virginia Mag. of History, xii, 453
Woodruff's Litchfield, Ct. Gen. Reg., 211–7
Storm
Fernald's Genealogical Exchange, iii, 26
Treman Genealogy
Storrs
Seymour, Conn., History, 565–6
Story
Bronsdon Genealogy, 205-8
Reese Genealogy, 123–8
Stoughton
Nash's Fifty Puritan Ancestors, 58–60
Stout
Fisher Family of N. J. (1890), 96–123
Jerseyman, ii (1905), 19–22
Lamb Family of N. J. (1904), app. 1–4
Pound and Kester Genealogy, 566, 580–3
Stover
Greene's History Boothbay, Me., 629
Stow
Blair Genealogy (1900), 165–71
Strachey
William and Mary Quar., iv, 192; v, 6
Strait
Crayon's Rockaway, N. J., Records, 189
Strange
Austin's R. I. Gen. Dictionary, 390
Stratchan
Richmond, Va., Times, June 12, 1904
See also under Strachan
Stratton
Hunt Family of N. J. (1906), 78–83
Richmond Times, April 8, 15; May 6, 1906
Stokes Genealogy, 288
Stratton-Whithed Families (1889), 16 p.
Street
Abbott, Jas. S., Memorial (1905), 41 p.
Treman Genealogy
Streeter
Kellogg's Hist. Bernardston, Mass., 509
Temple's History Framingham, 716
Stretcher
Sellers' Delaware Families, 1–22
Strettell
Keith's Pa. Prov. Councillors, pt. ii, 196–208
Stribling
McIlhany's Virginia Fams. (1903), 33–98
Vawter Family of Va., 215–36
West Virginia Hist. Mag., v, 114–8
Strider
Baltimore Sun, Oct. 15; Dec. 3, 1905
Striker
N. Y. Gen. Biog. Rec., xxxviii, 1–9
Stringham
Tucker Genealogy (1901), 172-4
Tucker Genealogy (1903)
Strong
Herkimer Genealogy, 98, 113–22
Strong Genealogy (1819), 4 pages
Treman Genealogy

Woodruff's Litchfield, Ct. Gen. Reg., 217–9
Strother
Baltimore Sun, Nov. 26; Dec. 10, 1905
Green's Culpeper County, Virg.
Richmond, Va., Times, Aug. 27, Sept. 24, 1905
Stuard
Stuard Family (1903), 14 pages
Stuart
Baltimore Sun, July 29; Aug. 5, 12, 1906
Stevens Genealogy (1906), 28
Walker Family of Virginia, 32–55
West Virginia Hist. Mag., v, 119–6
Stubbs
Stubbs Family of Va., 1902
Sturtevant
New Eng. Hist. and Gen. Reg., lv, 78
Sublett
Sublett Gen. (1896), 32 pages
Suddarth
Woods' History Albemarle Co., Va., 321
Summers
West Virginia Hist. Mag., iii, 228–34
Sumner
Kingsbury Genealogy (1906), 59–63
Wadsworth Family (1904), 15 pages
Sumter
Woods' History Albemarle Co., Va., 322
Super
Bean's Hist. Montgomery Co., Pa., 1115
Sutherland
Well's History of Newbury, Vt., 702
Sutphen
Clayton's Hist. of Union Co., N. J., 130
Symmes' Tennent, N. J., Church, 415
Sutton
American Ancestry, xii, 113
Baltimore Sun, Sept. 18, 1904
Sutton Family of N. J. (1900), 47 pages
Suydam
Suydam's Hendrick Rycken (1898), 41 p.
Swagler
Crumrine's Hist. Washington, Pa., 949
Swain
Hinchman's Nantucket Settlers, ii, 152–4, 304
Maulsby Family of Pa.
Maulsby Family, 125–7
Swan
Baltimore Sun, April 23, 1905
Bronsdon Genealogy, 117–9
Chesebrough Genealogy, 89–95
Seymour, Conn., History, 566–7
Treman Genealogy
Wheeler's Hist. Stonington, Ct., 609–17
Swann
Virginia Mag. of Hist., iii (1895), 154–6
Swart
Crumrine's Hist. Washington, Pa., 672
Swasey
Well's Ancestry (1900), 90–108
Well's History of Newbury, Vt., 703
See also under Swazey
Sweatnam
Forman Genealogy, 53–5

Sweet
Kewaunee, Wis., Owl for 1900 and 1901
Le Baron Genealogy, 176
Peoria County, Ill., History, 693
Sweetser
Wells Genealogy (1903), 147–51
Sweringen
See under Swearingen
Swetland
Eaton and Swetland Ancestry (1900), 21–7, 34–51
Swett
Carter's Hist. Pembroke, N. H., ii, 307
Greene's History Boothbay, Me., 630
Swift
Hinchman's Nantucket Set., ii, 169–75
Penn. Mag. of History, xxx, 129–58
Swift Family of Phila. (1906), 32 pages
Temple's History Framingham 718
Swinerton
Jenkins Family of Pa. (1904), 174
Swinney
Treman Genealogy
Swoope
Swope Genealogy, 364–6
Sykes
Gray Genealogy (1889), 79–87
Sylvester
Dennison Genealogy (1906), 25–111
Hosmer's History of Deer Isle, Me., 125
Well's History of Newbury, Vt., 704
Syme
William and Mary Quarterly, xi, 77
Symes
Hayden's Virginia Genealogies, 92a
Symonds
Hoyt's Salisbury, Mass., Fams., 597–602

Tabb
William and Mary Quar., xiii, 121–8, 168–75, 270–8; xiv, 50, 150–4
Taggert
Sterns' Our Kindred, 23, 34
Taintor
Converse Genealogy (1905), 133–41
Temple's History Framingham, 718
Talbot
Rodgers Family of Pa. (1876), 2–4
Tucker Genealogy (1901), 243–9
Tucker Genealogy (1903)
Talbott
Warfield's Maryland, 530
William and Mary Quarterly, x, 61
Talcott
Stiles' Wethersfield, Ct., ii, 693
Taliaferro
Baltimore Sun, July 30; Aug. 6, 1905
Clarke's King Wm. Co.,Va., Fams., 100–2
Richmond, Va., Times, Oct. 22, 1905
Willis Family of Va., 140–9
McIlhany's Virginia Families (1903)
Richmond, Va., Times, Aug. 13, 1905
Tallman
Wells Family of Ohio (1892), 24–30, 124

Talmage
Crayon's Rockaway, N. J., Rec., 117–20
Talman
Talman Fam., Troy, N. Y. (1901), chart
Tanner
Tanner Family of R. I. (1905), 216 pages
Tapley
Litchfield, Me., History (1897), 348
Tapley Genealogy (1900), 256 pages
Taplin
Tapley Genealogy
Well's History of Newbury, Vt., 705
Tappan
Antill Genealogy, 27–30
Tapscott
Hull Genealogy (1904), 19
Tarbell
New Eng. Hist. Gen. Reg., lxi, 70–5, 165–72, 299–302
Ramsdell's Hist. Milford, N. H., 944
Tarbox
Greene Family of R. I. (1905), 122–4
Tarleton
Tarleton Genealogy (1900), 244 pages
Tasker
Howard Genealogy (1897), 13–6
Tate
Boone Family (1902), 4 pages
McAllister Family of N. C.
McIlhany's Va. Fams. (1903), 100–7
Tatum
Clarke's King Wm. Co., Va., Fams., 102
Taylor
McIlhany's Virginia Families (1903)
Tayloe
Willis Family of Va., 129
Taylor
Baltimore Sun, Feb. 5, 1905
Crumrine's Hist. Washington, Pa., 952
Darlington Genealogy, 95–8
Genung Family of L. I.
Green's Culpeper County, Virg.
Harris Ancestry (1898)
Jerseyman, vii (1901), 24; viii (1902), 4–7, 9–13, 17–23, 34; ix, 1–13, 24–30, 33–9; x, 1–70
Keith's Pa. Prov. Councillors, pt. ii, 212–5
Le Baron Genealogy, 144–6
Litchfield, Me., History (1897), 349–51
Lowe Genealogy, 147–9
McGavock Family of Va.
McIlhany's Va. Fams. (1903), 215–20
Newhall Ancestry, 134
Ramsdell's Hist. Milford, N. H., 946–9
Richmond, Va., Times, July 10; Aug. 7; Nov. 27, 1904
Robertson and Taylor Gen., 225–63
Smedley Genealogy, 79–81, 105, 147
Stiles' Wethersfield, Ct., ii, 699–702
Taylor, John, Hadley, Mass., Memorial
Taylor Biographies (1902), 126 pages
Walker Family of Va. (1902)
White Genealogy (1900), 502–7, 702–51
William and Mary Quarterly, xii, 129–34
Woodruff's Litchfield, Ct. Gen. Reg., 219–21

Tayntor
See under Taintor
Teakle
Clarke's King Wm. Co., Va., Fams., 103–5
See also under Teackle
Teays
West Virg. Hist. Mag., iv, No. 4
Tebbets
Scale's History of Dover, N. H., 239
Tefft
Tefft Genealogy (1904), 102 pages
Teller
Clayton's Hist. of Union Co. N. J., 371
Temple
Baltimore Sun, April 1, 1906
Richmond, Va., Times, July 15, 1906
Smedley Genealogy, 222
Temple Genealogy, app. (1899), 162 p.
Temple's History Framingham, 719–21
Well's History of Newbury, Vt., 707
Tenney
Stackpole's Hist. Kittery Me., 760
Tenney Genealogy, 2d ed. (1904), 691 p.
Well's Hist. of Newbury, Vt., 708–11
Terhune
Harvey's Hud. and Berg. Co., N. J., 210
Terrell
Seymour, Conn., History, 567–8
Woods' Hist. Albemarle Co., V., 324–7
Terrill
William and Mary Coll. Quar., xiii, 263–5
Terry
Allen's History of Enfield, Ct., 38
Nash's Fifty Puritan Ancestors, 26
Tetherly
Stackpole's Hist. Kittery, Me., 760–2
Willis' Old Eliot, Me., vi, 72
Tew
Tew Family of R. I., chart
Tewksbury
Well's History of Newbury, Vt., 712
Thacher
Blair Genealogy (1900), 171–5
Thatcher
Rosbrugh Memorial (1880), 89–92
Thayer
Bates Gen. Notes, i (1903), 14 pages
Bates Genealogy, Notes No. 2, 1903
Hill Genealogy (1904), 34
New Eng. Hist. Gen. Reg., lx, 281–91
Seymour, Conn., History, 568–71
Woonsocket, R. I., Reporter for Nov. 19, 1902
Thom
Green's Culpeper County, Virg.
Thomas
Baltimore Sun, Aug. 20, 1905
Bean's Hist. Montgomery Co., Pa., 867
Boogher's Virg. Gleanings (1903), 283–8
Egle's Dauphin Co., Pa. (1883), 254–5
Le Baron Genealogy, 171–3
Mayer Genealogy, 142–5
Morse's Sketches of Perkins and Thomas (1898), 13–8
N. Y. Gen. Biog. Rec., xxxvi, 276–9
Pound and Kester Genealogy, 137–45

Sanford's Hist. Hopkinton, N. Y., 577–9
Smedley Genealogy, 179–83
Tapley Genealogy, 23
Thomas Family (1906), 19 pages
Woods' History Albemarle Co., Va., 327
Thompson
Carter's Hist. Pembroke, N. H., 11, 308
Converse Genealoy (1905), 830
Deer Island, Me., Press for 1900
Greene's Hist. Boothbay, Me., 631–4
Hanna's Ohio Valley Genealogies, 119
Hosmer's History of Deer Isle, Me., 46
Hull Genealogy (1904), 16
Jackson Genealogy (1890), 26
Jameson Genealogy
Landrum's Spartanburg, S. C., 417–9
Manning Genealogy, 351–3
Mayflower Descendant, ii (1900), 152–4
Old Northwest Gen. Quarterly, 176–8
Peoria County, Ill., History, 695
Schureman Family of N. J., 25, 31–4, 45–51, 68–81
Stackpole's Hist. Kittery, Me., 764–70
Thompson Family, chart
Thompson Family of Me. (1907), 293 p.
Treman Genealogy
Watson's Some Notable Families, 51
Well's History of Newbury, Vt., 713
Wheeler's Hist. Stonington, Ct., 618–20
Willis' Old Eliot, Me., vi, 74
Woods' Hist. Albemarle Co., Va., 328–30
Wood Family of Sackville, N. B., 25
Thomson
Acadienses, v, 306–24
Green's Culpeper County, Virg.
Hill Genealogy (1904), 55–7
Schureman Genealogy, 1902
So. Car. Hist. Mag., iii (1902), 97–113
Thornal
Clayton's Hist. of Union Co., N. J., 850
Thornburgh
Maulsby Genealogy, 49–55, 90–7
Thorndike
Warren Genealogy (1903), 56–62
Thorne
Cornell Genealogy, 378
Stokes Genealogy, 278
Thornton
Adam's Matthew Thornton of N. H., (1903), 13–9
Clarke's King Wm. Co., Va., Fams., 105–7
Page Genealogy, 2d ed. (1893), 214
Richmond, Va., Times, Oct. 23, 1904
Thornton Family of N. H. (1905), 34 p.
Willis Family of Va., 134–8
Throwgood
Baltimore Sun, July 21, 1907
Thorpe
Greene's History Boothbay, Me., 634
New Eng. Hist. Gen. Reg., lix, 392–6
Thrall
Old Northwest Gen. Quar., ix, 169–83; x, 83–5
Seymour, Conn., History, 571–2
Throckmorton
Baltimore Sun., Oct 13, 20, 27, Nov. 3, 1907

Jerseyman, x (1904), 26
Va. Magazine of History, viii, 83–9, 309–12; ix, 192–4; xiv, 445
William and Mary Coll. Quar., ii, 241–7; xiii, 66
Throop
Woodruff's Litchfield, Ct. Gen. Reg.,223
Throope
N. Y. Gen. Biog. Rec., xxxvi, 118–35, 207–12, 302–7; xxxvii, 35–49; 103–9
Thurlow
Litchfied, Me., History (1897), 352
Thurston
Thurston Fam., Newport, R. I. (1885),
Thurston Family of Newport, R. I. (1885), 9 p.
Thweatt
Va. Magazine of History, vii, 355
Tibbals
Crissey's History of Norfolk, Ct., 533
Tibbetts
Greene's History Boothbay, Me., 635–8
Litchfield, Me., History (1897), 353–7
Tibbitts
Salter Memorial (1900), 45–58
Ticknor
Hart's Memoir of Geo. Ticknor (1871), 3
Tidy
Stackpole's History Kittery, Me., 763
Tiernan
Tiernan Genealogy, 25 pages
Tiernan Genealogy (1901), 466 pages
Tilden
Baltimore Sun, Dec. 11, 1904
Tilghman
Keith's Pa. Prov. Councillors, pt. ii, 336–9, 398–416
Till
Keith's Pa.Prov.Councillors, pt.ii 194–5
Timanus
Baltimore Sun, Mar. 5, 1905
Timberlake
Richardson Family of Va., 17–9
Richmond, Va., Times, Jan. 14, 1906
Woods' History Albemarle Co., Va., 330
Timmons
Hanna's Ohio Valley Genealogies, 120
Timson
William and Mary Coll. Quar., iii, 204, 273; v, 3–5
Tinker
Tinker Genealogy (1900), 36 pages
Tinkham
Le Baron Genealogy, 73–5, 174
Titcomb
Hoyt's Salisbury, Mass., Fams., 602–5
Titsworth
Clayton's Hist. of Union Co., N. J., 134
Tobey
Stackpole's Hist. Kittery, Me., 770–9
Tobey Genealogy (1905), 350 pages
Willis' Old Eliot, Me., vi, 76–9
Todd
Bean's Hist. Montgomery Co., Pa., 660
Charleston, S. C., News, Aug. 6, 1905
Hall Memoranda (1902), 76–8

Harris Family of Pa. (1903), 41, 44, 61
Kittochtinny Magazine, i, 60–95, 172–88, 253–79, 357–83
McGavock Family of Va.
Nash's Fifty Puritan Ancestors, 79–87
Walker Family of Virginia, 55
Warfield's Maryland, 48
Tolbert
Rodgers and Talbot Fam. (1876), 4 p.
Tolles
Seymour, Conn., History, 572–4
Tolman
Dedham Hist.Reg.,xi, 144–6; xiv, 125–7
Tolman, James, Memorial (1869)
Tombs
Temple's History Framingham, 722
Tomkinson
Tomkinson Genealogy (1904), 132 p.
Tomlinson
Seymour, Conn., History, 574–9
Tomms
Temple's History Framingham, 722
Tompkins
Cornell Genealogy, 384
Crayon's Rockaway, N. J., Records, 154
Toothaker
Hosmer's History of Deer Isle, Me., 61
Litchfield, Me., History (1897), 357
Topliff
American Ancestry, xii, 162
New Eng. Hist. Gen. Reg., lviii, 117–21
Topliff Genealogy (1906), 56 pages
Topping
Old Northwest Gen. Quarterly, vii, 56
Torrey
Deer Island, Me., Press for 1900
Hosmer's Hist. of Deer Isle, Me., 49–51
Torsey
New Eng. Hist. Gen. Reg., lxi, 375–8
Towle
Parson's History of Rye, N. H., 546
Robie Genealogy (1900), 131 pages
Towle Genealogy (1903), 312 pages
Towles
Va. Mag. of Hist., viii, 320–2, 428–30; ix, 198–200, 324–6, 433–5
Towne
Ramsdell's Hist. Milford, N. H., 952–6
Towne
Temple's History Framingham, 723
Towne Genealogy (1901), 368 pages
Townley
Clayton's Hist. of Union Co., N. J., 148
Towns
Litchfield, Me., History (1897), 358–60
Townsend
Crumrine's Hist. Washington, Pa., 899
Genung Family of L. I.
Hall's Hist. of Atlantic City, N. J., 440
Underhill Society Report (1901), 14–9
Tracy
Evans Scioto Co., Ohio, History, 1245–7
Hyde and Dana Gen. (1904), 38–41
Jackson Genealogy (1905)
Nash's Fifty Puritan Ancestors, 106–9
Tracy Family of Lenox (1900)

Train
Sanford's Hopkinton, N. Y., 579
Temple's History Framingham, 724
Trask
New Eng. Hist. and Gen. Reg., lv, 321–
30, 385–8; lvi, 69–73, 199–202, 397–
401; lvii, 65–7, 384–7
Temple's History Framingham, 725
Trask Genealogy (1904), 33 pages
Travers
Richmond Times, Nov. 26, 1905, p. 6;
Jan. 7, 1906
Temple's History Framingham, 726
Travers Genealogy (1903), 147 pages
Travis
Temple's History Framingham, 726
Trayne
Temple's History Framingham, 724
Treadway
Temple's History Framingham, 726
Treadwell
New Eng. Hist. Gen. Reg., lx, 48–55,
191–8, 291–8, 386
Treadwell Genealogy (1906), 26 pages
Treat
Hall Memoranda (1902), 137–43
Hodge Genealogy (1900)
Stiles' Wethersfield, Ct., ii, 710–7
Treman Genealogy
Tredick
Tarleton Genealogy, 153–5
Trefethern
Parson's History of Rye, N. H., 547–52
Tremaine
Treman Genealogy (1901), 2129 pages
Treman
Treman Genealogy (1901), 2129 pages
Trescott
Hyde Park Hist. Rec., iii (1903), 55–76
Treworgy
Stackpole's Hist. Kittery, Me., 780–1
Trezevant
So. Car. Hist. Mag., iii (1902), 24–56
Trimble
Clarke's Old King Wm. Co., Va., Fam-
ilies, 25
Old Northwest Gen. Quar., vii, 74–6; ix,
195, 275; x, 1, 110
Smedley Genealogy, 280–2
Tripe
Stackpole's Hist. Kittery, Me., 781–2
Triplett
William and Mary Quarterly, x, 136
Tripp
Stevens and Tripp Fams. (1906), 33–43
Tripp Genealogy (1903), 133 pages
Trolinger
Stockard's History Alamance, N. C.
Troop
Bent Progenitors (1903), 55
Troth
Glenn's Colonial Mansions, ii, 390–3
Haines Family of N. J., 392–4
Trott
Stokes Family of N. J.
Treat Genealogy

Trout
McIlhany's Va. Fams. (1903), 112–31
Trowbridge
New Eng. Hist. Gen. Reg., lix, 291–7
Temple's History Framingham, 727–9
Warren Genealogy (1903), 156–9
Troxell
Dotterer Genealogy
Trucksess
Bean's Hist. Montgomery Co., Pa., 1196
True
Litchfield, Me., History (1897), 360–71
Trueblood
Morrison's Among Ourselves, i, 42–70
Pound and Kester Genealogy, 561–6
Trueman
Trueman's Chignecto Isthmus, Can., Set-
tlers
Truesdell
Carter's History Pembroke, N. H., i, 294
Truman
Moore Fam., Chester, Pa., 76–8, 148, 150
Smedley Genealogy, 202–4, 327–31
Treman Genealogy (1901), 2129 pages
Trumbull
Wheeler's Hist. Stonington, Ct., 621–23
Trundy
Hosmer's History of Deer Isle, Me., 97
Tryon
Stiles' Wethersfield, Ct., ii, 717
Woodruff's Litchfield, Ct., Gen. Reg., 225
Tuck
Ramsdell's Hist. Milford, N. H., 956
Tucker
Bellows Falls Times, March 23, 1905
Clayton's Hist. Union Co., N. J., 194, 343
Parson's History of Rye, N. H., 553
Ramsdell's Hist. Milford, N. H., 957–9
Seymour, Conn., 579–81
Stackpole's Hist. Kittery, Me., 782–4
Tucker Genealogy (1901), 305 pages
Virginia Hist. Mag. (1897), 360–3
Well's Hist. of Newbury, Vt., 714–8
William and Mary Quarterly, x, 205–7
Willis' Old Eliot, Me., vi, 80–2
Tuell
Handy's History of Sumner, Me., 190–5
Tully
Dorrance Genealogy, 23
Turnstall
Virg. Mag. of History, xiv, 444
Turberville
Richmond, Va., Times, March 18; April
15; Sept. 16, 1906
Turnbull
Tucker Genealogy (1903)
Turner
Baltimore Sun, Jan. 22, 1905; Aug. 25;
Sept. 15, 1907
Deer Island, Me., Press for 1900
Dinwiddie Genealogy (1902), 35–46
Handy's History of Sumner, Me., 183–9
Keith's Pa. Prov. Councillors, ii, 220–1
Landrum's Spartanburg, S. C., 406–8
Ramsdell's Hist. Milford, N. H., 959
Stockard's History of Alamance, N. C.

Treman Genealogy
Tussey
Stern's Our Kindred, 63
Tuttle
Abbott, Jas. S., Memorial (1905), 41 p.
Crayon's Rockaway, N. J., Records, 191
Dover, N. H., Enquirer, 1854 to 1868
Munson Genealogy, 83-7
Ramsdell's Hist. Milford, N. H., 960-2
Richmond, Va., Times, July 17, 1904
Tuttle Family (1871), 30 pages
Well's History of Newbury, Vt., 718
Tuxbury
Well's History of Newbury, Vt., 712
Twining
Twining Genealogy, 2d ed. (1905), 251 p.
Twitchell
Temple's History Framingham, 730
Twombly
Scales' History Dover, N. H., 314-8
Tyler
Carter's Hist. Pembroke, N. H., ii, 309
Deer Island, Me., Press for 1900
Hosmer's History Deer Isle, Me., 116-8
Richmond, Va., Times, Aug. 16, 1903
Tyler Letters, iii (1896), 209-17, 221-6b
William and Mary Quarterly, xii, 116
Tyng
Manchester, N. H., Hist. Quar., ii, 87
Tyson
Baltimore Sun, Jan. 22, 1905]
Shoemaker Genealogy, 76-9

Uber
Small Family of Penn. (1905)
Udall
New Eng. Hist. Gen. Reg., lx, 330
Udell
Fernald's Genealogical Exchange, i, 41,
   49, 57, 65, 73, 81
Uhler
Uhler Family of Pa. (1901), 35 pages
Underhill
Hull Genealogy (1904), 30
Underhill Society Annual Report (1900),
   24 pages; (1901) 32 pages
Underhill and Townsend Fams. (1904),
   8 pages
Underwood
Converse Genealogy (1905), 810
Temple's History Framingham, 730
Well's History of Newbury, Vt., 719
William and Mary Coll. Quar., x, 275
Upham
Newhall Ancestry, 110-33
Temple's History Framingham, 731
Upsall
New Eng. Hist. Gen. Reg. (1880), 28
Upson
Seymour, Conn., History, 581-3
Upton
Lowe Genealogy, 24-33
Urmston
Clayton's Hist. of Union Co, N, J., 252

Usher
Usher, Ellis, B., Biog. (1902), 14 pages
Usher, Hannah L., Biog. (1903)
Utter
Austin's R. I. Gen. Dict., 211

Vaiden
Clarke's King Wm. Co. Va., Fams., 178-
   83
Vail
New Eng. Hist. Gen. Reg., lviii, 310
Sanborn's Four Boston Fams. (1904), 7 p
Sayre Genealogy, 223-8
Vail Genealogy (1902), 371 pages
Woodruff's Litchfield, Ct.,Gen.Reg., 226
Valentine
Smedley Genealogy, 97, 184-7
Vallette
Bronsdon Genealogy, 162-76, 276-80
Vanartsdalen
Symmes' Tennent, N. J., Church, 419
Van Bibber
West Virg. Hist. Mag., iii (July 1903),
   213-25
Van Bierum
See Van Boerum
Van Boerum
See Booraem
Van Brunt
N. Y. Gen. Biog. Rec., xxxv, 33-7, 83-6
Van Buskirk
Harvey's Hud. and Berg. Co., N. J., 190
N. J. Hist. Soc. Proc. (1906), iii, 159-71;
   iv, 24-33, 75-89
Van Bussum
Harvey's Hud. and Berg. Co., N. J., 208
Vance
Crumrine's Washington, Pa., 953, 957
Evans' Scioto Co., Ohio, History, 1248
Keith's Pa. Prov. Councillors, pt.ii, 445-9
Kittochtinny Magazine, i, 422
Van Cleef
Treman Genealogy
Van Cortlandt
Barclay Genealogy, 123
Cornell Genealogy, 389
Roebling's Constant Journal, 424-33
Tucker Genealogy (1901), 186-8
Tucker Genealogy (1903)
Van Court
Sayre Genealogy, 318-22
Van Couwenhoven
Gustin Ancestry
Vandelinda
Harvey's Hud. and Berg. Co., N. J., 172
Vanderbilt
Clayton's Hist. of Union Co., N. J., 740
Vanderoef
Ferrier Genealogy, 40-2
Vanderslice
McGavock Family of Va.
Vandersloot
Vandersloot Genealogy (1901), 70 pages
See Vondersloot

Vanderveer
Van Brunt Genealogy, 51–3
Vandervoort
Crayon's Rockaway, N. J., Rec., 121–3
Van Deusen
Van Deusen Genealogy (1901), 182 p.
Van Dorn
Beekman's Monmouth, N. J., Set., 41–7
Red Bank Newspaper, about 1900
Van Duzer
Jessup Golden Wedding (1903), 25
Van Dyck
Harvey's Hud. and Berg. Co., N. J., 198
N. Y. Gen. Biog. Rec., xxxvii, 114–7
Van Harlingen
Schureman Family of N. J., 42, 65–7
Van Hoesen
New Amsterdam Year Book, ii, 5–7
Van Hoosear Genealogy, 5–7
Van Hoosear
Van Hoosear Genealogy (1902), 96 p.
Van Horn
Greene's History Boothbay, Me., 638
Lundy Genealogy, 458
Van Houten
Van Houten Genealogy (1897), 10 pages
Van Iveren
Pearson's Schenectady, N. Y.,Set.,124–7
Van Kleek
Van Kleek Genealogy (1900), 59 pages
Van Leer
Glenn's Colonial Mansions, ii, 328
Van Mater
Beekman's Monmouth, N. J., Set., 64–91
Van Meter
Deer Island, Me., Press for 1900
Vanmeter
Evans' Scioto Co., Ohio, History, 1249
Van Meter
Moorefield, Pa., Examiner, Jan. 10, 1905
Van Meter's Va. and Ky. Fams., 47–67
West Virg. Hist. Mag., ii, pt. ii, 1–18;
  iii, pt. i, iv, 224–31
Van Ness
Treman Genealogy
Van Nostrand
Symmes' Tennent, N. J., Church, 447
Van Orden
New Paltz Independent, Sept. 13, 1895
Van Pelt
Bean's Hist. Montgomery Co., Pa., 732
Van Rensselaer
Glenn's Colonial Mansions, i, 141–68
Van Rensselaer Family (1888), 21 pages
Van Riper
Labaw's Preakness, N. J., History, 53–7
Van Saen
Labaw's Preakness, N.J., History, 57–61
Van Saun
Labaw's Preakness, N.J., History, 57–61
Van Schaack
Treman Genealogy
Van Sweringen
Tiernan Genealogy (1901), 21–47
Van Tienhoven
N. Y. Gen. Biog. Records, xii, 50

Van Vlierden
N. Y. Gen. Biog. Record, xxxv, 69
Van Vliet
Russell Genealogy, 183
Van Voorhis
Crumrine's Hist. Washington, Pa., 695–7
Van Wagenen
Le Fevre's Hist. New Paltz, N. Y., 479
New Paltz, N. Y., Independent, Feb. 6,
  1903
Van Winkle
Labaw's Preakness, N.J., History, 63–5
Van Wyck
Brush-Bowers Genealogy (1904), 50–9
Van Ysselsteyn
Crall Ancestry
Varick
Treman Genealogy, 762, 783
Varnum
Treman Genealogy
Varnum Genealogy (1907)
Varrell
Parson's History, of Rye, N. H., 555–9
Vaughan
Meriwether Genealogy (1899), 164–70
Shannon Genealogy, 30–6, 49
Vaught
Pound and Kester Genealogy, 191–4
Vawter
Henderson Family of Va., 27–8
Richmond, Va., Times, June 4, 1905
Vawter Genealogy (1905), 442 pages
Venable
Baltimore Sun, Dec. 25, 1904
William and Mary Quartely, xv, 21–4
Verdery
Habersham Genealogy, 41–3
Vermilya
Benton (David) Ancestors (1906)
Vernon
Landrum's Spartanburg, S. C., 311–8
Lea Genealogy (1906)
Ver Planck
Herkimer Genealogy, 77
Viall
New Eng. Hist. and Gen. Reg., lv, 184–6
Vickers
Baltimore Sun, June 23, 1907
Viele
N. Y. Gen. and Biog. Rec., xxxiv, 1–3
Viets
Viets Genealogy (1902), 228 pages
Vincent
Wheeler's Hist. Stonington, Ct., 624–5
Visscher
Van Deusen Genealogy (1901), 143
Visscher Genealogy (1881), 2 pages
Vogdes
Glenn's Colonial Mansions, ii, 330–1
Vondersloot
Vondersloot Genealogy (1901), 70 pages
Voorhees
Clayton's Hist. of Union Co., N. J., 671
Labaw's Preakness, N. J., History, 83
Vorce
Vorce Genealogy (1901), 111 pages

Vought
Vought Family of N. J. (1907), 27 pages
Vredenburgh
Harvey's Hudson and Bergen Co., N. J., 103–5
Schureman Fam.,N.J.,26, 35, 51–3, 81–6

Waddams
Stiles' Wethersfield, Ct., ii, 721–4
Waddell
Well's History of Newbury, Vt., 720
Wade
Chappell Genealogy (1900), 285–95
Wadhams
Luzerne, Pa.,Legal Reg.,xii (1883), 63–8
Wadleigh
Hoyt's Salisbury, Mass., Families, 605
Wadley
Hinchman's Nantucket Sett., ii, 227–9
Wadsworth
Litchfield, Me., History (1897), 373–5
Wadsworth Family of Milton, Mass. (1904), 15 p.
Wady
Kewaunee, Wis., Owl, June, 1904, 291; Dec., 1905, 437
Waight
Temple's History Framingham, 732
Wainwright
Gamble's Family Data (1906), 87–96
Wait
Temple's History Framingham, 732
Wait Genealogy (1904), 55 pages
Waite
Evans' Scioto Co., Ohio, History, 1250
Greene Family of R. I. (1905), 278
Pocumtuck Valley, Mass., Hist., ii, 490
Well's Genealogy (1903)
Wakeman
American Ancestry, xii, 211
Walderne
New Eng. Hist. Gen. Reg. (1888), 186
Waldo
Waldo Genealogy (1902), 1121 pages
Waldron
Litchfield, Me., History (1897), 375
New Eng. Hist. and Gen. Reg., xliii, 60–4; xliv, 58–64
Parson's History of Rye, N. H., 560
Scales' Hist. Dover, N.H., 222–36, 405–8
Well's History of Newbury, Vt., 721
Wales
Vinton Genealogy, 312
Walker
Baltimore Sun, Mar. 3, 10, 17, 1907
Beidler Family of Pa., 193–201
Carter's History Pembroke, N. H., ii,310
Clarke's King Wm. Co., Va., Fams., 107
Crumrine's Hist. Washington, Pa., 741
Litchfield, Me., History (1897), 376–9
Moore Family of Chester, Pa., 86–8
New Eng. Hist. Gen. Reg., lvii, 350–6
Newhall Ancestry, 181–4
Page Genealogy, 2d ed. (1893), 124–5, 199–234

Parson's History of Rye, N. H., 560–3
Richmond, Va., Times, April 10, 1904; April 16, 1905
Scales' History of Dover, N. H., 318–20
Stackpole's Hist. Kittery, Me., 784–5
Temple's History Framingham, 733
Treman Genealogy
Walker Family of Maryland (1883), 24 p
Walker Family of Va. (1902), 722 pages
Walker Family of Woburn (1903), 9 p.
Wash., D. C., Hist. Bulletin, vi, vii, 64
Wood Genealogy (1901), 29
Woods' Hist. Albemarle Co., Va., 334–6
Walkup
Temple's History Framingham, 734–6
Wall
Jerseyman, ix (1903), 34–6
Shoemaker Genealogy, 45–7, 60
Wallace
Habersham Genealogy, 24
Hanna's Ohio Valley Genealogies, 121
Moore Family of Chester, Pa., 76, 145
New Eng. Hist. Gen. Reg., lvi, 185–7
Ramsdell's Hist. Milford, N. H., 964–70
Thornton Family of N. H. (1905), 29–31
Wallace Family of Md. (1902), 34 pages
Well's Hist. of Newbury, Vt., 721–4
William and Mary Quar., xiii, 177–82
Woods' History Albemarle Co., Va., 336
Waller
Clarke's King Wm.Co.,Va., Fams.,108–10
Martinsville, Va., Standard, April 2, 16, 1902
Richmond, Va., Times, April 16, 1905
Treman Genealogy
William and Mary Quarterly, x, 118–20; xiii, 175–7
Walley
Treman Genealogy
Wallingford
Dover, N. H., Enquirer, Feb. 21, Aug. 21, 1867
Ramsdell's Hist. Milford, N. H., 970
Wallis
Corliss' North Yarmouth, Me., 379
Lukens Family chart
Parson's History of Rye, N. H., 563
Waln
Dunwoody Genealogy (1899), 156–8
Phila. North American, Dec. 29, 1907
Walstone
New Eng. Hist. Gen. Reg., lix, 385
Walt
Bean's Hist. Montgomery Co., Pa., 921
Walter
Glenn's Amer. Genealogist, i, 64–81
Walters
Kewaunee, Wis., Owl for April, 1901
Walthall
Richmond, Va., Times, Feb. 4, 1906
Walton
Baltimore Sun, Nov. 20, 1904
Scales' History Dover, N. H., 239–42
Walton Family (1905), chart
Waltz
Waltz Genealogy (1884), 128 pages

Wampole
Sellers Genealogy, 126–31
Ward
Amer. Hist. Mag., iv (1899), 15, 21–4
Britton Ancestry (1901)
Gray Genealogy (1889), 169–71
Nash's Fifty Puritan Ancestors, 72–7, 171
Seymour, Conn., History, 583–6
Trask's Mem. of A. H.Ward (1863), 11 p.
Ward Family Reunion (1905), 49 pages
Warren Genealogy (1903), 174–8
White Genealogy (1900), 295–314
Wardell
N. Y. Gen. Biog. Rec., xxxvi, 20
Warden
Warden Genealogy (1901), 248 pages
Wardin
See Warden
Wardwell
Greene Family of R. I. (1905), 276
Wardwell Genealogy (1905), 22 pages
Ware
Litchfield, Me., History (1897), 380
Ware Genealogy (1901), 335 pages
Warfield
Warfield's Maryland, 83–91, 365–8, etc.
Waring
N. Y. Gen. and Biog. Rec., xxxiv, 272
Richmond, Va., Times, July 22; Aug. 12, 1906
Virg. Mag. of History, x, xi, 209
Warne
Crumrine's Hist. Washington, Pa., 600
Warner
Baltimore Sun, June 25, 1905
Habersham Gen.
Jameson Genealogy
Kellogg's Bernardston, Mass., 513–7
Lewis Family of Va. (1906)
Nash's Fifty Puritan Ancestors, 68
Peoria County, Ill., History, 699
Sanford's Hist. Hopkinton, N. Y., 580
Seymour, Conn., History, 586
Stiles' Wethersfield, Ct., ii, 727–52
Warner Family of Conn. (1892), 49 pages
Watson's A Royal Lineage
Wells Genealogy (1903)
Willis Family of Va., 115–7
Warren
Britton Ancestry, 1901
Carter's History Pembroke, N. H., ii,311
Mayflower Descendant, iii (1901), 45–51, 105–17
New Eng. Hist. Gen. Reg., lv, 70–8, 161–70
Roebling's Constant Journal, 434–61
Stackpole's Hist. Kittery, Me., 785–90
Temple's History Framingham, 736
Treman Genealogy
Tucker Genealogy (1901), 62
Tucker Genealogy (1903)
Warren Genealogy (1901), 39 pages
Warren Fam., Kittery, Me.(1902), 138 p.
Warren Fam., Weymouth (1903), 207 p.
Wells Genealogy (1903)

Warriner
Jenkins Family of Pa. (1904), 179
Warrington
Stokes Genealogy, 299
Wartman
Dotterer Genealogy
See also under Woertman
Washburn
Benjamin Genealogy, 78–92
Seymour, Conn., History, 586–89
Washburn Genealogy (1904), 10 pages
Washington
Conway's Barons of Potomack, 1892
Glenn's Colonial Mansions, ii, 19–84
Habersham Gen.
Lewis Family of Va., 1906
Newburgh, N.Y., Hist. Papers, xiii, 210–4
N. Y. Gen. and Biog. Rec., xxxiii, 200–8
Page Genealogy, 2d ed. (1893), 213–4
Richmond, Va., Times, Feb. 21, 1904
Washington Genealogy (1900), 14 pages
Washington Family Wills (1891), 19 p.
Washington Evening Star, Apr. 17, 30, 1889
William and Mary Quarterly, x, 113
Wasson
Crumrine's Hist. Washington, Pa., 887
Thornton Family of N. H. (1905), 16
Waterhouse
Peoria County, Ill., History, 700
Waterhouse Family of Me. (1906), 27 p.
Waterman
Hinchman's Nantucket Sett., ii, 224–6
Litchfield, Me., History (1897), 382
Waterman Family of Me. (1906), 100 p.
Waters
Baltimore Sun, Nov. 6, 20, 1904; Dec. 31, 1905; Jan. 7, 28, 1906
Benton (David) Ancestors (1906)
Flagg Genealogy (1903)
Tucker Genealogy (1901), 51
Virg. Mag. of History, ix, 428
Watkins
Sayre Genealogy, 302–4
Treman Genealgy
Warfield's Maryland, 411–6
Watrous
Hall Memoranda (1902), 168
Watson
Hall (of Ct.) Memoranda (1902), 27
Hanna's Ohio Valley Genealogies, 122
Jameson Genealogy
Litchfield, Me., History (1897), 383
Marston Genealogy (1873), 39–45
Scales' History of Dover, N. H., 250–3
Woods' Hist. Albemarle Co., Va., 337–40
Watt
Bean's Hist. Montgomery Co., Pa., 583
Fulton Genealogy, 147
Watts
Benton Genealogy (1901), 105–7
Hall Memoranda (1902), 87
Keith's Pa Prov. Councillors, pt. ii, 298–302
Richmond, Va., Times, Jan. 22, 1905

Waugh
Woodruff's Litchfield, Ct. Gen. Reg., 229–31

Way
New Eng. Hist. Gen. Reg., xliv, 151–3
Stacy's Medway Church, Ga., 276–8

Waymouth
Willis' Old Eliot, Me., vi, 83
See also under Weymouth

Wayne
Glenn's Colonial Mansions, ii, 281–340

Weare
New Eng. Hist. Gen. Reg. (1901), 56
Putnam's Hist. Mag. (1898), 245–51

Weaver
Bean's Hist. Montgomery Co., Pa., 574–6, 671
Glenn's Amer. Genealogist, i, 84
Jennings Genelogy, ii, 659–91

Webb
Bellows Falls Times, May 28, 1903
Crayon's Rockaway, N. J., Records, 270
Deer Island, Me., Press for Jan. 23 to March 6, 1901
Greenlaw's Gen. Advertiser, iv, 28
Hanna's Ohio Valley Genealogies, 123
Hosmer's Hist. of Deer Isle, Me., 122–5
Richmond, Va., Times, March 5, 1905
Stern's Our Kindred, 16–8
Stiles' Wethersfield, Ct., ii, 753–7

Webber
Greene's History Boothbay, Me., 639
Litchfield, Me., History (1897), 384
Putnam's Hist. Mag. (1899), 57–63, 115–8
Well's History of Newbury, Vt., 726

Webster
Benton (David) Ancestors (1906)
Buell Genealogy, 211
Kellogg's Hist. Bernardston, Mass., 518
Parson's History of Rye, N. H., 564–7
Sewall Genealogy (1904), 7–13, 18
Webster Genealogy (1897), 40 pages
Webster Genealogy (1904), 68 pages
Well's History Newbury, Vt., 727–9
Woodruff's Litchfield, Ct., Gen. Reg., 231–5

Wedgwood
Litchfield, Me., History (1897), 385

Wedgewood
Parson's History of Rye, N. H., 567

Weed
Deer Island, Me., Press for 1900
Hosmer's History Deer Isle, Me., 135–7
Stiles' Wethersfield, Ct., ii, 758

Weeks
Hall's History Greenland, N. H., 232–8
Pound and Kester Genealogy, 552–61
Stackpole's Hist. Kittery, Me., 790–2
Willis' Old Eliot, Me., vi, 86

Weers
Peoria County, Ill., History, 700

Weidman
Egle's Dauphin County, Pa. (1883), 256

Weidner
Dotterer Genealogy

Weigley
Egle's Dauphin Co., Pa. (1883), 353–4

Weinberger
Bean's Montgomery Co., Pa., 414–6

Weisel
Cumming Family of Md. (1905), chart

Welch
Crissey's Hist. of Norfolk, Ct., 466–94
Hanna's Ohio Valley Genealogies, 123–5
Manning Genealogy, 188
Pound and Kester Genealogy, 310–66
Stackpole's Hist. Kittery, Me., 792
Warfield's Maryland, 91
Welch MSS. in N. J. Hist. Soc. Lib.
Welch Family of Boston (1906), 73 p.

Weld
Jenkins Family of Pa. (1904), 177

Weldin
Stern's Our Kindred, 63

Welker
Dotterer Genealogy

Weller
Hodge Genealogy, 1900

Welles
Buell Genealogy, 44
Stiles' Wethersfield, Ct., ii, 760–80

Wellford
Page Genealogy, 2d ed. (1893), 187

Welling
Warfield's Maryland, 418
Warwick, N. Y., Advertiser, June 6, 1; 1889

Wellman
Brush-Bowers Gen. (1904), 110–2

Wells
Buell Genealogy, 31
Chesebrough Genealogy, 538
Hastings Genealogy (1899), 33–6
Hoyt's Salisbury, Mass., Fams., 808–20
Sayre Genealogy, 297–9
Stiles' Wethersfield, Ct., ii, 780–2
Treman Genealogy
Wells Family of Ohio (1892), 142 pages
Wells Family of Ipswich (1900), 8 pages
Wells Ancestry (1900), 214 pages
Wells Fam. Ipswich, Mass.(1903), 205 p.
Wells Fam. Greenfield, Mass.(1905), 65 p.
Well's Hist. of Newbury, Vt., 729–31

Welschance
Small Family of Penn. (1905)

Wemple
N. Y. Gen. Biog. Rec., xxxv, 190–8, 234 –40; xxxvi, 47–52, 91–7, 191–3, 248 –54

Wendell
Wendell Family (1907), 2 charts

Wenlock
Baltimore Sun, Jan. 21, 1906

Wentworth
Stackpole's Hist. Kittery, Me., 793–4
Treman Genealogy
Willis' Old Eliot, Me., vi, 87–9

Wentz
Bean's Hist. Montgomery Co., Pa., 1180

Wenzell
Temple's History Framingham, 738

Wesley
Wesley Ancestry (1885), 23 pages
West
Clarke's King Wm. Co., Va., Fams., 110
Hanna's Ohio Valley Genealogies, 125
New Eng. Hist. Gen. Reg., lx, 142–51
Newport, R. I., Mercury, June–Sept., 1904
Richmond, Va., Times, July 9, 1905
Sinnott Genealogy
Stern's Our Kindred, 142–7
Treman Genealogy
West Fam. of Duxbury (1906), 14 pages
Wheeler's Hist. Stonington, Ct., 626–35
William and Mary Quarterly, x, 65
Westbrook
N. Y. Gen. Biog. Record, xxxvii, 89
Westcott
Thayer Ancestors (1894), 128–31
Westervelt
Harvey's Hud. and Berg. Co., N. J., 99
Westervelt Genealogy (1905), 175 pages
Westfall
N. Y. Gen. Biog. and Rec., xxxiii, 10–4, 87–90
Westgate
Jennings Genealogy, ii, 692–726
Westman
Greene's History Boothbay, Me., 640
Westmoreland
Landrum's Spartanburg, S. C., 427
Weston
Kimball-Weston Memorial, 42–6
Litchfield, Me., History (1897), 387
Westover
Woodruff's Litchfield, Ct., Gen. Reg., 235–7
Wetherbee
Ramsdell's Hist. Milford, N. H., 975
Wetherill
Mayer Genealogy, 104–6
See Witherell
Wetmore
Acadienses, i, 243–9; ii, 90–7, 166–9; iii, 51–5; vi, 95–101
Hall Memoranda (1902), 69–71
Weyborne
Clapp Ancestors (1902), 61
Weymouth
Litchfield, Me., History (1897), 388–90
Stackpole's Hist. Kittery, Me., 794–6
Whaley
Eaton Ancestry (1900), 66–9
Whaley Genealogy (1901), 234 pages
Whalley
Dexter's Life Edw. Whalley (1876), 32 p.
Wharff
Litchfield, Me., History (1897), 390–2
Wharton
Glenn's Colonial Mansions, ii, 194–7
Keith's Pa. Prov. Councillors, pt. i, 25–8
Wheat
Wheat Genealogy (1903), 122 pages
Wheatley
Wheatley Genealogy (1902), 154 pages
Wheaton
Le Baron Genealogy, 139–41

Wheeler
Greene's History Boothbay, Me., 641
Nash's Fifty Puritan Ancestors, 91
Ramsdell's Hist. Milford, N.H., 976–8
Seymour, Conn, History, 589–96
Temple's History Framingham, 739–41
Treman Genealogy
Warden Genealogy, 13–8
Warren Genealogy (1903), 86–8
Well's History Newbury, Vt., 731
Wheeler's Hist. Stonington, Ct., 636–57
White Genealogy (1900), 434
Woods' History Albemarle Co., Va., 342
Wheelock
Converse Genealogy (1905), 181–4
Quinabaug Hist. Soc. Leaflet, 191–204
Wheelwright
Dennison Genealogy (1906), 127
Hoyt's Salisbury, Mass., Families, 607
Wells Genealogy (1903), 159–67
Whidden
Parson's History of Rye, N. H., 569
Whipple
Britton Ancestry (1901)
New Eng. Hist and Gen. Reg., xi, 360
Putnam's Hist. Mag. (1896), 217
Willis' Old Eliot, Me., vi, 90
Whitaker
Burhans Genealogy, 19–22
Whitbeck
Van Deusen Genealogy (1901), 19–25
Whitcher
Well's History of Newbury, Vt.
See Whittier
Whitcomb
Clapp Ancestors (1902), 63
Tucker Genealogy (1901), 49
Whitcomb Fam. of N. H. (1899), 19 p.
Whitcomb Fam. Dorchester (1904), 621 p.
White
Bellows Falls Times, March, 1904
Brookline Hist. Soc. Pubs., 1904
Carter's Hist. Pembroke, N. H., ii, 312–5
Evans' Scioto Co., Ohio, Hist., 125, 1–3
Hall Memoranda (1902), 121–6
Hill Genealogy (1904), 33
Hodge Genealogy (1900)
Kingsbury Genealogy (1904), 14–41
Landrum's Spartanburg, S. C., 419
New Eng. Hist. and Gen. Reg., lv, 22–31
Richmond, Va., Times, Sept. 4, 1904
Scales' Hist. of Dover, N. H., 320–2
Seymour, Conn., History, 596–9
Stockard's History of Alamance, N. C.
Stuart Genealogy (1894), 37–43
Treman Genealogy
Tucker Genealogy (1901), 92
Well's Hist. of Newbury, Vt., 734–9
White Fam. of Wenham (1900), 3 vols.
White Fam. of Taunton (1902), 493 p.
White Family Quarterly (1903)
White Fam. of Brookline, Mass. (1904), 38 pages
White Fam., Andover, Ct. (1905), 155 p.
White Fam. New Jersey (1907), 88 p.
Woods' Hist. Albemarle Co., Va., 343

Whitehead
Clayton's Hist. Union Co. N. J., 816
Cornell Genealogy, 376–7
N. Y. Gen. and Biog. Rec., xxxiii, 101–7
Shepard's John Whitehead (1902), 7 p.
William and Mary Quarterly, xi, 139–41
See Whithed
Whitehouse
Carter's Hist. Pembroke, N. H., ii, 315
Greene's History Boothbay, Me., 642
Whitelaw
Well's History of Newbury, Vt., 739
Whitesides
McIlhany's Virginia Families (1903)
Whitford
Peoria County, Ill., History, 702
Whithed
Stratton-Whithed Fams. (1889), 16 p.
See Whitehead
Whiting
Blair Family of Virg. (1898), 176–99
Dedham Hist. Reg.,xii, 110–5; xiii, 7–19
Hill Genealogy (1904), 72
Newhall Ancestry, 69–71
Old Northwest Gen. Quar., vii, 81
Robie and Whiting Gen. (1900), 131 p.
Whiting Family (1902), 8 pages
Whiting Family of Dedham (1902), 80 p.
Whitlock
Tuttle Genealogy (1871), 11–3
Whitman
Brush-Bowers Genealogy (1904), 45
New Eng. Hist. Gen. Reg., lviii, 310
Sanborn's Four Boston Fams. (1904),
    7 p.
Well's History of Newbury, Vt., 740
Whitmarsh
Whitmarsh Genealogy (1902), 10 pages
Whitmore
Farwell Family (1878), chart
Hosmer's History of Deer Isle, Me., 128
Seymour, Conn., History, 599
Temple's History Framingham, 742
Treman Genealogy
Whitmore Family Manor (1856), 14 p.
Whitmores of Ludson, Eng. (1873), 9 p.
Whitmores of Madeley, Eng.(1875),¦47 p.
Whitney
Hill Genealogy (1904), 38
Hoar's Wm. W. Rice (1897), 52–6, 72–83
Lawrence Genealogy (1904)
Litchfield, Me., History (1897), 393–5
Lowe Genealogy, 144
Merrick Genealogy, 434–8
Sayre Genealogy, 282–4
Stackpole's History Kittery, Me., 796–7
Temple's History Framingham, 743–5
Treman Genealogy
Whitridge
Pearson's Autobiog. of J. B. Whitridge
    (1902), 18 pages
Whitsitt
Amer. Hist. Mag., ix (1904), 58, 113, 231,
    352
Whitson
Moore Family of Chester, Pa., 127–130

Whittelsey
Treman Genealogy
Whittemore
Carter's Pembroke, N. H., ii, 317–23
Whittemore Genealogy (1878), 9 pages
Whittier
Hinchman's Nantucket Sett., ii, 234–6
Well's Hist. Newbury, Vt., 732–5
Whittle
Baltimore Sun, July 7, 1907
Whittlesey
Stiles' Wethersfield, Ct., ii, 786
Wiatt
William and Mary Coll. Quar., x, 59–61;
    xii, 35–45, 111–6
Wick
Woodruff Genealogy (1902), 144–6
Wickersham
Small Family of Penn., 222
Wickes
Thayer Ancestors (1894), 137–40
Wickham
N. Y. Gen. and Biog. Rec., xxxii, 135
Stiles' Wethersfield, Ct., ii, 787–92
Wickliffe
William and Mary Coll. Quar., x, 175–7
Widdifield
Lundy Genealogy, 137–45
Widener
Widener Genealogy (1906), 330 pages
Wiggin
Dover, N. H., Enquirer for April 8–29,
    1869
Tarleton Genealogy, 56
Wiggins
Crayon's Rockaway, N. J., Rec., 156–9
Wigglesworth
Wells Genealogy (1903)
Wightman
Acadiensis, vii, 115–27
Wikoff
Keith's. Pa. Prov. Councillors, pt. ii,
    299–302
Wilbur
Tucker Genealogy (1901), 115–7
Wilcox
Nash's Fifty Puritan Ancestors, 46–57
Richmond, Va., Times, Nov. 20, 1904
Treman Genealogy
Westerly, R. I., Sun for April, 1896
Wheeler's Hist. Stonington, Ct., 658–61
Wilcox Genealogy (1902), 36 pages
Wilcoxson
Nash's Fifty Puritan Ancestors, 142
Wild
See Wildes
Wilder
Ford's History of Clinton, Mass., 126
Hill Genealogy (1904), 66
White Genealogy (1900), 62–6, 457–
    623
Wilder Fam. of Pembroke, Me. (1889)
Wilder Fam. of Pembroke (1902), 10 p.
Wildes
Essex Inst. Hist. Coll., xlii, 129–52, 273–
    309

Wilhite
Baltimore Sun, Dec. 15, 1907
Wilkins
Carter's Hist. Pembroke, N. H., ii, 323–6
Landrum's Spartanburg, S. C., 364–9
Ramsdell's Hist. Milford, N. H., 979–81
Wilkinson
De Camp Genealogy (1896), 140–51
Willard
Acadiensis, v, 157–65
Johnson Narrative (1834), 1–2
Nash's Fifty Puritan Ancestors, 143–6
Stiles' Wethersfield, Ct., ii, 792–8
Temple's History Framingham, 745
Warren Genealogy (1903), 106–10
White Genealogy (1900), 82
Willcomb
Willcomb Fam. New Eng. (1902),302 p.
Willcox
William and Mary Quarterly, xi, 58–60
Willet
Willet Manuscript (1907)
Willet Family (1905), chart
Willets
Lundy Genealogy, 459
Stevenson Family of Long Island, 61
Willett
Abbott, Jas. S., Memorial (1905), 41 p.
Cornell Genealogy (1902), 28
Willey
Carter's Hist. of Pembroke, N. H., ii, 326
Litchfield, Me., History (1897), 396
Williams
Alston Genealogy, 429–87
Baltimore Sun, April 2, 1905
Bean's Hist. Montgomery Co., Pa., 809–13, 824
Brown Family of Pa. (1885), pt. ii, 1–21
Carter's History Pembroke, N. H., ii,327
Chesebrough Genealogy, 110–6
Clayton's Hist. of Union Co., N. J., 377
Green's Culpeper County Virg.
Gernhardt Genealogy, 285–99
Hamlin Genealogy (1900), 235–8
Lancaster Genealogy, 81, 88
Lawson's Genealogy (1903), 269–79
Litchfield, Me., History (1897), 396–9
McAllister Family of N. C.
Metcalf Genealogy (1898), 54–7
New Eng. Hist. Gen. Reg., lvi, 363; lvii, 75–82, 198–200
Peoria County, Ill., History, 703
Prindle Genealogy, 249–55
Shoemaker Genealogy, 56–8, 99
Slaughter's Life of Wm. Green, 60–6
Stackpole's Hist. Kittery, Me., 797–8
Stiles' Wethersfield, Ct., ii, 798–837
Temple's History Framingham, 746
Thayer Ancestors (1894), 143–5
Treman Genealogy
Wheeler's Hist. Stonington, Ct., 662–85
Williamson
McAllister Family of N. C.
Smedley Genealogy, 58–68, 117, 130, 233
William and Mary Quarterly, xii, 196
Williamson, Joseph, Memoir (1903), 9 p.

Williamson Fam. York, Pa. (1906), 71 p.
Willing
Keith's Pa. Prov,Councillors,pt.i, 89–114
Willis
Baltimore Sun, Aug. 26; Sept. 2, 9, 1906
Willis Family of Me. (1906), 115 pages
Willoby
Ramsdell's Hist. Milford, N, H., 982–4
Willoughby
Richmond, Va., Times, Oct. 1, 1905
Ramsdell's Hist. Milford, N. H.
See Willoby
Wills
Haines Family of N. J., 276–319
Hibbard Genealogy, 401–3
McKinney Family of Pa., 58–67
Willson
Lundy Genealogy, 113–37, 170–6, 326–45, 460–8
Old Northwest Quarterly, ix, 257
Wilmot
New Eng. Hist. Gen. Reg., lix, 67–73
Peoria County, Ill., History, 735
Wilmot Fam. of New Haven (1904), 9 p.
Wilson
Baltimore Sun, Oct. 28, 1906
Bean's Montgomery Co., Pa., 819, 971
Carter's Hist. of Pembroke, N. H., ii. 328
Crumrine's Hist. Washington, Pa., 482
Jameson Genealogy
Kittochtinny Magazine, i, 314–6
Litchfield, Me., History (1897), 399
New Eng. Hist. Gen. Reg., lxi, 36–41, 127–33
Ramsdell's Hist. Milford, N. H., 984
Sanford's Hist. Hopkinton, N. Y., 582–4
Stackpole's Hist. Kittery, Me., 798–802
Temple's History Framingham, 747
Treman Genealogy
Wells Family of Ohio (1892), 31–4
Willis' Old Eliot, Me., vi, 92–4
Wilson Fam. of Pelham, N. H. (1905), chart
Wilson Fam. of Boston (1907), 16 pages
Wiltbank
Penn. Mag. of History, xxix, 339–42
Winans
Clayton's Hist.Union Co., N. J., 381, 400
Woodruff Genealogy (1902), 118–20
Winch
Temple's History Framingham, 748–52
Winchester
Temple's History Framingham, 752
Winder
Winder Genealogy (1902), 112 pages
Yeardley Genealogy, 12–5
Windermuth
Wintermute Gen.
Wing
Anderson-Perrine Family, 106–10
Hinchman's Nantucket Settlers, ii, 183–8, 305
Kewaunee, Wis., Owl for Oct., 1901
Old Northwest Gen. Quarterly, v, 73–9
Sinnott Genealogy

Wingate
Benton (David) Ancestors (1906)
Dover, N.H., Enquirer, Jan.–Nov., 1857
Treman Genealogy
Wingfield
Downing Genealogy (1902), 133 pages
Woods' Hist. Albemarle Co., Va., 344–6
Wingo
Landrum's Spartanburg, S. C., 399–405
Winkley
Scales' History Dover, N. H., 305–8
Stackpole's Hist. Kittery, Me., 802–3
Winnie
Sanford's Hist. Hopkinton, N. Y., 586
See also under Winne
Winship
Winship Genealogy (1906), 37 pages
Winslow
Sinnott Genealogy
Winston
Green's Culpeper County Virg.
Meriwether Genealogy (1899), 113
Richmond, Va., Times, Oct. 18, 1903
Winston Family of Virginia (1900) chart
Winter
Egle's Dauphin Co., Pa. (1883), 256–8
Wintermute
Wintermute Gen. (1900), 335 pages
Winters
Winters Genealogy (1889), 186 pages
Winthrop
Glenn's Colonial Mansions, ii, 117
New Eng. Hist. Gen. Reg., lx, 223
Wirt
Swope Genealogy, 76–8, 102–5
Wirz
Wurtz Genealogy
Wise
Stackpole's Hist. Kittery, Me., 803–4
Vawter Genealogy, 237–41
Wishart
Crumrine's Hist. Washington, Pa., 544
Wisner
Ferrier Genealogy, 42–4
Wistar
Shourds' Fenwick's Colony, N. J., 360–3
Wiswall
Newhall Ancestry, 99
Witham
Willis' Old Eliot, Me., vi, 95
Witherell
Sanford's Hist. Hopkinton, N. Y., 584–6
Witherstine
Bentley Gleanings (1905), 105, 122–8
Withington
Clayton's Hist. of Union Co., N. J., 794
Topliff Genealogy (1906)
Witter
Preston Genealogy (1899)
Wheeler's Hist. of Stonington, 686–90
Wittum
Stackpole's Hist. Kittery, Me., 804
Wofford
Landrum's Spartanburg, S. C., 220–39
Wolcott
Hall Memoranda (1902), 160–8

Stiles' Wethersfield, Ct., ii, 838–47
Treman Genealogy
Woodruff's Litchfield, Ct., Gen. Reg., 240–53
Womack
Cody and Womack Genealogy, 21–3
Wood
Ames Genealogical Notes (1900), 20–1
Baltimore Sun Feb. 17, 24, 1907
Brush-Bowers Genealogy (1904), 47–9
Clayton's Hist. of Union Co., N. J., 815
Eastman Genealogy (1901), 137
Goodrich's Hist. Dryden, N. Y., 202–8
Hull Genealogy (1904), 20
Landrum's Spartanburg, S. C., 369–71
Newburgh, N. Y., Hist. Papers, x, 34–47
Newhall Ancestry, 142–9
Shourds' Fenwick's Colony, N. J., 71
Temple's History Framingham, 753
Treman Genealogy
White Genealogy (1900), 445–8
Wood Fam. of Concord (1901), 365 p.
Wood Fam. Alstead, N. H. (1902), 187 p
Wood Fam. Bucks Co., Pa. (1903), 85 p
Wood Fam. Sackville, N. B. (1904) 46 p.
Woods' Hist. Albemarle Co., Va., 347–51
Woodbridge
New Eng. Hist. Gen. Reg., liv, 201–3
Tucker Genealogy (1901), 83
Wheeler's Hist. Stonington, Ct., 691–4
Woodbury
Colby Family of N. H., 39–50, 123
Litchfield, Me., History (1897), 401–4
Underhill's Life of J. A. Woodbury (1903), 18 pages
Warren Genealogy (1903), 112–5
Woodbury Genealogy (1899), 24 pages
Woodbury's Old Planter in New Eng., (1885)
Woodbury Family (1904), 251 pages
Woodhouse
Stiles' Wethersfield, Ct., ii, 848
William and Mary Quarterly, ii, 262–4 (1903), 60
Woodhull
Symmes' Tennent, N. J., Church, 408
Woodhull Genealogy (1904), 425 pages
Woodman
Gamble's Family Data (1906), 131
Stackpole's Hist. Kittery, Me., 805–6
Woodnut
Glenn's Colonial Mansions, ii, 385–8
Wodruff
Landrum's Spartanburg, S. C., 349–53
N. J. Hist. Soc. Proc., ii (1900), 115–8
Peoria County, Ill., History, 704
Walker Family of Va. (1902)
Woodruff's Litchfield, Ct., Gen. Reg., 254–63
Woodruff Genealogy (1902), 152 pages
Woods
Robinson Family of Pa. (1902), 194–214
Woods' Hist. Albemarle Co., Va., 351–6
Woods-McAfee Fam., Va. (1905), 503 p.
Woodson
Richmond, Va., Times, March 27, 1904

William and Mary Quarterly, ix, 254–9; x, 44–8, 185–91; xi, 50–8
Woods' Hist. Albemarle Co., Va., 356
Woodward
Bean's Hist. Montgomery Co., Pa., 985
Dunwoody Genealogy (1899), 138–41
N. Y. Gen. Biog. Rec., xxxvii, 136–40, 218–24
Peoria County, Ill., History, 704
Smedley Genealogy, 68–71, 133
So. Car. Hist. Mag., viii, 29–41
Warfield's Maryland, 123–7
Woodworth
Treman Genealogy
Woodworth Genealogy (1901), 70 pages
Woody
Stockard's History of Alamance, N. C.
Woolsey
Cornell Genealogy, 31
Woolsey Fam. Record (1901), 256 pages
Woolson
Lancaster Genealogy, 32
Ramsdell's Hist. Milford, N. H., 988
Temple's History Framingham, 753
Wooster
Seymour, Conn., History, 599–605
Wootton
Baltimore Sun, May 12, 19, 26, June 2, 1907
Work
Crumrine's Hist. Washington, Pa., 823
Worley
Hanna's Ohio Valley Genealogies, 127
Worrell
Hanson's Old Kent County,Md., 169
Worster
Stackpole's Hist. Kittery, Me., 806–7
Wortendyke
Harvey's Hud. and Berg. Co., N. J., 91–3, 102
Worth
Manlsby Genealogy, 126
Manlsby Family of Pa.
Worth Family of Penn. (1879), 4 pages
Worthen
Forrest Genealogy, 22
Worthington
Ames Genealogy, 1898
Ames Genealogical Notes (1900), 23–5
Old Northwest Gen. Quar., vi, 37–40
Tower's Spencerman Sketches, iii, 234–52
Warfield's Maryland, 145–56, 369
Wrenshall
N. Y. Gen. and Biog. Rec., xxxiv, 97
Wright
Barber Genealogy (1890), 139–43
Bellows Falls Times, July, 1903
Benton (David) Ancestors (1906)
Emory's Colonial Fams. of Md., 1–163
Genung Family of L. I.
Jenkins Family of Pa. (1904), 164–6
Kellogg's Bernardston, Mass., 523–5
Lawson's Genealogy (1903), 235–43
McGinness and Scott Genealogy, 220–3
Nash's Fifty Puritan Ancestors, 122

New Eng. Hist. Gen. Reg., lviii, 39–41
Old Northwest Gen. Quarterly, vii, 1–11
Perkiomen Region, Pa., iii (1900), 127
Ramsdell's Hist. Milford, N. H., 990–4
Richmond, Va., Times, April 15, 1906
Sanford's Hist. Hopkinton, N. Y., 581
Stiles' Wethersfield, Ct., ii, 850–65
Temple's History Framingham, 754
Treman Genealogy
White Genealogy (1900), 428–33
Woodruff's Litchfield, Ct.,Gen.Reg., 239
Wright Family of Guilford, Ct. (1901),ne
Wright Fam., Guilford, Ct. (1901), 16 p.
Wyoming Hist. Soc. Proc., iii (1886), 21
Wyoming Hist.Soc.Proc.,iii (1886), 21–3
Wurts
Le Fevre's Hist. of New Paltz, N. Y., 464–6
Wurtz Genealogy (1889), 91 pages
Wyant
Seymour, Conn., History, 605–6
Wyatt
Baltimore Sun, April 16, 1905
Richmond, Va., Times, Feb. 28; March 20, 1904
William and Mary Quarterly, x, 59–61, 260–4
Wyche
William and Mary Coll. Quar., xiii, 256–60; xiv, 59–62, 103–7; xv, 42–5
Wyckoff
Forman Genealogy, 147
Symmes' Tennent, N. J., Church, 420–4
Wyley
Treman Genealogy
Wylie
Greene's History Boothbay, Me., 643–7
Wyman
Bellows Falls Times, April, 1905
Hill Genealogy (1904), 78
Wynkoop
Wynkoop Gen., 3d ed. (1904), 258 pages
Wynn
See Gwynn

Yale
Abbott, Jas. S., Memorial (1905), 41 p.
Yancey
Alston Genealogy, 301–3
Green's Culpeper County Virg.
Woods' History Albemarle Co., Va., 357
Yarnall
Moore Family of Chester, Pa., 149
Smedley Genealogy, 112, 175–7
Yarrington
Richardson Genealogy (1906)
Yates
Baltimore Sun, Aug. 19, 1906
Peoria County, Ill., History, 705
Va. Magazine of History, vii, 436
West Virg. Hist. Mag., ii, July, 44–51
Yates Family of Me. (1906), 47 pages
Yeakle
Bean's Hist. Montgomery Co., Pa., 520, 774, 818, 1078–82, 1157

Yeardley
Baltimore Sun, March 26, 1905; Apr. 15, 22, 29, 1906
Yearsley
Stern's Our Kindred, 8, 60
Yeaton
American Ancestry, xii, 9
Parson's History of Rye, N. H., 571
Yendell
New Eng. Hist. Gen. Reg., lviii, 309–11
Sanborn's Four Boston Fams. (1904),7 p.
Yerkes
Yerkes Genealogy (1904), 262 pages
Yoder
Keim and Allied Families, 643–5
Yonge
Yonge Ancestry in Eng. (1906), 25 p.
York
Hosmer's History of Deer Isle, Me., 58
Wheeler's Hist. Stonington, Ct., 695–703
Yost
Bean's Montgomery Co., Pa., 519, 998
Dotterer Genealogy
Penn.-German, vii, 337–41
Youmans
Treman Genealogy
Young
McGinness and Scott Genealogy, 145–69, 185–92

N. Y. Gen. Biog. Rec., xxxv, 257–65; xxxvi, 53–8, 97–102
Roberts Family of Maine, 14–8
Treman Genealogy
Youngs
Genung Family of L. I.
Youngs Genealogy (1907)
Yount
Dotterer Genealogy
Yundt
Dotterer Genealogy

Zabriskie
Harvey's Hud. and Berg. Co., N. J., 49–53
Zabriskie Homestead and Genealogy (1881), 100 pages
Zehring
Egle's Dauphin Co., Pa. (1883), 258–9
Zeigler
Peoria County, Ill., History, 706
Zieber
Perkiomen Region, Pa., iii, 67
Zimmerman
Dotterer Genealogy, 56, 112–7
Zouch
Virg. Mag. of History, xii, 429